Carmichael

INCLUDING

Nearly 200 Masterpieces of Journalism
from Daniel Defoe, Charles Dickens,
Victor Hugo, Mark Twain, and
Rudyard Kipling,
to Winston Churchill, Irvin S. Cobb,
H. G. Wells, Ernest Hemingway,
John Hersey, and Rebecca West

Together with
a Representative Selection
of Eyewitness Radio Reporting

* * * *

Each account is placed
in its full setting
by a biographical and historical
introduction and a well-authenticated
record of the consequences of the events.

* * * *

With a Preface by
Herbert Bayard Swope

A TREASURY OF

GREAT

REPORTING

"Literature Under Pressure"
from the Sixteenth Century
to Our Own Time
Edited by

Louis L. Snyder

PROFESSOR OF HISTORY
THE CITY UNIVERSITY OF NEW YORK

AND

Richard B. Morris

GOUVERNEUR MORRIS PROFESSOR OF HISTORY

COLUMBIA UNIVERSITY

2nd Edition, Revised and Enlarged

A Fireside Book Published by
Simon and Schuster · New York

8   9   10   11   12   13   14   15   16

To Ida Mae and Berenice

ISBN 0-671-75101-8 PBK.

LIBRARY OF CONGRESS CATALOG CARD NUMBER: 62–8901

MANUFACTURED IN THE UNITED STATES OF AMERICAS

Table of Contents

PREFACE

IF THIS anthology survives, even remotely, like Palgrave's, and becomes known as a Golden Treasury of the World's Great Reporting, the editors and authors will be content (or should be), the publishers will be pleased, and I shall be vindicated. From the outset I have been deeply impressed with the brilliant editorial conception of the two young but learned historians (these adjectives ought to make me popular with them!) who have assembled and interpreted these masterpieces of journalism. I am equally enthusiastic about their execution of the idea.

When they asked me to write the Preface I consented, thinking I might be as independent of the main theme of the book—as unrelated, even though not as brilliant, as Shaw is in his prefaces, and as Somerset Maugham (whom the cognoscenti call "Willie") is in his introductions.

However, my freedom of action is somewhat restrained, because, much to my delight, they have included a story of mine in their anthology, or as H. L. Mencken calls it, their chrestomathy.

Professors Snyder and Morris give us in this collection nearly two hundred of the greatest examples of "literature under pressure"—or, in the words of Matthew Arnold, "literature in a hurry." They remind us again, as Heywood Broun used to say, that every good reporter is writing literature for some future historian. (Joseph Pulitzer frequently added a sardonic footnote to Matthew Arnold's observation. He said that every reporter was a hope, every editor a disappointment.) But this book is more than a mere matter of "scissors and taste." The editors have done a truly creative job. They begin with a comprehensive and analytical introduction on the art and technique of reporting. They have also given us the historical and professional background of each story —the story behind the story—and they have added whenever necessary the aftermath and the significance. Under their guidance we range from Daniel Defoe, Victor Hugo, Rudyard Kipling, Winston Churchill, and Mark Twain to William Bolitho, John Gunther, Bill Shirer, Walter Duranty, Ernest Hemingway, Quentin Reynolds, John Hersey, Bill Laurence, and Rebecca West. I have named but a few of the immortals of the Fourth Estate whose greatest work is found in these pages.

There are some familiar stories here, and some classics, as well as some surprises. But, in the words of Sir Arthur Quiller Couch, "the best is still the best, though a hundred judges have declared it so."

This work follows the greatest rule of writing (and editing) that was ever laid down—that of the Red Queen in *Alice in Wonderland,* who, when asked how to tell a story, said: "Begin at the beginning, go through to the end and then stop."

The only story which Drs. Snyder and Morris did not include, and which merits attention on the score of its brevity and magnificent condensation, was the two-word story written by St. John in his Gospel, when he said: "Jesus wept." In those two words he told a great deal more than if he had used hundreds of words, because he allied himself to the imagination of his reader; and that is an enormous asset.

Sometimes I hear a newspaperman of the old school * say: "Whatever happened to the art of reporting? Remember?" Now we can truthfully answer that the winnowed best of it, from the sixteenth century to our own day, and from all countries and all media, including broadcasting, is included in this book.

Personally, I don't think reporting is as good now as it used to be. To this perhaps dogmatic and nostalgic generalization there are some notable and distinguished exceptions. Most of them are magnificently represented in this book.

I have been a newspaperman all my life, and a reporter during a large period of my activity. Once when I was so fortunate as to be a guest of Kipling, he said that a good reporter was the noblest work of God; that he wanted always to be known as a reporter, and that, because he thought I was showing promise, he was having me down to his house in Bateman's Burwash. Incidentally, while I was his guest, he never stopped excoriating America, but there was a reason for that, which I shall not go into now. In spite of his anti-Americanism he, too, was a GOOD reporter!

By including British reporting in this collection our authors illustrate

---

* A school located at 63 Park Row, New York.

that one thing British journalism has to teach us. We have independence; we have courage; we have freedom; but, from a mechanistic point of view, they know more about condensation than we do.

The American press tells a story six times: first, in the headlines; second, in the banks of the headlines; third, in the lead; fourth, in the details; fifth, in the captions over the pictures; and sixth, in the pictures themselves. And this list doesn't include the Index.

I think our headlines have gone too far afield. They seek tricks in semantics and fight repetition as though repetition were a plague. Sometimes it is the best way of gaining emphasis.

But, usually, the briefer, the more effective.

Personally, I am inclined to think that what is called in the trade a "label head" is important. Instead of seeking novelty of treatment, an old circulation dodge, I think it would be helpful if the head were to read, for example, "The Hiss Trial," then go on with the news of the day in a subhead. That sort of signpost would help the readers, instead of compelling them to swing through the whole paper for a recognizable symbol. And it would save space.

This is really a serious work and should become a standard textbook. It does not represent hastily considered judgments; it is based on the most thorough search for journalistic importance, effectiveness, and survival value that has been made within my knowledge. It should help make journalism a learned profession, and (see Peter Zenger) help keep it a free one.

I applaud the editors' insistence on "the interrogative state of mind," on "the perceptive faculties," and on "stamina plus an infinite adaptability to all circumstances" as fundamental to the art of good reporting. I commend to all students, practitioners, and teachers of journalism the discerning and inspiring editorial comments and analyses by Professors Snyder and Morris, and their "sense of history."

This book tends, on the whole, to support my view that the reporters are not so resourceful today as they used to be. (I repeat, there are some glorious exceptions to this *obiter dictum,* and the best of them are to be found in this book.)

I think too much emphasis these days is laid upon good writing instead of good getting. There are too many press agents who substitute for the reporter. And in the truer function of the reporter—swarming all over the story and making it wholly his—we had men who made journalistic history. No poll parrots they—no mere echoes of the songs sung by hired hands. They always insisted on seeing the central figure. If not, they would know the reason why! They refused to take "No!" for an answer. And they turned first to the "morgue"—an important step in any story. But it is a practice not always followed today.

That was the best method of obtaining accuracy—the prize element of good journalism. And that quality has been distorted and smeared by those who write with no pretense at verification.

There were giants in those days—and in the Table of Contents of this Treasury, you will find quite a few giants today. If I were stood up against a wall and compelled to answer as to what is the greatest characteristic of good journalism, I would say with my one-time chief *:

"Accuracy, terseness, accuracy." And I would add, as an afterthought, "Accuracy."

Journalism is a priestly mission. It has high dignity. I commend this book to its devotees as a sort of Bible. It will help those already in the ministry and bring proselytes to the service. And it will show why newspaper work is so eternally and so irresistibly seductive.

HERBERT BAYARD SWOPE

August 11, 1949

---

* Joseph Pulitzer, founder of the St. Louis *Post Dispatch* and The New York *World*.

INTRODUCTION

MATTHEW ARNOLD once observed that "journalism is literature in a hurry." Reporting, the very marrow of journalism, may well be considered literature in an even greater hurry. This *Treasury* presents nearly 200 of the greatest examples of reporting. In most cases, they were written under pressure, and yet they have managed to catch that added dimension of history.

Explanatory notes preceding and following each selection may serve to give these stories focus and relationship, to place them in the main stream of world journalism, and to fit the isolated events reported into the pattern of modern times.

A long line of great reporters, beginning with the newsletter writers who recorded notable events in the Age of Discovery and coming down to the reporters for the modern newspaper, world news syndicates, and radio news networks, find their place in this volume. Whether they give us accounts of "enterprise of great pith and moment" or choose to tell us of relatively minor happenings, their reports, vitalized by eloquence and insight, constitute a memorable evocation of historical eras and events. True, the forerunners of Daniel Defoe were preoccupied with witchcraft and the black arts, while the contemporaries of Rebecca West are concerned with atomic fission, but the major occurrences which were the subject of news stories in 1587 would, if they happened today, make the front page.

How the Editors Picked Their Stories

To GUIDE them in making selections of the newspaper, magazine, and radio reporting included in this *Treasury* the editors conducted an extensive poll of city editors, teachers of journalism, and radio newsmen and executives across the country. Pulitzer Prize awards for newspaper reporting, National Headliners' Club awards for radio reporting, and other accolades of the news-gathering profession were also taken into consideration. Plowing through the massive newspaper files of the British Museum, Paris' Bibliothèque Nationale, the Library of Congress, the New York Public Library, the Columbia University Graduate School of Journalism, and various newspaper morgues, the editors have also uncovered a few stories that never won a prize, that nobody recalled, but that yet bear the stamp of greatness upon them. The inclusion of sports, science, and labor stories is a tribute to the recent trend in the direction of news specialization.

Like Alice in Wonderland, the editors would not dream of pursuing white rabbits with pink eyes unless they took watches out of their waistcoat pockets and proceeded to scrutinize them. True, our curiosity has not been whetted by the banal and the commonplace, but at the same time we have tried to avoid overemphasizing the lurid, the sensational, the hostile, and the catastrophic, to refrain from confining our coverage to those that "eat the bread of wickedness and drink the wine of violence." For researchers in newspaper files this course is not the easiest to pursue. When John Milton observed that "evil news rides post, while good news baits," he was remarking upon a phenomenon by no means restricted to the age of Cromwell. As long as people will refuse to see "news" in the law-abiding, the conventional, the average, reporters will stick to the formula of "blood, money, and broads," continuing to fill the hybrid role of thrill purveyors and truth disseminators, serving, as Vincent Sheean so aptly phrases it, as professional observers "at the peep show of misery."

The editors have endeavored to include in this anthology selections that have depth and significance other than momentary. The rise of brutal militarism and the authoritarian state, the fight for freedom and the democratic way of life, the spread of bigotry and the search for tolerance, the respect for human personality in a world of increasing mechanization and centralized control, the struggle for a better economic and social order—these are some of the issues which determined the selection of much of the reportage included between these covers.

Reporting as Literature under Pressure

THE FIRST and most obvious difference between reporting and other types of chronicling is the difference of pace. The reporter must have the ability to produce a rapid-fire story under conditions hardly ideal for creative writing. And to keep doing so. He must carry the burden of unrelenting and monotonous regularity, intensified by the pressure of meeting a deadline. His perceptive powers must be keyed to the fast and exciting pace he has to maintain.

Charles Dickens fondly recalled his youthful newspaper experiences when he was forced to write his stories on the palm of his hand, "by the light of a dark lantern, in a post chaise and four, galloping through a wild country, and through the dead of the night, at the then surprising rate of fifteen miles an hour!" He confessed to having been upset "in almost every description of vehicle known in this country" and bemired on roads many miles from London, stranded in the company of exhausted horses and drunken postboys, with only one idea—meeting his paper's deadline. With a saddle for a seat and his knee for a desk, William Howard Russell, war correspondent of the London *Times,* wrote his story of the charge of the Light Brigade at Balaklava until the candle he used for a light "disappeared in the bottle like a stage demon through a trapdoor."

The change from horse-and-buggy and courier dispatch to jet planes and video has merely stepped up the reportorial pace. While the pressure has not been lifted, its degree varies with the kind of deadline the reporter has to meet. Newsmen for daily papers have to make hair-trigger literary decisions. Reporters for news weeklies or monthlies have time for greater reflection and more polished writing, but, with much of the pressure lifted, their reporting often lacks that impact of immediacy which is carried by top-flight newspaper stories. With the deadline postponed, the reporter has the opportunity to re-create his news event in time perspective, making his selection of essential facts on the basis of occurrences subsequent to the events he narrates. Around this point the reporter ceases to be a newsman and assumes the mantle of Clio. The editors have given priority to stories that carry a sense of urgency, but some pieces have been included that illustrate the work of reporters at less intense pressure levels.

The Perceptive Faculties

THERE IS no simple formula for the reporter who must work under pressure and yet produce a story with staying power. But there are certain essentials it would be disastrous to ignore. To begin with, great reporting must reveal perception, disclose its creator to be the possessor of "the seeing eye and the hearing ear," capable of discerning the deeper implications in the chance event he has witnessed. Vespucci had this perception when he recognized that what he looked upon was a New World, a fact that Columbus died without ever realizing. Schumann had this kind of perception when he hailed Chopin's piano variations on *"Là ci darem"* (which had been coolly received by the critics) with the words, "Hats off, gentlemen, a genius!" Such reportorial perception distinguishes a great novelist like Charles Dickens, who was also a great newspaper reporter. Dickens could discern the bizarre, the humorous, and the tragic in situations that to others seemed commonplace and dull.

Like the scientist-explorer, the critic of the arts, and the novelist, the great reporter must be able to see what is significant and distinctive about the event he is covering. Charles A. Dana demonstrated this kind of perception when he recognized that the June Days of 1848 in Paris were no mere demonstration of class anarchy, but rather the "fanaticism of an idea" galvanized by hunger. When Rebecca West attended the Nuremberg trials she observed that there emanated from the twenty-one Nazi defendants "a smell of corruption." Few are likely to forget her portrait of the banker Schacht in the dock, "A corpse frozen by *rigor mortis* into an attitude which would make it difficult to fit him into his coffin."

That "Interrogative State of Mind"

THE GENERAL PUBLIC, conditioned by the Hollywood stereotype, conceives of the reporter as combining the most acute detective talents of a Sherlock Holmes and the swashbuckling qualities of a D'Artagnan. It is, perhaps, significant that both of these gentlemen were fictional characters. The average reporter, assigned to the humdrum, tedious routine of news gathering, bears little resemblance to these glamorous personages. Nevertheless, although the conventional portrait is highly colored, the mythology has some basis in fact.

Great reporting is the product of what H. G. Wells has happily termed "an interrogative state of mind." The reporter must be constantly on the alert to question, to challenge, to probe. His acute powers of observation must be implemented by that *x* factor—the detective instinct. The *World* reporter who ripped a button off the trousers of Russell Sage's would-be assassin, leading to the culprit's arrest, possessed it. So did Daniel J. Kirwin, the star reporter of the old *Herald* staff. Assigned to cover the murder of the banker John Hawkins, Kirwin found blood on the floor covering, indicating that the corpse had been moved, noted that the banker's blood-stained hat had been hung upon the rack, obviously after the crime, and checked the movements of the victim's nephew, ascertaining that he had been absent from the Union Square Theater for forty-five minutes—time enough to commit the crime. Under the third degree, the nephew broke down and confessed.

This detective instinct has led newsmen into strange situations. Julius Chambers, famous for his stunts as a reporter on the staffs of the *Herald* and the old *World,* heard murder done over the telephone through a chance open wire, a connection that occurred only when the temperature went down to zero. Pursuing this lead, he spent months following abandoned wires, only to discover, when he located the murderer, who had killed his rival for a girl's affections, that evidence heard over the telephone was not admissible in a court of law. When the headless, armless, legless torso of a man was found in the East River, wrapped in oilcloth, Hearst's *Journal* staff went to work to solve the "Guldensuppe mystery." Other dismembered segments of the corpse turned up, each wrapped in a piece of the same oilcloth. From color prints made of this oilcloth pattern thirty members of the *Journal* staff scoured the city and eventually ran down the purchaser. As a result, a former mistress of the victim and her new lover were convicted.

Few newspapermen better exemplified that "interrogative state of mind" than a former managing editor of *The New York Times,* the encyclopedic Carr Van Anda. An accomplished Egyptologist, he set to work to decipher the hieroglyphics on the interior of Tutankhamen's tomb from a news photo. He did not rest until he had exposed certain forgeries on the inscribed slab and deduced from them that Horam-heb had murdered King Tut—not an exceptional incident even in those days. Equally master of Einsteinian physics and National League batting averages, Van Anda had that curiosity and acuteness of eye which stamped him the exceptional newspaperman. A more recent example: when the late S. Burton Heath, crack *World-Telegram* reporter, read a transcript of testimony given by a Federal judge in the surrogate's audit of the accounts of his deceased business partner, his eye noted certain suspicious items. By running these clues down, Heath forced Martin T. Manton, the presiding judge of the United States Circuit Court of Appeals, to resign from the bench. Subsequently that dignitary was sent to the Federal penitentiary.

Stamina Plus "an Infinite Adaptability to All Circumstances"

THE REPORTER must be prepared to take risks, to stay at his post of danger, and at times to operate on his last reserves of adrenalin. From the time, in 1883, when Frank Vizetelly was cut down in the Sudan as "Fuzzy Wuzzy" smashed British defenses, down to the recent murder of George Polk, broadcaster for CBS, killed as he tried to make contact with guerrilla forces in Greece, reporters, notably war correspondents, have found that they have chosen perilous careers. Rudyard Kipling, whose admiration for the courage and stamina of the war correspondent was matched by his contempt for the armchair strategist, summed up the qualities needed for that vocation: "The power of glib speech that neither man nor woman can resist when a meal or a bed is in question, the eye of a horse coper, the skill of a cook, the constitution of a bullock, the digestion of an ostrich, and an infinite adaptability to all circumstances. But many die before they attain to this degree." To send home dispatches included in this *Treasury*, men have risked jungle fever, Minié bullets, perils of the sea and air, and exposure to atomic explosions.

The Ideal of Objectivity

CARRIED AT the masthead of *Niles' Weekly Register*, the great American news magazine of the early nineteenth century, was this appropriate quotation from Shakespeare's *Henry VIII*:

> *I wish no other herald,*
> *No other speaker of my living actions,*
> *To keep mine honor from corruption,*
> *But such an honest chronicler.*

In praising the honest chronicler Shakespeare was paying tribute to the kind of reporting that is fair, accurate, and complete, disciplined by the reporter's own conscience and his awareness of the fact that it will be read by a critical public capable of being persuaded by the truth and of rejecting the bogus article. Admittedly, the ideal of complete objectivity has seldom been achieved either by reporters or by historians. Both types of chroniclers give us their selection of the facts, and every such selection is really subjective. Dr. Samuel Johnson "took care that the Whig dogs should not have the best of it," and many other reporters have been frank partisans. Homer Bigart, Pulitzer-Prize-winning reporter of the *New York Herald Tribune,* writing from behind the Iron Curtain, concedes that, although the reporter is required to "give both sides," the bias "creeps in." *

A century ago newspaper reporters took little pains to disguise their emotional reactions to an event. In its issue of February 18, 1815, Niles' *Register* reported the ending of the War of 1812 with the headline GLORIOUS NEWS and a subhead that was a stanza from *The Star-Spangled Banner.* The story began in this vein: "Who would not be an American? Long live the republic! Peace is signed in the arms of victory." No, clearly Hezekiah Niles was uninfected with the virus of neutrality. Great reporting is written in the midst of stirring action, not from the vantage point of an ivory tower. Once the reporter has determined what is true by sifting the evidence and discarding the false, there is no continuing obligation on his part to remain neutral. The great reporter is a partisan for the truth. The great reporter has a social conscience. In this book the great reporters are not neutral.

We rejoice that Victor Hugo's account of Napoleon the Little's December 4 Massacre constituted a passionate denunciation of "the murder of a people by one man," that young MacGahan could arouse the Western world with something of his own fiery indignation at the Turkish atrocities in Bulgaria, that Richard Harding Davis did not remain any more neutral in thought than did the Germans in action when they invaded Belgium in World War I and conducted themselves in Louvain "like men after an orgy."

Sometimes events are reported while controversy still flames at white heat. While the editors would agree with Lewis Gannett that truth cannot always be discovered "by seeking the mathematical middle ground between heated contestants," they are cognizant of the fact that truth is seldom either black or white, although sensationalists would paint it either way. Accordingly, they have sought to present both sides of many controversial news events. New York newsmen took diametrically opposing views on a vital point in the celebrated duel between Burr and Hamilton. Both accounts are included. The national capital at the time the Bonus Army was smashed seemed to a French reporter, Jules Sauerwein, like ancient Carthage, but to Lee McCardell, an American newspaperman, the routing of the veterans assumed the elements of more intimate, personal tragedy.

No single reporter can give the whole picture of a battle, a flood, a calami-

---

* Joseph G. Herzberg and members of the New York *Herald Tribune* staff, *Late City Editor,* Henry Holt, 1947.

tous fire. The testimony of many observers must be enlisted to re-create so grandiose and staggering a canvas. Waterloo is one of the best examples. Napoleon's personal behavior when disaster confronted him on that occasion is viewed in this book through hostile British eyes and through sympathetic French eyes. Henry Villard's stunning beat at Bull Run, really a preliminary story, is supplemented by William Howard Russell's later and more complete account of the "miserable, causeless panic," which Villard had barely hinted at. Whitelaw Reid clearly recognized Pickett's disastrous charge at Gettysburg for what it was—"a crushing defeat." A Southern reporter tried to retrieve a measure of glory for the Confederacy's dead heroes of that engagement. Accounts have been included of American and Japanese newsmen who reported phases of the recent war in the Pacific in dispatches amusingly at variance.

Techniques of Reporting

ERWIN D. CANHAM, editor of the *Christian Science Monitor,* makes the point that rhetoric is perhaps the least of the requisites for reporting. The most essential obligation of the reporter is to get the story right. Nevertheless, to have staying power great reporting must possess literary quality. Terseness and vitality distinguish such reporting, whose color is obtained without resorting to exaggeration (sports writers excepted, of course!), stooping to the bromidic, or employing fossil phraseology, empty verbiage, too often betraying a poverty of factual information and a lack of reportorial zeal. The kind of reporter we have been on the lookout for is the newsman who, as A. J. Liebling puts it, "uses metaphors as sparingly as a Montclair housewife employs garlic," but, while eschewing words that throb, nonetheless knows "where to find the right part of speech when he has to have it." Even sports writers in recent years, in the opinion of Stanley Woodward, are beginning to see the light and to avoid "the unholy jargon," that tendency to call things by names other than their own.

Over the past hundred years the structure of the news story has undergone drastic modification. It is today a commonplace of American journalism that a news story must illustrate hind-to-end writing. Unlike other literary forms, the climax is at the beginning. The lead, or opening paragraph or paragraphs, gives the reader the essential facts. The body of the story is merely detailed expository material, its paragraph structure a series of separate units without transitions connecting them with what went before or what is to follow, and arranged in decreasing importance. The body of the news story must meet the cutoff test. If at any point after the lead a deletion should be made in the story, the essential facts will still remain.

What is now the sacred cow of journalism was unknown to newsmen before the close of the nineteenth century. Take, for example, the magnificent news dispatch on the charge of the Light Brigade sent in by William

Howard Russell, a star war reporter, from the heights before Sebastopol. It began in leisurely style:

> If the exhibition of the most brilliant valor, of the excess of courage, and of a daring which could have reflected luster on the best days of chivalry can afford full consolation for the disaster of today, we can have no reason to regret the melancholy loss which we sustained in a contest with a savage and barbarian enemy.

Then Russell proceeded to describe the various phases of the battle, and, not until the very last paragraph, do we get a full realization of the catastrophic nature of the losses suffered by the 607 sabers of the Light Cavalry Brigade. Yet the story meets the basic criteria of editors today. It provides all the facts from every available source, and answers the traditional five reporter's questions: Who? What? When? Where? Why? Most important, from beginning to climactic concluding tabulation, it holds the reader's attention unflagging.

Another experienced reporter, Henry Morton Stanley, started off his dispatch announcing his discovery of Livingstone by reflecting upon how his prospects had improved in the course of the last two months of his African journey. Then came the electric sentence: "And the only answer to it all is Livingstone, the hero traveler, is alongside of me." But for the details of the perilous trip, we must read a long recital. The classic dialogue of the encounter between Stanley and Livingstone is reserved for the very last lines of the story. By postponing the answer to many questions about the course of his adventure Stanley maintained an atmosphere of tension down to the account of the climactic meeting at the very end of the dispatch.

These older techniques, still widely observed in British journalism, were geared to the gaslight era. But they were at times abused. The *New York Tribune* reporter of the Sullivan-Corbett fight in New Orleans in 1892 who wrote 2500 words or more before he said who won must have been a direct cause of the revolution in the technique of news writing. By the time of the Spanish-American War the modern news story, with its conventional lead and body structure, was widely used.

The lead has been aptly described by John C. Rogers, a *Herald Tribune* staff man, as "a sort of come-on. Like a woman's eyes or a barker's line, the lead must invite interest or the suitors and customers may turn away." The normal approach is the summary lead that gives the gist of the story. "Four men were killed and eighty-four persons went to hospitals with gunshot wounds, cracked heads, broken limbs, or other injuries received in a battle late this afternoon between police and steel strikers at the gates of the Republic Steel Corporation plant in South Chicago." This was the lead for *The New York Times* account of the Memorial Day Massacre in 1937. Gene Currivan started his *Times* story of the forced tour at Buchenwald in this fashion: "German civilians—1200 of them—were brought from the neighboring city of Weimar today to see for themselves the horror, brutality, and human indecency perpetrated against their 'neighbors' at the infamous Buchenwald concentration camp. They saw sights that brought tears to their eyes, and scores of them, including German nurses, just fainted away."

To avoid stuffiness and monotony reporters have found it expedient to introduce variations of the conventional lead, the most electrifying of these innovations being the cartridge lead effective in big stories. "The old San Francisco is dead" was the way Will Irwin began his account of the great earthquake. Jack Lait's story, leading off with these words : "John Dillinger, ace bad man of the world, got his last night—two slugs through the heart and one through the head," was calculated to hold the reader to the text as effectively as contact with a third rail. Or let us consider the lead for *Time* magazine's story on Pearl Harbor : "The U. S. Navy was caught with its pants down. Within one tragic hour—before the war had really begun—the U. S. appeared to have suffered greater losses than in the whole of World War I." Occasionally a direct quotation at the start can galvanize reader interest. "Herman Rosenthal has squealed again." What all the plunderworld was whispering served as the terse opening of Herbert Bayard Swope's sensational exposé of Police Lieutenant Becker's plot to murder a gambler.

Current fashions in news reporting indicate a perceptible trend away from the unimaginative application of the hind-to-end technique and the cutoff test, and the return to the literary styles of Messrs. Russell and Stanley. Not only is this true of news-magazine writers like John Hersey and Rebecca West, but the symptoms are manifest in the work of some of the best of contemporary newspaper reporters. "Here is the first and only eyewitness report on the opening chapter of the British expeditionary troops' advance in Norway south of Trondheim. It is a bitterly disillusioning and almost unbelievable story." With these words Leland Stowe launched into a superb account of British frustration in Norway and more than fulfilled the promise of his lead, but one has to read the entire story to get all the facts.

The same rules for writing a news story do not apply to the "feature" story, where the reporter takes a detail, perhaps from a major news story, and stresses "angles," often emotional or humorous, with the idea of both informing and entertaining. While the great bulk of reporting pieces in this anthology are news stories, "feature" stories are represented by such pieces as Ned Ward's account of his visits to Bedlam and Bridewell, the exposé by Harold Littledale of the *New York Post* of abuses in New Jersey's state prisons, and Alexander Woollcott's account of how Verdun Belle found her own. Nor do the conventional rules govern the interview story, where the reporter emphasizes what is said rather than what happens. Specimens of the art of reporting an interview have been culled from the writings of such experts as Horace Greeley and Frank Ward O'Malley of *The Sun*.

Sometimes, as in the case of the London *Daily Telegraph*'s interview with the Kaiser, the publication of the interview story can have a perceptible impact on historical forces.

No inconsiderable portion of great reporting is fortuitous, the result of the opportunity to be a spectator at the ringside of great events, some known in advance, for which preparations can be made, some tremendously unexpected. When the latter situation arises, the reporter must be equal to the emergency. On May 6, 1937, young Herbert Morrison stood behind a WSL sound truck at Lakehurst to describe the arrival of the dirigible *Hindenburg*. He started in a matter-of-fact way: "It is practically standing still now." Then he shouted: "It bursts into flames! It's falling on the mooring mast! It's one of the worst catastrophes in the world!" The rest was incoherent. Morrison was too hysterical to tell the whole story.

Many newsmen feel that the "treadmill stuff" is often a truer test of real reportorial talent. With this in mind we have given space in this anthology to some pieces that illustrate what Dwight Marvin of the Troy *Record* calls "the genius of small incidents, made great by great writers"—the sort of situation that a Charles Dickens or a Meyer Berger could handle superbly.

Genuflections to the Omitted

IN COMPILING this anthology of representative reporting and reporters the editors have omitted some outstanding stories, some through oversight, some through choice. News accounts, quoting eyewitness testimony, but largely nonnarrative in form, have not been selected. Nor have narrative accounts been included of events that never came off. We fought off the temptation to include Dr. Johnson's report for *The Gentleman's Magazine* of a notable speech in the House of Commons that the elder Pitt never made. Johnson blandly confessed: "That speech I wrote in a garret in Exeter Street. I never was in the gallery of the House of Commons but once." Boswell's hero, informally reporting Parliamentary debates and manufacturing eloquent speeches of political leaders at a time when official reports were forbidden, relied upon others for on-the-spot coverage. Reporting in similar vein has been attributed to the notorious Finnerty, whose fascinating account of Wilberforce's eulogy of the Irish potato is hilarious reading. But this speech was concocted out of whole cloth.

Despite their melodramatic appeal, hoaxes and stunts have been kept out of this anthology, even the notorious "moon hoax" of R. A. Locke, a reporter for the New York *Sun*, professing to give an account of the inhabitants of the moon, based on discoveries reported as having been made by Sir John Herschel at the Cape of Good Hope (1836). James Gordon Bennett, Jr., the thrill purveyor of his generation, devoted the entire front page of his November 9, 1874, issue of *The New York Herald* to an account of the sensational escape of the wild animals from the Central Park zoo. The reporter told of "awful combats between the beasts and the citizens," described "terrible scenes of mutilation," and headlines screamed : A SHOCKING SABBATH CARNIVAL OF DEATH. The hero of that occasion was Tammany's archfoe, Governor Dix, who, symbolically, shot a Bengal tiger on the streets of the town, while lions, leopards, and other jungle beasts were reported still at large. Persistent readers who read to the end of the account found out : "The entire story given above is a pure fabrication. Not one word of it is true." To readers of tales of our Atomic Age truth is indeed stranger than fiction, and the hoax no longer has the supreme fascination of an earlier day. While a hoax, then, may not be considered news, its impact may very well make news, and, accordingly, the *Treasury* allots space to an account of the panic that gripped the nation when Orson Welles led a Martian invasion of New Jersey that never materialized beyond the air waves.

An entire anthology could well be devoted to coverage of gossip reporting, not represented in this book. From the announcement in the London *Morning Post* in 1787 that the Prince of Wales' arrival at Brighton had "frightened away a number of old maids who used constantly to frequent that place!" down to the assiduity of American news magazinemen in ferreting out the details of the romance that culminated in the abdication of Edward VIII for "the woman I love," gossip reporting has enlisted some high-level talent. "You, sir, thrive by scandal and live by defamation," someone fairly charged an early English editor. Oliver Goldsmith was even more explicit. To him most reporters of his day were collectors of gossip. "They only collect their materials from the oracle of some coffeehouse, which oracle has himself gathered them the night before from a beau at a gaming table, who has pillaged his knowledge from a great man's porter, who had had his information from the great man's gentleman, who has invented the whole story for his own amusement the night preceding." Substitute Stork Club for coffeehouse and press agent for gentleman's gentleman, and you have identified quite a few current gossip outlets.

No more brilliant gossip reporter ever lived than Benjamin Disraeli, whose newspaper work in the 1830's aroused wide attention. Hedda Hopper and Louella Parsons had their counterparts in the Countess of Jersey and the Duchess of Sutherland, immortalized in Disraeli's last novel, *Endymion.* Once when the Duchess' rival entered a Mayfair drawing room one feline stooge of la Sutherland said in a very audible whisper : "You must be careful what you say before Lady Jersey. She reports for the papers."

The present anthology does not encompass the areas of reporting that critically evaluate creative effort, whether in the fields of music, the arts, literature, or the theater. Such critics are not really reporters, but in fact judges handing down decisions based upon the aesthetic standards of their day. It required great will power to omit George Bernard Shaw's account of how Eugène Ysaÿe was forced to play encores at the end of a violin recital ("He threw a bunch of thistles to the donkeys") or Dorothy Parker's summation of a Katharine Hepburn effort ("She ran the gamut of emotions from A to B"), or Hanslick's account of the performance of Wagner's *Die Meistersinger,* in which the composer's archenemy is portrayed as the ridiculous Beckmesser ("inextricable confusion—a composition painfully mannered and positively brutal in its effect"). We shall always relish the Baltimore *Sun*'s reference to the forthcoming appearance in 1837 of Paganini, the world-renowned violinist. "The man is a good fiddler beyond a doubt," that journal grudgingly conceded, "but there are some stories connected with the morality of Paganini which do not make him a second Joseph by a long shot."

Was Reporting "Better Then"?

FOR SEVERAL YEARS the editors have lived in the company of great reporting and have found no evidence indicating that the art is senescent. They cannot endorse the view of so recent a commentator as Ward Greene, who feels that reporting stories of our own day fail usually to "stand up," that newspaper stories were "better then." True, for bravura reporting few of the present generation can equal a Victor Hugo, a Russell, a Forbes, or a Richard Harding Davis. Nor do the current run of news stories sound quite the lurid note of the effusions of the roaring twenties, *The Front Page* era of Ben Hecht and Charles MacArthur. The cheering news is that rhetorical pyrotechnics and raucous sentimentality are disappearing from the better grade of news stories. Today reporters write with greater subtlety and depth than did most of their predecessors. They are better grounded in scientific and technical matters. They have better linguistic equipment when working in foreign countries, and they have by no means lost the touch for finding the social pulsebeat in their stories.

The generation that knew Dickens would take Rebecca West's London folk to their hearts. Something of the crusading ardor of a Horace Greeley or a Ray Stannard Baker still fires a John Gunther. Rudyard Kipling and Winston Churchill would recognize the hand of the master in A. D. Divine's story of Dunkirk. "Bull Run" Russell would tip his silk hat to Leland Stowe for his account of fiasco in Norway and to A. B. Austin for his reporting of the Dieppe raid, and the great Creelman would find history repeating itself in A. T. Steele's reporting of the rape of Nanking. The kind of detective ingenuity that A. B. Macdonald, reporter for the *Kansas City Star,* demonstrated in cracking a murder in Amarillo is guaranteed to elicit a "bravo" from Herbert Bayard Swope. Sweat and sacrifice and heroism still live in the news stories of an Ernest Hemingway, a Quentin Reynolds, and a Robert J. Casey.

Today's men and women of the working press are as responsive to the challenge of great events as were the star reporters of an earlier day. In the final analysis history is news reporting in slow motion. The reporter who seeks out the evidence at first hand is marching with the shock troops in the battalions of truth. He has "loosed the fateful lightning of a terrible, swift sword"—the truth that shall make men free.

THE EDITORS

July 15, 1949

Note for the Second Edition

This second edition of *A Treasury of Great Reporting* includes examples of superb reportage from the days of the Berlin Blockade to the recent trial of Adolph Eichmann in Jerusalem. The reporters of the Nuclear Space Age still live as dangerously as their predecessors. They still tell of stirring events, and they still manage to quicken the conscience of mankind. Although television has added an extra dimension to newscasting and commentary, it has, by making the news more personal and more immediate, heightened the interest of the general public in serious newspaper reporting in depth. The pieces that have been added to this anthology largely fall into this category. Like Relman Morin's report from Little Rock or A. M. Rosenthal's account of his visit to Auschwitz, these stories come to grips with moral issues, with human rights, with the elementary decencies for which a democratic society must continue to fight.

—LOUIS L. SNYDER
—RICHARD B. MORRIS

July 1, 1961

Pioneer Newsletter Correspondents of Modern Times Report the Evil and Lustful Confessions of a Midnight Sorceress

THE INVENTION of printing made the multiplication of copies a profitable business, and the reporting of news spread rapidly on the European continent. Before the newspaper was evolved, newssheets, reporting in letter form important events on both an international and a local plane, were widely circulated. Such newsletters appeared in Italy, Germany, and the Netherlands several generations before they were common in England. Columbus' great letter of 1493 announcing the results of his first expedition was distributed as a news broadside, as was the account of the naval victory over the Turks at Lepanto and the disaster to the Spanish Armada. With the first decade of the sixteenth century a continuous stream of newssheets poured from the presses on the Continent.

Pre-eminent in Europe for its news-gathering service was the house of Fugger, the great German banking firm, with its headquarters at Augsburg, which kept itself posted on world events by newsletters sent by correspondents from remote corners of the globe. Their international business connections assured the Fuggers inside information from politicians and clerics alike. News came through to them with amazing rapidity and was even smuggled through the lines of opposing armies. Amounting to a sort of Kiplinger service, these newsletters either were based on direct eyewitness reporting or were rewrites of published reports collected by those diligent forerunners of Reuters * and the Associated Press—two alert Augsburgers named Jeremias Crasser and his successor, Jeremias Schiffle.

Of the numerous newsletters that have survived in the Fugger collection at the Vienna National Library, perhaps the most engrossing is a firsthand account of the trial and confession in 1587 of Walpurga Hausmännin, a Dillingen midwife accused of practicing witchcraft for some thirty years and of being in league with the devil. To understand the state of mind that prompted this confession and the guillibility of those who acted upon it one would need the insight of Freud and the statistics of Kinsey. This Fugger newsletter, somewhat condensed, is translated from the original German.

---

* The first of the great collecting and distributing news agencies, founded by Julius Reuter, a Prussian, in 1849.

The witch Walpurga is tried and sentenced
for her wanton rendezvous with the devil

Victor von Klarwill, ed., *Fuggerzeitungen* (Vienna, 1923)

Walpurga Hausmännin, evil and wretched woman, now imprisoned and in chains, has, under solicitous questioning as well as torture, confessed her witchcraft and made the following admissions.

When, some thirty-one years ago, she had become a widow, she cut corn for Hans Schlumperger, of this town [Dillingen], along with his former servant named Bis im Pfarrhof. The latter she enticed with lewd speeches and gestures, and the pair agreed to meet, on a designated night, in her dwelling, there to indulge in lustful intercourse. However, when Walpurga sat at night in her chamber, awaiting him and thinking evil and fleshly thoughts, it was not the bound servant who turned up, but rather the Evil One, who, in the latter's guise and raiment, proceeded to indulge in fornication with her. Then he gave her a piece of money that looked like a thaler, but no one would accept it of her, for it was a bad coin and like lead. So she threw it away. After the act of fornication, she saw and felt the cloven foot of her whoremonger and observed that his hand was not natural but appeared to be made of wood. Scared out of her wits, she called upon the name of Jesus, upon which the Devil left her and vanished.

The very next night the Evil Spirit visited her again in the same shape and whored with her. He made her many promises to help her in her poverty and need, for which reason she yielded herself up to him body and soul. Thereafter the Evil One made a scratch below her left shoulder, demanding that she should sell her soul to him with the blood that had flown therefrom. He gave her a quill and, as she could not write, guided her hand. This script the Devil took with him, and whenever her thoughts assumed a pious character or she longed to attend church the Devil reminded her of it.

Furthermore, Walpurga confesses that she often rode on a pitchfork by night with her paramour and that at such devilish trysts she met a big man with a gray beard who sat in a chair like a great prince and was richly attired. This was the Great Devil, to whom she once more dedicated herself body and soul. Once when she heedlessly pronounced the name of Jesus, the Great Devil struck her in the face and (dreadful to relate) forced her to renounce God, Christianity, the saints, and the holy sacraments. Thereupon the Great Devil baptized her anew, naming her Höfelin, and her devil paramour, Federlin.

At these diabolical assignations she ate, drank, and slept with her paramour. Because she would not allow him to drag her along everywhere, he beat her cruelly. For food she often had a good roast or an innocent child, also well roasted, or a sucking pig, with red and white wine, but no salt.* Her paramour, Federlin, visited her in many different places in order to

---

* Supposed to be anathema to the Devil and witches alike.

cohabit with her, even in the street by night and while she lay in prison. She further confessed that her paramour gave her salves in a little box with which to injure people, animals, and even the precious fruit of the field.

Federlin compelled her to do away with young infants at birth, even before they had been taken to holy baptism. This she did whenever she had the chance. Her victims:

1 and 2. About ten years ago she had rubbed Anna Hämännin, who lived not far from Durstigel, with her salve on the occasion of her first childbirth and also otherwise so damaged her that mother and child remained together and died.

3. Dorothea, the stepdaughter of Christian Wachter, bore her first child ten years before. At its birth she applied pressure on its little brain so that it died. The Devil had specially bidden her to destroy the first-born.

[Forty other victims are cited in the confession.]

She rubbed with her salve and caused the death of Lienhart Geilen's three cows, Bruchbauer's horse, Max Petzel's cow two years ago, and Duri Striegel's cow three years ago [among others]. In short, she confessed to having destroyed a large number of cattle over and above these. A year ago she found bleached linen on the common and rubbed it with her salve, so that the pigs and geese ran over it and perished shortly thereafter.

Walpurga confessed that every year since she sold herself to the Devil she has on Saint Leonard's Day exhumed at least one or two innocent children. With her devil paramour and other companions she has eaten these and used their hair and their little bones for witchcraft. The other children she had slain at birth she was unable to

exhume because they had been baptized. The bones of these little children she employed to manufacture hail. Had not God mercifully prevented her, she would have caused still more and greater evils, Walpurga admitted.

After hearing this confession, the Judges and Jury of the Court of this Town of Dillingen, by virtue of the Imperial Prerogative and Rights of his Right Reverence, Herr Marquard, Bishop of Augsburg and Provost of the Cathedral, our most gracious Prince and Lord, finally returned a unanimous verdict that Walpurga Hausmännin was convicted under common law and the criminal code of the Emperor Charles V of the Holy Roman Empire of being an evil and notorious witch and sorceress and that she be punished and dispatched from life to death by burning at the stake. All her goods, chattels, and estate were condemned to the Treasury of our Most High Prince and Lord.

She was sentenced to be led, seated in a cart to which she is tied, to the place of execution, her body first to be torn five times with red-hot irons. The first time, outside the Town Hall, in the left breast and the right arm. The second time, at the lower gate, in the right breast. The third time, at the mill brook outside the hospital gate, in the left arm. The fourth time, at the place of execution, in the left hand. Considering that the condemned was a licensed and pledged midwife of the city of Dillingen for nineteen years and yet acted so vilely, her right hand, with which she did such knavish tricks, is to be cut off at the place of execution. After the burning her ashes are not to remain lying on the ground, but are to be carried to the nearest stream and dumped therein.

THE WITCH WALPURGA was burned at the stake at Dillingen on September 20, 1587. For more than a hundred years to come Europe and the New World as well were to be in the grip of the witchcraft frenzy. African natives, Pennsylvania "hex" women, and swastika-worshiping Nazis attest the power of the belief in sorcery and magic in the world of the twentieth century. A sensational twentieth-century example was the trial of John Blymyer in York County, Pennsylvania, reported by Dudley Nichols for the New York *World*, January 7 and 8, 1929. The child of an unlettered household, John claimed that he had been "powwowed for 'stummick fever' when a boy, and had seen his father break an evil spell on the bony family horse by cutting a tuft of hair from its tail and burning it in the fireplace." When he sought to take a lock of hair from an elderly farmer whom he believed to have hexed him, the latter resisted, and Blymyer killed him. Blymyer was sentenced to life imprisonment. "And thus have the powers of darkness been routed and the name of York kept fair," concluded Dudley Nichols.

A Reporter for *The London Spy* Finds Bedlam "an Almshouse for Madmen, a Showing Room for Whores, and a Sure Market for Lechers"

THE PERSONAL and intimate note in reporting was slow to appear in English journalism. The first English newspaper, the *London Gazette*,* was really a vehicle for official state papers, and the editorship was a government appointment. It was not until the overthrow of James II in 1688 that newspapers became an important factor in the life of the English people. Some newsmen, like Samuel Buckley, editor of *The Daily Courant*, and Daniel Defoe, publisher of *The Review*, were principally concerned either with reporting the more important political events of the day or with writing editorialized commentaries. There was room for another kind of reporting, reporting concerned less with events than with exposés of social and economic conditions. One of the pioneers in this field was Ned Ward, whose alehouse view of English social conditions titillated an entire generation. The success that greeted Ward's *Trip to Jamaica* encouraged him to undertake writing as a career. His newspaper, *The London Spy,* which appeared at monthly intervals between 1698 and 1700, caught fire at once. In an age when newsmen were little more than retailers of random information, Ward's paper proved him to be a master of anecdote and dialogue, an amazing reporter of the casual and picaresque. Audacious, impudent, and bawdy, Ward, a predecessor of Defoe, Addison, and Steele, had more in common with the modern gossip columnist, on the one hand, and the twentieth-century muckrakers, on the other, than with the more solid literary figures of eighteenth-century journalism.

Ward wrote to make money, and he made enough to buy himself a tavern. "The condition of an author is much like that of a strumpet," he complained. "The unhappy circumstances of a narrow fortune hath forced us to do that for our subsistence, which we are much ashamed of." His incisive portraits of vagrants, underworld characters, and alehouse patrons are comparable to Hogarth's later engravings. In his *Southwark Fair* Hogarth depicts an amazing collection of strolling theatrical people, gambling women, monkeys, bagpipers, trapeze artists, fire-eaters, and wrestlers. He sketches the rogue directing a country cousin while robbing him of his handkerchief and the artful villain decoying a couple of unthinking country girls to their ruin. There is much in Hogarth that was anticipated by Ned Ward in re-

---

* This paper originally appeared in 1665 as the *Oxford Gazette*.

porting his earlier tours through Bedlam,* London's notorious insane asylum and one of the world's oldest mental institutions, and Bridewell, a workhouse for the indolent and for petty criminals. Ward's pen portraits of alehouse customers—dinner spongers, cook teasers, pan soppers, plate twirlers, table whittlers, and spoon pinchers—contributed a truly Hogarthian argot to English journalism. The pioneer London reporter seemed to delight in writing of pimps and panders, thieves and chimneysweeps, informers and brothelkeepers, "spewed out of alleys, jails and garrets," and "liquored well with foggy ale."

Ward's accounts of Bedlam and Bridewell appeared, respectively, in the January and April, 1699, issues of *The London Spy*. In his first story Ned Ward tells us of a trip he took with a companion through London, going down toward Billingsgate, then over toward the docks, "where some salt water slaves, according to their well-bred custom, were pelting the sons of whores at one another, about the birth of their oyster boats." Then Ward visited the government office where servants for the plantations bound themselves to a term of service in America to pay their passage across the seas. Passing various other oddities on the way, Ward relates:

"Hell in an uproar"

The London Spy, January, 1699

Thus we prattled away our time, till we came in sight of a noble pile of building, which diverted us from our former discourse, and gave my friend the occasion of asking me my thoughts of this magnificent edifice. I told him I conceived it to be my Lord Mayor's palace, for I could not imagine so stately a structure could be designed for any quality inferior. He smiled at my innocent conjecture, and informed me this was *Bedlam,* a hospital for madfolk.

"In truth," said I, "I think they were mad that built so costly a college for such a crackbrained society."

"Come," [said his friend], "let us take a walk in, and view its insides."

Accordingly, we were admitted in through an iron gate, within which sat a brawny Cerberus of an indigo color, leaning upon a money box. We turned in through another iron barricade, where we heard such a rattling of chains, drumming of doors, ranting, hollering, singing, and running that I could think of nothing but Don Quevedo's vision,† where *the damned broke loose, and put hell in an uproar.*

The first whimsy-headed wretch of this lunatic family that we observed was a merry fellow in a straw cap,

---

* The term "Bedlam" is a corruption of Bethlehem, for Bedlam was originally a priory of the order of the Star of Bethlehem that was later converted into a hospital for lunatics.

† A reference to *The Visions* of Francisco Gómez de Quevedo y Villegas (1580–1645), a picaresque work translated into English by Sir Roger L'Estrange. Quevedo's third vision of Pluto's Lairs, or Hell, obviously inspired this passage.

who was talking to himself after this manner: that he had an army of eagles at his command. Then, clapping his hand upon his head, swore by his crown of moonshine he would battle all the stars in the skies but he would have some claret. In this interim came a gentleman to stare at him with a red face.

"No wonder," said his Aerial Majesty, "claret is so scarce. Look, there's a rogue who carries more in his nose than I, that am Prince of the Air, have had in belly this twelvemonth!"

"If you are Prince of the Air," said I, "why don't you command the Man in the Moon to give you some?" To which he replied:

"The Man in [the] Moon is a sorry rascal. I sent to him for a dozen bottles but the other day, and he swore by his bush his cellar had been dry this six months. But I'll be even with the rogue. I expect a cloud laden with claret to be sent to me by the sun every day. And if a spoonful of lees would save him from choking, the old drunken whore's-bird should not have a drop."

Another was holding forth with as much vehemence against kingly government as a brother of Commonwealth Doctrine rails against plurality of living. I told him he deserved to be hanged for talking of treason.

"Now," says he, "you're a fool, we madmen have as much privilege of speaking our minds within these walls as an ignorant dictator, when he spews out his nonsense to the whole parish. Prithee, come and live here, and you may talk what you will, and nobody will call you to question for it. Truth is persecuted everywhere abroad, and flies hither for sanctuary, where she

sits as safe as a knave in a church, or a whore in a nunnery. I can use her as I please, and that is more than you dare do. I can tell great men such bold truths as they don't love to hear, without the danger of a whipping post; and that you can't do. *For if ever you see a madman hanged for speaking truth, or a lawyer whipped for lying, I'll be bound to prove my cap a wheelbarrow.*"

We then took a walk into the Women's Apartment, to see what whimsical fegaries their wandering fancies would have them to entertain us withal.

The first that we looked in upon stood standing with her back against the wall, crying:

"Come, John, come. Your master's gone to 'Change. I believe the poor fool's afraid of forfeiting his indentures.* Did you ever see the like? Why, sure you won't serve your mistress so, John, will you? Hark, hark, run, you rogue; your master's come back to shop. Yes, you shall have a wife, you old rogue, with seven hundred pounds, and be married six years, and not get a child. Fie for shame, out upon't! A husband for a woman! A husband for the devil! Hang you! Rot you! Sink you! Confound you!"

And thus at last she ran raving on, to the highest degree of madness.

Having pretty well tired ourselves with the frantic humors and rambling ejaculations of the madfolk, we took a turn to make some few remarks upon the looseness of the spectators, amongst whom we observed abundance of intriguing. Mistresses we found were to be had of all ranks, qualities, colors, prices, and sizes from the velvet scarf to the Scotch-

---

* The written contract binding an apprentice might be forfeited for misconduct on his part.

plaid petticoat. Commodities of all sorts went off, for there wanted not a suitable Jack for every Jill. Every fresh-comer was soon engaged in an amour. Though they came in single, they went out by pairs. 'Tis a new Whet-Stones Park, now the old one is plowed up, where a sportsman at any hour in the day may meet with game for his purpose. 'Tis a convenience to London, as the Long Cellar to Amsterdam, where any stranger may purchase a purge for his reins at a small expense, and may have a pox by chance flung into the bargain.

All that I can say of it is this: *'Tis an almshouse for madmen, a showing room for whores, a sure market for lechers, and a dry walk for loiterers.*

* * *

The London Spy, April, 1699

We then turned into the gate of a stately edifice my friend told me was Bridewell, which to me seemed rather a prince's palace rather than a house of correction, till gazing round me, I saw in a large room a parcel of ill-looking mortals stripped to their shirts like haymakers, pounding a pernicious weed, which I thought, from their unlucky aspects, seemed to threaten their destruction.

"These," said I to my friend, "I suppose are the offenders at work. Pray what do you think their crimes may be?"

"Truly," said he, "I cannot tell you. But if you have a mind to know, ask any of them their offense, and they will soon satisfy you."

"Prithee, friend," said I to a surly bull-necked fellow who was thumping as lazily at his wooden anvil as a ship carpenter at a log in the King's yard at Deptford, "what are you confined to this labor for?"

My hempen operator, leering over his shoulder, cast at me one of his hanging looks, which so frightened me I stepped back for fear he should have knocked me on the head with his beetle.

"Why, if you must know, Mr. Tickle-Tail," says he, taking me, as I believe, being in black, for some country pedagogue, "I was committed hither by Justice Clodpate, for saying I had rather hear a blackbird whistle Walsingham, or a peacock scream against foul weather, than a parson talk nonsense in a church, or a fool talk Latin in a coffeehouse. And I'll be judged by you, that are a man of judgment, whether in all I said there be one word of treason to deserve whipping post."

The impudence of this canary bird so dashed me out of countenance, together with his unexpected answer, that like a man surfeited with his mistress' favors, I had nothing to say, but heartily wished myself well out of their company.

Going from the workroom to the common side, or place of confinement, where they are locked up each night, through the frightful grates of which uncomfortable apartment a ghastly skeleton stood peeping, that from his terrible aspect, *I thought some power immortal had imprisoned death, that the world might live forever.*

I could not speak to him without dread of danger, lest when his lips opened to give him an answer, he should poison the air with his contagious breath, and communicate to me the same pestilence which had brought his infected body to a dismal anatomy. Yet moved with pity towards so sad an object, I began to inquire into the causes of his sad appearance, who, after a penitential look that called for mercy and compassion, with much difficulty he raised his feeble voice a degree above silence. [He] told me he had been sick six weeks under that sad confinement, and had nothing to comfort him but bread and water, with now and then the refreshment of a little small beer.

I asked him further what offense he had committed that brought him under this unhappiness. To which he answered he had been a great while discharged of all that was charged against him, and was detained only for his fees, which, for want of friends, being a stranger to the town, he was totally unable to raise. I asked him what his fees amounted to. He told me:

"Five groats."

"Bless me," thought I, "what a rigorous uncharitable thing is this, that so noble a gift, intended when first given to so good an end, should be thus perverted! And what was designed to prevent peoples falling into misery, through laziness or ill courses, should now be corrupted by such unchristian confinement as to starve a poor wretch because he wants money to satisfy the demands of a mercenary Cerberus, when discharged of the prison by the court on such severe, nay barbarous, usage, is a shame to our laws, and unhappiness to our nation, and a scandal to Christianity."

From thence we turned into the Women's Apartment. We followed our noses, and walked up to take a view of the ladies, who we found were shut up as close as nuns, but, like so many slaves, were under the care and direction of an overseer, who walked about with a very flexible weapon of offense to correct such hempen journeywomen who were unhappily troubled with the spirit of idleness. These smelled as frowzily as so many goats in a Welsh gentleman's stable, or rather a litter of pis-tail children under the care of a parish nurse. They looked with as much modesty as so many Newgate saints canonized at the Old Bailey.

"Pray, sir," says one of them. "You look very wistfully at us. What do you think of us?"

"Why, truly," said I, "I think you have done something to deserve this punishment, or else you would not be here."

"If you'll believe me without blushing, I'll tell you the truth. I happened to live with an old rogue of a haberdasher, and when my mistress was out of the way, he used to tickle my lips with a pen feather. At last she caught us and had me before Justice Overdoe, who committed me hither, where I have had more lashes of my back than ever my belly deserved."

"Don't believe her, master," cries another. "She's as arrant a strumpet as ever earned her living at twopence a bout, and was committed hither for lying so long on her back that her rump grew to the bedclothes till she could not rise again."

My friend reconducted me back into the first quadrangle, and led me up a pair of stairs into a spacious chamber, where the court was sat [*sic*] in great grandeur and order—a grave gentleman, whose awful looks bespoke him some honorable citizen, being mounted in the judgment seat, armed with a hammer, like a 'change broker at Lloyd's Coffee House, and a woman under the lash in the next room, where the folding doors were opened, that the whole court might view the punishment. At last, down went the hammer, and the scourging ceased. Till I was undeceived, I thought that it sold there lashes by auction.

"Now," says my friend, "pray give me your thoughts of what you have seen, whether you think this sort of correction is a proper method to re-form women from their vicious prac-tices or not?"

"Why truly," said I, "if I must de-liver my opinion, according to my real sentiments, I only conceive it may make many whores, but that it can in no measure reclaim them."

[Ward declared that correction of this sort exposed young people unnec-essarily to shame, that it was indecent to expose the naked bodies of wom-en to the sight of men and boys, and that, since women's constitutions were weaker, it was not right to punish them like dogs.]

"I believe," replied my friend, "you are aiming to curry favor with the fair sex. This lecture to a town lady, if you had a mind to be wicked, would save you money in your pocket, though, in-deed, what you have urged seems no more than reasonable."

ESSENTIALLY SUPERFICIAL and shallow in his reporting, Ward nonetheless in these two excerpts revealed the tragic plight of the mentally unstable and the unfortunate lot of the unemployed of his day. In portraying the ghastly skeleton confined to a cell for failure to discharge inconsequential prison fees, *The London Spy* reporter was striking a blow against imprisonment for debt, a cause which had the journalist Defoe's wholehearted support. Charles Dickens, a great English reporter of a later century, gives us, in his *American Notes,* a picture of an American insane asylum that reveals how slight, if any, was the improvement in the care and treatment of the men-tally ill. He beheld "the moping idiot, cowering down with long disheveled hair ; the gibbering maniac with his hideous laugh and pointed finger ; the vacant eye, the fierce wild face, the gloomy picking of the hands and lips, and munching of the nails. There they were all without disguise, in naked ugliness and horror."

Equally memorable was the visit of a British reporter, William Howard Russell, to the New Orleans jail, which he found a "crowded and noisome place," where hardened criminals rubbed elbows with petty offenders, and debtors vied for attention with female lunatics "with disheveled hair and torn clothes," who, "with indecent gestures, were yelling to the wretched men opposite to them."

"The shame of the states" is the way the New York *Star*'s science editor, Albert Deutsch, has only recently characterized the treatment of the men-tally ill in America, after visiting thirty mental hospitals. In contrast, Deutsch found modern Bedlam "one of the finest hospitals I have ever seen, with the luxury service provided in a luxurious setting. Would that our so-called Bedlams in the U. S. A. even approximated it in service to patients."

Daniel Defoe and Dr. Johnson Interview

Some Ghosts

IN *The Gathering Storm* (1948) Winston Churchill pays tribute to the remarkable vitality of Daniel Defoe's reportorial techniques. "I have followed, as in previous volumes," writes Churchill, "as far as I am able, the method of Defoe's *Memoirs of a Cavalier* (1724), in which the author hangs the chronicle and discussion of great military and political events upon the thread of the personal experiences of an individual." Defoe, generally acknowledged to be the father of modern journalism, combined his reportorial gift with the fighting heart of a pamphleteer. The founder in 1704 of *The Review,* which thrice weekly inveighed against the evils of imprisonment for debt and bitingly satirized religious bigotry and political chicanery, and the creator of *Robinson Crusoe* and *Moll Flanders,* Defoe told his story in simple, unadorned language, not disdaining colloquialisms. His *Journal of the Plague Year,* published almost fifty years after the great London plague of 1665, was based not alone upon his personal eyewitness recollections when a mere child of six, but also upon interviews with numerous survivors and extensive research into the published accounts of others. No other reporter has so vividly portrayed the desolation of the town of London—its empty streets in which grass grew, its shut-up shops, its frightened populace, the rumbling of the dead cart, the bell always tolling, and the endless cry, "Bring out your dead!" His *Memoirs of a Cavalier,* an amazing evocation of the campaigns of the Thirty Years' War and the Civil War in England, reveals him to be a master of military tactics. Whether describing the career of a warrior, a pirate, a plunderworld citizen, or a fortuneteller, Defoe wrote it as though from lifelong experience.

Possessing the fresh ring of spontaneity that all great reporting should have is Defoe's notable story, *A True Relation of the Apparition of One Mrs. Veal.* The account of that lady's astonishing visitation to her friend, Mrs. Bargrave, at Canterbury on September 9, 1705, the day after her death, was reported very soon thereafter, appearing as a news pamphlet in 1706. "This relation," Defoe asserted, "is a matter of fact. It was sent by a Justice of the Peace at Maidstone to his friend in London, as here written, and it was attested by a sober gentlewoman, his kinswoman, who lived near Mrs. Bargrave, and had heard the story from Mrs. Bargrave's own mouth. This lady, who was not a person to be easily deceived, testified that Mrs. Bargrave was a pious and honest woman." The moral, added Defoe, is the reality of the life to come and the need of repentance and right living in the present world. Reportorial gems of that age invariably pointed a moral.

"This thing has very much affected me,"
Robinson Crusoe's creator confesses

Daniel Defoe, *A True Relation of the Apparition of One Mrs. Veal* (London, 1706)

This thing is so rare in all its circumstances, and on so good authority, that my reading and conversation have not given me anything like it. Mrs. Bargrave is the person to whom Mrs. Veal appeared after her death; she is my intimate friend, and I can avouch for her reputation for these last fifteen or sixteen years, on my own knowledge; and I can confirm the good character she had from her youth to the time of my acquaintance.

Now you must know Mrs. Veal was a maiden gentlewoman of about thirty years of age, and for some years last past had been troubled with fits, which were perceived coming on her by her going off from her discourses very abruptly to some impertinence. She was maintained by an only brother, and kept his house in Dover. Mrs. Veal was intimately acquainted with Mrs. Bargrave from her childhood. Mrs. Veal's circumstances were then mean; her father did not take care of his children as he ought, so that they were exposed to hardships; and Mrs. Bargrave in those days had as unkind a father, though she wanted neither for food nor clothing, whilst Mrs. Veal wanted for both, insomuch that she would often say:

"Mrs. Bargrave, you are not only the best, but the only friend I have in the world; and no circumstance in life shall ever dissolve my friendship."

Some time after Mr. Veal's friends got him a place in the customhouse at Dover, which occasioned Mrs. Veal by little and little to fall off from her intimacy with Mrs. Bargrave, though there never was any such thing as a quarrel; but an indifferency came on by degrees, till at last Mrs. Bargrave had not seen her in two years and a half; though about a twelvemonth of the time Mrs. Bargrave had been absent from Dover, and this last half year had been in Canterbury about two months of the time, dwelling in a house of her own.

In this house, on the eighth of September, 1705, she was sitting alone, in the forenoon, thinking over her unfortunate life, then took up her sewing work, which she had no sooner done but she hears a knocking at the door. She went to see who was there, and this proved to be Mrs. Veal, her old friend, who was in a riding habit; at that moment of time the clock struck twelve noon.

"Madam," says Mrs. Bargrave, "I am surprised to see you, you have been so long a stranger"; but told her she was glad to see her, and offered to salute her, which Mrs. Veal complied with, till their lips almost touched; and then Mrs. Veal drew her hand across her own eyes and said, "I am not very well," and so waived it. She told Mrs. Bargrave she was going a journey, and had a great mind to see her first.

"But," says Mrs. Bargrave, "how came you to take a journey alone? I am amazed at it, because I know you have a good brother."

"Oh," says Mrs. Veal, "I gave my brother the slip, and came away, because I had so great a desire to see you before I took my journey."

So Mrs. Bargrave went in with her into another room within the first, and Mrs. Veal set her down in an elbow-chair, in which Mrs. Bargrave was sitting when she heard Mrs. Veal knock. Then says Mrs. Veal,

"My dear friend, I am come to renew our old friendship again, and beg your pardon for my breach of it; and if you can forgive me, you are the best of women."

"Oh," says Mrs. Bargrave, "do not mention such a thing. I have not had an uneasy thought about it; I can easily forgive it."

"What did you think of me?" said Mrs. Veal. Says Mrs. Bargrave,

"I thought you were like the rest of the world, and that prosperity had made you forget yourself and me."

After all this discourse, which the apparition put in much finer words than Mrs. Bargrave said she could pretend to, and as much more than she can remember, for it cannot be thought that an hour and three quarters' conversation could be retained, though the main of it she thinks she does, she said to Mrs. Bargrave she would have her write a letter to her brother, and tell him she would have him give rings to such and such, and that there was a purse of gold in her cabinet, and that she would have two broadpieces given to her cousin Watson.

Talking at this rate, Mrs. Bargrave thought that a fit was coming upon her, and so placed herself in a chair just before her knees, to keep her from falling to the ground, if her fits should occasion it . . . and to divert Mrs. Veal . . . took hold of her gown sleeve sev-

eral times and commended it. Mrs. Veal told her it was a scoured silk, and newly made up.

Then Mrs. Veal asked for Mrs. Bargrave's daughter. She said she was not at home, "But if you have a mind to see her," says Mrs. Bargrave, "I'll send for her." "Do," says Mrs. Veal. On which she left her, and went to a neighbor's to see for her; and by the time Mrs. Bargrave was returning, Mrs. Veal was got without the door into the street, in the face of the beast market, on a Saturday (which is market day), and stood ready to part, as soon as Mrs. Bargrave came to her. She asked her why she was in such haste. She said she must be going, though perhaps she might not go her journey until Monday; * and told Mrs. Bargrave she hoped she should see her again at her cousin Watson's before she went whither she was going. Then she said she would take her leave of her, and walked from Mrs. Bargrave in her view, till a turning interrupted the sight of her, which was three quarters after one in the afternoon.

Mrs. Veal died the seventh of September, at twelve o'clock at noon, of her fits, and had not above four hours' sense before death, in which time she received the sacrament. The next day after Mrs. Veal's appearing, being Sunday, Mrs. Bargrave was so mightily indisposed with a cold and a sore throat that she could not go out that day; but on Monday morning she sent a person to Captain Watson's to know if Mrs. Veal was there. They wondered at Mrs. Bargrave's inquiry, and sent her word that she was not there, nor was expected. At this answer, Mrs. Bargrave told the maid she had cer-

---

* According to the register of St. Mary's, Dover, Mrs. Veal was buried on September 10. That would be Monday, and, possibly, the Monday of her "journey."

tainly mistook the name or made some blunder. And though she was ill, she put on her hood, and went herself to Captain Watson's, though she knew none of the family, to see if Mrs. Veal was there or not. They said they wondered at her asking, for that she had not been in town; they were sure, if she had, she would have been there.

Says Mrs. Bargrave, "I am sure she was with me on Saturday almost two hours."

They said it was impossible; for they must have seen her, if she had. In comes Captain Watson while they are in dispute, and said that Mrs. Veal was certainly dead, and her escutcheons * were making. This strangely surprised Mrs. Bargrave, when she sent to the person immediately who had the care of them, and found it true. Then she related the whole story to Captain Watson's family, and what gown she had on, and how striped, and that Mrs. Veal told her it was scoured. Then Mrs. Watson cried out,

"You have seen her indeed, for none knew but Mrs. Veal and myself that the gown was scoured."

And Mrs. Watson owned that she described the gown exactly; "for," said she, "I helped her to make it up." This Mrs. Watson blazed all about the town, and avouched the demonstration of the truth of Mrs. Bargrave's seeing Mrs. Veal's apparition; and Captain Watson carried two gentlemen immediately to Mrs. Bargrave's house to hear the relation from her own mouth. And when it spread so fast that gentlemen and persons of quality, the judicious and skeptical part of the world, flocked in upon her, it at last became such a task that she was forced to go out of the way; for they were in general extremely well

satisfied of the truth of the thing, and plainly saw that Mrs. Bargrave was no hypochondriac, for she always appears with such a cheerful air and pleasing mien that she has gained the favor and esteem of all the gentry, and it is thought a great favor if they can but get the relation from her own mouth.

All the time I sat with Mrs. Bargrave, which was some hours, she recollected fresh sayings of Mrs. Veal. And one material thing more she told Mrs. Bargrave—that old Mr. Breton allowed Mrs. Veal ten pounds a year, which was a secret, and unknown to Mrs. Bargrave till Mrs. Veal told her. Mrs. Bargrave never varies in her story, which puzzles those who doubt the truth or are unwilling to believe it. A servant in the neighbor's yard adjoining to Mrs. Bargrave's house heard her talking to somebody an hour of the time Mrs. Veal was with her. Mrs. Bargrave went out to her next neighbor's the very moment she parted with Mrs. Veal, and told her what ravishing conversation she had with an old friend.

I asked Mrs. Bargrave several times if she was sure she felt the gown. She answered modestly, "If my senses are to be relied on, I am sure of it." I asked her if she heard a sound when she clapped her hands upon her knees. She said she did not remember she did, but said she appeared to be as much a substance as I did, who talked with her.

"And I may," said she, "be as soon persuaded that your apparition is talking to me now as that I did not really see her; for I was under no manner of fear, and received her as a friend, and parted with her as such. I would not," says she, "give one far-

---

* Armorial shields draped in black for the funeral.

thing to make anyone believe it; I have no interest in it. Nothing but trouble is entailed upon me for a long time, for aught I know; and had it not come to light by accident, it would never have been made public."

This thing has very much affected me, and I am as well satisfied as I am of the best-grounded matter of fact. And why we should dispute matter of fact because we cannot solve things of which we have no certain or demonstrative notions seems strange to me. Mrs. Bargrave's authority and sincerity alone would have been undoubted in any other case.

DEFOE'S STORY did not entirely satisfy Sir Walter Scott. Modern reporters, Scott pointed out, would have cross-examined Mrs. Bargrave and would not have quit until Mrs. Veal's body had been dug up. But more recent scholarship has corroborated Defoe's account. The essential details actually occurred, and all the persons in the story have been identified. Defoe, on the basis of interviews with persons close to the visitation, possibly with Mrs. Bargrave herself, simply told the ghost story without embroidering. His readers wondered and believed, for, as Defoe put it, whether the apparition really was seen must continue to depend upon the evidence as to Mrs. Bargrave's veracity. This is a question for students of psychical research.

And who can say that the bill for the cleaning of Mrs. Veal's gown will not some day be found?

1762. A different ghost and a different reporter. That massive Tory, Samuel Johnson, with his generous heart and irascible temper, his hypochondriacal tendencies and his St. Vitus fidgets, accepted reportorial assignments to keep from starving. Ever since, as an Oxford student, he had been driven from the quadrangle at Christ Church by the sneering looks that foppish aristocrats cast at the holes in his shoes, he fought a continual battle with poverty. It was from Edward Cave of the *Gentleman's Magazine* that he first obtained regular employment when he sought work in London. The only magazine in the kingdom with a national circulation, it devoted considerable space to news coverage.

In the winter of 1762 reporter Johnson was called in to cover the case of the ghost that walked at Cock Lane. In the January issue of the *Gentleman's Magazine* he told how one Parsons, a parish clerk in Cock Lane, near Smithfield, claimed that his twelve-year-old child had been taken possession of by the ghost of a deceased gentlewoman of a respectable Norfolk family. An investigation, reported by Johnson, was begun almost at once. "The whole town of London think of nothing else," commented Horace Walpole, who himself rushed over to the scene of the phenomenon.

Boswell's hero detects an imposture in Cock Lane

Gentleman's Magazine (London), January, 1762

Between the hours of eleven and twelve at night, a gentleman was sent to the house of one Parsons, officiating parish clerk at St. Sepulchre's in Cock Lane, near West Smithfield, to be witness to the noises and other extraordinary circumstances attending the supposed presence of a spirit that for these two years past has been heard in the night, to the great terror of the family. The gentleman attended, and found the child in bed, and the spirit being at hand, several questions were put to it by the father. The gentleman, not caring to pronounce too hastily upon what appeared to him extraordinary, got some friends together, among whom were two or three clergymen, about twenty other persons, including two Negroes, and sat up another night.

They first thoroughly examined the bed, bedclothes, etc., and being satisfied that there was no visible appearance of a deceit, the child, with its sister, was put into bed, which was found to shake extremely by the gentleman who had placed himself at the foot of it.

Among others, the following questions were asked:

Whether her disturbance was occasioned by any ill-treatment from Mr. K[ent]? *Yes.*

Whether she was brought to an untimely end by poison? *Yes.*

In what was the poison administered, beer or purl. *Purl.*

How long before her death? *Three hours.*

Is the person called *Carrots* [her servant] able to give information about poison? *Yes.*

Whether she was K——'s wife['s] sister? *Yes.*

Whether she was married to K——? *No.*

Whether any other person than K—— were concerned in the poisoning? *No.*

Whether she could visibly appear to anyone? *Yes.*

Whether she would do so? *Yes.*

Whether she would go out of the house? *Yes.*

Whether she would follow the child everywhere? *Yes.*

Whether she was pleased in being asked questions? *Yes.*

Whether it eased her mind? *Yes.*

[Here a mysterious noise, compared to the fluttering of wings round the room, was heard.]

How long before her death had she told *Carrots* that she was poisoned? *One hour.*

[Here *Carrots*, who was admitted to be one of the company on Tuesday night, asserted that the deceased had not told her so, she being at that time speechless.]

How long did *Carrots* live with her? *Three or four days.* [*Carrots* attested to the truth of this.]

Whether if the accused should be taken up he would confess? *Yes.*

Whether she should be at ease in her mind if the man was hanged? *Yes.*

How long it would be before he would be executed? *Three years.*

How many clergymen were in the room? *Three.*

How many Negroes? *Two.*

Whether she could distinguish the person of any in the room? *Yes.*

Whether the color of a watch held up by one of the clergy was white, yellow, blue, or black? Answered *black.* [The watch was in a black shagreen case.]

At what time she would depart in the morning? *At four o'clock.*

Accordingly, at this hour the noise removed to the Wheatsheaf, a public house, at the distance of a few doors, in the bedchamber of my landlord and landlady, to the great affright and terror of them both.

Such is the manner of interrogating the spirit; the answer is given by knocking or scratching. An affirmative is one knock; a negative two. Displeasure is expressed by scratching.

As the impostor will probably soon be discovered, let this short detail suffice to show the tendency of it; the whole of the nonsense would fill a magazine.

IN THE FEBRUARY issue of *Gentleman's Magazine,* under the heading, "An Account of the Detection of the Imposture of Cock Lane," the learned reporter ran the ghost story down to earth.

Gentleman's Magazine (London), February, 1762

Having in our last given a short history of the imposture in Cock Lane, we are under a necessity of giving an account of the method taken for the detection of the fraud, which though in a great measure eluded by the cunning of the girl, who is the principal agent, and by the obstinacy of the father, who perhaps was the contriver of it; yet it had such an effect as to convince all present that the girl has some art of counterfeiting particular noises, and that there is nothing preternatural in the responses that are given to the querists on this occasion:

On the night of the first of February, many gentlemen, eminent for their rank and character, were, by the invitation of Rev. Mr. Aldrich, of Clerkenwell, assembled at his house, for the examination of the noises supposed to be made by a departed spirit, for the detection of some enormous crime.

About ten at night, the gentlemen met in the chamber, in which the girl, supposed to be disturbed by a spirit, had, with proper caution, been put to bed by several ladies. They sat rather more than an hour, and, hearing nothing, went downstairs, where they interrogated the father of the girl, who denied, in the strongest terms, any knowledge or belief of fraud.

The supposed spirit had before publicly promised, by an affirmative knock, that it would attend one of the gentlemen into the vault under the church of St. John, Clerkenwell, where the body is deposited, and give a token of her presence there by a knock upon her coffin. It was therefore determined to make this trial of the existence or veracity of the supposed spirit.

While they were inquiring and deliberating, they were summoned into the girl's chamber by some ladies, who were near her bed, and who had heard knocks and scratches. When the gentlemen entered, the girl declared that she felt the spirit like a mouse upon her back, and was required to hold her hands out of bed. From that time, though the spirit was very solemnly required to manifest its existence, by appearance, by impression on the hand or body of any present, by scratches, knocks, or any other agency, no evidence of any preternatural power was exhibited.

The spirit was then very seriously advertised that the person to whom the promise was made, of striking the coffin, was then about to visit the vault, and that the performance of the promise was then claimed. The company at one o'clock went into the church, and the gentleman to whom the promise was made went, with one more, into the vault. The spirit was solemnly required to perform its promise, but nothing more than silence ensued; the person supposed to be accused by the spirit then went down, with several others, but no effect was perceived. Upon their return, they examined the girl, but could draw no confession from her. Between two and three she desired, and was permitted, to go home with her father.

It is therefore the opinion of the whole assembly that the child has some art of making or counterfeiting particular noise, and that there is no agency of any higher cause.—*This account was drawn up by a gentleman of veracity and learning, and therefore we have thought it sufficient; though the impostor has been since more clearly detected, even to demonstration.*

By a pamphlet just published, entitled *The Mystery Revealed,* there is a vindication of Mr. K——, the person pointed at by this supposed ghost, by which the public is informed of the following particulars.

In the year 1756 Mr. K. was married to a young gentlewoman in Norfolk, with whom he lived happily for eleven months; but she dying in childbed, and the sister, who had lived as a companion to the deceased, continuing to assist Mr. K. in the public business which he then carried on in the country, they contracted such an intimacy together that when he quitted that business with a design to settle in London, she insisted on following him even on foot, if he would not procure her a more creditable conveyance.

As they were excluded by the canon law from marrying, they thought it, *in foro conscientiae,* no crime to indulge their mutual passion for each other, and, it is acknowledged, that they did cohabit together as man and wife, and that they mutually made their wills in favor of each other, by which agreement the young lady would have been a considerable gainer had she survived, her fortune being only £100, his a great deal more. Unfortunately for Mr. K., both the landlords, at whose houses he first lodged, were necessitous; both borrowed money of him, and both were sued by him for the payment of it. To this he ascribes the cause of the Cock Lane plot against him.

It appears that while they lodged at Parson's, the young lady grew pregnant, and that Dr. Cooper, of Northumberland Street, while she was but in the sixth month of pregnancy, was retained to attend her in her labor. This gentleman continued to visit her till she was taken ill of what he thought an eruptive fever, not knowing that she had never had the smallpox. As the lodgings where she was taken ill were very inconvenient, she was removed from thence with all the care that could be, Dr. Cooper attending her in the coach, and Mr. K. having provided a nurse, and prepared rooms for her reception at a house he had taken in Bartlet Street,

Clerkenwell. Here it was discovered that the distemper with which she was seized was the smallpox; and for the first four days, both the physician and the apothecary (Mr. Jones of Grafton Street) who attended her thought the symptoms rather favorable; but when maturation should have been performed, the pulse flagged, the fever sank, and the whole eruption put on a very warty and pallid appearance: and, in short, her death was pronounced almost certain three or four days before it happened, during which time a clergyman was called in, and every precaution taken that could be devised, as well for the care of her soul as for the preservation of her person. These facts are attested by Dr. Cooper and Mr. Jones. And the clergyman who attended her has often been heard to confirm this part of the narrative in every particular.

* * *

A FEW hints "to the renowned Society of Ghostmongers, and particularly to the Clergyman their Secretary," are conveyed by Dr. Johnson in closing. "We have no reason to imagine," he observes, "that the decoy duck in Cock Lane, so addicted to angry scratching, so intent upon revengeful purposes, so silly (though at the same time cunning) in the management of her little cheats, so palpably mistaken in many instances, and so evasive and prevaricating in others, we have, I say, no room to suppose that this little dabbler in necromancy is a celestial visitant, deputed hither, on a very important occasion, by the king of heaven." Johnson warns his readers to "look out the managers behind the screens," for "they are no spirits. They are as surely clothed with flesh and blood as you yourselves are, only guarding most cautiously against the light, because they too well know their deeds are evil, and therefore not careful of bearing a strict examination." To detect such frauds is a noble work, and when the impostors are exposed, they ought to be pilloried, Johnson concluded. The authorities agreed. Parsons was pilloried and sent to prison for two years. His accomplices received shorter sentences or were fined.

"Would not you, sir, start as Mr. Garrick does if you saw a ghost?" Johnson was once asked in the course of a discussion of the naturalness of Garrick's acting. "I hope not," the Doctor replied. "If I did, I should frighten the ghost."

An Editor Defies the Crown and Lays the Cornerstone for Freedom of the Press in America

WHEN, IN 1644, in his *Areopagitica*, John Milton asserted: "Give me the liberty to know, to utter, and to argue freely according to conscience, above all liberties," he was championing the cause of all early newspapermen. Editors spent almost as much time in jail as they did in the printing office. Defoe, a habitué of debtors' jail, was sentenced to a year in Newgate for a satire on religious intolerance. John Wilkes, another stouthearted reporter, was committed to the Tower and expelled from the House of Commons for daring to assert in his newspaper, *The North Briton*, in 1763, that the King, in a speech to Parliament, had not told the truth. American colonial newsmen fared no better. Before coming to this country, Benjamin Harris was pilloried, fined, and imprisoned for criticizing the King. His colonial venture, *Publick Occurrences*, the first newspaper in the English colonies, was suppressed four days after its initial appearance in 1690 for daring to report that the English armed forces had allied themselves with "miserable" savages. When James Franklin, the editor of *The New England Courant*, was jailed for attacking the colonial government, he had his half brother, Ben, then sixteen years old, and destined to be the most famous of colonial editors, carry on the enterprise in his own name. By this flimsy subterfuge he evaded the censors for a time.

None of these early newsmen served the cause of freedom more effectively than did that German immigrant, John Peter Zenger, whose *New-York Weekly Journal*, from its first issue in 1733, infused an independent and even truculent spirit into American colonial journalism. Backed by the ousted chief justice of New York, Lewis Morris, and by two prominent attorneys, James Alexander and William Smith, Zenger proceeded to attack the highhanded administration of Governor William Cosby. With grim, Swiftian humor he published mock advertisements of strayed animals recognizable as political foes. Although the major articles were undoubtedly contributed by his sponsors, Zenger was legally responsible for them. In the fall of 1734 the authorities ordered certain issues of the *Journal* containing doggerel rhymes burned. Arrested and remanded to prison when unable to furnish the excessive bail demanded, Zenger, during his ten months' confinement, arranged to have his paper appear every Monday, the business being managed by his wife, who received her instructions from her husband "through the Hole of the Door of the Prison."

In April term, 1735, Zenger was brought to trial for criminal libel. An information accused him of having declared that the liberties and property of the people of New York were in jeopardy, "men's deeds destroyed, judges arbitrarily displaced, new courts erected without consent of the legislature," trial by jury "taken away when a governor pleases," and men of property "denied the vote." Zenger pleaded not guilty. When his counsel, Smith and Alexander, attacked the judges for their bias, they were promptly disbarred. Then Andrew Hamilton of Philadelphia appeared for the prisoner, whose own report of the trial follows:

The trial of John Peter Zenger

A Brief Narrative of the Case and Tryal of John Peter Zenger (New York, 1736)

Mr. Hamilton: May it please Your Honor; I am concerned in this cause on the part of Mr. Zenger, the defendant. The information against my client was sent me, a few days before I left home, with some instructions to let me know how far I might rely upon the truth of those parts of the papers set forth in the information and which are said to be libelous. And though I am perfectly of the opinion with the gentleman who has just now spoke, on the same side with me, as to the common course of proceedings, I mean in putting Mr. Attorney upon proving that my client printed and published those papers mentioned in the information; yet I cannot think it proper for me (without doing violence to my own principles) to deny the publication of a complaint, which I think is the right of every freeborn subject to make, when the matters so published can be supported with truth; and therefore I'll save Mr. Attorney the trouble of examining his witnesses to that point; and I do (for my client) confess that he both printed and published the two newspapers set forth in the information, and I hope in so doing he has committed no crime.

Mr. Attorney: Then if Your Honor pleases, since Mr. Hamilton has con-

fessed the fact, I think our witnesses may be discharged; we have no further occasion for them.

Mr. Hamilton: If you brought them here, only to prove the printing and publishing of these newspapers, we have acknowledged that, and shall abide by it.

Mr. Chief Justice: Well, Mr. Attorney, will you proceed?

Mr. Attorney: Indeed, sir, as Mr. Hamilton has confessed the printing and publishing these libels, I think the jury must find a verdict for the King; for supposing they were true, the law says that they are not the less libelous for that; nay, indeed, the law says their being true is an aggravation of the crime.

Mr. Hamilton: Not so neither, Mr. Attorney, there are two words to that bargain. I hope it is not our bare printing and publishing a paper that will make it a libel. You will have something more to do before you make my client a libeler; for the words themselves must be libelous, that is, *false, scandalous, and seditious* or else we are not guilty.

Mr. Attorney: The case before the court is whether Mr. Zenger is guilty of libeling His Excellency the Governor of New York, and indeed the whole administration of the government. Mr. Hamilton has confessed the printing and publishing, and I think nothing is plainer than that the words in the information are *scandalous, and tend to sedition, and to disquiet the minds of the people of this province.* And if such papers are not libels, I think it may be said there can be no such thing as a libel.

Mr. Hamilton: May it please Your Honor; I cannot agree with Mr. Attorney: for though I freely acknowledge that there are such things as libels, yet I must insist at the same time that what my client is charged with is not a libel; and I observed just now that Mr. Attorney, in defining a libel, made use of the words *scandalous, seditious, and tend to disquiet the people;* but (whether with design or not I will not say) he omitted the word *false.*

Mr. Attorney: I think I did not omit the word *false.* But it has been said already that it may be a libel notwithstanding it may be true.

Mr. Hamilton: In this I must still differ with Mr. Attorney; for I depend upon it, we are to be tried upon this information now before the court and jury, and to which we have pleaded *Not Guilty,* and by it we are charged with printing and publishing *a certain false, malicious, seditious, and scandalous libel.* This word *false* must have some meaning, or else how came it there?

Mr. Chief Justice: You cannot be admitted, Mr. Hamilton, to give the truth of a libel in evidence. A libel is not to be justified; for it is nevertheless a libel that it is *true.*

Mr. Hamilton: I am sorry the court has so soon resolved upon that piece of law; I expected first to have been heard to that point. I have not in all my reading met with an authority that

says we cannot be admitted to give the truth in evidence upon an information for a libel.

Mr. Chief Justice: The law is clear that you cannot justify a libel. [Hamilton then cites cases to support his contention that the truth of a libel is admissible in evidence.]

Here the court had the case under consideration a considerable time, and every one was silent.

Mr. Chief Justice: Mr. Hamilton, the court is of opinion you ought not to be permitted to prove the facts in the papers: these are the words of the book, *"It is far from being a justificacation of a libel that the contents thereof are true, or that the person upon whom it is made had a bad reputation, since the greater appearance there is of truth in any malicious invective so much the more provoking it is."*

Mr. Hamilton: These are Star Chamber cases, and I was in hopes that practice had been dead with the court.

Mr. Chief Justice: Mr. Hamilton, the court have delivered their opinion, and we expect you will use us with good manners; you are not to be permitted to argue against the opinion of the court.

Mr. Hamilton: With submission, I have seen the practice in very great courts, and never heard it deemed unmannerly to——

Mr. Chief Justice: After the court have declared their opinion, it is not good manners to insist upon a point in which you are overruled.

Mr. Hamilton: I will say no more at this time; the court, I see, is against us in this point; and that I hope I may be allowed to say.

Mr. Chief Justice: Use the court with good manners, and you shall be allowed all the liberty you can reasonably desire.

Mr. Hamilton: I thank Your Honor. Then, gentlemen of the jury, it is to you we must now appeal, for witnesses to the truth of the facts we have offered, and are denied the liberty to prove; and let it not seem strange that I apply myself to you in this manner. I am warranted so to do both by law and reason. The last supposes you to be summoned *out of the neighborhood where the fact is alleged to be committed;* and the reason of your being taken out of the neighborhood is *because you are supposed to have the best knowledge of the fact that is to be tried.* And were you to find a verdict against my client, you must take upon you to say the papers referred to in the information, and which we acknowledge we printed and published, are *false, scandalous, and seditious;* but of this I can have no apprehension. You are citizens of New York; you are really what the law supposes you to be, *honest and lawful men;* and, according to my brief, the facts which we offer to prove were not committed in a corner; *they are notoriously known to be true;* and therefore in your justice lies our safety. And as we are denied the liberty of giving evidence, to prove the truth of what we have published, I will beg leave to lay it down as a standing rule in such cases *that the suppressing of evidence ought always to be taken for the strongest evidence;* and I hope it will have that weight with you.

It is true in times past it was a crime to speak truth, and in that terrible Court of Star Chamber many worthy and brave men suffered for so doing; and yet even in that court, and in those bad times, a great and good man durst say, what I hope will not be taken amiss of me to say in this place,

to wit, the practice of informations for libels is a sword in the hands of a wicked king, and an arrant coward to cut down and destroy the innocent; the one cannot, because of his high station, and the other dares not, because of his want of courage, revenge himself in another manner.

Mr. Attorney: Pray, Mr. Hamilton, have a care what you say, don't go too far neither, I don't like those liberties.

Mr. Hamilton: Sure, Mr. Attorney, you won't make any applications; all men agree that we are governed by the best of kings, and I cannot see the meaning of Mr. Attorney's caution, my well-known principles, and the sense I have of the blessings we enjoy under his present Majesty, makes it impossible for me to err, and, I hope, even to be suspected, in that point of duty to my king. May it please Your Honor, I was saying that notwithstanding all the duty and reverence claimed by Mr. Attorney to men in authority, they are not exempt from observing the rules of common justice, either in their private or public capacities; the laws of our mother country know no exemption.

I hope to be pardoned, sir, for my zeal upon this occasion: it is an old and wise caution *that when our neighbor's house is on fire, we ought to take care of our own.* For though, blessed be God, I live in a government where liberty is well understood and freely enjoyed, yet experience has shown us all (I'm sure it has to me) that a bad precedent in one government is soon set up for an authority in another; and therefore I cannot but think it mine and every honest man's duty that (while we pay all due obedience to men in authority) we ought at the same time to be upon our guard against power, wherever we apprehend that it may affect ourselves or our fellow subjects.

I am truly very unequal to such an undertaking on many accounts. And you see I labor under the weight of many years, and am borne down with great infirmities of body; yet old and weak as I am, I should think it my duty, if required, to go to the utmost part of the land where my service could be of any use in assisting to quench the flame of prosecutions upon informations, set on foot by the government, to deprive a people of the right of remonstrating (and complaining too) of the arbitrary attempts of men in power. Men who injure and oppress the people under their administration provoke them to cry out and complain; and then make that very complaint the foundation for new oppressions and prosecutions. I wish I could say there were no instances of this kind.

But to conclude: the question before the court and you, gentlemen of the jury, is not of small nor private concern, it is not the cause of a poor printer, nor of New York alone, which you are now trying. No! It may in its consequence affect every freeman that lives under a British government on the Main of America. It is the best cause. It is the cause of liberty; and I make no doubt but your upright conduct this day will not only entitle you to the love and esteem of your fellow citizens; but every man who prefers freedom to a life of slavery will bless and honor you as men who have baffled the attempt of tyranny, and, by an impartial and uncorrupt verdict, have laid a noble foundation for securing to ourselves, our posterity, and our neighbors that to which nature and the laws of our country have given us a right—the liberty both of exposing and opposing arbitrary power (in

these parts of the world, at least) by speaking and writing truth.

Mr. Chief Justice: Gentlemen of the jury. The great pains Mr. Hamilton has taken to show how little regard juries are to pay to the opinion of the judges, and his insisting so much upon the conduct of some judges in trials of this kind, is done, no doubt, with a design that you should take but very little notice of what I may say upon this occasion. I shall therefore only observe to you that, as the facts or words in the information are confessed: the only thing that can come in question before you is whether the words, as set forth in the information, make a libel. And that is a matter of law, no doubt, and which you may leave to the court. But I shall trouble you no further with anything more of my own, but read to you the words of a learned and upright judge in a case of the like nature.

"To say that corrupt officers are appointed to administer affairs is certainly a reflection on the government. If people should not be called to account for possessing the people with an ill opinion of the government, no government can subsist. For it is necessary for all governments that the people should have a good opinion of it. And nothing can be worse to any government than to endeavor to procure animosities; as to the management of it, this has been always looked upon as a crime, and no government can be safe without it be punished."

Mr. Hamilton: I humbly beg Your Honor's pardon; I am very much misapprehended if you suppose what I said was so designed.

Sir, you know I made an apology for the freedom I found myself under a necessity of using upon this occasion. I said there was nothing personal designed; it arose from the nature of our defense.

The jury withdrew, and in a small time returned, and being asked by the clerk whether they were agreed of their verdict, and whether John Peter Zenger was guilty of printing and pub-lishing the libels in the information mentioned, they answered by Thomas Hunt, their foreman: *Not Guilty.* Upon which there were three huzzas in the hall, which was crowded with people, and the next day I was discharged from my imprisonment.

SINCE IN THOSE DAYS the common law strictly construed criminal libel ("the greater the truth, the greater the libel"), Hamilton's plea for the right of the jury to inquire into the truth or falsity of the libel took the issue from hostile court to friendly jury. Zenger's acquittal may therefore be considered the first great victory for the freedom of the press, and it foreshadowed many later jury verdicts of "not guilty of publishing." His account of the trial aroused tremendous interest both in the colonies and in Great Britain and went through numerous editions. Ben Franklin's *Poor Richard* endorsed the verdict:

> *While free from Force the Press remains,*
> *Virtue and Freedom cheer our Plains.**

However, it took another half century before the British government enacted into law the precedent established in this case—the right of the jury in seditious libel to judge the truth of the matter published.

---

* Franklin lifted the verse from Matthew Green's poem, *The Spleen,* published posthumously in 1737.

Bostonians Send Out Invitations to a Tea Party

THE BRITISH GOVERNMENT was amazingly inept in handling the colonial press. The Stamp Act, one of the earliest revenue measures passed after the French and Indian War, served to unite newspaper publishers, as well as other professional men, in opposition to the government tax program. The *Pennsylvania Journal*, with skull and crossbones at its masthead, ran a streamer: "EXPIRING: In hopes of a resurrection to LIFE again." The radicals kept the propaganda initiative, and, by the eve of the American Revolution, twenty-three newspapers supported the cause of independence as against a mere seven that remained steadfast to George III, a loyalty usually buttressed by subsidies.

After 1765 the home government taxed and then retreated, only to tax again. The Stamp Act was repealed, but Parliament stoutly declared that it had "full power and authority to make laws and statutes of sufficient force and validity to bind the colonies . . . in all causes whatsoever." Every time a tax was passed, boycotts and violent resistance in America forced Parliament to back down. "What enforcing, and what repealing; what bullying and what submitting; what doing and undoing," thundered Edmund Burke in Parliament. Finally, in 1770, the ministry repealed the tax on all articles except tea, which was kept merely as a matter of principle. Then, in April, 1773, the government, in order to get its favorite trust, the East India Company, out of the red, handed it a monopoly of the tea trade with America, but, by allowing a refund on duties previously paid when the tea was exported from England to the colonies, actually made it possible for Americans to buy tea at a lower price than the same tea sold for in the mother country. As Franklin pointed out, the inventors of this noble piece of chicanery had no idea "that any people can act from any other principle but that of interest; and they believe" that this small reduction was "sufficient to overcome all the patriotism of an American." As usual, they reckoned without their customers.

In Boston, the merchants, many of them forced to be smugglers by the unfair laws of trade, were united against this menace of monopoly. Once competition in the tea market had been destroyed, they argued, prices could be manipulated for the benefit of the English stockholders. This monopoly would breed other monopolies, which in the end would stifle free enterprise in America.

Placards, conspicuously posted, notified Bostonians on the morning of November 29, 1773:

FRIENDS! BRETHREN! COUNTRYMEN!

That worst of plagues, the detested Tea, shipped for this Port by the East India Company, is now arrived in this Harbor. The Hour of Destruction or manly Opposition to the Machinations of Tyranny stare you in the Face. Every Friend to his Country, to himself, or to Posterity is now called upon to meet in Faneuil Hall, at Nine o'Clock THIS DAY (At which Time the Bells will ring) to make a united and successful Resistance to the last, worst, and most destructive Measure of Administration.

Two weeks of unceasing vigilance prevented any tea from being landed. Fearing that the customhouse officials would seize the tea and sell it secretly to raise money to pay the salaries of the governor and judges, the merchants held a last meeting on December 14 at the Old South Meeting House. The owner of the ship *Dartmouth*, which had a tea cargo, was ordered to clear his ship. Two days later he notified the townsmen that a clearance had been refused him. When he protested to Governor Hutchinson, that Tory worthy, himself a gifted if partisan reporter, told him that "he could not give a pass unless the vessel was properly qualified from the customhouse." Just as news of this run-around reached the meeting, a diversion took place which was colorfully reported in the December 23 issue of Boston's *News-Letter*, the most venerable of colonial newspapers still operating on the eve of the Revolution.*

A tea party at which "King" Hancock, Sam Adams, and their Mohawk braves pour

---

The Massachusetts Gazette and Boston News-Letter, December 23, 1773

Just before the dissolution of the meeting, a number of brave and resolute men, dressed in the Indian manner, approached near the door of the assembly, and gave the war whoop, which rang through the house and was answered by some in the galleries. But silence being commanded, and a peaceable deportment was again enjoined till the dissolution. The Indians, as they were then called, repaired to the wharf, where the ships lay that had the tea on board, and were followed by hundreds of people, to see the event of the transactions of those who made so grotesque an appearance.

They, the Indians, immediately repaired on board Captain Hall's ship, where they hoisted the chests of tea and when upon deck stove the chests and emptied the tea overboard. Having cleared this ship, they proceeded to Captain Bruce's and then to Captain Coffin's brig. They applied themselves so dexterously to the destruction of this commodity that in the space of three hours they broke up 342 chests, which was the whole number

---

* Founded in 1704, the *News-Letter* underwent numerous mergers, being known at the time of the Tea Party as *The Massachusetts Gazette and Boston News-Letter*, under the editorship of Richard Draper.

in those vessels, and discharged their contents into the dock. When the tide rose it floated the broken chests and the tea insomuch that the surface of the water was filled therewith a considerable way from the south part of the town to Dorchester Neck, and lodged on the shores.

There was the greatest care taken to prevent the tea from being purloined by the populace. One or two being detected in endeavoring to pocket a small quantity were stripped of their acquisitions and very roughly handled. It is worthy of remark that although a considerable quantity of goods were still remaining on board the vessels, no injury was sustained.

Such attention to private property was observed that a small padlock belonging to the captain of one of the ships being broke, another was procured and sent to him.

The town was very quiet during the whole evening and the night following. Those persons who were from the country returned with a merry heart; and the next day joy appeared in almost every countenance, some on occasion of the destruction of the tea, others on account of the quietness with which it was effected. One of the Monday's papers says that the masters and owners are well pleased that their ships were thus cleared.

* * *

THE IDENTITY of the Mohawk braves was one of the best-kept secrets of all time. One of the participants declared many years later that Sam Adams, leader of the Sons of Liberty, and John Hancock were among those who participated. Hancock's ruffles gave him away, as well as his voice, when he gave the countersign, "an Indian grunt and the expression *me know you.*"

The Tea Party has well been called "the boldest stroke which had yet been struck in America." Reactionary opinion in England, incensed at this defiance of property rights, called for stern measures. The "Coercive Acts" followed. Boston's port was closed, and the people of Massachusetts lost self-government. But only for a short time, for soon a united colonial people, in Continental Congress, planned measures to redress their grievances.

A logical aftermath of the Tea Party was a boycott on tea, from which "pestilential herb" Americans were weaned for all time. Coffee became king as colonists took to heart the admonition of the *New Hampshire Gazette:*

> *Rouse, every generous thoughtful mind,*
> *The rising danger flee;*
> *If you would lasting freedom find,*
> *Now, then, abandon tea!*

From the Rude Bridge That Arched the Flood
Isaiah Thomas Reports the Battle of Lexington

AFTER THE TEA PARTY Boston took on the appearance of an armed camp. Her port closed, her town overrun with redcoats, Boston turned for help to the countryside. Her cause was espoused by courageous newspapermen, chief among them the patriot Isaiah Thomas. Fearing that his paper, the *Massachusetts Spy*, attacked by the Loyalists as a "sedition foundry," would be suppressed, Thomas warned the authorities:

Should the liberty of the press be once destroyed, farewell the remainder of our invaluable rights and privileges! We may next expect padlocks on our lips, fetters on our legs, and only our hands left at liberty to slave for our worse than EGYPTIAN TASKMASTERS, OR—FIGHT OUR WAY TO CONSTITUTIONAL FREEDOM.

Learning that he was on the list of a dozen patriots to be captured and executed by the British military authorities, along with Sam Adams and Hancock, Thomas shipped his printing press and his fonts of type to Worcester. It was he who, on the night of April 18, 1775, displayed the lantern that signaled the start of Paul Revere's ride to warn the countryside that the British forces had got wind of a large store of powder and arms collected by the patriots at Concord and were about to march on that town. Thomas, who had discontinued publishing the *Spy* in Boston on April 6, started anew at Worcester on May 3 with what was the most sensational piece of reporting ever to herald the first issue of a newspaper. Carrying the streamer: AMERICANS! LIBERTY OR DEATH! JOIN OR DIE! the story recounted the opening engagement of the Revolution. An outstanding propaganda piece, the account carries much authority by virtue of the fact that Thomas joined the militia at Lexington at the break of day on the 19th, and was reporting events he himself had witnessed.

"The shot heard round the world"

Massachusetts Spy, May 3, 1775

AMERICANS! forever bear in mind the BATTLE OF LEXINGTON!—where British troops, unmolested and unprovoked, wantonly and in a most inhuman manner, fired upon and killed a number of our countrymen, then robbed, ransacked, and burnt their houses! nor could the tears of defenseless women, some of whom were in the pains of childbirth, the cries of helpless babes, nor the prayers of old age, confined to beds of sickness, appease their thirst for blood!—or divert them from their DESIGN of MURDER and ROBBERY!

The particulars of this alarming event will, we are credibly informed, be soon published by authority, as a Committee of the Provincial Congress have been appointed to make special inquiry and to take the depositions, on oath, of such as are knowing in the matter. In the meantime, to satisfy the expectations of our readers, we have collected from those whose veracity is unquestioned the following account, viz.

A few days before the battle, the Grenadier and Light-Infantry companies were all drafted from the several regiments in Boston; and put under the command of an officer, and it was observed that most of the transports and other boats were put together, and fitted for immediate service. This maneuver gave rise to a suspicion that a more formidable expedition was intended by the soldiery, but what or where the inhabitants could not determine. However, town watches in Boston, Charlestown, Cambridge, etc., were ordered to look well to the landing place.

About ten o'clock on the night of the eighteenth of April, the troops in Boston were disclosed to be on the move in a very secret manner, and it was found they were embarking on boats (which they privately brought to the place in the evening) at the bottom of the Common; expresses set off immediately to alarm the country, that they might be on their guard. When the expresses got about a mile beyond Lexington, they were stopped by about fourteen officers on horseback, who came out of Boston in the afternoon of that day, and were seen lurking in by-places in the country till after dark. One of the expresses immediately fled, and was pursued two miles by an officer, who when he had got up with him presented a pistol, and told him he was a dead man if he did not stop, but he rode on till he came up to a house, when stopping of a sudden his horse threw him off, having the presence of mind to holloo to the people in the house,

"Turn out! Turn out! I have got one of them!"

The officer immediately retreated and fled as fast as he had pursued. The other express, after passing through a strict examination, by some means got clear.*

The body of the troops, in the meantime, under the command of Lieutenant Colonel Smith, had crossed the river and landed at Phipp's Farm. They immediately, to the number of 1000, proceeded to Lexington, about six miles below Concord, with great silence. A company of militia, of about eighty men, mustered near the meetinghouse; the troops came in sight of them just before sunrise. The militia, upon seeing the troops, began to disperse. The troops then set out upon the run, hallooing and huzzaing, and coming within a few rods of them, the commanding officer accosted the militia, in words to this effect,

"Disperse, you damn'd rebels!— Damn you, disperse!"

Upon which the troops again huzzaed and immediately one or two officers discharged their pistols, which were instantaneously followed by the firing of four or five of the soldiers; and then there seemed to be a general discharge from the whole body. It

---

* Paul Revere later reported that it was he who, "after passing through a strict examination," escaped. His companion, Dr. Prescott, was the "express" who reached Concord.

is to be noticed they fired on our people as they were dispersing, agreeable to their command, and that we did not even return the fire.* Eight of our men were killed and nine wounded. The troops then laughed, and damned the Yankees, and said they could not bear the smell of gunpowder.

A little after this the troops renewed their march to Concord, where, when they arrived, they divided into parties, and went directly to several places where the province stores were deposited. Each party was supposed to have a Tory pilot. One party went into the jailyard and spiked up and otherwise damaged two cannon, belonging to the province, and broke and set fire to the carriages. Then they entered a store and rolled out about a hundred barrels of flour, which they unheaded and emptied about forty into the river. At the same time others were entering houses and shops, and unheading barrels, chests, etc., the property of private persons. Some took possession of the town house, to which they set fire, but was extinguished by our people without much hurt. Another party of the troops went and took possession of the North Bridge. About 150 provincials who mustered upon the alarm, coming toward the bridge, the troops fired upon them without ceremony and killed two on the spot! (Thus had the troops of Britain's king fired FIRST at two separate times upon his loyal American subjects, and put a period to two lives before one gun was fired upon them.) Our people THEN fired and obliged the troops to retreat, who were soon joined by their other parties, but finding they were still pursued the whole body retreated to Lexington,

both provincials and troops firing as they went.

During this time an express from the troops was sent to General Gage, who thereupon sent out a reinforcement of about 1400 men, under the command of Earl Percy, with two fieldpieces. Upon the arrival of this reinforcement at Lexington, just as the retreating party had got there, they made a stand, picked up their dead, and took all the carriages they could find and put their wounded thereon. Others of them, to their eternal disgrace be it spoken, were robbing and setting houses on fire, and discharging their cannon at the meetinghouse.

The enemy, having halted about an hour at Lexington, found it necessary to make a second retreat, carrying with them many of their dead and wounded. They continued their retreat from Lexington to Charlestown with great precipitation. Our people continued their pursuit, firing till they got to Charlestown Neck (which they reached a little after sunset), over which the enemy passed, proceeded up Bunker's Hill, and the next day went into Boston, under the protection of the *Somerset*, man-of-war of sixty-four guns.

A young man, unarmed, who was taken prisoner by the enemy, and made to assist in carrying off their wounded, says that he saw a barber who lives in Boston, thought to be one Warden, with the troops and that he heard them say he was one of their pilots. He likewise saw the said barber fire twice upon our people and heard Earl Percy give the order to fire the houses. He also informs that several

---

* Numerous depositions were later made by Americans who took part in the battle to the effect that one of their own officers ordered them to disperse before the British officer commanded it. No one will ever know who fired the first shot.

officers were among the wounded who were carried into Boston, where our informant was dismissed. They took two of our men prisoners in battle, who are now confined in barracks.

Immediately upon the return of the troops to Boston, all communication to and from the town was stopped by General Gage. The provincials, who flew to the assistance of their distressed countrymen, are posted in Cambridge, Charlestown, Roxbury, Watertown, etc., and have placed a guard on Roxbury Neck, within gunshot of the enemy. Guards are also placed everywhere in view of the town, to observe the motions of the King's troops. The Council of War and the different Committees of Safety and Supplies sit at Cambridge, and the Provincial Congress at Watertown. The troops in Boston are fortifying the place on all sides, and a frigate of war is stationed at Cambridge River, and a sixty-four-gun ship between Boston and Charlestown.

Deacon Joseph Loring's house and barn, Mrs. Mulliken's house and shop, and Mr. Joshua Bond's house and shop, in Lexington, were all consumed. They also set fire to several other houses, but our people extinguished the flames. They pillaged almost every house they passed by, breaking and destroying doors, windows, glass, etc., and carrying off clothing and other valuable effects. It appeared to be their design to burn and destroy all before them, and nothing but our vigorous pursuit prevented their infernal purposes from being put into execution. But the savage barbarity exercised upon the bodies of our unfortunate brethren who fell is almost incredible. Not content with shooting down the unarmed, aged, and infirm, they disregarded the cries of the wounded, killing them without mercy, and mangling their bodies in the most shocking manner.

We have the pleasure to say that notwithstanding the highest provocations given by the enemy, not one instance of cruelty that we have heard of was committed by our militia; but, listening to the merciful dictates of the Christian religion, they "breathed higher sentiments of humanity."

The public most sincerely sympathize with the friends and relations of our deceased brethren, who sacrificed their lives in fighting for the liberties of their country. By their noble intrepid conduct, in helping to defeat the force of an ungrateful tyrant, they have endeared their memories to the present generation, who will transmit their names to posterity with the highest honor.

* * *

THE PATRIOT version of an unprovoked attack, coupled with wanton atrocities, was spread broadcast long before General Gage's counter-version was known. But the end of May saw the *Newport Mercury* reporting British accusations that the Americans had engaged in gouging and scalping, and didn't "fight fair." Thomas' was the first of some excellent front-line reportorial pieces to appear during the Revolution. The *Pennsylvania Journal* carried a graphic account of the Battle of Princeton. The *New York Journal* ran an exciting story on the capture of Stony Point by "Mad Anthony" Wayne in 1779, and patriot newspapers devoted much attention to retailing atrocity tales, notable among them being the *New Jersey Gazette*'s account of the massacre at Cherry Valley, and the *New Hampshire Gazette*'s exposé

of barbarous conditions aboard British prison ships in New York. In recounting the burning of Kingston, the *New York Packet* of October 23,
1777, exclaimed: "Britain, how art thou fallen! Ages to come will not be
able to wipe away the guilt, the horrid guilt, of these and such like deeds,
lately perpetrated by thee." But none topped in reportorial excellence
Thomas' report of Lexington and Concord, which was widely reprinted in
other journals eager to give their readers the story of "the shot heard round
the world."

Lexington proved that the Americans could defeat the British. The initiative was in their hands, and by nightfall the approaches to Boston were
blocked, thus beginning the siege of that metropolis. Within a matter of
months Washington had forced the British to pull out. The *New-York
Mercury,* edited by Hugh Gaine, later a Tory turncoat, declared, "the proceedings of April 19 have united the colonies and continent. . . . All that is
attended to, besides plowing and planting, is making ready for fighting."
Lord Percy, whose timely reinforcements made it possible for the redcoats
to extricate a bleeding fragment from the rout, commented, "Whoever
looks upon them [the New Englanders] as an irregular mob will find himself much mistaken."

Isaiah Thomas had sounded the alarm. Journalist Tom Paine, using a
drumhead for a desk and the wintry campfire for a light, soon issued a
clarion call for independence and followed up with a realistic warning to
"summer soldier" and "sunshine patriot" alike that "these are the times
that try men's souls."

Pistol in Hand, the French Journalist, Desmoulins, Incites the Mob of Paris to Storm the Bastille

T HE WHOLE BUSINESS is now over," commented Arthur Young on June 27, 1789, "and the revolution complete." Convinced that the victory of constitutional government meant the end of the crisis, this acute British reporter left Paris at once, thereby missing the most stirring events of the French Revolution. For, taking advantage of a week-end recess of the National Assembly, Louis XVI suddenly dismissed his reform-minded finance minister, Necker, on July 11. When news reached Paris the next day, a sense of panic gripped businessmen and proletarians alike. That afternoon a twenty-nine-year-old lawyer-journalist, Camille Desmoulins by name, stood with a group of friends in the Palais-Royal, discussing the issues. His subsequent moves impelled Robespierre at a later time to hail him as the "first of all the revolutionaries" and "a republican by instinct." * Some four years after the event Desmoulins reported the incident in his own newspaper, Le Vieux Cordelier (The Old Friar), when he was seeking to clear himself of counterrevolutionary charges. The only conspiracy to which he pleaded guilty was that of conspiring for the past five years "to make France republican, happy, and prosperous," of conspiring to accomplish these ends even before July 12, 1789.

"Let all citizens follow my example!"

Le Vieux Cordelier (Paris), No. V, December 25, 1793

It was on the twelfth of July that, pistol in hand, I conspired, calling the nation to arms and to liberty. I was the first to take this national cockade, which you cannot attach to your hat without thinking of me.

It was just half-past two when I came to sound out the people. My anger against the despots had turned into despair. To my mind the gather-

ings of people, although deeply stirred, even dismayed, had no insurrectionary momentum.

Just then I observed three young men, hand in hand, moved by a more impetuous courage. I saw that they had come to the Palais-Royal for the same reason as I. Some passive citizens followed them.

"Gentlemen," I said to them, "here

* *Courrier Universel*, December 16, 1793.

is the beginning of a patriotic assemblage. One of us must do his duty and mount a table to address the people."

"Go ahead, get up here."

"I am willing."

Whereupon I was carried upon the table rather than allowed to mount it. Hardly had I got up on my feet when I saw myself surrounded by an immense crowd. Here is my short speech, which I shall never forget:

"Citizens! There is not a moment to lose. I have just come from Versailles. M. Necker is dismissed. His dismissal is the tocsin of a St. Bartholomew's for patriots! This evening all the Swiss and German battalions will sally forth from the Champs-de-Mars to cut our throats. We have only one recourse—to rush to arms and wear cockades as a means of recognizing each other."

I had tears in my eyes, and spoke with a feeling that I have never been able to recapture, no less describe. My proposal was received with wild applause. I continued:

"What colors will you have?"

Someone shouted: "Choose!"

"Will you have green, the color of hope, or the blue of Cincinnatus, the color of American liberty and democracy?"

Some voices were raised, "Green, the color of hope!"

At that I cried, "Friends! The signal is given. Watching me are spies and satellites of the police. At least I will not fall into their hands alive."

Then, drawing two pistols from my pocket, I exclaimed, "Let all citizens follow my example!"

Smothered with embraces, I stepped down. Some pressed me to their hearts. Others bathed me in their tears. A citizen of Toulouse, fearing for my life, vowed he would never abandon me. In the meantime, they had brought me a green ribbon, a piece of which I first put in my hand, distributing the rest among those crowding around me.

THE YOUNG JOURNALIST had set in motion a chain of events that ended with the miraculous capture of the Bastille two days later.

Desmoulins first wrote this account in 1790, and published it in his newspaper three years later. Though his letter to his father dated July 16, 1789, is not quite so detailed and some minor discrepancies have since been brought to light, the basic account stands up. With pardonable ego Desmoulins may, perhaps, have exaggerated its historical significance.

Desmoulins was a pioneer of modern French reporting. French censorship prior to 1789 had resulted in suppressing any note of personal journalism. But with the calling of the Estates-General, all that changed. In the spring and summer of 1789 literally hundreds of newspapers were born in Paris—some five hundred made their appearance in the French metropolis by 1792. Never before in history, even in the American Revolution, had newspapermen taken so active a role in the shaping of political events. Mirabeau, Brissot, Desmoulins, Marat, and Hébert represented all shadings of revolutionary opinion. Those favoring a limited monarchy along English lines took comfort from Mallet du Pan's solid journal, the *Mercure de France*. The more radical preferred the witty and even bloodthirsty sentiments of Desmoulins' *Révolutions de France et de Brabant*. Other leftists preferred Marat's *Ami du Peuple* (when attacked by Marat, Desmoulins said, "I will persist in praising you because I think we should defend liberty not only with men but also with dogs") or the unbridled yellow journalism, sinking to the depths of obscenity, of Hébert's *Père Duchesne*. All were modern newspapers, using headlines, exploiting interest in sex scandals (Marie Antoinette was a great boon to the gossip columnists), and printing stock-market quotations and theater notices.

Like the sorcerer's apprentice, Desmoulins and his confederates had started a flood they were unable to stop. The tide of revolutionary terror swept up him and his friends as victims. On December 5, 1793, Desmoulins began issuing the *Vieux Cordelier* to defend himself from counterrevolutionary charges and to support his hero, Danton. The extremists now turned on the Dantonists, whom they condemned as tired-out revolutionaries, playboys, and profiteers. With more courage than discretion, Desmoulins proceeded to attack the Terror, and his old schoolmate, Robespierre, assured his followers that once "a few more serpents were crushed" victory would lay within their grasp. Finally, Saint-Just carried the day. Danton, Desmoulins, and their followers were condemned to death. Characteristically, Desmoulins spent his last moments in jail dashing off a reply to Saint-Just's charges. With Danton he was led to his execution. According to an eyewitness, "three carts painted red, each drawn by two horses, and escorted by five or six gendarmes, passed at a foot's pace through a huge silent crowd, which could show no joy and dared show no sorrow." As Danton mounted the scaffold, he turned to the executioner and called out: "Don't forget to show my head to the people. It's worth the trouble."

Alexander Hamilton's *Evening Post* and Aaron Burr's *Morning Chronicle* Disagree on the Most Famous Duel in American History

ALEXANDER DID NOT have a moral right to the name Levine, since his mother, a young, hot-blooded West Indian beauty, had previously left the bed of her middle-aged husband, John Michael Levine, a prosperous Danish-Jewish planter, and had taken up with a handsome ne'er-do-well, James Hamilton. Their son, Alexander, was born at Nevis in 1757. His birth was the clinching evidence that gave Levine his divorce.

From his very first encounter with Aaron Burr, Hamilton seems to have developed a mortal antipathy to him. Both these young Revolutionary officers found their position defending Brooklyn Heights against Howe's fleet completely untenable. Defying General Knox, Burr turned to the troops and asked: "Do you wish to remain here and end up in a dungeon or hanged like dogs, or will you follow me who can bring you to safety?" Burr's daring, yet sensible, proposal carried the day and stole the show from the brilliant West Indian captain of artillery.

Actually, Burr and Hamilton were alike in many respects. Young, brilliant, with a flair for military strategy and an instinctive knowledge of men and politics, they were slight in stature, handsome and vivacious, dynamic personalities, devastating with the ladies, athirst for power, and not overly scrupulous in the means to attain it. After the Revolution these two top members of the New York bar not infrequently crossed swords. When, in the later period of Washington's administration, party divisions had arisen, Hamilton, serving as Secretary of the Treasury—his is probably the greatest economic mind America has produced—found himself, as leader of the Federalists, under attack from his enemies, the Republicans (Jefferson's party, not to be confused with the present party of that name), for his strong pro-British bias. Chief among his accusers was Aaron Burr.

After Hamilton left the Cabinet he almost fought a duel with Monroe, later President, with Burr as Monroe's second. Hamilton accused Monroe of a breach of faith in allowing the disclosure to be made of Hamilton's shocking affair with Mrs. Reynolds and of his having been systematically blackmailed to keep the episode quiet. Burr drew up a statement that brought the bitter exchange to a peaceful conclusion. Eliza Hamilton stood steadfast beside her husband.

Burr, whose "talents for intrigue" were fully recognized by Washington, was, as a result of the inept provisions of the election laws, tied in votes with Jefferson in the presidential election of 1800. The final choice was thrown into the lap of the House of Representatives, strongly Federalist in character and extremely hostile to Jefferson. When Hamilton heard that the leaders of his party were planning to vote for Burr, whom he regarded as a Bonaparte, his wrath knew no bounds. He attacked Burr with reckless vehemence, castigating him as "the Catiline of America."

Once Jefferson was seated in the presidency, he was understandably determined to undermine politically his Vice-President, Burr, whom he considered a double-crosser. Seeing no real prospect of succeeding to the presidency, Burr sought the governorship of New York. When he failed to get the Jeffersonian nomination, he solicited the aid of embittered Federalists. Hamilton, alarmed, now denounced his old enemy as "a man of irregular and unsatiable ambition," a dangerous and despicable person, who ought not to be trusted. Burr coolly bided his time. After being trounced in the election, he wrote Hamilton, demanding satisfaction for remarks that exceeded the bounds of fair comment. Hamilton equivocated, and, in terms of the so-called code of honor then prevailing, Burr had no recourse save to challenge him to a duel.

The first eyewitness report of the encounter on the west bank of the Hudson comes from the New York *Morning Chronicle*, founded by Burr and his partisans; the second, from the *Evening Post*, which Hamilton himself had founded and which has continued in existence to the present day. On the day of the funeral, the Federalist editor, William Coleman, suspended publication of the *Post*—the only time in its history, according to Allan Nevins, that it missed an issue because of a death. For a week all its news columns carried heavy black borders. In addition to preparing newspaper copy on Hamilton's death, Coleman was "at some pains to collect all the information on the subject that was to be had from authentic sources," and supplemented the *Post* accounts with a documentary volume on Hamilton's death.

Pistols for two—coffee for one

New York *Morning Chronicle*, July 18, 1804

Colonel Burr arrived first on the ground, as had been previously agreed; when General Hamilton arrived the parties exchanged salutations, and the seconds proceeded to make their arrangements. They measured the distance, ten full paces, and cast lots for the choice of position as also to determine by whom the word should be given, both of which fell to the second of General Hamilton. They then proceeded to load the pistols in each other's presence, after which the parties took their stations. The gentleman who was to give the word then explained to the parties the rules which were to govern them in firing, which were as follows:

"The parties being placed at their stations—the second who gives the word shall ask them whether they are ready; being answered in the affirmative, he shall say 'present,' after this the parties shall present and fire when they please—if one fires before the other, the opposite second shall say one, two, three, fire—and shall then fire or lose his fire."

He then asked if they were prepared, being answered in the affirmative, he gave the word *present,* as had been agreed upon, and *both parties took aim* * *and fired in succession,* the intervening time is not expressed, as the seconds do not precisely agree on that point. The fire of Colonel Burr took effect, and General Hamilton almost instantly fell. Colonel Burr then advanced toward General Hamilton with a manner and gesture that appeared to General Hamilton's friend to be expressive of regret, but without speaking, turned about and withdrew, being urged from the field by his friend as has been subsequently stated, with a view to prevent his being recognized by the surgeon and bargeman, who were then approaching. No further communication took place between the principals, and the barge that carried Colonel Burr immediately returned to the city. We conceive it proper to add that the conduct of the parties in this interview was perfectly proper, as suited the occasion.

* * *

New York *Evening Post,* July 19, 1804

In the interviews that have since taken place between the gentlemen that were present, they have not been able to agree in two important facts that passed there—for which reason nothing was said on those subjects in the paper lately published as to other particulars in which they were agreed.

Mr. P[endleton] expressed a confident opinion that General Hamilton did not fire first—and that he did not fire at all *at Colonel Burr.* Mr. V[an] N[ess] seemed equally confident in opinion that General H. did fire first—and of course that it must have been at his antagonist.

General Hamilton informed Mr. P. at least ten days previous to the affair that he had doubts whether he would not receive and not return Mr. Burr's first fire. Mr. P. remonstrated against this determination, and urged many considerations against it, as dangerous to himself and not necessary in the particular case, when every ground of accommodation, not humiliating, had been proposed and rejected. He said he would not decide lightly, but take time to deliberate fully. It was incidentally mentioned again at their occasional subsequent conversations, and on the evening preceding the time of the appointed interview, he informed Mr. P. he had made up his mind *not to fire at Colonel Burr the first time, but to receive his fire, and fire in the air.* Mr. P. again urged him upon this subject, and repeated his former arguments. His final answer was in terms that made an impression on Mr. P.'s mind which can never be effaced. "My friend, it is the effect of a religious

---

* By mutual agreement of the seconds this account was modified to read: "both parties presented," which implied merely an "elevation of the arm" (New York *Evening Post,* July 18, 1804).

scruple, and does not admit of reasoning; it is useless to say more on the subject, as my purpose is definitely fixed."

His last words before he was wounded afford a proof that his purpose had not changed. When he received his pistol, after having taken his position, he was asked if he would have the hairspring set. His answer was, *"Not this time."*

After he was wounded, and laid in the boat, the first words he uttered after recovering his power of speech were (addressing himself to a gentleman present, who perfectly well remembers it), *"Pendleton knows I did not mean to fire at Colonel Burr the first time."*

The pistol had been used by General Hamilton, laying loose over the other apparatus in the case which was open; after having been some time in the boat, one of the boatmen took hold of it to put it in the case. General Hamilton, observing this, said, *"Take care of that pistol—it is cocked. It may go off and do mischief."* This is also remembered by the gentleman alluded to.

This shows that he was not sensible of having fired at all. If he had fired *previous* to receiving the wound, he would have remembered it, and therefore have known that the pistol could not go off; but if *afterwards* it must have been the effect of an involuntary exertion of the muscles produced by a mortal wound, in which case he could not have been conscious of having fired.

Mr. P. having so strong a conviction that if General Hamilton had fired first, it could not have escaped his attention (all his anxiety being alive for the effect of the first fire, and having no reason to believe the friend of Colonel Burr was not sincere in the contrary opinion), he determined to go to the spot where the affair took place, to see if he could not discover some traces of the course of the ball from General Hamilton's pistol. He took a friend with him the day after General Hamilton died, and after some examination they fortunately found what they were in search of. They ascertained that the ball passed through the limb of a cedar tree, at an elevation of about twelve feet and an half, perpendicularly from the ground, between thirteen and fourteen feet from the mark on which General Hamilton stood, and about four feet wide of the direct line between him and Colonel Burr, on the right side; he having fallen on the left. The part of the limb through which the ball passed was cut off and brought to this city, and is now in Mr. Church's possession.

No inferences are pointed out as resulting from these facts, nor will any comments be made. They are left to the candid judgment and feelings of the public.

* * *

William Coleman, *A Collection of the Facts and Documents Relative to the Death of Alexander Hamilton* (New York, 1804)

It was nearly seven in the morning when the boat which carried General Hamilton, his friend Mr. Pendleton, and the surgeon mutually agreed on, Dr. Hosack, reached that part of the Jersey shore called the Weahawk. There they found Mr. Burr and his friend Mr. Van Ness, who, as I am told, had been employed since their arrival, with coats off, in clearing away the bushes, limbs of trees, etc., so as to make a fair opening.

The parties in a few moments were at their allotted situations. When Mr. Pendleton gave the word, *Mr. Burr raised his arm slowly, deliberately took his aim, and fired.* His ball entered General Hamilton's right side. As soon as the bullet struck him, he raised himself involuntarily on his toes, turned a little to the left (at which moment his pistol went off), and fell upon his face. Mr. Pendleton immediately called out for Dr. Hosack, who, in running to the spot, had to pass Mr. Van Ness and Colonel Burr; but Van Ness had the cool precaution to cover his principal with an umbrella, so that Dr. Hosack should not be able to swear that he saw him on the field. What passed after this the reader will have in the following letter from Dr. Hosack himself, in answer to my note:

"August 17th, 1804
"Dear Sir,

"To comply with your request is a painful task; but I will repress my feelings while I endeavor to furnish you with an enumeration of such particulars relative to the melancholy end of our beloved friend Hamilton, as dwell most forcibly on my recollection.

"When called to him, upon his receiving the fatal wound, I found him half sitting on the ground, supported in the arms of Mr. Pendleton. His countenance of death I shall never forget. He had at that instant just strength to say, 'This is a mortal wound, Doctor'; when he sunk away, and became to all appearance lifeless. I immediately stripped up his clothes, and soon, alas! ascertained that the direction of the ball must have been through some vital part. His pulses were not to be felt; his respiration was

entirely suspended; and upon laying my hand on his heart, and perceiving no motion there, I considered him as irrecoverably gone. I however observed to Mr. Pendleton that the only chance for his reviving was immediately to get him upon the water.

"We therefore lifted him up, and carried him out of the wood, to the margin of the bank, where the bargemen aided us in conveying him into the boat, which immediately put off. During all this time I could not discover the least symptom of returning life. I now rubbed his face, lips, and temples, with spirits of hartshorn, applied it to his neck and breast, and to the wrists and palms of his hands, and endeavored to pour some into his mouth. When we had got, as I should judge, about fifty yards from the shore, some imperfect efforts to breathe were for the first time manifest. In a few minutes he sighed, and became sensible to the impression of the hartshorn, or the fresh air of the water. He breathed; his eyes, hardly opened, wandered, without fixing upon any objects. To our great joy he at length spoke: 'My vision is indistinct,' were his first words. His pulse became more perceptible; his respiration more regular; his sight returned.

"Soon after recovering his sight, he happened to cast his eye upon the case of pistols, and observing the one that he had had in his hand lying on the outside, he said, 'Take care of that pistol; it is undischarged, and still cocked; it may go off and do harm.— *Pendleton knows* (attempting to turn his head towards him) *that I did not intend to fire at him.*' 'Yes,' said Mr. Pendleton, understanding his wish, 'I have already made Dr. Hosack acquainted with your determination as to that.' Perceiving that we approached the shore, he said, 'Let Mrs.

Hamilton be immediately sent for. Let the event be gradually broken to her; but give her hopes.'

"Looking up, we saw his friend Mr. Bayard standing on the wharf in great agitation. He had been told by his servant that General Hamilton, Mr. Pendleton, and myself, had crossed the river in a boat together, and too well he conjectured the fatal errand, and foreboded the dreadful result. Perceiving, as we came nearer, that Mr. Pendleton and myself only sat up in the stern sheets, he clasped his hands together in the most violent apprehension; but when I called to him to have a cot prepared, and he at the same moment saw his poor friend lying in the bottom of the boat, he threw up his eyes and burst into a flood of tears and lamentation. Hamilton alone appeared tranquil and composed. We then conveyed him as tenderly as possible up to the house. The distresses of this amiable family were such that till the first shock was abated, they were scarcely able to summon fortitude enough to yield sufficient assistance to their dying friend.

"During the night he had some imperfect sleep; but the succeeding morning his symptoms were aggravated, attended, however, with a diminution of pain. His mind retained all its usual strength and composure. The great source of his anxiety seemed to be in his sympathy with his half-distracted wife and children. He spoke to me frequently of them. 'My beloved wife and children,' were always his expressions. But his fortitude triumphed over his situation, dreadful as it was. Once, indeed, at the sight of his children brought to the bedside together, seven in number, his utterance forsook him. He opened his eyes, gave them one look, and closed them again till they were taken away. As a proof of his extraordinary composure of mind, let me add that he alone could calm the frantic grief of their mother. *'Remember, my Eliza, you are a Christian,'* were the expressions with which he frequently, with a firm voice, but in a pathetic and impressive manner, addressed her. His words, and the tone in which they were uttered, will never be effaced from my memory. At about two o'clock, as the public well knows, he expired.

"I am, Sir,

"Your friend and humble servant,

                "DAVID HOSACK

"Wm. Coleman, Esq."

After his death, a note which had been written the evening before the interview was found addressed to the gentleman who accompanied him to the field; thanking him with tenderness for his friendship to him, and informing him where would be found the keys of certain drawers in his desk, in which he had deposited such papers as he had thought proper to leave behind him; together with his last will.

ON AUGUST 4, the *Evening Post* reported that a coroner's inquest found that "Aaron Burr, Esq., Vice-President of the United States, was guilty of the murder of Alexander Hamilton."

For weeks the *Morning Chronicle* and the *Evening Post* debated *in extenso* the question of whether Hamilton actually planned to shoot. The opposing seconds almost fought a duel themselves. The facts are that Hamilton had no heart in the duel his reckless course had provoked, and it is abundantly clear that he never had the least intention of hitting Burr. From the point of view of Burr's later reputation, Hamilton would have done both Burr and the nation a great service if he had ended his foe's career at Weehawken. As for Hamilton himself, his death made him a martyr who was to enjoy a transfiguration seldom paralleled in American history. To this cause the *Western Telegraph* contributed a Scottish ballad "On the Murder of Hamilton," which included this stanza:

> *Oh! wo betide ye, Aaron Burr!*
> *May mickle curse upo' ye fa'!*
> *Ye've killed as brave a gentleman*
> *As e'er liv'd in America.*

"Peter Porcupine" Reports from Jail How
Workers Wage Futile War on the Machines

FEW JOURNALISTS could hate with the consuming fire of William Cobbett, the great English radical of his generation. He hated landlords. He hated London stockbrokers. He hated big government. He regarded tea and potatoes as instruments of the devil. He pursued his enemies with a quill dipped in bile. "Miscreant" and "reptile" were mild epithets when Cobbett was wound up.

The son of an ordinary day laborer, Cobbett emigrated to America after a brief military career and published pamphlets under the pseudonym of "Peter Porcupine." Antagonized by the excesses of the French Revolution, he denounced American liberals (Tom Paine was his especial bête noire) with all the passion of an unreconstructed Tory and jingo. The first thing he knew, he was on the losing end of a libel suit for $5000. "With this I depart for my native land, where neither the moth of Democracy nor the rust of Federalism doth corrupt and where thieves do not, with impunity, break through and steal five thousand dollars at a time," was Cobbett's parting barb.

Something happened to Cobbett when he returned to England. He became more and more sympathetic to the cause of the small farmer and the worker. His newspaper, the *Political Register,* wholeheartedly espoused the cause of political democracy and manifested increasing alarm at the reactionary trend of events as Britain mobilized to curb Napoleon. More concerned with winning the war for democracy at home than with defeating Napoleon or going to war with America, Cobbett remarked: "We like to hear the lion roar, for then we know he is hurt."

Toward the latter part of 1811 working-class discontent suddenly exploded all over industrial England. Although the American nonimportation measures and Napoleon's Continental system may have been the immediate cause of the "scarcity of work," labor attributed its plight to its new enemy, the machine, which it proceeded to smash with unrestrained fury. In the April 18, 1812, issue of the *Political Register* Cobbett, writing from jail, where he had been confined for a slashing attack on the flogging of soldiers, summarized the reports of the London papers and subjected these dispatches to a withering blast. These reports were the inspiration for Ernst Toller's fiery tragedy, *The Machine Wreckers.*

Cobbett on the Luddite Riots

Cobbett's Weekly Political Register, April 18, 1812

SCARCITY IN FRANCE,
and
RIOTS IN ENGLAND

The smothering system has prevailed so long in England that, really, at last, the world knows but little of what passes here, and even we ourselves do not know much of it. As far as lies in my power this base system shall be thwarted. I will make all known that comes to my knowledge, because it is for the good of the country. I will not only not lend my aid to the long-practiced imposture; but I will do all that I can to expose that imposture, supported by means of a servile and corrupt press, the most efficient instrument in the delusion, the debasement, and the enslaving of a people.

There is, it appears, a scarcity of grain in France; and, it is well known, that there is a scarcity in England. Our hired newspapers have noticed both; and it is my intention to let the world see what they have said of both; what their tone has been when speaking of the scarcity in England, compared to what it has been when speaking of the scarcity in France; how they blow hot and cold with the same mouth; how impatient they are to see insurrections in France; and how they are for instant punishment of every creature who dares complain in England.

But, it may be said, "why not let them alone with their falsehoods?" Why? Why, because falsehoods ought never to pass undetected; falsehoods ought never to pass in the world for truth. These falsehoods have, too, a tendency to injure the cause of freedom; they have a tendency to prolong the sufferings of Europe; they ought, therefore, to be exposed to all the parties concerned.

[Cobbett cites a report in *The Courier* of April 8 to the effect that the scarcity in France exists and has been produced by the war. "We are told that the people of France hate the war, and hate Bonaparte because he continues the war."]

When the hireling of *The Courier* was writing so blithely about the scarcity in France, and about the disaffection towards the Emperor and his family, it little thought how soon it would have to give account of transactions like those at Manchester, Carlisle, Bristol, Truro, Leeds, etc. He hoped, I suppose, like the hireling of *The Times* newspaper, that he should have "no such disturbances to record, but those which would take place in France." This brave, liberal, and Christianlike hope has been disappointed; and these hired personages have been compelled to record distresses and disturbances in England instead of distresses and disturbances in France. The accounts which I myself have received from Carlisle, where the poor woman was shot, and from Manchester, where some of the people were sabered, are very different indeed from those published by *The Times* and *The Courier*. But I do not choose to make use of my own intelligence. I do not choose to expose myself to the charge of sending exaggerated statements to the continents of Europe and America. I will take the accounts which the hirelings themselves have been pleased to give us, and let the world judge from them.

"There have been riots at Manchester, Carlisle, and other places. At all but the first, on account of the high price of provisions; at Manchester, on account of an attempt to send a flattering address to the Prince Regent. In treating upon the subject of the riot (at Carlisle), it is our intention merely to state the leading facts. The late proceedings of the populace, we believe, originated in three cases: the very low wages of our manufacturing poor, the dearness of every necessary of life, and the late artificial scarcity, which has been produced by agents from Liverpool, etc., who have bought up, at very advanced prices, all the grain in the market. On Saturday last the bread corn was bought up in a few minutes; consequently, many of the heads of families were disappointed and obliged to return home empty. Apprehensions being entertained that the same agents were at work in buying up potatoes, some carts loaded were seized by the populace, who sold them at reduced prices. Early on Monday morning great quantities of corn were brought from depots of the corn buyers to the port of Sandsfield, five miles distant. The populace, unable to endure the sight of so much grain passing by their doors, whilst themselves and families were in want, proceeded to the vessels, and pressed several carts, loaded them, and were about to return, when the magistrates and the soldiers of the 55th arrived. We understand that the magistrates, after having promised that the markets in future should be duly regulated, and the propositions of advancing the wages of the manufacturing poor should have their con-

sideration, the populace relinquished their booty and returned home. The populace appeared perfectly satisfied with the assurances of the magistrates, who are said to have promised to use every exertion to prevent forestalling. All terminated quietly at Sandsfield, except that some of the magistrates and officers were assailed in the suburbs, on their return, by women and boys with a few stones.

"The soldiers were marched up to the market place, and followed by an immense concourse of people; many, no doubt, attracted by curiosity. Some of the officers were hissed and hooted at on their retiring, when they suddenly wheeled, *drew their swords, and ran to their men, who were still under arms, and ordered them to clear away the place,* by *which many were wounded.* The mob, as if momentarily appalled, did not further incommode them, and the officers went to mess, leaving the soldiers under arms. After the lapse of a few minutes, the populace assembled in great numbers before the messroom, broke the windows, and threatened vengeance to the officers. On this the Riot Act was read. Some rounds, it is stated, were afterwards fired, by *which a woman was killed* (said in other papers to have been with child) and *several men wounded;* and most of the houses in the market place exhibited some mark of the firing.

"On Tuesday the examination of thirty-eight persons was held, who, with the exception of two or three, who were charged with having thrown stones, were all discharged. On that day the coroner's inquest was taken on the unfortunate woman, when the jury, after long deliberation and continued differences of opinion, returned a verdict of accidental death.

"All is now quiet."

RIOTS IN YORKSHIRE

LEEDS, APRIL 11—Last Sunday night, about twelve o'clock, a number of armed men, with their faces covered, entered the workshop of Mr. Smith, of Snowgatehead, near Holmfirth, in the neighborhood of Huddersfield, and broke all his dressing frames and shears. They proceeded from thence to Horn Coat, about a mile distant, entered the dressing shop of Mr. Joseph Brook, and not content with breaking his frames and shears, which they entirely destroyed, they broke and demolished his household furniture and all the windows. From thence they proceeded to Reins, near Honley, about three miles further, where they arrived about two o'clock, and entered the workshop of Mr. James Brook, and broke one frame, which was all he had, and which had been taken down about five weeks. At the earnest entreaty of Mr. Brook, they were prevailed upon not to break his shears.

"We regret to have to record one of the worst cases which has occurred since the commencement of that terrible system of depredation, which has spread alarm through this manufacturing district, both as it respects the number concerned in it and their wanton and outrageous conduct. On Thursday night, about twelve o'clock, the extensive cloth manufactory of Mr. Joseph Foster, of Horbury, near Wakefield, was surrounded by a large body of armed men, who, after securing all the approaches to the premises, proceeded to break into that part of the mill appropriated to the dressing of cloth, where they completely destroyed all the shears and frames; the former were not merely snipped, but absolutely broken in pieces. They then demolished all the windows, and, as if

actuated by the most diabolical frenzy, broke into those parts of the premises against which these depredators do not pretend to have any ground of complaint, the scribbling mill and weaving shops, and materially injured the machinery, and wantonly damaged a quantity of warp ready for the loom, destroyed not merely the glass of the window, but the frames, which were of cast iron, the windows of the dyehouses, the countinghouse, and even the dwelling houses contiguous to the workshop shared the same fate.

"At the commencement of these dreadful outrages, a detachment from the main body invested the dwelling house occupied by Mr. Foster's sons; they literally shivered the door in pieces, and broke both the window and frame, proceeded to the lodging room of the young men, and demanded the keys of the building, under pain of instant death. They dragged two of them out of bed, and tied them together, making them lie naked upon the floor: the other they compelled to accompany them with the keys, but this last outrage was quite unnecessary, as many practicable breaches had been already made in the building, and a considerable progress made in the work of destruction. The dwelling house occupied by the bookkeeper was also broken into, and his family treated with the most brutal violence; and to complete the full measure of their guilt, they afterwards set fire to the building, but which was happily extinguished, after their departure, before it communicated to the main body of the building, but not before very considerable damage had been done.

"These lawless men, having accomplished their object, assembled in a neighboring field, when the leader called over their numbers, to which each individual answered. Having ascertained that their whole number was there, said, 'the work is done, all is well, disperse'; which order was obeyed."

Such are the accounts that have been published respecting these riots. It was natural enough for the editor of *The Times* to express his disappointment at having to record riots of this sort in England, when he so fondly and humanely hoped that he should have to record no disturbances except such as would take place in France. There appears to have been some serious work at Carlisle. We are told that "many were wounded" before the attack upon the messroom; and that, afterwards, "a woman was killed, several men wounded, and that most of the houses in the market place exhibited some marks of firing." Now, seeing that this was the case, and seeing that soldiers are called out upon all such occasions, as at Nottingham, Manchester, etc., I beg leave to suggest to the hirelings of *The Times,* the *Post,* and *The Courier* whether they are not rather indiscreet in railing so vehemently against the use of troops for similar purposes in France; seeing that ignorant people, the "lower classes," the "populace," the "mob,"

may not be able to see why the invectives made use of against the employment of a military force in that country should not be applicable to the employment of a military force, for similar purposes, in this country.

The Times, in speaking of the extent of the danger from the riots, coolly observes: "we would not wish the public to apprehend more from them, or in them, than there really is. They are mere Mob Riots, which, resulting from *disorderly force,* are to be suppressed by *a force that is ordered and organized."* With what perfect coolness, with what *sang-froid,* with what a disregard of the lives of the people this must have been written! The man who wrote this must look upon the mass of the people as little better than brutes, and must regard the soldiers as raised and kept in pay for the purpose of making war upon them. You hear from him no expression of sorrow at the death of this poor woman, who has, perhaps, left a family of children. All is defiance on his part: all hostility towards the people. Is this the sort of feeling that an Englishman ought to have upon the perusal of news like this? He, alas! knows not what it is to feel hunger and to hear children crying for bread.

WHAT WE NOW call technological unemployment was keenly felt by British workmen as the Industrial Revolution unfolded. Cobbett, noting the deterioration in the conditions of labor, declared: "I wish to see the poor men of England what the poor men of England were when I was a boy." Notwithstanding, he had no objection to the introduction of machinery, which he felt was beneficial to mankind. In the *Political Register* of 1816 he asked: "If we indulge ourselves in a cry against machines, where are we to stop? Is not the flail a machine? The corn could be rubbed out in the hand and winnowed by the breath; but then 999 out of every thousand of us must starve, and the few that remained must become as savages." To Cobbett the villains of the piece were not the machines, but unfair taxation, inflated paper currency, and the national debt. His acceptance of the ma-

chine did not imply any endorsement of the cruel suppression of the workers' demonstrations. "The hirelings call aloud for sending forth penal statutes and troops to put you down," he observed. "I send you the most
persuasive arguments my mind can suggest and all the kindest wishes of
my heart."

The London *Post* Exults After Napoleon's
Downfall at Waterloo, and a French Reporter
Defends the Emperor

EVEN DURING the relatively short Peace of Amiens, when the Allied powers had an armed truce with Bonaparte, the London *Morning Post* carried on its own private and implacable war against the Corsican adventurer. With its peculiarly British "Be damned to you" savor and its reputation for presenting top-flight reportorial talent, the *Post* during the Napoleonic Wars was England's greatest paper. The momentum of its auspicious start on the eve of the American Revolution with a series of stories by the renowned and cantankerous Dr. Samuel Johnson, reporting his tour of the Hebrides, was maintained in the years that followed. Essayist Charles Lamb first won his spurs as a society reporter for the *Post,* going down to Margate to gather news of the "fashionable arrivals."

But it was the *Post* columnist, Coleridge, who really raised the war whoop against Napoleon. British officials charged that an article of his entitled "A Comparison of France under Napoleon with Rome under the First Caesars" led to the rupture of the Peace of Amiens. Certainly Napoleon, quick to throttle the press in lands under his sway, bitterly resented the *Post* attack. While Coleridge was visiting Italy, then under Napoleonic rule, Bonaparte issued an order for his arrest. Warned in time, the poet managed to get aboard a ship, which was chased by a French cruiser almost all the way into an English port. Napoleon's "vindictive appetite was omnivorous," Coleridge commented, "and preyed equally on a Duc d'Enghien and the writer of a newspaper paragraph." Continental papers took heart from the *Post*'s great fight, and, once the dead hand of Napoleonic censorship was removed, opposition papers sprang up, none more famous than the *Mercure rhénan,* edited by the Rhinelander journalist, Joseph Goerres.

At the time of Napoleon's disastrous retreat from Moscow the *Post*'s abuse reached its apogee. A typical comment:

> MURAT—Say, Sire! Shall we fight, or run away,
> Or shall we return, and seek Marshal Ney?
> BONEY—Why, Sir! do you fight—I'll run away,
> And as for returning—if possible—Ney!

It was only human, then, for the *Post* to rejoice at Wellington's victory at Waterloo, reported June 22, 1815, under eight headlines—a number equal to that used to describe the Armistice in the *Morning Post* of November 12, 1918—and equally natural that the *Post* should go out of its way to imply cowardice on the part of Bonaparte on that occasion. The *Post*'s account represents an outstanding piece of coverage of the Napoleonic Wars. Front-line correspondents, like Henry Crabb Robinson, who sent dispatches to *The Times* on Napoleon's campaign in Germany in 1807, were generally unsuccessful in getting to the right spot at the right time. Robinson missed out in Spain on the battle of Corunna, in 1809, arriving after it was all over. A comparison of the *Post* story of June 22, 1815, below, with George Wilkins Kendall's account of the capture of Mexico City epitomizes the great development that took place in the art of battle reporting in the thirty years that followed Waterloo.

> *"One of the most splendid and comprehensive victories ever obtained . . . by British valor"*

London *Morning Post*, June 22, 1815

GREAT AND GLORIOUS NEWS—ANNIHILATION OF BONAPARTE'S WHOLE ARMY—HIS OWN NARROW PERSONAL ESCAPE—CAPTURE OF THE TRAITOR'S PERSONAL STAFF AND CARRIAGE, AND TWO HUNDRED AND TEN PIECES OF CANNON

With hearts gratefully elated and all due thanks to Heaven for the event, we have this day the supreme happiness of announcing one of the most splendid and comprehensive victories ever obtained even by British valor or the illustrious Wellington himself. Its consequences we do not hesitate to announce completely decisive of the fate of Bonaparte, whose army has been completely overthrown, in a general and most tremendous battle, with the loss of the whole of his artillery, while coward at heart, always principally regardful of his own personal safety, he himself narrowly effected his escape.

The honorable Major Percy arrived between eleven and twelve o'clock last night, in a post chaise and four, with two of Napoleon's eagles captured in battle, which were displayed from the windows of the carriage. He was the bearer of dispatches from the Duke of Wellington, dated Waterloo, the nineteenth instant, which state that after the brilliant actions of the sixteenth and seventeenth, His Grace drew up his army in line, which, on the eighteenth, was attacked with desperate vigor by Bonaparte, with the whole of his force. The conflict which ensued was long, dreadful, and most sanguinary, but it gloriously terminated in the complete overthrow of the Tyrant's army, with the loss of two hundred and ten pieces of cannon, 150 by the British, and sixty by the Prussian army, the greater part of Bonaparte's baggage, and nearly the whole of his personal staff.

This much is stated in the dispatches of our illustrious chief; in addition to which, Major Percy informs that on finding his army overthrown and all his hopes destroyed, the vanquished Napoleon, who beheld the last desperate efforts of his troops from a scaffolding situated on an eminence, betook himself to rapid flight on horseback, leaving his carriage and nearly the whole of his personal staff in the possession of the British. The conflict was of so tremendous a description that few prisoners were made; and the Allied Armies were left in pursuit of the shattered remains of the enemy's force, without the slightest prospect of the Tyrant being ever able to rally again, or in any respect to retrieve his fallen fortunes. What renders this great and splendid achievement the more gratifying to us is the proud circumstances of its having been accomplished chiefly by British valor, though every praise is due to the Prussian Chief for his vigorous and cordial cooperation; and under Heaven we trust that the overthrow of the Tyrant, if not already effected, will be accomplished before either the Russian or Austrian armies come up, and without further aid from any of our Allies. Britain, therefore, may indeed be now truly considered as at the summit of glory. Having saved herself by her own exertions, she has saved Europe by her example and support, and to her generous and noble sacrifices will Europe and the whole world be indebted for the overthrow and annihilation of the curse and scourge of the human race—upon which great and godlike event we may now venture to congratulate the British public and the whole race of civilized man.

Colonels Gordon and Canning, belonging to the Duke of Wellington's staff, were both killed close to the person of that illustrious hero, whose own person, always exposed to the greatest danger, is held sacred by Heaven for the general good of the nations of the earth.

The Park and Tower guns will be fired at ten o'clock this morning in honor of the splendid event which it is our pride and happiness this day to record, and an *Extraordinary Gazette* will be published before noon.

Major Percy, on his arrival with the dispatches, first went to Lord Bathhurst's office; but not finding His Lordship there, he proceeded to Lord Harrowby's in Grosvenor Square, where all the Cabinet were assembled, and there delivered the dispatches and the eagles with which he was entrusted, amidst the universal and ecstatic cheerings of the populace.

We shall stop the press to give the official particulars of the dispatches.

* * *

IN IDOLIZING Wellington as "the greatest warrior of the age," the *Post* did less than full justice to the military genius of Napoleon, who inaugurated a revolution in the art of war and, stressing mobility and audacity, astounded Europe with a *Blitzkrieg* that time after time, down through 1809, hurled the combined powers of his enemies headlong to defeat. Finally overreaching himself in Russia in 1812, Napoleon was defeated the following year at Leipzig, in what was appropriately called the Battle of Nations —the greatest battle fought in Europe or America until the First World War. Her manpower depleted after twenty years of warfare, France could no longer stand up against a united Europe. Napoleon was sent to Elba in

1814. Except for the scare of the Hundred Days caused by his escape, that was the end. Waterloo was an anticlimax.

A more sympathetic account of Napoleon's conduct at Waterloo came from the pen of an unnamed French reporter who covered the battle. On November 4, 1815, the London *Times,* on the threshold of a career unrivaled in English journalism, reprinted the account, which originally appeared in Paris. To *The Times* the story gave further illustration of Napoleon's "characteristic traits, his obstinacy, ferocity, and promptitude," and hardly supports the charge of cowardice under fire.

A French reporter's view: "Then the tragedy is ended"

The Times (London), November 4, 1815

It was a dreadful night. The rain fell in torrents and was most oppressive to the troops, bivouacked as they were in the midst of mire, and not having had any time to construct any temporary shelter.

Daylight having appeared, the French took their arms and were surprised to perceive that the English remained not only where they had been the night before, but appeared as if resolved to defend their position. Bonaparte, who had been afraid that they would escape during the night, was much pleased at finding them when he awoke and, not being able to restrain his transport, said to some persons near him at the moment he discovered the enemy:

"Ah! I have them, then—these English!"

Without further consideration, and with that imprudent eagerness which constitutes one of his characteristics, he summoned the columns which had halted in the rear, and without gaining any information, without knowing either the position or the strength of the enemy, without ascertaining that the Prussian army was sufficiently

kept in check by General Grouchy's corps, he resolved on an immediate attack.

Scarcely were the French troops formed when Bonaparte, who had taken his station on a hill not far from the farmhouse at which he slept, sent orders to begin the attack. He walked to and fro with his arms folded over his breast, at a short distance from his staff. The weather was stormy and continued so through the day.

Towards noon, the first discharge of cannon took place from the French line, and a large body of riflemen were dispatched to begin the action. After fighting about an hour, the English seemed to give way a little and the French pressed forward. At every point the one fought the other with equal ardor, and the artillery made frightful havoc.

The points, at which the two English wings had taken their station, having been carried, the French army passed the ravine and approached the positions, which vomited a deluge of balls and grapeshot upon them. The charges, which had been ordered, were immediately executed. The French cavalry darted forward to seize the artillery, but was assailed in its turn by the cavalry of the enemy, and the carnage on both sides was horrible. Neither one side nor the other would yield an inch of ground. Fresh columns advanced, the charges were renewed, and the position was thrice on the point of being forced, but thrice, after performing prodigies of valor, the French were arrested in their progress. They now began to exhibit symptoms of hesitation and inquietude. Several dismounted batteries were put into retreat. A considerable number of wounded soldiers were detached from the main body and spread alarm as to the issue of the battle. Profound silence had succeeded to the acclamations and cries of joy with which soldiers, certain of marching to victory, had before been rending the air. With the exception of the infantry of the guard, all the troops were engaged and exposed in a most destructive fire. The action continued with unabating violence, yet without any decisive result.

It was near seven o'clock when Bonaparte, who had until then remained on the hill, from which he clearly saw all that was passing, contemplated with a look of ferocity the hideous scene of butchery beneath him. The more numerous the difficulties which occurred, the more obstinate did he appear. He was indignant at obstacles which he had so little foreseen, and far from thinking that it was wrong to sacrifice an army, which placed unbounded confidence in him, he incessantly sent fresh troops, with orders to charge and force their way in spite of every resistance. He was several times told that appearances were bad and that the troops were exhausted, but his only answer was: "Forward, forward!"

A general sent information that he could not maintain his position, on account of being dreadfully annoyed by a battery, and asked what he was to do.

"To take the battery," said Bonaparte, turning his back on the aide-de-camp.

An English officer who was wounded and made a prisoner was brought to him. He made several inquiries, and among the rest, what was the strength of the English army. The officer told him that it was very strong and would almost immediately be reinforced by 60,000 men.

"So much the better," said he. "The more we meet, the more we shall conquer."

He dispatched several messengers with dispatches, which he dictated to a secretary, and repeated many times in a tone of distraction: "*The victory is mine—remember to say that.*"

It was at this period, when all his attempts had been abortive, that information was brought to him of Prussian columns debouching on his right flank and threatening his rear; but he would not believe these reports, and constantly answered that these Prussian troops were no other than those of General Grouchy. It was not long, however, before he was undeceived by the violence of the enemy's attack. Part of the Sixth Corps was sent to sustain this new shock, till Grouchy's corps arrived, which was every minute expected. The Prussian corps which now appeared in the field at so critical a moment was that of General Bülow.

Bonaparte, without altering his resolution in any way, was of the opinion that the moment had come to decide the day. He formed, for this purpose, a fourth column, almost entirely composed of the guards. The veterans marched up the hill with the intrepidity which might be expected of them.

The whole army resumed its vigor, and the combat was resumed throughout the line. The guards made repeated charges and were as often repulsed. Overpowered by the irresistible discharge of artillery, which seemed every moment to increase, these invincible grenadiers saw their ranks constantly thinned; but they closed together with perfect coolness. Nothing arrested their progress but death.

The hour of their defeat, however, was come. Enormous masses of infantry supported by an immense force of cavalry, to which the French could oppose no resistance, as their own was entirely destroyed, poured down upon them from all sides with a degree of fury which made all idea of quarter, on either part, out of the question.*

It was in vain that Bonaparte attempted to make a final effort by bringing into action some battalions of the guards which had not yet been employed, and which he himself headed.†

All was useless. Intimidated by what passed around them, this feeble reserve soon yielded, and with the rest fled back like a torrent. The artillerymen abandoned their cannon; the soldiers of the wagon train cut the traces of their horses; the infantry, the cavalry, and every other species of soldiery formed one confused, intermingled mass, partly flying across the roads, partly across the fields. The generals were lost in this crowd; the corps had no longer any regular commander, and not a single battalion existed behind which the rest could rally. The disorder was increased by the darkness of night.

At this time everyone was ignorant of Bonaparte's fate, for he had suddenly disappeared. The general report was that he had fallen in the heat of battle. This intelligence being conveyed to a well-known general, he replied in the words of Megret, after the death of Charles XII at Fredrikshald: "Then the tragedy is ended." (*Voilà la pièce finie.*) Others said that while making a charge at the head of his guards, he had been dismounted and taken prisoner. The same uncertainty prevailed as to Marshal Ney and most of the principal officers.

A great number of persons affirmed that they had seen Bonaparte pass through the crowd and that they knew him by his gray greatcoat and horse. This proved to be the fact. When the

---

* Reporting the stubborn fight put up by the veterans of Napoleon's Imperial Guard, Colonel Sir Augustus Frazer, commanding Royal Horse Artillery, wrote: "I have seen nothing like that moment, the sky literally darkened with smoke, the sun just going down, and which till then had not for some hours broken through the gloom of a dull day, the indescribable shouts of thousands, where it was impossible to distinguish friend and foe. Every man's arm seemed to be raised against that of every other. Suddenly, after the mingled mass had ebbed and flowed, the enemy began to yield, and cheerings and English huzzas announced that the day must be ours."

† This statement was contradicted by Walter Scott in his *Notes on the Battle of Waterloo.* Napoleon, said Scott, harangued the guards from "a remote spot," and Ney, not Napoleon, led the guards. "It is remarkable that, during the whole carnage, none of Bonaparte's suite was killed or wounded, whereas scarcely one of the Duke of Wellington's personal attendants escaped unhurt." More recent students of the battle, notably John Codman Ropes, John Holland Rose, and Captain A. F. Becke, give Ney chief credit for rushing from band to band, brandishing a broken sword, and taunting his men, "Cowards! Have you forgotten how to die?" The facts in dispute are clarified by a participant in the engagement, Sergeant-Major Edward Cotton of the Seventh Hussars, who states: "The first, or leading, column [of the Imperial Guard] was led by Napoleon in person, until the front lines came abreast of where the highroad is cut through the bank beyond the orchard of La Haye-Sainte, a prominent point about two hundred yards to their left of the Genappe road, which they left obliquely on their right; here the Emperor gave them in charge of Ney" (*A Voice from Waterloo* [6th ed., revised, London, 1862], p. 112).

last battalion of the guard which he led into action were overthrown, he was carried away with them and surrounded on all sides by the enemy. He then sought refuge in an orchard adjoining the farm of Cailon, where he was afterwards met by two officers of the guard, who were, like him, endeavoring to evade the enemy. To them he made himself known, and they passed together over the plain, upon which were scattered various Prussian parties. These, however, luckily for the fugitives, were employed in plundering the captured equipage. Bonaparte was recognized on several occasions in spite of the darkness of night, and the soldiers whispered to each other as he passed:

"Look! There is the Emperor!"

These words seemed almost to alarm him, and he hurried forward through the multitude. Where were now the acclamations which used to greet his ear the moment he appeared in the midst of his troops?

AFTER WATERLOO Napoleon was banished to the volcanic island of St. Helena in mid-Atlantic. Six years later the lonely, sick, embittered exile died. "It is my wish," he wrote in his will, "that my ashes shall be laid to rest on the banks of the Seine among the French people whom I have loved so well." Only the words, "Here lies," were cut on his tombstone, which needed no name.

There is a story that George IV of England, who had been feuding with his wife Caroline, daughter of the Duke of Brunswick, for a great many painful years, when told of the death of Napoleon in the words: "Sire, your greatest enemy is dead," exclaimed joyfully,

"Is she, by God!"

Two Newspapers of Paris Defy a Despot and Touch Off the Bloody June Days of 1830

A TRUE BOURBON, Charles X of France "never learned anything and never forgot anything." By his absolutist policy he was bent on blotting out the tradition of revolutionary resistance. Determined to restore reaction, he restricted the suffrage and suspended the liberty of the press. But he had reckoned without the fourth estate, by now a powerful force in the life of the French nation. On July 25, 1830, forty-four Paris newsmen, including Thiers of the *National* and Baude of the *Temps,* protested. "The government has this day lost the character of legality which commands obedience," they declared. "As for ourselves, we resist. It is for France to judge how far her own resistance should extend." Defying a police order forbidding their publication, a number of French newspapers, including the *Temps,* appeared on the streets. Crowds began to form, crying *"Vive la Charte!"* ("Long live the Constitution!") The authorities, badly scared, decided to suppress the incorrigible newspapers. The historic incident was reported by *Le Globe* of Paris:

"The editors of the National *and the* Temps *have this morning resisted"*

Le Globe (Paris), July 27, 1830

The *Constitutionnel* and the *Débats* have not been published this morning.

The editors of the *National* and the *Temps* have this morning resisted the officers who came to break up their presses. They did not resist by open force, but the officers, who were attended with a big display of military force, were obliged to force the doors. The presses were then defaced despite the protests of the proprietors. Since this morning the *gendarmerie* has been stationed on the boulevards and about the Exchange.

THIS *opéra bouffe* before the *Temps* office was witnessed by Louis Blanc, a Socialist newspaperman and editor. In his *History of Ten Years,* a reportorial narrative of the stirring decade, 1830–40, Blanc gives us some colorful details omitted in the terse press account of the incident.

57

Louis Blanc, *The History of Ten Years, 1830-40* (London, 1844-45)

The *Temps,* of all the journals, had been most critical. An invasion of its premises was due momentarily. About noon a detachment of mounted *gendarmerie* drew up in order of battle before the gate. Upon the announcement of the approach of the *commissaire,* M. Baude had the doors of the printing house locked, and the gates opening on the street thrown wide open. The workmen, the contributors, and all those employed on the paper in any capacity drew up in two files. M. Baude stationed himself between them, bareheaded. All stood silent. Passers-by, curiosity aroused, stopped. The gendarmes were obviously uneasy.

The *commissaire* arrived. Obliged to pass between the two files of men who stood mute and impassive on either hand, he became excited, turned pale, and, approaching M. Baude, politely stated the object of his mission.

"It is by virtue of the *ordonnances,* Monsieur," said M. Baude firmly, "that you have come to destroy our presses. Well, then, in the name of the law I call on you to forbear."

The *commissaire* sent for a locksmith. He came, and, just as the doors of the printing house were about to be forced open, M. Baude stopped the man, and, producing a copy of the Code, read him the section relating to the punishment for robbery accompanied by housebreaking. The locksmith uncovered his head to show his respect for the law. Upon being ordered again by the *commissaire* to proceed and appearing about to obey, M. Baude called out ironically,

"Oh, go ahead! It's only a matter of the galleys."

At the same time, preparing to appeal from the *commissaire* to the assize courts, he drew out of his pocket a notebook to enter the names of the witnesses present. The notebook passed from hand to hand, and everyone inscribed his name. The terrified locksmith threw up the job and was loudly cheered. Another was sent for. He tried to carry out the orders, but suddenly found that his tools were gone. Then they got hold of the smith employed to rivet the irons on the convicts. These proceedings, which consumed several hours, were witnessed by a multitude of people, who were given an example of disobedience combined with respect for the law.

THE REACTION of the Parisian populace to these absolutist acts was spontaneous. Surging to the barricades, they fought the feebly led government troops in the narrow streets. At the very beginning of the outbreak the French press was physically unprepared to give the events full coverage,* but an on-the-spot account was forwarded to the London *Times* :

---

* The well-known Paris newspaper, *Galignani's Messenger,* reported on July 31: "The state of the metropolis for the last two days has been such as to render the publication of the *Messenger* impracticable, and obliges us even today, although affairs have assumed a more favorable aspect, to limit our impression to half a sheet and defer the great mass of interesting matter to our next."

"We have changed our government, but not our consciences"

The Times (London), August 2, 1830

A letter of the twenty-ninth of July, accompanying the express [from Paris], says:

"The most horrible carnage has taken place in Paris—yesterday till eight o'clock in the evening, and today till noon. The number of killed and wounded is considerable on both sides, but the Royal Guard was at length repulsed on all points, and the three-colored flag is hoisted on the Tuileries. It could never have been supposed that there was such invincible courage in the population of the capital. Everyone flew to arms, and this morning Paris could have resisted 100,000 men. The Royal Guard is now posted along the road to Saint-Cloud; but it appears that, having received reinforcements from Beauvais, it will attempt another attack this night.

"Calais, July 31, 4 P.M.—The mail coach has just arrived, with the royal arms painted out. It brings neither letters nor passengers from Paris, and the conductor is unfortunately intoxicated. He brings, however, a confirmation of this morning's news—that a provisional government is established, to whom the army has submitted."

IN THE Paris dispatches great stress was placed upon the idealism of the insurgents. The reporter for the Paris paper, *Constitutionnel,* only recently suppressed, gave free reign to typical Parisian sentimentality in his account.

Constitutionnel (Paris), July 30, 1830

Examples of the heroism and probity of the Parisian are innumerable, and all equally worthy of eternal remembrance. We would not willingly omit one of them, but the task is above the strength of the press itself, which we may justly denominate the French Hercules. We are only going to cite those which we have been able to collect in haste at the present moment.

This morning, the thirtieth, at the corner of Rue Montmartre and the boulevard, some citizens, who were clearly simple workingmen, marched along, commanded by one of their comrades, who had been appointed their chief on account of his age, good sense, and experience. On the point of their weapons were fixed loaves of bread and some fowls, which had been regularly distributed among them. Several members of this troop, finding themselves opposite a wine vault, went off to get some spirits, but soon returned to their ranks at the order of their commander.

"Today," said he to them, "not one drop of brandy—not one drop of wine, without water, must any of us drink. We must carry all drunkards to the guardhouse." All the brave men who accompanied him set up an immediate cry, "Our captain is right!" and went their way, ready to fight even fasting, ready to meet death without any other stimulus than their generous and ardent love for their country and for liberty.

At the gates of the Tuileries an individual who was found pillaging made himself a general on his own authority, and planted sentinels with orders to shoot every man who was found leaving the spot. The order was executed, and everybody caught carrying off stolen goods was severely chastised and compelled to surrender what he had taken. Some new trousers were found in one of the barracks of the *gendarmerie*. Some thoughtless individuals put these trousers on over those which they were themselves wearing. The trousers were immediately torn to pieces by their comrades. There was a unanimous cry amongst them: "We came here to conquer, not to rob." Here some poor workmen, having forced the shop of a gunsmith, who had already surrendered his cash and powder, sought for more in all quarters, even among his furniture. In one of his drawers they found some money. One of them shut the drawer instantly and said, "This is not what we were looking after."

Two brave mechanics, whose names we are sorry that we could not learn, having been among the first to enter that part of the Tuileries which the Duchess of Berry inhabited, found a casket of bronze containing a large sum of gold. Staggering under the weight of their load, they entered the court of the Louvre and asked a citizen to help them protect this treasure. The three then repaired to the Hôtel de Ville, where the precious burden was deposited without either asking for or receiving any reward.

An officer of the National Guard requested an ordinary mechanic to prevent people from carrying anything away from the Tuileries. "Be quiet, my captain," he answered. "We have changed our government, but not our consciences."

WITHIN THREE days Charles X was forced to abdicate, and the liberal-minded Duke of Orléans, Louis Philippe, was made "lieutenant general of the kingdom." The middle class supported him, but Louis Philippe determined to face the populace and win it to his side. For the full story, the account by the Paris correspondent of the London *Times* is supplemented by the recollections of that ubiquitous reporter of the insurrection, Alexandre Dumas. Novelist, soldier of fortune, and editor of *La France Nouvelle* and *Les Mousquetaires*, in turn, the quadroon d'Artagnan of the July Days was in the thick of the uprising at virtually every stage. A mounted National Guardsman, he attempted to take the Hôtel de Ville, dodged grapeshot behind one of the bronze lions of the Palais Mazarin, and entered the Tuileries with the invading forces. Dispatched by Lafayette to capture the royal powder magazine at Soissons and bring the powder to Paris—an almost impossible and, as events proved, entirely unnecessary feat—Dumas carried it off with only two companions, but not before threatening to blow out the brains of the military commander in the best style of Athos, Porthos, and Aramis, whom he immortalized some fourteen years later in *The Three Musketeers*. But before considering Dumas' story of the establishment of the constitutional regime, later included in his history of the reign, let us examine the vivid account of the procession to the Hôtel de Ville sent in by a London *Times* reporter.

The D'Artagnan of the July Days reports
Louis Philippe's break with divine-right
monarchy

The Times (London), August 4, 1830

PARIS, AUGUST 1—During the night of the thirtieth of July, the Duke of Orléans came to Paris and received at half-past eight in the morning the commissioners appointed to wait upon him by the meeting of the deputies.

His Royal Highness' proclamation was expressed in a manner worthy of commendation, and was calculated to calm the most distrustful. However, the assembled deputies thought they might take upon themselves to draw up a proclamation also and carry it in a body to the Palais-Royal. The deputies passed through an immense crowd and were greeted with the loudest applause. This first representation of a public authority appearing in the midst of disorder brought with it hope and security.

Before the deputies the barricades fell. The Prince received them with extreme affability and with an expression of his sentiments which produced a marked effect on everyone. When His Royal Highness signified his intention of proceeding on horseback to the Hôtel de Ville, all the deputies consented to accompany him. The ride was long and wearisome, across the barricades, and in the scorching heat of the sun. But what a spectacle! What transports! and what an immense concourse of people!

> *"Vive la Charte!"*
> *"Vive la liberté!"*
> *"Vive le Duc d'Orléans!"*

were acclamations which resounded for nearly two hours, the time which the procession took in moving to the Hôtel de Ville. On entering the grand hall, the Prince embraced M. de Lafayette.

To ALEXANDRE DUMAS the procession to the Hôtel de Ville was a much more tense occasion, for the radicals of Paris wanted to establish a republic, with the patriarch, the Marquis de Lafayette, as president.

Alexandre Dumas, *Le dernier roi* (Paris, 1852)

A deputation from the Chamber was sent to the Duc d'Orléans; first, to congratulate him, and, second, to escort him to the Hôtel de Ville. The Chamber of Peers and the Chamber of Deputies were already won over to his cause. There only remained to win over the Hôtel de Ville—that fortress wherein the great popular goddess, Revolution, had taken refuge at every outbreak for the past nine hundred years.

Again Revolution had returned, and when the power came to the Duke he was forced to go to her to have it consecrated.

They set out. The Duke on horseback, uneasy within, but outwardly calm. M. Laffitte * followed, and, as he could not walk because of a sprained leg, and could not ride in a carriage due to the unpaved streets, he was carried in a sedan chair by Savoyards. From the Palais-Royal to the river's edge, all went well. This was the middle-class quarter, and the middle classes cheered their chosen leader. But once the Pont-Neuf was passed, they were in the people's domain, and marks of enthusiasm gave way to an icy silence. At the Place de Grève they found a state of open revolution. Noting men with bare arms, the ground littered with the straw of the recent encampment, and traces of fighting, elsewhere obliterated, but here carefully preserved, one could hardly have realized that in another quarter the battle was over and that the people had abdicated in favor of the Chamber of Peers, the Chamber of Deputies, and the Palais-Royal. No. The people, sullen, uneasy, watchful, seemed to have taken refuge at the Hôtel de Ville.

The Duke dismounted. Before him yawned the somber vault of the Hôtel de Ville like the mouth of an abyss. Looking quite pale, he went up the steps, disappearing with his small retinue into its gloomy recess. It was a small mouthful for the stony monster that devoured him.

Awaiting his royal visitor at the top was M. de Lafayette.

Chance made me a spectator of the Duke's reception. I had just come from Soissons, where, by General Lafayette's order, I had gone to collect six thousand pounds of powder.

The situation was critical. In going to seek the people's approval in the people's palace, the Duc d'Orléans had made a break, complete and final, with divine-right monarchy. It was the consummation of fifteen years of plotting. It was the consecration of revolt in the person of a prince of the blood.

The declaration was read to the Chamber. When the reader came to these words, "A jury for offenses of the press," the man who was to make the famous September laws leaned over to Lafayette and said:

"That is a useless clause, my dear general, for, as I hope, there will be no more offenses of the press."

When the reading was finished, he placed his hand on his heart and answered:

"As a Frenchman I grieve for the evil done to the country and for the blood that has been spilled. As a prince I am happy to contribute to the happiness of the nation."

Just then a man in the uniform of a general pressed through the crowd and came face to face with the prince. It was General Dubourg, the man who had contributed so effectively to the revolution, a man never heard of before and never mentioned since.

"You have made a sacred promise, Monseigneur," said the general to the prince. "See that you keep it; for"— and he pointed to the square filled with excited people—"if you forget it, the people now gathered in the Place de Grève will know how to remind you."

The prince started, grew red in the face, and said in a moving voice:

"Monsieur, you do not know me. I am an honest man, and when I have a duty to carry out I am not to be won by prayers or moved by threats."

Then, turning to Lafayette, he said a few words in a tone that could only

---

* Jacques Lafitte, a French statesman and financier, who supported Louis Philippe and was later rewarded for his services by being made prime minister.

be heard by those standing close by. Almost at the same instant and as though to make a diversion, the scene took on some grandeur. Lafayette drew him toward the window, put a tricolor flag in his hand, and showed him to the populace in the sacred shadow of the national colors.

The crowd burst into cheers.*

*   *   *

THE OCCASION REMINDED Dumas of a similar scene enacted in July of 1790, exactly forty years before, when Louis XVI accepted the liberal monarchical constitution. Only two and a half years later Louis XVI went to the scaffold, but it took a full eighteen years, to quote Dumas, "to conduct Louis Philippe from triumph to exile."

---

* A week later Louis Philippe was proclaimed King of the French.

Charles Dickens Reports a Spy Hanged by Puppets and a Highwayman Beheaded in Rome

O N DECEMBER 27, 1845, *Punch* carried an announcement of the launching of a new morning paper "of Liberal politics" whose editor was to be Charles Dickens. This was not Dickens' first newspaper experience, for he had previously served as a reporter for the *Mirror of Parliament* and *The Morning Chronicle*, covering debates in the House of Commons. Flinging himself into his new work with characteristic energy, the restless genius (within four months Dickens quit the paper) surrounded himself with a brilliant staff. The initial number of his paper, *The Daily News*, appeared on January 21, 1846, on page six of which was the first installment of "Travelling Letters Written on the Road, by Charles Dickens." These letters, republished and amplified as *Pictures from Italy*, reveal an amazing keenness of eye, an inordinate zest for life, an ability to recognize humor or horror where others saw only the commonplace, that stamp this sinewy writer as one of the greatest reporters of all time. Describing an incident during his visit to Genoa, Dickens wrote:

"The General dead! And the spy hanged!"

The Daily News (London), February 26, 1846

The Theater of Puppets, or Marionetti—a famous company from Milan—is, without any exception, the drollest exhibition I ever beheld in my life. I never saw anything so exquisitely ridiculous. They *look* between four and five feet high, but are really much smaller; for when a musician in the orchestra happens to put his hat on the stage, it becomes alarmingly gigantic, and almost blots out an actor. They usually play a comedy and a ballet. The comic man in the comedy I saw one summer night is a waiter at an hotel. There never was such a locomotive actor since the world began. Great pains are taken with him. He has extra joints in his legs; and a prac- tical eye, with which he winks at the pit, in a manner that is absolutely insupportable to a stranger, but which the initiated audience, mainly composed of the common people, receive (so they do everything else) quite as a matter of course, and as if he were a man. His spirits are prodigious. He continually shakes his legs and winks his eye. And there is a heavy father with gray hair, who sits down on the regular conventional stage bank, and blesses his daughter in the regular conventional way, who is tremendous. No one would suppose it possible that anything short of a real man could be so tedious. It is the triumph of art.

In the ballet, an Enchanter runs

away with the Bride, in the very hour of her nuptials. He brings her to his cave, and tries to soothe her. They sit down on a sofa (the regular sofa! in the regular place, O. P. Second Entrance!), and a procession of musicians enter; one creature playing a drum, and knocking himself off his legs at every blow. These failing to delight her, dancers appear. Four first; then two; *the* two; the flesh-colored two. The way in which they dance; the height to which they spring; the impossible and inhuman extent to which they pirouette; the revelation of their preposterous legs; the coming down with a pause on the very tips of their toes, when the music requires it; the gentleman's retiring up, when it is the lady's turn; the final passion of a *pas de deux;* and the going off with a bound!—I shall never see a real ballet, with a composed countenance again.

I went, another night, to see these Puppets act a play called *St. Helena, or the Death of Napoleon.* It began by the disclosure of Napoleon, with an immense head, seated on a sofa in his chamber at St. Helena; to whom his valet entered, with this obscure announcement:

"Sir Yew ud se on Low!" * (the *ow*, as in cow).

Sir Hudson (that you could have seen his regimentals!) was a perfect mammoth of a man, to Napoleon; hideously ugly; with a monstrously disproportionate face, and a great clump for the lower jaw, to express his tyrannical and obdurate nature. He began his system of persecution, by calling his prisoner "General Buonaparte"; to which the latter replied, with the deepest tragedy,

"Sir Yew ud se on Low, call me not thus. Repeat that phrase and leave me! I am Napoleon, Emperor of France!"

Sir Yew ud se on, nothing daunted, proceeded to entertain him with an ordinance of the British government, regulating the state he should preserve, and the furniture of his rooms: and limiting his attendants to four or five persons.

"Four or five for *me!*" said Napoleon. "Me! One hundred thousand men were lately at my sole command; and this English officer talks of four or five for *me!*"

Throughout the piece, Napoleon (who talked very like the real Napoleon, and was forever having small soliloquies by himself) was very bitter on "these English officers" and "these English soldiers": to the great satisfaction of the audience, who were perfectly delighted to have Low bullied; and who, whenever Low said "General Buonaparte" (which he always did: always receiving the same correction), quite execrated him. It would be hard to say why; for Italians have little cause to sympathize with Napoleon, heaven knows.

There was no plot at all, except that a French officer disguised as an Englishman came to propound a plan of escape; and being discovered, but not before Napoleon had magnanimously refused to steal his freedom, was immediately ordered off by Low to be hanged. In two very long speeches, which Low made memorable by winding up with "Yas!"—to show that he was English—which brought down thunders of applause. Napoleon was so affected by this catastrophe that he fainted away on the spot and was carried out by two other puppets. Judging from what followed, it would appear that he never recovered the

---

* Sir Hudson Lowe, British governor of St. Helena, who enforced the regulations regarding Napoleon's exile with frigid formality.

shock; for the next act showed him, in a clean shirt, in his bed (curtains crimson and white), where a lady, prematurely dressed in mourning, brought two little children, who kneeled down by the bedside, while he made a decent end; the last word on his lips being "Vatterlo."

It was unspeakably ludicrous. Bonaparte's boots were so wonderfully beyond control, and did such marvelous things of their own accord; doubling themselves up, and getting under tables, and dangling in the air, and sometimes skating away with him, out of all human knowledge, when he was in full speech—mischances which were not rendered the less absurd by a settled melancholy depicted on his face. To put an end to one conference with Low, he had to go to a table and read a book; when it was the finest spectacle I ever beheld, to see his body bending over the volume, like a bootjack, and his sentimental eyes glaring

obstinately into the pit. He was prodigiously good in bed, with an immense collar to his shirt, and his little hands outside the coverlet. So was Dr. Antommarchi, represented by a puppet with long lank hair, like Mawworm's,* who, in consequence of some derangement of his wires, hovered about the couch like a vulture, and gave medical opinions in the air. He was almost as good as Low, though the latter was great at all times—a decided brute and villain, beyond all possibility of mistake.

Low was especially fine at the last, when, hearing the doctor and the valet say, "The Emperor is dead!" he pulled out his watch, and wound up the piece (not the watch) by exclaiming, with characteristic brutality,

"Ha! ha! Eleven minutes to six! The General dead! and the spy hanged!"

This brought the curtain down, triumphantly.

DESPITE ADVENTURES with a postilion "as wild and savagely good-looking a vagabond as you would desire to see," but who favored slow-motion travel, Dickens resumed his journey through Italy. Visiting Romeo and Juliet's Verona, he found the house of the Capulets had "now degenerated into a most miserable little inn," whose yard, ankle-deep in dirt, was filled with "a brood of splashed and bespattered geese," with "a grim-visaged dog, viciously panting in a doorway, who would certainly have had Romeo by the leg the moment he put over the wall." At Rome, Dickens attended the carnival, observing "the handsome Roman women" showing off in their barouches "at this time of general license" and great vans of pretty girls moving through confetti-filled streets. Then came the "extraordinary" spectacle—the "last gay madness" of the carnival—the lighting of tapers everywhere until the street was ablaze, and then everybody had but one engrossing object, to extinguish other people's candles and to keep his own alight, and taunts of *"Senza moccolo!"* (without a light!) mingled with peals of laughter.

But a more gruesome sight attracted the reportorial talent of Charles Dickens. It seems that a highwayman had waylaid a Bavarian countess traveling as a pilgrim to Rome, had robbed her, and had beaten her to death

---

* A character in Isaac Bickerstaffe's play, *The Hypocrite.*

with her own pilgrim's staff. Newly married, he gave some of her apparel to his bride, who, suspicions aroused, confessed to a priest. Four days after committing the murder, the highwayman was picked up and kept in prison for some nine months.

"A little patch of black and white, for the long street to stare at, and the flies to settle on"

Charles Dickens, *Pictures from Italy* (London, 1846)

On Friday, as he was dining with the other prisoners, they came and told him he was to be beheaded next morning, and took him away. It was very unusual to execute in Lent; but his crime being a very bad one, it was deemed advisable to make an example of him at that time, when great numbers of pilgrims were coming towards Rome, from all parts, for the Holy Week. I heard of this on the Friday evening, and saw the bills up at the churches, calling on the people to pray for the criminal's soul. So, I determined to go and see him executed.

The beheading was appointed for fourteen and a half o'clock, Roman time: or a quarter before nine in the forenoon. I had two friends with me; and as we did not know but that the crowd might be very great, we were on the spot by half-past seven. The place of execution was near the church of San Giovanni Decollato (a doubtful compliment to Saint John the Baptist), in one of the impassable back streets without any footway of which a great part of Rome is composed— a street of rotten houses which do not seem to belong to anybody, and do not seem to have ever been inhabited, and certainly were never built on any plan, or for any particular purpose, and have no window sashes, and are a little like

deserted breweries, and might be warehouses but for having nothing in them. Opposite to one of these, a white house, the scaffold was built. An untidy, unpainted, uncouth, crazy-looking thing, of course: some seven feet high, perhaps: with a tall gallows-shaped frame rising above it, in which was the knife, charged with a ponderous mass of iron, all ready to descend, and glittering brightly in the morning sun, whenever it looked out, now and then, from behind a cloud.

There were not many people lingering about; and these were kept at a considerable distance from the scaffold by parties of the Pope's dragoons. Two or three hundred foot soldiers were under arms, standing at ease in clusters here and there; and the officers were walking up and down in twos and threes, chatting together, and smoking cigars.

At the end of the street was an open space, where there would be a dust heap, and piles of broken crockery, and mounds of vegetable refuse, but for such things being thrown anywhere and everywhere in Rome, and favoring no particular sort of locality. We got into a kind of washhouse belonging to a dwelling house on this spot; and standing there in an old cart, and on a heap of cart wheels piled against the wall, looked, through a large grated window, at the scaffold, and straight down the street, beyond it, until, in consequence of its turning off abruptly to the left, our perspective was brought to a sudden termination, and had a corpulent officer, in a cocked hat, for its crowning feature.

Nine o'clock struck, and ten o'clock struck, and nothing happened. All the bells of all the churches rang as usual. A little parliament of dogs assembled in the open space and chased each other in and out among the soldiers. Fierce-looking Romans of the lowest class, in blue cloaks, russet cloaks, and rags uncloaked, came and went and talked together. Women and children fluttered on the skirts of the scanty crowd. One large muddy spot was left quite bare, like a bald place on a man's head. A cigar merchant, with an earthen pot of charcoal ashes in one hand, went up and down, crying his wares. A pastry merchant divided his attention between the scaffold and his customers. Boys tried to climb up walls and tumbled down again. Priests and monks elbowed a passage for themselves among the people and stood on tiptoe for a sight of the knife: then went away. Artists, in inconceivable hats of the middle ages, and beards (thank heaven!) of no age at all, flashed picturesque scowls about them from their stations in the throng. One gentleman (connected with the fine arts, I presume) went up and down in a pair of Hessian boots, with a red beard hanging down on his breast, and his long and bright red hair plaited into two tails, one on either side of his head; which fell over his shoulders in front of him, very nearly to his waist, and very carefully entwined and braided!

Eleven o'clock struck; and still nothing happened. A rumor got about,

among the crowd, that the criminal would not confess; in which case, the priests would keep him until the Ave Maria (sunset); for it is their merciful custom never finally to turn the crucifix away from a man at that pass, as one refusing to be shriven, and consequently a sinner abandoned of the Saviour, until then. People began to drop off. The officers shrugged their shoulders and looked doubtful. The dragoons, who came riding up below our window, every now and then, to order an unlucky hackney coach or cart away, as soon as it had comfortably established itself and was covered with exulting people (but never before), became imperious and quick-tempered. The bald place hadn't a straggling hair upon it; and the corpulent officer, crowning the perspective, took a world of snuff.

Suddenly, there was a noise of trumpets. "Attention!" was among the foot soldiers instantly. They were marched up to the scaffold and formed round it. The dragoons galloped to their nearer stations too. The guillotine became the center of a wood of bristling bayonets and shining sabers. The people closed round nearer, on the flank of the soldiery. A long straggling stream of men and boys, who had accompanied the procession from the prison, came pouring into the open space. The bald spot was scarcely distinguishable from the rest. The cigar and pastry merchants resigned all thoughts of business for the moment and, abandoning themselves wholly to pleasure, got good situations in the crowd. The perspective ended, now, in a troop of dragoons. And the corpulent officer, sword in hand, looked hard at a church close to him, which he could see, but we, the crowd, could not.

After a short delay, some monks

were seen approaching to the scaffold from this church; and above their heads, coming on slowly and gloomily, the effigy of Christ upon the cross, canopied with black. This was carried round the foot of the scaffold, to the front, and turned towards the criminal, that he might see it to the last. It was hardly in its place, when he appeared on the platform barefooted; his hands bound; and with the collar and neck of his shirt cut away, almost to the shoulder. A young man—six and twenty—vigorously made, and well shaped. Face pale; small dark mustache; and dark brown hair.

He had refused to confess, it seemed, without first having his wife brought to see him; and they had sent an escort for her, which had occasioned the delay.

He immediately kneeled down, below the knife. His neck fitting into a hole, made for the purpose, in a cross plank, was shut down, by another plank above; exactly like the pillory. Immediately below him was a leathern bag. And into it his head rolled instantly.

The executioner was holding it by the hair, and walking with it round the scaffold, showing it to the people, before one quite knew that the knife had fallen heavily, and with a rattling sound.

When it had traveled round the four sides of the scaffold, it was set upon a pole in front—a little patch of black and white, for the long street to stare at, and the flies to settle on. The eyes were turned upward, as if he had avoided the sight of the leathern bag, and looked to the crucifix. Every tinge

and hue of life had left it in that instant. It was dull, cold, livid, wax. The body also.

There was a great deal of blood. When we left the window, and went close up to the scaffold, it was very dirty; one of the two men who were throwing water over it, turning to help the other lift the body into a shell, picked his way as through mire. A strange appearance was the apparent annihilation of the neck. The head was taken off so close, that it seemed as if the knife had narrowly escaped crushing the jaw, or shaving off the ear; and the body looked as if there were nothing left above the shoulder.

Nobody cared or was at all affected. There was no manifestation of disgust, or pity, or indignation, or sorrow. My empty pockets were tried, several times, in the crowd immediately below the scaffold, as the corpse was being put into its coffin. It was an ugly, filthy, careless, sickening spectacle; meaning nothing but butchery, beyond the momentary interest, to the one wretched actor. Yes! Such a sight has one meaning and one warning. Let me not forget it. The speculators in the lottery station themselves at favorable points for counting the gouts of blood that spurt out, here or there; and buy that number. It is pretty sure to have a run upon it.

The body was carted away in due time, the knife cleansed, the scaffold taken down, and all the hideous apparatus removed. The executioner: an outlaw *ex officio* (what a satire on the punishment!) who dare not, for his life, cross the Bridge of St. Angelo but to do his work: retreated to his lair, and the show was over.

DICKENS STANDS here self-revealed as the great reporter of the law and its abuses. An inveterate champion of the underdog, Dickens never forgot his experiences as a Bow Street reporter. An opponent of imprisonment for debt, the creator of Pickwick and Mr. Micawber was largely instrumental in its eventual abolition. Who could forget his devastating exposé of the prison system—Newgate in *Sketches by Boz*, Fleet Street in *Pickwick Papers*, and the condemned cell ecstasy of Fagin? Against capital punishment he continued to wield a potent pen. It is no coincidence that *The Daily News* in March, 1846, carried a series of articles by Dickens attacking the death penalty. "Though every other man who wields a pen should turn himself into a commentator on the Scriptures, not all their united efforts," Dickens asserted, "could persuade me . . . executions are a Christian law." And whoever reads the account of the beheading of the Italian highwayman would not be likely to forget the lottery speculators picking their lucky numbers by the blood spurting from the guillotined carcass. Nor did Dickens himself ever forget this experience. A dozen years later, in *A Tale of Two Cities,* he summoned up all his reportorial skill to re-create that lurid atmosphere in the scene in which Sydney Carton goes to the guillotine.

General Scott Enters the Halls of the Montezuma

T HE CUP OF FORBEARANCE has been exhausted." In these words President
Polk announced, on May 11, 1846, that a Mexican force had crossed
the Rio Grande, killed some American troopers, and captured the rest. At
last had come the incident ardent expansionists, champing at the bit ever
since Mexico had refused to accept our annexation of Texas, had awaited.
Zach Taylor's early victories in Mexico alarmed Polk, who considered "Old
Rough and Ready" a dangerous presidential rival. Accordingly, he stripped
him of his infantry and sent Winfield Scott on an expedition to capture
Mexico City. Not since the days of Hernando Cortez had a comparable
military exploit been achieved. Seizing Vera Cruz on March 27, 1847, Scott,
with twenty thousand men, heavily outnumbered, pushed into the formidable mountains, cutting himself off from supplies and reinforcements.

Accompanying this expedition was a Yankee reporter, George Wilkins
Kendall, who, a number of years before, had, along with Francis Lumsden,
founded the New Orleans *Picayune,* so named from the small coin. Warfare
against Mexico was not a new story to him. In 1841 he had joined the ill-
fated Santa Fe expedition, fighting for the independent state of Texas and
ending up in a prison in Mexico City, which he compared to the "Black
Hole" of Calcutta. Belligerently anti-Mexican after that experience, Kendall took the first opportunity to join Taylor. He reported how Jeff Davis'
impetuous Mississippians, supported by Sherman's grape and canister, won
the day at Buena Vista. But as soon as the Scott campaign was organized
he attached himself as a voluntary aide to the staff of General Worth and
participated in all the fighting on this expedition. Using a system of couriers and boats, "Mr. Kendall's express" got the news back to New Orleans
before any of his competitors and even ahead of the official dispatches.

Before Mexico City formidable obstacles awaited Scott's forces. "A
single failure," Kendall observed, "cut off as they were from all hope of
reinforcements, would bring the Mexicans upon the invaders in such overwhelming numbers that even the most obstinate and enduring valor would
not be able to withstand them." After defeats at Contreras and Churubusco,
Santa Anna, a veteran double-crosser, not uninfluenced by Yankee dollars,
agreed to an armistice, which Kendall in his dispatches vehemently denounced. When news of the truce reached the capital, angry crowds gathered before the palace, according to an eyewitness who retailed the story
to Kendall, crying out, "Death to the wooden-legged tyrant!" "Down with
the traitor who wants to sell us out!" Santa Anna crossed up the Americans,
and the blood bath continued. At last, on September 13, Chapultepec, a
rocky eminence commanding the western approaches to Mexico City, fell
after desperate resistance to Americans, who, like medieval knights,

mounted the walls on scaling ladders to carry the Castillo. To escape gringo bayonets, many retreating Mexicans, chiefly young cadets, Kendall reported, dashed over the precipice "in the extremity of their fright." Kendall himself was wounded in the knee, but rode ahead without stopping. The fall of Chapultepec opened the way to an attack on the western gate of the capital. Kendall's announcement of the victory appeared in the *Picayune* on October 14:

George Wilkins Kendall, New Orleans Picayune *correspondent, describes the fall of Mexico City*

New Orleans *Daily Picayune*, October 14, 1847

CITY OF MEXICO, SEPTEMBER 14, 1847 —Another victory, glorious in its results and which has thrown additional luster upon the American arms, has been achieved today by the army under General Scott—the proud capital of Mexico has fallen into the power of a mere handful of men compared with the immense odds arrayed against them, and Santa Anna, instead of shedding his blood as he had promised, is wandering with the remnant of his army no one knows whither.

The apparently impregnable works on Chapultepec, after a desperate struggle, were triumphantly carried; Generals Bravo and Mouterde, besides a host of officers of different grades, taken prisoners; over 1000 noncommissioned officers and privates, all their cannon and ammunition, are in our hands; the fugitives were soon in full flight towards the different works which command the entrances to the city, and our men at once were in hot pursuit.

General Quitman, supported by General Smith's brigade, took the road by the Chapultepec aqueduct toward

the Belén gate and the Ciudadela; General Worth, supported by General Cadwalader's brigade, advanced by the San Cosme aqueduct toward the *garita* * of that name. Both routes were cut up by ditches and defended by breastworks, barricades, and strong works of every description known to military science. Yet the daring and impetuosity of our men overcame one defense after another, and by nightfall every work to the city's edge was carried.

General Quitman's command, after the rout at Chapultepec, was the first to encounter the enemy in force. Midway between the former and the Belén gate, Santa Anna had constructed a strong work; but this was at once vigorously assaulted by General Quitman, and aided by a flank fire from two of Duncan's guns, which General Worth had ordered to approach as near as possible from the San Cosme road, the enemy was again routed and in full flight. They again made a stand from their strong fortifications at and near the Belén *garita*, opening a tremendous fire not only of round shot,

* Gate.

grape, and shell, but of musketry; yet boldly General Quitman advanced, stormed, and carried the works, although at great loss, and then every point on this side the city was in our possession. In this onslaught two of our bravest officers were killed—Captain Drum and Lieutenant Benjamin.

Meanwhile General Worth was rapidly advancing upon San Cosme. At the English burying ground the enemy had constructed a strong work. It was defended by infantry for a short time, but could not resist the assault of our men. The affrighted Mexicans soon fled to another line of works nearer the city, and thus General Worth was in possession of the entrance to San Cosme. As his men advanced toward the *garita,* the enemy opened a heavy fire of musketry from the housetops, as well as of grape, canister, and shell from their batteries, thus sweeping the street completely. At this juncture the old Monterey game, of burrowing and digging through the houses, was adopted. On the right, as our men faced the enemy, the aqueduct offered a partial shelter; on the left, the houses gave some protection; but many were still killed or wounded by the grape which swept every part, as well as by the shells which were continually bursting in every direction. About eight o'clock the work of the pickax and the crowbar, under the direction of Lieutenant G. W. Smith, of the Sappers and Miners, had fairly commenced, and every minute brought our men nearer the enemy's last stronghold.

In the meantime two mountain howitzers were fairly lifted to the top of one of the houses and into the cupola of the church, from which they opened a plunging and most effective fire, while one of Duncan's guns, in charge of Lieutenant Hunt, was run

up under a galling fire to a deserted breastwork, and at once opened upon the *garita.* In this latter daring feat, four men out of eight were either killed or wounded, but still the piece was most effectively served. The work of the Miners was still going on. In one house which they entered, by the pickax, a favorite aide of Santa Anna's was found. The great man had just fled, but had left his friend and his supper. Both were well cared for—the latter was devoured by our hungry officers; the former, after doing the honors of the table, was made a close prisoner. Just as the dark was setting in, our men had dug and mined their way almost up to the very guns of the enemy, and now, after a short struggle, they were completely routed and driven out with the loss of everything. The command of the city by the San Cosme route was attained.

During the night, General Quitman commenced the work of throwing up breastworks and erecting batteries, with the intention of opening a heavy cannonade upon the Ciudadela with the first light this morning. At ten o'clock at night General Worth ordered Captain Huger to bring up a twenty-four-pounder and a ten-inch mortar to the *garita,* or gate, of San Cosme and, having ascertained the bearings and distance of the grand plaza and palace, at once opened upon these points. The heavy shells were heard to explode in the very heart of the city. At a little after midnight Major Palacios, accompanied by two or three members of the municipal council of the city, arrived at General Worth's headquarters, and in great trepidation informed him that Santa Anna and his grand army had fled, and that they wished at once to surrender the capital! They were referred to the commander-in-chief, and immediately started for Tacubaya; but in the meantime the firing upon the town ceased.

At seven o'clock this morning General Scott, with his staff, rode in and took quarters in the national palace, on the top of which the Stars and Stripes was already flying. An immense crowd of blanketed *leperos*, the scum of the capital, were congregated in the plaza as the commander-in-chief entered it. They pressed upon our soldiers and eyed them as though they were beings of another world. So much were they in the way, and with such eagerness did they press around, that General Scott was compelled to order our dragoons to clear the plaza.* They were told, however, not to injure or harm a man in the mob—they were all our friends!

About five minutes after this, and while General Worth was returning to his division near Alameda, he was fired upon from a house near the Convent of San Francisco. Some of the cowardly Polkas, who had fled the day previous without discharging their guns, now commenced the assassin game of shooting at every one of our men they saw, from windows, as well as from behind the parapets on the *azoteas* or tops of the houses. In half an hour's time our good friends, the *leperos*, in the neighborhood of the hospital of San Andrés and the Church of Santa Clara, also commenced discharging muskets and throwing bottles and rocks from the *azoteas*. I have neglected to mention that, just previous to this, Colonel Garland had been severely wounded by a musket fired by some miscreant from a window.

For several hours this cowardly war upon our men continued, and during this time many were killed or wounded. It was in this species of fighting that Lieutenant Sidney Smith received his death wound. The division of General Twiggs in one part of the city, and General Worth in another, were soon actively engaged in putting down the insurrection. Orders were given to shoot every man in all the houses from which the firing came, while the guns of the different light batteries swept the streets in all directions. As the assassins were driven from one house they would take refuge in another; but by the middle of the afternoon they were all forced back to the barriers and suburbs. Many innocent persons have doubtless been killed during the day, but this could not be avoided. Had orders been given at the outset to blow up and demolish every house or church from which one man was fired upon, the disturbances would have been at once quelled. As it is, I trust that the lesson the rabble and their mischievous leaders have received today may deter them from future outrages.

On entering the palace General Scott at once named General Quitman governor of Mexico—a most excellent

---

* In his account of *The War between the United States and Mexico*, which he had Carl Nebel handsomely illustrate, Kendall adds this supplementary information: "Among them were hundreds of liberated convicts, many of whom had arms concealed under their ragged vestments, besides a number of the national guard, who, changing their uniforms, and throwing the universal blanket of the country over their shoulders, now mingled with the throng of the more worthless. They had left their arms, either at their own houses or at points designated, and were ready to open upon the invaders at the first signal. One condition upon which the convicts were liberated the preceding night was that they should stir up resistance against the invaders, and the *ladrones* and many of the lower orders of the national guard had a double object in view in keeping up hostilities—the opportunity to gratify their deep hatred of foreigners by a system of assassination they were led to believe justifiable. and to plunder the more wealthy of their own countrymen at the same time."

appointment. Some wag immediately proclaimed aloud in the plazas as follows: "General John A. Quitman, of Mississippi, has been appointed governor of Mexico, *vice* General José María Tornel, resigned—*very suddenly!*" It seems that the valiant Tor- nel ran off at an early hour, and his magnificent house has been converted into a hospital for our wounded officers.

Yours, etc.,

G. W. K.

THE OFFICER ingenious enough to install the mountain howitzers in the church cupola was a young lieutenant named Ulysses Simpson Grant. He was but one of an all-star cast of younger players who covered themselves with glory in this performance, among them Captains Robert E. Lee and George B. McClellan, distinguishing themselves in the great outflanking operations. Of Stonewall Jackson at Chapultepec, Kendall wrote: "I never saw a man work as hard as young Jackson, tearing off harness and dragging out dead and kicking horses."

The war ended, Kendall outdid himself with his news beat of the signing of the Treaty of Guadalupe Hidalgo (ceding Texas, Arizona, New Mexico, and California), in February, 1848, and signed by an emissary previously repudiated by the American government. A copy of the treaty was brought to New Orleans by chartered steamer, outracing the government's own boat as well as that of Kendall's competitor, James L. ("Mustang") Franer, of the New Orleans *Delta*. Kendall then went to Europe for a well-deserved rest. But the year was 1848, and the place he chose for a vacation was Paris. One June day, as he was getting a shave in the Palais-Royal, revolution suddenly burst out all around him. Kendall dodged bullets and climbed Montmartre to view the June Days. His graphic dispatches, though expressing the view that France was not yet ready for democracy, were avidly read by New Orleans' heavy French population and kept the *Picayune*'s circulation at record heights.

A February Revolt Brings a Republic to France, but the Bloody Strife of the July Days Forecasts Its Early Doom

I N HIS NEWSPAPER *Le Mois*, Alexandre Dumas, only a short time after the accession of Louis Philippe, predicted that the King's government, resting as it did upon "the aristocracy of ownership," would fall, for that aristocracy was "each day sapped by internal dissensions." Mercilessly caricatured in the press by Honoré Daumier, the King gravitated toward reaction, and the last years of his reign were dominated by the archconservative, François Guizot. A widespread depression in the years 1846–47 increased unrest and revolutionary agitation. When the government prohibited a great public banquet that had been planned by the opposition party for February 22, 1848, revolution once more broke out in Paris.

"Mourir pour la patrie!"

The Times (London), February 26, 1848

PARIS, FEBRUARY 24—I write in the midst of alarm and excitement indescribable. In two words—the change of ministry will not satisfy the people, who are now, I believe, unanimous.

The King has been required to abdicate in favor of the Count de Paris, under the regency of the Duchess of Orléans.

At ten o'clock a column of six hundred or eight hundred people of all ranks, who had been fighting, passed up the boulevard. Among them were evidently many of the *communistes,* and, possibly, some of those malefactors who will mix in all popular movements. The bearing and attitude of this column was terrible. The subsequent act of one of the party justified the apprehension which their appearance suggested.

Although M. Guizot had returned from the ministry, the Hôtel des Affaires Étrangères remained occupied and guarded by troops. About ten o'clock a young man walked up to the officer in command and blew his brains out with a pistol. Seeing him fall, his soldiers without orders fired on the people, of whom four or five were killed.

The report of this discharge, at the moment when we flattered ourselves that all was tolerably well over, created a painful sensation. Twenty minutes afterwards, however, a most touching and melancholy procession arrived, and, as far as I could perceive, turned alarm into rage.

The buzz of an approaching multitude coming from the Boulevard des Capucines was heard, and a low song of death, *Mourir pour la patrie,* was chanted by the throng instead of the victorious *Marseillaise.* Mingled with this awful and imposing chorus, the noise of wheels could be heard. A large body of the people slowly advanced. Four in front carried torches. Behind them came an open cart surrounded by torchbearers. The light was strong, and discovered four or five dead bodies, partly undressed, which appeared to have been carefully ranged in the cart.

When the head of the column reached the corner of the Rue Lepelletier, the song was changed to a burst of fury which will not soon be forgotten by those who heard it. The procession halted at the office of the *National,* and the whole party burst into a unanimous shriek or cry of *Vengeance!* You know how sonorous is that word when pronounced in French. The dead bodies in the cart were those of the men who fell under the fire of the soldiers above-mentioned.

The night was an awful one. The noise of workmen appeared to break on the stillness. Having heard a similar one in 1830, I guessed what was going on. Barricades—one immensely strong at the end of the Rue Richelieu—were in progress of construction. This has continued up to this moment (half-past ten). Every tree on the whole line of the boulevard has been felled. Every one of the superb lampposts has been thrown down, and all converted into barricades.

At the corner of every street is a barricade—gentlemen, shopkeepers, clerks, workmen, all laboring at the work with an eagerness and an earnestness beyond description.

The King must go further than he has, or defend his position to the last extremity.

Half-past one—I am informed that the Palace of the Tuileries, which has been attacked by the people, is likely to fall into their power. I am equally told that the King has abdicated in favor of the Count de Paris, but that this will not satisfy the people, who now call for a reversal of the dynasty and the formation of a provisional government. If this be true "the Republic" is not far off.

Three o'clock—It is all true. The King formally abdicated in the Chamber of Deputies at one o'clock and then proceeded to Neuilly under an escort of cuirassiers.

The people took possession of the Tuileries without resistance and gutted it. The throne has just been carried up the boulevard. The tricolored flag has been superseded by a red flag.

* * *

THE PROVISIONAL revolutionary government ignored Louis Philippe's decree of abdication in favor of his grandson and proclaimed a republic. The ex-monarch's flight from the country under the pseudonym of plain "Mr. Smith" was reported from Paris and Newhaven (start and finish) in news dispatches to the London *Times,* but some of the choicest details of the journey were later recounted by Victor Hugo in his *Choses vues* (*Things Seen*). Hugo, a fighting liberal and humanitarian, was among that numerous group of journalists and men of letters, including Balzac and Dumas, who helped in no small measure in shaping the course of the '48 Revolution in Paris. Alphonse de Lamartine headed the right-wing republicans and Louis Blanc the radicals. Hugo, when the revolt broke out, had only just

been elected to the legislature (2500 more votes were cast for him than for
Louis Napoleon Bonaparte, who had recently slipped back to France).
Eschewing extremism from both left and right, Hugo, on February 24, when
the Revolution was at its height, mounted the mayoralty building in his
Paris precinct to announce the abdication of Louis Philippe and the establishment of a new liberal ministry under a queen regent. Thence he tore over
to the Place de la Bastille, climbed the base of the July Column, and tried
to talk down a howling mob of twenty thousand in fighting mood. "Neither
king nor queen. No masters!" the crowd shouted menacingly. When a
worker leveled his rifle at him, Hugo reported: "I gazed at him steadily."

As the London *Times'* story indicates, Louis Philippe pushed his luck
pretty far.

The Times (London), March 2, 1848

PARIS, FEBRUARY 28—When the people appeared on the Place Carrousel
the King was still in the court of the
Tuileries on horseback. He had just
time to save himself, without change
of clothes or money, and go with the
Queen through the garden to the Place
de la Concorde. They intended to go
to the Chamber of Deputies, but when
they reached the Obélisque a rush
took place, and though surrounded by
officers it appeared probable that they
would be captured; and then they
escaped with difficulty through the
press, and got away in a carriage by
the Champs-Elysées. When at Neuilly,
the National Guard clubbed together
to give them enough pocket money to
continue their journey!

* * *

FOR THAT journey through France we are indebted to Hugo's account.

"Mr. Smith" takes French leave when
les misérables *start the '48 Revolution*

Victor Hugo, *Choses vues* (sixth edition, Paris, 1887)

It was M. Crémieux who bore the sad
tidings to King Louis Philippe: "Sire,
you must leave Paris."

The King had already abdicated.
The fatal signature had been affixed.
He looked straight at M. Crémieux.

The sharp firing in the Palais-Royal
could be heard. The Municipal Guards
of the Château d'Eau were proceeding
to attack the barricades in the Rue de
Valois and the Rue Saint-Honoré.

Every moment wild shouting broke
out and drowned the reports of the
musketry. It was apparent that the
populace was approaching. From the
Palais-Royal to the Tuileries it is but
a stride for the Giant who is called
Revolt.

Extending his hand in the direction
whence came the ominous shouts, M.
Crémieux repeated his warning:
"Sire, you must leave."

Without saying a word in reply and without removing his eyes from M. Crémieux, the King took off his general's hat, which he handed to someone beside him at random, doffed his uniform bearing the heavy silver epaulets, and said, without rising from the great armchair in which he had reclined, as if exhausted, for several hours:

"A round hat, a frock coat."

These were procured. In an instant he was nothing but an elderly tradesman.

Then he cried out in an excited tone:

"My keys, my keys!"

The keys were not forthcoming.

Meanwhile the noise increased. The firing seemed to get closer. The terrible din increased.

The King kept repeating: "My keys, my keys!"

At length the keys were found and brought to him. He locked a portfolio which he carried in his arms, and a still larger portfolio assigned to the care of his valet. He displayed a feverish agitation. Around him all was hurry-skurry. The princess and the valets could be heard calling out: "Quick, quick!" The Queen alone was cool and proud.

They started. They traversed the Tuileries. The King gave his arm to the Queen, or, to be more accurate, the Queen gave her arm to the King. The Duchess de Montpensier was supported by M. Jules de Lasteyrie, the Duke de Montpensier by M. Crémieux. Said the Duke to M. Crémieux:

"Remain with us, M. Crémieux. Do not leave us. Your name may be useful to us."

In this manner they reached the Place de la Révolution. There the King turned pale.

He looked around for the four carriages which he had commanded from his stables. They were not there.

At the entrance to the stables the driver of the first carriage had been shot, and at the time the King was seeking them in the Place Louis XV, the people were burning them in the Place du Palais-Royal.

At the foot of the obelisk a small hackney carriage with one horse was stopped.

In the carriage were four women holding four children on their knees.

The four ladies were Mesdames de Nemours and de Joinville and two ladies of the court. The four children were the King's grandsons.

Hurriedly opening the door, the King commanded the four ladies:

"Get out, all of you, all of you."

These were the only words he spoke.

The firing became more and more alarming. The surging of the mob entering the Tuileries could now be heard.

In the twinkling of an eye the four ladies were standing on the pavement, the same pavement whereon the scaffold of Louis XVI had been erected.

The King mounted or rather plunged into the empty carriage. The Queen followed him. Madame de Nemours mounted in front. The King still retained his portfolio under his arm, but had the larger, a green one, placed inside the cab. This was accomplished with some difficulty. Finally, M. Crémieux pushed it in with his fist.

"Go on," ordered the King.

The cab started. They took the Neuilly road.

Thuret, the King's valet, mounted behind. But he could not hold to the bar which occupied the place of a bracket seat, and he attempted to bestride the horse, but ended by running on foot. The carriage passed him.

Thuret ran as far as Saint-Cloud, thinking to find the King there. But he found that he had proceeded to the Trianon.

Just then the Princess Clémentine and her husband, the Duke of Saxe-Coburg, arrived by railway.

"Quick, madame," said Thuret. "Let us take the train and go to the Trianon. The King is there."

In this way Thuret proceeded to rejoin the King.

Meanwhile, at Versailles the King had succeeded in procuring a berlin and a kind of omnibus. He occupied the carriage with the Queen; his suite the omnibus. They hired post horses and set out for Dreux.

Resuming his journey, the King now took off his false hair and put on a cap of black silk, which he pulled down to his eyes. His beard had not been trimmed since the previous day. He had had no sleep. He was unrecognizable. He turned to the Queen, who remarked: "You look a hundred years old!"

There are two roads to Dreux. That to the right is the better, well paved, and is the road generally taken. The other is full of ruts and is the longer.

The King ordered: "Postilion, take the left road."

This was a shrewd move, as he was hated at Dreux and some people were waiting on the highroad with hostile intentions. In this manner he escaped danger.

The *sous-préfet* of Dreux, who had been notified of his approach, joined him and handed him twelve thousand francs—half in notes, and half in silver in bags.

Leaving the omnibus behind to follow as best it could, the berlin proceeded towards Evreux. The King knew that about a league from the town there lived a faithful adherent, M. de ——.

It was dark when the carriage reached the mansion.

Thuret descended, and rang for a long time. At last someone appeared.

Thuret asked for M. de ——.

He was away. It was winter. M. de —— was in town.

His farmer, who had opened the door, explained this to Thuret.

"It does not matter," replied Thuret. "I have here an old lady and gentleman, friends of his, who are very tired. Just open the doors for us."

"I have not got the keys," said Renard.

The King was worn out by fatigue, suffering, and hunger. Renard saw the old man and had compassion on him.

"Monsieur et madame," he repeated. "Pray come in. I cannot open the château for you, but I can open the farmhouse. Come in. Meanwhile I will go in search of my master at Evreux."

The King and Queen alighted. Renard conducted them to the lower room in the farm. Within, a good fire blazed. The King was chilled to the bone.

"I am very cold," he remarked, and added: "I am very hungry."

Renard asked: "Monsieur, would you like some onion soup?"

"Very much," said the King.

They made some onion soup, and produced the remains of the farm breakfast, something that looked like cold stew, and an omelet.

The King and Queen seated themselves at table and everyone with them —Renard, the farmer, his sons from the plow, and Thuret the valet.

The King ate greedily what they put before him. The Queen did not eat a thing.

In the midst of the meal the door

opened. The newcomer was M. de ——, who had hurried out from Evreux.

Recognizing Louis Philippe, he exclaimed: "The King!"

"Silence!" cried the King.

But it was too late.

M. de —— reassured him. Renard was a worthy fellow. They might trust him. All the people at the farm could be depended upon.

"Well," said the King, "I must leave at once. How shall I proceed?"

"Where do you wish to go?" inquired Renard.

"Which is the nearest seaport?"

"Honfleur."

"Well, then, I will make for Honfleur."

"All right," said Renard.

"How far is it from here?"

"Twenty-two leagues."

The King was alarmed, and exclaimed: "Twenty-two leagues!"

"You will reach Honfleur tomorrow morning," Renard assured him.

Renard had a trap in which he was accustomed to go to market. He was a breeder and seller of horses. To this vehicle he now harnessed a pair of strong animals.

The King settled himself on one side, Thuret on the other. As coachman, Renard seated himself in the center. Placing a bag of corn across the apron, they started on their way. It was seven o'clock at night.

The Queen did not leave for another two hours, traveling in the carriage with the post horses.

The King had put the bank notes in his pocket. The moneybags worried him.

"More than once the King was on the point of telling me to throw them away," Thuret recalled to me later, when narrating these details.

Their passage through Evreux was not without some trouble. At the end of the town, near St. Taurin's Church, were some people collected, who proceeded to stop the carriage.

Seizing the bridle, a man stated: "They say the King is escaping this way."

Another man held a lantern to the King's face.

Finally, some kind of officer of the National Guard, who had for some moments been scrutinizing the harness in a suspicious manner, cried out:

"Hold everything! It is Père Renard. I know him, citizens."

Then, turning to Thuret, he added in a low voice: "I recognize your companion in the corner. Get away as fast as you can!"

Thuret has since told me: "He spoke just in time, for, as I feared he was going to cut the traces, I was about to stab him. I had my knife open in my hand."

Renard whipped his horses, and they left Evreux behind them.

They kept on all night. From time to time they halted at the inns upon the road, and Renard baited his horses.

He advised Thuret: "Get down. Be as much at your ease as you can. Talk familiarly to me." He also "tutoyed" the King.

Pressing his black cap down almost upon his nose, the King maintained a profound silence.

At seven A.M. they reached Honfleur. The horses had come twenty-two leagues, without rest, in twelve hours. They were exhausted.

"It is time," pronounced the King.

From Honfleur the King reached Trouville, where he hoped to conceal himself in a house formerly occupied by M. Duchâtel when he came to bathe on his vacations. But the house was shut up. He was obliged to take shelter with a fisherman.

In the morning General Rumigny came in, and all was nearly lost—an officer had recognized him on the quay.

At last the King was ready to embark. The provisional government greatly assisted him.

Nevertheless, at the very last moment, a commissary of police, desirous of demonstrating his great zeal, presented himself on board the vessel in which the King was, in plain sight of Honfleur and the bridge.

Between decks he kept staring at the old gentleman and lady who were seated in a corner, looking as if they were intent upon their slender baggage.

Nonetheless, he made no move.

Suddenly the captain took out his watch and asked:

"*M. le Commissaire de Police*, do you intend to remain on board or go ashore?"

"Why do you ask?" replied the commissary.

"Because if you are not in France in fifteen minutes you will be in England in the morning."

"You are about to sail, then?"

"Immediately."

It was a very downcast commissary who made his decision to leave, after having vainly attempted to hunt down his prey.

The vessel sailed.

Within sight of Honfleur she nearly foundered when she collided with a large ship, which carried away a portion of the mast and bulwarks, the weather being foul and the night dark. These injuries were repaired as well as possible, and the next morning the King and Queen were in England.

* * *

The Times (London), March 4, 1848

NEWHAVEN, SUSSEX, MARCH 3—We are gratified at being able to state that the ex-King and Queen of the French have arrived in England.

On leaving Paris they proceeded to Versailles, where they hired a common vehicle to take them to Dreux. Here they put up at the house of a person on whose fidelity they could rely, where they passed the night. This friend, whom we understand to be a farmer, procured disguises for the royal fugitives and suite, the King habiting himself in an old cloak and an old cap, having first shaved his whiskers, discarded his wig, and altogether so disguised himself as to defy the recognition even of his most intimate friends. The other disguises were also complete. [The reporter then summarizes the route from Dreux to Honfleur, and thence to Trouville, where the party was delayed by bad weather.]

On Thursday afternoon the gentleman who sheltered the dethroned monarch and his consort at Honfleur engaged a French fishing boat to convey the fugitives from Honfleur to Havre, and fearing that in this small vessel the features of the King might be recognized, the gentleman engaged a person to interpret French to the King, who, to render his disguise more complete, passed as an Englishman. Nothing of moment transpired on the passage to Havre, where the *Express* was waiting with her steam up, and at nine o'clock on Thursday evening the royal fugitives and suite set sail for England. The vessel reached the offing of Newhaven Harbor at seven o'clock this morning, but owing to the state of the tide she could not enter the harbor till nearly twelve o'clock. Meanwhile, however, General Dumas and General Rumigny (members of the ex-King's party) landed in boats, General Dumas proceeding to London with the intelligence of Louis Philippe's arrival, whilst General Rumigny repaired to the Bridge Inn and gave directions to prepare the best apartments for some guests about to land on the pier. This, of course, was done, but having ascertained that the guests were no less than the ex-King and Queen of the French, the landlady laid carpets from the entrance door to the sitting room, and every arrangement was made to render the apartments as comfortable as their size would admit.

Shortly before twelve o'clock the royal fugitives landed on the quay, and the moment the King set his foot on the shore he emphatically exclaimed, "Thank God, I am on British ground."

* * *

Two YEARS LATER "Mr. Smith" died in England, a broken man. "During the eighteen years of his reign," commented the London *Daily News*, "not one single great or generous idea germinated in his soul." The explanation of the Revolution that catapulted him from the throne was simple. To Louis Blanc there was "only one cause, poverty." But the remedy was more obscure.

The February Revolution in Paris was followed by mass uprisings in Germany, Austria, and Italy. In Vienna Metternich, the high priest of world reaction since 1815, was forced to flee in a laundry wagon. In Berlin the troops of the Prussian King, Frederick William IV, fired on "my dear Berliners." Carl Schurz, later to gain fame in America as a soldier, a statesman, and a newspaper editor (with Clemenceau he covered the events of the Reconstruction era for the New York press), reported that the people gathered before the palace, chanting "Jesus, My Refuge!" From Milan, the London *Times* correspondent, Michael B. Honan, reported the uprising of the masses, now openly avowing their "long-concealed detestation of Austria."

In France a moderate provisional government, with a sprinkling of socialists, yielded to the demands of the people of Paris by issuing a decree guaranteeing work for all citizens and by establishing "national workshops," Louis Blanc's pet project. Incompetent direction contributed to the collapse of this work-relief program, and unemployment and poverty were the twin specters that stalked the streets of Paris. When the National Assembly set up General Cavaignac as a "republican dictator," backed by the National Guard, and proceeded to shut down the workshops, the bloodiest street fighting Europe had ever seen broke out toward the end of June. The first detailed story of the June Days appeared in Horace Greeley's *New York Tribune* on July 14, 1848, under the headline: "THE FOUR DAYS OF BLOOD: Full Particulars of the Horrid Scene." The account that followed stressed the dangerous and terroristic character of the radical

forces, "the *ouvriers* and the dregs of the population of Paris," and credited
them with acts of dreadful butchery, including the disemboweling of National Guardsmen. Again, as in the previous Paris uprisings, the best stories
were sent out by foreign correspondents stationed in Paris, for, as the
Tribune explained, "the journals of Paris were not able to appear, except
in single leaves, and even these in limited numbers." Although ample record of the gory details is found in *Galignani's Messenger* for June 29, 1848,
perhaps the most balanced, certainly the most sympathetic, account of the
abortive workmen's revolt was sent in by a young American newspaper reporter who had arrived in Paris in the midst of the June Days.

Greeley's reporter of the Paris revolt had known the pinch of want himself. Born in New Hampshire, Charles A. Dana had been forced by family
circumstances to go to work at the age of twelve and had stood by when
his employer was ruined by the Panic of 1837. After completing his studies
at Harvard, he joined Brook Farm, an experiment in communal living near
West Roxbury, Massachusetts, and stayed until a disastrous fire terminated
the venture. Greeley then engaged him for the *Tribune,* starting him off at
ten dollars a week and advancing him to fourteen dollars. During 1848 and
1849 he traveled through Europe, supporting himself by writing as many as
five letters a week, which appeared in the *Tribune* and newspapers in other
cities as well.

In the August 17 issue of the *Tribune* a French correspondent reported
how, when the revolt started on June 23, he went to his post as a National
Guardsman and remained on duty four days and four nights. He did not see
his lodgings again until the twenty-seventh, "when, fatigued to death, and
without having changed my clothes or taken off my boots during those four
days, I greeted the long-deserted bed with real rapture." In the midst of
the tumult, Charles A. Dana reached Paris and "sat hemmed and blockaded in his room, by the strictness of the measures of the siege; and we
found and greeted each other for the first time, when the civil war was at
an end," the Frenchman added. "I desired to leave him the office of describing to his countrymen beyond the Atlantic the first powerful impressions
which he had experienced on European soil; and on the other hand I was
too much exhausted, too much excited about these events, so overpowering
and so incalculable in their consequences, to take up the pen and attempt
to pronounce judgment upon them." A neophyte in French politics, Dana
proved worthy of the veteran newsman's confidence. His first story:

Charles A. Dana, Tribune *correspondent,*
reports the cry: "All we want is work!"

New York Tribune, July 24, 1848

PARIS, JUNE 29, 1848—The public papers will give you lengthy details upon the terrible events which have just taken place in Paris. These events are so multiplied and varied in their character that it is impossible to grasp them in their totality and give any exact statement in regard to them. The most distorted and erroneous accounts are spreading in every direction, and each party will give its own coloring to what has taken place instead of seeking to discover the exact truth and making it known. I will not undertake to give you a history of the crisis through which this great capital has just passed. I doubt whether any one can do it at present, for, as I understand, the recent events are too varied to be summed up and reduced to order so soon after their occurrence. I will, therefore, simply state what I have seen myself and acts of which I can guarantee the authenticity. I will write a mere episode of the late crisis, and leave you to form as good an idea of the whole as you can from the fragment which I send you.

[Dana describes his trip from Boulogne to Paris. At Amiens large numbers of National Guardsmen were thrown around the railroad station. Others were crowded into the railway carriages. Cavalry were keeping back workers who had gathered in the square before the station. "I had time to go among the workmen and ascertain the sentiments that animated them. 'All we want,' said they, 'is work; politics do not concern us much. We want employment by which to gain a living. For these last four months since the Revolution took place, we

have been able to obtain no work, and we are without bread.' "]

As we approached Paris all was perfectly quiet. The inhabitants in the little villages through which we passed did not seem unusually excited, and yet a desperate conflict was going on in the capital—the center and head of the nation. We arrived at length at Saint-Denis, about two leagues distant from Paris. Here the National Guards got out, formed into columns, and marched into Paris by some circuitous route. The part of the capital which the railroad entered was in the hands of the insurgents, and persons were placed at Saint-Denis to inform them of the danger. The insurgents would have attacked them, or any armed men, but not travelers without arms. There was consequently no danger for us to proceed, and we did so. The train could not enter the city, and it stopped just outside the walls at a large depot where the Railroad Company had its workshops. This outer depot, with its yards, was surrounded by a high wall, and a body of soldiers were stationed inside as a guard. The part of the city is called La Chapelle, and was in the hands of the insurgents, although they were scattered thinly over it, and had but a few barricades and a small force in it.

[Leaving the train, Dana and some fellow travelers entered a cabaret.]

Some workmen in blouses were in the place, and others came and went. We soon learned that a part of them were among the insurgents and had come there to obtain something to eat and drink.

As I had no other opportunity of seeing or conversing with the men engaged in the insurrection except on that evening and the next morning, I will enter into some details of what I heard and saw. It may give you some idea of the character of those engaged in the late outbreak and the spirit that animated them. From the public prints you cannot obtain any impartial information. The conservative papers will denounce the insurgents as a body of plunderers who wished merely to destroy and pillage, while the ultraradical papers are either suppressed or are silent.

At one of the tables sat a young man in a blouse, a workman, who had been engaged in the affray during the day. I entered into a conversation and asked him what his political principles were. "I am," said he, "a Socialist and Democratic Republican. I do not want that the rich should prey upon the poor; I want the association of labor and capital; that the laborer should have a share of the profits, and that the rich man should not take all the profits to himself and make a fortune out of the labor of the poor man." He appeared to be a gay, good-natured fellow, laughing and talking with a good deal of lightness of the events of the day.

A National Guard in uniform, and with his gun, entered, who wished, as I learned, to gain admission to the railroad depot. He sat down at the table, called for a glass of wine, and he and the workman in blouse soon got into conversation. "I know you," said the workman. "You are an *ouvrier* (a workman), a good fellow, but you fight on the wrong side." "No, indeed," answered the National Guard, "your party is a party of brigands." Hereupon arose an altercation which waxed quite warm. "Tomorrow we shall gain the day," said the workman in blouse. "No," answered the National Guard,

"you are beaten already and tomorrow you will be finished." The controversy went on and became pretty violent, when the workman in blouse, giving his hand to the National Guard, said, "Well, we will not quarrel about it. You are a good fellow. We shall see."

The French character combines great extremes. You find violence and often ferocity on one side, and on the other great good humor and kindness. Above all, you find everywhere an extraordinary degree of courage and a strong sentiment of honor.

I was very desirous of entering the city, but not wishing to separate from my party, I began to inquire the possibility of finding a more comfortable resting place. A workman in the cabaret said he had a lodging near by, with two beds in it, which he would give up to our party—that four could sleep there if we choose to lie two upon a bed. We had been told previously, upon inquiring as to the possibility of entering the city, that there was a barricade at the end of the street not far distant from the cabaret, and that if we passed that way the insurgents might take us for soldiers and fire upon us. My friends decided upon running no risk, and remained. I decided upon going, as my guide assured me he could take us by a road where there were no barricades. It was near one o'clock when we set out; the night was fine, and all was quiet save that now and then the silence was broken by a musketshot. My guide led me through several streets and at length to the house where he had his lodgings. We crossed a courtyard, entered a rear building, went up two pairs of stairs, passed through a large room filled with looms, and came at length to a room with a couple of beds in it. "I am," said he, "a weaver of shawls. This is my workshop. In four months I have not gained four farthings. My workmen are literally starving, and I set up the little cabaret at which you supped in order to gain a few sous from the workmen belonging to the railroad."

I was up at 3½ o'clock. While I was dressing, a workman came in who had been sleeping in a neighboring room and asked for a bag of caps which he had left there. "Are you going to return to work again today?" asked my host of him. "Yes," was his laconic answer. We all went downstairs together. The man who asked for the caps was a quiet, intelligent-looking person, but there was a firmness and determination in his face which showed that the affair with him was a serious one. Wishing to know the motives that animated him, I entered into a conversation and at length asked him who and what he was fighting against.

"I fight," said he, "against the rich, against the bad rich who starve the poor. They withdraw their money from circulation. They take our labor from us and reduce us to starvation. I might as well die by a bullet as to die from hunger."

By the time I returned [to the railroad depot] it was six o'clock. The report of firearms was constant, the barricades began to be manned, and the troops and National Guards were preparing to move upon them. I obtained a handcart, got my baggage upon it, found a man to draw it, and started off with my guide again. We could not make the circuitous route we had made on foot and were forced to go nearer to the scene of action. We passed near a number of barricades, turning up generally the first corner above them. These barricades were built of the paving stones, dug up by the insurgents and piled across the streets, forming a kind of stone wall, broad at the base and slanting toward

the top. Those which I saw were not more than four or five feet high.

As the morning advanced, the firing became more general; but no regular attack was made by the troops of the National Guards upon the quarter through which I was passing. I saw only one barricade which was defended. Four men with their muskets were lying behind it; and some more screened behind the adjoining houses.

I got safely into the city, and after changing my dress, I went to the office of the *Démocratie Pacifique*. By this time it was ten o'clock. Orders had been issued to place sentinels in every street and let no one pass, so as to prevent men or supplies from going or being transported from any part of the city to the insurgents' quarters. I found myself completely blockaded in the house and could not stir out. This was Sunday, the twenty-fifth; the next morning, Monday, the twenty-sixth, I obtained a pass from the Division Militaire to cross the river and return. This enabled me to see some parts of Paris where order reigned. Paris looked like a vast camp; troops of the line and National Guards were marching to and fro; companies were sleeping on bundles of straw after the fatigues of the night; soldiers were cooking at fires made up in the street. The cavalry horses were drinking from the elegant fountains in the Place de la Révolution —the life of the camp appeared to be the only life left in Paris.

Next morning after the battle was over, and the insurgents had surrendered or fled, I visited the upper portion of the boulevards toward the Place de la Bastille, the place itself, and the street of Faubourg Saint-Antoine. The entrance of the latter street was the center of the conflict. On the left a house was battered down and smoking in ruins. The other houses were pierced with cannon balls, window shutters torn off, the windows all broken, and the walls showing the marks of thousands of musket balls.

I entered the street. On all the window shutters was written, "Death to Thieves." This was done by the insurgents. I inquired of four or five shopkeepers whether they had been pillaged, and I found that not any of them had lost anything. The insurgents respected scrupulously the property of people, and committed not an act of robbery as far as I could learn. The shopkeepers here are as much opposed to the insurgents as in any part of Paris and would have been very ready to denounce any act of pillage. They seemed grateful for the scrupulous manner in which their property had been respected. Acts of cruelty, useless executions, were committed on both sides under the terrible excitement of the conflict; but I am glad to say that low acts of stealing and plunder did not take place. Men do not fight as the insurgents fought merely to steal. It is the fanaticism of an idea, the hatred of class or party only, which can fire men with such desperation, or else some terrible necessity which urges them on.

IN A SOMBER STORY date-lined Paris, July 27, 1848,* Dana described that city as "the place of expiation of the world." "If the history of Paris is gloomy," he added, "how much more so her present condition. From the hilltop [of Montmartre] you can see the dark and filthy quarters of the poor, and the narrow streets, whose walls still bear the traces of the battle of June. In those quarters are crowded the hundreds of thousands of men, women, and children who, in prosperous times, live on the verge of starvation and now are literally starving." Warning of increasing class tension, Dana declared: "The whole social body seems set afloat like a mass of struggling atoms, tossed no one of them can tell whither or wherefore, with no apparent ending except to fall violently upon each other." Dana predicted that "if the *bourgeoisie* do not discover some means of improving the condition of the masses through practical, industrial reforms, French society will be shaken to its foundations, and the *bourgeoisie* will in the end be conquered by violence, as were the aristocracy and the Church in the Revolution of 1793."

In an editorial in the *New York Tribune* of April 24, 1849, Dana, one day to become the great editor of the New York *Sun,* struck this moderate note: "Let no man be frightened by the terms 'social' and 'Socialist' as adopted by the democratic journals of France. They are Socialists not as propagandists of any societary theory or system, but as believers together that the condition of the toiling, suffering millions ought to be, may be ameliorated, and that it is the pressing duty of governments to effect such amelioration." When Louis Napoleon was elected the first President of France (December 10, 1848), Dana charged that France had voted for him "as it were in intoxication," and warned: "I have no faith in the sincerity of Louis Napoleon's adherence to the Republic. There is no doubt that he would much rather be Emperor than President."

---

* *New York Tribune,* August 14, 1848.

Victor Hugo Denounces Louis Napoleon's December Fourth Massacre as "The Murder of a People by One Man"

P ARIS IS PERFECTLY QUIET," was the report by "Submarine Telegraph" to the London *Times,* date-lined 9:30 A.M., December 4, 1851. But at 5 P.M. that same day the Paris correspondent telegraphed: "The insurrection broke out in earnest."

These terse dispatches informed the world that the first of the modern Fascist dictators, a true prototype of Mussolini and Hitler, had seized power.

Elected President of the Republic in December, 1848, Louis Napoleon, nephew of the great Bonaparte, quickly strove for total power. Curtailing the franchise, muzzling the press, manipulating the army in order the better to control it, Louis Napoleon was ready for his *coup d'état.* On December 2, 1851, he arrested the leading members of the opposition, dispersed the legislature, seized the printing shops of Paris, and captured the bell towers to stifle the revolutionary summons of the tocsin. Paris, momentarily stunned, soon rushed to the barricades. Of the horrible massacre of December 4, not one line appeared in the censored Paris press.

Unfortunately for Louis Napoleon, there was one eyewitness to this butchery who would not be silenced. Victor Hugo's reportorial genius had been proved in his youth, when he wrote *The Last Day of a Condemned Man* (1829). This fictionalized autobiography, based on a visit to the place of execution of felons, captured the psychological oppression of those last moments and "the horrible throng, with its hyena cry." Now Hugo was at the height of his powers. With rare courage he served as a leader of the underground Committee of Resistance. In his *Napoleon the Little* (1852) Hugo recorded these fateful days, but, twenty-five years later, provided a more extended treatment in his *History of a Crime; The Testimony of an Eyewitness,* from which this inspired selection is excerpted. No story filed by a foreign correspondent who managed to elude Louis Napoleon's censorship measured up, for intimate detail and full coverage, to the account Hugo later wrote.

"It is death in pellets"

Victor Hugo, *Histoire d'un crime; déposition d'un témoin* (Paris, 1877)

Suddenly a window, looking straight into hell, was violently thrown open. Had Dante been peering through the gloom, he would have recognized the eighth circle of his poem in the fatal Boulevard Montmartre.

A hideous spectacle—Paris in the clutches of Bonaparte!

The armed men massed together on the boulevard felt a sudden frenzy incite them. They were no longer men, but demons. For them there was no longer a banner, law, humanity, or country. For them France had ceased to exist, and Murder rode rampant through their souls. The division of the robber Schinderhannes, the brigades of the murderers Mandrim, Cartouche, Poulailler, Trestaillon, and Tropmann, advanced through the gloom, shooting down and murdering on all sides—for we cannot attribute the terrible scenes that were enacted in that melancholy eclipse of faith and honor to the French Army.

History has handed down to us the accounts of many terrible massacres, but there was some reason for each of them. St. Bartholomew and the dragonnades had their origin in religious differences. The Sicilian Vespers and the Butcheries of September were the offspring of patriotism. In each case they crushed the enemy or rooted out the foreigner; but the carnage of the Boulevard Montmartre was a useless crime for which no reason could be assigned. And yet a reason, and a very terrible one, did exist. Let us say what it was. There are two mighty powers in the state—the Law and the People. A man murders the law. He feels the

hour of retribution draw near, and there is nothing left for him to do but to slay the people.

And he does so.

The second of December was the risk, the fourth was the method to make things secure.

Rising indignation had to be stifled by abject terror.

Louis Bonaparte achieved that glory, and at the same time reached the pinnacle of his infamy. Let us tell how he did it, and recall what history did not see—the murder of a people by one man!

On a sudden, at a given signal, by a musket fired—it does not matter where or by whom—a deadly fire of grape was opened on the crowd. Grapeshot is a crowd of itself; it is death in pellets. It knows not where it comes from or whither it is going; it slays, and passes on. And yet it has a species of soul. It acts with premeditation and executes a design. The movement was an unexpected one. It was like a handful of thunderbolts dashed upon the people. Nothing could be more simple. It had all the easiness of the solution of a riddle. The grapeshot annihilated the populace.

What are you doing there? Die. Are you passing through the street? It is a crime. Why do you oppose the government? Government is a cutthroat. It has stated that it will do a certain thing: it has begun it; it must be carried out. If society is to be saved, the people must be destroyed.

In an instant there was a series of murders extending for a quarter of a mile along the boulevard. Eleven pieces of cannon demolished the Hôtel Sallandrouze. One shot pierced right through twenty-eight houses. The Baths of Jouvence were riddled. Tortoni's was destroyed. One whole quarter of Paris was a scene of terrified fright. The air was full of cries of anguish.

Death, sudden death, was on all sides. No one expected anything. People were falling on all sides. Whence did it come?

"From on high," said a *Te Deum* of bishops.

"From below!" said the truth. "From a spot worse than the veriest depth of hell!"

It was the conception of a Caligula executed by a Papavoine.

Xavier Durrie came on the boulevard. He said afterwards, "I took sixty steps, and I stumbled against sixty corpses." Then he realized it was a heinous crime to be in the street. It was also a crime to be in your own house. The murderers entered the houses and slaughtered the inmates.

Adde, of the library on the Boulevard Poissonnière, was on his doorstep; they killed him. At the same moment—for the murder was a widely extended one—far away in the Rue de Lancry, the owner of No. 5, M. Thirion de Montauban, was at his door; they killed him. In the Rue Tiquetonne, a child of seven years of age, named Boursier, was passing by; they killed him. Mlle. Soulac, 196, Rue du Temple, opened her window; they killed her. In the same street, at No. 97, two women, Mesdames Vidal and Raboisson, dressmakers, were in their own house; they killed them. Of the foot passengers, Mlle. Gressier, living at No. 209 Faubourg Saint-Martin, Madame Guilard, of 77, Faubourg Saint-Denis, and Madame Garnier, of No. 6 Boulevard Bonne-Nouvelles, fell under the shower of grape—the first on the Boulevard Montmarte, and the others on the Boulevard Saint-Denis. They were only wounded, and endeavored to rise to their feet; but the soldiers with shouts of fiendish laughter looked on, and they fell down again. This time they were dead.

No one escaped. The muskets and pistols were used at point-blank range. The New Year was drawing near, and there were shops full of New Year's gifts. A child of thirteen years of age, flying before the fire of the soldiers, took refuge in a shop in the Arcade Sauveur, and hid himself under a heap of toys. He was seized and slaughtered, his murderers with a laugh enlarging the wounds with their sabers. A woman told me, "You could hear the little creature's cries all through the arcade." The 75th Regiment of the Line took the barricade of the Porte Saint-Denis. There had been no resistance, only butchery afterwards. Massacre stalked (a horrible but an expressive word) in the boulevards and in all the streets. It was like a devilfish extending its long snaky arms. Should they fly? Wherefore? Hide themselves? To what end? Death was pursuing you farther than you could fly.

In the Rue Pagevin a soldier said to a foot passenger, "What are you doing here?"

"Returning home," was the reply.

The soldier killed him.

Colonel Espinasse shouted out, "After the bayonet, the artillery."

Colonel Rochefort cried out, "Pierce, bleed, saber!" Then he added, "It will save noise and powder."

At the corner of the Rue du Sentier, an officer of spahis waved his sword in the air and shouted, "You do not understand your orders. Fire at the women!"

A pregnant woman ran across the road. She fell, and the soldiers, running up, finished her with the butt ends of their muskets. Another woman, frightened out of her wits, was about to turn a corner of the street. She carried a child in her arms. Two soldiers took aim at her. One cried, "At the woman!" and hit his mark. The child rolled on the pavement. Then the other cried, "At the child!" fired, killing it.

A man well known in the scientific world, Dr. Germain Sée, declared that in one single house—that of the Baths of Jouvence—there were under a penthouse in the courtyard nearly eighty wounded, chiefly old men, women, and infants. Dr. Sée gave them assistance before all others.

"There was in the Rue Mardier," said an eyewitness, "a perfect string of corpses, which began from the Rue Neuve Saint-Eustache. Before the Maison Odier there were twenty-six bodies. Before the Hôtel de Montmorency, thirty. Before the Variétés, fifty-two, of which eleven were women. In the Rue de la Grange Batelière were three naked corpses. No. 19, Rue du Faubourg Montmartre, was full of dead and wounded bodies.

A woman, running at the top of her speed with her hair disheveled and her arms stretched out, was flying down the Rue Poissonnière, shrieking, "They're killing us! they're killing us!"

The soldiers were joking among themselves. "I'll bet," said one, "that I knock her over."

I wished to know what to believe. In order to state that certain crimes had been committed, it was necessary that they should be proved. I therefore went to the spot of the murder.

In certain states of agony, feeling grows dead. We do not think, or if we do think it is blindly, and we only hope that events may end one way or the other. The death of others inspires you with so much horror that you long for your own dissolution, if at least by dying you could serve any good end. Your memory reverts to those men whose deaths have caused popular commotions and risings, and you feel that you have but one ambition left —to be a dead body that has been of some use.

I walked on, therefore, filled with gloomy thoughts. I wended my way to the boulevards. I saw a fiery furnace. I heard the peals of thunder. Jules Simon, a man who in those terrible days risked his valuable life freely, came toward me. He stopped me.

"Where are you going?" he asked. "You will get yourself killed. What is it you want?"

"Just that," I told him.

We shook hands, and I continued on my way.

I reached the boulevard. The scene was indescribable. I have seen this crime. I have seen this tragedy, this butchery. I have seen this blind stream of death, and the fall, upon every side of me, of the murdered people; and it is for this reason that I can sign this book as an EYEWITNESS.

Destiny has its designs. It watches mysteriously over the future historian. She permits him to mingle with carnage and destruction, but she will not permit him to die, since she wishes him to report these events.

THESE PAGES that take fire are corroborated by the London *Times* correspondent, who estimated the death total as mounting to eight hundred. French democracy was crushed, but the workers of Paris would never forget "the day of the massacre of the boulevards."

"Hugo is mad," Montalembert cried out when, on Bastille Day, five months before the massacre, Victor Hugo had challenged the monarchists in the Chamber:

"You are all dead! You do not belong in our century, in our world!" When the uproar had subsided, he added: "Because we have had a Napoleon the Great, must we have a Napoleon the Little?"

The fight against "Napoleon the Little" soon took on the character of an epic duel, with Hugo, after the massacre, continuing to pour out a stream of withering sarcasm from enforced exile, in which he was joined by other French political refugees, including Dumas and Louis Blanc. "What the lion would not have dared, the ape has done!" he exclaimed. "What the eagle would have feared to seize in its talons, the parrot has clutched in its claws! What Louis XI would have failed in, what Richelieu would have hurled himself against in vain, what Napoleon would have been unequal to —in one single day, between the dark and the dawn, the absurd has become possible; axioms have become chimeras, and everything that was a lie has become a living fact."

But Hugo continued to sustain the hope of all French liberals that this "stunted Tiberius" would fall. "Do you not hear, in the shadows beyond, that muffled sound?" he asked. "Do you not hear someone moving backward and forward? Do you not see that the breathing from behind makes the canvas tremble?" "The Republic is not dead," Hugo would say. "The Republic is our religion."

From the Heights Before Sebastopol a London *Times* Reporter Sees Six Hundred British Cavalrymen Ride into the Valley of Death

TELL THE EXACT TRUTH."

With these words, John Thaddeus Delane, editor of *The Times* of London, sent a young Irishman, William Howard Russell, to report the Crimean War. After a farewell dinner given him by Dickens and Thackeray, Russell took passage to Malta, little knowing that the dispatches he was to send from the theater of war were soon to bring him international fame as a war correspondent.

The war that Russell reported was fought by Britain, in alliance with Turkey, France, and Sardinia, to maintain the power balance in Europe and to thwart a Russian push to the Mediterranean. The allied forces carried the war directly to Russia by invading her southern flank and landing on the Crimean peninsula. The conception was bold; its execution was marred by scandalous incompetence.

The common soldiers who survived the terrible winter of 1854–55 were not likely ever to forget the experience. Eight soldiers died of exposure and sickness to every one killed in actual combat. Their encampment was on an open plateau, described by Russell as "a vast, black waste of soddened earth, when it was not covered with snow, dotted with little pools of foul water, and seamed with brown-colored streamlets strewn with carcasses of horses." Here they shivered through the winter, without overcoats, adequate shelter, or decent food. Russell shook British stay-at-homes out of their customary complacency by charging that "all the pictures ever drawn of plague and pestilence, from the work of the inspired writer who chronicled the woes of infidel Egypt down to the narratives of Boccaccio, Defoe, or Moltke, fall short of individual 'bits' of disease and death which anyone may see in half a dozen places during an hour's walk in Balaklava." Medical care was scandalous. "The commonest accessories of a hospital are wanting," Russell declared. "The sick appear to be tended by the sick and the dying by the dying." Then he dispatched this memorable challenge: "Are there no devoted women among us able and willing to go forth and minister to the sick and suffering soldiers?" Florence Nightingale, who with a small staff of nurses went to the front and set up a pioneer medical service, proved that the reporter's appeal was not lost on the women of England. On reading Russell's dispatches, John Bright commented: "The Angel of Death has been abroad throughout the land. You may almost hear the beating of his wings." Parliament, goaded to action by an infuriated public, overthrew the Aberdeen ministry, held responsible for the mismanagement of the campaign. But, actually, as the Duke of Newcastle told Russell later on, "it was you who turned out the government."

Though the "glorious catastrophe" at Balaklava occurred on October 25, 1854, the first account intimating the nature of the disaster appeared in *The Times* almost three weeks later:

William Howard Russell reports the charge of the Light Brigade, "that thin red streak topped with a line of steel"

The Times (London), November 11, 1854

THE ATTACK ON BALAKLAVA
(By Submarine and British Telegraph)

We have received from our correspondent at Marseilles the following dispatch, which had reached that port by the French post steamer which left Constantinople on the thirtieth ult.:

"Your correspondent in the army before Sebastopol writes on the twenty-eighth that 607 light infantry were engaged in the affair of the twenty-fifth, and that only 198 returned.

"Eight hundred cavalry were engaged, of whom only two hundred returned.

"Nine officers were killed, twenty-one wounded, and four were missing.

"The 17th Lancers were almost destroyed.

"We require reinforcements."

THEN, AS "all the world wondered," the full story of the "noble six hundred," destined to become a classic of military reporting, appeared two days later. Russell subsequently explained why he was able to record so photographically the sensational events at Balaklava. "Alma was a long, straggling, smoky battlefield, of which the view was interrupted and broken, so that it was impossible to see it from any point. Inkerman was fought in fog and mist. But the field of Balaklava," he recalled, "was as plainly seen from the verge of the plateau where I stood as the stage and those upon it are seen from the box of a theater."

The Times (London), November 13, 1854

HEIGHTS BEFORE SEBASTOPOL, OCTOBER 25—If the exhibition of the most brilliant valor, of the excess of courage, and of a daring which would have reflected luster on the best days of chivalry can afford full consolation for the disaster of today, we can have no reason to regret the melancholy loss which we sustained in a contest with a savage and barbarian enemy.

I shall proceed to describe, to the best of my power, what occurred under my own eyes, and to state the facts which I have heard from men whose veracity is unimpeachable, reserving to myself the exercise of the right of private judgment in making public and in suppressing the details of what occurred on this memorable day.

The position we occupied in reference to Balaklava was supposed by most people to be very strong—even impregnable. Our lines were formed by natural mountain slopes in the rear, along which the French had made very formidable intrenchments. Below those intrenchments, and very nearly in a right line across the valley beneath, are four conical hillocks, one rising above the other as they recede from our lines. On top of each of these hills the Turks had thrown up earthen redoubts, defended by 250 men each, and armed with two or three guns—some heavy ship guns—lent by us to them, with one artilleryman in each redoubt to look after them. These hills cross the valley of Balaklava at the distance of about two and a half miles from the town. Supposing the spectator then to take his stand on one of the heights forming the rear of our camp before Sebastopol, he would see the town of Balaklava, with its scanty shipping, its narrow strip of water, and its old forts on his right hand. Immediately below he would behold the valley and plain of coarse meadowland, occupied by our cavalry tents, and stretching from the base of the ridge on which he stood to the foot of the formidable heights on the other side. He would see the French trenches lined with Zouaves a few feet beneath, and distant from him, on the slope of the hill, a Turkish redoubt lower down, then another in the valley, then

in a line with it some angular earthworks, then, in succession, the other two redoubts up Canrobert's Hill.

At the distance of two or two and a half miles across the valley there is an abrupt rocky mountain range of most irregular and picturesque formation, covered with scanty brushwood here and there, or rising into barren pinnacles and plateaus of rock. In outline and appearance, this position of the landscape is wonderfully like the Trossachs.* A patch of blue sea is caught in between the overhanging cliffs of Balaklava as they close in the entrance to the harbor on the right. The camp of the Marines pitched on the hillsides more than one thousand feet above the level of the sea is opposite to you as your back is turned to Sebastopol and your right side towards Balaklava. On the road leading up the valley, close to the entrance of the town and beneath these hills, is the encampment of the 93rd Highlanders.

The cavalry lines are nearer to you below, and are some way in advance of the Highlanders, and nearer to the town than the Turkish redoubts. The valley is crossed here and there by small waves of land. On your left the hills and rocky mountain ranges gradually close in toward the course of the Chernaya, till at three or four miles' distance from Balaklava the valley is swallowed up in a mountain gorge and deep ravines, above which rise tier after tier of desolate whitish rock garnished now and then by bits of scanty herbage, and spreading away towards the east and south, where they attain the alpine dimensions of Tschatyr Dagh. It is very easy for an enemy at the Belbek, or in command of the road of Mackenzie's Farm, Inkerman, Simferopol, or Bakhchisarai, to debouch through these gorges at any time upon

* A picturesque wooded glen of Scotland, immortalized by Scott's *The Lady of the Lake*.

this plain from the neck of the valley, or to march from Sebastopol by the Chernaya and to advance along it towards Balaklava, till checked by the Turkish redoubts on the southern side or by the fire from the French works on the northern side, i.e., the side which in relation to the valley of Balaklava forms the rear of our position.

[Russell reports that at seven o'clock word came that the Russians had dispossessed their "despised enemy," the Turks, from redoubt No. 1, and were opening fire on redoubts 2, 3, and 4. At the first news of the advance of the enemy, Sir Colin Campbell, in command of Balaklava, had drawn up the 93rd Highlanders in front of the road to the town. When the Russians advanced, the Turks fired a few rounds and "bolted." The French light infantry then advanced, followed by a small escort of Hussars. As the Turks retired from redoubt No. 2, the Cossacks attacked them with sword and lance. "The Turks betake themselves towards the Highlanders, where they check their flight and form into companies placed on the flanks of the Highlanders."]

As the Russian cavalry on the left of their line crown the hill, across the valley they perceive the Highlanders drawn up at the distance of some half mile, calmly awaiting their approach. They halt, and squadron after squadron flies up from the rear, till they have a body of some 1500 men along the ridge—Lancers and Dragoons and Hussars. Then they move *en échelon* in two bodies, with another in reserve. The cavalry who have been pursuing the Turks on the right are coming up the ridge beneath us, which conceals our cavalry from view. The heavy brigade in advance is drawn up in two columns. The first column consists of

the Scots Grays and of their old companions in glory, the Enniskilleners; the second of the 4th Royal Irish, of the 5th Dragoon Guards, and of the 1st Royal Dragoons. The Light Cavalry Brigade is on their left in two divisions also. The silence is oppressive; between the cannon bursts, one can hear the champing of bits and the clink of sabers in the valley below. The Russians on their left drew breath for a moment, and then in one grand line dashed at the Highlanders. The ground flies beneath their horses' feet —gathering speed at every stride they dash on towards that thin red streak topped with a line of steel. The Turks fire a volley at eight hundred yards, and run. As the Russians come within six hundred yards, down goes that line of steel in front, and out rings a rolling volley of Minié musketry. The distance is too great. The Russians are not checked, but still sweep onwards with the whole force of horse and man, through the smoke, here and there knocked over by the shot of our batteries above. With breathless suspense everyone awaits the bursting of the wave upon the line of Gaelic rock; but ere they came within 150 yards, another deadly volley flashes from the leveled rifles, and carries death and terror into the Russians. They wheel about, open files right and left, and fly back faster than they came.

"Bravo Highlanders! well done!" shout the excited spectators; but events thicken. The Highlanders and their splendid front are soon forgotten. Men scarcely have a moment to think of this fact that the 93rd never altered their formation to receive that tide of horsemen.

"No," said Sir Colin Campbell, "I did not think it worth while to form them even four deep!"

The ordinary British line, two deep,

was quite sufficient to repel the attack of these Muscovite chevaliers. Our eyes were, however, turned in a moment on our own cavalry. We saw Brigadier General Scarlett ride along in front of his massive squadrons. The Russians —evidently *corps d'élite*—their light-blue jackets embroidered with silver lace, were advancing on their left at an easy gallop, towards the brow of the hill. A forest of lances glistened in their rear, and several squadrons of gray-coated dragoons moved up quickly to support them as they reached the summit. The instant they came in sight the trumpets of our cavalry gave out the warning blast which told us all that in another moment we would see the shock of battle beneath our very eyes. Lord Raglan, all his staff and escort, and groups of officers, the Zouaves, the French generals and officers, and bodies of French infantry on the height, were spectators of the scene as though they were looking on the stage from the boxes of a theater. Nearly everyone dismounted and sat down, and not a word was said.

The Russians advanced down the hill at a slow canter, which they changed to a trot and at last nearly halted. The first line was at least double the length of ours—it was three times as deep. Behind them was a similar line, equally strong and compact. They evidently despised their insignificant-looking enemy, but their time was come.

The trumpets rang out through the valley, and the Grays and Enniskilleners went right at the center of the Russian cavalry. The space between them was only a few hundred yards; it was scarce enough to let the horses "gather way," nor had the men quite space sufficient for the full play of their sword arms. The Russian line brings forward each wing as our cavalry advance and threaten to annihilate them as they

pass on. Turning a little to their left, so as to meet the Russians' right, the Grays rush on with a cheer that thrills to every heart—the wild shout of the Enniskilleners pierced through the dark masses of the Russians. The shock was but for a moment. There was a clash of steel and a light play of sword blades in the air, and then the Grays and the redcoats disappear in the midst of the shaken and quivering columns. In another moment we see them merging and dashing on with diminished numbers, and in broken order, against the second line, which is advancing against them to retrieve the fortune of the charge.

It was a terrible moment. "God help them! They are lost!" was the exclamation of more than one man, and the thought of many. With unabated fire the noble hearts dashed at their enemy —it was a fight of heroes. The first line of Russians which had been smashed utterly by our charge, and had fled off at one flank and towards the center, were coming back to swallow up our handful of men. By sheer steel and sheer courage Enniskillener and Scot were winning their desperate way right through the enemy's squadrons, and already gray horses and redcoats had appeared right at the rear of the second mass, when, with irresistible force, like one bolt from a bow, the 1st Royals, the 4th Dragoon Guards, and the 5th Dragoon Guards rushed at the remnants of the first line of the enemy, went through it as though it were made of pasteboard, and dashing on the second body of Russians, as they were still disordered by the terrible assault of the Grays and their companions, put them to utter rout. This Russian horse in less than five minutes after it met our dragoons was flying with all its speed before a force certainly not half its strength.

A cheer burst from every lip—in the enthusiasm officers and men took off their caps and shouted with delight, and thus keeping up the scenic character of their position, they clapped their hands again and again.

And now occurred the melancholy catastrophe which fills us all with sorrow. It appears that the Quartermaster General, Brigadier Airey, thinking that the Light Cavalry had not gone far enough in front when the enemy's horse had fled, gave an order in writing to Captain Nolan, 15th Hussars, to take to Lord Lucan, directing His Lordship "to advance" his cavalry nearer to the enemy. A braver soldier than Captain Nolan the army did not possess. He was known to all his arm of the service for his entire devotion to his profession, and his name must be familiar to all who take interest in our cavalry for his excellent work published a year ago on our drill and system of remount and breaking horses. I had the pleasure of his acquaintance, and I know he entertained the most exalted opinions respecting the capabilities of the English horse soldier. Properly led, the British Hussar and Dragoon could in his mind break square, take batteries, ride over columns of infantry, and pierce any other cavalry in the world, as if they were made of straw. He thought they had not had the opportunity of doing all that was in their power, and that they had missed even such chances as they had offered to them—that, in fact, they were in some measure disgraced. A matchless rider and a first-rate swordsman, he held in contempt, I am afraid, even grape and canister. He rode off with his orders to Lord Lucan. He is now dead and gone.

God forbid I should cast a shade on the brightness of his honor, but I am bound to state what I am told occurred when he reached His Lordship. I should premise that, as the Russian cavalry retired, their infantry fell back towards the head of the valley, leaving men in three of the redoubts they had taken and abandoning the fourth. They had also placed some guns on the heights over their position, on the left of the gorge. Their cavalry joined the reserves, and drew up in six solid divisions, in an oblique line, across the entrance to the gorge. Six battalions of infantry were placed behind them, and about thirty guns were drawn up along their line, while masses of infantry were also collected on the hills behind the redoubts on our right. Our cavalry had moved up to the ridge across the valley, on our left, as the ground was broken in front, and had halted in the order I have already mentioned.

When Lord Lucan received the order from Captain Nolan and had read it, he asked, we are told, "Where are we to advance to?"

Captain Nolan pointed with his finger to the line of the Russians, and said, "There are the enemy, and there are the guns, sir, before them. It is your duty to take them," or words to that effect, according to the statements made since his death.

Lord Lucan with reluctance gave the order to Lord Cardigan to advance upon the guns, conceiving that his orders compelled him to do so. The noble Earl, though he did not shrink, also saw the fearful odds against him. Don Quixote in his tilt against the windmill was not near so rash and reckless as the gallant fellows who prepared without a thought to rush on almost certain death.

It is a maxim of Decker that "cavalry never act without support," that "infantry should be close at hand when cavalry carry guns, as the effect is only instantaneous," and that it is necessary to have on the flank of a line of cavalry some squadrons in column, the attack on the flank being most dangerous. The only support our Light Cavalry had was the reserve of Heavy Cavalry at a great distance behind them—the infantry and guns being far in the rear. There were no squadrons in column at all, and there was a plain to charge over before the enemy's guns were reached of a mile and a half in length.

At 11:10 our Light Cavalry Brigade rushed to the front. They numbered as follows, as well as I could ascertain:

	MEN
4th Light Dragoons	118
8th Irish Hussars	104
11th Prince Albert's Hussars	110
13th Light Dragoons	130
17th Lancers	145
Total	607 sabers

The whole brigade scarcely made one effective regiment, according to the numbers of continental armies; and yet it was more than we could spare. As they passed towards the front, the Russians opened on them from the guns in the redoubts on the right, with volleys of musketry and rifles.

They swept proudly past, glittering in the morning sun in all the pride and splendor of war. We could hardly believe the evidence of our senses! Surely that handful of men were not going to charge an army in position? Alas! it was but too true—their desperate valor knew no bounds, and far indeed was it removed from its so-called better part —discretion. They advanced in two lines, quickening their pace as they closed towards the enemy. A more fearful spectacle was never witnessed than by those who, without the power to aid, beheld their heroic countrymen rushing to the arms of death. At the distance of 1200 yards the whole line of the enemy belched forth, from thirty iron mouths, a flood of smoke and flame, through which hissed the deadly balls. Their flight was marked by instant gaps in our ranks, by dead men and horses, by steeds flying wounded or riderless across the plain. The first line was broken—it was joined by the second, they never halted or checked their speed an instant. With diminished ranks, thinned by those thirty guns, which the Russians had laid with the most deadly accuracy, with a halo of flashing steel above their heads, and with a cheer which was many a noble fellow's death cry, they flew into the smoke of the batteries; but ere they were lost from view, the plain was strewed with their bodies and with the carcasses of horses. They were exposed to an oblique fire from the batteries on the hills on both sides, as well as to a direct fire of musketry.

Through the clouds of smoke we could see their sabers flashing as they rode up to the guns and dashed between them, cutting down the gunners as they stood. The blaze of their steel, as an officer standing near me said, was "like the turn of a shoal of mackerel." We saw them riding through the guns, as I have said; to our delight we saw them returning, after breaking through a column of Russian infantry, and scattering them like chaff, when the flank fire of the battery on the hill swept them down, scattered and broken as they were. Wounded men and dismounted troopers flying towards us told the sad tale—demigods could not have done what they had failed to do. At the very moment when they were about to retreat, a regiment of lancers was hurled upon their flank. Colonel Shewell, of the 8th Hussars, saw the danger, and rode his few men straight at them, cutting his way through with fearful loss. The other regiments turned and engaged in a desperate encounter. With courage too great almost for credence, they were breaking their way through the columns which enveloped them, when there took place an act of atrocity without parallel in the modern warfare of civilized nations. The Russian gunners, when the storm of cavalry passed, returned to their guns. They saw their own cavalry mingled with the troopers who had just ridden over them, and to the eternal disgrace of the Russian name the miscreants poured a murderous volley of grape and canister on the mass of struggling men and horses, mingling friend and foe in one common ruin. It was as much as our Heavy Cavalry Brigade could do to cover the retreat of the miserable remnants of that band of heroes as they returned to the place they had so lately quitted in all the pride of life.

At 11:35 not a British soldier, except the dead and dying, was left in front of these bloody Muscovite guns. Our loss, as far as it could be ascertained in killed, wounded, and missing at two o'clock today, was as follows:

	Went into Action Strong	Returned from Action	Loss
4th Light Dragoons	118	39	79
8th Hussars	104	38	66
11th Hussars	110	25	85
13th Light Dragoons	130	61	69
17th Lancers	145	35	110
	607	198	409

ONE HUNDRED AND NINETY-EIGHT—that was "all that was left of them, left of six hundred," whom Tennyson was inspired by Russell's story to memorialize. Killed by the first shot fired was Captain Nolan, and Lord Lucan was slightly wounded. In short, as Russell forthrightly concluded, "our Light Brigade was annihilated by their own rashness, and by the brutality of a ferocious enemy."

In the Crimean War Britain maintained her record of losing all the battles except the last, which was the pay-off. The Russians burned the fortress town of Sebastopol and at length capitulated. The Black Sea was opened to the commerce of all the world, an agreement which Russia soon flouted. In fact, the victory proved a hollow one, for less than a generation later the Great Powers found it necessary to intervene once more to check Russia's growing influence in the Balkans after her defeat of Turkey in 1878.

"Balaklava" Russell Protests the Conduct of the
Plunder-Drunk Besiegers of Lucknow

BRITISHERS IN INDIA in the 1850's were sitting on a powder keg. With the control of that immense domain still vested in a private business corporation, the East India Company, friction between European ruler and exploited native was incessant. The Company's position became increasingly vulnerable owing to its heavy reliance upon underpaid sepoys, or native troops, to maintain order at a period when Indian nationalist feeling was becoming intensified. Native princes, fearful that they would be deposed as the British rule was steadily extended in India, were a further unstabilizing factor. But the spark that ignited the conflagration was the introduction of the Minié rifle, with its greased cartridges. The sepoys charged that they were being defiled by having to bite off the ends of cartridges that, they asserted, were greased with the fat of cows (sacred to Hindus) and pigs (*verboten* to Moslems).* A savage mutiny that spread from Bengal up the Ganges Valley in 1857 found Hindus and Moslems, historic antagonists, fighting side by side. Soon reports of massacres, rape, and mutilation at Cawnpore and Delhi inflamed even the staid *Times* of London to demand "ample vengeance."

Again Delane, the editor of *The Times,* turned to Russell to track down the truth. When Lord Clarendon heard of the assignment he shrewdly observed: "Imagine all the mischief in store for us from that fellow, who, of course, will want a second crop of Crimean laurels grown upon the ruins of everybody's reputation." In fact, a forecast of the objectivity of Russell's dispatches was given by the correspondent himself aboard ship en route to India, when he said, "If we, who are the governors of the people, do not govern ourselves and protect the people, what redress have they, and what have we to expect?"

Although the mutiny was largely suppressed before Russell's arrival in India, Sir Colin Campbell still had important mopping-up operations ahead for his forces, not the least of which was the recapture of Lucknow, a rallying point of the revolt. Russell's dispatches, condensed in his published *Diary in India* (1860), instead of inflaming the public to wild revenge by accounts of native atrocities, constituted a biting exposé of counteroutrage perpetrated on the natives in putting down the uprising. Of the results of the siege Russell had not the slightest doubt, but the cruelty revealed on both sides appalled him. "Conduct warfare on the most chivalrous prin-

---

* At a court-martial in 1857 Colonel Abbott, an inspector general of ordnance, gave evidence that "the tallow might or might not have contained the fat of cows."

ciples, there must ever be a touch of murder about it, and the assassin will lurk under fine phrases."

Under the date line, March 9, 1859, Russell reported two interviews—one with Sir Colin Campbell, who told him of the plan by which Sir James Outram was to command the rear of the enemy's line and to take their works in flank and reverse; the other with an acquaintance who had just participated in the fighting with Outram.

"And the assassin will lurk under fine phrases"

William Howard Russell, *My Diary in India in the Year 1858–9* (London, 1860)

Later I saw one who had come from Outram's camp, and he told us of the great success of the day, and of the fine advance made by the right corps, a wing of an army. Alas! that he should have to tell, too, of the disgusting termination to the attack on the Chuckerwallah Kothie, the yellow house on the race course, in which some few sepoys made a resistance, which a national Tyrtaeus * or Dibdin † would have chanted in noble song. Their enemies called it foolish and fanatic. What could they do more than fight to the last, and kill or wound every man who approached them?

As they had killed a British officer of a Sikh ‡ regiment and several men, and wounded more, the troops were withdrawn from the house, and a heavy fire of artillery was opened on it. After the walls had been perforated in all directions with shot and shell, so that it seemed impossible for the little garrison to have escaped, a detachment of Sikhs rushed into the house—some of the sepoys were still alive, and they were mercifully killed; but for some reason or other which could not be explained, one of their number was dragged out to the sandy plain outside the house. He was pulled by the legs to a convenient place, where he was held down, pricked in the face and body by the bayonets of some of the soldiery, whilst others collected fuel for a small pyre, and, when all was ready, *the man was roasted alive!*

There were Englishmen looking on; more than one officer saw it. No one offered to interfere! The horror of this infernal cruelty was aggravated by an attempt of the miserable wretch to escape when half burned to death. By a sudden effort he leaped away and, with the flesh hanging from his bones, ran for a few yards ere he was caught, brought back, put on the fire again, and held there by bayonets till his remains were consumed.

"And his cries, and the dreadful scene," said my friend, "will haunt me to my dying hour."

"Why didn't you interfere?"

"I dared not. The Sikhs were furious. They had lost Anderson; our own men encouraged them, and I could do nothing." §

* Ancient Greek elegiac poet.
† Writer of English naval songs.
‡ A militaristic Hindu sect, some of whose followers were used to crush the sepoys.
§ "I saw the charred bones, some days after, on the plain."—W. H. R.

FIVE DAYS later Russell reported the plundering of Lucknow; discipline among the armed forces completely collapsed once the fight was won:

Imagine courts as large as the Temple gardens, surrounded with ranges of palaces, or at least of buildings well stuccoed and gilded, with fresco paintings here and there on the blind windows, and with green jalousies and Venetian blinds closing the apertures which pierce the walls in double rows. In the body of the court are statues, lines of lampposts, fountains, orange groves, aqueducts, and kiosks with burnished domes of metal.

Through these, hither and thither, with loud cries, dart European and native soldiery, firing at the windows, from which come now and then dropping shots or hisses a musket ball. At every door there is an eager crowd, smashing the panels with the stocks of their firelocks, or breaking the fastenings by discharges of their weapons. The buildings which surround the courts are irregular in form, for here and there the lines of the quadrangle are broken by columned fronts and lofty porticoes before the mansions of the ministry, or of the great officers of the royal household, which are resplendent with richly gilt roofs and domes.

Here and there the invaders have forced their way into the long corridors, and you hear the musketry rattling inside; the crash of glass, the shouts and yells of the combatants, and little jets of smoke curl out of the closed lattices. Lying amid the orange groves are dead and dying sepoys; and the white statues are reddened with blood.

Leaning against a smiling Venus is a British soldier shot through the neck, gasping, and at every gasp bleeding to death! Here and there officers are running to and fro after their men, persuading or threatening in vain. From the broken portals issue soldiers laden with loot or plunder. Shawls, rich tapestry, gold and silver brocade, caskets of jewels, arms, splendid dresses. The men are wild with fury and lust of gold —literally drunk with plunder. Some come out with china vases or mirrors, dash them to pieces on the ground, and return to seek more valuable booty. Others are busy gouging out the precious stones from the stems of pipes, from saddlecloths, or the hilts of swords, or butts of pistols and firearms. Some swathe their bodies in stuffs crusted with precious metals and gems; others carry off useless lumber, brass pots, pictures, or vases of jade and china.

The scene of plunder was indescribable. The soldiers had broken up several of the storerooms, and pitched the contents into the court, which was lumbered with cases, with embroidered cloths, gold and silver brocade, silver vessels, arms, banners, drums, shawls, scarfs, musical instruments, mirrors, pictures, books, accounts, medicine bottles, gorgeous standards, shields, spears, and a heap of things, the enumeration of which would make this sheet of paper like a catalogue of a broker's sale. Through these moved the men, wild with excitement, "drunk with plunder." I had often heard the phrase, but never saw the thing itself before. They smashed to pieces the fowling pieces and pistols to get at the gold mountings and the stones set in the stocks. They burned in a fire, which they made in the center of the court, brocades and embroidered shawls for the sake of the gold and silver. China, glass, and jade they dashed to pieces in pure wantonness; pictures they ripped up, or tossed on the flames; furniture shared the same fate. Suddenly a fellow rushed at us with the long chain of a luster, made of long green and blue prisms, in his hand, shouting out, "Look here! Look here! Holy mother of Moses, what will you give me for this iligant shtring of imeralds and jewls?" Nor would he really believe our assurance that it was worthless.

By this time, twenty men—mostly English, but some Sikhs—were in the court. The explosion of their rifles, as they burst open locks and doors, had attracted stray marauders. More than one quarrel, which came nigh to bloodletting, had already arisen: things looked threatening. We could do no good: and, as a Mustee * sapper just happened to look in, we laid hold of him to carry our jade bowls, and got into the outer court, in which there was, on a larger scale, a repetition of the same scene as we had just left.

Oh, the toil of that day! Never had I felt such exhaustion. It was horrid enough to have to stumble through endless courts which were like vapor baths, amid dead bodies, through sights worthy of the Inferno, by blazing walls which might be pregnant with mines, over breaches, in and out of smoldering embrasures, across frail ladders, suffocated by deadly smells of rotting corpses, of rotten ghee,† or vile native scents; but the seething crowd of camp followers into which we emerged in Hazratgang ‡ was something worse. As ravenous, and almost as foul, as vultures, they were packed in a dense mass in the street, afraid or unable to go into the palaces, and, like the birds they resembled, waiting till the fight was done to prey on their plunder.

"Everybody talks about your letters and everybody praises them," Charles Dickens wrote to Russell. Indeed, Russell's courageous dispatches to *The Times* served to quench the spirit of revenge at home. While the massacre by the sepoys was, admittedly, "the acts of barbarous savages," Russell asked whether the actions of the British were "those of civilized Christians." "All these kinds of vindictive, unchristian, Indian torture, such as sewing Mohammedans in pigskins, smearing them with pork fat before execution and burning their bodies, and forcing Hindus to defile themselves, are disgraceful and ultimately recoil on ourselves." The Indian Mutiny resulted in the British Government taking over the administration of India from the East India Company. Russell, in these words, impliedly approved the transfer from Company to Crown:

"I believe that India is the talisman by which England is the greatest power in the world, and that by its loss we lose the magic and prestige of the name which now holds the world in awe," declared *The Times* correspondent. "Let us govern India by superior intelligence, honesty, virtue, morality, not by the mere force of heavier metal," were Russell's final words on the Indian issue.

---

* A half-caste,
† A semifluid butter made in India.
‡ A road leading to the tomb of Amjad Ali Shah, the capture of which on March 14th lead to the occupation of the whole of the enemy's defense lines at Lucknow.

Brigham Young Admits to Fifteen Wives

THE TWO-HOUR INTERVIEW granted by Brigham Young to Horace Greeley in the summer of 1859, when the nationally famous newspaper editor (emulating his own slogan: "Go West, young man!") stopped over at Salt Lake City en route to California, made journalistic history. While interviews had previously been used to take unofficial depositions from prisoners or witnesses, a public official was invariably present. The older newspaper interviews were generally not reported between quotation marks, but indirectly.* The informal interview, possibly initiated by Greeley and best exemplified by the account of his meeting with Brigham Young, revealed intimate details in the lives of celebrities. For a time this technique was denounced as "the most perfect contrivance yet devised to make journalism an offense, a thing of ill savor in all decent nostrils."

The ruthless and domineering leader of the Latter-day Saints and quondam journeyman house painter was then fifty-eight years old and at the height of his reputation. Accepting the inspiration of Joseph Smith, Young had for long years demonstrated his brilliant administrative talents in building up the Mormon Church. He had personally led the exodus of the remnant of Israel from the Middle West and had fixed upon the Great Salt Lake Valley region because its apparent barrenness was calculated to discourage intrusion by the Gentiles. A despot who brooked no outside interference with his Church, Young had brought the economic life of his obedient followers under centralized control and preserved his system basically intact in the face of intense nation-wide hostility. Fanatically opposed to liquor (but he put the Church into the liquor business), gambling, and card playing, he nevertheless had radical views on sexual behavior. He had an indeterminate number of wives—fifteen when Greeley called upon him, but possibly as many as twenty-seven in all before he died—and fifty-six children. Owing to his personal wealth, his family burdens did not rest too heavily upon his shoulders.

When Greeley launched the *New York Tribune* in 1841, his avowed object was to found "a journal removed alike from servile partisanship on the one hand, and from gagged, mincing neutrality on the other." The *Tribune* soon became the "political Bible" of the North, renowned for its condemnation of slavery, business monopolies, and the exploitation of labor. With an absent-minded manner, an amazing indifference to dress, and a squeaking voice, the bewhiskered editor was a "natural" for every cartoonist in the land. His desk was invariably a chaotic heap of papers, his drawers bursting with forgotten memos, and his hat and pockets bulged with notes. In his illegible handwriting he would dash off a story at railroad speed, but

---

* For a slight variant of this older form, see Dr. Johnson's account of the interview concerning the Cock Lane ghost, pp. 15-19.

new compositors found it difficult to decipher his pothooks. It is told that one new hand, an Irishman, asked the foreman of the composing room the meaning of one of Greeley's sentences. "I can't make out the sense o' this," he declared. " ' 'Tis five, 'tis fifty; fifty 'tis, 'tis five.' What does Mr. Greeley mane by that?" Greeley had been quoting *Hamlet*: "That he is mad, 'tis true: 'tis true 'tis pity; And pity 'tis 'tis true."

Though its lead is slow-moving, the interview that appeared in the *Tribune* of August 20, 1859, is amazingly informative on some of the chief topics of interest of that day:

Horace Greeley Finds Salt Lake City a Man's Town

New York Tribune, August 20, 1859

TWO HOURS WITH BRIGHAM YOUNG

SALT LAKE CITY, UTAH, JULY 13, 1859 —My friend Dr. Bernhisel, M.C.,* took me this afternoon, by appointment, to meet Brigham Young, President of the Mormon Church, who had expressed a willingness to receive me at two P.M. After some unimportant conversation on general topics, I stated that I had come in quest of fuller knowledge respecting the doctrines and polity of the Mormon Church and would like to ask some questions bearing directly on these, if there were no objection. President Young avowed his willingness to respond to all pertinent inquiries. The conversation proceeded substantially as follows:

H. G.: Am I to regard Mormonism (so-called) as a new religion, or as simply a new development of Christianity?

B. Y.: We hold that there can be no true Christian Church without a priesthood directly commissioned by and in immediate communication with the

* Mormon Church.

Son of God and Saviour of mankind. Such a church is that of the Latter-day Saints, called by their enemies Mormons; we know no other that even pretends to have present and direct revelations of God's will.

H. G.: Then I am to understand that you regard all other churches professing to be Christian as the Church of Rome regards all churches not in communion with itself—as schismatic, heretical, and out of the way of salvation?

B. Y.: Yes, substantially.

H. G.: What is the position of your church with respect to slavery?

B. Y.: We consider it of divine institution and not to be abolished until the curse pronounced on Ham shall have been removed from his descendants.

H. G.: Are any slaves now held in this territory?

B. Y.: There are.

H. G.: Do your territorial laws uphold slavery?

B. Y.: Those laws are printed—you can read for yourself. If slaves are brought here by those who owned them in the States, we do not favor their escape from the service of those owners.

H. G.: Am I to infer that Utah, if admitted as a member of the Federal Union, will be a slave state?

B. Y.: No, she will be a free state. Slavery here would prove useless and unprofitable. I regard it generally as a curse to the master. I myself hire many laborers and pay them fair wages; *I could not afford to own them.* I can do better than subject myself to an obligation to feed and clothe their families, to provide and care for them in sickness and health. Utah is not adapted to slave labor.

H. G.: Let me now be enlightened with regard more especially to your church polity: I understand that you require each member to pay over one tenth of all he produces or earns to the Church.

B. Y.: That is the requirement of our faith.

H. G.: What is done with the proceeds of this tithing?

B.Y.: Part of it is devoted to building temples and other places of worship; part to helping the poor and needy converts on their way to this country; and the largest portion to the support of the poor among the Saints.

H. G.: Is none of it paid to bishops and other dignitaries of the Church?

B. Y.: Not one penny.

H. G.: How, then, do your ministers live?

B. Y.: By the labor of their own hands, like the first Apostles. *I am the only person in the Church who has not a regular calling apart from the Church's service.*

H. G.: Can you give any rational explanation of the aversion and hatred with which your people are generally regarded by those among whom they have lived and with whom they have been brought directly into contact?

B. Y.: No other explanation than is afforded by the crucifixion of Christ and the kindred treatment of God's ministers, prophets, and saints in all ages.

H. G.: How general is polygamy among you?

B.Y.: I could not say. Some of those present [heads of the Church] have each but one wife; others have more; each determines what is his individual duty.

H. G.: What is the largest number of wives belonging to any one man?

B. Y.: I have fifteen; I know no one who has more; but some of those sealed to me are old ladies whom I regard rather as mothers than wives, but whom I have taken home to cherish and support.

H. G.: Does not Christ say that he who puts away his wife, or marries one whom another has put away, commits adultery?

B. Y.: Yes; and I hold that no man should ever put away a wife except for adultery—not always even for that. Such is my individual view of the matter. I do not say that wives have never been put away in our church, but that I do not approve of that practice.

Such is, as nearly as I can recollect, the substance of nearly two hours' conversation. [President Young] spoke readily, not always with grammatical accuracy, but with no appearance of hesitation or reserve, and with no apparent desire to conceal anything. He was very plainly dressed in thin summer clothing, and with no air of sanctimony or fanaticism. In appearance, he is a portly, frank, good-natured, rather thick-set man of fifty-five,* seeming to enjoy life, and be in no particular hurry to get to heaven. His associates are plain men, evidently born and reared to a life of labor, and looking as little

---

* Since Young was born in 1801, Greeley was in error.

like crafty hypocrites or swindlers as any body of men I ever met.

I have a right to add here, because I said it to the assembled chiefs at the close of the above colloquy, that the degradation (or, if you please, the restriction) of woman to the single office of childbearing and its accessories is an inevitable consequence of the system here paramount. I have not observed a sign in the streets, an advertisement in the journals, of this Mormon metropolis, whereby a woman proposes to do anything whatever. No Mormon has ever cited to me his wife's or any woman's opinion on any subject; no Mormon woman has been introduced or has spoken to me; and, though I have been asked to visit Mormons in their houses, no one has spoken of his wife (or wives) desiring to see me, or his desiring me to make her (or their) acquaintance, or voluntarily indicated the existence of such a being or beings.

One remark made by President Young I think I can give accurately, and it may serve as a sample of all that was offered on that side. It was in these words, I think exactly:

"If I did not consider myself competent to transact a certain business without taking my wife's or any woman's counsel with regard to it, I think I ought to let that business alone."

The spirit with regard to woman, of the entire Mormon, as of all other polygamic systems, is fairly displayed in this avowal. Let any such system become established and prevalent, and woman will soon be confined to the harem, and her appearance in the street with unveiled face will be accounted immodest. *I joyfully trust that the genius of the nineteenth century tends to a solution of the problem of woman's sphere and destiny radically different from this.*

H. G.

CALLED BY Allan Nevins the nation's "greatest editor, perhaps its greatest popular educator," Horace Greeley, in this interview, justifies consideration as one of America's top-flight reporters as well. Taking his stand on the side of woman's rights, Greeley had fired the opening gun in the campaign against the Mormon marriage system. Three years later Congress prohibited polygamy for the future in the territories, and ultimately the Mormons bowed to the sentiment of the country.

Garibaldi and His Thousand Redshirts

Win Palermo

THE MOST ROMANTIC military exploit of modern times was the conquest of Sicily by Garibaldi and his thousand redshirts. The hero of the *Risorgimento* (Italian Resurrection) was a fiery, foolhardy, and courageous ex-Staten Island candlemaker who settled down in Italy in 1854 after his enforced exile in America. For several years he observed the progress being made in unifying Italy under the House of Savoy by Count Cavour, whose temperament was in every way the antithesis of his. At last Garibaldi was ready to strike. Italy's William Tell assembled a thousand poorly equipped men, wearing bright-red woolen shirts and red hats, and set sail from Genoa the night of May 5, 1860, to invade the kingdom of Naples, then under the despotism of Francis II, who had recently succeeded to the throne on the death of his notorious father, Ferdinand II ("King Bomba"). Luckily escaping Neapolitan cruisers lying in wait to intercept him, Garibaldi landed at Marsala, which was amazingly defenseless, considering that it was the likeliest landing place. After a month of forced marches, sleepless nights, and exposure to mountain rains and semitropical sun, the band of scarecrows came to the gates of Palermo.

This expedition was covered by a number of first-class newspapermen, including Frank Vizetelly, an artist and war correspondent, representing the *Illustrated London News*, D. F. Botto, a reporter for *Il Mondo Illustrato*, and Carlo Arrivabene, for the London *Daily News*. But none surpassed in authority and reportorial excellence the Hungarian-born Nandor Eber, the London *Times* correspondent, whose accounts were later a basic source for George Macaulay Trevelyan's classic treatment, *Garibaldi and the Thousand* (1909). Eber reported the hatred of the people for everything Neapolitan and the prevailing confidence in Garibaldi's ultimate victory. On May 23 he wrote from Messina: "Every one of us looked out anxiously for the coast of Sicily, as if the traces of an insurrection could be seen, like the eruption of a volcano, from afar." Here is Eber's great dispatch from Palermo:

*How the volcano of revolution erupted in
Sicily, as told by Eber, the Hungarian,
London Times correspondent*

The Times (London), June 8, 1860

THE INSURRECTION IN SICILY
(From Our Special Correspondent)

PALERMO, MAY 27—It is two P.M., and I am writing to you with the bombshells flying above my head through the air. When the landing of Garibaldi produced the first fit of terror at Naples, the youthful Bourbon sent to his brave fleet concentrated in the Bay of Palermo the order to bomb his faithful Palermitans and reduce their town to ashes if they should dare to rise against his paternal authority. The Palermitans had been treated once already in this paternal manner by the illustrious father of the present sovereign, who, as you remember, figures in history as King Bomba for having given these souvenirs of his love to every large town of his kingdom. Whoever has been in a town which is bombarded will tell you that it is very unpleasant, especially if you have not got the means of answering in a condign manner, and yet Palermo has risen this morning.

This morning at daybreak Garibaldi appeared at the eastern gates of Palermo, and, after a comparatively bloodless struggle, entered them. By ten A.M. the greater part of the town was in his hands. The Neapolitans were driven into a number of strong positions round the Royal Palace, to the southwest of the town, and to the northwest of the Mole, their line of retreat, and, not being able to do anything more, the ships have opened their fire, always the last remedy. Of the events since yesterday I can speak as an eyewitness. They will prove to you that Garibaldi's star, so far from being in the decline, seems rising brighter every day, and that if Sicily becomes free it will be owing to him.

* * *

EBER THEN REVIEWS Garibaldi's strategy : to capture the town by surprising posts in "the lower and comparatively ill-defended" part and then gradually to work his way from street to street. Although Eber tries to maintain a pretense of neutrality, it was he, according to Colonel Türr, Garibaldi's Hungarian aide, who advised Garibaldi to choose the Termini gate, which was the least strongly defended. Any other gate probably would have been fatal. Orders were issued.

The different bands gradually worked their way towards the summit of the pass. I was mounted on a regular Rosinante, with a halter passed round the jay, and provided with a saddle which seemed to have been formed to fit on the vertebrae of my lean black charger.

The road up to the pass winds along rows of gigantic cactus hedges, which give a thoroughly Eastern character to the country. It was just sunset when we arrived on the top, where, through a gap, we could see the bay and town of Palermo and the sea beyond, looking more like a fairy picture than reality. All the mountains, with their rugged points naturally of a reddish tint, seemed to have drunk in the rays of the setting sun, and exhibited that rosy color which I had thought hitherto a special gift of the plain of Attica. While you had this charming scene before you, you looked behind, as it were, into the hearts of the mountains. It was one of the finest spots I ever saw, and all the country was fragrant with spring flowers, the perfume of which came out with redoubled vigor as soon as the sun had set. It proved a bad road for the expedition, that mountain pass, but it was lovely to look upon.

In order to entertain the Neapolitans with the idea that all was safe on that side, the usual large fires were kindled on the tops of the mountains and kept up long after our departure by men left behind for that purpose. Garibaldi went up to look at the position underneath, or, perhaps, to indulge in that kind of reverie to which he is subject in such solemn moments, and which ends in a concentration of all his faculties on the sole aim he has before him.

The evening gun in the fort had been long re-echoed by the mountains, and the moon had risen clear and bright above our heads, giving a new charm to this lovely scenery, before we stirred.

DESCENDING SINGLE FILE, Garibaldi's forces approached the gates, but their noise aroused the defenders, and they were received by "a well-sustained fire, not only in front, but from the houses on their flanks." But, fortunately, Neapolitan aim was poor. "I never saw so little damage done by so much shooting," commented Eber. Rushing the sandbag barricade at bayonet point, and dashing across the *stradone,* a furious *salto* in which the *Times* reporter played a heroic role, Garibaldi and his followers reached the market place.

One must know these Sicilians to have an idea of the frenzy, screaming, shouting, crying, and hugging; all would kiss his hands and embrace his knees. Every moment brought new masses, which debouched in troops from one of the streets, anxious to have their turn. As the *Cacciatori* gradually cleared the lower part of the town, most of the inhabitants came to have a look, and give a greeting to the Liberator of Palermo and Sicily.

The entrance was effected about half-past five A.M., and by noon more than one half of the town was clear of the troops. But two hours before this was effected the citadel had opened its fire on the town, at first moderately enough, but soon after with great vigor, firing large thirteen-inch shells,

red-hot shot, and every other projectile calculated to do the greatest possible damage. About noon or so the ships in the harbor opened their fire, and between the two they contrived to destroy a great number of houses in the lower part of the town, killing and wounding a large number of people of all ages and both sexes. Two of the large shells were sent right into the hospital and exploded in one of the wards. Everywhere you perceived ruins and conflagration, dead and wounded, not a few of whom must have perished among the ruins of their houses. If the object of the Neapolitans was to inspire terror, they certainly succeeded. Whoever could took refuge in whatever he thought the most bombproof place, and those who could not you saw crying, praying, and wringing their hands in the streets. It was a pitiable sight, indeed, and it did more harm to inoffensive people than to those who might have retaliated.

* * *

"THE NEAPOLITAN MONARCHY has buried itself under a heap of ruins of dead bodies," Eber reported on May 30. The next day he sent this dispatch:

The Times (London), June 13, 1860

PALERMO, MAY 31—Anyone in search of violent emotions cannot do better than set off at once for Palermo. However *blasé* he may be, or however milk-and-water his blood, I promise it will be stirred up. He will be carried away by the tide of popular feeling, or else the impetuosity and variation of this torrent will produce in him a reaction such as he rarely felt.

The popular proverb has it that no day resembles its predecessor. Here almost every hour changes the state of affairs, and with the state of affairs the feelings of 200,000 people change from one extreme to another almost without the slightest transition. One moment all is triumph and hope, and the next all is terror and dejection. One instant the town resounds with cheers, the next you see numbers prostrated before the shrines of Madonnas and saints which are to be found in almost every corner. Now and then, between the two fits, there is a short lull—a kind of exhaustion which is soon followed by another attack of hope or fear.

In the afternoon Garibaldi made a tour of inspection round the town. I was there, but find it really impossible to give you even a faint idea of the manner in which he was received everywhere. It was one of those triumphs which seem to be almost too much for a man. The most wonderful thing I ever saw in this way was the reception of Napoleon and Victor Emmanuel at Milan, just about a year ago, and I am almost inclined to think that the one yesterday was more extraordinary. The entry of the sovereigns was something more formal, which prevented the full expression of popular enthusiasm. They were on horseback and surrounded by their guards, while the popular idol, Garibaldi, in his red flannel shirt, with a loose colored handkerchief round his neck, and his worn wide-awake,* was walking on foot among those cheering, laughing, crying, mad thousands; and all his few followers could do was to prevent him from being bodily carried off the ground. The people threw themselves forward to kiss his hands, or, at least, to touch the hem of his garment, as if it contained the panacea for all their past and perhaps coming suffering. Children were brought up, and mothers asked on their knees for his blessing; and all this while the object of this idolatry was as calm and smiling as when in the deadliest fire, taking up the children and kissing them, trying to quiet the crowd, stopping at every moment to hear a long complaint of houses burned and property sacked by the retreating soldiers, giving good advice, comforting, and promising that all damages should be paid for.

Had Garibaldi and the town only to

---

* A soft-brimmed felt hat.

do with the troops, the thing would be easy enough; but it is the bombardment which makes the position more difficult. From the specimen we had on the first day one can see what might be done if it was continued for any length of time. King Bomba II might fulfill his threat of converting the town into a heap of ruins, and bury hundreds of inoffensive inhabitants among them, especially if the soldiers continue, as they have hitherto done, to burn every house they sack.

One might write volumes of horrors on the vandalism already committed, for every one of the hundred ruins has its story of brutality and inhumanity. Were there not so many of the officers of the ships who have strolled about the town and seen them with their own eyes, I should be almost afraid of writing them down, so incredible do they sound. It is, above all, in the quarters to the right and left of the Royal Palace, mostly inhabited by the poorer classes and thickly crowded with monasteries, that the horrors can be witnessed by everyone who walks up. Anyone can do so by using his senses. In these small houses a dense population is crowded together even in ordinary times. The fear of the bombardment crowded them even more. A shell falling on one, and crushing and burying the inmates, was sufficient to make people abandon the neighboring one and take refuge a little further on, shutting themselves up in the cellars. When the Royalists retired they set fire to those of the houses which had escaped the shells, and numbers were thus burned alive in their hiding places. All about the neighborhood of the Albergeria the air is charged with the exhalations of the corpses imperfectly covered by the ruins, and with that greasy smell occasioned by the burning of an animal body.

If you can stand the exhalation, try and go inside the ruins, for it is only there that you will see what the thing means and you will not have to search long before you stumble over the charred remains of a human body, a leg sticking out here, an arm there, a black face staring at you a little further on. You are startled by a rustle. You look round and see half a dozen gorged rats scampering off in all directions, or you see a dog trying to make his escape over the ruins. Myriads of flies rise up at your approach, and you hurry out, in order to escape their disgusting and poisonous contact.

I only wonder that the sight of these scenes does not convert every man in the town into a tiger and every woman into a fury. But these people have been so long ground down and demoralized that their nature seems to have lost the power of reaction.

* * *

TRULY, AS Eber observed, "an epic poem could be written about what the 1062 Italians and five Hungarians did in Sicily during these last twenty days." Victorious at Palermo, Garibaldi took Sicily, sailed to Naples, and at Volturno defeated an army twice the size of his forces. Then, in November, 1860, the Dictator of Sicily and Naples resigned, sailed back to his farm on Caprera "with a large bag of seed corn and a small handful of lira notes," and left Victor Emmanuel the constitutional monarch of the new kingdom of Italy. In discarding the idea of a republic, the Italians, according to the London *Times,* had become "not only moderate but practical in their political conduct."

A Southern Planter Puts His Human Chattels

on the Auction Block

FOR SALE. LONG COTTON AND RICE NEGROES.

A GANG OF 460 NEGROES, accustomed to the culture of Rice and Provisions; among whom are a number of good mechanics and house servants. Will be sold on the 2nd and 3rd of March next, at Savannah, by

JOSEPH BRYAN

TERMS OF SALE—One third cash; remainder by bond, bearing interest from day of sale, payable in two equal installments, to be secured by mortgage on the Negroes, and approved personal security, or for approved city acceptance on Savannah or Charleston. Purchasers paying for papers.

The Negroes will be sold in families, and can be seen on the premises of JOSEPH BRYAN, in Savannah, three days prior to the day of sale, when catalogues will be furnished.

THE ABOVE ADVERTISEMENT appeared in the Savannah *Republican,* February 28, 1859, and in numerous other leading Southern newspapers. Commenting editorially, the Savannah paper called this "one of the largest lots of Negroes ever offered in the state, and it therefore presents many inducements to purchasers."

Horace Greeley, head of the nationally influential *New York Tribune,* seized upon this sale to promote the antislavery cause and assigned a reporter to cover the auction. A few years earlier, readers of *The New York Times* learned from Frederick Law Olmsted (who, because of his extensive coverage of the South, was really the number-one roving reporter of antebellum days) of the backwardness of plantation life and the resentment of the poorer whites toward Negro labor competition. But his objective reporting lacked the sensationalism of the *Tribune* story, which was well calculated to raise abolitionist blood pressure to a dangerous level.

The master whose "generosity" to his ex-slaves is ironically depicted was Pierce Butler, an absentee planter who was compelled by the Panic of 1857 to dispose of a considerable portion of his estate. Just ten years before, he had emerged the victor in a long and bitter divorce action brought against his wife, Fanny Kemble, who chose freedom in England and the resumption of her stage career to the slave system of a Georgia plantation which she had quickly come to abhor. The slave trader, Joseph Bryan, of a distinguished Southern family, was the prosperous beneficiary of the inflated prices that slave labor commanded on the eve of the Civil War. Slave traders, considered a compound of unscrupulous horse trader, tavernkeeper, garrulous, cheap politician, and hard-drinking gambler, had little standing in the South. Hating the traders because of their fear of being separated from their loved ones and from old associations, slave mothers frightened unruly pickaninnies into obedience by saying:

"De spekilatah is comin' and I'se gwine ter let 'im hab yo', sho'!"

The *Tribune* story appeared in the March 9, 1859, issue:

A Tribune *reporter sees a slave market in action and notes the vendor's munificence*

New York Tribune, March 9, 1859

AMERICAN CIVILIZATION ILLUSTRATED

A GREAT SLAVE AUCTION

HUMAN FEELINGS OF NO ACCOUNT

The largest sale of human chattels that has been made in Star-Spangled America for several years took place on Wednesday and Thursday of last week, at the race course near the city of Savannah, Georgia. The lot consisted of four hundred and thirty-six men, women, children, and infants, being that half of the Negro stock remaining on the old Major Butler plantations which fell to one of the two heirs to that estate.

The sale had been advertised largely for many weeks, and as the Negroes were known to be a choice lot and very desirable property, the attendance of buyers was large. The breaking up of an old family estate is so uncommon an occurrence that the affair was regarded with unusual interest throughout the South. For several days before the sale every hotel in Savannah was crowded with Negro speculators from North and South Carolina, Virginia, Georgia, Alabama, and Louisiana, who had been attracted hither by the prospects of making good bargains. Nothing was heard for days, in the barrooms and public rooms, but talk of the great sale.

The office of Joseph Bryan, the Negro broker who had the management of the sale, was thronged every day by eager inquirers in search of information. Little parties were made up from the various hotels every day to visit the race course, distant some three miles from the city, to look over the chattels, discuss their points, and make memoranda for guidance on the day of sale. The buyers were generally of a rough breed, slangy, profane, and bearish, being, for the most part, from the back-river and swamp plantations, where the elegancies of polite life are not perhaps developed to their fullest extent.

The Negroes came from two plantations, the one a rice plantation near Darien and the other a cotton plantation.

None of the Butler slaves have ever been sold before, but have been on these two plantations since they were born.

The slaves remained at the race course, some of them for more than a week and all of them for four days before the sale. They were brought in thus early that buyers who desired to inspect them might enjoy that privilege, although none of them were sold at private sale. For these preliminary days their shed was constantly visited by speculators. The Negroes were examined with as little consideration as if they had been brutes indeed; the buyers pulling their mouths open to see their teeth, pinching their limbs to find how muscular they were, walking them up and down to detect any signs of lameness, making them stoop and bend in different ways that they might be certain there was no concealed rupture or wound; and, in addition to all this treatment, asking them scores of questions relative to their qualifications and accomplishments. All these humiliations were submitted to without a murmur, and in some instances with good-natured cheerfulness—where the slave liked the appearance of the proposed buyer and fancied that he might prove a kind "mas'r."

The following curiously sad scene is the type of a score of others that were there enacted:

"Elisha," chattel No. 5 in the catalogue, had taken a fancy to a benevolent-looking middle-aged gentleman who was inspecting the stock, and thus used his powers of persuasion to induce the benevolent man to purchase him, with his wife, boy, and girl, Molly, Israel, and Sevanda, chattels Nos. 6, 7, and 8.

"Look at me, mas'r. Am prime rice planter; sho' you won't find a better man den me; no better on de whole plantation; not a bit old yet. Do mo' work den ever. Do carpenter work, too, little. Better buy me, mas'r. I'se be good sarvant, mas'r. Molly, too, my wife, sa, fus'-rate rice hand; mos' as good as me. Stan' out yer, Molly, and let the gen'lem'n see."

Molly advances, with her hands crossed on her bosom, and makes a quick short curtsy, and stands mute, looking appealingly in the benevolent man's face. But Elisha talks all the faster.

"Show mas'r yer arm, Molly—good arm dat, mas'r—she do a heap of work mo' with dat arm yet. Let good mas'r see yer teeth, Molly—see dat, mas'r. Teeth all reg'lar, all good—she'm young gal yet. Come out yer, Israel, walk aroun' an' let the gen'lem'n see how spry you be."

Then, pointing to the three-year-old girl who stood with her chubby hand to her mouth, holding onto her mother's dress, and uncertain what to make of the strange scene:

"Little Vandy's on'y a chile yet; make prime gal by-and-by. Better buy us, mas'r, we'm fus'-rate bargain"—and so on. But the benevolent gentleman found where he could drive a closer bargain and so bought somebody else.

The sentiment of the subjoined characteristic dialogue was heard more than once repeated:

"Well, Colonel, I seen you looking sharp at shoemaker Bill's Sally. Going to buy her?"

"Well, Major, I think not. Sally's a good, big, strapping gal, and can do a heap o' work; but it's five years since she had any children. *She's done breeding, I reckon.*"

The buyers, who were present to the number of about two hundred, clustered around the platform; while the Negroes, who were not likely to be immediately wanted, gathered into sad groups in the background to watch the progress of the selling in which they were so sorrowfully interested. The wind howled outside, and through the open side of the building the driving rain came pouring in. The bar downstairs ceased for a short time its brisk trade. The buyers lit fresh cigars, got ready their catalogues and pencils, and the first lot of human chattels are led upon the stand, not by a white man, but by a sleek mulatto, himself a slave, and who seems to regard the selling of his brethren, in which he so glibly assists, as a capital joke. It had been announced that the Negroes would be sold in "families," that is to say, a man would not be parted from his wife, or a mother from a very young child. There is perhaps as much policy as humanity in this arrangement, for thereby many aged and unserviceable people are disposed of, who otherwise would not find a ready sale.

The expression on the faces of all who stepped on the block was always the same and told of more anguish than it is in the power of words to express. Blighted homes, crushed hopes, and broken hearts was the sad story to be read in all the anxious faces.

The auctioneer brought up Joshua's Molly and family. He announced that Molly insisted that she was lame in her left foot and perversely would walk lame, although, for his part, he did not believe a word of it. He had caused her to be examined by an eminent physician in Savannah, which medical light had declared that Joshua's Molly was not lame, but was only shamming. However, the gentlemen must judge for themselves and bid accordingly. So Molly was put through her paces, and compelled to trot up and down along the stage, to go up and down the steps, and to exercise her feet in various ways, but always with the same result, the left foot *would* be lame. She was finally sold for $695.

Whether she really was lame or not, no one knows but herself, but it must be remembered that to a slave a lameness, or anything that decreases his market value, is a thing to be rejoiced over. A man in the prime of life, worth $1600 or thereabouts, can have little hope of ever being able, by any little savings of his own, to purchase his liberty. But let him have a rupture, or lose a limb, or sustain any other injury that renders him of much less service to his owner, and reduces his value to $300 or $400, and he may hope to accumulate that sum, and eventually to purchase his liberty. *Freedom without health is infinitely sweeter than health without freedom.*

And so the Great Sale went on for two long days, during which time there were sold 429 men, women, and children. The total amount of the sale foots up to $303,850—the proceeds of the first day being $161,480, and of the second day $142,370.

Leaving the race buildings, where the scenes we have described took place, a crowd of Negroes were seen gathered eagerly about a man in their midst. That man was Mr. Pierce M. Butler of the free city of Philadelphia, who was solacing the wounded hearts of the people he had sold from their firesides and their homes, by doling out to them small change at the rate of a dollar a head. To every Negro he had sold, who presented his claim for the paltry pittance, he gave the munificent stipend of one whole dollar in specie; he being provided with two canvas bags of twenty-five-cent pieces, fresh from the mint, to give an additional glitter to his munificent generosity.

AFTER THE AUCTION the slaves could look forward to shipment to the respective plantations of their new masters. William H. Seward, later Lincoln's Secretary of State, witnessed a cargo of slaves shipping out of Norfolk for New Orleans in 1846. Down to the steerage a well-dressed man led a long line of seventy-five slaves—men, women, and children—each carrying a bag, bundle, or bandbox containing all their possessions. "As I stood looking at this strange scene," Seward reported, "a gentleman stepped up to my side and said: 'You see the *curse* that our forefathers bequeathed to us. Oh, they don't mind it; they are cheerful; they enjoy this transportation and travel as much as you do.' The captain of our boat, seeing me intensely interested, turned to me and said: 'Oh, sir, do not be concerned about them. They are the happiest people in the world!' I looked, and there they were— slaves, ill-protected from the cold, fed capriciously on the commonest food —going from all that was dear to all that was terrible, and still they wept not. And these were 'the happiest people in the world'! The sable procession was followed by a woman, a white woman, dressed in silk and furs and feathers. She seemed [to be] the captain's wife. She carried in her hand a Bible!"

God's Angry Man Grants an Interview

WAR BETWEEN RIVERS and mountains which must have shaken the earth itself to its center." In these words Thomas Jefferson described the passage of the Potomac through the Blue Ridge at Harpers Ferry. And at this scenic spot, on Sunday, October 16, 1859, John Brown, commander-in-chief of the "Provisional Army" (18 men in all) struck an astonishing blow for the liberation of the slaves. He hoped, in seizing the Federal arsenal, to secure sufficient arms for a full-dress insurrection. After having attained his objective, he should have stripped the arsenal and fled to the hills. Instead, he committed the fatal error of lingering on the scene with his ridiculously small force.

Harpers Ferry had its Paul Revere—John D. Starry, a local physician, who put spurs to his horse and roused the citizens of Charlestown, eight miles away. The uprising that the South had been fearing ever since Nat Turner's Insurrection in Virginia in 1831 appeared to have come to pass, and the militia was called out. Brown's forces retreated from their positions at the bridge and in the town to the fire-engine house within the armory, taking with them some prominent townsmen as hostages. Brown's own son was mortally wounded and died in the night.

"If you must die, die like a man," Brown told him.

An aroused Federal government sent Colonel Robert E. Lee, a son of "Light-Horse Harry" Lee of Revolutionary fame and soon to distinguish himself as a Confederate general, with a detachment of marines. Lee ordered the engine-house door broken down with sledgehammers and called upon the insurgents to give up. When Brown refused, Lee ordered his men to the attack, which he subsequently reported as follows:

The fire engines within the house had been placed by the besieged close to the doors. The doors were fastened by ropes, the spring of which prevented their being broken by the blows of the hammers. The men were therefore ordered to drop their hammers, and, with a portion of the reserve, to use as a battering ram a heavy ladder, with which they dashed in part of the door and gave admittance to the storming party. The fire of the insurgents up to this time had been harmless. At the threshold one marine fell mortally wounded. The rest, led by Lieutenant Green and Major Russell, quickly ended the contest. The insurgents that resisted were bayoneted. Their leader, John Brown, was cut down by the sword of Lieutenant Green, and our citizens were protected by both officers and men. The whole was over in a few minutes.

To the scene sped one of James Gordon Bennett's reporters, who sent on to *The New York Herald* an account of Brown's examination after his capture. The self-appointed liberator had been removed from the engine room to the office of the armory, where he was questioned by Lee, "Jeb" Stuart.

Governor Wise of Virginia, Senator J. M. Mason, Congressman Vallandigham of Ohio, Colonel Lewis Washington, Andrew Hunter, and Congressman James Faulkner of Virginia. The first four were destined to play
important roles in the Confederacy, and Vallandigham was to become a
leader of the Northern fifth column.

"Whom the gods would destroy"—
John Brown's retort recorded by a
James Gordon Bennett newsman

The New York Herald, October 21, 1859

THE HARPERS FERRY OUTBREAK

VERBATIM REPORT OF THE QUESTION-
ING OF OLD BROWN BY SENATOR MA-
SON, CONGRESSMAN VALLANDIGHAM,
AND OTHERS

From Our Special Correspondent
HARPERS FERRY, OCTOBER 19, 1859
—"Old Brown," or "Osawatomie
Brown," as he is often called, the hero
of a dozen fights or so with the "border ruffians" of Missouri, in the days
of "bleeding Kansas," is the head and
front of this offending [*sic*]—the
commander of the abolition filibuster
army. His wounds, which first were
supposed to be mortal, turn out to be
mere flesh wounds and scratches, not
at all dangerous in their character. He
has been removed, together with
Stephens, the other wounded prisoner,
from the engine room to the office of
the armory, and they now lie on the
floor, upon miserable shakedowns,
covered with some old bedding.

Brown is fifty-five years of age,
rather small-sized, with keen and restless gray eyes, and a grizzly beard and
hair. He is a wiry, active man, and
should the slightest chance for an escape be afforded, there is no doubt
that he will yet give his captors much

trouble. His hair is matted and tangled, and his face, hands, and clothes
are smutched and smeared with blood.

Colonel Lee stated that he would
exclude all visitors from the room if
the wounded men were annoyed or
pained by them, but Brown said he
was by no means annoyed; on the contrary, he was glad to be able to make
himself and his motives clearly understood. He converses freely, fluently,
and cheerfully, without the slightest
manifestation of fear or uneasiness,
evidently weighing all his words, and
possessing a good command of language. His manner is courteous and
affable, and he appears to make a favorable impression upon his auditory,
which, during most of the day yesterday, averaged about ten or a dozen
men.

When I arrived in the armory,
shortly after two o'clock in the afternoon, Brown was answering questions
put to him by Senator Mason, who had
just arrived from his residence at
Winchester, thirty miles distant, Colonel Faulkner, member of Congress who
lives but a few miles off, Mr. Vallandigham, member of Congress of Ohio,
and several other distinguished gentlemen. The following is a verbatim report of the conversation:

Mr. Mason: Can you tell us, at

least, who furnished money for your expedition?

Mr. Brown: I furnished most of it myself. I cannot implicate others. It is by my own folly that I have been taken. I could easily have saved myself from it had I exercised my own better judgment rather than yielded to my feelings. I should have gone away, but I had thirty-odd prisoners, whose wives and daughters were in tears for their safety, and I felt for them. Besides, I wanted to allay the fears of those who believed we came here to burn and kill. For this reason I allowed the train to cross the bridge and gave them full liberty to pass on. I did it only to spare the feelings of these passengers and their families and to allay the apprehensions that you had got here in your vicinity a band of men who had no regard for life and property, nor any feeling of humanity.

Mr. Mason: But you killed some people passing along the streets quietly.

Mr. Brown: Well, sir, if there was anything of that kind done, it was without my knowledge. Your own citizens, who were my prisoners, will tell you that every possible means were taken to prevent it. I did not allow my men to fire, nor even to return a fire, when there was danger of killing those we regarded as innocent persons, if I could help it. They will tell you that we allowed ourselves to be fired at repeatedly and did not return it.

A Bystander: That is not so. You killed an unarmed man at the corner of the house over there [at the water tank] and another besides.

Mr. Brown: See here, my friend, it is useless to dispute or contradict the report of your own neighbors who were my prisoners.

Mr. Mason: If you would tell us who sent you here—who provided the means—that would be information of some value.

Mr. Brown: I will answer freely and faithfully about what concerns myself —I will answer anything I can with honor, but not about others.

Mr. Vallandigham (member of Congress from Ohio, who had just entered): Mr. Brown, who sent you here?

Mr. Brown: No man sent me here; it was my own prompting and that of my Maker, or that of the devil, whichever you please to ascribe it to. I acknowledge no man [master] in human form.

Mr. Vallandigham: Did you get up the expedition yourself?

Mr. Brown: I did.

Mr. Mason: What was your object in coming?

Mr. Brown: We came to free the slaves, and only that.

A Young Man (in the uniform of a volunteer company): How many men in all had you?

Mr. Brown: I came to Virginia with eighteen men only, besides myself.

Volunteer: What in the world did you suppose you could do here in Virginia with that amount of men?

Mr. Brown: Young man, I don't wish to discuss that question here.

Volunteer: You could not do anything.

Mr. Brown: Well, perhaps your ideas and mine on military subjects would differ materially.

Mr. Mason: How do you justify your acts?

Mr. Brown: I think, my friend, you are guilty of a great wrong against God and humanity—I say it without wishing to be offensive—and it would be perfectly right for anyone to interfere with you so far as to free those you willfully and wickedly hold in bondage. I do not say this insultingly.

I think I did right and that others will do right who interfere with you at any time and all times. I hold that the golden rule, "Do unto others as you would that others should do unto you," applies to all who would help others to gain their liberty.

Lieut. Stewart: But you don't believe in the Bible.

Mr. Brown: Certainly I do.

Mr. Vallandigham: Have you had any correspondence with parties at the North on the subject of this movement?

Mr. Brown: I have had correspondence.

A Bystander: Do you consider this a religious movement?

Mr. Brown: It is, in my opinion, the greatest service a man can render to God.

Bystander: Do you consider yourself an instrument in the hands of Providence?

Mr. Brown: I do.

Bystander: Upon what principle do you justify your acts?

Mr. Brown: Upon the golden rule. I pity the poor in bondage that have none to help them; that is why I am here; not to gratify any personal animosity, revenge, or vindictive spirit. It is my sympathy with the oppressed and the wronged, that are as good as you and as precious in the sight of God. [Brown then proceeded to deny that he ever took any slaves against their will, to justify secrecy as necessary to success, and, when told of Gerrit Smith's published letter criticizing moral suasion as hopeless and advocating an insurrection in the South as the only effective way of Negro emancipation, declared:] I should concur with it. *I agree with Mr. Smith that moral suasion is hopeless.* I don't think the people of the slave states will ever consider the subject of slavery in its true light till some other argument is resorted to than moral suasion.

Mr. Vallandigham: Did you expect a general rising of the slaves in case of your success?

Mr. Brown: No, sir; nor did I wish it; I expected to gather them up from time to time and set them free.

Mr. Vallandigham: Did you expect to hold possession here till then?

Mr. Brown: Well, probably I had quite a different idea. I do not know that I ought to reveal my plans. I am here a prisoner and wounded, because I foolishly allowed myself to be so. You overrate your strength in supposing I could have been taken if I had not allowed it. [Brown admitted that he had purchased the arms that enabled him to seize the armory, but refused to say just where he had obtained them.]

Reporter of the Herald: I do not wish to annoy you; but if you have anything further you would like to say I will report it.

Mr. Brown: I have nothing to say, only that I claim to be here in carrying out a measure I believe perfectly justifiable, and not to act the part of an incendiary or ruffian, but to aid those suffering great wrong. *I wish to say, furthermore, that you had better—all you people at the South—prepare yourselves for a settlement of that question that must come up for settlement sooner than you are prepared for it.* The sooner you are prepared, the better. You may dispose of me very easily. I am nearly disposed of now; but this question is still to be settled—this Negro question, I mean; the end of that is not yet

Q.: Brown, suppose you had every nigger in the United States, what would you do with them?

A.: Set them free.

Q.: Your intention was to carry them off and free them?

A.: Not at all.

A Bystander: To set them free would sacrifice the life of every man in this community.

Mr. Brown: I do not think so.

Bystander: I know it. *I think you are fanatical.*

Mr. Brown: And I think you are fanatical. "Whom the gods would destroy they first make mad," and you are mad.

Q.: Was it your only object to free the Negroes?

A.: Absolutely our only object.

Q.: But you demanded and took Colonel Washington's silver and watch?

A.: Yes; *we intended freely to appropriate the property of slaveholders to carry out our object.* It was for that, and only that, and with no design to enrich ourselves with any plunder whatever.

Q.: Did you know Sherrod in Kansas? I understand you killed him.

A.: I killed no man except in fair fight; I fought at Black Jack Point and Osawatomie, and if I killed anybody, it was at one of these places.

* * *

HOMICIDAL MANIAC or saintly martyr—the verdict of history is still suspended over the head of John Brown. The South did not forget that in the Pottawatomie massacre in Kansas in 1856 * Brown and his gang had wiped out the family of a mild proslavery man, splitting open their heads and chopping off their arms and fingers. Emotionally unstable, the apostle of direct action possessed an indubitable streak of insanity. His violent and irresponsible coup did more than any other single action to feed the flames of secession in the South.

From the time of his capture until his execution Brown showed courage and dignity. Governor Wise remarked after the interview: "They are themselves mistaken who take him to be a madman. He is a fanatic, vain and garrulous, but firm, truthful, and intelligent." In pointing out that the South was just as fanatical as he was on the subject of slavery and in prophesying that the issue would shortly come up for settlement, Brown was justified by the course of events. In his last speech, delivered at his trial for treason, he reinforced the moral position he took at the interview. "I am yet too young to understand that God is any respecter of persons. I believe that to have interfered as I have done—as I have always freely admitted I have done—in behalf of His despised poor was not wrong, but right."

Many in the North, like Lincoln, rejected the solution of violence offered by Brown and the more rabid abolitionists. Others felt differently. On the day after the execution *The Springfield Republican* commented: "John Brown still lives." To Emerson, John Brown had "made the gallows glorious like the cross." Walt Whitman's sympathy was expressed in the poem, *Years of Meteors*:

---

* Brilliantly reported in the Leavenworth *Kansas Weekly Herald,* June 7, 1856.

> *I would sing how an old man, with white hair,*
> *mounted the scaffold in Virginia,*
> *(I was at hand, silent I stood with teeth shut*
> *close, I watch'd,*
> *I stood very near you old man when cool and*
> *indifferent, but trembling with age and your*
> *unheal'd wounds, you mounted the scaffold)* . . .

The execution was sensationally exploited by *Frank Leslie's Illustrated Newspaper,* whose issues of December 10 and 17, 1859, carried the account of Dr. Rawlings, staff correspondent, and sketches made on the spot by a staff artist. "The most important paper we have yet issued," *Leslie's* boasted.

Abe Lincoln in Illinois Bids a Farewell That Proves Tragically Prophetic

O N FEBRUARY 11, 1861, Lincoln bade farewell to his friends in Springfield and began his journey to the Eastern states that culminated in his inauguration. Six states of the South had already seceded from the Union. Buchanan, nervous, hesitant, impotent, was still in office. Lincoln had grave doubts about his own ability to resolve the crisis, and, while not a pious man, was undoubtedly sincere in his statement that without divine assistance "I cannot succeed." During the Lincoln-Douglas debates Lincoln had crawled one day into an empty boxcar with Henry Villard, the journalist for the *New Yorker Staats-Zeitung,* and scouted the rumors that he was a presidential possibility. "Just think of such a sucker as me as President," he laughed, his long arms hugging his bony knees.

This same Henry Villard was later correspondent of the Associated Press at Springfield and covered Lincoln's farewell remarks for *The New York Herald.* The version of the speech subsequently published in his *Memoirs* varies in minor details from the *Herald* text, but the latter seems to have more literary flavor and a greater ring of extemporaneousness about it.

Villard's *Herald* story appeared in the February 12, 1861 (Lincoln's birthday), issue:

"Not knowing when or whether I ever may return"

The New York Herald, February 12, 1861

SPRINGFIELD, ILLINOIS, FEBRUARY 11 —President-elect Lincoln, accompanied by his lady and a number of friends, left his hotel at half-past seven A.M. and rode up to the Great Western depot. Over a thousand persons of all classes were assembled in the depot building and on each side of the festivity-decorated special train to bid farewell to their honored townsman. The President-elect took his station in the waiting room and allowed his friends to pass by him and take his hand for the last time. His face was pale and quivered with emotion so deep as to render him almost unable to utter a single word.

At eight o'clock precisely he was conducted to the cars by Mr. Wood and Mr. Baker, of the *Journal.* After exchanging a parting salutation with his lady, he took his stand on the platform, removed his hat, and, asking silence, spoke as follows to the multitude that stood in respectful silence and with their heads uncovered:

MR. LINCOLN'S PARTING WORDS

"My friends: No one not in my situation can appreciate my feeling of sadness at this parting. To this place and to the kindness of these people, I owe everything. Here I have been a quarter of a century and have passed from a young man to an old man. Here my children have been born, and one is buried. I now leave, not knowing when or whether I ever may return, with a task before me greater than that which rested upon Washington. Without the assistance of that Divine Being who ever attended him, I cannot succeed. With this assistance, I cannot fail. Trusting in Him who can go with me, and remain with you, and be everywhere for good, let us confidently hope that all will yet be well. In that same Almighty Being I place my reliance for support, and I hope you, my friends, will all pray that I may receive that divine assistance without which I cannot succeed, but with which success is certain.* To His care commending you as, I hope, in your prayers you will commend me, I bid you an affectionate farewell."

Toward the conclusion of his remarks himself and audience were moved to tears. His exhortation to pray elicited choked exclamations of "We will do it; we will do it!" As he turned to enter the cars three cheers were given, and a few seconds afterwards the train moved slowly out of the sight of the silent gathering.†

* * *

VILLARD ACCOMPANIED the tour and wired his report from the next station at which the train stopped. He also wired: "Refreshments for the thirsty are on board. The cheers are always for Lincoln and the Constitution. The President-elect continues reserved and thoughtful, and sits most of the time alone in the private saloon prepared for his special use." Lincoln had left for the White House on a journey that was "to give him a place among the immortals."

Again, to crowds greeting him at Columbus, Lincoln confessed his sense of humility at the heavy tasks before him. Face to face with indifferent and even hostile crowds in New York, he stiffened his backbone. Speaking to the people above the head of Fernando Wood, New York's prosecessionist mayor, Lincoln declared: "So long, then, as it is possible that the prosperity and liberties of this people can be preserved within this Union, it shall be my purpose at all times to preserve it." At his inaugural he declared that "the central idea of secession is the essence of anarchy," and yet he appealed to all his countrymen: "We are not enemies, but friends. We must not be enemies. The mystic chords of memory, stretching from every battlefield and patriot grave to every living heart and hearthstone all over this broad land, will yet swell the chorus of the Union when again touched, as surely they will be, by the better angels of our nature."

Villard recounts how, as the train traveled east, Lincoln disappointed many who saw him for the first time, who noted his shrill, high-pitched

---

* The Nicolay and Hay edition of Lincoln's *Works* omits this sentence.

† According to other accounts, Lincoln climbed up on the rear platform of the train and stood waving as the train pulled out.

voice, his "most unprepossessing features, the gawkiest figure, and the most awkward manners." Very tall, he stooped a little and walked sham-blingly. Walt Whitman, who saw him when he came to New York, recog-nized the nobility of that figure: "His dress of complete black, stovepipe hat pushed on the head, dark-brown complexion, seam'd and wrinkled yet canny-looking face, black bushy head of hair, disproportionately long neck." To do justice to the figure of Lincoln one would require, in Whit-man's opinion, "the eyes and brains and finger-touch of Plutarch and Aeschylus and Michelangelo, assisted by Rabelais."

In Illinois, where people had come to know him, they had come to love him. His gentleness, his kindness, his unfailing humor, his fabulous anec-dotal ability, helped him through the trying days and lifted him above his depressing home background, the shrewish wife he had married in des-peration. On one of the blackest days of the war Lincoln turned to Andrew Gregg Curtin of Pennsylvania and told him that the somber military report he had just received reminded him of what had once happened to the son of a neighbor of his out in Illinois. His two boys, John and Jim, went out to gather apples. John climbed the tree and shook the fruit off; Jim gath-ered the apples. Just then a boar, grubbing in the orchard, waddled up and began to eat the falling apples faster than they could be gathered up. Jim caught the boar by the tail. It squealed and snapped at the lad's legs, and, between rushes of the boar, he yelled up to John: "I—want—you—to—come—down—here—and—help—me—to—let—go—of—this—darned hog's tail." "And, Curtin," concluded the President, "that's just what I want of you and the rest. I want you to pitch in and help me let go of the hog's tail that I have got ahold of."

B. S. Osbon, of the New York *World*, Sees the Stars and Stripes Hauled Down Over Fort Sumter as Civil War Comes to America

E ARLY IN THE MORNING of April 12, 1861, the curtain went up on the "tragedy of the century." At 3:20 A.M. General Beauregard's aides personally delivered to Major Robert Anderson, the commander at Fort Sumter, the Union citadel in Charleston Harbor, the general's message:

"We have the honor to notify you that he will open the fire of his batteries on Fort Sumter within one hour from this time."

Anderson walked with the aides to their boat, shook their hands, and declared:

"If we never meet in this world again, God grant that we may meet in the next."

Shortly thereafter the Confederate batteries opened fire. After a gallant thirty-four-hour defense, while Union naval vessels stood outside the harbor without firing a shot in his behalf, Anderson was forced to surrender. In his own words, his "quarters were entirely burned, the main gates destroyed by fire, the gorge walls seriously impaired, the magazine surrounded by flames and its door closed from the effects of the heat, four barrels and three cartridges of powder only being available and no provisions remaining but pork." * The spectacle of the garrison standing doggedly by its guns moved the attackers to a chivalrous tribute. Beauregard reported: "Our brave troops, carried away by their naturally generous impulses, mounted the different batteries, and at every discharge from the fort cheered the garrison for its pluck and gallantry, and hooted the fleet lying inactive just outside the bar."

The South was jubilant at the success of this reckless deed. The Charleston *Mercury* of April 13 featured the story of the first day's bombardment:

FT. SUMTER BOMBARDMENT

SPLENDID PYROTECHNIC EXHIBITION

FORT MOULTRIE IMPREGNABLE

THE FLOATING BATTERY AND STEVENS' BATTERY A SUCCESS

NOBODY HURT ON OUR SIDE

"It may be a drama of but a single act," that paper commented. On news of the surrender, the Montgomery *Advertiser* of the next day reported that

---

* A photograph taken by Mathew B. Brady, the renowned cameraman of the Civil War, revealed Fort Sumter a mass of ruins. Shot, shell, and dismounted cannon were scattered about like leaves of the forest.

"the face of every Southern man was brighter, his step lighter, and his bearing prouder than it had been before."

From the deck of the revenue cutter *Harriet Lane,* one of a dozen craft sent to take supplies and reinforcements to Fort Sumter, B. S. Osbon, of the New York *World,* witnessed the start of the Civil War. En route home, Osbon transferred to the *Baltic* to interview the embittered Major Anderson, who told him that a junior officer had raised the white flag of surrender without permission, giving the South an easy victory. Osbon was the first to tell the North the story of Fort Sumter. His sensational beat began to appear in the *World* on April 13, the day after the attack started:

"The ball is opened. War is inaugurated"

New York *World,* April 13, 1861

THE WAR BEGUN

CHARLESTON, APRIL 12—*The ball is opened. War is inaugurated.*

The batteries of Sullivan's Island, Morris Island, and other points were opened on Fort Sumter at four o'clock this morning. Fort Sumter has returned the fire, and a brisk cannonading has been kept up.

The military are under arms, and the whole of our population are on the streets. Every available space facing the harbor is filled with anxious spectators.

The firing has continued all day without intermission.

Two of Fort Sumter's guns have been silenced, and it is reported that a breach has been made in the southeast wall.

The answer to General Beauregard's demand by Major Anderson was that he would surrender when his supplies were exhausted; that is, if he was not reinforced.

CHARLESTON, APRIL 12, 3 P.M.—Civil war has at last begun. A terrible fight is at this moment going on between Fort Sumter and the fortifications by which it is surrounded. The issue was submitted to Major Anderson of surrendering as soon as his supplies were exhausted, or of having fire opened on him within a certain time. He refused to surrender, and accordingly at twenty-seven minutes past four o'clock this morning Fort Moultrie began the bombardment by firing two guns.

Major Anderson has the greater part of the day been directing his fire principally against Fort Moultrie, the Stevens and floating battery, these and Fort Johnson being the only ones operating against him. The remainder of the batteries are held in reserve.

The Stevens battery is eminently successful and does terrible execution on Fort Sumter. Breaches, to all appearances, are being made in the several sides exposed to fire. Portions of the parapet have been destroyed, and several of the guns there mounted have been shot away.

The excitement in the community is indescribable. With the first boom of the gun, thousands rushed from their beds to the harbor front, and all day every available place has been thronged by ladies and gentlemen, viewing the solemn spectacle through their glasses. Most of these have relatives in the several fortifications, and many a tearful eye attested the anxious affection of the mother, wife, and sister, but *not a murmur came from a single individual.*

Business is entirely suspended. Only those stores are open necessary to supply articles required by the army.

Troops are pouring into the town by hundreds, but are held in reserve for the present, the force already on the islands being ample. The thunder of the artillery can be heard for fifty miles around, and the scene is magnificently terrible.

New York *World,* April 15, 1861

CHARLESTON, APRIL 13, 12 M.—Major Anderson is hemmed in by ruins and fire. Every building in Fort Sumter is burning. He has blown up one or two to arrest the flames. This does not in any wise diminish his strength. He has been compelled to cease firing altogether.

Major Anderson's flag has been shot away and now waves from a pole on the ramparts.

CHARLESTON, APRIL 13, P.M.—The Federal flag was again hoisted over Fort Sumter, when Porcher Miles, with a flag of truce, went to the fort. In a few minutes the Federal flag

was again hauled down by Major Anderson and a white one unfurled.

The bells are ringing out a merry peal, and our people are engaged in every demonstration of joy.

The visitors reported that Major Anderson surrendered because his quarters and barracks were destroyed and he had no hope of reinforcements. The fleet lay idly by during the thirty hours of the bombardment, and either could not or would not help him; besides, his men were prostrate from overexertion.

Everyone is satisfied with the victory and happy that no blood was shed.

THIS STORY BROUGHT Osbon an offer of twenty-five dollars a week on the *Herald,* which seemed like fabulous riches compared to the nine dollars the *World* had been paying their star reporter. At the siege of New Orleans, Osbon was on the quarterdeck with Farragut, whom he warned to climb down from the rigging just before it was carried away by a shell, a fragment of which cut off most of the newsman's luxuriant red beard. But Osbon got himself into much hotter water when a newspaper, a member of a syndicate for which he was writing, published an advance story of a naval battle off the North Carolina coast before the battle occurred. Forced to stand trial for treason, he was at length acquitted and his reputation for trustworthiness completely vindicated.

The Osbon story on Fort Sumter galvanized the North into action, quickly dissipating the naïve idea that the war was over. Whether or not Lincoln had provoked the South into making the attack by sending naval vessels to the relief of the fort ("A declaration of war," Jefferson Davis stigmatized Lincoln's act), the North rallied behind him. Douglas, Lincoln's recent campaign opponent, came out from an interview with the President with the ringing statement: "There are only two sides to the question. Every man must be for the United States government or against it. There can be no neutrals in this war; only patriots or traitors."

On April 14, 1865, exactly four years and a day after the surrender, Major General Robert Anderson, summoned from retirement, personally hoisted the Stars and Stripes over Fort Sumter. "I thank God that I have lived to see this day," he fervently declared.

Two Civil War Correspondents Shock the North
With Their Firsthand Accounts of Disaster
at Bull Run

O F ALL THE DAYS OF THE WAR," wrote Walt Whitman, "there are two especially I can never forget. Those were the day following the news, in New York and Brooklyn, of that first Bull Run defeat, and the day of Abraham Lincoln's death." The humiliation of Bull Run, he added, caused the North to recoil "from its extreme of superciliousness" and plunge "to the depth of gloom and apprehension."

Although Union short-term volunteers were still green, unprepared for field operations, the army deferred to Northern clamor for a quick victory and began the invasion of Virginia in July of '61. At Bull Run, on July 21, the Federals met the Confederates under Generals Beauregard and Joseph E. Johnston, turned their flank, and appeared to have won the day. Then Confederate reinforcements poured in. The Union troops became panicky, broke ranks, and retreated to Washington, a confused and demoralized mob.

A galaxy of brilliant journalists reported the battle, including Henry Villard for *The New York Herald*, E. H. House and William A. Croffutt, for the *Tribune*, E. C. Stedman for the *World*, William Howard Russell for the London *Times*, and the photographer, Mathew B. Brady. In his *Memoirs* (1904) Villard attests the cockiness of the Union officers prior to the engagement.

"Well, Captain," Villard asked a Zouave officer, "you are all ready for the fray?"

"Yes," he replied, "there is nothing like being always ready for the 'damned rebs.' "

"The leer from his eyes and a certain unsteadiness in the saddle indicated plainly that he had braced himself up internally for the fight," Villard added.

When the retreat started, Villard tried to locate General McDowell, but one of Hunter's staff officers told him:

"You won't find him. All is chaos in front. The battle is lost. Our troops are all giving way and falling back without orders."

To score a beat on the rival reporters, Villard saddled his horse and made his way through the line of retreat, choked by supply vehicles, to Washington. En route he passed a regiment of Pennsylvania three-month men, who had insisted on marching away from the front as their term of service had expired the previous day. Later on he recognized Colonel Ambrose E. Burnside, riding hatless, swordless, and alone bestride a fine black charger. "I am hurrying ahead to get rations for my command," Burnside volunteered, but this properly struck Villard as preposterous, for such duties were not performed by regimental commanders. Villard's prejudice against Burnside, conceived on that day, died hard.

After an eighteen-hour ride Villard reached Washington, sent along a six-hundred-word telegram (the limit permitted by newspapers in those days), and then, after a brief rest, secured additional eyewitness details from Captain Fry of the War Department. Some of Fry's barbed comments on the New York regiments were deleted by the newspaper. Villard's beat was featured in *The New York Herald* of July 20, 1861:

The New York Herald's *Henry Villard*
scores a stunning beat

The New York Herald, July 20, 1861

CENTERVILLE, SIX AND A HALF MILES FROM MANASSAS JUNCTION, THURSDAY, JULY 18, 5 P.M.—I have just returned from the thickest of an action of considerable moment, between a portion of the rebel forces and the Fourth Brigade of General Tyler's division, composed of the Second and Third Michigan, the First Massachusetts, and Twelfth New York Volunteer regiments, under command of Colonel Richardson; and as the aide of General McDowell, who will carry the official report of the affair to General Scott, and who offers the only means of communication with Washington this evening, is about starting, I have only time to send you the following brief particular of today's operation.

At eleven o'clock General Tyler proceeded to make a reconnaissance in force, with Captain Ayres' (late Sherman's) battery, four companies of cavalry, and Colonel Richardson's brigade, composed as above stated. Advancing up the road to Bull's Run for about two miles, the column came to an opening, after passing through a long stretch of timber, when sight was caught of a strong body of the enemy. General Tyler immediately ordered Captain Ayres' battery to advance and open on them, which they did from a commanding elevation. Eight shells had been thrown, when suddenly a volley was fired upon us from a hidden battery, about a mile down the road.

Our howitzers then threw some grapeshot into the timber, when at once a terrific series of volleys of musketry was poured out from the woods upon the troops outside. At the same time a battery commenced playing upon us from an elevation in the rear. Shot of every description flew about us for some minutes like hail; but it being, fortunately, nearly all aimed too high, hardly anyone was struck outside the woods.

A retreat was now ordered, when

infantry, cavalry, and artillery fell back behind our battery on the hill. The Twelfth New York and a portion of the First Massachusetts broke ranks and scattered in different directions, in their hasty retreat, for some distance through the woods, in the rear of the battery.

Our troops fought under great disadvantage. Not one rebel ventured out of the woods during the action. *The affair was not an attack, but merely a reconnaisance* to discover the position and strength of the enemy.

HEADQUARTERS OF THE GRAND ARMY, CENTERVILLE, JULY 19, 8 A.M.—*Much of the haste and confusion of the re-treat was due to the inefficiency and cowardice of some of the officers.*

I can personally testify to the more than ordinary coolness and gallantry shown by Colonel Richardson during the action. A shower of rifle balls was constantly aimed at him, but they did not for a moment deter him from doing his whole duty. General Tyler also showed great courage on the occasion. He was exposed to the enemy's fire for nearly four hours.

The representatives of the press stood their ground as well as any, in spite of the shot, shell, and rifle balls that kept whizzing past them for hours.

* * *

The New York Herald, July 22, 1861

FAIRFAX COURTHOUSE, July 21—I am en route to Washington with details of a great battle.

We have carried the day.

The rebels accepted battle in their strength, but are totally routed.

Losses on both sides considerable.

* * *

The New York Herald, July 23, 1861

THE DISASTER AT BULL'S RUN

WASHINGTON, JULY 22, 1861—Our troops, after taking three batteries and gaining a great victory at Bull's Run, were eventually repulsed and commenced a retreat on Washington.

After the latest information was received from Centerville, at half-past seven o'clock last night, a series of unfortunate events took place which have proved disastrous to our army. Many confused accounts are prevalent, but facts enough are known to warrant the statement that we have suffered severely on account of a most unfortunate occurrence, which has cast a gloom over the retreating army and excited the deepest melancholy throughout Washington.

Our Union forces were advancing upon the enemy and taking his masked batteries gradually but surely, by driving the rebels towards Manassas Junction, when they seem to have been reinforced by twenty thousand men under General Johnston, who, it is understood, then took command and immediately commenced driving us back. We were retreating in good order, the rear well covered with a solid column, when *a panic among our troops suddenly occurred, and a regular stampede took place.*

WHILE Villard's early dispatches constituted a journalistic beat of the first magnitude, it remained for Russell of the London *Times* to give the dramatic details of the rout and to supplement and amplify the *Herald* account. Russell had come to America with pronounced antislavery sentiments and with no special predilection for the cause of the Southern Confederacy. Interviewing Mr. Lincoln at the White House, he came away with the feeling that the President was far "more willing to temper justice with mercy" than to take "a harsh view of men's nature." Lincoln's remark to Russell was more prophetic than he intended. "The London *Times*," declared the President, "is one of the greatest powers in the world. In fact, I don't know anything which has much more power—except perhaps the Mississippi." Russell's sensational account of cowardice and demoralization in the summer of '61, which won him the sobriquet "Bull Run," appeared in *The Times* on August 6:

"Bull Run" Russell describes the stampede— "a miserable, causeless panic"

The Times (London), August 6, 1861

JULY 22, 1861—I sit down to give an account—not of the action yesterday, but of what I saw with my own eyes, hitherto not often deceived, and of what I heard with my own ears, which in this country are not so much to be trusted. Let me, however, express an opinion as to the affair of yesterday. In the first place, the repulse of the Federalists, decided as it was, might have had no serious effects whatever beyond the mere failure—which politically was of greater consequence than it was in a military sense—but for the disgraceful conduct of the troops. The retreat on their lines at Centerville seems to have ended in a cowardly rout—a miserable, causeless, panic. Such scandalous behavior on the part of soldiers I should have considered impossible, as with some experience of camps and armies I have never even in alarms among camp followers seen the like of it.

[The Federalists were advancing steadily and seemed to have won a decisive advantage.] As I turned down into the narrow road, there was a forward movement among the large four-wheeled tilt wagons, when suddenly there arose a tumult in front of me at a small bridge across the road, and then I perceived the drivers of a set of wagons with the horses turned towards me, who were endeavoring to force their way against the stream of vehicles setting in the other direction. By the side of the new set of wagons there were a number of commissariat men and soldiers, whom at first sight I took to be the baggage guard. They looked excited and alarmed and were running by the side of the horses—in front the dust quite obscured the view. At the bridge the currents met in wild disorder.

"Turn back! Retreat!" shouted the men from the front, "we're whipped, we're whipped!" They cursed and tugged at the horses' heads and struggled with frenzy to get past. I got my horse up into the field out of the road and went on rapidly towards the front. Soon I met soldiers who were coming through the corn, mostly without arms; and presently I saw firelocks, cooking tins, knapsacks, and greatcoats on the ground, and observed that the confusion and speed of the baggage carts became greater and that many of them were crowded with men or were followed by others who clung to them. The ambulances were crowded with soldiers, but it did not look as if there were many wounded. Negro servants on led horses dashed frantically past; men in uniform, whom it were a disgrace to the profession of arms to call "soldiers," swarmed by on mules, chargers, and even draft horses, which had been cut out of carts or wagons, and went on with harness clinging to their heels, as frightened as their riders. Men literally screamed with rage and fright when their way was blocked. On I rode, asking all, "What is all this about?" and now and then, but rarely, receiving the answer, "We're whipped"; or, "We're repulsed."

I was just about to ask one of the men for a light, when a sputtering fire on my right attracted my attention, and out of the forest or along the road rushed a number of men. The gunners seized the train of the nearest piece to wheel it round upon them; others made for the tumbrels and horses as if to fly, when a shout was raised, "Don't fire; they're our own men"; and in a few minutes on came pell-mell a whole regiment in disorder. I rode across one and stopped him.

"We're pursued by cavalry," he gasped. "They've cut us all to pieces."

As he spoke a shell burst over the column; another dropped on the road, and out streamed another column of men, keeping together with their arms, and closing up the stragglers of the first regiment. I turned, and to my surprise saw the artillerymen had gone off, leaving one gun standing by itself. They had retreated with their horses. It was now well established that the retreat had really commenced, though I saw but few wounded men and the regiments which were falling back had not suffered much loss. No one seemed to know anything for certain. Even the cavalry charge was a rumor.

Suddenly the guns on the hill opened, and at the same time came the thuds of artillery from the wood on the right rear. The stampede then became general. What occurred at the hill I cannot say, but all the road from Centerville for miles presented such a sight as can only be witnessed in the track of the runaways of an utterly demoralized army. Drivers flogged, lashed, spurred, and beat their horses, or leaped down and abandoned their teams and ran by the side of the road; mounted men, servants, and men in uniform, vehicles of all sorts, commissariat wagons thronged the narrow ways. At every shot a convulsion, as it were, seized upon the morbid mass of bones, sinew, wood, and iron, and thrilled through it, giving new energy and action to its desperate efforts to get free from itself. Again the cry of "Cavalry" arose. In silence I passed over the long bridge. Some few hours later it quivered under the steps of a rabble of unarmed men. The Federalists, utterly routed, had fallen back upon Arlington to defend the capital, leaving nearly five batteries of artillery, eight thousand muskets, immense quantity of stores and baggage, and their wounded and prisoners in the hands of the enemy!

"Let the American journals tell their stories in their own way. I have told mine as I know it." And that Russell certainly did. A storm of vilification descended upon him. Although his story was endorsed one hundred per cent by General Sherman, Russell was savagely attacked by Bennett's *Herald,* which charged, "as for running away, Mr. Russell himself set the example, and riding a foaming steed, was foremost in the line of retreat." Russell wrote to John Bigelow: "I'm not kilt yet, tho' the *Herald* is doing its best to get me assassinated. I got exactly the same sort of language, minus the ruffianly threats and insults, because I told the truth in the Crimea and India."

But despite his slashing exposé of Union army morale, Russell was recalled by the London *Times* for daring to reveal a certain measure of sympathy for the Northern cause. His employers, stubborn in their support of the Confederacy almost to perversity, left American news coverage in the hands of the more pliable Charles Mackay. Later on in the course of the war Mackay observed that the battles up to that time had had no effect on the war's progress and that "they proved nothing but the courage of the combatants." The editors changed the word "nothing" to "anything" and probably aroused more anti-British indignation in the North than had flared up since the Boston Massacre.*

The cold facts about Bull Run were sobering. General Sherman spoke bluntly to Lincoln: "What we need," Sherman said, "is cool, thoughtful, hard-fighting soldiers—no more hurrahing, no more humbug."

---

* Alone among London dailies supporting the North was *The Daily News,* whose feature writer, Harriet Martineau, an expert on American life and probably the first woman in England to take to the regular work of daily journalism, tried to redress the balance in appraising the Civil War in America.

Karl Marx and Friedrich Engels Report a Labor Rally in Britain

BRITISH OPINION on the American Civil War divided along class lines. Tory aristocrats naturally sympathized with Southern planters, and industrialists, seeking free access to Southern cotton, envisaged a huge market for their products in a separate Southern Confederacy. But to British labor, Union victory spelled the abolition of slavery, an event they and humanitarian British leaders like Cobden and Bright ardently desired. At first, upper-class views prevailed in Britain, and the South was accorded the status of a belligerent, an act the North regarded as deliberately unfriendly.

Suddenly a naval incident occurred that almost precipitated war. Late in 1861 headstrong Captain Charles Wilkes, the hero of an Antarctic expedition, seized the two Confederate commissioners, Mason and Slidell, aboard the British mail steamer *Trent*, bound for Southampton. An aroused Britannia, who herself had never respected the "freedom of the seas," suddenly demanded that this "insult to the flag" be avenged. The navy was put on a war footing and troops were sent to Canada. Secretary of State Seward's conciliatory offer to deliver the Confederate envoys to the British soothed the ruffled lion. Yet, perhaps more influential in curbing British temper was the acute realization that labor would not tolerate war with America.

When a huge workers' rally was held in London late in January, 1862, not least of those who attended was a German correspondent for the Vienna *Presse*. This newsman was no stranger to workers' meetings. The reporter who once declared that "capitalism produces its own gravediggers," and had urged the workmen of the world to unite as they had "nothing to lose but their chains," Karl Marx, was a shrewd observer of the course of the war in America, and naturally proabolition. In his *Capital* he had insisted that "labor cannot emancipate itself in the white skin where in the black it is branded."

For over a decade Marx had contributed articles to the *New York Tribune,* reviewing European conditions, a connection he ended in 1862. Meantime, he had accepted an assignment to serve as English correspondent for *Die Presse,* a leading Viennese journal with a strong middle-class circulation. However, all his articles and dispatches appear to have been written in close collaboration with Friedrich Engels, his lifelong friend and coauthor of *The Communist Manifesto.* Engels, as Edward M. Earle, a foremost military expert, has pointed out, was a strategist of the front rank. He had previously written daily reports of the military campaigns

in Hungary during the Kossuth revolution, which Karl Marx had published
in his *Neue Rheinische Zeitung,* and later on he prepared for London's
Pall Mall Gazette a series of articles in which he forecast the strategy that
led to Moltke's decisive victory at Sedan during the Franco-Prussian War.
Marx could not have failed to relish the chance to report this great pro-
Union rally, which substantiated his own opinion that "at least the *working classes* of England" were on the side of the North.

The Marx-Engels dispatch, date-lined London, January 28, 1862, appeared in the February 2 issue of *Die Presse*:

Pioneers of modern Socialism see tides of English opinion turn against the American Confederacy in the Civil War

Die Presse (Vienna), February 2, 1862

It is notorious that the working class,
so preponderant in a society that,
within living memory, no longer includes a *peasantry,* is unrepresented in
Parliament. Despite that fact, it is not
without political influence. No important change, no decisive step has ever
been taken in this country without
pressure from without, whether it was
the opposition party applying such
pressure against the government or the
government applying the pressure
upon the opposition. By *pressure from
without* the Englishman understands
huge, extraparliamentary demonstrations, which naturally cannot be
staged without the wholehearted co-
operation of the working class. Pitt, in
his anti-Jacobin war, demonstrated
that he knew how to use the masses
against the Whigs. The Catholic emancipation, the Reform Bill, the abolition of the Corn Laws, the Ten Hours

Bill, the war against Russia, the re-
jection of Palmerston's Conspiracy
Bill *—all these were the fruit of
stormy extraparliamentary demonstrations, in which the working class,
sometimes artificially incited, sometimes acting spontaneously—now as a
persona dramatis, now as the chorus—
played the principal role or, depending upon the circumstances, the noisy
role. All the more striking is the English working class' attitude toward the
American Civil War.

The misery that the stoppage of
factories and cutting of working time,
brought on by the blockade of the
slave states, has produced among the
workers in the northern manufacturing districts is unbelievable and daily
on the increase. The rest of the working class do not suffer to the same extent; but they still suffer severely from
the reaction on the remaining fields of

* Marx alludes to these great reforms: the admission of Roman Catholics to most political
offices (1829); the extension of the franchise to the middle class (1832); the repeal of the
Corn Laws, forbidding the importation of wheat when the average price of wheat at home
was below a stated figure (1846); the limitation of the hours of labor of women and children
in textile factories to ten hours daily (1847). Palmerston's Conspiracy Bill (1858) would
have provided criminal penalties for certain kinds of trade-union activity.

production of the crisis in the cotton industry, from the curtailment of the export of their own products to the American North as a result of the Morrill Tariff,* and from the elimination of exports to the South as a result of the blockade.

At this very moment English intervention in America has accordingly become a bread-and-butter issue for the working class. Nor have its "natural superiors" scorned any means of inflaming its anger against the United States. The sole surviving great and widely circulated workers' organ, *Reynolds' Weekly Newspaper,* has been purchased expressly to mouth weekly for six months in wild diatribes the *coeterum censeo* of English intervention. Now, the working class is fully aware that the government only waits for the intervention cry from below, for the *pressure from without,* to put an end to the American blockade and to English misery. Under these circumstances the obstinacy with which the working class keeps silent, only to break that silence to speak against intervention and *for* the United States, is admirable. This is new, brilliant evidence of the indestructible excellence of the English masses, of that excellence which is the secret of England's greatness and which, to borrow the hyperbolic language of Mazzini, made the English common soldier seem a demigod during the Crimean War and the Indian insurrection.

This report of a great *workers' meeting* that took place yesterday in Marylebone, most populous district of London, illustrates the "policy" of the working class.

The chairman, Mr. Steadman, opened the meeting by observing that it was up to the English people to decide upon the nature of the *reception* of Messrs. Mason and Slidell. "Did these gentlemen come here on a voyage to free the slaves from their chains or to forge a new link for those very chains?"

Mr. Yates: "The working class don't dare keep silent. The two gentlemen who are sailing across the ocean to our land are the agents of slaveholding and tyrannical states. In open rebellion against the lawful Constitution of their country, they are coming here to persuade our government to recognize the independence of the slave states. The working class must go on record now lest the English government believe that we are not concerned with its foreign policy. Had our government acted honestly, it would have supported the North heart and soul in putting down this fearful rebellion."

Then, after a detailed defense of the Northern states, the speaker made this motion:

"This meeting resolves that the agents of the rebels, Mason and Slidell, now en route to England from America, are completely unworthy of the moral support of the working class of this country, since they are slaveholders as well as the confessed agents of that tyrannical faction, at once in rebellion against the American republic and sworn enemy of the social and political rights of the working class in all countries."

Mr. Whyune seconded the motion.

At this point Mr. Nichols, a self-declared resident *"of the extreme North of the United States,"* but in fact an *advocatus diaboli,* sent to the meeting by Messrs. Yancey and

---

* American tariff rates were boosted in 1861 and revised upward during the war to the highest thus far in the history of the nation.

Mann,* rose to protest against the motion.

"I am here because here freedom of speech prevails. With us at home, the government has permitted no man to open his mouth for three months. Liberty has been crushed not only in the South, but also in the North. The war has many foes in the North, but they dare not speak. No less than two hundred newspapers have been suppressed or destroyed by the mob. The Southern states have the same right to secede from the North as the United States had to separate from England."

Despite the eloquence of Mr. Nichols, the motion was carried unanimously. Notwithstanding, he sprang up again, shouting: "If they reproached Messrs. Mason and Slidell with being slaveholders, the same thing would apply to Washington and Jefferson."

In a detailed reply Mr. Beale proceeded to refute Nichols, and then to offer a second motion:

"In view of the ill-concealed efforts of *The Times* and other misleading journals to represent English public opinion on all American affairs falsely; to embroil us in war with millions of our kinsmen on any pretext whatso-ever, and to take advantage of the momentary perils of the republic to defame democratic institutions, this meeting considers it the very special duty of the workers, unrepresented in the Senate of the nation, to declare their sympathy with the United States in their titanic struggle for the maintenance of the Union; to denounce the shameful dishonesty and advocacy of slaveholding on the part of *The Times* and aristocratic journals of similar ilk; to express themselves most emphatically in favor of the strictest policy of nonintervention in American affairs and for the settlement of all matters in dispute by commissioners or courts of arbitration, nominated by both sides; to denounce the war policy of the organ of the stock-exchange swindlers, and to express the warmest sympathy with the strivings of the abolitionists for a final solution of the slave question."

This motion was adopted unanimously, as was the final motion "to forward to the American government *per medium* of Mr. Adams † a copy of the resolutions framed, as an expression of the feelings and opinions of the working class of England."

* * *

Such demonstrations forced the Palmerston government to back down. But, perhaps even more influential, as Marx himself pointed out, in keeping England from actively intervening in behalf of King Cotton, was the new role of King Wheat, supplied to Britain from America's Northwest. Britain chose wheat and peace instead of cotton and war.

At the end of 1862 the workingmen of Manchester addressed a letter to Lincoln, urging "immediate and total emancipation." Lincoln, in reply, expressed sympathy with the acute sufferings of British labor—the blockade had caused great unemployment in the textile towns, with some thirty per cent of the population in certain areas forced to seek charity—and declared his confidence that "whatever else may happen, whatever misfortune may

---

* Confederate commissioners in England.
† Charles Francis Adams, American minister to England.

befall your country or my own, the peace and friendship which now exist
between the two nations will be, as it shall be my desire to make them,
perpetual." Before replying, Lincoln had issued his Emancipation Proclamation, for which he invoked "the considerate judgment of mankind and
the gracious favor of Almighty God."

Whitelaw Reid Records Pickett's Charge at Gettysburg as a Southern Newsman Tells of the "Overwhelming Heartbreak"

W OULD YOU LIKE (if you feel able) to equip yourself with horse and outfit, put substitutes in your place in the office, and join Hooker's army in time for the fighting?" When the managing editor of the *Cincinnati Gazette* addressed this dispatch to reporter Whitelaw Reid, he expected only one answer. And he was not disappointed. Intuitively, the youthful war correspondent, onetime antislavery writer from Xenia, Ohio, realized that something big was brewing. Under the pseudonym of "Agate" Reid had only recently gained laurels for his front-line coverage of the Battle of Shiloh (a ten-column report, widely reprinted, of that chaotic battle, involving 150,000 troops, advancing and retreating on a five-mile line through densely wooded terrain). Hooker, shadowing Lee, demanded that the troops at Harpers Ferry be placed under him, else he be relieved of his command. Lincoln, by choosing the latter alternative and supplanting Hooker by Meade, astonished the North. When news reached Frederick that Meade, an "unknown," had replaced the brilliant Union general, "it was a dismal day," reported Charles Carleton Coffin, the war correspondent of the *Boston Journal*. But Coffin conceded that the new plain-spoken commander—"tall, slim, gray-bearded," wearing a slouch hat and a blue blouse, with his pantaloons tucked into his boots—had the respect of his own men "because he was always prepared to endure hardships."

Meantime, news that dashing "Jeb" Stuart (called "the best cavalryman ever foaled in North America") had crossed the Potomac below Washington threw that city into panic. On June 30 Reid wrote: "Washington was again like a city besieged, as after Bull Run." In the presence of hectic preparations and general alarm, he reported seeing a sight that, in his own words, "should blacken evermore every name concerned." In the face of cries for reinforcements, with Stuart's cavalry "swarming about the very gates of the Capitol," "there came sprucely marching down the avenue, in all their freshness of brilliant uniforms and unstained arms, with faultlessly appareled officers and gorgeous drum-major, and clanging band, and all the pomp and circumstance of glorious war," a New England "nine months' regiment, mustering over nine hundred bayonets whose term of service had that day expired!"

En route to the battlefield, Reid observed haste and improvisation everywhere. If Baltimore was in a "panic," then Frederick was "pandemonium."

Drunken soldiers beneath Reid's window were making the night hideous, brawling, swearing, and stealing horses. Taking to the saddle at Frederick, Reid shook off the camp followers and reached the main Union army at Gettysburg. His epochal dispatch, date-lined "Field of Battle, near Gettysburg, July 2," took up fourteen columns in the *Cincinnati Gazette*.

Standing on Cemetery Hill, the center of the Union line and the point most exposed to rebel fire, Reid observed the batteries all about him, troops moving into position, new lines forming, old lines extending. "No sound comes up from the deserted town, no ringing of bells, no voices of children, no hum of busy trade. Only now and then a blue curl of smoke rises and fades from some high window; a faint report comes up, and perhaps the hiss of a Minié is heard. The houses are not wholly without occupants."

Reid's report of the ebb and flow of the great battle on Wednesday and Thursday was based on eyewitness evidence and checked by interviews with four Union generals. Of the "iron" column under General Howard that held the left on Cemetery Hill, going in 1820 strong, coming out with seven hundred men, "Agate" observed: "Who shall say that they did not go down into the very valley of the Shadow of Death on that terrible afternoon?" But the Union forces held. Finally, on Friday, Longstreet reluctantly, at Lee's insistence, ordered Pickett to charge Cemetery Hill. Reid's account:

Cincinnati Gazette: *"It was a crushing defeat"*

Cincinnati Gazette, July 5, 1863

Ascending the high hill to the rear of Slocum's headquarters, I saw such a sight as few men may ever hope to see twice in a lifetime. Around our center and left, the rebel line must have been from four to five miles long, and over that whole length there rolled up the smoke from their two hundred and fifty guns. The roar, the bursting bombs, the impression of magnificent power, "all the glory visible, all the horror of the fearful field concealed," a nation's existence trembling as the clangor of those iron monsters swayed the balance—it was a sensation for a century!

About two the fire slackened a little, then broke out deadlier than ever, till, beaten out against our impenetrable sides, it ebbed away and closed in broken, spasmodic dashes.

The great, desperate, final charge came at four. The rebels seemed to have gathered up all their strength and desperation for one fierce, convulsive effort, that should sweep over and wash out our obstinate resistance. They swept up as before, the flower of their army to the front, victory staked upon the issue. In some places they literally lifted up and pushed back our lines, but that terrible "position" of ours!—wherever they entered it, enfilading fires from half a score of crests swept away their columns like merest chaff. Broken and hurled back, they easily fell into our hands, and on the center and left the last half-hour brought more prisoners than all the rest.

So it was along the whole line; but it was on the Second Corps that the flower of the rebel army was concentrated; it was there that the heaviest shock beat upon and shook and even sometimes crumbled our line.

We had some shallow rifle pits, with barricades of rails from the fences. The rebel line, stretching away miles to the left, in magnificent array, but strongest here—Pickett's splendid division of Longstreet's corps in front, the best of A. P. Hill's veterans in support—came steadily and, as it seemed, resistlessly sweeping up. Our skirmishers retired slowly from the Emmetsburg road, holding their ground tenaciously to the last. The rebels reserved their fire till they reached this same Emmetsburg road, then opened with a terrific crash. From a hundred iron throats, meantime, their artillery had been thundering on our barricades.

Hancock was wounded; Gibbon succeeded to the command—approved soldier, and ready for the crisis. As the tempest of fire approached its height, he walked along the line, and renewed his orders to the men to reserve their fire. The rebels—three lines deep—came steadily up. They were in point-blank range.

At last the order came! From thrice six thousand guns there came a sheet of smoky flame, a crash of leaden death. The line literally melted away; but there came the second, resistless still. It had been our supreme effort—on the instant we were not equal to another.

Up to the rifle pits, across them, over the barricades—the momentum of their charge, the mere machine strength of their combined action swept them on. Our thin line could fight, but it had not weight enough to oppose to this momentum. It was pushed behind the guns. Right on came the rebels. They were upon the guns, were bayoneting the gunners, were waving their flags above our pieces.

But they had penetrated to the fatal point. A storm of grape and canister tore its way from man to man and marked its track with corpses straight down their line! They had exposed themselves to the enfilading fire of the guns on the western slope of Cemetery Hill; that exposure sealed their fate.

The line reeled back—disjointed already—in an instant in fragments. Our men were just behind the guns. They leaped forward upon the disordered mass; but there was little need for fighting now. A regiment threw down its arms, and, with colors at its head, rushed over and surrendered. All along the field smaller detachments did the same. Webb's brigade brought in eight hundred taken in as little time as it requires to write the simple sentence that tells it. Gibbon's old division took fifteen stands of colors.

Over the fields the escaped fragments of the charging line fell back—the battle there was over. A single brigade, Harrow's (of which the Seventh Michigan is part), came out with fifty-four less officers, 793 less men than it took in! So the whole corps fought—so, too, they fought further down the line.

It was fruitless sacrifice. They gathered up their broken fragments, formed their lines, and slowly marched away. It was not a rout, it *was* a bitter, crushing defeat. For once the Army of the Potomac had won a clean, honest, acknowledged victory.

THE STRATEGIC significance of the charge was grasped by Frank A. Haskell, then aide-de-camp to General Gibbon. "Upon the ability of the two trefoil divisions to hold the crest and repel the assault depended not only their own safety or destruction, but also the honor of the Army of the Potomac and defeat or victory at Gettysburg," that eyewitness participant asserted. "We were there waiting, and ready to do our duty—that done, results could not dishonor us." How near defeat they really were was revealed by Reid. Short of ammunition, had not a reserve ammunition train been brought up in the nick of time, "we would have been left to cold steel." The future editor of the *New York Tribune* maintained that forty thousand fresh troops hurled upon the retreating Confederates could have ended the campaign along with the battle. But there were no reserves. The fight was over.

How did Pickett's charge appear to Confederate newsmen across the battlefield at Gettysburg? Date-lined, "In Camp, near Hagerstown, Maryland, July 8, 1863," the reporter for the Richmond *Enquirer*, in retreat with Lee's main army, sent on this eloquent account (somewhat condensed) to soften the blow to the folks back home:

The Richmond Enquirer: *"Who would recall them from this bed of glory?"*

Richmond *Enquirer*, July 12, 1863

The sun rises, clouds obscure its brightness as if loath to look upon the scene to witness such inhumanity, but from which no people are exempt who ever left a history or benefited the human race. The conflict began ere Tubal Cain first worked in brass, and will continue till a higher virtue than man has ever reached shall govern events.

The morning is now wearing away —at times a cannon shot breaks the quiet, and a shell comes screaming through the air—now and then the skirmishers break forth, varying from the sharp, quick crack of a single rifle to perfect volleys. Hour after hour thus passes, and the battle is not yet begun. Our troops are taking position —Ewell is on the left. Hill holds the center, and Longstreet is on the right.

Long lines of men are moving across yonder fields, or marching through that piece of wood.

But where is that division which is to play so conspicuous a part in this day's tragedy? They are in line of battle, just fronting that frowning hill, from which heavy batteries are belching forth shell and shrapnel with fatal accuracy. The men are lying close to the ground. Hours pass, and the deadly missiles come thick and fast on their mission to death. See that shattered arm; that leg shot off; that headless body, and here the mangled form of a young and gallant lieutenant. That hill must be carried to rout the enemy; a terrible chastisement has been inflicted upon him; with immense loss he had been driven from his position two days previous—this is his stronghold.

This captured, rout is inevitable. It is a moment of great emergency; if unshrinking valor or human courage can carry those heights, it will be done.

General Pickett receives the order to charge those batteries at the opportune moment. The cannonade still goes on with intense fury; our batteries are handled with great skill. This battery and that limber up, advance to the front, wheel into action, and again the roar of cannon becomes almost deafening. Our shells seem to burst with terrible accuracy. Now a caisson of the enemy's is blown up—quickly another follows—their fire slackens—the order comes to advance. That flag which waved amid the wild tempest of battle at Gaines' Mill, Frazier's Farm, and Manassas never rose more proudly. Kemper, with as gallant men as ever trod beneath that flag, leads the right; Garnett, with his heroes, brings up the left; and the veteran Armistead, with his brave troops, moves forward in support. The distance is more than half a mile. As they advance the enemy fire with great rapidity. Shell and solid shot give place to grape and canister. The very earth quivers beneath the heavy roar. Wide gaps are made in this regiment and that brigade. Yet they close up and move steadily onward.

That flag goes down. See how quickly it again mounts upward, borne by some gallant man who feels keenly the honor of his old commonwealth in this hour which is to test her manhood. The line moves onward, straight onward—cannons roaring, grape and canister plunging and plowing through the ranks—bullets whizzing as thick as hailstones in winter, and men falling as leaves fall when shaken by the blasts of autumn.

In a double-quick, and with a shout which rises above the roar of battle, they charge. Now they pour in volleys of musketry. They reach the works. The contest rages with intense fury. Men fight almost hand to hand. The red cross and gridiron wave defiantly in close proximity. The enemy are slowly yielding—a Federal officer dashing forward in front of his shrinking columns, and, with flashing sword, urges them to stand. General Pickett, seeing the splendid valor of his troops, moves among them as if courting death by his own daring intrepidity. The noble Garnett is dead, Armistead wounded, and the brave Kemper, with hat in hand, still cheering on his men, falls from his horse into the ranks of the enemy. His men rush forward, rescue their general, and he is borne mortally wounded from the field.

Where is the gallant Williams? The First is there, but his clear voice is no longer heard. He has fallen lifeless, and there goes his horse now riderless. There stand the decimated ranks of the Third; and Mayo, though struck, stands firm with his faithful men, animating them to yet more daring deeds; but Callcott, the Christian soldier, who stood unmoved amid this carnival of death, has fought his last battle.

The fight goes on—but few are left; and the shrinking columns of the enemy gain confidence from the heavy reinforcements advanced to their support. They, too, are moving in large force on the right flank. This division, small at first, with ranks now torn and shattered, most of its officers killed or wounded, no valor able to rescue victory from such a grasp, annihilation or capture inevitable, slowly, reluctantly, fell back. It was not given to these few remaining brave men to accomplish human impossibilities. The enemy dared not follow them beyond their works.

Night now approaches. The wounded are being borne off to their respective hospitals; many with slight wounds plodded along, leaving the ambulances to their less fortunate comrades. With night the battle closed, our army holding the same position from which it had driven the enemy two days previous. One by one the stars came out in the quiet sky, and over that field of carnage hung the sweet influences of the Pleiades. In the series of engagements a few pieces of artillery and eight thousand prisoners were captured by our army. Our loss in killed, wounded, and missing, supposed about ten thousand, whilst the enemy, we understand, acknowledges a loss of thirty thousand. The army of northern Virginia—with zeal unabated, courage intrepid, devotion unchilled, with unbounded confidence in the wisdom of that great chieftain who has so often led them to victory—stands ready to advance their standards farther into the enemy's country, or repel any new invasion of the Confederacy. Though many a Virginia home will mourn the loss of some noble spirit, yet, at the name of Pickett's division and the battle of Gettysburg, how the eye will glisten and the blood course quicker, and the heart beat warm, as among its noble dead is recalled the name of some cherished one. They bore themselves worthy of their lineage and their state. Who would recall them from their bed of glory? Each sleeps in a hero's grave!

THE FINAL WORD on the "overwhelming heartbreak" was penned by George Edward Pickett in a letter to his sweetheart:

Well, it is all over now. The battle is lost, and many of us are prisoners, many are dead, many wounded, bleeding, and dying. Your Soldier lives and mourns and, but for you, my darling, he would rather, a million times rather, be back there with his dead, to sleep for all time in an unknown grave.

Blood on the Moon

THE SCENE, Ford's Theater in Washington; the play, *Our American Cousin*; the time, 10:15 P.M., April 14, 1865.

"The American cousin had just been making love to a young lady who says she'll never marry but for love," wrote Julia Adelaide Shephard to her father, "but when her mother and herself find out that he has lost his property they retreat in disgust at the left hand of the stage while the American cousin goes out at the right. We are waiting for the next scene." *

The next scene was unforgettable. An assassin entered the box in which Mr. Lincoln and his party were seated, raised his derringer, and shot the President in the back of the head. Chaos ensued.

The Associated Press correspondent, Lawrence A. Gobright, was seated in his office that evening, when someone rushed in with a report of the tragedy. He sent out a short "special," the first newspaper story on the event, and hurried over to the theater. Entering the President's box, he found blood upon Lincoln's chair and secured possession of the pistol John Wilkes Booth † had used. He then called a hack and drove to Seward's residence, found everybody overwrought, and returned to his office to write his story, which, he later recounted, he based upon "details from witnesses at the theater who came into the office." The dispatches that appeared in the *New York Tribune* are given in the order received, the fullest being Gobright's AP dispatch near the end.

Gobright, AP correspondent, reports the assassination of Lincoln

New York Tribune, April 15, 1865

HIGHLY IMPORTANT
THE PRESIDENT SHOT
SECRETARY SEWARD ATTACKED

First Dispatch

To the Associated Press
WASHINGTON, FRIDAY, APRIL 14, 1865
—The President was shot in a theater tonight, and perhaps mortally wounded.

Second Dispatch

To Editors: Our Washington agent orders the dispatch about the President "stopped." Nothing is said about the truth or falsity of the dispatch.

---

* Quoted by Carl Sandburg, *Abraham Lincoln: The War Years,* IV (New York, 1939), p. 280.

† While driving along Pennsylvania Avenue that spring day, Lincoln had stopped his carriage at Ford's Theater, torn off a bit of the white margin of a newspaper, written on it a few lines to the effect that he would be happy to occupy the box on the night of April 14, and sent the message in to the manager's office. Some years afterwards the manager, in going through a trunk filled with papers, found John Wilkes Booth's letter accepting the renewal of his contract for the following year. It was written on a single sheet, folded twice, and inside the folds was hidden the message on the newspaper margin that Lincoln had sent in.

Third Dispatch

Special Dispatch to the *New York Tribune*

The President was just shot at Ford's Theater. The ball entered his neck. It is not known whether the wound is mortal. Intense excitement.

Fourth Dispatch

Special Dispatch to the *New York Tribune*

The President expired at a quarter to twelve.

Fifth Dispatch

To the Associated Press

WASHINGTON, APRIL 15, 12:30 A.M.— The President was shot in a theater tonight, and is perhaps mortally wounded.

The President is not expected to live through the night.

Secretary Seward was also assassinated.

No arteries were cut.

Particulars soon.

Sixth Dispatch

Special Dispatch to the *New York Tribune*

WASHINGTON, FRIDAY, APRIL 14, 1865 —Like a clap of thunder out of a clear sky spread the announcement that President Lincoln was shot while sitting in a box at Ford's Theater. The city is wild with excitement. A gentleman who was present thus describes the event:

At about 10½ o'clock, in the midst of one of the acts, a pistol shot was heard, and at the same instant a man leaped upon the stage from the same box occupied by the President, brandished a long knife, and shouted, *"Sic semper tyrannis!"* then rushed to the rear of the scenes and out of the back door of the theater. So sudden was the whole thing that most persons in the theater supposed it a part of the play. and it was some minutes before the fearful tragedy was comprehended. The man was pursued, however, by someone connected with the theater to the outer door and seen to mount a horse and ride rapidly away. A regiment of cavalry have started in all directions, *with orders to arrest every man found on horseback.*

Scarce had the news of this horror been detailed when couriers came from Secretary Seward's, announcing that he also had been assassinated. The following are authentic particulars:

Seventh Dispatch

Special Dispatch to the *New York Tribune*

WASHINGTON, FRIDAY, APRIL 14, 1865 —The President attended Ford's Theater tonight, and about ten o'clock an assassin entered his private box and shot him in the back of the head. The ball lodged in his head, and he is now lying insensible in a house opposite the theater. No hopes are entertained of his recovery. *Laura Keene claims to have recognized the assassin as the actor, J. Wilkes Booth.* A feeling of gloom like a pall has settled on the city.

Assassination of Secretary Seward

About the same hour a horseman rode up to Secretary Seward's, and, dismounting, announced that he had a prescription to deliver to the Secretary in person. Major Seward and Miss Seward were with their father at the time. Being admitted, the assassin delivered the pretended prescription to the Secretary in bed, and *immediately cut his throat from ear to ear.* Fortunately the jugular vein was not severed, and it is possible Mr. Seward may survive.

Secretary Stanton was undisturbed at his residence. Thus far, no murderous demonstrations are reported. It is deemed providential that General Grant left tonight for New Jersey. He was publicly announced to be present at the theater with the President. *Ten thousand rumors are afloat, and the most intense and painful excitement pervades the city.*

Eighth Dispatch

Special Dispatch to the *New York Tribune*

WASHINGTON, FRIDAY, APRIL 14, 1865 —The assassin is said to have gained entrance to the President's box by sending in his card, requesting an interview. The box was occupied by Mrs. Lincoln and Colonel Parker of General Grant's staff. The villain drew his pistol across Mrs. Lincoln's shoulder and fired. Colonel Parker sprang up and seized the assassin, but he wrested himself from his grip and sprang down upon the stage as described. His spur caught in the American flag as he descended and threw him at length. He unloosed the spur and dashed to the rear, brandishing his knife and revolver.

Ninth Dispatch

To the Associated Press

WASHINGTON, FRIDAY, APRIL 14, 1865 —President Lincoln and wife, with their friends, this evening visited Ford's Theater for the purpose of witnessing the performance of *Our American Cousin.*

It was announced in the papers that General Grant would also be present, but he took the late train of cars for New Jersey.

The theater was densely crowded, and everybody seemed delighted with the scene before them. During the third act, and while there was a temporary pause for one of the actors to enter, a sharp report of a pistol was heard, which merely attracted attention, but suggested nothing serious, until a man rushed to the front of the President's box, waving a long dagger in his right hand, and exclaiming, *"Sic semper tyrannis,"* and immediately leaped from the box, which was on the second tier, to the stage beneath, and ran across to the opposite side, making his escape amid the bewilderment of the audience from the rear of the theater, and, mounting a horse, fled.

The screams of Mrs. Lincoln first disclosed the fact to the audience that the President was shot, when all present rose to their feet, rushing toward the stage, many exclaiming:

"Hang him, hang him!"

The excitement was of the wildest possible description, and of course there was an abrupt termination to the theatrical performance.

There was a rush toward the President's box, when cries were heard:

"Stand back and give him air."

"Has anyone stimulants?"

On a hasty examination, it was found that the President had been shot through the head above and back of the temporal bone, and that some of the brains were oozing out.

He was removed to a private house opposite to the theater, and the Surgeon General of the army and other surgeons sent for to attend his condition.

On an examination of the private box, blood was discovered on the back of the cushioned rocking chair on which the President had been sitting, also on the partition and on the floor. A common single-barreled pocket pistol was found on the carpet.

A military guard was placed in front of the private residence to which the President had been conveyed. An immense crowd was in front of it, all deeply anxious to learn the condition of the President. It had been previously announced that the wound was mortal, but all hoped otherwise. The shock to the community was terrible.

At midnight the Cabinet, together with Messrs. Sumner, Colfax, and Farnsworth, Judge Curtis, Governor Oglesby, General Meigs, Colonel Hay, and a few personal friends, with Surgeon General Barnes and his immediate assistants, were around his bedside.

The President was in a state of syncope, totally insensible, and breathing slowly. The blood oozed from the wound at the back of his head. The surgeons exhausted every possible effort of medical skill, but all hope was gone.

Tenth Dispatch

Special Dispatch to the *New York Tribune*

WASHINGTON, APRIL 15, 1 A.M.—One of our reporters is just in from the Presidential Mansion, who says an orderly reports the President still is breathing, but beyond all probable recovery.

Eleventh Dispatch

Special Dispatch

WASHINGTON, FRIDAY, APRIL 14, 1865, 1¼ A.M.—The President is slowly dying. The brain is slowly oozing through the ball hole in his forehead. He is of course insensible. There is an occasional lifting of his hand, and heavy stertorous breathing; that's all.

Mrs. Lincoln and her two sons are in a room of the house opposite the Ford Theater, where the President was taken, and adjoining that where he is lying. Mr. Sumner is seated at the head of the bed. Secretary Stanton, Welles, Dennison, Usher, and McCullock, and Mr. Speed are in the room. A large number of surgeons, generals, and personal family friends of Mr. Lincoln fill the house. All are in tears. Andy Johnson is here. He was in bed in his room at the Kirkwood when the assassination was committed. He was immediately apprised of the event, and got up. The precaution was taken to provide a guard of soldiers for him, and these were at his door before the news was well through the avenue. Captain Rathbone of Albany was in the box with the President. He was slightly wounded.

We give the above dispatches in the order in which they reached us, the first having been received a little before midnight, for we know that every line, every letter, will be read with the intensest interest. There are none in all this broad land today who love their country, who wish well to their race, that will not bow down in profound grief at the event it has brought upon us. For once all party rancor will be forgotten, and no right-thinking man can hear of Mr. Lincoln's death without accepting it as a national calamity. We can give in these, its first moments, no thought of the future. God, in His inscrutable providence, has thus visited the nation; the future we must leave to Him.

Later.—The accounts are confused and contradictory. One dispatch announces the President died at 12½ P.M. Another, an hour later, states that he is still living, but dying slowly. We go to press without knowing the exact truth, but presume there is not the slightest ground for hope.

* * *

"I CAN NEVER FORGET the alarm and horror of that night," Gobright recalled a few years later. "The streets were crowded with persons, talking over the startling and shocking events. It was feared that a wide-extended conspiracy existed, and it was not known where the stroke would next fall. Thousands of people feared to retire to their beds. Meantime, military guards were stationed throughout the city, and mounted patrols were rapidly in motion."

The President's deathbed scene was reported by an army surgeon in attendance—Dr. Charles Sabin Taft, an uncle of William Howard Taft. Mrs. Lincoln, he narrated, frantically turned to the dying man:

" 'Love,' she exclaimed, 'live for but one moment to speak to me; one—to speak to our children.'

"Then, to the doctor: 'Oh, shoot me, doctor, why don't you shoot me, too? I cannot live. I begged him not to go.'

"When it was announced that the great heart had ceased to beat, Mr. Stanton said in solemn tones:

" 'He now belongs to the ages.' "

While political enemies smeared Vice-President Johnson and the radicals with being behind the assassination, there is not a shred of evidence to justify the charge. In fact, in view of the extent of fifth-column activity in the North throughout the war (the exposé of the treasonable activities of the Order of the Sons of Liberty by Felix Grundy, a Federal spy, may be compared with the recent revelations of Fascists in our midst by John Roy Carlson in *Under Cover* [1943]) and the unaccountably negligent protection of the President's person, it was remarkable that he had escaped an assassin's bullet as long as he did. Lincoln was greatly exercised over the traitors at large in the North. "Must I shoot a simple-minded soldier boy who deserts while I must not touch a hair of a wily agitator who induces him to desert?" he once asked.

Hysteria and incompetence permitted Booth and an accomplice, David E. Herold, to escape. The dramatic story of the tracking down of the assassins was written for the New York *World* by George Alfred Townsend, a Delaware newsman and man of letters who began his reportorial career on *The Philadelphia Inquirer*, worked for *The New York Herald* as a war correspondent, and became a nation-wide celebrity as a result of this story. In at the kill himself, Townsend begins his report by recounting the early stages of the chase from a swamp in St. Mary's County, Maryland, to Garrett's farm, near Port Royal, on the Rappahannock. The real hero of the chase was La Fayette Baker, chief of the United States Secret Service. At his order a squad of troopers, commanded by E. J. Conger and L. B. Baker, closed in on the assassin. A Confederate officer who had assisted Booth in crossing the Potomac gave the hunters the lead to Booth's whereabouts. Let Townsend take up the story from this point.

The hunters close in for the kill—the
New York World's *George Alfred*
Townsend joins in the chase

New York *World,* April 29, 1865

Taking this captain * along for a guide, the worn-out horsemen retraced, although some of the men were so haggard and wasted with travel that they had to be kicked into intelligence before they could climb to their saddles. The objects of the chase thus at hand, the detectives, full of sanguine purpose, hurried the cortege so well along that by two o'clock early morning, all halted at Garrett's gate.

In the dead stillness, Baker dismounted and forced the outer gate; Conger kept close behind him, and the horsemen followed cautiously. They made no noise in the soft clay, nor broke the all-foreboding silence anywhere, till the second gate swung open gratingly; yet even then no hoarse nor shrill response came back, save the distant croakings, as of frogs or owls, and the whiz of some passing night hawk. So they surrounded the pleasant old homestead, each horseman carbine in poise, adjusted under the grove of locusts, so as to enclose the dwelling with a circle of fire. After a pause, Baker rode to the kitchen door on the side and, dismounting, rapped and hallooed lustily. An old man, in drawers and nightshirt, hastily undrew the bolts and stood on the threshold, peering into the darkness.

[The old man told La Fayette Baker that Booth and Herold had gone, but his young son confessed that they were in the barn. The troopers, with cocked pistols at the informer's head, approached the barn.]

The troops, dismounted, were stationed at regular intervals around it and, ten yards distant at every point, four special guards placed to command the door and all with weapons in supple preparation, while Baker and Conger went directly to the door. It had a padlock on it, and the key of this Baker secured at once. In the interval of silence that ensued, the rustling of planks and straw was heard inside, as of persons rising from sleep.

At the same moment, Baker hailed: "To the persons in this barn. I have a proposal to make; we are about to send into you the son of the man in whose custody you are found. Either surrender him your arms and then give yourselves up, or we'll set fire to the place. We mean to take you both, or have a bonfire and a shooting match."

No answer came to this of any kind. The lad, John M. Garrett, who was in deadly fear, was here pushed through the door by a sudden opening of it, and immediately Lieutenant Baker locked the door on the outside. The boy was heard to state his appeal in an undertone. Booth replied:

"Damn you! Get out of here. You have betrayed me."

At the same time he placed his hand in his pocket as for a pistol. A remonstrance followed, but the boy slipped out and over the reopened portal, re-

* The Confederate officer.

porting that his errand had failed and that he dared not to enter again. The boy was placed at a remote point and the summons repeated by Baker.

A bold, clarion call came from within, so strong as to be heard at the house door:

"Who are you and what do you want with us?"

Baker again urged: "We want you to give up your arms and become our prisoners."

"But who are you?" hallooed the same strong voice.

Baker—That makes no difference. We know who you are and we want you. We have here fifty men, armed with carbines and pistols. You cannot escape.

There was a long pause, and then Booth said: "Captain, this is a very bad case, I swear. Perhaps I am being taken by my own friends." No reply from the detectives.

Booth—Well, give us a little time to consider.

Baker—Very well. Take time.

Here ensued a long and eventful pause. What thronging memories it brought to Booth we can only guess. In this little interval he made the resolve to die; but he was cool and steady to the end. Baker, after a lapse, hailed for the last time:

"Well, we have waited long enough. Surrender your arms and come out, or we'll fire the barn."

Booth answered thus: "I am but a cripple, a one-legged man. Withdraw your forces one hundred yards from the door and I will come. Give me a chance for my life, Captain. I will never be taken alive."

Baker—We did not come here to fight, but to capture you. I say again, appear, or we fire the barn.

Then, with a long breath, which could be heard outside, Booth cried,

in sudden calmness, still invisible as we were to him:

"Well, then, my brave boys, prepare a stretcher for me."

There was a pause, repeated, broken by low discussions within between Booth and his associate, the former saying, as if in answer to some remonstrance or appeal, "Get away from me. You are a damned coward, and mean to leave me in my distress, but go, go. I don't want you to stay. I won't have you stay." Then he shouted aloud:

"There's a man inside who wants to surrender."

Baker—Let him come, if he will bring his arms.

Here Herold, rattling at the door, said, "Let me out. Open the door. I want to surrender."

Baker—Hand out your arms, then.

Herold—I have not got any.

This was said in a whining tone and with an almost visible shiver. Booth cried aloud at this hesitation, "He hasn't got any arms. They are mine, and I have kept them."

Baker—Well, he carried the carbine, and he must bring it out.

Booth—On the word and honor of a gentleman, he has no arms with him. They are mine, and I have got them.

At this time Herold was quite up to the door, within whispering distance of Baker. The latter told him to put out his hands to be handcuffed, at the same time drawing open the door a little distance. Herold thrust forward his hands, when Baker, seizing him, jerked him into the night and straightway delivered him over to a deputation of cavalrymen. The fellow began to talk of his innocence and plead so noisily that Conger threatened to gag him unless he ceased. Then Booth made his last appeal, in the same clear, unbroken voice:

"Captain, give me a chance. Draw

off your men, and I will fight them singly. I could have killed you six times tonight, but I believe you to be a brave man and would not murder you. Give a lame man a show."

Ere he ceased speaking, Colonel Conger, slipping around to the rear, drew some loose straws through a crack, and lit a match upon them. They were dry and blazed up in an instant, carrying a sheet of smoke and flame through the parted planks and heaving in a twinkling a world of light and heat upon the magazine within. The blaze lit up the black recesses of the great barn until every wasp's nest and cobweb in the roof was luminous, flinging streaks of red and violet across the tumbled farm gear in the corner, plows, harrows, hoes, rakes, sugar mills, and making every separate grain in the high bin adjacent gleam like a mote of precious gold. They tinged the beams, the upright columns, the barricades, where clover and timothy, piled high, held toward the hot incendiary their separate straws for the funeral pile. They bathed the murderer's retreat in a beautiful illumination, and while in bold outline his figure stood revealed, they rose like an impenetrable wall to guard from sight the hated enemy who lit them. Behind the blaze, with his eye to a crack, Conger saw Wilkes Booth standing upright on a crutch. He likens him in this instant to his brother, Edwin, whom he says he so much resembled that he half believed, for the moment, the whole pursuit to have been a mistake. At the gleam of the fire Wilkes dropped his crutch and his carbine, and on both hands crept up to the spot to espy the incendiary and shoot him dead. His eyes were lustrous like fever, and swelled and rolled in terrible beauty, while his teeth were fixed and he peered with vengeance in his look. The

fire that made him visible concealed his enemy. A second he turned glaring at the fire, as if to leap upon it and extinguish it, but it had made such headway that this was a futile impulse and he dismissed it. As calmly as upon a battlefield a veteran stands amidst a hail of ball and shell and plunging iron, Booth turned at a man's stride and pushed for the door, carbine in poise, and the last resolve of death, which we name despair, set on his high bloodless forehead.

As so he dashed, intent to expire not unaccompanied, a disobedient sergeant, at an eyehole, drew upon him the fatal bead. The barn was all glorious with conflagration, and in the beautiful ruin this outlawed man strode like all we know of wicked valor, stern in the face of death. A shock, a shout, a gathering up of his splendid figure as if to overtip the stature God gave him, and John Wilkes Booth fell headlong to the floor, lying there in a heap, a little life remaining.

"He has shot himself," cried Baker, unaware of the source of the report, and rushing in, he grasped his arms to guard against any feint or strategy. A moment convinced him that further struggle against prone flesh was useless. Booth did not move, nor breathe nor gasp. Conger and two sergeants now entered and, taking up the body, they bore it in haste from the advancing flames and laid it without upon the grass, all fresh with heavenly dew.

"Water," cried Conger, "bring water."

When this was dashed into his face, he revived a little and stirred his lips. Baker put his ear close down and heard him say:

"Tell Mother—I die—for my country."

* * *

ASIDE FROM Booth, nine persons were implicated in the assassination. Four were hanged, including Herold, four imprisoned, and a jury failed to convict the ninth suspect, John H. Surratt. Booth was finally buried in an unmarked grave in the Booth family plot in Greenmount Cemetery, Baltimore. Despite positive identification of the corpse, a widespread legend gained ground that the assassin had escaped. At various times he was reported lurking in London, Paris, in far-off India, and, finally, was rumored to have committed suicide in Oklahoma in 1903.

Lincoln's death, five days after Appomattox, was a national calamity. A genuine liberal, averse to vindictive measures, Lincoln might very well have brought about a general conciliation with the defeated South had he been permitted to complete his term. Only a few weeks before, he had counseled the nation to go forward, "with malice toward none, with charity for all." But with his death, a passion for retribution dictated drastic and oppressive policies that Lincoln would have unalterably opposed.

Mark Twain Covers a Grand Bull Drivers' Convention in Washoe City

IN THE SUMMER of 1862, Joseph Thompson Goodman, the editor of the influential Western newspaper, the *Territorial Enterprise* of Virginia City, Nevada, glanced through a story sent in by a young mining prospector. Signed "Josh," the piece burlesqued a Fourth-of-July oration delivered by a local jurist, whose clichés were so notorious that the reporter didn't bother to attend the gathering. "I was sired by the great American eagle," the orator began—with more in similar vein. "Josh" was hired at once (none too soon, as he was stone-broke), and the folks in the land of Washoe, the western part of the Nevada Territory, were soon introduced to a new journalistic personality, Samuel Langhorne Clemens.

As a reporter Clemens was in every way the direct antithesis of Henry Morton Stanley. He was never stuffy and was utterly without pomposity and pretense and extremely casual about his reportorial labors. Yet his mastery of hyperbole and satire ideally equipped him to perpetuate on paper the crude, boisterous, and lawless life on the mining frontier where the silver fever was endemic. Judged by Eastern reportorial standards, Mark Twain's reporting was undisciplined, casual, and perhaps a bit imaginative, but there was an essential veracity about it. It was the kind of reporting the West loved. "Information appears to stew out of me naturally," Mark confessed, "like the precious ottar of roses out of the.otter. Sometimes it has seemed to me that I would give worlds if I could retain my facts; but it cannot be. The more I calk up the sources, and the tighter I get, the more I leak wisdom." In *The Celebrated Jumping Frog of Calaveras County*, written in the summer of 1865, Mark Twain provided a characteristic description of Nevada. "The country looks something like a singed cat," he pointed out, "owing to the scarcity of shrubbery, and also resembles that animal in the respect that it has more merits than its personal appearance would seem to indicate. . . . It has no character to speak of," resembling in this, "many, ah! too many, chambermaids in this wretched world." Answering the question, "what diseases do they die of mostly?" Mark stated matter-of-factly that Nevadans "used to die of conical balls, and cold steel, mostly, but here lately erysipelas and the intoxicating bowl have the bulge on those things."

Sam Clemens was assigned to cover the proceedings of the territorial legislature, and he soon began a friendly feud with Clement T. Rice, a reporter for the Virginia City *Union*, whom he ridiculed as "the Unreliable." On one occasion Clemens sent the *Enterprise* a satirical account of the activities of the Washoe delegation in the legislature, which was published

under the heading "The Grand Bull Drivers' Convention." While a copy of
the issue in which this article was written is not extant, it was republished
soon thereafter in the *Placer Weekly Courier*, and has only recently been
unearthed by Effie Mona Mack in the course of researches for her volume
on *Mark Twain in Nevada*.

"A suspicion crossed my mind that they were partially intoxicated"

Placer Weekly Courier (Forest Hill, Placer County, Nevada), January 17, 1863

CARSON, MIDNIGHT, DECEMBER 23—
On the last night of the session, Hon.
Thomas Hannah announced that a
Grand Bull Drivers' Convention
would assemble in Washoe City, on
the twenty-second, to receive Hon.
Jim Sturtevant and the other members
of the Washoe delegation. I journeyed
to the place yesterday to see that the
ovation was properly conducted. I
traveled per stage. The Unreliable of
the *Union* went also—for the purpose
of distorting the facts. The weather
was delightful. It snowed the entire
day. The wind blew such a hurricane
that the coach drifted sideways from
one toll road to another, and sometimes utterly refused to mind her helm.
It is a fearful thing to be at sea in a
stagecoach. We were anxious to get to
Washoe by four o'clock, but luck was
against us. We were delayed by stress
of weather; we were hindered by the
bad condition of the various toll roads;
we finally broke the afterspring of the
wagon, and had to lay up for repairs.
Therefore we only reached Washoe at
dusk. Messrs. Lovejoy, Howard, Win-
ters, Sturtevant, and Speaker Mills
had left Carson ahead of us, and we
found them in the city. They had not
beaten us much, however, as I could
perceive by their upright walk and un-
tangled conversation.

At six P.M., the Carson City Brass
Band, followed by the Committee of
Arrangements, and the Chairman of
the Convention, and the delegation,
and the invited guests, and the citizens
generally, and the hurricane, marched
up one of the most principal streets,
and filed in imposing procession into
Foulke's Hall. The delegation, and the
guests, and the band were provided
with comfortable seats near the Chairman's desk, and the constituency occupied the body pews. The delegation
and the guests stood up and formed a
semicircle, and Mr. Gregory introduced them one at a time to the constituency. Mr. Gregory did this with
much grace and dignity, albeit he affected to stammer and gasp, and hesitate, and look colicky, and miscall the
names, and miscall them again by way
of correcting himself, and grab desperately at invisible things in the air—all
with a charming pretense of being
scared.

The Hon. John K. Lovejoy arose in
his place and blew his horn. He made
honorable mention of the legislature
and the Committee on Internal Im-
provements. He told how the fountains
of their great deep were broken up,
and they rained forty days and forty
nights, and brought on a flood of toll
roads over the whole land. He ex-

plained to them that the more toll roads there were, the more competition there would be, and the roads would be good, and tolls moderate in consequence.

Mr. Speaker Mills responded to the numerous calls for him, and spoke so well in praise of the Washoe delegation that I was constrained to believe that there really was some merit in the deceased.

The Chairman, Mr. Gaston, introduced Colonel Howard, and that gentleman addressed the people in his peculiarly grave and dignified manner. The constituency gave way to successive cataracts of laughter, which was singularly out of keeping with the stern seriousness of the speaker's bearing. He spoke about ten minutes, and then took his seat, in spite of the express wish of the audience that he should go on.

Hon. Jim Sturtevant next addressed the citizens, extemporaneously. He made use of the very thunder which I meant to launch at the populace. Owing to this unfortunate circumstance, I was forced to keep up an intelligent silence during the session of the convention.

After this the assemblage broke up and adjourned to take something to drink. At nine o'clock the band again summoned the public to Foulke's Hall, and I proceeded to that place. I found the Unreliable there, and George Hepperly. I had requested Mr. Hepperly, as a personal favor, to treat the Unreliable with distinguished consideration and I am proud and happy to acknowledge he had done so. He had him in charge of two constables.

The hall had been cleared of the greater part of its benches, and the ball was ready to commence. The citizens had assembled in force, and the sexes were pretty equally represented in the proportion of one lady to several gentlemen. The night was so infernally inclement—so to speak—that it was impossible for ladies who lived at any considerable distance to attend. However, those that were there appeared in every quadrille, and with exemplary industry. I did not observe any wallflowers—the climate of Washoe appears to be unsuited to that kind of vegetation.

In accordance with the customs of the country, they indulged in the plain quadrille at this ball. And notwithstanding the vicissitudes which I have seen that wonderful national dance pass through, I solemnly affirm that they sprung some more new figures on me last night. However, the ball was a very pleasant affair. We could muster four sets and still have a vast surplusage of gentlemen—but the strictest economy had to be observed in order to make the ladies hold out.

The supper and the champagne were excellent and abundant, and I offer no word of blame against anybody for eating and drinking pretty freely. If I were to blame anybody, I would commence with the Unreliable —for he drank until he lost all sense of etiquette. I actually found myself in bed with him with my boots on. However, as I said before, I cannot blame the cuss; it was a convivial occasion, and his little shortcomings ought to be overlooked. When I went to bed this morning, Mr. Lovejoy, arrayed in fiery red night clothes, was dancing the war dance of his tribe (he is President of the Paiute Association) around a spittoon, and Colonel Howard, dressed in a similar manner, was trying to convince him that he was a humbug. A suspicion crossed my mind that they were partially intoxicated, but I could not be sure about it on account of everything appearing to turn

around so. I left Washoe City this
morning at nine o'clock, fully persuaded that I would like to go back

there again when the next convention
meets.

* * *

SHORTLY AFTER this article appeared, Sam Clemens began to sign his pieces
"Mark Twain," after the call of the leadsman on the Mississippi, when he
had sunk his line to the two-fathom knot. "By the mark, twain" signified
that the boat had twelve feet of water under her—a comforting assurance.
Once the *Daily Alta California* ran a story to the effect that "Mark Twain"
meant two chalk marks the bartender in a Virginia City saloon used to
record on the wall back of the bar whenever Sam Clemens, who "drank for
the pure and unadulterated love of the ardent," had invited a guest to join
him. Mark Twain was impelled to deny the libel. The inside story appeared
in the *Daily Alta California* of June 9, 1877:

Dear Sir:

"Mark Twain" was the *nom de plume* of one Captain Isaiah Sellers, who used to
write river news over it for the New Orleans *Pica; ne*. He died in 1863 and as he could
no longer need that signature, I laid violent hands upon it without asking permission of
the proprietor's remains. That is the history of the *nom de plume* I bear.

Yours,

Samuel L. Clemens

Soon Mark Twain's *Enterprise* stories were copied all over the West
Coast and he was on his way to becoming a national literary figure. Writing
his mother at this time, he declared: "I am proud to say I am the most
conceited ass in the Territory."

London's Star Reporter, Archibald Forbes, Sees Paris Strangled by Prussians and Revolutionaries

FRANCE WOULD NEVER forget it—*l'année terrible* (1870–71), the year that witnessed the hated Prussian conqueror take over the city and then a bloody class war almost completely crush it. To add to her cup of bitterness, France, in her war with Prussia, did not have the sympathy of the Western world, which considered her the aggressor. "On the head of Louis Napoleon rests the tremendous crime of embroiling Europe in bloodshed," *Reynolds'*, Britain's labor paper, declared, while *The Morning Advertiser* condemned Napoleon the Little's "iron despotism." And, although the Communist Auguste Blanqui might thunder in his newspaper, *La Patrie en danger*, published during the siege, that "all the world is prepared to die on the barricades," he overestimated France's martial spirit in that war.

Top-flight British and American reporters covered the Franco-Prussian War. The *New York Tribune*'s George Washburn Smalley headed a joint staff of *Tribune* and London *Daily News* men. Moncure Conway was at the front line for the New York *World*, along with Murat Halstead of the *Cincinnati Commercial*. From inside Paris Henry Vizetelly and Henry Labouchère thrilled the readers of London's *Daily News* with accounts of the siege, sent out by balloon post and carrier pigeon.

Although Louis Napoleon capitulated at Sedan on September 2, 1870, the war was carried on by a newly proclaimed French republican government. Two German armies swept on Paris and laid siege to the city, which did not capitulate until January 28, 1871. Every reporter with the Prussian armies wanted to get inside the beleaguered city ahead of the armed forces, but actually the first person to enter the city was Archibald Forbes, the London *Daily News* reporter, whose sudden appearance startled his Paris newspaper colleagues, including another *Daily News* reporter using the pseudonym of "Besieged Resident," "quite as much as Friday did Robinson Crusoe." His eighteen hours of on-the-spot coverage was hailed as one of the two great beats of the war (the other was the first story of the French defeat at Sedan, which the British newsman Holt White sent to *The Pall Mall Gazette*).

"Paris is utterly cowed; fairly beaten"

The Daily News (London), February 4, 1871 (*By Special Dispatch*)

FROM OUR SPECIAL CORRESPONDENT WITH THE HEADQUARTERS OF THE CROWN PRINCE OF SAXONY, PARIS, FEBRUARY 1—Leaving Saint-Denis yesterday forenoon, I rode through the Prussian foreposts to the neutral ground without interruptions, and so on to the Porte La Chapelle. Here the gates were closed, but a great crowd had collected in expectation of their presently opening. Everybody on the German side laughed at the quixotry of my attempt to enter. The crowd was orderly, civil, and very patient, too. Many people had loaves and cabbages. After waiting half an hour, an officer appeared on the wall, and exclaimed, *"À la Porte de Santois."* We all therefore made to the right, I, being mounted, beating the others. This gate was open, but an officer was stationed there to examine passes. I rode slowly, looking straight between my horse's ears, and somehow nobody stopped me. Once inside, I came in upon sundry mobs of semidrunken National Guards, and the cry was, "Down with the Prussian!"

Matters got serious. The clamor spread, and men tried to clutch at my bridle. I thought it wiser to be bold, and turned on the first man who had shouted, and proclaimed that I was an Englishman, come if possible to do good, not harm, and thus succeeded in diverting attention to my assailant. Then I rode on unmolested through to the Rue Arnaud, where were massed several battalions of the National Guard, apparently to receive their pay; then through the Boulevard de Magenta, and so straight on to the American Legation, in the Champs-Elysées.

"Paris is utterly cowed; fairly beaten"—so said the first Englishman I met; and his opinion was mine. Yet Paris was orderly and decent, and with a certain solemn, morose self-restraint was mastering the tendency to demonstrate. The streets were crowded, almost wholly with men in uniform. Civilians were few and far between. Many shops were open, but many also were closed. There was no want of hardware in Paris. You might have bought enough and to spare of anything except edibles. Drink was plentiful enough, but except near the gate I saw not a soul drunk. The food shops had nothing to show. There were confitures and preserves, jellies, etc., but solid comestibles were conspicuous by their absence. In one shop I saw several large shapes of stuff that looked like lard. When I asked what it was, I found it was horse fat. The bakers' shops were closed: the grating down over the butchers'.

And oh, the number of funerals! One, two, three; I met six altogether in the course of my ride. Sad with an exceeding great sadness; such was what I found as regards Paris long before I reached the American Legation. Self-respecting, too, in her misery; not blatant; not disposed to collect in jabbering crowds. Each man went his way with chastened face and listless gait.

I spoke with a soldier of the line. Yes, he had had enough of it. *Sacré!* They had nearly killed him, these terrible Prussians, and he was very hungry. When would the gates open for food? Food began to be with me a personal question. I had nearly filled my wallet with newspapers, and only stowed away, for an exigency, a few slices of ham. Did even the rarest geological or mineralogical specimen make such a sensation as these slices of ham? When I at length reached my quarters the servant woman asked permission to take the meager plateful out and show it as a curiosity to her companions; and after the ham was eaten, stray visitors came in, attracted by the tidings, and begged for a look at the unwonted viands.

The whole city is haunted with the chaste odors which horseflesh gives out in cooking; odors which I learned to appreciate at Metz. They permeate the deserted British Embassy, where, asserting my privileges as a Briton, I stabled my horse; they linger in the corridors of the Grand Hôtel, and fight with the taint from wounds in evil cases. The Grand Hôtel is one huge hospital. Half Paris seems converted into hospitals, if one may judge by the flags. They were more than were needed until the southern bombardment began; and then, when the hospitals, ambulances, orphanages, and madhouses on the south side had to be evacuated, there was a squeeze on this side of the water.

The pinch for food is worse than ever, pending the result of the negotiations for its supply. The day before yesterday the hungry broke into the reserved store of posted provisions in the Halle, smashed all obstacles, and looted the place. Meat other than horseflesh is absolutely not to be procured. I was assured that if I offered £50 down in bright shining gold for a veritable beefsteak, I should have no claimant for the money! The last cow that changed hands "for an ambulance" fetched £80. Those left cannot now be bought for money. The bread is not bad. The difficulty is to get it. Only people say there is nothing else to do but wait outside the bakers' and the butchers'. I saw huge throngs at both as I rode through Paris, and chiefly women, waiting silently in the cold. What must it have come to when the Parisians are so utterly crushed!

To ADD TO THE PERILS of the city populace, typhoid and other dread diseases were on the rise. Fatalities mounted rapidly, rising to a total of 4465 for the single week ending January 23, 1871, according to a *Daily News* correspondent inside Paris.

In a dispatch date-lined Lagny (a suburb of Paris), February 2, Forbes wrote: "I was inside Paris. How was I to get out? It was clear I was no use there—quite *de trop*, in fact." Forbes left the city, evading challenge. When he spotted a cordon of soldiers at the Vincennes gate he began to whistle and looked the other way. His next notable dispatch described the entry of the Germans into Paris, and reveals that, like most Britons, Forbes was pro-Prussian in this conflict. The courtesies he had received at Prussian headquarters contrasted with the rather ruthless treatment accorded him at the hands of the Paris proletariat.

"I speak from sore-boned experience"

The Daily News (London), March 3, 1871

PARIS, WEDNESDAY EVENING, MARCH 1 —All Paris was there, as you may have seen on a day when there was a grand imperial pageant. Ladies in dainty dresses and high-heeled boots tripped about; chevaliers of France with the ribbons in their buttonholes gratified their curiosity at the expense of their honor. The windows were so full that I imagine some of them must have been let for money. But it was the conduct of what may be designated the mob that disgusted me most. Touch a German soldier they dared not. They cowered—half a hundred of the white-blooded hounds—before a solitary uhlan strolling his horse listlessly about. But let them only catch an unfortunate civilian, and then just mark their valor. Fortunately, they were too limp and vague to know how to take life adroitly, else many a murder might have been done in Paris this afternoon.

Say you I speak from prejudice? My prejudice, if I had any, was fain to lie the other way. I speak from sore-boned experience. As I walked down the Champs-Elysées, the Crown Prince of Saxony with his staff rode by. His guest for many a week before, I would have eaten dirt had I not raised my hat to His Royal Highness. He returned my salute, and, beckoning to me, shook hands, and a short conversation ensued.

After I had taken my leave, Count Urztheim, his aide-de-camp, rode after me to communicate from the Prince a piece of information which he was kind enough to think would be of interest to me. My companion and myself soon found that this episode had gained us the marked attention of about a hundred of the hungry prowlers after heroic seizures on which no risk was attendant. We thought little of the demonstration at first, and tried to lose our suite by turning back in the rear of the Bavarians, and halting there, but our unconcern seemed but to aggravate the patriots. After much consultation a little party came forward and civilly requested us to accompany them to a certain post. Although apprehensive of the consequences, we were unwilling to appeal to the Bavarian officers, and so be the possible means of precipitating a fracas; we therefore complied. No sooner were we outside the German quarter than the tactics were changed. My friend was torn away from me, and for many hours I saw no more of him. Cries of *"Mouchard," "Sacré Prussien," "Cochon,"* assailed me.

Somebody hit me over the head with a stick; another kicked me from behind; yet another tripped me up. I went down, and the patriots jumped on me with sabots. I struggled up and, hitting out right and left, made my way to an officer of the National Guard. He laughed and turned away. Then they got me down again, striking each other in their eagerness to have a blow at me. Some clamored, "To the Seine with him," but others, the majority, were for the police station. Thither, accordingly, I was conducted in a novel fashion, on my back and dragged by the legs, a distance of some three hundred yards. Needless to say that my coat was in ribbons, my head was cut, my back bumped into bruises, my legs torn nearly out of the sockets. Great powers! how I longed, as they dragged me along, for a single section of the old Royal Dragoons, or that I might have a chance at but three of the cowards at a time! Chucked inside the police station like a bale of goods, I was conveyed by a back door, and in the pleasing companionship of a drunken woman, a blouse who had stolen a lump of putty, and a tatter- demalion who had been seen selling a couple of cigars to a German, to a certain prefect, a venerable gentleman in a white tie. I sent a note to the British Embassy, whence emanated with creditable alacrity the porter, an official whom I had learned to look upon as the British Embassy incarnate. The benevolent prefect released me, and I was glad to slink home in my soiled and tattered clothes.

* * *

FORBES HAD COME to esteem the Parisians just about as highly as they regarded him. In ironic vein he enumerated some of the "heroic" feats of the people of Paris. They had stripped women naked who had fraternized with the enemy; they had sacked a café where a few German officers supped; they had deodorized the public buildings occupied by the conquerors. "Paris remained the virtual mistress of the field." But, Forbes asked, "where were the stunted, thin-faced, evil-eyed, scraggy-necked, knob-jointed, white-livered horde of miscreants that had yelled and whistled and sworn and shrunk into their clumsy sabots when a German looked their way?" Considering the Paris rough to be a cross between a cat and a rabbit, Forbes in his critical reporting of the conduct of that city's proletariat lacked that warm quality of human sympathy which distinguished the writing of a Hugo.

Nonetheless, the stark cruelty of the class war that broke out in liberated Paris in March—a climax to the four-month siege—impelled Forbes, against his normal sympathies, to take the side of the underdog. Paris, accustomed since 1789 to taking the lead, now set up a workers' government. A group of left-wing republicans * proclaimed Paris a "commune," adopted the red flag, and called for proletarian revolution. But the Thiers government at Versailles, using returning French troops, proceeded to put down the uprising with a fierce energy never shown in the war against the Prussians. Before the struggle ended, the Archbishop of Paris, one of the hostages taken by the Communards, was executed and the city set aflame. Even women and children fought. *Harper's Weekly* carried gruesome stories of *les pétroleuses,* the Communard women who were believed to have gone about with gasoline, setting indiscriminate fires. Forbes' dispatch reporting the Bloody Week, May 21–28:

---

* This heterogeneous group of revolutionaries, consisting of socialists, anarchists, utopians, and radical republicans, is generally referred to as the Communards, although Forbes consistently labels them Communists.

"We want but a Nero to fiddle"

The Daily News (London), May 26, 1871

THE FIGHTING IN PARIS
SCENES AND INCIDENTS
OF THE STRUGGLE
(From our Special Correspondent)

PARIS, TUESDAY, MAY 23—We are in a veritable state of siege. Yesterday afternoon, by devious paths and eccentric dodges, that I might avoid the double risks of being shot and compelled to labor on the barricades, I reached the Gare du Nord, which, of course, was closed, as also were all the gates round the *enceinte*. There seemed one chance to get a letter outside. I selected a railway employee of acute aspect and short of an arm, and promised him a goodly reward if he could walk down the line and reach Saint-Denis with my dispatches. He accepted the task, put the letters in his boots, and departed, promising to return at eight and report his success or failure. He has not come back. He may have been shot; he may have been made a prisoner; he may have got to Saint-Denis and found it impossible to return. I live in hope, dashed with apprehension.

After dispatching him, I started to revisit the localities close to the fighting. There was no great difficulty till I reached the neighborhood of the Church of Notre-Dame-de-Lorette. At the foot of the rue of the same name there was one barricade facing us. A National Guardsman was guarding the approach. First he ordered me to go back, then to run forward. I ran forward and found myself in the center of an extraordinary triangle. Another barricade faced up the Rue Saint-

Lazare. There was yet another across the neck of the Rue Faubourg-Montmartre. Men were squatting behind the latter; two exchanging shot with the Versaillists. I ran across the front of the barricade on the Rue Saint-Lazare and got under cover of the church. Here another barricade brought me up, and I was arrested, and informed that I must take a musket and go to work to defend the barricade. The work was not in my line; if it had been I should have objected very strongly, for the place was nothing but a mantrap, the barricades being so ingeniously constructed that the rear was open to the fire that might pass over the other two. My protestations that I was a foreigner, and a neutral, ultimately prevailed, and I was allowed to go the way I came, but had to abandon for the time my intention of getting farther to the west, and so I returned to the Gare du Nord.

In the evening, soon after eight o'clock, the firing died out almost everywhere, and there was a dead calm. The barricades—there were barricades everywhere—had for the most part been finished, and one might pass most of them without fearing to be requisitioned as a navvy. I made my way down the Rue Lafayette, making occasional detours for strategical reasons. What strange people these Parisians are! It was a fine evening, and the scene in the narrow streets was like Duke's Place in Aldgate on a summer Sunday afternoon. Men and women were placidly sitting on chairs by their street doors, gossiping leisurely about the events of the day. The children played round the barricades; their mothers scarcely looked up as the *générale* beat or the distant report of the bursting of a shell came on the light night wind.

Reaching the Hôtel de la Chaussée d'Antin, where I have quarters, I found, as I had expected, that it had been a very hot corner during the afternoon. It is close to the Boulevard Haussmann, which had been continuously swept with shell all the afternoon. A fragment had invaded the privacy of a friend whom I had left in the Hôtel, and had fallen before him on his desk as he wrote. The reason of the temporary lull was not very apparent—perhaps the Versaillists were eating a late dinner. About ten the din began again. Shell after shell burst close to us in the Boulevard Haussmann, and there came the loud noise of a more distant fire, which seemed to be sweeping the barricade. In the intervals of the shellfire was audible the steady grunt of the mitrailleuses, and I could distinctly hear the pattering of the balls as they rained down the adjacent Boulevard Haussmann. This dismal din, so perplexing and bewildering, continued all night. A friend sleeping in the room above me was awakened by the smashing of the button of a shell through his window. It dented a hole in the roof above his bed and fell on his pillow.

Daybreak brought no cessation of the noise. Looking out, and cautiously, up the Boulevard Haussmann, I saw before me a strange spectacle of desolation. Lampposts, kiosks, and trees were shattered and torn down. The road was strewn with the green boughs of trees which had been cut by the storm of shot and shell. The Versaillists had a battery in position at an emplacement close to the Caserne de la Pépinière, and had possession of a slight barricade, lower down, within four hundred yards of the eastern end of the boulevard, at the Rue Taitbout. It was held as an outpost, and over it the battery was firing steadily with shrapnel shell and mitrailleuse in the eastern end of the boulevard, where a few National Guards still prowled in doorways, throwing a shot now and then at the barricade. Communist sergeants were rushing about the side streets and the Rue de Lafayette, ordering everybody to close their windows but to open their jalousies, this seemingly being regarded as a precaution against Versaillist sympathizers firing on them from the houses. One thing is remarkable in this curious episode of fighting. There has been no attempt on the part of the National Guards to occupy the houses and fire from them at the advancing Versaillists. They have been content to utilize barricades and such cover as the streets casually afforded. The Versaillists, on the other hand, are said to occupy the houses and fire freely from them; as to the truth of this I know not of my own knowledge, but I do know that they expose themselves very little indeed; and that, except in a few instances, they have done nothing in the way of hand-to-hand fighting.

About six o'clock I went for a walk —a morning walk just at present is not to be indulged in in Paris without considerable circumspection. My idea of the operations of the night had been that the Versaillists, having desisted from active advancing operations, had maintained a close and heavy fire down the Boulevard Haussmann and the Boulevard des Italiens, to prevent the concentration of the Communists and the construction of obstacles to further progress in the morning. This was correct as to the former boulevard, but I was quite wrong as to the latter. Getting out into the Great Boulevard by side streets, I found it lined with detachments of National Guards, a large proportion of whom were very drunk, while all were quite at their ease. The barricade at the end of the Rue de la Paix, which had been knocked about from the Madeleine direction yesterday, was restored, strengthened, and armed with mitrailleuses. Nay, more, I was assured by Communist officers that the mitrailleuse fire, which had been so steady throughout the night, had been delivered by their side from this barricade, and that it had driven the Versaillists away from the Madeleine, so that they could not sweep the long boulevard as it had seemed to me they were doing. There was some confirmation of this in the fact that the boulevard was quite a happy haven of safety, and had only been cut up by the shelling of the day before and by occasional vagrant abuses which seemed to come from the direction of the Trocadéro. I did myself the honor to partake of coffee with a hospitable but particularly drunken squad of National Guardsmen, and then struck down the Palais-Royal to ascertain how it had fared with the Rue de Rivoli and Rue Saint-Honoré. I found several of the cross streets much shattered with shellfire, which was slowly dropping still, but the barricades at the Place du Palais-Royal were armed and intact, and it was obvious that the big barricade at the Place de la Concorde and of the Rue de Rivoli was still held by the Nationals, sure evidence that the Versaillists were not in possession of the Place de la Concorde. This ascertained, I proceeded westward along the Rue Saint-Honoré, which has been seriously injured by shellfire from the Trocadéro. It is crossed with frequent barricades, and was strongly held by detachments of drunken and resolute men.

I penetrated as far as the head of the Rue Saint-Honoré where it runs into the Rue Royale, and there was witness to one of the strangest, cross-question and crooked-answer spectacles I ever saw. The Versaillists were in the Rue Faubourg-Saint-Honoré, which is a continuation, on the western side of the Rue Royale, of the Rue Saint-Honoré, behind the barricade at the end of which I was standing. The Versaillists were in the Corps Législatif across the water, and were firing over the bridge and the Place de la Concorde into the big Federal barricade across the end of the Place Royale. In one sense, then, the Versaillists in the Rue Faubourg-Saint-Honoré were behind the defenders of this barricade; but then our barricade at the head of the Rue Saint-Honoré neutralized them there, and so the deadlock seemed a fixture. One thing I established for certain, and that was that the Versaillists were not in the Place de la Concorde.

About ten there came the sound of a terrible fire behind [Forbes'] hotel, and I managed, at some risk, to obtain ocular proof that the Versaillists had carried the Church of Notre-Dame-de-Lorette and the mantrap barricades in which I had got involved yesterday, and were now fighting their way along the Rue de Châteaudun, so as to get into the Rue de Lafayette, on the eastward considerably of my hotel. Meanwhile a heavy fire was maintained down the Boulevard Haussmann, so that our hotel seemed imminently about to be surrounded. As I returned to its front, and prowled forward cautiously into the Rue de Lafayette, and looked up eastward to the barricades across the Rue de Lafayette, and continued across the Rue de Châteaudun, I saw the Federals firing furiously down the latter street. After considerable resistance they broke, and the Versaillists gained the barricade. I saw the red breeches surrounding it as they poured out of the Rue de Châteaudun.

Now they are (one o'clock) firing westward along the Rue de Lafayette into the Boulevard Haussmann, while other Versaillist troops are pressing down the Boulevard Haussmann, firing like furies, and covered by a shell-fire falling in their front. Thus the Federals in the Boulevard Haussmann, a mere handful but very obstinate, are taken front and rear, and must slide out of the crux, to all appearance by the New Opera, from the summit of which still flies the red flag. They are taken in flank, too, for a fire is pouring down on them by the Rue de la Chaussée d'Antin, from the Church of the Trinity. Balls are whistling past my window; a shell has just shattered the lamppost at the junction of the Rue de Lafayette with the Boulevard Haussmann. I see Federal after Federal sneaking away by the cover afforded by the Opera House. Every minute I expect to see the Versaillists come in sight round the corner, marching down the Boulevard Haussmann. One thing is certain, I can't get away eastward anyhow, I am hemmed in between three fires, if not four. There is not a soul in the street, even the women, who are so fond of shell fragments, are under cover now. I hear the bugle sounding, whether it is a Versaillist or a Federal bugle, I cannot tell. It is reported that the Versaillists have carried Montmartre; if so, all is nearly over. There is a report that they have the Gare du Nord, too. Another shell has just broken the windows on my ground floor. I am on the second floor. Dombrowski was alive this morning.

Half-past two P.M.

Contrary to my anticipation, the Versaillists are not yet round the corner; that is, they have not got so far down the Boulevard Haussmann as the corner of the Rue de Lafayette, where I am writing, and the red flag still waves from the top of the New Opera House. The shells and mitrailleuses are whistling past the corner where I am ensconced, in one continual whistle, and the clash of broken glass is incessant. For a time it seemed as if the fighting were confined to this particular spot. It is hottest here still, but I hear them at it on the Great Boulevard also, and there is musketry fire also to the eastward. I don't like my position, but to change it would to all appearance be out of the frying pan into the fire.

It is impossible to define the situation. All is chaos, at least for the moment. What a beautiful day it is! Such a day as one would like to be lying on the grass, under a hawthorn hedge, looking at the young lambs skipping about; not cowering in a corner, dodging shot and shell, in this undignified manner, and without any matches wherewith to light one's pipe.

Half-past three

The Federals are still sticking to their fighting in the Boulevard Haussmann, and around the Opéra, but the Versaillists are streaming eastward up the Rue de Lafayette, and have carried the barracks de Bonne-Nouvelle, in the Rue du Faubourg-Poissonnière. Down it they have a clear road into the Boulevard Poissonnière, and will probably be at the Porte Saint-Martin in a very short time. Meanwhile my Federal friends on the barricade at the end of the Rue Halévy, opening on the Boulevard Haussmann, are making a furious fight of it, replying up the Chaussée d'Antin to the Versaillists at the Church of the Trinity. They have got a cannon and a mitrailleuse off the Boulevard des Italiens, and they are not giving these pieces much time to cool. Their courage is something surprising. The house at the right-hand corner of the Boulevard Haussmann and the Rue de Lafayette has caught fire. Pleasant prospect, if the fire gains head, for one who is sheltered by its gable, as I am. The red flag is still flying over against us on the top of the Opera House, but I fear its lease is a short one.

Five o'clock

The firing is furious and confusing all round. At the Opera House it is especially strong. I see troops and man after man skulking along the parapet of its roof. They have packs on, so I think they are Versaillists; but I cannot see their breeches and so cannot be certain. The *drapeau rouge* still waves from the statue on the summit of the New Opera House. The Federals are massed now at the top of the Rue Lafitte and firing down toward the boulevards. This must mean that the Versaillists are on the boulevards now. On account of the Versaillist fire the Federals cannot well come out into the Rue de Provence, and everywhere they seem between the devil and the deep sea. The people in the Porte Cochère are crying bravo and clapping their hands, because they think the Versaillists are winning.

Twenty minutes past five

They were Versaillists that I saw on the parapet of the New Opera. There is a cheer; the people rush out into the fire and clap their hands. The tricolor is waving on the hither end of the Opera House. I saw the man stick it up. The red flag still waves at the other end. A ladder is needed to remove it. Ha! you are a good plucky one, if all the rest were cowards. You deserve to give the army a good name. A little grig of a fellow in red breeches, he is one of the old French linesman breed. He scuttles forward to the corner of the Rue Halévy in the Boulevard Haussmann, takes up his post behind a tree, and fires along the Boulevard Haussmann towards the Rue Taitbout. When is a Frenchman not dramatic? He fires with an air; he loads with an air; he fires again with a flourish, and is greeted with cheering and clapping of hands. Then he beckons us back dramatically, for he meditates firing up the Rue de Lafayette, but changes his mind and blazes away again up Haussmann. Then he turns and waves on his fellows as if he were on the boards of a theater, the Federal bullets cutting the bark and leaves all around him. He is down. The woman and I dart out from our corner and carry him in. He is dead, with a bullet through the forehead.

Twenty-five minutes to six

The scene is intensely dramatic. A Versaillist has got a ladder and is mounting the statue of Apollo on the front elevation of the New Opera House. He tears down the *drapeau rouge* just as the Versailles troops stream out of the Chaussée d'Antin across the Boulevard Haussmann, and down the Rue Meyerbeer and the continuation of the Chaussée d'Antin. The people rushed from their houses with bottles of wine; money was showered into the streets. The women fell on the necks of the sweaty, dusty men in red breeches, and hugged them amid shouts of *"Vive la ligne."* The soldiers fraternized warmly; drank and pressed forward. Their discipline was admirable. They formed in companies behind the next barricade and obeyed the officer at once when he called them from conviviality. Now the wave of Versaillists is over us for good, and the red breeches are across the Great Boulevard and going at the Place Vendôme. Everybody seems wild with joy, and Communist cards of citizenship are being torn up wholesale. It is not *citoyen* now under pain of suspicion. You may say *monsieur* if you like.

Ten P.M.

Much has been done since the hour at which I last dated. The Versaillist soldiers, pouring down in one continuous stream by the Chaussée d'Antin, horse, foot, and artillery, crossed the Great Boulevard, taking the insurgents in flank, not without considerable fighting and a good deal of loss, for the Federals fought like wildcats wherever they could get the ghost of a cover. Anxious to ascertain whether there was any prospect of an Embassy bag to Versailles, I started up the now quiet Boulevard Haussmann, and by tacks and dodges got down into the Rue de Miromesnil, which debouches in the faubourg opposite the Palace of the Elysée. Shells were bursting very freely in the neighborhood, but the matter was urgent, and I pressed on up to the Rue du Faubourg-Saint-Honoré, and looked round the corner for a second. Had I looked a second longer, I should not have been writing these lines. A shell splinter whizzed past me as I drew back, close enough to blow my beard aside. The street was a pneumatic tube for shellfire. Nothing could have lived in it. I fell back, thinking I might get over to the Embassy as the firing died away, and waited in the entry of an ambulance

for an hour. There were not a few ambulances about this spot. I saw, for a quarter of an hour, one wounded man carried into the one I was near every minute, for I timed the stretchers by my watch. Looking into others, I could see the courtyards littered with mattresses and groaning men. A few but not many corpses, chiefly of National Guards, lay in the streets, behind the barricades, and in the gutters.

As I returned to the Hôtel de la Chaussée d'Antin, I had to cross the line of artillery pouring southward from the Church of the Trinity, and so down the Rue Halévy, toward the quarter where the sound indicated hot fighting was still going on. The artillerymen received a wild ovation from the inhabitants of the Chaussée d'Antin. The men gave them money, the women tendered them bottles of wine. All was *gaudeamus*. Where, I wonder, had the people secreted the tricolor all these days of the Commune? It now waved from every window, and flapped in the still night air, as the shouts of *"Vive la ligne"* gave it a lazy throb.

Wednesday

And so evening wore into night, and night became morning. Ah! this morning! Its pale flush of aurora bloom was darkest, most somber night for the once proud, now stricken and humiliated, city. When the sun rose, what saw he? Not a fair fight—on that within the last year Sol has looked down more than once. But black clouds flouted his rays—clouds that rose from the Palladium of France. Great God! that men should be so mad as to strive to make universal ruin because their puny course of factiousness is run! The flames from the Palace of the Tuileries, kindled by damnable petroleum, insulted the soft light of the morning and cast lurid rays on the grimy recreant Frenchmen who skulked from their dastardly incendiarism to pot at countrymen from behind a barricade. How the place burned! The flames reveled in the historical palace, whipped up the rich furniture, burst out the plate-glass windows, brought down the fantastic roof. It was in the Prince Imperial's wing facing the Tuileries Gardens where the demon of fire first had his dismal sway. By eight o'clock the whole of the wing was nearly burned out. As I reached the end of the Rue Dauphine the red belches of flames were bursting out from the corner of the Tuileries facing the private gardens and the Rue de Rivoli: the rooms occupied by the King of Prussia and his suite on the visit to France the year of the Exhibition. There is a furious jet of flame pouring out of the window where Bismarck used to sit and smoke. Crash! Is it an explosion or a fall of flooring that causes this burst of black smoke and red sparks in our faces? God knows what hell devices may be within that burning pile; it were well surely to give it a wide berth.

And so eastward to the Place du Palais-Royal, which is still unsafe by reason of shot and shell from the neighborhood of the Hôtel de Ville. And there is the great archway by which troops were wont to enter into the Place du Carrousel—is the fire there yet? Just there, and no more; could the archway be cut, the Louvre, with its artistic riches, might still be spared. But there are none to help. The troops are lounging supine in the rues; intent—and who shall blame weary, powder-grimed men?—on bread and wine. And so the devastator leaps from chimney to chimney, from window to window. He is over the arch-

way now, and I would not give two hours' purchase for all the riches of the Louvre. In the name of modern vandalism, what means that burst of smoke and jet of fire? Alas for art; the Louvre is on fire independently. And so is the Palais-Royal and the Hôtel de Ville, where the rump of the Commune are cowering amidst their incendiarism; and the Ministry of Finance, and many another public and private building besides.

I turn from the spectacle sad and sick, to be sickened yet further by another spectacle. The Versaillist troops collected about the foot of the Rue Saint-Honoré were enjoying the fine game of Communist hunting. The Parisians of civil life are caitiffs to the last drop of their thin, sour, white blood. But yesterday they had cried *"Vive la Commune!"* and submitted to be governed by this said Commune. Today they rubbed their hands with livid currish joy to have it in their power to denounce a Communist and reveal his hiding place. Very eager at this work are the dear creatures of women. They know the ratholes into which the poor devils have got, and they guide to them with a fiendish glee which is a phase of the many-sided sex. *Voilà!* the braves of France returned to a triumph after a shameful captivity! They have found him, the miserable! Yes, they drag him out from one of the purlieus which Haussmann had not time to sweep away, and a guard of six of them hem him round as they march him into the Rue Saint-Honoré. A tall, pale, hatless man, with something not ignoble in his carriage. His lower lip is trembling, but his brow is firm, and the eye of him has some pride and defiance in it. They yell—the crowd—"Shoot him; shoot him!"—the demon women most clamorous, of course. An arm goes into the air; there are on it the stripes of a noncommissioned officer, and there is a stick in the fist. The stick falls on the head of the pale man in black. Ha! the infection has caught; men club their rifles, and bring them down on that head, or clash them into splinters in their lust for murder. He is down; he is up again; he is down again; the thuds of the gunstocks on him sounding just as the sound when a man beats a cushion with a stick. A certain British impulse, stronger than consideration for self, prompts me to run forward. But it is useless. They are firing into the flaccid carcass now, thronging about it like blowflies on a piece of meat. His brains spurt on my boot and plash into the gutter, whither the carrion is bodily chucked, presently to be trodden on and rolled on by the feet of multitudes and wheels of gun carriages.

Womanhood, then, is not quite dead in that band of bedlamites who had clamored "Shoot him." Here is one in hysterics; another, with wan, scared face, draws out of the press an embryo bedlamite, her offspring, and, let us hope, goes home. But surely all manhood is dead in the soldiery of France to do a deed like this. An officer—one with a bull throat and the eyes of Algiers—stood by and looked on at the sport, sucking a cigar meanwhile.

The merry game goes on. Denouncing becomes fashionable, and denouncing is followed in the French natural sequence by braining. Faugh! let us get away from the truculent cowards and the bloody gutters, and the yelling women, and the Algerian-eyed officers. Here is the Place Vendôme, held, as I learn on credible authority, by twenty-five Communists and a woman, against all that Versailles found it in its heart to do, for hours. In the shattered Central Place Versaillist sentries are stalking about the ruins of the column. They have accumulated, too, some forces in the rattrap. There is one corpse in the gutter buffeted and besmirched—the corpse, as I learn, of the Communist captain of a barricade who held it for half an hour single-handed against the braves of France, and then shot himself. The braves have, seemingly, made sure of him by shooting him and the clay, which was once a man, over and over again.

And how about the chained wildcats in the Hôtel de Ville? Their backs are to the wall, and they are fighting now, not for life, but that they may do as much evil as they can before their hour comes—as come it will before the minute hand of my watch makes many more revolutions. The Versaillists do not dare to rush at the barricades around the Hôtel de Ville; they are at once afraid of their skins and explosions. But they are mining, circumventing, burrowing, and they will be inside the cordon soon. Meanwhile the holders of the Hôtel de Ville are pouring out death and destruction over Paris in miscellaneous wildness. Now it is a shell in the Champs-Elysées; now one in the already shattered Boulevard Haussmann; now one somewhere about the Avenue Reine Hortense. It is between the devil and the deep sea with the people in the Hôtel de Ville. One enemy with weapons in his hand is outside; another, fire, and fire kindled by themselves, is inside. Will they roast, or seek death on the bayonet point?

It is hard to breathe in an atmosphere mainly of petroleum smoke. There is a sun, but his heat is dominated by the heat of the conflagrations. His rays are obscured by the lurid, blue-black smoke that is rising with a greasy fatness everywhere into the air. Let us out of it, for goodness' sake. I take horse, and ride off by the river brink toward the Point-du-Jour, leaving at my back the still loud rattle of the firing and the smoke belches. I ride on to the Point-du-Jour through Dombrowski's "second line of defense" by the railway viaduct. Poor Dombrowski! a good servant to bad masters. I should like to know his fate for certain. Versaillists have told me that they saw him taken prisoner yesterday morning, dragged on to the Trocadéro, and there shot in cold blood in the face of day, looking dauntlessly into the muzzles of the chassepots. Others say he is wounded and a prisoner.

As I ride up the broad slope of the avenue between Viroflay and Versailles, I pass a very sorrowful and dejected company. In file after file of six each march the prisoners of the Commune—there are over two thousand of them together—patiently, and it seems to me with some consciousness of pride they march, linked closely arm in arm. Among them are many women, some of them the fierce barricade Hecates, others mere girls, soft and timid, who are here seemingly because a parent is here too. All are bareheaded and foul with dust, many powder-stained too, and the burning sun beats down on bald foreheads. Not the sun alone beats down, but the flats of sabers wielded by the dashing Chasseurs d'Afrique, who are the escort of these unfortunates. Their experiences might have taught them decency to the captives. No saber blades had descended on their pates in that long, dreary march from Sedan to their German captivity; they were the prisoners of soldiers. But they are prisoners now no longer, as they caper on their wiry

Arab stallions, and in their pride of cheap victory, they belabor unmercifully the miserables of the Commune. In front are three or four hundred prisoners, lashed together with ropes, and among these are not a few men in red breeches, deserters taken red-handed. I marvel that they are here at all, and not dead in the streets of Paris.

As I drive along the green margin of the placid Seine to Saint-Denis, the spectacle which the capital presents is one never to be forgotten. On its white houses the sun still smiles. But up through the sunbeams struggle and surge ghastly swart waves and folds and pillars of dense smoke; not one or two, but I reckon them on my fingers till I lose the count. Ha! there is a sharp crack, and then a dull thud on the air. No artillery that, surely some great explosion, which must have rocked Paris to its base. There rises a convolvulus-shaped volume of whiter smoke, with a jetlike spurt, such as men describe when Vesuvius bursts into eruption, and then it breaks into fleecy waves and eddies away to the horizon all round as the ripple of a stone thrown into a pool spreads to the margin of the water. The crowds of Germans who sit by the Seine, stolidly watching, are startled into a burst of excitement—the excitement might well be world-wide. "Paris the beautiful" is Paris the ghastly, Paris the battered, Paris the burning, Paris the blood-spattered, now. And this is the nineteenth century, and Europe professes civilization, and France boasts of culture, and Frenchmen are braining one another with the butt ends of muskets, and Paris is burning. We want but a Nero to fiddle.

IN A STORY TO *The Daily News*, date-lined Paris, Quartier Latin, May 26, a correspondent reported cold-blooded "horrible assassination" at the Panthéon, where troops butchered captured Communards. "After what I have seen in France," the reporter concluded, "I can only pray that God may grant that the English character shall always remain the same." The final stand of the Communards took place at Père Lachaise cemetery, where some eighteen thousand perished in the orgy of revenge. "The Commune," observed the leftist *Reynolds'*, "has made Paris another Moscow for the victors." But the more conservative *West End News* shouted that France would have no stable government until "Paris is erased from the list of cities."

The New York Times Exposes Boss Tweed

B OSS" TWEED was neither the first plunderer of the public till in New York City nor the last. Before him came Samuel Swartwout, a Collector of the Port of New York, who fled to Europe with over a million dollars in stolen loot. Then Fernando Wood, an unscrupulous demagogue and Tweed's immediate predecessor, amply demonstrated just how corrupt a mayor could be. But of all the plunderers, Tweed was the most brazen.

Elected to the Common Council in 1852, William Marcy Tweed became one of the "Forty Thieves" whose bank accounts were fattened from streetcar franchises, city-land sales, and bounties appropriated by the city during the Civil War for substitutes of drafted men. Tweed went on to Congress and the New York State Senate. The Grand Sachem of the Tammany Society, whose symbol now was the head of a tiger—borrowed from Tweed's old volunteer fire company—Tweed and his crew were swept into power in 1868. A. Oakey ("The Elegant One") Hall became Mayor; Peter B. ("Brains") Sweeny, Chamberlain; and Richard B. ("Slippery Dick") Connolly, Controller. Tweed forced through a new city charter that created a Board of Audit for the city to control the municipal treasury. The Board comprised Hall, Sweeny, and Connolly in their official capacities, together with Tweed, who had had himself appointed Commissioner of Public Works.

In the overthrow of the Tweed Ring honors are divided between *The New York Times* and Thomas Nast of *Harper's Weekly*. Founded in 1851 by Henry Jarvis Raymond and George Jones, the *Times* had already won a reputation for objective news reporting, living up to Raymond's ideals: "We do not mean to write as if we were in a passion, unless that shall really be the case; and we shall make it a point to get in a passion as rarely as possible." *Harper's* was at that time the most important weekly in America, its Nast cartoons powerfully implemented by editorials from the pen of George William Curtis.

On July 8, 1871, the *Times* unlimbered its big guns, although its sensational exposé was tucked away in an inner page. It seems that ex-sheriff James O'Brien, a rival of Tweed's, after pocketing some of the loot himself, turned over to the *Times* transcripts of the Controller's records. Tweed frantically sent Controller Connolly to bribe George Jones of the *Times*, reputedly offering him five million dollars to forego the publication of the documents.

"I don't think the devil will ever make a higher bid for me than that," Jones declared.

"Why, with that sum you could go to Europe and live like a prince," Connolly rejoined.

"Yes," said Jones, "but I should know that I was a rascal."*

The *Times* exposé:

"What are you going to do about it?"

The New York Times, July 8, 1871

Reliable and incontrovertible evidence of numerous gigantic frauds on the part of the rulers of the city has been given to the public from time to time. Few, if any, of the frauds, however, which have been thus exposed will be found to be of greater magnitude or of a more shameful character than those which are presented in this article. The facts which are narrated are obtained from what we consider a good and trustworthy source, and the figures which help to explain them are transcribed literally from the books in the Controller's office. If Controller Connolly can prove them to be inaccurate he is heartily welcome to do so.

[A wealth of evidence is presented to show that amazing frauds were perpetrated in the rental of armories. Long-unoccupied buildings were selected by the "Ring" and rented for armory purposes, although entirely unsuitable. When Tweed's partner, James H. Ingersoll, rented a building for an armory, he proceeded to lock it up to make sure that it remained unused.]

During the year 1869, with the exception of the Eighty-fourth, there were no changes made in the location of the different regiments, and but little repairs were attempted, and yet, within thirty days, commencing March 12, 1870, more than HALF A MILLION DOLLARS were paid out of the City Treasury for "repairs on armories and drill rooms." The checks representing this amount were drawn in favor of Ingersoll and Watson, A. Garvey, Keyser and Co., but they were all returned from the bank bearing the indorsement of James H. Ingersoll. [Among the outstanding cases of fraudulent rentals was that in the amount of $16,500 paid for stable lofts that would not bring $2500 in the real-estate market.]

In addition to this, Ingersoll and Watson have been drawing Five Thousand Dollars a year for an indefinite period for an armory that never had any existence. It is described as being at No. 53 Chrystie Street, but the most diligent inquiry through the building and the neighborhood has failed to elicit the fact that any part of the premises has ever been used for military purposes. The building is in a wretched neighborhood, in the rear of Ingersoll and Watson's store, at No. 71 Bowery. The upper floors are let to different parties and are all occupied; the store and basement have been unoccupied since the first of May, up to which time they were occupied by a tobacco manufactory—so that the pretext that any part of the building has ever been used as an armory is glaringly false and fraudulent.

The following is a recapitulation of the amounts paid as rent for the armories now occupied, compared with what *should* be paid:

* Nast spurned a bribe of half a million dollars.

Yearly Rent   *Worth*
Total: $190,600 $46,600
Unoccupied Armories for which
Rent is Paid ... [Total] Yearly
Rent, $85,500

Who are responsible for these frauds? First, Mayor Hall and Controller Connolly, who pass upon these claims and sign checks for their payment—knowing them to be fraudu-

lent. Second, William M. Tweed and Peter B. Sweeny, who pocket their share of the proceeds—knowing it to have been fraudulently obtained. Third, James H. Ingersoll, Joseph B. Young, Clerk to the Board of Supervisors, and Stephen C. Lynes, Jr., the present City Auditor, whose agency in these matters is as palpable as it is shameful.

* * *

SINCE BRIBERY FAILED, Tammany sought revenge by instituting a suit to eject the *Times* from the premises it had held undisputed possession of for fourteen years, but other New York papers rallied to its defense. (Several newspapers on Tweed's payroll were compelled to suspend after the exposé.) When Tweed cynically asked, "What are you going to do about it?" he was quickly shown by an aroused public. Tammany's bitterest foe was Thomas Nast, the cartoonist. "Every stroke of his pen cuts like a scimitar," it was truly said. Devastating cartoons depicted the Tammany Tiger on the loose, with Tweed watching from his regal seat as the Tiger attacked a young girl (the republic) lying prostrate in the arena; a group of vultures waiting for the storm to blow over ("Let us *Prey*"); each member of the Ring pointing to the other, " 'Twas Him," in answer to the question: "Who Stole the People's Money?"; finally, the panicky Ring members shouting "Stop, Thief!" and running frantically by the side of decent citizens to track down the crooks. Stung to the quick, Tweed threw out all Harper textbooks from the public schools, replacing them with products of a Tammany-owned publishing company.

The *Times* story of July 8 had outlined the Ring's essential technique: phony leases, padded bills, false vouchers, unnecessary repairs, outrageous kickbacks, raised accounts. On July 22 the *Times,* under a front-page headline, THE SECRET ACCOUNTS: PROOFS OF UNDOUBTED FRAUDS BROUGHT TO LIGHT, published a set of accounts "copied with scrupulous fidelity from Controller Connolly's books." Purporting to show the amounts paid during 1869 and 1870 for repairs and furniture for the new courthouse, they spoke for themselves. The warrants were nominally drawn in different names, but all were indorsed to the Ring's agent, "Ingersoll and Co." On one day alone furniture was supposed to have been supplied to the amount of $129,469.48! In all, the Ring had pilfered anywhere from $75,000,000 to $200,000,000. A mere fraction of the loot was restored to the city treasury. Tweed, convicted, died in Ludlow Street Jail, a broken man.* Others, like Connolly, lived lives of luxury in Paris. Sweeny made partial restitution and put the onus of theft upon his dead brother.

---

* When first arrested, Tweed escaped from jail, only to be later captured in Spain by an official who identified him by means of a Nast cartoon.

Horatio Seymour might cynically observe that "our people want men in office who will not steal but who will not interfere with those who do," but the crusade of the newspapers for civic decency belied his comment. The very next year the New York *Sun*, through its Washington correspondent, A. M. Gibson, exposed the notorious star-route abuses, by which compensation was given to mail carriers for mail never delivered. Again the *Times* fired its heavy artillery, and a house cleaning finally took place in the Post Office Department. During the same period, the *St. Louis Democrat* exposed the Whisky Ring, organized in St. Louis to defraud the government of the revenue tax, and implicated several Grant appointees. A fearless press had at last turned the tide against the plunderers.

Two Reporters See "Our Lady of the Lamp"

and Her Crumpled-Tempered Cow Bring

Calamity to·Chicago

A PAGE-ONE ADVERTISEMENT in the *Chicago Tribune* for October 8, 1871, contained this timely injunction from the Mutual Security Insurance Company: *"Fire—fire, prepare for fall and wintry fires."* That was the last issue of the *Tribune* until October 12, for the great fire that broke out the night of the eighth destroyed its new "fireproof" building together with the business section of the city. That same issue had the first story on the fire under the headline: "THE FIRE FIEND. TERRIBLY DESTRUCTIVE CONFLAGRATION LAST NIGHT." There was no issue of the *Tribune* again for four days, when it appeared with a grateful acknowledgment to the *Cincinnati Commercial* for quickly rushing a complete font of type.

The start of the fire was witnessed by a great American journalist, Horace White, then editor of the *Chicago Tribune,* later on, with Carl Schurz and Edwin L. Godkin, a member of the brilliant triumvirate that took over the destinies of the New York *Evening Post* and *The Nation*. White ended his long journalistic career as editor-in-chief of the *Post*. White's vivid account first appeared in an out-of-town paper in the form of a letter to Murat Halstead, nationally known editor of the *Cincinnati Commercial*.

The Great Fire

Cincinnati Commercial, October 11, 1871

I had retired to rest, though not to sleep, when the great bell struck the alarm, but fires had been so frequent of late and had been so speedily extinguished that I did not deem it worth while to get up and look at it or even to count the strokes on the bell to learn where it was. The bell paused for fifteen minutes before giving the general alarm which distinguishes a great fire from a small one. When it sounded the general alarm I rose and looked out. There was a great light to the southwest of my residence, but no

greater than I had frequently seen in the quarter, where vast piles of pine lumber have been stored all the time I have lived in Chicago, some eighteen years. But it was not pine lumber that was burning this time. It was a row of wooden tenements in the south division of the city, in which a few days ago were standing whole rows of the most costly buildings which it hath entered into the hearts of architects to conceive.

I watched the increasing light for a few moments. Red tongues of light began to shoot upward. My family were all aroused by this time, and I dressed myself for the purpose of going to the *Tribune* office to write something about the catastrophe. Once out upon the street, the magnitude of the fire was suddenly disclosed to me.

The dogs of hell were upon the housetops of La Salle and Wells Streets, just south of Adams, bounding from one to another. The fire was moving northward like ocean surf on a sand beach. It had already traveled one eighth of a mile and was far beyond control. A column of flame would shoot up from a burning building, catch the force of the wind, and strike the next one, which in turn would perform the same direful office for its neighbor. It was simply indescribable in its terrible grandeur. Vice and crime had got the first scorching. The district where the fire got its first firm foothold was the Alsatia of Chicago. Fleeing before it was a crowd of bleareyed, drunken, and diseased wretches, male and female, half naked, ghastly, with painted cheeks, cursing and uttering ribald jests as they drifted along.

I went to the *Tribune* office, ascended to the editorial rooms, took the only inflammable thing there, a kerosene lamp, and carried it to the basement, where I emptied the oil into the sewer. This was scarcely done when I perceived the flames breaking out of the roof of the courthouse, the old nucleus of which, in the center of the edifice, was not constructed of fireproof material as the new wings had been. As the flames had leaped a vacant space of nearly two hundred feet to get at this roof, it was evident that most of the business portion of the city must go down, but I did not reflect that the city waterworks, with their four great pumping engines, were in a straight line with the fire and wind. Nor did I know then that this priceless machinery was covered by a wooden roof. The flames were driving thither with demon precision.

Billows of fire were rolling over the business palaces of the city and swallowing up their contents. Walls were falling so fast that the quaking of the ground under our feet was scarcely noticed, so continuous was the reverberation. Sober men and women were hurrying through the streets from the burning quarter, some with bundles of clothes on their shoulders, others dragging trunks along the sidewalks by means of strings and ropes fastened to the handles, children trudging by their sides or borne in their arms. Now and then a sick man or woman would be observed half concealed in a mattress doubled up and borne by two men. Droves of horses were in the streets, moving by some sort of guidance to a place of safety. Vehicles of all descriptions were hurrying to and fro, some laden with trunks and bundles, others seeking similar loads and immediately finding them, the drivers making more money in one hour than they were used to see in a week or a month. Everybody in this quarter was hurrying toward the lake shore. All the streets crossing that part of Michigan Avenue which fronts on the lake (on which my own residence stood) were crowded with fugitives hastening towards the blessed water.

ANOTHER NEWSMAN, John R. Chapin, a special artist for *Harper's Weekly,* whose art editor he became, made a magnificent sketch of the conflagration. His letter to *Harper's* accompanying the sketch was first-rate reporting.

Harper's Weekly, October 28, 1871

To the Editor of Harper's Weekly:

I confess that I felt myself a second Nero as I sat down to make the sketch which I send herewith of the burning of Chicago. In the presence of such a fearful calamity, surrounded by such scenes of misery and woe, having within a brief hour barely escaped with my life from the burning hotel, knowing that under my eye human life was being destroyed, wealth swept away, and misery entailed upon untold thousands of my fellow men, nothing but the importance of preserving a record of the scene induced me to force my nervous system into a state sufficiently calm to jot down the scenes passing before me.

No man can describe a battle so well as he who was far away from it. I shall not, therefore, pretend to give a description of anything more than that which I witnessed; and I trust that I shall be forgiven the use of the personal pronoun in view of the necessity of narrating my own experience in order to convey my impressions to others.

I arrived in Chicago for the first time on Saturday, the seventh instant, and stopped at the Sherman House. During the afternoon of that day a friend drove me around through the business portion of the city to show me the magnificent buildings which covered the area now a heap of ashes. At the *Tribune* building we were shown through that immense structure that we might see how completely *fireproof* it was.

An alarm of fire during the evening caused no anxiety, for it was a thing of frequent occurrence. Yet the morning brought us intelligence that twenty acres in the southwestern part of the city had been swept as with the besom of destruction. We, together with thousands of others, went out in the afternoon to see the ruins. In the evening, returning from church with a young and dear friend, we parted at the hotel door with a promise to meet on the morrow. In a few hours we were homeless wanderers and did not meet again.

Retiring to my room, I read until half-past ten, and at that hour went to bed and to sleep. I had heard the alarm of fire at ten o'clock; but, notwithstanding a high wind—a gale, indeed—was blowing, I felt no uneasiness, but dropped off to slumber with a mind full of engagements for the morning, which never were to be fulfilled. I had slept about two or three hours when I was awakened by a rattling of a key in my door, as though someone was trying to enter. Calling out "Who's there? What do you want?" and receiving no answer, I again fell asleep, but was again awakened by the sound of the tramping of feet and confusion in the hall, and by a dull roar, which I supposed was the sound of wheels on the Nicholson pavement. I rose and went to the window, threw open the blinds, and gazed upon a sheet of flame towering one hundred feet above the top of the hotel and upon a shower of sparks as copious as drops in a thunderstorm. [Chapin quitted the building.]

Hesitating but an instant to gaze into the face of the awful but sublime monster that was pursuing me, I turned and fled through the fiery shower—whither I knew not—but away from the fire. Coming to the river, I recognized to the left of me the entrance to the tunnel on Washington Street, and hastened toward it. It was filled already with a crowd of fugitives, all flying, with their backs and arms loaded with what they had gathered in the despair of the moment, seeking a place of safety.

The scenes witnessed among this crowd were painful, and in many instances humorous and ludicrous in the extreme—or would have been under other circumstances. Helping now a poor mother who was struggling along with an infant and half a dozen older children, anon assisting an old woman staggering under her burden of household stuff, we at length reached the other side and emerged into a place of safety.

Here for the first time I realized the magnitude of the danger and the awful nature of the calamity. As far as the eye could see toward the south the flames extended in one unbroken sheet, while they were advancing (a wall of fire from one to two hundred feet in height) with terrible rapidity. One glance was sufficient to convince the most hopeful that the city was doomed. A gale of wind was blowing from the southwest and urging the fire onward over the wealthiest and handsomest portion of the place. No human power could stay its progress, and no effort was made. The slightest change of wind to the southward would have driven the sparks across to the west side and, falling among the frame buildings of which that portion is mainly composed, would have cut off the escape of tens of thousands toward the prairie.

Dripping with perspiration from my exertions, yet feeling the chill of the blast, I dared not stand for a moment, but wandered from street to street, until I met a gentleman, his wife, and three children, who, like myself, had been driven out shelterless, who kindly directed me to the Mallory House, where I was permitted to change my clothing; and now, more warmly clad, I started out to help, if I could, all that I could. I soon found myself on the Randolph Street Bridge, the point whence my sketch was taken.

No language which I can command will serve to convey any idea of the grandeur, the awful sublimity, of the scene. For nearly two miles to the right of me the flames and smoke were rising from the ruins and ashes of dwellings, warehouses, lumberyards, the immense gasworks; and the view in that direction was bounded by an elevator towering one hundred and fifty feet in the air, which had withstood the fire of the night before, but which was now a living coal, sending upward a sheet of flame and smoke a thousand feet high.

Following the line of fire northward, the next prominent object was the Nevada House, a large brick hotel of six or seven stories in height by about one hundred feet square. For a long time this stood surrounded by the fire, and it seemed likely to resist the attack of the flames; but soon a slight column of smoke climbed up the farther corner, a light tongue of flame followed, and in three minutes thereafter the whole structure was toppling to the ground. Before us we looked upon a sight which it is impossible to describe. Everyone knows how inadequate is human language to express the grandeur of Niagara—we can only *feel* it. And yet Niagara sinks into insignificance before that towering wall of whirling, seething, roaring flame which swept on, on—devouring the most stately and massive stone buildings as though they had been the cardboard playthings of a child.

Across Lake Street the surging fire extends, and laps the cornices of the tall warehouses filled with wealth. The signs smoke, then blaze, and catch the window frames, and in another moment the interior is a mass of fire, which rushes upward to join the mad whirl of the storm above. Now it has reached the river; and if the bridge can be saved, it can be confined to its present limits. Anxious eyes watch the bridge yonder. The crowd surges back and forth—and "Ah! there's a stream! It will be saved!" A few moments of suspense, and someone says, "The elevator is on fire." "No; that's the reflection of the fire." Every eye is turned that way with the utmost anxiety. The smoke is so dense that we can hardly see. It blows aside, and what was the reflection of the fire is now a lurid glare of flame. It is doomed. Two, three minutes more, and it is a monstrous pyramid of flame and thick, black smoke, solid as stone. "My God! look there! there are men on *top*." "No!" "Wait a moment until the smoke clears away." "Yes, there are—three, *five*. They're lost! See! they are suffocating. They have crept to the corner. O God! is there no help for them? What are they doing? They are drawing something up; 'tis a rope." They fasten it; and just as the flames burst out around them the first one slides over the parapet and down, followed by one after another until the whole are saved, thank God! A universal cry of relief goes up from the crowd, and we turn to other points.

Let those readers who are familiar with New York imagine Broadway to be the river, and the East River to be the lake; then imagine the *whole* of the

city from the Battery to Grand Street in flames—one half of that space covered with such buildings as the Herald Building, Times Building, City Hall, and such blocks as Stewart's, the Metropolitan and St. Nicholas Hotels, all burning with such a blaze as swept upward from Barnum's Museum; add to this a gale of wind as severe as any you ever experience in the city—and they can form some faint conception of the scene which I have been attempting to describe, but to which no human language can do justice.

And who shall attempt to depict the scenes of misery, the agony of suffering, among that mass of people which was surging back and forth, to and fro, in every direction, on the west side? In every doorway were groups and families, on the curbs, in the gutters, everywhere—in the depots, in the stores, wherever there was a shelter, and where there was none—they could be seen huddled around their little all that the flames had spared, with misery depicted on their countenances and with despair in their hearts. I leave these scenes to more powerful pens than mine, for I too had my load of painful anxiety to bear. Where was the young friend with whom I had parted the night before? He had been burned out and was homeless. 'Twas in vain to seek him from among those thousands. Late in the afternoon I was reluctantly compelled, for the sake of my family, who knew that I had been stopping at the Sherman, to leave for someplace where I could telegraph of my safety. Seeking out the Indianapolis Depot, I purchased my ticket and awaited the opportunity to depart. Hour after hour passed in the presence of scenes of misery, the fire all the time spreading northward, until, at 7:25 P.M., we started away from the doomed city out on to the prairie. As we got away and looked back we could realize the extent of the territory, and I send you a sketch of the scene as it appeared from the windows of the train. Forty miles away we still saw the brilliant flames looming above the doomed city.

JOHN R. CHAPIN

EDITOR WHITE paid tribute to the poor who helped the rich and the rich who helped the poor, to the cartmen who worked for nothing as well as to those who demanded $150 a load. "It takes all sorts of people to make a great fire," he commented.

According to tradition, the fire had an ignoble beginning. Late on Sunday evening, October 8, a Mrs. Leary went into a stable on Dekoven Street, on the West Side near the river, to milk a cow, carrying with her a kerosene lamp. Kicked over by the cow, the lamp scattered its burning fluid over hay and straw. The little fire was fanned into fury by a high wind. Soon the flames sprang from house to house, from square to square, until the great city was afire.

John Hay, onetime Lincoln secretary, later to become an eminent American Secretary of State, was at the time of the fire an editorial writer on the staff of the *New York Tribune*. In a letter to his newspaper, he described a visit to the little warped and weatherbeaten shanty whence "came a woman with a lamp to the barn behind the house, to milk the cow with the crumpled temper, that kicked the lamp, that spilled the kerosene, that fired the straw, that burned Chicago."

"My emotions not being satisfactory from a front view of the shanty," wrote Hay, "I went around to the rear, and there found the Man of the House sitting with two of his friends. His wife, Our Lady of the Lamp—freighted with heavier disaster than that which Psyche carried to the bedside of Eros—sat at the window, knitting. I approached the Man of the House, and gave him good day. He glanced up with sleepy, furtive eyes. He seemed fearful that Chicago was coming down upon him for prompt and integral payment of that $200,000,000 his cow had knocked over."

Mrs. Leary claimed that the account of the starting of the fire was an invention. The *Chicago Journal* had given this report of an interview with her:

REPORTER: Are you the lady of the house?
MRS. LEARY: I am, sir.
REPORTER: Have you lived here long?
MRS. LEARY: Going on five years.
REPORTER: Do you own this place?
MRS. LEARY: I do.
REPORTER: Did the fire start in your barn?
MRS. LEARY: It did.
REPORTER: What was in it?

MRS. LEARY: Five cows, a horse, and about two tons of hay in the loft.

REPORTER: Is your husband an expressman?

MRS. LEARY: Indade, he is not. We all knocked our living out of those five blessed cows, and I never had a cint from the parish in all my life, and the dirty *Times* had no business to say it, bad cess to it.

REPORTER: How about that kerosene-lamp story?

MRS. LEARY: There is not a word of truth in the whole story. I always milked my cows by daylight, and never had a lamp of any kind or a candle about the barn. It must have been set afire. Two neighbors at the far end of the alley saw a strange man come up about half-past nine in the evening. He asked them was the alley straight through. They told him it was, and he went through. It was not five minutes till they saw the barn on fire. Before we had time to get out the horse or any of the cows it was all gone, and the fire was running in every direction. The boys turned to and saved the house. I hope to die if this isn't every word of it true. If you was a priest I wouldn't tell it any different.

Mrs. Leary had nothing more to say. Further questioning was useless.

The conflagration destroyed two thirds of the city's buildings, with property damage mounting near the $200,000,000 mark. One hundred thousand people were left homeless. Some 250 lost their lives. Rainfall finally ended the ravages after twenty-seven hours of horror and destruction. Three weeks after the fire a *Chicago Tribune* reporter made a tour of the city, and ended his story with these words: "There remains only a sense of desolation and ruin, so great and terrible that one can linger no longer, but gropes his way as best he can back to the light, and the homes of men."

Chicago was down, but by no means out. Her gallant spirit was epitomized by the *Chicago Tribune* comment: "But to a blow, no matter how terrible, Chicago will not succumb."

Henry Morton Stanley Raises the Stars and Stripes over Lake Tanganyika for the *Herald* and Finds a Sick Old Man Who Sought the Fountains of Herodotus

IN MARCH of 1866 a Scottish explorer-missionary named David Livingstone landed on the shore of East Africa near the mouth of the river Ruvuma. Shortly thereafter he disappeared into the bush. From that time until he died in 1873 at a remote African village seven hundred miles from the coast only one white man was to see him again. Livingstone's explorations in Africa had a double purpose—to find the source of the Nile and to bring the slave trade to an end. During this period Arab traders had penetrated into the heart of the dark continent, not only to secure copper and ivory, but also native men, women, and children. "I have been led on from one step to another," Livingstone declared, "by the overruling providence of the great Parent," in order to achieve "a great good for Africa."

To resolve all doubts concerning Livingstone's fate and to build up newspaper circulation, James Gordon Bennett, Jr., the enterprising young proprietor of *The New York Herald*, commissioned one of his star reporters to equip an expedition to search for the lost explorer. The man to whom he turned was Henry Morton Stanley. Born in North Wales in 1841, the son of a cottager, Stanley was reared in a workhouse, shipped as a cabin boy to New Orleans, and enrolled as a volunteer in the Confederate Army. Taken prisoner at Shiloh, he secured release from prison camp by enlisting in the Federal artillery. Switching sides was not too difficult for this outsider, who had no feeling whatsoever for the ideological issues of the war. "I had a secret scorn," he confessed later on, "for people who could kill one another for the sake of African slaves. There were no blackies in Wales, and why a sooty-faced nigger from a distant land should be an element of disturbance between white brothers was a puzzle to me." This shocking bit of self-revelation came with strange irony from a man who was to risk his life to rescue the greatest of all the friends of the slaves in Africa.

Stanley joined *The New York Herald* in 1868 and quickly made a reputation by his sensational stories of war in Abyssinia. In his best-selling travel book, *How I Found Livingstone* (1872), Stanley tells us the circumstances surrounding his assignment. Summoned to Bennett's quarters at the Grand Hotel in Paris on October 16, 1869, he learned from his chief that he was to find the missing explorer. "Draw a thousand pounds now," said Bennett, "and when you have gone through that, draw another thousand, and when that is spent, draw another thousand, and so on; but FIND LIVINGSTONE."

Stanley's expedition from Zanzibar into the interior of Africa was an epoch in African exploration. The meeting of reporter and explorer at Ujiji on November 10, 1871, made one of the most famous newspaper stories of all time. The first news that Stanley's expedition had been crowned with success came in a dispatch from the London correspondent to the *Herald*, published on July 2, 1872, which read:

It is with the deepest emotions of pride and pleasure that I announce the arrival this day of letters from Mr. Stanley, Chief of the *Herald* Exploring Expedition to Central Africa. I have forwarded the letters by mail. Knowing, however, the importance of the subject and the impatience with which reliable news is awaited, I hasten to telegraph a summary of the *Herald* explorer's letters, which are full of the most romantic interest, while affirming, emphatically, the safety of Dr. Livingstone.

In the story of the meeting, which the *Herald* published in full five weeks later, Stanley maintained almost to the very last paragraph a sense of high adventure, excitement, and acute tension, revealing himself at the same time as an indomitable, even ruthless, newspaper personality, not above some obviously insincere genuflections to the chauvinism of *Herald* readers.

"Dr. Livingstone, I presume?"

The New York Herald, August 10, 1872

BUNDER * UJIJI, ON LAKE TANGAN-YIKA, CENTRAL AFRICA, NOVEMBER 23, 1871—Only two months gone, and what a change in my feelings! But two months ago, what a peevish, fretful soul was mine! What a hopeless prospect presented itself before your correspondent! Arabs vowing that I would never behold the Tanganyika; Sheik, the son of Nasib, declaring me a madman to his fellows because I would not heed his words. My own men deserting, my servants whining day by day, and my white man endeavoring to impress me with the belief that we were all doomed men! And the only answer to it all is Livingstone,

* Anglo-Indian for harbor.

the hero traveler, is alongside of me, writing as hard as he can to his friends in England, India, and America, and I am quite safe and sound in health and limb. Wonderful, is it not, that such a thing should be, when the seers had foretold that it would be otherwise —that all my schemes, that all my determination, would avail me nothing? But probably you are in as much of a hurry to know how it all took place as I am to relate. So, to the recital.

September 23 I left Unyanyembe, driving before me fifty well-armed black men, loaded with the goods of the expedition, and dragging after me one white man. Several Arabs stood by my late residence to see the last of me and mine, as they felt assured there was not the least hope of their ever seeing me again. Shaw, the white man, was pale as death, and would willingly have received the order to stop behind in Unyanyembe, only he had not quite the courage to ask permission, from the fact that only the night before he had expressed a hope that I would not leave him behind, and I had promised to give him a good riding donkey and to walk after him until he recovered perfect health. However, as I gave the order to march, some of the men, in a hurry to obey the order, managed to push by him suddenly, and down he went like a dead man. The Arabs, thinking doubtless that I would not go now because my white subordinate seemed so ill, hurried in a body to the fallen man, loudly crying at what they were pleased to term my cruelty and obstinacy; but, pushing them back, I mounted Shaw on his donkey, and told them that I must see the Tanganyika first, as I had sworn to go on. Putting two soldiers, one on each side of him, I ordered Shaw to move on and not to play the fool before the Arabs, lest they should triumph over us. Three or four black laggards, loath to go, received my dogwhip across their shoulders as a gentle intimation that I was not to be balked after having fed them so long and paid them so much. And it was thus we left Unyanyembe. Not in the best humor, was it? However, where there is a will there is a way.

Once away from the hateful valley of Kwihara, once out of sight of the obnoxious fields, my enthusiasm for my work rose as newborn as when I left the coast. But my enthusiasm was short-lived, for before reaching camp I was almost delirious with fever.

* * *

IN ADDITION to the perils of jungle fever, Stanley had to deal with deserting and mutinous natives, whom he chained and flogged. Shaw, the Englishman, fell by the road and was sent back to the coast by carriers. When his rebellious guide leveled his gun at Stanley, a faithful porter dashed it aside. Stanley summarized the route for his readers:

It is possible for any of your readers so disposed to construct a map of the road on which the *Herald* expedition was now journeying, if they draw a line 150 miles south by west from Unyanyembe, then 150 miles west northwest, then ninety miles north, half east, then seventy miles west by north, and that will take them to Ujiji. [Stanley resumed his account with an extract from his journal, dated November 3, 1871:]

"Near Isinga met a caravan of eighty Waguha direct from Ujiji, bearing oil, and bound for Unyanyembe. They report that a white man was left by them five days ago at Ujiji. He had the same color as I have, wears the same shoes, the same clothes, and has hair on his face like I have, only his is white. This is Livingstone. Hurrah for Ujiji! My men share my joy, for we shall be coming back now directly; and, being so happy at the prospect, I buy three goats and five gallons of native beer, which will be eaten and drank directly."

Two marches from Malagarazi brought us to Uhha. Kawanga was the first place in Uhha where we halted. It is the village where resides the first *mutware,* or chief, to whom caravans have to pay tribute. To this man we paid twelve and a half dhoti,* upon the understanding that we would have to pay no more between here and Ujiji. Next morning, buoyed up by the hope that we should soon come to our journey's end, we had arranged to make a long march of it that day. We left Kawanga cheerfully enough. The country undulated gently before us like the prairie of Nebraska, as devoid of trees almost as our own plains. The top of every wave of land enabled us to see the scores of villages which dotted its surface, though it required keen eyes to detect at a distance the beehive and straw-thatched huts from the bleached grass of the plain. We had marched an hour, probably, and were passing a large village, with populous suburbs about it, when we saw a large party pursuing us, who, when they had come up to us, asked us how we dared pass by without paying tribute to the king of Uhha.

"We have paid it!" we said, quite astonished.

"To whom?"

"To the Chief of Kawanga."

"How much?"

"Twelve and a half dhoti."

"Oh, but that is only for himself. However, you had better stop and rest at our village until we find all about it."

But we halted in the middle of the road until the messengers they sent came back. Seeing our reluctance to halt at their village, they sent men also to Mionvu, living an arrow's flight from where we were halted, to warn him of our contumacy. Mionvu came to us, robed most royally, after the fashion of Central Africa, in a crimson cloth, arranged togalike over his shoulder and depending to his ankles, and a brand-new piece of Massachusetts

* A length of loincloth.

sheeting folded around his head. He greeted us graciously—he was the prince of politeness—shook hands first with myself, then with my head men, and cast a keen glance around, in order, as I thought, to measure our strength. Then seating himself, he spoke with deliberation something in this style:

"Why does the white man stand in the road? The sun is hot; let him seek the shelter of my village, where we can arrange this little matter between us. Does he know not that there is a king in Uhha, and that I, Mionvu, am his servant? It is a custom for us to make friends with great men, such as the white man. All Arabs and Wanguana stop here and give us cloth. Does the white man mean to go on without paying? Why should he desire war? I know he is stronger than we are here, his men have guns, and we have but spears and arrows; but Uhha is large and has plenty of people. The children of the king are many. If he comes to be a friend to us he will come to our village, give us something, and then go on his way."

The armed warriors around applauded the very commonplace speech of Mionvu because it spoke the feelings with which they viewed our bales. Certain am I, though, that one portion of his speech—that which related to our being stronger than the Wahha—was an untruth, and that he knew it, and that he only wished us to start hostilities in order that he might have a good reason for seizing the whole. But it is not new to you, of course, if you have read this letter through, that the representative of the *Herald* was held of small account here, and never one did I see who would care a bead for anything that you would ever publish against him. So the next time you wish me to enter Africa I only hope you will think it worth while to send with me one hundred good men from the *Herald* office to punish this audacious Mionvu, who fears neither *The New York Herald* nor the Star-Spangled Banner, be the latter ever so much spangled with stars.

I submitted to Mionvu's proposition, and went with him to his village, where he fleeced me to his heart's content. His demand, which he adhered to like a man who knew what he was about, was sixty dhoti for the king, twelve dhoti for himself, three for his wife, three each to three *makko*, or subchiefs, one to Mibruri's little boy; total, eighty-five dhoti, or one good bale of cloth. Not one dhoti did he abate, though I talked until six P.M. from ten A.M. I went to bed that night like a man on the verge of ruin. However, Mionvu said that we would have to pay no more in Uhha.

Pursuing our way next day, after a four hours' march, we came to Kahirigi, and quartered ourselves in a large village, governed over by Mionvu's brother, who had already been advised by Mionvu of the windfall in store for him. This man, as soon as we had set the tent, put in a claim for thirty dhoti, which I was able to reduce, after much eloquence, lasting over five hours, to twenty-six dhoti. I am short enough in relating it because I am tired of the theme; but there lives not a man in the whole United States with whom I would not gladly have exchanged positions had it been possible. I saw my fine array of bales being reduced fast. Four more such demands as Mionvu's would leave me, in unclassic phrase, "cleaned out."

After paying this last tribute, as it was night, I closed my tent and, lighting my pipe, began to think seriously upon my position and how to reach Ujiji without paying more tribute. It was high time to resort either to battle or to a strategy of some kind, possibly to striking into the jungle; but there was no jungle in Uhha, and a man might be seen miles off on its naked plains. At least this last was the plan most likely to succeed without endangering the prospects almost within reach of the expedition. Calling the guide, I questioned him as to its feasibility, first scolding him for leading me to such a strait. He said there was a Mguana, a slave of Thani Bin Abdullah, in the Coma, with whom I might consult. Sending for him, he presently came, and I began to ask him for how much he would guide us out of Uhha without being compelled to pay any more Muhongo. He replied that it was a hard thing to do, unless I had complete control over my men and they could be got to do exactly as I told them. When satisfied on this point, he entered into an agreement to show me a road—or rather to lead me to it—that might be clear of all habitations as far as Ujiji, for twelve dhoti, paid beforehand. This cloth was paid to him at once.

At half-past two A.M. the men were ready, and, stealing silently past the huts, the guide opened the gates, and we·filed out one by one as quickly as possible. The moon was bright, and by it we perceived that we were striking across a burned plain in a southerly direction, and then turned westward, parallel with the highroad, at a distance of four miles, sometimes lessening or increasing that distance as circumstances compelled us. At eight A.M. we halted for breakfast, having marched nearly six hours within the jungle which stretched for miles around us.

We were only once on the point of being discovered, through the mad freak of a weakbrained woman who was the wife of one of the black soldiers. We were crossing the knee-deep Rusizi when this woman, suddenly and without cause, took it into her head to shriek and shout as if a crocodile had bitten her. The guide implored me to stop her shrieking, or she would alarm the whole country, and we would have hundreds of angry Wahha about us. The men were already preparing to bolt—several being on the run with their loads. At my order to stop her noise she launched into another fit of hysterical shrieking, and I was compelled to stop her cries with three or four sharp cuts across her shoulders, though I felt rather ashamed of myself; but our lives and the success of the expedition were worth more, in my opinion, than a hundred of such women. As a further precaution she was gagged and her arms tied behind her, and a cord led from her waist to that of her liege lord's, who gladly took upon himself the task of looking after her, and who threatened to cut her head off if she made another outcry.

On the second morning, after crossing the Sunuzzi and Rugufu Rivers, we had just started from our camp, and as there was no moonlight the head of the column came to a village, whose inhabitants, as we heard a few voices, were about starting. We were all struck with consternation, but consulting with the guide, we dispatched our goats and chickens, and leaving them in the road, faced about, retraced our steps, and after a quarter of an hour struck up a ravine, and descending several precipitous places, about half-past six o'clock found ourselves in Ukaranga—safe and free from all tribute-taking Wahha.

Exultant shouts were given—equivalent to the Anglo-Saxon hurrah—upon our success. Addressing the men,

I asked them, "Why should we halt when but a few hours from Ujiji? Let us march a few hours more and tomorrow we shall see the white man at Ujiji, and who knows but this may be the man we are seeking? Let us go on, and after tomorrow we shall have fish for dinner and many days' rest afterwards, every day eating the fish of the Tanganyika. Stop; I think I smell the Tanganyika fish even now."

This speech was hailed with what the newspapers call "loud applause; great cheering," and "Ngema—very well, master"; "Hyah Barak-Allah—Onward, and the blessing of God be on you."

We strode from the frontier at the rate of four miles an hour, and, after six hours' march, the tired caravan entered the woods which separated the residence of the Chief of Ukaranga from the villages on the Mkuti River. As we drew near the village we went slower, unfurled the American and Zanzibar flags, presenting quite an imposing array. When we came in sight of Nyamtaga, the name of the Sultan's residence, and our flags and numerous guns were seen, the Wakaranga and their Sultan deserted their village en masse and rushed into the woods, believing that we were Mirambo's robbers, who, after destroying Unyanyembo, were come to destroy the Arabs and bunder of Ujiji; but he and his people were soon reassured, and came forward to welcome us with presents of goats and beer, all of which were very welcome after the exceedingly lengthy marches we had recently undertaken.

Rising at early dawn, our new clothes were brought forth again that we might present as decent an appearance as possible before the Arabs of Ujiji, and my helmet was well chalked and a new puggree folded around it, my boots were well oiled and my white flannels put on, and altogether, without joking, I might have paraded the streets of Bombay without attracting any very great attention.

A couple of hours brought us to the base of a hill, from the top of which the Kirangozi said we could obtain a view of the great Tanganyika Lake. Heedless of the rough path or of the toilsome steep, spurred onward by the cheery promise, the ascent was performed in a short time. I was pleased at the sight; and, as we descended, it opened more and more into view until it was revealed at last into a grand inland sea, bounded westward by an appalling and black-blue range of mountains, and stretching north and south without bounds, a gray expanse of water.

From the western base of the hill was a three hours' march, though no march ever passed off so quickly. The hours seemed to have been quarters, we had seen so much that was novel and rare to us who had been traveling so long on the highlands. The mountains bounding the lake on the eastward receded and the lake advanced. We had crossed the Ruche, or Linche, and its thick belt of tall matted grass. We had plunged into a perfect forest of them and had entered into the cultivated fields which supply the port of Ujiji with vegetables, etc., and we stood at last on the summit of the last hill of the myriads we had crossed, and the port of Ujiji, embowered in palms, with the tiny waves of the silver waters of the Tanganyika rolling at its feet, was directly below us.

We are now about descending—in a few minutes we shall have reached the spot where we imagine the object of our search—our fate will soon be decided. No one in that town knows we are coming; least of all do they know

we are so close to them. If any of them ever heard of the white man at Unyanyembe they must believe we are there yet. We shall take them all by surprise, for no other but a white man would dare leave Unyanyembe for Ujiji with the country in such a distracted state—no other but a crazy white man, whom Sheik, the son of Nasib, is going to report to Syed or Prince Burghash for not taking his advice.

Well, we are but a mile from Ujiji now, and it is high time we should let them know a caravan is coming; so "Commence firing" is the word passed along the length of the column, and gladly do they begin. They have loaded their muskets half full, and they roar like the broadside of a line-of-battle ship. Down go the ramrods, sending huge charges home to the breech, and volley after volley is fired. The flags are fluttered; the banner of America is in front, waving joyfully; the guide is in the zenith of his glory. The former residents of Zanzita will know it directly and will wonder—as well they may—as to what it means. Never were the Stars and Stripes so beautiful to my mind—the breeze of the Tanganyika has such an effect on them. The guide blows his horn, and the shrill, wild clangor of it is far and near; and still the cannon muskets tell the noisy seconds. By this time the Arabs are fully alarmed; the natives of Ujiji, Waguha, Warundi, Wanguana, and I know not whom hurry up by the hundreds to ask what it all means—this fusillading, shouting, and blowing of horns and flag flying. There are Yambos shouted out to me by the dozen, and delighted Arabs have run up breathlessly to shake my hand and ask anxiously where I come from. But I have no patience with them. The expedition goes far too slow. I should like to settle the vexed question by one personal view. Where is he? Has he fled?

Suddenly a man—a black man—at my elbow shouts in English, "How do you do, sir?"

"Hello, who the deuce are you?"

"I am the servant of Dr. Livingstone," he says; and before I can ask any more questions he is running like a madman towards the town.

We have at last entered the town. There are hundreds of people around me—I might say thousands without exaggeration, it seems to me. It is a grand triumphal procession. As we move, they move. All eyes are drawn towards us. The expedition at last comes to a halt; the journey is ended for a time; but I alone have a few more steps to make.

There is a group of the most respectable Arabs, and as I come nearer I see the white face of an old man among them. He has a cap with a gold band around it, his dress is a short jacket of red blanket cloth, and his pants—well, I didn't observe. I am shaking hands with him. We raise our hats, and I say:

"Dr. Livingstone, I presume?"

And he says, "Yes."

*Finis coronat opus.**

IN HIS TRAVEL book Stanley felt impelled to embroider the circumstances of the meeting, with the result that a stilted, wooden dialogue of doubtful authenticity is preserved. When he wrote the letter to the *Herald* on November 23, 1871, he admitted that he neglected to observe the kind of trousers Livingstone was wearing. But a year later he was able to repair that lapse in his memory. The doctor had on "a pair of gray tweed trousers." His enlarged version of the meeting with the explorer:

I would have run to him, only I was a coward in the presence of such a mob—would have embraced him, but that I did not know how he would receive me; so I did what moral cowardice and false pride suggested was the best thing—walked deliberately to him, took off my hat, and said:

"Dr. Livingstone, I presume?"

"Yes," said he, with a kind, cordial smile, lifting his cap slightly.

I replaced my hat on my head, and he replaced his cap, and we both grasped hands. I then said aloud: "I thank God, doctor, I have been permitted to see you."

He answered, "I feel thankful that I am here to welcome you."

Yes, it was a stroke of inspiration when Stanley cut the original story at the place he did!

On March 14 of the following year Livingstone's journal briefly records: "Mr. Stanley leaves." Less reticent, but equally convinced of the significance of his mission, Stanley records: "We walked side by side; the men lifted their voices in a song. I took long looks at Livingstone to impress his features thoroughly on my memory." Then Stanley begged Livingstone to turn back. "You have done what few men could do," were Livingstone's last words in reply—the last he ever spoke to a white man—"far better than some great travelers I know. And I am grateful to you for what you

---

* The end crowns the work.

have done for me. God guide you safe home and bless you, my friend." To this valedictory Stanley replied: "And may God bring you safely back to us all, my dear friend. Farewell."

News of Stanley's expedition found British scientists skeptical. "It must be Livingstone," remarked the great orientalist, Rawlinson, in a letter to the London *Times,* "that has discovered Stanley." But at length Stanley was given his day in court. The pundits and the professors listened to his learned paper on the results of Livingstone's recent explorations, and even Rawlinson publicly conceded "the great value attached by the Royal Geographical Society to Mr. Stanley's services."

Livingstone, though broken in health, was still fired by a desire to find the ancient fountains of Herodotus, believed to be the source of the Nile, but he was fated to die in the course of a new expedition into the interior. In a letter to *The New York Herald,* one of his last statements before he died, he reiterated his fight against the slave trade and made a remark soon to be inscribed upon his grave. "All I can say in my solitude is, may Heaven's rich blessing come down on everyone—American, English, Turk—who will help to heal this open sore of the world." Thoroughly sold on the future of Africa, Stanley devoted many of the remaining years of his life to further explorations, notably in the Congo. His stories of pigmies, Amazons, cannibals, exotic animals, rubber-producing plants, and other wonders of the dark continent served to precipitate the undignified "scramble for Africa" among the great powers.

Mark Twain Delivers a Persian Potentate to London and Conjugates the Word "Shah"

I N 1867 the owners of the *Alta California*, San Francisco's pioneer paper,* commissioned Mark Twain to travel to the Mediterranean and the Holy Land and report what he saw. His weekly letters in the Sunday *Alta* were the basis for *The Innocents Abroad*, which appeared in 1869 and established Mark Twain's literary reputation. The defiantly American attitude of the ex-river pilot and quondam silver prospector, his uncompromising democracy, and his uninhibited colloquial style won him an enormous reading public. But despite the demands upon him as a public lecturer, despite attractive assignments from newspapers to continue his hilarious travels abroad, Mark Twain did not abandon his editorial career. For several years he served as editor and part owner of the Buffalo *Express*, and throughout the rest of his life he continued to write newspaper pieces.

When he was in England in the summer of 1873, Mark Twain was prevailed upon by *The New York Herald* to cover the approaching visit of the Shah of Persia to Britain. For weeks Continental and English newspapers had regaled their readers with the accounts of the European tour of the Oriental potentate. The Shah's visitation provided a perfect field day for Mark Twain's own special brand of humorous first-person reporting. In all, he wrote five stories, appearing in the *Herald* on July 1, 4, 9, 11, and 19, 1873, under the following headlines:

O'SHAH
MARK TWAIN SETS OUT TO IMPRESS "THE KING OF KINGS"

THE SHAH
MARK TWAIN EXECUTES HIS CONTRACT AND DELIVERS
THE PERSIAN TO LONDON

SHA-DOINGS
PERSIAN POTENTATE BEING "IMPRESSED" BY JOHN BULL

SHAH'D
MARK TWAIN HOOKS THE PERSIAN OUT OF THE ENGLISH CHANNEL

T-SHAH!
MARK TWAIN GIVES THE ROYAL PERSIAN A "SEND-OFF"

A somewhat condensed version of the series:

---

* The newspaper first appeared in Monterey on August 15, 1846, as the *Californian*, then, with the discovery of gold, was removed to Yerba Buena (now San Francisco), was merged with the *California Star*, and was issued thereafter as the *Alta California*.

*"Shah, O'Shah, Shah'd, T-Shah! The only
way whereby you may pronounce the Shah's
title correctly is by taking a pinch of snuff"*

The New York Herald, July 1, 4, 9, 11, 19, 1873

LONDON, JUNE 18, 1873—"Would you like to go over to Belgium and help bring the Shah to England?"

I said I was willing.

"Very well, then. Here is an order from the Admiralty which will admit you on board Her Majesty's ship *Lively*, now lying at Ostend, and you can return in her day after tomorrow."

That was all. That was the end of it. Without stopping to think, I had in a manner taken upon myself to bring the Shah of Persia to England. I could not otherwise regard the conversation I had just held with the London representative of *The New York Herald*. The amount of discomfort I endured for the next two or three hours cannot be set down in words. I could not eat, sleep, talk, smoke with any satisfaction. The more I thought the thing over the more oppressed I felt. What was the Shah to me, that I should go to all this worry and trouble on his account? Where was there the least occasion for taking upon myself such a responsibility? If I got him over all right, well. But if I lost him? if he died on my hands? if he got drowned? It was depressing, any way I looked at it. In the end I said to myself, "If I get this Shah over here safe and sound I never will take charge of another one." And yet, at the same time I kept thinking: "This country has treated me well, stranger as I am, and this foreigner is the country's guest—that is enough, I will help him out; I will fetch him over; I will land him in

London, and say to the British people, 'Here is your Shah; give me a receipt.' "

I felt easy in my mind now, and was about to go to bed, but something occurred to me. I took a cab and drove downtown and routed out that *Herald* representative.

"Where is Belgium?" said I.

"Where is Belgium? I never heard such a question!"

"That doesn't make any difference to me. If I have got to fetch this Shah I don't wish to go to the wrong place. Where is Belgium? Is it a shilling fare in a cab?"

He explained that it was in foreign parts—the first place I have heard of lately which a body could not go to in a cab for a shilling.

I said I could not go alone, because I could not speak foreign languages well, could not get up in time for the early train without help, and could not find my way. I said it was enough to have the Shah on my hands; I did not wish to have everything piled on me. Mr. Blank was then ordered to go with me. I do like to have somebody along to talk to when I go abroad.

When I got home I sat down and thought the thing all over. I wanted to go into this enterprise understandingly. What was the main thing? That was the question. A little reflection informed me. For two weeks the London papers had sung just one continual song to just one continual tune, and the idea of it all was "how to impress the Shah." These papers had told all about the St. Petersburg splendors, and had said at the end that splendors would no longer answer; that England could not outdo Russia in that respect; therefore some other way of impressing the Shah must be contrived. And these papers had also told all about the Shahstic reception in Prussia and its attendant military pageantry. England could not improve on that sort of thing—she could not impress the Shah with soldiers; something else must be tried. And so on. Column after column, page after page of agony about how to "impress the Shah." At last they had hit upon a happy idea—a grand naval exhibition. That was it! A man brought up in Oriental seclusion and simplicity, a man who had never seen anything but camels and such things, could not help being surprised and delighted with the strange novelty of ships. The distress was at an end. England heaved a great sigh of relief; she knew at last how to impress the Shah.

My course was very plain, now, after that bit of reflection. All I had to do was to go over to Belgium and impress the Shah. I failed to form any definite plan as to the process, but I made up my mind to manage it somehow. I said to myself, "I will impress this Shah or there shall be a funeral that will be worth contemplating."

[Mark Twain and his companion took the train to Dover.]

We stepped aboard the little packet and steamed away. The sea was perfectly smooth, and painfully brilliant in the sunshine. There were no curiosities in the vessel except the passengers and a placard in French setting forth the transportation fares for various kinds of people. The lithographer probably considered that placard a triumph. It was printed in green, blue, red, black, and yellow; no individual line in one color, even the individual letters were separately colored. For instance, the first letter of a word would be blue, the next red, the next green, and so on. The placard looked as if it had the smallpox or something. I inquired the artist's name and place of business, intending to hunt him up and kill him when I had time; but no one could tell me. In the list of prices first-class passengers were set down at fifteen shillings and fourpence, and dead bodies at one pound ten shillings and eightpence—just double price! That is Belgian morals, I suppose. I never say a harsh thing unless I am greatly stirred; but in my opinion the man who would take advantage of a dead person would do almost any odious thing. I publish this scandalous discrimination against the most helpless class among us in order that people intending to die abroad may come back by some other line.

[Arrived at Ostend, Mark Twain idled about until it was time to board the *Lively*, which was to carry the Shah's brother and the Grand Vizier. The Shah himself was scheduled to be conveyed in the *Vigilant*, accompanied by Sir Henry Rawlinson, the Persian scholar and the Queen's special ambassador. An impressive assemblage awaited the arrival of the Shah's train from Brussels.]

Now the train was signaled, and everybody got ready for the great event. The Belgian regiment straightened itself up, and some two hundred Flounders * arrived and took conspicuous position on a little mound. I was a little afraid that this would impress the Shah; but I was soon occupied with other interests. The train of thir-

---

* By which Mark Twain meant the people of Flanders. "I feel sure I have eaten a creature of that name or seen it in an aquarium or a menagerie, or in a picture or somewhere."

teen cars came tearing in and stopped abreast the ships. Music and guns began an uproar. Odd-looking Persian faces and felt hats (brimless stovepipes) appeared at the car windows.

Some gorgeous English officials fled down the carpet from the *Vigilant*. They stopped at a long car with the royal arms upon it, uncovered their heads, and unlocked the car door. Then the Shah stood up in it and gave us a good view. He was a handsome, strong-featured man, with a rather European fairness of complexion; had a mustache, wore spectacles, seemed of a good height and graceful build and carriage, and looked about forty or a shade less. He was very simply dressed—brimless stovepipe and close-buttoned dark-green military suit, without ornament. No, not wholly without ornament, for he had a band of two inches wide worn over his shoulder and down across his breast, scarf fashion, which band was one solid glory of fine diamonds.

A Persian official appeared in the Shah's rear and enveloped him in an ample quilt—or cloak, if you please— which was lined with fur. The outside of it was of a whitish color and elaborately needleworked in Persian patterns like an India shawl. The Shah stepped out, and the official procession formed about him and marched down the carpet and on board the *Vigilant* to slow music. Not a Flounder raised a cheer. All the small fry swarmed out of the train now.

The Shah walked back alongside his fine cabin, looking at the assemblage of silent, solemn Flounders; the correspondent of the London *Telegraph* was hurrying along the pier and took off his hat and bowed to the "King of Kings," and the King of Kings gave a polite military salute in return. This was the commencement of the excite-

ment. The success of the breathless *Telegraph* man made all the other London correspondents mad, every man of whom flourished his stovepipe recklessly and cheered lustily, some of the more enthusiastic varying the exercise by lowering their heads and elevating their coattails. Seeing all this, and feeling that if I was to "impress the Shah" at all, now was my time, I ventured a little squeaky yell, quite distinct from the other shouts, but just as hearty. His Shahship heard and saw and saluted me in a manner that was, I considered, an acknowledgment of my superior importance. I do not know that I ever felt so ostentatious and absurd before. All the correspondents came aboard, and then the Persian baggage came also, and was carried across the ship alongside of ours. When she could hold no more we took somewhere about a hundred trunks and boxes on board our vessel. Two boxes fell into the water, and several sailors jumped in and saved one, but the other was lost. However, it probably contained nothing but a few hundred pounds of diamonds and things.

At last we got under way and steamed out through a long slip, the piers on either side being crowded with Flounders; but never a cheer. A battery of three guns on the starboard pier boomed a royal salute, and we swept out to sea, the *Vigilant* in the lead, we right in her wake, and the baggage ship in ours. Within fifteen minutes everybody was well acquainted; a general jollification set in, and I was thoroughly glad I had come over to fetch the Shah.

LONDON, JUNE 19, 1873—Leaving Ostend, we went out to sea under a clear sky and upon smooth water—so smooth, indeed, that its surface was scarcely rippled.

[Mark Twain then describes the

naval spectacle, including the salute from the thirty-five-ton guns of the *Devastation,* "the mightiest war vessel afloat."]

When we first sailed away from Ostend I found myself in a dilemma. I had no notebook. But "any port in a storm," as the sailors say. I found a fair, full pack of ordinary playing cards in my overcoat pocket—one always likes to have something along to amuse children with—and really they proved excellent to take notes on, although bystanders were a bit inclined to poke fun at them and ask facetious questions. But I was content; I made all the notes I needed. The aces and low "spot" cards are very good indeed to write memoranda on, but I will not recommend the king and jacks.

Referring to the seven of hearts, I find that this naval exhibition and journey from Ostend to Dover is going to cost the government £500,000. Got it from a correspondent. It is a round sum.

Referring to the ace of diamonds, I find that along in the afternoon we sighted a fresh fleet of men-of-war coming to meet us. The rest of the diamonds, down to the eight spot (nines and tens are no good for notes), are taken up with details of that spectacle. Most of the clubs and hearts refer to matters immediately following that, but I really can hardly do anything with them because I have forgotten what was trumps.

The Duke of Edinburgh and Prince Arthur received the Shah in state and then all of us—princes, Shahs, ambassadors, Grand Viziers, and newspaper correspondents—climbed aboard the train and started off to London just like so many brothers.

From Dover to London it was a sight to see. Seventy miles of human beings in a jam—the gaps were not worth mentioning—and every man, woman, and child waving hat or handkerchief and cheering. I wondered—could not tell—could not be sure—could only wonder—would this "impress the Shah"? I would have given anything to know. But—well, it ought—but—still one could not tell.

And by and by we burst into the London railway station—a very large station it is—and found it wonderfully decorated and all the neighboring streets packed with cheering citizens. Would this impress the Shah? I—I— well, I could not yet feel certain.

The Prince of Wales received the Shah—ah, you should have seen how gorgeously the Shah was dressed now —he was like the sun in a total eclipse of rainbows—yes, the Prince received him, put him in a grand open carriage, got in and made him sit over further and not "crowd," the carriage clattered out of the station, all London fell apart on either side and lifted a perfectly national cheer, and just at that instant the bottom fell out of the sky and forty deluges came pouring down at once!

The great strain was over, the crushing suspense at an end. I said, "Thank God, this will impress the Shah."

Now came the long files of Horse Guards in silver armor. We took the great Persian to Buckingham Palace. I never stirred till I saw the gates open and close upon him with my own eyes and knew he was there. Then I said:

"England, here is your Shah; take him and be happy, but don't ever ask me to fetch over another one."

This contract has been pretty straining on me.

LONDON, JUNE 21, 1873—After delivering the Shah at the gates of that unsightly pile of dreary grandeur known as Buckingham Palace I cast all responsibility for him aside for the time being, and experienced a sense of relief and likewise an honest pride in my success such as no man can feel who has not had a Shah at nurse (so to speak) for three days.

[Mark Twain then proceeds to describe the Guildhall Ball and the appearance of the Shah at the opera.]

As regards the momentous occasion of the opera, this evening, I found myself in a grievous predicament, for a republican. The tickets were all sold long ago, so I must either go as a member of the royal family or not at all. After a good deal of reflection it seemed best not to mix up with that class lest a political significance might be put upon it. We are all gone mad, I do believe. Eleven hundred five-shilling lunatics and a hundred two-guinea maniacs. The *Herald* purchased a ticket and created me one of the latter, along with two or three more of the staff.

At last came the long-expected millennium himself, His Imperial Majesty the Shah, with the charming Princess of Wales on his arm. He had all his jewels on, and his diamond shaving brush in his hat front. He shone like a window with the westering sun on it.

We are certainly gone mad. We scarcely look at the young colossus who is to reign over 70,000,000 of people and the mightiest empire in extent which exists today. We have no eyes but for this splendid barbarian, who is lord over a few deserts and a modest ten million of ragamuffins—a man who has never done anything to win our gratitude or excite our admiration, except that he managed to starve a million of his subjects to death in twelve months. If he had starved the rest I suppose we would set up a monument to him now.

LONDON, JUNE 26, 1873—I suppose I am the only member of the Shah's family who is not wholly broken down and worn out; and, to tell the truth, there is not much of me left. If you have ever been limited to four days in Paris or Rome or Jerusalem and been "rushed" by a guide you can form a vague, faraway sort of conception of what the Shah and the rest of us have endured during these late momentous days. If this goes on we may as well get ready for the imperial inquest.

[Mark Twain then reports the spectacle of the grand fleet at Portsmouth.] The crash and roar of these great guns was as unsettling a sound as I have ever heard at short range. I took off my hat and acknowledged the salute, of course, though it seemed to me that it would have been better manners if they had saluted the Lord Mayor, inasmuch as he was on board.

LONDON, JUNE 30, 1873—For the present we are done with the Shah in London. He is gone to the country to be further "impressed." True, his engagement is not yet completed, for he is still billed to perform at one or two places; but curiosity is becoming sated, and he will hardly draw as good houses as heretofore. Whenever a star has to go to the provinces it is a bad sign.

This must be a dreary, unsatisfactory country to him, where one's desires are thwarted at every turn. Last week he woke up at three in the morning and demanded of the Vizier on watch by his bedside that the ballet dancers be summoned to dance before him. The Vizier prostrated himself upon the floor and said:

"O king of kings, light of the world, source of human peace and contentment, the glory and admiration of the age, turn away thy sublime countenance, let not thy fateful frown wither thy slave; for behold the dancers dwell wide asunder in the desert wastes of London, and not in many hours could they be gathered together."

The Shah could not even speak, he was so astounded with the novelty of giving a command that could not be obeyed. He sat still a moment, suffering, then wrote in his tablets these words:

"Mem.—Upon arrival in Teheran, let the Vizier have the coffin which has just been finished for the late general of the household troops—it will save time."

He then got up and set his boots outside the door to be blacked and went back to bed, calm and comfortable, making no more to-do about giving away that costly coffin than I would about spending a couple of shillings.

If the mountains of money spent by civilized Europe in entertaining the Shah shall win him to adopt some of the mild and merciful ways that prevail in Christian realms it will have been money well and wisely laid out. If he learns that a throne may rest as firmly upon the affections of a people as upon their fears; that charity and justice may go hand in hand without detriment to the authority of the sovereign; that an enlarged liberty granted to the subjected need not impair the power of the monarch; if he learns these things Persia will be the gainer by his journey, and the money which Europe has expended in entertaining him will have been profitably invested. That the Shah needs a hint or two in these directions is shown by the language of the following petition, which has just reached him from certain Parsees residing here and in India. [The petition denounces the poll tax and certain economic and legal discriminations against the Parsees in Persia suffering under the Moslem yoke.]

We are all sorry to see the Shah leave us, and yet are glad on his account. We have had all the fun and he all the fatigue. He would not have lasted much longer here. I am just reminded that the only way whereby you may pronounce the Shah's title correctly is by taking a pinch of snuff. The result will be "t-Shah!"

As HUCKLEBERRY FINN later remarked about Mark Twain, "he told the truth, mainly. There was things which he stretched, but mainly he told the truth." No more accurate epitome can be found of Mark Twain's autobiographical reporting.

Neither the Shah nor any other royal personage ever succeeded in turning Mark Twain's head. His daughter, Jean, once commented on an invitation to Mark to dine with the Kaiser. "Papa," she declared, "the way things are going, pretty soon there won't be anybody left for you to get acquainted with but God."

Mark Twain's handling of the "King of Kings" was thoroughly consistent with his attitude toward royalty. As Huck Finn succinctly observed to Jim, "All I say is, kings is kings, and you got to make allowances. Take them all around, they're a mighty ornery lot. It's the way they're raised." In *A Connecticut Yankee at King Arthur's Court* (1889) the view is expressed that "there is nothing diviner about a king than there is about a tramp, after all." In his *Notebook* (1935) Mark Twain was even more uninhibited. "There was never a throne which did not represent a crime" is one characteristic utterance, and, again, "There are shams and shams; there are frauds and frauds, but the transparentest of all is the sceptered one."

An unreconstructed democrat, Mark Twain in his later years was somewhat pessimistic about the survival of the democratic way of life. "Strip the human race absolutely naked," he confessed in his *Notebook,* "and it would be a real democracy. But the introduction of even a rag of tiger skin, or a cow tail, could make a badge of distinction and be the beginning of monarchy." American snobbery came in for barbed comment. "In public we scoff at titles and hereditary privileges, but privately we hanker after them, and when we get the chance we buy them for cash and a daughter." He believed that the American republic was inevitably drifting toward centralization and monarchy. In 1908 he felt he had no choice. "I shall vote for the continuance of the monarchy," he declared at that time. "That is to say, I shall vote for Mr. Taft."

A Young American Reporter, Januarius Aloysius MacGahan, Provides the Spark that Ignites the Russo-Turkish War

JAMES GORDON BENNETT, JR., go-getting, flashy, ruthless, was the great thrill purveyor of the 1870's. The man who sent Stanley to find Livingstone was constantly on the lookout for intrepid newsmen to explore frozen wastes and penetrate remotest jungles. With the addition of Januarius Aloysius MacGahan to the staff of foreign correspondents working for *The New York Herald*, Bennett gave irrefutable proof of his genius as a talent scout.

An Ohio farm boy of Irish ancestry, MacGahan gained his reputation during the Franco-Prussian War by interviewing such notables as Gambetta, Louis Blanc, and Victor Hugo. His friendliness toward Dombrowski, the Communard leader, during the siege of Paris almost cost him his life, which was spared through the timely intercession of the American minister.

In 1873 the *Herald* sent MacGahan to penetrate the iron curtain that an expanding Russia had dropped over her Asiatic lands, and, specifically, to report a Cossack expedition into Central Asia to reduce Turkestan, the only remaining state in that area that refused to recognize her supremacy. Russia's main objective was the Moslem stronghold of Khiva. In pursuit of the Russian army, MacGahan took the dangerous trail alone, except for an old Tartar interpreter, a treacherous guide, a servant, and six horses. Driving across wild stretches of sand, suffering the agonies of almost unendurable thirst, he caught up at last with the Russian rear guard, only to be forbidden to proceed further. Escaping surveillance, MacGahan plunged across the shifting sands, with the polestar as his guide, and a troop of Cossacks in hot pursuit. After a journey of a month's duration, acclaimed in Central Asia "as by far the most wonderful thing that had ever been done there," he arrived at the headquarters of the Russian General Kaufmann. Hard upon his heels rode the fast-charging cavalrymen, driving six hundred miles across the desert to arrest him. At this point MacGahan did some fast talking and managed to keep out of jail.

On June 10, 1873, MacGahan entered Khiva with the Russian troops, but the cursory dispatch, date-lined June 11, which did not appear in *The New York Herald* until August 4, gave no hint of the desperate chase or of the Arabian night's entertainment that the reporter had experienced the previous evening. The dispatch summarized Russian casualties, revealed that forty thousand slaves had been set free by the conquerors, and pictured Khiva as "a dirty, squalid town," and the palace of the Khan as "shabby." What he did not tell the readers that day was that the palace had been the scene of one of the nerviest exploits ever credited to any American reporter.

When he was not writing under pressure, MacGahan told the story at length in his book published the following year, entitled *Campaigning on the Oxus, and the Fall of Khiva.* Among "the crowd of weeping and distracted women" in the conquered city, the American reporter noted a young girl, about eighteen, whose beauty, calm demeanor, and "noble appearance" convinced him that she was the sultana of the Khivan harem. Several times she turned her eyes imploringly to him. "I never in my life before so much regretted my ignorance of an unknown tongue," confessed the young Ohioan. Haunted by the dark-eyed beauty, he determined to help her if he could, and at midnight he crept past the sentinels, entered the palace court, revolver in hand, and made his way to the harem.

Through a hopeless labyrinth of intricate passages MacGahan advanced. For a while he thought he was trapped in a dungeon, but later investigation revealed that "imprisonment is a refinement of cruelty unknown at Khiva. They cut off people's noses, ears, and heads, whip them, stone them to death, but never imprison them." Once he struck a match to light the small piece of candle he carried, and found to his horror that he was on the verge of a deep well. Another time he entered a small room and, noting a pile of black earth in one corner, stooped down and picked up a handful, but dropped it in terror. It was gunpowder. "There was enough powder in that little room," MacGahan declared, "to blow the whole palace to atoms." At last he came to the chambers of the beauty in distress, and, using sign language, managed to convey to her that she had nothing to fear from the Russians. When he took leave of her, "she kissed hands to me, and then disappeared in the dark corridor." The next morning, when food was sent into the harem, it was found to be empty. The women had all escaped! The exemplary restraint which the twenty-nine-year-old newsman had demonstrated in the circumstances made the story even more extraordinary.

MacGahan's greatest reportorial feats were not performed for Bennett's *Herald,* for, after reporting the Carlist War in Spain and an Arctic expedition, MacGahan broke with Bennett. However, he did not have to wait long for an assignment. In the summer of 1876 the London *Daily News,* that great organ of the Liberal party, commissioned him to go to the field and investigate the alleged atrocities committed by the bashi-bazouks in Bulgaria.

For centuries the people of the Balkans had chafed under Turkish rule. In 1875 Herzegovina revolted, and in May of the following year insurrection flared up in Bulgaria. To crush these revolts the Turks resorted to terrorist measures. On June 23, 1876, *The Daily News* published a letter

from its "Own Correspondent" resident at Constantinople, Sir Edwin
Pears, with the following startling lead:

Dark rumors have been whispered about Constantinople during the last month of
horrible atrocities committed in Bulgaria. The local newspapers have given mysterious
hints about correspondence from the interior which they have been obliged to suppress.
I have hitherto refrained from mentioning these rumors, or from stating what I have
heard, but they are now gradually assuming definiteness and consistency, and cruelties
are being revealed which place those committed in Herzegovina and Bosnia altogether
in the background.

This particular dispatch inspired Gladstone to open fire upon the Disraeli
ministry, but Disraeli persisted in referring to the "Bulgarian atrocities"
as "a Russian trap to call for the expulsion of the Turks from Europe."
When the British minister at Constantinople, Sir Henry Elliot, exhibited
what even the Prime Minister privately conceded to be a "lamentable want
of energy" in tracking down these rumors, and went so far as to whitewash
Turkish conduct, *The Daily News* decided upon an independent investigation.

MacGahan reached Philippopolis, the center of the district in which the
atrocities were perpetrated, on July 23, and, in company with Eugene
Schuyler, the American Consul General for Turkey, proceeded at once to
interview survivors. His sensational letters to *The Daily News,* date-lined
July 28 to August 26, were, according to the editors of that paper, "republished more extensively than any letters ever before by the daily and
weekly press." To meet the demand, the newspaper soon published them in
pamphlet form, from which this condensation is taken.

"These Turks have no pity, no compassion,
no bowels"

*The Turkish Atrocities in Bulgaria: Letters of the Special Commissioner of "The Daily
News," J. A. MacGahan, Esq.* (London, 1876)

PHILIPPOPOLIS, JULY 28—I came with
the mission of investigating and making a report. I think I came in a fair
and impartial frame of mind. I had
determined to see for myself wherever
it was possible; to make inquiries, to
weigh and compare statements, to
carefully sift evidence and get at the
plain unvarnished truth, and not allow
my mind to be influenced by unsup-
ported assertions on either side.

I have scarcely more than begun the
investigation, and the frame of mind I
had resolved to maintain at any haz-
ard has already passed away. I fear I
am no longer impartial, and I certainly
am no longer cool. There are certain
things that cannot be investigated in
a judicial frame of mind. There are
facts which, when perceived, send the
blood through the veins with an angry
rush and cause the muscles to contract

in sudden anger. There are things too horrible to allow anything like calm inquiry; things the vileness of which the eye refuses to look upon, and which the mind refuses to contemplate. There are facts which repel and revolt; facts which, when you go about among them, fly in your face.

Such is the nature of the facts I came to investigate. I have already investigated enough to feel convinced that, except from a purely statistical point of view, further investigation would be unnecessary. The atrocities admitted on all hands by those friendly to the Turks, and by the Turks themselves, are enough and more than enough. I do not care to go on heaping up the mournful count. When you are met in the outset of your investigation with the admission that sixty or seventy villages have been burned; that some fifteen thousand people have been slaughtered, of whom a large part were women and children, you begin to feel that it is useless to go any further. When, in addition to this, you have the horrid details of the violent outrages committed upon women, the hacking to pieces of helpless children, and spitting them upon bayonets; and when you have these details reported you by the hundreds, not by Bulgarians, but by the different consuls at Philippopolis and the German officials on the railway, as well as Greeks, Armenians, priests, missionaries, and even Turks themselves, you begin to feel that any further investigation is superfluous.

PEŠTERA, AUGUST 1—We have just passed through the village of Raddovo on our way here, where we stop for the night before continuing tomorrow to Batak. Raddovo was apparently a very flourishing little place, and, to tell the truth, it has suffered less, perhaps, than the majority of the towns that were left to the tender care of the bashi-bazouks. It was a village of 160 houses, of which not one is left standing, and the inhabitants are now living under sheds of straw, constructed in nooks and corners of the black and crumbling walls. They gathered around us when we stopped in the middle of the once flourishing place, and timidly told us their story. They had offered no resistance at all to the bashi-bazouks, but simply ran away when they heard the Turks were coming. Having received timely notice, they had nearly all escaped, and only twenty-two men had been killed in all. The women and children had all been saved.

When the people returned to their smoking homes, they found themselves completely ruined. There was not a stick of furniture nor a cooking utensil left, and all their cattle, sheep, and horses had been driven off. Their harvests were still standing in the fields, and they are unable to gather and save them without their cattle, which the Turks refuse to restore. Unless the poor people can get back their cattle, gather their harvests, and rebuild their houses, they will be in a state of destitution by next winter fearful to think of.

TATAR PAZARDZHIK, AUGUST 2—Since my letter of yesterday I have supped full of horrors. Nothing has yet been said of the Turks that I do not now believe; nothing could be said of them that I should not think probable and likely. There is, it would seem, a point in atrocity beyond which discrimination is impossible, when mere comparison, calculation, measurement, are out of the question, and this point the Turks have already passed. You can follow them no further. The way is blocked up by mountains of hideous facts, beyond which you cannot see and do not care to go. You feel that it is time to turn back; that you have seen enough.

But let me tell you what we saw at Batak. [MacGahan describes the deserted village, with its silent mill wheels, its slopes barren of cattle, a place "as lonely as a graveyard."]

As we approached, our attention was directed to some dogs on a slope overlooking the town. We turned aside from the road, and, passing over the debris of two or three walls, and through several gardens, urged our horses up the ascent towards the dogs. They barked at us in an angry manner, and then ran off into the adjoining fields. I observed nothing peculiar as we mounted, until my horse stumbled, when, looking down, I perceived he had stepped on a human skull, partly hid among the grass. It was quite dry and hard, and might, to all appearances, have been there for two or three years, so well had the dogs done their work. A few steps further there was another, and beside it a part of a skeleton, likewise white and dry. As we ascended, bones, skeletons, and skulls became more frequent, but here they had not been picked so clean, for there were fragments of half-dry, half-putrid flesh still clinging to them. At last we came to a kind of little plateau or shelf on the hillside, where the ground was nearly level, with the exception of a little indentation where the head of a hollow broke through. We rode towards this with the intention of crossing it, but all suddenly drew rein with an exclamation of horror, for right before us, almost beneath our horses' feet, was a sight that made us shudder. It was a heap of skulls, intermingled with bones from all parts of the human body, skeletons nearly

entire, rotting clothing, human hair, and putrid flesh, lying there in one foul heap, around which the grass was growing luxuriantly. It emitted a sickening odor like that of a dead horse, and it was here the dogs had been seeking a hasty repast when our untimely approach interrupted them.

There was not a roof left, not a whole wall standing; all was a mass of ruins, from which arose, as we listened, a low plaintive wail, like the "keening" of the Irish over their dead, that filled the little valley and gave it voice. We had the explanation of this curious sound when we afterwards descended into the village. We looked again at the heap of skulls and skeletons before us, and we observed that they were all small, and that the articles of clothing, intermingled with them and lying about, were all parts of women's apparel. These, then, were all women and girls. From my saddle I counted about a hundred skulls, not including those that were hidden beneath the others in the ghastly heap, nor those that were scattered far and wide through the fields. The skulls were nearly all separate from the rest of the bones; the skeletons were nearly all headless. These women had all been beheaded.

We descended into the town. Within the shattered walls of the first house we came to was a woman sitting on a heap of rubbish, rocking herself to and fro, and wailing a kind of monotonous chant, half sung, half sobbed, that was not without a wild discordant melody. This was the explanation of the curious sound we had heard when up on the hill. As we advanced there were more and more; sitting on the heaps of stones that covered the floors of their houses; others walking up and down before their doors, wringing their hands and repeating the same despairing wail. There were few tears in this universal mourning. It was dry, hard, and despairing. As we proceeded, most of them fell into line behind us, and they finally formed a procession of four or five hundred people, mostly women and children, who followed us about, wherever we went, with mournful cries. Such a sound as their united voices sent up to heaven I hope I never hear again.

The number of children killed in these massacres is something enormous. They were often spitted on bayonets, and we have several stories from eyewitnesses who saw little babes carried about the streets, both here and at Otluk-kui, on the point of bayonets. The reason is simple. When a Mohammedan has killed a certain number of infidels he is sure of paradise, no matter what his sins may be. Mohammed probably intended that only armed men should count, but the ordinary Mussulman takes the precept in broader acceptation, and counts women and children as well. Here in Batak the bashi-bazouks, in order to swell the count, ripped open pregnant women and killed the unborn infants.

We asked about the skulls and bones we had seen up on the hill upon first arriving in the village. These, we were told, were the bones of about two hundred young girls, who had first been captured and reserved for a fate worse than death. They had been kept till the last; they had been in the hands of their captors for several days—for the burning and pillaging had not all been accomplished in a single day—and during this time they had suffered all it was possible that poor, weak, trembling girls could suffer at the hands of brutal savages. Then, when the town had been pillaged and burned, when all their friends had been slaughtered,

these poor young things, whose very wrongs should have insured their safety, whose very outrages should have insured them protection, were taken, in the broad light of day, beneath the smiling canopy of heaven, coolly beheaded, then thrown in a heap there, and left to rot.

Mr. Disraeli was right when he wittily remarked that the Turks usually terminated their connection with people who fell into their hands in a more expeditious manner than by imprisoning them. And so they do. Mr. Disraeli was right. At the time he made that very witty remark * these young girls had been lying there many days.

PHILIPPOPOLIS, AUGUST 10—When we were at Panagyurishte we were shown in the ruins of the church, before the place where the altar had stood, a black spot, speckled with calcined bones, on which lay a bouquet of flowers. This was the remains of a priest, Theodor Poff, eighty-five years of age, who had been seized and tortured in the hopes of obtaining money; mutilated and maltreated in ways which only the foul imagination of a Turk could invent, then killed and burned here before the altar. In another place we were shown a black spot where an old blind man, Dondje Stregleyoof, was beaten half to death, and then thrown senseless on a heap of wood and burned alive.

There was an old man here, Zivatko Boyadjieff by name, a public benefactor, a liberal contributor to the School Fund, who in winter supported half the widows and orphans of the place, who was renowned for his charities to Christian and Turk alike. He was likewise seized, tortured, and maltreated. His eyes were put out, and after undergoing the most fearful tor-

---

* Disraeli's remark, which was quoted against him ever after, was made on July 10.

ments he was thrown on a heap of wood, fainting or dead, the people do not know which, and burned. They seized the priest Nestor and cut off his fingers, one by one, to extort money, and as the poor man had none to give them, they continued by cutting off his hands, and finally his head. We were shown in the yard of a neat little cottage, embowered in trees, a grave, beside which a young woman was kneeling as we passed. It was the grave of a young man of eighteen, who had just returned home from school when the troubles began, after an absence of two years, and who had taken no part in the outbreak. They had seized him, and in mere sport cut off his hands one by one, in the presence of his mother, then killed him.

What made these acts more terrible was that many of them were committed in the presence of weeping relatives—wife, mother, brothers, sisters of the victims. And they were repeated by the hundred. It would take a volume to tell all of the stories that were repeated to us.

These Turks have no pity, no compassion, no bowels. They have not even the pity of wild beasts. Even the tiger will not slay the young of its own species. But the Turks, these strong-bearded men, picked infants up out of their cradles with their bayonets, tossed them in the air, caught them again, and flung them at the heads of the shrieking mothers. They carried little babes about the streets on the points of their bayonets, with the poor little heads and arms drooping around the barrels of their guns, and the blood streaming down over their hands. They cut off the heads of children, and compelled other children to carry the still bleeding heads in their arms.

Hundreds of women came to us recounting what they had seen and what they had suffered. Not a woman in the place seemed to have escaped outrage. They all confessed it openly. In other places where these things occurred the women have shown a hesitation to speak. In some cases they denied they had been outraged, and we afterward learned they confessed to others that they had been. At Avrat-Alan a deputation of ladies called upon Mr. Schuyler to make their complaints, and he was somewhat astonished to find they had very little to say. Upon going away, however, they left him a letter, signed by them all, saying that scarcely a woman in the place had escaped outrage. They could not bring themselves to tell him viva voce; but thinking that, as he was investigating here in an official capacity, he ought to know, they had decided to write to him.

Here, however, they did not hesitate to speak out. Outrages were committed so publicly, so generally, that they feel it would be useless to try to hide their shame, and they avow it openly. These acts were committed not only in the houses, but in the streets, in the yards, in the courts, for the Turks have not even the decency which may accompany vice. They have not even the modesty of vileness; they have not even the shame of nature. Mothers were outraged in the presence of their daughters; young girls in the presence of their mothers, of their sisters and brothers. One woman told us, wringing her hands and crying, that she and her daughter, a girl of fifteen, had been violated in the same room; another that she was violated in the presence of her children. A girl of eighteen avowed, shuddering and bowing her face in her hands, that she had been outraged by ten soldiers. A woman who came to us on crutches, with a bullet in her ankle, said she had been violated by three soldiers while lying wounded on the ground, groaning in agony. Young, delicate, fragile little creatures, ten and twelve years old, were treated in the most brutal manner.

And yet Sir Henry Elliot and Mr. Disraeli will keep prating to us about exaggeration, forsooth! The crimes that were committed here are beyond the reach of exaggeration. There were stories related to us that are maddening in their atrocity; that cause the heart to swell in a burst of impotent rage that can only find vent in pitying, useless tears. We were told of a young girl of sixteen outraged by three or four bashi-bazouks in the presence of her father, who was old and blind. Suddenly she saw one of them preparing, in mere sport, to kill the poor old man, and she sprang forward with a shriek, threw her arms around his neck, weeping, and trying to shield him with her own delicate body. It was all in vain. The bullet sped on its course, and the father and daughter— the sweet young girl and the blind old man—fell dead in each other's arms.

If I tell what I have seen and heard it is because I want the people of England to understand what these Turks are, and if we are to go on bolstering up this tottering despotism; if we are to go on carrying this loathsome, vice-stricken leper about on our shoulders, let us do it with open eyes and a knowledge of the facts; let us see the hideous things we are carrying.

* * *

Mac gahan's sensational newsletters opened England's eyes. On September 6, hardly two weeks after the final dispatch from MacGahan, Gladstone published a devastating pamphlet, entitled *Bulgarian Horrors and the Question of the East,* in which he congratulated *The Daily News* on its enterprising reportorial work in the Balkans and declared that "it is even possible that, but for the courage, determination, and ability of this single organ, we might, even at this moment, have remained in darkness, and Bulgarian wretchedness might have been without its best and brightest hope." When the British government sent Walter Baring to make an official on-the-spot report, he confirmed MacGahan's information and denounced the massacre as "the most heinous crime of the century." By conservative estimates some 12,000 Bulgarians were slain. Harold Temperley, a noted student of diplomatic history, investigated the question as recently as 1931, when, in a paper read before the British Academy, he held that MacGahan's findings were sustained "in the light of historical criticism."

MacGahan's stories whipped up world-wide indignation against the Turks and provided a spark that ignited the Russo-Turkish War and led to an independent Bulgaria. His *Daily News* dispatches from the Russian lines, notably on the siege of Plevna, are magnificent examples of battle reporting. With equal objectivity he excoriated Turkish cruelty and Russian inefficiency, and blamed the tsarist forces for being unprepared to take care of the survivors when Plevna finally fell. "In the pools of water lie corpses half decayed; pale, withered hands and feet stick out of the soil on all sides, and horrible, dead, mummified faces stare at one from every little hollow in the ground." "Plevna is one vast charnel house," MacGahan concluded, "surpassing in horror anything that can be imagined."

MacGahan himself fell victim to a fatal illness contracted during the war, and died at Constantinople in 1878, when he was only thirty-four years of age. The Tsar is reputed to have said that, had MacGahan lived, his letters would have made him the ruler of Bulgaria, where he was long revered as that country's liberator.

With Constantinople in danger, Sultan Abdul-Hamid II, appropriately characterized as "a creature half fox, half rat," sued for peace, and the independence of "Greater Bulgaria" was recognized. But by the Congress of Berlin in 1878 Bulgaria was greatly reduced in size. The Great Powers did not drive the "unspeakable Turk" out of Europe, "bag and baggage," as Gladstone had demanded, and Britain, in standing by Turkey and thwarting Russia, had, as World War I was to prove, put her money on the wrong horse.

Terror Reigns in Whitechapel as Jack the
Ripper Strikes

THOMAS DE QUINCEY, in a celebrated essay "On Murder, Considered as One of the Fine Arts," reports at length the "immortal" murders committed by John Williams in London's East End in the year 1812. When, in the course of one hour, that fantastic criminal "exterminated all but two entire households, and asserted his own supremacy above all the children of Cain," he threw the East End of London into a frenzy that lasted for weeks. Again Williams struck, and still again, always observing the maxim "that the best person to murder was a friend; and, in default of a friend, which is an article one cannot always command, an acquaintance," as in neither case would the prospective victim be on guard. Finally, after a bloody reign of terror, Williams was trapped by circumstantial evidence (a ship carpenter's mallet left at the scene of one of his murders), but he cheated his executioners by hanging himself by his braces in his cell.

Williams' repetitive pattern of homicides, all bearing the same hallmark, set some kind of record for well over sixty years. Then, in the same East End of London, at that time one of the most completely evil places in the world, De Quincey's model homicidal maniac was outdone by a series of "perfect" crimes successfully executed. To Whitechapel crime was an old story. In its narrow, twisting streets, blackened by the night fog, an army of denizens and criminals, including the High Pip terrorists and the vicious Blind Beggars, plied their trade among the poor and forgotten dregs of humanity. In the late hours a regiment of Amazons, members of the world's oldest profession, walked the streets.

Here, on Osborne Street in the heart of Whitechapel, on Easter Monday, 1888, the body of Emma Smith, a blowzy prostitute, was found. The murderer, who apparently knew something about anatomy, did a businesslike job of mutilation on the corpse. In late August another lady of easy virtue was found similarly carved up, and the next month there were two more. After the fourth murder the police at Scotland Yard received a taunting message:

This is the fourth. I will murder 16 more and then give myself up.

Jack the Ripper

By this time all Whitechapel was swept by panic. The gentlemen of Scotland Yard huffed and puffed in a frenzied hunt for the phantom who seemed immune to the ordinary odds of fate. One dim-witted detective tried to catch the criminal by photographing the eyeballs of the victim in the then unexploded belief that the image of the fiend would still be there.

Other policemen dressed themselves in feminine clothing and wigs to masquerade as streetwalkers and went on fruitless pilgrimages in the alleys of Whitechapel. Someone had to profit by all the commotion—this time it was the carpenters, who developed a lucrative business of securing and bolting doors. In the meantime Jack the Ripper sent letters written in blood to the police, ridiculing their efforts to find him. "Decent women," he informed them, with proper humility, "are perfectly safe."

The London *Times* followed the course of the murders with a series of brilliantly impartial observations and ingenious conjectures. The condensed version here of the Ripper stories includes several characteristically British letters to the Editor of *The Times*.

"I send you half the kidne I took from one woman, prasarved it for you"

The Times (London), August 10, September 1, 10, 11, 20, October 1, 2, 3, 9, 10, 15, 19, 25, November 10, 13, 1888

August 10—Yesterday afternoon M. G. Collier, Deputy Coroner for the Southeastern Division of Middlesex, opened an inquiry respecting the death of a woman who was found on Tuesday last with thirty-nine stabs on her body at Grove-Yard Buildings, Whitechapel.

Dr. T. R. Killeen said the deceased had been dead for some three hours. The left lung was penetrated in five places, and the right lung was penetrated in two places. The heart, which was rather fatty, was penetrated in one place. The liver was healthy but was penetrated in five places, the spleen in two, and the stomach—which was perfectly healthy—was penetrated in six places.

It was one of the most dreadful murders anyone could imagine. The man must have been a perfect savage to inflict such a number of wounds on a defenseless woman in such a way.

September 1—Another murder of the foulest kind was committed in the neighborhood of Whitechapel in the early hours of yesterday morning, but by whom and with what motive is at present a complete mystery. At a quarter to four o'clock Police Constable Neill when in Bucks Row, Whitechapel, came upon the body of a woman lying on a part of the roadway, and on stooping to raise her up in the belief that she was drunk, he soon discovered that her throat was cut almost from ear to ear.

The police have no theory with respect to the matter except that a gang of ruffians exists in the neighborhood which, blackmailing women of the "unfortunate" class, takes vengeance on those who do not find money for them. They base the surmise on the fact that within twelve months two other women have been murdered in the district by almost similar means.

September 10—Whitechapel and the whole of the East of London have again been thrown into a state of intense excitement by the discovery early on Saturday morning of the body of a woman who had been murdered in a similar way to Mary Ann Nichols at Bucks Row on Friday week. In fact, the similarity in the two cases is startling, as the victim of the outrage had her head almost severed from her body and was completely disemboweled. This latest crime, however, even surpasses the other in ferocity.

The police believe that the murder has been committed by the same person who perpetrated the three previous ones in the district and that only one person is concerned in it. This person might be, is doubtless, laboring under some terrible form of insanity, and it is feared that unless he can speedily be captured more outrages of a similar class will be committed.

September 11—The latest reports as to the search for the murderer are not of a hopeful character.

September 20—No further arrest in connection with the Whitechapel murders had been made up to last night and the police are still at fault.

October 1—In the early hours of yesterday morning two more horrible murders were committed in the East End of London, the victims in both cases belonging, it is believed, to the same unfortunate class. No doubt seems to be entertained by the police that these terrible crimes were the work of the same fiendish hands which committed the outrages which had already made Whitechapel so painfully notorious.

In the first-mentioned case the body was found in a gateway leading to a factory, and although the murder compared with the other may be regarded as of an almost ordinary character— the unfortunate woman only having her throat cut—little doubt is felt

from the position of the corpse that the assassin intended to mutilate it. He seems, however, to have been interrupted by the arrival of a cart.

The murder in the City was committed in circumstances which show that the assassin, if not suffering from insanity, appears to be free from any fear of interruption while at his dreadful work. The deceased was found lying on her back with her head inclined to the left side. Her left leg was extended, the right being bent, and both her arms were extended. The throat was terribly cut; there was a large gash across the face from the nose to the right angle of the cheek, and part of the right ear had been cut off. There were also other indescribable mutilations. It is stated that some anatomical skill seems to have been displayed in the way in which the lower part of the body was mutilated.

At three o'clock yesterday afternoon a meeting of nearly a thousand persons took place in Victoria Park. After several speeches upon the conduct of the Home Secretary and Sir Charles Warren,* a resolution was unanimously passed that it was high time both officers should resign and make way for some officers who would leave no stone unturned for the purpose of bringing the murderers to justice, instead of allowing them to run riot in a civilized city like London.

October 1—Letter to the Editor of *The Times:*

"Sir: I beg to suggest the organization of a small force of plain-clothes constables mounted on bicycles for the rapid and noiseless patrolling of streets and roads by night. Your obedient servant,

"Fred. Wellesley"

---

* Commissioner of Police of the metropolis.

October 2—Two communications of an extraordinary nature, both signed "Jack the Ripper," have been received by the Central News Agency. The first stated that in the "next job" he did the writer would "clip the lady's ears off" and send them to the police. The second communication was a postcard to Scotland Yard: "I was not coddling, dear old Boss, when I gave you the tip. You'll hear about Saucy Jacky's work tomorrow. Double event this time. Number One squealed a bit; couldn't finish it straight off. Had not time to get ears for police."

October 2—Letter to the Editor of *The Times:*
"Sir: With regard to the suggestion that bloodhounds might assist in tracking the East End murderer, as a breeder of bloodhounds and knowing their power, I have little doubt that, had a hound been put upon the scene of the murder while fresh, it might have done what the police have failed in. I am, sir, your obedient servant,
                                 "Percy Lindley"
Letter to the Editor of *The Times:*
"Sir, I cannot help thinking that these Whitechapel murders point to one individual, and that individual insane. He may be an earnest religionist with a delusion that he has a mission from above to extirpate vice by assassination. I was myself all but the victim of an assassin who believed he had a mission to destroy me as the impersonation of all that was evil and hindered the progress of mankind. I have, &c,
                          "Edgar Sheppard, M.D."
Letter to the Editor of *The Times:*
"As a magistrate of more than thirty years' experience among the criminal population of London, as well as much intercourse with the working classes, I have no hesitation in saying that the best way to detect crime of a heinous character is to offer at once a large and substantial reward.
"I have the honor to remain your obedient servant,
                                 "Henry White,
                          Magistrate of Middlesex"

October 3—Great satisfaction was expressed yesterday throughout the City at the promptness with which the Lord Mayor has offered a reward for the discovery and conviction of the murderer or murderers of the woman who was found butchered in Mitre-square.
Up to a late hour last night no arrests had been made. No clues have been discovered, but it is fully believed that the lurking place of the murderer is not very far from the scene of his atrocious crimes.

October 3—Letter to the Editor of *The Times:*
"Sir: Will you allow me to recommend that all the police boots should be furnished with a noiseless sole and heel, of India rubber or other material, to prevent the sound of their measured tread being heard at night, which would enable them to get closer to a criminal before he would be aware of their approach? Yours faithfully,
                                 "L. R. Thomson"

October 9—It is stated by a news agency that definite instructions have been issued to the police that they are not to remove the body of a murdered victim but to send notice immediately to a veterinary surgeon in the Southwest district, who holds several trained bloodhounds in readiness to be taken to the spot where the body may be found and to be at once put on the scent.

October 10—Sir Charles Warren witnessed a private trial of bloodhounds in one of the London parks at an early hour yesterday morning.

October 15—Last Friday Mr. George Lusk, who is a member of the Whitechapel Vigilance Committee, received the following letter:

"I write you in black ink, as I have no more of the right stuff. I think you are all asleep in Scotland Yard with your bloodhounds, as I will show you tomorrow night. I am going to do a double event, but not in Whitechapel. Got rather too warm there. Had to shift. No more till you hear me again.

"JACK THE RIPPER"

October 19—Mr. George Lusk has received several letters purporting to be from the perpetrator of the Whitechapel murders. It is stated that a letter delivered shortly after five o'clock on Tuesday evening was accompanied by a cardboard box containing what appeared to be a portion of a kidney. The letter was in the following terms:

"From Hell. Mr. Lusk. Sir, I send you half the kidne I took from one woman, prasarved it for you, tother piece I fried and ate it; it was very nice. I may send you the bloody knif that took it out if you only wate while longer.

[Signed] "CATCH ME
WHEN YOU CAN, Mr. Lusk"

Dr. Openshaw, who is pathological curator of the London Hospital Museum, examined the contents of the cardboard box and pronounced it to be a portion of a human kidney—a "ginny" kidney, that is to say, one that had belonged to a person who had drunk heavily.

It is stated that Sir Charles War-ren's bloodhounds were out for practice at Tooting yesterday morning and were lost. Telegrams have been dispatched to all metropolitan police stations stating that if seen anywhere information is to be immediately sent to Scotland Yard.*

October 25—The following petition to the Queen was freely circulated among the women of the laboring classes of East London:

To Our Most Gracious Sovereign Lady Queen Victoria.

Madam: We, the women of East London, feel horror at the dreadful sins that have been lately in our midst and grief because of the shame which has befallen the neighborhood. From the inquests we have learned much of the lives of those of our sisters who have lost a firm hold on goodness and are living sad and degraded lives. We call on your servants in authority to close bad houses within whose walls such wickedness is done, and men and women ruined in body and soul. We are, Madam, your loyal and humble subjects.

November 10—During the early hours of yesterday morning another murder of a most revolting and fiendish character took place in Spitalfields. The scene of this last crime is at No. 26 Dorset Street. As an instance of the poverty of the neighborhood it may be mentioned that nearly the whole of the houses in this street are common lodginghouses, and the one opposite where this murder was enacted has accommodations for some three hundred men and is fully occupied every night.

The poor woman lay on her back on the bed, entirely naked. Her throat

---

* *The Times* inexplicably failed to add the pertinent fact that the two capricious bloodhounds answered to the names "Champion Barnaby" and "Burgho."

was cut from ear to ear, right down to the spinal column. The ears and nose had been cut clean off. The breasts had also been cut cleanly off and placed on a table which was by the side of the bed. The stomach and abdomen had been ripped open while the face was slashed about so that the features of the poor creature were beyond all recognition. The kidneys and heart had also been removed from the body and placed on the table by the side of the breasts. The liver had likewise been removed and laid on the right thigh. The lower portion of the body and the uterus had been cut out, and these appeared to be missing. A more horrible or sickening sight could not be imagined.

November 13—During yesterday several arrests were made, but after a short examination in all cases the persons were set at liberty, as it was felt certain they had no connection with the crime.

As will be seen from our Parliamentary report, Sir Charles Warren tendered his resignation on Thursday last.

JACK THE RIPPER was never caught. In the early months of 1889 other killers began to imitate him, and the result was confusion multiplied. He may have killed precisely twenty women, as he said he would, and then, satiated, quit his nefarious avocation.

Who was this fabulously successful murderer? Was he a religious maniac? Medical student? Artist? Sculptor? Physician? There have been all sorts of conjectures. Some armchair detectives point knowingly to the fact that just two years before Jack the Ripper appeared on the streets of Whitechapel, Robert Louis Stevenson had published his gruesome allegory, *Dr. Jekyll and Mr. Hyde*. Others are certain that the Ripper was a student or young professor maddened by the doom of venereal disease caught from one of the East End prostitutes. Still others believe that he was a lunatic Russian physician escaped from an asylum or an American collector of female body organs.

One man definitely saw the Ripper. A bag of grapes found at the body of a victim was identified by a fruitstand owner named Parker as having been bought for the girl a few hours earlier by a man of about thirty, approximately five feet seven inches tall, stockily built, and of dark complexion. The police promptly paid Parker to close his fruit stall and wander through the streets in search of the killer. On the eighth night, just at dusk while the lamplighters were making the rounds, Parker saw the Ripper, dressed in a black greatcoat reaching down to his knees and wearing a black slouch hat. Parker instantly called for help.

It was too late. Jack the Ripper, reacting with the instincts of a hunted animal, vanished into the cloak of London's all-embracing fog.

Ray Stannard Baker Sees Coxey's Army Halted at the Steps of the Capitol

IT WAS TIME to "quit raising corn" and to "begin raising hell," Kansas farmers were told by radical agitators. A great many people felt that way. In 1892 workers had been shot down by Pinkerton men when open labor warfare flared up in the Homestead Strike of the Carnegie Steel Works. The following year a panic spelled soup kitchens in the cities and hard times on the farms. "Populism," the party of social protest and cheap currency, seemed on the march. A shrewd forty-year-old businessman from Massillon, Ohio, a congenital reformer and paper-money agitator, Jacob Sechler Coxey, joined forces with a Pacific Coast labor organizer named Carl Browne, a tall, bearded Westerner, wearing the kind of costume, commented one reporter, that "a bad actor would use in playing the role of a wild and woolly cowboy." Coxey and Browne gathered together an industrial army of the unemployed (about a hundred strong), the "Commonweal of Christ," and marched out of Massillon on a chilly Easter Sunday, with flags flying and followed by nearly half as many reporters as "soldiers." Accompanying Coxey were his wife and young son, little Legal Tender Coxey. Their objective was Washington. All over the West industrial armies were grouping to converge on the Federal capital. Trains were stolen, and the countryside was kept in a state of feverish anxiety.

Covering Coxey's march from Massillon was a young newspaper reporter on the staff of the Chicago *Record* (afterward the Chicago *Daily News*). Ray Stannard Baker, who had only shortly before demonstrated his grasp of social problems in his reporting of a strike of waiters in a Chicago restaurant, sent on this comment in a dispatch to the *Record,* date-lined Alliance, Ohio, March 28: "When such an ugly and grotesque fungus can grow so prominently on the body politic there must be something wrong. The national blood is out of order, and Coxey, Browne, and the other Commonwealers seem, seriously considered, to be but the eruption on the surface."

Instead of the army of a hundred thousand men Coxey had confidently predicted, he had a mere five hundred when he arrived in Washington in time for a May Day demonstration. When Coxey's Army marched up Pennsylvania Avenue it was cheered by an enormous crowd. As the marchers approached the Capitol, they were barred by a phalanx of police from curb to curb. The decisive moment had arrived. Would they fight or would they quit? Here is Baker's answer, contained in this condensed dispatch to the *Record,* date-lined May Day, 1894:

"The campaign of the army of peace has ended in war"

Chicago *Record,* May 2, 1894

Coxey's eventful march from Massillon to the marble steps of the national Capitol closed today in riot and bloodshed. The campaign of the army of peace has ended in war. For the first time in the six weeks during which the Commonweal has been plodding steadily eastward a written law of the land has been willfully violated, and for the first time there has been a collision with the authorities.

As a result Carl Browne lies in a cell at the police station tonight and General Coxey, who only escaped arrest because he was less dashing and impetuous than his fellow reformer, is racking his brains for a plan to support the band of penniless wanderers whom he has gathered from all over the country. Furthermore, the good-roads and noninterest-bearing-bonds bills * are no nearer passage than they were a month ago.

In today's exciting incidents the army proper took no part. The contest was wholly between three hundred armed police officers and the doughty twin reformers. Twenty thousand spectators enjoyed the excitement, and at least a score of them paid for their pleasure with broken heads or black eyes.

A gray-haired member of Congress who watched the riot from a portico of the Capitol said after the mob was dispersed: "The events of this first of May will live in history as the manifestation of a widespread discontent among the laboring classes of the country. I think now that the climax has been reached and the furor for industrial armies will gradually subside. This belief that the enactment of new laws by Congress is a panacea for all our national ills is a dangerous symptom. The wise heads of the country have got to give it close and thoughtful attention."

It has been a long day. Early this morning Carl Browne ordered his horse and rode out to Brightwood Park, where the army was encamped. The bugler was just puckering up his lips to blow the assembly for breakfast when the marshal arrived. The men rushed forward, fell into line before the wagons, and Commissary Marshal Blinn served each of them with six hardtack crackers, a piece of bread, and a cup of coffee. When the breakfast had been swallowed the command to fall in was given.

Commune Marshal Schrum, assisted by several Commonwealers, issued to each man a "war club of peace," consisting of an oak stick four feet long with a white banner surmounted by a tiny flag fluttering at the end. Browne made a little speech. "The greatest ordeal of the march is at hand," he said. "The eyes of the world are on you and you must conduct

---

* Coxey, aiming to end unemployment, proposed a good-roads bill, calling for an issue of $500,000,000 of legal-tender notes to be used in constructing roads throughout the country, workmen to be employed at $1.50 for an eight-hour day. The opposition of Governor Greenhalge of Massachusetts was typical. The bill, he maintained, was immoral, for unemployment was an act of God. Coxey's proposals became the core of the later New Deal approach.

yourselves accordingly." Browne then ordered the commune marshals to form their men for the parade.

Five mounted policemen swung into line at the head of the column. Most of the men had spent hours getting ready for the great occasion. But any improvement in the appearance of the marchers was counterbalanced by the faded and torn banners and battered commissary wagons. Immediately beside the Chicago commune rode Christopher Columbus Jones in a hackney cab. He is a little man with a long nose, and his high hat, ruffled with its experience, comes down over his head.

By the time the procession swung into Pennsylvania Avenue the crowd had grown so great that it was with difficulty that the mounted police escort, now increased to twenty-five, could clear a way for the army.

At last the procession stopped with Coxey's carriage near the B Street entrance to the grounds. Browne dismounted and forced his way back. The general saw him. Rising from his seat, he stooped over and kissed his wife, as if he realized something of the terrible ordeal to follow.

Coxey leaped nimbly to the ground, and in a moment he and Browne were swallowed up in a wild surging mob of men which lifted them from their feet and bore them bodily across the street to the Capitol grounds. More than a hundred mounted policemen who were stationed around the B Street entrance rode into the crowd with the intention of capturing the two Commonwealers, but they might as well have attempted to arrest a cyclone. The mob forced one of them against the stone wall which bounds the Capitol plaza and threw his horse

violently to the ground. At this point the man from Calistoga shouted to Coxey to jump over the wall, but the general lost his footing and in a moment he was at the bottom of a pack of writhing, struggling humanity. Browne leaped quickly into the grounds with the mob after him. Here the policemen saw him and forced their horses over the wall. A wild rush through the shrubbery took place, men and women rolling and tumbling over one another in the wild scramble.

The mounted policemen lost their heads and, not being able to see Browne, they drew their clubs and began striking everyone within reach. Women and children were ruthlessly ridden down. A Commonwealer who had some way escaped from the ranks stood behind a tree and struck a policeman a terrific blow in the back with his war club of peace. The next officer that came up saw the attack and clubbed the Commonwealer into insensibility and let him lie where he had fallen.

Just as Browne reached the corner of the steps he was seized by an officer. Without a moment's indecision the man from Calistoga swung his arm quickly around and sent the policeman spinning far out into the crowd. The next moment he was seized from behind, and a clenched fist struck him several blows in the face. In the struggle that followed his clothing was badly torn, and a string of his dead wife's beads, which he always wore around his throat, was scattered.* An inoffensive Negro named Johnson crowded up to watch the struggle, and one of the policemen struck him a blow with his club.

Two mounted policemen closed

---

* Ray Stannard Baker picked up a few of the beads and, later that day, brought them to Browne in his cell in the District Jail. "You're the only friend I've got left in the world," Browne blubbered.

down upon the Negro and hit him repeatedly until he sank to the ground with his head terribly lacerated. Browne, together with Christopher Columbus Jones, who had been arrested trying to assist his friend in the fight, was taken to the police station.

All this time Coxey had been struggling through the crowd toward the central steps of 'the Capitol. He had asked a policeman to help him, and the two wormed their way through the mob like sparrows through a wheat field. Before anyone knew it Coxey was bounding up the east front entrance to the Capitol. He was up to the tenth step before he was recognized. Then the officers closed in above him, and his further passage was barred. The great crowd now recognized him, and a shout went up. Coxey turned to the crowd and raised his hat. He was deadly pale. Captain Garden of the Capitol police stepped to one side of him, and Lieutenant Kelly of the city police was at his other arm. The other officers formed solidly about him. The crowd below was kept back by menacing clubs.

"What do you want to do here?" asked Captain Garden.

"I wish to make an address," responded General Coxey, his voice showing intense emotion.

"But you cannot do that," said Captain Garden, quietly but firmly.

"Then can I read a protest?" asked Coxey.

There was a moment's hesitation. Coxey drew from his pocket a typewritten manuscript and began to unfold it. There was a movement among the officers. Captain Garden quietly took Coxey by the left arm, and Lieutenant Kelly took him by the right. They moved down the steps, the solid rank of officers following. Coxey thus was impelled downward and forward. He was not pulled or put under arrest, but firmly pushed along until he reached his carriage. Here a big Negro tried to strike an officer and was badly beaten.

The army, which had stood quietly in place under the command of Jesse Coxey during the entire melee, was now ordered to march. The column moved forward like a funeral procession to its new camping place on M Street, near the James Creek Canal.

The Senate adjourned today on account of Senator Stockbridge's death, and many of the Senators watched the riot from the Capitol portico. While the House was nominally in session, most of the members were outside enjoying the excitement.

In his protest this afternoon General Coxey said:

"The Constitution of the United States guarantees to all citizens the right to peacefully assemble and petition for redress of grievances, and, furthermore, declares that the right of free speech shall not be abridged. We stand here today to test these guarantees of our Constitution. We chose this place of assemblage because it is the property of the people and if it be true that the right of the people to peacefully assemble upon their own premises and with their petitions has been abridged by the passage of laws in direct violation of the Constitution, we are here to draw the eyes of the nation to this shameful fact."

General Coxey talked to a reporter at the new camp. "I was careful to walk on the sidewalk and trespass upon no local regulations when I went up to the steps," he said. "This is the beginning of the movement; that is all."

BUT COXEY was wrong. The end was anticlimax. Coxey, Browne, and Jones were given twenty days for carrying banners, and Coxey and Browne were fined five dollars for walking on the grass. In this way panicky authorities flouted the constitutional right of petition. But the movement soon played out. Easterners gave the army of tramps and unemployed a chilly reception. Having spanked Coxey, the government then proceeded to issue a blanket injunction against Eugene Debs and his workers, who had begun the Pullman Strike (which Baker also reported),* thus breaking a temporary paralysis of the entire American railroad system. Together, these two disturbances caused the most extensive troop movements since the Civil War. Coxey and Debs had made the conservatives hysterical. Taft's comment to his wife on the Pullman Strike was characteristic: "It will be necessary for the military to kill some of the mob before the trouble can be stayed. They have only killed six as yet. This is hardly enough to make an impression."

Still spry when interviewed in 1948 at the age of ninety-four, Coxey announced an entirely different, more conservative objective: "I'm going to live to be a hundred."

The Lansing, Michigan, newsman who reported Coxey's march on Washington went on to achieve fame as a feature writer for *McClure's Magazine,* a militant reform organ, joining such famous muckrakers as Ida Tarbell, Lincoln Steffens, and William Allen White. As a political reporter Baker was unusually penetrating. Covering William Howard Taft's Cooper Union speech in February, 1908, Baker reported that a man in the audience put to him the following question:

"What is a man going to do who is out of work and starving?"

Taft's rejoinder: "God knows; I don't."

In charge of press relations for the American peace delegation at the Paris Conference, Baker came to know and reverence Woodrow Wilson, and produced a Pulitzer-acclaimed biography of that war leader.

---

* Baker wrote a number of powerful strike stories; perhaps the most brilliant was his account of the firing by soldiers on the Pullman strikers at Hammond, Indiana, July 8, 1894, during which melee one man was killed, seven wounded, "and not one of them a striker."

James Creelman Exposes Cold-Blooded Massacre

by the Japanese at Port Arthur

AT THE END of the nineteenth century Nippon's war lords began to flex their muscles. Their attempt to dominate Korea led to war with China. Ill-organized, inefficient, overconfident, the Chinese were defeated in less than a year by an enemy whom they had contemptuously rated as "dwarfs."

Outstanding among the newsmen who reported the victory of modern times against the Middle Ages was James Creelman. This Montreal boy, who ran away from home at the age of twelve and turned up in New York with a nickel in his pocket, fought his way up the reportorial ladder. Joining the *Herald* staff in 1878 and later editing the Paris edition of that paper, Creelman interviewed Tolstoy, the redoubtable Hippolyte of Haiti, and other headliners, but broke with Bennett when the latter refused to let him have a by-line. In 1894 Pulitzer sent him to cover the Sino-Japanese War.

Creelman gave readers of the New York *World* an unforgettable picture of the Chinese commanders, "with huge spectacles, heroes of many a classical debate, and surrounded by the painted, embroidered, and carved monsters of mythological war." "Wholly ignorant of modern military science," they "awaited the coming of the trim little up-to-date soldiers of Japan with all the scorn of learned foolishness." Creelman saw the Japanese clear Korea of Chinese troops and reported the climax at Pingyang, when three hundred Manchurian cavalrymen, mounted on snow-white horses, charged down the valley "with their long black lances set and pennons dancing from shining spear points." "Not a man stirred in the Japanese line" until the riders were within two hundred feet, when Nipponese infantry and artillery opened up and "horses and riders went down together and were hurled in bloody heaps." Then began the Japanese invasion of Manchuria, culminating in the attack on Port Arthur. "Our army is advancing in the name of civilization to overthrow barbarism!" Japanese Field Marshal Oyama declared.

After Port Arthur fell on November 21, 1894, weeks passed without word from Creelman. On November 24 news arrived of the killing of a war correspondent by the Chinese. *The World* feared it was Creelman; *The Illustrated London News* felt it might be their man, Vizetelly. It turned out to be a Japanese newsman. Then on December 10 came word that a backstabbing fellow correspondent had accused Creelman of being a Chinese spy. At last, Creelman's dispatches began to get through. His pen portrait of the Japanese division commander, Yamaji, stands out in the material he sent on about the Port Arthur attack:

"*A sight that would damn the fairest nation on earth*"

James Creelman, *On the Great Highway: The Wanderings and Adventures of a Special Correspondent* (Lothrop Publishing Company, Boston, 1901)

All was ready for the battle of Port Arthur, and the Japanese army was already moving through the night into position for an attack upon the sixteen great modern forts at daybreak.

The little group of saddle-weary foreign correspondents stood around a heap of blazing wood while their horses were being fed by the excited coolies. The wide valley flamed and roared with the campfires of the invading host, and thousands of dust-covered coolies moved in the darkness with the ammunition and food. I anxiously watched a small man pacing slowly before a smoldering fire around which were gathered a few whispering staff officers. His head was bowed, and his hands were locked behind his back as he moved. It was General Yamaji, the terrible little division commander —he who deliberately plucked out his own eye at school to show his comrades that he was not a coward. Our fate depended upon this man, for he was the real general of the attacking forces, the stout old field marshal being a political rather than a military element in the situation.

Yamaji turned away from the fire and, with a surly nod of the head to his officers, mounted his horse. The staff followed his example. I swung myself into the saddle and joined the general as he pushed forward with the right wing of the army across the head of the valley and around the face of the western hills, in preparation for the turning movement which was to be the key of the battle.

We were carried along in the darkness with a horrible sense of universal motion, on the edges of giant earth seams and steep precipices, with the artillery clanging and grinding, and the ponderous siege batteries groaning over the loose stones in the dry river beds; horses plunging and stumbling, with mountain guns strapped on their backs; the swift clatter of the cavalry sweeping backward and forward with news of the enemy, the steady tramp and murmur of the infantry; the crawling lines of coolies attending the fighting men; now and then a horse and rider rolling down over the rocks; frightened steeds shying at campfires; a procession of ammunition boxes carried along like black coffins; occasionally a glimpse of a ravine with rivers of bayonets gleaming at the bottom of it; anxious and hungry skirmishers creeping on their bellies along the ridges of the distant peaks—and yet, a curious hush over it all—the sense of a secret to be kept.

Not a sign of a flag, the roll of a drum, nor the note of a bugle; nothing but the rush of human feet, the beat of hoofs, the crunching of wheels, and the clank of cold steel.

It made a man grow cold to be near Yamaji and see the gleam in that one eye. There were sounds of voices around him as the swift messengers came and went in the gloom, but it was a strange babble of Asiatic accents, falling weirdly upon the ears of a New York newspaper writer, borne along atomlike in that human torrent. Yamaji stood out on the wall of the redoubt in plain sight, as silent and unmoved as a carved image, while showers of shattered rock and earth fell about him. It was a face to study— cold, stoical, Asiatic. The battle seemed to bore him; it was too easy. There was not enough bloodshed. His one eye searched the scene like the eye of a machine. Once he smiled and showed his yellow teeth—a ghastly smile.

Yet only a few days before I saw Yamaji release the little singing birds in the Talienwan forts lest they might starve in their cages—so strangely is mercy and cruelty compounded in the human heart.

ON DECEMBER 12, 1894, the people of America were astounded to read this front-page *World* story under the headline A JAPANESE MASSACRE:

New York *World*, December 12, 1894

YOKOHAMA, JAPAN, DECEMBER 11— The Japanese troops entered Port Arthur on November 21 and massacred practically the entire population in cold blood.

The defenseless and unarmed inhabitants were butchered in their houses and their bodies were unspeakably mutilated. There was an unrestrained reign of murder which continued for three days. The whole town was plundered with appalling atrocities.

It was the first stain upon Japanese civilization. The Japanese in this instance relapsed into barbarism.

All pretense that circumstances justified the atrocities are false. The civilized world will be horrified by the details.

The foreign correspondents, horrified by the spectacle, left the army in a body.

CREELMAN

*   *   *

THE JAPANESE tried to get Creelman to kill the story by offering him a bribe, but to no avail. American public opinion, hitherto friendly to Japan, underwent an immediate *volte-face*. In the Senate an American treaty with Japan was held up. Creelman later amplified the original dispatch:

On the Great Highway (Boston, 1901)

Then began the meaningless and unnecessary massacre which horrified the civilized world and robbed the Japanese victory of its dignity.

As the triumphant troops poured into Port Arthur they saw the heads of their slain comrades hanging by cords, with the noses and ears shorn off. There was a rude arch at the entrance to the town decorated with these bloody trophies. It may have been this sight which roused the blood of the conquerors, and banished humanity and mercy from their hearts; or it may have been mere lust of slaughter. The world can judge for itself. But the Japanese killed everything they saw.

Unarmed men, kneeling in the streets and begging for life, were shot, bayoneted, or beheaded. The town was sacked from end to end, and the inhabitants were butchered in their own houses.

A procession of ponies, donkeys, and camels went out of the western side of Port Arthur with swarms of terrified men and children. The fugitives waded across a shallow inlet, shivering and stumbling in the icy water. A company of infantry was drawn up at the head of the inlet and poured steady volleys at the dripping victims; but not a bullet hit its mark.

The last to cross the inlet were two men. One of them led two small children. As they staggered out on the opposite shore a squadron of cavalry rode up and cut down one of the men. The other man and the children retreated into the water and were shot like dogs.

All along the streets we could see the pleading storekeepers shot and sabered. Doors were broken down and windows torn out.

The sound of music—the first we had heard since the invasion began— drew us back to the drill ground, where all the Japanese generals were assembled to congratulate the field marshal —all save Nogi, who was pursuing the enemy among the hills. What cheering and handshaking! What solemn strains from the band! And all the while we could hear the rattle of volleys in the streets of Port Arthur, and knew that the helpless people were being slain in cold blood and their homes pillaged.

That was the coldest night we had known. The thermometer suddenly went down to twenty degrees above zero. I found my way up the valley to Suishiyeh, although I was so tired that I twice had to lie down on the roadside. There was nothing to eat in the little house where I slept, but the field marshal sent me a bottle of Burgundy. For two weeks I had not taken my boots off.

In the morning I walked into Port Arthur with the correspondent of the London *Times*. The scenes in the streets were heart-rending. Everywhere we saw bodies torn and mangled, as if by wild beasts. Dogs were whimpering over the frozen corpses of their masters. The victims were mostly shopkeepers. Nowhere the trace of a weapon, nowhere a sign of resistance. It was a sight that would damn the fairest nation on earth.

There was one trembling old woman, and only one, in that great scene of carnage, her wrinkled face quivering with fear, and her limbs trembling as she wandered among the slain. Where was she to go? What was she to do? All the men were killed, all the women were off in the frozen hills, and yet not an eye of pity was turned upon her, but she was jostled and laughed at until she turned down a bloodstained alley, to see God knows what new horror.

FORTY-THREE YEARS elapsed between the Port Arthur outrage and the Rape of Nanking.* The Japanese merely gave the screw another grisly turn.

As for Port Arthur and the rest of the strategic Liaotung Peninsula, the Big Powers insisted that Japan return this territory to China. Russian imperialism, concerned with a trans-Siberian railway and egged on by Kaiser Wilhelm II, whose classic "Willy-Nicky" letters to Tsar Nicholas II warned the Russians against the "Yellow Peril," temporarily thwarted

---

* See below, p. 520.

Japanese imperialism. Once Japan was out, Russia lost no time in getting a lease on Port Arthur, which she converted into a supposedly impregnable naval base, only to lose it some years later to the Japanese after a year-long siege, among the bloodiest in history, reported by American newsmen as "a story of death unparalleled in war."

Nippon was on the march.

"Say to the Whole of France that I Am Innocent!" Cries a French Artillery Captain on His Day of Degradation

THE DREYFUS AFFAIR had all the elements of a sensational detective story on a national scale. On the surface it appeared to be an imbroglio of what Thomas Carlyle would have called "despicable personalities," but actually it was a significant chapter in the history of France.

The facts of the celebrated case are familiar. In the fall of 1894 Alfred Dreyfus, a captain of artillery attached to the French General Staff, was arrested and accused of having sold important French military secrets to the Germans. On being found guilty by a court-martial, he was stripped of his commission in a public degradation and condemned to solitary confinement on Devil's Island, the notorious convict settlement near French Guiana. In the fearful heat of the tropics this was in reality a disguised sentence of lingering death.

Dreyfus was a Jew. Many bigoted French nationalists, seeking a scapegoat for their country's troubles, derived considerable satisfaction from the conviction of the Jewish officer. But the case was as much antidemocratic as it was anti-Semitic. The real issue, it appeared, was the maintenance of a caste system, not only in the army, but in French society. Various political factions rallied to the one side or the other. Monarchists, clericals, and anti-Semites joined hands to contend vociferously that Dreyfus was guilty.

The complicating and disturbing factor was that Dreyfus was innocent. Echoes of the struggle between the Dreyfusards and anti-Dreyfusards were heard all over the earth. "The name of this Franco-Hebrew captain has been spoken," wrote William Harding of the Associated Press, "and his fate discussed by the trappers of the Yenisei, by the Peruvian silver miners, by the alcaldes of Guatemala, by the priests of Tibet, and by the gamblers of Monte Carlo." It was true. Every cabinet from Calcutta to the Hague had felt the vibrations and weighed the consequences of the Dreyfus affair ; every schoolboy from Hong Kong to Brooklyn heard something about the trials of Dreyfus, of Esterhazy, and of Zola.

A saving factor in an incredibly nasty situation—the railroading of an innocent man—was the admirable behavior of a group of great French journalists who had a jealous regard for the honor of France. Émile Zola, Jean Jaurès, Georges Clemenceau, Anatole France, and Léon Blum rallied the reporters of the world to the defense of Dreyfus by the simple expedient of digging out the truth. Eventually, at the second court-martial of Rennes from August 7 to September 9, 1899, some three hundred newspapermen assembled from all parts of the world saw, heard, thought, dreamed, discussed, and wrote of nothing but Dreyfus for five weeks.

Literally millions of words were written on the Dreyfus case by talented journalists, but perhaps the finest piece of reporting to come out of the affair was the story below, written by an unknown French newspaperman for *L'Autorité* (Paris) on the day of the degradation of Dreyfus, January 5, 1895. Note that the reporter was an unfriendly witness, but between the lines of his story there appear shadows of doubt as to the condemned man's guilt.

Three years later, when the sentence on Dreyfus was undergoing review in the Court of Assizes, a court of appeal, the counsel for the defense read this news story to the crowded audience. One of the reporters present was Jean Jaurès, the brilliant Socialist parliamentarian, who believed Dreyfus to be "a living witness to military lies, to political cowardice, and to the crimes of authority." "For me, convinced that Dreyfus was innocent," wrote Jaurès, "I scarcely need to say that the reading was poignant. On all the auditors, and even on the enemies of Dreyfus, that reading visibly produced a profound impression. In order to understand all the courage of that cry of innocence which burst from the tormented man, it is necessary to realize into what a tempest of hate and scorn that cry was thrown. That cry of innocence, so troubled, for a moment shook the conscience; and over that assembly, which was boiling with the coarse disorder of hatred, there passed a sigh of tragic mystery."

Dreyfus hears the mob cry: "Death to the traitor!"

L'Autorité (Paris), January 6, 1895

The first stroke of nine sounds from the school clock. General Darras lifts his sword and gives the command, which is repeated at the head of each company:

"*Portez armes!*"

The troops obey.

Complete silence ensues.

Hearts stop beating, and all eyes are turned toward the corner of the vast square, where Dreyfus had been shut up in a small building.

Soon a little group appears: it is Alfred Dreyfus who is advancing, between four artillerymen, accompanied by a lieutenant of the Republican guard and the oldest noncommissioned officer of the regiment. Between the dark dolmans of the gunners we see distinctly the gold of the three stripes and the gold of the cap bands: the sword glitters, and even at this distance we behold the black sword knot on the hilt of the sword.

Dreyfus marches with steady step. "Look, see how the wretch is carrying himself," someone says.

The group advances towards General Darras, with whom is the clerk of the court-martial, M. Vallecale.

There are cries now in the crowd. But the group halts.

A sign from the officer in command, the drums beat, and the trumpets blow, and then again all is still; a tragic silence now.

The artillerymen with Dreyfus drop back a few steps, and the condemned man stands well out in full view of us all.

The clerk salutes the general, and turning towards Dreyfus reads distinctly the verdict: "The said Dreyfus is condemned to military degradation and to deportation to a fortress."

The clerk turns to the general and salutes. Dreyfus has listened in silence. The voice of General Darras is then heard, and although it is slightly tremulous with emotion, we catch distinctly this phrase:

"Dreyfus, you are unworthy to wear the uniform. In the name of the French people, we deprive you of your rank."

Thereupon we behold Dreyfus lift his arms in air, and, his head well up, exclaim in a loud voice, in which there is not the slightest tremor:

"I am innocent. I swear that I am innocent. *Vive la France!*"

In reply the immense throng without clamors, "Death to the traitor!"

But the noise is instantly hushed. Already the adjutant whose melancholy duty it is to strip from the prisoner his stripes and arms has begun his work, and they now begin to strew the ground.

Dreyfus makes this the occasion of a fresh protest, and his cries carry distinctly even to the crowd outside:

"In the name of my wife and children, I swear that I am innocent. I swear it. *Vive la France!*"

But the work has been rapid. The adjutant has torn quickly the stripes from the hat, the embroideries from the cuffs, the buttons from the dolman, the numbers from the collar, and ripped off the red stripe worn by the prisoner ever since his entrance into the Polytechnic School.

The saber remains: the adjutant draws it from its scabbard and breaks it across his knee. There is a dry click, and the two portions are flung with the insignia upon the ground. Then the belt is detached, and in its turn the scabbard falls.

This is the end. These few seconds have seemed to us ages. Never was there a more terrible sensation of anguish.

And once more, clear and passionless, comes the voice of the prisoner: "You are degrading an innocent man!"

He must now pass along the line in front of his former comrades and subordinates. For another the torture would have been horrible. Dreyfus does not seem to be affected, however, for he leaps over the insignia of his rank, which two gendarmes are shortly to gather up, and takes his place between the four gunners, who, with drawn swords, have led him before General Darras.

The little group, led by two officers of the Republican Guard, moves toward the band of music in front of the prison van and begins its march along the front of the troops and about three feet distant from them.

Dreyfus holds his head well up. The public cries, "Death to the traitor!" Soon he reaches the great gateway, and the crowd has a better sight of him. The cries increase, thousands of voices demanding the death of the wretch, who still exclaims: "I am innocent! *Vive la France!*"

The crowd has not heard, but it has seen Dreyfus turn toward it and speak.

A formidable burst of hisses replies to him, then an immense shout which rolls like a tempest across the vast courtyard:

"Death to the traitor! Kill him!"

And then outside the mob heaves forward in a murderous surge. Only by a mighty effort can the police restrain the people from breaking through into the yard, to wreak their swift and just vengeance upon Dreyfus for his infamy.

Dreyfus continues his march. He reaches the group made up of the press representatives.

"You will say to the whole of France," he cries, "that I am innocent!"

"Silence, wretch," is the reply. "Coward! Traitor! Judas!"

Under the insult, the abject Dreyfus pulls himself up. He flings at us a glance full of fierce hatred.

"You have no right to insult me!"

A clear voice issues from the group:

"You know well that you are not innocent. *Vive la France!* Dirty Jew!"

Dreyfus continues his route.

His clothing is pitiably disheveled. In the place of his stripes hang long dangling threads, and his cap has no shape.

Dreyfus pulls himself up once more, but the cries of the crowd are beginning to affect him. Though the head of the wretch is still insolently turned toward the troops, his legs are beginning to give way.

The march round the square is ended. Dreyfus is handed over to the two gendarmes, who have gathered up his stripes, and they conduct him to the prison van.

Dreyfus, completely silent now, is placed once more in prison. But there again he protests his innocence.

* * *

In his own investigation of the affair, a courageous and honest officer of the General Staff, Major Picquart, established the fact that the man who had betrayed his country was actually Major Esterhazy, the grandson of an illegitimate member of the French branch of the Austrian house of Esterhazy. A scoundrel, gambler, and dissolute cad, Esterhazy brazenly requested an appearance before a court-martial to meet what he called "this shameful accusation." The hearing developed into a farce, with judges, prosecution, and the accused forming a united front. Acquitted on January 11, 1898, by unanimous vote, Esterhazy emerged from the courtroom a free man as the crowds shouted: "Long live France! Down with the Jews!"

The acquittal of Esterhazy was a turning point in the Dreyfus case, for it angered a meek-looking gentle man with a voice of thunder. Émile Zola had known terrible poverty in a Parisian attic as well as glittering success as a distinguished novelist. Although he studiously avoided public life, he was fascinated by the case of the Jewish captain that was convulsing French politics and social life. Just two days after the acquittal, Zola published in the newspaper *L'Aurore* (Paris) an impassioned letter beginning with the words *J'accuse* and addressed to the President of the Republic. Zola's fiery letter amounted in effect to an accurate recapitulation of the facts in the case down to that very day. It was a smashing success, a thunderclap that shook the world. "It was a breast bared," wrote one observer, "an indignant conscience calling other consciences to its aid." To Anatole France it was "a moment in the conscience of mankind." For his pains Zola was convicted of libel, his name was struck from the rolls of the Legion of Honor, and he was forced to leave France and live in exile in England for more than a year.

One sensation succeeded another in the famous case. As befits an absorbing drama, eventually the hero was rewarded and the villain punished. Dreyfus was restored to the army and promoted in rank. Zola died before the affair was ended; his remains were buried with great pomp in the Panthéon, the Westminster Abbey of France. The honor of France was vindicated by the dismissal of the officers in the conspiracy against Dreyfus.

On February 17, 1908, an enterprising reporter for the *Philadelphia Press* found Esterhazy in an attic in London, dying alone, and in poverty. "He was huddled up in an old armchair and clad in a well-worn light-brown overcoat, crouching over the fire, seeking to get warmth to his thin, attenuated frame. The gray-bearded old man, with his hair prematurely silvered and shoulders bowed, looked what he is—an outcast from society, whose only desire is to be left alone and to eke out his own life." This was the same scoundrel who as a trusted staff officer in Paris had written to his mistress: "All these grotesque French generals still wear the mark of the Prussian boot on their behinds."

Thus ended the greatest detective story in history. The Dreyfus case turned out to be not a "great Jewish conspiracy" to deliver France to the enemy, but a momentous political battle in which republican and democratic ideas won a striking victory against the forces of reaction.

Stephen Crane Pins the Red Badge of Courage
on Surgeon Gibbs

EVERYTHING IS QUIET. There is no trouble here. There will be no war," Frederic Remington, the well-known artist, wired William Randolph Hearst from Cuba. Hearst's reply is apocryphal:

"You furnish the pictures, and I'll furnish the war."

The revolution in Cuba, the end product of a combination of Spanish misrule and a depression owing to an American tariff against Cuban sugar, was made to order for the circulation war between Hearst's *Journal* and Pulitzer's *World*. After the swashbuckling newsman Richard Harding Davis had inflamed public opinion by reporting the harsh rule of the Spanish Commander, General Valeriano ("The Butcher") Weyler, taking up the entire front page and half of the second of an issue of the *Journal* with a sensational story of the execution of Adolfo Rodríguez, a twenty-year-old insurgent, the battle of the "yellows" was kept up until this country was at war with Spain. The culminating incident, the sinking of the warship *Maine* in Havana Harbor on February 15, 1898, was attributed by Hearst without a particle of proof to "an enemy's secret infernal machine."

Of all the reportorial talent to observe the campaign in Cuba, the outstanding literary figure was a Pulitzer correspondent named Stephen Crane. Only a few years before, this half-starved young writer had been eking out a miserable existence doing reportorial bits for the *Tribune* and the *Herald*. Then came *The Red Badge of Courage* (1895), Crane's great novel of the common soldier in the turmoil of the Civil War—a masterpiece of battle reporting. Genius, observed William Dean Howells, seemed to "spring to life fully armed."

Crane lived violently. He married the madam of a Jacksonville bawdyhouse; almost lost his life on a filibustering expedition to Cuba in 1896, when his vessel sank off the Florida coast and he spent fifty hours in an open boat; rushed over to Greece to cover the war with Turkey; and, for a few moments, settled down to writing in England. "Very typically American," H. G. Wells found him at this time. "Long and spare, with very straight hair and straight features, and long quiet hands and hollow eyes, moving slowly and speaking slowly."

This master of descriptive writing ("The red sun was pasted in the sky like a wafer"—a good sample) was not particularly successful in emulating the romantic, chesty school of reporting fashionable with Rudyard Kipling and Richard Harding Davis. His best work in Cuba was not in the reporting of battles, but in writing about soldiers and soldiering. Crane's great moment came in June of '98, when a detachment of marines landed on the eastern bank of Guantánamo Bay below Santiago. Crane was sick. Surgeon Gibbs gave him quinine and advised him to clear out. But, sick or not, he had come to see the war and was going to report it if he died in the attempt. His story of the first American casualties in the fighting in Cuba made *The World*'s front page. His newspaper account was straightforward, informative, but hardly inspired.

A World *correspondent immortalizes an*
incident on the shores of Guantánamo Bay

New York *World,* June 13, 1898

Special Cable Dispatch to *The World*

ON BOARD *The World* DISPATCH BOAT *Triton,* OFF GUANTÁNAMO, VIA PORTO ANTONIO, JAMAICA, JUNE 12—For thirteen hours the marines, under Lieutenant Colonel Huntington, who landed from the *Panther* and raised Old Glory over the battered fortifications of the Spanish at the mouth of Guantánamo Harbor, sustained an attack made by the Spaniards.

Four of our men are killed and one wounded. The killed are:

Assistant Surgeon John Blair Gibbs of Richmond, Va.

Sergeant Charles H. Smith, of Smallwood.

Private William Dunphy, of Gloucestèr, Mass.

Private James McColgan, of Stoneham, Mass.

Corporal Glass was slightly wounded on the head.

The advance pickets under Lieutenants Neville and Shaw are thought to be prisoners.

The attack began at three o'clock Saturday afternoon. It lasted with almost continuous skirmishing until this morning.

It is not known how great was the Spanish loss. Their dead and wounded were carried off. It is thought from blood splashes found after the fighting that their loss was heavy.

The Spaniards advanced upon our outposts through thick tropical underbrush and began firing.

Sergeant Smith, who was at the extreme picket post relieving the guard, fell at the first fire.

The firing at first was desultory. The Spaniards drove in the outposts, a part of Captain Spicer's company.

They fell back upon the camp, where the fighting was continued until five o'clock, when the Spaniards were repulsed.

Captain McCalla landed reinforcements from the marines of the *Marblehead* in the launch. Ensign Sullivan afterward went close to the shore in the launch, trying to draw the enemy's fire, but failed to accomplish this.

The bodies of Privates McColgan and Dunphy were found in the brush. Each was shot in the head. The large cavities caused by the bullets, which inside a range of five hundred yards have a rotary motion, indicate that they were killed at close range. Their bodies were stripped of shoes, hats, and cartridges and horribly mutilated.

The marines received the attack upon the camp formed into three sides of a hollow square. The country about was craggy, cut with ravines, and covered with a tropical thicket. The Spaniards up to midnight attacked from the cover of this undergrowth.

The afternoon was cloudy and the night windy. After sunset it grew very dark. At night the enemy was discoverable only by the flashes of their arms, save when occasionally the searchlights of the ships sweeping along the deep foliage discovered a party of the Spaniards.

Whenever this happened the guns of the marines lined along the camp and the machine gun of the launch of the *Marblehead* volleyed at the assailants.

The launch pushed up the bay along the shore, firing upon the Spaniards with her gun. It is believed that her fire was deadly.

About midnight the Spaniards charged up the hill from the southwest upon the camp. Upon repeated volleys of bullets they broke and retreated. So close did they come that revolvers were used..

Three Spaniards got to the edge of the camp, where Colonel José Campina, the Cuban guide, fired upon

them. They turned and ran helter-skelter down the hills.

It was during this assault that Assistant Surgeon Gibbs was killed. He was shot in the head in front of his own tent. He fell into the arms of Private Sullivan, and both dropped. A second bullet threw dust in their faces. Surgeon Gibbs lived ten minutes, but did not regain consciousness.

Firing was kept up by small squads of Spaniards. The marines had lain upon their arms, and some of them, worn out with the fatigue of two days' labor and fighting almost without rest, had fallen asleep. At dawn all were aroused in anticipation of a second assault, but one was not made.

When daylight made it possible to use field guns, three twelve-pounders opened upon the few Spaniards then visible, who fled.

Our men behaved well and are praised by their officers. The great majority of them had never before been under fire, and though a night attack is especially trying, not one of them flinched.

They themselves give credit for courage to the Spaniards, whom they express a desire to meet again.

BUT TO Crane the death of Surgeon Gibbs was much more than a name on a casualty list. It inspired one of his finest pieces of writing. In *Wounds in the Rain* (1900), a collection of Cuban sketches published at the end of the war, Crane amplified those intense moments during the Spanish attack on the camp, those ten minutes during which Surgeon Gibbs lived after he had been fatally wounded.

Stephen Crane, *Wounds in the Rain*. From Volume IX of *The Works of Stephen Crane,* edited by Wilson Follett, by permission of Alfred A. Knopf, Inc. Copyright, 1900, by Frederick A. Stokes; copyright, 1928, by Mary Alice Ludwig.

One day, our dispatch boat found the shores of Guantánamo Bay flowing past on either side. It was at nightfall, and on the eastward point a small vil-

lage was burning, and it happened that a fiery light was thrown upon some palm trees so that it made them into enormous crimson feathers. The water was the color of blue steel; the Cuban woods were somber; high shivered the gory feathers. The last boatloads of the marine battalion were pulling for the beach. The marine officers gave me generous hospitality to the camp on the hill.

That night there was an alarm, and amid a stern calling of orders and a rushing of men, I wandered in search of some other man who had no occupation. It turned out to be the young assistant surgeon, Gibbs. We foregathered in the center of a square of six companies of marines. There was no firing. We thought it rather comic. The next night there was an alarm; there was some firing; we lay on our bellies; it was no longer comic.

On the third night the alarm came early; I went in search of Gibbs, but I soon gave over an active search for the more congenial occupation of lying flat and feeling the hot hiss of the bullets trying to cut my hair. For the moment I was no longer a cynic. I was a child who, in a fit of ignorance, had jumped into the vat of war.

I heard somebody dying near me. He was dying hard. It took him a long time to die. He breathed as all noble machinery breathes when it is making its gallant strife against breaking, breaking. But he was going to break. He was going to break. It seemed to me, this breathing, the noise of a heroic pump which strives to subdue a mud which comes upon it in tons. The darkness was impenetrable. The man was lying in some depression within seven feet of me. Every wave, vibration, of his anguish beat upon my senses. He was long past groaning. There was only the bitter strife for air which

pulsed out into the night in a clear penetrating whistle with intervals of terrible silence in which I held my own breath in the common unconscious aspiration to help. I thought this man would never die. I wanted him to die. Ultimately he died.

At the moment the adjutant came bustling along erect amid the spitting bullets. I knew him by his voice.

"Where's the doctor? There's some wounded men over there. Where's the doctor?"

A man answered briskly: "Just died this minute, sir." It was as if he had said: "Just gone around the corner this minute, sir."

Despite the horror of this night's business, the man's mind was somehow influenced by the coincidence of the adjutant's calling aloud for the doctor within a few seconds of the doctor's death. It—what shall I say? It interested him, this coincidence.

The day broke by inches, with an obvious and maddening reluctance. From some unfathomable source I procured an opinion that my friend was not dead at all—the wild and quivering darkness had caused me to misinterpret a few shouted words. At length the land brightened in a violent atmosphere, the perfect dawning of a tropic day, and in this light I saw a clump of men near me. At first I thought they were all dead. Then I thought they were all asleep. The truth was that a group of wan-faced, exhausted men had gone to sleep about Gibbs' body so closely and in such abandoned attitudes that one's eye could not pick the living from the dead until one saw that a certain head had beneath it a great dark pool.

CRANE WAS CITED for his bravery under fire at Guantánamo. His last days on the Cuban front proved an anticlimax. With Leonard Wood and Richard Harding Davis he recklessly ascended San Juan Hill. Reporting "T. R.'s" ride to glory with his Rough Riders, Crane made the mistake of telling the truth about the conduct of New York's Seventy-first, and Pulitzer found himself assailed by Hearst for slandering the heroism of New York's sons. Dazed by quinine, broken in health, Crane returned to New York and then went on to England. In the winter of 1900, wasting away with tuberculosis, Crane went to his last bivouac with Surgeon Gibbs.

Creelman of the *Journal* Leads the Charge
at El Caney

SOME REPORTERS in Cuba wrote the news. James Creelman made the news. His personal exploit at El Caney turned out to be one of the best news stories of the war. Riding along Santiago's outer picket lines, Creelman cabled the *Journal* a preliminary story on the preparations for the great attack.

Copyboy Hearst consoles his bleeding reporter: "I'm sorry you're hurt, but wasn't it a splendid fight?"

New York *Journal*, July 1, 1898

WHEELER'S HEADQUARTERS AT THE FRONT, JUNE 28, BY THE *Journal*'s DISPATCH BOAT *Simpson* TO KINGSTON, JUNE 30—We are almost ready for the last dread scene of agony on the intrenched green slopes that guard the doomed Santiago.

Two barriers of barbed wire surround the city on the land side, with six heavily guarded openings. The American army is gradually stretching out across the hills on the eastern side of Santiago, within five miles of the cannon-crowded hillside which must be taken before the city can be captured.

No man who has not gone over this trail, no man who was not in the terrible downpour of rain which drenched our army to the skin this afternoon, can understand the suffering of our troops and the heroism with which they bore it.

Cavalrymen dismounted, infantrymen from Colorado, Michigan, and Massachusetts toiled hour after hour through jungles of cactus, poisonous vines, and high grass that cuts like razor edges.

The blistering tropic sunlight makes the skyline of distant hills shimmy and waver prismatically before the eyes. From the stagnant pools strange gray mists float upward, and vultures with outstretched wings look greedily down from above vegetation torn and trampled underfoot by our troops.

A horribly sour breath rises from the earth. Curious stenches steal from hidden places in the jungle.

Thousands of gigantic land crabs, splotched with yellow and red, wriggle and twist themselves along the sides of the roads with leprous white claws clicking viciously—a ghastly, dreadful sight to young soldiers fresh from New York, Boston, and Detroit.

Ragged Cubans slip noiselessly through the undergrowth or sprawl under the shade of huge gossamer trees, watching with childish pleasure the steady onpush of their American defenders.

The heat is almost intolerable. The sun is like a great yellow furnace torturing everything living, and turning everything dead into a thousand mysterious forms of terror.

A fierce light swims in waves before the eyes of the exhausted soldiers. This morning a young infantryman reeled and fell in the road almost under my mule's feet. When I helped him to his feet he smiled and said:

"It's all right. I never struck such a place as this, but I must get to the front before the fight begins. I had to lie to get into the army, for I am only seventeen years old."

Five minutes later he was trudging along gallantly.

Two hours later the first great tropic rainstorm we have encountered fell from the sky, not slantwise, but straight down. It was the first actual test of the army in the most dreadful experience of the tropics. For three hours the great, cold torrent swept down from the clouds, drenching the soldiers to the skin, soaking their blankets and carrying misery into all our vast camps reaching out on either side of the trail, extinguishing campfires and sending rivers of mud-red water swirling along the narrow road, dashing over rocks where the trail inclined downward. Through this filthy flood our army streamed onward, splashing in the mud and water or huddling vainly for shelter under trees.

An hour before the heat was so great that men reeled and swooned, but now came one of the mysterious transitions of the tropics.

The whole army shivered. As I rode along I could see robust men shaking from head to foot, their skins turned gray and white. Millions of land crabs came chattering and squirming from under poisonous undergrowth, and the soldiers crushed them under their heels.

Every man who had quinine swallowed a dose. Officers, splashed with mud to their hips, hurried here and there, urging the men to strip naked when the rain was over and dry their clothes at the campfires.

Presently thousands of men were standing about naked, while the sun drew up the thick vapors from the earth and vicious tropical flies stung their white skins.

One thought which seemed to run like an electric current through the army was anxiety to get to the front.

Soldiers everywhere begged to have their regiments put in the first line of attack. The weather is nothing to them. The possibility of disease is nothing to them. Exposure and hunger do not trouble them. They want to fight. You can see it in their faces. You can hear it in their talk.

The most wonderful thing is that, in spite of the surroundings, less than one per cent of the army is sick. This, I believe, is the lowest death record of any army in the world.

I saw a touching scene during the great storm today. While the giant gusts of rain were beating down on the earth groups of soldiers stood unsheltered around the graves of Rough Riders on the little trail where they died so heroically. There may be a monument erected to these men, but there can never be a nobler tribute than this.

As the poor fellows pressed around Hamilton Fish's grave the rain cataracted from their hat rims and ran in little rivulets over the mound.

* * *

BUT THE FATES decreed that Creelman's next story would appear under the by-line of his boss, William Randolph Hearst. On July 1, 1898, the very same day that Teddy charged up San Juan Hill, General Lawton, in command of some seven thousand troops, prepared to capture the Spanish blockhouse at El Caney. Receiving an inside tip at midnight, Creelman slipped away from his fellow correspondents and made the top of a small hill from which the stone fort at El Caney was clearly visible. Crawling forward to an adjacent hill, Creelman caught up with General Chaffee, of whom he later wrote: "I never saw a finer soldier, and never a more warlike face." Bullets came uncomfortably close. One clipped a button from the general's breast. It seemed better to be shot at fighting than to die watching. The only man to know the back road up the hill, Creelman suggested a bayonet charge and offered to lead the way if Chaffee would send troops to a depression on the hillside where they would be partly sheltered until they were within close rushing distance. "Hardly the business of a correspondent," admitted the *Journal* reporter. Ordinarily a very formal person ("Mr. Creelman" even to his closest associates), Creelman in the next few moments "ceased to be a journalist" and found himself a hero.

New York *Journal,* July 4, 1898

THE HEROIC CAPTURE OF CANEY TOLD BY THE *JOURNAL'S* EDITOR-IN-CHIEF

Special Cable Dispatch to the New York Journal—WITH THE ARMY IN FRONT OF SANTIAGO, JULY 1, MIDNIGHT, VIA KINGSTON, JAMAICA, JULY 3—Tonight, as I write, the ambulance trains are bringing in the wounded soldiers from the fierce battle around the little inland village of Caney.

Siboney, the base of the army, is a hospital and nothing more. There is no saying when the slaughter will cease. The tents are crowded with wounded, and the hard-worked surgeons are busy with their mechanical work. There is an odor of anesthetics and the clatter of ambulances in the one narrow street

Under the fierce firing of far-heavier artillery forces than it was supposed

the Spaniards had, the American infantry and dismounted cavalry have done their work, and done it nobly.

I have been at the artillery positions all day to see what our guns could or could not do. There is no question of skill or courage of American gunners. Their work was as near perfect as gunnery gets to be, but there was no artillery to speak of.

The War Department has furnished the necessary heavy guns, but they remain in the rear because of the difficulty of transportation from the coast.

I set out before daybreak this morning on horseback with Honore Laine, who is a colonel in the Cuban Army, and has served for months as the *Journal's* correspondent in Cuba. We rode over eight miles of difficult country which intervenes between the army based on the coast and the fighting line which is being driven forward toward Santiago.

ARRIVED AT THE FRONT, Hearst witnessed the American batteries assisting
the advance on the line of Santiago's defenses. The Spaniards soon found
the range and made the attackers most uncomfortable. Through his glasses
Hearst could make out the infantry advancing toward El Caney.

The infantry firing was ceaseless, our
men popping away continuously, as a
string of firecrackers pops. The Spaniards fired in volleys whenever our
men came in sight of the open spaces.

Many times we heard this volley
fire and saw numbers of our brave fellows pitch forward and lie still on the
turf while the others hurried on to the
next protecting clump of bushes.

For hours the Spaniards had poured
their fire from slits in the stone fort,
from their deep trenches, and from
the windows of the town. For hours
our men answered back from trees and
brush and gullies. For hours cannon at
our side banged and shells screamed
through the air and fell upon fort and
town. And always our infantry advanced, drawing nearer and closing up
on the village, till at last they formed
under a group of mangrove trees at the
foot of the very hill on which the stone
fort stood.

With a rush they swept up the slope,
and the stone fort was ours.

Then you should have heard the
yell that went up from the knoll on
which our battery stood. Gunners, drivers, Cubans, correspondents, swung their hats and gave a
mighty cheer. Immediately our battery stopped firing for fear we would
hurt our own men, and dashing down
into the valley hurried across to take
up a position near the infantry, who
were now firing on Caney from its new
position before the musketry firing
ceased and the Spaniards, broken into
small bunches, fled from Caney in the
direction of Santiago.

Laine and I hurried up to the stone
fort and found that James Creelman,
the *Journal* correspondent with the infantry column, had been seriously
wounded and was lying in the Twelfth
Infantry hospital.

Our men were still firing an occasional shot, and from blockhouses and
isolated trenches from which the Spaniards could not easily retreat, flags of
truce were waving. Guns and side arms
were being taken away from such
Spaniards as had outlived the pitiless
fire, and their dead were being dumped
without ceremony into the trenches
after the Spanish fashion.

When I left the fort to hunt for
Creelman I found him, bloody and
bandaged, lying on his back on a
blanket on the ground, but shown all
care and attention that kindly and
skillful surgeons could give him. His
first words to me were that he was
afraid he could not write much of a
story, as he was pretty well dazed, but
if I would write for him he would dictate the best he could. I sat down
among the wounded and Creelman
told me his story of the fight. Here
it is:

"The extraordinary thing in this
fight of all the fights I have seen is the
enormous amount of ammunition
fired. There was a continuous roar of
musketry from four o'clock morning
until four o'clock afternoon.

"Chaffee's brigade began the fight
by moving along the extreme right,
with Ludlow down in the low country
to the left of Caney. General Chaffee's
brigade consisted of the Seventeenth,
Seventh, and Twelfth Infantry and
was without artillery. It occupied the
extreme right.

"The formation was like two sides

of an equilateral triangle, Ludlow to the south and Chaffee to the east.

"Ludlow began firing through the brush, and we could see through the palm trees and the tangle of bushes the brown and blue figures of our soldiers in a line a mile long, stealing from tree to tree, from bush to bush, firing as they went.

"Up here on the heights, General Chaffee, facing Caney, moved his troops very early in the morning, and the battle opened by Ludlow's artillery firing on the fort and knocking several holes in it. The artillery kept up a steady fire on the fort and town and finally demolished the fort. Several times the Spaniards were driven from it. But each time they returned before our infantry could approach it.

"Our artillery had but four small guns, and though they fired with great accuracy, it was ten hours before they finally reduced the stone fort on the hill and enabled our infantry to take possession.

"The Twelfth Infantry constituted the left of our attack, the Seventeenth held the right, while the Seventh, made up largely of recruits, occupied the center.

"The Spaniards fired from loopholes in the stone houses of the town, and, furthermore, were massed in trenches on the east side of the fort. They fought like devils.

"From all the ridges around about a stream of fire was kept on Chaffee's men, who were kept wondering how they were being wounded. For a time they thought General Ludlow's men were on the opposite side of the fort and were firing over it.

"The fact was the fire came from heavy breastworks on the northwest corner of Caney, where the principal Spanish force lay, with their hats on sticks to deceive our riflemen. From this position the enemy poured in a fearful fire. The Seventeenth had to lie down flat under the pounding, but even then men were killed.

"General Chaffee dashed about with his hat on the back of his head like a magnificent cowboy, urging his men on, crying to them to get in and help their country with a victory.

"Smokeless powder makes it impossible to locate the enemy. You wonder where the fire comes from. When you stand up to see you get a bullet.

"We finally located the trenches and could see the officers moving about, urging their men. But one by one their heads went up, while their faces disappeared behind the breastworks. The enemy was making a turning movement to the right.

"To turn the left of the Spanish position it was necessary to get a blockhouse, which held the right of our line. General Chaffee detailed Captain Clarke to approach and occupy this blockhouse as soon as the artillery had sufficiently harried its Spanish defenders.

"Clarke and Captain Haskell started up the slope. I told them I had been on the ridge and knew the condition of affairs, so I would show them the way.

"We pushed right up to the trench around the fort, and getting out our wire cutters severed the barbed wire in front of it. I jumped over the several strands and got into the trench.

"It was a horrible, blood-splashed thing, and an inferno of agony. Many men lay dead, with gleaming teeth, and hands clutching their throats. Others were crawling there alive.

"I shouted to the survivors to surrender, and they held up their hands.

"Then I ran into the fort, and found there a Spanish officer and four men alive, while seven lay dead in one room. The whole floor ran with blood. Blood splashed all the walls. It was a perfect hogpen of butchery.

"Three poor wretches put their hands together in supplication. One had a white handkerchief tied on a stick. This he lifted and moved it toward me. The officer held up his hands, while the others began to pray and plead.

"I took the guns from all and threw them outside the fort. Then I called some of our men and put them in charge of the prisoners.

"I then got out of the fort, ran around to the other side, and secured the Spanish flag.* I displayed it to our troops, and they cheered lustily.

"Just as I turned to speak to Captain Haskell I was struck by a bullet from the trenches on the Spanish side."

Such was the graphic story Creel-man told as he lay wounded and in pain.

General Chaffee moved on and took the breastworks, and Caney was ours. Banks, the color sergeant of the Twelfth Infantry, raised the American flag over the town.

General Chaffee says he is much astonished at the number of men lost in the besieged town, as it did not contain over a thousand Spanish. Some twenty-five of these were killed and fifty wounded, while one hundred and fifty were taken prisoners. The killed and wounded on our side exceeded these figures.

The Twelfth lost heavily. Lieutenant Churchman was shot through the breast and Sergeant Miller, of the first company, was killed.

The Spanish flag captured from the Spanish stone fort I will forward to the *Journal* by mail.

W. R. HEARST

IN HIS VOLUME of reporting stories, *On the Great Highway* (1901), Creelman tells how he staggered to a hammock in a compartment of the fort, "hearing my own blood drip," was carried down the hill and laid among the wounded, while "bullets sang above the heads of the surgeons" as they bent over their patients. Creelman continues:

The heat was terrific. Things swam in the air. There was a strange yellow glare on everything. Voices of thunder seemed to come from the blurred figures moving to and fro. A horse twenty feet high stamped the earth with his feet and made the distant mountaintops rock. Little fiery blobs kept dropping down from somewhere, and the world was whirling upside down. Someone was being killed? Who was being killed? Whose sword was lost? Why was that general standing on one leg and having all his buttons shot off? Copy! copy! an hour to spare before the paper goes to press!

Someone knelt in the grass beside me and put his hand on my fevered head. Opening my eyes, I saw Mr. Hearst, the proprietor of the New York *Journal*, a straw hat with a bright ribbon on his head, a revolver at his belt, and a pencil and notebook in his hand. The man who had provoked the war had come to see the result with his own eyes, and, finding one of his correspondents prostrate, was doing the work himself. Slowly he

---

* In an account of the incident written for the *Review of Reviews*, November, 1898, Creelman declared: "Suddenly I thought of the flag. It was the thing that I had come to get. I wanted it for the *Journal*. The *Journal* had provoked the war, and it was only fair that the *Journal* should have the first flag captured in the greatest land battle of the war."

took down my story of the fight. Again and again the tinging of Mauser bullets inter-rupted. But he seemed unmoved. That battle had to be reported somehow.

"I'm sorry you're hurt, but"—and his face was radiant with enthusiasm—"wasn't it a splendid fight? We must beat every paper in the world."

After a previous *Journal* exploit, when reporter Karl Decker rescued beauteous Evangelina Cisneros, daughter of a Cuban insurgent leader, from jail, Governor Sadler of Missouri urged that Hearst send five hundred of his reporters to free the island.* Five hundred Creelmans would without doubt have shortened the war!

---

* New York *Journal,* October 13, 1897.

Winston Churchill, Alone Save for a Huge

Vulture, Makes His Escape from the Boers

SOME OF THE most brilliant reporting of modern times was inspired by
British military heroics in Africa as the nineteenth century came to a
close. When, in the 1880's, the British control of the Nile was threatened
by an Arab revolt in the Sudan and General "Chinese" Gordon was trapped
in Khartoum, Frederic Villiers, an artist and war correspondent for the
Weekly Graphic, who inspired Kipling's portrait of the war correspondent
in *The Light that Failed* (1891), reported how he was caught in the broken
square at Tamai, and confessed: "How I got out of that fight I hardly know
to this day." The London *Daily Telegraph*'s reporter, Bennet Burleigh,
who rode about in the broken line, described the ferocious enemy charge:
"I saw Arab after Arab, through whose bodies our bullets had plowed their
way, charging down on the square, with the blood spouting in pulsating
streams from them at every throb." Two days before relief forces came in
sight of Khartoum, Gordon and his garrison of eleven thousand were massacred.

The British never forgot. When they had mustered an adequate force,
they sent Colonel Kitchener south to settle the score. At Omdurman, on
September 2, 1898, Kitchener's army, outnumbered two to one, with only
two British brigades (the rest Egyptian), met the reckless dervishes, as
these militant Arabs were called, head on. After the natives had charged in
vain against the British squares, the Twenty-first Lancers turned to the
attack.

We are indebted to a twenty-four-year-old British officer serving with
the Twenty-first Lancers for an unforgettable word picture of that cavalry
charge, which he sent in to the London *Morning Post.* A descendant of
Britain's greatest military hero, the Duke of Marlborough, whose biographer he became, Winston Churchill had, at the age of twenty-one, already
created a sensation in England by his front-line news dispatches to the
Daily Graphic on the Cuban revolution. Then, attached to the Malakand
Field Force, he sent to *The Daily Telegraph* a series of incisive accounts
from the Indian frontier. At Omdurman Churchill reported a mass of dervishes some forty yards from him, "wild with excitement, dancing about
on their feet, shaking their spears up and down." "The whole scene seemed
to flicker," he commented. "I have an impression, but it is too fleeting to
define, of brown-clad Lancers mixed up here and there with this surging
mob." Suddenly he found himself alone. When a dervish sprang at him and
wielded his spear, Churchill showed some of that poise which pulled him
through many a later military crisis. "I shot him at less than a yard," he

reported. "He fell on the sand, and lay there dead. How easy to kill a man! But I did not worry about it."

Colonel Lionel James, later of the London *Times,* who covered the campaign for Reuters, recalled how Churchill offered his story of the charge of the lancers to him on condition that the news agency should specifically mention his presence in the cavalry clash. George Steevens, the renowned *Daily Mail* reporter, observed at that time: "Churchill will go far! He has every property that makes for success. He has blood, brain, rich friends behind him, and audacity."

That audacity was soon to be put to the test again. Hardly had the battle-weary correspondent returned to England from Omdurman when he found his country at war with the Boers. These patriarchal farmers of Dutch descent resisted incorporation into an all-British South Africa, an objective devoutly desired by the British, particularly after gold had been discovered in that area in 1885. The British considered the war a pushover, and London newspaper publishers sent their star reporters to the war scene to record anticipated military victories. The highest priced among the correspondents was Winston Churchill, who, at the age of twenty-five, commanded the unprecedented figure of £250 a month to report the war for the London *Morning Post.*

On October 31, 1899, Churchill arrived in Natal, which the Boers had invaded.

It took just two weeks for Churchill to appreciate how serious the British military position had become. When the armored train on which he was riding was derailed, he was captured, marched sixty miles to the railhead at Elandslaagte, and then dispatched with other prisoners to Pretoria, to be formally imprisoned. As a war correspondent Churchill was in a vulnerable position, for he had been helping the British armed forces in their vain effort to elude the trap at the time he was caught, and under the laws of war he might have been shot out of hand. This the Boers refrained from doing. Still Winston protested on the ground that he was a noncombatant and his arrest therefore illegal. Upon reading the protest the state attorney, a promising young lawyer named Jan Smuts, destined to become the greatest figure in modern South African history, objected. "Winston Churchill noncombatant? Impossible," was his curt comment.

The next we hear of Churchill is from Portuguese East Africa.

"I am very weak, but I am free"

Pearson's Illustrated War News, December 30, 1899

HOW I ESCAPED FROM PRETORIA

BY WINSTON CHURCHILL

The Morning Post has received the following telegram from Mr. Winston Spencer Churchill, its war correspondent, who was taken prisoner by the Boers and escaped from Pretoria.

LOURENÇO MARQUES, DECEMBER 21, 10 P.M.—I was concealed in a railway truck under great sacks.

I had a small store of good water with me.

I remained hidden, chancing discovery.

The Boers searched the train at Komati Poort, but did not search deep enough, so after sixty hours of misery I came safely here.

I am very weak, but I am free.

I have lost many pounds, but I am lighter in heart.

I shall also avail myself of every opportunity from this moment to urge with earnestness an unflinching and uncompromising prosecution of the war.

On the afternoon of the twelfth the Transvaal Government's Secretary for War informed me that there was little chance of release.

I therefore resolved to escape the same night, and left the State Schools Prison at Pretoria by climbing the wall when the sentries' backs were turned momentarily.

I walked through the streets of the town without any disguise, meeting many burghers, but I was not challenged in the crowd.

I got through the pickets of the Town Guard, and struck the Delagoa Bay Railroad.

I walked along it, evading the watchers at the bridges and culverts.

I waited for a train beyond the first station.

The out 11:10 goods train from Pretoria arrived, and before it had reached full speed I boarded with great difficulty, and hid myself under coal sacks.

I jumped from the train before dawn, and sheltered during the day in a small wood, in company with a huge vulture, who displayed a lively interest in me.

I walked on at dusk.

There were no more trains that night.

The danger of meeting the guards of the railway line continued, but I was obliged to follow it, as I had no compass or map.

I had to make wide detours to avoid the bridges, stations, and huts.

My progress was very slow, and chocolate is not a satisfying food.

The outlook was gloomy, but I persevered, with God's help, for five days.

The food I had to have was very precarious.

I was lying up at daylight, and walking on at nighttime, and, meanwhile, my escape had been discovered and my description telegraphed everywhere.

All the trains were searched.

Everyone was on the watch for me.

Four wrong people were arrested.

But on the sixth day I managed to board a train beyond Middelburg, whence there is a direct service to Delagoa.

WHEN HE ARRIVED at Lourenço Marques, he went to the consulate. "Sorry," said the secretary, "the Consul is very busy."

"Just tell him Mr. Churchill of *The Morning Post* is calling."

The Consul fell over backwards in welcoming the visitor.

Churchill's audacious exploit tickled the British and infuriated the Boers, who believed that all this came from allowing prisoners to read Mill's *On Liberty,* and who had offered a reward of £25 for Churchill, "dead or alive."

Churchill warned his countrymen: "We are fighting a formidable adversary." He urged the need of a large-scale effort, at least a quarter of a million men, to put down the fierce Boer horsemen who were more than a match for the untrained British infantrymen. On his advice, large armies, commanded by Roberts and Kitchener, were dispatched, and the Boers were ultimately vanquished.

Although he was soon to launch upon a notable parliamentary career, Churchill's heart was always in front-line reporting. On a later occasion he contrasted the scenes at each end of a telegraph wire when the machine clicks off exciting news. His observation is characteristic:

How different are the scenes. The club on an autumn evening—its members, grouped anxiously around, discussing, wondering, asserting; the noise of traffic outside; the cigarette smoke and electric lights within. And, only an hour away along the wire, the field with the bright sunlight shining on the swirling muddy waters; the black forbidding rocks; the white tents of the brigade up the valley; a long streak of vivid green rice crop by the river; and in the foreground the brown-clad armed men.

I can never doubt which is the right end to be at. It is better to be making the news than taking it; to be an actor rather than a critic.

When, during World War II, General Eisenhower appealed to King George to keep the impulsive Churchill from participating in the D-Day engagement, His Majesty was forced to advise the Prime Minister that if the latter insisted on going, then the King would have to go at the head of his troops.

The events reported in *The World Crisis* (1923–29) and *The Gathering Storm* (1948) gave Churchill his chance to demonstrate a rare combination of skills—to play a chief role in the making of the news and then to demonstrate outstanding capacities in reporting it. The result: top-flight reporting and great historical literature at one and the same time.

Carry Nation Moves on Sodom-Manhattan and Tries Out Her System of "Hatchetation" in the Big City

H ER FIRST HUSBAND died in the agony of delirium tremens, and Carry * Nation never forgot it. In the mind of the eccentric little woman from Medicine Lodge, Kansas, there started a chain reaction that finally culminated in an explosion twenty-five years later. Beginning in minor-league style, Mrs. Nation organized a crusade against drink that carried her from the sun-parched plains of Kansas to the hellholes of New York.

At 9:45 on the morning of December 27, 1900, Mrs. Nation, now the president of the Barber County Women's Christian Temperance Union, began large-scale operations. This was her first big-city raid. Entering the saloon in the basement of the Carey Hotel in Wichita, Kansas, and without a word of warning, she pulled two large stones from a bundle of papers in her hand and promptly sent one of them whizzing through a large oil painting of Cleopatra at the Roman bath. Before the bartenders could recover from their astonishment, the redoubtable little Amazon threw the second large stone through a $1500 mirror situated directly back of the bar. Now thoroughly aroused by crusading zeal, she destroyed all the bottled goods she could reach. Within minutes Mrs. Nation was in the county jail, where she issued a triumphant statement:

"I came to the governor's town to destroy the finest saloon in it, hoping thus to attract attention to the flagrant violation of a Kansas law." †

Carry Nation's grand idea was fissionable. Soon other women came up with the same or similar plan. Mrs. Nation purchased several dozen bright and shiny hatchets, armed her followers with them, and, as "Home Defenders," began to move on dens of iniquity. Practicing what she called "hatchetation," she toured large cities throughout the country to preach the gospel of temperance. Her fame as the "Smasher" spread. Barkeepers snatched her hatchets, adorned them with blue ribbons, and hung them over their bars as trophies. Those who were not sufficiently alert found their mirrors and bottles smashed. The entire nation rocked with laughter at this display of slapstick comedy, but Carry Nation carried on with indomitable will and inflexible purpose.

In the late summer of 1901, Mrs. Nation finally reached that model for

---

* That is the way her unlettered father entered her name in the family Bible.

† Although Kansas had adopted a prohibition amendment in 1880 by a vote of 92,302 to 84,304, enforcement was resisted in certain localities, such as Wichita, where saloons operated under a system of city fines, collected in lieu of licenses.

modern Sodoms—Manhattan. Here she did no smashing, but under the shrewd and not disinterested guidance of New York reporters, she graced the city "with two visits of equal lunacy," described below in accounts from the New York *World*.

John L. Sullivan takes a powder: "Not on your life! Tell her I'm sick in bed!"

New York *World*, August 29, 1901

Here is what Carry Nation did during a six-hour stay on Manhattan Island yesterday:

Gave Police Commissioner Murphy the most uncomfortable quarter of an hour in his life.

Scared Chief Devery into dodging her.

Gave John L. Sullivan a bad attack of the frights.

Kept Acting Mayor Guggenheimer in a state of nervous agitation.

Had a row with her manager and left town as happy as a lark.

With a two-foot hatchet strapped to the girdle under her linen jacket, her beaded black poke bonnet pushed down firmly on her head, her broad jaw set at its most pugnacious angle, the Smasher strode into Colonel Murphy's room at Headquarters at eleven A.M., plumped into a chair close to him, and in ringing tones demanded:

"Don't you think New York is an awful bad place?"

"I don't think anything of the kind," testily said the Colonel.

"Yes, it is," insisted the Smasher. "It's full of hellholes and murder factories."

"Stop right there. I don't want to listen to you or to hear that kind of

talk in this place," almost shouted the Commissioner.

"You won't listen to me?" queried the Smasher in surprise. "Why, I came here a-purpose to discuss these matters with you. Do you mean to say you won't discuss these murder shops, these hellholes, these sinks of depravity in New York?"

"That's just what I mean."

"Now, now, now," said Mrs. Nation patronizingly, "I want to know why the saloons are permitted to open on Sunday."

"I won't discuss that matter with you."

Mrs. Nation laid a pudgy forefinger on the Colonel's arm. He angrily brushed it away, but in her sweetest tones the Smasher went on:

"I only came here to do New York good. I want to do good for humanity. I want to do something for you."

"You don't know what you're talking about," said the Colonel, in a rage. "Go back to Kansas. If you want to do something, why don't you do it for your husband?"

"I have no husband now," said the Smasher in a tone of regret. "I supposed you knew all about."*

"Oh, yes," said the Commissioner, with a grin. "All I have to say is that

* Carry's second husband, David Nation, divorced her for desertion that same year after many years of constant bickering.

I congratulate Mr. Nation. He ought to be a happy man now."

Unabashed, the Smasher took hold of the saloon question again.

"I won't sit here and be lectured. I don't want to talk to you. You are not in your right mind," said the Colonel.

"Do you think I am crazy?" shouted the now-furious Smasher.

"Yes, I do."

"You say, then, just what those wicked, riotous, rum-soaked, bedeviled Republicans in Kansas City say. They say that when they know that forty hellholes are closed in Topeka."

Murphy beckoned to Detective Linden to eject Mrs. Nation. Linden hesitated, and the Joint Smasher, undaunted, added new misery by saying:

"Now, father, be calm. I want to talk with you without quarreling."

"Don't call me father," said Murphy in a voice of agony.

"I will call you father. You are old enough to be my father. I'm only fifty-four and you are at least eighty, and I'll call you father anyway. Now, father, do you think a little 'hatchetation' would do a lot of good in New York?"

"If you violate the law I'll have you locked up," shouted the Commissioner.

The Smasher kept a crafty eye on Linden, and as she saw the detective had got his nerve up to the ejecting point she bounced out of her chair, saying:

"Now, father, we could have had a nice long talk if you didn't quarrel with me. We will all of us have to give an account of our stewardship—remember that."

All this time Deputy Commissioner Devery was hiding in a corner where he could listen without being seen. As the Smasher went out she passed a man smoking a cigarette. Turning to him, she shouted:

"You horrid, nasty man! Don't you know that your fate will be an eternal smoking?"

"Now take me to see John L. Sullivan," said the Smasher to her manager. "He once said some mean things about me."

Up to the Forty-second Street saloon formerly owned by the ex-champion the Smasher went. The saloon was recently closed, but John L. still had a room on the upper floor. A messenger took up word to the pugilist, who said:

"Not on your life. Tell her I'm sick in bed."

Word came from City Hall that the Joint Smasher was coming, and, much perturbed, Acting Mayor Guggenheimer called in the policeman at the door and said:

"If Carry Nation comes here don't let her in. Tell her the Mayor's office cannot be used for advertising purposes."

The Smasher, however, did not visit the City Hall. Instead she had a pleasant row with her manager. He had contracted for her to deliver a lecture last night at Ocean City, New Jersey. She had contracted to lecture tonight at College Green, Ohio, and at Dyckman, Illinois, tomorrow night. So she took the one P.M. train for Ohio while the manager fretted and fumed.

Mrs. Nation will return to New York Saturday and will lecture in Carnegie Hall Sunday.

Proprietor Caddigan, of the Hoffman House, was in a nervous frenzy last night. He did not know that Mrs. Nation had left the city, and jokers had told him she intended to invade the café at nine P.M., smash the famous $10,000 painting, _Nymphs and Satyr_, and rip to pieces the $100,000 worth of art treasures. Mr. Caddigan posted a man at all the entrances until someone told him Mrs. Nation was on her way to Ohio.

MRS. NATION fulfilled her engagements in the Midwest and then returned to New York on Sunday, September 1, 1901. How she was barred from the Democratic Club, precipitated a riot in three saloons, and came to grief at Devery's corner was described in this report.

New York *World*, September 2, 1901

A deafening medley of voices that merged into a terrific "Hurrah for Carry Nation!" A mob of thousands, beating this way and that, tearing, trampling each other for a sight of that squat, determined little figure, marching on with the exaltation of a conquering hero, and the Kansas Smasher was steered straight into the arms of three burly New York policemen and promptly "pinched."

It happened at Devery's corner, Twenty-eighth Street and Eighth Avenue, at 5:30 yesterday afternoon. The dauntless Carry unmolested had:

Precipitated a riot in three saloons.

Invaded two Sunday concert halls.

Paraded the highways and byways with a tumultuous rabble at her heels.

It was only when she invaded the district of the Big Chief * that the arm of the law became effective.

"I am not disturbing the peace," asserted Mrs. Nation indignantly, whisking about in her Quakerish linen gown with its quaint cape, and fixing on the bluecoats an invincible eye.

"You are raising a crowd and creat-ing a riot, and I arrest you," was the response of one of her captors, while the two others closed in about her and the procession started for the West Twentieth Street Station.

At Twenty-fourth Street, satisfied by Mrs. Nation's friends that she was about to return to her hotel, the policemen released her and put her on a car amid a volley of "Hurrahs!"

Mrs. Nation arrived from Danbury, Illinois, at 9:30 yesterday morning to fulfill her lecture engagement at Carnegie Hall last night. She went immediately to the Victoria Hotel, loudly declaring that she had traveled in a "saloon on wheels."

Giving herself only time to exchange her linen duster for a fresh white piqué frock (plain in cut and finished with the invariable cape, with a small hatchet in her buttonhole) and fortifying herself with a service at the Cathedral, the crusader started out to purify New York. With characteristic directness she went straight to the Democratic Club.

* * *

---

* The "Big Chief" was William S. Devery, a former captain of police, who at this time was Police Commissioner Murphy's first deputy. Devery's political headquarters was at a pump located at Twenty-eighth Street and Eighth Avenue. It is reasonable to assume that reference to his "district" meant the area of his political control in 1901, although apparently he was not then the district "leader" under Tammany, which post he obtained the very next year. In 1903, a reformed man, he ran as an independent anti-Tammany candidate for mayor against McClellan, the candidate of Charles Murphy, the Tammany leader whom Devery despised. Ironically, Carry Nation again visited Devery's headquarters in the 1903 campaign under happier circumstances, praised him, applauded him, not as a Republican or Democrat, but as a Prohibitionist! He took it all gallantly and, in deference to the Smasher, even ordered his followers to cease smoking! But, of course, like many others, he was only kidding "the old battle-ax."

"I want to get in," she said to the servant who barred her path.

"No ladies admitted!"

"But I want to see a member who can admit me," went on the imperturbable Carry, while a crowd gathered about the steps.

"I'm one, madam," from an elderly gentleman just inside the door, "and I repeat it is against the rules."

"Break 'em," responded the Smasher, one foot on the threshold.

The Superintendent rushed forward to the rescue.

"Have you got anything in here you don't want me to see? I would like to hold a Sunday-school lesson and a Bible reading in here."

"The club was not organized for that purpose," put in the Superintendent hastily.

"Don't you know," and she pushed her way past, only to be politely thrust out again, "that God said it isn't good for men to be alone?"

"Who are you, madam?" in wrathful tones.

"I'm Carry Nation, and I tell you that this must be a mighty bad place if you can't let a woman in."

At Fiftieth Street and Seventh Avenue Mrs. Nation saw the side door of a saloon open, and dashed in, attended by a crowd that filled the place.

"Oh me! Oh my!" she cried, making way for the "barkeep," who, paralyzed with terror at the unexpected onslaught, turned a sickly white.

"Look at him! Look at his white face! Nervous, ain't you?" and with a gleeful laugh Carry launched out for a bottle of whisky and raised it to hurl it to the floor, but the man was too quick for her, and disarmed, she turned to the loungers drinking at the tables.

"Ain't you 'shamed, boy, to be drinking up what you ought to give to your family?" she inquired from a bulletheaded youth.

"Ain't got none," was the laconic reply.

"Give her a highball, Peter, and I'll stand treat," cried a voice from the rear before the employees of the place could come to their senses and endeavor to clear the place.

The Smasher's progress down Broadway after this escapade was a veritable triumphal procession.

A short luncheon, and Mrs. Nation was in fine fettle for her afternoon campaign.

"Take me to some more hellholes," she demanded of her escort. Darting into a saloon at Twenty-ninth Street and Sixth Avenue, she cried:

"Ain't this against the law? Where are the police? I am Carry Nation, and I protest against the selling of that hell broth."

"We are selling lemonade," insisted the barkeeper.

"Lemonade!" echoed the reformer scornfully. "It's beer!" and walking over to a table where some sailors were drinking, she seized one of the steins and took a sip. "I know the taste of beer as well as you do, and you men are disgracing Uncle Sam's uniform every drop you drink."

At Thirty-first Street and Sixth Avenue she effected an entrance and intrepidly faced the danger of a rough handling.

Her further progress was "tipped off." Wide-open places were mysteriously closed at a moment's notice, and the Smasher was confronted by a series of closed doors, with anxious faces peeping from behind drawn curtains.

Half a dozen times en route she was obliged to take a car to escape the crowds, but her enthusiasm never flagged, and while her escort lagged and faltered she never turned a hair.

At the Apollo Music Garden—the French quarter of Eighth Avenue, with a legend that reads *Entrée libre au Café Chantant*—she went in search of women sinners, but quiet reigned and an irritable proprietor turned her out of his "private house."

Further down she investigated The Abbey, No. 416, another music hall, with similar results. It was here that the crowds running from every direction swelled into a mighty sea of humanity that brought about her encounter with the police.

Mrs. Nation did not confine her attention to the saloon abuse and cigarettes. She discovered in the lobby of the Victoria Hotel a subject for her hatchet that roused her to fury.

"Look at that image," she cried, pointing to a figure of Diana, clothed simply in a bow and arrow—"she ain't got a thing on. Where's the hotel proprietor?"—and she rushed up to the desk.

"There's a woman over there," she announced to the astonished clerk, "without any apparel on her. It ain't respectable. Would you like your wife to see that?" pointing an accusing finger. "Now, I'd like you to put a little something on her right away or there may be a little 'hatchetation' around here."

The clerk hurriedly promised the matter should be looked to, and Carry retired to rest for her lecture.

Corsets came in for her denunciation from the platform of Carnegie, where her talk was constantly interrupted by shouts of laughter, storms of applause, and audible comment. She bade girls avoid making their "hearts and livers into one solid lump." She likened herself to Moses, who, she said, was the first smasher when he broke up the golden calf.

Today she goes to Steeplechase Park, Coney Island, and will make the Bowery her chief concern while here.

* * *

FROM THE DAYS of Fanny Wright, who fought against slavery, Lucy Stone, who demanded the vote, and Dorothea L. Dix, whose passion was prison reform, America has been under unceasing attack by the strong-willed woman-with-a-mission. A picturesque precursor of the prohibition era, Carry Nation anticipated the coming of Volsteadism. Her direct antithesis in objective was the explosive and defiant Isadora Duncan, who through her perfection of the art of the dance carried on open warfare against the "curse of Puritanism," preached the beauty of the human body, and demanded that America tear aside the veil of prudery and rid itself of sex inhibitions. In his book, *Impresario* (1946), Sol Hurok tells how Isadora, while dancing in Boston's Symphony Hall, in the midst of that New England which she despised as "enslaved by its Brahminism," suddenly stopped and pointed to the replicas of the Greek statues that adorned the walls:

"These are not Greek gods—they are false! And you are as false as those plaster statues! You don't know what beauty is!"

Whereupon the temperamental dancer tore her tunic down to bare one of her breasts and cried out: "This—this is beauty!"

The reactions of her Boston audience have never been satisfactorily recorded in prose.

The World's First Airplane Flight Is Reported

Exclusively by the Norfolk *Virginian-Pilot*

GREEK MYTHOLOGY has it that Icarus, son of Daedalus, fled on wings to escape the resentment of Minos, but the sun melted the wax that cemented his wings and he crashed to his death in the Aegean Sea.

Late in the autumn of 1878 a father came home with an object partly concealed in his hands. Suddenly he tossed it into the air. His sons, Orville and Wilbur Wright, observed that "instead of falling to the floor," as they had expected, "it flew across the room till it struck the ceiling, where it fluttered awhile, and finally sank to the floor." "A toy so delicate lasted only a short time in the hands of small boys," the Wright brothers later recollected, but the memory of this helicopter was "abiding." Soon they began building helicopters and experimenting with kiteflying, but as they grew older, they were forced to give up this "fascinating sport as unbecoming to boys of our ages." Nevertheless, they read avidly of the experiments in gliding of Otto Lilienthal, a German, who was killed in 1896 as the result of an accident owing to insufficient control of the equilibrium of his glider. Lilienthal had guided and balanced his machine by shifting the weight of his body. The proprietors of a bicycle-repair business in Ohio, the young Wright brothers set about the task of developing a system in which the center of gravity remained constant and the equilibrium was maintained by varying the air pressure through adjustment of the angles of the wings.

The Wrights first tried out a machine designed to be flown as a kite, with a man on board, in winds of from fifteen to twenty miles an hour. But, not getting sufficient wind power, they tried flying the machine as a kite without a man on board, operating the levers through cords from the ground. This experiment "inspired confidence in the new system of balance."

In the early winter of 1903 the brothers assembled for the first time their power-driven craft, with a wingspread of thirty-three feet. Cotton cloth from a department store formed the sails of the double wings. Without wheels, the plane slid along the ground on ash skids similar to those of a sleigh. This primitive, rickety contraption was moved to the barrier reefs off the North Carolina coast, where the roaring seas sweep in south of Hatteras and winds can be counted upon to give lift to a plane's wings. At Kill Devil Hill, near Kittyhawk, the Wrights constructed a crude monorail track to aid the take-off. They tuned up the puny twelve-horsepower engine with its four-cylinder gasoline motor, which they fervently hoped would sustain the 745-pound biplane. Invitations were extended to people living in the vicinity, but, the Wrights recalled, "not many were willing to face the rigors of a cold December wind in order to see, as they no doubt thought, another flying machine *not* fly."

Only fragmentary accounts of these experimental flights reached the outside world. A few days before, on December 8, 1903, Samuel P. Langley, the secretary of the Smithsonian Institute and the best known among Americans interested in aviation, had plunged into the Potomac River below Washington in a power-driven airplane that he had constructed at a cost of $70,000. Dozens of newsmen saw Langley's failure; none was present at the scene of the Wrights' triumph. The only newspaper in America to give the flight serious coverage was the Norfolk *Virginian-Pilot*. The writer of this story tried to sell it first to other papers, but found them too skeptical to buy it. The account, published in part below, appeared in the issue of December 18, 1903, the morning after the successful flights at Kittyhawk.

Twelve seconds that changed the world

Norfolk *Virginian-Pilot*, December 18, 1903

The problem of aerial navigation without the use of a balloon has been solved at last.

Over the sand hills of the North Carolina coast yesterday, near Kittyhawk, two Ohio men proved that they could soar through the air in a flying machine of their own construction, with the power to steer and speed it at will.

This, too, in the face of a wind blowing at the registered velocity of twenty-one miles an hour.

Like a monster bird, the invention hovered above the breakers and circled over the rolling sand hills at the command of its navigator and, after soaring for three miles, it gracefully descended to earth again, and rested lightly upon the spot selected by the man in the car as a suitable landing place.

While the United States government has been spending thousands of dollars in an effort to make practicable the ideas of Professor Langley, of the Smithsonian Institute, Wilbur and Orville Wright, two brothers, natives of Dayton, Ohio, have, quietly, even secretly, perfected their invention and put it to a successful test.

They are not yet ready that the world should know the methods they have adopted in conquering the air, but the *Virginian-Pilot* is able to state authentically the nature of their invention, its principles and its chief dimensions.

The idea of the box kite has been adhered to strictly in the basic formation of the flying machine.

A huge framework of light timbers, thirty-three feet wide, five feet deep, and five feet across the top, forms the machine proper.

This is covered with a tough, but light canvas.

In the center, and suspended just below the bottom plane, is the small gasoline engine which furnished the motive power for the propelling and elevating wheels.

These are two six-bladed propellers, one arranged just below the center of the frame, so gauged as to exert an upward force when in motion, and the other extends horizontally to the rear from the center of the car, furnishing the forward impetus.

Protruding from the center of the car is a huge, fan-shaped rudder of canvas, stretched upon a frame of wood. This rudder is controlled by the navigator and may be moved to each side, raised, or lowered.

Wilbur Wright, the chief inventor of the machine, sat in the operator's car, and when all was ready his brother unfastened the catch which held the invention at the top of the slope.

The big box began to move slowly at first, acquiring velocity as it went, and when halfway down the hundred feet the engine was started.

The propeller in the rear immediately began to revolve at a high rate of speed, and when the end of the incline was reached the machine shot out into space without a perceptible fall.

By this time the elevating propeller was also in motion, and keeping its altitude, the machine slowly began to go higher and higher until it finally soared sixty feet above the ground.

Maintaining this height by the action of the under wheel, the navigator increased the revolutions of the rear propeller, and the forward speed of the huge affair increased until a velocity of eight miles was attained.

All this time the machine headed into a twenty-one-mile wind.

The little crowd of fisherfolk and coast guards, who have been watching the construction of the machine with unconcealed curiosity since September, were amazed.

They endeavored to race over the sand and keep up with the thing in the air, but it soon distanced them and continued its flight alone, save the man in the car.

Steadily it pursued its way, first tacking to port, then to starboard, and then driving straight ahead.

"It is a success," declared Orville Wright to the crowd on the beach after the first mile had been covered.

But the inventor waited. Not until he had accomplished three miles, putting the machine through all sorts of maneuvers en route, was he satisfied.

Then he selected a suitable place to land and, gracefully circling, drew his invention slowly to the earth, where it settled, like some big bird, in the chosen spot.

"Eureka!" he cried, as did the alchemists of old.

The success of the Wright brothers in their invention is the result of three years of hard work. Experiment after experiment has been made and failure resulted, but each experiment had its lesson, and finally, when the two reappeared at Kittyhawk last fall, they felt more confident than ever.

The spot selected for the building and perfecting of the machine is one of the most desolate upon the Atlantic seaboard. Just on the southern extremity of that coast stretch known as the graveyard of American shipping, cut off from civilization by a wide expanse of sound water and seldom in touch with the outer world save when a steamer once or twice a week touches at the little wharf to take and leave government mail, no better place could scarcely have been selected to maintain secrecy.

And this is where the failures have grown into success.

The machine which made yesterday's flight easily carried the weight of a man of 150 pounds, and is nothing like so large as the ill-fated *Buzzard* of Potomac River fame.

It is said the Wright brothers intend constructing a much larger machine, but before this they will go back to their homes for the holidays.

Wilbur Wright, the inventor, is a well-groomed man of prepossessing appearance. He is about five feet, six inches tall, weighs about 150 pounds, and is of swarthy complexion. His hair is raven-hued and straight, but a piercing pair of deep-blue eyes peer at you over a nose of extreme length and sharpness.

His brother, Orville, on the other hand, is a blond, with sandy hair and fair complexion, even features, and sparkling black eyes. He is not quite as large as Wilbur, but is of magnificent physique.

The pair have spent almost the entire fall and winter and early spring months of the past three years at Kittyhawk, working upon their invention, leaving when the weather began to grow warm and returning in the early fall to work.

Their last appearance was on September 1, and since then they have been actively engaged upon the construction of the machine which made yesterday's successful flight.

ALTHOUGH HIS ACCOUNT of the historic event correctly gauged the solution to the problem of aerial navigation, the *Virginian-Pilot* reporter awkwardly garbled one of the most important facts of the story (for which he deserved an ear-chewing session with his city editor)—the length of the first flights. At two points in his report he speaks of a three-mile flight and quotes Orville Wright as announcing success after the "first mile."

As a matter of fact, there were four flights and none came near the reported three-mile flight. The first was made by Orville Wright at 10:30 in the morning. After running the motor for a few minutes he released the wire that held the machine to the monorail. The plane headed slowly forward into a twenty-seven (not twenty-one!)-mile wind, with Wilbur Wright running at the side, holding the wing to balance the machine on the track. After a forty-foot run the plane lifted. *The plane remained in the air at ten feet for just twelve seconds,* and suddenly made an erratic descent just 120 feet from the point at which it had soared into the air, probably because the front elevator was overbalanced. The second and third flights lasted just a little longer. At noon the same day came the fourth and last flight by Wilbur Wright, who covered 852 feet and remained in the air just fifty-nine seconds. After this flight, a sudden gust of wind turned the plane over, damaging its power plant and ending for the time the possibility of further flight. These facts are substantiated by the Wrights' own words:

The first flight lasted only twelve seconds, a flight very modest compared to that of birds, but it was, nevertheless, the first in the history of the world in which a machine carrying a man had raised itself by its own power into the air in free flight, had sailed forward on a level course without reduction of speed, and had finally landed without being wrecked. The second and third flights lasted a little longer, and the fourth lasted fifty-nine seconds, covering a distance of 852 feet over the ground against a twenty-mile wind.

It was almost four years before America became aware of what the Wrights had done. Then the press began to report at greater length the resumption of their experiments at Kittyhawk. In the meantime the Wrights received no popular encouragement; their friends thought them near lunatics, and even their father laughed at them.

Wilbur Wright died of typhoid in 1912 at a time when the airplane was scarcely more than a mechanical freak. Orville retired into a world of introspection while nations poured money and materials into the development of military aviation. Angered by disputes over the priority of his flight, Orville, in 1928, removed the original Wright plane from the Smithsonian Institute and gave it to the South Kensington Museum in London. After Orville's death it was returned to the United States.

When asked during World War II if he was sorry he had developed the airplane, Orville answered:

"No. I feel about it much as I do about fire. I regret its damage but I am glad the human race discovered it."

Orville Wright died on January 30, 1948, removing from the air age the last of the two brothers who gave man wings.

A Correspondent of the Paris *Journal* Sees Blood

Flow on the Hardened Snow of St. Petersburg

THE WAR WITH Japan that broke out in 1904 revealed Russia to be a colossus with feet of clay. Plagued by mismanagement and corruption, the gigantic Russian armies suffered a series of humiliating defeats. On the domestic front, revolutionary discontent reached the fever stage.

At this point a Greek Orthodox priest of somewhat mysterious background named Father Gapon, the leader of the government unions, urged his followers to seek relief directly from the "Little Father." Accordingly, on Sunday, January 22, 1905, a procession of several thousand workingmen, led by Father Gapon in priestly attire and carrying a crucifix, marched with ikons through the streets of St. Petersburg, chanting religious songs. Unarmed, the crowd sought to present a petition to "their Tsar," Nicholas II, asking for a redress of grievances. The petition read:

> Sire, we, workingmen and inhabitants of St. Petersburg, our wives and our children and our helpless old parents, come to thee, sire, to seek for truth and defense. We have become beggars; we have been oppressed; we are burdened by toil beyond our powers; we are scoffed at; we are not recognized as human beings; we are treated as slaves. . . . We are choked by despotism and irresponsibility, and we are breathless. . . . Let everyone be free and equal in the right of election. . . . Directly and openly as to a father, we speak to thee, sire . . . for all the toiling classes of Russia.

Although the Tsar was away at Tsarskoe Selo, the various approaches to the Winter Palace were strongly guarded by detachments of infantry, uhlans, and Cossacks. Shortly before noon, the demonstrators began to converge upon the palace from different directions. Then the Cossacks and the uhlans charged. What happened was reported by a British correspondent, who included in his dispatch a quotation from the story written by the Paris *Journal* newsman. Back home, the rewrite men added comments by Jaurès, the French Socialist leader and journalist, and by England's poet, Swinburne:

Swinburne advises the Tsar to make a cowardly escape

London *Weekly Times and Echo*, January 29, 1905

The storm which has been gathering over St. Petersburg for the last few days has burst. The appeal which the people this afternoon attempted to make to the Tsar was heard only by the troops, who replied with volleys.

The meeting in the Palace Square was called for noon, but it was not the intention of the authorities to allow the public to assemble anywhere near the palace. On Vassili Ostrov the workmen bound for the palace found their way blocked at every point by Cossacks, uhlans, and men of the Finland regiment. The workmen, however, were equally resolute in their intention to get to the palace, and some conflicts occurred. How the masses of workingmen succeeded in eluding the soldiers and police is unknown, but towards noon, notwithstanding the injunctions of a formidable guard of troops, hundreds had assembled in the immense square before the Emperor's residence. They witnessed the arrival of several members of the court and the departure of the Dowager Empress for Tsarskoe Selo. The crowd gradually became more dense as the men poured in from the main avenues, and soon the lower ends of the Nevsky, Oorskaya, and Gogol Streets were filled with workingmen, who stood in groups, discussing their grievances.

Soon the driblets of men had formed a crowd of serious proportions. Those in front were unable to move forward or backward. The men of the Pavloski Regiment were posted at several points near the square out of sight of most of the crowd, but a square cordon of cavalry barred further progress in the direction of the palace. Everyone felt that the decisive moment had arrived. The appeal made to the troops by those who were pressed forward was disregarded, and two blank volleys were fired. The crowd still pressed forward, and then the soldiers loaded with ball and fired. Men dropped dead or wounded, and the crowd wavered. Their confusion was heightened by a charge of the Cossacks. The crowd were still unable to get back more than a few paces, and the Cossacks charged again. This time the cavalry wedge was driven more deeply into the heart of the crowd, and there were angry cries and frenzied gesticulations from the helpless mass. Curses and excited cries for vengeance attended the efforts of the military to clear the square. Attention was next directed to the dispersal of the crowd along the famous Nevsky Prospect from the Moscow Railway Station to Mikaelovska Street. Here several blank volleys sufficed to send the people down the side streets in compact masses. In the meantime the troops in the Palace Square had succeeded in driving the people back to the great open square surrounding the Cathedral of St. Isaac, and into the Admiralty Square. The troops fired into the crowd more than once. Several were killed, and large numbers were wounded, and the crowd rushed wildly in all directions.

The first trouble began at eleven o'clock, when the military tried to turn back some thousands of Putilov strikers * at one of the bridges connecting the island, which is the great industrial quarter, with the central portions of the city. The same thing happened almost simultaneously at the other bridges, where the constant flow of workmen pressing forward refused to be denied access to the common rendezvous in the Palace Square. The Cossacks at first used their knouts, then the flat of their sabers, and finally they fired. The strikers in the front ranks fell on their knees and implored the Cossacks to let them pass, protesting that they had no hostile intentions. They refused, however, to be intimidated by blank cartridges, and

---

* The use of the term "strikers" instead of the more accurate "demonstrators" may be attributed to the reporter's carelessness.

orders were given to load with ball.

The passions of the mob broke loose like a bursting dam. The people, seeing the dead and dying carried away in all directions, the snow on the streets and pavements soaked with blood, cried aloud for vengeance. A great mass meeting was held at the headquarters of the Workmen's Union. The speakers denounced the military, inveighed against the government, and attacked the Tsar himself. The crowd, responding, howled: "Down with monarchy!"

Meanwhile the situation at the palace was becoming momentarily worse. The troops were reported to be unable to control the vast masses which were constantly surging forward. Reinforcements were sent, and at two o'clock, here also, the order was given to fire. Men, women, and children fell at each volley, and were carried away in ambulances, sledges, and carts. It was no longer a workmen's question. The indignation and fury of every class was aroused. Students, merchants, all classes of the population alike are inflamed. At the moment of writing firing is going on in every quarter of the city. Several officers have been severely injured on the Nevsky Prospect. Their swords were taken from them and their epaulets torn off. Panic and consternation reign supreme. The troops are apparently reckless, firing right and left, with or without reason. The rioters continue to appeal to them, saying: "You are Russians! Why play the part of bloodthirsty butchers?" One infantry regiment is reported to have refused to fire on the rioters. As the killed and wounded are borne away, men reverently raise their caps and many shout: "Hurrah! Well done!" in honor of those stricken down.

"Painful and tragic events are fol-lowing each other precipitately," telegraphed the correspondent of the Paris *Journal*. "I have seen blood flow in streams on the hardened snow. I have seen police agents, sword in hand, slash blindly about them. I have seen their revolvers used wildly against the crowd. I have seen whole companies of infantry discharging murderous volleys on the shrieking crowd. And on all sides the dead with the wounded falling upon them, and the horrible pell-mell, in which women and children covered with blood fall in the snow. It is not a strike. It is a revolution."

Father Gapon has issued the following letter to the people:

"Dear Comrades and Fellow Workmen: There is no Tsar now. Innocent blood has flowed between him and the people. Long live the struggle for freedom! I bless you all. Tomorrow I shall be with you; today I am too busy.
"Father George"

The manner in which the dead were buried is described by all St. Petersburg as unworthy of a Christian government. No funerals were allowed, and not even the presence of near relatives was permitted. Two bodies were put into each coffin, and a large number of coffins were laid upon a lumber sledge and dragged to the Uspensky Burial Ground at dead of night. No member of the public was admitted. In addition to the gravediggers and the police, there were two spies and two sleigh drivers.

According to the statements of eyewitnesses, Father George Gapon, who led the workmen's procession from the Narva Triumphal Gate, is uninjured. The procession numbered 15,000 men, headed by two priests wearing their vestments and carrying crosses in their hands. Father Gapon, escorted by his bodyguard, walked by the side of the holy pictures, the portrait of the Emperor, and other priestly rulers. He wore ordinary clothes, and intended to put on his vestments later. The demonstrators marched singing "God save Thy people." The command to fire was given to the troops, and was immediately followed by a volley. The holy pictures and the portrait of the Emperor were pierced with bullets, and the priest at the head of the procession was wounded. Father Gapon, who, like the others, was thrown to the ground, crawled into a neighboring house.

Among the positively authenticated horrors of the rioting is the case of an aged general, whose sledge was stopped by the infuriated people as he was driving in the direction of the troops. The crowd asked: "Are you going to order them to fire on us?" The general told the coachman to drive on, and was instantly struck on the head by a well-dressed man wearing a sable fur coat. He was then thrown out of the sledge and beaten and trampled to death.

Five thousand people have been arrested. They include one hundred lawyers, who are now on their way to Siberia without even the formality of a trial. Arrests have taken place hourly, and no fewer than 158 women have been arrested. Women—some of them ladies of refinement and education—were dragged from their beds during the night and lodged in prison.

The Boyevaya Organizatsiya (fighting organization) of the terrorist party, says the Paris *Aurore,* has condemned the Tsar to death, charging him with having given orders for the people to be fired upon when the latter believed that it was going to a peaceful meeting.

"The Russian Revolution," says M. Maxim Gorky, the well-known author

and reformer, "has commenced, and it will lead to terrible bloodshed. The result of the awful proceedings on Sunday is that the prestige which the Tsar held with Russia's working classes exists no more. All they wanted to do was to present their petition to the Emperor. If the Emperor had come out of his palace and appeared before them, and if his troops had not been there, all would have ended with cheering, and with the multitude falling on their knees to praise him.

"I myself had a narrow escape from death. I certainly should not have been here today if the troops had fired properly. A friend was shot dead right by my side."

Gorky on Tuesday left St. Petersburg for Riga, where his wife, who is an actress under the stage name of Andreeva, lies dying. On his arrival at Riga he was arrested.

The Tsar is reported to have been seized with a fit of despair after the Neva incident of last week. He was induced to go to Tsarskoe "to recover from his emotion," and was kept in ignorance of Sunday's events. [Since then] the Tsaritsa has expressed her desire to place her children in a place of safety, and the Tsar has been contemplating the possibility, according to circumstances, of starting for the Crimea or Denmark. The Grand Dukes Vladimir and Alexander, adopting a violent and threatening attitude, opposed these plans, on the ground that the Tsar's departure would mean financial ruin, and the vengeance of the mob for themselves.

M. Jaurès, the distinguished French Socialist, writes: "Hypocritical absolutism, incapable and vicious, could find no other reply than murder to the just and moderate demands of millions of men. Between the Tsar and his people there flows a river of blood.

There can be no doubt now that he is not only aware of it all, but authorizes it all. It is he who is the murderer."

Mr. Swinburne contributed a characteristic sonnet to *The Pall Mall Gazette* on "Tsar Louis XVI." The following are the last four lines:

*Fly coward, and while time is thine
    to fly:
Cherish awhile thy terror-shortened
    breath;
Not as thy grandsire died, if justice
    give
Judgment, but slain by judgment thou
    shalt die.*

"RED SUNDAY" horrified the world and aroused the embittered workers. The following month the Grand Duke Sergius, the uncle of the Tsar and governor general of Moscow, was blown up in the Kremlin by a bomb thrown by the Social Revolutionary Kaliaev. In June a great mutiny broke out in the Black Sea fleet, and in October a paralyzing railway strike developed into a general strike. The Tsar reluctantly granted a constitution and established an Imperial Parliament.

"It makes me sick to read the news!" Nicholas II wrote to his wife. "Nothing but new strikes in schools and factories, murdered policemen, Cossacks, and soldiers, riots, disorder, mutinies. But the ministers, instead of acting with quick decision, only assemble in council like a lot of frightened hens and cackle about providing united ministerial action."

"Red Sunday" and the Revolution of 1905 were the stormy prelude to 1917, when the Russian people struck down the government that recognized only the rifle, saber, and knout as means of communicating with them.

Jack London Sees a City Die Before His Eyes, and Will Irwin, Three Thousand Miles Away, Covers the Same Story for the New York *Sun*

O N THE EVENING of April 16, 1906, Enrico Caruso sang Don José in *Carmen* at the Grand Opera House of San Francisco. At 5:13 the next morning there was a terrific rumble and roar as the earth writhed in agony. Caught in the Palace Hotel, Caruso recounted later: "I waked up, feeling my bed rocking as though I am in a ship. From the window I see buildings shaking, big pieces of masonry falling. I run into the street. That night I sleep on the hard ground—my legs ache yet from so rough a bed."

In the wake of the tremor, with bewildering speed came one of the most disastrous fires of modern times. Gas mains were smashed, electric-power lines cut, railroad trains overturned. Loss of life was counted in the hundreds. 225,000 people were made homeless, as the $7,000,000 City Hall and some 28,000 other buildings collapsed or were destroyed by fire.

Early press reports had listed the twenty-four-year-old John Barrymore, about to embark on an Australian tour, among the missing. John, according to his biographer, Gene Fowler, persuaded a newsman to tag onto the close of a news-service bulletin to New York a message for his sister, Ethel. Barrymore reported that he had been thrown out of bed by the tremor and had wandered dazedly to the street, where an army sergeant put a shovel in his hand and made him work amid the ruins for twenty-four hours. When Ethel read this piece of fiction to uncle John Drew and asked if he believed it, that famous actor replied: "Every word. It took an act of God to get him out of bed, and the United States Army to put him to work."

Early in 1906 Jack London, a native San Franciscan, sailor, stoker, mill hand, janitor, and friend of the underdog, expressed a wish to work, crowbar in hand, shoulder to shoulder with intellectuals and workers, "to get a solid pry now and again" and set the whole edifice of society rocking. "Someday," he prophesied, "when we get a few more hands and crowbars to work, we'll topple it over, along with all its rotten life and unburied dead, its monstrous selfishness and sodden materialism."

The San Francisco earthquake, hard upon London's prediction, accomplished in a few moments more than all the crowbars London and his friends could have wielded in a generation. This master of swift and vivid action, one of the fabulously successful writers of modern times, happened to be near the scene and wrote a vivid firsthand account of the disaster. In a biography of her husband, Charmian London recounts the circumstances of the writing assignment. Jack was so deeply shaken by the catastrophe that he declared: "I'll never write about this for anybody. What use trying? One could only string big words together, and curse the futility of them." Soon came frantic wires from *Collier's Weekly*, asking for a 2500-word description of the earthquake and fire. The offer of twenty-five cents a word was too attractive for the narrator of the Klondike gold rush to ignore.

London dashed off the article. His wife snatched his scribbled sheets and swiftly typed them. The story was sent out over the wires, and, "just for luck," Jack mailed the manuscript simultaneously. Wild daily messages from *Collier's* followed for a week to come. "Why doesn't your story arrive?" "Must have your story immediately!" "Holding presses at enormous expense. What is the matter? Must have your story for May-fifth number."

The report arrived in time for the May 5 issue and was published under a banner title: THE STORY OF AN EYEWITNESS, BY JACK LONDON, COLLIER'S SPECIAL CORRESPONDENT. A blurb at the head told how the story was planned:

Upon receipt of the first news of the earthquake, *Collier's* telegraphed to Mr. Jack London, who lives only forty miles from San Francisco, requesting him to go to the scene of disaster and write the story of what he saw. Mr. London started at once, and has sent the following dramatic description of the tragic events he witnessed in the burning city.

"San Francisco is gone!"—*Jack London*

Collier's Weekly, May 5, 1906

The earthquake shook down in San Francisco hundreds of thousands of dollars' worth of walls and chimneys. But the conflagration that followed burned up hundreds of millions of dollars' worth of property. There is no estimating within hundreds of millions the actual damage wrought. Not in history has a modern imperial city been so completely destroyed. San Francisco is gone! Nothing remains of it but memories and a fringe of dwelling houses on its outskirts. Its industrial section is wiped out. Its social and residential section is wiped out. The factories and warehouses, the great stores and newspaper buildings,

the hotels and the palaces of the nabobs, are all gone. Remains only the fringe of dwelling houses on the outskirts of what was once San Francisco.

Within an hour after the earthquake shock the smoke of San Francisco's burning was a lurid tower visible a hundred miles away. And for three days and nights this lurid tower swayed in the sky, reddening the sun, darkening the day, and filling the land with smoke.

On Wednesday morning at a quarter past five came the earthquake. A minute later the flames were leaping upward. In a dozen different quarters south of Market Street, in the working-class ghetto, and in the factories, fires started. There was no opposing the flames. There was no organization, no communication. All the cunning adjustments of a twentieth-century city had been smashed by the earthquake. The streets were humped into ridges and depressions and piled with debris of fallen walls. The steel rails were twisted into perpendicular and horizontal angles. The telephone and telegraph systems were disrupted. And the great water mains had burst. All the shrewd contrivances and safeguards of man had been thrown out of gear by thirty seconds' twitching of the earth crust.

By Wednesday afternoon, inside of twelve hours, half the heart of the city was gone. At that time I watched the vast conflagration from out on the bay. It was dead calm. Not a flicker of wind stirred. Yet from every side wind was pouring in upon the city. East, west, north, and south, strong winds were blowing upon the doomed city. The heated air rising made an enormous suck. Thus did the fire of itself build its own colossal chimney through the atmosphere. Day and night this dead calm continued, and yet, near to the flames, the wind was often half a gale, so mighty was the suck.

The edict which prevented chaos was the following proclamation by Mayor E. E. Schmitz:

"The Federal Troops, the members of the Regular Police Force, and all Special Police Officers have been authorized to KILL any and all persons found engaged in looting or in the commission of any other crime.

"I have directed all the Gas and Electric Lighting Companies not to turn on gas or electricity until I order them to do so; you may therefore expect the city to remain in darkness for an indefinite time.

"I request all citizens to remain at home from darkness until daylight of every night until order is restored.

"I warn all citizens of the danger of fire from damaged or destroyed chimneys, broken or leaking gas pipes or fixtures, or any like cause."

Wednesday night saw the destruction of the very heart of the city. Dynamite was lavishly used, and many of San Francisco's proudest structures were crumbled by man himself into ruins, but there was no withstanding the onrush of the flames. Time and again successful stands were made by the fire fighters, and every time the flames flanked around on either side, or came up from the rear, and turned to defeat the hard-won victory.

An enumeration of the buildings destroyed would be a directory of San Francisco. An enumeration of the buildings undestroyed would be a line and several addresses. An enumeration of the deeds of heroism would stock a library and bankrupt the Carnegie medal fund. An enumeration of the dead—will never be made. All vestiges of them were destroyed by the flames. The number of the victims of the earthquake will never be known. South of Market Street, where the loss of life was particularly heavy, was the first to catch fire.

Remarkable as it may seem, Wednesday night, while the whole city crashed and roared into ruin, was a quiet night. There were no crowds. There was no shouting and yelling. There was no hysteria, no disorder. I passed Wednesday night in the part of the advancing flames, and in all those terrible hours I saw not one woman who wept, not one man who was excited, not one person who was in the slightest degree panic-stricken.

Before the flames, throughout the night, fled tens of thousands of homeless ones. Some were wrapped in blankets. Others carried bundles of bedding and dear household treasures. Sometimes a whole family was harnessed to a carriage or delivery wagon that was weighted down with their possessions. Baby buggies, toy wagons, and gocarts were used as trucks, while every other person was dragging a trunk. Yet everybody was gracious. The most perfect courtesy obtained. Never in all San Francisco's history were her people so kind and courteous as on this night of terror.

All the night these tens of thousands fled before the flames. Many of them, the poor people from the labor ghetto, had fled all day as well. They had left their homes burdened with possessions. Now and again they lightened up, flinging out upon the street clothing and treasures they had dragged for miles.

They held on longest to their trunks, and over these trunks many a strong man broke his heart that night. The hills of San Francisco are steep, and up these hills, mile after mile, were the trunks dragged. Everywhere were trunks, with across them lying their exhausted owners, men and women. Before the march of the flames were flung picket lines of soldiers. And a block at a time, as the flames advanced, these pickets retreated. One of their tasks was to keep the trunk pullers moving. The exhausted creatures, stirred on by the menace of bayonets, would arise and struggle up the steep pavements, pausing from weakness every five or ten feet.

Often after surmounting a heartbreaking hill, they would find another wall of flame advancing upon them at right angles and be compelled to change anew the line of their retreat. In the end, completely played out, after toiling for a dozen hours like

giants, thousands of them were compelled to abandon their trunks. Here the shopkeepers and soft members of the middle class were at a disadvantage. But the workingmen dug holes in vacant lots and back yards and buried their trunks.

At nine o'clock Wednesday evening I walked down through miles and miles of magnificent buildings and towering skyscrapers. Here was no fire. All was in perfect order. The police patrolled the streets. Every building had its watchman at the door. And yet it was doomed, all of it. There was no water. The dynamite was giving out. And at right angles two different conflagrations were sweeping down upon it.

At one o'clock in the morning I walked down through the same section. Everything still stood intact. There was no fire. And yet there was a change. A rain of ashes was falling. The watchmen at the doors were gone. The police had been withdrawn. There were no firemen, no fire engines, no men fighting with dynamite. The district had been absolutely abandoned. I stood at the corner of Kearney and Market, in the very innermost heart of San Francisco. Kearney Street was deserted. Half a dozen blocks away it was burning on both sides. The street was a wall of flame. And against this wall of flame, silhouetted sharply, were two United States cavalrymen sitting their horses, calmly watching. That was all. Not another person was in sight. In the intact heart of the city two troopers sat their horses and watched.

Surrender was complete. There was no water. The sewers had long since been pumped dry. There was no dynamite. Another fire had broken out further uptown, and now from three sides conflagrations were sweeping down. The fourth side had been burned earlier in the day. In that direction stood the tottering walls of the Examiner Building, the burned-out Call Building, the smoldering ruins of the Grand Hotel, and the gutted, devastated, dynamited Palace Hotel.

The following will illustrate the sweep of the flames and the inability of men to calculate their spread. At eight o'clock Wednesday evening I passed through Union Square. It was packed with refugees. Thousands of them had gone to bed on the grass. Government tents had been set up, supper was being cooked, and the refugees were lining up for free meals.

At half-past one in the morning three sides of Union Square were in flames. The fourth side, where stood the great St. Francis Hotel, was still holding out. An hour later, ignited from top and sides, the St. Francis was flaming heavenward. Union Square, heaped high with mountains of trunks, was deserted. Troops, refugees, and all had retreated.

It was at Union Square that I saw a man offering a thousand dollars for a team of horses. He was in charge of a truck piled high with trunks from some hotel. It had been hauled here into what was considered safety, and the horses had been taken out. The flames were on three sides of the square, and there were no horses.

Also, at this time, standing beside the truck, I urged a man to seek safety in flight. He was all but hemmed in by several conflagrations. He was an old man and he was on crutches. Said he: "Today is my birthday. Last night I was worth thirty thousand dollars. I bought five bottles of wine, some delicate fish, and other things for my birthday dinner. I have had no dinner, and all I own are these crutches."

I convinced him of his danger and started him limping on his way. An hour later, from a distance, I saw the truckload of trunks burning merrily in the middle of the street.

On Thursday morning, at a quarter past five, just twenty-four hours after the earthquake, I sat on the steps of a small residence of Nob Hill. With me sat Japanese, Italians, Chinese, and Negroes—a bit of the cosmopolitan flotsam of the wreck of the city. All about were the palaces of the nabob pioneers of Forty-nine. To the east and south, at right angles, were advancing two mighty walls of flame.

I went inside with the owner of the house on the steps of which I sat. He was cool and cheerful and hospitable. "Yesterday morning," he said, "I was worth six hundred thousand dollars. This morning this house is all I have left. It will go in fifteen minutes." He pointed to a large cabinet. "That is my wife's collection of china. This rug upon which we stand is a present. It cost fifteen hundred dollars. Try that piano. Listen to its tone. There are few like it. There are no horses. The flames will be here in fifteen minutes."

Outside, the old Mark Hopkins residence, a palace, was just catching fire. The troops were falling back and driving refugees before them. From every side came the roaring of flames, the crashing of walls, and the detonations of dynamite.

I passed out of the house. Day was trying to dawn through the smoke pall. A sickly light was creeping over the face of things. Once only the sun broke through the smoke pall, blood-red, and showing quarter its usual size. The smoke pall itself, viewed from beneath, was a rose color that pulsed and fluttered with lavender shades. Then it turned to mauve and yellow and dun. There was no sun. And so dawned the second day on stricken San Francisco.

An hour later I was creeping past the shattered dome of the City Hall. Than it there was no better exhibit of the destructive force of the earthquake. Most of the stones had been shaken from the great dome, leaving standing the naked framework of steel. Market Street was piled high with the wreckage, and across the wreckage lay the overthrown pillars of the City Hall shattered into short crosswise sections.

This section of the city, with the exception of the Mint and the Post Office, was already a waste of smoking ruins. Here and there through the smoke, creeping warily under the shadows of tottering walls, emerged occasional men and women. It was like the meeting of the handful of survivors after the day of the end of the world.

On Mission Street lay a dozen steers, in a neat row stretching across the street, just as they had been struck down by the flying ruins of the earthquake. The fire had passed through afterward and roasted them. The human dead had been carried away before the fire came. At another place on Mission Street I saw a milk wagon. A steel telegraph pole had smashed down sheer through the driver's seat and crushed the front wheels. The milk cans lay scattered around.

All day Thursday and all Thursday night, all day Friday and Friday night, the flames still raged.

Friday night saw the flames finally conquered, though not until Russian Hill and Telegraph Hill had been swept and three quarters of a mile of wharves and docks had been licked up.

The great stand of the fire fighters was made Thursday night on Van Ness Avenue. Had they failed here, the comparatively few remaining houses of the city would have been swept.

Here were the magnificent residences of the second generation of San Francisco nabobs, and these, in a solid zone, were dynamited down across the path of the fire. Here and there the flames leaped the zone, but these fires were beaten out, principally by the use of wet blankets and rugs.

San Francisco, at the present time, is like the crater of a volcano, around which are camped tens of thousands of refugees. At the Presidio alone are at least twenty thousand. All the surrounding cities and towns are jammed with the homeless ones, where they are being cared for by the relief committees. The refugees were carried free by the railroads to any point they wished to go, and it is estimated that over one hundred thousand people have left the peninsula on which San Francisco stood. The government has the situation in hand, and thanks to the immediate relief given by the whole United States, there is not the slightest possibility of a famine. The bankers and businessmen have already set about making preparations to rebuild San Francisco.

* * *

WHILE SAN FRANCISCO was on fire a newsman on the city staff of the New York *Sun* was at his desk, impatiently waiting for reports from the stricken city. Dispatches were few and brief. But Will Irwin was a lusty and talented reporter who had worked on the San Francisco *Chronicle* and knew the city intimately. Without sleep for hours on end, he sat at his desk and wrote extended accounts of the disaster, based on fragmentary dispatches, deductions, and, most of all, on his own great knowledge of the city. For eight days he ground out his narrative without reference to book or map, and later the stories were borne out to be remarkably accurate. It was an extraordinary feat to tell the story not in dry figures but in terms of people and places that every Easterner longed to see but now would never have the chance. "It was," commented a rival paper, "an unusual example of that imaginative reconstruction of the truth of an event which, whether based upon his own observed facts or the reports of others, every great reporter achieves at his creative best."

"The City That Was"—Will Irwin

New York *Sun*, April 21, 1906

The old San Francisco is dead. The gayest, lightest-hearted, most pleasure-loving city of this continent, and in many ways the most interesting and romantic, is a horde of huddled refugees living among ruins. It may rebuild; it probably will; but those who have known that peculiar city by the Golden Gate and have caught its flavor of the Arabian Nights feel that it can never be the same. It is as though a petty, frivolous woman had passed through a great tragedy. She survives, but she is sobered and different. If it rises out of the ashes it must be a modern city, much like other cities and without its old flavor.

The city lay on a series of hills and the lowlands between. These hills are really the end of the Coast Range of mountains which lie between the interior valleys and the ocean to the south. To its rear was the ocean; but the greater part of the town fronted on two sides on San Francisco Bay, a body of water always tinged with gold from the great washings of the mountain, usually overhung with a haze, and of magnificent color changes. Across the bay to the north lies Mount Tamalpais, about five thousand feet high, and so close that ferries from the water front took one in less than half an hour to the little towns of Sausalito and Belvedere, at its foot.

It is a wooded mountain, with ample slopes, and from it on the north stretch away ridges of forest land, the outposts of the great Northern woods of *Sequoia sempervirens*. This mountain and the mountainous country to the south brought the real forest closer to San Francisco than any other American city.

Within the last few years men have killed deer on the slopes of Tamalpais and looked down to see the cable cars crawling up the hills of San Francisco to the north. In the suburbs coyotes will steal in and rob hen roosts by night. The people lived much out-of-doors. There is no part of the year, except a short part of the rainy season, when the weather keeps one from the woods. The slopes of Tamalpais are crowded with little villas dotted through the woods, and these minor estates run far up into the redwood country. The deep coves of Belvedere, sheltered from the wind by Tamalpais, held a colony of "arks," or houseboats, where people lived in the rather disagreeable summer months, coming over to business every day by ferry. Everything invites out-of-doors.

The climate of California is peculiar; it is hard to give an impression of it. In the first place, all the forces of nature work on laws of their own in that part of California. There is no thunder or lightning; there is no snow, except a flurry once in five or six years; there are perhaps half a dozen nights in the winter when the thermometer drops low enough so that there is a little film of ice on exposed water in the morning. Neither is there any hot weather. Yet most Easterners remaining in San Francisco for a few days remember that they were always chilly.

For the Gate is a big funnel, drawing in the winds and the mists which cool off the great, hot interior valleys of the San Joaquin and Sacramento. So the west wind blows steadily ten months of the year, and almost all the mornings are foggy. This keeps the temperature steady at about fifty-five degrees—a little cool for comfort of an unacclimated person, especially indoors. Californians, used to it, hardly ever think of making fires in their houses except in the few exceptional days of the winter season, and then they rely mainly upon fireplaces. This is like the custom of the Venetians and the Florentines.

But give an Easterner six months of it, and he learns to exist without a chill in a steady temperature a little lower than that to which he is accustomed at home. After that one goes about with perfect indifference to the temperature. Summer and winter San Francisco women wear light tailor-made clothes, and men wear the same fall-weight suits all the year round. There is no such thing as a change of clothing for the seasons. And after becoming acclimated these people find the changes from hot to cold in the normal regions of the earth hard to bear. Perhaps once in two or three years there comes a day when there is

no fog, no wind, and a high temperature in the coast district. Then there is hot weather, perhaps up in the eighties, and Californians grumble, swelter, and rustle for summer clothes. These rare hot days are the only times when one sees on the streets of San Francisco women in light dresses.

Along in early May the rains cease. At that time everything is green and bright and the great golden poppies, as large as the saucer of an after-dinner coffee cup, are blossoming everywhere. Tamalpais is green to its top; everything is washed and bright. By late May a yellow tinge is creeping over the hills. This is followed by a golden June and a brown July and August. The hills are burned and dry. The fog comes in heavily, too; and normally this is the most disagreeable season of the year. September brings a day or two of gentle rain; and then a change, as sweet and mysterious as the breaking of spring in the East, comes over the hills. The green grows through the brown, and the flowers begin to come out.

As a matter of fact, the unpleasantness of summer is modified by the certainty that one can go anywhere without fear of rain. And in all the coast mountains, especially the seaward slopes, the dews and the shelter of the giant underbrush keep the water so that these areas are green and pleasant all summer.

In a normal year, the rains begin to fall heavily in November; there will be three or four weeks of steady downpour and then a clear and green week. December is also likely to be rainy; and in this month people enjoy the sensation of gathering for Christmas the mistletoe which grows profusely on the live oaks, while the poppies are beginning to blossom at their feet. By the end of January the rains come lighter. In the long spaces between rains there is a temperature and a feeling in the air much like that of Indian summer in the East. January is the month when the roses are at their brightest.

So much for the strange climate, which invites out-of-doors and which has played its part in making the character of the people. The externals of the city are—or were, for they are no more—just as curious. One usually entered the city by way of San Francisco Bay. Across its yellow flood, covered with the fleets from the strange seas of the Pacific, San Francisco presented itself in a hill panorama. Probably no other city in the world could be so viewed and inspected at first sight. It rose above the passenger, as he reached dockage, in a succession of hill terraces.

At one side was Telegraph Hill, the end of the peninsula, a height so abrupt that it had a two-hundred-foot sheer cliff on its seaward frontage. Further along lay Nob Hill, crowned with the Mark Hopkins mansion, which had the effect of a citadel, and in later years by the great, white Fairmount. Further along was Russian Hill, the highest point. Below was the business district, whose low site caused all the trouble.

Except for the modern buildings, the fruit of the last ten years, the town presented at first a disreputable appearance. Most of the buildings were low and of wood. In the middle period of the seventies, when a great part of San Francisco was building, there was some atrocious architecture perpetrated. In that time, too, everyone put bow windows on his house, to catch all the morning sunlight that was coming through the fog, and those little houses, with bow windows and fancywork all down their fronts, were characteristic of the middle-class residence districts.

Then the Italians, who tumbled over Telegraph Hill, had built as they listed and with little regard for streets, and their houses hung crazily on a side hill which was little less than a precipice. For the most part, the Chinese, although they occupied an abandoned business district, had remade the houses Chinese fashion, and the Mexicans and Spaniards had added to their houses those little balconies without which life is not life to a Spaniard.

Yet the most characteristic thing after all was the coloring. For the sea fog had a trick of painting every exposed object a sea gray which had a tinge of dull green in it. This, under the leaden sky of a San Francisco morning, had a depressing effect on first sight and afterward became a delight to the eye. For the color was soft, gentle, and infinitely attractive in mass.

The hills are steep beyond conception. Where Vallejo Street ran up Russian Hill it progressed for four blocks by regular steps like a flight of stairs. It is unnecessary to say that no teams ever came up this street or any other like it, and the grass grew long among the paving stones until the Italians who live thereabouts took advantage of this to pasture a cow or two. At the end of the four blocks, the pavers had given it up and the last stage to the summit was a winding path. On the very top a colony of artists lived in little villas of houses whose windows got the whole panorama of the bay. Luckily for these people, a cable car climbed the hill on the other side, so that it was not much of a climb to home.

With these hills, with the strangeness of the architecture, and with the green-gray tinge over everything, the city fell always into vistas and pictures, a setting for the romance which hung over everything, which has always hung over life in San Francisco since the padres came and gathered the Indians about Mission Dolores.

And it was a city of romance and a gateway to adventure. It opened out on the mysterious Pacific, the untamed ocean, and most of China, Japan, the South Sea islands, Lower California, the west coast of Central America, Australia that came to this country passed in through the Golden Gate. There was a sprinkling, too, of Alaska and Siberia. From his windows on Russian Hill one saw always something strange and suggestive creeping through the mists of the bay. It would be a South Sea island brig, bringing in copra, to take out cottons and idols; a Chinese junk with fanlike sails, back from an expedition after sharks' livers; an old whaler, which seemed to drip oil, back from a year of cruising in the Arctic. Even the tramp windjammers were deep-chested craft, capable of rounding the Horn or circumnavigating the globe; and they came in streaked and picturesque from their long voyaging.

In the orange-colored dawn which always comes through the mists of that bay, the fishing fleet would crawl in under triangular lateen sails, for the fishermen of San Francisco Bay are all Neapolitans who have brought their costumes and their customs and sail with lateen rigs shaped like the ear of a horse when the wind fills them and stained an orange brown.

Along the water front the people of these craft met. "The smelting pot of the races," Stevenson called it; and this was always the city of his soul. There are black Gilbert Islanders, almost indistinguishable from Negroes; lighter Kanakas from Hawaii or Sa-

moa; Lascars in turbans; thick-set Russian sailors; wild Chinese with unbraided hair; Italian fishermen in tam-o'-shanters, loud shirts, and blue sashes; Greeks, Alaska Indians, little bay Spanish-Americans, together with men of all the European races. These came in and out from among the queer craft, to lose themselves in the disreputable, tumbledown, but always mysterious shanties and small saloons. In the back rooms of these saloons South Sea island traders and captains, fresh from the lands of romance, whaling masters, people who were trying to get up treasure expeditions, filibusters, Alaskan miners, used to meet and trade adventures.

There was another element, less picturesque and equally characteristic, along the water front. For San Francisco was the back eddy of European civilization—one end of the world. The drifters came here and stopped, lingered awhile to live by their wits in a country where living after a fashion has always been marvelously cheap. These people haunted the water front or lay on the grass on Portsmouth Square.

That square, the old plaza about which the city was built, Spanish fashion, had seen many things. There in the first burst of the early days the vigilance committee used to hold its hangings. There in the time of the sand-lot riots Dennis Kearney, who nearly pulled the town down about his ears, used to make his orations which set the unruly to rioting. In these later years Chinatown lies on one side of it and the Latin Quarter and the Barbary Coast on the other.

On this square men used to lie all day long and tell strange yarns. Stevenson lay there with them in his time and learned the things which he wove into *The Wrecker* and his South

Sea stories, and now in the center of the square there stands the beautiful Stevenson monument; stands or stood —one finds his tenses queerly mixed in writing of this city which is and yet is no more. In later years the authorities put up a municipal building on one side of this square and prevented the loungers, for decency's sake, from lying on the grass. Since then some of the peculiar character of the old square has gone.

The Barbary Coast was a loud bit of hell. No one knows who coined the name. The place was simply three blocks of solid dance halls, there for the delight of the sailors of the world. On a fine busy night every door blared dance music from orchestras, steam pianos, and gramophones, and the cumulative effect of the sound which reached the street was at least strange. Almost anything might be happening behind the swinging doors. For a fine and picturesque bundle of names characteristic of the place, a police story of three or four years ago is typical. Hell broke out in the Eye Wink Dance Hall. The trouble was started by a sailor known as Kanaka Pete, who lived in the What Cheer House, over a woman known as Iodoform Kate. Kanaka Pete chased the man he had marked to the Little Silver Dollar, where he turned and punctured him. The by-product of his gun made some holes in the front of the Eye Wink, which were proudly kept as souvenirs, and were probably there until it went out in the fire. This was low life, the lowest of the low.

Until the last decade almost anything except the commonplace and the expected might happen to a man on the water front. The cheerful industry of shanghaing was reduced to a science. A stranger taking a drink in one of the saloons which hung out over the water might be dropped through the floor into a boat, or he might drink with a stranger and wake up in the forecastle of a whaler bound for the Arctic. Such an incident is the basis for Frank Norris' novel, *Moran of the Lady Letty,* and although the novel draws it pretty strong, it is not exaggerated. Ten years ago the police and the foreign consuls, working together, stopped this.

Kearney Street, a wilder and stranger Bowery, was the main thoroughfare of these people. An exiled Californian, mourning over the city of his heart, said yesterday:

"In a half an hour on Kearney Street I could raise a dozen men for any wild adventure, from pulling down a statue to searching for the Cocos Island treasure."

This is hardly an exaggeration.

These are a few of the elements which made the city strange and gave it the glamour of romance which has so strongly attracted such men as Stevenson, Frank Norris, and Kipling. This lay apart from the regular life of the city, which was distinctive in itself.

The Californian is the second generation of a picked and mixed stock. The merry, the adventurous, often the desperate, always the brave, deserted the South and New England in 1849 to rush around the Horn or to try the perils of the plains. They found there, already grown old in the hands of the Spaniards, younger sons of hidalgos and many of them of the proudest blood of Spain. To a great extent the pioneers intermarried with Spanish women; in fact, except for a proud little colony here and there, the old Spanish blood is sunk in that of the conquering race. Then there was an influx of intellectual French people, largely overlooked in the histories of the early days; and this Latin leaven has had its influence.

Brought up in a bountiful country, where no one really has to work very hard to live, nurtured on adventure, scion of a free and merry stock, the real, native Californian is a distinctive type; as far from the Easterner in psychology as the extreme Southerner is from the Yankee. He is easygoing, witty, hospitable, lovable, inclined to be unmoral rather than immoral in his personal habits, and above all easy to meet and to know.

Above all there is an art sense all through the populace which sets it off from any other part of the country. This sense is almost Latin in its strength, and the Californian owes it to the leaven of Latin blood. The true Californian lingers in the north; for southern California has been built up for "lungers" from the East and Middle West and is Eastern in character and feeling.

With such a people life was always gay. If they did not show it on the streets, as do the people of Paris, it was because the winds made open cafés disagreeable at all seasons of the year. The gaiety went on indoors or out on the hundreds of estates which fringed the city. It was noted for its restaurants. Perhaps the very best for people who care not how they spend their money could not be had there, but for a dollar, seventy-five cents, fifty cents, a quarter, or even fifteen cents the restaurants afforded the best fare on earth at the price.

If one should tell exactly what could be had at Coppa's for fifty cents or at the Fashion for, say thirty-five, no New Yorker who has not been there would believe it. The San Francisco French dinner and the San Francisco free lunch were as the Public Library to Boston or the stockyards to Chi-

cago. A number of causes contributed to this consummation. The country all about produced everything that a cook needs and that in abundance—the bay was an almost untapped fishing pound, the fruit farms came up to the very edge of the town, and the surrounding country produced in abundance fine meats, all cereals and all vegetables.

But the chefs who came from France in the early days and liked this land of plenty were the head and front of it. They passed on their art to other Frenchmen or to the clever Chinese. Most of the French chefs at the biggest restaurants were born in Canton, China. Later, the Italians, learning of this country where good food is appreciated, came and brought their own style. Householders always dined out one or two nights a week, and boardinghouses were scarce, for the unattached preferred the restaurants. The eating was usually better than the surroundings.

Meals that were marvels were served in tumbledown little hotels. Most famous of all restaurants was the Poodle Dog. There have been no less than four restaurants of this name, beginning with a frame shanty, where, in the early days, a prince of French cooks used to exchange ragouts for gold dust. Each succeeding restaurant of the name has moved further downtown; and the recent Poodle Dog stands—or stood—on the edge of the Tenderloin in a modern five-story building. And it typified a certain spirit that there was in San Francisco.

For on the ground floor there was a public restaurant where there was served the best dollar dinner on earth. It ranked with the best, and the others were in San Francisco. Here, especially on Sunday night, almost everybody went to vary the monotony of home cooking. Everyone who was anyone in the town could be seen there off and on. It was perfectly respectable. A man might take his wife and daughter there.

On the second floor there were private dining rooms, and to dine there, with one or more of the opposite sex, was risqué but not especially terrible. But the third floor—and the fourth floor—and the fifth! The elevator man of the Poodle Dog, who has held the job for many years and never spoke unless spoken to, wore diamonds and was a heavy investor in real estate. There were others as famous in their way—The Zinka, where at one time everyone went after the theater; and Tate's, which has lately bitten into that trade; the Palace Grill, much like the grills of Eastern hotels, except for the price; Delmonico's, which ran the Poodle Dog neck and neck in its own line, and many others, humbler but great at the price.

The city never went to bed. There was no closing law, so that the saloons kept open nights and Sundays at their own sweet will. Most of them elected to remain open until three o'clock in the morning at least. Yet this restaurant life does not exactly express the careless, pleasure-loving character of the people. In great part their pleasures were simple, inexpensive, and out-of-doors. No people were fonder of expeditions into the country, of picnics —which might be brought off at almost any season of the year—and often long tours in the great mountains and forests. And hospitality was nearly a vice.

As in the early mining days, if they liked the stranger the people took him in. At the first meeting the local man probably had him put up at the club; at the second, he invited him home to dinner. As long as he stayed he was being invited to week-end parties at ranches, to little dinners in this or that restaurant, and to the houses of his new acquaintances, until his engagements grew beyond hope of fulfillment. There was rather too much of it. At the end of a fortnight a stranger with a pleasant smile and a good story left the place a wreck. This tendency ran through all grades of society—except, perhaps, the sporting people who kept the tracks and the fighting game alive. These also met the stranger— and also took him in.

Centers of hospitality were the clubs, especially the famous Bohemian and the Family. The latter was an offshoot of the Bohemian, which had been growing fast and vying with the older organization for the honor of entertaining pleasing and distinguished visitors.

The Bohemian Club, whose real founder is said to have been the late Henry George, was formed in the seventies by a number of newspaper writers and men working in the arts or interested in them. It had grown to a membership of 750. It still kept for its nucleus painters, writers, musicians, and actors, amateur and professional. They were a gay group of men, and hospitality was their avocation. Yet the thing which set this club off from all others in the world was the midsummer High Jinks.

The club owns a fine tract of redwood forest fifty miles north of San Francisco, on the Russian River. There are two varieties of big trees in California: the *Sequoia gigantea* and the *Sequoia sempervirens*. The great trees of the Mariposa grove belong to the *gigantea* species. The *sempervirens,* however, reaches the diameter of sixteen feet, and some of the greatest trees of this species are in the Bohemian Club grove. It lies in a cleft of the mountains; and up on one hillside there runs a natural out-of-doors stage of remarkable acoustical properties.

In August the whole Bohemian Club, or such as can get away from business, go up to this grove and camp out for two weeks. And on the last night they put on the Jinks proper, a great spectacle with poetic words, music, and effects done by the club, in praise of the forest. In late years this has been practically a masque or an opera. It costs about $10,000. It takes the spare time of scores of men for weeks; yet these seven hundred businessmen, professional men, artists, newspaper workers, struggle for the honor of helping out on the Jinks; and the whole thing is done naturally and with reverence. It would hardly be possible anywhere else in this country; the thing which makes it possible is the art spirit which is in the Californian. It runs in the blood.

Someone has just been collecting statistics which proves this point. *Who's Who in America* is long on the arts and on learning and comparatively weak in business and the professions. Now someone who has taken the trouble has found that more persons mentioned in *Who's Who* by the thousand of the population were born in Massachusetts than in any other state; but that Massachusetts is closely crowded by California, with the rest nowhere. The institutions of learning in Massachusetts account for her preeminence; the art spirit does it for California. The really big men nurtured on California influence are few, perhaps; but she has sent out an amazing number of good workers in painting, in authorship, in music, and especially in acting.

"High society" in San Francisco had settled down from the rather wild spirit of the middle period; it had come to be there a good deal as it is

elsewhere. There was much wealth; and the hills of the western addition were growing up with fine mansions. Outside of the city, at Burlingame, there was a fine country club centering a region of country estates which stretched out to Menlo Park. This club had a good polo team, which played every year with teams of Englishmen from southern California and even with teams from Honolulu.

The foreign quarters are worth an article in themselves. Chief of these was, of course, Chinatown, of which everyone has heard who ever heard of San Francisco. A district six blocks long and two blocks wide, when the quarter was full, housed 30,000 Chinese. The dwellings were old business blocks of the early days; but the Chinese had added to them, rebuilt them, had run out their own balconies and entrances, and had given it that feeling of huddled irregularity which makes all Chinese-built dwellings fall into pictures. Not only this; they had buried to a depth equal to three stories under the ground, and through this ran passages in which the Chinese transacted their dark and devious affairs—as the smuggling of opium, the traffic in slave girls, and the settlement of their difficulties.

There was less of this underground life than formerly, for the Board of Health had a cleanup some time ago; but it was still possible to go from one end of Chinatown to the other through secret underground passages. The Chinese lived there their own life in their own way. The Chinatown of New York is dull beside it. And the tourist, who always included Chinatown in his itinerary, saw little of the real life. The guides gave him a show by actors hired for his benefit. In reality the place had considerable importance in a financial way. There were clothing and cigar factories of importance, and much of the tea and silk importing was in the hands of the merchants, who numbered several millionaires. Mainly, however, it was a Tenderloin for the house servants of the city—for the San Francisco Chinaman was seldom a laundryman; he was too much in demand at fancy prices as a servant.

On the slopes of Telegraph Hill dwelt the Mexicans and Spanish, in low houses, which they had transformed by balconies into a resemblance of Spain. Above, and streaming over the hills, were the Italians. The tenement quarter of San Francisco shone by contrast with that of New York, for while these people lived in old and humble houses they had room to breathe and a high eminence for light and air. Their shanties clung on the side of the hill or hung on the very edge of the precipice overlooking the bay, on the edge of which a wall kept their babies from falling. The effect was picturesque, and this hill was the delight of painters. It was all more like Italy than anything in the Italian quarter of New York and Chicago— the very climate and surroundings, wine country close at hand, the bay for their lateen boats, helped them.

Over by the ocean and surrounded by cemeteries in which there are no more burials, there is an eminence which is topped by two peaks and which the Spanish of the early days named after the breasts of a woman. At its foot was Mission Dolores, the last mission planted by the Spanish padres in their march up the coast, and from these hills the Spanish looked for the first time upon the golden bay.

Many years ago someone set up at the summit of this peak a sixty-foot cross of timber. Once a high wind blew it down, and the women of the Fair family then had it restored so firmly that it would resist anything. As it is on a hill it must have stood. It has risen for fifty years above the gay, careless, luxuriant, and lovable city, in full view from every eminence and from every valley. It must stand tonight above the desolation of ruins.

* * *

Irvin S. Cobb Writes 600,000 Words on the Harry K. Thaw Murder Trial—Sensation of the pre-Kinseyan Era

New York *Sun,* June 26, 1906

Stanford White, the architect, was shot and killed last night by Harry Thaw, of Pittsburgh, on the roof of the Madison Square Garden at the performance of *Mamzelle Champagne,* a new musical summer show that opened last night.

Mr. White had been spending the evening at the Manhattan Club and went over to the roof garden to see how a theatrical performance would go on top of this big building which he himself had designed.

It was 11:05 when Mr. White arrived at the roof and was escorted to a table and chair about two feet from the stage on the left-hand side. A sextet billed as the "Big Six" were dancing and singing in the chorus of a song that Harry Short was leading in.

A tall young man walked down the aisle between the tables at this time and, approaching White, drew a revolver.

Raising it with great deliberation to the level of his shoulder, he fired one shot and then, after a short interval, two more close together. A host of persons in the house saw White roll from his chair to the floor, toppling over the table in front of him as he did.

After he had fired the shots Thaw looked down at the prostrate form of the architect and said:

"You deserve this. You have ruined my wife!"

THUS BEGAN what was perhaps the most spectacular criminal case in American history and the Sunday supplement's juiciest crime story for several decades. There were all sorts of sordid overtones and undertones to this sensational murder of Stanford White, architectural genius, by Harry Kendall Thaw on account of Evelyn Nesbit, that season's glamour girl. Stanford White, *bon vivant,* gourmet, and epicure, had tasted fame as the designer of the Memorial Arch in Washington Square and various clubhouses, university buildings, and business structures. His murderer was the offspring of one of the wealthiest and most strait-laced families in Pittsburgh. Reared in a strict environment, Thaw was guarded by companions who were enjoined to keep him from evil influence and "the girls." The result might have been expected: Thaw became one of New York's most notorious playboys.

Florence Evelyn Nesbit was a girl of flowerlike beauty, with a wealth of golden hair and great brown eyes. The lush prose of Irvin S. Cobb, who thought her the most exquisitely lovely human being he had ever seen, described her as having "the slim, quick grace of a fawn, a head that sat on her flawless throat as a lily on its stem, eyes that were the color of blue-brown pansies and the size of half dollars, a mouth made of rumpled rose petals." As an artist's model, Evelyn had posed for Charles Dana Gibson's *Eternal Question,* a popular portrait that adorned half the dens and studios of the country. Smitten the moment he laid eyes on her and boasting that she was his "by right of discovery," Stanford White showered his wealth upon the beautiful girl. Then Harry Thaw met Evelyn and fell desperately in love. His family, properly horrified, issued an ultimatum—leave that woman or get along on $2500 a year. This dire tragedy was averted when the two were married and the family was reconciled.

After the marriage Thaw was enraged to learn from his bride that she had been seduced by Stanford White before Thaw married her. Whereas under similar conditions today a husband might turn to the Kinsey Report, in those days he was more likely to reach for a shotgun. Infuriated, unbalanced by brooding, the Pittsburgh playboy stalked his enemy to the tables of Madison Square Garden and snuffed out his life with three pistol shots.

Harry Thaw was brought to trial in early 1907. Some eighty reporters, special writers, and artists were present to cover the continuing story. Throughout the nation, from the smallest village to the greatest metropolis, the public insatiably demanded more and more lurid details of the assassination. Irvin S. Cobb later revealed that he wrote in longhand a total of more than 600,000 words of running report—enough words to make eight sizable summer novels. There was something to write about every minute, from the vast sums spent on the defense to the battle of the insanity experts over the Exaggerated Ego, the Dementia Americana, the Brain Storm, and the rest of the alienists' jargon. The Thaw case, according to Cobb, "had in it wealth, degeneracy, rich old wasters; delectable chorus girls and adolescent artists' models; the behind-the-scenes of Theaterdom and the Underworld, and the Great White Way; the abysmal pastimes and weird orgies of overly aesthetic artists and jaded debauchees." It was a dizzy, bedaubed, bespangled bacchanalia that enthralled newspaper readers from the Bowery to the Gold Coast.

Here is Irvin S. Cobb's sensational report of Evelyn Nesbit on the stand during Thaw's first trial. Judged by atomic-age standards, this may be corny reporting, but it is typical of the era of Floradora girls, gramophones, and electric hansoms, and historically valuable as a commentary on a fabulous decade.

"*You have ruined my wife!*"

New York *Evening World*, February 7, 1907

A pale, slim little woman on the witness stand this afternoon laid bare the horrors of a life such as few women have led, in her effort to save Harry Thaw from the electric chair. The woman was his wife. For nearly two hours during the morning session and for an equal length of time in the afternoon she traced her history from childhood.

Men and women wept as the life story was unfolded, sometimes artlessly, sometimes with thrilling dramatic force and fervor.

Harry Thaw sobbed unrestrainedly as his wife half whispered the story of her degradation when she was a slip of fifteen. It was a public rending of a woman's soul, but a powerful argument to substantiate the claim of the defense that brooding over the wrongs his girl-wife had suffered shifted the mental balance of Harry Thaw.

The news that Evelyn Nesbit was on the witness stand spread over the city during the morning session and the fragmentary reports of her testimony aroused intense interest. While the court was resting at noon a crowd of probably ten thousand persons gathered around and inside the Criminal Courts Building.

There were riotous scenes as the tide of humanity beat against the immovable police lines. A few slipped through —a sufficient number to fill the courtroom to the limit of its capacity. Those who gained entrance heard a story confirming all the rumors that have gained currency about Evelyn Nesbit and Stanford White since the night Harry Thaw ended the architect's life on the roof of Madison Square Garden.

Evelyn Nesbit held nothing back; she told it all. How as a child, hungry for childhood's playthings, she had carried the weight of a whole shiftless household on her shoulders; how, with all the wiles of the serpent, her elderly seducer had brought hideous shame to her; how, when the chance of honorable wedlock came to her, she bared her secrets to the young lover; how the dreadful news had maddened him; how finally she had seen Stanford White, the seducer, slain by Harry Thaw, the husband.

"Call Mrs. Evelyn Thaw," said Mr. Delmas, chief counsel for the defense of Harry Thaw, as soon as the trial was resumed today.

She came, white and cold and outwardly calm, in her little, plain blue frock, her white turndown collar, her big, schoolboy tie, and her black velvet hat. A court officer let her in by the side door, and she slipped down the paneled aisle back of the jury box and halted alongside the witness chair and put one of her small hands, with a yellow glove, upon the Book that the usher held out to her. She was sworn to tell the truth, the whole truth, and nothing but the truth, so help her God.

The biggest scene in New York's biggest murder trial was at hand.

She slipped into the big oaken chair yawning for her and nestled herself there almost like a tired child. Her hands dropped into her lap. There was something pitiably small and paltry and weak about the girl sitting there ready to crucify herself for the sake of her husband.

He was twenty feet away from her, directly in front of her, with his elbows on the counsel table. He never looked her way. Sweat was dripping in big soggy drops off the ends of his stiff hair.

In a low, sweet voice, plaintive but perfectly steady, she made her first answers to Delmas' smoothly modulated questions.

"You are the wife of the defendant, Harry Thaw?" asked the counsel for the prisoner.

"Yes."

"When were you born?"

"December 25, 1884."

The witness said that she and her husband went to the Madison Square Garden on the night of June 25. They got there after nine. They had left the Café Martin shortly after nine.

"While you were at the Café Martin did you see Stanford White?"

"Yes."

"Did you ask for a pencil while at the table?"

"Yes."

"Then you wrote something on a paper?"

"Yes."

"What did you do with the paper on which you wrote?"

"I passed it to my husband."

"Did the writing refer to the presence of Stanford White?"

The witness responded in the affirmative, but the question was ruled out.

The witness then told of driving from the Café Martin in a cab to Madison Square Garden. Harry Thaw stopped by the aisle. Almost immediately after sitting down, the prisoner got up and walked out. He was away from his wife about five minutes. He returned and sat talking with the witnesses for half an hour.

"What did you see then?"

"I saw Stanford White seated at a table towards which we were going."

"Did you see your husband then?"

"He was behind me. I saw him a moment before I saw Mr. White."

"What was he doing?"

"He was standing with his arm outstretched."

"Did you see a revolver?"

"I heard three shots."

"What did you do?"

"I cried to Mr. McCaleb, 'My God, he has shot him!' "

"Describe his manner as he approached you."

"I cannot. All I remember was that he was coming toward me."

"What did he say?"

"He kissed me and said, 'Dearie, I think I have saved your life.' "

"What did you say?"

"I said, 'Harry, Oh, Harry, why did you do it? What have you done?'

"He answered, 'All right, dearie, I have probably saved your life.'

"I was taken away in a cab and do not remember much of what happened after that. It was all confusion."

Well as the girl-wife bore up under the beginning of the ordeal, she made you think of some weak, trapped creature whose frightened heart jumped inside its ribs—like a brown hare in a deadfall or a bird in a net that is still only because it has worn itself out with hopeless struggling.

The way she patted her bracelet watch—the only jewel she wore— alone betrayed the lightness of the grip she had upon her tortured nerves.

A deep frown made a cleft in her forehead. Never until she reached the recital of the tragedy did the telltale tremor creep into her sweet voice. As soon as Delmas had caused her to tell the story of the shooting he switched away abruptly on a new tack, taking up the subject of the marriage of the girl and thus getting close to the real kernel of the defense.

She said she had been married to the defendant in Pittsburgh in April, 1903. Josiah Thaw and Mr. Holman, Mrs. Thaw's stepfather, were present. Mrs. Thaw said that Thaw had first proposed to her in Paris in June, 1902. She had refused to marry him at the time.

Mr. Delmas asked with solemn emphasis:

"In stating your reasons to him, Thaw, why you would not marry him, did you state a reason based upon an event earlier in your life as a basis for refusing him?"

"I said just, 'Because.' He repeated the request, 'Why don't you marry me?' Again I replied, 'Because.' Then he came over to me and placed his hands on my shoulders and looked me straight in the eyes. He said, 'Evelyn, is it because of Stanford White?' I replied, 'Yes.' Then he sat down and told me he was my friend, and that if I did not marry him he would never marry anyone at all. Then I cried."

Then Mrs. Thaw went ahead and told of her meetings with White.

"It was a girl friend who first introduced me to Stanford White. It was in 1901, when I was sixteen years and some months old. This girl and I got into a cab and drove to the Waldorf, where I had an errand. Then we drove to a dingy doorway on West Twenty-ninth Street; and the girl told the driver to stop at the door. We got out, my girl friend leading the way."

"When was this?"

"In August, 1901."

"You were how old?"

"Sixteen years. My hair was down my back, and I had on short dresses."

"You say that your mother dressed you up for the occasion?"

"Yes."

Mrs. Thaw described her climb up the steps. She said the wide door slammed behind them as they climbed the stairs. The girl said she halted twice, alarmed, but her friend reassured her. At length they came, she said, to White's studio. White met them on the stairs and took them into a room where a table was set for four people.

"The room was very gorgeous," said Mrs. Thaw. "It was beautifully decorated."

"There was another gentleman there?" asked Delmas.

"Yes."

"You must not tell his name."

"I will not."

"You wore short dresses, did you, and your hair was down your back?"

"Yes, my skirts were down to my shoetops."

"You told Mr. Thaw all about this at the time he proposed to you?"

"Yes, I am repeating to you what I told Mr. Thaw at the time he first proposed to me, when he questioned me about Mr. White."

"You all sat down to luncheon in the studio?"

"Yes, and pretty soon the man who was with Mr. White got up and went away. He said he was going away on business.

"Then Mr. White took me and the young lady upstairs to a room in which there was a big velvet swing. We got in the swing and he pushed it so that it flew way up in the air. The swing went so high that our feet kicked through a big Japanese umbrella.

"This luncheon and the swinging fun was in the afternoon," went on the girl under Delmas' prompting. "After a while Mr. White's gentleman friend came back. It was suggested that we go for a drive in the park. We told Mr. White good-by and went downstairs. We drove around the park together in an electric hansom—just the two of us, myself and the girl friend. Then we went to a dentist, where the girl had her teeth fixed. Then I went home and told my mamma all that happened.

"The next time I saw Mr. White was after he had written a letter to my mother."

"Did you see this letter?"

"Yes."

"Did you state to Mr. Thaw in that conversation what the contents of that letter were?"

"Yes, I did."

"Afterward you became familiar with Mr. White's writing?"

"Yes."

The District Attorney objected to this testimony, but it got in.

"Mr. Thaw asked me to tell him everything," continued the witness, "and I did. This letter of Mr. White's asked my mother to call at No. 160 Fifth Avenue. I remember this very distinctly. Mr. Thaw asked me to tell him what was in the letter, and I told him as much of it as I could remember."

"What else was in the letter?"

"Well, Mr. White wrote my mother that if I had any teeth which needed fixing to send me to the dentist and he would pay the bill. He told my mother he would have her dentist's bills paid also. Stanford White said he had had the teeth fixed of nearly all the girls of the *Floradora* company.

"He said," continued Mrs. Thaw, "in his letter that it was not at all unusual. The next time I saw Mr. White at the same studio where I first met him. Again we had luncheon. This was several weeks after the first luncheon.

"My mother gave me a new dress for this luncheon, and a red cape and a red hat. I put on this red cape because she said I was going to a party and must be nicely dressed. She wouldn't tell me where the party was to take place.

"I was put in a cab and started away for the studio. As I was crossing Twenty-fourth Street I saw a man coming out of Park and Tilford's. It was Stanford White. He put me in a hansom and drove me to Madison Square Garden. We went up in the tower to Mr. White's apartment.

"There was another young man there. We had a nice little luncheon. All Mr. White would let me have was a chocolate éclair and a glass of champagne. We stayed there having a nice time until about twelve o'clock that night, or maybe it was one o'clock.

"I asked Mr. White to take me home to my mother, and he took me home all the way to my door and up to my mother. There were three parties like this in the tower at the Garden.

"After one of them Mr. White called on my mother and asked her if she did not want to go to Pittsburgh and visit her friends. My mother said she couldn't bear to go away and leave me alone in New York. Mr. White told her to go ahead and have a nice time and he would look after me and see that nothing happened to me.

"Then Mamma went to Pittsburgh. The day after she left Mr. White sent a carriage for me. He telephoned that I was to come to his studio in East Twenty-second Street and have some photographs taken. I got dressed about ten o'clock in the morning.

"I went down to the carriage door and drove to the studio. When I got there the door opened by itself. I think this was in September, 1901. I went upstairs to the studio. Mr. White was there. There was another man there I knew on the top landing. In the studio there was another man whom I also knew, one a photographer."

"Did you tell Mr. Thaw what took place in that studio?"

"Yes, I told him all about it. In the studio was a lot of clothing, including a gorgeous kimono. They told me to dress up in the things and they photographed me many times. I posed until I got very tired.

"Then Mr. White told the other man to go out and get something to eat. We had a lunch then, after which I put on my street dress in a private room and Mr. White and I had our lunch together. The others had gone. Mr. White gave me only one glass of champagne. Then he sent me home. Nothing had happened except that while I was dressing he had called to me to ask if I needed any help in dressing. I said no.

"The next night Mr. White asked me to come to a party in his studio in West Twenty-fourth Street. I went there after the theater. There was no one there except Mr. White. He said the others had thrown him down. 'That's too bad,' I said, 'for now we cannot have any party.'

" 'Oh, yes,' he said, 'you stay. I want you to see the rest of the apartment. There are three very pretty rooms.' Then he took me into a bedroom. In this room there was a little table on which there was a little bottle of champagne. He gave me one glass.

"He showed me all around the room, which was full of curious and strange things. When we got through looking at the things he said, 'Why don't you drink the champagne?' So I drank it. Then there came a drumming in my ears. Everything began to swim around me. After that everything turned black.

"When I came to again, I was in the bed, all undressed. My clothes were all scattered. Mr. White was alongside of me. He was entirely undressed. I began to scream. He jumped up and put on a big kimono. There were mirrors all around the room. I screamed and screamed. He begged me to be quiet.

"As I got out of bed, I began to scream more than ever, I screamed and screamed."

"Where was Mr. White when you regained consciousness?"

"He was in bed beside me."

"When you got out of bed, what did Mr. White do?"

"He got out, got down on the floor, and took the hem of my dress and told me not to mind. He said he couldn't help it. I was so nice and young and slim. He told me that I must never get fat, as he did not like fat girls. He said they were loathsome. I asked him if everybody did as he had done. He said yes. He told me that it was all that made life worth living, but that I must always keep quiet about ourselves. He told me I was so sweet and pretty that he was unable to keep away from me and that he loved me.

"He made me swear that I must never tell my mother. He said that some of the girls in the theater were foolish and talked about it. He said women in society were clever. He said I must be just as clever. He said he would always be good to me. He kept me there all night, talking like that. I would keep screaming, but he would quiet me and tell me that everything was all right."

By this time dozens in the courtroom were sobbing. Harry Thaw, with his face in his handkerchief, was weeping aloud. His shoulders shook and his hands trembled. Agony was written deep in every line of his wife's face, but she broke down only once.

"What was the effect on Mr. Thaw

when you told him about all this?" said Mr. Delmas.

"He broke down and sobbed and wept," ran on Mrs. Thaw, herself half sobbing. "He clenched his hands before his face and bit his nails, crying, 'The coward, the coward!' We sat up all night while I told him all about this."

"Did he say anything about your mother?"

"Yes; he said that she ought to have known better than allow me to take flowers and presents from an old married man and then go out with him."

"Did Mr. Thaw persist in his request that you marry him?"

"Yes; about two months after I had told him all about this he again urged me to become his wife. He said it wasn't my fault; that I had been deceived by Mr. White, and that he considered me as good and pure as if I had never met him.

"I told Mr. Thaw that even if I did marry him friends of Stanford White would always laugh at him and sneer at him. I told him some of the girls at the theater had already said mean things about me. I said, 'Harry, I can't marry you because I am a ruined girl. As soon as I am well of this operation I have just undergone I will learn to dance and go back on the stage.'"

Harry Thaw had stopped weeping. His wife was now calmer, too. There were tortured lines in her drawn, pitiable face, and there were unutterable words of pathos in her vibrant, shaking voice.

THE JURY FAILED to agree. At a second trial Thaw, choosing to plead insanity, missed the death house at Sing Sing by a margin of inches and went instead to the State Asylum for the Criminal Insane at Matteawan, a few miles farther up the Hudson River. Here he distinguished himself on one Easter morning at breakfast by having placed at the table for every inmate, including the violent ones, a lovely Bermuda lily and a nice fresh vanilla éclair—his own favorite food. When Thaw escaped from Matteawan in 1913 and made a cross-country flight in the summer sun, Jack Lait, the reporter, contributed a bonus-winning lead to his story: "Harry Thaw arrived in Chicago last night, brown as a nut." Thaw remained free, appearing in the sensational press as the central figure of sporadic scandals. He died in 1947, unhonored and unsung, except for long obituaries recalling the details of the assassination of Stanford White.

Evelyn, divorced from Harry Thaw, floated out of the spotlight and became an entertainer in the cafés of the hinterland and water-front honky-tonks. For a time buxom presidents of women's clubs and do-gooders considered it a favorite indoor sport to denounce Evelyn Nesbit for "capitalizing her shame," but eventually the once-famed beauty was consigned to oblivion.

The Thaw-White episode has a parallel in the notorious pre-Civil War shooting by Dan Sickles, "Yankee King of Spain," of Philip B. Key, son of the author of *The Star-Spangled Banner*. That Dumas-like hero, America's most fabulous lover, with a brood of illegitimate children to his credit, chose this melodramatic method of avenging his honor, which had been sullied when his young and beautiful bride, Teresa, carried on an extramarital affair with Key. The case first raised the unwritten law as a defense. Edwin M. Stanton, the successful defense attorney, correctly appraised public sentiment by pleading: "And may the Lord who watches over the home and family guide the bullet and direct the stroke!" Thaw's behavior was even more extreme, as he took the law into his own hands to exact retribution for something that had happened prior to his marriage.

Frank Ward O'Malley of *The Sun* Writes a
Celebrated Sob Story

U NDER THE SLIGHTLY intoxicating influence of shoptalk an able reporter
was said to have made the very profound remark that the tear-impel-
ling article is the most difficult kind of story for a good reporter to write or
a bad reporter to avoid trying to write. To this another equally proficient
newsman added that good reporters write a "sob story" only when it grips
them like an octopus and demands to be written; then they merely perform
the function of jotting down the facts and let the reading public do the
weeping.

Frank Ward O'Malley, of the old New York *Sun,* possessed a vein of
structural humor that delighted his readers, but at the same time he was
a master of the sob-story technique. Born in Pittston, Pennsylvania, on
November 30, 1875, he studied architecture, drawing, painting, and sculpture as a young man, and came to New York in 1902 as an illustrator and
contributor of light verse. Art finally palled on O'Malley, whereupon he
went to *The Sun* as a humorist and special writer. His work was so outstanding that he became widely and somewhat reverently known among
newsmen as "O'Malley of *The Sun.*"

This is O'Malley's famous story of the killing of Policeman Gene Sheehan,
one of those tragic and completely unnecessary murders which appear too
often in metropolitan crime. It is told as a straightforward report in the
words of the policeman's mother. O'Malley was just thirty-two years old
when he wrote this minor masterpiece. Old-timers still tell how a Westches-
ter commuter rose to his feet in 1907 and read this story aloud to a coach
of strangers, the dramatic lines making him choke before he could finish
the report. To ultrasophisticated ears it may not ring precisely true, but
O'Malley's story has a unique quality that stands out among the yellowed
clippings of newspaper morgues.

A policeman walks east to death

New York *Sun,* October 23, 1907

Mrs. Catherine Sheehan stood in the
darkened parlor of her home at 361
West Fifteenth Street late yesterday
afternoon and told her version of the
murder of her son Gene, the youthful policeman whom a thug named
Billy Morley shot in the forehead
down under the Chatham Square ele-

vated station early yesterday morning. Gene's mother was thankful that her boy hadn't killed Billy Morley before he died, "because," she said, "I can say honestly even now that I'd rather have Gene's dead body brought home to me, as it will be tonight, than to have him come to me and say, 'Mother, I had to kill a man this morning.'

"God comfort the poor wretch that killed the boy," the mother went on, "because he is more unhappy tonight than we are here. Maybe he was weak-minded through drink. He couldn't have known Gene or he wouldn't have killed him. Did they tell you at the Oak Street station that the other policeman called Gene Happy Sheehan? Anything they told you about him was true, because no one would lie about him. He was always happy, and he was a fine-looking young man and he always had to duck his helmet when he walked under the gas fixture in the hall as he went out the door.

"He was doing dance steps on the floor of the basement after his dinner yesterday noon for the girls—his sisters, I mean—and he stopped of a sudden when he saw the clock and picked up his helmet. Out on the street he made pretend to arrest a little boy he knows who was standing there—to see Gene come out, I suppose—and when the little lad ran away laughing, I called out, 'You couldn't catch Willie, Gene; you're getting fat.'

" 'Yes, and old, Mammy,' he said, him who is—who was only twenty-six —'so fat,' he said, 'that I'm getting a new dress coat that'll make you proud when you see me in it, Mammy.' And he went over Fifteenth Street, whistling a tune and slapping his leg with a folded newspaper. And he hasn't come back again.

"But I saw him once after that, thank God, before he was shot. It's strange, isn't it, that I hunted him up on his beat late yesterday afternoon for the first time in my life. I never go around where my children are working or studying—one I sent through college with what I earned through dressmaking and some other little money I had, and he's now a teacher; and the youngest I have at college now. I don't mean that their father wouldn't send them if he could, but he's an invalid, although he's got a position lately that isn't too hard for him. I got Gene prepared for college, too, but he wanted to go right into an office in Wall Street. I got him in there, but it was too quiet and tame for him, Lord have mercy on his soul; and then, two years ago, he wanted to go on the police force, and he went.

"After he went down the street yesterday I found a little book on a chair, a little list of the streets or something that Gene had forgot. I knew how particular they are about such things, and I didn't want the boy to get into trouble, and so I threw on a shawl and walked over through Chambers Street toward the river to find him. He was standing on a corner someplace down there near the bridge, clapping time with his hands for a little newsy that was dancing; but he stopped clapping, struck, Gene did, when he saw me. He laughed when I handed him a little book and told that was why I'd searched for him, patting me on the shoulder when he laughed—patting me on the shoulder.

" 'It's a bad place for you here, Gene,' I said. 'Then it must be bad for you, too, Mammy,' said he; and as he walked to the end of his beat with me —it was dark then—he said, 'They're lots of crooks here, Mother, and they know and hate me and they're afraid of me'—proud, he said it—'but maybe they'll get me some night.' He patted me on the back and turned and walked east toward his death. Wasn't it strange that Gene said that?

"You know how he was killed, of course, and how—now let me talk about it, children, if I want to. I promised you, didn't I, that I wouldn't cry any more, or carry on? Well, it was five o'clock this morning when a boy rang the bell here at the house and I looked out the window and said, 'Is Gene dead?' 'No, ma'am,' answered the lad, 'but they told me to tell you he was hurt in a fire and is in the hospital.' Jerry, my other boy, had opened the door for the lad and was talking to him while I dressed a bit. And then I walked downstairs and saw Jerry standing silent under the gaslight, and I said again, 'Jerry, is Gene dead?' And he said, 'Yes,' and he went out.

"After a while I went down to the Oak Street station myself, because I couldn't wait for Jerry to come back. The policemen all stopped talking when I came in, and then one of them told me it was against the rules to show me Gene at that time. But I knew the policeman only thought I'd break down, but I promised him I wouldn't carry on, and he took me into a room to let me see Gene. It was Gene.

"I know today how they killed him. The poor boy that shot him was standing in Chatham Square, arguing with another man, when Gene told him to move on. When the young man wouldn't but only answered back, Gene shoved him, and the young man pulled a revolver and shot Gene in the face, and he died before Father Rafferty of St. James got to him. God rest his soul. A lot of policemen heard the shots, and they all came running with their pistols and clubs in their hands. Policeman Laux—I'll never forget his name or any of the others that ran to help Gene—came down the Bowery

and ran out into the middle of the Square where Gene lay.

"When the man that shot Gene saw the policemen coming he crouched down and shot at Policeman Laux, but thank God he missed him. Then policemen named Harrington and Rourke and Moran and Kehoe chased the man all around the streets there, some heading him off when he tried to run into that street that goes off at an angle—East Broadway is it?—a big crowd had come out of Chinatown now and was chasing the man too, until Policemen Rourke and Kehoe got him backed up against a wall. When Policeman Kehoe came up close the man shot his pistol right at Kehoe, and the bullet grazed Kehoe's helmet.

"All the policemen jumped at the man then, and one of them knocked the pistol out of his hand with a blow of a club. They beat him, this Billy Morley, so Jerry says his name is, but they had to because he fought so hard. They told me this evening that it will go hard with the unfortunate murderer, because Jerry says that when a man named Frank O'Hare, who was arrested this evening charged with stealing cloth or something, was being taken to headquarters, he told Detective Gegan that he and a one-armed man who answered to the description of Morley, the young man who killed Gene, had a drink in a saloon at Twenty-second Street and Avenue A and that when the one-armed man was leaving the saloon he turned and said, 'Boys, I'm going out now to bang a guy with buttons.'

"They haven't brought me Gene's body yet. Coroner Shrady, so my Jerry says, held Billy Morley, the murderer, without letting him get out on bail, and I suppose that in a case like this they have to do a lot of things before they can let me have the body here. If Gene only hadn't died before Father Rafferty got to him I'd be happier. He didn't need to make his confession, you know, but it would have been better, wouldn't it? He wasn't bad, and he went to Mass on Sunday without being told; and even in Lent, when we always say the rosary out loud in the dining room every night, Gene himself said to me the day after Ash Wednesday, 'If you want to say the rosary at noon, Mammy, before I go out, instead of at night when I can't be here, we'll do it.'

"God will see that Gene's happy to-night; won't He, after Gene said that?" the mother asked as she walked out into the hallway with her black-robed daughters grouped behind her. "I know He will," she said, "and I'll ——" She stopped, with an arm resting on the banister to support her. "I —I know I promised you girls," said Gene's mother, "that I'd try not to cry any more, but I can't help it." And she turned toward the wall and covered her face with her apron.

* * *

THE GREAT O'MALLEY left *The Sun* to write humorous and other yarns for *The Saturday Evening Post* and Mencken's and Nathan's *American Mercury* until his death in 1932. But in all newspaper shops *The Sun*'s ace retained his reputation as the master "straight" reporter, who could catch the spirit of an event, great or small, and pass it on to the newspaper reader by means of "a magnificent talent for ringmastering words."

The Daily Telegraph Interviews
Kaiser Wilhelm II, Who Lays Bare Germany's
Plans for a Navy to Challenge Britain

EACH TIME WILHELM II, the loudest of the Hohenzollerns, bellowed about German strength and the close alliance between himself, God, and Germany, the world came closer and closer to war. His worst *faux pas* of the year 1908 was the famous *Daily Telegraph* affair, an incredible mistake that raised a storm of protest in both England and Germany and nearly led to the Kaiser's abdication.

On October 28, 1908, *The Daily Telegraph* of London published an account of an interview between the Kaiser and an unnamed British subject —one of the most significant interviews in the history of journalism. This story was plain dynamite. While appearing to present himself as a lover of peace, the Kaiser, through his own words, showed himself to be a blustering warmonger, anxious to allay British anxiety over Germany's big navy plans by using an argument that was a characteristic blending of distorted historical fact and offensive flattery.

But let us start at the beginning.* In the late fall of 1907, when the Kaiser was paying a few weeks' visit to his good English friend, Colonel Stuart-Wortley, the owner of Highcliffe Castle, he told his host of all he had done for England and how he had been misunderstood there. When he saw the British army officer again, during the military maneuvers at Alsace in September, 1908, at a time when Anglo-German relations were at low ebb, he "expressed his personal desire that the utmost possible publicity should be given in England to Anglophile views held by himself and his house." Colonel Stuart-Wortley convinced the Kaiser that the best approach to the problem was to publish an interview in *The Daily Telegraph* in an attempt to pacify the British press and British public opinion. Then Stuart-Wortley, using the Kaiser's statements, composed a rough draft of an interview with an unspecified interlocutor. With the help of an expert journalist, E. Harold Spender, then on the staff of the London *Daily News,* Stuart-Wortley whipped the interview into final form and on September 23 submitted it to the Kaiser. "No one will ever know the source from which the communiqué came," he assured Wilhelm.

---

* There have been so many versions of the circumstances surrounding *The Daily Telegraph* affair that the editors have gone to the most reliable source for the facts given here—the secret dispatches of the German Foreign Office: *Die diplomatischen Akten des Auswärtigen Amtes* (*Die Grosse Politik der europäischen Kabinette, 1871–1914*), Berlin, 1921–25, Deutsche Verlagsgesellschaft für Politik und Geschichte, Band XXIV, pp. 167-210. In view of the fact that versions of the interview vary widely, the editors have used here the actual text appearing in the London *Daily Telegraph* on October 28, 1908.

Wilhelm was delighted, pronouncing the article to be well written, and a faithful report of what he had said. Then began an extraordinary comedy of errors as the interview bumped along channels to the pressroom of *The Daily Telegraph.* The Kaiser sent it through Ambassador von Jenisch to Chancellor von Bülow, with word that Bülow was to read it, "suggest any desirable alterations on the margin of the existing English text," and then send it straight back to him, not through the Foreign Office, "keeping it a secret from as many others as is at all possible." Jenisch—a diplomat—did not read the article and did as he was told.

Chancellor von Bülow was at his summer home at Norderney, on the shore of the North Sea, and was not tempted to read another hackneyed "Kaiser speech." He sent it off to Berlin with the superscription "Confidential" and the instruction "Revise carefully" on the margin. In Berlin it was opened by the deputizing Undersecretary Stemrich, who took good care not to read the typescript, but passed it on instead to Privy Councilor Klehmet. The latter, a very conscientious bureaucrat, read the typescript, and at first felt "very dubious about the advisability of publication." But, thought Klehmet, who was he to stand in the way of the Emperor's express wish "when the Chancellor on his side has conveyed no sense of uneasiness?" Klehmet corrected two important misstatements and suggested several changes in diction.

Back went the interview to Herr Stemrich, who signed his name without reading the typescript; thence it went back to Norderney, where Bülow gave it a cursory glance and signed it as it stood with Klehmet's corrections, which he described "as alterations which strike me as desirable." When the typescript reached Berlin, it was marked "Urgent" by the Secretary of State, who "had no time to take cognizance of the contents." Then, like a football, the interview went back to Bülow, who remarked that he had just seen it himself, then to Jenisch, then to the Kaiser, then to his English friend, Stuart-Wortley—and finally to *The Daily Telegraph.*

Despite Wilhelm's protestations of friendship for England during the Boer War, the British could hardly have forgotten the Kaiser's congratulatory telegram to President Kruger of the Boer Republic on the occasion of the Boer repulse of a British invasion of the Transvaal in 1896. The Kaiser's visit to Tangier in 1905 to protest the partition of North Africa between France and England, now bound in an *entente cordiale,* was still fresh in the minds of most readers. Then came the German Navy Bill of 1906, which Britain promptly answered by a treaty with Russia. To allay suspicion of Germany, the Kaiser dragged in a red herring—the Oriental menace, particularly aiming at the Anglo-Japanese alliance, then six years old.

Here it is—*The Daily Telegraph* interview, one of the biggest news stories of modern times.

"You English are mad, mad, mad as March hares"

London *Daily Telegraph*, October 28, 1908

We have received the following communication from a source of such unimpeachable authority that we can without hesitation comment on the obvious message which it conveys to the attention of the public.

Discretion is the first and last quality requisite in a diplomatist, and should still be observed by those who, like myself, have long passed from public into private life. Yet moments sometimes occur in the history of nations when a calculated indiscretion proves of the highest public service, and it is for that reason that I have decided to make known the substance of a lengthy conversation which it is my privilege to have had with His Majesty the German Emperor. I do so in the hope that it may help to remove that obstinate misconception of the character of the Kaiser's feelings toward England which, I fear, is deeply rooted in the Englishman's breast. It is the Emperor's sincere wish that it should be eradicated. He has given repeated proofs of his desire by word and deed. But, to speak frankly, his patience is sorely tried, now that he finds himself so continually misrepresented, and has so often experienced the mortification of finding that any momentary improvement of relations is followed by renewed outbursts of prejudice and a prompt return to the old attitude of suspicion.

As I have said, His Majesty honored me with a long conversation, and spoke with impulsive and unusual frankness.

"You English," he said, "are mad, mad, mad as March hares. What has come over you that you are so completely given over to suspicions quite unworthy of a great nation? What more can I do than I have done? I declared with all the emphasis at my command, in my speech at Guildhall, that my heart is set upon peace, and that it is one of my dearest wishes to live on the best of terms with England. Have I ever been false to my word? Falsehood and prevarication are alien to my nature. My actions ought to speak for themselves, but you listen not to them but to those who misinterpret and distort them. That is a personal insult which I feel and resent. To be forever misjudged, to have my repeated offers of friendship weighed and scrutinized with jealous, mistrustful eyes, taxes my patience severely. I have said time after time that I am a friend of England, and your press—or, at least, a considerable section of it—bids the people of England refuse my proffered hand and insinuates that the other holds a dagger. How can I convince a nation against its will?

"I repeat," continued His Majesty, "that I am the friend of England, but you make things difficult for me. My task is not of the easiest. The prevailing sentiment among large sections of the middle and lower classes of my own people is not friendly to England. I am, therefore, so to speak, in a minority in my own land, but it is a minority of the best elements as it is in England with respect to Germany. That is another reason why I resent your refusal to accept my pledged word that I am the friend of England. I strive without ceasing to improve relations, and you retort that I am your archenemy. You make it hard for me. Why is it?"

Thereupon I ventured to remind His Majesty that not England alone, but the whole of Europe had viewed with disapproval the recent action of Germany in allowing the German consul to return from Tangier to Fez, and in anticipating the joint action of France and Spain by suggesting to the Powers that the time had come to Europe to recognize Mulai Hafiz as the new Sultan of Morocco.

His Majesty made a gesture of impatience.

"Yes," he said, "that is an excellent example of the way in which German action is misrepresented. First, then, as regards to the journey of Dr. Vassel. The German government, in sending Dr. Vassel back to his post at Fez, was only guided by the wish that he should look after the private interests of German subjects in that city, who cried for help and protection after the long absence of a consular representative. And why not send him? Are those who charge Germany with having stolen a march on the other Powers aware that the French consular representative had already been in Fez for several months before Dr. Vassel set out? Then, as to the recognition of Mulai Hafiz. The press of Europe has complained with much acerbity that Germany ought not to have suggested his recognition until he had notified to Europe his full acceptance of the Act of Algeciras,* as being binding upon him as Sultan of Morocco and succes-

sor of his brother. My answer is that Mulai Hafiz notified the Powers to that effect weeks ago, before the decisive battle was fought. He sent, as far back as the middle of last July, an intentional communication to the governments of Germany, France, and Great Britain, containing an explicit acknowledgment that he was prepared to recognize all the obligations towards Europe which were incurred by Abd-al-Aziz during his sultanate. The German government interpreted that communication as a final and authoritative expression of Mulai Hafiz's intentions, and therefore they considered that there was no reason to wait until he had sent a second communication before recognizing him as the *de facto* Sultan of Morocco, who had succeeded to his brother's throne by right of victory in the field."

I suggested to His Majesty that an important and influential section of the German press had placed a very different interpretation upon the action of the German government, and, in fact, had given it their effusive approbation precisely because they saw in it a strong act instead of mere words, and a decisive indication that Germany was once more about to intervene in the shaping of events in Morocco.

"There are mischiefmakers," replied the Emperor, "in both countries. I will not attempt to weigh their relative capacity for misrepresentation. But the facts are as I have stated. There has been nothing in Germany's recent action with regard to Morocco which runs contrary to the explicit declara-

---

* The International Conference at Algeciras, Spain, met in 1906 under the chairmanship of Theodore Roosevelt, who was called in at the earnest and repeated appeals of the Kaiser. The following measures were adopted: Morocco's independence was recognized; her finances were to be managed by a bank under international control; the "Open Door" principle was accepted; order was to be maintained by the formation of a police force under French control; and customs and traffic in arms were entrusted for the most part to France. Though Germany won in principle at Algeciras, France won in practical results.

tion of my love of peace which I made both at Guildhall and in my latest speech at Strasbourg."

His Majesty then reverted to the subject uppermost in his mind—his proved friendship for England. "I have referred," he said, "to the speeches in which I have done all that a sovereign can to proclaim my good will. But, as actions speak louder than words, let me also refer to my acts. It is commonly believed in England that throughout the South African War Germany was hostile to her. German opinion undoubtedly was hostile—bitterly hostile. But what of official Germany? Let my critics ask themselves what brought to a sudden stop, and, indeed, to absolute collapse, the European tour of the Boer delegates, who were striving to obtain European intervention? They were feted in Holland, France gave them a rapturous welcome. They wished to come to Berlin, where the German people would have crowned them with flowers. But when they asked me to receive them—I refused. The agitation immediately died away, and the delegation returned empty-handed. Was that, I ask, the action of a secret enemy?

"Again, when the struggle was at its height, the German government was invited by the governments of France and Russia to join with them in calling upon England to put an end to the war. The moment had come, they said, not only to save the Boer Republics, but also to humiliate England to the dust. What was my reply? I said that so far from Germany joining in any concerted European action to put pressure upon England and bring about her downfall, Germany would always keep aloof from politics that could bring her into complications with a sea power like England. Posterity will one day read the exact terms of the telegram—now in the archives of Windsor Castle—in which I informed the sovereign of England of the answer I had returned to the Powers which then sought to compass her fall. Englishmen who now insult me by doubting my word should know what were my actions in the hour of their adversity.

"Nor was that all. Just at the time of your Black Week, in the December of 1899, when disasters followed one another in rapid succession, I received a letter from Queen Victoria, my revered grandmother, written in sorrow and affliction, and bearing manifest traces of the anxieties which were preying upon her mind and health. I at once returned a sympathetic reply. Nay, I did more. I bade one of my officers procure for me as exact an account as he could obtain of the number of combatants in South Africa on both sides and of the actual position of the opposing forces. With the figures before me, I worked out what I considered to be the best plan of campaign under the circumstances, and submitted it to my General Staff for their criticism. Then, I dispatched it to England, and that document, likewise, is among the state papers at Windsor Castle, awaiting the severely impartial verdict of history. And, as a matter of curious coincidence, let me add that the plan which I formulated ran very much on the same lines as that which was actually adopted by Lord Roberts, and carried by him into successful operation. Was that, I repeat, the act of one who wished England ill? Let Englishmen be just and say!

"But, you will say, what of the German navy? Surely, that is a menace to England! Against whom but England are my squadrons being prepared? If England is not in the minds of those Germans who are bent on creating a powerful fleet, why is Germany asked to consent to such new and heavy burdens of taxation? My answer is clear. Germany is a young and growing empire. She has a world-wide commerce which is rapidly expanding, and to which the legitimate ambition of patriotic Germans refuses to assign any bounds. Germany must have a powerful fleet to protect that commerce and her manifold interests in even the most distant seas. She expects those interests to go on growing, and she must be able to champion them manfully in any quarter of the globe. Germany looks ahead. Her horizons stretch far away. She must be prepared for any eventualities in the Far East. Who can foresee what may take place in the Pacific in the days to come, days not so distant as some believe, but days, at any rate, for which all European Powers with Far Eastern interests ought steadily to prepare? Look at the accomplished rise of Japan; think of the possible national awakening of China; and then judge of the vast problems of the Pacific. Only those Powers which have great navies will be listened to with respect when the future of the Pacific comes to be solved; and if for that reason only Germany must have a powerful fleet. It may even be that England herself will be glad that Germany has a fleet when they speak together on the same side in the great debates of the future."

Such was the purport of the Emperor's conversation. He spoke with all the earnestness which marks his manner when speaking on deeply pondered subjects. I would ask my fellow-countrymen who value the cause of peace to weigh what I have written, and to revise, if necessary, their estimate of the Kaiser and his friendship for England by His Majesty's own words. If they had enjoyed the privilege, which was mine, of hearing them spoken, they would doubt no longer either His Majesty's firm desire to live on the best of terms with England or his growing impatience at the persistent mistrust with which his offer of friendship is too often received.

IN ORDER to understand what happened to the Kaiser after this interview was published one must have had the privilege of observing a self-satisfied man after dinner carefully light up a fragrant cigar and then, after a few minutes of delightful puffing, have it explode in his face. The reaction in both England and France was exactly the opposite of what Wilhelm had so confidently expected. He had hoped to disarm England's suspicions and improve the relations between the two countries. Instead the British lion growled. The English doubted his sincerity; they ridiculed and resented the idea that his advice had helped them win the Boer War; they noted his admission that the prevailing sentiment in Germany was unfriendly to England.

Even the politically immature German people sensed that something was wrong and became alarmed. A tempest of indignation broke out in Germany. The long-accumulated bitterness about the Kaiser's willful and tactless behavior was expressed in almost revolutionary manner. Liberals and Socialists combined to protest against the dangers of his personal rule. Chancellor von Bülow, who at bottom was not sorry that the Kaiser was learning a lesson, went before an infuriated Reichstag and apologized for his headstrong royal master. His defense of his sovereign had a schoolmaster's air about it that Wilhelm II could not abide and never forgave. Wilhelm the Irrepressible, deeply chagrined, had a nervous collapse and promised that he would use more reserve in private conversation henceforth.

"When was there an opportunity more favorable than the present one to extort parliamentary government?" declared a Social Democrat. But the German liberals were too timid to make a decisive move, and the opportunity passed by.

Only a few weeks before this interview Austria had formally annexed the provinces of Bosnia and Herzegovina, a fatal step on the road to World War I.

Herbert Bayard Swope of *The World* Breaks the Becker Case and Tears New York Wide Open

L ORD NORTHCLIFFE called him "the greatest reporter in the world." Woodrow Wilson said that "he had the fastest mind with which I ever came into contact." Walter Lippmann judged him to be "a fascinating devil." Stanley Walker, himself a first-rate newsman, described him as "an inexorable whirlwind." "He is as easy to ignore," wrote Walker, "as a cyclone. His gift of gab is a torrential and terrifying thing. He is probably the most charming extrovert in the Western world."

This was Herbert Bayard Swope, the executive editor of the old New York *World* in the fabulous twenties. Of all the dynamic journalists in this rugged decade, Swope stood out "like a snorting Caesar in a company of Caspar Milquetoasts." Six feet one inch tall, two hundred pounds, his face a striking crimson, he raged and stormed through the newspaper world, bringing to *The World* the highest circulation in its history. Two years after he left it, Joseph Pulitzer's old journal was no more.

Swope hit the top in journalism in 1912, when, almost singlehanded, he tilted lances with the "System"—New York City's alliance of police and underworld, and cracked the celebrated Rosenthal-Becker case. It was one of the great crime stories of all time. *The World* was the first paper to print the revelations of Herman Rosenthal, the gambler, about police protection. What happened in the sensational case is told by Swope himself in his "FIRST COMPLETE STORY OF NEW YORK'S AMAZING MURDER: HOW POLICE LIEUTENANT BECKER PLOTTED THE DEATH OF GAMBLER ROSENTHAL TO STOP HIS EXPOSÉ," presented here in condensed form.

"I want to have him croaked!"

New York *World*, October 27, 1912

"Herman Rosenthal has squealed again."

Through the pallid underworld the sibilant whisper ran. It was heard in East Side dens; it rang in the opium houses in Chinatown; it crept up to the semipretentious stuss and crap games of the Fourteenth Street region, and it reached into the more select circles of uptown gambling where business is always good and graft is always high.

Rosenthal had squealed once too often.

This time his action was a direct affront to the "System." He had publicly defied it. He had set it, through its lieutenant, at naught. He had publicly thrown down the gantlet, and it was snatched up, to be returned in the form of four bullets crashing into his head while he stood in the heart of the city under a blaze of lights that enabled bystanders to follow every move of the four assassins, who, their job having been done, and well done, swarmed above the gray automobile that had brought them to their work, and fled, secure, as they thought, from successful pursuit because they were acting under the sheltering hand of Police Lieutenant Charles Becker, who had issued the order to Jack Rose:

"I want Herman Rosenthal croaked!"

But in his death Herman Rosenthal found a thousand tongues where he had been but one. His murder cried in accusation a thousandfold stronger than any he could have made. In his death he gave life to the grudge that he had been nursing in his heart. He vitalized the fierce hatred he felt for the powers that had preyed upon him, and now the people of the state of New York demand that two lives shall pay forfeit for every bullet fired at the man who was not permitted to tell his story.

In this drama of life, which reads so clearly that it would seem to be a work of art—an unreal thing rather than a real story lived by real people —three figures loomed.

Around them the plot is spun. Without them the action lags. Of them one is dead by murder, one is about to pay the penalty for this crime by death in the electric chair, and the third in fear and trembling awaits his summons— sure it will come—from the friends of those subordinate actors in the tragedy whom he surrendered to the law.

Rosenthal squeals; Becker, the police blackmailer, and Rose, his creature, enter upon the stage at the rise of the curtain and are never once away from it until the final fall.

And behind this trio hangs the vast impalpable spectacle, the "System," in whose labyrinthian maze men are killed, others are robbed, and women are made slaves—each a sacrifice to the greater glory of the "System."

Becker was of the "System," by the "System," and for the "System." He lived and had his being through the grace he found in its eyes. Like Caesar, all things were rendered unto Becker in the underworld, and as it was his to take, so, too, was it his to give. Nothing escaped him. Like Briareus he had a hundred arms, and each of them reached into the pocket of whoever was engaged in an occupation that needed quiet and darkness rather than the light of day and the eyes of the public.

It was not a common type of man who could attain this position of power in the Police Department of the city of New York. He is big in girth and stature. He stands five feet eleven and weighs 190 pounds. His shoulders are broad and his chest deep. He is dark in hair and skin. His nose is straight and big, jutting out uncompromisingly over a long upper lip, a mouth like the cut of a knife, and a chin that sticks out squarely at the end of a jaw that looks like a granite block.

He is forty-two years old. He was born in Callicoon, New York, which was the place of nativity of the redoubtable Dr. Frederick A. Cook, the self-made hero of polar exploration. Becker joined the police force in 1893. His career has been a troublous one since then.

The System is many-sided. It can be gently kind as well as fiercely protective. It takes care of its own, and its own takes care of it. Becker wanted to be a hero. Becker was a good soldier in the System's cause; therefore, Becker a hero should be.

He was presented with a medal of police heroism for rescuing James Butler from a rushing tide at the foot of West Tenth Street one July morning. Proudly Becker wore his medal and the accompanying bronze star on his sleeve for two years. Then came the exposé.

Butler made an affidavit, fully corroborated, that he was an old lifesaver and an expert swimmer and that he had jumped into the river at the request of Becker, who promised him five dollars for doing so, but never paid the money.

Becker began to be talked about as a coming man in police circles.

On June 22, 1911, Charles Becker, who had been made a lieutenant four years before, was detailed to the command of Special Squad No. 1, known as the "Strong-Arm Squad." From then on his history is written in blackmail and murder, in money and blood.

In ten months following his elevation to the most conspicuous position in the New York Police Department Becker, receiving a salary of $2250 and supporting himself and his wife in a luxurious manner, rolled up bank deposits approximating $100,000.

Here enters on the scene Jack Rose, Becker's man Friday—Rose, the humble; Rose, the obsequious; Rose, the fawning, who, at the last, was to turn and rend the man for whom he had committed blackmail, perjury, and murder.

Rose's real name is Jacob Rosenschwig. He is thirty-seven years old. He was born in Russian Poland, and he seems ashamed of it. He was reared on the East Side just at the time that that melon of the city had discovered that America was indeed an Eldorado —for those who wished to make it so.

Money was to be had for the asking —if the asking was hard enough.

In appearance Rose is one man in ten thousand. You need see him only once never to forget him. He has not a hair on his body. His face and head are as smooth and bare as a billiard ball, and from this resemblance he gained the sobriquet of "Billiard Ball Jack." The gambling fever was deep in his blood. He would rather gamble than eat—and he often did.

Rosenthal need not be described. He is dead. The murder tore a corner off the underworld and brought to view the rats, the wolves, the preyers, and the preyed scurrying away from the light that they so feared.

At that time Herman Rosenthal was running a gambling house in Forty-fifth Street. Rosenthal was always a hustler. He was a moneymaker. Rosenthal the loose-tongued, Rosenthal the babbler, in spite of his unpopularity, which was largely due to the fact that he often talked too much about things that he ought not to talk about at all, was credited with certain powers both in and out of the department.

He had watched Becker's rise closely. Rosenthal described himself as not being a "lover of cops." But he saw in Becker a chance to help himself and at the same time help Becker.

Like the little drops of water, one friction succeeded another between Rosenthal and Becker. Becker made a raid on a crap game during which his press agent, one Charles Plitt, Jr., shot and killed a Negro named Waverly Carter. At the time Becker's money was pretty well tied up. Besides, he had heard that Rosenthal had made a "killing," so he told Rose to tell Rosenthal that he would like to get $500 for the purposes of Plitt's defense.

Rosenthal's refusal to give Becker the money, coupled with the pressure being put upon him at headquarters, caused the relations between the two to buckle, if not break.

Becker knew Rosenthal was dangerous, and he set himself a task of covering his enemy's every move. On a day late in June Becker telephoned for Rose to hurry down to the Union Square Hotel, where the two were in the habit of meeting almost daily, either there or at Luchow's. Becker was much disturbed. He said:

"This —— Rosenthal is going further than I ever thought he was. He is trying to prove that I was his partner. He is peddling the story to the newspapers. He is getting really dangerous. He must be stopped."

"That ought to be easy enough," Rose said, not realizing for a moment the sinister meaning that Becker sought to convey.

"Jack," responded the policeman, "I want you to go after this fellow Jack Zelig down in the Tombs. We framed him on a charge of carrying a gun. Give him a hundred dollars and tell him that if he wants to save himself you will get him out and that he is to send his gang after Rosenthal."

"What do you mean," asked Rose, "get them to beat him up?"

"No," answered Becker with scorn. "I don't want him beaten up. I want him croaked, murdered, his throat cut, dynamited, anything that will take him off the earth. There's a fellow who is too mean to live. There is no other way of handling the job. I WANT YOU TO HAVE HIM CROAKED!"

And as if realizing that the abruptness of his proposition had startled Rose, and fearing that a sufficient cause had not been presented to enlist the collector's sympathy in the undertaking, Becker went on, laying his hands on Rose's shoulders:

"Why, Jack, you haven't any idea the kind of man that Rosenthal is. I would be ashamed to tell you the things that he said about you and your wife and your children."

The shot struck home. Rose's dormant willingness was vitalized into life. He agreed that something ought to be done, but he wasn't at all sure as to the method suggested by Becker —murder. He temporized, but Becker would have none of it.

So Rose, who in the meanwhile, under the direction of Becker, had enlisted the sympathy, support, and active co-operation of "Bridgie" Weber, and with Weber, of course, Harry Vallon, arranged the bail bond for Zelig in $10,000. Sam White, another East Side gambler, was among those who subscribed and who later was accused of knowing why Zelig's freedom was desired.

Rose knew four of Zelig's men who traveled together—Frank Muller, alias "Whitey" Lewis; Harry Horowitz, alias "Gyp the Blood"; Louis Rosenberg, alias "Lefty Louie"; and Frank Ciroficci, alias "Dago Frank." All were mankillers, if not in deed, then in spirit, and two of them had real notches on their guns. They knew he came from Zelig and that he had been responsible for getting Zelig out on bail to await trial on a second offense of carrying concealed weapons, which if substantiated meant imprisonment for fourteen years. They knew, too, that Rose, through Becker, could, if he wished, have the charge vitiated; so they felt grateful for what he had done for their chief, and eager to oblige him so that he could do more.

Certainly they would do the job, and glad to do it. But Rose had no stomach for murder and he sought to fight it off. Becker gave him no rest. Once, twice, three times between the date of Rose's conversation with the gunmen and the final murder Becker came to him with reproaches that the job had not yet been done.

"*Now,*" he said, "*I want some action or it will be worse for everybody. This fellow is getting so dangerous that there is no telling what may happen. Go after him anywhere. Kill him anyplace you find him. Break into his house if you have to. I'll take care of everybody that's in it. Not a thing will happen.*"

Two days later, in the first week of July, Becker ordered Rose to meet him at One Hundred and Twenty-fourth Street and Seventh Avenue, where the policeman was to raid a Negro crap game. Rose was there and with him came his errand runner—lobbygow—Sammy Schepps. Schepps was sent down to Weber's poker room at Forty-second Street and Sixth Avenue to bring Weber and Vallon to the place. Schepps himself was not allowed to be present. He was not trusted with the secrets, and so he had to wait a half a block away—and in that wait lies the cause of Becker being where he is today and of Rose, Weber, and Vallon being accepted as state's witnesses.

Becker's words were powerful. Rose and Schepps drove up to the Southern Boulevard apartment house where "Dago Frank" and "Lefty Louie" and their wives had been living and told them to hold themselves in readiness for action that night.

Three of them—"Lefty Louie," "Gyp the Blood," and "Dago Frank" —were stationed in front of the Garden Restaurant at Fiftieth Street and Seventh Avenue, where Rosenthal and his wife, accompanied by Jack Sullivan, had been trailed. It was three o'clock in the morning. They were ready to do their work, but either through fancy or some real cause Jack Rose's nerve failed him and he came up on the run from his position a block away to inform the gunmen that they were being shadowed by Burns detectives working for District Attorney Whitman, and that if an attack were made upon Rosenthal there would be no opportunity for a getaway.

"The next day," Rose swore on the witness stand, "I met Becker and he asked me what was the matter with the Rosenthal job. He wanted to know why it had not been pulled off at the Garden Restaurant as planned. I told him about the detectives, and he said:

"'Tell them there isn't anything to be scared of. They don't need to be frightened off by any detective. Why, you tell them that they can shoot Rosenthal in front of any policeman and they'll be all right. I tell you there won't be any trouble about it at all.'

"On July 13," Rose continued, "Becker telephoned me that Rosenthal had made an affidavit for the *Morning World*. Becker said he was going to try to prevent its publication, but he said he didn't know if he could do it, and he said the whole trouble was my fault because of the delay. I told him that I was going to the Sam Paul outing the next day and I would have a long talk with Vallon and Weber, and all the details would be planned. The next day we went to the outing. We all bought *The World*. We read Rosenthal's affidavit and, more than that, we read the statement that had come from Whitman down at Newport. Then we knew that it was really serious.

"On Monday afternoon, July 13, Becker got me on the telephone at the Lafayette Baths and told me that

Jack Sullivan had just told him that Whitman had made good on *The World*'s story and had seen Rosenthal at noon and that a secret engagement had been made to put Rosenthal before the Grand Jury the next morning. And Becker said that Sullivan had found out that Rosenthal had given up the names of Abe Hahlo, Dollar John Lang, and Abe the Rebler, three East Side gamblers. These men were to swear that Becker had been in partnership with Rosenthal and that Becker had been getting graft through me."

Rose left the Lafayette Baths about nine o'clock to go to the Sam Paul Association, when he met Harry Vallon and Jack Sullivan. Rose ordered an automobile and dropped in, with Sullivan, at the Madison Square Garden, where the so-called "King of the Newsboys" met Lieutenant Becker and attended a prize fight. Rose and Vallon drove to Dora Gilbert's home, where they had several drinks. They succeeded in getting from her an affidavit bitterly hostile to Rosenthal, which Becker proposed to use to discredit the gambler.

This duty having been complied with, a roundup of the murderers was begun. Rose and Vallon telephoned to certain places where knowledge of the four could be obtained and left directly.

The red car which Rose had hired at the Sam Paul Association lost a tire on the trip from Dora Gilbert's apartment to Tom Sharkey's saloon. So the first thing that Rose did when he arrived there was to telephone to the Café Boulevard for Libby and Shapiro's car—the gray murder car, No. 41313.

Here the details were supplied from Rose's narrative:

"Vallon, Schepps, and myself got in. The car was driven by Willie Shapiro. We went up to the Seventh Avenue place where 'Dago Frank' had moved. I often saw all the boys there. When we got in front of the house I sent Schepps to ring the bell. A head popped out of the window, and I recognized 'Dago Frank.' He came downstairs and got in, and I asked him where the rest of the boys were, and he told me they had gone downstairs ahead.

"We drove down to Forty-third Street and Sixth Avenue. There, in front of the poker room, stood 'Bridgie' Weber, 'Lefty,' 'Whitey,' and 'Gyp.' We all went upstairs. Weber told the Negro waiter to bring us something to eat and drink. The rest did so, but I didn't seem to have any appetite. After giving the order to the waiter Weber went out. We knew where he had gone and why. He had gone to find Herman Rosenthal and then he was coming back to tell us where he was.

"I found myself hoping that Weber wouldn't locate him. I wanted to give him another chance. I thought of his wife and how she was worrying every day about Herman, and it broke me all up.

"Just as I was trying to think of some way to stall it off for a little while Weber came rushing back and leaned over the table and whispered,

" *'Rosenthal is at the Metropole now.'*

"Even if I had wanted to, before I could say a word, everybody got up and went out—'Gyp,' 'Lefty,' 'Whitey,' 'Dago,' Weber, and Vallon. Schepps started to, but I asked him to wait with me."

That Monday night there had been a heavy feeling about Mrs. Rosenthal's heart and she sought to dissuade her husband from leaving her. "Don't go out, Herman," she said. "I'm dreadfully worried about you. Everybody tells me you're in great danger. So stay at home with me at least for tonight."

He was a marked man. Everyone in that neighborhood knew him and everyone expected that those he attacked would square matters with him. He passed a group of gamblers who had just walked up from the Hotel Knickerbocker, and they stopped and told him that he had been the sole topic of conversation and that if he was a wise man he would go home.

With a cheery "Good night," which, if it were assumed, did not show it in the tone, Rosenthal went on. It was then about one o'clock. He entered the restaurant.

The first man he saw there and the first man to see him was "Bridgie" Weber. Then he lost sight of him, for a good reason. It was then that Weber hurried over for the agents of death, who were waiting impatiently for the final word.

Rosenthal talked as he always did of his grievances. So filled was he with this subject that he had become a nuisance to his friends. Twice he left his table, once to go into the hallway to speak to a friend named Morris Luban, who had beckoned to him, and the other time to go to the side door and purchase some newspapers, which had just appeared on the street, it being then about a quarter of two.

It has never been established whether Rosenthal was sent to or whether he walked to his fate, without being lured to it. He had returned to his table and thrown the newspapers down before him and said in a tone of pride:

"That's what the newspapers think of me. Look at that!" and he showed his companions how his story had been given a prominent position on the front page.

Then, refusing another drink and saying that he promised his wife to be home early, Rosenthal threw a dollar down on the table to pay an eighty-cent check and started out. Some of those present think that just at this time it was that a stranger approached him and said:

"Herman, somebody wants to see you outside."

Rosenthal passed through the opening formed by the folded back circular door, and as his foot touched the pavement four shots rang out. Four men had been standing on the sidewalk, facing the café door. They stood close together. As Rosenthal emerged they acted in unison. The right arms of three of them snapped up, the left arm of one, and as the pistols spoke Rosenthal toppled forward and fell without a groan. As he was falling, the left-handed man pulled his trigger again and sent a bullet crashing into the top of the victim's head. The impact was so powerful that the body turned half around and fell on its side and the eyes stared straight up at the brilliant arc lights, the brows set in an expression of bewilderment, with the mouth parted in a fearful grin. There was a jagged hole in the left cheek, and the dropping jaw and relaxed muscles that let the joints twist horribly showed that medical assistance was unnecessary, and on the crown of his head was the great jagged wound made by the last bullet.

Seven policemen were within five hundred feet of the murder, yet the four men made their flight in safety.

Before the body had settled down the four men had run to a gray car standing on the other side of the street in the shadow of the George M. Cohan Theater, pointing east, clambered aboard, and fled.

They were the adventurers, recruited by Jack Rose two hours earlier, who had come to the scene when "Bridgie" Weber gave the word that the trap had been baited.

Then they had piled out of the poker room, and the four had gotten into the same gray car that had brought them there and had moved on to the Metropole. Each of them knew Herman Rosenthal, and so the possibility of error was minimized. They had taken up their station not five feet from the café entrance, to be sure that their prey would not escape them, nor had he.

One officer had been in the Metropole all the time. He was Policeman File, who had jumped for the street at the flash of the first gun and who had stumbled over the body of the dead man, but from whom the murderers were able to escape because of the bystanders, who made it dangerous for File to shoot.

"They've murdered Herman Rosenthal!"

This time it was no whisper that spread through the underworld. It was a cry that staggered the city. It ran the length of Broadway and flashed through the East Side. It stirred the community as it had never been stirred before, for never had a crime of violence given such a direct defiance to law and order.

*   *   *

IF THE IRREPRESSIBLE Herbert Bayard Swope had not acted swiftly upon receiving word of Rosenthal's murder, the police might have been able to cover the trail of the gunmen. But within an hour Swope had gotten District Attorney Charles Seymour Whitman out of bed and had brought him posthaste to the West Forty-seventh Street station. The prodded District Attorney saw to it that the police record finally had written into it the real number of the getaway automobile. Police Lieutenant Becker was present.

Rose later swore that he had asked Becker at this time whether he had seen Rosenthal's body. "Sure," he quoted Becker as saying, "I went to the back room and had a look at him. It was a pleasing sight to me to look at the Jew there. If Whitman had not been there I would have cut his tongue out and hung it somewhere as a warning to other squealers. Now the only thing to do is to sit tight and don't worry."

It didn't work out that way. On July 29, Rose, convinced that he was being "thrown to the wolves" and promised immunity by Whitman, confessed full details of the plot. Lieutenant Becker went to the electric chair, accompanied by Dago Frank, Gyp the Blood, Lefty Louie, and Whitey Lewis.

His perfect handling of the case made Whitman Governor of New York. But, throughout, the District Attorney was steered by Swope, who even wrote his statements for him. It was a classic story in newspaper enterprise.

After the Rosenthal-Becker case Herbert Bayard Swope went on to make further newspaper history. In late September, 1914, he scored a beat by obtaining, with the aid of Admiral von Tirpitz, an exclusive interview with the German hero, Kapitän-Leutnant von Weddingen, commander of the *U-9*, which had sunk the British cruisers *Cressy, Hogue,* and *Aboukir*.

In 1917 Swope was awarded the first Pulitzer Prize in reporting for his series of articles: "Inside the German Lines."

This was the heyday of personalized journalism. At the Peace Conference Swope was the first to get the outline of the terms of the treaty of peace and the first to get a copy of the Covenant of the League of Nations. To the editors of this volume he revealed how he obtained the first authentic summary of the original document and published it a day before it was read at a plenary session of the Peace Conference on April 10, 1919. "I asked the President to give me a revised and amended draft," Swope told us. "He replied: 'Sorry, I may not give it to you, but if you drop in at Colonel House's office at five-thirty this afternoon, he will not be in.'" A rival newspaper, the European edition of *The New York Herald,* published the draft with this bow to Swope: "Mr. Herbert Bayard Swope, the special correspondent of the New York *World,* has scored the great journalistic success of the Conference by obtaining an analytical synopsis of the new document. By courtesy of Mr. Swope the *Herald* is enabled today to reproduce the salient passages of the new version of the Covenant."

Richard Harding Davis Sees the German Army
Goose-Step Through the Streets of Brussels

AFTER THE Franco-Prussian War of 1870–71 the elder von Moltke warned Germany that she must prepare for a war on two fronts. Several schemes were devised, but it was not until 1905 that Count Alfred von Schlieffen, Chief of the German General Staff, developed a plan calling for a defensive war against Russia, while a swift advance was to be made on the Channel ports and Paris through Belgium and southern Holland, and then a concentrated attack in the east. At the outset of World War I, Moltke, a nephew of the great conqueror of France in 1870–71, put a modified Schlieffen Plan into effect. The Germans invaded Belgium with the purpose of swinging like a hammer in a wide arc on Paris. Speedily mobilized, exceptionally well equipped, diabolically efficient, the invaders smashed through the little country whose neutrality had been guaranteed in 1839 by the European powers in a document that the Germans now regarded as a "scrap of paper." The Belgian army, though it resisted fiercely, was scattered within two weeks.

The German surge into Brussels was witnessed by a top-flight American war correspondent, Richard Harding Davis, who was so well established as a journalist that he could command a salary from the fabulous Hearst reputed to have been $3000 a month. A prolific writer of fiction, plays, and narratives embodying his war experiences, ranging from the Greco-Turkish War (1897) to World War I, he enjoyed enormous popularity as the glamour boy of war correspondents. A whole generation of Americans, from domesticated dowagers to thrill-happy youngsters, sought vicarious adventure in his dramatic prose. Other newsmen dubbed him the "knight-errant of the nineties." As the original firm-jawed Gibson man with a dimple in his chin, he set the pattern of virility for the men and boys of his day.

Germans were marching through the Belgian capital as Richard Harding Davis wrote his story. The wires were down to Antwerp and Ostend, and Davis was unable to leave Brussels. He had obtained papers from the Belgians giving him permission to depart, but the Germans, while giving him the same privilege, stipulated that he should remain in the city until their turning movement was completed. Although virtually a prisoner in Brussels, Davis, with typical ingenuity, arranged for a young English courier to get his message to the outside world. The messenger, E. A. Dalton by name, dressed in riding breeches, puttees, and a dark coat, left Brussels at dusk. For companions he had long lines of German infantry. Keeping to the main road, he was able to get short lifts from wagons or automobiles. When he came to the point where the main body of Germans turned off from the road to Ghent and where he was apt to be challenged, he hid in the undergrowth beside the road and crept along on his hands and knees for a mile before daring to emerge onto the highway again. He finally reached Ostend, boarded a government refugee boat, and crossed to Folkestone with the message he had given his word to deliver.

This dispatch is the newsman's favorite piece of reporting of World War I, and, in fact, one of the great war reports of all time. In the words of Arno Dosch-Fleurot it is "a picture of imperialism itself coming down the road." It inspired Fairfax Downey, the biographer of Richard Harding Davis, to comment: "The measured beat and swinging rhythm of its sentences seemed to echo the marching tread of all the hordes of history sweeping relentlessly, interminably over conquered kingdoms."

"Like a river of steel it flowed, gray and ghostlike"

The News Chronicle, London, August 23, 1914

BRUSSELS, FRIDAY, AUGUST 21, 2 P.M. —The entrance of the German army into Brussels has lost the human quality. It was lost as soon as the three soldiers who led the army bicycled into the Boulevard du Régent and asked the way to the Gare du Nord. When they passed the human note passed with them.

What came after them, and twenty-four hours later is still coming, is not men marching, but a force of nature like a tidal wave, an avalanche or a river flooding its banks. At this minute it is rolling through Brussels as the swollen waters of the Conemaugh Valley swept through Johnstown.

At the sight of the first few regiments of the enemy we were thrilled with interest. After for three hours they had passed in one unbroken steel-gray column we were bored. But when hour after hour passed and there was no halt, no breathing time, no open spaces in the ranks, the thing became uncanny, inhuman. You returned to watch it, fascinated. It held the mystery and menace of fog rolling toward you across the sea.

The gray of the uniforms worn by both officers and men helped this air of mystery. Only the sharpest eye could detect among the thousands that passed the slightest difference. All moved under a cloak of invisibility. Only after the most numerous and severe tests at all distances, with all materials and combinations of colors that give forth no color, could this gray have been discovered. That it was selected to clothe and disguise the German when he fights is typical of the German staff in striving for efficiency to leave nothing to chance, to neglect no detail.

After you have seen this service uniform under conditions entirely opposite you are convinced that for the German soldier it is his strongest weapon. Even the most expert marksman cannot hit a target he cannot see. It is a gray green, not the blue gray of our Confederates. It is the gray of the hour just before daybreak, the gray of unpolished steel, of mist among green trees.

I saw it first in the Grand Palace in front of the Hôtel de Ville. It was impossible to tell if in that noble square there was a regiment or a brigade. You saw only a fog that melted into the stones, blended with the ancient house fronts, that shifted and drifted, but left you nothing at which you could point.

Later, as the army passed below my window, under the trees of the Botanical Park, it merged and was lost against the green leaves. It is no exaggeration to say that at a hundred yards you can see the horses on which the uhlans ride, but you cannot see the men who ride them.

If I appear to overemphasize this disguising uniform it is because of all the details of the German outfit it appealed to me as one of the most remarkable. The other day when I was with the rear guard of the French Dragoons and Cuirassiers and they threw out pickets, we could distinguish them against the yellow wheat or green gorse at half a mile, while these men passing in the street, when they have reached the next crossing, become merged into the gray of the paving stones and the earth swallows them. In comparison the yellow khaki of our own American army is about as invisible as the flag of Spain.

Yesterday Major General von Jarotsky, the German Military Governor of Brussels, assured Burgomaster Max that the German army would not occupy the city, but would pass through it. It is still passing. I have followed in campaigns six armies, but excepting not even our own, the Japanese, or the British, I have not seen one so thoroughly equipped. I am not speaking of the fighting qualities of any army, only of the equipment and organization. The German army moved into this city as smoothly and as compactly as an Empire State Express. There were no halts, no open places, no stragglers.

This army has been on active service three weeks, and so far there is not apparently a chin strap or a horseshoe missing. It came in with the smoke pouring from cookstoves on wheels, and in an hour had set up post-office wagons, from which mounted messengers galloped along the line of columns, distributing letters, and at which soldiers posted picture postcards.

The infantry came in in files of five, two hundred men to each company; the Lancers in columns of four, with not a pennant missing. The quick-firing guns and fieldpieces were one hour at a time in passing, each gun with its caisson and ammunition wagon taking twenty seconds in which to pass.

The men of the infantry sang *Fatherland, My Fatherland.* Between each line of song they took three steps. At times two thousand men were singing together in absolute rhythm and beat. When the melody gave way the silence was broken only by the stamp of iron-shod boots, and then again the song rose. When the singing ceased, the bands played marches. They were followed by the rumble of siege guns, the creaking of wheels, and of chains clanking against the cobblestones and the sharp bell-like voices of the bugles.

For seven hours the army passed in such solid columns that not once might a taxicab or trolley car pass through the city. Like a river of steel it flowed, gray and ghostlike. Then, as dusk came and as thousands of horses' hoofs and thousands of iron boots continued to tramp forward, they struck tiny sparks from the stones, but the horses and the men who beat out the sparks were invisible.

At midnight pack wagons and siege guns were still passing. At seven this morning I was awakened by the tramp of men and bands playing jauntily.

Whether they marched all night or not I do not know; but now for twenty-six hours the gray army has rumbled by with the mystery of fog and the pertinacity of a steam roller.

* * *

IN THE MEANTIME the German press reported the fall of Brussels in calm and confident dispatches. In its special war edition of August 21, 1914, the *Neue Preussische Zeitung* (Berlin) announced at the top of its front page:

In the last few hours we have received the news that German troops have entered Brussels. The telegram is short and convincing, just as we have come to expect from our High Command:

GERMAN TROOPS HAVE ENTERED BRUSSELS.

On the next day the *Neue Preussische Zeitung* gave further details:

Neue Preussische Zeitung (Berlin), August 22, 1914

The coming of the German troops was kept a secret from the people of Brussels until the last minute. The proclamation of the Burgomaster hit the people like a clap of thunder. The Burgomaster went out to meet the troops and upon their appearance had a white flag held aloft. He then talked with a German officer and received from the latter the assurance that nothing would happen to the people if they would give up all acts of violence towards the Germans. The entry of the Germans led to scenes of panicky fright among the people in the villages near Brussels. Brussels itself is like a dead city; in the environs the people are in great fear that they will be held responsible and punished energetically because of the destruction of German business houses in Brussels.

The bad conscience of the people of Brussels is indicated by the fact that in the last few days they have hurriedly removed all barricades and barbed-wire defenses, for the understandable order came that it was useless to defend the open city.

Brussels is completely cut off from the outer world. The citizens are in deathly fear, which is heightened through continually misleading newspaper reports. Until the last day the newspapers stated that the Germans were reluctant to fight. Even noble families had begun to flee from their castles, and they sat, just like the poor folk, on their baggage in the North Station, in order to escape via Ostend to England. Railway service was soon halted; moreover, it became impossible to obtain automobiles.

ALTHOUGH IMPRESSED by its efficiency, Richard Harding Davis was not convinced that the German army would smash through to victory. After writing his classic dispatch, he gave an accurate prophecy of the future of the German war machine:

To perfect this monstrous engine, with its pontoon bridges, its wireless, its hospitals, its airplanes that in rapid alignment sailed before it, its field telephones that, as it advanced, strung wires over which for miles the vanguard talked to the rear, all modern inventions had been prostituted. To feed it millions of men had been called from homes, offices, and workshops; to guide it, for years the minds of the highborn, with whom it is a religion and a disease, had been solely concerned.

It is, perhaps, the most efficient organization of modern times; and its purpose only is death. Those who cast it loose upon Europe are military-mad. And they are only a very small part of the German people. But to preserve their class they have in their image created this terrible engine of destruction. For the present it is their servant. But, "Though the mills of God grind slowly, yet they grind exceeding small." And, like Frankenstein's monster, this monster, to which they gave life, may turn and rend them.

First of the Dashing War Correspondents Sees the Germans Put Louvain to the Torch and Leave It an Empty Blackened Shell

O N AUGUST 4, 1914, just three days after the outbreak of World War I, President Wilson proclaimed a policy of neutrality. Shortly thereafter the President urged the American people to be "neutral in fact as well as in name," but soon a succession of incidents stirred up a burning resentment against Germany among many Americans and strong feeling for the underdogs. Hardly had the war begun before trained German propagandists popped up like mushrooms throughout the country. But their obvious and heavy-handed efforts were thwarted by the kind of stories reputable American war correspondents began to send home about the conduct of German troops in the field. Many Americans were aroused to silent fury by Richard Harding Davis' account of the horrors of Louvain, reprinted below.

It was a grim story. On August 20, 1914, German troops, led by such famous regiments as the Death's Head and Zeiten Hussars, entered the Belgian city of Louvain with bands playing and singing *Watch on the Rhine* and *Hail to the War Lord*. As a not very subtle method of impressing the populace, the infantry was marched through in formal goose step, with boots striking heavy blows on the earth as they fell in unison. Dumfounded by the din—the tramp of feet, the clatter of horses' hoofs, the sharp echoes from the house walls, and the rumble of the guns—the people looked on in silence. As if on review before the Emperor, the gray-green surge of overwhelming military might, eyes front, poured through the town.

That night the cafés and restaurants began to fill up with hungry officers and men. At first they paid in cash for everything they bought. Then somebody started the ugly rumor that a German officer had been wounded by a sniper. There seemed to be substantiation for the report when a wounded officer was borne very conspicuously on a litter through the streets, followed by the dead body of his assailant.

When the sniping continued, the German military authorities tried to stop it by leading large bands of Belgians, indiscriminately chosen, to execution. Unnerved, the occupation troops began to throw torches into houses suspected of harboring snipers. Soon the whole city was aflame.

"That night the Germans were like men after an orgy," reports Richard Harding Davis

New York Tribune, August 31, 1914

LONDON, AUGUST 30—I left Brussels on Thursday afternoon and have just arrived in London. For two hours on Thursday night I was in what for six hundred years has been the city of Louvain. The Germans were burning it, and to hide their work kept us locked in the railroad carriages. But the story was written against the sky, was told to us by German soldiers incoherent with excesses; and we could read it in the faces of women and children being led to concentration camps and of citizens on their way to be shot.

The Germans sentenced Louvain on Wednesday to become a wilderness, and with the German system and love of thoroughness they left Louvain an empty blackened shell. The reason for this appeal to the torch and the execution of noncombatants, as given to me on Thursday morning by General von Lutwitz, military governor of Brussels, was this: on Wednesday while the German military commander of the troops of Louvain was at the Hôtel de Ville talking to the Burgomaster, a son of the Burgomaster with an automatic pistol shot the chief of staff and German staff surgeons.

Lutwitz claims this was the signal for the civil guard, in civilian clothes on roofs, to fire upon the German soldiers in the open square below. He said also the Belgians had quick-firing guns, brought from Antwerp. As for a week the Germans had occupied Louvain and closely guarded all approaches, the story that there was any gunrunning is absurd.

Fifty Germans were killed and wounded. For that, said Lutwitz, Louvain must be wiped out. So in pantomime with his fist he swept the papers across his table.

"The Hôtel de Ville," he added, "was a beautiful building; it is a pity it must be destroyed."

Ten days ago I was in Louvain when it was occupied by Belgian troops and King Albert and his staff. The city dates from the eleventh century, and the population was 42,000. The citizens were brewers, lacemakers, and manufacturers of ornaments for churches. The university once was the most celebrated in European cities, and still is, or was, headquarters of the Jesuits.

In the Louvain college many priests now in America have been educated, and ten days ago over the green walls of the college, I saw hanging two American flags. I found the city clean, sleepy, and pretty, with narrow twisting streets and smart shops and cafés set in flower gardens of the houses, with red roofs, green shutters, and white walls.

Over those that faced south had been trained pear trees, their branches heavy with fruit spread out against the walls like branches of candelabra. The Town Hall was very old and very beautiful, an example of Gothic architecture, in detail and design more celebrated even than the Town Hall of Bruges or Brussels. It was five hundred years old, and lately had been repaired with great taste and at great cost.

Opposite was the Church of St. Pierre, dating from the fifteenth century, a very noble building, with many chapels filled with carvings of the time of the Renaissance in wood, stone, and iron. In the university were 150,000 volumes.

Near it was the bronze statue of Father Damien, priest of the leper colony in the South Pacific, of which Robert Louis Stevenson wrote. All these buildings now are empty, exploded cartridges. Statues, pictures, carvings, parchments, archives—all are gone.

No one defends the sniper. But because ignorant Mexicans when their city was invaded fired upon our sailors, we did not destroy Vera Cruz. Even had we bombarded Vera Cruz, money could have restored it. Money can never restore Louvain. Great architects, dead these six hundred years, made it beautiful, and their handiwork belonged to the world. With torch and dynamite the Germans have turned these masterpieces into ashes, and all the Kaiser's horses and all his men cannot bring them back again.

When by troop train we reached Louvain, the entire heart of the city was destroyed and fire had reached the Boulevard Tirlemont, which faces the railroad station. The night was windless, and the sparks rose in steady, leisurely pillars, falling back into the furnace from which they sprang. In their work the soldiers were moving from the heart of the city to the outskirts, street by street, from house to house.

In each building, so German soldiers told me, they began at the first floor, and when that was burning steadily passed to the one next. There were no exceptions—whether it was a store, chapel, or private residence it was destroyed. The occupants had been warned to go, and in each deserted shop or house the furniture was piled, the torch was stuck under it, and into the air went the savings of years, souvenirs of children, of parents, heirlooms that had passed from generation to generation.

The people had time only to fill a pillowcase and fly. Some were not so fortunate, and by thousands, like flocks of sheep, they were rounded up and marched through the night to concentration camps. We were not allowed to speak to any citizen of Louvain, but the Germans crowded the windows, boastful, gloating, eager to interpret.

We were free to move from one end of the train to the other, and in the two hours during which it circled the burning city war was before us in its most hateful aspect.

In other wars I have watched men on one hilltop, without haste, without heat, fire at men on another hill, and in consequence on both sides good men were wasted. But in those fights there were no women and children, and the shells struck only vacant stretches of veldt or uninhabited mountainsides.

At Louvain it was war upon the defenseless, war upon churches, colleges, shops of milliners and lacemakers; war brought to the bedside and fireside; against women harvesting in the fields, against children in wooden shoes at play in the streets.

At Louvain that night the Germans were like men after an orgy.

There were fifty English prisoners, erect and soldierly. In the ocean of gray the little patch of khaki looked pitifully lonely, but they regarded the men who had outnumbered but not defeated them with calm but uncurious eyes. In one way I was glad to see them there. Later they will bear witness as to how the enemy makes a wilderness and calls it war. It was a most weird picture.

On the high ground rose the broken spires of the Church of St. Pierre and the Hôtel de Ville, and descending like steps were row beneath row of houses, those on the Boulevard de Jodigne. Some of these were already cold, but others sent up steady, straight columns of flame. In others at the third and fourth stories the window curtains still hung, flowers still filled the window boxes, while on the first floor the torch had just passed and the flames were leaping. Fire had destroyed the electric plant, but at times the flames made the station so light that you could see the second hand of your watch, and again all was darkness, lit only by candles.

You could tell when an officer passed by the electric torch he carried strapped to his chest. In the darkness the gray uniforms filled the station with an army of ghosts. You distinguished men only when pipes hanging from their teeth glowed red or their bayonets flashed.

Outside the station in the public square the people of Louvain passed in an unending procession, women bareheaded, weeping, men carrying the children asleep on their shoulders, all hemmed in by the shadowy army of gray wolves. Once they were halted, and among them were marched a line

of men. They well knew their fellow townsmen. These were on their way to be shot. And better to point the moral an officer halted both processions and, climbing to a cart, explained why the men were to die. He warned others not to bring down upon themselves a like vengeance.

As those being led to spend the night in the fields looked across to those marked for death they saw old friends, neighbors of long standing, men of their own household. The officer bellowing at them from the cart was illuminated by the headlights of an automobile. He looked like an actor held in a spotlight on a darkened stage.

It was all like a scene upon the stage, so unreal, so inhuman, you felt that it could not be true, that the curtain of fire, purring and crackling and sending up hot sparks to meet the kind, calm stars, was only a painted backdrop; that the reports of rifles from the dark rooms came from blank cartridges, and that these trembling shopkeepers and peasants ringed in bayonets would not in a few minutes really die, but that they themselves and their homes would be restored to their wives and children.

You felt it was only a nightmare, cruel and uncivilized. And then you remembered that the German Emperor has told us what it is. It is his Holy War.

THE BURNING of Louvain was a featured story in the press of most of the world, but German newspapers soft-pedaled the incident. Instead, there was a long series of angry reports on "the barbaric deeds of the Belgians against the Germans." A sample, from the *Berliner Tageblatt,* August 12, 1914:

German refugees from Belgium are still coming to our office and reporting to us the terrible but true stories of Belgium fanaticism. A German butcher in the Rue Saint-Pierre in Brussels was literally cut to pieces by a wild mob. The crazed people shouted that they would give him a death in keeping with his trade. Of a German family of seven children in Brussels, three children were trampled to death in the mob. One German woman had her eye gouged out. Another woman, who managed to save herself but not her children, went insane on the journey to Germany. Her fellow passengers reported that she threw herself from the train and killed herself.

The Moltke-Schlieffen Plan seemed to be working. The Germans moved inexorably forward. Nine days after Davis' account of Louvain a correspondent of the London *Daily Mail* wired from Amiens:

This is a pitiful story I have to write. Would to God it did not fall to me to write it! But the time for secrecy is past. Only by realizing what has happened can we nerve ourselves for the effort we must make to retrieve it. . . . I write with the Germans advancing incessantly, while all the rest of France believes they are still held near the frontier. . . . Our small British force could not stand before a volume so powerful, so immense. It has been scattered all over the country, so I learn from officers—staff officers among them—and men met here and there. . . . As the captain of the dragoons said, "They are everywhere."

Then, at the end of the first week of September, the steam roller was stopped and turned back at the Marne by "Papa" Joffre's taxicab army.

To make the British public aware of the critical conditions on the western front and to end that apathy with which many Englishmen began the war ("To Hell with Servia!" *John Bull* had declared in early August), British reporters quickly matched Davis in reporting horror stories. *The Daily News* of London started a series called "Under the Heel of the Hun," while Horatio Bottomley filled *John Bull* with sensational accounts, such as one dated October 3, 1914, beginning: "It is our bounden duty to call up before the eye of imagination the scenes of butchery, rape, and rapine which everywhere have marked the progress of the German arms," and ending with the affirmation: "There shall be no peace till the crimes of Louvain and Rheims are compensated to the full in money, in blood, and in kind; no peace till the German fleet is destroyed or surrendered; no peace till the dishonored sword of Kaiser Wilhelm is broken across his craven back, and he is driven like Cain of old from the habitations of men."

One thing was clear. The Allies were determined to fight it out. "Let us see the thing through," declared H. G. Wells, vocalizing popular sentiment.

Will Irwin Denounces the Germans of World War I

for Using Poison Gas at Ypres

CHEMICAL WARFARE is not new to the twentieth century. The Greek historian, Thucydides, records two instances of the use of burning sulphur and pitch in the Peloponnesian Wars. Throughout classical times as well as during the Middle Ages such devices were tried, including the employment of Greek fire. With the increased mobility of war and the resultant possibilities of wider range of action, the opportunities for using such weapons in a primitive form disappeared. But at the Hague Conference of 1899 and again at the Hague Convention of 1907, the participating governments, including Imperial Germany, pledged themselves not to use irritant or poison gas in any future conflicts.

On April 22, 1915, the German military violated these clear-cut agreements by discharging chlorine from cylinders on the western front. The attack came as a staggering surprise to unprotected French and Canadian troops, and, if followed through, it might well have won the war.

This sensational story was covered for the *New York Tribune* by Will Irwin, who had already made journalistic history by his story of the 1906 San Francisco earthquake.*

*The Hague Convention becomes another
scrap of paper*

New York Tribune, April 25, 1915

NORTH OF FRANCE, APRIL 24—There is no doubt that the action which has been proceeding about Ypres for a week, and which will probably be known in history as the second battle of Ypres, is the hardest and the hottest which has yet developed on the extreme western front. Indeed, no battle of the war has developed so much action on so concentrated a front. It is the third desperate attempt of the Germans since this war began to break through the combined British and Belgian lines and take the all-important city of Calais.

This series of attacks and counterattacks running along the whole line developed into that general attack on the British lines with Calais for objective which the Germans probably had been planning ever since matters began to come to a deadlock in the Carpathians. The Germans, making full use of their artillery, launched infantry attacks in their old manner—close-locked. As formerly, the British

* See page 274.

322

and French slaughtered them heavily with machine-gun and rifle fire. Then on Thursday the Germans suddenly threw in that attack with asphyxiating bombs, which will doubtless become famous in this war. It succeeded in breaking the line of French near Bixschoote, although not to such an extent as the Germans claim in today's communiqué.

The nearest British support was a part of the Canadian contingent. Fighting with desperate bravery, the Canadians succeeded in recovering part of the lost ground. They are still at it today. On a favorable wind the sound of cannonading can be heard as far away as the coast towns.

The nature of the gases carried by the German asphyxiating shells remains a mystery. Whatever gas it is, it spreads rapidly and remains close to the ground. It is believed not to be specially deadly—one that rather overpowers its victims and puts them *hors de combat* without killing many. Its effect at Bixschoote may have been due to panic caused by the novelty of the device. Its composition and manner of discharge are probably no mystery to the scientific artillerymen of the Allies. That such devices might be used in war has been known for a long time, but the positive prohibitions of the Hague Conference have prevented the more civilized nations of Europe from going far with experiments in this line.

IN HIS NEXT dispatch, Irwin revised his opinion on the deadliness of the poison gas:

New York Tribune, April 27, 1915

BOULOGNE, APRIL 25—The gaseous vapor which the Germans used against the French divisions near Ypres last Thursday, contrary to the rules of the Hague Convention, introduces a new element into warfare. The attack of last Thursday evening was preceded by the rising of a cloud of vapor, greenish gray and iridescent. That vapor settled to the ground like a swamp mist and drifted toward the French trenches on a brisk wind. Its effect on the French was a violent nausea and faintness, followed by an utter collapse. It is believed that the Germans, who charged in behind the vapor, met no resistance at all, the French at their front being virtually paralyzed.

Everything indicates long and thorough preparation for this attack. The work of sending out the vapor was done from the advanced German trenches. Men garbed in a dress resembling the harness of a diver and armed with retorts or generators about three feet high and connected with ordinary hose pipe turned the vapor loose towards the French lines. Some witnesses maintain that the Germans sprayed the earth before the trenches with a fluid which, being ignited, sent up the fumes. The German troops, who followed up this advantage with a direct attack, held inspirators in their mouths, thus preventing them from being overcome by the fumes.

In addition to this, the Germans appear to have fired ordinary explosive shells loaded with some chemical which had a paralyzing effect on all the men in the region of the explosion. Some chemical in the composition of these shells produced violent watering of the eyes, so that the men overcome by them were practically blinded for some hours.

The effect of the noxious trench gas seems to be slow in wearing away. The men come out of their nausea in a state of utter collapse. Some of the rescued have already died from the aftereffects. How many of the men, left unconscious in the trenches when the French broke, died from the fumes it is impossible to say, since those trenches were at once occupied by the Germans.

This new form of attack needs for success a favorable wind. Twice in the day that followed the Germans tried trench vapor on the Canadians who made on the right of the French position a stand which will probably be remembered as one of the heroic episodes of this war. In both cases the wind was not favorable, and the Canadians managed to stick through it. The noxious, explosive bombs were, however, used continually against the Canadian forces and caused some losses.

* * *

ADDITIONAL FACTS on this first use of poison gas in World War I were given by a correspondent for the London *Chronicle,* who wrote of "a thick curtain of smoke, which advanced like the yellow wind of northern China." According to this correspondent, among those who escaped nearly all coughed and spat blood, the chlorine attacking the mucous membrane. The dead turned black at once. The attacking Germans made no prisoners. "Whenever they saw a soldier whom the fumes had not quite killed they snatched away his rifle and threw it in the Yser and advised him ironically to lie down 'to die better.' "

In his dispatches to the *New York Tribune* Will Irwin failed to include the salient news that he himself had been a victim of the gas attack, a fact which he revealed later in his book of reminiscences, *The Making of a Reporter* (1942):

Our train was going to load up and back out. I fell to and helped with the stretchers. In my absorption, I noticed a peculiar smell, to which I paid little attention. I found myself coughing and the air seemed to burn. And after an eternity we backed out for Boulogne. . . .

I was fighting illness. There was something the matter with my throat. Memory is a confusion of trains loading and unloading the wounded, shell cases and gas cases together, of new cots filling the halls and vestibules of the Casino, of nurses working until they staggered. . . .

Gas masks began to arrive. . . . Women volunteers set to work night and day on primitive muslin mouth pads stuffed with absorbent cotton, treated with chemicals held in place by elastics.

I realized that something more than incipient tonsillitis was afflicting my throat But it was no time or place to be ill. I dragged around haunting the hospitals until presently I felt a little better.*

---

* From *The Making of a Reporter,* published by G. P. Putnam's Sons. Copyright, 1942, by Will Irwin.

The German press immediately began to boast of this "triumph of chemistry." The *Frankfurter Zeitung* (April 25, 1915) made it clear that from the German point of view the use of poison gas was a repayment in kind:

It is indeed possible that our bombs and shells rendered it impossible for the enemy's troops to remain in their trenches or artillery positions.

It is even probable that, in point of fact, projectiles emitting poisonous gases were employed by us, for the German army command has permitted no doubt to exist that, as a reply to the treacherous projectiles of the English and French, which have been constantly observed for many weeks, we on our side also would employ gas bombs, or whatever one may call them.

The German army command, moreover, referred to the fact that from German chemistry considerably more effective substances might be expected, and our army command was right.

Why the Germans did not immediately seize the opportunity offered by the use of poison gas to launch a decisive all-out attack along the various war fronts remains one of the great surprises of World War I. One explanation is that they found some difficulty in combining infantry attacks with cylinder charges depending upon a favorable wind. Within a few days the Allies were equipped with a crude form of respirator, thus effectively disposing of the danger of a knockout blow. Then came language the Germans could understand—retaliatory gas attacks. It was all enormously discouraging.

Rudyard Kipling Talks for the "Lost Hounds" of the Sea at Jutland

RUDYARD KIPLING'S career as a newspaperman began at the immature age of seventeen, when he talked himself onto the payroll of the Lahore *Civil and Military Gazette.* "I represented fifty per cent of the 'editorial staff' of the one daily paper of the Punjab," he recollected, adding, "and a daily paper comes out every day even though fifty per cent of the staff have fever." Working at times with a temperature of 104, arguing with native compositors who followed copy without knowing a single word of English, with resultant "glorious and sometimes obscene misprints," young Kipling covered local events—races, bridge openings, floods, communal riots, and murder trials, and one "really filthy job," of checking the percentage of lepers among the butchers who supplied beef and mutton to the European community of Lahore. At one divorce trial that Kipling reported, counsel asked respondent if she had ever expressed a desire to dance on her husband's grave. Until then she had denied every charge. "Yess," she hissed, "and I jolly-damn-well *would,* too."

Equipped with a keen eye and an exceptional memory (in reporting Kipling took few notes—just names, dates and addresses—"If a thing didn't stay in my memory, I argued it was hardly worth writing out"), Kipling soon stirred the world with his sketches of India. The voice of imperialist Britain, this superlatively gifted writer was constantly besieged by the world press to report spot events. His greatest opportunity arose during World War I, when he reported for the London *Daily Telegraph* certain phases of the Battle of Jutland—from the point of view of tonnage and armament one of the great naval battles of all time.

In the late spring of 1916 the German fleet, led by Admiral von Scheer, made an audacious sally out of the North Sea, parallel with the coast of Schleswig-Holstein and Jutland. Answering that challenge, Admiral Jellicoe's main battle fleet swept down from the North, while Admiral Beatty's battle-cruiser fleet began feeling for the enemy. On the afternoon of May 31, British scouts made contact with the enemy about one hundred miles off the Jutland coast. At half-past three Beatty's cruisers engaged the enemy's battle cruisers, which soon ran to rejoin the main fleet. The British fought the Germans on a parallel course until the German battle fleet came into sight, when Beatty, outgunned, withdrew to the protection of the British battle fleet. Hitherto the enemy had had the advantage of fighting in a mist while the British hulls stood out clear in the afternoon light. But by a turning movement the British had the enemy to the westward of them, where their ships made a better mark. The day was closing and the weather thickened. Covered by destroyers, in a great screen of gray smoke, the German main fleet got away. As darkness fell, the British fleet lay between the enemy and his home ports, but when dawn came no trace of the enemy to the southward could be found. Apparently the Germans had changed course and broken for home astern the British main fleet, which had tried in vain to bring the Germans to general action and smash them decisively with their gunpower superiority.

Kipling's account of the battle, republished in *Sea Warfare* (1916), sought to stress the importance of individual and group destroyer action. He interviewed the crews of destroyers to record their experiences. The tales he heard moved him to observe: "Have you ever noticed that men who do Homeric deeds often describe them in Homeric language?" adding, "The sentence 'I looked round for useful employment' is worthy of Ulysses when 'there was an evil sound at the ships of men who perished and of the ships themselves broken at the same time.' " In this masterful account one sees the author of *Captains Courageous,* and of salty ballads of ocean and engine room, rising to the challenge. It was only natural that the creator of the beast stories of *The Jungle Books* should see the destroyers as "lost hounds" returning after an unchecked night "among the wild life of the dark."

Two "furious days" when "there was an evil sound at the ships of men who perished"

London *Daily Telegraph,* October 19, 23, 26, 31, 1916. From *Sea Warfare:* Copyright, 1915, 1916, 1917, by Rudyard Kipling. Reprinted by permission of Mrs. George Bambridge and Doubleday & Co., Inc.

When the German fleet ran for home, on the night of May 31, it seems to have scattered—"starred," I believe, is the word for the evolution—in a general *sauve qui peut,* while the Devil, livelily represented by our destroyers, took the hindmost. Our flotillas were strung out far and wide on this job. One man compared it to hounds hunting half a hundred separate foxes.

I take the adventures of several couples of destroyers who, on the night of May 31, were nosing along somewhere towards the Schleswig-Holstein coast, ready to chop any Hun stuff coming back to earth by that particular road. The leader of one line was *Gehenna,* and the next two ships astern of her were *Eblis* and *Shaitan,* in the order given. There were others, of course, but with the exception of one *Goblin* they don't come violently into this tale. There had been a good deal of promiscuous firing that evening, and actions were going on all round. Towards midnight our destroyers were overtaken by several three- and four-funnel German ships (cruisers, they thought) hurrying home. At this stage of the game anybody might have been anybody—pursuer or pursued. The Germans took no chances, but switched on their searchlights and opened fire on *Gehenna*. Her acting sublieutenant reports: "A salvo hit us forward. I opened fire with the afterguns. A shell then struck us in a steampipe, and I could see nothing but steam. But both starboard torpedo tubes were fired."

Eblis, Gehenna's next astern, at once fired a torpedo at the second ship in the German line, a four-funneled cruiser, and hit her between the second funnel and the mainmast, when "she appeared to catch fire fore and aft simultaneously, heeled right over to starboard, and undoubtedly sank." *Eblis* loosed off a second torpedo and turned aside to reload, firing at the same time to distract the enemy's attention from *Gehenna*, who was now ablaze fore and aft. *Gehenna's* acting sublieutenant (the only executive officer who survived) says that by the time the steam from the broken pipe cleared he found *Gehenna* stopped, nearly everybody amidships killed or wounded, the cartridge boxes round the guns exploding one after the other as the fires took hold, and the enemy not to be seen. Three minutes or less did all that damage. *Eblis* had nearly finished reloading when a shot struck the davit that was swinging her last torpedo into the tube and wounded all hands concerned. Thereupon she dropped torpedo work, fired at an enemy searchlight which winked and went out, and was closing in to help *Gehenna*, when she found herself under the noses of a couple of enemy cruisers. "The nearer one," he says, "altered course to ram me, apparently." The Senior Service writes in curiously lawyerlike fashion, but there is no denying that they act quite directly. "I therefore put my helm hard

aport and the two ships met and rammed each other, port bow to port bow." There could have been no time to think and, for *Eblis'* commander on the bridge, none to gather information. But he had observant subordinates, and he writes—and I would humbly suggest that the words be made the ship's motto for evermore—he writes, "Those aft noted" that the enemy cruiser had certain marks on her funnel and certain arrangements of derricks on each side which, quite apart from the evidence she left behind her, betrayed her class. *Eblis* and she met. Says *Eblis:* "I consider I must have considerably damaged this cruiser, as twenty feet of her side plating was left in my foc's'le." Twenty feet of ragged rivet-slinging steel, razoring and reaping about in the dark on a foc's'le that had collapsed like a concertina! It was very fair plating, too. There were side-scuttle holes in it —what we passengers would call portholes. But it might have been better, for *Eblis* reports sorrowfully, "by the thickness of the coats of paint [duly given in thirty-seconds of the inch] she would not appear to have been a very new ship."

New or old, the enemy had done her best. She had completely demolished the *Eblis'* bridge and searchlight platform, brought down the mast and the forefunnel, ruined the whaler and the dinghy, split the foc's'le open above water from the stem to the galley which is abaft the bridge, and below water had opened it up from the stem to the second bulkhead. She had further ripped off *Eblis'* skin plating for an amazing number of yards on one side of her, and had fired a couple of large-caliber shells into *Eblis* at point-blank range, narrowly missing her vitals. Even so, *Eblis* is as impartial as a prize court. She reports that the second shot, a trifle of eight inches, "may have been fired at a different time or just after colliding." But the night was yet young, and "just after getting clear of this cruiser an enemy battle cruiser grazed past our stern at high speed" and again the judgmatic mind—"I think she must have intended to ram us." She was a large three-funneled thing, her center funnel shot away, and "lights were flickering under her foc's'le as if she was on fire forward." Fancy the vision of her, hurtling out of the dark, redlighted from within, and fleeing on like a man with his throat cut!

As an interlude, all enemy cruisers that night were not keen on ramming. They wanted to get home. A man I know who was on another part of the drive saw a covey bolt through our destroyers; and had just settled himself for a shot at one of them when the night threw up a second bird coming down full speed on his other beam. He had bare time to jink between the two as they whizzed past. One switched on her searchlight and fired a whole salvo at him point-blank. The heavy stuff went between his funnels. She must have sighted along her own beam of light, which was about a thousand yards.

"How did you feel?" I asked.

"I was rather sick. It was my best chance all that night, and I had to miss it or be cut in two."

"What happened to the cruisers?"

"Oh, they went on, and I heard 'em being attended to by some of our fellows. They didn't know what they were doing, or they couldn't have missed me sitting, the way they did."

After all that *Eblis* picked herself up, and discovered that she was still alive, with a dog's chance of getting to port. But she did not bank on it. That grand slam had wrecked the bridge, pinning the commander under the wreckage. By the time he had extricated himself he "considered it advisable to throw overboard the steel chest and dispatch box of confidential and secret books." These are never allowed to fall into strange hands, and their proper disposal is the last step but one in the ritual of the burial service of His Majesty's ships at sea. *Gehenna,* afire and sinking, out somewhere in the dark, was going through it on her own account. This is her Acting Sublieutenant's report: "The confidential books were got up. The First Lieutenant gave the order: 'Every man aft,' and the confidential books were thrown overboard. The ship soon afterwards heeled over to starboard and the bows went under. The First Lieutenant gave the order: 'Everybody for themselves.' The ship sank in about a minute, the stern going straight up into the air."

But it was not written in the Book of Fate that stripped and battered *Eblis* should die that night as *Gehenna* died. After the burial of the books it was found that the several fires on her were manageable, that she "was not making water aft of the damage," which meant two thirds of her were, more or less, in commission, and, best of all, that three boilers were usable in spite of the cruiser's shells. So she "shaped course and speed to make the least water and the most progress towards land." On the way back the wind shifted eight points without warning—and, what with one thing and another, *Eblis* was unable to make port till the scandalously late hour of noon on June 2, "the mutual ramming having occurred about 11:40 P.M. on May 31." She says, this time without any legal reservation whatever, "I cannot speak too highly of the courage, discipline, and devotion of the officers and ship's company."

Her recommendations are a Compendium of Godly Deeds for the Use of Mariners. They cover pretty much all that man may be expected to do. There was, as there always is, a first lieutenant who, while his commander was being extricated from the bridge wreckage, took charge of affairs and steered the ship first from the engine room, or what remained of it, and later from aft, and otherwise maneuvered as requisite, among doubtful bulkheads. In his leisure he "improvised means of signaling," and if there be not one joyous story behind that smooth sentence I am a Hun!

EVERYONE IMPROVISED, Kipling reported, even the two remaining quartermasters—"mutinous dogs, both of 'em"—one wounded in the right hand and the other in the left. Between them they took the wheel all the way home, refusing to be relieved during the thirty-six hours before the ship returned to port. "So *Eblis* passes out of the picture," Kipling commented, with "never a moan or complaint from a single wounded man." But the *Gehenna* went down. Her crew hung on the rafts until picked up by the *Shaitan,* in bad shape herself, having been rammed by the *Goblin,* when that British destroyer was attacked by a German cruiser and knocked out of control. To add to the mess, an unknown destroyer rammed the *Shaitan*'s aft, cutting off several feet of her stern and leaving her rudder jammed hard over. Finally, that disabled little destroyer was sunk by gunfire from her own ships.

Kipling, in these words, summarizes this phase of the battle:

So you see, in that flotilla alone there was every variety of fight, from the ordered attacks of squadrons under control, to single ship affairs, every turn of which depended on the second's decision of the men concerned; endurance to the hopeless end; bluff and cunning; reckless advance and red-hot flight; clear vision and as much of blank bewilderment as the Senior Service permits its children to indulge in. That is not much. When a destroyer who has been dodging enemy torpedoes and gunfire in the dark realizes about midnight that she is "following a strange British flotilla, having lost sight of my own," she "decides to remain with them," and shares their fortunes and whatever language is going.

If lost hounds could speak when they cast up next day, after an unchecked night among the wild life of the dark, they would talk much as our destroyers do.

*   *   *

BOTH SIDES claimed victory; the Germans because they had inflicted greater losses, the British because the German fleet was forced to return to Kiel and to remain there for the duration of the war, only to be scuttled by the Germans themselves at Scapa Flow in 1919. At Jutland Great Britain maintained her command of the seas. Squeezed by the British naval blockade, which was now intensified, the Germans took the measure of desperation—unrestricted submarine warfare, which brought America into the war.

H. G. Wells Unveils the Tank

IN THE BLEAK, gray dawn, lying obliquely upon the slope and on the very lip of the foremost trench," the war correspondent first saw his land ironclad—"long, narrow, and very strong steel frameworks carrying the engine, and borne by eight pairs of big pedrail wheels, each about ten feet in diameter," with "thick stumpy feet," like "the legs of caterpillars." Capable of crossing a thirty-foot trench, of shooting out a stream of rifle bullets with unerring precision, this mechanism left in its wake dead and wounded men. With these oracular words, H. G. Wells, the prophet of doom, warned readers of *The Strand Magazine* in 1903 of the shape of war to come.

Then came World War I, and the British, spurred on by Winston Churchill from his post in the Admiralty, and against the advice of old army men, developed the tank, the major tactical innovation of the war. Its initial appearance in battle was brilliantly reported by Philip Gibbs and Beach Thomas. Reporting for *The Daily Sketch* of September 18, 1916, on Tommy Atkins' "new toy," Philip Gibbs wrote: "When our soldiers first saw these strange creatures lolloping along the roads and over old battlefields, taking trenches on the way, they shouted and cheered wildly, and laughed for a day afterwards." For the badly scared Germans it was a terrifying experience. The Ministry of Munitions felt that the tank's true progenitor should be given the opportunity of a personal unveiling. Joseph Reinach, the French writer, pulled the leg of innumerable British officers by passing off long extracts of H. G. Wells' old *Strand* story as eyewitness accounts of the genuine article. Wells commented: "The filiation was indeed quite traceable. They were my grandchildren—I felt a little like King Lear when first I read about them." Here is Mr. Wells' interview with that monster of his fertile imagination.

"The filiation was indeed quite traceable.
They were my grandchildren"

London *Daily Chronicle*, December 18, 1916

The young of even the most horrible beasts have something piquant and engaging about them, and so I suppose it is in the way of things that the land ironclad which opens a new and more dreadful and destructive phase in the human folly of warfare should appear first as if it were a joke. Never has any such thing so completely masked its wickedness under an appearance of genial silliness. The Tank is a creature to which one naturally flings a pet name; the five or six I was shown wandering, rooting, and climbing over obstacles, round a large field near X, were as amusing and disarming as a litter of lively young pigs.

At first the War Office prevented the publication of any pictures or descriptions of these contrivances except abroad; then abruptly the embargo was relaxed, and the press was flooded with photographs. The reader will be familiar now with their appearance. They resemble large slugs with an underside a little like the flattened rockers of a rocking horse, slugs between twenty and forty feet long. They are like flat-sided slugs, slugs of spirit, who raise an inquiring snout, like the snout of a dogfish, into the air. They crawl upon their bellies in a way that would be tedious to describe to the general reader and unnecessary to describe to the inquiring specialist. They go over the ground with the sliding speed of active snails. Behind them trail two wheels, supporting a flimsy tail, wheels that strike one as incongruous as if a monster began kangaroo and ended doll's perambulator. (These wheels annoy me.) They are not steely monsters; they are painted the drab and unassuming colors that are fashionable in modern warfare, so that the armor seems rather like the integument of a rhinoceros. At the sides of the head project armored cheeks, and from above these stick out guns that look like stalked eyes. That is the general appearance of the contemporary Tank.

It slides on the ground; the silly little wheels that so detract from the genial bestiality of its appearance dandle and bump behind it. It swings round about its axis. It comes to an obstacle, a low wall let us say, or a heap of bricks, and sets to work to climb with its snout. It rears over the

obstacle, it raises its straining belly, it overhangs more and more, and at last topples forward; it sways upon the heap and then goes plunging downward, sticking out the weak counterpoise of its wheeled tail. If it comes to a house or a tree or a wall or suchlike obstruction it rams against it so as to bring all its weight to bear upon it— it weighs *some* tons—and then climbs over the debris. I saw it, and incredulous soldiers of experience watched it at the same time, cross trenches and wallow amazingly through muddy exaggerations of shell holes. Then I repeated the tour inside.

Again the Tank is like the slug. The slug, as every biological student knows, is unexpectedly complicated inside. The Tank is as crowded with inward parts as a battleship. It is filled with engines, guns, and ammunition, and in the interstices, men.

"You will smash your hat," said Colonel Stern. "No; keep it on, or else you will smash your head."

Only Mr. C. R. W. Nevinson could do justice to the interior of a Tank. You see a hand gripping something; you see the eyes and forehead of an engineer's face; you perceive that an overall bluishness beyond the engine is the back of another man. "Don't hold that," says someone; "it is too hot. Hold on to that." The engines roar, so loudly that I doubt whether one could hear guns without; the floor begins to slope and slopes until one seems to be at forty-five degrees or thereabouts; then the whole concern swings up and sways and slants the other way. You have crossed a bank. You heel sideways. Through the door which has been left open you see the little group of engineers, staff officers, and naval men receding and falling away behind you. You straighten up and go uphill. You halt and begin to rotate. Through the open door, the green field, with its red walls, rows of work sheds, and forests of chimneys in the background, begins a steady processional movement. The group of engineers and officers and naval men appears at the other side of the door and farther off. Then comes a spring downhill. You descend and stretch your legs.

About the field other Tanks are doing their stunts. One is struggling in an apoplectic way in the mud pit with a cheek half buried. It noses its way out and on with an air of animal relief.

They are like jokes by Heath Robinson. One forgets that these things have already saved the lives of many hundreds of our soldiers and smashed and defeated thousands of Germans.

Said one soldier to me: "In the old attacks you used to see the British dead lying outside the machine-gun emplacements like birds outside a butt with a good shot inside. *Now,* these things walk through."

*   *   *

ONCE THE AIRPLANE has located and destroyed the big guns, Wells pointed out, tanks can advance, destroying machine guns, completing the destruction of barbed wire, and holding prisoners immobile. "Then the infantry will follow to gather in the sheaves." Provided the tanks had the air ascendancy, upon which Wells always insisted, he could imagine no way of checking a mass tank offensive.

While the Allies were not prepared to exploit the tank offensive immediately after the initial shock had stunned the Germans, they finally got it rolling during what the Germans called their "black days" of July 18 and August 8, 1918, when Allied tanks rolled forward at Soissons and Amiens and helped seal the defeat of Germany.

The lesson in land armaments was not entirely forgotten. Writing in 1916, Wells predicted: "The race for sea power before 1914 was mere child's play to the breeding of engineering monstrosities for land warfare that must now follow any indeterminate peace settlement." Commenting on the "cheerful amusement" the sight of a tank aroused, Wells declared: "I cannot believe that men are so insensate and headstrong as to miss the plain omens of the present situation," for, he warned, if tanks do not make mankind pause, "then they are the grimmest jest that ever set men grinning." This was the kind of jest that challenged the imagination of the postwar German general staff, which, following H. G. Wells' conception, combined tanks with aerial weapons, while the French were fatally wedded to the Maginot mentality.

A New York *Evening Post* Reporter Exposes
Monstrous Abuses in New Jersey's State Prison

THE FIRST BUILDING of the New Jersey State Prison at Trenton had been constructed in 1835 and was still standing in 1917, a symbol of society's vengeance on its unfortunates. Like trapped animals, convicts were placed in pitch-black dungeons that were in effect sealed tombs. The death rate from tuberculosis was high, for the corridors were so wet in spring and autumn that the keepers had to wear rubber footwear to protect their own health.

In early 1917 Harold A. Littledale, an enterprising reporter of the New York *Evening Post,* made an extensive investigation of the Trenton prison and emerged with an astonishing story to confront Governor-elect Walter E. Edge. It was a tale of horror.

Prisoners with midnight in their hearts

New York *Evening Post,* January 12, 1917. Copyright, 1917, New York Evening Post Co.

Bad prisons breed crime, and the New Jersey State Prison at Trenton is among the worst in the country. It is bad in its structure, bad in its influence, and bad in its management. By comparison Sing Sing is a cozy corner, for Trenton is monstrous, medieval, unhealthy, and overcrowded.

It is hard to believe that in the twentieth century, one hundred years after Elizabeth Fry visited Newgate * and the English convict ships, man's inhumanity to man should express itself as it does express itself at Trenton. It is hard to believe that for infractions of the rules men are placed face to the wall for punishment and deprived of their meals. It is hard to believe that their labor is farmed out to private contractors for a pittance while their families are in want. It is hard to believe that the state's wards are cast into dungeons. It is hard to believe that women are placed with men. It is hard to believe that the insane mingle with the sane, the consumptive with the healthy, the pervert with the pure. But this, and much more, obtains at Trenton; this and much more exists and is sanctioned and is permitted to be.

Here is the indictment:

It is a fact that two, three, and even four men are confined together in the same cell in violation of the law.

It is a fact that dungeons exist and that men are incarcerated therein and given only bread and water twice a day.

It is a fact that men have been

---

* In the early nineteenth century the chief prison of London, Newgate, was in a disgraceful state of privation, filthiness, and neglect. Appalled by the horrible conditions, Elizabeth Fry (1780–1845), a courageous philanthropist, demanded and obtained a measure of reform.

chained to the walls of underground dungeons.

It is a fact that every day a man serves in a dungeon is added to his minimum sentence.

It is a fact that women convicts are confined with men, and that cell 55, wing 4, is kept apart for that purpose.

It is a fact that women prisoners eat, sleep, and live in their cells and work on sewing machines in the corridor outside their cells.

It is a fact that there is no dining hall and that men are fed in their cells or in the corridor.

It is a fact that the cries of convicts protesting against their food have been heard by those who passed through the streets outside.

It is a fact that these wards of the state save the scraps of one meal to eat at the next.

It is a fact that the men have only half an hour's recreation a week and that the recreation yard for fourteen women convicts is larger than the recreation yard for 1200 men.

It is a fact that many cells are dark and ill-ventilated.

It is a fact that in the newest wing seventy cells are so damp that they cannot be used, and that on occasions the corridor is so wet that the keepers have to wear rubbers.

It is a fact that a cell building erected in 1835 is in use today.

It is a fact that the state's wards were confined up to last Monday in an old wing that the State Board of Health had condemned as unfit for human habitation.

It is a fact that consumptives circulate with the well, exposing them to contagion.

It is a fact that the degenerate, the pervert, and the homosexual are placed with other convicts, with what result can well be imagined.

It is a fact that the first offender is thrown with the habitual criminal.

It is a fact that a youth was released in December who came to the prison a boy of thirteen years, wearing short trousers.

It is a fact that men are punished by being put face to the wall and that sometimes they are kept there all day without food.

It is a fact that convicts may not receive fruit.

It is a fact that a commodious bathhouse, with hot- and cold-water supply, is used only two months in the year.

It is a fact that for ten months in the year the convicts are given only a bucket of water once a week in which to bathe, that after bathing they must wash their clothes in this water and then wash out their cells.

It is a fact that the lights in the cells are extinguished at 8:30 P.M., and that on Sunday evenings there is no light at all.

It is a fact that the hospital is too small and its equipment inadequate.

It is a fact that the management of the prison is vested in a Board of Inspectors who meet only once a month, and whose members are from scattered parts of the state.

It is a fact that the Board of Inspectors of six members appointed six committees, a chairmanship for each member, creating so much more interference.

It is a fact that paroles can be granted by two independent bodies— the Board of Inspectors and the Court of Pardons.

It is a fact that a salaried schoolteacher is employed, but that there is no schoolroom or furniture, in violation of the law.

It is a fact that three chaplains are employed, but that the chapel seats only 350 persons, while the prison population is usually in excess of 1300.

It is a fact that the salaried moral instructor is the Reverend Thomas R. Taylor, father of Leon R. Taylor, ex-Speaker of the Assembly, and that he was appointed by his son while Acting Governor of the state.

It is a fact that contract labor exists, if not in violation of the law, certainly against the spirit of it.

It is a fact that some of the shops where convicts are employed by private contractors are ill-ventilated and dark.

It is a fact that one contract shop is in the cellar.

It is a fact that more than one hundred men are employed on a contract in violation of the law.

It is a fact that much space is given over to these private contractors for use as storerooms.

It is a fact that the Board of Inspectors turns the convicts over for work on the public roads at the rate of $1.25 a day, which is paid by the taxpayers, but that the board turns the convicts over to private contractors at thirty-five cents a day.

It is a fact that free light, heat, and power are furnished to the contractors.

It is a fact that goods made in the prison for private contractors are not marked "Manufactured in New Jersey State Prison," and that this is a violation of the law.

It is a fact that while the contract shops are put in operation daily, the shop, equipped at a cost of more than $12,000 to make socks and underwear for inmates of state institutions, is idle and has been idle for some months, and that the salaried instructor has nothing to do.

It is a fact that the graded and meriting system was recommended in 1911 and that nothing was done.

It is a fact that the employment of a dietarian was recommended in 1911 by the State Commissioner of Charities and Corrections and that nothing was done.

It is a fact that the keepers are underpaid and overworked.

It is a fact that the powers of the Principal Keeper (Warden) are little more than those of janitor.

It is a fact that convicts are supposed to be paid 2½ cents a day for their work in prison and that they do not get it.

That, then, is the New Jersey State Prison at Trenton, where 1300 men are confined at a net cost in 1915 (the last available report) of more than $253,000. That is how the state's wards are kept. That is how they are punished. That is how they are "reformed." That is how society is "protected." That is the state of affairs in this year of grace, 1917. Is it really one hundred years since Elizabeth Fry found men and women shut together, found them in rags, found them dirty, and inveighed so against the malice and all uncharitableness that the English conscience was stirred and the era of reform begun? In the state of New Jersey today is there no Elizabeth Fry who will come forward and fight this thing? Or is it "mollycoddling" convicts to permit them to see the sun in the day, to give them better food, to give them light in their cells at night that they may read or study as they would, to provide them with dining halls where they might eat like human beings instead of having their food thrust into their cages as if they were wild and dangerous beasts, to end forever the vicious system of contract labor as Chapter 372 of the Laws of 1911 intended it should be ended, to permit them to receive fruit from their friends who wish to bring them fruit, to try to bring out the good that is in each and every one of them, for good there is in all of them, and it is like pure gold. If this is "mollycoddling" convicts it is best to leave them as they are with midnight in their hearts.

LITTLEDALE'S DRAMATIC REPORT, attributing the evils to a muddled system of management, stirred up a hornets' nest in the state of New Jersey. The new governor immediately appointed a commission to investigate the charges, and within three weeks he found a report on his desk listing a series of eleven basic reforms, such as bricking up the dungeons, separate confinement of prisoners, establishment of a psychiatric clinic, and introduction of a grades and merit system.

Like John Howard of England, who in 1769 began his ceaseless labors in behalf of prison reform, Littledale achieved results by awakening the public conscience to a sense of guilt for its inhumanity. For his exposé he was awarded the 1918 Pulitzer Prize in reporting.

Floyd Gibbons Chooses His Torpedo and Scores

a Clean Beat on the Sinking of the *Laconia*

FLOYD GIBBONS was the most colorful and picturesque of the war reporters. There was nothing soft or gentle about him. He was a hard-swinging, battling Irishman, full of humor and inconsistency. He always took good care of Gibbons, but he passed a lot of it around too."

This tribute to a fellow newsman, written by Frazier Hunt, aptly summarizes what other reporters thought of Floyd Gibbons. A restless extrovert, Gibbons had had an active career. When he heard the challenging news that Pancho Villa, the revolutionary bandit, intended to kill on sight any gringos found in Mexico, Gibbons promptly headed alone for the Mexican hills and called the bad man's bluff. With a kind of comic-opera ingenuity he fitted out a boxcar, attached it to the bandit's train, and from this primitive trailer he witnessed three of Villa's biggest battles. Receiving the War Department's permission to join General Pershing's punitive expedition to Colonia Dublan, he rode with the American cavalry units that crossed the border. He had convictions along with his courage: his critical study of inefficient American militia mobilization on the Mexican border in 1916 stirred up a great controversy throughout the United States.

Floyd Gibbons was not only a great reporter; he was also a lucky one. In early 1917 the Imperial German government announced that after February 1 she would resume her campaign of unrestricted submarine warfare and that she would have her submarines sink without warning any ship entering a forbidden zone in the waters of the North Atlantic. This was a situation made to order for Floyd Gibbons. Walter Howey, the fabulous city editor of *The Chicago Tribune*, decided to send Gibbons, then his star reporter, to England to get news through the censorship proving that England had paid in blood for her lack of preparedness.

At this moment the German Ambassador, von Bernstorff, was handed his papers in Washington and was preparing to return to Germany on the *Frederick VII*. In order to safeguard Gibbons' voyage across the Atlantic, the *Tribune* suggested that he travel with the Ambassador. Anticipating the possibility that the Germans might commit an overt act Gibbons rejected the advice and deliberately picked the *Laconia*, an eighteen-thousand-ton Cunarder whose route lay through the submarine zone. His considerate employers thereupon equipped him with a special life preserver, a large fresh-water bottle, electric flashlights, and a flask of brandy. Never in the history of reporting had a newspaperman approached a submarine sinking so well prepared.

Gibbons' hunch was justified. The *Laconia* sailed for France on February 17, 1917. Just eight days later a German U-boat surfaced on the Atlantic and sent two torpedoes crashing into the side of the British passenger ship. Here is Gibbons' account of the sinking, pounded out hastily after he was rescued.

"It was bedlam and nightmare"

The Chicago Tribune, February 26, 1917

QUEENSTOWN, FEBRUARY 26 [VIA LONDON]—I have serious doubts whether this is a real story. I am not entirely certain that it is not all a dream and that in a few minutes I will wake up back in stateroom B 19 on the promenade deck of the Cunarder *Laconia* and hear my cockney steward informing me with an abundance of "and sirs" that it is a fine morning.

It is now a little over thirty hours since I stood on the slanting decks of the big liner, listened to the lowering of the lifeboats, heard the hiss of escaping steam and the roar of ascending rockets as they tore lurid rents in the black sky and cast their red glare over the roaring sea.

I am writing this within thirty minutes after stepping on the dock here in Queenstown from the British mine sweeper which picked up our open lifeboat after an eventful six hours of drifting and darkness and baling and pulling on the oars and of straining aching eyes toward the empty, meaningless horizon in search of help. But, dream or fact, here it is:

The Cunard liner *Laconia,* 18,000 tons' burden, carrying seventy-three passengers—men, women, and children—of whom six were American citizens—manned by a mixed crew of 216, bound from New York to Liverpool, and loaded with foodstuffs, cotton, and raw material, was torpedoed without warning by a German submarine last night off the Irish coast. The vessel sank in about forty minutes.

Two American citizens, mother and daughter, listed from Chicago and former residents there, are among the dead. They were Mrs. Mary E. Hoy and Miss Elizabeth Hoy. I have talked with a seaman who was in the same lifeboat with the two Chicago women, and he has told me that he saw their lifeless bodies washed out of the sinking boat.

The American survivors are Mrs. F. E. Harris of Philadelphia, who was the last woman to leave the *Laconia;* the Reverend Father Wareing of St. Joseph's Seminary, Baltimore; Arthur T. Kirby of New York, and myself.

A former Chicago woman, now the wife of a British subject, was among the survivors. She is Mrs. Henry George Boston, the daughter of Granger Farwell of Lake Forest.

After leaving New York, passengers and crew had had three drills with the lifeboats. All were supplied with life belts and assigned to places in the twelve big lifeboats poised over the side from the davits of the top deck.

Submarines had been a chief part of the conversation during the entire trip, but the subject had been treated lightly, although all ordered precautions were strictly in force.

After the first explanatory drill on the second day out from New York, from which we sailed on Saturday, February 17, the "abandon ship" signal, five quick blasts on the whistle, had summoned us twice to our life belts and heavy wraps (with a flask and a flashlight) and to a roll call in front of our assigned boats on the top deck.

On Sunday we knew generally we were in the danger zone, though we did not know definitely where we were —or at least the passengers did not.

In the afternoon, during a short chat with Captain W. R. D. Irvine, the ship's commander, I had mentioned that I would like to see a chart and note our position on the ocean. He replied, "Oh, would you?" with a smiling, rising inflection that meant "It is jolly well none of your business."

Prior to this my cheery early-morning steward had told us that we would make Liverpool by Monday night, and I used this information in another question to the Captain.

"When do we land?" I asked.

"I don't know," replied Captain Irvine; but my steward told me later it would be Tuesday, after dinner.

The first cabin passengers were gathered in the lounge Sunday evening, with the exception of the bridge fiends in the smoke room.

Poor Butterfly was dying wearily on the talking machine, and several couples were dancing.

About the tables in the smoke room the conversation was limited to the announcement of bids and orders to the stewards. Before the fireplace was a little gathering which had been dubbed the Hyde Park corner—an allusion I don't quite fully understand. This group had about exhausted available discussion when I projected a new bone of contention.

"What do you say are our chances of being torpedoed?" I asked.

"Well," drawled the deliberative Mr. Henry Chetham, a London solicitor, "I should say four thousand to one."

Lucien J. Jerome, of the British diplomatic service, returning with an Ecuadorian valet from South America, interjected: "Considering the zone and the class of this ship, I should put it down at two hundred and fifty to one that we don't meet a sub."

At this moment the ship gave a sudden lurch sideways and forward. There was a muffled noise like the slamming of some large door at a good distance away. The slightness of the shock and the meekness of the report compared with my imagination were disappointing. Every man in the room was on his feet in an instant.

"We're hit!" shouted Mr. Chetham.

"That's what we've been waiting for," said Mr. Jerome.

"What a lousy torpedo!" said Mr. Kirby in typical New Yorkese. "It must have been a fizzer."

I looked at my watch. It was 10:30 P.M.

Then came the five blasts on the whistle. We rushed down the corridor leading from the smoke room at the stern to the lounge, which was amidships. We were running, but there was no panic. The occupants of the lounge were just leaving by the forward doors as we entered.

It was dark on the landing leading down to the promenade deck, where the first-class staterooms were located. My pocket flashlight, built like a fountain pen, came in handy on the landing.

We reached the promenade deck. I

rushed into my stateroom, B 19, grabbed my overcoat and the water bottle and special life preserver with which the *Tribune* had equipped me before sailing. Then I made my way to the upper deck on that same dark landing.

I saw the chief steward opening an electric switch box in the wall and turning on the switch. Instantly the boat decks were illuminated. That illumination saved lives.

The torpedo had hit us well astern on the starboard side and had missed the engines and the dynamos. I had not noticed the deck lights before. Throughout the voyage our decks had remained dark at night and all cabin portholes were clamped down and all windows covered with opaque paint.

The illumination of the upper deck, on which I stood, made the darkness of the water, sixty feet below, appear all the blacker when I peered over the edge at my station boat, No. 10.

Already the boat was loading up and men and boys were busy with the ropes. I started to help near a davit that seemed to be giving trouble, but was stoutly ordered to get out of the way and get into the boat.

We were on the portside, practically opposite the engine well. Up and down the deck passengers and crew were donning life belts, throwing on overcoats, and taking positions in the boats. There were a number of women, but only one appeared hysterical— little Miss Titsie Siklosl, a French-Polish actress, who was being cared for by her manager, Cedric P. Ivatt, appearing on the passenger list as from New York.

Steam began to hiss somewhere from the giant gray funnels that towered above. Suddenly there was a roaring swish as a rocket soared upward from the captain's bridge, leaving a comet's tail of fire. I watched it as it described a graceful arc in the black void overhead, and then, with an audible pop, it burst in a flare of brilliant colors.

There was a tilt to the deck. It was listing to starboard at just the angle that would make it necessary to reach for support to enable one to stand upright. In the meantime electric floodlights—large white enameled funnels containing clusters of bulbs— had been suspended from the promenade deck and illuminated the dark water that rose and fell on the slanting side of the ship.

"Lower away!" Someone gave the order, and we started down with a jerk towards the seemingly hungry rising and falling swells.

Then we stopped with another jerk and remained suspended in mid-air while the man at the bow and the stern swore and tussled with the lowering ropes. The stern of the lifeboat was down, the bow up, leaving us at an angle of about forty-five degrees. We clung to the seats to save ourselves from falling out.

"Who's got a knife, a knife, a knife!" shouted a sweating seaman in the bow.

"Great God, give him a knife!" bawled a half-dressed, jibbering Negro stoker, who wrung his hands in the stern.

A hatchet was thrust into my hand and I forwarded it to the bow. There was a flash of sparks as it crashed down on the holding pulley. One strand of the rope parted and down plunged the bow, too quick for the stern man. We came to a jerky stop with the stern in the air and the bow down, but the stern managed to lower away until the dangerous angle was eliminated.

Then both tried to lower together.

The list of the ship's side became greater, but, instead of our boat sliding down it like a toboggan, the taffrail caught and was held. As the lowering continued, the other side dropped down and we found ourselves clinging on at a new angle and looking straight down on the water.

Many feet and hands pushed the boat from the side of the ship, and we sagged down again, this time smacking squarely on the pillowy top of a rising swell. It felt more solid than mid-air, at least. But we were far from being off. The pulleys stuck twice in their fastenings, bow and stern, and the one ax passed forward and back, and with it my flashlight, as the entangling ropes that held us to the sinking *Laconia* were cut away.

Some shout from that confusion of sound caused me to look up, and I really did so with the fear that one of the near-by boats was being lowered upon us.

A man was jumping, as I presumed, with the intention of landing in the boat, and I prepared to avoid the impact, but he passed beyond us and plunged into the water three feet from the edge of the boat. He bobbed to the surface immediately.

"It's Duggan," shouted a man next to me.

I flashed a light on the ruddy, smiling face and water-plastered hair of the little Canadian, our fellow saloon passenger. We pulled him over the side. He spluttered out a mouthful of water and the first words he said were:

"I wonder if there is anything to that lighting three cigarettes on the same match? I was up above trying to loosen the rope to this boat. I loosened it and then got tangled up in it. The boat went down but I was jerked up. I jumped for it."

His first reference concerned our deliberate tempting of fates early in the day when he, Kirby, and I lighted three cigarettes from the same match and Duggan told us he had done the same thing many a time.

As we pulled away from the side of the ship, its receding terrace of lights stretched upward. The ship was slowly turning over. We were opposite that part occupied by the engine rooms. There was a tangle of oars, spars, and rigging on the seat and considerable confusion before four of the big sweeps could be manned on either side of the boat.

The jibbering, bulletheaded Negro was pulling directly behind me, and I turned to quiet him as his frantic reaches with his oar were hitting me in the back. In the dull light from the upper decks I looked into his slanting face, eyes all whites and lips moving convulsively. Besides being frightened the man was freezing in the thin cotton shirt that composed his entire upper covering. He would work feverishly to get warm.

"Get away from her; get away from her," he kept repeating. "When the water hits her hot boilers, she'll blow up, and there's just tons and tons of shrapnel in the hold!"

His excitement spread to other members of the crew in the boat. The ship's baker, designated by his pantry headgear, became a competing alarmist, and a white fireman, whose blasphemy was nothing short of profound, added to the confusion by cursing everyone.

It was the giveaway of nerve tension. It was bedlam and nightmare.

Seeking to establish some authority in our boat, I made my way to the stern and there found an old, white-haired sea captain, a second cabin passenger, with whom I had talked before. He was bound for Nova Scotia with codfish. His sailing schooner, the *Secret,* had broken in two, but he and his crew had been taken off by a tramp and taken back to New York.

He had sailed from there on the *Ryndam,* which, after almost crossing the Atlantic, had turned back. His name is Captain Dear.

"The rudder's gone, but I can steer with an oar," he said. "I will take charge, but my voice is gone. You'll have to shout the orders."

There was only one way to get the attention of the crew, and that was by an overpowering blast of profanity. I did my best and was rewarded by silence while I made the announcement that in the absence of the ship's officer assigned to the boat, Captain Dear would take charge.

We rested on our oars, with all eyes on the still lighted *Laconia.* The torpedo had struck at 10:30 P.M., according to our ship's time. It was thirty minutes afterward that another dull thud, which was accompanied by a noticeable drop in the hulk, told its story of the second torpedo that the submarine had dispatched through the engine room and the boat's vitals from a distance of two hundred yards.

We watched silently during the next minute, as the tiers of lights dimmed slowly from white to yellow, then to red, and nothing was left but the murky mourning of the night, which hung over all like a pall.

A mean, cheese-colored crescent of a moon revealed one horn above a rag bundle of clouds in the distance. A rim of blackness settled around our little world, relieved only by general leering stars in the zenith, and where the *Laconia*'s lights had shone there re-

mained only the dim outline of a blacker hulk standing out above the water like a jagged headland, silhouetted against overcast sky.

The ship sank rapidly at the stern until at last its nose stood straight up in the air. Then it slid silently down and out of sight like a piece of disappearing scenery in a panorama spectacle.

Boat No. 3 stood closest to the ship and rocked about in a perilous sea of clashing spars and wreckage. As the boat's crew steadied its head into the wind, a black hulk, glistening wet and standing about eight feet above the surface of the water, approached slowly and came to a stop opposite the boat and not six feet from the side of it.

"What ship was dot?" The correct words in throaty English with the German accent came from the dark hulk, according to Chief Steward Ballyn's statement to me later.

"The *Laconia,*" Ballyn answered.

"Vot?"

"The *Laconia,* Cunard line," responded the steward.

"Vot does she weigh?" was the next question from the submarine.

"Eighteen thousand tons."

"Any passengers?"

"Seventy-three," replied Ballyn, "men, women, and children, some of them in this boat. She had over two hundred in the crew."

"Did she carry cargo?"

"Yes."

"Vell, you'll be all right. The patrol will pick you up soon," and without further sound, save for the almost silent fixing of the conning-tower lid, the submarine moved off.

* * *

THERE WAS NO assurance of an early rescue, despite the promise of the German U-boat commander. The lifeboat bobbed about like a cork on the swells. After six hours in the open boat, the wet and bedraggled survivors were picked up by British jack-tars of the mine sweeper H.M.S. *Laburnum*.

Gibbons and the rescued survivors were landed at Queenstown that night. The newsman, acting by instinct, rushed to a typewriter. "I cabled the story," he said later, "and put the question up to the American public for an answer."

Gibbons' report of the sinking of the *Laconia*, the testimony of an eye-witness, was published on February 26, 1917, synchronously with the delivery of President Wilson's address to Congress in joint session. In his speech the President took a position, no longer realistic—that Germany, in implementing her campaign of unrestricted submarine warfare, had not yet committed an "overt act" that would make action by the United States imperative. Gibbons' dramatic news story made it clear that the President's stand was already outdated.

"We make absolutely no distinction in sinking neutral ships within the war zone," Herr Zimmermann, the German Foreign Secretary, had warned. "Our determination is unshakable since that is the only way to end the war." This was an intimation that American vessels, like those of other neutrals, must comply with U-boat rulings or take the consequences. On March 12, 1917, the unarmed steamer *Algonquin*, with a crew of twenty-seven, of whom ten were Americans, was shelled and sunk without warning by a German submarine. A few days later three unarmed American vessels, the *City of Memphis, Illinois,* and *Vigilancia,* were also sunk. Count Reventlow, a German publicist, welcomed these sinkings thus in the *Deutsche Tageszeitung:* "It is good that American ships have been obliged to learn that the German prohibition is effective, and that there is no distinctive treatment for the United States." German contempt for American feeling could scarcely go further.

On April 2, 1917, President Wilson, visibly pale and deeply affected by the awesome character of his task, appeared before Congress and asked for a declaration of war against Germany:

When I addressed the Congress on the twenty-sixth of February last I thought that it would suffice to assert our neutral rights with arms, our right to use the seas against unlawful interference, our right to keep our people safe against unlawful violence. But armed neutrality, it now appears, is impracticable.

Floyd Gibbons himself went on to produce some of the great reporting of World War I. All America appreciated the grim, typically American humor of his story of the grizzled marine sergeant who went over the top, shouting to his buddies: "Come on, you sons o' bitches, do you want to live forever?" Anxious to experience the sensation of being wounded in battle, the unarmed reporter went along on a charge and in fact stopped three German machine-gun bullets, one of which tore one of his eyes from its socket. This was firsthand reporting with a vengeance. The loss of an eye at Belleau Wood was not much compared to the total of dead and wounded newspapermen in World War II, but it distinguished Floyd Gibbons as one of the two American correspondents who were wounded in the First World War.

The Turks Use Swords for Reasons of Economy
and Horrify the World by the Armenian Atrocities

DURING THE YEAR 1915 a stream of horrifying, but authentic, accounts of assassinations and forced marches of Armenians in Turkish lands poured from the presses of such Armenian papers as *Gotchnag* of New York, *Arev* of Baku, *Balkanian Mamoul* of Ruschuk, and *Horizon* of Tiflis. The November, 1915, issue of the London Armenian journal, *Ararat*, reported the incident, later to be immortalized by Franz Werfel in *The Forty Days of Musa Dagh* (1933), wherein, at the melodramatic very last moment, rescue came to a fragment of the Armenian people who, on their craggy fortress, had held out against extermination by the Turks in World War I. "The single happy incident in the national tragedy of the Armenians in the Ottoman Empire," Arnold Toynbee called it, in a sensational Blue Book he prepared for the British government.

Armenian-Turkish tension was no new story. "They would rather be crucified than circumcised" was how one observer epitomized the traditional stand of Armenians against Moslems. As early as 1885 entire Armenian villages were laid waste. When the Great Powers protested to the Sultan, he brusquely resented such "interference" in the internal affairs of the Sublime Porte. Again, when massacres flared up ten years later, *The Daily News* of London and the New York *World* endeavored, by firsthand coverage, to arouse the conscience of the Christian world. When the Young Turks forced out Sultan Abdul-Hamid II in 1908 the Armenians threw themselves wholeheartedly into service under the new regime. Their reward was the terrible Adana massacres, in which the Young Turks were directly implicated.

Fearing that Armenian fidelity to the Turkish cause would rapidly disintegrate, the Turkish government decided, when World War I came, to liquidate this minority on the dubious but convenient ground of military necessity. Early in 1916 Eleanor Franklin Egan published in *The Saturday Evening Post* an alleged text of the Ottoman government's proclamation ordering the deportations of Armenians, which she had copied on the margins of the inner pages of a book she pretended to be reading when Turkish officials searched her at the frontier. "I will not leave here so much as the odor of the Armenians," one Turkish official declared, in carrying out the deportation order.

That the Turks had, considerably earlier, begun their ruthless program of elimination was made clear in a sensational dispatch to the American press, dated August 14, 1915, from Henry Wood, the United Press correspondent at Constantinople, and condensed herewith:

"It is impolite to interfere"

United Press, August 14, 1915

For nearly three months now, the 2,000,000 Armenians of Turkey have been undergoing at the hands of the Young Turk government a renewal of the atrocities of Abdul-Hamid that so far has fallen short only of actual massacre.

So critical is the situation that Ambassador Morgenthau, who, alone, is fighting to prevent wholesale slaughter, has felt obliged to ask the co-operation of the ambassadors of Turkey's two allies. Baron von Wangenheim, the German Ambassador, and Margrave Pallavicini, the Austrian representative at Constantinople, have responded at least to the degree of joining with Ambassador Morgenthau in endeavoring to convince the Turkish government what a serious mistake it would be for Turkey to permit again a renewal of all the atrocities of the old Turkish regime.

In the meantime, the position of the Armenians and the system of deportation, dispersion, and extermination that is being carried out against them beggars all description.

Although the present renewal of the Armenian atrocities has been under way for three months, it is only just now that reports creeping into Constantinople from the remotest points of the interior show that absolutely no portion of the Armenian population has been spared.

It now appears that the order for the present cruelties was issued in the early part of May, and was at once put into execution with all the extreme genius of the Turkish police system— the one department of government for which the Turks have ever shown the greatest aptitude both in organization and administration. At that time sealed orders were sent to the police of the entire empire. These were to be opened on a specified date that would ensure the orders being in the hands of every department at the moment they were to be opened. Once opened, they provided for a simultaneous descent at practically the same moment on the Armenian population of the entire empire.

At Brusa, in Asiatic Turkey, the city which it is expected the Turks will select for their capital in the event of Constantinople falling, I investigated personally the manner in which these orders were carried out. From eyewitnesses in other towns I found that the execution of them was everywhere identical.

At midnight, the police authorities swooped down on the homes of all Armenians whose names had been put on the proscribed list sent out from Constantinople. The men were at once placed under arrest, and then the houses were searched for papers which might implicate them either in the present revolutionary movement of the Armenians on the frontier or in plots against the government which the Turks declare exist. In this search, carpets were torn from the floors, draperies stripped from the walls, and even the children turned out of their beds and cradles in order that the mattresses and coverings might be searched.

Following this search, the men were then carried away, and at once there began the carrying out of the system of deportation and dispersion which has been the cruelest feature of the present anti-Armenian wave. The younger men, for the most part, were at once drafted into the army. On the authority of men whose names would be known in both America and Europe if I dared mention them, I am told that hundreds if not thousands of these were sent at once to the front ranks at the Dardanelles, where death in a very short space of time is almost a certainty. The older men were then deported into the interior, while the women and children, when not carried off in an opposite direction, were left to shift for themselves as best as they could.

The terrible feature of this deportation up to date is that it has been carried out on such a basis as to render practically impossible in thousands and thousands of cases that these families can ever again be reunited. Not only wives and husbands, brothers and sisters, but even mothers and their little children have been dispersed in such a manner as to preclude practically all hope that they will ever see each other again.

Of all the terrible vengeances so far meted out by the Turks in the present anti-Armenian crusade, none appear to have equaled that inflicted on the population of the city of Zeitun. Twenty thousand Turks from Thrace were taken to Zeitun and established in the houses that for generations had belonged to the Armenian families. The latter were then scattered to the four winds of the empire.

I talked with eyewitnesses who, coming to Constantinople from the interior, had seen this miserable population being dispersed and deported. They were being herded across the country by soldiers in groups ranging from fifty to several hundred. Old men who were unable to maintain the fast pace set by the mounted soldiers were beaten till they fell dead in their tracks. Children who were likewise too tender to stand the terrible strain dropped out by the wayside, while the mothers were driven relentlessly on with no hopes of ever again being able to find their little ones. Other mothers with babies in arms, unable to see the latter die under their very eyes, unable to give them the nourishment necessary to sustain life, and unable to bear the agony of leaving them by the wayside to an unknown fate, dropped them in wells as they passed, thus ending the sufferings of the little ones and having at least the consolation of knowing their fate.

FRESH MASSACRES took place in 1916. A German eyewitness reported how the Armenian settlement at Mush was burned to the ground, a model for a later Lidice. "Every officer boasted of the number he had personally massacred as his share in ridding Turkey of the Armenian race." The dead Armenians, dumped in the town of Harput, remained long unburied, with dogs and vultures licking their bodies. Testimony was unearthed by neutral observers that the eyebrows of Armenians were plucked out, their breasts cut off, their nails torn off—"all done at nighttime, and in order that the people may not hear their screams and know of their agony soldiers are stationed around the prisons beating drums and blowing whistles." "Now let your Christ help you," the Turkish soldiers sneered.

Describing the horrors that blighted Mesopotamia, Henri Barby, a

French war correspondent for *Le Journal* of Paris, who had previously covered the campaigns in Serbia and brought to light evidence of war atrocities by the Austro-Hungarian armies, sent to his paper an account of an interview with Dr. H. Toroyan, an Armenian physician formerly in the service of the Turkish army.

Le Journal (Paris), July 13, 1916

Along the burning banks of the distant Euphrates, between sultry Mesopotamia and the Badiet-esh-Sham, the desolate desert of Syria, are encamped the several thousands of deported Armenians who have escaped the great massacre.

Their condition there is such that no words can express the horror of it. That is the unanimous testimony of the rare travelers who have succeeded in visiting the camps where the unhappy victims are dying off, between Aleppo and Bagdad. They are subjected to frightful sufferings—without shelter either against the deadly cold of last winter or against the terrific heat of the present summer, which grows more pitiless every day—and daily they are perishing in great numbers, though those struck down by death are the least to be pitied.

I am now in a position to cite unimpeachable testimony as to the facts of these unheard-of atrocities.

A Turkish army physician, Dr. H. Toroyan—an Armenian by birth, as appears by his name—was commissioned by the Young Turkish government to visit the exiles' camps. The horrors of which he was a helpless witness in the course of his mission, and the hideous scenes at which he was present, affected him so deeply that he determined to make his way out of Turkey, at the risk of his life, in order to reveal to the civilized world the barbarity and infamy of the guilty parties—that is, of the present rulers

of Turkey and their accomplices.

Dr. Toroyan, in spite of the almost insurmountable difficulties with which he had to contend, succeeded in escaping and reaching Caucasia. There I met him, and his first words with me were these:

"My unhappy countrymen deported to Mesopotamia have besought me to make an appeal on their behalf to the whole civilized world, to the Caucasian Armenians in particular, and above all to the Armenians in America, whose women and children are dying every day—decimated by suffering, hunger, and disease and subjected to the devilish cruelty of the zaptiahs who are in charge of their place of exile."

He proceeded to show me the notes which he had taken day by day in the course of his tour of inspection down the Euphrates. It is a long series of awful pictures—stories of murders and tortures and revolting rapes. The bestial instincts of human nature are unleashed in the presence of tears and blood. The Turkish butchers amused themselves by massacring men "for pleasure" and hunting women like beasts of the field.

It was on November 25, 1915, that Dr. Toroyan left Djerablus and began to descend the Euphrates on a raft. At Djerablus he saw a convoy of Armenians from Syria and twenty-five Armenian families from Aintab, who were being driven along by gendarmes toward the military tribunal under blows of the lash. Other Armenian families were coming in from Kaisaria and Konya by railway. From the moment they left the train they became the victims of the most atrocious outrages. The Chechens carried off three hundred women and girls (the prettiest) in order to sell them as slaves.

But I will let Dr. Toroyan tell his own story:

"This camp," he continued, "was still congested when I left it, with Armenians from Adana and Cilicia. Most of them were women and girls. Two of them whom I knew well but only recognized with difficulty, to so lamentable a condition were they reduced, cast themselves at my feet:

" 'Tell the gallant soldiers [of the Allies] to come quickly to Mesopotamia,' they cried to me between their sobs. 'We are worse than dead.' "

The doctor went down on his raft with the current as far as Meskeneh. There he landed and, escorted by two Turkish gendarmes, paid a visit to the Armenian camp.

"The poor people were in rags which barely covered their bodies," he said, "and had nothing to shelter them against the weather. I asked my gendarmes what all the strange little mounds of earth were which I saw everywhere, with thousands of dogs prowling round about them.

" 'Those are the graves of the infidels!' they answered calmly.

" 'Strange, so many graves for such a little village.'

" 'Oh, you do not understand. Those are the graves of these dogs—those who were brought here first, last August. They all died of thirst.'

" 'Of thirst? Was there no water left in the Euphrates?'

" 'For whole weeks together we were forbidden to let them drink.'

"I arrived at last at the extremity of this vast field of graves. There were two old men there, crouched on the ground, sobbing. I questioned them: 'Where are you from?' They made no answer. They were stupefied by suffering. Perhaps they had lost the power of speech. Further on, however, another exile, prostrate on the ground, in the midst of other victims belonging to the same family, did give me an answer. I learned that the camp contained five thousand Armenians from Mersin and other Cilician towns.

"But now my two gendarmes came up to me. They pointed to a girl: 'Effendi, let us take her and carry her with us to Bagdad.' Without waiting for my answer they called the poor girl. She approached, shrieking with terror. She said several words to me in French. Before she was deported she had been a schoolmistress at Smyrna. She was dying of hunger. I tried to learn from her precise details about the martyrdom of the exiles, but she could answer nothing but: 'Bread! Bread!' Then she fainted and fell down unconscious.

" 'She is dead! The schoolmistress, too, has died of hunger!' piteous voices cried around us. But the gendarmes were anxious to take advantage of their victim's unconsciousness to gain possession of her. Already they had seized her and were carrying her toward our raft. I stopped them. Then I poured several drops of brandy between the poor girl's lips, and she came to herself again.

"A mother came to implore me. She offered her honor and her life if I would save her son, who was in agony, devoured by a fever. I gave her a little aspirin.

"And now they crowded round me in thousands—these poor emaciated beings with hollow cheeks and eyes, either dulled or unnaturally bright.

From every side they flocked together with all the haste they could, and surrounded me with a tumult of despairing cries: 'Bread! Medicine!'

"The gendarmes rushed at them. Into this pitiful crowd they struck at random with kicks and blows as hard as they could. I left the scene, desperate at my powerlessness to alleviate this infinite suffering.

"I saw two women, one of them old, the other very young and very pretty, carrying the corpse of another young woman. I had scarcely passed them when cries of terror arose. The girl was struggling in the clutches of a brute who was trying to drag her away. The corpse had fallen to the ground, the girl, now half unconscious, was writhing by the side of it, the old woman was sobbing and wringing her hands.

"I could not interfere. I had the strictest orders. Shaking with rage and indignation, I took refuge on my raft, which was moored to the riverbank.

"In the middle of the night I was awakened by desperate shrieks. My two gendarmes, who had remained on shore, had seized some Armenian girls. It was their intention to violate them, and they were striking savagely at the exiles who were trying to interfere. The tumult, which I heard without seeing it, continued. At last the gendarmes returned, the boatman unmoored the raft and bent to his oars. We were starting. The great river boat glided over the smooth water. Suddenly the gendarmes shouted and guffawed as if they were watching a fine farce:

"'The girl! The girl we had to-night!'

"I looked, and saw floating on the surface a corpse which they had recognized and which I recognized, too. It was the schoolmistress from Smyrna, the poor girl to whom I had spoken only a few hours before. It was she who, in the darkness, had been the victim of these two wild beasts."

* * *

ONLY A MILITARY DEFEAT for the Turks could end the atrocities. On March 11, 1917, General Frederick Stanley Maude led his British forces into Bagdad, the chief city of Mesopotamia, thus shattering the dream of Pan Germans for a Berlin-to-Bagdad Railway. In his *Seven Pillars of Wisdom* (1926) Colonel Lawrence describes the riotous welcome afforded the conquerors. The steps and stairs of the Town Hall were packed with a swaying mob, "embracing, dancing, singing. Damascus went mad with joy. The men tossed up their tarbushes to cheer, the women tore off their veils. Householders threw flowers, hangings, carpets, into the road before us; their wives leaned, screaming with laughter, through the lattices and splashed us with bath dippers of scent." A far more somber sight met the eyes of Edmund Candler, whose account of a refugee camp at Bagdad appeared in the London *Times,* June 21, 1917. A veteran traveler in the Orient, Candler had been a London *Times* and *Mail* correspondent on the western front in the first years of World War I and subsequently covered the campaigns in Mesopotamia for *The Times.* Candler later confessed in an article in *Blackwood's* that the sights he saw convinced him of the "senselessness" of the "disease" of war. Here are some of those sights.

THE ARMENIAN TRAGEDY
REFUGEES' STORIES IN BAGDAD
WHOLESALE MASSACRES
By Edmund Candler

BAGDAD, APRIL—One of the best things that are being done in Bagdad is the salvage of Armenian women and children who have survived the massacre and who are now living in Mussulman families. These are being gathered into homes financed by the British government, and their own community are looking after them.

I visited one of these institutions yesterday. The inmates were all young, many of marriageable age, and there were a great number of children under six who have already forgotten their language and their faith.

The bald statements of what they have suffered and seen is damning and an unanswerable arraignment against the Turkish government. The first girl I saw was a child of ten from a village near Erzurum. She and her family had started on donkeys with a few of their belongings, but in three days the Kurds had left them nothing, and they had to walk. The Turks had issued a proclamation in all the villages that the Armenians were to be sent away to a colony that was being prepared for them, and that their property was to be kept under the care of the government during the war and then restored. This was more than a year ago. The gendarmes were very pleasant to them in their homes, and told them that they were to be given new land to cultivate, and that their journey would not be long. The first assurance, as they guessed, was visionary. In the second the gendarmes did not lie.

For many of them it was all over on the third day. Two or three hundred of the men were separated from the women and killed at a distance, shot or cut down with a sword. After that the same sort of thing happened nearly every day. The guards were very haphazard; there was no system. Some of the women were pushed into the river; others thrust over precipices. Twelve hundred left the two villages near Erzurum; four hundred only reached Ras-el-Ain. The survivors were all women and children; there was not a man among them or a male child over the age of nine.

I met a refugee from the Karahisar district who, with six companions, had been saved by some Armenian women he found established in a Bedouin camp. Eight hundred families in all had left Karahisar. Half of these were capsized and drowned on Arab boats on the Euphrates. The survivors, when they reached Deir-ez-Zor, were placed in an internment camp. While here, they approached the mutessarif, hoping to purchase their release. They offered him three thousand liras. It was not enough. They made a second collection; every piaster they could raise was thrown into the pool. This time the sum was nearly five thousand liras, and the mutessarif accepted the bribe on condition that they should sign a paper, "We, the Armenians of——, give this sum willingly to the Turkish army."

But it did not save them. The hated gendarmes accompanied them on the march, and nine miles from the city the massacre began. Sticks and stones and knives and daggers were employed, and a few merciful bullets. But, as always happens, the assassins tired of their work; even the physical part of it was exhausting, and the last act was postponed from day to day. In the end a tired gendarme gave them the hint to go. The night was dark, and the guard more careless than usual, and the last remnants of the party, fifty-five in all, made their escape.

Another man I heard of was the sole survivor of a group of refugees who disappeared between Ras-el-Ain and Nisibin. They were taken into the desert and formed in line, as in a Chinese execution, to be dispatched with the sword. There was no shortage of ammunition, I was told, but the sword was employed for reasons of economy. While waiting for his turn, it occurred to the Armenian that a bullet would be an easier death. So he broke from the line. In the confusion the gendarmes missed him. It was almost dusk; he hid in the brushwood; by a miracle he escaped and found his way to Bagdad.

The main features of the massacres are much the same. The emigrants, if they are not killed on the road, are taken to some depot, where they are kept a few days. Here they find a large camp of two or three thousand or more. Soon notice comes from Constantinople that the refugees of a certain district have been allotted land for cultivation, and they are told they must start on their journey again. This, they know, is probably the death sentence, but they nourish a thin hope. For the first half day they are generally safe, as murder on a large scale is deprecated near a town. Nobody, for instance, saw anyone killed in Trebizond; but a few days after the Armenians had left the city their bodies came floating down the river. The desert is a nonconductor. What is done there leaves only vague rumor.

Few Armenian women were so fortunate [as a Bagdad refugee whose honor was respected]. Many were killed with as little scruple as the men. Plainness or good looks were fatal in different ways. The old and ugly died by violence or were starved; the young were taken into the families of the Turks. A traveler now in Bagdad was given a letter by an official at Ras-el-Ain to deliver to the gendarme in charge of the road.

"Choose a pretty one for me," he wrote, "and leave her in the village outside the town."

At Aleppo and Ras-el-Ain German officers stalked side by side with these specters of famine and murder and death, and not a finger was raised or a word said. "It is impolite to interfere" is the German watchword.

THE ARMENIAN ATROCITIES (in all, perhaps 800,000 were exterminated) were the prologue to Belsen, Buchenwald, and Dachau, for the Germans observed with genuine scientific absorption the experiment of their ally with the technique of mass murder. American Ambassador Henry Morgenthau was thoroughly justified in his charge that "Germany could, but would not, prevent" the outrages. Corroboration for this charge was provided by a German war correspondent, Dr. Harry Stürmer, who, writing later on from Switzerland, accused Germany of "the most shameless cowardice" and attacked German officers for complicity in the atrocities, for being, in fact, "more eager than some of the Turkish officials of local districts" to carry out the instructions to exterminate or expel the Armenians. Stürmer cited the case "of two traveling German officers who came to a little village in further Asia Minor, where some Armenians had taken refuge in the interior of a house, refusing to be driven away like animals. Guns had been placed in position to drive them out of their shelter and fire on women and children. These German officers then, without any orders, took up the matter as a sporting affair, and seized the occasion to show their skill in artillery practice." The Armenian journal *Mschak* of Tiflis charged that German officers at Erzurum kidnaped Armenian girls as their share of the booty, an accusation repeated to the London *Times* by its Bucharest correspondent.

When the war ended, the Armenians looked to the Allies to retrieve some of their losses. "Your Wilson came from Washington," said the chairman of their delegation at Versailles, "but he was sent by God." They demanded a port on the Mediterranean and a protectorate under a friendly Western power, independent of Turkey. But the Great Powers let them down, and the Treaty of Lausanne of 1923 was a stunning victory for a revived Turkish power. "An abject, cowardly, and infamous surrender," Lloyd George called it.

Death Comes to Mata Hari: a Serpent in Woman's Form Falls Before a Firing Squad

A SPECTATOR who had seen Mata Hari dance described her in these words:

> You can scarcely credit the mystic frenzy produced by her lascivious attitudes. Her nervous tremors, her violent contortions, were terribly impressive. There was something in the performance of the solemnity of an idol, something of the loathsome horror of a writhing reptile. From her great somber eyes, half closed in sensuous ecstasy, there gleamed an uncanny light, like phosphorescent flames. She seemed to embrace an invisible being in her long shapely arms. To witness this spectacle was to receive the impression that one had actually been present at the metamorphosis of a serpent taking a woman's form.

MATA HARI, born Gertrud Margarete Zelle on August 7, 1876, in the little Dutch village of Teeuwarden, was a lustrous-eyed, golden-skinned Eurasian. Married at eighteen to a Dutch officer named Captain McLeod, she had journeyed to Java, where she had learned to dance naked on the purple granite altar of the Kanda Swany. Returning to Europe, she adopted the vocation of courtesan and the avocation of stage dancer. With a seductive power over men, she flitted from one conquest to another, enticing some of the most noted figures of Europe to her love nests. In her private house at Neuilly, a fashionable suburb of Paris, she received magistrates, artists, diplomats, and generals. According to Harry J. Greenwall, Paris correspondent of the London *Daily Express*, Mata Hari had for a lover the German Crown Prince, who took her to the maneuvers in Silesia. In Holland, says Greenwall, her lover was Prime Minister van der Linden, in France the Minister of War. Until drink and dissipation coarsened her, she was a creature of rare beauty.

A gifted liar, cunning and resourceful, Mata Hari at the outbreak of World War I became attached to the German spy service. By the simple expedient of getting her French lovers roaring drunk, she extracted information that may have cost the lives of many Allied soldiers. She very nearly succeeded in opening the gates of Paris to the Germans. Eventually this "most notorious woman in the world" was caught and condemned to death.

Before the court the "Red Dancer" showed a cool lack of concern about her fate, intimating that life meant nothing to her. "She made a great impression," wrote one eyewitness, "standing as straight as a ramrod, and sweeping her judges with flashing glances from her pale forget-me-not eyes." She boasted of her numerous conquests among officers, and said: "The officer is a sort of artist." Several high-placed Frenchmen testified in

her behalf, insisting that in the privacy of her boudoir they had discussed
such innocuous subjects as Javanese art, but *never* military secrets. Her
lawyer, Maître Clunet, fell on his knees before President Poincaré and
begged for mercy for his client. The President of France shook his head.
"Old friend," he said to the weeping Clunet. "I cannot. For France's sake,
I cannot." The venerable barrister, seventy-five years of age, then sought
to save Mata Hari's life by proclaiming that she was *enceinte,* that he was
the culprit, and that the law did not permit the execution of a pregnant
woman. The lovely spy only laughed.

It is a truism that in all ages resolute attackers have spared no efforts
to send their spies and secret agents within the walls of the enemy's city.
The Old Testament presents a famous example: "And Joshua saved Rahab
the harlot alive, and her father's household, and all that she had; and she
dwelleth in Israel even unto this day; because she hid the messengers which
Joshua sent to spy out Jericho." Mata Hari was not so fortunate.

The account of Mata Hari's execution that follows was written in Paris
on October 18, 1917, by Henry G. Wales, a staff correspondent of the International News Service.

*"For a fraction of a second it seemed she
tottered there, on her knees, gazing directly
at those who had taken her life"*

International News Service, October 19, 1917

PARIS, OCTOBER 18, 1917—Mata Hari,
which is Javanese for Eye-of-the-
Morning, is dead. She was shot as a
spy by a firing squad of Zouaves at the
Vincennes Barracks. She died facing
death literally, for she refused to be
blindfolded.

Gertrud Margarete Zelle, for that
was the real name of the beautiful
Dutch-Javanese dancer, did appeal to
President Poincaré for a reprieve, but
he refused to intervene.

The first intimation she received
that her plea had been denied was
when she was led at daybreak from her
cell in the Saint-Lazare prison to a
waiting automobile and then rushed
to the barracks where the firing squad
awaited her.

Never once had the iron will of the
beautiful woman failed her. Father
Arbaux, accompanied by two sisters
of charity, Captain Bouchardon, and
Maître Clunet, her lawyer, entered her
cell, where she was still sleeping—a
calm, untroubled sleep, it was remarked by the turnkeys and trusties.

The sisters gently shook her. She
arose and was told that her hour had
come.

"May I write two letters?" was all
she asked.

Consent was given immediately by
Captain Bouchardon, and pen, ink,
paper, and envelopes were given to her.

She seated herself at the edge
of the bed and wrote the letters
with feverish haste. She handed them

over to the custody of her lawyer.

Then she drew on her stockings, black, silken, filmy things, grotesque in the circumstances. She placed her high-heeled slippers on her feet and tied the silken ribbons over her insteps.

She arose and took the long black velvet cloak, edged around the bottom with fur and with a huge square fur collar hanging down the back, from a hook over the head of her bed. She placed this cloak over the heavy silk kimono which she had been wearing over her nightdress.

Her wealth of black hair was still coiled about her head in braids. She put on a large, flapping black felt hat with a black silk ribbon and bow. Slowly and indifferently, it seemed, she pulled on a pair of black kid gloves. Then she said calmly:

"I am ready."

The party slowly filed out of her cell to the waiting automobile.

The car sped through the heart of the sleeping city. It was scarcely half-past five in the morning and the sun was not yet fully up.

Clear across Paris the car whirled to the Caserne de Vincennes, the barracks of the old fort which the Germans stormed in 1870.

The troops were already drawn up for the execution. The twelve Zouaves, forming the firing squad, stood in line, their rifles at ease. A subofficer stood behind them, sword drawn.

The automobile stopped, and the party descended, Mata Hari last. The party walked straight to the spot, where a little hummock of earth reared itself seven or eight feet high and afforded a background for such bullets as might miss the human target.

As Father Arbaux spoke with the condemned woman, a French officer approached, carrying a white cloth.

"The blindfold," he whispered to the nuns who stood there and handed it to them.

"Must I wear that?" asked Mata Hari, turning to her lawyer, as her eyes glimpsed the blindfold.

M. Clunet turned interrogatively to the French officer.

"If Madame prefers not, it makes no difference," replied the officer, hurriedly turning away.

Mata Hari was not bound and she was not blindfolded. She stood gazing steadfastly at her executioners, when the priest, the nuns, and her lawyer stepped away from her.

The officer in command of the firing squad, who had been watching his men like a hawk that none might examine his rifle and try to find out whether he was destined to fire the blank cartridge which was in the breach of one rifle, seemed relieved that the business would soon be over.

A sharp, crackling command, and the file of twelve men assumed rigid positions at attention. Another command, and their rifles were at their shoulders; each man gazed down his barrel at the breast of the woman which was the target.

She did not move a muscle.

The underofficer in charge had moved to a position where from the corners of their eyes they could see him. His sword was extended in the air.

It dropped. The sun—by this time up—flashed on the burnished blade as it described an arc in falling. Simultaneously the sound of the volley rang out. Flame and a tiny puff of grayish smoke issued from the muzzle of each rifle. Automatically the men dropped their arms.

At the report Mata Hari fell. She did not die as actors and moving picture stars would have us believe that people die when they are shot. She did not throw up her hands nor did she plunge straight forward or straight back.

Instead she seemed to collapse. Slowly, inertly, she settled to her knees, her head up always, and without the slightest change of expression on her face. For the fraction of a second it seemed she tottered there, on her knees, gazing directly at those who had taken her life. Then she fell backward, bending at the waist, with her legs doubled up beneath her. She lay prone, motionless, with her face turned towards the sky.

A noncommissioned officer, who accompanied a lieutenant, drew his revolver from the big, black holster strapped about his waist. Bending over, he placed the muzzle of the revolver almost—but not quite—against the left temple of the spy. He pulled the trigger, and the bullet tore into the brain of the woman.

Mata Hari was surely dead.

* * *

THIS NEWS report effectively dissolves the legend that Mata Hari faced the firing squad while she was clad only in a fur coat, which she opened at the last moment to reveal her naked body to the executioners.

Nobody claimed the body of the beautiful dancer, once so ardently admired. It was thrust into a plain wooden coffin, lifted to a truck, and driven away with two gendarmes sitting on the coffin and smoking their pipes. The corpse was taken to the operating theater of a Paris hospital and there dissected.

John Reed, American Radical, Witnesses the Storming of the Winter Palace on a Day That Shook the World

JOHN REED was a classmate of Walter Lippmann at Harvard, a member of the staff of the *Lampoon,* captain of the water-polo team, song leader at football games, manager of the dramatic club, and writer of lyrics for the Hasty Pudding Show. It was clear that the uninhibited young Westerner was headed straight for Wall Street, a million dollars, and a cozy, well-ordered bourgeois life. After graduation from Harvard he did the conventional thing by shipping on a cattle boat to Europe. Wandering then over the Continent, he returned to Greenwich Village, New York's home of romance and rebellion.

In 1913, when Reed was just twenty-six, the editors of the *Metropolitan Magazine* and the New York *World* sent him to Mexico to cover the hellbent-for-destruction riding of Francisco Villa. Young Reed's dispatches from Mexico added up to war reporting not surpassed even by the great Richard Harding Davis. The ordinarily calm Walter Lippmann was said to have written Reed: "If all history had been reported as you are doing this, Lord! I say that, with Jack Reed, reporting begins." Lippmann was speaking of paragraphs like this one:

Almost every hundred yards along the road were little heaps of stones, surmounted by wooden crosses—each one the memorial of a murder. And occasionally a tall whitewashed cross uprose in the middle of a side road, to protect some little desert rancho from the visits of the devil. Black, spiny chaparral the height of a mule's back scraped the side of the coach; Spanish bayonets and the great barrel cactus watched us like sentinels from the skyline of the desert. And always the mighty Mexican vultures circled over us, as if they knew we were going to war.

Four years later, the young revolutionary poet plunged into the chaos of the Bolshevik Revolution. In his *Ten Days That Shook the World* he records what he "had to see for himself." In broad, sweeping strokes he traced the steps by which the Bolsheviks seized power. To John Reed his own work was "a slice of intensified history—history as I saw it." To Lenin it was "a truthful and most vivid exposition." To Granville Hicks, his biographer, it was "the drama of great events, clearly understood and objectively recounted. The poet in him made every detail vivid; the revolutionary made every detail significant."

Reed had come to a Russia seething with discontent. On March 15, 1917, the Romanov dynasty, which had withstood many revolutionary assaults by using the sword, pistol, and rope, had come suddenly to an inglorious end with the abdication of Nicholas II. The revolution took place, said one of its leaders, Milyukov, "because history does not know of another government so stupid, so dishonest, so cowardly, so treacherous as the government now overthrown." The provisional government, under the leadership of Prince Lvov, a liberal aristocrat, sought to carry on the war against Germany and to transform Russia into a modern democracy without attacking the rights of property. A superhuman task, it was never accomplished.

The new government survived only seven months. The Russian people, defeated, starved, exhausted, embittered, yearned for peace. Discipline at the front evaporated, and thousands of troops deserted. Peasants seized the estates; workingmen occupied the factories. Into this chaotic situation stepped a small group of determined men who had studied the dynamics of popular control and who directed the vast, surging mood of indignation into the channels of a second revolution, this time overthrowing the bourgeois state in favor of a proletarian dictatorship. It was done under superbly effective leadership. Vladimir Ilyich Ulyanov, known under the pseudonym Lenin, provided the genius for direction without which the revolution could not have been successful. Leon Bronstein, known as Trotsky, a penetrating writer and volcanic orator, had studied Karl Marx in the British Museum, but always with a manual on military tactics near by. These two took over control of the soviets (councils) of soldiers, workingmen, and peasants' delegates and the Bolshevik party, which was to guide the revolution. The cause was helped immeasurably by two slogans that effectively condensed Bolshevik philosophy: "Peace, Land, Bread!" and "All Power to the Soviets!" "The provisional government," said Trotsky, "is nothing more than a pitiful, helpless half government which awaits the motion of a historical broom to sweep it away."

Lenin had been in hiding since July, but now, in early November, he was in Petrograd with the blessing of the Germans, who had taken him there on a sealed train in the hope that he would lead another revolution. By November 6, the Bolsheviks, without firing a shot, had quietly and systematically taken over the key buildings of Petrograd, including the telegraph, the telephone, and all other government offices, with the exception of the Winter Palace and the offices of the general staff. Lenin set November 7 as the date for the insurrection. Early that morning Kerensky, then Prime Minister of the provisional government, went to the front with the avowed purpose of bringing back loyal troops to crush the revolt. The other members of the government decided to await his return at the Winter Palace, which thereby became the crucial point of the revolution.

John Reed's account of the storming of the Winter Palace, condensed here, is literature written under pressure, which merits the accolade of great reporting.

"Like a black river, filling all the streets, without song or cheer we poured through the Red Arch"

From *Ten Days That Shook the World,* by John Reed, by permission of International Publishers. 1934

Wednesday, November 7, I rose very late. The noon cannon boomed from Peter-Paul as I went down the Nevsky. It was a raw, chill day. In front of the State Bank some soldiers with fixed bayonets were standing at the closed gates.

"What side do you belong to?" I asked. "The government?"

"No more government," one answered with a grin, "*Slava Bogu!* Glory to God!" That was all I could get out of him.

The streetcars were running on the Nevsky, men, women, and small boys hanging on every projection. Shops were open, and there seemed even less uneasiness among the street crowds than there had been the day before. A whole crop of new appeals against insurrection had blossomed out on the walls during the night—to the peasants, to the soldiers at the front, to the workmen of Petrograd.

I bought a copy of *Rabotchi Put,* the only newspaper which seemed on sale, and a little later paid a soldier fifty kopecks for a secondhand copy of *Dien.* The Bolshevik paper, printed on large-sized sheets in the conquered office of the *Russkaya Volia,* had huge headlines: ALL POWER—TO THE SOVIETS OF WORKERS, SOLDIERS, AND PEASANTS! PEACE! BREAD! LAND!

Just at the corner of the Ekaterina Canal, under an arc light, a cordon of armed sailors was drawn across the Nevsky, blocking the way to a crowd of people in columns of fours. There were about three or four hundred of them, men in frock coats, well-dressed women, officers—all sorts and conditions of people.

Like a black river, filling all the streets, without song or cheer we poured through the Red Arch, where the man just ahead of me said in a low voice: "Look out, comrades! Don't trust them. They will fire, surely!" In the open we began to run, stooping low and bunching together, and jammed up suddenly behind the pedestal of the Alexander Column.

After a few minutes' huddling there, some hundreds of men, the army seemed reassured and without any orders suddenly began again to flow forward. By this time, in the light that streamed out of all the Winter Palace windows, I could see that the first two or three hundred men were Red Guards, with only a few scattered soldiers. Over the barricade of firewood we clambered, and leaping down inside gave a triumphant shout as we stumbled on a heap of rifles thrown down by the *yunkers* who had stood there. On both sides of the main gateway the doors stood wide open, light streamed out, and from the huge pile came not the slightest sound.

Carried along by the eager wave of men, we were swept into the right-hand entrance, opening into a great bare vaulted room, the cellar of the east wing, from which issued a mass of corridors and staircases. A number of huge packing cases stood about, and upon these the Red Guards and soldiers fell furiously, battering them open with the butts of their rifles, and pulling out carpets, curtains, linens, porcelain plates, glassware. One man went strutting around with a bronze clock perched on his shoulder; another found a plume of ostrich feathers, which he stuck in his hat. The looting was just beginning when somebody cried, "Comrades! Don't touch anything! Don't take anything! Property of the people!" Many hands dragged the spoilers down. Damask and tapestry were snatched from the arms of those who had them; two men took away the bronze clock. Roughly and hastily the things were crammed back in their cases, and self-appointed sentinels stood guard. It was all utterly spontaneous. Through corridors and up staircases the cry could be heard growing fainter and fainter in the distance, "Revolutionary discipline! Property of the people."

We crossed back over to the left entrance, in the west wing. There order was also being established. "Clear the palace!" bawled a Red Guard, sticking his head through an inner door. "Come, comrades, let's show that we're not thieves and bandits. Everybody out of the palace except the Commissars, until we get sentries posted."

Two Red Guards, a soldier and an officer, stood with revolvers in their hands. Another soldier sat at a table behind them, with pen and paper. Shouts of "All out! All out!" were heard far and near within, and the army began to pour through the door, jostling, expostulating, arguing. As each man appeared he was seized by the self-appointed committee, who went through his pockets and looked under his coat. Everything that was plainly not his property was taken

away, the man at the table noted it on his paper, and it was carried into a little room. The most amazing assortment of objects were thus confiscated; statuettes, bottles of ink, bedspreads worked with the imperial monogram, candles, a small oil painting, desk blotters, gold-handled swords, cakes of soap, clothes of every description, blankets. One Red Guard carried three rifles, two of which he had taken away from *yunkers;* another had four portfolios bulging with written documents. The culprits either sullenly surrendered or pleaded like children. All talking at once, the committee explained that stealing was not worthy of the people's champions; often those who were caught turned around and began to help go through the rest of the comrades.

We asked if we might go inside. The committee was doubtful, but the big Red Guard answered firmly that it was forbidden. "Who are you anyway?" he asked. "How do I know that you are not all Kerenskys?" (There were five of us, two women.)

In the meanwhile unrebuked we walked into the palace. There was still a great deal of coming and going, of exploring newfound apartments in the vast edifice, of searching for hidden garrisons of *yunkers* which did not exist. We went upstairs and wandered through room after room. This part of the palace had been entered also by other detachments from the side of the Neva. The paintings, statues, tapestries, and rugs of the great state apartments were unharmed; in the offices, however, every desk and cabinet had been ransacked, the papers scattered over the floor, and in the living rooms beds had been stripped of their coverings and wardrobes wrenched open. The most highly prized loot was clothing, which the working people needed.

In a room where furniture was stored we came upon two soldiers ripping the elaborate Spanish leather upholstery from chairs. They explained it was to make boots with.

The old palace servants in their blue and red and gold uniforms stood nervously about, from force of habit repeating, "You can't go in there, *barin!* It is forbidden——"

All this time, it must be remembered, although the Winter Palace was surrounded, the government was in constant communication with the front and with provincial Russia. The Bolsheviki had captured the Ministry of War early in the morning, but they did not know of the military telegraph office in the attic, nor of the private telephone line connecting it with the Winter Palace. In that attic a young officer sat all day, pouring out over the country a flood of appeals and proclamations; and when he heard that the palace had fallen, put on his hat and walked calmly out of the building.

Interested as we were, for a considerable time we didn't notice a change in the attitude of the soldiers and Red Guards around us. As we strolled from room to room a small group followed us, until by the time we reached the great picture gallery where we had spent the afternoon with the *yunkers,* about a hundred men surged in after us. One giant of a soldier stood in our path, his face dark with sullen suspicion.

"Who are you?" he growled. "What are you doing here?" The others massed slowly around, staring and beginning to mutter. *"Provocatori!"* I heard somebody say. "Looters!" I produced our passes from the Military Revolutionary Committee. The soldier took them gingerly, turned them upside down, and looked at them without comprehension. Evidently he could not read. He handed them back and spat on the floor. *"Bumagi!* Papers!" said he with contempt. The mass slowly began to close in, like wild cattle around a cowpuncher on foot. Over their heads I caught sight of an officer, looking helpless, and shouted to him. He made for us, shouldering his way through.

"I'm the Commissar," he said to me. "Who are you? What is it?" The others held back, waiting. I produced the papers.

"You are foreigners?" he rapidly asked in French. "It is very dangerous." Then he turned to the mob, holding up our documents. "Comrades!" he cried. "These people are foreign comrades—from America. They have come here to be able to tell their countrymen about the bravery and the revolutionary discipline of the proletarian army!"

"How do you know that?" replied the big soldier. "I tell you they are provocators! They say they have come here to observe the revolutionary discipline of the proletarian army, but they have been wandering freely through the palace, and how do we know they haven't got their pockets full of loot?"

"Pravilno!" snarled the others, pressing forward.

"Comrades! Comrades!" appealed the officer, sweat standing out on his forehead. "I am Commissar of the Military Revolutionary Committee. Do you trust me? Well, I tell you that these passes are signed with the same names that are signed to my pass!"

He led us down through the palace and out through a door opening onto the Neva quay, before which stood the usual committee going through pockets. "You have narrowly escaped," he kept muttering, wiping his face.

We came out into the cold, nervous night, murmurous with obscure armies on the move, electric with patrols. From across the river, where loomed the darker mass of Peter-Paul, came a hoarse shout. Underfoot the sidewalk was littered with broken stucco, from the cornice of the palace where two shells from the battleship *Avrora* had struck; that was the only damage done by the bombardment.

It was now about three in the morning. On the Nevsky all the street lights were again shining, the cannon gone, and the only signs of war were Red Guards and soldiers squatting around fires. The city was quiet—probably never so quiet in its history; on that night not a single holdup occurred, not a single robbery.

ON OCTOBER 17, 1920, just before his thirty-third birthday, John Reed was dead of typhus. A few days later he was buried in Red Square near the Kremlin wall, one of the few American heroes of the Soviet Union.

Lincoln Steffens has given us an unforgettable picture of the young poet. "He was bitten by a sick louse, a doomed parasite. Jack would have made a song of that, a laughing song. When John Reed came, big and growing, handsome outside and beautiful inside, when that boy came down from Cambridge to New York, it seemed to me that I had never seen anything so near to pure joy. No ray of sunshine, no drop of foam, no young animal, bird or fish, and no star, was as happy as that boy was. If only we could keep him so, we might have had a poet at last who would see and sing nothing but joy.

"I don't know just what it was that finally caught and took the joy of this poet and turned him into a poem. He became a fighter; out for a cause; a revolutionist at home here, and in Russia a communist. He didn't smile any more.

"To a poet, to a spirit like Jack Reed, the communist, death in Moscow must have been a vision of the resurrection and the life of man."

Steffens himself caught some of that vision. Sent with William Bullitt by Lloyd George and Wilson to see if the Red leaders would agree to a conference with the Allies, he returned to Paris "bug-eyed with wonder," William Allen White later recalled. "I have seen the future, and it works!" he declared impressively, climaxing his story of the wonders of the new Russia with the exclamation: "Gentlemen, I tell you they have abolished prostitution!" At this point Herbert Bayard Swope of *The World* is reputed to have interjected:

"My God, Steff! What did you do!"

Sergeant Alexander Woollcott Sees Verdun Belle

Find Her Own

ALL HELL had broken loose on the western front, but Sergeant Alexander Woollcott, then correspondent for *Stars and Stripes,* a weekly newspaper by enlisted men for enlisted men, was more interested in his terrific argument with Arthur Ruhl, *Collier's Weekly* war correspondent. Ducking a burst of shellfire, the two men fell flat. While still reclining on his belly, Woollcott turned and said: "I have never heard anything so preposterous. To me Maude Adams as Peter Pan was gay and spirited and altogether charming as the silver star on top of the tree on Christmas morning."

The thirty-one-year-old Woollcott, according to his biographer, Samuel Hopkins Adams, was the least military figure in the A.E.F. "His uniform, soiled, sagging, and corrugated with unexpected bulges, looked as if he had just emerged from the delousing plant. His carriage was grotesque." He went into action with a frying pan strapped around his waist and an old gray shawl across his shoulders.

But from the pen of this obese and myopic, slightly ludicrous, figure came some of the best reporting of World War I. Whether he was discussing a telephone man rigging his wires under fire, a French curé sticking to his nearly destroyed village, "Wild Bill" Donovan, Father Duffy, or the Lost Battalion, Alexander Woollcott invariably got some of his own effervescent enthusiasm into his stories. One of his best reports, produced under high pressure, was the story of Verdun Belle, a mongrel bitch who refused to abandon her platoon.

*Stars and Stripes readers learn of happy
family reunion, human and canine*

Stars and Stripes, June 14, 1918

This is the story of Verdun Belle, a trench dog who adopted a young leatherneck, of how she followed him to the edge of the battle around Château-Thierry, and was waiting for him when they carried him out. It is a true story.

Belle is a setter bitch, shabby white, with great splotches of chocolate brown in her coat. Her ears are brown and silken. Her ancestry is dubious. She is undersize and would not stand a chance among the haughtier breeds they show in splendor at Madison Square Garden back home. But the marines think there never was a dog like her since the world began.

No one in the regiment knows

whence she came, nor why. When she joined the outfit in a sector near Verdun, she singled out one of the privates as her very own and attached herself to him for the duration of the war. The young marine would talk long and earnestly to her, and everyone swore that Belle could "compree" English.

She used to curl up at his feet when he slept, or follow silently to keep him company at the listening post. She would- sit hopefully in front of him whenever he settled down with his laden mess kit, which the cooks always heaped extra-high in honor of Belle.

Belle was as used to war as the most weather-beaten poilu. The tremble of the ground did not disturb her, and the whining whir of the shells overhead only made her twitch and wrinkle her nose in her sleep. She was trench-broken. You could have put a plate of savory pork chops on the parapet, and nothing would have induced her to go up after them.

She weathered many a gas attack. Her master contrived a protection for her by cutting down and twisting a French gas mask. At first this sack over her nose irritated her tremendously, but once, when she was trying to claw it off with her forepaws, she got a whiff of the poisoned air. Then a great light dawned on Belle, and after that, at the first *alerte,* she would race for her mask. You could not have taken it from her until her master's pat on her back told her everything was all right.

In the middle of May, Belle presented a proud but not particularly astonished regiment with nine confused and wriggling puppies, black and white or, like their mother, brown and white, and possessed of incredible appetites. Seven of these were alive and kicking when, not so very many days ago, the order came for the regiment to pull up stakes and speed across France to help stem the German tide north of the troubled Marne.

In the rush and hubbub of marching orders, Belle and her brood were forgotten by everyone but the young marine. It never once entered his head to leave her or her pups behind. Somewhere he found a market basket and tumbled the litter into that. He could carry the pups, he explained, and the mother dog would trot at his heels.

Now the amount of hardware a marine is expected to carry on the march is carefully calculated to the maximum strength of the average soldier, yet this leatherneck found extra muscle somewhere for his precious basket. If it came to the worst, he thought, he could jettison his pack. It was not very clear in his mind what he would do with his charges during a battle, but he trusted to luck and Verdun Belle.

For forty kilometers he carried his burden along the parched French highway. No one wanted to kid him out of it, nor could have if they would. When there followed a long advance by camion, he yielded his place to the basket of wriggling pups, while he himself hung on the tailboard.

But then there was more hiking, and the basket proved too much. It seemed that the battle line was somewhere far off. Solemnly, the young marine killed four of the puppies, discarded the basket, and slipped the other three into his shirt.

Thus he trudged on his way, carrying those three, pouched in forest green, as a kangaroo carries its young, while the mother dog trotted trustingly behind.

One night he found that one of the black and white pups was dead. The road, by this time, was black with hurrying troops, lumbering lorries jostling the line of advancing ambulances, dust-gray columns of soldiers moving on as far ahead and as far behind as the eye could see. Passing silently in the other direction was the desolate procession of refugees from the invaded countryside. Now and then a herd of cows or a little cluster of fugitives from some desolated village, trundling their most cherished possessions in wheelbarrows and baby-carts, would cause an eddy in the traffic.

Somewhere in this congestion and confusion, Belle was lost. In the morning there was no sign of her, and the young marine did not know what to do. He begged a cup of milk from an old Frenchwoman, and with the eye-dropper from his kit he tried to feed the two pups. It did not work very well. Faintly, the veering wind brought down the valley from far ahead the sound of the cannon. Soon he would be in the thick of it, and there was no Belle to care for the pups.

Two ambulances of a field hospital were passing in the unending caravan. A lieutenant who looked human was in the front seat of one of them, a sergeant beside him. The leatherneck ran up to them, blurted out his story, gazed at them imploringly, and thrust the puppies into their hands.

"Take good care of them," he said. "I don't suppose I'll ever see them again."

And he was gone. A little later in the day, that field hospital was pitching its tents and setting up its kitchens and tables in a deserted farm. Amid all the hurry of preparation for the big job ahead, they found time to worry about those pups. The problem was food. Corned willy was tried and found wanting.

Finally, the first sergeant hunted up a farm-bred private, and the two of them spent that evening chasing four nervous and distrustful cows around a pasture, trying vainly to capture enough milk to provide subsistence for the new additions to the personnel.

Next morning the problem was still unsolved. But it was solved that evening.

For that evening a fresh contingent of marines trooped by the farm, and in their wake—tired, anxious, but undiscouraged—was Verdun Belle. Ten kilometers back, two days before, she had lost her master and, until she should find him again, she evidently had thought that any marine was better than none.

The troops did not halt at the farm, but Belle did. At the gate she stopped dead in her tracks, drew in her lolling tongue, sniffed inquiringly the evening air, and like a flash—a white streak along the drive—she raced to the distant tree where, on a pile of discarded dressings in the shade, the pups were sleeping.

All the corps men stopped work and stood around and marveled. For the onlooker it was such a family reunion as warms the heart. For the worried mess sergeant it was a great relief. For the pups it was a mess call, clear and unmistakable.

So, with renewed faith in her heart and only one worry left in her mind, Verdun Belle and her puppies settled down on detached service with this field hospital. When, next day, the reach of the artillery made it advisable that it should move down the valley to the shelter of a fine hillside château, you may be sure that room was made in the first ambulance for the three casuals.

This was the Château of the Guardian Angel, which stands on the right of the Paris-Metz road, just north of

La Ferté as you hike toward Château-Thierry.

In a grove of trees beside the house the tents of the personnel were pitched, and the cots of the expected patients ranged side by side. The wounded came—came hour after hour in steady streams, and the boys of the hospital worked on them night and day. They could not possibly keep track of all the cases, but there was one who did. Always a mistress of the art of keeping out from underfoot, very quietly Belle hung around and investigated each ambulance that turned in from the main road and backed up with its load of pain to the door of the receiving room.

Then one evening they lifted out a young marine, listless in the half stupor of shell shock. To the busy workers he was just Case Number Such-and-Such, but there was no need to tell anyone who saw the wild jubilance of the dog that Belle had found her own again at last.

The first consciousness he had of his new surroundings was the feel of her rough pink tongue licking the dust from his face. And those who passed that way on Sunday last found two cots shoved together in the kindly shade of a spreading tree. On one the mother dog lay contented with her puppies. Fast asleep on the other, his arm thrown out so that one grimy hand could clutch one silken ear, lay the young marine.

Before long they would have to ship him on to the evacuation hospital, on from there to the base hospital, on and on and on. It was not very clear to anyone how another separation could be prevented. It was a perplexing question, but they knew in their hearts they could safely leave the answer to someone else. They could leave it to Verdun Belle.

Stephen Bonsal Beards the Wounded
Tiger in His Lair

THE PEACE CONFERENCE in Paris at the end of World War I proved to be a three-ringed circus of colliding temperaments. Woodrow Wilson, the idol of Europe and its moral conscience, was politically the loneliest man in the City of Light. Aloof, imperious, at odds even with his closest advisers, he was continually outgeneraled by Clemenceau and Lloyd George, who resorted to the transparent trick of yielding on the most preposterous propositions, which they never intended to win, and then extracting concessions from the American President because of their "conciliatory" attitude.

Père de la Victoire, Georges Clemenceau was president of the conference and its most persistent gadfly. The Tiger was then seventy-eight years old, a survivor of that French generation which had been roundly beaten by Bismarck's Prussia and never forgot it. A veteran of the Paris Commune of 1871 and a defender of Dreyfus, he had earned the name "Tiger" for his tooth-and-nail fight against injustice. Clemenceau's tremendous love of country was matched only by his fierce hatred for Germany, which he wanted punished as "a uniquely sinful nation." Making no bones about France's peace aims, Clemenceau declared: "The greater the sanguinary catastrophe which devastated and ruined the richest regions of France, the more ample and more splendid shall be the reparation." He demanded that after his death he be buried "standing up marching toward Germany." The idealism of Wilson frankly bored him. Of Wilson's Fourteen Points he said: "Wilson has Fourteen; the Good Lord himself had only Ten."

Between the two giants stood the diminutive wizard from Wales, Lloyd George. What he lacked in technical equipment he more than made up for in shrewdness. "What am I to do between a man who thinks he is Jesus Christ and another who thinks he is Napoleon?"

On February 19, 1919, Clemenceau was shot by a man named Cotton as he was leaving his house on the Rue Franklin for a conference with Balfour and House at the Crillon. Seven shots were fired at close quarters, but only one took effect. This bullet, which lodged close to vital organs, was never extracted and caused Clemenceau great pain for the remaining ten years of his life. The Tiger refused to dignify the incident as an attempt at assassination and spoke of it as an "accident." At the preliminary hearing of the would-be assassin, he testified:

> When I think of the men who are continually sniping at me from ambush, I am tempted to say that this brave fellow who faced my walking stick with nothing in the

way of a weapon save a machine-gun revolver should have conferred upon him some prize of valor, some Grand Cross or other. But I must not be impulsive; the women and children and all the innocent bystanders who might have been hurt while the fellow was aiming at my miserable old carcass should be considered. Then his poor marksmanship must be taken into account. We have just won the most terrible war in history, yet here is a Frenchman who at point-blank range misses his target six times out of seven. Of course the fellow must be punished for the careless use of a dangerous weapon and for poor marksmanship. I suggest that he be locked up for about eight years, with intensive training in a shooting gallery.*

This story and the account that follows are from Stephen Bonsal's *Unfinished Business* (1944), a diary of the Peace Conference, awarded the 1944 Pulitzer Prize in history. Colonel Bonsal, an ace correspondent, who was whisked by Colonel House from a damp cellar on the western front to the Peace Conference, served as an official aide and interpreter. His journal is invaluable eyewitness reporting of the peacemaking after World War I.

"I have lived in a world where it was good form to shoot a democrat"

From *Unfinished Business*, by Stephen Bonsal. Copyright, 1944, reprinted by permission of Doubleday and Company, Inc.

I accompanied Colonel House to his [Clemenceau's] lair in the Rue Franklin, named after our Benjamin. The Tiger was seated in an armchair because his wound does not permit him to lie down. He was wrapped in an old army blanket, and the same unchanged foulard was twisted around his neck. He had on his characteristic skullcap and gray gloves. He was as gay as a cricket and announced that he would attend the meeting of the Council on Monday, although no one, least of all the worried doctors, thinks he will be able to do so. When House mentioned the opinion of the medicos the Tiger roared with laughter: "They are a gang of jackasses!" he shouted, "and who knows this better than I? Was I not a member of their gang for

twenty years? Listen, *mes amis,* to a frank confession: I am responsible for many crimes, indeed for downright murders. Not in war, as many suppose, but in the piping days of peace, during the years I practiced what they call the healing art, in Montmartre."

He drew the Colonel to him and went on in English: "The slogan now is full speed ahead. As I cannot lie down since that madman shot me [the *attentat* took place three days before], I just naturally will not let anybody else lie down. I shall insist upon a little speed being turned on. I am confident that if we 'Americans' and the British and French would only get together we could push through the Peace Treaty with Germany in a very few days and then we would be at

* Cotton was later given a sentence of ten years in prison.

liberty to take up the arrangements with Austria, Turkey, and the Bulgars —and those fellows should not detain us for long."

Unfortunately at this moment Signor Sonnino burst into the room and began to talk about Italy's claims, which he feared could not be properly formulated until we could see the situation more clearly. Here the Tiger groaned and for the first time admitted he was in pain. To me he whispered, "It feels like an Italian stiletto," and then he turned and began to tease his patient and adoring nurse, Sister Théoneste, with his bizarre views on heaven and hell.

In the following ten days I was sent by Colonel House, during the absence of Mr. Wilson in America the ranking member of our delegation, almost every evening to lay before M. Clemenceau the developments of the day and to receive any communications he might care to make to his fellow negotiators. The Tiger had turned the sickroom topsy-turvy with his eccentricities. To the complaining sisters who nursed him with such devotion, he had an answer that turned away their wrath:

"Before the 'accident' I was only a tired old patient and had to knuckle under; now I'm a martyr, and you've got to put up with me."

One of these eccentricities was to sleep from nine in the evening until midnight; then, bright as a button, he was ready for business, and despite the protest of the doctors, his sickroom was thronged.

"I must make a peace," said M. Clemenceau to me in one of these midnight sessions, "based upon my belief and upon my own experience of the world in which we have to live. My responsibility is personal and nontransferable. When called to the

bar of history, I cannot say, 'Well, I made these arrangements to conform to Mr. Wilson's viewpoint.' *Mr. Wilson has lived in a world that has been fairly safe for democracy; I have lived in a world where it was good form to shoot a democrat.* After a few weeks of sparring I became convinced that your President wanted the same things that I did, although we were very far apart as to the ways and the means by which we could reach the desired end.

"When he first developed his program, it seemed to me perfectly Utopian. I said to him, 'Mr. Wilson, if I accepted what you propose as ample for the security of France, after the millions who have died and the millions who have suffered, I believe, and indeed I hope, that my successor in office would take me by the nape of the neck and have me shot at daylight before the donjon of Vincennes.' After that we began to get together.

"Once I said to him, 'Mr. Wilson, have you ever seen an elephant cross a swinging bamboo bridge?' Mr. Wilson said he had not. 'Well, I'll tell you how he goes about it. First, he trots down into the stream to see if the foundations are all right; then he comes back and puts one foot on the bridge. If the result is reassuring, he ventures its mate. Then he gives the bridge a sharp jolt. If it stands that, he gives it his trust and advances. Now that's my idea about your bridge leading to the new Jerusalem. I may be, as they say I am, a springing tiger where my personal fortunes are concerned, but where the safety of France is at stake —well, there never was an elephant more careful or more cautious than I am going to be.'

"I never said, as widely reported" (the Paris papers were filled with suggestions to this effect at the time), insisted Clemenceau in my talk with him this evening [February 28], "that Wilson was pro-German, but I did think and I probably said, as I generally say what I think, that many of his plans and proposals were unduly and most unwisely helpful to the Germans in their present and unregenerate state. I confess that from my first cable contact with it Wilsonism alarmed me, and that is why on the eve of the conference I announced in the Chamber, '*It will be more difficult to make peace than it was to make war.*' Now who can deny that in peacemaking France is meeting with great opposition from all her Allies who were so noble and considerate while the battle was on? During the long war years we sustained the heaviest losses, we suffered the most, and now what is our fate at the conference?

"We are blocked in our plea for security; only our undoubted claim to Alsace goes uncontested. For the little else we may obtain we shall have to fight and fight hard. I mean to do that very thing, and Wilson knows it. There is one bright spot in the dark prospect. Wilson is as frank with me as I am with him. We have both placed our cards on the peace table."

There is, it is true, one criticism of Mr. Wilson to which M. Clemenceau often returns, as indeed he did today, which seems to me not without foundation. "I told your President that, in my judgment, the grave fault of his attitude is that he eliminated sentiment and endeavored to efface all memory of the past. A grave, a very grave fault it seems to me. It was then I would say, 'I am the last, the only survivor of the Protest of Bordeaux—against the infamy of the treaty that the Prussians imposed at the point of the bayonet. M. le Président, I speak for our glorious dead who fell in the two wars. For myself I can hold my tongue, but not for them.' "

In one of the many rude discussions that took place between the Tiger and Lloyd George, Mr. Wilson, the Presbyterian elder, was by many accounts compelled to intervene to prevent the fisticuffs that seemed imminent. As he retired to his corner, the little Welshman said: "Well! I shall expect an apology for these outrageous words."

"You shall wait for it as long as you wait for the pacification of Ireland," was the hot reply.

Only one thing at this moment can be vouched for as certain, and that is that the relations between the Entente Powers and their chiefs, consecrated by the death of millions of youths, are strained; indeed, they are near the breaking point.

* * *

DESPITE CONSTANT FRICTION between the four major Allied Powers at the Paris Conference, a treaty was finally agreed upon, to which a protesting German delegation affixed its signature in the Hall of Mirrors at Versailles on June 28, 1919. For both Clemenceau and Wilson the treaty-making marked the climax of their political careers and the zenith of their reputations.

Wilson was heartsick over the compromises in the Versailles Treaty. Embittered by "the little group of willful men" in the Senate led by Henry Cabot Lodge, who wanted to amend that document, Wilson, on September 3, 1918, set out from Washington to carry his case to the people. On September 25 he delivered his fortieth speech at Pueblo, Colorado, where he was given a great ovation. That night he collapsed. His face drooped on one side; his left arm and leg were paralyzed for a time. Rushed back to Washington, he carried on the battle for the treaty from his sickroom in the White House. No Republican reservations were acceptable to him. It had to be the League of Nations, or nothing. The Senate chose the latter alternative. No better summation of Wilson's place in history has ever been penned than William Allen White's four-line epitaph:

> God gave him a great vision
> The Devil gave him an imperious heart
> The proud heart is still
> The vision lives

Clemenceau found the French people similarly lacking in gratitude. Intense French nationalists considered the Treaty of Versailles as much too moderate. The voters rejected the Tiger when he ran for the presidency of the republic in 1920, preferring Paul Deschanel, and Clemenceau soon heard himself called, not *Père de la Victoire,* but *Perd la Victoire!* (Loser of the Victory).

Ben Hecht Makes Chicago Front Page with His Story of Carl Wanderer, Who Was Glad That He Killed the "Ragged Stranger"

NEWSPAPER WRITING, as the late Henry Justin Smith once told a class in journalism, "is hard, and it grinds your brains to powder. You don't burn yourself up, though. You get hardened like steel. And your literary style becomes like steel, too." To the man who gets his biggest kick out of writing, making the front page is the stuff of life. "Talk about your fiction!" said Carl Sandburg. "Man, that first page today has human stuff on it that puts novels in the discard."

One of the men who made the front page was Ben Hecht—newspaperman, author, scenarist, playwright. Born in New York City on February 28, 1893, Hecht as a young man turned his eyes westward. Proud of his uncle who was a strong man in a circus, young Hecht spent his summer vacations touring the West as an acrobat in a small circus. He got his first newspaper job on the *Chicago Journal* in 1910, and four years later was off on a brilliant career in the fabled local room of the *Chicago Daily News*. In 1918 he represented the *Daily News* in Berlin, returning in 1919 to begin a daily short column, stories later collected as *A Thousand and One Afternoons in Chicago*. Again and again Hecht showed an uncanny ability to picture the strange jumble of events in strokes as vivid and touching as the brushmarks of a novelist. His vitality and roaring gusto made him a legend in the newsrooms of the nation. "He is short and stubby," said Henry F. Pringle, "with sharp blue-gray eyes and stringy black hair. He looks tough. He is."

Chicago in the early twenties was noted for the existence of the multimillionaire Al Capone, ten thousand speakeasies, Thompson submachine guns and sawed-off shotguns, and an epidemic of gangland killings such as no civilized modern city had ever seen before or since. It was perfect territory for the talents of Ben Hecht. One of his best stories was a front-page report of one of the most famous murders in the history of Chicago—the case of the ragged stranger.

At first it was just another murder that called for a single sentence of comment over morning coffee. A young war veteran, Carl Oscar Wanderer, had returned home to Chicago, married his childhood sweetheart, and gone to work in his father's butchershop. The first news reports told how, on the evening of June 21, 1920, Wanderer had taken his young wife to the Pershing Theater to see *The Sea Wolf*. On the way home the couple had been followed by a ragged young gunman who attempted a holdup in the vestibule of the Wanderer home. In true cinema style, the war veteran drew his gun and shot it out with the holdup man. In the scuffle, the bride was fatally wounded. Wanderer was still pumping bullets into the already dead body of the gunman when a policeman, attracted by the noise, arrived on the scene.

The coroner's jury, which brought in a verdict against John Doe, the unknown tramp, made it a special point to express its condolences to Wanderer on the loss of his wife and also to congratulate him for his red-blooded courage in snuffing out the life of a menace to society. But in the meantime, the *Chicago Daily News,* sniffing a story, sent young Ben Hecht to interview the hero. Hecht's report, according to John Craig, his city editor at the time, was the best Hecht story of the old days. "It carried no by-line," said Clem Lane, current city editor of the *Daily News.* "In that era of the newspaper business, by-lines were few and far between."

"Well, I got him. I got him anyway"

Chicago Daily News, June 22, 1920

Carl Wanderer, freshly shaved and his brown suit neatly pressed, stood looking over the back porch of his home at 4732 North Campbell Avenue. His wife, who was murdered last night by a holdup man in the doorway downstairs, lay in their bedroom.

Wanderer looked at his gold watch, and his hand was steady. He smiled blankly at the back porches in front of him and, with his eyes grown cold, repeated, "Well, I got him. I got him anyway."

At two o'clock this afternoon there are scheduled two inquests, one over the body of Mrs. Carl Wanderer and the other over the body of the stickup man. Wanderer, standing two feet away from the man who had killed his wife, opened fire with his .45.

Last October Wanderer was discharged from service as a first lieutenant. He came back from France with a *Croix de guerre* and a DSC. He had for a year been the best pistol shot in his battalion—the 17th machine-gun battalion.

Campbell Avenue is a quiet, snug neighborhood, and in the morning children play under the trees in the back yards. Wanderer, putting his gold watch back in his pocket, went on talking in a quiet, tense voice.

"The first shot blew him across the hallway," he said. "Then I couldn't see him. But I knew where he'd landed and I let him have three more. I got him but——"

The machine gunner and owner of a *Croix de guerre* stopped talking, and a young husband in a brown suit with eyes reddened from tears finished the sentence. "If I'd only gotten him sooner. Just a nickel's worth sooner."

Later the husband said, "There isn't much to tell. We'd been to a movie and this man followed us, I suppose. I was going to turn on the light in the vestibule so as to see the keyhole, when I heard a voice, 'Don't

turn on the light.' I reached for my
gun. I knew what the fellow was up
to. But he got cold feet. He never
asked us to put our hands up, but
began shooting right off the bat. I was
a few seconds late. I don't know why.
But I got him. He got what was coming to him."

Outside, neighbors sat on their
sunny porch steps and stared at the
house at 4732. The street was again
quiet and peaceful, as if tragedy had
never visited it. A gray hearse motored
up in front of the address, and the
neighbors discussed the life of the
couple as it had been before last night.
One of them said, "She told me only
yesterday she was going to be a
mother, and was so happy."

Through a card found in the clothes
of the assailant he was tentatively
identified at the hospital as Edward

Masters, who, the police say, is a well-
known slugger and gunman. The card
bore the name of the John Robinson
circus and indicated that he had at
one time been an employee of the
commissary department of the circus.
He also wore a newspaper driver's
badge, which bore the number 706.

Captain Michael Evans of the
bureau of identification made an effort
to identify the dead slayer of Mrs.
Wanderer through fingerprints. He
said later, however, that the prints did
not correspond with any on record. It
is thought the man was an ex-convict,
but that he came here from another
city. The manager of the circulation
department of a morning paper
viewed the man and said that he believed he had formerly been employed
on a wagon driven by one of the newspaper's employees.

THIS WAS ONLY Part I of an unfinished story. In fulfilling his assignment,
Hecht had gone straight to Wanderer's home, where he was astonished to
find the bereaved husband, on the morning after the murder of his wife,
seemingly unconcerned. During the interview Hecht conceived a strong dislike for Wanderer, and something of his feeling found its way between the
lines of his brief story. The police either caught the hint or came to their own
conclusions, for in short order they proved that both guns found at the
murder scene had been in Wanderer's possession the day before.

Wanderer soon broke down under searching questioning and confessed
that he had killed not only the ragged stranger but also his pregnant wife.
It seems that the war hero, preferring the more interesting life of a lieutenant in the army, was in deadly fear of the bonds of domesticity. He had
picked up the first likely-looking tramp he could find on the street, convincing him that his wife carried a roll of bills big enough to choke a horse,
and together they had planned the bogus holdup. What finally trapped
Wanderer were the usual murderer's mistakes—bringing two guns, both
of which could be traced to him, and then using only one to shoot both his
wife and the tramp.

"When tried for the murder of his wife," wrote Alexander Woollcott, the
connoisseur of juicy crimes, "Wanderer was defended by foxy lawyers who
were capable of maintaining in one breath that the confession had been
extracted by brute force, that Wanderer was crazy as a coot, and anyway
it had all been done by a couple of other fellows." The jury found Wan-

derer guilty of the murder of his wife, but limited the penalty. A second, and considerably tougher, jury found him guilty of slaying the ragged stranger and condemned him to death.

Wanderer's behavior pattern of bravado and scorn persisted to the end. On the gallows he sang a popular song loudly as the noose was being adjusted over his head. This stimulated Alexander Woollcott to a whimsical conclusion for a sordid tale: "From one of the crowd of reporters watching the execution came the audible comment that Wanderer deserved hanging for his voice alone."

Warrior's Requiem

AMERICA IN 1921, convalescing from the storms and stresses of World War I, was like a suddenly liberated vacationist, feverishly turning to new fads, playthings, trivialities, and scandals, anything to forget the recent blood bath and all its horrors. But in the midst of the cacophony of gin parties the entire nation paused to pay reverent tribute to its Unknown Soldier. The body arrived home from France on Admiral Dewey's old flagship, to be received with solemn ceremonies at the Capitol, an impressive military funeral, and entombment at Arlington National Cemetery.

This outpouring of the national heart was witnessed and well reported by many newsmen in Washington. But Kirke Larue Simpson, a native of San Francisco and a member of the Washington staff of the Associated Press, surpassed his colleagues with a magnificent series of day and night reports on November 9, 10, and 11, 1921, for which he was awarded the 1922 Pulitzer Prize in reporting. Simpson himself knew something of war: he had served with the First California Volunteer Infantry in the Philippine campaigns during the Spanish-American War and the Philippine Insurrection, 1898–99. In stately prose he described the preparations to receive the body and the final services when the unknown warrior was laid to rest in a majestic shrine among the quiet hills of Arlington. The third of his famous articles: "BUGLES SOUND TAPS FOR WARRIOR'S REQUIEM," reprinted here, was the number-one favorite reportorial piece of newsmen and teachers of journalism polled by the editors of this book.

Kirke L. Simpson: "America's unknown dead from France sleeps tonight"

The Associated Press, November 9, 10, 11, 1921

Under the wide and starry skies of his own homeland America's unknown dead from France sleeps tonight, a soldier home from the wars.

Alone, he lies in the narrow cell of stone that guards his body; but his soul has entered into the spirit that is America. Wherever liberty is held close in men's hearts, the honor and the glory and the pledge of high endeavor poured out over this nameless one of fame will be told and sung by Americans for all time.

Scrolled across the marble arch of the memorial raised to American soldier and sailor dead, everywhere, which stands like a monument behind his tomb, runs this legend: "We here highly resolve that these dead shall not have died in vain."

The words were spoken by the martyred Lincoln over the dead at Gettysburg. And today with voice strong with determination and ringing with deep emotion, another President echoed that high resolve over the coffin of the soldier who died for the flag in France.

Great men in the world's affairs heard that high purpose reiterated by the man who stands at the head of the American people. Tomorrow they will gather in the city that stands almost in the shadow of the new American shrine of liberty dedicated today. They will talk of peace; of the curbing of the havoc of war.

They will speak of the war in France, that robbed this soldier of life and name and brought death to comrades of all nations by the hundreds of thousands. And in their ears when they meet must ring President Harding's declaration today beside that flag-wrapped, honor-laden bier:

"There must be, there shall be, the commanding voice of a conscious civilization against armed warfare."

Far across the seas, other unknown dead, hallowed in memory by their countrymen, as this American soldier is enshrined in the heart of America, sleep their last. He, in whose veins ran the blood of British forebears, lies beneath a great stone in ancient Westminster Abbey; he of France, beneath the Arc de Triomphe, and he of Italy under the altar of the fatherland in Rome.

And it seemed today that they, too, must be here among the Potomac hills to greet an American comrade come to join their glorious company, to testify their approval of the high words of hope spoken by America's President. All day long the nation poured out its heart in pride and glory for the nameless American. Before the first

crash of the minute guns roared its knell for the dead from the shadow of Washington Monument, the people who claim him as their own were trooping out to do him honor. They lined the long road from the Capitol to the hillside where he sleeps tonight; they flowed like a tide over the slopes about his burial place; they choked the bridges that lead across the river to the fields of the brave, in which he is the last comer.

As he was carried past through the banks of humanity that lined Pennsylvania Avenue a solemn, reverent hush held the living walls. Yet there was not so much of sorrow as of high pride in it all, a pride beyond the reach of shouting and the clamor that marks less sacred moments in life.

Out there in the broad avenue was a simple soldier, dead for honor of the flag. He was nameless. No man knew what part in the great life of the nation he had filled when last he passed over his home soil. But in France he had died as Americans always have been ready to die, for the flag and what it means. They read the message of the pageant clear, these silent thousands along the way. They stood in almost holy awe to take their own part in what was theirs, the glory of the American people, honored here in the honors showered on America's nameless son from France.

Soldiers, sailors, and marines—all played their part in the thrilling spectacles as the cortege rolled along. And just behind the casket, with its faded French flowers on the draped flag, walked the President, the chosen leader of a hundred million, in whose name he was chief mourner at his bier. Beside him strode the man under whom the fallen hero had lived and died in France, General Pershing, wearing only the single medal of Victory that every American soldier might wear as his only decoration.

Then, row on row, came the men who lead the nation today or have guided its destinies before. They were all there, walking proudly, with age and frailties of the flesh forgotten. Judges, Senators, Representatives, highest officers of every military arm of government, and a trudging little group of the nation's most valorous sons, the Medal of Honor men. Some were gray and bent and drooping with old wounds; some trim and erect as the day they won their way to fame. All walked gladly in this nameless comrade's last parade.

Behind these came the carriage in which rode Woodrow Wilson, also stricken down by infirmities as he served in the highest place of the nation, just as the humble private riding in such state ahead had gone down before a shell or bullet. For that dead man's sake, the former President had put aside his dread of seeming to parade his physical weakness and risked health, perhaps life, to appear among the mourners for the fallen.

There was handclapping and a cheer here and there for the man in the carriage, a tribute to the spirit that brought him to honor the nation's nameless hero, whose commander-in-chief he had been.

After President Harding and most of the high dignitaries of the government had turned aside at the White House, the procession, headed by its solid blocks of soldiery and the battalions of sailor comrades, moved on with Pershing, now flanked by Secretaries Weeks and Denby, for the long road to the tomb. It marched on, always between the human borders of the way of victory the nation had made for itself of the great avenue; on over the old bridge that spans the

Potomac, on up the long hill to Fort Myer, and at last to the great cemetery beyond, where soldier and sailor folk sleep by the thousands. There the lumbering guns of the artillery swung aside, the cavalry drew their horses out of the long line and left to the foot soldiers and the sailors and marines the last stage of the journey.

Ahead, the white marble of the amphitheater gleamed through the trees. It stands crowning the slope of the hills that sweep upward from the river, and just across was Washington, its clustered buildings and monuments to great dead who have gone before, a moving picture in the autumn haze.

People in thousands were moving about the great circle of the amphitheater. The great ones to whom places had been given in the sacred enclosure and the plain folk who had trudged the long way just to glimpse the pageant from afar, were finding their places. Everywhere within the pillared enclosure bright uniforms of foreign soldiers appeared. They were laden with the jeweled order of rank to honor an American private soldier, great in the majesty of his sacrifices; in the tribute his honors paid to all Americans who died.

Down below the platform placed for the casket, in a stone vault, lay wreaths and garlands brought from England's King and guarded by British soldiers. To them came the British Ambassador in the full uniform of his rank to bid them keep these tributes from overseas safe against that hour.

Above the platform gathered men whose names ring through history —Briand, Foch, Beatty, Balfour, Jacques, Diaz, and others—in a brilliant array of place and power. They were followed by others, Baron Kato from Japan, the Italian statesmen and officers, by the notables from all countries gathered here for tomorrow's conference, and by some of the older figures in American life too old to walk beside the approaching funeral train.

Down around the circling pillars the marbled box filled with distinguished men and women, with a cluster of shattered men from army hospitals, accompanied by uniformed nurses. A surpliced choir took its place to wait the dead.

Faint and distant, the silvery strains of a military band stole into the big white bowl of the amphitheater. The slow cadences and mourning notes of a funeral march grew clearer amid the roll and mutter of the muffled drums.

At the arch where the choir awaited the heroic dead, comrades lifted his casket down and, followed by the generals and the admirals, who had walked beside him from the Capitol, he was carried to the place of honor. Ahead moved the white-robed singers, chanting solemnly. Carefully, the casket was placed above the banked flowers, and the Marine Band played sacred melodies until the moment the President and Mrs. Harding stepped to their places beside the casket; then the crashing, triumphant chords of *The Star-Spangled Banner* swept the gathering to its feet again.

A prayer, carried out over the crowd by amplifiers so that no word was missed, took a moment or two, then the sharp, clear call of the bugle rang "Attention!" and for two minutes the nation stood at pause for the dead, just at high noon. No sound broke the quiet as all stood with bowed heads. It was much as though a mighty hand had checked the world in full course. Then the band sounded, and in a mighty chorus rolled up the words of *America* from the hosts within and

without the great open hall of valor.

President Harding stepped forward beside the coffin to say for America the thing that today was nearest to the nation's heart, that sacrifices such as this nameless man, fallen in battle, might perhaps be made unnecessary down through the coming years. Every word that President Harding spoke reached every person through the amplifiers and reached other thousands upon thousands in New York and San Francisco.

Mr. Harding showed strong emotion as his lips formed the last words of the address. He paused, then with raised hand and head bowed, went on in the measured, rolling periods of the Lord's Prayer. The response that came back to him from the thousands he faced, from the other thousands out over the slopes beyond, perhaps from still other thousands away near the Pacific, or close-packed in the heart of the nation's greatest city, arose like a chant. The marble arches hummed with the solemn sound.

Then the foreign officers who stand highest among the soldiers or sailors of their flags came one by one to the bier to place gold and jeweled emblems for the brave above the breast of the sleeper. Already, as the great prayer ended, the President had set the American seal of admiration for the valiant, the nation's love for brave deeds and the courage that defies death, upon the casket.

Side by side he laid the Medal of Honor and the Distinguished Service Cross. And below, set in place with reverent hands, grew the long line of foreign honors, the Victoria Cross, never before laid on the breast of any but those who had served the British flag; all the highest honors of France and Belgium and Italy and Rumania and Czechoslovakia and Poland.

To General Jacques of Belgium it remained to add his own touch to these honors. He tore from the breast of his own tunic the medal of valor pinned there by the Belgian King, tore it with a sweeping gesture, and tenderly bestowed it on the unknown American warrior.

Through the religious services that followed, and prayers, the swelling crowd sat motionless until it rose to join in the old, consoling *Rock of Ages,* and the last rite for the dead was at hand. Lifted by his hero-bearers from the stage, the unknown was carried in his flag-wrapped, simple coffin out to the wide sweep of the terrace. The bearers laid the sleeper down above the crypt, on which had been placed a little of the soil of France. The dust his blood helped redeem from alien hands will mingle with his dust as time marches by.

The simple words of the burial ritual were said by Bishop Brent; flowers from war mothers of America and England were laid in place.

For the Indians of America Chief Plenty Coos came to call upon the Great Spirit of the Red Men, with gesture and chant and tribal tongue, that the dead should not have died in vain, that war might end, peace be purchased by such blood as this. Upon the casket he laid the coupstick of his tribal office and the feathered war bonnet from his own head. Then the casket, with its weight of honors, was lowered into the crypt.

A rocking blast of gunfire rang from the woods. The glittering circle of bayonets stiffened to a salute to the dead. Again the guns shouted their message of honor and farewell. Again they boomed out; a loyal comrade was being laid to his last, long rest.

High and clear and true in the echoes of the guns, a bugle lifted the old, old notes of taps, the lullaby for the living soldier, in death his requiem. Long ago some forgotten soldier-poet caught its meaning clear and set it down that soldiers everywhere might know its message as they sink to rest:

> *Fades the light;*
> *And afar*
> *Goeth day, cometh night,*
> *And a star,*
> *Leadeth all, speedeth all,*
> *To their rest.*

The guns roared out again in the national salute. He was home, The Unknown, to sleep forever among his own.

WHILE AGREEING that Kirke Simpson's report was "one of the classics of modern journalism," Herbert Bayard Swope reminded the editors of another masterpiece inspired by the same occasion, one less informative, to be sure, but with more depth, written in a larger focus. H. G. Wells' story of the ceremonies at Arlington appeared in Mr. Swope's *World* on November 12, 1921, appropriately, too, the day of the opening of the Disarmament Conference, which Wells was covering for *The World* and *The Chicago Tribune.* "A great story," Mr. Swope conceded. "It had to be, considering the astounding cost per word we had to pay for it!"

H. G. Wells: "Poor Hans and poor Ivan lie rotting yet"

New York *World*, November 12, 1921

Britain, France, and Italy and now the people of the United States have honored and buried the bodies of certain Unknown Soldiers, each according to their national traditions and circumstances. Canada, I hear, is to follow suit.

So the world expresses its sense that in the Great War the only hero was the common man. Poor Hans and poor Ivan lie rotting yet under the soil of a hundred battlefields, bones, and decay, rags of soiled uniform, and fragments of accouterments, still waiting for monuments and speeches, yet they too were mother's sons, kept step, obeyed orders, went singing into battle, and knew the strange intoxication of soldierly fellowship and the sense of devotion to something much greater than themselves.

In Arlington Cemetery soldiers of the Confederate South lie honored equally with the Federal dead, the right or wrong of their cause altogether forgotten and only their sacrifice remembered. A time will come when we shall cease to visit the crimes and blunders and misfortunes of their governments upon the common soldiers and poor folk of Germany and Russia, when our bitterness will die out and we shall mourn them as we mourn our own, as souls who gave their lives and suffered greatly in the universal misfortune.

A time will come when these vast personifications of conflict, the Unknown British Soldier, the Unknown American Soldier, the Unknown French soldier, etc., will merge into that of a still greater personality, the embodiment of 20,000,000 separate bodies and many million broken lives, the Unknown Soldier of the Great War.

It would be possible, I suppose, to work out many things concerning him. We could probably find out his age and his height and suchlike particulars very nearly. We could average figures and estimates that would fix such matters within a very narrow range of uncertainty. In race and complexion, I suppose he would be mainly North European; North Russian, German, Frankish, North Italian, British, and American elements would all have the same trends towards a tallish, fairish, possibly blue-eyed type; but also there would be a strong Mediterranean streak in him, Indian and Turkish elements, a fraction of Mongolian, and an infusion of African blood—brought in not only through the American colored troops but by the free use by the French of their Senegalese.

None of these factors would be strong enough to prevent his being mainly Northern and much the same mixture altogether as the American citizen of 1950 is likely to be. He would be a white man with a touch of Asia and a touch of color. And he would be young—I should guess about twenty-one or twenty-two—still boyish, probably unmarried rather than married, with a father and mother alive and with the memories and imaginations of the home he was born in still fresh and vivid in his mind when he died. We could even, I suppose, figure in general terms how he died. He was struck in daylight amid the strange noises and confusion of a modern battlefield by something out of the unknown—bullet, shell fragment, or the like. At the moment he had been just a little scared—everyone is a little scared on a battlefield—but much more excited than scared and trying hard to remember his training and do his job properly. When he was hit he was not so much hurt at first as astonished. I should guess that the first sensation of a man hard hit on a battlefield is not so much pain as an immense chagrin.

I suppose it would be possible to go on and work out how long it was before he died after he was hit, how long he suffered and wondered, how long he lay before his ghost fell in with that immense still muster in the shades, those millions of his kind who had no longer country to serve nor years of life before them, who had been cut off as he had been cut off suddenly from sights and sounds and hopes and passions. But rather let us think of the motives and feelings that had brought him, in so gallant and cheerful a frame of mind, to this complete sacrifice.

What did the Unknown Soldier of the Great War think he was doing when he died? . . . He was still too young a man to have his motives very clear. . . . I cannot imagine many English boys using their last breath to say "Rule Britannia!" or "King George for Merry England!" Some of our young men swore out of vexation and fretted; some, and it was not always the youngest, became childish again and cried touchingly for their mothers; many maintained the ironical flippancy of our people to the end; many died in the vein of a young

miner from Durham with whom I talked one morning in the trenches near Martinpuich, trenches which had been badly "strafed" overnight. War, he said, was a beastly job, "but we've got to clean this up." That is the spirit. I believe that was far nearer to the true mind of the Unknown Soldier than any tinpot *viva*ing of any flag, nation, or empire whatever.

I believe that when we generalize the motives that took the youth who died in the Great War out of the light of life and took them out at precisely the age when life is most desirable, we shall find the dominant purpose was certainly no narrow devotion to the "glory" or "expansion" of any particular country but a wide-spirited hostility to wrong and oppression. . . .

So far as the common men in every belligerent country went, the war was a war against wrong, against force, against war itself. Whatever it was in the thoughts of the diplomatists, it was that in the minds of the boys who died. In the minds of the young and generous millions, who are personified in the Unknown Soldier of the Great War, in the minds of the Germans and Russians who fought so stoutly, quite as much as the Americans, British, French, or Italians, the war *was a war to end war.*

And that marks our obligation.

Every speech that is made beside the graves of these Unknown Soldiers who die now in the comradeship of youthful death, every speech which exalts patriotism above peace, which hints at reparations and revenges, which cries for mean alliances to sustain the tradition of the conflict, which exalts national security over the common welfare, which wags the "glorious flag" of this nation or that in the face of the universal courage and tragedy of mankind is an insult and an outrage upon the dead youth who lies below. He sought justice and law in the world as he conceived these things, and whoever approaches his resting place unprepared to serve the establishment of a world law and world justice, breathes the vulgar cants and catchwords of a patriotism outworn and of conflicts that he died to end, commits a monstrous sacrilege and sins against all mankind.

* * *

"A BEASTLY JOB, but we've got to clean this up." How accurately that epitomizes H. G. Wells' own attitude toward war and the future of mankind. At the end of a year of extensive newspaper work—fifty-two articles in twelve months—Wells summarized his credo: "I do believe there is a better life for such creatures as we are, and betterment for our race and an escape from the meanness, the dullness, the petty doomed life of this time." "My imagination," he added, "takes refuge from the slums of today in a world like a great garden, various, orderly, lovingly cared for, dangerous still but no longer dismal, secure from dull and base necessities." Through extension of the scientific spirit and through social and economic reconstruction, Wells felt such a world to be attainable. "To live under the rule of King George or President Coolidge and under the sway of current customs, habits, and usages can be made tolerable by the recognition of their essential transitoriness and their ultimate insignificance. And in no other way can it be made tolerable to anyone with a sense of beauty and a passion for real living," was Wells' parting thought.

A Passionate Little Frenchman with Bald Head and Assyrianlike Beard Goes into the Business of Murder for Profit

"THE CAREER OF Henri Désiré Landru," wrote Webb Miller, "reads like a tale from the Middle Ages. He was perhaps the most monstrous criminal character of modern annals."

Born in Paris in 1865, Landru was the son of a respectable businessman who became insane in later life and committed suicide. As a youth Henri was *"un petit garçon, très doux, très timide et très caressant."* But this shy, sweet little lad developed into an impudent swindler and eventually into a multiple murderer. At the outbreak of World War I he hit upon the idea of wholesale love-making as a lucrative business. Using the time-tested method of matrimonial advertisements, he came into contact with hundreds of women whose husbands had been killed or were at the front. These lonely women enjoyed the violent love-making of the passionate little man with the remarkably shaped bald head and Assyrianlike beard. His method consisted of exaggerated flattery and attentiveness. To middle-aged women with sagging breasts, dyed hair, and wrinkled cheeks he wrote letters singing praises to their "wonderful hair" and "seductive eyes." His own eyes, large and serpentlike, had an uncanny attraction for women. In his murder villa, ready for instant use, he had an extensive collection of love letters carefully filed.

During the five years of an active career of murder, Landru maintained a separate home for his wife and son. A good husband and family man, he provided well for his little family. He explained his absences at the murder scene—Villa Gambais—by saying that he was out of Paris "on business trips."

Eventually the police caught up with the middle-aged Lothario and his wholesale business of seduction and murder. The lover of some two hundred and eighty-three women, Landru had hacked ten of his thirteen "fiancées" to pieces and had burned their bodies piecemeal in his cookstove in Villa Gambais. Dr. Paul, the celebrated criminologist, produced two hundred and fifty-six fragments of human bones from the stove, of which he declared one hundred and forty-seven to be fragments of human skulls. Experts found that soot in the chimney of the villa contained a high element of fat.

William Bolitho's eyewitness account of the trial of Henri Landru does full justice to one of the most grotesque stories in the history of mass murder. "Of all the people I have met in the last twenty years," wrote Walter Duranty in 1935, "and there have been some high-sounding names among them, I think William Bolitho had the finest intellect. He taught me nearly all about the newspaper business that is worth knowing. I have never met anyone who could see further through a brick wall than he could, or who was better, to use a newspaper phrase, at 'doping out the inside facts of any situation.' "

At the beginning of World War I, William Bolitho Ryall, who was then eighteen, worked his way to England from his native South Africa and enlisted in the British army. Early in 1916 he became a junior lieutenant in France, generally turning up at spots where the fighting was hot and the British losses were heavy. During the postwar years he was correspondent for *The Manchester Guardian* and the New York *World*. The mental range of this gifted young man went far beyond the limits of mere newspaper reporting. With a brilliant insight, an intuitive sense of the underlying realities of any situation, and, above all, an ability to express himself in beautifully flowing prose, he quickly rose to the top of his profession. His book *Twelve Against the Gods* (1929) was an enormous success in America, where he dropped his last name, Ryall, in favor of plain William Bolitho.

The Trial of Bluebeard: William Bolitho

William Bolitho, *Murder for Profit*. Copyright, 1926, by Harper and Brothers

At last the trial arrived, and we may turn our attention to Landru's great antagonist—Society. The daily badgering of the monster in his cage by the examining magistrate had lasted from April 13, 1919, to November, 1921. But all this racking had not drawn out of the man a secret, the only one the examiners hoped for, how he had disposed of his corpses. The villa at Gambais had been excavated and sacked from rafters to cellar, without any result but a handful of charred bones which only cranks in the anatomy school could swear were not rabbits' bones. The kitchen stove, on which the spiritual eyes of 30,000,000 people were fixed ever since Salmon the reporter had playfully hinted that Landru might have used it as a private

incinerator, had been dismounted and brought as a trophy; on Landru's own suggestion, the discomfited experts had scraped the soot out of the chimney for analysis, with no better result.

So much preliminary drumming on the likelihood of enormous crowds at the opening of the case had the contrary effect: on the first day and until the truth was incautiously published by the reporters, the court was only moderately full. It was a hall the size of a meetinghouse, distempered in a grim shade of green, whose only ornament was a huge gas chandelier, gummy and long unused. The weather was cold, the light hard. In front of the judge's bench was a table covered with "material evidence," the heavier parts of which were stacked far into the body of the court, so that the witnesses on their way to the stand had to pick their way among the burst mattresses, the dismounted iron bedsteads, past a rusty stove, and look at the silky Gilbert across a square rod of false hair, cardboard boxes of bones, jewelry that all looked sham, books, and iron bric-a-brac, the lesser spoils of Landru's victims. The front of the court thus had the sordid and depressing air of a house removal. At the other end, there was a dock strongly barred off where throughout the trial the ticketless public stood in a slab: pale-faced rogues, gamboge-tressed women without hats, truant workmen, and inquisitive middle-class women from Paris, all day obsessed with the wish to gain a place nearer the front. In front of them were twenty rows of school benches, where the reporters of the world press scribbled and quarreled.

On the third day the court changed: the whole of leisured Paris came to fight for places; a special train was run from the Gare d'Orsay in time for the opening. Both the cavernous corridors and the wet street outside were thick all day with a crowd that pushed like a panic to a theater to get in. The sovereign people itself had come to enjoy the function of judging. A place inside, instead of being the present of a magistrate, was only to be won, like all the other privileges of a democracy, by competition, and became a trophy of ferocity in a woman, or cunning strength in a man. The successful part of the nation, once inside, consolidated positions, squeezed up beside the judge on his bench, forced its way beside the jurymen, and occupied every window ledge. The principle of representation was abandoned; society moved itself to share in the condemnation and punishment of the offender.

From this confined rabble at every significant point of the trial rose various sounds, ignoble roars of laughter, infamous grumblings, and yells of delight and excitement. It was never quiet. The ordinary machinery of justice clogged, only with the greatest hardship managed to enter into action at all. The jurymen took two hours and the assistance of a platoon of police to get to their box. The judge, though he had a private entrance, was often late. The reporters, unofficial delegates of our world civilization, abandoned their earlier composure in the crush and, fearing to be excluded from the function by which they earned their living, scuffled with the mob and fought their colleagues each for his own hand with no less determination.

The French dock is a long bench, raised to the same level as the judge's desk. In this, above the fleshly figure of his counsel, Moro-Giafferi, was the profile of Landru, russet and bleached bone. The horrible patina of the jail was on his naked cranium, which seemed to shine in the wintry light from a window behind. His coat, which he never removed, was a mackintosh of the military cut fashionable when he was arrested: a shade lighter than his beard, which was trimmed in the shape of a fan. In the street he might have passed as one of those innumerable petty speculators that dealt in army stores. But on his dais framed by the broad blue gendarmes, with the aura of his iniquity, he seemed unlike any human seen before, as Napoleon might have appeared on the day of his anointing. His skull was certainly strange with its dead color and incandescence. His nose was the greatest rarity, as thin and transparent at the bridge as a sheet of greased paper. When he sat and listened to the long requisitories, he could be taken for an actor in his carefully attentive pose, but so thin and delicate that one could notice the outline of the small, sharp elbow through his sleeve. We saw his full face but rarely: when he entered, stumbling and blinking through the side door that ended the stone stairs from the prison yard every morning; and sometimes when he turned to the roaring arena to protest. Then we caught a glimpse of his cavernous eyes, which never lost their abstraction even when he was shouting. Usually his manner was chosen and finicky, but after a few minutes in this style he would drop back into the Paris twang. When Fernande Segret was giving her evidence he closed his eyes; once when the rough Attorney General, coming to the matter of Thérèse Marchadier's pet dogs, which were found strangled with a waxed thread under an oleander clump at Gambais, rushed at him the question: "Is that how you killed all your victims, Landru?"—he seemed scared, and shook.

Once, at the eighth repetition of the question, 'What became of this woman, Landru?' he lost his temper and stood up, shaking his long, large hands with rage. He had many poses. He seemed sometimes like a fox, with his snout finding danger in the air; sometimes he seemed false; sometimes he seemed like a wood insect, with undefined antennae that felt their way along the board in front of him. Sometimes he would pause and slowly take out, wipe and don a pair of gilt spectacles before an answer; then he seemed simply a prematurely old man. Usually he was obviously immersed in a private dream; but he took great pleasure in the whirling combats between the hairy prosecutor and his sleek Corsican defender. He had a

weakness for minor details, on which he extended himself, until he suddenly remembered some warning he had had of the danger of these tactics and sat down.

The judge, after a few days' browbeating, treated him with consideration. Both of them were interested in the crowd; the judge stroking his beard with his soft white hand, the accused sideways, without completely turning his head, as if he were eavesdropping. As in all multiple-murder trials, the evidence was largely a repetition, each new victim had been met in the same way, traced in the same way, perhaps killed in the same way, it may be by this abominable new weapon of a waxed thread round the neck while asleep, which no agonizing effort could disengage. Probably, too, Landru disposed of their bodies in the same way; like Pel and Soleillant, dissecting them minutely, then burning the pieces to ashes in a red-hot stove, then no doubt by the aid of his motorcar strewing their few pounds of relics in the hedges of distant lanes.

The witnesses stepped after each other monotonously; concierges in Sunday clothes, little old women with dingy reticules, dry-eyed sisters, mustached detectives with long and precise records of their failures. The crowd, subtly changing every day, ceased to pay any attention to these. It fed its thousand eyes on the figure in the dock, which grew lighter and more transparent every day, like a discarded carapace. Landru fell into somnolences that lasted hours, during which the heaps of papers in front of him had obviously no part in the reverie. The classic attitude of the mass murderer towards his punishment. Maître Moro-Giafferi, who at first had difficulty in inducing his client to resign the first role to him, composed dramatic tantrums, revolved his black professional sleeves at the more honestly bad-tempered red advocate opposite, then, having had his effect, subsided, and put on pince-nez. The judge, badly handled by indignant reporters in the press every morning, let an elegant melancholy creep over him, and little by little abandoned any effort to cow the crowd, which every day grew wilder and more primitive as the great moment of condemnation approached—and as the stage element in its composition gradually gained the majority.

Caricaturists, who in the first days had timidly made their sketches using their knees as easels, now boldly advanced among the undergrowth of *pièces de conviction,* blocking the defense's view of the witness rail, and drew Landru to the life at three feet from his eyes. This seemed to please him and amuse him; at a sign from one of the artists he would turn his head at the angle they wanted. And a more encumbering breed, the press photographers, doggedly impudent, lugged their ungainly apparatus into similar good positions and took time exposures of the court. To no avail— for the ration of winter light, already insufficient for their purpose, was now always barred off by the backs of those who had climbed into the window ledges. Most photographers having failed, the cameramen took to the expedient of hanging incandescent lamps of great power over the prisoner's bench, when the court was not sitting, so that at any rate the great moment and the most interesting expression would not escape them and the millions for whom they deputized.

So the time arrived: the jury after all these days had nothing before them but a coincidence; but it was enough. Ten women (the prosecution fixed on this number somewhat arbitrarily) who had known, loved, and followed Landru had vanished. In his possession were their papers, their birth certificates, their marriage papers, all the paraphernalia with which the human anthill tries to fix separate personality, without which there could be no emigration from France. Against this Moro-Giafferi could only weakly hint that possibly Landru had shipped them to the brothels of South America, where common superstition has it there come no newspapers. The man himself, in his extremity, had never dared to make such a defense. He relied on the weary romanticism of "an honorable man will never tell a woman's secret," which, carefully weighed by the stony jurymen, came to much the same thing. But to this the terrible quietus of the prosecution struck mortally: What? Women of over fifty? Women whose false hair, false teeth, false bosoms, as well as identity papers you, Landru, have kept, and we captured? The jury retired.

In these moments, while prisoner and judges were withdrawn, the court crowd, this assembly of a modern people which had just sacrificed 1,500,000 of its young men to preserve its institutions and its culture, was extraordinary. It had been waiting from an early hour to keep its place, and in its joy at success gave itself over to a debauch. These thousand compressed bodies were the elect of all Paris, all France, arrived by their abilities to the most coveted spectacle of the century: the sight of Landru's condemnation. They could not move, but within the inches of everyone's power, they rioted with abandon. The shrill cries of women at the daring contacts of their neighbors, the screams, the high giggles of chorus girls, the shouts of rage or pleasure of the men, combined in a chorus. It filled the street outside, and filtered no doubt to the ears of the man waiting in the cold cell somewhere beneath, wrapping himself close in the warm quilt of his sentimental daydreams. It was not the cold formula of a delegated justice, but the voice of outraged society itself, doing its own justice.

A thousand incidents kept the crowd alive while the tedious jury kept it in waiting. Girls pulled by the legs tumbled from their perch in the windows, strong men forced themselves from three places distant upon each other and revenged their dignity on some enemy with blows, which falling generously on the people between were returned, or saluted with bellows of pain. At last the jury, ill at ease and silent, filed back, and the door opened for Landru. Immediately there was a frenzy. As the man stood half bowed forward to catch his fate and his sentence, at precisely the right moment the photographers fired their illlumi-

nation. There was a great glare of light over him. From every part of the massed hall arms protruded upward with black boxes, cameras which aimed at him. And as though in the throes of an eruption, figures shot themselves out of the crowd level with hands waving and their faces distorted with the effort of their struggle. One man (according to some it was the dean of the Comédie Française) actually succeeded in leaping to one of the advocate's benches, and stood there, hilarious, with opera glasses to his eyes, greedily scanning the lost criminal's expression.

When the court was empty, the servants found the floor strewn like a holiday beach with bitten sandwiches, papers, bottles, and other unmentionable, unmistakable traces of their presence which human beings, alas, must leave on a spot where they have been long hours kept immobile without privacy.

* * *

FOR AN ACCOUNT of the execution of Landru we turn to the story by Webb Miller, who was, like Bolitho, an eyewitness of the trial and finale of the famous case. One of the most talented of America's foreign correspondents, Miller was born in Pokagon, Michigan, in 1892. After teaching rural school from 1910–11, he turned to newspaper reporting, his occupation taking him from the publicized "Front Page" room in Chicago to forty-one countries in America, Europe, Africa, and Asia. He had grandstand seats at the pursuit of Pancho Villa, the Sinn Fein outbreak in Ireland, the British front in Flanders, Verdun, the Argonne, the Riff War, the Gandhi salt riots in India, the Italo-Ethiopian War, the abdication of Edward VIII, and a host of other headline events. In his fine autobiography, *I Found No Peace* (1936), he confessed that "the sordidness, brutality, horror, hypocrisy, intolerance, and inhumanity which existed in the relations between human beings often sickened and discouraged me." A man of abnormal shyness and great sensitivity, Webb Miller was killed in a London blackout accident in May, 1940.

The Execution: Webb Miller

On the night of February 24, [1922], together with half a dozen French reporters, I caught the electric train to Versailles. We went to the courthouse, obtained crudely mimeographed green *laissez-passers* for the execution, and retired to the Hôtel des Réservoirs with five bottles of cognac to await dawn.

At four A.M. word came that M. Deibler, the famous executioner who performed all the executions throughout France, had arrived with his apparatus. Anatole Deibler, shy, wistful, goat-bearded, had performed more than three hundred executions. His salary was 18,000 francs per year (a little over $1000 at the 1936 rate of exchange). He suffered from a weak heart and could not walk upstairs, but this did not seem to interfere with his gruesome vocation. He lived in a small house near Versailles under the name of M. Anatole, consorted very little with his neighbors, and led a retiring existence. He kept the guillotine in a shed outside his house. When performing an execution he wore white gloves and a long white "duster."

We hurried to the prison. Four hundred troops had drawn cordons at each end of the street and permitted only the possessors of the little green mimeographed tickets to pass. According to the French law, executions must occur in the open street in front of the prison door. On the damp, slippery cobblestones beside the streetcar tracks workmen were rapidly erecting the guillotine a dozen feet outside the towering gate of Versailles prison. It was still quite dark. The only light came from the workmen's old-fashioned lanterns with flickering candles and the few electric street lights. The workmen bolted the grisly machine together and adjusted its balance with a carpenter's level. Deibler hauled the heavy knife to the top of the uprights.

Nearly one hundred officials and newspapermen gathered in a circle around the guillotine; I stood about fifteen feet away. News arrived from inside the prison that Landru, whose long black beard had been cut previously, asked that he be shaved.

"It will please the ladies," he said to his jailers.

His lawyer and a priest went into his cell. He refused the traditional cigarette and glass of rum always offered just before executions.

Landru wore a shirt from which the neck had been cut away, and a pair of cheap dark trousers. That was all— no shoes or socks. He would walk to the guillotine barefooted.

As his arms were strapped behind him his lawyer whispered, "Courage, Landru." "Thanks, Maître, I've always had that," he replied calmly.

Just as the first streaks of the chilly February dawn appeared, a large closed van drawn by horses arrived and backed up within a few feet of the right side of the guillotine. Deibler's assistants, wearing long smocks, pulled two wicker baskets from the van. They placed the small round basket carefully in front of the machine where the head would fall. Two assistants placed another basket about the size and shape of a coffin close beside the guillotine. Into that the headless body would roll.

The cordon of troops halted a streetcar full of workmen on their way to work. They decided to open the cordon to permit the car to proceed, and it slowly rumbled past within a few feet of the grim machine. Staring faces filled the windows.

The guillotine underwent a final test. Deibler raised the lunette, the half-moon-shaped wooden block which was to clamp down upon Landru's neck. Then he lowered it, and the heavy knife shot down from the top of the uprights with a crash which shook the machine. The lunette and knife were raised again. All was ready.

Suddenly the huge wooden gates of the prison swung open. The spectators became silent and tense. Three figures appeared, walking rapidly. On each side a jailer held Landru by his arms, which were strapped behind him. They supported and pulled him forward as fast as they could walk. His bare feet pattered on the cold cobblestones, and his knees seemed not to be functioning. His face was pale and waxen, and as he caught sight of the ghastly machine, he went livid.

The two jailers hastily pushed Landru face foremost against the upright board of the machine. It collapsed, and his body crumpled with it as they shoved him forward under the wooden block, which dropped down and clamped his neck beneath the suspended knife. In a split second the knife flicked down, and the head fell with a thud into the small basket. As an assistant lifted the hinged board and rolled the headless body into the big wicker basket, a hideous spurt of blood gushed out.

An attendant standing in front of the machine seized the basket containing the head, rolled it like a cabbage into the larger basket, and helped shove it hastily into the waiting van. The van doors slammed, and the horses were whipped into a gallop.

When Landru first appeared in the prison courtyard I had glanced at my wrist watch. Now I looked again. Only twenty-six seconds had elapsed.

* * *

LANDRU WAS NO MECHANICAL MONSTER, but a human being of flesh and blood, a latter-day representative of the breed of Cain. How can one explain the motivations of this most notorious technician in a forbidden trade? What strange and sudden changes could make a mass murderer out of a mild bookkeeper? William Bolitho sought an answer in sociological terms. It was, as always, a combination of twisted personality and sadistic environment. Landru appeared in the Paris of the Peace Conference days, just emerging from the hypnotic nightmare of a four-year spree in mass betrayals and mass slaughter. "In huge Paris," wrote Bolitho, "there was talk of death, and purpose which is life. There were drums in the air, which made it a frenzy to be alone. Age, sex, and time were in complicity with Landru. He was the male, master of the secret."

The seedy little murderer gave jaded Parisians exactly what they wanted —blood and sex and crime. They fought greedily for glimpses of the cornered criminal on trial, laughed uproariously at his jokes, and commiserated with him in his misfortunes. Tens of thousands on the boulevards and in the cafés gaily repeated his caustic aphorisms spat out at his accusers. Others in deadly fear of sexual impotence marveled at his proud and perhaps egotistical confession that he had had relations with two hundred and sixty-three women. Henri Landru, the romantic poet and manicured multi-murderer, had captured the imagination of a frustrated and bewildered people. It was an exercise in mass hysteria.

William Bolitho Describes Sarah Bernhardt's
Last Scene

WHEN THE GREAT ACTRESS, Sarah Bernhardt, was touring the West, she was interviewed by Sam Davis, then a Nevada reporter for the Carson *Appeal,* the *San Francisco Examiner,* and the Associated Press. Deeply impressed by the way he had handled her story, the emotional actress said good-by as her train was about to leave. First she kissed him on both cheeks, then on the lips, and then she said: "The right cheek for the *Appeal,* the left for the *Examiner,* and the lips, my dear friend, for yourself."

Davis' reply deserves to be included in a treasury of the world's great retorts: "Madame," he said, "I also represent the Associated Press, which serves three hundred and eighty papers west of the Mississippi."

The burial of Sarah Bernhardt was witnessed by William Bolitho, who perpetuated the event in another example of his masterful reportorial technique. For a brief moment the gifted reporter caught the extraordinary vitality, the impetuous charm, and the wonderful voice of that greatest actress of our times, now "a poor, old woman, going to the rest she had well deserved," but once described by the critic Jules Lemaître as "one of the most gracious apparitions who ever vaulted, for the consolation of men, on the changing surface of this world of miracles."

"Her art was not separate from her; nor to be put off at the end"

New York *World,* April 3, 1923

The air was steady and bright, the day they buried Sarah Bernhardt. The crowd heard the wheel creakings as she passed, and smelled the loads of costly roses like heavy incense in their faces. Even those at the back, who could see nothing, had this satisfaction: they grumbled less than is usual at so great a show. From the pavement we saw people in the window balconies and on the roofs. Something of our emotion must have reached them, for they nudged each other and seemed to smile.

Sarah Bernhardt was always her own stage manager. She planned to make her last appearance on the mortal stage the best of all her parts. All her life she meditated it. Once in a dream, she saw herself buried abroad, far from Paris; this would have ruined all. Ever afterwards she carried with her on all her travels, a rosewood coffin, lined with white satin; packed in an unwieldly case. She was sure at least of this. Like the simplest woman of her city, she trusted no foreigners in such essential matters.

Everyone sees death differently; some as a black ghost; some as a hope; or a bankruptcy, or a dreamless relief. Sarah thought of it as a supreme tragedy to be played in triumph. That is as good a way as another. She was an actress in the inward places of her heart. Though she had worked for seventy years, and had tasted all joys, and known all possible sorrows, she forgot her fatigue when she thought of the stage set for her final performance. Now everything had been set out as she had directed: the huge, battered case, that had lumbered behind her on all her travels, was waiting in the hall for its final journey, next to the mound of trunks that never would serve her any more. The priest was beside her bed, the moment was near. Before she let herself sink, she went over methodically, meticulously, the setting she had made for her great Exit. Service in the dark, little church of Saint François de Sales, that tiny hiding place for peace in the worldly Plaine Monceau. The long route allegorical of her life, down the stately Boulevard Malesherbes, through the midday crowd of the rich Rue Royale, across the glorious Place de la Concorde; through the long Rue de Rivoli, from the palaces at one end to the narrow streets where working housewives would be doing their morning shopping; a moment's pause beside her own theater; then slowly on, to the City of the Dead, Père Lachaise, there to lie forever in the past, beside Rachel and her elders.

She could hear from not far below in the street, the reporters, her last critics, discussing the decision of the Hôtel de Ville to bury her in state. And workgirls, on their way to the factory, asking how she did. The last House was full; waiting impatiently for her. At noon she felt this, and said, half impatiently, as if it were an actor who was late, *"Comme mon agonie est longue!"* How unpunctual is Death. Nothing remained now to do but to play that supreme role for which she had so well prepared. It would not be tiring. Some light through the shutter slats, of a spring sun, comforted her. By an unexpected chance, the season would help her out. And with her last breath she said, *"Je veux des fleurs, beaucoup de fleurs."* The last touch; more flowers than she had ever had for a gala night.

Three blows of a sexton's staff on the stone pavement of the aisle; signal in France for the raising of the curtain; given as she had appointed as her coffin came through the door.

All the first-night crowd were there; all that had a name in fashion, riches, art; following her funeral procession, coactors in her greatest production. There were the flowers she had asked: more than she had dreamed of. They filled the place before the porch; waist-high; weighed down seven coaches. All the details of her strange fancy had been carried out. It was a stage play; a playing to the gallery. Small critics may mistake her, and regret; or stupidly blame. Her death was a pageant she had planned; for she was an actress, not merely in her trade, but in her soul. Her art was not separate from her; nor to be put off at the end. Her whole life, loves, miseries, was a well-constructed play, a romantic legend of the sort she most admired. The Paris streets were her last gallery; crushed on a five-mile route to see Sarah play her fifth act.

Her life and death were as single-purposed as a saint; and with the same ruling purpose; to give all to her fellows. Flattery and the rewards of her profession, she felt no more than a billionaire thinks of new gains on the curb; and money was no more in her thoughts than is the need for his daily bread to a monk. What she had, she gave freely, the last morsel; to her family, to a countless crowd of parasites she pitied and protected; to her companions, to the public. She wished they might have pleasure in her going.

But in this last part, played before a vaster gallery than ever she had in life, she had to ask our indulgence. The enchantments of her voice were mute forever; her graces and gestures were taken from her. And in spite of the roses that banked over and covered it, as she the greatest actress of our times passed, in a narrow black coffin drawn by black, silver-spangled horses, the stage illusion was at last stripped from her, and we knew that we were looking at the funeral of a poor, old woman, going to the rest she had well deserved. It was not the curtain she had planned; it was a greater one; and Sarah's last scene touched emotions that she never had in the days of her fresh glories.

* * *

IN THE PRIME of life when writing this prose ode to death, Bolitho little knew that his own days were numbered. Deciding to settle down to enjoy the fruits of a successful writing career, he bought a little château near Avignon in southern France and set eagerly about the pleasant pursuit of raising South African fruits and plants in its lovely gardens. One day he suffered an attack of acute appendicitis, which was wrongly diagnosed by a local doctor. He was finally rushed in a local ambulance to the operating table in Avignon, but it was too late. After thirty-six hours of agony he was dead from peritonitis. He was not yet forty.

"There has passed," commented Heywood Broun, "the most brilliant journalist of our time. Bolitho's best was far and away beyond the topmost reach of any newspaper competitor."

The *World* Takes Its Readers into the Secrets of the Ku Klux Klan

D. W. GRIFFITH's sensational film, *The Birth of a Nation* (1914),* served to invest with a spurious glamour a revived Klan which, drawing its inspiration from the old KKK of Reconstruction days, was founded in 1915 and blossomed forth under the impetus of prodigious promotion and notoriety. Frederick Lewis Allen, the historian of the twenties, tells how emotions of group loyalty and antagonism were inflamed during the war and then, suddenly denied their intended expression, found a kind of perverted release in the persecution of elements which, to the dominant white Protestant group, seemed alien and "un-American."

By using white robes and hoods, flaming crosses, and an elaborate ceremonial hocus-pocus, the Klan exerted an irresistible appeal to bored and frustrated small-towners thirsting for adventure or anxious to get away from their wives at night. Innate cruelty, arrested development, naïve love of the mystical, and the attraction of what Charles Merz, of *The New York Times,* once called that "Sweet Land of Secrecy"—these were the dominant impulsions of many who flocked to the banners of the Klan. To venture forth, panoplied as a Knight of the Invisible Empire, was far more exciting than talking politics at the cracker barrel.

On October 10, 1920, a startling front-page story broke in the New York *World.* Date-lined Atlanta, Georgia, the day before, the story began:

> The old Ku Klux Klan of Reconstruction days has been revived. Hooded night-riders in long, flowing white gowns parade the thoroughfares and bypaths of the South in the dark hours when innocent people are abed.

The *World*'s executive editor, Herbert Bayard Swope, was riding again, this time armed with a double-barreled shotgun—one barrel primed for the bedsheeted bigots, the other for the connivers at outrageous peonage practices on turpentine plantations, in lumber mills, and on the roads (Samuel D. McCoy's *World* stories from Florida in 1923 had a lot to do with the elimination of these terroristic methods). Assisting Swope were such top-flight newsmen as Rowland Thomas, Charles S. Hand, and Ned McIntosh. The exposé reached a climax with a series of stories beginning on September 6, 1921, each having the lead: "What Is the Ku Klux Klan?" The *World* stripped bare the commercialism of Klan leadership, with the top dog, William Joseph Simmons, a fake colonel, as Imperial Wizard, and under him King Kleagles heading Realms, Grand Goblins lording it over Domains,

---

* A twelve-reeler, which proved to be one of the greatest financial successes in film history.

membership peddlers, bearing the honorific title of plain Kleagles, and membership open to supporters of its race and religious hate credo willing to put up ten dollars, four of which the peddlers kept, a goodly portion of the rest going into Atlanta headquarters. The *World* printed a complete roster of the officers and the names and addresses of the sales force. "Wholly mercenary in its motive" was Simmons' ironic counterblast at the *World*.

Attacking "the right to hate in concert, in secret, and in disguise," Swope continued on the offensive. In the winter of 1922–23 the *World* reported a reign of terror in Morehouse Parish, Louisiana, where, despite evidence of the torture and murder of marked victims, a grand jury refused to indict. Other newsmen were inspired to take up the cudgels.* In Vincennes, Indiana, Thomas H. Adams, an editor, brought about the arrest of Grand Dragon D. C. Stephenson, on a charge of rape and murder. "Keep the swine from killing me!" the jailed Klan leader soon whined.† The Klan's bold invasion of the Northern states soon occupied the attention of numerous gifted reporters, among them, Lindsay Denison. His report in the New York *Evening World* of May 3, 1923, under the headline: 10,000 IN MOONLIT FIELD FACE KLAN'S MYSTIC CIRCLE GUARDED BY ARMED MEN, from which this excerpt is taken, effectively re-creates the spirit of "honorable Klannishness" that pervaded that noble order.

Bigotry in bedsheets

New York *World*, May 3, 1923

The Knights of the Ku Klux Klan, Invisible Empire, held a "klavern" on the farm of John Hobbs, a half mile east of Middlebush, a hamlet five miles out of New Brunswick, New Jersey, early this morning. It couldn't have been earlier, for the proceedings which were supposed to be nearly over at midnight did not begin until then. It was not until nearly half-past two o'clock that the sixty-two-foot cross flared up against the sky and faded out again and the small army of Klansmen from every county in New Jersey started streaming out over the roads toward home.

With all the theatric effect of white robes and Alice-in-Wonderland terminology, the deepest impression of last night's ceremonies upon the outsiders had to do with the numbers in which they turned out. The Klan estimate of members of the order present was ten thousand. Unofficial observers guessed it as from ten thousand to six thousand.

There was not a road in Somerset County that was not at some time after dark traversed by long trails of automobile headlights; sometimes one counted ten or fifteen cars; at other times there were fifty or sixty. There

---

* Leonard L. Cline wrote a brilliant account of the Morehouse Parish trials ("The Mer Rouge Case"), which appeared in the Baltimore *Sun*, January 7, 1923.
† The Grand Dragon was convicted and imprisoned for life.

was never a time between ten o'clock and midnight when the main streets of New Brunswick were not filled with slow-moving processions. They blinked and glared their way through the lanes and highways, often losing their bearings so that columns passed each other on the same road. They were in fine limousines, in delivery trucks, in speed cars, in milk wagons, in touring cars, and in great omnibuses.

Somewhere behind each car, on the end of the mudguard, on the license-plate rack, or on the spare-tire case, hung a white streamer. Sometimes it was a silken knotted ribbon like the decoration of a bridal car; more often it was merely a strip of cheesecloth, and frequently it was a bunch of cotton waste tied with string.

On the brightly lighted business streets of New Brunswick the significance of the white streamer was quickly recognized. It put a stop for an hour or two to ordinary night activities of the town, while whispering groups gathered back from the curb in the comparative shadows of the curb line and store doors. Comment was not always friendly.

The Klansmen had meant to keep their meeting secret. No one except twelve invited guests "from the alien world," one *The Evening World* writer, who had been invited weeks ago with a pledge to hold their knowledge in confidence, were supposed to know there was to be a "Klavern." But, after the attack of anti-Klansmen on a recruiting meeting at Bound Brook, ten miles from New Brunswick, night before last, there was not a taxicab driver, hotel clerk, bootlegger, or night policeman in Somerset or Middlesex County who was not eager to be the first to tell strangers about the Middlebush meeting. There

are many Negroes in New Brunswick's population. They vanished from the streets soon after ten o'clock.

The guests of the Publicity Committee were separated in the traffic jam in front of the Pennsylvania Railroad Station in New Brunswick. Two of us, with a committeeman, found ourselves in a motorbus marked Long Branch and Red Bank, filled with men who were obviously fisherfolk, truck growers, garagekeepers, and workmen, and here and there an austere, thin-lipped person in a high collar who might have been a bank clerk or a rising young lawyer. The lumbering bus got off the road three times and there was plenty of time to get acquainted.

It was a good-natured company. There were just two topics of conversation aside from neighborhood gossip that a stranger could not always get a drift of. One was what each man's wife would say to him when he got home along about daylight—he having promised to be in about midnight. The other was the awe and horror which the gathering of the Klans must be producing at the roadsides upon which the travelers peered through the steam-coated windows.

One thing was clear then and remained clear throughout the night. The members of the Klan take themselves very seriously, even in their friendly chat. It is no frolicsome lark for them. They are quite sure that they "are getting this country on the right road at last." They keep saying it.

"Where's Jim?" asked a man in a sheepskin coat; "thought he was coming."

"Why, say, I thought you knew," was the answer. "His wife wouldn't let him."

"Why, what's the matter with her?" asked the inquirer, "always thought she was a kinder sensible woman."

The other man whispered something.

"Is that so? Well, now, do you know I never knew she follered the Pope? What do you know about that!"

They let us out in a field overgrown with low underbrush through which the lights of hundreds of cars could be seen twinkling. The road ahead was jammed with cars. More were piling in behind. It was a little after eleven o'clock.

A man apparently having authority took the committeeman off into the dark and whispered with him. They brought papers to the headlight of the bus and discussed them. The man of authority said he guessed he'd have to take us in. We set out across the underbrush until we came to a woven wire fence. On the other side of it, out of a stubble field, appeared eight or ten stocky-looking youths. Some of them had handkerchiefs tied across the lower half of the face; others wore no concealment.

Every one of them carried a club, a twisted weapon from three to four feet long, often knotted, twisted, and gnarled with the bark on. They shooed us down outside of the fence for half a mile until a gate was reached.

"Where is G-1?" shouted the voice of a clubman at the gate after the committeeman had whispered affectionately in his ear. Like an echo, the call went out and over the farm. "G-1?" "Is G-1 down there?" "Where did G-1 go?"

A group of figures in white robes, white capes with a figured circle on the left breast or on both breasts, and high-pointed caps with "N. J." embroidered on the sides came flitting hurriedly down the farm lane. Four of them indicated different directions in which "G-1" might be found. The others said they didn't know.

In a pocket formed by parked automobiles at the end of the lane stood a dignified elderly man with a marvelously pleasant voice of powerful carrying power [*sic*]. He was dressed in a business suit of trim-cut gray. He was not masked. He had a pleasant face.

"I am G-1," he said. The Klansmen of the party stopped as if shot. "Who are these men, aliens?"

"No, sir," said Gibson [a New York businessman who was a Klansman], "they are invited witnesses."

"Ah," commented G-1, with courteous gravity. "Authorized aliens but not to be naturalized."

Then, with the utmost kindliness but with definite command in every note of his voice, he told the visitors just when they could get off and where —or rather where they could not get off. He said he would blow a whistle three times when he wanted to see them again.

"I may not permit you to see the opening work," he said. "But from the time the aliens are brought in until they rise from kneeling you may see and hear all that happens. It is understood that you will use no names of any whom you recognize; the photographers will take no pictures of uncovered faces or of automobile license plates."

A robed messenger dashed through the automobile line and whispered. G-1 disappeared with him. A moment later ten, fifteen, thirty youths appeared and galloped back toward the front gate, dragging clubs behind them. There was some shouting back at the gate. It was soon quieted. There was a wait of half an hour except for the droning voice over beyond the automobiles reciting a ritual. A deep chorus of concerted replies and two verses of a hymn in which the words "Klansmen stand together . . . for ever and for aye" could be made out.

A whistle sounded. A robed man stepped out and said, "G-1 says 'bring 'em in.' "

On the other side of the automobile screen was a circle of white-robed figures inclosing a space of perhaps three or four acres. To the east of it rose against the moonlit sky the poles of a cross, the upright apparently sixty feet high. Beneath it was a rostrum. On it stood an imposing white-robed figure.

Standing or kneeling on one knee in a row at his feet were twenty closely guarded, robed men. Many had red-lined capes turned back. The invited visitors were led in back of the robed men, triple and quadruple lines of men in dark clothes with handkerchief masks. All along the woods at the edge of the cornfield stalked clubmen.

We were told the person on the rostrum was the Exalted Cyclops. It was explained that he was the master of ceremonies. He had a tiny electric droplight over the desk by which he read the ritual. His voice was strong and more penetrating than that of G-1, but was also impressive.

In the center of the great ring was an altar at which another robed figure stood. The Exalted Cyclops addressed him as "Nighthawk," if one's ears served right, and told him to look into the matter of the "aliens" who were to be naturalized.

"I have your orders, sir," said Nighthawk, and with arms folded on his breast he stalked out to the rear.

There followed a sonorous colloquy between the Exalted Cyclops and one

he addressed as Kotop, who appeared at the altar. The wording of the mutual expressions of patriotism, devotion to clean living and to mutual adherence sprinkled along the way of this antiphony was remarkable in its musical cadence and the clear simplicity of its diction.

A gasoline-lighted small torch appeared at the altar. The Kotop was instructed to usher in the "aliens awaiting naturalization." The cross-bearer—they spoke of him, I think, as a "Klextor"—with an assistant carrying the tank of illuminating gas, marched over to the edge of the ring.

The unmistakable pipe-organ tones of the voice of G-1 was [sic] heard reciting the lines of "God give us men," followed by some preliminary instructions.

Then a dark column of men poured through a gap in the line. From a distance of three hundred feet they looked like a huddled flock of frightened herded prisoners. They were in columns of fours. The committeemen told us there were two thousand of them.

They were marched across the rear of the circle, which now became a square, and were lined up like soldiers at inspection, in widely separated ranks. The Exalted Cyclops announced that they would be "subjected to the Eye of Scrutiny."

All the robed members marched in single file in and around them, putting the eyeholes in their hoods close to the faces of the "aliens."

After half an hour ten hapless persons whose features or speech or appearance of general intelligence seemed to have indicated that the Eye of Scrutiny did not like them were plucked out and escorted in a hollow square before the rostrum. The Exalted Cyclops informed them that they

had been found lacking in the essential qualities of Klansmen; he assured
them a mistake might have been made
and that they would be received into
the order later if they were all right.
They were then escorted off the premises by an additional guard of clubmen.

Facing east, north, south, and west
on the sides of the big square, addresses on the high purposes of the
Invisible Empire were made to the
"aliens," who marched from place to
place, stumbling through the corn
stubble. It was impressed upon them
that only men of undoubted loyalty to
the government, to God, to their fellow
Klansmen were desired. They were invited, if they felt themselves unfit, to
withdraw before it was too late, because if their unfitness were discovered later they would, without fear or
favor, be ejected from the order.

At the end of the instructions the
"aliens" were massed across the altar
from the cross, and oaths and obligations were read to them, to which they
swore successively with their right
hands on their hearts and their left
hands uplifted. Those who followed
the reading of the pledges noted that
they emphasized especially "white supremacy," adhesion to the law of government of the community, state, and
nation, unswerving and unquestioning, demanded the separation of
church and state, free schools and free
seats in schools, and that no prejudice
of church or fraternal organization
should stand between Klansman and
his duty to the government, the Invisible Empire, and his fellow Klansmen.

The words "white supremacy" were
the nearest to a direct reference to the
reputed object of the Klan, to combat
in all things the Negro, the Catholic,
the Jew, and the foreign-born generally.

At the end of a prayer the great
cross was lighted. A strong breeze was
setting in to the south. The upright
and the arm to the south blazed up
so they were seen, it was learned later,
seven miles away. The north arm
merely smoldered.

At half-past three o'clock this morning automobiles were still going
through New Brunswick like traffic at
Forty-second Street and Broadway at
three o'clock in the afternoon.

* * *

ON OCTOBER 6, 1921, the Richmond *Times-Dispatch* declared: "All who
love the South will join in the benediction '*Requiescat in pace.*'" But more
than a benediction was needed to kill the Klan. Hard fighting lay ahead,
and Swope saw it. The day after Denison's story appeared, the New York
legislature took up a *World*-drawn bill to strip secrecy from the operations
of the Klan, imposing heavy penalties upon violators. The very next day
the bill passed, and a legislator from Rockland County took the occasion to
congratulate the *World* for fighting "most consistently of all papers the
growth of this organization that has for its principle the arraigning of
classes and creeds against one another." His name was James A. Farley.

Did the *World* campaign of pitiless publicity help stifle the Klan? The
statistics of membership would support an affirmative answer. Early in
1926 *The New York Times* felt justified in asserting that "the Ku Klux
Klan is definitely on the wane," and by 1930 its membership had shrunk
from four and a half million in 1924 to a mere nine thousand. In a *New*

Yorker piece on "The Downfall of Fascism in Black Ankle County," Joseph Mitchell facetiously recounted what happened when the prospective victims of the Klan met force with force. Mr. Catfish Giddy and other leaders of the movement got cold feet and quit. Then Mrs. Catfish Giddy "ripped up her husband's robes and told her friends he was so fat she found enough material in it for two pillowcases, an apron, and a tablecloth." Once the movement had been courageously exposed as a heartless racket, the good sense of the American people was soon brought into play to dissipate its force. From time to time levies upon that ample fund of good sense may still be exigent, for the Klan continues in its erratic course to stage occasional revivals.

An Eclipse of the Sun Inspires a

Pulitzer Prize Story

A ND IT SHALL come to pass in that day, saith the Lord God, that I will cause the sun to go down at noon, and I will darken the earth in the clear day."

Thus spoke the Prophet Amos in predicting an eclipse in Assyria in 762 B.C. Many years earlier a Chinese king, Chung K'ang, severely punished two of his astronomers for failing to predict that "the sun and the moon would not meet harmoniously." From the days of Pindar to Mark Twain's *Connecticut Yankee*, eclipses have continued to challenge the imagination of men.

The eclipse that occurred in 1923 was in itself a normal solar obscuration, but it inspired a masterpiece of reporting. This story, written by Magner White, was awarded the 1924 Pulitzer Prize in reporting.

Rehearsal for blackout

San Diego, California, *Sun,* September 10, 1923. (The Scripps-Howard Newspapers)

The biggest shadow in the world— 235,000 miles high, 105 miles wide, and 75 miles thick in its densest part —fell across San Diego today, the shadow of the moon as it crossed the face of the sun.

The heavenly appointment was carried out as predicted, 120 years since the last time, 120 years until the next time.

One hundred and twenty years ago, scared Indians fled over the hills at the sight, or the more civilized ones knelt before shrines in the comparatively new San Diego mission and received the comfort of padres, wise in the mysteries of the heavens.

Today, white successors to the Indians gazed from housetops, land points, and from airplanes at the sight. Some, calm in the meager knowledge

of science, were unafraid; others trembled like the Indians of old as the earth's satellite blotted out the sun, leaving only its pearly corona flashing through the blackness like a halo in the sky.

Indian ceremonies of yesterday on the hills found their counterpart in a "Fete of the Sun" at Coronado, where five hundred actors dramatized the awe of the multitude during the eventful moments of the midnight that came at noon.

Smoked glasses and exposed films by the thousands were turned toward the phenomenon. Scientists strained every eye nerve, keenly aware of the tremendous possibilities for discovery that attended the fleeting moments.

Clouds and fog of the early morning added five hundred per cent to

the inky depth of the shadow. Whatever was lost to science by the meanness of weather conditions was gained
in impressiveness for the lay spectator.

Traveling twenty-five miles a minute, the shadow came.

The moon, which had been unseen
in the morning fog, began to encroach
on the sun's apparent rim. The contact was signaled immediately by a
sudden "turning down" of the sun's
light, more sensed than visualized.

Behind its prepared glasses, San
Diego presented its composite face to
the fiery convergence.

Toward the gazing city, at the top
of the 235,000-mile shadow, was the
greatest mystery in the neighboring
heavens, something the eye of mortal
man has never looked upon—the
"other side" of the moon, the coldest
and deadest side of one of the solar
system's coldest and deadest orbs.

Steadily the moon moved on, obscuring more of the sun's face, and the
shadows deepened ominously.

Nervous scientists twisted thumb-
screws and made final adjustments of
their costly instruments all along the
coast, from Point Loma to Ensenada.

Airplanes laden with scientific instruments whirred overhead, exploring
the outskirts of the speeding shadow,
tiny spots that grew dimmer as the
moon continued her encroachment on
the sun's blazing rim.

Sudden cool gusts of wind, released
from the command of solar energy,
swept in from the sea as darkness fell.

In the residential districts and on
suburban farms chickens, puzzled by
the abrupt night, took to their roosts;
and cattle stirred restlessly in the
yards, the routine of their lives distorted by the happening in the sky.

Animals in Ringling Brothers circus, waiting for the afternoon performance, paced their cages and roared
and whined, disturbed by this sudden
lighting up within a few hours of
morning.

Noon whistles sounded—the first
time a noon whistle ever sounded in
San Diego during an eclipse of the
sun. Midnight at midday! Paradox of
120 years.

The black pattern weaves, from
lacy dimness to deeper gloom. Imaginative forebodings become deeper,
shaking at the foundations of the
security the human being feels in
ordinary times; suggesting, in the
thought which we hide from each other
through sheer bravado, that perhaps
this time something may happen
that never happened before, something disastrous, something gigantic
and overwhelming that will take no
account of mankind's limited past
experience.

And now still darker. The Mistress
Moon moves on in her eternal path,
prompt in her appointment. Tiny humans on the globe below, the Earth—
how inconsequential before this relentless, dogged power of the solar
bodies moving in their orbits.

Darker! The real shadow is coming! Incredible speed. It bursts in
from the sea, going twenty-five miles
a minute.

Night is upon us.

What is this fear we can't keep
down? The hint of the infinite night
—a world with no sun!

Our friends give us ghastly smiles,
pale lilies they are. Shadow bands
stripe the earth; quivering crescents
of light flit on the sides of buildings.

The city glows in puny artificial
light.

The blot in the sky is now complete.
The sun is gone!

A tiny streak shoots out from behind the blot—a solar prominence. A
scientist tells us that "tiny streak" is

80,000 miles long! Blazing and glowing at a heat beyond human imagination. It is a real hell-fire. One lick of its tongue across this earth——!

Oh, war—thou feeble destructionist!

And yet this is a small demonstration we are witnessing. The Indians of Pala in 1806 and we mental aborigines of 1923 are all together as much less than nothing before this sight of the heavens—and yet it is nothing in the universe. The burning of vast stars, such as the giant sun that exploded last winter and consumed itself in a space thousands of times greater than our entire solar system, was a greater characteristic of the magnitude of the universe than is this temporary darkening of a small strip of our planet.

But this terrible awe. Children on the doorsteps catch it and cry out at the darkness.

Why is everything else so still? We realize it all of a sudden—there is not a laugh in the city!

By telephone we get a picture of "Quaint Tijuana" during these three minutes. There is no wickedness there now.

The saloons have no customers during this sample of absolute night. Painted women stand in their doorways and look out on the heavens for the first time, perhaps, in years with wondering minds. Before the spectacle they are moved inwardly with misgivings. The background of childhood superstition and those years, long ago, of contact with churches comes to the front.

Their poor souls, dormant and obscured by the fast life, begin to scratch inside their broken bodies—and the pain of that passing experience is sweet, because it is so rare.

"What makes it? What makes it?"

The universe has played a dark card—and that card is a trump card, for Tijuana, quick with arguments for worldly ways, has no answer to the riddle of the universe.

Ah, it's lighter now. The gloom is passing. It lifts, speeds by, and again the shadows are lacy.

The crescents are back on the sides of buildings.

The sun shoots a glaring signal from around the edge of the moon. The sun is escaping from the interloper. The inexorable laws of space that forced this illusion are now destroying it.

Boundaries of the densest portions of the black night are fleeing eastward and to the south, across Mexico.

Breezes slowly die as the sun's rays resume control of the terrestrial temperature.

Soon it is morning of the "night that came in the day."

Puzzled chickens flock down from their roosts. Cows go back to their grazing. Street lights are turned off. Frightened children are reassured.

San Diego drifts back into its marts and households.

Tijuana shakes its languor.

The spell is gone, gone for 120 years.

When the shadow returns, we shall not see it. We shall be with the Pala Indians of 1806.

And the event will be the all-absorbing topic then to those strange creatures whom we may never meet except in our imaginations—our children's grandchildren.

W. O. McGeehan Describes the Battle of the Century—The Dempsey-Firpo Fight

PAUL GALLICO, one of the masters of the art of sports reporting, pointed out that there is rarely anything pretty about prize fighting. "The ring is a dirty game and it smells bad. But it is exciting, colorful, Rabelaisian, earthy. It attracts the rabble and the unwashed. It stinks of bodies and liniment and leather and blood and it appeals to the so-called lowest instincts of humankind. But they are still humankind's instincts and therefore important."

Boxing—the art of hitting without getting hit—was reported by Homer in his *Iliad* and by Virgil in his *Aeneid*. The ancient Olympic games featured bouts between highly trained boxing champions, some of whom wore the swollen cauliflower ear as an honored mark of their profession. Fighting with a cestus, an iron-studded gauntlet of leather, "no man ever had a losing streak of more than one," Arthur Daley points out. The old-style bare-knuckle fighting was as brutal as a gouging match on the frontier. Philip Hone, a celebrated New York diarist, tells of one bout a century ago in which two bruisers "thumped and battered each other for the gratification of a brutal gang of spectators" for almost three hours, until, after being knocked down eighty-one times, one of the contestants fell dead in the ring. In the mining towns sports reporters made a special point of it when the referee "failed to be killed."

John L. Sullivan, "the Boston Strong Boy," was the last heavyweight champion to fight with his fists. It was during his reign that the transition was made from bare knuckles to padded gloves. When Gentleman Jim Corbett knocked out John L., in 1892, the vanquished boxer announced to the crowd: "If I had to be licked I'm glad it was by an American. Yours truly, John L. Sullivan."

Corbett, Fitzsimmons, Jeffries, Johnson, and Willard each held the title in turn. Then in 1919 a new heavyweight sensation, with dark eyes and beautifully proportioned body, appeared on the pugilistic horizon. Jack Dempsey, "the Manassa Mauler," was utterly without mercy in his profession of slugging men into unconsciousness. Using a bobbing and weaving style of attack, the snarling tiger knocked out Jess Willard, breaking his jaw in thirteen places before being declared the winner in the third round.

On September 14, 1923, Dempsey met an Argentine giant, Luis Angel Firpo, called "the Wild Bull of the Pampas," at the Polo Grounds in New York. The champion weighed 192½ pounds, Firpo 216½. The fight lasted less than two rounds. But during this brief time some 85,000 spectators were treated to what was probably the most thrilling bout in boxing annals.

Fortunately this epic sports event received the attention of a masterful sports historian. That the brilliant W. O. McGeehan was "the greatest sports writer that ever lived" was the generous verdict of Paul Gallico. A sentimental Irishman, William O'Connell McGeehan was born in San Francisco and gradually worked his way to *The New York Herald* to become one of the top sports writers of his day. He added many phrases to the sports argot—phrases of an ironically descriptive nature, differing from the slapstick slang then in vogue—among them "the cauliflower industry" and "the manly art of modified murder." To him the New York State boxing commissioners were "the Iron Dukes." "Prize fighting is not a sport," he once wrote. "It is a business. As a business it is probably as honest as American politics or the average business and probably a little more honest than the stock market."

"They told me yesterday that Firpo could not understand the English count beyond six"

The New York Herald, September 14, 1923

The Manassa matador dropped the Wild Bull of the Pampas, but not until the matador was gored by the bull so that he will remember it for many a day. Fifty-seven seconds after the bell rang for the second round at the Polo Grounds last night, Luis Angel Firpo, the hope and pride of Latin America, rolled over near the ropes at the south side of the ring inert, unconscious—knocked out.

But what happened before this was as hard to follow as the shifting colors of a kaleidoscope. It was the most savage heavyweight bout that ever was staged, while it lasted. The first round was startlingly like that sanguinary affair at Toledo when Dempsey knocked out Jess Willard and won his championship.

Seven times Dempsey dropped the Argentine giant last night, and seven times the giant pulled himself up to his feet. He came up each time fighting, and lashing savagely but blindly at the champion. It was a right to the jaw that dropped Firpo the first time. The other six times the giant was felled by volleys of blows, on the head, on the body, all over his huge bulk. As he dropped for the fourth time it seemed that he could not rise.

Charles Schwegler, the old prize fighter, who was at the bell, rose in his chair and counted. Firpo turned his seemingly sightless eyes in the direction of the bell as the counter shouted "Nine!" He dragged himself upward painfully and slowly, only to be knocked down again and again.

But every time the Argentino came up he lashed at the champion. Some of these blows landed, for Dempsey seemed reckless and determined to carry the fight to the Argentino to the end. He rushed in, disregarding the clublike right of the giant.

Certainly Luis Angel Firpo had been given even more punishment than Willard had received at Toledo. The blood was gushing from his mouth as he reeled into his corner. His ribs were red where Dempsey had pounded him. Yet under that bloody smear the mask of a face remained just as expressionless as ever.

Near the ringside the pack sensed the fact that it would be over in the second round. They crowded closer to the ring. At the bell starting the bout Dempsey, with his teeth bared in that ring snarl and the face suggesting the wolf, rushed out of his corner. He battered Firpo against the ropes.

Then there was a gasp as though all the spectators had caught the same fear. Firpo swung that cave man's right of his and caught the champion under the chin. Dempsey reeled against the ropes, groggy. Then he slipped through them on the south side of the ring in among the typewriters and telegraph instruments.

The man at the bell bawled his count. He reached the count of three when Dempsey was pushed back into the ring. The champion looked a bit wobbly. His eyes seemed to be glazed for just a fraction of a second. His jaw was sunk, and he looked bewildered. But that was just for a fleeting instant. The scowl came back again, and Dempsey settled down to his killing of the Wild Bull.

The champion's head cleared quickly. He drove Firpo over onto the corner where his manager, Jack Kearns, sat pale and shaking at the narrow escape of the champion. A right to the jaw sent Firpo to the mat again for a short time. The champion stepped across the prostrate body of the giant and waited.

For the last time Firpo arose from that dirty bit of white canvas early in the second round. Even then he did not rise like a beaten man. The blood gushed from the battered lips, but the eyes behind the narrow lids were gleaming like the points of white-hot

needles. His stout heart was still full of fight. He lashed with that clublike left to find that vulnerable place at the base of Dempsey's brain. But the blows glanced off Dempsey's head. The champion pressed close and lashed a right and left to the Argentino's jaw. Firpo's brown pillars of legs started to crumble beneath him. As he started to sink Dempsey drove a final right hook to the jaw. Firpo, the hope of Latin America, sagged face downward to the mat close to the ropes.

On the other side of the ring the man at the bell started to count, waving his arms. Referee Gallagher bent over the prostrate giant, waving his arms and shouting the numbers into his ear. They told me yesterday that Firpo could not understand the English count beyond six. This time he could not hear anything. He was out. There was no motion but his spasmodic breathing and a feeble attempt to raise that ponderous right arm. It happened so quickly that the crowd did not even cheer.

Dempsey stood a little back from the fallen giant as he fell for the last time. He listened for the final count just a little wobbly on his own clean-cut legs. As it went to eight he licked his lips in a wolfish fashion. At "ten" he rushed to his corner into the arms of his younger brother and Johnny Dempsey. Then he raised his gloves in acknowledgment of the cheering that finally came.

This was no boxing match. It was a fight, and a most primitive one at that.

Only in the jungle would you find a replica of the rapidly shifting drama that over 85,000 at the Polo Grounds saw last night. A pair of wolves battling in the pines of the North Woods, a pair of cougars in the wastes of the Southwest, might have staged a faster and more savage bout, but no two human beings.

Firpo recovered quickly enough as they dragged him from his stool. The mask of a face was cleared again, and it was as expressionless as ever. There was no look of dejection there, there was no indication of humiliation in those features.

Jack Dempsey fought his own fight. In his heart he valued this Latin just a bit too cheaply and he almost lost his championship because of it. He carried the fight to Firpo and seemed to drive him mad. It was apparent that he might have picked Firpo to pieces at long range, but he rushed in. He showed what the French call the will to use the bayonet. That made it a fight the like of which probably has not been seen since heavyweights first started to battle.

In the dressing room of Dempsey, besieged with the admirers of the champion, Jack Kearns said: "Of course we will fight him again. We will fight anybody."

* * *

"THERE WAS a big question before the fight," wrote Ring Lardner, "as to whether or no the Wild Bull could take it. He took it and took it plenty and came back for more, and got it. They ain't nobody living that could take what he took before he finally took that left and right in succession and became the tame cow of the pampas."

Ring Lardner furthermore noted that another question was settled, namely can Dempsey take it? "Jack was on the receiving end of four or five of the most murderous blows ever delivered in a prize ring, but he came back after each one and fought all the harder. He never lost sight of the main idear, that he must get this guy and get him quick. He didn't get him none too quick and if the fight had went a round longer they would have been wholesale deaths from heart disease with maybe some of the victims in Dempsey's corner. It was a FIGHT."

Heywood Broun Discovers that the Ruth Is
Mighty and Shall Prevail

To HELL WITH Babe Ruth!" In banzai charges Japanese during the Pacific war uttered this blasphemous attack on a national idol, on the theory that they would undermine American morale.

He was unforgettable, even when he struck out. He was beyond challenge the most popular athletic hero in the history of American sports. When Babe Ruth stood up to bat, slowly and deliberately waving his huge bludgeon, the worshiping crowds of sports fans were transported to the heights of Mt. Olympus. He was color itself—a fellow with a huge frame, a tremendous head on a barrel-shaped torso, the wrists of a giant, the legs of a bantamweight, and a round, moonface with little, glittering eyes. When the Babe connected and trotted around the bases, taking mincing steps, there was always a great, reverent roar from the stands.

The sports writers stayed up late composing new names and superlatives for him: The Sultan of Swat, the Behemoth of Swing, the Mammoth of Maul, the Bambino, the Colossus of Clout. Paul Gallico described him as "one of the ugliest men I have ever known—kneaded, rough-thumbed out of earth, a golem, a figurine that might have been made by a savage." To John Kieran he was the Paul Bunyan of baseball: "He stood out among the ordinary heroes of the diamond as Gulliver towered above the Lilliputians. Even his escapades were colossal. He never did anything by half measures. Those who knew him best can still gape with wonder or rock with laughter in recalling his off-the-record feats through his hilarious career."

The son of a Baltimore saloonkeeper, George Herman Ruth was brought up in St. Mary's Industrial School, an institution for delinquents. A priest at the school recommended him to Jack Dunn, the manager of the Baltimore Orioles, who took him on in 1914 at an annual salary of $600. The gangling youth soon found to his amazement that by playing the game that gave him the greatest pleasure in the world he could earn fantastic sums. He began his big-league career as a southpaw pitcher for the Boston Red Sox and later came to the New York Yankees. A peerless slugger, he clouted a total of 714 home runs and earned as much as $80,000 a season for his services.

It was a never-dimming miracle of this inexplicable country, wrote Paul Gallico, that this half brute could emerge from the filth and ashes "to shine more brightly than any phoenix as the beloved hero of the nation, rich beyond maddest fantasies." The Babe's exploits both on and off the playing field were legendary. He earned a total of more than $2,000,000 and spent most of it. He once admitted: "I lost $35,000 on one horse race alone."

After earning $40,000 in one season he had to borrow money from the Yankee club to pay his way to training camp the following spring. When he bought a new car and promptly turned it upside down in a culvert, he was informed by the car-agency manager that mechanics would be sent out at once to repair the damage. "Hell, no!" roared the Babe. "Don't bother. Just send me another car." After making a movie in Cuba, he collected a check for $25,000, which he kept in his vest pocket and hauled out to show to those who doubted his story. The paper finally wore out, the promoters ran into difficulty, and the $25,000 check became a soiled scrap. The Babe thought it a great joke on himself.

Joe Williams, the sports reporter, tells the story of a memorable day in St. Paul when Queen Marie of Rumania happened to be in town at the same time as the Babe, then on a vaudeville tour. To his business manager the situation was a "natural." The King of Swat was to meet the Queen of Rumania. Everything was all set. The Mayor was to make the introduction at City Hall. The Queen, no shy violet, appeared precisely on time. No Ruth. Thirty minutes later, and still no Ruth. Walsh, his business manager, phoned his hotel.

"Aw, them foreign dames give me a pain," grumbled Ruth. "You keep 'em."

Ban Johnson, the late president of the American League, once commented: "Ruth has the mind of a fifteen-year-old boy." His stomach was considerably larger. On one notable occasion during a training swing through the South, the Babe ate twelve railroad-station hot dogs and drank eight bottles of yellow soda pop. The resultant stomach-ache was felt around the world. The entire nation was gripped in an amazing deathwatch, but the Babe survived.

It was said that the Babe couldn't even remember the names of his teammates. He greeted everyone, friends and acquaintances and strangers, young or old, with the same welcome: "Hello, kid."

Babe Ruth's mighty exploits were immortalized in a famous baseball story by Heywood Broun, one of the best of American sports writers. A giant of a man with an ability to write mellifluous prose, Broun later turned from sports to assume the burdens of the world on his ample shoulders. As adept at dramatic criticism as in sports reporting, Broun once panned Geoffrey Steyne as "the worst actor on the American stage." The next time his victim appeared before the footlights Heywood greeted him with this terse salvo at the very end of his review: "Mr. Steyne's performance was not up to his usual standard."

The Sultan of Swat steals a World Series show

New York *World*, October 12, 1923

The Ruth is mighty and shall prevail. He did yesterday. Babe made two home runs, and the Yankees won from the Giants at the Polo Grounds by a score of four to two. This evens up the World Series, with one game for each contender.

It was the first game the Yankees won from the Giants since October 10, 1921, and it ended a string of eight successive victories for the latter, with one tie thrown in.

Victory came to the American League champions through a change in tactics. Miller Huggins could hardly fail to have observed Wednesday that terrible things were almost certain to happen to his men if they paused anyplace along the line from first to home.

In order to prevent blunders in base running he wisely decided to eliminate it. The batter who hits a ball into the stands cannot possibly be caught napping off any base.

The Yankees prevented Kelly, Frisch, and the rest from performing tricks in black magic by consistently hammering the ball out of the park or into sections of the stand where only amateurs were seated.

Though simplicity itself, the system worked like a charm. Three of the Yankees' four runs were the product of homers, and this was enough for a winning total. Erin Ward was Ruth's assistant. Irish Meusel of the Giants also made a home run, but yesterday's show belonged to Ruth.

For the first time since coming to New York, Babe achieved his full brilliance in a World Series game. Before this he has varied between pretty good and simply awful, but yesterday he was magnificent.

Just before the game John McGraw remarked:

"Why shouldn't we pitch to Ruth? I've said before, and I'll say it again, we pitch to better hitters than Ruth in the National League."

Ere the sun had set on McGraw's rash and presumptuous words, the Babe had flashed across the sky fiery portents which should have been sufficient to strike terror and conviction into the hearts of all infidels. But John McGraw clung to his heresy with a courage worthy of a better cause.

In the fourth inning Ruth drove the ball completely out of the premises. McQuillan was pitching at the time, and the count was two balls and one strike. The strike was a fast ball shoulder-high, at which Ruth had lunged with almost comic ferocity and ineptitude.

Snyder peeked at the bench to get a signal from McGraw. Catching for the Giants must be a terrific strain on the neck muscles, for apparently it is etiquette to take the signals from the bench manager furtively. The catcher is supposed to pretend he is merely glancing around to see if the girl in the red hat is anywhere in the grandstand, although all the time his eyes are intent on McGraw.

Of course the nature of the code is secret, but this time McGraw scratched his nose, to indicate: "Try another of those shoulder-high fast ones on the Big Bam and let's see if we can't make him break his back again."

But Babe didn't break his back, for he had something solid to check his terrific swing. The ball started climbing from the moment it left the plate. It was a pop fly with a brand-new gland and, though it flew high, it also flew far.

When last seen the ball was crossing the roof of the stand in deep right field at an altitude of 315 feet. We wonder whether new baseballs conversing together in the original package ever remark: "Join Ruth and see the world."

In the fifth Ruth was up again, and by this time McQuillan had left the park utterly and Jack Bentley was pitching. The count crept up to two strikes and two balls. Snyder sneaked a look at the little logician deep in the dugout. McGraw blinked twice, pulled up his trousers, and thrust the forefinger of his right hand into his left eye. Snyder knew that he meant, "Try the Big Bozo on a slow curve around his knees and don't forget to throw to first if you happen to drop the third strike."

Snyder called for the delivery as directed, and Ruth half topped a line drive over the wall of the lower stand in right field. With that drive the Babe tied a record. Benny Kauff and Duffy Lewis are the only other players who ever made two home runs in a single World Series game.

But was McGraw convinced and did he rush out of the dugout and kneel before Ruth with a cry of "Maestro" as the Babe crossed the plate? He did not. He nibbled at not a single word he has ever uttered in disparagement of the prowess of the Yankee slugger. In the ninth Ruth came to bat with two out and a runner on second base. By every consideration of prudent tactics an intentional pass seemed indicated.

Snyder jerked his head around and observed that McGraw was blowing his nose. The Giant catcher was puzzled, for that was a signal he had never learned. By a process of pure reasoning he attempted to figure out just what it was that his chief was trying to convey to him.

"Maybe he means if we pitch to Ruth we'll blow the game," thought Snyder, but he looked toward the bench again just to make sure.

Now McGraw intended no signal at all when he blew his nose. That was not tactics, but only a head cold. On the second glance, Snyder observed that the little Napoleon gritted his teeth. Then he proceeded to spell out with the first three fingers of his right hand: "The Old Guard dies, but never surrenders." That was a signal Snyder recognized, although it never had passed between him and his manager.

McGraw was saying: "Pitch to the big bum if he hammers every ball in the park into the North River."

And so, at Snyder's request, Bentley did pitch to Ruth, and the Babe drove the ball deep into right center; so deep that Casey Stengel could feel the hot breath of the bleacherites on his back as the ball came down and he caught it. If that drive had been just a shade to the right it would have been a third home run for Ruth. As it was, the Babe had a great day, with two home runs, a terrific long fly, and two bases on balls.

Neither pass was intentional. For that McGraw should receive due credit. His fame deserves to be recorded along with the men who said, "Lay on, MacDuff," "Sink me the ship, Master Gunner, split her in twain," and "I'll fight it out on this line if it takes all summer." For John McGraw also went down eyes front and his thumb on his nose.

BABE RUTH was too much for the baffled Giants. The American League Yankees won the 1923 World Series from the National League champions by a final score of four games to two.

During the 1932 World Series between the New York Yankees and the Chicago Cubs the Babe performed his greatest feat. The Windy City team, with Root pitching, was giving Ruth an unmerciful riding. He had already hit one home run when he came to bat in the latter part of the game. The entire Cub bench came to the front of the dugout to hurl choice epithets at him. When Ruth missed the first pitch, the Chicago fans roared, whereupon he held up one finger so that everyone could see it. When he swung again and missed, the crowd rocked with laughter and the Cub players hurled more insults. The Babe held up two fingers. Then there were two pitches, pitches wide of the mark.

At this point came the magnificent gesture. With his forefinger extended, the Babe pointed to the flagpole in center field to show the pitcher, the Cubs, and the crowd where he was going to wallop the next ball for a home run. He blasted the next ball straight and true out of the park at exactly the point he had predicted. It was an amazing feat, and it is already being denied by baseball historians.

The Babe's legs gave out at forty, and he retired. He never got the chance to manage a big-league ball club; it was said that nobody could be sure that Ruth could manage himself. When, in the summer of 1948, the Big Fellow died, after a prolonged and cruel illness, some 80,000 fans filed past his bier as he lay in state at Yankee Stadium, "the House that Ruth Built." "It is part of our national history," the *New York Post*'s Jimmy Cannon commented, "that all boys dream of being Babe Ruth before they are anyone else."

Walter Duranty Reports a Moscow Trial

ONE EVENING in the summer of 1924 Walter Duranty, the British-born foreign correspondent of *The New York Times,* was sitting at home in Moscow when about 9:30 a telephone message came from the acting chief of the Press Department of the Foreign Office, requesting his presence at once. Instantly alert because the voice was full of excitement, Duranty immediately left to meet his caller.

"I am taking you to a trial," the acting chief informed him. "Only two other correspondents will be admitted. It is the trial of our greatest enemy; we have caught him red-handed. Tonight the Supreme Military Tribunal of the USSR will pass judgment on its archenemy, Boris Savinkov, Kerensky's War Minister, who planned the killing of Count Mirbach and the attempted assassination of Lenin and the revolt at Yaroslavl in 1918; the man who more than anyone brought about the Franco-British intervention and the Polish War. He came into Russia secretly, in disguise and with false papers, but we caught him; and tonight he will be judged."

Duranty came out of the courtroom with one of the greatest stories of his brilliant career. A correspondent attached to French headquarters during World War I, he had been sent to the Baltic region by *The New York Times* and soon became the world's best-known correspondent on Russia and Russian affairs. In 1932 he was awarded the Pulitzer Prize for the best correspondence of the year for his series of dispatches on the working out of the Five Year Plan. When John Gunther in 1935 published his bestselling *Inside Europe* he quite properly titled his chapter on Russia: "Duranty's Inferno."

"The greatest theatrical performance
I ever attended"

The New York Times, August 30, 1924

MOSCOW, AUGUST 29—Boris Savinkov, archconspirator, archterrorist, supporter of Kerensky, and the bitterest enemy of the Soviet regime, has returned to Russia only to be trapped and to become the central figure in a scene of the greatest dramatic tension, which was enacted last night and early this morning.

Lifting the veil, the Supreme Military Tribunal last night permitted a few chosen spectators to see the final stage of his trial. The trial went on far past midnight. They heard the tired old revolutionary defy the judges and defy death. The court condemned him But the prisoner's indifference to the verdict of death—for he was the revolutionary, the terrorist, up to the last moment—and his willingness to confess that he had erred in his judgment of the Soviet's stability moved the judges to grant him the right to appeal.

The result was that today the Central Executive Committee exercised clemency and commuted the death sentence to ten years' imprisonment.

General Savinkov it was who planned the most outstanding assassinations of the old Social Revolutionary murder gang. They killed Minister Plehve and Grand Duke Sergius at the Kremlin gate. They wounded General Dubassov, and only an accident prevented them from blowing up the cruiser *Rurik* and killing Chukhnin, commander of the war port of Sebastopol.

There were a score of other killings or attempted killings in those days, and behind them all was this little man with the big head with its Napoleonic features and the soul of a fanatic, for he was the incarnation of the murderous conspiracy. He was Kerensky's Minister of War, and when he saw the tide running then toward the Bolsheviki he returned to his old game of deadly plot and murder. The abortive coups of Kornilov and Kanedin were inspired by him. With the aid of French gold he raised an insurrection against the Soviet power in Yaroslavl. His orders armed with a revolver the girl Fanny Kaplan, who so nearly killed Lenin in the summer of 1918.

From Poland and Paris, General Savinkov directed a dozen murders of Bolsheviki leaders, and attack upon attack of semibrigand partisans against Soviet Russia. Then he weakened and returned to his fatherland, and into the lion's mouth, with a forged passport under the name of Stepanov. Immediately the Bolsheviki

caught him, and last night they judged him. Never have I seen such a tremendous drama.

Like true artists, the Russians prepare their stage effects unconsciously. I received my precious communication from the Soviet Foreign Office to be ready for "a most interesting story." Accompanied by two other foreign correspondents, I drove with a Foreign Office official to an unknown destination. It was the building where Krasnachokov, director of one of the biggest Soviet banks, was condemned to five years' imprisonment for abuse of his position. There, while the guards, armed to the teeth and with bayonets fixed, took the official papers to an inner room for verification, he revealed what was the scene awaiting upstairs.

Not a line had appeared in the press. Not an iota of this stupendous story—to Russia—had leaked out to the public. In the courtroom were barely two hundred persons, representing all the influential officials of the Soviet regime now in Moscow. Acting Premier Kamenev was there with his beautiful wife, as was Kurski, the Minister of Justice; Krassikov, President of the Supreme Court; Minjiniki Elyava, Premier of the Caucasian Federation, and Béla Kun, once dictator of Red Hungary.

It was the keenest first-night audience that Moscow could offer. Every man and woman was agog with expectation, intensely conscious of the unrivaled treat before them and prepared to enjoy its piquancy to the uttermost. Nor were they disappointed.

The court entered—three youngish men in uniform, with the supreme judge of the Military Tribunal, Ulrich, in the center. Then came the guards and soldiers and, surprisingly, two sailors—and the prisoner.

He was a small man, quite bald, about forty-five, who walked with rather weak and faltering steps. He was dressed in a cheap double-breasted gray sack suit, with a starched white collar and shirt and a thin black tie. His face suggested the pictures of young Napoleon, but was cadaverous and drawn, with deep shadows under the eyes. Savinkov was quite unafraid, and glanced around with the curiosity of a man taking his last look at human beings and their funny little life.

"Make your final statement," said Ulrich, the preliminary examinations having been held *in camera*.

General Savinkov arose from the wooden bench and turned his eyes on the spectators, lazily surveying them. Stanislavski would have turned green with envy just to watch him, for this was a nature that art cannot rival. Like Regulus of old, Savinkov had left ease and safety to face death, and now the final moment had come. He, a Russian, must speak to Russians in a worthy manner before he died.

Just as the tension became almost unbearable, he began to speak in a low, weak voice, but one which was quite audible throughout the small courtroom.

"I am not afraid to die," he began. "I know your sentence already, but I do not care. I am Boris Savinkov, revolutionary and friend of revolutionaries, to be judged now by your revolutionary court.

"I am here by my fault, my unwilling fault. You represent the Russian people, the workers and the peasants. Judge me for my faults, my unwilling faults, toward Russia."

Then Savinkov told the story of his life as a conspirator against the Tsar. He told it either with consummate art or with utter sincerity. Speaking simply in words that every person in the audience could understand, for to them he addressed himself rather than to the judges, he reviewed his terrorist adventures, the death of Plehve, Sergius, and the rest; told how he lived always cut off from human life, cut off from the workers and peasants, always under the shadow of a shameful death, always utterly apart from men and women who lived and loved in the sunlight.

Often, Savinkov paused so long that the whole room quivered with emotion. Was it sincerity? Was it weakness? Was it art?

"Then came the triumph of the idea to which I have devoted my life, the triumph of revolution."

His voice deepened as he turned toward the auditors with a pathetic, hopeless gesture of both hands.

"Then you, who now represent revolutionary Russia, seized the reins," he went on. "I turned against you for four reasons. First, my life's dream had been the Constituent Assembly. You smashed it, and iron entered my soul. I was wrong. Our Russia isn't ready for self-government. You knew it, and I didn't. I admit my fault.

"Second, the Brest Litovsk peace, which I regarded as a shameful betrayal of my country. Again I was wrong, and you were right. History has proved it, and I admit my fault.

"Third, I thought that Bolshevism couldn't stand, that it was too extreme, that it would be replaced by the other extreme of monarchism, and that the only alternative was the middle course. Again I was proved wrong, and again I admit it.

"Fourth, the most important reason, I believed that you didn't represent the Russian masses, the workers and peasants. I lived always in the watertight compartment of the conspirator. I knew nothing of the feelings of the Russian masses. But I thought that they were against you, and so I, who have given my life to their services, set myself against you, also."

General Savinkov then told, in accents that carried conviction to nearly all who heard him, how he was faced in Paris by an appalling problem. Perhaps he had been wrong in estimating the feelings of the Russian people; perhaps the Bolsheviki did represent them.

"People came and told me about Russia," he said; "that the peasants and workers were happy under the Bolshevist regime. And I half believed them. Others said the opposite—that my country was groaning under a cruel tyranny. And I half believed that also, until my position became unbearable. I must know the truth or die, I said, and so I came along of my own free will, without bombs or revolvers, without plots or supporters, with only one object—to learn the truth, to see it with my own eyes, to hear it with my own ears.

"Now I know, and my life is cheap as the price of that knowledge. I say here before your court, whose sentence I know already, surrounded by your soldiers, of whom I have no fear, that I recognize unconditionally your right to govern Russia. I ask not your mercy. I ask you only to let your revolutionary conscience judge a man who has never sought anything for himself, who has devoted his whole life to the cause of the Russian people. But I add this: before coming here to say that I recognize you, I have gone through worse suffering than the utmost you can do to me."

The last words were uttered in the same low voice as the rest. Then Savinkov sat down, opened a cheap cardboard box of cigarettes, asked for a light from a guard, and began to smoke. The presiding judge, Ulrich, announced a fifteen minutes' interval.

When the judges, guards, and the prisoner withdrew, evidently nine tenths of the audience believed in Savinkov's sincerity. *The New York Times* correspondent asked the opinion of Kurski, the Minister of Justice.

"I think he is telling the truth," Kurski replied. "And what is more, our investigations have shown no attempt on his part to start terrorist activities here, or to get in touch with anti-Bolshevist organizations. For one thing, there are no such organizations in existence, though he may not know that. Anyway, I believe he is honest."

Béla Kun did not agree.

"Savinkov is a bold fellow, who has always carried his life in his hands," he said. "But he is a romantic creature, not a Marxist. He has been tracked and threatened a thousand times and has lived ever in an atmosphere of murder and sudden death. Now he is up against it, and, like the true romantic, gives us a beautiful story."

The judges, guards, and prisoner reentered the hall. The second act was tragically short.

"We have heard your statement," said Ulrich. "Have you anything more to say before judgment is passed upon you?"

Savinkov stood up, a little lonelier and more worn than ever.

"I know your sentence," he said, "and I don't care. I am not afraid of it, nor of death. But one thing I do fear—that the Russian people will misjudge me and misunderstand my life and its purpose. I never was an enemy of the Russian people. I devoted my life to serve them. I have made mistakes, but I die unashamed and unafraid."

He sat down as the audience was inclined to applaud this their worst enemy.

"I WILL ALWAYS THINK of it as the greatest theatrical performance I ever attended," Duranty wrote later. "Savinkov's final speech was the greatest piece of oratory I have ever heard. I say this deliberately, although I have heard speeches by men who are reputed great orators. It was like the last speech from the scaffold with which condemned criminals about to die in old Britain, whether they were kings or highwaymen or poor devils who had stolen a sheep, used to regale an appreciative audience."

With the exception of Duranty and two colleagues, no foreigners were present at the trial, which infuriated the diplomatic corps when they heard of it and won him a dozen invitations to dinner in the next three days.

Though Duranty did not know it at the time, the Savinkov trial was the forerunner of a series of sabotage and treason trials that attracted world-wide attention. To foreign observers these affairs seemed excessively theatrical and the courtroom confessions seldom very convincing. In October, 1930, a group of engineers under the leadership of a Professor Ramsin was arrested on a charge of plotting to undermine the economic structure of the USSR and to overthrow its government. Ramsin and his associates publicly confessed to all the charges brought against them; they were condemned to death, but the sentence was afterward commuted to imprisonment for ten years. In March, 1933, at the Moscow trials forty-one engineers working for the Metropolitan-Vickers Company in Moscow were brought to trial for sabotage. One by one they proceeded to the microphone and, with astonishing readiness, enumerated their wrecking activities, although they were men of the highest professional standing. The engineers were acquitted and deported from Russia.

In August, 1936, Zinoviev and Kamenev and other survivors of the old Trotskyite group were taken into custody and accused of the murder nearly two years before of Sergei Kirov, one of Stalin's junior favorites, and of planning to murder Stalin. The defendants fluently confessed their sins, but were executed together with a hundred others. On June 11, 1937, a Supreme Military Tribunal sentenced Marshal Tukhachevsky and seven other ranking generals of the Red Army to death on charges of "military conspiracy with an unfriendly power," obviously meaning Germany. The former heroes of the Civil War promptly confessed their treason and were shot to death within twenty-four hours. The last of the great trials took place in March, 1938, when Rykov, President of the Council of Commissars, Bukharin, the editor of *Pravda,* Yagoda, the former chief of the Ogpu, and others were executed for treason.

The exaggerated self-immolation and confessions of the accused in the trials and purges mystified the Western world. Inside Russia they were accepted as a necessary concomitant "for the construction of a new society."

"Skeets" Miller of the Louisville *Courier-Journal*
Describes a National Battle for One
Obscure Human Life

IT BEGAN innocently enough. Young Floyd Collins, a native of the Kentucky countryside, was always prowling underearth in search of new cavern wonders to attract tourists. On a cold winter's day in early 1925 he found a marvelous coliseum, a great new cavern, in Sand Cave, a few miles from Mammoth Cave. Suddenly, when less than one hundred feet from daylight, he was caught in a cave-in that pinned his foot under a six-ton boulder. The young man lay imprisoned in a huge, natural tomb, with rocks, gravel, and mud covering him to the hips.

That's all there was to it, except that the alarm eventually reached into the homes and hearts of the entire nation. When William Burke ("Skeets") Miller, a diminutive reporter for the Louisville *Courier-Journal,* arrived at Sand Cave to cover the story, he found several friends of the trapped man warming themselves at a fire and wondering how soon Collins would extricate himself. The enterprising newsman promptly organized rescue squads and crawled on his belly like a snake down into a black, slippery passage to interview the trapped man. This series of dispatches lived up to the best traditions of the *Courier-Journal*'s great editor, fire-breathing "Marse Henry" ("To Hell with the Hapsburgs and Hohenzollerns") Watterson.

Here are two of the stories on the Floyd Collins tragedy, for which Miller was awarded the 1926 Pulitzer Prize in reporting:

The saga of Floyd Collins

Courier-Journal (Louisville), February 2, 3, 1925

CAVE CITY, KENTUCKY, FEBRUARY 2—
Floyd Collins is suffering torture almost beyond description, but he is still hopeful he will be taken out alive, he told me at 6:20 o'clock last night on my last visit to him.

Until I went inside myself I could not understand exactly what the situation was. I wondered why someone

couldn't do something quick, but I found out why.

I was lowered by my heels into the entrance of Sand Cave. The passageway is about five feet in diameter. After reaching the end of an eighty-foot drop I reached fairly level ground for a moment.

From here on I had to squirm like

a snake. Water covers almost every inch of the ground, and after the first few feet I was wet through and through. Every moment it got colder. It seemed that I would crawl forever, but after going about ninety feet I reached a very small compartment, slightly larger than the remainder of the channel.

This afforded a breathing spell before I started again on toward the prisoner. The dirty water splashed in my face and numbed my body, but I couldn't stop.

Finally I slid down an eight-foot drop and, a moment later, saw Collins and called to him. He mumbled an answer.

My flashlight revealed a face on which is written suffering of many long hours, because Collins has been in agony every conscious moment since he was trapped at ten o'clock Friday morning.

I saw the purple of his lips, the pallor on the face, and realized that something must be done before long if this man is to live.

Before I could see his face, however, I was forced to raise a small piece of oilcloth covering it.

"Put it back," he said. "Put it back —the water."

Then I noticed a small drip-drip-drip from above. Each drop struck Collins' face. The first few hours he didn't mind, but the constant dripping almost drove him insane. His brother had taken the oilcloth to him earlier in the day.

This reminded me of the old water torture used in ages past. I shuddered.

Here I was at the end of the journey, and I saw quickly why it was that workmen who had penetrated as far as I had accomplished but little. I was exhausted, as they had been. I was numb from head to foot. Chills

raced through my body. I missed the fresh air. I came to know in this brief time what Collins had suffered, but I could not comprehend fully. I felt certain I would get out. Collins has hopes, nothing more. I was in no physical pain. Collins' foot, held by a six-ton rock in a natural crevice, is never without pain.

I tried to squirm over Collins' body to reach the rock, but his body takes up nearly all the space. I squeezed in, hunting for some way to help him, until he begged me to get off.

"It hurts—hurts awful," he said.

Collins is lying on his back, resting more on the left side, so that his left cheek rests on the ground. His two arms are held fast in the crevice beside his body, so that he really is in a natural strait jacket.

I was behind Lieutenant Robert Burdon of the Louisville Fire Department, and followed by Homer Collins, brother of the victim, and Guy Turner. Homer Collins had brought with him some body harness to place around his brother, and we finally succeeded in putting it on him.

The prisoner helped as best he could by squirming and turning as much as possible, and finally we were ready to haul away on the rope attached to Collins. We pulled as much as we could, and it seemed as though we made headway. It was estimated we moved the prisoner five inches.

Perhaps we did, but I can hardly realize it. All of us were on the point of collapse, and after a short time our strength failed. We couldn't do any more.

We saw that the blankets and covering which Collins' brother had brought to him were in place and that he was resting as comfortably as we could make him.

Then we left near his head a lantern

well filled with oil. It isn't much, but the tiny light it throws means much in that relentless trap and it may bring some bit of consolation to a daring underground explorer whose chance for life is small.

We said farewell, and the last man started backward. I found soon that the trip out is worse than the one in. I encountered difficulty in crawling backward for a time, but practice soon enabled me to make progress.

Every foot it seemed the dirty water would splash in my face. I didn't mind it on my body any more, because I was numb to it. Frequently I had to go back up an incline, and the water would flow down to my neck, but, as I said, I already was as cold as I could get.

It was with the utmost relief that I came to the small compartment about midway from the entrance which affords to the rescuer his only resting place. I found that by working my head down to my feet and by easing my feet backward I could face about.

This aided a great deal, and within twenty minutes I came in sight of lights at the entrance. But, before reaching it, I discovered that two members of the party were unable to proceed farther and I spent what little strength remained in me to get them out.

SAND CAVE, CAVE CITY, KENTUCKY, FEBRUARY 3—Death holds no terror for Floyd Collins, he told me when I fed him tonight, more than 115 hours after he was trapped in Sand Cave, but he does not expect to die in the immediate future.

"I believe I would go to heaven," Collins said as I placed a bottle of milk to his lips, "but I can feel that I am to be taken out alive and—with both of my feet."

I have been in the cave three times since 5:30 o'clock this afternoon at the head of as many rescue parties. I am small and able to get back to the prisoner with the least possible difficulty. I am confident we are working now on a plan that will save Collins' life, and Collins shares my views.

Our plan is simple. I lead the way into the small, narrow, and extremely cold passageway and squirm back more than one hundred feet.

Thirteen other men crawl in behind me and pass a small chip hammer along to me. With this I work as best I can, enlarging the cave, and, as soon as I have succeeded in getting loose a large piece, I pass it back to the men behind me and, in this way, it is relayed out to the entrance.

It is terrible inside. The cold, dirty water numbs us as soon as we start in. We have come to dread it, but each of us tells ourselves that our suffering is as nothing compared to Collins'.

His patience during long hours of agony, his constant hope when life seemed nearing an end, is enough to strengthen the heart of anyone.

Collins doesn't know it, but he is playing a very, very big part in his own rescue.

Late this afternoon it was decided that Collins might possibly be rescued by drilling through the side of a hill and tunneling through behind him. The work was started by seven drillers of the Kentucky Rock Asphalt Company, but it was halted after a short time. It was feared that vibrations would dislodge huge rocks above Collins and crush him to death.

It was then decided to send rescuers in to him. I went first, starting in at 5:30 o'clock. In the next hour we made more progress than had been made in any single attempt before, and our waning confidence came back.

Time after time large and small rocks were passed along the human chain and out of the cave, which trapped Collins at ten o'clock Friday morning after the first attempt to explore it.

A minute seems an hour in there, and the water-sharpened rocks cut like a knife. But the numbness has its compensations. It keeps one from feeling the cuts and bruises.

All of us were exhausted, finally, and the word was passed back to crawl out. The air outside revived us quickly.

* * *

DAY AFTER DAY, the plight of Floyd Collins made page-one news. Millions of Americans who had never given a second thought to disasters claiming hundreds of lives kept their thoughts glued to the cave. Anyone who shared the dread of being buried alive could understand Floyd's hideous torment and could feel his breath fighting for air.

Inside the cave frantic rescue workers clawed away at the debris about Collins. Outside, in the mud and the cold, a throng of curious onlookers milled about a makeshift city of hundreds of pitched tents. State troopers with menacing guns restrained the mobs. Beyond Kentucky all America watched. "Be courageous, calm, and don't worry," wired one observer from far away. "Trust in God, and all will be well."

For seventeen days the nation shared the captive's horror. Crack miners from Southern pits sank a shaft from above as a final resort, even though it might precipitate an avalanche. Down below, the floor of the cave uplifted and cut off Floyd from his rescuers. "In millions of American homes," wrote one reporter, "the suspense became personal, the sound of the miners' boring was an audible throb."

The ending was an unhappy one. On February 17, 1925, *The New York Times* announced in a three-column page-one headline:

FIND FLOYD COLLINS DEAD IN
CAVE TRAP ON 18TH DAY; LIFE-
LESS AT LEAST 24 HOURS; FOOT
MUST BE AMPUTATED TO GET BODY OUT

Too many people would have got hurt had they tried to get Floyd Collins' body out. So they just filled in the cave with timbers and cement and let him stay right there where the cave had trapped him.

H. L. Mencken Finds a Place on Earth Where "Darwin Is the Devil, Scopes Is the Harlot of Babylon, and Darrow Is Beelzebub in Person"

Be it enacted—that it shall be unlawful for any teacher in any of the universities, normals, and all other public schools in the state, which are supported in whole or in part by the public school funds of the state, to teach the theory that denies the story of the divine creation of man as taught in the Bible, and to teach instead that man has descended from a lower order of animals.

THIS STATUTE was passed by the legislature of the state of Tennessee on March 21, 1925. It was a climax in a struggle that had split American Protestants into two warring camps. On the one side were the fundamentalists—those who believed in the letter of the Bible and who refused to accept any teaching that conflicted with it. On the other side were the modernists (or liberals), who, like the medieval scholastics, tried to reconcile faith with reason. The Tennessee legislature, dominated by fundamentalists, decided to deliver a powerful blow to the body of the modernists.

A few strong-minded liberals in the small town of Dayton, Tennessee, decided to put the law to a test. They persuaded John Thomas Scopes, a teacher of biology at the local high school, to allow himself to be caught red-handed in the act of teaching evolution to his pupils. Thus began a drama that was soon ballyhooed by an irreverent press into a great national circus occupying the attention of the entire world through the summer days of 1925. William Jennings Bryan, the Great Commoner—famous orator, leader of the free-silver forces, thrice-defeated candidate for President of the United States, former Secretary of State, and zealous, indefatigable champion of the Bible—volunteered his services to the prosecution. Clarence Darrow, agnostic and liberal—a pleader of unpopular causes, the criminal lawyer who only recently had saved Richard Loeb and Nathan Leopold, wealthy young Chicago thrill slayers, from execution—accepted the appeal of the Civil Liberties Union to become chief counsel for Scopes. It was a natural—the battle of the century between Bryan, the unreconstructed fundamentalist, and Darrow, the hard-bitten friend of the underdog.

The hot spotlight of national publicity glared down on the sleepy little town of Dayton as the battle of the giants got under way. Gaunt Gothic Americans flocked to the scene from the surrounding mountains, eager to learn about this high-falutin' talk of monkeys and even more determined to defend their way of life against the outlanders. It was a kind of Tennessee

Roman holiday, with all the world eavesdropping. Hot-dog and lemonade stands were set up in the streets. Book hawkers offered tracts on evolution at cut rates. Revivalists had a field day, posting such signs as this:

DO YOU WANT TO BE A SWEET ANGEL?

FORTY DAYS OF PRAYER.

ITEMIZE YOUR SINS.

COME CLEAN!

Bryan strode into Dayton as the shining knight in armor of the fundamentalists. Among the mass of gratuitous advice was this hint from Billy Sunday, the revivalist: "If man evolved from a monkey, why are there so many monkeys left? Why didn't they all evolve into humans?" Aimee Semple McPherson, the highly publicized evangelist of the gaudy Four-Square Gospel shrine in California, telegraphed "the lionhearted champion of the Bible":

CONSTANT PRAYER DURING WEEK ALL NIGHT PRAYER SATURDAY NIGHT STOP SUNDAY AFTERNOON BIBLE PARADE MASS MEETING AND TRIAL WITH HANGING AND BURIAL OF MONKEY TEACHERS TENNESSEE CAN COUNT ON US

An even more encouraging wire came from Smackover, Arkansas:

MY DEAR BROTHER BRYAN FIGHT THEM EVOLUTIONS UNTIL HELL FREEZES OVER AND GIVE THEM A ROUND OF THE ICE GOD BLESS YOU IN YOUR TIME OF TRIALS AND GIVE YOU WISDOM AND GRACE TO DO WHAT DEAR JESUS WILL SMILE UPON

YOUR UNACQUAINTED BROTHER

HAPPY GORDON MEAD

Into the supercharged atmosphere of Dayton came a mercurial newspaperman from Baltimore, who found a happy hunting ground for his peculiar talents. From the end of World War I to the brisk days of the New Deal, Henry Louis Mencken turned the blasts of his highly personal rhetoric on what he felt to be the stuffy spiritual, moral, and cultural institutions of the republic. Thoroughly enjoying the bizarre aspects of the American scene, he lashed out in all directions in a style composed of unequal parts of Boccaccio, Erasmus, Rabelais, and Mencken. He was fascinated by the stupidity of the common man and by the prevalence of mental vacuity in what he was fond of calling the "Bible Belt" or "Cow States." "The time-serving demagogues in public office," comments *Newsweek*, "the bigots in the pulpits, the editorial puritans, the pedagogical practitioners of timidity, gentility, and sanctimony in our institutions of learning, the bluenoses who imposed Prohibition upon the country, the prudes and Philistines and peasants who set themselves in vulgar opposition to culture—these felt the Mencken whiplash." A whole generation of college students swore by or at the Wagnerian rhythm of Mencken's prose. This was the reporter sent by the Baltimore *Evening Sun*, along with

the *Sunpapers'* Essary, Kent, Hyde, and Duffy, to cover the Scopes trial in
Tennessee. Nothing could have made Mencken happier. He took the opportunity to investigate the Holy Roller cult in the mountains behind
Dayton, where the yearning mountaineers' souls needed nightly reconver-
sion.

Deep in "the Coca-Cola belt"

The Sun, Baltimore, July 13, 1925

DAYTON, TENNESSEE, JULY 13—There
is a Unitarian clergyman here from
New York, trying desperately to horn
into the trial and execution of the infidel Scopes. He will fail. If Darrow
ventured to put him on the stand the
whole audience, led by the jury, would
leap out of the courthouse windows
and take to the hills. Darrow himself,
indeed, is as much as they can bear.
The whisper that he is an atheist has
been stilled by the bucolic make-up
and by the public report that he has
the gift of prophecy and can reconcile
Genesis and evolution. Even so, there
is ample space about him when he
navigates the streets. The other day a
newspaperwoman was warned by her
landlady to keep out of the courtroom
when he was on his legs. All the local
sorcerers predict that a bolt from
heaven will fetch him in the end. The
night he arrived there was a violent
storm, the town water turned brown,
and horned cattle in the lowlands were
afloat for hours. A woman back in the
mountains gave birth to a child with
hair four inches long, curiously bobbed
in scallops.

The Book of Revelation has all the
authority, in these theological up-
lands, of military orders in time of
war. The people turn to it for light
upon all their problems, spiritual and
secular. If a text were found in it denouncing the antievolution law, then

the antievolution law would become
infamous overnight. But so far the
exegetes who roar and snuffle in the
town have found no such text. Instead
they have found only blazing ratifica-
tions and reinforcements of Genesis.
Darwin is the devil with seven tails
and nine horns. Scopes, though he is
disguised by flannel pantaloons and a
Beta Theta Pi haircut, is the harlot
of Babylon. Darrow is Beelzebub in
person, and Malone is the Crown
Prince Friedrich Wilhelm.

I have hitherto hinted an Episco-
palian down here in the Coca-Cola
belt is regarded as an atheist. It
sounds like one of the lies that journalists tell, but it is really an understatement of the facts. Even a
Methodist, by Rhea County standards, is one a bit debauched by pride
of intellect. It is the four Methodists
on the jury who are expected to hold
out for giving Scopes Christian burial
after he is hanged. They all made it
plain, when they were examined, that
they were freethinking and independent men, and not to be run amuck by
the superstitions of the lowly. One
actually confessed that he seldom read
the Bible, though he hastened to add
that he was familiar with its principles. The fellow had on a boiled shirt
and a polka-dot necktie. He sits somewhat apart. When Darrow withers to
a cinder under the celestial blowpipe,

this dubious Wesleyan, too, will lose a few hairs.

Even the Baptists no longer brew a medicine that is strong enough for the mountaineers. The sacrament of baptism by total immersion is over too quickly for them, and what follows offers nothing that they can get their teeth into. What they have is a continuous experience of the divine power, an endless series of evidence that the true believer is a marked man, ever under the eye of God. It is not enough to go to a revival once a year or twice a year; there must be a revival every night. And it is not enough to accept the truth as a mere statement of indisputable and awful fact; it must be embraced ecstatically and orgiastically, to the accompaniment of loud shouts, dreadful heavings and gurglings, and dancing with arms and legs.

This craving is satisfied brilliantly by the gaudy practices of the Holy Rollers, and so the mountaineers are gradually gravitating toward the Holy Roller communion, or, as they prefer to call it, the Church of God. Gradually, perhaps, is not the word. They are actually going in by whole villages and townships. At the last count of noses there were 20,000 Holy Rollers in these hills. The next census, I have no doubt, will show many more. The cities of the lowlands, of course, still resist, and so do most of the county towns, including even Dayton, but once one steps off the state roads the howl of holiness is heard in the woods, and the yokels carry on an almost continuous orgy.

A foreigner in store clothes going out from Dayton must approach the sacred grove somewhat discreetly. It is not that the Holy Rollers, discovering him, would harm him; it is simply that they would shut down their boil-

ing of the devil and flee into the forests. We left Dayton an hour after nightfall and parked our car in a wood a mile or so beyond the little hill village of Morgantown. Far off in a glade a flickering light was visible and out of the silence came a faint rumble of exhortation. We could scarcely distinguish the figure of the preacher; it was like looking down the tube of a dark field microscope. We got out of the car and sneaked along the edge of a mountain cornfield.

Presently we were near enough to see what was going on. From the great limb of a mighty oak hung a couple of crude torches of the sort that car inspectors thrust under Pullman cars when a train pulls in at night. In their light was a preacher, and for a while we could see no one else. He was an immensely tall and thin mountaineer in blue jeans, his collarless shirt open at the neck and his hair a tousled mop. As he preached he paced up and down under the smoking flambeaux and at each turn he thrust his arms into the air and yelled, "Glory to God!" We crept nearer in the shadow of the cornfield and began to hear more of his discourse. He was preaching on the day of judgment. The high kings of the earth, he roared, would all fall down and die; only the sanctified would stand up to receive the Lord God of Hosts. One of these kings he mentioned by name—the king of what he called Greece-y. The King of Greece-y, he said, was doomed to hell.

We went forward a few more yards and began to see the audience. It was seated on benches ranged round the preacher in a circle. Behind him sat a row of elders, men and women. In front were the younger folk. We kept on cautiously, and individuals rose out of the ghostly gloom. A young mother sat suckling her baby, rocking as the preacher paced up and down. Two scared little girls hugged each other, their pigtails down their backs. An immensely huge mountain woman, in a gingham dress cut in one piece, rolled on her heels at every "Glory to God." On one side, but half visible, was what appeared to be a bed. We found out afterward that two babies were asleep upon it.

The preacher stopped at last and there arose out of the darkness a woman with her hair pulled back into a little tight knot. She began so quietly that we couldn't hear what she said, but soon her voice rose resonantly and we could follow her. She was denouncing the reading of books. Some wandering book agent, it appeared, had come to her cabin and tried to sell her a specimen of his wares. She refused to touch it. Why, indeed, read a book? If what was in it was true, then everything in it was already in the Bible. If it was false, then reading it would imperil the soul. Her syllogism complete, she sat down.

There followed a hymn, led by a somewhat fat brother wearing silver-rimmed country spectacles. It droned on for a half a dozen stanzas, and then the first speaker resumed the floor. He argued that the gift of tongues was real and that education was a snare. Once his children could read the Bible, he said, they had enough. Beyond lay only infidelity and damnation. Sin stalked the cities. Dayton itself was a Sodom. Even Morgantown had begun to forget God. He sat down, and the female aurochs in gingham got up. She began quietly, but was soon leaping and roaring, and it was hard to follow her. Under cover of the turmoil we sneaked a bit closer. A couple of other discourses followed, and there were two or three hymns. Suddenly a change of mood began to make itself

felt. The last hymn ran longer than the others and dropped gradually into a monotonous, unintelligible chant. The leader beat time with his book. The faithful broke out with exultations. When the singing ended there was a brief palaver that we could not hear and two of the men moved a bench into the circle of light directly under the flambeaux. Then a half-grown girl emerged from the darkness and threw herself upon it. We noticed with astonishment that she had bobbed hair. "This sister," said the leader, "has asked for prayers." We moved a bit closer. We could now see faces plainly and hear every word.

What followed quickly reached such heights of barbaric grotesquerie that it was hard to believe it real. At a signal all the faithful crowded up to the bench and began to pray—not in unison, but each for himself. At another they all fell on their knees, their arms over the penitent. The leader kneeled, facing us, his head alternately thrown back dramatically or buried in his hands. Words spouted from his lips like bullets from a machine gun—appeals to God to pull the penitent back out of hell, defiances of the powers and principalities of the air, a vast impassioned jargon of apocalyptic texts. Suddenly he rose to his feet, threw back his head, and began to speak in tongues—blub-blub-blub, gurgle-gurgle-gurgle. His voice rose to a higher register. The climax was a shrill, inarticulate squawk, like that of a man throttled. He fell headlong across the pyramid of supplicants.

A comic scene? Somehow, no. The poor half-wits were too horribly in earnest. It was like peeping through a knothole at the writhings of a people in pain. From the squirming and jabbering mass a young woman gradually detached herself—a woman not uncomely, with a pathetic homemade cap on her head. Her head jerked back, the veins of her neck swelled, and her fists went to her throat as if she were fighting for breath. She bent backward until she was like a half of a hoop. Then she suddenly snapped forward. We caught a flash of the whites of her eyes. Presently her whole body began to be convulsed—great convulsions that began at the shoulders and ended at the hips. She would leap to her feet, thrust her arms in air, and then hurl herself upon the heap. Her praying flattened out into a mere delirious caterwauling, like that of a tomcat on a petting party.

I describe the thing as a strict behaviorist. The lady's subjective sensations I leave to infidel pathologists. Whatever they were they were obviously contagious, for soon another damsel joined her, and then another and then a fourth. The last one had an extraordinarily bad attack. She began with mild enough jerks of the head, but in a moment she was bounding all over the place, exactly like a chicken with its head cut off. Every time her head came up a stream of yells and barking would issue out of it. Once she collided with a dark, undersized brother, hitherto silent and stolid. Contact with her set him off as if he had been kicked by a mule. He leaped into the air, threw back his head, and began to gargle as if with a mouthful of BB shot. Then he loosened one tremendous stentorian sentence in the tongues and collapsed.

By this time the performers were quite oblivious to the profane universe. We left our hiding and came up to the little circle of light. We slipped into the vacant seats on one of the rickety benches. The heap of mourners was directly before us. They bounced into us as they cavorted. The smell that they radiated, sweating there in that obscene heap, half suffocated us. Not all of them, of course, did the thing in the grand manner. Some merely moaned and rolled their eyes. The female ox in gingham flung her great hulk on the ground and jabbered an unintelligible prayer. One of the men, in the intervals between fits, put on his spectacles and read his Bible.

Beside me on the bench sat the young mother and her baby. She suckled it through the whole orgy, obviously fascinated by what was going on, but never venturing to take any hand in it. On the bed just outside the light two other babies slept peacefully. In the shadows, suddenly appearing and as suddenly going away, were vague figures, whether of believers or of scoffers I do not know. They seemed to come and go in couples. Now and then a couple at the ringside would step back and then vanish into the black night. After a while some came back. There was whispering outside the circle of vision. A couple of Fords lurched up in the wood road, cutting holes in the darkness with their lights. Once someone out of sight loosed a bray of laughter.

All this went on for an hour or so. The original penitent, by this time, was buried three deep beneath the heap. One caught a glimpse, now and then, of her yellow bobbed hair, but then she would vanish again. How she breathed down there I don't know; it was hard enough ten feet away, with a strong five-cent cigar to help. When the praying brothers would rise up for a bout with the tongues their faces were streaming with perspiration. The fat harridan in gingham sweated like a longshoreman. Her hair got loose and fell down over her face. She fanned herself with her skirt. A powerful mortal she was, equal in her day to obstetrics and a week's washing on the same morning, but this was worse than a week's washing. Finally, she fell in a heap, breathing in great, convulsive gasps.

We tired of it after a while and groped our way back to our automobile. When we got to Dayton, after eleven o'clock—an immensely late hour for these parts—the whole town was still gathered on the courthouse lawn, hanging upon the disputes of theologians. The Bible champion of the world had a crowd. The Seventh Day Adventist missionaries had a crowd. A volunteer from faraway Portland, Oregon, made up exactly like Andy Gump, had another and larger crowd. Dayton was enjoying itself. All the usual rules were suspended and the curfew bell was locked up. The prophet Bryan, exhausted by his day's work for Revelations, was snoring in his bed up the road, but enough volunteers were still on watch to keep the battlements manned.

Such is human existence among the fundamentalists, where children are brought up on Genesis and sin is unknown. If I have made the tale too long, then blame the spirit of garrulity that is in the local air. Even newspaper reporters, down here, get some echo of the call. Divine inspiration is as common as the hookworm. I have done my best to show you what the great heritage of mankind comes to in regions where the Bible is the beginning and end of wisdom, and the mountebank Bryan, parading the streets in his seersucker coat, is pointed out to sucklings as the greatest man since Abraham.

* * *

THREE DAYS LATER William O. McGeehan, the sports writer, who covered the Scopes trial for the *New York Herald Tribune,* reported that in the midst of a booming peroration by Dudley Field Malone, "Mr. H. L. Mencken fell off his chair with a crash that startled the courtroom."

"It is a jedgment," said one of the sisters. "The walls are falling in, and Mr. Mencken is the first to go, and he won't go to glory, either."

The great scene of the trial came on the seventh day, when Bryan and Darrow locked horns in a savage encounter under extraordinary circumstances. Immediately preceding the cross-examination, Darrow insisted that a sign ten feet long with huge letters READ YOUR BIBLE! be removed from in front of the jury. A prosecution attorney objected, saying "It is time for us to tear up all the Bibles, throw them into the fire, and let the country go to hell." A court officer rapped for order: "People, this is no circus. There are no monkeys up here. This is a lawsuit. Let us have order." Bryan made an unctuous little speech: "If having that up there during the trial makes our brother to offend, I would take it down during the trial."

The crowd was so great in the afternoon that Judge Raulston had removed the court to the lawn. There under the maple trees hundreds of spectators formed fundamentalist and modernist cheering sections. The weather was oppressively hot and humid. All the participants stripped to their shirt sleeves—Bryan in a pongee shirt, Darrow with lavender suspenders, and Judge Raulston with judicial galluses.

Bryan started out calmly and confidently, but he was soon stung to anger by the relentless, barbed questioning of Darrow. Finally, in a burst of fury he and Darrow both came to their feet and shook fists at one another. Although publicly humiliated, Bryan refused to acknowledge defeat.

Here is *The New York Times'* report of the main event—the intellectual battle of the century between William Jennings Bryan, the plumed knight of the fundamentalists, and Clarence Darrow, the agnostic with lavender galluses.

Monkey business in Tennessee

The New York Times, July 21, 1925

At last it has happened. After days of ineffective argument and legal quibbling, with speeches that merely skirted the edges of the matter which everyone wanted discussed in this Scopes antievolution trial, William Jennings Bryan, fundamentalist, and Clarence Darrow, agnostic and pleader of unpopular causes, locked horns today under the most remarkable circumstances ever known to American court procedure.

It was on the courthouse lawn, where Judge Raulston had moved so that more persons could hear, with the Tennessee crowds whooping for their angry champion, who shook his fist in the quizzical, satiric face of Mr. Darrow, that Mr. Bryan was put on the stand by the defense to prove that the Bible need not be taken literally.

With an airplane whizzing overhead, Mr. Darrow asked Mr. Bryan about Jonah and the whale, Joshua and the sun, where Cain got his wife, the Flood, and the Tower of Babel, until the youthful Attorney General Stewart, desperately trying to bring the performance within legal bounds, asked, "What is the meaning of all this harangue?"

"To show up fundamentalism,"

shouted Mr. Darrow, lifting his voice in one of the few moments of anger he showed, "to prevent bigots and ignoramuses from controlling the educational system of the United States."

Mr. Bryan sprang to his feet, his face purple, and shook his fist in the lowering, gnarled face of Mr. Darrow, while he cried:

"To protect the word of God from the greatest atheist and agnostic in the United States."

A roar of applause broke from the crowd under the trees and Mr. Darrow, looking down at them, called out sarcastically:

"Why don't you folks cheer?"

At the end of a day so crowded with unexpected happenings all Dayton tonight is holding its head, overcome by the drama of the unprecedented trial.

Mr. Darrow was cited in contempt as soon as court opened this morning for his defiance of the judge on Friday, and ordered to show cause why he should not be punished.

In the afternoon he apologized to Judge Raulston, who in a talk that was almost a prayer, his voice shaken with emotion, brought Mr. Darrow to the "mourner's bench," forgave him, and told him to go back home and learn in his heart the words of the man who said, "Come unto Me and receive eternal life."

All morning the crowds packed into the courtroom to hear what everybody assumed would be the final argument of the case, until in the afternoon the building was jammed. Judge Raulston did not wish to shut anybody out, and in order that all might hear he moved to a platform built against the wall of the courthouse, under the maple trees, where a week ago Mr. Bryan delivered a sermon. On the benches in front nearly everyone could get a seat, and hundreds stood, forming themselves into opposing modernist and fundamentalist cheering sections, although liberals present were in a small minority.

It was a striking scene. Judge Raulston sat at a little table in the center, with the state attorneys at his left and the defense at his right, while about them were a few newspapermen and fortunate persons who managed to squeeze by the guard. In front was a sea of upturned faces, waiting for what they presumed would be an ordinary argument, faces which became eager when Mr. Darrow announced that he would call Mr. Bryan as a witness for the defense.

And then for nearly two hours, while those below broke into laughter or applause or cried out encouragement to Mr. Bryan, Mr. Darrow goaded his opponent. In a blue shirt and suspenders he leaned against the edge of his table, Bible in hand, and asked Mr. Bryan if he really believed that the serpent had always crawled on its belly because it tempted Eve, and if he believed that Eve was made from Adam's rib.

Mr. Bryan started off as sweetly as a cooing dove. He wanted to confound this agnostic Darrow, he told the court; he wanted to testify to his faith in the revealed word of God and show that scientists did not know what they were talking about.

He overruled the objection of Attorney General "Tom" Stewart, who saw his lawsuit vanishing in the battle smoke of debate, but as Mr. Darrow prodded him with all the power of his logical mind, the admissions wrung from Mr. Bryan roused him to anger, and in a burst of fury he denounced Mr. Darrow as having only the purpose of casting slurs on the Bible.

"I have merely the purpose of showing up your fool ideas that no intelligent Christian believes in," shouted Mr. Darrow, stung to anger, and the judge, in the midst of confusion as both antagonists rose to their feet and shook their fists at each other, adjourned the court.

Mr. Darrow drew from Bryan that he knew little of comparative religion, very little of geology, nothing of physiology, and hardly anything that would interest a man seeking light on the vast questions of evolution and religion on which he has written for years. He took refuge again and again in his faith in the written word of the Bible. If what science he had learned did not agree with that he did not believe it and did not want to know.

"I have all the information I need to live by and die by," he declared vehemently.

But his insistence upon the literal acceptance of the Bible was weakened somewhat, for he admitted when questioned about Joshua making the sun stand still that it was one of those things that "anybody can put his own construction upon," and explained that although there was no doubt that the earth moved around the sun the Bible was "inspired by the Almighty, and He may have used language that could be understood at that time."

The problem of what was meant by "days" in the Genesis account of creation was also one on which Mr. Bryan said things pleasing to Mr. Darrow, for he admitted that "days" probably meant "periods," and that creation might have lasted for millions of years.

All those under the trees were completely absorbed in the conflict between the two men, each representing a point of view as to religion so diametrically opposed. It was as if all the voices of these two great divisions of religious thought, rationalism and faith, were debating in the persons of Mr. Darrow and Mr. Bryan. It was a burning vital issue to those people of Rhea County who were present, and to the little group of liberals who clustered in front.

Jonah and the whale should be taken literally, said Mr. Bryan, for he believed "in a God who can make a whale and can make a man, and make both do what He pleases."

"You don't know whether it was the ordinary mine-run of fish, or made for that purpose?" asked Mr. Darrow with quiet sarcasm.

"You may guess," replied Mr. Bryan, calmly, fanning himself with a palm-leaf fan, "an evolutionist guess."

"You are not prepared to say whether that fish was made especially to swallow a man or not?"

"The Bible doesn't say, so I'm not prepared to say," replied Mr. Bryan, and that was his attitude on nearly every question raised. It was a miracle, and one miracle was just as easy to believe as another, said Mr. Bryan.

"A miracle is a thing performed beyond what man performs," he said. "When you get beyond what man can do, you get within the realm of miracles, and it is just as easy to believe in the miracle of Jonah as any other miracle in the Bible."

The attorneys for the state were chuckling over the way Mr. Bryan was acquitting himself by this time, but they did not look so pleased as the afternoon wore on.

Joshua and the sun was another miracle that Mr. Darrow wanted to know about. How did it happen that the sun stood still, when the earth moves around the sun?

It was the language of the day, Mr. Bryan said, and if anything stopped it must have been the earth.

"Now, Mr. Bryan, have you ever pondered what would have happened to the earth if it had stood still?"

"No," replied Mr. Bryan. "The God I believe in could have taken care of that, Mr. Darrow."

"Don't you know it would have been converted into a molten mass of matter?"

"You testify to that when you get on the stand," retorted Mr. Bryan. "I will give you a chance," he said, for he had announced that he would call all the defense counsel if they called him, much to the delight of everyone present.

Then they got onto the flood, and attempted to fix the date of it by the Bible, and against the opposition of Mr. Stewart, Mr. Bryan told the court to let Mr. Darrow have all the latitude he wanted.

"I am going to have some latitude when he gets through," he said grimly.

"You can have latitude and longitude," said Mr. Darrow.

"These gentlemen have not had much chance," said Mr. Bryan, rising to his feet from the witness chair. "They did not come here to try this case. They came here to try revealed religion. I am here to defend it, and they can ask me any questions they please."

The applause from the yard brought a snort of disgust from Mr. Darrow, and in reproach for what Mr. Bryan called his insults, he raised his fist and shouted at him:

"You insult every man of science and learning in the world because he does not believe in your fool religion."

Judge Raulston calmed them both, and Mr. Stewart again stepped forward to protest.

"I have a public duty to perform under my oath," said the earnest young attorney general, who, with his case, had been crowded into the background. "I ask the court to stop it."

"How long ago was the flood, Mr. Bryan?" asked Mr. Darrow, and the debate was on again. They figured it up with the help of Bishop Usher's chronology, as being 2348 B.C. Mr. Bryan thought the fish might have lived, but everything else was destroyed.

"Don't you know there are any number of civilizations that are traced back to more than five thousand years?" asked Darrow.

"I know we have people who trace things back according to the number of ciphers they have," replied Bryan; "but I am not satisfied they are accurate. I am satisfied by no evidence that I have found, that would justify me in accepting the opinions of these men against what I believe to be the inspired word of God."

There was a civilization before the flood, said Mr. Bryan, but when he was asked if he knew a scientific man in the world who believed that all the animals and all the races now inhabiting the world had come here since the flood, he took refuge in saying that he was more interested in what Christians were doing now than in what happened in the past.

"You have never had any interest in the age of the various races and people and civilizations and animals that exist upon the earth today, is that right?" asked Mr. Darrow.

"I have never felt a great deal of interest in the effort that has been made to dispute the Bible by the speculation of men, or the investigations of men," replied Mr. Bryan.

The mild manner in which the "evangelical leader of the prosecution," as Mr. Malone has called him, seated himself in his chair, was vanishing rapidly. His face flushed under Mr. Darrow's searching words, and he writhed in an effort to keep himself from making heated replies. His eyes glared at his lounging opponent, who stood opposite him, glowering under his bulging brow, speculatively tapping his arm with his spectacles. No greater contrast in men could be imagined. The traps of logic fell from Mr. Darrow's lips as innocently as the words of a child, and so long as Mr. Bryan could parry them he smiled back, but when one stumped him he took refuge in his faith and either refused to answer directly or said in effect:

"The Bible states it; it must be so."

"Have you ever investigated to find out how long man has been on the earth?" asked Darrow.

"I have never found it necessary," said Mr. Bryan.

Mr. Bryan's complete lack of interest in many of the things closely connected with such religious questions as he has been supporting for many years was strikingly shown again and again by Mr. Darrow. He had never made a study of the ancient civilizations of China, or Egypt, he did not know that they couldn't go back beyond the time of creation as given in the Bible.

Mr. Bryan was of the opinion that he had heard of records of archeologists which describe the flood, but he did not know that there were many old religions with traditions of the flood. The origins of religion had not interested him much, either.

"The Christian religion has satisfied me," he said, "and I have never felt it necessary to look up some competitive religions."

The word competitive interested Mr. Darrow, and Bryan finally qualified it by saying he meant "religious unbelievers" in the Christian religion. The religions of Confucius and Buddha he did not regard as competitive, because he thought them inferior, and he insisted on telling Mr. Darrow what he thought of both. He did not know, however, how old the religions of Confucius, Buddha, or Zoroaster were.

"I think it much more important to know the differences between them than to know their age."

Mr. Darrow asked him if he knew how many men were on earth at various times, and when told he was the first man Mr. Bryan had ever met who was interested in it, he asked:

"Mr. Bryan, am I the first man you ever heard of who has been interested in the age of human societies and primitive man?"

He asked Mr. Bryan if he did not know there were thousands of books in the libraries on the subjects he had been asking about, and Mr. Bryan said he did not, but would take his word for it. He said he hadn't read much on primitive man, and when Mr. Darrow asked him if he had ever in

his life tried to find out about the civilizations of the earth, how long they had existed, he replied:

"No, sir, I have been so well satisfied with the Christian religion that I have spent no time trying to find arguments against it."

"You don't care how old the earth is, how old man is, and how long the animals have been here?"

"I am not so much interested in that," said Mr. Bryan.

And then he drew from Mr. Bryan the admission that he had never studied anything on the subject he had written about.

"You have never made an investigation to find out?" he was asked.

"No, sir, I have never," Mr. Bryan answered.

Mr. Bryan said that Buddhism was a religion of agnosticism, because he had seen in Rangoon that the Buddhists were to send a delegation to the agnostics' congress to be held in Rome.

After more colloquy about the Tower of Babel and some more objections from Mr. Stewart, General Ben McKenzie said the defense would no more file Colonel Bryan's testimony as part of the record for the Appellate Court than they would file a rattlesnake.

Mr. Darrow, Dudley Field Malone, and Arthur Garfield Hays burst out as one man:

"We will file it, we will file it."

"File it from Dan to Beersheba," Mr. Bryan said in his deep rumble.

* * *

On the morning of July 21, Judge Raulston mercifully put an end to the unequal struggle. It was clear that Bryan, now old and flabby, could not possibly win a clear-cut victory over the wily Darrow. Unable to get any scientific evidence before the jury, Scopes' lawyers saw that their only hope lay in taking the fight up to the Tennessee Supreme Court. Scopes was quickly found guilty and fined one hundred dollars, which the Baltimore *Sunpapers* paid.

Bryan was closer to death than he had realized. During the trial, H. L. Mencken had reported that "there was a vague, unpleasant manginess about Bryan's appearance . . . the hair was gone behind his ears, in the obscene manner of the late Samuel Gompers." It was a shrewd observation. The Great Commoner died a week after the trial.

A brilliant post-mortem story on Bryan was sent in to the *St. Louis Post-Dispatch* by Paul Y. Anderson, which had this lead:

"In a rambling old white house on the outskirts of Dayton, where the maples rustle placidly and the fragrance of the harvest lingers on the air, rests today the majestic clay which was William Jennings Bryan.

"Little groups of men lie in the grass under the maples and converse in subdued tones. At intervals people tiptoe into the house, stay a minute and emerge. A cricket sings among the petunias in the side yard. A rocking chair creaks momentarily on the long front porch."

In Dayton, Ohio, a fiery cross was burned "in memory of William Jennings Bryan, the greatest Klansman of our time." It was an undeserved slur.

Damon Runyon Reports
the Ruth Snyder-Judd Gray
"Dumbbell Murder" Case

IRREVERENT CRITICS of their own colleagues, quick to spot fakers and windbags, reporters are equally generous in acclaiming real journalistic talent. Most of them agree enthusiastically that if there ever was a newspaperman's newsman it was Damon Runyon, reporter, sports writer, and creator of Broadway fiction in his more imaginative moments. Arthur Brisbane said flatly that he was "the best reporter in the world." A British critic wrote: "Seriously, though in a minor sphere, Runyon is comparable to Shakespeare and Milton as an improvisator of language." These flashes from his sports stories illustrate the Damon Runyon touch:

What a football player—this man Red Grange! Say it again. He is melody, and symphony, on the football field. He is crashing sound. He is poetry. He is brute force. [1925]

The popular impression was that the old sachem of smack, George Herman Ruth, wasn't feeling any too sprightly. Behold the Babe, then, walking up to the old saucer, or plate, unassisted, and knocking off two doubles and a single for himself. Can it be that the Babe is slowing up? [1928]

In a wild, crazy brawl that is a throwback to the time of the cave man, Max Baer, of California, becomes heavyweight champion of the world tonight. Grinning and babbling like a veritable madman and fighting with insane fury, the black-haired ex-butcher boy hammered the grotesque face and huge body of Primo Carnera, the Italian giant, until the referee, Arthur Donovan, calls a halt after two minutes and sixteen seconds of the eleventh round have elapsed. [1934]

The son of a printer-philosopher of Pueblo, Colorado, young Damon, then only thirteen years old, saw his first pieces in print under his own name in the Pueblo, Colorado, *Adviser,* which was temporarily under his father's editorship. After working on newspapers in Denver and San Francisco, Runyon landed in New York in 1911, and almost overnight became a star reporter on sports. According to his biographer, Ed Weiner, he was assigned to cover the 1913 World Series between the New York Giants and the Philadelphia Athletics. Regaining consciousness on a train five hundred miles west of New York "with symptoms that needed no definition," he from that moment put whisky out of his life. A great reporter emerged from that decision.

Runyon was at his best in the courtroom. He found the same popular interest in a murder trial that he observed in any city at a big football game, baseball series, or prize fight. "The thrills," he wrote, "are just as numerous as in any sporting event I ever saw, with something new popping up at every turn. The game of murder trial is played according to very strict rules, with stern umpires called judges to prevent any deviation from the rules."

One of Runyon's great reports was his coverage of the Hall-Mills murder case (1926), in which a New Jersey pastor, Reverend Edward Wheeler Hall, was murdered together with his sweetheart, Mrs. Eleanor Mills: "Out of the grave came the heart of the dead dominie today in the form of musty-letters that fairly smoked with his love for the little choir singer." Other newsmen say that his best story was his report of the "Daddy" Browning divorce case (1927): "That gallused old codger, 'Daddy' Browning, and his flapper wife, the celebrated 'Peaches,' go to bat with their matrimonial pains and aches. . . . A rattle of applause broke out among the spectators as Daddy Browning came down the aisle, walking first on one foot and then on the other." Some reporters insist that Runyon hit the heights with his report of the trial of Al Capone for income-tax evasion (1931): "Capone was quietly dressed this morning, bar a hat of pearly white, emblematic, no doubt, of purity." *

We settle for Runyon's story, condensed herein, of the Ruth Snyder-Judd Gray murder case (1927) as his greatest courtroom report. The liquidation of Albert Snyder by his giddy, gaudy, addlepated wife and her myopic, corset-salesman cavalier was an essentially commonplace crime, but precisely for that reason it caught the imagination of the American public as have few crimes of this crime-packed century. Jack the Ripper and the Monster of Düsseldorf were vague shadows who went in for fancy mayhem, and the public quickly tired of their baroque crimes, but Mrs. Snyder and Judd Gray were the people next door. "Indeed," said Alexander Woollcott, "Ruth Snyder was so like the woman across the street that many an American husband was soon haunted by an unconfessed realization that she also bore an embarrassing resemblance to the woman across the breakfast table." With the exception of the Harry K. Thaw trial for the murder of Stanford White and the Bruno Richard Hauptmann trial for the kidnaping and murder of the Lindbergh baby, the Snyder-Gray case consumed more newsprint than any other *cause célèbre* of the twentieth century.

---

* Damon Runyon died on December 10, 1946, a victim of cancer. The memorial fund established by his friends in his name to combat the disease has won strong national support.

Murder in the worst degree

International News Service, April 19, 27, 28, May 9, 1927

A chilly-looking blonde with frosty eyes and one of those marble, you-bet-you-will chins, and an inert, scare-drunk fellow that you couldn't miss among any hundred men as a dead setup for a blonde, or the shell game, or maybe a gold brick.

Mrs. Ruth Snyder and Henry Judd Gray are on trial in the huge weather-beaten old courthouse of Queens County in Long Island City, just across the river from the roar of New York, for what might be called for want of a better name, The Dumb-bell Murder. It was so dumb.

They are charged with the slaughter four weeks ago of Albert Snyder, art editor of the magazine, *Motor Boating,* the blonde's husband and father of her nine-year-old daughter, under circumstances that for sheer stupidity and brutality have seldom been equaled in the history of crime.

It was stupid beyond imagination, and so brutal that the thought of it probably makes many a peaceful, home-loving Long Islander of the Albert Snyder type shiver in his pajamas as he prepares for bed.

They killed Snyder as he slumbered, so they both admitted in confessions—Mrs. Snyder has since repudiated hers—first whacking him on the head with a sash weight, then giving him a few whiffs of chloroform, and finally tightening a strand of picture wire around his throat so he wouldn't revive.

This matter disposed of, they went into an adjoining room and had a few drinks of whisky used by some Long Islanders, which is very bad, and talked things over. They thought they had committed "the perfect crime," whatever that may be. It was probably the most imperfect crime on record. It was cruel, atrocious, and unspeakably dumb.

They were red-hot lovers then, these two, but they are strangers now.

Mrs. Snyder, the woman who has been called a Jezebel, a lineal descendant of the Borgia outfit, and a lot of other names, came in for the morning session of court stepping along briskly in her patent-leather pumps, with little short steps.

She is not bad-looking. I have seen much worse. She is thirty-three and looks just about that, though you cannot tell much about blondes. She has a good figure, slim and trim, with narrow shoulders. She is of medium height, and I thought she carried her clothes off rather smartly. She wore a black dress and a black silk coat with a collar of black fur. Some of the girl reporters said it was dyed ermine; others pronounced it rabbit.

They made derogatory remarks about her hat. It was a tight-fitting thing called, I believe, a beret. Wisps of her straw-colored hair straggled out from under it. Mrs. Snyder wears her hair bobbed, the back of the bobbing rather ragged. She is of the Scandinavian type. Her parents are Norwegian and Swedish.

Her eyes are blue-green and as chilly-looking as an ice-cream cone. If all that Henry Judd Gray says of her actions the night of the murder is true, her veins carry ice water. Gray says he dropped the sash weight after slugging the sleeping Snyder with it once and that Mrs. Snyder picked it up and finished the job.

Gray, a spindly fellow in physical build, entered the courtroom with quick, jerky little steps behind an officer, and sat down between his attorneys, Samuel L. Miller and William L. Millard. His back was to Mrs. Snyder, who sat about ten feet distant. Her eyes were on a level with the back of his narrow head.

Gray was neatly dressed in a dark suit, with a white starched collar and subdued tie. He has always been a bit on the dressy side, it is said. He wears big, horn-rimmed spectacles, and his eyes have a startled expression. You couldn't find a meeker, milder-looking fellow in seven states, this man who is charged with one of the most horrible crimes in history.

He occasionally conferred with his attorneys as the examination of the talesmen was going forward, but not often. He sat in one position almost the entire day, half slumped down in his chair, a melancholy-looking figure for a fellow who once thought of "the perfect crime."

Mrs. Snyder and Gray have been "hollering copper" on each other lately, as the boys say. That is, they have been telling. Gray's defense goes back to old Mr. Adam, that the woman beguiled him, while Mrs. Snyder says he is a "jackal," and a lot of other things besides that, and claims that he is hiding behind her skirts.

Some say Mrs. Ruth Snyder "wept silently" in court yesterday. It may be so. I could detect no sparkle of tears against the white marble mask, but it is conceivable that even the very gods were weeping silently as a gruff voice slowly recited the blonde woman's own story of the murder of her husband by herself and Henry Judd Gray.

Let no one infer she is altogether without tenderness of heart, for when they were jotting down the confession that was read in the courtroom in Long Island City, Peter M. Daly, an assistant district attorney, asked her:

"Mrs. Snyder, why did you kill your husband?"

He wanted to know.

"Don't put it that way," she said, according to his testimony yesterday. "It sounds so cruel."

"Well, that is what you did, isn't it?" he asked in some surprise.

"Yes," he claims she answered, "but I don't like that term."

A not astonishing distaste, you must admit.

"Well, why did you kill him?" persisted the curious Daly.

"To get rid of him," she answered simply, according to Daly's testimony; and indeed that seems to have been her main idea throughout, if all the evidence the state has so far developed is true.

She afterward repudiated the confession that was presented yesterday, with her attorneys trying to bring out from the state's witnesses that she was sick and confused when she told her bloody yarn five weeks ago.

The woman, in her incongruous widow's weeds, sat listening intently to the reading of her original confession to the jury, possibly the most horrible tale that ever fell from human lips, the tale of a crime unutterably brutal and cold-blooded and unspeakably dumb.

Her mouth opened occasionally as if framing words, and once she said, not quite distinctly, an unconscious utterance, which may have been a denial of some utterance by the lawyer or perhaps an assurance to her soul that she was not alive and awake.

Right back to old Father Adam,

the original, and perhaps the loudest "squawker" among mankind against women, went Henry Judd Gray in telling how and why he lent his hand to the butchery of Albert Snyder.

She — she — she — she — she — she — she — she. That was the burden of the bloody song of the little corset salesman as read out in the packed courtroom in Long Island City yesterday.

She — she — she — she — she — she. 'Twas an echo from across the ages and an old familiar echo, at that. It was the same old "squawk" of Brother Man whenever and wherever he is in a jam, that was first framed in the words:

"She gave me of the tree, and I did eat."

It has been put in various forms since then, as Henry Judd Gray, for one notable instance close at hand, put it in the form of eleven long typewritten pages that were read yesterday, but in any form and in any language it remains a "squawk."

"She played me pretty hard." . . . "She said, 'You're going to do it, aren't you?' " . . . "She kissed me." . . . She did this. . . . She did that. . . . Always she—she—she—she—she ran the confession of Henry Judd.

And "she"—the woman accused— how did she take this most gruesome squawk?

Well, on the whole, better than you might expect.

You must remember it was the first time she had ever heard the confession of the man who once called her "Momsie." She probably had an inkling of it, but not its exact terms.

For a few minutes her greenish-blue eyes roared with such fury that I would not have been surprised to see her leap up, grab the window sash weight that lay among the exhibits on the district attorney's table, and perform the same offices on the shrinking Gray that he says she performed on her sleeping husband.

She "belabored him," Gray's confession reads, and I half expected her to belabor Gray.

Her thin lips curled to a distinct snarl at some passages in the statement. I thought of a wildcat and a female cat, at that, on a leash. Once or twice she smiled, but it was a smile of insensate rage, not amusement. She once emitted a push of breath in a loud "phew," as you have perhaps done yourself over some tall tale.

The marble mask was contorted by her emotions for a time, she often shook her head in silent denial of the astounding charges of Gray, then finally she settled back calmly, watchful, attentive, and with an expression of unutterable contempt as the story of she—she—she—she ran along.

Contempt for Henry Judd, no doubt. True, she herself squawked on Henry Judd, at about the same time Henry Judd was squawking on her, but it is a woman's inalienable right to squawk.

As for Henry Judd, I still doubt he will last it out. He reminds me of a slowly collapsing lump of tallow. He sat huddled up in his baggy clothes, his eyes on the floor, his chin in hand, while the confession was being read. He seems to be folding up inch by inch every day.

He acts as if he is only semiconscious. If he was a fighter and came back to his corner in his present condition, they would give him smelling salts.

The man is a wreck, a strange contrast to the alert blonde at the table behind him.

The room was packed with women yesterday, well-dressed, richly befurred women from Park Avenue, and Broadway, and others not so well dressed from Long Island City, and the small towns farther down the island. There were giggling young schoolgirls and staid-looking matrons, and my friends, what do you think? Their sympathy is for Henry Judd Gray!

I made a point of listening to their opinions as they packed the hallways and jammed the elevators of the old courthouse yesterday and canvassed some of them personally, and they are all sorry for Gray. Perhaps it is his forlorn-looking aspect as he sits inert, numb, never raising his head, a sad spectacle of a man who admits he took part in one of the most atrocious murders in history.

There is no sympathy for Mrs. Snyder among the women and very little among the men. They all say something drastic ought to be done to her.

If you are asking a medium-boiled reporter of murder trials, I couldn't condemn a woman to death no matter what she had done, and I say this with all due consideration of the future hazards to long-suffering man from sash weights that any lesser verdict than murder in the first degree in the Snyder-Gray case may produce.

It is all very well for the rest of us to say what *ought* to be done to the blonde throwback to the jungle cat that they call Mrs. Ruth Brown Snyder, but when you get in the jury room and start thinking about going home to tell the neighbors that you have

voted to burn a woman—even a blonde woman—I imagine the situation has a different aspect. The most astonishing verdict that could be rendered in this case, of course, would be first degree for the woman and something else for the man. I doubt that result. I am inclined to think that the verdict, whatever it may be, will run against both alike—death or life imprisonment.

Henry Judd Gray said he expects to go to the chair, and adds that he is not afraid of death, an enviable frame of mind, indeed. He says that since he told his story to the world from the witness stand he has found tranquillity, though his tale may have also condemned his blonde partner in blood. But perhaps that's the very reason Henry Judd finds tranquillity.

He sat in his cell in the county jail over in Long Island yesterday, and read from one of the epistles of John.

"Marvel not, my brethren, if the world hate you. We know that we have passed from death unto life, because we love the brethren. He that loveth not his brother abideth in death. Whosoever hateth his brother is a murderer: and ye know that no murderer hath eternal life abiding in him."

A thought for the second Sunday after Pentecost.

In another cell, the blonde woman was very mad at everybody because she couldn't get a marcel for her bobbed locks, one hair of which was once stronger with Henry Judd Gray than the Atlantic cable.

THE JURY of Long Islanders, which left its box at 5:20 on the afternoon of May 9, 1927, made short shrift of the accused. Just an hour and thirty-seven minutes later, at 6:57, the twelve men delivered their verdict—murder in the first degree for both, no mercy. On Friday, May 13, the penalty was set at death in the electric chair.

In the mode and manner prescribed by the laws of the state of New

York, Ruth Brown Snyder and Henry Judd Gray were executed at Sing Sing Prison soon after eleven P.M. on January 13, 1928.

Gene Fowler wrote a shocking story of the executions for the *New York American:*

"Jesus have mercy!" came the pitiful cry. Ruth's blue eyes were red with much weeping. Her face was strangely old. The blonde bobbed hair, hanging in stringy bunches over her furrowed brow, seemed almost white with years of toil and suffering as the six dazzling, high-powered lights illuminated every bit of Ruth's agonized lineaments. . . .

Tightly corseted by the black leather bands, Ruth was flabby and futile as the blast struck her. Her body went forward as far as the restraining thongs would permit.

The tired form was taut. The body that once throbbed with the joy of her sordid bacchanals turned brick red as the current struck. Slowly, after half a minute of the death-dealing current, the exposed arms, right leg, throat, and jaws bleached out again.

One more sensation was to emerge from the death house. A photographer of the New York *Daily News* obtained entrance to the execution chamber as a newspaperman and a legal witness. Although, like all those present, he had been put on his honor by Warden Lewis E. Lawes not to attempt to take any pictures, he had a specially devised camera strapped to his ankle. He got a picture, only a little blurred, of Ruth Snyder in the electric chair at the instant of death. The next morning this horrible portrait was splashed across the whole front page of *The Daily News*.

Was this awesome stunt news to which the public was entitled or a deplorable descent into vulgarity? *The Daily News* proclaimed piously that the photograph accurately portrayed what capital punishment was like and at the same time was a devastating comment on the wages of sin. Other newspapers replied that it might have been a good stunt but that it was rotten journalistic ethics. "The Ruth Snyder picture," commented Stanley Walker, then city editor of the *New York Herald Tribune*, "is regarded by the men who take news pictures as perhaps the most damaging blot upon their professional history. There is a strong sense of honor, an undefined code which forbids shyster practices, even among this group of hard-boiled buccaneers."

It is proverbial that executions involving women invariably run into difficulties. A case in point is that of Edith Thompson, an Englishwoman hanged twenty-five years ago for helping her lover dispose of her husband. Mrs. Thompson fainted before her execution, but her limp body was dragged to the gallows. The execution was so gruesome that the hangman tried to commit suicide, one of the wardresses present went mad, and the chaplain collapsed with a nervous breakdown.

Edwin L. James Sees a Hundred Thousand Frenchmen Greet Young Charles Augustus Lindbergh, Jr., After an Epoch-Making Flight from New York to Paris

IT WAS MAY 20, 1921. Inside a single-engined monoplane sat a tall, lanky pilot, winging his way across the stormy Atlantic "into the brilliant light of history and to unimagined fame." Unlike the gigantic aircraft that now fly on schedule to Europe, this little plane had no lights, no heat, no radio, no automatic pilot, no deicers.

Charles Augustus Lindbergh, Jr., was the son of a member of Congress who had been distinguished for his liberalism. A former stunt flier at county affairs and circuses, young Lindbergh had been a pilot for the air-mail service between St. Louis and Chicago. In 1919 Raymond Orteig, a New York hotel man, offered a prize of $25,000 for the first nonstop flight between New York and Paris, a distance of 3600 miles. For eight years there had been no contestants for what seemed an impossible task. At the beginning of 1927 a number of able pilots on both sides of the Atlantic made ready. Sponsored by a group of St. Louis businessmen, young Lindbergh came to New York only to find Richard E. Byrd and his three-man crew, and Chamberlin and Levine, ready to take off.

At 7:40 A.M. on the morning of May 20, 1927, Lindbergh lifted his 220-horsepower plane, *The Spirit of St. Louis,* carrying a huge load of 451 gallons of gasoline and twenty gallons of oil, from Roosevelt Field in a miraculous take-off. Never before had an engine of such small horsepower lifted so heavy a load. Lindbergh later described what happened on the flight (*The New York Times,* May 23, 1927):

As you know, we (that's my ship and I) took off rather suddenly. We had been told that we might expect good weather mostly during the whole of the way. But we struck fog and rain over the coast not far from the start.

As all aviators know, in a sleetstorm one may be forced down in a few minutes. It got worse and worse. There, above and below me, on both sides, was that driving storm. I made several detours trying to get out of it, but in vain. I flew as low as ten feet above the water and then mounted up to ten thousand feet. Along toward morning the storm eased off, and I came down to a comparatively low level.

Shortly after leaving Newfoundland I began to see icebergs. There was a low fog and even through it I could make out the bergs clearly. It began to get very cold, but I was well prepared.

Within an hour after leaving the coast it became dark. Then I struck clouds and decided to try to get over them. For a while I succeeded, at a height of ten thousand feet. I flew at this height until early morning. The engine was working beautifully and I was not sleepy at all. I felt just as if I was driving a motorcar over a smooth road, only it was easier.

Then it began to get light and the clouds got higher. I went under some and over others. There was sleet in all of those clouds, and the sleet began to cling to the plane. That worried me a great deal and I debated whether I should keep on or go back. I decided I must not think any more about going back.

Lindbergh made it—after nearly thirty-four hours of flying. He later described the reception accorded him in Paris as the most dangerous part of the trip. "Never in my life have I seen anything like that human sea!" The account of that epochal occasion, written for *The New York Times* of May 23, 1927, by Edwin L. James, then its chief European correspondent, today its managing editor, explains why James could not succeed (as Ambassador Herrick did) in carrying out the letter of his cabled instructions from his home office to "isolate Lindbergh."

"Not since the Armistice has such a sight been seen here"

The New York Times, May 23, 1927

PARIS, MAY 21—Lindbergh did it. Twenty minutes after ten o'clock tonight suddenly and softly there slipped out of the darkness a gray-white airplane, as 25,000 pairs of eyes strained toward it. At 10:24 *The Spirit of St. Louis* landed and lines of soldiers, ranks of policemen, and stout steel fences went down before a mad rush as irresistible as the tides of the ocean.

"Well, I made it," smiled Lindbergh, as the little white monoplane came to a halt in the middle of the field and the first vanguard reached the plane. Lindbergh made a move to jump out. Twenty hands reached for him and lifted him out as if he were a baby. Several thousands in a minute were around the plane. Thousands more broke the barriers of iron rails round the field, cheering wildly.

As he was lifted to the ground Lindbergh was pale, and with his hair unkempt he looked completely worn out. He had strength enough, however, to smile, and waved his hand to the crowd. Soldiers with fixed bayonets were unable to keep back the crowd.

United States Ambassador Herrick was among the first to welcome and congratulate the hero.

A *New York Times* man was one of the first to reach the machine after its graceful descent to the field. Those first to arrive at the plane had a picture that will live in their minds for the rest of their lives. His cap off, his famous locks falling in disarray around his eyes, "Lucky Lindy" sat peering out over the rim of the little cockpit of his machine.

It was high drama. Picture the

scene. Almost if not quite 100,000 people were massed on the east side of Le Bourget field. Some of them had been there six and seven hours.

Off to the left the giant phare lighthouse of Mount Valérien flashed its guiding light three hundred miles into the air. Closer on the left Le Bourget Lighthouse twinkled, and off to the right another giant revolving phare sent its beams high into the heavens.

Big arc lights on all sides with enormous electric glares were flooding the landing field. From time to time rockets rose and burst in varied lights over the field.

Seven-thirty, the hour announced for the arrival, had come and gone. Then eight o'clock came, and no Lindbergh; at nine o'clock the sun had set, but then came reports that Lindbergh had been seen over Cork. Then he had been seen over Valentia, in Ireland, and then over Plymouth.

Suddenly a message spread like lightning, the aviator had been seen over Cherbourg. However, remembering the messages telling of Captain Nungesser's flight, the crowd was skeptical.

"One chance in a thousand!" "Oh, he cannot do it without navigating instruments!" "It's a pity, because he's a brave boy!" Pessimism had spread over the great throng by ten o'clock.

The stars came out, and a chill wind blew.

Suddenly the field lights flooded their glares onto the landing ground, and there came the roar of an airplane's motor. The crowd was still, then began a cheer, but two minutes later the landing glares went dark, for the searchlight had identified the plane and it was not Captain Lindbergh's.

Stamping their feet in the cold, the crowd waited patiently. It seemed quite apparent that nearly everyone was willing to wait all night, hoping against hope.

Suddenly—it was 10:16 exactly—another motor roared over the heads of the crowd. In the sky one caught a glimpse of a white-gray plane and for an instant heard the sound of one. Then it dimmed, and the idea spread that it was yet another disappointment.

Again landing lights glared and almost by the time they had flooded the field the gray-white plane had lighted on the far side nearly half a mile from the crowd. It seemed to stop almost as it hit the ground, so gently did it land.

And then occurred a scene which almost passed description. Two companies of soldiers with fixed bayonets and the Le Bourget field police, reinforced by Paris agents, had held the crowd in good order. But as the lights showed the plane landing, much as if a picture had been thrown on a moving-picture screen, there was a mad rush.

The movement of humanity swept over soldiers and by policemen and there was the wild sight of thousands of men and women rushing madly across half a mile of the not-too-even ground. Soldiers and police tried for one small moment to stem the tide, then they joined it, rushing as madly as anyone else toward the aviator and his plane.

The first people to reach the plane were two workmen of the aviation field and half a dozen Frenchmen.

"Cette fois, ça va!" they cried. (This time, it is done.)

Captain Lindbergh answered: "Well, I made it."

An instant later he was on the shoulders of half a dozen persons who tried to bear him from the field.

The crowd crushed about the aviator, and his progress was halted until a squad of soldiers with fixed bayonets cleared a way for him.

It was two French aviators—Major Pierre Weiss and Sergeant de Troyer —who rescued Captain Lindbergh from the frenzied mob. When it seemed that the excited Frenchmen and -women would overwhelm the frail figure which was being carried on the shoulders of half a dozen men, the two aviators rushed up with a Renault car and, hastily snatching Lindy from the crowd, sped across the field to the commandant's office.

Then followed an almost cruel rush to get near the airman. Women were thrown down and a number trampled badly. The doors of the small building were closed, but the windows were forced by enthusiasts, who were promptly ejected by the soldiers.

Spurred on by reports spread in Paris of the approach of the aviator, other thousands began to arrive from the capital.

The police estimate that within half an hour after Captain Lindbergh landed there were probably 100,000 storming the little building to get a sight of the idol of the evening.

Suddenly he appeared at a window, waving his helmet. It was then that, midst cheers for him, came five minutes of cheering for Captain Nungesser.

While the gallant aviator was resting in the Aviators' Club, part of the crowd turned toward his airplane. It had landed in the pink of condition. Before the police could intervene the spectators, turned souvenir-mad, had stripped the plane of everything that could be taken off, and some were even cutting pieces of linen from the wings when a crowd of soldiers with fixed bayonets quickly surrounded *The Spirit of St. Louis* and guarded it

while mechanics wheeled it into a shed, but only after it had been considerably marred.

While the crowd was waiting, Captain Lindbergh was taken away from the field about midnight, to seek a well-earned repose.

The thing that Captain Lindbergh emphasized more than anything else to the American committee which welcomed him, and later to newspapermen, was that he felt no special strain. "I could have gone one half again as much," he said with conviction.

Not since the Armistice of 1918 has Paris witnessed a downtown demonstration of popular enthusiasm and excitement equal to that displayed by the throngs flocking to the boulevards for news of the American flier, whose personality has captured the hearts of the Parisian multitude.

Thirty thousand people had gathered at the Place de l'Opéra and the Square du Havre, near Saint-Lazare station, where illuminated advertising signs flashed bulletins on the progress of the flier. In front of the office of the Paris *Matin* in the Boulevard Poissonnière the crowds quickly filled the streets, so that extra police details had the greatest difficulty in keeping the traffic moving in two narrow files between the mobs which repeatedly choked the entire street.

From the moment when the last evening editions appeared, at 6:30 o'clock, until shortly after nine there was a curious reaction, due to the fact that news seemed to be at a standstill. The throngs waited, hushed and silent, for confirmation.

It was a tense period when the thought in every mind was that they were witnessing a repetition of the deception which two weeks ago turned victory into mourning for the French aviators Nungesser and Coli. Suppose the news flashed from the *Empress of France* that the American flier was seen off the coast of Ireland proved false, as deceiving as the word flashed that Nungesser's *White Bird* had been sighted off Nova Scotia!

During a long, tense period no confirmation came. The people stood quietly, but the strain was becoming almost unbearable, permeating through the crowd. Pessimistic phrases were repeated. "It's too much to think it possible." "They shouldn't have let him go." "All alone, he has no chance if he should be overcome with exhaustion."

To these comments the inevitable reply was, "Don't give up hope. There's still time."

All this showed the French throng was unanimously eager for the American's safety and straining every wish for his ultimate victory.

A Frenchwoman dressed in mourning and sitting in a big limousine was seen wiping her eyes when the bulletins failed to flash confirmation that Lindbergh's plane had been sighted off Ireland. A woman selling papers near by brushed her own tears aside, exclaiming:

"You're right to feel so, madame. In such things there is no nationality —he's some mother's son."

Something of the same despair which the crowds evinced two weeks ago spread as an unconfirmed rumor was circulated that Lindbergh had been forced down. Soon after nine o'clock this was turned to a cheering, shouting pandemonium when *Le Matin* posted a bulletin announcing that the Lindbergh plane had been sighted over Cherbourg.

To THOSE UNFAMILIAR with his mechanical skill Lindbergh was an ingenious lad who had implausibly survived an epoch-making but slightly irrational feat. Actually it was an extraordinary achievement of calculated precision—this crossing of the Atlantic by air only three miles off course in three thousand miles. Although some sixty others had preceded him in transatlantic flights by plane and dirigible, Lindbergh was the first to make the flight entirely alone and to land exactly where he had planned. "There's one thing I'd like to get straight about this flight," said Lindbergh. "They call me 'Lucky,' but luck isn't enough. As a matter of fact, I had what I regarded and still regard as the best existing plane to make the flight from New York to Paris. I had what I regard as the best engine, and I was equipped with what were in the circumstances the best possible instruments for making such efforts."

Royally feted in Paris, Brussels, and London, Lindbergh returned to the United States to face the greatest and most frenzied ovation in the nation's history. Four million people lined the streets of New York to welcome him with almost hysterical joy. The City Fathers had to appropriate $16,000 and the services of two thousand white wings to cart away some 1800 tons of paper, ticker tape, and confetti. Newspapers went all out to describe the fantastic greeting, using some 25,000 tons of newsprint to satisfy an avid public. Editorial comment was extraordinary: the *New York Herald Tribune* observed that "Lindbergh is a work of art, and like a picture or a poem, he either thrills you or he doesn't."

Within three weeks the modest young hero received some 3,500,000 letters, a good portion of which proposed marriage. Offers in excess of $5,000,-000 rained down on him, including one from a movie company suggesting $1,000,000 for an exclusive film in which he would actually be married. Thousands of poems were written in his honor; a mountain in Colorado was named Mount Lindbergh; his brief speeches were compared to Lincoln's Gettysburg Address. The nation indulged in an orgy of delirious hero-worship.

Then a curious thing happened. Alienated by the constant invasions of his privacy, Lindbergh changed from a shy, stalwart young man into a hard, glum, reticent feudist with press and public. Soon his status "wavered between crowd adoration and its only possible sequel, crowd hate," comments Dixon Wecter. The tragic kidnaping of his first-born son in 1932 was a severe shock from which he apparently never recovered. In the late thirties his popularity suffered a precipitous decline when he went beyond the field of aviation and began to dabble with political ideologies. The archapostle of isolation and appeasement in America, Lindbergh got way out on a limb and had trouble getting back.

Louis Stark of *The New York Times* Describes the Execution of Sacco and Vanzetti, a Shoemaker and a Fish Peddler

IT STARTED OUT as a simple case of pay-roll murder, but before long it developed into a *cause célèbre,* and its repercussions have not yet subsided.

On April 15, 1920, two shoe-factory employees, Frederick Parmenter, the paymaster for the Slater and Morrill shoe factory, and Alexander Berardelli, his guard, were shot down on the main street of South Braintree, Massachusetts. The two murderers, described by witnesses as "Italians," escaped with pay-roll boxes containing $15,776.51. Three weeks later two suspects were arrested—Nicola Sacco, an edge trimmer in a shoe factory, and Bartolomeo Vanzetti, a fish peddler.

At the time of the murder Nicola Sacco was twenty-eight years old. He had come to the United States at the age of seventeen and had learned the trade of shoeworker. Earning from sixty to eighty dollars a week, he was the fastest worker of the three thousand men in his factory and was rated "of good character" by his employer. He named his son Dante "because Dante is a big man in my country." In his spare time he took part in radical meetings.

Vanzetti in 1920 was thirty-four years old. A student and prize scholar at a Catholic school in Italy, he had come to America at the age of twenty. A philosophical anarchist, a dreamer, and an idealist, he contributed frequently to radical papers. He once wrote that as a result of reading Saint Augustine and *The Divine Comedy,* "humanity and equality of rights began to afflict my heart."

What happened to these two men must be judged in the light of the tense, anti-Red climate of opinion that prevailed at the termination of World War I. Shortly before their arrest, Sacco and Vanzetti had arranged a mass meeting of protest against the alleged brutality of Department of Justice agents toward a fellow radical who had leaped to his death from a New York building while undergoing questioning. An additional black mark on their record was the fact that both men had been active in strikes.

Heatedly protesting their innocence, Sacco and Vanzetti furnished alibis for the day of the murders. Of some 675 talesmen called for service on the jury, at least three hundred insisted that they had conscientious scruples against the death penalty. The trial judge, Webster Thayer, warned jurors against evading their obligations as citizens, and called on them to do their duty with the courage of American soldiers on the battlefield. Friends of the defendants interpreted this as "courage to convict," for, they asserted, no courage was needed to acquit, and the prosecution charged that many talesmen feared that the "Black Hand" would burn down their houses if they voted guilty.

At the trial the defense introduced the radicalism of the defendants as an explanation of certain actions alleged to show "consciousness of guilt." The severe grilling by the prosecutor, some rather prejudicial remarks of the judge, and weaknesses in the evidence combined to create a widespread belief that the defendants were being punished for radicalism rather than for murder. In July, 1921, the two men were convicted of murder in the first degree and were sentenced to death.

Then began an amazing six-year Golgotha for the shoemaker and the fish peddler. The Sacco-Vanzetti case leaped out of the Massachusetts courtroom into the minds and lives of millions throughout the world. In Paris, Anatole France, Romain Rolland, and Henri Barbusse wrote appeals for Sacco and Vanzetti, the case was discussed before the Chamber of Deputies, and a bomb attempt was made on the life of Ambassador Herrick. A general strike in Uruguay was attributed directly to the Sacco-Vanzetti case. Threats against American consular officials were made in Peru, Cuba, Spain, Mexico, even in Japan. In the United States liberals of all shades hastened to the defense of the two Italians, convinced that the men had been convicted "by atmosphere, not by evidence." Mrs. Louis Brandeis, wife of the Supreme Court Justice, placed her home at the disposal of Mrs. Sacco. There were great demonstrations to stay execution or beg for mercy. It was charged that Judge Thayer had denounced the defendants as "bastards" and "anarchists" in conversation outside the courtroom and had then ruled that he was not prejudiced against them. A witness, Daly, swore that Ripley, the jury foreman, had said, prior to his call as a juror: "Damn them, they ought to hang, anyway." Walter Lippmann, moved to action by a masterly analysis of the trial made by Professor Felix Frankfurter of the Harvard Law School, took an entire page of the New York *World* for a strong editorial entitled: "Doubts That Will Not Down."

The more "Massachusetts justice" was attacked, the more obstinate was the reaction. A commission under the chairmanship of President Abbott Lawrence Lowell of Harvard examined the evidence and gave the court a clean bill of health. Governor Alvan T. Fuller of Massachusetts refused to intervene. One of the last desperate steps to save the condemned men was an appeal to the venerable Supreme Court Justice, Oliver Wendell Holmes, who held that he could not stay execution, for want of jurisdiction.

From Vanzetti's cell came a remarkable statement:

If it had not been for these things, I might have live out my life talking at street corner to scorning men. I might have died unmarked, unknown, a failure. Now we are not a failure. This is our career and our triumph. Never in our full life could we hope to do such a work for tolerance, for justice, for man's understanding of men as we do by accident. Our words—our lives—our pains—nothing! The taking of our lives—lives of a good shoemaker and a poor fish peddler—all! That last moment belongs to us—that agony is our triumph.

To this "American Dreyfus Case" there was no happy ending, for the two men were destined to die in the electric chair. On the last day of his life Vanzetti penned this eloquent message to the son of his friend Sacco:

August 21, 1927. From the Death House of Massachusetts State Prison
My dear Dante:

I still hope, and we will fight until the last moment, to revindicate our right to live and to be free, but all the forces of the State and of the money and reaction are deadly against us because we are libertarians or anarchists.

I write little of this because you are now and yet too young to understand these things and other things which I would like to reason with you.

But, if you do well, you will grow and understand your father's and my case and your father's and my principles, for which we will soon be put to death. . . .

Remember and know also, Dante, that if your father and I would have been cowards and hypocrits and rinnegetors of our faith, we would not have been put to death. They would not even have convicted a lebbrous dog; not even executed a deadly poisoned scorpion on such evidence as they framed against us. They would have given a new trial to a matricide and abitual felon on the evidence we presented for a new trial. . . .

. . . If we will be executed after seven years, four months and seventeen days of unspeakable tortures and wrong, it is . . . because we were for the poor and against the exploitation and oppression of the man by the man. . . .

The day will come when you will understand the atrocious cause of the above written words, in all its fullness. Then you will honor us. . . .

Bartolomeo

On August 22, 1927, the day before the executions, there was turmoil in Paris such as had not been witnessed since the World War. Forty were hurt in a Sacco-Vanzetti demonstration in London. There were riotous demonstrations before American consulates all over the earth. Congressman Fiorello La Guardia flew to Boston to see the Governor and emerged saying the condemned men had one chance in a thousand. Justices Taft and Stone refused to intervene.

The emotional strain of the last day before the executions was caught in a series of brilliant reports by Louis Stark of *The New York Times*, who had given the case close attention since its inception, and who, in the years that followed, continually brought *Times* readers up to date on the facts. Stark's four-thousand-word résumé of the case, written upon assignment for *The New York Times* on March 5, 1922, is probably the most objective analysis of the case to appear in a newspaper. On the evening of the execution, Stark arrived at the prison at ten o'clock and began filing details of the preparations. "The story of the electrocutions," he informed the editors of this book in a letter describing the scene, "was written in a room close to the execution chamber at Charlestown Prison. The small room assigned to the reporters was in the utmost confusion. The noise was almost deafening. Telegraph keys were clicking away and typewriters were banging furiously. The Morse operators were the coolest of the fifty men and women in the room. Our nerves were stretched to the breaking point. Had there not been a last-minute reprieve on August 10? Might there be one now?"

Only one reporter, W. E. Playfair of the Associated Press, was permitted to attend the executions, since the state law designated one representative of the press as a witness, and the assignment had been handed him six years before, upon the conviction of Sacco and Vanzetti. From the details furnished by Playfair and several assistants who remained on the streets observing the police and the crowds, Stark fed this dispatch to *The New York Times*.

"Doubts that will not down"

The New York Times, August 23, 1927

CHARLESTOWN STATE PRISON, MASSACHUSETTS, TUESDAY, AUGUST 23— Nicola Sacco and Bartolomeo Vanzetti died in the electric chair this morning, carrying out the sentence imposed on them for the South Braintree murders of April 15, 1920.

Sacco marched to the death chair at 12:11 and was pronounced lifeless at 12:19.

Vanzetti entered the execution room at 12:20 and was declared dead at 12:26.

To the last they protested their innocence, and the efforts of many who believed them guiltless proved futile, although they fought a legal and extralegal battle unprecedented in the history of American jurisprudence.

With them died Celestino F. Madeiros, the young Portuguese, who won seven respites when he "confessed" that he was present at the time of the South Braintree murder and that Sacco and Vanzetti were not with him. He died for the murder of a bank cashier.

The six years' legal battle on behalf of the condemned men was still on as they were walking to the chair and after the current had been applied, for a lawyer was on the way by airplane to ask Federal Judge George W. Anderson in Williamstown for a writ of habeas corpus.

The men walked to the chair without the company of clergy. Father Michael J. Murphy, Prison Chaplain, waited until a minute before twelve and then left the prison.

Sacco cried, "Long live anarchy!" as the prison guards strapped him into the chair and applied the electrodes. He added a plea that his family be cared for.

Vanzetti at the last made a short

address, declaring his innocence.
Madeiros walked to the chair in a
semistupor caused by overeating. He
shrugged his shoulders and made no
farewell statement.

Warden William Hendry was almost overcome by the execution of the
two men, especially that of Vanzetti,
who shook his hand warmly and
thanked him for all his kindnesses.

The Warden was barely able to
whisper the solemn formula required
by law:

"Under the law I now pronounce
you dead, the sentence of the court
having been legally carried out."

The words were not heard by the
official witnesses.

After Governor Fuller had informed
counsel for the two condemned radicals that he could take no action, their
attorney, Michael A. Musmanno,*
made a dash to the prison in an automobile and tried to make another call
on Sacco and Vanzetti, but Warden
Hendry refused, as the legal witnesses were just about to pass into the
execution chamber.

The witnesses gathered in the Warden's office an hour before midnight.
They were instructed as to the part
they would take.

At 11:38 all but the official witnesses were asked to leave the Warden's office. Led by Warden Hendry,
the official witnesses walked toward
the rotunda of the prison. He rapped
three times on the inner door. A key
grated in the lock. Just then Mr. Musmanno dashed in breathlessly.

"Please, Warden," he said, touching Mr. Hendry on the arm, "a last request."

"No, no," the Warden said, sternly,

slightly unnerved at the last-minute
interruption. Mr. Musmanno turned
away, weeping. He had refused to accept as a farewell gift a book from
Vanzetti because he felt that the men
could be saved.

"I only tried to see them the last
time," said Musmanno through tears.

The witnesses walked through the
prison and entered the death house
with the Warden. They took their
places, and then Madeiros was escorted into the chamber. He walked
without support, attended by two
guards, one at each side. He was
strapped in the chair at 12:03 and at
12:09 he was pronounced dead.

He was officially pronounced dead
by Dr. George Burgess MacGrath,
Medical Examiner of Norfolk County,
and Dr. Howard A. Lothrop, Surgeon-
in-Chief of the Boston City Hospital.
Stethoscopes were also applied to Madeiros' chest by Dr. Joseph I. Mac-
Laughlin, the prison physician, and
Colonel Frank P. Williams, Surgeon
General of the Massachusetts National Guard. The same procedure was
followed in the case of Sacco and Vanzetti.

Sacco, whose cell was next to that
of Madeiros, was the next. A guard
opened his door. Sacco was ready. His
face was pale from his long confinement. Without a word he took his
place between his guards. Walking
slowly but steadily he traversed the
seventeen steps into the death chamber. He required no support and sat
down in the chair. As the guards were
finishing their work Sacco cried out in
Italian:

"Long live anarchy!"

In English he shouted:

---

* Michael Angelo Musmanno, then "a vivacious young man with flowing brown hair and
streaming black Windsor tie," who had been sent from Pittsburgh to Boston by the Sons
of Italy to ask the Governor for clemency; more recently a judge of the International War
Crimes Trial, who made a searching investigation of the facts surrounding the death of Hitler.

"Farewell my wife and child, and all my friends!"

He has two children, Dante, fourteen, and Inez, six, but his difficulty in speaking English and the excitement of the occasion were responsible for the slip.

"Good evening, gentlemen," he said jerkily. Then came his last words: "Farewell, Mother."

Warden Hendry waited until Sacco apparently was satisfied that there was no more to say. Then he gave the signal. Sacco was pronounced dead at 12:19:02.

Vanzetti's door was opened. He, too, was calm. He shook hands with the two guards and kept step with them. He had four more steps to the death chair than Sacco. On entering the chamber he spoke to the Warden, shaking hands and saying:

"I want to thank you for everything you have done for me, Warden."

Vanzetti spoke in English. His voice was calm throughout. There was not the slightest tremor or quaver.

Then, addressing the witnesses, he said:

"I wish to tell you that I am innocent, and that I never committed any crime but sometimes some sin."

They were almost the same words he addressed to Judge Webster Thayer in the Dedham courtroom last April when he was sentenced to die during the week of April 10, the sentence having been deferred because the Governor's Advisory Commission was working on the case.

"I thank you for everything you have done for me," he went on, calmly and slowly. "I am innocent of all crime, not only of this, but all. I am an innocent man."

Then he spoke his last words:

"I wish to forgive some people for what they are doing to me."

Vanzetti stepped into the chamber at 12:20:30. At 12:26:55 he was declared dead.

Before midnight Warden Hendry told reporters how he broke the news to Sacco and Vanzetti.

"I simply told them it was my very painful duty to convey to them the information that they were going to die shortly after midnight," he said. "I told them that their lawyers had informed me that they had done all they could and had failed."

Father Michael J. Murphy, Prison Chaplain, again offered the men his services, but they refused his offer of the last rites. Earlier in the day the Chaplain visited the men and on coming from the death house said:

"I offered them the consolation of religion, but all three preferred to die as they had lived—outside the pale. They can call on me at any time before the execution, and I will hear their confessions and give communion."

Warden Hendry received two telegrams, one addressed to himself, which he did not make public, and another addressed to Sacco. After reading the Sacco telegram the Warden refused to make known its contents to the prisoner, explaining that he did not know the writer.

The telegram read:

"Take heart, men. It is justice that dies. Sacco and Vanzetti will live in history." It was signed Epstein and sent from New York.

The police, despite their elaborate precautions, had a surprise about an hour before midnight, when it was discovered that someone had penetrated the lines thrown around the prison for blocks and made his way to the very entrance of the Warden's office, where he had passed an envelope to one of the regular guards and strolled off.

The envelope contained a two-page letter, the contents of which the Warden withheld. An investigation was begun at once to learn how the mysterious messenger had gained entrance to the guarded area.

The police broke up a meeting of nearly five hundred Italians in Salem Street, in the North end, as midnight approached. They threatened to hold a demonstration in front of the Bunker Hill Monument, and also threatened to hold a protest meeting before the State House and on the Common.

Mounted police charged a crowd of several thousand that gathered just outside the roped-off area surrounding the jail at the hour of execution. Two hundred Sacco and Vanzetti sympathizers had congregated in Thompson Square to join a parade out to Bunker Hill. Policemen afoot were unable to control the excited crowd. The charge of the mounted police drove men, women, and children back in a wave. Several persons were crushed. Two women were arrested, charged with sauntering and loitering.

More than one thousand cars were blocked in a traffic jam along Main Street, obstructing the passage of pedestrians and police. The street became a tangled mass of automobiles and other vehicles. There was a terrific din as policemen shouted orders, the ironshod hoofs of their mounts clattered over pavements and hundreds of automobilists shouted their sirens continuously.

Charlestown Prison was armed and garrisoned as if to withstand a siege. Machine guns, gas and tear bombs, not to mention pistols and riot guns, constituted the armament, and to man it were five hundred patrolmen, detectives, and state constables besides the usual prison guard.

A weird and martial picture was presented when motion-picture photographers held aloft flaming calcium torches, lighting up a passing detail of mounted state police with a ghastly flicker and silhouetting their silent figures against the grim gray of the prison walls.

Mrs. Rose Sacco and Miss Luigia Vanzetti called three times at the death house during the day. Their last visit was at seven o'clock in the evening, when they remained five minutes and departed weeping. Gardiner Jackson and Aldini Felicani of the Defense Committee, who accompanied the women, arranged with Warden Hendry for the transfer of their bodies to the relatives.

Mrs. Sacco and Miss Vanzetti arrived at the prison for the first time in the day at eleven A.M. Dr. Joseph I. MacLaughlin, the prison physician, was in the death house at the time and Vanzetti introduced his sister to him. The two women were downcast. They pressed their faces close to the heavily barred cell doors under the eyes of the guards.

An hour passed, and the interview ended with tearful farewells. Farewell embraces were not permitted. There were handclasps and faces were pressed to the cell doors. The bars are an inch thick and an inch apart and heavily meshed.

Madeiros at noon seemed quite calm and smoked many cigarettes. Vanzetti worked on a letter to his father. Sacco paced up and down his cell. But when Michael A. Musmanno of defense counsel called on Sacco and Vanzetti at 2:30 P.M. he found them depressed and ready for death. They told him they were convinced no power on earth would save them. Sacco begged to see his wife again. Vanzetti regretted that his sister had come from Italy to be with him in his last moments of agony. He was sorry that her last memory of him would be clouded with knowledge of the gray prison, the death cell, and the electric chair.

At 3:10 P.M. the two women returned to the death house in an automobile driven by Miss Edith Jackson of New Haven. Mrs. Sacco, who has always presented a tearless and composed face to the public, wept for the first time as she approached the gate. Miss Vanzetti's arm supported her as the two passed into the death house for the second time in the day. They greeted the men through the wire mesh and remained an hour. Sacco spoke of his children and Vanzetti of his old home in Italy. The women were weeping as they stepped into the automobile.

William G. Thompson, former counsel of Sacco and Vanzetti, called then late in the day. Mr. Thompson had returned from his summer home at South Tamworth, New Hampshire, at the request of Vanzetti and visited both men at the death house. He spent nearly an hour there. When he left he said that Sacco and Vanzetti had reasserted that they were absolutely innocent of the South Braintree murders. He declared also that there was no truth in the report that he had been offered an opportunity to inspect the files of the Department of Justice and had refused.

The conversation with Vanzetti, said Mr. Thompson, was partly on the man's political and philosophical beliefs. He declined to discuss the report of Governor Fuller or that of the Advisory Commission other than to say that, having read both documents with care, he found nothing in them which altered his opinion "that these two men are innocent and their trial was in a very real sense unfair."

Mr. Thompson left, and half an hour later Mrs. Sacco and Miss Vanzetti arrived for their third and final visit to the condemned men. They were in an automobile with Gardiner Jackson and Aldini Felicani of the Defense Committee. The men stepped out, while the women waited. Jackson and Felicani asked Warden Hendry for permission to have the women see their unfortunate relatives for the last time. The request was granted. Mr. Jackson and Mr. Felicani arranged for the bodies of the two men to be turned over to Mrs. Sacco and Miss Vanzetti.

* * *

THE EXECUTIONS touched off a wave of bitter demonstrations throughout the world. The Socialist leader, Norman Thomas, remarked: "I do not know what the feelings of these men have been upon going to their death after seven long years, but I do know that tonight the cruelty, the stupidity, the obstinacy of men has taken two otherwise noble and humble men and made of them symbols. Men looking back through the ages will remember them as we remember John Brown."

Impartial students of the law who examined the voluminous case record agreed that Sacco and Vanzetti had been convicted on insufficient evidence, that the presiding judge was guilty of gross prejudice, and that President Lowell's Committee of Inquiry had conducted the investigation in a one-sided manner. In his book *The Best Is Yet* (1945), Morris L. Ernst, attorney for the American Civil Liberties Union, wrote: "I am sure I know

the gang who did the job. Sacco and Vanzetti had nothing to do with it."
Louis Stark's concluding comment on the case: "The tragedy of the Sacco-
Vanzetti case is the tragedy of three men—Judge Thayer, Governor Fuller,
and President Lowell—and their inability to rise above the obscene battle
that raged for seven long years around the heads of the shoemaker and the
fish peddler."

Harlem Says "Bye-Bye, Honey" to Florence Mills

NEW YORK'S HARLEM is one of the great Negro centers of the world and one of the most densely populated areas on earth. With the wisdom of the ages the people of Harlem have learned to withstand the blows of prejudice and discrimination that long since might have broken a people of lesser fiber. Yielding to no one in their pride as Americans, they nevertheless have their own traditions, mores, and emotions. There is little to compare with Lenox Avenue engulfed in a wave of joy on a victorious Joe Louis night—unless it be the other end of the emotional scale. The sorrow of Harlem is a majestic thing to behold.

In the era of the Fabulous Twenties, Harlem took Florence Mills, the talented little dancer, to its great heart. Born in Washington thirty-two years before, she came home in October, 1927, from a triumphant Continental tour with Lou Leslie's *Blackbirds*. Everyone in Harlem, from corner ragamuffins to distinguished intellectuals, knew Florence Mills, and everyone gloried in her great success. Few knew that she had been ill. As she came off the ship, with a bouquet of American roses in her arms, she was met by her old mother, who embraced her warmly and said with maternal intuition: "Baby, you've come home to die!" A month later Florence Mills was dead.

A Boston reporter, W. A. Macdonald, saw how Harlem expressed its grief for the loss of Florence Mills. Here is a condensed version of his story, which was the personal nomination of Louis M. Lyons of the *Boston Globe* and the Nieman Foundation for inclusion in this *Treasury*.

"Baby, you've come home to die!"—
W. A. Macdonald's Boston Evening
Transcript *story*

Boston Evening Transcript, November 7, 1927

On Saturday night the line outside the undertaking chapel in Harlem was still there. Only now it was longer than it had been since the body of Florence Mills was brought there in the middle of the week. It began for the day in the middle of the morning; it dissolved for the night at two o'clock in the morning of Sunday. There it was on Saturday before the stone building at the corner of Seventh Avenue and One Hundred and Thirty-seventh Street, where a cardboard sign on the door said: "REMAINS OF MISS MILLS ON VIEW AT ONE O'CLOCK. THE FAMILY." There were no police there then be cause the crowd was small. It grew so fast that the doors were opened two hours before the cardboard's time. They wanted all to go in at once, but quiet-voiced young men at the door ordered that it form in line.

Mostly these were colored people; a few were white. Mostly they were poor; their clothes showed that. They moved slowly into the chapel and down the aisle. There were old women, young women, pretty girls, children. An elderly Negress complained from the steps that white people had come saying they were from out of town and had been admitted while "They push we out." Someone hushed her. This was the fourth day that this line had passed through the chapel. A white truck driver in a soiled leather jacket took the butt of a cigar from his mouth as he went in. A tall young policeman, his bright hair gleaming in the dim light, walked down the aisle, his hands on the shoulders of a little colored boy to whom he leaned down and spoke. Except for the sound of shuffling feet the room was still.

Thousands by thousands the people of Harlem were looking for the last time at Florence Mills. It was such a fleeting look. In the great copper coffin lay the figure of the little dancer, her dress silver, her thin legs in gray. Her dark, short face was a rounded square.

Two tall white candles burned above the metal coffin. One stood at the head, one at the foot. The melted wax had formed in corrugations down their sides. In the background were banks of flowers. A hundred thousand dollars' worth of flowers before the day was over. From all over the world that knew her came the flowers by cable, by telegraph, by messengers direct from those who had selected their tribute with loving care. Hour by hour the thousands moved before them. They waited, slowly moving,

outside the building in the cold rain of dreary morning; they were patiently going on through the clearing afternoon; they were strengthening their line through the cold evening under the stars in the sky above Harlem. At seven o'clock at night they extended through One Hundred and Thirty-Seventh Street for nearly a block. And more were coming all the time.

Meantime Harlem was going on with its other life. It is the greatest Negro city in the world. From just north of Central Park up to the end of Manhattan, more than two hundred thousand Negroes are gathered in an unbroken community, most of which was to be crowded into the streets about the Mother Zion African Methodist Episcopal Church for the funeral on Sunday. Up and down Seventh Avenue strolled the life of Harlem, stepping a little more quickly as the cold wind nipped. People gathered in the theaters, where Florence Mills had sung and danced; they laughed at actors of their own color. Girls of the chorus did their stuff for the appreciation of good-humored audiences. A pair of Negroes on one stage played a silent, tricky poker game while the audience exploded with laughter. And the manager, standing in the back of the darkened house, laid a hand on a man's sleeve. "Success never changed her; you know that. When she was here she was always the same. She never wanted any special favor, any star's dressing room even after she began to make a hit. She might have been one of the chorus if you saw her backstage. You know that. She never owned an automobile, for all the money she made. She would take her nickel and walk to the subway. She didn't ride in taxicabs. And she was a fine woman.

"She and her husband were a happy

couple. And they went everywhere together. One thing about Florence Mills, she always did her best. When she was in the Harlem theaters she always did her best. She was a hard worker, no gay parties, never spoiled, and she was good to her mother." The manager paused; he was deeply moved. "You know that," he said. "Well, you want to see the show."

It is midnight when Harlem begins to gather at the night clubs. Here was a club that had been going only a month, and it was filling with people at midnight. They were gay people; they sat briefly at the tables and then took to the floor. Or they hung in seated groups and talked. Everyone knew Florence Mills here. Not two weeks ago she was here with her husband.

"No, I haven't been to see her," said one man with a quiet voice. "I wanted to remember her as I saw her here. There will never be another Florence Mills." He waited for a moment. "She was a great woman." Jazz welled up from the orchestra.

And then about two o'clock in the morning began a dance tune that was different from the rest. Swaying couples moved slowly on the floor in the press. Smoke from hundreds of cigarettes spired upwards from the tables. The dance music was slow; it was the long, deliberate beat of the tom-tom; it was measured and savage and professional. The couples, pressed close together, danced to its deliberate beat. It was a dirge!

On Sunday morning groups gathered at homes in Harlem. They were her friends; they talked about her. No tears came—but almost. The crowd gathered again at the chapel. The funeral was set for one o'clock, but the crowd was there at half-past ten. Thousands upon thousands it

grew. People leaned out of the windows as far as the eye could see. They gathered on fire escapes and on rooftops. Downstairs the floor was reserved for those who had cards of admission, of which nine thousand had been issued. The capacity of the church is 2350.

Out of the organ came a soft thread of sound. Then at two o'clock, faint in the distance, *The Rock of Ages* found its way into the crowded church. It stopped, and the Chopin march rose and swelled and diminished and grew again. Slowly, oh so slowly, down the aisle with the music came forty girls, bareheaded and wearing their outdoor coats, and their arms were burdened with the white and crimson of flowers.

A sound like wind and storm on sea was the crowd outside.

The girls who bore the flowers stood in rank. They were pretty. They were friends of Florence Mills. Some of them stifled sounds as they took their breath. Through the church ran a quiver of crying.

The Carolina choir from one of the theaters sang *Deep River*. The burden of the music was carried by a tall young woman whose deep contralto rose from the humming underbeat of the choir.

The gust of noise through the doors was the storm of the crowd outside. A hundred thousand, a hundred and fifty thousand people were there in a colored sea five blocks long. Once a gust of laughter came from the sea. The pastor spoke of the loss to the race, an actress gifted by nature, a personality striking and charming, a woman whose success had never spoiled her poise and dignity, a daughter who had never forgotten her mother.

Juanita Stinnette, of the stage team of Chapelle and Stinnette, stood forth to begin a song that her partner had written for the funeral. The singer wavered and regained control. Louder and louder she went on. She was leaning toward the bank of flowers that hid the casket. She was addressing the little dancer who lay therein. High and loud rang the last note. Down in a heap went the singer, screaming. The white gloves of an usher covered her mouth as they bore her out. A quiver ran through the church. From outside came the noise of the crowd.

There was more music. The congregation rose as the pastor read the service. Ashes to ashes and dust to dust. People struggled with their coats. The bearers lifted the great copper coffin. High above the heads of the people the bank of roses moved slowly down the aisle. The people pushed out into the greater crowd outside. Block after block it jostled for position. Along One Hundred and Thirty-seventh Street to the corner of Seventh Avenue moved the procession and past the corner where all traffic was stalled on the avenue. As it passed through that crowded sea the hats of Harlem came off. You could see it as a great movement along the avenue. An airplane roared overhead. The police whistles shrilled, sharp, imperative; automobiles moved slowly at the sound.

Florence Mills, to whom the little chorus girl, leaning over the casket, had said, "Bye-bye, honey," rode up Seventh Avenue.

*   *   *

Russell Owen Reports the First Airplane
Flight Over the South Pole

YOU ARE A FOOL to go on a trip that is to last so long, you will get only a half a dozen good stories, and you will be forgotten when you return." This was the reaction of one of his colleagues when Russell Owen, specialist on exploration stories for *The New York Times,* announced that his managing editor had selected him to go along with the Byrd Antarctic expedition in 1928–29. Owen himself, however, was convinced that the Antarctic offered unlimited opportunities for news, "where there is frozen beauty beyond belief and where there are storms which drink from the human system the warmth of life." He was right.

Richard Evelyn Byrd, American naval officer, aviator, and explorer, with his pilot, Floyd Bennett, had flown in a Fokker monoplane over the North Pole on May 9, 1926, the first conquest of the North Pole by air. In the fall of 1928 Byrd led a carefully prepared scientific expedition to the Antarctic, establishing a base that he named Little America, from which he was to make the first flight over the South Pole. This was the expedition Owen was to report for *The New York Times.*

In those early days of short-wave radio development it did not seem possible that Owen would be able to get much news to the United States, nine thousand miles away. But day after day he sent back as much as three or four thousand words. This successful reporting feat, which marked the beginning of the commercial development of short-wave communication, won Owen the 1930 Pulitzer Prize in reporting.

Here is Owen's report of the most dramatic part of the expedition—Byrd's flight across the South Pole.

"Like a cork in a washtub"

The New York Times, November 29, 1929

LITTLE AMERICA, ANTARCTICA, NOVEMBER 29—Conqueror of two Poles by air, Commander Richard E. Byrd flew into camp at 1:10 o'clock this morning, having been gone eighteen hours and fifty-nine minutes. An hour of this time was spent at the mountain base, refueling.

The first man to fly over the North and South Poles and the only man to fly over the South Pole stepped from his plane and was swept up on the arms of the men in camp who for more than an hour had been anxiously watching the southern horizon for a sight of the plane.

Deaf from the roar of the motors, tired from the continual strain of the flight and the long period of navigation under difficulties, Commander Byrd was still smiling and happy. He had reached the South Pole after as hazardous and as difficult a flight as had ever been made in an airplane, tossed by gusts of wind, climbing desperately up the slopes of glaciers a few hundred feet above the surface.

His companions on the flight stumbled out stiff and weary also, but so happy that they forgot their cramped muscles. They were also tossed aloft, pounded on the back, and carried to the entrance of the mess hall.

Bernt Balchen, the calm-eyed pilot who first met Commander Byrd in Spitzbergen and who was with him on the transatlantic flight, came out first. There was a little smudge of soot under the nose, but the infectious smile, which has endeared him to those who know him, was radiant.

He was carried away, and then came Harold June, who, between intervals of helping Balchen and attending to fuel tanks and lines and taking pictures, found time to send the radio bulletins which told of the plane's progress.

And after him Captain Ashley McKinley was lifted from the doorway, beaming like the Cheshire cat because his surveying camera had carried on its work all the way.

Men crowded about them, eager for the story of what they had been through, catching fragments of sentences. It had evidently been a terrific battle to get up through the mountains and the plateau.

"We had to dump a month and a half of food to do it," said Commander Byrd. "I am glad it wasn't gas. It was nip and tuck all the way."

"Yes," chuckled Balchen. "Do you remember when we were sliding around those knolls, picking the wind currents to help us, and there wasn't more than three hundred feet under us at times? We were just staggering along, with drift and clouds and all sorts of things around us."

When the plane approached the mountains on the way south, Commander Byrd picked out the Livingston Glacier, a large glacier somewhat to the west of the Axel Heiberg Glacier, as the best passageway.

The high mountains shut them in all around as they forced their way upwards, Byrd conserving his fuel to the utmost, coaxing his engines, picking up the upcurrents of air as best he could to help the plane ride upward.

Clouds swirled about them at times, puffballs of mist driven down the glacier; drift scurried beneath them; it was a wicked place for an airplane to be, hemmed in by a wall of the towering peaks on either side.

This was the time when they had to lighten ship, and Byrd, looking around for what could be spared, decided to dump some food. There was a dump valve in the fuselage tank, but he had determined to go through and did not know what winds he might face at the top of the glacier. So food was thrown overboard, scattered over the ridged and broken surface of the Livingston Glacier.

"It is an awful-looking place," Commander Byrd said.

They finally reached the hump at an elevation of 11,500 feet, as indicated by the barometer, although it might have been a little more, because of the difference in pressure inland.

But there was little space under the staggering plane, buffeted by the winds that eddied through the gigantic gorge. Once at the top, Byrd could level off for a time and then gain altitude.

Then there came into view the long sweep of the mountains of the Queen Maud range, stretching to the southeast, and the magnificent panorama of the entire bulwark of mountains along the edge of the Polar Plateau.

"It was the most magnificent sight I have ever seen," Commander Byrd said. "I never dreamed there were so many mountains in the world. They shone under the sun, wonderfully tinted in color, and in the sea a bank of clouds hung over the mountains, making a scene I shall never forget."

Over the plateau the Commander set his course for the Pole. They had had a beautiful wind all the way into the mountains which held them up, but the fight to get over the edge of the plateau had used a lot of gasoline and there was some doubt as to whether there was enough to get back.

But Commander Byrd determined to go on. If they had favorable winds, coming back they would be all right, but if as much time was consumed coming in as going out, they would run out of gasoline.

He took the chance and won. Flying over the plateau with long sweeping slopes leading up to the mountains, with wind drifting snow from them along the surface, it was very difficult to estimate the drift of the plane.

But by constant attention to the drift meter Commander Byrd was able to get enough sights on the surface below to keep the plane on its course and correct the inevitable tendency in all long-distance flights of swerving to one side or the other.

Between the mountains and the Pole at one point he saw a new range of mountains, apparently between the trails followed by Captain Roald Amundsen and Captain Robert F. Scott. But the mountains far to the west, the continuation of the range running up the western side of the Barrier, were, as Commander Byrd described them, "simply magnificent."

Everyone rather hoped that mountains would be seen at the other side of the Pole from Little America, but there was nothing in sight there.

When Commander Byrd's calculations showed that he had reached the vicinity of the Pole he ran along a line at an angle to his course and then swung in a wide circle, as he did at the North Pole, to make sure of coming within striking distance of that infinitesimal spot on the earth's surface.

Some time was spent in that maneuver, and then the plane was again set on a course for Little America.

The accuracy of the navigation was strikingly shown on this part of the flight, as it was necessary to navigate the entire distance home. By means of the sun compass, the Commander hit the Axel Heiberg Glacier exactly and slid down that to the Barrier.

To understand what that means, try to realize being over a vast plain, nearly four hundred miles from the place where the mountains were entered, with an encircling rim of majestic peaks all looking different from the south from what they had looked on the way in. Captain Amundsen remarked on this vastly different aspect on his return journey.

But the course, as laid, brought the plane flying high over the Polar Plateau to the mouth of the Axel Heiberg Glacier, and Bernt Balchen kept a good elevation on the way down.

Even so, it was a rough ride, for in the narrow gorge of this glacier, which Captain Amundsen ascended on his way to the Pole, the wind eddies tossed the plane around "like a cork in a washtub," as Balchen said, the high peaks sticking up all around them. It was the hardest part of the trip from the flying point of view.

When the Barrier was reached the plane headed for the base laid down on a previous flight, and a landing there was made at five o'clock this morning [noon, New York time].

June landed the plane here because he had been here on the previous flight, and also took off and made a splendid job of it. More gasoline was put into the tanks, and, when the plane was in the air again, Commander Byrd headed to the east toward Carmen Land.

What he had seen there on the previous flight interested him, and his interest was repaid. He not only traced out more definitely the course of the Charles Bob Mountains, but he also saw another range far to the east.

The camp had been out of touch with the plane for some time after the Pole was reached, although the signals from the locked radio key came in and showed that it was in the air.

Men had waited up all night in the mess hall, clustering about the radio room to get the news of the progress of the flight.

As the reports indicated the slow time the plane was making on the way in, there was some anxiety, and mechanics checked and rechecked figures to estimate the amount of flying time the plane had with the gasoline in the tanks when it left and what ground speed it was making.

There was some gloom as the slow progress inland was recorded and then, as a long interval came between messages before the Pole was reached, everyone wondered what was keeping June so busy.

Finally came the message that the plane was in the vicinity of the Pole, and there was a sigh of relief and men lay down on their bunks and tried to get a little sleep.

The whine of the plane's transmitter for the loud-speakers in each house was a reassurance rather than an annoyance, and if the sound had ceased probably everyone would have started up instantly.

As it was, the fluctuations in the signals made sleep almost impossible.

The other two expert pilots in camp, Captain Alton U. Parker and Dean Smith, were "flying the plane" all the way, showing by their tense expressions how they were linked with the men in the cockpit of the *Floyd Bennett*, fighting their way through the mountains.

One man lay down on the wooden bench in front of the loud-speaker and went to sleep, and when the signal strength died down at one time he jumped up as if pricked with a pin. It was an anxious night in camp, for everyone here realized what those men in the plane were facing in the climb through the rifts in the mountains.

There was a pleasant omen in the weather, however. It had been somewhat overcast to the north when the plane took off and there was a strong wind, but William C. (Cyclone) Haines and Henry Harrison, the meteorologists, after taking balloon runs and receiving word from the geological party inland as to the conditions near the mountains, decided that the flight could be made.

After the plane started, the conditions steadily grew better and there was a dead calm at Little America and a clear sky with only a thin line of sea smoke to the north over the sea. Better landing conditions could not have been asked for.

In the meantime the plane had

taken off at the mountains, and Commander Byrd flew east for a time so as to see over into Carmen Land. Then he set a course for Little America, and, in addition to navigating all the way, flew the plane himself for a time.

By starting so far east of the course for the camp, he placed himself out of reach of any aid from the flags laid down by the geological and supporting parties of the dog-team trail.

There was a constant tendency to fly to the east, but Commander Byrd was sure that his course lay further west and held the plane in that direction.

He hit the trail about forty miles north of Little America, in a direct course for the camp, and word was sent in from the plane that they would arrive in a short time.

Everybody here tumbled out of the houses and clustered on the snow near the Fairchild plane, where two deep trenches marked the resting places of the *Floyd Bennett*'s skis.

They watched the horizon. After what seemed to be hours a thin line appeared in the southern sky and grew rapidly to the size where it could be identified as the plane.

With a tail wind it came booming in, flying high and then sliding down rapidly to a few hundred feet over the camp. The men below waved their hats and cheered, jumping up and down and yelling with joy.

The plane crossed the camp at eight minutes past ten o'clock and two minutes later had made a wide circle over the bay and landed. It taxied up to its resting place, mechanics beckoning to Balchen and June in the cockpit to steer them, and slid into its hole.

One of the most difficult flights in the history of aviation had ended, and the conquest of both Poles by air had been accomplished.

The adventurous thought born in the mind of a young Virginian several years ago had been fulfilled—the North Atlantic had been spanned and the North and South Poles encircled by airplanes.

* * *

FOR HIS GREAT reporting of the Byrd Antarctic expedition Russell Owen was wined and dined upon his return. He wrote later that he loved the assignment, though it brought him some of the most heartbreaking experiences that can happen to a man who enters on an adventure in the spirit of idealism. In his own words:

There was some tripe in the stories which I sent north, but it was unavoidable. No one can realize the situation in which a reporter finds himself with forty-one other men on a polar expedition. He is the outcast, the subject of anathema, the nincompoop who sits in front of a typewriter and stares at the wall, while other men are freezing their fingers and toes and wielding snow shovels. We each did our work well, but I doubt if any of them realized how difficult mine was. For each of those forty-one men stood behind me and looked over my shoulder while I wrote—it all went on the bulletin board. If I mentioned a name it caused caustic comment from those who also wanted their names included.

Most of the men on that expedition are my friends, and I think that they eventually understood what I was trying to do. But it took many months and much unhappiness and patience to win their esteem I was proud of that expedition, despite its shortcomings. It might have accomplished much more, but as a newspaper saga it was worth while.

In his account of the Fabulous Twenties, *Only Yesterday* (1931), Frederick Lewis Allen took a somewhat dim view of Admiral Byrd's flight to the South Pole: "In the larger centers of population there was manifest a slight tendency to yawn: his exploit had been overpublicized, and heroism, however gallant, lost something of its spontaneous charm when it was subjected to scientific management and syndicated in daily dispatches."

A *Kansas City Star* Reporter Turns Detective

and Solves a Murder in Amarillo

O N THE MORNING of June 27, 1930, A. D. Payne, a prominent Amarillo, Texas, lawyer, who had been in the habit of riding from home to his downtown office, three miles away, announced that he was going to walk down for exercise. He left the family coupé to be used that day by his wife and two of their three children, a son, A. D., Jr., and a daughter, Bobbie Jean.

Just as he was leaving, his daughter asked if she might walk down with him, and he consented.

That little whim saved the child's life, for after Mrs. Payne had driven the car six blocks the whole front of it became filled with smoke. Her son, sitting on the seat beside her, exclaimed:

"Mother, that smells exactly like the smoke of that powder fuse I found in the back yard and burned."

To this the mother replied:

"Daddy told me to drive faster if the car smoked."

Those were her last words. A moment later there was an explosion that shook the entire neighborhood. Mrs. Payne shot upward through the roof of the car and forward a distance of forty feet. The little boy, frightfully injured, was hurtled out through the top of the car, but he lived.

It was an old story, celebrated alike in Greek tragedy and modern Sunday supplement—a man tires of his wife and tries to commit the "perfect crime." What made this story one of the most unusual in the annals of American murder was the dramatic suddenness with which the mystery was cleared away when a reporter, trained to ferret out news details, succeeded where experienced criminal investigators had failed. Ordinarily a newsman stands by as an observer and chronicles the developments in the solution of a murder mystery. But not A. B. Macdonald of the *Kansas City Star*. For his work on this case Macdonald was awarded the 1931 Pulitzer Prize in reporting. Here is his story.

"I love that girl. She is as pure as the driven snow"

Kansas City Star, August 24, 1930

When A. D. Payne murdered his wife in Amarillo, Texas, he believed he had planned and executed the "perfect crime."

Payne is a lawyer. He has been a college man, a schoolteacher, and principal of a city high school. He has taken a college course in criminology. In his law practice he has defended criminals and studied their crimes.

For ten months Payne was continuously and patiently planning the murder of his wife and children. His trained mind worked out five different schemes of murder, but in each there was a flaw that might direct suspicion toward him and he abandoned it. He was not going to bungle the job. He was not going to slay his wife and children until he had found a way so perfect that the crime could not be fastened upon him.

At last he hit upon the idea of blowing up the wife and two of their children with dynamite. This plan he carried out, and it was so perfectly done that five weeks afterward the death of Mrs. Payne was as much a mystery as it was the day it occurred. The sheriff of the county, and his deputies, the entire police force of the city, several detectives sent to Amarillo by insurance companies, and nearly all the newspaper reporters of that city had worked upon the case, trying to unravel it. They had followed every clue they could find. They had chased every rumor to its origin, and they were baffled.

Gene Howe is editor and half owner of the only two newspapers in Amarillo, the *News* and the *Globe*. He was deeply interested in the Payne case from the first. He believed the death of Mrs. Payne was a murder. His papers offered a reward of $500 to anyone who would find evidence sufficient to find and convict the murderer.

Howe writes a column or two a day in his *Evening Globe* under the name of "Old Tack." One day there appeared a paragraph stating that "Old Tack" would have himself appointed a deputy sheriff and work to solve the Payne case. This was meant as a joke, but it had an unexpected result. It brought Payne himself into Howe's newspaper office. He came to thank Howe for the interest he was taking in trying to find out who slew his "dear wife." He urged Howe to go ahead on the mystery; he tendered any assistance he could give and he offered a reward of $5000 to anyone who could clear up the puzzle.

This set Howe to thinking along a new line. He wrote the *Star* and asked that someone be sent to work on the mystery.

The *Star* wired Howe that I would come, and that same day Howe called Payne by telephone and told him that the *Star* was sending a reporter.

"That's fine," said Payne. "When he gets here bring him to see me and the children. I will give him all the help I can."

I reached Amarillo late the afternoon of August 2. Howe met me at the train.

My first question was: "What do you think of it?"

"I don't know," he replied. "Sometimes I think Payne killed her and again I think that he did not. I am completely baffled. So are all the authorities. Ninety per cent of the people here suspect Payne killed her, but there isn't a shred of proof."

She was heavily insured and so was each of the three children, with Payne as the beneficiary, and Payne's life was heavily insured for the benefit of his wife and children, and nearly all the policies carried "double indemnity." For some reason I did not believe that this insurance alone was motive enough for Payne to kill his wife and children.

"There may be a woman in the case," I suggested.

"That is just about impossible," Mr. Howe said. "Payne was a devoted husband. He and his wife were so much in love with each other it was a subject of talk all through the neighborhood. He was always home at night. Almost every evening they took a walk together and often they held hands as they walked."

Payne welcomed us cordially. We sat and talked. There was something about him that made me suspect him. He was nervous. His long fingers kept fidgeting and pulling at his cheeks and chin. Behind his thin-lipped mouth I felt there was a cruel, heartless nature. I never once thought he was innocent after I first saw him and heard his even-toned voice; it seemed unnatural.

No matter what question was asked him he always dwelt on how he loved his wife, how much she loved him, and how they just lived for each other. He overdid that.

His eldest daughter, who will be fourteen next February, was getting dinner. Every once in a while she would come to the door and gaze in at us where we sat talking, and I imagined that there was a frightened look in her eyes.

Last March Mrs. Payne opened a closet door and a shotgun exploded. The charge of birdshot tore through her hand. Payne spent a full hour explaining to us his theory that the gun had been standing on a sewing machine and as she opened the door it jarred the gun and it fell and went off. I did not believe that. I could not imagine any way that gun could go off unless it was set as a trap, with a string to the doorknob. Mr. Howe let the gun drop a dozen times on its butt from the height of the sewing machine, and its hammer would not fall. The

more Payne talked, setting the gun on the machine, jarring it off, the more I became convinced he had set that trap.

Near noon Payne's little girl, Bobbie Jean, came in with a Bible under her arm. "This is our little girl coming from Sunday school," said Payne.

I asked Bobbie Jean about her escape from death. She sat in a chair, answering my questions. Once her father corrected her: "No, honey, it wasn't that way, don't you remember, it was this way": and he began to set her right.

Into the face of the child came a look of fright and fear, as she looked at her father and heard him correcting her. She burst into tears, and sobs choked her. Her sister hurried in from the kitchen, nervously wringing her hands, and tears were in her eyes.

I could see that the whole household was on high tension, and that the two girls had been coached by Payne to tell their stories a certain way. Little Bobbie Jean had forgotten and told the truth. I felt then, and I know now, that both knew their father had killed their mother, and were in mortal fear lest they might say something that would disclose it.

Something convinced me that there was a strange woman somewhere in the background. It came into my mind that if that were true she would probably have called him by telephone at his office, or he would have called her, or, possibly, she might have come to his office to see him, and, if so, his stenographer might know about it.

With that in mind I decided to see every stenographer that had worked for him. I asked him if he had ever been enamored of another woman.

"No," he said emphatically, "I was never untrue to my dear wife even in thought, let alone in deed."

He gave me a list of his different

stenographers, and I wrote down what he said of each:

"I had several different stenographers in the last year. The first one was Vera Holcomb. She stayed with me only a short while. I don't know what became of her. The next was Verona Thompson. She came to work for me last August a year ago, and I let her out in December. She is twenty-four or twenty-five years old, just an ordinary-looking woman. No man would ever get sweet on her. The next was Mabel Bush, who lives on Pierce Street. She's young and very attractive, a redhead full of pep and wide-awake. She is only about nineteen or twenty. My stenographer now is Miss Ocie Humphries."

Nothing suspicious in that as it reads, but in the way he spoke it there appeared a design to steer us away from suspicion that Miss Thompson might have any attraction that would lure him, while Miss Bush was dangerously alluring.

Payne said, several days later, that when Howe and I left his house that Sunday, he felt certain that he had convinced us of his innocence and that we would write vindications of him.

But as we were leaving his home Mr. Howe had asked me:

"What do you say about it?"

"He's guilty," I said. "He killed her, and those little girls know it. There's a woman in it, and I believe that Thompson girl knows all about it."

We waited for her a minute or two in the reception room of the Maples apartments. She was staring at me wide-eyed and very serious. She said afterward that she thought I was a detective from New York or Chicago. I noticed, instantly, that there was something about her that might be thought very attractive by many men. She had a shapely form and when she smiled she showed a row of teeth as white as pearls, while her eyes were brilliant. She was that type of working girl who knows how to dress attractively and to be agreeable to men.

I knew it would be useless to beat around the bush. My first question was:

"Verona, how many times has Payne taken you out to lunch?"

"Many times," she answered, without a moment's hesitation. "But there was always another girl with us."

I took another shot in the dark. It occurred to me that if Payne had been in hotels with her he would not dare to do that in Amarillo, but that he would take her to some other town, and that probably would be the wild oil town of Borger, where no questions are asked of couples who might come in that way. Still, they might not have been at Borger, and I wanted her to think that I knew all about where they had been, so my next question was:

"And have you been out in the Panhandle with him?"

She thought I meant the town of Panhandle, and she replied:

"Yes, I've been to Panhandle with him."

"And to Borger?"

"Yes, to Borger."

"Do you think he killed her?" she asked.

"Yes, I think so."

She shook her head and said: "My! It was an awful thing, wasn't it?"

After we reached the street Mr. Howe said: "That's the woman he killed her for."

"Yes, that's the woman."

* * *

WHEN Verona Thompson confessed that Payne had been making violent love to her for months before his wife was killed, Payne broke down.

"I am the meanest man that ever lived," he cried. "I love that girl, Verona Thompson. She is as pure as the driven snow!"

Payne was tried and sentenced to the chair. Shortly before the time set for his execution, he killed himself in his cell by setting off a tiny explosive charge strapped to his chest.

Two Reporters See the Bonus Army Smashed

THE SUMMER OF 1932 marked the worst period of the depression era. The failure of the government to provide relief of some sort had brought large numbers of people, once self-supporting, to the verge of destitution. Veterans of World War I, reduced to the ignominy of selling apples on street corners, decided to do something about it. Possessing certificates calling for a bonus in 1945, payment to be calculated on the length of each man's service during the war, they asked for an immediate bonus on the ground that they needed money now more than they would ever need it again. Many honestly believed that they were collecting a lawful debt.

In early June disgruntled veterans began to descend on Washington. Many brought their wives, children, and all their possessions. Soon encampments of tents, huts, and hovels, without adequate sanitary facilities, were scattered throughout the capital. Congressmen, refusing to face the issue squarely, played politics, holding out hope to the veterans but taking no steps to meet their demands. The District of Columbia authorities were in a dilemma: they were reluctant to use police force to evict the squatters from their improvised shanty town, but they regarded the occupation as a menace to public health. Nothing was done for two months.

The scene at Washington in the middle of June was described by the noted French journalist, Jules Sauerwein, foreign correspondent for the Paris paper, *Matin*.

Jules Sauerwein: "Washington today recalls ancient Carthage"

The New York Times, June 19, 1932

WASHINGTON, JUNE 17—For whoever may have a little imagination, Washington today recalls ancient Carthage. Beyond the city, on the banks of the Potomac, in the immense marshy field of the tributary, Anacostia, 17,000 men are encamped just as, in ancient times, were the mercenaries of Hasdrubal. They demand money, but not the arrears of a few months. On the contrary, their claim goes back four-

teen years and extends for a dozen years in the future. They are veterans who, not content with their pension, although seven or eight times higher than that of other countries, desire cash from the state today by its sacrificing $2,000,000,000—all that it would pay them as a premium for mobilization up to 1945.

I passed an hour in this camp of revolt, which, this morning, had rather

the air of a camp of despair. Rain having fallen in torrents during the night,
many of these unfortunates had slept
in a veritable marsh. With a previ-
sion of the bad weather they had tried
to organize themselves in the region
reserved for Pennsylvania Avenue. It
was a conglomeration of tented huts
made of tattered cloth fixed up on old
boards with packing boxes serving as
props. Under one of these pitiful shelters men are mournfully lying shivering with fever. They try to comfort
themselves by jokes. They have placed
at the door a sign, "The Lame, Sick,
and Lazy."

Under a fragile pavilion, which
seems to have been made of old pajamas, two Negroes are under a single
blanket. Traced on a poster which
trembles in the wind, we read, "Don't
cry, little girl, I will come back." I
enter into conversation with them.
They are obstinate and angry. One of
them produces a letter from his family.

"Read what my wife writes: 'If now
you have made your expedition you
return without money, you would better stay where you are, for the entire
town is laughing at you.'"

A group gathers around us, and a
young man, apparently a leader in this
section, declares in a decisive way:

"We shall remain here, if we have
to, all summer. We shall build a city.
Tomorrow eight hundred more comrades will arrive from New York. We
are sure to succeed with the House of
Representatives and the others. Here
are my headquarters. You see that it
is already a solid building."

And he pointed to a large iron bed-
stead planted right in the middle of
the field and around which they were
beginning to raise brick walls. I
thought of the six hundred who had
already gone to the hospital in a week.
There should have been thousands.

"HISTORIANS of the future will record that the collapse of American democracy reached its final stage in 1932 and that thereupon dictatorship began.
The sly man in the White House, Herbert Hoover, prepares to strike at our
liberty."

Thus began the lead editorial of the *Bonus Expeditionary Force News*
on July 28, 1932. While America was spared the fulfillment of the prophecy,
the warning that the President was "prepared to strike" was quickly borne
out. That very afternoon a military expedition occupied Washington for
the first time since the War of 1812. Federal troops, under the command
of General Douglas MacArthur, routed thousands from their makeshift
hovels, won the battle of Anacostia flats, and drove the veterans out of
Washington. "It was a good job, quickly done," remarked General Mac-
Arthur.

For the following story of the conflict in Washington and the scenes
attending the expulsion of the veterans, Lee McCardell of the Baltimore
Evening Sun was awarded honorable mention for the 1933 Pulitzer Prize
in reporting.

Lee McCardell: For General Glassford, "a big bottle of ginger ale"; for the veterans, gas bombs

Baltimore *Evening Sun*, July 29, 1932

WASHINGTON, JULY 29—The bonus army was retreating today—in all directions.

Its billets destroyed, its commissary wrecked, its wives and babies misplaced, its leaders lost in the confusion which followed its rout last night by troops of the Regular Army, the former soldiers tramped the streets of Washington and the roads of Maryland and Virginia, foraging for coffee and cigarettes.

Some of the former soldiers said they planned a rendezvous at Johnstown, Pennsylvania. How to reach this rallying point was a puzzling question. Most of the men had no money. And the hitchhiking business was bad—very bad.

Near the scene of the worst fighting yesterday, a good many veterans were still camping out today. Troops were moving into town late in the day to oust the last of them, while several small columns of bonus seekers packed their few belongings on their backs and headed north without waiting for them.

Police were apprehensive that some of these marching groups still had ambitions to picket the White House, but they all went plodding on, quiet, sullen, and disheartened.

There were plenty of wild stories going the rounds today about the consequences of the rioting, but they boiled down in fact to about this: twenty men are still held by the po-

lice and four times that many, held for a while by the police or the soldiers, have been turned loose with warnings to be good.

The latest casualty list showed about fifty or fifty-five wounded or gassed in the fighting. The best estimate of the number of veterans in all the Washington camps when the row broke out seems to be General Glassford's,* and he puts the figure at six thousand. A very much smaller number was engaged in the downtown rioting.

This afternoon the nine hundred veterans still encamped in Camp Bartlett, which was left undisturbed yesterday, began pulling out for Johnstown.

Some four hundred of the refugee bonus seekers who crossed the border into Virginia in their flight last night were firmly escorted back to the District line this morning. But they couldn't get in; the Washington officials have barred the way to re-entry. The marchers stuck there on the boundary; they couldn't go either way. They waited aimlessly for something to happen. Finally the District let them in.

Commander Edward McK. Johnson of the Maryland state police moved headquarters up to the District of Columbia line, directing his men to see that no bonus marchers lingered in that state.

The commanders of the Virginia

---

* Brigadier General Pelham Davis Glassford, retired, was Major and Superintendent of the Metropolitan Police Department of Washington, D.C., from November, 1931, to October, 1932.

state police and state militia hurried from Richmond to Alexandria, Virginia, six miles from Washington, and directed authorities to keep the veterans on the move.

Few of the bonus marchers had had any sleep last night. And many of them had been worn out by the scramble to get out of the way of cavalry sabers, bayonets, and tear-gas bombs.

The battle really had ended shortly after midnight, when, from the dusty brow of a low hill behind their camp on the Anacostia flats, the rear guard of the Bonus Expeditionary Force fired a final round of Bronx cheers at the tin-hatted infantrymen moving among the flames of Camp Marks.

The powerful floodlights of Fire Department trucks played over the ruins of the camp. In the shadows behind the trucks four troops of cavalry bivouacked on the bare ground, the reins of their horses hooked under their arms.

The air was still sharply tainted with tear gas.

The fight had begun, as far as the Regular Army was concerned, late yesterday afternoon. The troops had been called out after a veteran of the Bonus Army had been shot and killed by a Washington policeman during a skirmish to drive members of the Bonus Army out of a vacant house on Pennsylvania Avenue, two blocks from the Capitol.

The soldiers numbered between seven hundred and eight hundred men. There was a squadron of the Third Cavalry from Fort Myer, a battalion of the Twelfth Infantry from Fort Washington, and a platoon of tanks (five) from Fort Meade. Most of the police in Washington seemed to be trailing after the soldiers, and traffic was tied up in 115 knots.

The cavalry clattered down Pennsylvania Avenue with drawn sabers.

The infantry came marching along with fixed bayonets.

All Washington smelled a fight, and all Washington turned out to see it.

Streets were jammed with automobiles.

Sidewalks, windows, doorsteps were crowded with people trying to see what was happening.

"Yellow! Yellow!"

From around the ramshackle shelters which they had built on a vacant lot fronting on Pennsylvania Avenue, just above the Capitol, the bedraggled veterans jeered.

And other words less polite.

The cavalrymen stretched out in extended order and rode spectators back on the sidewalks. The infantry started across the lot, bayonets fixed.

Veterans in the rear ranks of a mob that faced the infantry pushed forward. Those in front pushed back. The crowd stuck. An order went down the line of infantrymen. The soldiers stepped back, pulled tear-gas bombs from their belts, and hurled them into the midst of the mob.

Some of the veterans grabbed the bombs and threw them back at the infantry. The exploding tins whizzed around the smooth asphalt like devil chasers, pfutt-pfutt-pfutt. And a gentle southerly wind wafted the gas in the faces of the soldiers and the spectators across the street.

Cavalrymen and infantrymen jerked gas masks out of their haversacks. The spectators, blinded and choking with the unexpected gas attack, broke and fled. Movie photographers who had parked their sound trucks so as to catch a panorama of the skirmish ground away doggedly, tears streaming down their faces.

The police tied their handkerchiefs around their faces.

"Ya-a-a-ah!" jeered the veterans.

But more gas bombs fell behind them. The veterans were caught in the back draft. They began to retreat. But before they quit their shacks they set them on fire. The dry wood and rubbish from which the huts were fashioned burned quickly. The flames shot high. Clouds of dirty brown smoke blanketed the avenue.

A few of the routed veterans hung back.

"I got all my money in my shack," yelled one ragged fellow.

"Get back!" said a mounted trooper, riding into the man. "Get back!"

Across the grass of a quadrangular park toward the river—and another packing-box village—trudged the veterans, crowded by cavalrymen who occasionally whacked them over the shoulders with the flat of their sabers.

All the accumulated profanity of their army service was poured out by the soldiers on the retreating veterans. Most of the veterans were middle-aged, with lined and weather-beaten faces. Many of the regulars were youngsters with the bloom of boyhood still on their cheeks.

The veterans took their time about the retreat. And the regulars didn't press them any more than was necessary.

Below the park the mob piled up again along the curb of another vacant square which the shambling shacks of the Bonus Army had converted into an idler's paradise.

The cavalry was drawn up in the street, facing the mob. The veterans cursed and jeered and taunted the troopers. Now and then one of the ragged army would attempt to dodge through the line. The troopers wheeled about and forced them back.

The infantry was still mopping up the first campsite and replenishing its tear-gas-bomb supply and chasing stragglers of the Bonus Army out of the park.

Veterans with soiled American flags over their shoulders—they had taken their flags along with them in their first retreat—paraded the gutter under the cavalry horses' noses.

"Now, hit me, you yellow b——," they invited.

"You God —— bums," screamed a middle-aged woman in the front rank of the mob, shaking her fist at the cavalrymen.

A brickbat clipped a horse's shin. The animal shied. The Bonus Army jeered.

"Tin soldiers! Where did you learn to ride? On a hobbyhorse?"

"Yello-o-ow!"

"If we had guns——"

"Jeez, if we had guns!"

Most of the troopers take their razzing good-naturedly. The younger ones grin with embarrassment. Only the older cavalrymen show signs of impatience.

"No, no, no!" shouts an officer, holding up his hand to a trooper who starts to ride against a man carrying a flag.

The mob jeers.

A squad of cavalry circles back through the park, pulls up under a low-branched tree, and pulls two fugitives out.

Ambulances dash up and down the street madly. Most of the casualties are policemen, bonus soldiers, and bystanders who have been knocked out by gas.

The veterans catch more of the gas bombs this time than they did before. One bonus soldier has a bushel basket with which he pockets the cans as fast as they are thrown and hurls them back.

"We've had that before," the veterans yell. "You lousy rats."

The cavalry rides forward, big bays prancing, threatening sabers to the fore.

"Move on! Get out! Get going!"

A man with a motorized popcorn wagon can't get his engine started.

"Come on—you're gonna get more if you don't."

"I can't get it started, mister," wails the popcorn man.

"You better had—it won't be any good to you if you don't."

And now the infantrymen are advancing again. They stop and readjust their gas masks. The cavalrymen take turns slipping their heavy sabers into the scabbards under their right knee and pulling on their gas masks, too. The police get out their handkerchiefs.

"They're gonna give us more gas, the yellow bums."

Veterans with automobiles parked in the jungle behind the mob begin to crank up their machines. Others grab rolls of bedding from their shacks. A tin disk sails through the air down at the west end of the square. Another devil chaser pfutt-pfutts across the surface of the street.

But the breeze is still blowing from the south and the gas drifts back against the attacking party. Newspaper reporters and photographers cut and run for fresh air.

"Get out of that," yells a trooper.

"Me?"

"You!"

"I live here—this is my home," whimpers the man in the doorway.

"I don't give a damn who lives there—get out, I say."

"Can I take my things—I've got all my things in here?"

There's a quaver in his voice.

"Make it quick—two minutes."

To be sure the fellow doesn't double-cross him, the trooper rides up and watches him through the window of the shack, yelling to him to "hurry up!"

A member of the Bonus Army, somewhat the worse for a serious hangover, finds it difficult to steer a straight course down the middle of one street. He wants to turn.

He argues:

"I don't have to——"

A cavalry saber flashes.

Whack!

"Beat it!"

"I don't have to——"

Whack! Whack!

The father of a family of six—four of them little girls—can't decide what to load onto his decrepit automobile and what to abandon. He goes calmly about the business of roping orange crates on the bumper of his car and baskets of tomatoes on the fenders. His wife has her arms full of clothes. The children, packed into the back seat, are impatient to get on.

The mob has halted across one street down which the cavalrymen are driving them. Cobblestones and half bricks whizz through the air. The cavalry throw their arms up over their faces.

A dozen ragged white and colored tramps, presumably members of the Bonus Army, stand in the bed of a heavy motor truck, watching the advancing horsemen and the brickbat barrage.

"Out of there with you!"

"We ain't with them!"

"Get out!"

Slam! Whack! Smash!

Somebody got a saber over the head.

The men on the truck topple over each other, rolling out into the street.

In a filling station across the way a man—a newspaper reporter—is using a telephone.

"Out of there!" yells the trooper.

The man at the phone hangs on.

The trooper tosses a gas bomb into the station. The man comes out.

Here's another shower of stones. Sock! A full brick has struck a cavalry corporal beside the head. The blow almost rocks him out of his saddle. He clinches his knees and keeps his seat.

Are those white faces peering covertly from the windows of that Negro house? And aren't there a good many of them?

The cavalry turn their horses into the alleys.

The veteran suffering from a hangover has somehow managed to get on the wrong side of the dead line.

"Don't you belong over there?" asks a trooper.

"I want to——"

"Get over there where you belong!"

The horse rears in the dazed man's face.

He intends to state his case.

"I want to——"

Whack!

He doesn't seem to mind the saber, so the trooper kicks his horse and the animal runs the man over where he belongs—according to the trooper.

At the intersection at the end of the block the mob is solid again and howling.

Back up the street comes the rattle-rumble of caterpillar wheels. The tanks are moving up.

The veterans have deserted their camp now. The infantrymen peek into the tumble-down shacks for stragglers.

Most of these shelters are foul-smelling hovels. Liberal applications of disinfectant hasn't made them smell any better. And an odor of gas is beginning to stick to everything.

For a brief instant, before the infantrymen begin to touch off the shacks' straw and canvas, this lot is a pathetic kind of no man's land: piles of potatoes abandoned by the retreating veterans; half-eaten plates of slum; cook shacks with improvised ice boxes; rusty pots and pans; a bake oven partly filled with potatoes; baskets of onions; kettles of cabbage; a pair of woman's worn pink mules and black satin slippers in the straw of one dugout; clothing—all sorts of it; not much bedding, but plenty of ratty-looking mattresses; bottles of medicine; neat piles of magazines; odd pieces of greasy, bulging overstuffed furniture wedged into odd corners; rocking chairs; alarm clocks; a broken-down hatrack; enough odds and ends of scrapped automobiles to start a junk yard.

Somebody seems to have carefully emptied all the improvised contribution boxes before the retreat—slotted tin cans and milk bottles hung out here and there to catch stray pennies for the tobacco fund.

Meanwhile the infantrymen have applied the torch. The whole camp goes up in smoke.

The blazing camp sends out a great yellow glow that lights up the sky. The wind freshens and the smoke drifts into the faces of the watching Bonus Army. Motorboats with loud radios come chug-chugging in toward shore to watch the fire.

At half-past twelve General MacArthur returns with Secretary of War Hurley. The dapper Secretary of War is attired in white sport shoes and pants and a flapping felt hat and smokes his cigarette in a debonair fashion.

The Secretary and the General return to Washington.

General Miles opens his coat collar and settles himself on the back seat of his automobile to keep the death-watch.

The infantrymen are moving in toward the cliff now. Their bayonets and the skeletons of a hundred ancient bedsteads are silhouetted against the blaze.

From behind the smoke on the cliff comes the yell: "Yellow-w-w-w-w."

But the war is over. Camp Marks has been destroyed.

The bridge to Washington is under military guard.

At the soda fountain of a drugstore near the bridge on the Anacostia side General Glassford orders:

"A big bottle of ginger ale."

* * *

ALMOST ALL THE NATION's newspapers expressed the opinion that President Hoover was justified in expelling the Bonus Expeditionary Force from Washington. The disorder was generally attributed to radical elements, but some editorial writers blamed vote-seeking politicians for the assembling of the Bonus Army at the capital. General MacArthur announced to the press that delayed military action might have "threatened the institutions of our country" and led to "insurgency and insurrection." The men had become "a bad-looking mob animated by the spirit of revolution," he added.

Others were not so sure. Representative Fiorello La Guardia of New York informed President Hoover by wire: "Soup is cheaper than tear bombs and bread better than bullets in maintaining law and order in these times of depression, unemployment, and hunger." The popular humorist, Will Rogers, wrote: "They [the veterans] hold the record for being the best behaved of any fifteen thousand hungry men assembled anywhere in the world. Just think what fifteen thousand clubwomen would have done to Washington even if they wasn't hungry. The Senate would have resigned and the President committed suicide." Norman Thomas called the President's action "a bad case of nervous irritation mixed with fear." Senator Black denounced the attack as "unnecessary and ill-timed," and Senator Borah was too embittered to talk at all.

"Calvin's Dead, Aurora"

TIME, that postwar phenomenon among news magazines, with its tight, nervous, sardonic style, and its rapid-fire, often snide, usually irreverent characterizations of people of importance, soon carved out for itself a niche in reportorial history. In its issue of January 5, 1933, it published a memorable story. An ex-President had died, and John Shaw Billings, onetime *Brooklyn Daily Eagle* reporter, then national-affairs editor of *Time* magazine, and more recently editorial director of all Time, Inc., publications, told the story in straightforward, simple prose, subtly evoking some of the homely democracy of the little white towns of New England.

John Shaw Billings tells Time *readers of the passing of that "Puritan in Babylon"*

Courtesy of *Time*, Copyright Time, Inc., 1933

Early one afternoon last week Senator Carter Glass was warmly expounding his bank-reform bill on the Senate floor when Senator Swanson, his Virginia colleague, nudged him, whispered something. For a moment Senator Glass looked dumfounded. Then in a quavering voice he announced: "Mr. President, I have just been apprised of a fact very, very distressing to the nation generally and to me particularly. Former President Coolidge has just dropped dead. I think the Senate should immediately adjourn." Numb with shock, the Senate adjourned.

At the White House President Hoover was lunching with Secretary of State Stimson. Chief Usher Irwin Hood ("Ike") Hoover tiptoed into the dining room. Into the President's ear he whispered the news: "Mr. Coolidge has died of heart failure." After a stunned moment, the President pushed back his chair, laid down his napkin, strode to his office. There he hastily dispatched a special message to Congress, issued a proclamation for thirty days of public mourning. Within five minutes, down to half-staff came the White House flag. Down came the flags of Washington, of the nation.

The House, after it had heard the news by word of mouth, continued in session an hour to receive the President's message. It read: "It is my painful duty to inform you of the death today of Calvin Coolidge. . . . There is no occasion for me to recount his eminent services. . . . His entire lifetime has been one of single devotion to our country. . . ." Then the House, too, adjourned.

At Plymouth, Vermont, Miss Aurora Pierce, long-time Coolidge housekeeper, heard a tap on the homestead window. Allen Brown, a neighbor, was outside. She raised the sash to hear him say: "Calvin's dead, Aurora." She sat down in the room in which the thirtieth President of the United States had taken the oath from his father at 2:47 A.M., August 3, 1923, and let her tears run in silent grief.

In New York President-elect Roosevelt got word by telephone from a press association in the study of his home. He was "inexpressibly shocked" at the death of the man who had defeated him for the vice-presidency in 1920.

On the New York Stock Exchange, hundreds of brokers got the news simultaneously from their office tickers. They stared blankly, incredulously, at each other. Trading slacked off uncertainly with falling prices. The day closed with a brief little rally—a farewell salute to the man whose name had been given to the greatest bull market in history.

At "The Beeches," his Northampton home, Calvin Coolidge had gotten up that morning as usual at seven A.M. At the breakfast table he grumbled over the lack of news in the papers. At 8:30 he was at his office (Coolidge & Hemenway) on Main Street, reading his mail, attending to minor personal business. What he thought was another attack of indigestion—he had been doctoring himself with soda for three weeks—made him feel uncomfortable. At about ten o'clock he said to Harry Ross, his secretary: "Well, I guess we'll go up to the house."

As they entered Mrs. Coolidge was just going out shopping. Said her husband: "Don't you want the car?" "No," she replied, "it's such a nice day I'd rather walk." Mr. Coolidge sat talking with Secretary Ross—about the Plymouth place, last year's pa'tridge shooting, hay fever. He strolled to the kitchen to get a drink of water. He put a stray book neatly back into the case. He evened up pens on the desk. He idly fingered a jigsaw puzzle with his name on it. He went "down cellar," watched the furnaceman shovel coal. About noon he disappeared upstairs, presumably to shave, as so many New Englanders do about midday.

Returning a few minutes later, Mrs. Coolidge went upstairs to summon him for luncheon. In his dressing room she found him lying on the floor on his back in his shirt sleeves. To him death had come fifteen minutes before, swiftly, easily, without pain. For "Cause" the official death certificate said: "Coronary Thrombosis."

That night the body of Calvin Coolidge lay on its own bed in its own room. Outside the window a half-moon played tricks with night mists rising from the Mount Tom meadows. Beyond the mist and the moonlight a people mourned the loss of its greatest private citizen, its only ex-President. . . . Smith College girls, just back from the holidays, went to the Calvin Theater as usual, saw *Under-Cover Man* on the screen. Northampton's Mayor Bliss announced that the city's merchants would draw their shades but keep their doors open during the funeral. Said he: "I'm not going to ask them to close because I don't think Calvin Coolidge would want it. He knew what they've been through. Every nickel counts with them. He wouldn't want them to lose a sale."

Next night a plain bronze casket stood before the fireplace of "The Beeches" living room. On it was engraved: "Calvin Coolidge—1872–1933." . . . Far away through the same night with many a long whistle there roared a thirteen-car special bearing the great of Washington to Northampton.

Saturday was a gray leaden day. . . . It began to drizzle coldly as mourners with special tickets moved into the church. . . .

At Plymouth, one hundred miles north, Sexton Azro Johnson had a new grave ready in the Hillside Cemetery where lie six generations of the Coolidges. Twenty motorcars made the trip through a wet, cheerless afternoon. Their tires droned a dirge on the ruddy mud. From the last road the coffin was carried up the knoll to Plymouth's notched stony "God's Acre." Mourners followed in single file. Across the road in respectful silence villagers who had known Calvin Coolidge since his birth in yonder farmhouse watched their stark outline against the gray tapestry of winter clouds. The rain changed to hail. Someone held an umbrella over Mrs. Coolidge. Down from Salt Ash Mountain whipped a blast of icy wind, flapping the brown canvas canopy over the grave, drenching the floral wreaths. Bareheaded in the storm, Mr. Penner pronounced the committal. The wind snatched at his strongly spoken words, whittled them away. . . . "Earth to earth, ashes to ashes, dust to dust." The winches creaked. Down into the earth went all that remained of Calvin Coolidge to sleep between his father and his son. His widow turned away as the gravediggers started to shovel in brown, rain-soaked earth. For the first time tears overflowed her grave gray eyes.

The night snow fell, blotting out all trace of the new grave.

* * *

To THE EDITOR of *The Emporia Gazette,* William Allen White, Coolidge was "a Puritan in Babylon." In a sordid decade of materialism he served as "a tremendous shock absorber," and "his emotionless attitude" was "an anesthetic to a possible national conviction of sin." With Coolidge as leader, White concluded: "What a generation!"

Three Newspapermen Cover
the Reichstag Fire Incident

O N THE NIGHT OF FEBRUARY 27, 1933, just a few days before the March
5 elections, which were to confirm Adolf Hitler's chancellorship, the
Reichstag building in Berlin was gutted by fire. While police dragged an
incoherent, hysterical, half-naked Dutchman named Marinus van der
Lubbe from the flaming building, Nazi No. 2, Hermann Göring, blandly
announced to the world that the Communists had set the fire as a signal
for revolution. Hitler himself, with an air of pious indignation, proclaimed
the burning as "a sign from heaven!"

As a matter of fact, the Nazis had started the fire themselves—on the
simple principle that the end justifies the means. As the new Chancellor,
Hitler had only three Nazis in his cabinet as against eight belonging to the
Von Papen-Hugenberg group, at the moment his most powerful enemy. He
desperately needed a clear majority of Reichstag seats in the coming March
5 elections. It was certain that of the six hundred deputies in the new
Reichstag the Communists were bound to get about one hundred. The
Nazis claimed about two hundred and fifty, not a clear majority. Hence, if
the critical hundred seats of the Communists were wiped out, the battle
for power would be won.

A raid on the Karl Liebknecht house, the headquarters of the Communist
party in Berlin, was supposed to incriminate the Communists in a conspiracy to revolt and give the pretext for suppressing them, but it was a
failure. The Nazis had to think of something else, as the date for the
nation-wide elections was rapidly approaching.

What the Nazis thought of was described in a dispatch, three days late
but reasonably accurate, in one of the world's great newspapers, the *Frankfurter Zeitung*. This was one of the last free reports of Germany's famous
independent newspaper before it was engulfed in the wave of Nazi coordination.

The Frankfurter Zeitung *reports a fire*

Frankfurter Zeitung, March 1, 1933

"The dome of the Reichstag building
is burning in brilliant flames!"

This was the telephone message of a
resident of the Place of the Republic
at ten o'clock in the evening of February 27, which brought the alarm to
reporters in Berlin. At the Brandenburger Tor several thousand persons

were already pressing against police barriers set up in a wide circle around the Reichstag building standing impressively in the darkness. But from the cupola, with its golden decorations which light up the area during the day, great, crackling flames now reached into the night sky.

At first it seemed that the Berlin fire department, which appeared at the scene with astonishing speed, would be successful in short order in isolating the fire which endangered the surrounding buildings in a strong wind. But a good hour after the discovery of the fire the enormous throng, now stretching to the edge of the Tiergarten, to the Brandenburger Tor, and to both banks of the Spree, saw the flames mount to the crown of the cupola. At midnight thick, black smoke still poured upward from the dome.

The police have already learned that the fire was started by arson. A young, twenty-year-old Dutch Communist has been arrested inside the Reichstag and, according to the police, has already confessed. Brought to the police station at the Brandenburger Tor, he was immediately interrogated. On his person was found an identification card of the Dutch Communist party bearing the name van der Lubbe. He immediately confessed that he had started the fire in the Reichstag. Apparently this is the same arsonist who attempted to set the Palace on fire last Saturday evening.

At 11:30 P.M. all members of the Berlin and foreign press, who until then had been waiting outside the Reichstag, were led by firemen and police into the interior of the building to see for themselves the great damage done by the fire. Over the steps and through the entrance there was a maze of thick and thin fire hose leading to the reception hall. Although not touched by the flames, this hall presented a chaotic appearance, its thick, red carpets covered by a foot of water, fire apparatus strewn everywhere, and burned objects dragged from the plenary hall scattered about. Smoke was still pouring through the doors of the meeting hall. One could see from a distance that this latter hall was but a mass of ruins, from which flames continually blazed. The entire roof of the hall hangs precariously, showing the skeleton of its construction, and its collapse momentarily is feared. In addition, a number of rooms on the second floor have been damaged, including the press quarters, the reception room of the Reichsrat, the restaurants, and the workrooms of the Reichstag delegates. Everywhere there is extraordinarily heavy water damage. The meeting hall itself is as good as destroyed.

It has been established that approximately twenty bundles of incendiary materials had been scattered throughout the entire building, although not all of these were set on fire. The fires were started with the same type of charcoal torch found in the timberwork of the Palace after the attempt to destroy it.

There is some doubt as to whether the imprisoned man could have done it all himself.

During the attempts to extinguish the fire the area was visited by Chancellor Hitler, who was accompanied by Dr. Goebbels and Prince Wilhelm August, Vice-Chancellor von Papen, and numerous other ministers. Also present were Police President von Levetzow, Lord Mayor Salm, District Commander Schomburg, and other authorities. Important governmental talks took place at the Reichs Ministry until far into the night.

THE *Frankfurter Zeitung* unwittingly went to the heart of the issue when it spoke of "some doubt as to whether the imprisoned man could have done it all himself." In the meantime the press was being prepared for the business of substantiating a lie on a stupendous scale—a Nazi specialty. The official *Preussische Pressedienst* announced that "this act of incendiarism is the most monstrous act of terrorism carried out by Bolshevism in Germany." The *Vossische Zeitung* stated on March 1 that "the government is of the opinion that the situation is such that a danger to the state and nation existed and still exists."

Hitler and the Nazis then proceeded to destroy what remained of the German republic. Pacifists, liberals, democrats, and Communists were crushed along with a million marks' worth of glass and masonry. "When Germany awoke," wrote a British reporter, Douglas Reed, "a man's home was no longer his castle. He could be seized by private individuals, could claim no protection from the police, could be indefinitely detained without preferment of charge; his property could be seized, his verbal and written communications overheard and perused; he no longer had the right to foregather with his fellow countrymen, and his newspapers might no longer freely express their opinions." The Germany of the Weimar Constitution had gone up in flames, and from the ashes arose the stench of Hitler's Third Reich.

At this point let us turn to the brilliant account of the arson de luxe and the subsequent trial by John Gunther, the reporter of continents. Sometimes, John Gunther recently confessed to Robert Van Gelder, he wakes up in the middle of the night and thinks: "My God, suppose I hadn't written it!" He was talking about *Inside Europe,* one of his famous "inside" books which have achieved enormous popularity.

John Gunther's inside story on the Weimar Republic turned to dust and ashes

John Gunther, *Inside Europe*. Published by Harper and Brothers. Copyright, 1933, 1934, 1935, 1936, 1937, 1938, 1940, by John Gunther

The fire produced exactly what the Nazis hoped for.

The one hundred Communist deputies were arrested. A state of virtual siege was proclaimed. The provisions of the Constitution guaranteeing individual liberty were suppressed. Plans for a Communist outbreak were "revealed." Germany rose with a roar.

There was intense public excitement. The Nazis stormed the country, and Hitler was able to maneuver himself into a dictatorship for four years, affix himself to power immovably.

The true story of the fire is not so well known today as it might be. The Nazis did their job so well that, whereas everyone well informed instantly suspected them of complicity, there was much puzzlement as to details. Even today there are mysteries, subsidiary mysteries, not entirely clear. Let us deal with them.

During the night of the fire a Dutch half-wit named Marinus van der Lubbe was arrested when police found him in the burning ruins. There were no witnesses except the police to his arrest. The first statements about the Dutchman, issued by Göring, were false. It was said that he had a membership card of the Communist party on his person, a leaflet urging common action between Socialists and Communists, several photographs of himself, and a passport. Obliging fellow! He did possess the passport, but not the other documents, as the trial subsequently proved.

His career and movements were closely traced. He had set three other fires—minor ones—in Berlin just before the Reichstag fire. In 1929 he had joined something called the Dutch Communist Youth Organization, a secessionist group. Two years later he was expelled from this as a worthless and stupid fellow. He never belonged to the Communist party itself. Van der Lubbe's itinerary the few days before the fire was well established. As late as the night of February 17-18 he slept at Glinow, near Potsdam. He could not have got to Berlin before the nineteenth or twentieth. Yet inside a week he, an unknown hobo, either (*a*) so insinuated himself into the graces of the rigidly articulated Communist party as to be given the dangerous and delicate job of firing the Reichstag, or (*b*) was hired to do it by someone else.

When it became clear, even in Germany, that the van der Lubbe explanation simply would not hold water, the mystery thickened. The police got to the point of having to admit that van der Lubbe had confederates. But how, carrying incendiary material, could enough of them possibly have penetrated the Reichstag walls, doorways, or windows in the middle of Berlin without being seen?

The German authorities themselves let the cat out of the bag, and an astounding cat it proved to be. It was announced that the incendiaries had presumably entered and escaped from the building by means of an underground tunnel leading from the Reichstag basement to the palace of the speaker of the Reichstag—Göring—across the street. Originally this tunnel was part of the Reichstag's central heating system. Until an official communiqué revealed its existence not a dozen persons in Berlin had ever heard of it. So one aspect of the mystery was solved. The incendiaries, whoever they were, got in and out of the Reichstag building—through Göring's back yard. Incredible information!

An ostrich sticks its head in the sand—well-meaning but stupid ostrich. There is an obverse of the ostrich process. A man may naïvely and stridently call attention to something he wishes to conceal, hoping thereby to lessen interest in it. A squirrel hides a nut under a tree. Then he squats and points at it, showing where it is. Disingenuously a man may reveal what is embarrassing to him, hoping to modify the terms of the embarrassment.

Long before the trial opened the accusation that the Nazis themselves had burned the building had impressed the world. A mock trial was held in London. The *Brown Book*, telling part of the story—but inaccurately—was published by *émigrés* and widely circulated. Moreover, a secret nationalist memorandum, written to the order of a prominent deputy named Oberfohren, was passed from hand to hand. Oberfohren was a nationalist, a Junker, one of Papen's men. He asserted flatly that the Nazis were the incendiaries. In June, a Nazi detachment searched his flat; mystery for some time surrounded Oberfohren's whereabouts. Then it was announced that he had "shot himself."

The half-wit van der Lubbe was not the only person arrested. Ernst Torgler, chairman of the Communist *bloc* in the Reichstag, gave himself up to the police when he heard the announcement incredible to his ears that he was accused of complicity; subsequently three Bulgarian Communists, Dimitrov, Popov, and Tanev, were arrested, when a waiter who had served them in a Berlin café told the police that their activities had been "suspicious." Dimitrov was in Munich, not Berlin, on the night of the fire, as an incontrovertible alibi proved; nevertheless, he was held for five months until the trial, without a scrap of evidence against him.

I covered the trial in Leipzig and Berlin during its first six weeks. The court sat for fifty-seven days, and provided superlative drama. The trial was neither a farce nor a frame-up. The behavior of the police and judicial authorities before the trial was outrageous, but once the proceedings reached the courtroom there was a difference. The court got itself into a curious dilemma, of having to pretend to be fair even while exercising the greatest animus against the defendants, and little by little this necessity —caused mostly by the pressure of foreign opinion—to simulate justice led to some modicum of justice in the courtroom.

When the trial opened, I think, the judges like many people in Germany genuinely thought that van der Lubbe was a Communist and that the Communists were guilty. The prosecution thought so too and, assuming that the trial would be quick and easy, it made no serious effort to fabricate a "good" case. As the hearings went on it became evident even to the judges that there was no case at all. The evidence of the prosecution was a mystifying confusion of inaccuracies, contradictions, and plain lies. But once the trial started, it couldn't be stopped. With dreadful pertinacity, with true Teutonic thoroughness, the court plodded on, deeper every day in a morass of evidence that ineluctably proved just what it didn't want proved—the innocence of the accused. The prosecution, panicky, began to produce incredible cranks as witnesses, whom even the judges couldn't stomach; the judges, nervous, threw Dimitrov out of court whenever his questions became too intolerably pointed—which was often.

No one, of course, counted on the brilliant gallantry of Dimitrov. This Bulgarian revolutionary had, moreover, brains. Unerringly he picked every flaw in the testimony of a dishonest witness; unerringly he asked just those questions most damaging to the prosecution. He turned the trial into a public forum. The trial started as an attempt to pin the guilt of the Reichstag arson on the defendants. Dimitrov turned it before long into an action precisely opposite: one seeking to clear the Nazis of the same charge.

Once the court was forced into calling every relevant witness, like porters and workmen in the Reichstag building, the floodgates were open. Hot little clues dodged out. Lubbe, inert, apathetic, testified—in one of his few lucid moments—that he had been "with Nazis" the night before the fire. A gateman testified that a Nazi deputy, Dr. Albrecht, left the burning building, in great excitement, as late as ten P.M. A servant in Göring's house, Aldermann, testified that he heard, on several nights before the fire, mysterious sounds in the underground tunnel. Thus the fire—got hot.

THE CLASH BETWEEN Göring and Dimitrov was recorded by an unnamed special correspondent of the London *Times,* who gave an unforgettable picture of the exploding Premier of Prussia and the impudent, irrepressible revolutionary.

A London Times *correspondent sees Dimitrov make Göring's face turn red*

The Times (London), November 6, 1933

BERLIN, NOVEMBER 5—General Göring, Premier of Prussia, Reich Air Minister, Speaker of the Reichstag, General of Reichswehr and Police, shouting, "You'll be sorry yet if I catch you when you come out of prison, you crook!"—the presiding Judge of the Supreme Court ordering, "Out with him!"—Dimitrov, with overwhelming physical and moral forces against him, struggling with a foreign tongue but, as uncowed as ever, being hustled out of the court for the fifth time—this, the most remarkable of all the remarkable scenes that the trial of "van der Lubbe and associates" has yielded, held all spectators spellbound yesterday morning.

General Göring, called as witness, entered the courtroom soon after ten o'clock with a large following of ADC's in police, air service, and Nazi uniform, and of officials in plain clothes. He was in the plain brown uniform which most prominent Nazis now wear. The court was crowded for the occasion, several ministers and members of the diplomatic corps being present. Dimitrov's suspension had been raised "in view of the importance of the evidence."

General Göring spoke for about two hours. His statement had two parts— the first, a vigorous and eloquent attack on Communism; the second, a description of what he had seen in the burning Reichstag and the measures he had taken. He declared that he was convinced, "and knew as by clairvoyance," that the Communist party was responsible for the fire; that there had been a number of incendiaries, and that of these all but van der Lubbe had escaped by the underground passage connecting the Reichstag with the Reichstag engine house and with his, the Speaker's, official residence; and he told the Supreme Court that whatever its verdict he would punish the culprits.

[At this point *The Times* summarized Göring's testimony of the events of early 1933 and his share in them, with emphasis upon the night of the fire. "I am convinced," concluded Göring, "that a number of people fired the Reichstag. I must further affirm that, though it is the task of the court to ascertain the culprits, it is my task to ascertain the wirepullers of the whole terrible agitation. Let the trial end as it will, I will find the guilty and lead them to their punishment."]

Dimitrov then rose in exercise of his right to question witnesses, and a hush descended on the court as the two men faced each other. It was the lull before the storm.

Dimitrov said: "You have repeatedly stated your conviction that the Communists are guilty of this fire, and you, as Premier of Prussia, are head of the police and judiciary. May not this conviction of yours have influenced the whole police and judicial investigation, have guided it into this one channel, and closed all other channels of investigation?"

General Göring answered: "If I did influence the investigation in this direction, then it was the right direction." Raising his voice he said: "It was a political crime, and I was certain that the criminals are in your party."

There was a chorus of "Bravo" from the public, and Dimitrov, giving the applauders a contemptuous glance, said: "Yes, of course, bravo, bravo, bravo." Then he asked: "Does the witness know that this criminal party rules the sixth part of the earth, that the Soviet Union has diplomatic, political, and economic relations with Germany, and that its orders give thousands of German workers bread?"

General Göring, brandishing his fists, shouted: "What happens in Russia is of no interest to me. I have only to deal with the German Communist party and with the foreign crooks who come here to fire the Reichstag."

In the increasing tumult questions, answers, and the admonitions of the judge began to overlap. The judge told Dimitrov he was provoking the witness, and forbade him to make Communist propaganda. Dimitrov answered: "But he's making National Socialist propaganda," and asked "if it were known that this Communist party rules the best and greatest country in the world." The judge loudly forbade further questions, but meanwhile General Göring shouted: "I know that you behave yourself brazenly. You come here, fire the Reichstag, and then behave with this impudence in the face of the German people. Your place is the gallows."

In the hubbub it was just possible to hear Dimitrov say: "Are you afraid of these questions, Herr Minister President Göring?" and General Göring, raising his voice above the din, shout: "I am not afraid of you at all, you crook. I'm not here to be questioned by you." Meanwhile, Dimitrov was being hustled out of court, and General Göring shouted after him: "You'll be sorry yet if I catch you when you come out of prison."

* * *

THE *Times* correspondent failed to mention Dimitrov's final speech when, imperturbable as ever in the face of the executioner's ax or Göring's private vengeance, he demanded of the court that he be compensated for his lost time.

The court had to acquit Torgler, Dimitrov, Popov, and Tanev. Van der Lubbe was sentenced to death and duly decapitated. The feeble Dutchman died with his lips sealed, taking to his grave the secret of how he and the incendiaries worked.

It is of passing interest to note that while Dimitrov was fighting for his life, he was supported by organizations and individuals all over the world, who smothered Berlin in a paper storm of protest. This was the same Dimitrov who eventually became the Communist Premier of Bulgaria. In September, 1947, occurred one of those tragic incidents which demonstrate that the intolerance of the extreme left differs little from that of the extreme right. Dimitrov had Nikola Petkov, leader of the peasant opposition party in Bulgaria, arrested and tried on treason charges. Petkov was quickly found guilty and sentenced to death.

Once again the same organizations and individuals who in 1933 had interceded with the Nazis on Dimitrov's behalf now poured out protests to him in Sofia to spare the life of his political opponent. One might have expected Dimitrov, who had once been face to face with Göring and death, to heed the cries for mercy. But there was no magnanimity in Dimitrov's soul. The survivor of the Reichstag-fire trial ordered the sentence to be carried out. This was the man who at his own trial played Faust to Göring's Mephistopheles.*

---

* In early July, 1949, Moscow announced that Dimitrov had died of diabetes in a sanitarium near the Russian capital. The body lay in state, with Joseph Stalin himself standing solemnly in a guard of honor beside the casket of the hero of the Reichstag trial. A special refrigerator was ordered from Denmark to insure the preservation of the corpse.

San Francisco Chronicle Reporter Sees the Police Arrive Too Late to Save Anything But the Dead Clay of the Murderers

O N AN EVENING in late November, 1933, an infuriated mob stormed a California jail, dragged John M. Holmes and Thomas H. Thurmond, white men, from their cells and hanged them in willful defiance of the laws of the land. The men had already confessed to the kidnaping and murder of Brooke L. Hart, son of a San Jose merchant. They begged for their lives in vain. Thus, by mob action, Holmes and Thurmond became cold statistics in the recent social history of the United States. Since 1882 more than four thousand persons, three out of every four of them Negroes, had been lynched, a grievous blot on the nation's honor.

For his account of the California lynchings, Royce Brier, of the *San Francisco Chronicle,* was awarded the 1934 Pulitzer Prize in reporting. His story was written as a finishing touch to eleven hours of strenuous and extremely dangerous work, during which he was blinded by tear gas and menaced by the mob, which threatened to string up newspapermen alongside the kidnapers. There is little in horror fiction to compare with this straight report of human beings obsessed with lynch lust.

"Fine, that is swell!" Westbrook Pegler's
reaction to the California lynchings

San Francisco Chronicle, November 27, 1933

SAN JOSE, NOVEMBER 26—Lynch law wrote the last grim chapter in the Brooke Hart kidnaping here tonight. Twelve hours after the mutilated body of the son of Alex J. Hart, wealthy San Jose merchant, was recovered from San Francisco Bay a mob of ten thousand infuriated men and women stormed the Santa Clara County Jail, dragged John M. Holmes and Thomas H. Thurmond from their cells, and hanged them in historic St. James Park.

Swift, and terrible to behold, was the retribution meted out to the confessed kidnapers and slayers. As the pair were drawn up, threshing in the throes of death, a mob of thousands of men and women and children screamed anathemas at them.

The siege of the County Jail, a three-hour whirling, howling drama of lynch law, was accomplished without serious injury either to the seizers or the thirty-five officers who vainly sought to defend the citadel.

The defense of the jail failed because Sheriff Emig and his forces ran out of tear-gas bombs. Bombs kept the determined mob off for several hours.

Help from San Francisco and Oakland officers arrived too late to save the Hart slayers.

"Don't string me up, boys. God, don't string me up," was the last cry of Holmes as the noose was put about his neck in the light of flash lamps.

Thurmond was virtually unconscious with terror as the mob hustled him from the jail, down the alley, and across the street to his doom.

Great cheers from the crowd of onlookers accompanied the hoisting of the two slayers. Some women fainted, some were shielded from the sight by their escorts, but the gamut of human nature was here in the park. Old women with graying hair and benign faces expressed satisfaction at the quick end of the murderers, and young women with hardened faces broke down and wept.

King Mob was in the saddle and he was an inexorable ruler.

And here was a sovereign whose rise in invincible power stunned San Jose and will stun the nation and the world.

Brooke Hart's torn body was found in the water this morning. Barricades went up before the County Jail, and the crowd gathered and stayed all the day. It was a good-natured crowd. It knew the deputies and the police and the state highway patrolmen who stood guard. It bandied words with them.

There had been talk of an organized mob, and as the crowd grew in the evening there was no organization. There was shouting, and good nature still ruled.

"This crowd won't do anything," was the constant reiteration of Sheriff Emig's deputies.

Yet as their words of confidence were being spoken there flashed, like a prairie fire, the word through San Jose—eleven o'clock! Eleven o'clock!

The constant bombardment of that hour on the ear was monotonous and ominous.

Indeed, when that hour came the mob was well on its way to its prey, and they were dangling from limbs before midnight.

It was shortly before nine o'clock that the front line at the barricade made its first move of violence. Ten or fifteen patrolmen and deputies were against the barricade, which was not more than thirty feet from the jail door.

There was some pushing from behind, and the good-natured jeering, which had prevailed for almost an hour, took on a deeper tone of muttering. Strangely enough, there was little shouting of "lynch them" at this critical stage. It was a growl which was not unlike the throaty shouting in an African film.

Newspapermen stood behind the barriers, a few deputies stood about. Cameramen snapped flashlights.

Suddenly that front line lunged.

The police locked arms to hold them back. There were fifteen police and a hundred men exerting pressure against them. They swayed for a moment, locked in one another's embrace.

The police shouted orders, but they were mere shrill nothings as the mob behind began a deep rumble, dreadful in its menace.

Out of this twinkling of struggle, while the men behind the barriers held their breath, came a blast like that of a gun. The mob was temporarily quelled and uncertain, staggering back. "Shooting! Shooting!" went up the cry.

But it was a tear-gas bomb which had exploded.

The police suddenly gave way, taking one officer who had been burned back into the jail. The mob, after a moment of uncertainty, surged forward but was still a little cautious.

Out of the jail poured five or six deputies armed with tear-gas sticks. Again the leaders of the mob, those who must bear the brunt, staggered back.

But even as they staggered they jeered, and the first shouts of "lynch 'em," stabbed through the tumult.

"We'll get 'em now, boys. . . . Bring 'em out. . . . Bring 'em out. . . ." And another dreadful cry went up, a kind of chant which lasted but a minute: "Brooke Hart—Brooke Hart—Brooke Hart—Brooke Hart."

This chant, all of these shouts and screams were choked off in an instant as the first tear-gas bombs were fired.

"Boom—boom—boom," went the bombs. Again smoke, blue and lazy, drifted in the night air of the besieged jail, as lazy in the arc light as cigar smoke before a hearth.

The crowd broke and ran, women and children went screaming out beside the courthouse, handkerchiefs went to eyes everywhere, and the jail for a moment stood deserted, a grim old fortress which seemed in that moment impregnable.

"That's the end of it," everyone said, deputies, newspapermen, everyone.

And everyone, unable to plumb the depth of fury which has swayed San Jose for seventeen days, was wrong.

This was about nine o'clock.

The women and children had run, but there were hardy spirits who stayed. They were the leaders, they were the men who ultimately hanged Holmes and Thurmond.

They couldn't get in close to the jail. The lazy smoke burned their eyes. But they could stand off and throw rocks, and throw rocks they did.

The first rock came soon after the gas started to dissipate. A new post-office building is being built near by. There was tile aplenty about and bricks. There was also a vantage point from which to throw.

Sixty seconds after the first stone came, a steady shower was beating a tattoo on the stone wall of the jail, clanking against the steel door, making musical tinkles as it struck the bars.

Every rat-a-tat on stone or steel brought cheers from the crowd, and when a window in the jail fell the cheers were redoubled. The sound of a smashing window seemed by some alchemy to get them all, and they roared at the tops of their two hundred voices.

The alleyway before the jail door was now wholly untenable for human beings.

The scene in so far as concerned the pavement was not unlike the front steps of a church during the World War. Debris was everywhere. It was no man's land—no mistaking that.

Now not all of the officers on guard were besieged in the County Jail. Across the alley in Sheriff Emig's office were ten or twelve San Jose police officers, also armed with tear gas.

The situation was complicated by the splitting of forces in this manner, but once accomplished, nothing could be done about it.

The officers fired out the side windows and even sent a bomb out the front window of the courthouse, but the crowd seemed to survive this gas, and went about choking.

The leaders in the front-line trenches, so to speak, most of them boys between eighteen and twenty-three, were not dispersed by any of these bombs.

They stuck. There was some grim and terrible determination in them to get Holmes and Thurmond. There were scarcely more than fifty of them.

After about an hour of this rain of missiles at the jail, the leaders seemed to realize that they were getting nowhere. You can't knock a jail down with bricks.

It was then, about ten o'clock or shortly afterward, that the first settled attack was made on the steel door.

From the post-office construction job came a nine-inch iron pipe, weighing several hundred pounds, but there were willing hands to lift it.

Into the lazy smoke went fifteen or twenty men, charging from the crowd across the no man's land straight for the ancient steel doors of this jail, which had stood unbreeched since 1866.

"Boom," went the great pipe against the doors.

"Yeeoweeeeeeh," went a strange animal cry from the throats of the onlookers.

"Bang—bang—bang," went the tear-gas bombs from the second story of the jail.

"Ping," went a rock through the arc light at the corner of the jail, and the greatest cheer of all rent the air.

An eerie gloom swam in the courthouse alleys. It was like a stage set for the deepest of blue lights, and here was transpiring a drama the like of which has seldom been seen in America—a drama of a life brutally ended and two more to end.

There was no mistaking this mob now. It was out for Thurmond and Holmes, and nothing short of an army would stop it.

Who held that first iron pipe doesn't matter. They are known in San Jose, but ask someone who was there.

Here was the darkness and here was the mob out in the street. A policeman at the corner tooted his whistle. He was directing traffic. If the courthouse had blown up, if the sky had fallen, that policeman would still toot his whistle, directing traffic at the corner of St. James and First Streets.

He kept on sending 'em down First Street by the courthouse. Traffic was in a terrible snarl. All about the courthouse, about St. James Park to the east, wandered thousands, youngsters and their girls, women with children in their arms, men and their wives, nice old ladies with their daughters.

They milled about, went up as close to the howling front-line boys as possible, wandered away, wondering if they would get them or if they wouldn't get them.

It was a carnival, nothing less, and, after all, you couldn't drum up a straw of sympathy for Jack Holmes and Thomas Thurmond in this valley city.

But what was going on in the front lines? Darkness like a blanket wrapped the alleyway and the boxlike old prison.

Out of the darkness leaped another sound, the ominous sound the iron-pipe battering ram made on the steel door. Cheers, cheers, cheers, and more blasting of the tear-gas bombs, more staggering back by the men who held the ram.

Somebody said help is coming. San Francisco's and Oakland's inexhaustible supply of peace officers were speeding this way in automobiles and on motorcycles.

Armed with gas, more gas, and more gas, armed with riot guns.

It must have got about by telepathy, traveled to the front lines as surely as though an army had phones hooked up to the bombproofs.

"Get 'em! Get 'em! The cops are coming!" galvanized the mob and the leaders to more strenuous efforts. Still the bricks beat like an interminable tropic rain on the jail walls and bars and the steel door. Still the scene was plunged in darkness, blue darkness in which the slowly drifting smoke of the tear gas seemed to take the reflection from the very sky.

The third ram went into action. The leaders leaned as they strained at the great pipe, and in the darkness lunged at the door again. This time the double door gave way. It gave way with a tremendous crash, which stirred an entire block to frenzy.

Into the front corridor went the leaders with their ram. Screaming madly for vengeance, they had come to close quarters with the defenders, men they had known all their lives.

Across the corridor is a heavy barred grating, with a door. This door was open. The ram went through the grating, tearing it from its moorings. On went the ram to the brick wall behind, where it stopped.

In the darkness below, in the no man's land of a few minutes before, surged the mob, sending up yells in waves like the ocean surf. It was a steady drum of sound, in which words were indistinguishable.

In the second-story window at this moment appeared two of the leaders. "We're getting 'em. . . . We're bringing 'em down."

If it was possible the sound from below rose to a greater volume. Those below could not get into the jail. There wasn't room for them in the narrow corridors and cells.

And while the crowd screamed, here was the scene inside a jail occupied by men who had stood by valiantly, whatever may be said, against overwhelming odds.

They all knew one another—remember that—the mob and the officers. This was not a masked job.

Howard Buffington, veteran jailer, wept. He knew he was helpless before these men. They ran up the stairways, through the jail. No one could shoot them down. What is the law? No one had been hurt yet. Joe Walsh and Felix Cordray, all of them veterans, were helpless.

The mob knew where their prisoners were, and there was little chance of mistake. The mob leaders knew Thurmond and Holmes personally.

They went to Thurmond's cell on the third floor, the old northeast cell of David Lamson. Buffington went along with the leaders. They took the keys from Buffington. Thurmond, in mortal terror, was clinging to the grating in the toilet of his cell.

Then there occurred a scene probably never enacted before in a lynching in the history of America.

The leaders prayed for Thurmond's soul.

They knelt in that jail cell, five or six of them, in the midst of the turmoil and the shouting, and they prayed to God Almighty for the man who was so soon to meet that God.

They arose with the whimpering prisoner, arms grasping him on either side, and he stumbled down the stairs. He stumbled along tongue-tied with his last great terror.

The scene in the Holmes cell on the second floor of the prison was a different one. No one prayed for Holmes, the so-called leader of the Brooke Hart slaying.

Holmes was also concealed in the washroom off his cell, and when the crowd went in he denied he was Holmes.

With a last bravado he shouted: "I'm not Holmes."

But his destroyers laughed in his face. Too many of them knew him well. One man struck him in the face. "By God, you are!" shouted the men jammed in his cell. He fell to the floor. Grasping him by the feet they dragged him down the steps and out into the open, where Thurmond had just arrived.

For a moment there was bedlam about the jail. A few on the outskirts of the crowd shouted that one was the wrong man. There was some doubt at first that two men had been taken. But those next to the men knew whom they had.

There had been some howling in the jail for Tony Serpa, a youth recently convicted of manslaughter, when he had been charged with murder. It was a short-lived cry. The mob leaders were not to be diverted from their purpose.

The snarling mob with the half-unconscious prisoners did not tarry before the jail. They moved with a kind of mindless precision down the alley beside the courthouse to First Street, and across that street to St. James Park.

That movement across First Street seemed instantaneous. One moment the men were in the jail alley; there was yet a ray of hope for them, even though policemen were wandering away in a bewildered manner. The next moment the mob had the prisoners in the park, and their end had come.

A great murmuring went up from the thousands who had thus far taken little part in the actual seizure of Holmes and Thurmond. These spectators, men, women, and children,

streamed like a mighty surf toward the park.

They climbed the statue of William McKinley, and they milled about, gorging the entire west side of the big park.

There was not the remotest doubt where the sympathy of these people lay.

"String 'em up!" came from a thousand throats, from women as well as men, from grammar-school boys, from businessmen with spectacles, and from workingmen in rough garb.

There was some delay in getting a rope, some impatience from the crowd. Several men started climbing trees, and every man was given a cheer. The light was dim in the park, but there were a couple of arc lights and hundreds of flashlights.

After a delay of almost fifteen minutes, ropes were produced, and Thurmond, who was at the south end of the park, was the first man to be hanged. He was benumbed with fear, and his crazed mutterings were without meaning.

Thurmond was hanged to a low limb. As his body was slowly hoisted, the crowd broke into frantic cheering. Someone in that crowd must have had the technique of hangman's knots. Thurmond thrashed as he hung there, swaying to and fro, seeming to bend his body at the hips in a last spasm of life.

For perhaps three minutes he swayed there, his face blackening slowly, his tongue extended, although he was obviously unconscious.

"Brookie Hart—Brookie Hart," cried his executioners to the man who could no longer hear them.

The taunts went on as the man's body dangled at the end of the rope, slowly turning, now this way and now that, as though some mocking power were giving all a full view of him.

The crowd ran hither and thither, children scampering through the crowd to get the best view. Some children in arms were held twenty-five feet from the dangling man as the mob of onlookers milled about and gave vent to cries of triumph.

Holmes' execution followed that of Thurmond by a few minutes. In a despairing voice, which was nevertheless clear, he kept denying that he was Holmes, but the crowd knew better and those immediately about him did not bother to fling his words back at him.

Holmes, his bloody face turned on his captors, took death with more stamina than did Thurmond. As the rope was let down from a limb, he begged:

"Don't string me up, boys. . . . Don't string me up."

"Yes, I'm Holmes," he gasped, and held his head up, and in the next instant the noose dropped over it, and with a cheer his body was flung into the air.

Holmes did not struggle as long as did Thurmond. It seemed that that last relinquishment of hope had taken the life from him. The rope about his neck, too, seemed to have left him nothing but reflexes to cause motion.

There was a report that both nooses were the hangman's knots which crush into the skull behind the ear, and destroy consciousness.

While Thurmond still dangled, his feet even with the faces of the crowd, Holmes was thrown far into the air. The crowd gasped for a moment as it observed that his body was stark-naked.

Now, as the men swung there, both playthings of the winds and the twisted ropes, many who had cried for their execution turned away. Several women fainted in the crowd, but there were thousands who did not faint; there were hundreds who looked on with smiles.

And the burden of all the talk was: "Well, there won't be any kidnaping in this county for a long time."

The dead men swung there. Some of the more violent spirits were for cutting them down and burning them with gasoline. Thurmond's trousers were stripped from him, and some of the mob set fire to his rubber coat, which burned for a few minutes.

The bodies hung in the park for almost an hour. Shortly before midnight came squads of San Francisco police officers. The crowd ran. These were the police for whom Sheriff Emig called when he ran out of tear gas about half an hour before his prisoners were seized. They were too late to save anything but the dead clay of the murderers.

"THE HOLIDAY OF HATRED, violence, and death was ended," commented the San Francisco *Examiner*. This fine tag line is a reminder that the San Jose lynchings touched off an old-fashioned news battle between two San Francisco papers, the *Chronicle* and the *Examiner*, both of which came out of the contest with honors. Royce Brier of the *Chronicle* had had charge of the Hart kidnaping story from its inception, and three days before the finding of young Hart's body had scored a beat on the organization of a secret group of vigilantes. He predicted that no action would be taken against the kidnapers until the body was found. Within a matter of hours Brier had two telephone wires kept open direct to his city desk and for four hours during the lynching he gave the *Chronicle* a running account of the developments. The *Chronicle* published thirteen editions that night.

In the meantime, Reginald Clampett and Lennie Kullman, of the *Examiner,* also covered the story on the scene. William C. Wren, current managing editor of the *Examiner,* who shared in the writing of the story, informed the editors of this volume:

> The story was a composite of the work of several reporters. Kullman was stationed in a telephone booth right in the jail yàrd while the mob was storming the jail. It was the only telephone there, and he was getting the fumes of the tear gas thrown by the deputies at the mob, but he held the phone open from beginning to end of the attack on the jail and the lynching. Clampett was in the park across the street from the jail and phoned a running account of the lynching through Kullman.

The *Chronicle* and *Examiner* accounts were first-rate coverage.

It may be of incidental interest to note that at this time the acidulous sports writer Westbrook Pegler was about to shift his energies to the business of crusading columnist. The San Jose affair provided him with a perfect diving board for the plunge. His reaction to the lynching of Thurmond and Holmes was: "Fine, that is swell!" It was his red-blooded debut into the field of what he called "cosmic thought." At the same time Governor James Rolph, Jr., of California, was quoted as saying that he would like to turn over all jail inmates serving sentences for kidnaping into the custody of "those fine patriotic San Jose citizens, who know how to handle such a situation."

Heywood Broun was appalled by this condonation and actual praise for the lynchers. "In the beginning it seemed to me," he wrote, "that if this thing were so monstrously and obviously evil it would be enough to say calmly and simply: 'Here is one more sadistic orgy carried on by a psychopathic mob under the patronage of a moronic governor of a backward state.'" Broun lashed this "obscene, depraved, and vile" business. "To your knees, Governor," he advised, "and pray that you and your commonwealth be washed clean of this bath of bestiality into which a whole community has plunged!"

Low-Man-on-a-Totem-Pole H. Allen Smith
Visits a Nudist Colony

I N THE SUMMER OF 1933 H. Allen Smith, of the New York Bureau of the United Press, was given an assignment that enabled him to get a good look at life in the raw. His exposé, a fascinating story of a nudist colony at Highland, New York, is one of the few news reports ever written by a newsman who was stark-naked at the time of composition.

"I sat nude on a large rock," he explained later, "with my portable on my knees, when I wrote it. This distinction, however, probably is of dubious value. I need only mention that mosquitoes were there in vast numbers."

Nakedness bared

United Press Associations, August 17, 1933

All arguments to the contrary, it is very embarrassing to have a young woman walk up to you stark-naked and tell you that nudism is going to sweep the nation.

The shed-your-pants apostles at this particular nudist camp are serious about it. They appear to feel nudism will do wonders for this world.

This is your correspondent's first visit to a nudist camp, and this one, operated by Miss Jane Gay, who apparently cuts her own hair, is a little dandy.

There is a man here known only as Button-Button—a short German fellow who gives the impression of a bushel basket full of hickory nuts when viewed from the side. He is bald, and on top of his head is a wen, about the size of a ping-pong ball and a half. Because of this wen, the nudists call him Button-Button. And whenever he approaches in complete undress, they all begin singing: *When the Moon Comes Over the Mountain.*

Button-Button, however, is a serious sort of fellow. He doesn't resent the gibes.

"I figure," he told the United Press, "that if they have fun making the joke with me it is their own business, and I am not one to interfere with other people's business."

The camp is far off any traveled highway and overlooks a splendid lake. There were about twenty-five nudists present today, but the average on week ends is eighty. The nudists do not court publicity. But once a newspaperman gets in and convinces them that he is on a liver-and-carrots diet, they can be congenial. In fact, they can pester you to death.

Firmly intending to spend two days in their midst, this correspondent was not in the camp ten minutes before he had stripped. It all seemed perfectly natural—walking back and forth in front of the dining hall without so much as a pair of shorts on.

Then came Miss Gronlin. She came

around the corner, very blonde and very handsome. And she didn't even have shoes on. Your correspondent, a bird lover, became intensely interested in a thrush which was going into a power dive over Bear Mountain.

She didn't go on about her business, this Miss Gronlin. She came right up and said: "Are you Mr. Smith?"

Your correspondent never tells a lie.

"I am Miss Gronlin," she said, and she laid a hand on my arm. "Please come and go swimming. The lake is wonderful."

"Miss Gronlin," your correspondent told her firmly, "I am not used to this business."

"Oh, that's all right," she burst forth, "the water isn't so deep in places."

Well, the swim was great fun, and we rowed a boat, and asked after the fish in the lake, and found out that nudism is going to sweep the country, and that vegetables are very good for one, and that really there ain't no reason why people should object to nudism. What with Germany and all,

and that the sloping, grassy hill over there to the west is a swell place to take off your clothes and gallop like a horse, and that sometimes some nutty people stray into this camp.

There were perhaps ten other men and women engaged in aquatic sports sans-culottes.

A Miss Emery, who has charge of the dining room, came down to the pier and ripped off what little clothing she wore. She stretched her arms, yawned, and started off on a classical dance—one of those here-we-go-gathering-nuts-in-May dances.

After completing it, Miss Emery did a sort of Immelmann roll into the water, and your correspondent, fearing for her life, swam rapidly toward her. She seemed, however, perfectly capable of swimming in deep water, and was exceptionally good at floating on her back.

Standing on the dock, Miss Emery, still as naked as the day she was born (as was your correspondent), explained that the idea of this nudist camp is health.

The sun, she said, is good for one.

FROM THIS POINT H. Allen Smith went on to become one of America's more insane humorists. Fred Allen described him lovingly and accurately as "the screwball's Boswell" and "a jetsam journalist." "In the year 1939," Smith later confessed, "I wrote a novel and ruptured myself and in 1940 I became a subscriber to *Fortune* magazine. Though I am now clearly entitled to write my autobiography, this is not it." Since then Smith has entertained his public with a number of hilarious books, including a book of recollections appropriately called *Low Man on a Totem Pole* (1944).

Jack Lait Sees the FBI Liquidate
Public Enemy No. 1

UNTIL THEN he was just another insignificant Midwest hoodlum, but in May, 1933, John Dillinger declared war on the United States. With supreme contempt for the law the Indiana bad boy held up banks, used machine-gun bullets to cut down policemen, and on one notable occasion that brought him extraordinary national popularity he broke out of a foolproof prison by the simple expedient of flourishing a wooden pistol whittled from a washboard. "Mad-dog Dillinger," he was tabbed by the sensational press, and as "Public Enemy No. 1" he was catapulted to world-wide notoriety.

When Dillinger made the serious error of shooting down an agent of the Federal Bureau of Investigation he signed his own death warrant. Word went out from Washington to get Dillinger and nothing was to stand in the way. The subsequent man hunt for the toughest killer of his generation made the front pages and stayed there. Here was gangster fiction come to life: Dillinger fighting his way out of traps, Dillinger contemptuously raiding police arsenals, Dillinger dining with his father, Dillinger still looting banks, Dillinger altering his face and fingerprints. In the meantime G-men, hard with another kind of toughness, stalked this human jackal relentlessly.

They finally caught up with him in Chicago on a hot day in late July, 1934. Ironically, it was a New York editor who beat the entire Chicago press on the story of Dillinger's end. A gravel-voiced, hard-boiled, shrewd expert in the tough-guy school of prose, Jack Lait had himself been a Chicago newspaperman from 1901 to 1921, covering the rise of the Chicago gangs and living through the rough-and-tumble days immortalized by Hecht and MacArthur in *The Front Page*. "I had spent the flower of my youth in the Windy Burg," Lait wrote later. "There my name had become a household word, I knew everyone, and there I addressed at least ten thousand cops by their first name." A favor for one of these cops paid off, for the cop's son telephoned Lait in New York and urged him to come to Chicago at once. On a hunch Lait heeded the mysterious summons, which brought him within a few feet of the spot where G-men shot down Dillinger. Keeping a wire open to New York, Lait furnished a remarkable running account of the end of a bloody trail.

Dillinger "gets his"

International News Service, July 23, 1934

John Dillinger, ace bad man of the world, got his last night—two slugs through his heart and one through his head. He was tough and he was shrewd, but he wasn't as tough and shrewd as the Federals, who never close a case until the end. It took twenty-seven of them to end Dillinger's career, and their strength came out of his weakness—a woman.

Dillinger was put on the spot by a tip-off to the local bureau of the Department of Justice. It was a feminine voice that Melvin H. Purvis, head of the Chicago office, heard. He had waited long for it.

It was Sunday, but Uncle Sam doesn't observe any NRA * and works seven days a week.

The voice told him that Dillinger would be at a little third-run movie house, the Biograph, last night—that he went there every night and usually got there about 7:30. It was almost 7:30 then. Purvis sent out a call for all men within reach and hustled all men on hand with him. They waited more than an hour. They knew from the informer that he must come out, turn left, turn again into a dark alley where he parked his Ford-8 coupé. Purvis himself stood at the main exit. He had men on foot and in parked inconspicuous cars strung on both sides of the alley. He was to give the signal. He had ascertained about when the feature film, *Manhattan Melodrama,* would end. Tensely eying his wrist watch he stood. Then the crowd that always streams out when the main picture finishes came. Purvis had seen Dillinger when he was brought through from Arizona to Crown Point, Indiana, and his heart pounded as he saw again the face that has been studied by countless millions on the front pages of the world.

Purvis gave the signal. Dillinger did not see him. Public Enemy No. 1 lit a cigarette, strolled a few feet to the alley with the mass of middle-class citizens going in that direction, then wheeled left.

A Federal man, revolver in hand, stepped from behind a telegraph pole at the mouth of the passage. "Hello, John," he said, almost whispered, his voice husky with the intensity of the classic melodrama. Dillinger went with lightning right hand for his gun, a .38 Colt automatic. He drew it from his trousers pocket.

But, from behind, another government agent pressed the muzzle of his service revolver against Dillinger's back and fired twice. Both bullets went through the bandit's heart.

He staggered, his weapon clattered to the asphalt paving, and as he went three more shots flashed. One bullet hit the back of his head, downward, as he was falling, and came out under his eye.

Police cleared the way for the police car which was there in a few minutes. The police were there not because they were in on the capture, but because the sight of so many mysterious men around the theater had scared the

---

* National Recovery Administration, a New Deal Agency that, among other functions, regulated hours of work in industry.

manager into thinking he was about to be stuck up and he had called the nearest station.

When the detectives came on the run, Purvis intercepted them and told them what was up. They called headquarters and more police came, but with instructions to stand by and take orders from Purvis.

Dillinger's body was rushed to Alexian Brothers' hospital in a patrol wagon. There were no surgeons in it. But the policeman knew he was dead, and at the entrance of the hospital, where a kindly priest in a long cassock had come to the door to see who might be in need of help, the driver was ordered to the morgue.

I was in a taxi that caught up with the police car at the hospital, and we followed across town to the old morgue. No one bothered us, though we went fifty miles an hour.

There was no crowd then. We pulled in. Strong arms carried the limp, light form of the man who had been feared by a great government through that grim door of many minor tragedies. It lay on a rubber stretcher.

In the basement, the receiving ward of the last public hospice of the doomed, they stripped the fearsome remains.

What showed up, nude and pink, still warm, was the body of what seemed a boy, the features as though at rest and only an ugly, bleeding hole under the left eye, such as a boy might have gotten in a street fight. His arms were bruised from the fall and the bumping in the wagon.

But under the heart were two little black, bleeding holes, clean and fresh. These could not have been anything but what they were. That part of John Dillinger did not look as though it was a boy's hurt— it was the fatal finish of a cold-blooded killer and not half of

what he had given Officer O'Malley in East Chicago, Indiana, in the bank robbery when he cut the policeman almost in half with a machine gun.

The marks of the garters were still on the skin of his sturdy calves, the only part of him that looked like any part of a strong man. His arms were slender, even emaciated. But his legs were powerful-looking. His feet were neat and almost womanish, after the white socks and dudish white shoes had been taken from them.

His clothes were shabby with still an attempt at smartness. The white shirt was cheap, the gray flannel trousers, and the uninitialed belt buckle were basement-counter merchandise, his maroon-and-white print tie might have cost half a dollar.

In his pockets were $7.70 and a few keys and a watch in which was the picture of a pretty female.

Two women bystanders were caught in the line of fire and wounded slightly as the Federal men blazed away. They were Miss Etta Natalsky, forty-five, and Miss Theresa Paulus, twenty-nine, both residents of the neighborhood.

Miss Natalsky was taken to the Columbus Memorial Hospital with a wound in the leg and Miss Paulus to the Grant Hospital, but her wound, also in the leg, was found to be only superficial.

The notorious desperado had resorted to facial surgery to disguise himself, and it was only by his piercing eyes—described by crime experts as "the eyes of a born killer"—that he was recognized.

In addition to the facial alterations, he had dyed his hair a jet black from its natural sandy shade, and he wore gold-rimmed glasses.

Identification of the fallen man was confirmed by Purvis on the spot.

Later, at the morgue, an attempt was made to identify the body from finger-prints, but the tips of the fingers had been scarred, as if with acid.

A recent wound in the chest, which had just healed, was revealed in the morgue examination. It was believed this was a memento of a recent bank robbery.

Dr. Charles D. Parker, coroner's physician, remarked on the alteration in the slain man's features. Scars which he carried on each cheek Dillinger had had smoothed out by facial surgery. Purvis, after closely examining the changed features, said:

"His nose, that originally was pro-nounced 'pug,' had been made nearly straight. His hair had been dyed re-cently."

Souvenir hunters among the excited crowds that swarmed to the scene of the shooting frantically dipped news-papers and handkerchiefs in the patch of blood left on the pavement.

Traffic became so jammed that streetcars were rerouted, police lines established, and all traffic finally blocked out of the area.

Unsatiated by their morbid milling around the death spot, the crowds a little later rushed to the morgue to view the body. Denied admittance, they battled police and shouted and yelled to get inside. More than two thousand at one time were struggling to force the doors.

I have indisputable proof that the bureau had information that Dillinger had been here for at least three days. It was the first definite location of the hunted murderer since the affray in the Little Bohemia (Wisconsin) lodge.

"We didn't have time to get him then, but we had time enough this time," Purvis said.

Evidently Purvis not only had

enough time, but used it with the tra-ditional efficiency of his department. There has always been open rancor between the Chicago police and the Federals, who have several times done them out of rewards. The Federals are not permitted to accept rewards.

But the East Chicago force—Dil-linger had slaughtered three of their outfit in two raids, and the "coinci-dence" of their presence "when the tip came in" is obvious.

That Dillinger suspected nothing is proven by nothing as much as that the safety catch on his magazine gun was set. It was a new, high-type weapon, so powerful that its slugs would pene-trate the bulletproof vests of the sort that Dillinger himself had worn in other spots. The number had been filed off. Close examination indicated it had never been fired. It was fully loaded, and a clip of extra cartridges was in a pocket.

He had no other possible instrument of offense or defense, this desperado, except a slender penknife on the other end of a thin chain that held his watch.

All his possessions lay on the marble slab beside the rubber stretcher in the basement of the morgue as the in-ternes pawed his still warm face and body as they threw his head to this side and that, slung him over on his face, and dabbed the still-wet blood from where the bullets had bitten into him.

I wondered whether, a few brief minutes earlier, they would have had the temerity to treat John Dillinger's flesh so cavalierly.

They pointed to the scar on his shinbone, the one which had been so heavily broadcast as maiming and even killing Dillinger. It was a little bit of a thing and looked more like the result of a stone bruise than a volley from the muzzle of outraged society.

They flopped him over on the slab, quite by a clumsy accident, because the body didn't turn easily within the stretcher, what with its gangly, rubbery legs, and its thin, boneless arms. And as what was left of Dillinger clumped like a clod, face down, upon the slab which had held the clay of hoboes and who knows, a still warm but spent hand knocked off the straw hat which had fallen off his head in the alley and been trampled upon. And a good ten-cent cigar. Strangely intact.

The man who had killed him stood two feet away, smoking a cigar of the same brand. I must not mention his name. Purvis says "keep that a trade secret." With John ("Happy Jack") Hamilton and George ("Baby Face") Nelson, Dillinger's lieutenants, still at large, perhaps that is a fair enough precaution.

The Bureau of Identification men were on the job in a jiffy. They proved up the fingerprints, though they had been treated with a biting acid in an effort to obliterate the telltale. But the deltas and cores were unmistakable.

Behind the ears were well-done scars of a face-lifting job by a skillful plastic specialist. A mole on the forehead had been trimmed off rather well. His hair, by rights sandy, had been painted a muddy black with a poor grade of dye.

So had his mustache. The one identifying mark known around the globe as the Dillinger characteristic was there. And even in death he looked just like the Dillinger we all knew from the photographs. Probably the last breath of his ego.

Dillinger was a ladies' man. He didn't want to be picked up and identified by a rube sheriff. But, still, he wanted to whisper to a new sweetie in the confidences of the night:

"Baby, I can trust you—I'm John Dillinger!"

And she would look, and—he was! That mustache!

Having gone to astonishing lengths to change his inconspicuous identifying marks, with the necessary aid and advice of expert medical men, he had still refused to shave off that familiar trade-mark that every newspaper reader could see with eyes shut.

A scar on his chin had been reopened and smoothed up some, but not very convincingly. The droop at the left corner of his mouth was unmistakably intact. But the most striking facial change was in the tightening of the skin on his chin, almost completely killing his dimple, which was almost as widely known as his mustache.

Gold-rimmed eyeglasses fell off his face as he toppled over. These, one of the most amateurish of elements in disguise, did change his appearance decisively, the officers tell me.

The Federal office, as usual, issued contradictory statements and frankly admitted that certain information would not be given out.

Of the twenty-seven men who worked with Purvis, one was Captain Tim O'Neill of East Chicago, and four others were O'Neill's men. Purvis said they were there quite by chance and he had taken them in on the big adventure. A second statement also gave forth that Purvis had seen Dillinger enter as well as leave the theater.

As Dillinger emerged, walking near him were two youngish women, one of them wearing a red dress. Hundreds were leaving the house at the time, and almost any number of women would naturally have been near him. But the one with the red dress hurried up the alley, and four Federals made a formation between her and Dillinger before the first shot was fired. It is my theory that she was with Dillinger and that she was the tip-off party or in league with Purvis.

LAIT'S HUNCH WAS CORRECT: it was the "woman in red" who had betrayed Badman Dillinger. She was later deported to Europe. Reporter Lait went on to become a $52,000-a-year hustling Hearst man. As editor of the tabloid New York *Daily Mirror,* he doubled his paper's circulation (to 1,054,000 daily, 2,206,000 Sunday) in the face of some of the toughest competition in the country. In the meantime, as king of the hacks, he pounded out a total of 1500 short stories, seventeen books, eight plays, and a syndicated column for six hundred newspapers.

Sit-Down Strikes and a Memorial Day Massacre

Become Front-Page News

T HE ADMINISTRATION of Franklin D. Roosevelt inaugurated a New Deal for labor. The passage in 1933 of the National Industrial Recovery Act, which guaranteed to labor the right to bargain through representatives of its own choosing, a right reiterated by the National Labor Relations Act (Wagner Act) of 1935, stirred labor to what has aptly been characterized as "a frenzy of organizing." Because of the conservatism of the American Federation of Labor, organized along craft lines, labor leaders desirous of forming industrial unions formed the Committee for Industrial Organization (CIO), which seceded from the A. F. of L. By 1936, under the generalship of Philip Murray, the CIO began to invade the automobile and steel industries. The year 1937 began with a bitter struggle to organize the motor industry and culminated in the tragic "massacre" on Memorial Day, when the workers felt the lash of Republic Steel.

The highly mechanized auto industry, dominated by the Big Three, had hitherto proved a formidable bastion against organized labor. When, years before, Henry Ford had introduced the assembly-line technique he had not reckoned that someday labor would use the device as a surprise weapon against Big Business, for, by mere refusal to work or by slowing down assembly-line operations, a very few men could throw a monkey wrench into the whole machinery of production. In India Gandhi had on many occasions demonstrated the effectiveness of passive resistance. In fact, as early as 1906 a stay-in strike was run by the Wobblies (IWW) at the General Electric plant in Schenectady. But the real impetus to the sit-down came from Italy and France. In Italy sit-down strikes were first used on a wide scale before they were suppressed by Mussolini and his Black Shirts. French workers employed the same tactics in 1936. But two years earlier, at Akron, Ohio, a couple of baseball teams representing workers from two rubber plants sat down on the bases and the diamond because the umpire was not a union man. The game was resumed when a union member put on the umpire's mask and shouted:

"Batter up!"

The spectacular sit-downs at General Motors, which lasted forty-four days and involved 40,000 workers directly and 110,000 indirectly, were aimed not so much at the size of the pay envelope and the insecurity of working conditions, but rather as a protest against the conveyor-belt system and the speed-up. The strikers, according to Herbert Harris, an acute observer of labor conditions, "expressed the pent-up resentment of men in revolt against being dehumanized, against being only a badge, a number, a robot in thrall to a vast and intricate succubus of machinery, draining them of energy, threatening to cast them on the scrap heap after a few short years." When, late in December, 1936, William S. Knudsen, then executive vice-president of General Motors, suggested to the union that it seek adjustment of grievances with local plant managers, the workers muttered: "It's the merry run-around again." Rumors spread that the company was planning to remove tools and dies to less strongly unionized areas. The next move was made by the workers.

At Flint, Michigan, on New Year's eve, 1936, a few hundred workers seized a number of General Motors plants and caused a complete stoppage of production. Although owning nearly $200,000 worth of General Motors stock, Judge Edward Black saw nothing improper about issuing an injunction commanding the workers to vacate his company's property and forbidding picketing. When the workers defied this order, a clash with the police took place. At this point, Governor Frank Murphy, instead of trying to eject the workers by force, sent national guardsmen to the scene to prevent further strife pending union-management negotiations. This prolonged two-way siege was reported for *The New York Times* readers by Louis Stark, dean of labor reporters, and Russell B. Porter.

"When they tie a can to a union man,
Sit-down! Sit-down!"

The New York Times, December 31, 1936, January 1, 3, 11, 12, 13, 17, 1937

FLINT, MICHIGAN, DECEMBER 30— Backed by the John L. Lewis Committee for Industrial Organization, the United Automotive Workers of America today started its campaign to include the nation's automobile industry within its ranks. It struck at the center of General Motors operations and halted activities in three of its unit plants here. Affecting operations at all but one of the five General Motors units in Flint, Fisher Body Plant No. 1 was closed late tonight by a sit-down strike.

Returning from their usual lunch hour at ten P.M., an undetermined number of men refused to return to work and all operations ceased. Nearly three hundred women em-

ployed on the night shift immediately left the plant.

There was no disorder in the Fisher plants. Of the 1200 at work in Plant No. 2 when the sit-down began, fewer than five hundred remained in the plant tonight. Food was taken to them by other members of the union, with full permission of the company.

FLINT, MICHIGAN, DECEMBER 31— With 33,400 workers idle, seven General Motors plants shut down, and five more affected by strikes called by the United Automotive Workers of America in its campaign to make a closed shop of the automobile industry, formal notice was served on the union tonight by the corporation that no conference to discuss collective bargaining would be considered until the union's sit-down strikers vacated all General Motors plants.

In Flint, the center of the corporation's operations, the strikers have closed plants in four divisions, throwing 14,600 men out of work. The daily General Motors pay roll in Flint is about $350,000.

Several hundred strikers remained in the two Fisher Body plants tonight, having taken full possession of the No. 1 plant, which employs seven thousand men and which supplies all bodies used by the Buick Motor Company.

Taking command of the main gates at this plant, the strikers also took over the company cafeteria and prepared their own food during the day.* They held possession of the main entrance to the plant, and no one was allowed to enter or leave without permission. Company policemen stood by in idleness, making no attempt to interfere.

FLINT, MICHIGAN, JANUARY 3—Earlier last evening the officers had announced that the strikers would be removed, with the use of tear- and emetic-gas bombs if necessary, from the plants which they have held since Wednesday. The first move, the announcement had said, was to be at the No. 1 plant.

Sheriff Thomas Wolcott, who deputized a hundred Flint city policemen and sixty company guards late in the afternoon to enforce the injunction, went to the No. 1 plant last night to make a final appeal to the men to leave voluntarily. He said he was "laughed out" of the plant. The men, he added, greeted his appeal with boos and cat-calls.

Threescore or more pickets marched in single file in front of the No. 1 plant. Picketing was forbidden in the injunction, but the pickets said they would resist any attempt to arrest them.

FLINT, MICHIGAN, JANUARY 10 †— Several hundred men, women, and children stamped up and down in the snow [in front of the struck plants] to keep warm as a color guard of World War veterans who have formed "Union War Veterans Post No. 1" raised an American flag on the second floor of the building to the notes of a bugle.

The sit-down strikers, in the work clothes that they wore when the strike was called last week, leaned from the window.

Children and women who form the union auxiliary committee paraded past the strikers, who cheered and waved their hands. At the head of the parade was six-year-old Albert Dewar, Jr., carrying a pasteboard placard with the words, "My daddy is a union man." His father is a Chevrolet employee.

Other banners bore the slogans, "Our daddies will win," "We are behind our daddies 100 per cent," "We can't lose," "This is a new day."

At the rear of the procession was Kermit Johnson, a Chevrolet worker, carrying his infant son James, whose hands rested on the handle of a banner which bore the words:

"My daddy strikes for us little tykes."

---

* It was reported on January 4 that the sit-down strikers that day disposed of sixty gallons of veal stew for lunch and fifty-four gallons of meat balls and spaghetti for dinner.
† Louis Stark reporting.

24 HURT IN FLINT STRIKE RIOT:
POLICE BATTLE STREET MOBS:
GOVERNOR RUSHES TO SCENE

———

MILITIA MOBILIZES

———

TROOPS READY AS AUTO STRIKERS IN
PLANT REPEL GAS ATTACK

FLINT, MICHIGAN, JANUARY 12—
After more than five hours of hand-
to-hand fighting with the police, in
which at least twenty-four persons
were injured by bullets, stones, clubs,
knives, and tear-gas bombs, a siege
was on this morning at the Fisher
Body Plant No. 2, where "sit-down"
strikers are defying the courts and the
state authorities.

Governor Murphy, who rushed to
Flint by automobile, was in conference at the Hotel Durant on steps to
be taken to end the fighting. Under his
orders a company of the 125th Regiment of the Michigan Guard was mo-
bilizing for riot duty at the Flint armory, prepared to prevent further
bloodshed and rioting.

In addition it was reported that
four state policemen, in response to
appeals by Flint officials for aid,
would soon arrive to enter the fray.

The police meanwhile could do little more than hold their lines against
some eight hundred strikers, pickets,
and sympathizers who were being directed by the broadcasting apparatus
of a sound truck parked near the plant
gate. Virtually every window in the
two-story factory building appears to
have been broken. The street before
the plant, which is opposite the Chevrolet factory in Chevrolet Avenue,
was littered with debris. Rioters had
torn up stretches of the asphalt pavements to obtain missiles to hurl at the
police. At another point along the ave-

nue, curbstones had been pried up
and had been broken into pieces by
the strikers.

That some of the strikers were
armed was held certain, because at one
point a message was shouted from the
sound truck:

"Go home and get your guns and
come back again."

The wounded, however, were believed to have been injured mostly by
fragments of exploding tear-gas shells
fired by the police, and by missiles,
rather than by gunfire.

Of those hurt twenty persons were
taken to hospitals, among them five
policemen.

The trouble began when about four
hundred "sit-downers," who have
been occupying the second floor of
the plant since December 30, swarmed
suddenly from their positions and
overpowered the plant policemen, taking possession of the entire building.
As the disturbance spread, a riot call
was sounded, bringing the city policemen to the plant. The first officers arrived with supplies of tear-gas bombs,
hoping to quell the disorder with these.

Streams from the fire hoses brought
into play by the rioters drove the policemen back from the windows, however, so that the gas bombs were ineffective.

Meanwhile a crowd of about two
hundred strikers, who were outside the
plant, charged the gates, overcame police resistance, and joined their comrades inside.

The police reported that, despite
the odds against them, they had not
yet used their revolvers.

FLINT, MICHIGAN, JANUARY 12 *—
[Two thousand National Guardsmen
are reported massed.] When this reporter made a trip this afternoon

———

* Russell B. Porter reporting.

through the occupied factory, now completely controlled by the stay-in strikers, neither city nor company police were visible at the gate or in the adjacent street where last night's fight took place.

The strike committee in charge announced that it would evacuate the plant on orders from the National Guard if assured that the strikers would get a square deal.

"If they give us assurances that they will not let strikebreakers run the plant as soon as we get out and will not let the company move out stock, we will go out peacefully," said the leader of the group. "Otherwise, they'll have to take us out. That right, boys?"

A chorus of muttered assents came from a group of husky young strikers gathered around their leader near the dismantled final assembly line for Chevrolet bodies.

They showed various weapons, homemade blackjacks, clubs, door hinges, but denied that they had any machine guns or other firearms in the plant, as reported in the city. They said they had somewhat fewer than two hundred men in the plant now, a sizable reduction from the five to six hundred understood to have occupied the factory at the beginning of the sit-down strike two weeks ago.

[On January 15, 1937, announcement was made by Governor Frank Murphy: "We have arrived at a peace."] *

* * *

DETROIT, JANUARY 16 †—About 650

sit-in strikers marched out of the Fleetwood and Cadillac plants to the music of a band donated by the Detroit Musicians Union, affiliated with the American Federation of Labor.

While company guards and city police looked on, the strikers, marching at a double-quick pace, left through the gates that had been opened wide. They carried their lunch buckets and personal belongings. One or two had battered suitcases, others blankets, and one man carried a roll of newspapers of the last ten days which he apparently treasured.

At the gates the strikers embraced their wives and children while several hundred union associates cheered them enthusiastically. The strikers returned their cheers, waved their caps, and shouted greetings to their friends.

While a parade began to form, the band played union songs. The singing was led from a sound truck by Walter Reuther of the West Side local, the favorite appearing to be a union version of *Hinky-Dinky Parlez-Vous*, with this chorus:

> *The boss is shaking at the knees,*
> *Parlez-vous.*
> *The boss is shaking at the knees,*
> *Parlez-vous.*
> *The boss is shaking at the knees,*
> *He's shaking in his BVD's,*
> *Hinky-dinky parlez-vous.*

"Today it is General Motors, tomorrow Ford," said Leo Krycski, organizer for the CIO.

KRYCSKI WAS RIGHT, but bitter fighting lay ahead in the months to come before Ford capitulated. In May Walter Reuther and Richard Franken-

---

* The agreement between UAW and General Motors called for recognition of the former as the bargaining representative of its own members; the forty-hour week with time and-a-half overtime pay, and a promise that the speed-up system would be studied with a view to its modification.

† Louis Stark reporting.

stein, UAW officials, were beaten up when they sought to distribute leaflets at Ford's River Rouge plant. Some hundred and fifty men converged on them, they were ordered "to get the hell off of there," and when they attempted to withdraw were slugged and kicked down a flight of iron steps.

The sit-down had served its purpose. America's leading industrial giant had been forced to bargain collectively with labor. Not only in motors, but also in rubber, steel, textiles, oil refining, shipbuilding, and other trades some half million workers "sat down" in the ten months following September 1, 1936. In those days the strikers' favorite song was:

> *When they tie a can to a union man,*
> *Sit-down! Sit-down!*
> *When they give him the sack, they'll take him back,*
> *Sit-down! Sit-down!*
>
> *When the speed-up comes, just twiddle your thumbs,*
> *Sit-down! Sit-down!*
> *When the boss won't talk, don't take a walk,*
> *Sit-down! Sit-down!*

In 1939 the Supreme Court emphatically denounced the sit-down strike as "illegal." Following this decision, American labor ceased to resort to this technique of desperation.

The struggle of the CIO to organize the steel industry began in the summer of 1936. By February, 1937, the Steel Workers' Organizing Committee claimed 150,000 members, and in the spring of 1937 they scored an impressive victory—recognition by U. S. Steel as the bargaining agency of its own members, a wage boost of ten per cent, and a forty-hour work week with time and a half for overtime. But "Little Steel" was far less malleable, and, under the leadership of Republic Steel, was determined to fight the union to the bitter end. In fact, the struggle proved long and bloody. As early as May 27, 1935, Dwight L. Buchanan, star reporter of the Canton *Repository*, recounted an altercation that had taken place the previous day between company police and strikers at its Canton, Ohio, plant, resulting in the hospitalization of fourteen persons. According to Buchanan's account, heavily armed company police leaped from an armored truck and fired upon a crowd of persons lining the sidewalk, including women and children who had gathered to watch strikers stone autos emerging from the plant. Then company guards bombarded the street with tear-gas bombs.

Reinforcing Republic's terroristic tactics was an amazing espionage system. Spencer B. McCulloch, a reporter for the *St. Louis Post-Dispatch*, in a feature story on "Tom Girdler, Steel's No. 1 Strikebreaker," in the issue of June 29, 1937, charged that for ten years prior to 1925 Girdler ruled Aliquippa, Pennsylvania, a steel-plant center of thirty-one nationalities, with an iron hand and an all-seeing eye. Organizers, suspected organizers— in fact, anyone who didn't look right—were taken into custody, sometimes beaten, and put on the next train back to Pittsburgh. McCulloch further asserted: "An elaborate system of espionage permeated not only the plants but extended into the schools, churches, lodges, and even the homes. Nothing was too small to pass unnoticed. The most innocuous remark was apt to be carried to the boss, perhaps twisted in the telling." This type of private police system was later condemned by a Senate investigating committee as a threat to civil liberties as well as an impediment to collective bargaining.

Memorial Day Massacre: "We must do our duty"

The New York Times, May 31, 1937

4 KILLED, 84 HURT
AS STRIKERS FIGHT
POLICE IN CHICAGO

———

STREET MOB HALTED

———

1000 MARCHERS FAIL IN EFFORT TO
CLOSE REPUBLIC PLANT

CHICAGO, MAY 30—Four men were killed and eighty-four persons * went to hospitals with gunshot wounds, cracked heads, broken limbs, or other injuries received in a battle late this afternoon between police and steel strikers at the gates of the Republic Steel Corporation plant in South Chicago.

The clash occurred when about one thousand strikers tried to approach the Republic company's plant, the only mill of the three large independent steel manufacturers in this area attempting to continue production. About 22,000 steelworkers are on strike in the Chicago district.

The union demonstrators were armed with clubs, slingshots, cranks and gear-shift levers from cars, bricks,

steel bolts, and other missiles. Police charged that some of the men also carried firearms.

The riot grew out of a meeting held by steel-mill workers in protest against the action of police, who turned them back Friday night when they attempted to approach the Republic plant.

The march was organized at this meeting, held outside CIO headquarters at One Hundred and Thirteenth Street and Green Bay Avenue, three blocks from the plant. The strikers said they were going to march through the main gate entrance in an effort to force closing of the mill.

Heading the march were strikers from the Youngstown Sheet and Tube Company and Inland Steel Company plants in the Calumet district. They had been invited to the mass meeting and had volunteered to lead the march on the Republic, where about 1400 workers were said to be still on the job.

The union men chose a time when the police were changing shifts, hoping, the police said, to catch them dis-

* The next day's *Times* revised the casualty list to five killed and ninety persons hospitalized. Of the latter, twenty-nine strike demonstrators were wounded by gunfire and twenty-six policemen injured by missiles hurled by the strikers.

organized. But Captain James L. Mooney, Captain Thomas Kilroy, and Lieutenant Healy, expecting trouble, kept all their 160 men on hand.

Carrying banners and chanting "CIO, CIO," the strikers drew within a block and a half of the gate to find the police lined up awaiting them. Captain Kilroy stepped forward and asked the crowd to disperse.

"You can't get through here," he declared. "We must do our duty."

Jeers greeted his words. Then the demonstrators began hurling bricks, stones, and bolts.

The police replied with tear gas. The crowd fell back for a moment, choking, and then, the police say, began firing at the officers. The officers fired warning shots and, when, according to police, the strikers continued firing, they returned it.

Men began dropping on both sides. The strikers fell back before the police bullets and swinging police clubs.

Police wagons then raced onto the field and began picking up the injured. Some were taken to the Republic plant's emergency hospital, some to the South Chicago Hospital, and some to the Bridewell Hospital.

Most of the policemen who were injured were struck by steel bolts hurled by the strikers or shot from their slings.

By the Associated Press

CHICAGO, MAY 30—As a result of today's steel-strike battle thirty to forty of the strike crowd, some of them nursing gunshot wounds, were under arrest, but had not been booked on any specific charge.

Captain Mooney, who was in active charge of the police detail which halted the strikers, said his men received no order to draw their guns, but did so to protect themselves.

He declared that he and Captain Kilroy told the mob to disperse peaceably or its members would be arrested for unlawful assembly. The leaders of the march held a short conference, he added, and then ordered the sympathizers to press onward.

Immediately, the captain said, the crowd began to throw rocks, bolts, or anything handy, knocking down several officers. The officers tried to halt the front flank by using their riot sticks, he asserted, but one or two shots were fired by the sympathizers. He said he had the statements of twenty policemen to prove that the shots came from the mob.

"Our policemen drew their guns then," he went on, "without orders from anyone, because they were interested primarily in saving their own lives. They did not shoot into the crowd until several warning shots went unheeded." *

Dr. S. J. Nickamin, staff physician at the South Chicago Hospital, who was in the receiving room when the injured were brought in, declared they looked as if they came from a "*virtual massacre.*"

A. G. Patterson, financial secretary of Local 65 of the CIO in South Chicago, said he was on the scene of the riot because before the trouble he had been designated by the strikers as a Red Cross worker to treat those who might be hurt.

"Two leaders of the march were up ahead, carrying American flags," he said, "All were going along, and then the riot broke out spontaneously. Someone started to scuffle with a policeman. Then I heard several shots. Men and women were slugged all

---

* A corroborating statement by Captain Prendergast appeared in the *Chicago Daily News,* June 1, 1937.

around me. Police released tear gas. "I was blinded and fell in a heap with a bunch of others. I got up and saw the fellow next to me was shot in the stomach. I grabbed him, but the police took him away in a patrol wagon. The whole thing didn't last more than five or six minutes."

Pete Rimac, who runs a store on the edge of the field in which the fighting took place, said he watched the affray from a second-floor window.

"Between four hundred and five hundred shots were fired in about three minutes," he asserted. "The policemen had been lined up single file for about five blocks across the field when the marchers met them. When the crowd tried to press through, the officers closed around them and the riot broke out. I saw scores of men and women fall."

Frank A. Lauerman, superintendent of public relations for the Republic company, announced that the company planned to make no statement because the riot did not occur at the plant or on company property.

The New York Times, June 1, 1937

Joseph Hickey, one of the victims in the Burnside Hospital, who was cut and bruised on his head, told of the riot.

"I went to the meeting, and they decided to make a picket line at the front of the company," he said. "I went out with the rest of them and started to walk over to the plant. I was about one hundred yards behind the head of the line when the uproar began. They were like trapped rats, panic-stricken, terrified.

"I saw a woman fall as she was being clubbed by the policemen. She was bleeding and looked like she was dying. I ran over to help her and leaned down to pick her up, when the police hit me over the head. I was out after that."

Chicago Daily News, June 1, 1937

Peter Mrkonjich, who was shot in the left arm, also gave an account of the battle:

"After the meeting," he said, "we went out to form the picket line. I was walking along in the line when the shooting broke out about half a block away from me.

"Women, children, men, were running and falling and screaming like madmen. I turned and ran, too, but when I went just a few feet a bullet hit me in the arm. Some motorist picked me up and took me to the hospital."

A check today showed thirty-two persons still remained in hospitals.

* * *

THE *Chicago Daily News* of June 2 reported that twoscore of pickets appeared in Municipal Court "still in their stained clothing and bandages." They were freed on bond.

For four bitter years "Little Steel" continued to fight the CIO, until in 1941 almost all of the Independent steel companies capitulated and signed agreements with the union.

A. T. Steele of the *Chicago Daily News* Spends

Four Days of Hell in China

MERELY ANOTHER "China Incident," the Japanese called their large-scale military operations from 1931 to 1941 involving hundreds of thousands of soldiers. Defying the Stimson Doctrine (1931), which announced unequivocally that the United States would not recognize any change of political status in China brought about by force, Rising Sun militarists rushed ahead. As if to test the limits of American, Russian, British, and Chinese patience, they opened a new phase of conquest in 1937, issuing the implicit challenge: "Stop us if you dare!" Once again, without a declaration of war, they moved large forces into China, seized railways, highways, and key cities, slaughtered the Chinese who resisted, and then pressed on.

In the middle of December, 1937, the invaders reached Nanking. The Japanese assault on and capture of the city and the triumphant entry of their army was witnessed by A. T. Steele, of the *Chicago Daily News,* who reported that spectacle of butchery and confusion, of terror, panic, savagery, and suffering. For comparable acts of horror one would have to turn to the burning and sacking of Jerusalem by Nebuchadnezzar the Chaldean in 586 B.C., the destruction of Carthage by Scipio Aemilianus the Roman in 146 B.C., or the obliteration of Lidice in Czechoslovakia by Karl Hermann Frank the German in 1942. For the sons of Nippon, Nanking was a repeat performance—their previous record for bestiality, set at Port Arthur in 1894, had been recorded by James Creelman.* Steele, who was born in Toronto, got his start as a reporter on the *Boise Capital News,* was a correspondent in China for *The New York Times* and the Associated Press before joining the *Chicago Daily News,* and has since joined the staff of the *New York Herald Tribune*

The rape of Nanking

Chicago Daily News, December 15, 17, 18, 1937

NANKING (VIA THE USS *Oahu*), DECEMBER 15—"Four days in hell" would be the most fitting way to describe the siege and capture of Nanking.

I have just boarded the gunboat *Oahu* with the first group of foreigners to leave the capital since the attack began. The last thing we saw as we left the city was a band of three hun-

* See page 227.

dred Chinese being methodically executed before the wall near the water front, where already corpses were piled knee-deep.

It was a characteristic picture of the mad Nanking scene of the last few days.

The story of Nanking's fall is a story of indescribable panic and confusion among the entrapped Chinese defenders, followed by a reign of terror by the conquering army which cost thousands of lives, many of them innocent ones.

While the behavior of the Chinese before the city's abandonment was deplorable in many ways, it was mild compared to the excesses of the invading force.

All foreigners in Nanking are safe.

Japanese brutality at Nanking is costing them a golden opportunity to win the sympathy of the Chinese population, whose friendship they claim to be seeking.

After the complete collapse of Chinese morale and the blind panic which followed, Nanking experienced a distant sense of release when the Japanese entered, feeling that the behavior of the Japanese could not possibly be worse than that of their own defeated army. They were quickly disillusioned.

The Japanese could have completed the occupation of the remainder of the city almost without firing a shot, by offering mercy to the trapped Chinese soldiers, most of whom had discarded their arms and would surrender. However, they chose the course of systematic extermination.

It was like killing sheep. How many troops were trapped and killed it is difficult to estimate, but it may be anywhere between five thousand and twenty thousand.

With the overland routes cut off, the Chinese swarmed to the river through the Ksiakwan gate, which became quickly choked. Emerging via this gate today I found it necessary to drive my car over heaps of bodies five feet high, over which hundreds of Japanese trucks and guns had already passed.

Streets throughout the city were littered with the bodies of civilians and abandoned Chinese equipment and uniforms. Many troops who were unable to obtain boats across the river leaped into the river to almost certain death.

Japanese looting made the Chinese looting, which had preceded it, look like a Sunday-school picnic. They invaded foreign properties, among them the residence of the American ambassador, Nelson T. Johnson.

In the American-operated University Hospital they relieved the nurses of watches and money. They stole at least two American-owned cars, ripping off the flags. They even invaded the camps of refugees, stripping many poor of the few dollars they owned.

This account is based on the observations of myself and other foreigners remaining in Nanking throughout the siege.

I saw Chinese troops needlessly applying the torch to whole blocks of homes and shops around the city walls, dispossessing thousands in a futile attempt to impede the Japanese attack.

I saw a terrific two-day bombardment of Nanking's defenses, which finally softened and shattered Chinese resistance.

I heard the din of cannonading and machine-gunning accompanying the final Japanese assault on the strongly held south gate, where towering torches of flame lit up the battlefield.

Later I saw a scene of butchery outside that gate where the corpses of at least one thousand soldiers lie in every conceivable posture of death, amid a confusion of fallen telephone and power lines and charred ruins—apparently trapped by the closing of the gates.

I saw Chinese troops looting shop-windows, but later I saw the Japanese troops outdo them in a campaign of pillage which the Japanese carried out not only in the shops but in homes, hospitals, and refugee camps.

I saw Chinese multitudes beginning their retreat through the city's north gate, the only remaining exit. Then I saw that hurried but orderly withdrawal become a pell-mell rush and, finally, a milling panic as the last line of escape was cut off.

I saw hundreds of Chinese tear off their uniforms in the street, some donning civilian clothes, others running away in their underwear. Many came to me and to other foreigners, imploring protection and offering guns and money in exchange.

I saw fear-crazed troops attempt to force their entry into the headquarters of the international committee and, when refused, begin to toss guns, revolvers, and machine guns over the walls into the hands of the startled missionaries, who gingerly stowed them away for surrender to the Japanese.

These things, too, I saw:

A frightened soldier crawling under a German flag; hundreds of wounded crawling and limping through the streets, beseeching every passer-by for assistance; Japanese soldiers impressing coolies and donkeys into service to carry their loot; Japanese machine gunners moving through the streets in the moonlight, killing anyone who ran and some who did not; Japanese systematically searching houses and seizing many plain-clothes suspects, scores of these bound men

being shot one by one while their condemned fellows sat stolidly by, awaiting their turn.

I saw the Japanese beating and jabbing helpless civilians, and in the hospitals I saw many civilians suffering from bayonet wounds.

I saw the dead scattered along every street, including some old men who could not possibly have harmed anyone; also mounds of the bodies of executed men.

I saw a grisly mess at the north gate, where what once had been two hundred men was a smoldering mass of flesh and bones.

Outside the gate I saw rope ladders, strips of clothing and blankets hanging from the wall, where many escaped from the city after finding the gate choked, only to fall into a deadlier trap.

The safety zone created in the heart of fortified Nanking by the committee of foreigners was built on a foundation of colossal nerve, for from the first it was evident that neither side would respect it fully. Nevertheless, while a score of shells fell inside the zone and the area was occasionally sprayed by stray bullets and shrapnel, it was probably safer than other parts of the country.

The pathetic aspect of the picture was the way the Chinese of this once intensely nationalistic capital flocked to foreigners for protection. Ten years ago, when Generalissimo Chiang Kai-shek's nationalist army marched into Nanking, shouting antiforeign slogans, a display of the American flag would have been an invitation to death. Now thousands of Chinese would give anything short of their lives to get under the protection of a foreign flag.

For those four chaotic days between the collapse of the Chinese defense and the occupation of Nanking the Chinese population submitted themselves meekly and eagerly to the orders and suggestions of the few foreign missionaries and merchants running the international committee, which then was the sole administrative organ in the city.

Even trapped soldiers, hysterical with fear, besieged the committee headquarters with abject supplications for foreign protection against the approaching enemy.

It is noticeable that, despite the complete demoralization of the Chinese soldiery, they did not turn on the foreigners who would have been an easy prey for looting. The same cannot be said for the Japanese, who flouted foreign rights and repeatedly raided foreign properties plainly marked with embassy notices and flags.

All of us did some service in carrying wounded to the hospitals. The streets were full of them, and the piteous pleading for assistance was difficult to resist.

Hemingway and Matthews Watch Franco Conduct
a Dress Rehearsal for World War II

FOR ERNEST HEMINGWAY, the ten years he spent studying the ritual of bullfighting in a country he came to love deeply served him in good stead in reporting the more gory conflict that broke out on July 17, 1936, when Francisco Franco, an obese little Spanish general, led a rebellion against his government from Morocco. To Max Eastman, Hemingway's handling of gored matadors in his *Death in the Afternoon* bordered on the synthetic. "Bull in the Afternoon," Eastman called it. The enraged two-hundred-pound novelist then up and socked Max with the latter's *Enjoyment of Laughter*. For everyone, it was fun in the afternoon.

As a war reporter Hemingway had already won front rank for his masterly account of Caporetto in World War I. In *A Farewell to Arms* (1929), the best American novel of World War I, he had poignantly depicted one of the most memorable military panics in all history.

The dress rehearsal for World War II, the Spanish Civil War found the Nazis and Italian Fascists fighting beside the Insurgents, while liberal and leftist supporters from all over the world, including an elite nucleus of Communist leaders, backed the armed forces of the Spanish Republic. Ernest Hemingway was intensely active both in the recruiting of volunteers to fight Franco and in front-line reporting. But his coverage of the war for the North American Newspaper Alliance was merely one phase of his reportorial role. In Robert Jordon of *For Whom the Bell Tolls* (1940), he created a hero with a social purpose, "a feeling of consecration to a duty toward all the oppressed of the world." Jordan recognizes that there is injustice on both sides, but that only in the victory of his side is there hope for mankind. Jordan's readiness to lay down his life for the cause may well have been inspired by this story of Jay Raven, which Hemingway sent back from Madrid while hope of ultimate victory was still strong.

The author of For Whom the Bell Tolls
interviews a countryman from Pennsylvania,
"where once we fought at Gettysburg"

The New York Times, April 25, 1937. Reprinted by permission of the North American Newspaper Alliance, Inc., and Ernest Hemingway.

MADRID, APRIL 24—The window of the hotel is open and, as you lie in bed, you hear the firing in the front line seventeen blocks away. There is a rifle fire all night long. The rifles go "tacrong, carong, craang, tacrong," and then a machine gun opens up. It has a bigger caliber and is much louder— "rong, cararibg, rong, rong."

Then there is the incoming boom of a trench-mortar shell and a burst of machine-gun fire. You lie and listen to it, and it is a great thing to be in a bed with your feet stretched out gradually warming the cold foot of the bed and not out there in University City or Carabanchel. A man is singing hard-voiced in the street below and three drunks are arguing when you fall asleep.

In the morning, before your call comes from the desk, the roaring burst of a high-explosive shell wakes you. You go to the window and look out to see a man, his head down, his coat collar up, sprinting desperately across the paved square. There is the acrid smell of high explosive you hoped you'd never smell again.

In a bathrobe and bathroom slippers, you hurry down to the marble stairs and almost into a middle-aged woman, wounded in the abdomen, who is being helped into the hotel entrance by two men in blue workmen's smocks.

On the corner, twenty yards away, is a heap of rubble, smashed cement, and thrown-up dirt, a single dead man, his torn clothes dusty, and a great hole in the sidewalk from which the gas from a broken main is rising, looking like a heat mirage in the cold morning air.

"How many dead?" you ask a policeman.

"Only one," he says. "It went through the sidewalk and burst below. If it had burst on the solid stone of the road there might have been fifty."

A policeman covers the body; they send for someone to repair the gas main, and you go in to breakfast. A charwoman, her eyes red, is scrubbing the blood off the marble floor of the corridor. The dead man wasn't you nor anyone you know, and everyone is very hungry in the morning after a cold night and a long day the day before up at the Guadalajara front.

"Did you see him?" asked someone else at breakfast.

"Sure," you say.

"That's where we pass a dozen times a day—right on that corner." But everyone has the feeling that characterizes war. It wasn't me, see? It wasn't me.

The Italian dead up on the Guadalajara weren't you, although Italian dead, because of where you had spent your boyhood, always seemed, still, like our dead. No. You went to the front early in the morning in a miserable little car with a more miserable little chauffeur who suffered visibly the closer he came up to the fighting. But at night, sometimes late, without lights, with the big trucks roaring past, you came on back to sleep in a bed with sheets in a good hotel, paying a dollar a day for the best rooms on the front.

The smaller rooms in the back, on the side away from the shelling, were considerably more expensive. After the shell that lighted on the sidewalk in front of the hotel, you got a beautiful double corner room on that side, twice the size of the one you had had, for less than a dollar. It wasn't me they killed. See? No. Not me. It wasn't me any more.

Then, in a hospital given by the American Friends of Spanish Democracy, located out behind the Morata front along the road to Valencia, they said, "Raven wants to see you."

"Do I know him?"

"I don't think so," they s
he wants to see you."

"Where is he?"

"Upstairs."

In the room upstairs they were giving a blood transfusion to a man with a very gray face who lay on a cot with his arm out, looking away from the gurgling bottle and moaning in a very impersonal way. He moaned mechanically and at regular intervals, and it did not seem to be he that made the sound. His lips did not move.

"Where's Raven?" I asked.

"I'm here," said Raven.

The voice came from a high mound covered by a shoddy gray blanket. There were two arms crossed on the top of the mound with a wide blanket across the eyes.

"Who is it?" asked Raven.

"Hemingway," I said. "I came up to see how you were doing."

"My face was pretty bad," he said. "It got sort of burned from the grenade, but it's peeled a couple of times and it's doing better."

"It looks swell," I said. "It's doing fine."

I wasn't looking at it when I spoke.

"How are things in America?" he asked. "What do they think of us over there?"

"Sentiment's changed a lot," I said. "They're beginning to realize the government is going to win the war."

"Do you think so?"

"Sure," I said.

"I'm awfully glad," he said. "You know, I wouldn't mind any of this if I could just watch what was going on. I don't mind the pain, you know. It never seemed important really. But I was always awfully interested in things and I really wouldn't mind the pain at all if I could just sort of follow things intelligently. I could even be of some use. You know, I didn't mind the war at all. I did all right in the war. I got hit once before and I was back and rejoined the battalion in two weeks. I couldn't stand to be put away. Then I got this."

He had put his hand in mine. It was not a worker's hand. There were no calluses and the nails on the long, spatulate fingers were smooth and rounded.

"How did you get it?" I asked.

"Well, there were some troops that were routed and we went over to sort of re-form them, and we did; and then we had quite a fight with the Fascists, and we beat them. It was quite a bad fight, you know, but we beat them and then someone threw this grenade at me."

Holding his hand and hearing him tell it, I did not believe a word of it. What was left of him did not sound like the wreckage of a soldier, somehow. I did not know how he had been wounded, but the story did not sound right. It was the sort of way everyone would like to have been wounded. But I wanted him to think I believed it.

"Where did you come from?" I asked.

"From Pittsburgh. I went to the university there."

"What did you do before you joined up here?"

"I was a social worker," he said.

Then I knew it couldn't be true, and I wondered how he had really been so frightfully wounded; and I didn't care. In the war that I had known, men often lied about the manner of their wounding. Not at first; but later. I'd lied a little myself in my time, especially late in the evening. But I was glad he thought I believed it, and we talked about books. He wanted to be a writer, and I told him about what had happened north of Guadalajara and promised to bring some things from Madrid next time we got out that way. I hoped maybe I could get a radio.

"They tell me John Dos Passos and

Sinclair Lewis are coming over, too," he said.

"Yes," I said. "And when they come I'll bring them up to see you."

"Gee, that will be great," he said. "You don't know what that will mean to me."

"I'll bring them," I said.

"Will they be here pretty soon?"

"Just as soon as they come I'll bring them."

"Good boy, Ernest," he said. "You don't mind if I call you Ernest, do you?"

The voice came very clear and gentle.

"Hell, no," I said. "Please. Listen, old-timer, you're going to be fine. You'll be a lot of good, you know. You can talk on the radio."

"Maybe," he said. "You'll be back?"

"Sure," I said. "Absolutely."

"Good-bye, Ernest," he said.

"Good-bye," I told him.

Downstairs they told me he'd lost both eyes and was also badly wounded all through the legs and in the feet.

"He's lost some toes, too," the doctor said, "but he doesn't know that."

"I wonder if he'll ever know it."

"Oh, sure he will," the doctor said. "He's going to get well."

And it still isn't you that gets hit, but it is your countryman now. Your countryman from Pennsylvania, where once we fought at Gettysburg.

Then, walking along the road, with his left arm in an airplane splint, walking with the gamecock walk of the professional British soldier that neither ten years of militant party work nor the projecting metal wings of the splint could destroy, I met Raven's commanding officer, Jock Cunningham, who had three fresh rifle wounds through his upper left arm (I looked at them, one was septic) and another

rifle bullet under his shoulder blade that had entered his left chest, passed through, and lodged there.

He told me, in military terms, the history of the attempt to rally retiring troops on his battalion's right flank, of his bombing raid down a trench which was held at one end by the Fascists and at the other end by the government troops, of the taking of this trench and, with six men and a Lewis gun, cutting off a group of some eighty Fascists from their own lines, and of the final desperate defense of their impossible position his six men put up until the government troops came up and, attacking, straightened out the line again.

He told it clearly, completely convincingly, and with a strong Glasgow accent. He had deep, piercing eyes, sheltered like an eagle's; and, hearing him talk, you could tell the sort of soldier he was. For what he had done he would have had a VC in the last war. In this war there are no decorations. Wounds are the only decorations, and they don't award wound stripes.

"Raven was in the same show," he said. "I didn't know he'd been hit. Ay, he's a good mon. He got his after I got mine. The Fascists we'd cut off were very good troops. They never fired a useless shot when we were in that bad spot. They waited in the dark there until they had us located and then opened with volley fire. That's how I got four in the same place."

We talked for a while, and he told me many things. They were all important, but nothing was as important as that what Jay Raven, the social worker from Pittsburgh with no military training, had told me was true. This is a strange new kind of war where you learn just as much as you are able to believe.

* * *

"THERE ARE FOUR COLUMNS converging on the city and a fifth waits within," the Insurgent General Mola frankly boasted in a radio address. To be in Madrid under siege was a terrifying experience. Herbert L. Matthews, *New York Times* correspondent, reported on October 13, 1937, how, as a motion-picture theater across the square from his hotel began to empty, a six-inch high-explosive shell came screaming down to kill and maim several in the crowd and "start another of those terrific night bombardments"—six hundred shells in all crashing into the center of the city that night. His car was standing directly in front of the building, "the most vulnerable spot in the city. Ernest Hemingway and I dashed down to see if we could move the car to safety, but the square was an inferno." As it turned out, the car was not even scratched. "Everyone feels the great day is coming soon and these shells are harbingers of what the near future holds in store for this city," Matthews commented.

As the pace of the Fascist air raids was stepped up, Barcelona was singled out for cruel and unusual punishment.

Barcelona bombing leaves Herbert L. Matthews dazed: "I have never seen so many weeping women"

The New York Times, March 18, 1938

BARCELONA, MARCH 17—Barcelona has lived through twelve air raids in less than twenty-four hours, and the city is shaken and terror-struck. Human beings have seldom had to suffer as these people are suffering under General Francisco Franco's determined effort to break their spirit and induce their government to yield.

I have just come back from the principal morgue, which is at the Clinical Hospital, and there I counted 328 dead lying side by side. Those were more or less whole bodies. Then there are the others in hospitals and, above all, those who lie in the ruins of dozens of buildings and whose bodies never will be recovered.

The destruction is in one sense haphazard, for the bombs are dropped anywhere at all, without any attempt at specific objectives. However, there is an obvious plan, that every part of the city, from the richest to the poorest, shall get its full measure of tragedy.

Spaniards are meeting this trial—and it is the greatest that their people have had to bear in the whole war—with the stoicism and the dignity of their race, but they are only human, and this is terribly hard to bear. Foreigners are deserting their hotels for the frontier as fast as they can get conveyance, for there is a genuine sense of impending disaster here among those who have escaped so far.

One sees such occurrences as a British newspaperman giving his wife some money in case "something silly happens." A chambermaid said to me this morning:

"We are all going to be killed—all."

A clerk at a drugstore sighed as he handed over some headache medicine. "Oh, for a plane to fly to France," he said. "I don't want to die."

7:40, 10:25, 1:55—those were tragic moments during the day. It was not necessary to send many planes each time. Fearful damage done in the last-mentioned raid required only five heavy bombers.

The account of what happened today is an unmitigated succession of horrors, and one feels helpless trying to convey the horror of all this in cold print, which people read and throw away.

One comes back from the scenes dazed: men, women, and children buried alive, screaming in the wreckage of their houses like trapped animals. *I have never seen so many weeping women.*

This bombing is meant to strike terror, demoralize the rear guard, and weaken resistance, because human beings are not built to withstand such horror. It is true they are stricken by terror, all right—terror that freezes the blood and makes one either hysterical or on the verge of hysteria. But then, too, one would not be human if it did not cause rage—deep, burning rage. These people would like to return the compliment.

A tram was wrecked and everyone in it killed or wounded. A truck was still burning, and something black that had been a human being had just been taken out. And there was the noise—ambulances dashing up with whistles blowing, women screaming and struggling hysterically, men shouting. Up the block a house was burning fiercely.

And all around, everywhere we went, were wrecked houses, dead and wounded, and those intangibles of fear, horror, and fury.

I watched them take two wounded persons from a building in the first bombing this morning. Both had been completely buried. A woman was screaming so weakly that we thought she was a child until they extricated her limp body. She seemed dead then, but they rushed her away to a hospital.

The other was a fifteen-year-old boy. By some miracle he had not been crushed, although I could see from his hair down to his bare feet he had been completely buried. His body did not seem to be hurt, but something else was, for he could not control his muscles—the twitching of his face or shuddering.

There are those freakish things which happen to intensify the horror. There is that house where nothing remains on the fifth floor except some clothes hanging on a rack. In another place a corner of the kitchen has somehow escaped, and we could see that the housewife had not had time to wash the dishes. Once a funeral passed along a street where bombs had fallen. There could have been no fitter symbol.

But life must go on. They have been repairing car tracks and clearing wreckage. After each raid they do it. Then they wait for the next.

It is surely the most savage and most ruthless punishment any modern city has taken.

The raid at 1:55 this afternoon left Barcelona shaking under the strain.

The writer was in a restaurant, eating lunch. All of us got up hastily to dash toward the back as the building shook, and I watched in amazement as the windows bent inward under the strain without breaking.

One takes what humor one can out

of this tragedy; otherwise it would be hard to remain sane. For my own part I did not find it amusing to see a great hulking fellow who was eating with his girl jump up and beat her to the kitchen by three strides. Another thing, at which everybody laughs ruefully today, is the way everybody jumps at any unusual noise—the horns of cars that sound sirenlike, the banging of doors, the roar of automobile motors. I even saw a cat jump as if it had an electric shock when a shopkeeper suddenly lowered his blinds.

There is one remark I heard this afternoon that sticks, for it was not said in jest:

"It may not be the end of the war, but it feels like the end of the world!"

* * *

JUST ONE MONTH LATER, with disaster mounting, Hemingway reported the fighting on the Lérida front. "Sometimes in war there is a deadliness," he observed, "which makes all walking upright within a certain range either foolishness or bravado. But there are other times, before things really start, when it's like the old days when you walked around in the bull ring just before the fight." To Hemingway this feeling of danger "was something as valid as the dust you breathed or the rain that settled the dust finally and beat on your face in the open car." Reporting that shells were coming in close, he concluded, "as the smoke blew away ahead and settled through the trees, you picked an armful of spring onions from a field beside the trail that led to the main Tortosa road. They were the first onions of this spring and, peeling, one found they were plump and white and not too strong. The Ebro Delta has a fine rich land, and where the onions grow, tomorrow there will be a battle."

With battle came defeat. By the following spring the Loyalists had lost Barcelona. Ill-equipped, deserted by the Western democracies, they gave up in March, 1939.

For Matthews the Spanish Civil War was a lesson in political realism. On an earlier assignment he had watched Italian bombers and Black Shirts cut the Negus' forces in Ethiopia to pieces. He had come out of the campaign with the Italian War Cross and an indistinct conception of what Fascism meant. "The right or wrong of it did not interest me greatly." In Spain he changed his mind. What he saw convinced him beyond the shadow of a doubt that Fascism was the negation of human decency.

Bob Considine Sees a Pregnant Package of Coiled Venom Cut a Nazi Superman Down to Size

JOE LOUIS, the young Negro pugilistic sensation from Detroit, proved to be an expert in calculated slaughter. With a shuffling style and the fastest pair of hands of any heavyweight, he struck like a coiled rattler, and with effects about as deadly. On the evening of September 24, 1935, while 84,831 fans roared themselves hoarse at the Yankee Stadium, the Brown Bomber, now champion of the world, battered Max Baer into a bloody hulk. Dan Parker, sports columnist of the New York *Daily Mirror,* described the end of that bout:

> One sensed that the finish was imminent as the bell called the gladiators out for the fourth. Louis was as fresh as the charming bride he had wed that afternoon. Max was cut up, weary, and heavy of limb. Joe knew he had his man ready for the kill and took his time about it. He started off with more left jabs to the head.
>
> Louis jabbed Max into position with four lefts and then crossed his right. It landed flush on Baer's chin, and he dropped to one knee. Livermore's Loud-Speaker * was as quiet as a church mouse. He had had enough, and faded out of the pugilistic picture doing an Al Jolson. It would have been poetic justice if, as he knelt on one knee, he had cried: "Mammy!"

Joe Louis seemed to be unbeatable. Then came one of the greatest upsets in the annals of pugilism—on the night of June 19, 1936, Max Schmeling, the Black Uhlan of the Rhine, knocked out the Negro wonder in the twelfth round. Louis had gone into the ring a ten-to-one favorite, and the sports writers had referred to the beetle-browed German as "the condemned man." After the bout Damon Runyon soliloquized: "Louis is young. This thing tonight may be the thing needed to teach him that you can't take anything for granted in pugilism. He will be back again, because he is a great fighter." "He jes' whipped me, Ma," was the Brown Bomber's laconic comment.

Louis was indeed back again on the night of June 22, 1938. What happened in the ring that night when he faced the apostle of Aryan supremacy was recorded for posterity by Bob Considine of INS. Considine started his career in Washington, quickly rising from lowly messenger in the U. S. Treasury Department to special-feature writer for the *Washington Post,* and then sports editor of the *Washington Herald.* Since then he has become one of the most widely read syndicated sports columnists for INS, best known, perhaps, as Babe Ruth's official biographer.

---

* A resident of Livermore, California, Max Baer, to put it very mildly, was inclined to be loquacious upon all subjects, including his own fighting ability.

The Louis-Schmeling fight

International News Service, June 22, 1938

Listen to this, buddy, for it comes from a guy whose palms are still wet, whose throat is still dry, and whose jaw is still agape from the utter shock of watching Joe Louis knock out Max Schmeling.

It was a shocking thing, that knockout—short, sharp, merciless, complete. Louis was like this:

He was a big lean copper spring, tightened and retightened through weeks of training until he was one pregnant package of coiled venom.

Schmeling hit that spring. He hit it with a whistling right-hand punch in the first minute of the fight—and the spring, tormented with tension, suddenly burst with one brazen spang of activity. Hard brown arms, propelling two unerring fists, blurred beneath the hot white candelabra of the ring lights. And Schmeling was in the path of them, a man caught and mangled in the whirring claws of a mad and feverish machine.

The mob, biggest and most prosperous ever to see a fight in a ball yard, knew that here was the end before the thing had really started. It knew, so it stood up and howled one long shriek. People who had paid as much as $100 for their chairs didn't use them—except perhaps to stand on, the better to let the sight burn forever in their memories.

There were four steps to Schmeling's knockout. A few seconds after he landed his only punch of the fight, Louis caught him with a lethal little left hook that drove him into the ropes so that his right arm was hooked over the top strand, like a drunk hanging to a fence. Louis swarmed over him and hit with everything he had—until Referee Donovan pushed him away and counted one.

Schmeling staggered away from the ropes, dazed and sick. He looked drunkenly toward his corner, and before he had turned his head back Louis was on him again, first with a left and then that awe-provoking right that made a crunching sound when it hit the German's jaw. Max fell down, hurt and giddy, for a count of three.

He clawed his way up as if the night air were as thick as black water, and Louis—his nostrils like the mouth of a double-barreled shotgun—took a quiet lead and let him have both barrels.

Max fell almost lightly, bereft of his senses, his fingers touching the canvas like a comical stew-bum doing his morning exercises, knees bent and the tongue lolling in his head.

He got up long enough to be knocked down again, this time with his dark unshaven face pushed in the sharp gravel of the resin.

Louis jumped away lightly, a bright and pleased look in his eyes, and as he did the white towel of surrender which Louis' handlers had refused to use two years ago tonight came sailing into the ring in a soggy mess. It was thrown by Max Machon, oblivious to the fact that fights cannot end this way in New York.

The referee snatched it off the floor and flung it backwards. It hit the ropes and hung there, limp as Schmeling. Donovan counted up to five over Max, sensed the futility of it all, and stopped the fight.

The big crowd began to rustle restlessly toward the exits, many only now accepting Louis as champion of the world. There were no eyes for Schmeling, sprawled on his stool in his corner.

He got up eventually, his dirty gray-and-black robe over his shoulders, and wormed through the happy little crowd that hovered around Louis. And he put his arm around the Negro and smiled. They both smiled and could afford to—for Louis had made around $200,000 a minute and Schmeling $100,000 a minute.

But once he crawled down in the belly of the big stadium, Schmeling realized the implications of his defeat. He, who won the title on a partly phony foul, and beat Louis two years ago with the aid of a crushing punch after the bell had sounded, now said Louis had fouled him. That would read better in Germany, whence earlier in the day had come a cable from Hitler, calling on him to win.

It was a low, sneaking trick, but a rather typical last word from Schmeling.

* * *

ANOTHER YEAR. Another night. The Dark Destroyer fought his first farewell fight, trying vainly for ten somnolent rounds to catch up with Jersey Joe Walcott, his wraithlike and shadowy foe. Suddenly Walcott got fancy once too often. As *The New York Times* sports reporter, Arthur Daley, commented, "He zigged when he should have zagged." A paralyzing Louis right, and it was curtains for Jersey Joe!

A Foreign Correspondent, G. E. R. Gedye,

Reports the Convulsive Weeping of a People

Condemned to Serfdom

IN 1938 THE CROOKED CROSS of Nazidom snuffed out the life of two small nations. Eugene Lennhoff, onetime editor of the Vienna *Telegraph,* described the tension of those last five hours before Schuschnigg took to the air to announce that Austria had capitulated to Hitler. "We are yielding to force," the Austrian Chancellor proclaimed. "And so I take my leave of the Austrian people with a heartfelt wish: 'God save Austria!'" But God did not save Austria, although mass murder was avoided.

Only a few months before, at Prague, at the palace of the Hradschin, high up on the cliffs overlooking the Moldau, a British newsman, George E. R. Gedye, was ushered into the office of President Beneš of the Czechoslovak Republic. In a confidential interview Beneš struck a cheerful note:

I've seen you many times in the last ten years, Mr. Gedye. You have put before me so many problems. You have laughed at my optimism sometimes. And now look back —was I not right? You asked me, would the Hungarians move against us? What would we do if the Hapsburgs were restored? Where would we stand when the Little Entente collapsed? How could we go on if France dropped us? How could we face a German invasion? And each time I told you, *"Rest assured—nothing will happen. Just exactly nothing."* And I told you why. Well, was I not right? Has anything happened? Yes, I'm an optimist, a reasoned optimist—a reasonable optimist. And I tell you again today, when the world's press is uttering jeremiads again about Czechoslovakia, the same thing that I have told you before—*nothing will happen.* We have taken the necessary measures, and we have taken care that it is known. Let the cares of Central Europe slip quite easily off your shoulders, my poor, worried friend. Nothing will happen.

Mr. Beneš reckoned without Hitler and Henlein, the latter an obscure teacher from the Sudetenland, chosen to act as pathbreaker for the Nazi juggernaut. Henlein, charging "atrocities against Germans," stirred the German minority in Czechoslovakia into a state of frenzy, and demanded the return of the Sudetenland to the *Vaterland* in the name of "racial justice."

To these demands British Prime Minister Neville Chamberlain was strangely obsequious. Determined to avoid war at all costs, the British apostle of appeasement made a series of peace pilgrimages to Hitler, excursions that turned out to be exercises in humiliation. On September 29, 1938, the representatives of Germany, Italy, Great Britain, and France met at

Munich and sold Czechoslovakia down the river. To Chamberlain Munich spelled "peace in our time."

George E. R. Gedye, the same capable British newsman who had been assured by President Beneš that "nothing will happen," was present in Prague on September 21, 1938, when, what Vincent Sheean condemned as "the cowardly, treacherous, and unnecessary sacrifice" of Czechoslovakia to Hitler's appetite first became apparent to the Czech people. Beginning his career as a clerk, Gedye later turned to free-lance journalism and then worked for the London *Times, Daily Express,* and *Telegraph.* By 1929, when he became Central European correspondent of *The New York Times,* he had earned a world-wide reputation as an expertly informed reporter. In 1939, a year after writing this dispatch, he was forced to flee the Czechoslovak Republic to avoid arrest under a Gestapo warrant. In *Betrayal in Central Europe* (1939) Gedye told the whole story of the Munich incident, one of the great double crosses of twentieth-century diplomacy.

Crooked cross and double cross

The New York Times, September 22, 1938

PRAGUE, CZECHOSLOVAKIA, THURSDAY, SEPTEMBER 22—Last night at 7:30, after twenty-four hours of agonizing pressure, the Czechoslovak people learned that their state had been wrecked—just twenty years after it had been created—by those who brought it into existence, Great Britain and France.

A communiqué issued by the government announced that it had agreed to cede Sudeten German territory to the Reich. It declared Britain and France had insisted that "only by territorial sacrifice on our part could security and peace be assured.

"They informed us that they could not extend aid in the event we were attacked by Germany and they were of the opinion such a conflict would have been inevitable had Czechoslovakia refused to cede the territories of the German population," the com-

muniqué said, adding that the government had had no alternative but to accept.

Despite the censorship that was being applied—not, as had been expected, to protect the state from an external enemy during a war but to protect the government while it was agreeing to the final surrender—people had begun in the afternoon to suspect what was happening.

Even before the news got out in detail, demonstrations started that at first were quiet and full of pathos. By ten o'clock last night the capital bore the aspect of a city in the full swing not so much of a revolution as of a great national regeneration.

It was above all a furious demonstration against the government and one of trust in President Eduard Beneš and the army, although there were a number of Communist clenched fists raised and a few isolated Fascist threats against the President.

The demonstrations began spontaneously and the first ones were made with moving and touching dignity. They were carried out in front of cafés and hotels, and each demonstration ended with the singing of the national anthem while all heads were bared. The police, who were present in force, far from interfering, stood at salute as the national anthem was sung.

Many of the demonstrators, both men and women, wept unashamedly. More than one police officer standing near this correspondent was seen to pass his sleeves across his eyes.

On the sidewalks stood sad and red-eyed onlookers, watching the masses who marched, carrying the national colors, without any noticeable distinction of class or age. It was an unforgettable spectacle of a nation stricken down in peacetime, moved with great sorrow and vast anger.

On one street corner a news dealer told the writer:

"I have no London newspapers for sale tonight. The entire stock was bought up instantly after the news came out by a man who paid fifteen crowns each for them, tore them to shreds, ground them with his heel, spat on them, and turned away weeping."

In Prague it is estimated several hundred thousand persons took part in the demonstrations against the government and against capitulation.

Masses singing the national anthem and shouting for the commander-in-chief of the army, General Jan Syrovy, made their way down the Vaclavske Namesti to the Karel Bridge and swept across it, winding their way uphill toward the Hradschin Palace.

Halfway up they were confronted by strong detachments of mounted and foot police. The procession was headed by an automobile containing men displaying the national flag, and as they caught sight of it all the police sprang to attention, saluted, and fraternized with the crowd, allowing it to sweep on and offering no obstacle.

Arriving at the Hradschin gates, the crowd halted. Moving speeches were made by several impromptu speakers, the burden of which was trust in President Beneš and such phrases as "We have been betrayed by our allies and by cowards within our own camp." "Away with the cowardly government!" "No capitulation!" and "We will defend our republic at the side of our own army."

In many factories on the outskirts of the city workers downed their tools before the end of the working day and marched into the city to take part in the demonstrations.

There was one dramatic moment when the crowds on the Vaclavske Namesti heard a voice from a loudspeaker—which had just been voicing government warnings against joining demonstrations—declaiming furiously against the government and calling for a stouthearted defense of the republic. After some minutes the voice stopped abruptly in the middle of a sentence.

The explanation was that part of the crowd had forced its way into the broadcasting center and one man had got before the microphone to voice public sentiment before someone had thought of cutting off the current.

Similar spontaneous demonstrations in which all party distinctions vanished occurred in Ostrau, Pilsen, Olmütz, and hundreds of other towns and villages.

The crowds showed particular enthusiasm in demonstrating outside barracks. In Prague officers and soldiers were carried on the crowds' shoulders.

In Brno, an industrial area, German democratic elements joined with the Czechs in demonstrations with the slogan: "No surrender! We will defend ourselves to the last against the Nazi invaders. Away with the government of capitulators!"

More than 100,000 copies of a leaflet calling on the citizens of the republic to hold fast and defend their frontiers were circulated here last night, signed by eighty-five influential parliamentarians of all parties, secretaries of trade-unions, and leaders of cultural and economic bodies.

Together with the leaflets was issued an appeal to President Beneš urging him to use his authority "against the enemies within our ranks." The appeal asked the President to come forward, relying on the full support of the whole nation, which trusted in him, and to take the direction of affairs into his own hands.

"We know," the appeal said, "that you stand firm still—as firm as our army by its guns on the fortifications. Draw your support from the whole nation, which will never capitulate."

The leaflet, addressed to "our fellow citizens," began:

"The die is not yet cast. Czechoslovak democracy has not capitulated. A people does not capitulate. The government is not the nation.

"We have not yet lost one single rifle, one single gun, one airplane, or any of our fortifications. On the contrary, in the new unity of the whole people and its determination not to yield to the Nazis we have gained tremendous strength.

"Away with the enemies of the republic and the friends of the Nazis! The democrats of the world will stand by those who fight for their own, for

truth and justice. Let us show the world our readiness to defend ourselves.

"Parliament alone has the right to decide the republic's fate. We demand the immediate assembling of Parliament, which will reject the capitulation.

"Long live the Czechoslovak Republic, its loyal army and its first commander-in-chief, President Beneš! Firm stands the President, firm stands the army, and firm stands the nation!"

The dramatic and tragic events leading up to last night's tremendous demonstrations began with the demand at midnight Tuesday by the British and French Ministers here that President Beneš give them an audience immediately.

Apparently someone had blundered in handling the Czech reply to the Anglo-French demands for the acceptance of the London plan. It was to have been sent to London and Paris in code for transmission to the respective governments yesterday morning. Someone, however, allowed the document—which in essence was a polite refusal of the plan—to be handed in clear language to the two Ministers, who immediately telephoned its contents to their respective capitals and received instructions to reject the note and renew the pressure.

At 2:15 A.M. President Beneš received the Ministers, who handed him a note couched in extremely harsh terms insisting that there must be full and immediate surrender to the London plan, which involved the republic's dismemberment and the loss of its frontiers that for more than a thousand years have marked the historic provinces in which Czechs and Germans have lived side by side. The British and French insistence that they should be torn apart in accordance with Chancellor Adolf Hitler's will was inexorable.

As the Cabinet's deliberations went on throughout the night there were calls from the two legations at intervals of something like an hour to know whether the business was not yet finished.

At four A.M. the committee of the Cabinet's political ministers met under Dr. Beneš' presidency in the Hradschin Palace. At six there was a full Cabinet meeting. President Beneš declined to exercise his privilege of attending it.

Premier Milan Hodža had to tell his ministers that the British and French diplomats had informed him that the country was now faced with a united front of Germany, Hungary, and Poland and that unless its surrender was immediate and complete an invasion by all three armies would begin either yesterday or today.

Nobody, the Premier was told, would lift a finger to save Czechoslovakia, and she would disappear from the map entirely under complete partition.

The Cabinet ministers gloomily studied their maps, which showed them a country entirely surrounded by enemies save for a short strip bordering on Rumania. Hungary's enmity was of no particular consequence, it was felt, but Poland's was fatal.

Soon after nine o'clock yesterday morning the Cabinet Council decided to surrender.

* * *

ALSO PRESENT IN PRAGUE on that memorable night when the meaning of Munich finally seeped into the consciousness of the Czech people was a gifted American journalist, Vincent Sheean, whose news sense had many times brought him to the right spot at the right time. In his book *Not Peace But a Sword* (1939) Sheean told how he had been out in the Sudetenland all day, returning to Prague just after the loud-speakers had delivered the message of capitulation. On the crowded streets in the center of the city he saw women weeping convulsively, men with set, silent faces, boys standing in groups singing:

For a moment it seemed as if the population of Prague had merely turned out into the street, stunned and grief-stricken, for lack of anything better to do. The blow was so crushing that the bewildered people could not realize it all at once. They moved aimlessly, here and there, without direction, most often without speaking. . . . Never have I seen an assembly of people so instinctively moved to grief. . . .

Many thousands of people were weeping all through the night. I even saw a policeman in tears. A less belligerent or revolutionary mass demonstration has never taken place, and yet it was reported in the German press and wireless that night and the next day as a "Red Riot in Prague." Those who witnessed it, in whole or in part, know that it was a truly spontaneous expression of the grief of a people; in years of experience in such matters I have never seen anything like it. . . .

All night the people marched, sang, and wept, with those occasional chords from the loud-speaker sounding over their misery. At three o'clock in the morning, when I went to bed, there was some diminution in numbers, but the demonstration was still going on. It was still going on the next morning at a quarter to ten, when I got up.

Three different British correspondents, at different moments on that evening, congratulated Sheean bitterly on being an American, an eloquent testimony to their sense of shame at the dismemberment and annihilation of Czechoslovakia.

When in September, 1948, Beneš died, some seven months after accepting a Communist government to avert civil war, Anne O'Hare McCormick commented in *The New York Times:* "What happened to him at Munich happened twice. . . . The final decision was implicit in the first. Munich was the beginning of the tragedy that is not yet played out, and Czechoslovakia stands at the heart of it, victim of so many greater mistakes than her own."

A Philadelphia Reporter Beholds the Weirdest
Exhibition of Mass Hysteria in American History

At EIGHT P.M. Eastern standard time on the evening of October 31, 1938, Orson Welles and a little group of actors who called themselves the Mercury Theater on the Air appeared before the microphone in a New York studio of the Columbia Broadcasting System. The radio actors presented a freely adapted version of H. G. Wells' imaginative novel, *The War of the Worlds* (1898). The idea was to present an old-fashioned story appropriate for Halloween, but the script was devilishly realistic, as indicated by a few brief excerpts from the broadcast:

ANNOUNCER TWO: Ladies and gentlemen, I have a grave announcement to make. Incredible as it may seem, both the observations of science and the evidence of our eyes lead to the inescapable assumption that those strange beings who landed in the Jersey farmlands tonight are the vanguard of an invading army from the planet Mars. The battle which took place tonight at Grovers Mill has ended in one of the most startling defeats ever suffered by an army in modern times; seven thousand men armed with rifles and machine guns pitted against a single fighting machine of the invaders from Mars. One hundred and twenty known survivors. The rest strewn over the battle area from Grovers Mill to Plainsboro, crushed and trampled to death under the metal feet of the monster. . . .

THE SECRETARY OF THE INTERIOR: Citizens of the nation: I shall not try to conceal the gravity of the situation that confronts the country, nor the concern of your government in protecting the lives and property of its people. . . .

ANNOUNCER: I'm speaking from the roof of the Broadcasting Building, New York City. The bells you hear are ringing to warn the people to evacuate the city as the Martians approach. . . . Streets are all jammed. Noise in crowds like New Year's Eve in city. Wait a minute. . . . Enemy now in sight above the Palisades. Five great machines. First one is crossing a river. I can see it from here, wading in the Hudson like a man wading through a brook. . . .

George M. Mawhinney, rewrite man of the *Philadelphia Inquirer*, was at his desk at eight P.M. in the evening of the broadcast, when a reader telephoned to inquire if the paper had heard of a big explosion near Trenton. The caller was informed that the *Inquirer* had not. Soon the switchboard operator was overwhelmed by hysterical callers demanding information.

Assigned to the story, Mawhinney at first was inclined to handle it as an item of local interest by writing a few bright and sprightly paragraphs. But within a few minutes he had to revise his estimate of its importance. All the major news services and a number of special services taken by the *Inquirer* began sending flashes from all over the country. The rewrite man knew now that he had a story of national scope and one of the biggest of his career.

As the wires burned and the telephones clanged the newsman composed his story. The entire writing, with the exception of a few inserts and additions, was completed within an hour. With an eye-catching lead, a rapid-fire series of brief accounts covering the fantastic developments in local areas, and a smashing climax, Mawhinney produced a journalistic gem.

An invasion from the planet Mars

Philadelphia Inquirer, November 1, 1938

Terror struck at the hearts of hundreds of thousands of persons in the length and breadth of the United States last night as crisp words of what they believed to be a news broadcast leaped from their radio sets—telling of catastrophe from the skies visited on this country.

Out of the heavens, they learned, objects at first believed to be meteors crashed down near Trenton, killing many.

Then out of the "meteors" came monsters, spreading destruction with torch and poison gas.

It was all just a radio dramatization, but the result, in all actuality, was nation-wide hysteria.

In Philadelphia, women and children ran from their homes, screaming. In Newark, New Jersey, ambulances rushed to one neighborhood to protect residents against a gas attack. In the deep South men and women knelt in groups in the streets and prayed for deliverance.

In reality there was no danger. The broadcast was merely a Halloween program in which Orson Welles, actor-director of the Mercury Theater on the Air, related, as though he were one of the few human survivors of the catastrophe, an adaptation of H. G. Wells' *The War of the Worlds*.

In that piece of fiction men from Mars, in meteorlike space ships, come to make conquest of earth. The circumstances of the story were unbelievable enough, but the manner of its presentation was apparently convincing to hundreds of thousands of persons—despite the fact that the program was interrupted thrice for an announcement that it was fiction, and fiction only.

For the fanciful tale was broadcast casually, for all the world like a news broadcast, opening up serenely enough with a weather report.

The realism of the broadcast, especially for those who had tuned in after it had started, brought effects which none—not the directors of the Federal Radio Theater Project, which sponsored it, nor the Columbia Broadcasting Company, which carried it over a coast-to-coast chain of 151 stations, nor Station WCAU, which broadcast it locally—could foresee.

Within a few minutes newspaper offices, radio stations, and police departments everywhere were flooded with anxious telephone calls. Sobbing women sought advice on what to do;

broken-voiced men wished to know where to take their families.

Station WCAU received more than four thousand calls and eventually interrupted a later program to make an elaborate explanation that death had not actually descended on New Jersey, and that monsters were not actually invading the world.

But calm did not come readily to the frightened radio listeners of the country.

The hysteria reached such proportions that the New York City Department of Health called up a newspaper and wanted advice on offering its facilities for the protection of the populace. Nurses and physicians were among the telephone callers everywhere. They were ready to offer their assistance to the injured or maimed.

Hundreds of motorists touring through New Jersey heard the broadcast over their radios and detoured to avoid the area upon which the holocaust was focused—the area in the vicinity of Trenton and Princeton.

In scores of New Jersey towns women in their homes fainted as the horror of the broadcast fell on their ears. In Palmyra some residents packed up their worldly goods and prepared to move across the river into Philadelphia.

A white-faced man raced into the Hillside, New Jersey, police station and asked for a gas mask. Police said he panted out a tale of "terrible people spraying liquid gas all over Jersey meadows."

A weeping lady stopped Motorcycle Patrolman Lawrence Treger and asked where she should go to escape the "attack."

A terrified motorist asked the patrolman the way to Route 24. "All creation's busted loose. I'm getting out of Jersey," he screamed.

"Grovers Mill, New Jersey," was mentioned as a scene of destruction. In Stockton more than a half-hundred persons abandoned Colligan's Inn after hearing the broadcast and journeyed to Groveville to view the incredible "damage." They had misheard the name of the hypothetical town of "Grovers Mill," and believed it to be Groveville.

At Princeton University, women members of the geology faculty, equipped with flashlights and hammers, started for Grovers Corners. Dozens of cars were driven to the hamlet by curious motorists. A score of university students were phoned by their parents and told to come home.

An anonymous and somewhat hysterical girl phoned the Princeton Press Club from Grovers Corners and said: "You can't imagine the horror of it! It's hell!"

A man came into the club and said he saw the meteor strike the earth and witnessed animals jumping from the alien body.

The Trenton police and fire telephone board bore the brunt of the nation's calls, because of its geographical location close to the presumed scene of catastrophe. On that board were received calls from Wilmington, Washington, Philadelphia, Jersey City, and Newark.

North of Trenton most of New Jersey was in the midst of a bad scare.

A report spread through Newark that the city was to be the target of a "gas-bomb attack." Police headquarters were notified there was a serious gas accident in the Clinton Hills section of that city. They sent squad cars and ambulances.

They found only householders, with possessions hastily bundled, leaving their homes. The householders returned to their homes only after emphatic explanations by the police.

Fifteen persons were treated for shock in one Newark hospital.

In Jersey City one resident demanded a gas mask of police. Another telephoned to ask whether he ought to flee the area or merely keep his windows closed and hope for the best.

Many New Yorkers seized personal effects and raced out of their apartments, some jumping into their automobiles and heading for the wide-open spaces.

Samuel Tishman, a Riverside Drive resident, declared he and hundreds of others evacuated their homes, fearing "the city was being bombed."

He told of going home and receiving a frantic telephone call from a nephew.

Tishman denounced the program as "the most asinine stunt I ever heard of" and as "a pretty crumby thing to do."

The panic it caused gripped impressionable Harlemites, and one man ran into the street declaring it was the President's voice they heard, advising: "Pack up and go North, the machines are coming from Mars."

Police in the vicinity at first regarded the excitement as a joke, but they were soon hard pressed in controlling the swarms in the streets.

A man entered the Wadsworth Avenue station uptown and said he heard "planes had bombed Jersey and were headed for Times Square."

A rumor spread over Washington Heights that a war was on.

At Caldwell, New Jersey, an excited parishioner rushed into the First Baptist Church during evening services and shouted that a tremendous meteor had fallen, causing widespread death, and that north Jersey was threatened with a shower of meteors. The congregation joined in prayer for deliverance.

Reactions as strange, or stranger, occurred in other parts of the country. In San Francisco, a citizen called police, crying:

"My God, where can I volunteer my services? We've got to stop this awful thing."

In Indianapolis, Indiana, a woman ran screaming into a church.

"New York is destroyed; it's the end of the world," she cried. "You might as well go home to die."

At Brevard College, North Carolina, five boys in dormitories fainted on hearing the broadcast. In Birmingham, Alabama, men and women gathered in groups and prayed. Women wept and prayed in Memphis, Tennessee.

Throughout Atlanta was a widespread belief that a "planet" had struck New Jersey, killing from forty to seven thousand persons.

At Pittsburgh one man telephoned a newspaper that he had returned to his home in the middle of the broadcast and found his wife in the bathroom, clutching a bottle of poison.

"I'd rather die this way than like that," she screamed before he was able to calm her.

Another citizen telephoned a newspaper in Washington, Pennsylvania, that a group of guests in his home playing cards "fell down on their knees and prayed," and then hurried home.

At Rivesville, West Virginia, a woman interrupted the pastor's sermon at a church meeting with loud outcries that there had been "an invasion." The meeting broke up in confusion.

Two heart attacks were reported by Kansas City hospitals, and the Associated Press Bureau there received calls of inquiry from Los Angeles, Salt Lake City, Beaumont, Texas, and St. Joseph, Missouri.

Minneapolis and St. Paul police switchboards were deluged with calls from frightened people.

Weeping and hysterical women in Providence, Rhode Island, cried out for officials of the electric company there to "turn off the lights so that the city will be safe from the enemy."

In some places mass hysteria grew so great that witnesses to the "invasion" could be found.

A Boston woman telephoned a newspaper to say she could "see the fire" from her window, and that she and her neighbors were "getting out of here."

The broadcast began at eight P.M. Within a few minutes after that time it had brought such a serious reaction that New Jersey state police sent out a teletype message to its various stations and barracks, containing explanations and instructions to police officers on how to handle the hysteria.

These and other police everywhere had problems on their hands as the broadcast moved on, telling of a "bulletin from the Intercontinental Radio News Bureau" saying there had been a gas explosion in New Jersey.

"Bulletins" that came in rapidly after that told of "meteors," then corrected that statement and described the Mars monsters.

The march of the Martians was disastrous. For a while they swept everything before them, according to the pseudo-bulletins. Mere armies and navies were being wiped out in a trice.

Actually, outside the radio stations, the Martians were doing a pretty good job on the Halloween imaginations of the citizenry. The radio stations and the Columbia Broadcasting Company spent much of the remainder of the evening clearing up the situation. Again and again they explained the whole thing was nothing more than a dramatization.

In the long run, however, calm was restored in the myriad American homes which had been momentarily threatened by interplanetary invasion. Fear of the monsters from Mars eventually subsided.

There was no reason for being afraid of them, anyway. Even the bulletins of the radio broadcast explained they all soon died. They couldn't stand the earth's atmosphere and perished of pneumonia.

* * *

AFTER IT WAS ALL OVER, there was a lot of sheepish laughing. For Orson Welles, onetime boy wonder of the entertainment world and possessor of an unusually fine dramatic talent, the incident was a press agent's dream come true. To others the incident was not funny. The chairman of the Federal Communications Commission called the program "regrettable." In her column, "On the Record," in the *New York Herald Tribune,* November 2, 1938, Dorothy Thompson declared haughtily that "nothing whatever about the dramatization was in the least credible, no matter at what point the listener might have tuned in." Heywood Broun, in the *New York World-Telegram* on the same day, wrote: "Jitters have come home to roost. We have just gone through a laboratory demonstration of the fact that the peace of Munich hangs heavy over our heads, like a thundercloud." Broun was certain that the course of world history had affected national psychology.

The General Education Board set aside a special grant for the study of this strange exhibition of mass hysteria. With all the scientific research tools now available the underlying psychological causes for the panic of 1938 were examined. In 1940 the Princeton University Press published Hadley Cantril's book-length study of the incident, with emphasis upon the nature and extent of the panic, how the stimulus was experienced, descriptions of reactions, the historical setting, and individual cases. The author came to the conclusion that skepticism and knowledge must be spread more widely among common men by more extensive educational opportunities. "And if this final critical ability is to be used more generally by common men, they must be less harassed by the emotional insecurities which stem from underprivileged environments."

This was not the last of the H. G. Wells' fantasy. In February, 1949, radio station HCQRX in Quito, Ecuador, broadcast its own version of the invasion-from-Mars program. Here again the program hurried along from one false news flash to another, with Ecuadorian place names filled in. At first the Quiteños reacted like their North American cousins, pouring hysterically into the streets and calling for help. But when they learned the truth they refused to take it with shamefaced silence. An enraged mob stormed the three-story El Comercio building that housed the radio station, hurled gasoline and flaming balls of paper into the interior, and watched in silence as fifteen people trapped inside died in the fire. By the time police and soldiers, who had rushed off to repel the "Martians," returned, the newspaper building, its equipment, and the radio station were wrecked.

A Radio Announcer Sees Thirty-Three Pigboat

Men Snatched From the Bottom of the Sea

O<small>N</small> MAY 23, 1939, the U. S. submarine *Squalus,* disabled by a watery inflow from an open induction valve, sank in the Atlantic twelve miles from the tip of Cape Ann, Gloucester. As the entire nation waited for news, thirty-three haggard men were rescued from their underwater tomb by the use of an ingenious rescue elevator. Shaped something like a huge electric-light bulb, and rigged to permit manipulation by use of air-pressure lines and water ballast, the ten-ton rescue chamber rode down a cable to a hatch opening and was attached to the submarine by suction and fastened from the inside. It was the most dramatic rescue in submarine history.

At the moment when the diving bell was being reeled to the surface after its first descent, Jack Knell, a local announcer for the Columbia Broadcasting System, was bobbing about in a thirty-foot cruiser as close to the *Falcon,* the rescue ship, as the Coast Guard would allow. Without sleep for sixty hours and broadcasting under extreme nervous tension and suspense, the young announcer turned in an exciting air report, which won for him the National Headliners' Club Award for the best radio reporting of a news event in 1938–39.

Up periscope!

This is Jack Knell, speaking to you through short-wave transmitter WAAU, operating on 2190 kilocycles. We are at the present time in a small boat, riding at anchor at a spot approximately fifty yards from the scene of rescue operations of the sunken submarine *Squalus,* sixteen miles due north from the Portsmouth Navy Yard. We have seen and are seeing one of the most thrilling sights of our lives today. We are seeing history in the making.

About one hour ago, that huge ten-ton diving bell disappeared from view as it sank to the bottom of the sea. We spent anxious minutes awaiting its return to the surface, and just a few moments ago, before we came on the air, that immense bell broke the surface of the water. Its huge, pear-shaped bulk is now bobbing around in the water close to the side of the rescue ship, *Falcon.* The men aboard the *Falcon* are maneuvering the bell toward the stern of the ship by means of long poles. They seem to have it in the desired position now, and two men are astride the bell, working on the hatch cover in an attempt to unscrew the bolts which keep the cover tightly closed against the sea and the tremendous pressure down there, 250 feet below the surface.

One of the men is rising from his crouched position now, and the men aboard the rescue ship are leaning tensely over the side. . . . I think they're about to open the cover now . . . yes . . . the hatch cover of the diving bell is open! They're reaching down inside the bell now . . . and . . . there's a man's head. . . . They're helping someone out of the bell now. . . . He's climbing out of the bell under his own steam. . . . He's stepping across the top of the bell and is boarding the *Falcon*. . . . The first survivor rescued from the sunken submarine *Squalus* is out and safely aboard the rescue ship . . . and now here's another man coming out of the bell. He's being helped aboard the *Falcon*, although he seems to be able to make it without assistance . . . and here's another . . . and another. . . . These men seem to be in remarkably good condition, despite the tremendous strain they've been under. . . . Another man is out now, and they're reaching inside to aid another. . . . We may have lost count during the excitement of seeing these

men emerge from that bell alive and well, but I think that's the sixth man to come out of the bell . . . and here . . . here's the seventh.

Seven men have come out of that big, white, pear-shaped diving bell. We don't know if they have all been brought out of the sunken submarine or if some of them went down with the bell to control it. But there you are. . . . We've seen and have attempted to describe to you the actual rescue of the first seven survivors from the ill-fated submarine *Squalus*, which is lying at the bottom of the sea in approximately 250 feet of water. Undoubtedly the bell will immediately be sent down again in an attempt to bring up more of the men trapped down there, but it's a long job, taking at least an hour for the round trip, so we're going to sign off from this point for the time being, but we'll be on hand to bring you the eyewitness account of the rescue as the bell comes up again. Keep tuned to this network for further developments. This is Jack Knell, speaking to you through short-wave transmitter WAAU, operating on 2190 kilocycles. . . . This is the Columbia Broadcasting System.

* * *

AFTER KNELL's graphic broadcast the rescue chamber continued lifesaving journeys down and up the cable to the stricken submarine. In midevening, on the fourth and last descent, the contact by which the chamber dropped and rose again became entangled, with eight submarine men and two operators trapped inside. After four hours of anxious waiting, divers cleared away the tangle and the last survivors were brought to the surface. Twenty-six shipmates were left behind in the flooded compartments.

Walter Winchell Engineers the
Surrender of the President of Murder, Inc.

H E WAS A BLAND, stockily built little man, with soft liquid eyes and a curious smile that seemed to betray his shyness. But this disarming exterior concealed the heart of a ferocious killer. When he was a young lad his poverty-stricken East Side mother had called him by the fond diminutive, "Lepkeleh," or "Little Louis," and the name stuck, although later the wise guys of the underworld gave him such monikers as "Lepke," "The Judge," or "Judge Louis."

Such was the criminal cunning and ruthlessness of Louis "Lepke" Buchalter that he progressed from a chiseler of pushcart peddlers to the role of successor to the beer barons and alcohol kings who had made the Prohibition Twenties a murderous era. Streamlining the crude methods of his predecessors, he built his gangster machine into a vast organization of vice, racketeering, and extortion that, from 1928 to 1940, terrorized both bosses and workers in the fur, garment, leather, baking, and trucking industries of metropolitan New York. His industrial *saboteurs,* who were paid a standard rate of from $125-$150 a week, used a variety of weapons—bludgeons, pistols, icepicks, blackjacks, and destructive acids, the last a handy means for blinding recalcitrant businessmen.

Lepke seemed to be lawproof. Between 1922 and 1933 he was arrested no fewer than eleven times. No convictions. His system was devilishly simple —he ordered the extermination of any potential witnesses against him. "You're forty-five years old?" he asked one of them. "You have lived too long." From sixty to eighty men fell victim to the gruesome efficiency of Murder, Inc. "Former Lepke aids and gunmen," reported Meyer Berger, "made corpses on Catskill, Brooklyn, and Bronx landscapes. They were burned with gasoline, buried in quicklime, shot, stabbed with icepicks, garroted—all on the orders of the little man with the fawnlike stare and the uneasy and diffident front."

Even Lepke's luck couldn't last. In 1936 the untouchable crime director was arrested on a charge of racketeering in the fur industry, only to be freed at once on $10,000 bail by Martin T. Manton, senior judge of the United States Circuit Court of Appeals, who was later convicted for the crime of selling justice. Lepke jumped bail.

Then began an intensive man hunt to bring the killer to bay. The Board of Estimate of New York City at the request of District Attorney Thomas

E. Dewey offered a reward of $25,000 for Lepke "dead or alive." This sum was matched by J. Edgar Hoover and the Federal Bureau of Investigation, without the qualifying clause. A special squad of police was formed in New York to guard witnesses, while a large band of FBI agents descended on the city to watch for the killer. When his attempts to negotiate a deal fell through, Lepke in desperation decided to surrender to the Federal authorities in the belief that an indictment for smuggling narcotics was far preferable to a murder rap by racket-buster Dewey. How to give himself up was the immediate problem. Lepke would take no chances on being trapped like Dillinger. He decided to surrender to Walter Winchell on the ground that the G-men wouldn't shoot him on sight if he were with so celebrated a newspaperman as well as a close friend of Hoover, the top FBI man.

Any one of several thousand newsmen looking for Lepke would have given his lower right bicuspid for an eyewitness story of Lepke's capture. In engineering the surrender Winchell scored the most sensational beat of his fabulously successful career. Throughout the trial of Bruno Richard Hauptmann for the murder of the Lindbergh baby, he had time after time scooped his colleagues. When Giuseppe Zangara attempted to shoot President-elect Franklin D. Roosevelt in Miami, killing Mayor Anton Cermak of Chicago in the process, Winchell obtained the only interview with the assassin. "I'm Walter Winchell," he informed an overwhelmed sheriff. "Get me in there, and I'll put your name in every paper in the world." These authentic news beats and the ability to "smell" a story a continent away won for him an unchallenged position as the most widely distributed columnist in the nation, with many hundreds of papers printing his articles for an incredible 25,000,000 readers. To this impressive record he added the highest rating ever assigned to a news commentator on the air waves, as well as a solid reputation as the reporter who has done more to rouse the conscience of America against intolerance and totalitarianism than any other journalist of his time. "If there never was a Walter Winchell, somebody would have had to invent him," Heywood Broun once said.

Waiting for Lepke

New York *Daily Mirror*, August 26, 1939

NEW YORK, AUGUST 25 (INS)—The surrender of public enemy "Lepke" Buchalter to the government last night took place while scores of pedestrians ambled by, and two police radio cars waited for the lights to change,

near Twenty-eighth Street and Fifth Avenue.

The time was precisely 10:17 P.M., and the search for the most wanted fugitive in the nation was over. The surrender was negotiated by this reporter, whom G-man John Edgar Hoover authorized to guarantee "safe delivery."

After a series of telephone talks with persons unknown, and with the head of the FBI, Lepke appeared to drop out of the sky, without even a parachute. The time was 10:15. The scene was Madison Square between Twenty-third and Twenty-fourth Streets, where we had halted our car as per instructions.

The following two minutes were consumed traveling slowly north on Fourth Avenue and west on Twenty-seventh Street to Fifth Avenue, where the traffic lights were red—and to the next corner at Twenty-eighth Street, where Mr. Hoover waited alone, unarmed and without handcuffs, in a government limousine. Hoover was disguised in dark sunglasses to keep him from being recognized by passers-by.

The presence of two New York police cruisers, attached to the Fourteenth Precinct, so near the surrender scene startled Hoover as well as Lepke. The G-man later admitted he feared "a leak."

Lepke, who was calmer than this chauffeur, was on the verge of rushing out of our machine into Hoover's arms. The police cruisers, ironically, were the first observed by this reporter in two hours of motoring to complete the surrender.

Not until the final seconds was there a sign of uniformed law. But it was too late. The long arm of the government had reached out and claimed another enemy. The Federal Bureau of Investigation and the city of New York had saved $50,000—the reward offered.

While pausing alongside one police car at the Twenty-seventh Street intersection for the lights, Lepke, who

was wearing spectacles as part of his disguise, threw them to the corner pavement. They crashed noisily. Two passers-by, middle-aged men with graying temples, stopped and looked up at a building.

Apparently they thought a window had broken above. They never realized that the man for whom every cop in the land was searching was within touching distance.

After parking our car behind a machine which was parked behind Hoover's, we shut off the ignition and escorted Lepke into Hoover's car.

"Mr. Hoover," we said, "this is Lepke."

"How do you do?" said Mr. Hoover affably.

"Glad to meet you," replied Lepke. "Let's go."

"To the Federal Building at Foley Square," commanded Hoover. His colored pilot turned swiftly south.

Lepke was a little excited. He seemed anxious to talk—to talk to anybody new—after being in the shadows for over two years with so many hunted men.

"You did the smart thing by coming in, Lepke," comforted Hoover.

"I'm beginning to wonder if I did," Lepke answered. "I would like to see my wife and kids, please?"

Mr. Hoover arranged for them to visit him shortly after Lepke was booked, fingerprinted, and Kodaked. He had $1700 on him. He gave $1100 to the boy and $600 to the jailer—for "expenses."

When the government car reached Fourteenth Street, we got out and went to the first phone to notify our editor, who groaned:

"A fine thing! With a World War starting!"

The negotiations which led to Lepke's surrender began in this manner. On Saturday night, August 5 last, a voice on the phone said:

"Don't ask me who I am. I have something important to tell you. Lepke wants to come in. But he's heard so many different stories about what will happen to him. He can't trust anybody, he says. If he could find someone he can trust, he will give himself up to that person. The talk around town is that Lepke would be shot while supposedly escaping."

"Does he trust me?" we inquired.

"Do you really mean that?" said the voice anxiously.

"Sure," we assured. "I'll tell John Edgar Hoover about it and I'm sure he will see to it that Lepke receives his constitutional rights and nobody will cross him."

"O.K., put it on the air tomorrow night if you can get that promise," and then he disconnected.

We wrote a brief radio paragraph which was addressed to Lepke, "if you are listening now," which said we would try to get him assurance of a safe delivery. The next afternoon, Sunday, we phoned Mr. Hoover and read him the paragraph.

"You are authorized to state," said Hoover, "that the FBI will guarantee it!"

Hoover and his assistant director, Clyde Tolson, came to the studio and witnessed our microphoning. They remained for the repeat broadcast to the coast an hour later—in case another phone call came in.

For two nights, voices contacted us by phone and said:

"You're doing very well. You'll hear more later. If he agrees to come in, he will do it through you. But he may change his mind. Good-by."

And then all the dickering abruptly stopped—until last Tuesday night. Then a person we had never seen be-fore, or since, approached us at Fifty-third Street and Fifth Avenue and said: "Where can you be reached on a pay-station phone in an hour?"

We went to the nearest phone booth, where the stranger marked down the number and instructed: "This is about Lepke. This time it's important. Please be here in an hour."

He hastened away, hailed a passing cab, and taxied north.

When we so reported to Mr. Hoover, after what seemed to him like too much stalling, he was exasperated. For the first time in our seven years of knowing him, he barked at us:

"This is a lot of bunk, Walter. You are being made a fool of and so are we. If you contact those people again, tell them the time limit is up! I will instruct my agents to shoot Lepke on sight."

Promptly an hour later, right on the button, that pay-station phone tinkled. We didn't give the voice a chance to talk. "I just spoke to Hoover," we said breathlessly. "He's fed up. If Lepke doesn't surrender by four P.M. tomorrow, Hoover says no consideration of any kind will ever be given him. For every day he stays away it may mean an extra two years added to his sentence."

The voice interrupted: "He's coming in, but you simply have to wait until he can arrange things. He's willing to come in, but it can't be tomorrow. Maybe the next night. Where can you be reached tomorrow night at six?"

We gave him another phone number. He said he'd call—and the call came. But it didn't seem to be the same voice. This time the instructions included: "Drive up to Proctor's Theater in Yonkers."

How sure could we be that the

"meet" was for the surrender of Lepke? We weren't sure at all. But we hoped to convince the G-men that we weren't being made any "goat-between"! And so we motored up to Yonkers, and before we reached Proctor's Theater a car loaded with strangers—faces we don't recall ever seeing before—slowly drew alongside. We heard a voice say, "That's him."

One of the men got out, holding his handkerchief to his face as though he intended to blow into it. He got into our car, sat alongside, and kept the kerchief to his face throughout the brief conversation.

"Go to the drugstore on the corner of Nineteenth Street and Eighth Avenue," he instructed. "There are some phone booths there. Get in one and appear busy. About nine P.M. somebody will come up to you and tell you where to notify the G-men to meet you."

At 8:55 P.M. we were in that drugstore. We ordered a coke. The boy behind the counter looked at us as though we seemed familiar. Perhaps we imagined it. At any rate, we didn't get a chance to appear busy in the phone booth. A face met ours as we turned to look through the open door. The stranger jerked his head as though to telegraph "Come here." We

joined him outside and walked to our car slowly.

"Go back in there and tell Hoover to be at Twenty-eighth Street on Fifth Avenue between 10:10 and 10:20," he instructed.

We did so. When we returned to the car, the man was at the wheel. He drove slowly, to kill time, for more than an hour. Up and down Eighth Avenue, Ninth, Tenth, in and out of side streets, down to Fourteenth, back to Twenty-third, and east to Madison Square, where he stopped the car and said:

"Just wait here—and good luck."

And so saying he left hurriedly. We took the wheel, turned our eyes left, and noticed many people across the street lounging around. It was very humid. Our clothes were dripping. The butterflies started to romp inside of us.

Suddenly a figure approached our car in haste. Out of the nowhere, it seems. He opened the door, got in, and said: "Hello. Thanks very much."

We released the brake and stepped on the gas. "We'll be with Mr. Hoover in a minute or two," we said. "He's waiting in his car at Twenty-eighth Street."

"Yes, I know," said Lepke. "I just passed him."

WITH LEPKE safely bedded down for the night, J. Edgar Hoover asked: "Walter, what can I do for you?" To which the reporter replied: "First of all this reward isn't going to be paid to anybody. This is my gift to the government. I'll take a one-edition beat. I don't want to be greedy." It soon developed that the man from the *Daily Mirror,* who had been trying in vain to lose weight, had shed six pounds and an inch at the waistline from forty-eight hours of high tension and loss of sleep. Some rival newsmen found Winchell's scoop a little tough to take, but there was widespread agreement that this was one of the most extraordinary feats in the history of American reporting. Typical was an editorial in the *Brooklyn Eagle* that held that Winchell had performed "an outstanding public service, for which the community should be grateful."

Six months after this dramatic surrender Lepke went to Leavenworth under a fourteen-year term for narcotics and anti-trust violations. Then a jury in General Sessions convicted him of extortion on thirty-six counts and sentenced him to thirty years in New York State prison. The Federal sentence took precedence. In 1941 Lepke was brought back to New York to stand trial for the murder of Joseph Rosen, a Brooklyn storekeeper who had been shot to death in September, 1936. The boss racketeer was reported to have told his gunmen that "Rosen is shooting off his mouth that he is going to Dewey." This time Lepke was found guilty and was sentenced to death.

Once again there began a bitter wrangle between state and Federal authorities for Lepke's person, with the issue finally resolved when Attorney General Biddle turned the gangster over to New York State. Six times his attorneys saved Lepke from execution, finally appealing all the way up to the U. S. Supreme Court on the ground that their client was improperly released from Federal prison. On March 5, 1944, a thoroughly whipped cur went to the chair in Sing Sing's death house, plaintively protesting his innocence. Thomas E. Dewey, who gained national acclaim as the nemesis of Murder, Inc., went on to become Governor of New York and the standard-bearer of that party which made two unsuccessful attempts to obtain for him a lease on the residence at 1600 Pennsylvania Avenue.

Leland Stowe Exposes "One
of the Costliest Military Bungles in
Modern British History"

THE MIDDLE OF APRIL, 1940, marked the end of the "Twilight War." Suddenly the German juggernaut crashed into Norway. Germans who, as hungry children, had been taken into Norwegian homes during the famine years after World War I now returned in Nazi uniforms as strutting conquerors. Working hand in glove with the invading Nazis to throttle his own country was Norwegian Vidkun Quisling, who gave history a new synonym for "traitor." *

The German invasion was perfectly timed and prepared. Aroused from an eight-month trance, the British felt impelled to make a show of strength. To meet the thundering hordes the British landed a small force of territorials at ports flanking Trondheim, the key to central Norway. What had happened to this token army was first buried in a black censorship.

Then Leland Stowe flashed a report to America about the desperate situation. It was a clean beat, the unvarnished story of the 1500 British troops sent in against crack German forces, without air support or artillery. At the beginning of World War II, a New York newspaper told Stowe that he was too old to cover the war for them. Scarcely old and tottering at thirty-nine, Stowe promptly went to the *Chicago Daily News,* which sent him to the battle fronts to become one of the outstanding reporters of the war. Behind him was a brilliant record. For his coverage of the sessions of the Reparation Commission at Paris in 1930 he won a Pulitzer Prize. The Reichstag-fire trial, the war in Spain, and the Russo-Finnish conflict were each in turn handled in a distinguished manner by Stowe. In World War II he served with the armies of seven different countries and reported from forty-four different nations and colonies. This kind of front-line reporting brought him the University of Missouri School of Journalism Medal for outstanding war correspondence in 1941.

---

* "Quisling," commented the London *Times,* "has the supreme merit of beginning with a *q,* which (with one august exception) has long seemed to the British mind to be a crooked, uncertain, and slightly disreputable letter, suggestive of the questionable, the querulous, the quavering, of quaking quagmires and quivering quicksands, of queasiness, quackery, qualms, and Quilp." The "august exception," as H. L. Mencken points out, is *queen.*

Too little and too late

Chicago Daily News, April 25, 1940

GÄDDEDE, NORWEGIAN-SWEDISH FRONTIER, APRIL 25—Here is the first and only eyewitness report on the opening chapter of the British expeditionary troops' advance in Norway north of Trondheim. It is a bitterly disillusioning and almost unbelievable story.

The British force which was supposed to sweep down from Namsos consisted of one battalion of Territorials and one battalion of the King's Own Royal Light Infantry. These totaled fewer than 1500 men. They were dumped into Norway's deep snows and quagmires of April slush without a single antiaircraft gun, without one squadron of supporting airplanes, without a single piece of field artillery.

They were thrown into the snows and mud of sixty-three degrees north latitude to fight crack German regulars—most of them veterans of the Polish invasion—and to face the most destructive of modern weapons. The great majority of these young Britishers averaged only one year of military service. They have already paid a heavy price for a major military blunder which was not committed by their immediate command, but in London.

Unless they receive large supplies of antiaircraft guns and adequate reinforcements within a very few days, the remains of these two British battalions will be cut to ribbons.

Here is the astonishing story of what has happened to the gallant little handful of British expeditionaries above Trondheim:

After only four days of fighting, nearly half of this initial BEF contingent has been knocked out—either killed, wounded, or captured. On Monday, these comparatively inexperienced and incredibly underarmed British troops were decisively defeated. They were driven back in precipitate disorder from Vist, three miles south of the bomb-ravaged town of Steinkjer.

As I write, it is probable that the British field headquarters has been withdrawn northward and that the British vanguard has been compelled to evacuate one or several villages. Steinkjer was occupied by the Germans Tuesday.

I was in Steinkjer Monday evening just before the British lines were blasted to pieces. I was the only newspaper correspondent to enter the burning town and the only correspondent to visit British advance headquarters and to pass beyond to the edge of the front's heavy firing zone.

A score of buildings were flaming fiercely on the town's water front from a bombing two hours earlier. In the midst of the smoky ruins I heard machine-gun cracking at high tempo in the hills just beyond the town. Shell explosions rapped the valley regularly with angry echoes. This was the first sustained battle between German and British troops on Norwegian soil. Already the conflict was snarling hot.

A battalion of six hundred Territorials was fighting desperately to hold Vist, the point of their farthest southwest advance toward Trondheim. As Monday's twilight closed they were completely done in. For hours they had been torn and broken under the terrible triple onslaught of German infantry, trimotored bombers, and naval firing from destroyers at the head of Breitstadfjord.

Within two hours the British troops were in flight. They had no chance whatever of standing off from bombs and three- or six-inch shells with nothing but Bren machine guns and rifles. Before eleven o'clock that night I talked with the nerve-shattered survivors of the British battalion. We found two truckloads of them several miles above their headquarters and on their way north away from the front.

One of the officers told me that the battalion had lost more than two hundred in killed and that one entire company had been captured. He could not estimate the number of missing, but said that perhaps 150 of the battalion's six hundred might be rallied later on.

"We have simply been massacred," he declared. "It is the planes. We have no planes to fight back with, and we have no antiaircraft guns. It is just like Russians against the Finns, only worse—and we are the Finns."

A subofficer greeted me gratefully when he learned that I was a reporter.

"For God's sake, tell them we have got to have airplanes and antiaircraft guns," he pleaded.

"We were completely at the mercy of the Jerries. Their bombers flew low over us, at five hundred feet. They scattered us. We were up to our hips in snow.

"Then they dropped signal flares so their artillery knew our positions. Last night our wounded were crying in the woods, but we couldn't get to them or do anything. We had not even got proper clothes to fight with in the snow. Without white capes the Jerries just spotted us and mowed us down every time the bombers drove us out."

Paul Melander, a Swedish photographer, and I saw these things together. We were the only newsmen to spend nearly twenty-four hours in the British sector and to reach the edge of the firing zone on that front.

Although almost exhausted from lack of sleep, the British officers maintained remarkable calm. But this was a small military machine with vital cogs missing. Able to bomb at will, the Germans had seriously disrupted the organization of the little British expeditionary vanguard in their first four days at the front.

Forty British fighting planes at present could probably clear the skies over the entire Allied Norwegian fighting zones and all vital sections of their rear guard north of Trondheim. The British troops are praying that these fighters will arrive soon before it is too late.

Following the British defeat near Vist, we were told that Norwegian troops had been compelled to take over virtually all the north front above Trondheim. North of Trondheim the military initiative is now held by alert, aggressive, and first-class German troops. It is guaranteed by Nazi warplanes which are flying constantly at less than one thousand feet over the Allies' Norwegian sector and which bomb their objectives as easily as a marksman picks off clay pigeons.

Three times in one day German planes roared over my head at only five hundred or six hundred feet, and twice I was in buildings where key Norwegian commands were located. I thought the Nazis' espionage service—with its formidable network throughout Scandinavia—had already betrayed these locations. Providentially, this had not happened and no bombs were dropped. So these two

Norwegian control centers escaped. But without the Allies' aircraft and antiaircraft guns such miracles cannot endure for long.

This is merely an illustration of the tremendous initiative which has been handed to the Germans north of Trondheim by one of the costliest and most inexplicable military bungles in modern British history.

It has been handed to them by those high British authorities who thrust 1500 young Territorials into the snow and mud below Namsos ten days ago without a single antiaircraft gun or a single piece of artillery.

By THE END of April the British Expeditionary Force, outnumbered, outpowered, and cut to ribbons, was forced to withdraw. "Fortune had been cruelly against us," commented Winston Churchill in *The Gathering Storm,* where he tells how his full-scale "Operation Hammer" had been rejected by the Chiefs of Staff. Churchill conceded that Britain's finest troops, the Scots and Irish Guards, had been baffled by "the vigor, enterprise, and training of Hitler's young men," and concluded: "We, who had command of the sea and could pounce anywhere on an undefended coast, were outpaced by the enemy moving by land across very large distances in the face of every obstacle." For Britain there was one consolation. In their desperate grapple with the British navy in the Norwegian operation the Germans had ruined their own fleet, which could no longer be counted upon to support an invasion of England.

Leland Stowe's sensational report was shocking news to the British people. The dispatch played an important part in bringing about a change of British leadership at a critical moment of the war. Neville Chamberlain's "Hitler has missed the bus" had backfired. Britain, which had tried appeasement and complacency with disastrous results, now sought realistic and aggressive leadership. "The stroke of catastrophe and the spur of peril were needed to call forth the dormant might of the British nation. The tocsin was about to sound," Churchill commented. Winston was ready. On May 10, 1940, he became British Prime Minister.

"I was sure I should not fail," Churchill later confessed, adding, "I slept soundly and had no need for cheering dreams."

A. D. Divine Sees the Strangest Fleet in British History Achieve the Miracle of Dunkirk

IN 401 B.C., the young Greek historian Xenophon joined the expedition of the younger Cyrus against his brother, Artaxerxes II of Persia. After the battle of Cunaxa, in which Cyrus lost his life, the Greek army found itself in the heart of an unknown country, more than a thousand miles from home, and in the presence of a powerful enemy. There was nothing to do but retreat northward up the Tigris Valley through the wilds of Kurdistan, where savage mountain tribes would harass them in guerrilla attacks, and through the highlands of Armenia and Georgia to the lands of friendly Greek colonies on the Euxine.

Xenophon, who mainly directed the retreat, told the story of the march of the ten thousand Greeks in his *Anabasis*, or the "Upcountry March." Ultimately the Greeks reached Chrysopolis (Scutari), opposite Byzantium, with their backs to the Bosporus, and made their way home.

Many a British schoolboy who learned his Greek battles at Eton or Harrow recalled the details of the *Anabasis* when in late May and early June, 1940, a considerably larger army than Xenophon's escaped from Hitler's Europe and retreated gloriously into the textbooks of history.

On May 14, 1940, a BBC announcer, in precise and well-modulated tones, informed the British radio audience: "The Admiralty have made an order requesting all owners of self-propelled pleasure craft between thirty and one hundred feet in length to send all particulars to the Admiralty within fourteen days from today." Just two weeks later the House of Commons was warned "to prepare for hard and heavy tidings."

All hell had broken loose on the Continent as the Allies gave up as lost the Battle of Flanders. In ordering the Belgian army to surrender King Leopold had left the flanks of the Allies wide open. The German spearheads had axed through to the Channel, and now the whole British Expeditionary Force, plus assorted French, Poles, and Belgians, was caught in a trap. Intoxicated by the smell of victory, the Germans smashed in for the kill. There was no choice for the British—they had to be evacuated from the Continent or they would be annihilated. They opened the flood sluices around Dunkirk to guard the last port of escape to the sea. While French divisions fought across the tortured landscape in fire and flood, the bulk of an entrapped army of half a million men backed on Dunkirk. It was a desperate race to escape butchery.

German bombers had destroyed the docks at Dunkirk and a pall of smoke hung over the city. The East Mole, just wide enough for three men to walk abreast, and the open beaches were all that remained.

What happened during the following days, from May 29 to June 4, amazed the entire world. From a huge room carved out of the chalk under Dover Castle, Vice-Admiral Bertram Ramsay, with a staff of sixteen men, guided "Operation Dynamo." "There," wrote Edward R. Murrow, "above the port used by Caesar's galleys when they ran the cross-channel ferry, in a room where the words scrawled by prisoners taken from Napoleon's ships are still visible, Ramsay ran the show and demonstrated again the British genius for improvisation." From England there set out a rescue armada of motorboats, navy whalers, lifeboats, French fishing boats, Dutch schuits, Channel ferries, sloops, mine sweepers, drifters, destroyers. This strange fleet was manned by a motley crew of seagoing taxicab drivers and bankers. Many of the skippers went out with no more than a few bearings penciled on scraps of paper, while others steered by the flames from Dunkirk. Some lost their lives as destroyers cut their craft in two in the darkness, and others were battered, bruised, and broken by German fighter planes. In the meantime protecting warships and RAF bombers fashioned a wall of flame between the retreating forces around Dunkirk and the pursuing Germans.

On the evening of June 4, 1940, the Admiralty issued a communiqué that told the story of Dunkirk:

The Times (London), June 4, 1940

The most extensive and difficult combined operation in naval history has been carried out during the past week.

British, French, and Belgian troops have been brought back safely to this country from Belgium and northern France in numbers which, when the full story can be told, will surprise the world.

The withdrawal has been carried out in face of intense and almost continuous air attack and increasing artillery and machine-gun fire.

The success of this operation was only made possible by the close co-operation of the Allies and of the Services, and by never-flagging determination and courage of all concerned.

The rapid assembly of over six hundred small craft of all types was carried out by volunteers. These showed magnificent and tireless spirit.

The Admiralty cannot speak too highly of the services of all concerned. They were essential to the success of the operation and the means of saving thousands of lives.

The withdrawal was carried out from Dunkirk and from beaches in the vicinity. The whole operation was screened by naval forces against any attempt by the enemy at interference by sea.

In addition to almost incessant bombing and machine-gun attacks on Dunkirk, the beaches and the vessels operating off them, the port of Dunkirk and the shipping plying to and fro were under frequent shellfire. This was to some extent checked by bombardment of the enemy artillery positions by our naval forces. Naval bombardment also protected the flanks of the withdrawal. Losses have been inflicted upon both these forces.

The operation was rendered more difficult by shallow water, narrow channels, and strong tides. The situation was such that one mistake in the handling of a ship might have blocked a vital channel or that part of the port of Dunkirk which could be used. Nor was the weather entirely in favor of the operation. On two days a fresh northwesterly wind raised a surf which made work at the beaches slow and difficult. Only on one forenoon did ground mist curtail enemy air activity.

A withdrawal of this nature and magnitude, carried out in face of intense and almost continuous air attack, is the most hazardous of all operations. Its success is a triumph of Allied sea and air power in face of the most powerful air forces which the enemy could bring to bear from air bases close at hand.

THIS WAS, perhaps, as dramatic a communiqué as could have been expected from the British Admiralty, past masters of understatement. When "the full story" was told it was far more exciting. Most authoritative was the account written by Arthur Durham Divine, a British war correspondent of the Kemsley newspapers, world traveler and naval analyst, who told of the part he and Mrs. Miniver's husband, and many another boating enthusiast, played in the epic of Dunkirk.

"I am still amazed about the whole Dunkirk affair"

A. D. Divine, "*Miracle at Dunkirk*," by permission of the author's agent, Ann Watkins, Inc., and the *Reader's Digest*, December, 1940

I am still amazed about the whole Dunkirk affair. There was from first to last a queer, medieval sense of miracle about it. You remember the old quotation about the miracle that crushed the Spanish Armada, "God sent a wind." This time "God withheld the wind." Had we had one onshore breeze of any strength at all, in the first days, we would have lost a hundred thousand men.

The pier at Dunkirk was the unceasing target of bombs and shellfire throughout, yet it never was hit. Two hundred and fifty thousand men embarked from that pier.

The whole thing from first to last was covered with that same strange feeling of something supernatural. We muddled, we quarreled, everybody swore and was bad-tempered and made the wildest accusations of inefficiency and worse in high places. Boats were badly handled and broke down, arrangements went wrong.

And yet out of all that mess we beat the experts, we defied the law and the prophets, and where the government and the Board of Admiralty had hoped to bring away 30,000 men, we brought away 335,000. If that was not a miracle, there are no miracles left.

When I heard that small boats of all sorts were to be used at Dunkirk I volunteered at once. Within two hours of my first telephone call I was on my way to Sheerness. From Sheerness I acted as navigator for a party of small boats round to Ramsgate, and at Ramsgate we started work.

I was given a motorboat about as long as my drawing room at home, thirty feet. She had one cabin forward and the rest was open, but she had twin engines and was fairly fast. For crew we had one sublieutenant, one stoker, and one gunner. For armament we had two Bren guns—one my own particular pet which I had stolen—and rifles. In command of our boat we had a real live Admiral—Taylor, Admiral in charge of small boats.

We first went out to French fishing boats gathered off Ramsgate, boats from Caen and Le Havre, bright little vessels with lovely names—*Ciel de France, Ave Maria, Gratia Plena, Jeanne Antoine*. They had helped at Calais and Boulogne and in the preceding days at Dunkirk, and the men were very tired, but when we passed them new orders they set out again for Dunkirk.

They went as the leaders of the procession, for they were slow. With them went a handful of Dutch schuits, stumpy little coasting vessels commandeered at the collapse of Holland, each flying the white ensign of the Royal Navy, sparkling new, and each fitted out with a Lewis gun. Next went coasters, colliers, paddle steamers that in time of peace had taken trippers around the harbor for a shilling, tugs towing mud scows with brave names like *Galleon's Reach* and *Queen's Channel*.

There was a car ferry, surely on its first trip in the open sea. There were yachts; one the *Skylark*—what a name for such a mission! There were dockyard tugs, towing barges. There were sloops, mine sweepers, trawlers,

destroyers. There were Thames firefloats, Belgian drifters, lifeboats from all around the coast, lifeboats from sunken ships. I saw the boats of the old *Dunbar Castle*, sunk eight months before. Rolling and pitching in a cloud of spray were open speedboats, wholly unsuited for the Channel chop.

There was the old *Brighton Belle* that carried holiday crowds in the days before the Boer War. She swept mines in the Great War, and she swept mines in this war through all the fury of last winter.

There was never such a fleet went to war before, I think. As I went round the western arm of the harbor near sunset, passing out orders, it brought my heart into my throat to watch them leave. They were so small! Little boats like those you see in the bight of Sandy Hook fishing on a fine afternoon. Some were frowzy, with old motorcar tires for fenders, and some of them were bright with paint and chromium—little white boats that were soon lost to view across the ruffled water. And as they went there came round from the foreland a line of fishing boats—shrimp catchers and what not, from the east coast—to join the parade.

When this armada of oddments was under way, we followed with the faster boats—Royal Air Force rescue launches, picket boats, and the like—and with us went an X-lighter, a flatboat, kerosene-powered, built for landing troops at Gallipoli and a veteran of *that* evacuation more than twenty years ago.

It was the queerest, most nondescript flotilla that ever was, and it was manned by every kind of Englishman, never more than two men, often only one, to each small boat. There were bankers and dentists, taxi drivers and yachtsmen, longshoremen, boys, engineers, fishermen, and civil servants. There were bright-faced Sea Scouts and old men whose skins looked fiery red against their white hair. Many were poor; they had no coats, but made out with old jerseys and sweaters. They wore cracked rubber boots. They were wet, chilled to the bone, hungry; they were unarmed and unprotected, and they sailed toward the pillars of smoke and fire and the thunder of the guns, into waters already slick with the oil of sunken boats, knowing perfectly well the special kind of hell ahead. Still, they went, plugging gamely along.

I had a feeling, then and after, that this was something bigger than organization, something bigger than the mere requisitioning of boats. In a sense it was the naval spirit that has always been the foundation of England's greatness, flowering again and flowering superbly. I believe 887 was the official figure for the total of boats that took part over the ten days of the evacuation. But I think there were more than a thousand craft in all. I myself know of fishermen who never registered, waited for no orders, but, all unofficial, went and brought back soldiers. Quietly, like that.

It was dark before we were well clear of the English coast. It wasn't rough, but there was a little chop on, sufficient to make it very wet, and we soaked the Admiral to the skin. Soon, in the dark, the big boats began to overtake us. We were in a sort of dark traffic lane, full of strange ghosts and weird, unaccountable waves from the wash of the larger vessels. When destroyers went by, full tilt, the wash was a serious matter to us little fellows. We could only spin the wheel to try to head into the waves, hang on, and hope for the best.

Mere navigation was dangerous in the dark. Clouds hung low and blotted out the stars. We carried no lights, we had no signals, no means of recognition of friend or foe. Before we were halfway across we began to meet the first of the returning stream. We dodged white, glimmering bow waves of vessels that had passed astern, only to fall into the way of half-seen shapes ahead. There were shouts in the darkness, but only occasionally the indignant stutter of a horn. We went "by guess and by God."

From the halfway mark, too, there were destroyers on patrol crossing our line of passage, weaving a fantastic warp of foam through the web of our progress. There were collisions, of course. Dover for days was full of destroyers with bows stove in, coasting vessels with great gashes amidships, ships battered, scraped, and scarred. The miracle is that there were not ten for every one that happened.

Even before it was fully dark we had picked up the glow of the Dunkirk flames, and now as we drew nearer the sailing got better, for we could steer by them and see silhouetted the shapes of other ships, of boats coming home already loaded, and of low dark shadows that might be enemy motor torpedo boats.

Then aircraft started dropping parachute flares. We saw them hanging all about us in the night, like young moons. The sound of the firing and the bombing was with us always, growing steadily louder as we got nearer and nearer. The flames grew, too. From a glow they rose up to enormous plumes of fire that roared high into the everlasting pall of smoke. As we approached Dunkirk there was an air attack on the destroyers and for a little the night was brilliant with bursting bombs and the fountain sprays of tracer bullets.

The beach, black with men, illumined by the fires, seemed a perfect target, but no doubt the thick clouds of smoke were a useful screen.

When we got to the neighborhood of the mole there was a lull. The aircraft had dispersed and apparently had done no damage, for there was nothing sinking. They had been there before, however, and the place was a shambles of old wrecks, British and French, and all kinds of odds and ends. The breakwaters and lighthouse were magnificently silhouetted against the flames of burning oil tanks—enormous flames that licked high above the town. Further inshore and to the east of the docks the town itself was burning furiously, but down near the beach where we were going there was no fire and we could see rows of houses standing silent and apparently empty.

We had just got to the eastward of the pier when shelling started up. There was one battery of 5.9's down between La Panne and Nieuport that our people simply could not find and its shooting was uncannily accurate. Our place was in the corner of the beach at the mole, and as they were shelling the mole, the firing was right over our heads. Nothing, however, came near us in the first spell.

The picture will always remain sharp-etched in my memory—the lines of men wearily and sleepily staggering across the beach from the dunes to the shallows, falling into little boats, great columns of men thrust out into the water among bomb and shell splashes. The foremost ranks were shoulder-deep, moving forward under the command of young subalterns, themselves with their heads just above the little waves that rode in to the sand. As the front ranks were dragged aboard the boats, the rear ranks moved up, from ankle-deep to knee-deep, from knee-deep to waist-deep, until they, too, came to shoulder-depth and their turn.

Some of the big boats pushed in until they were almost aground, taking appalling risks with the falling tide. The men scrambled up the sides on rope nets, or climbed hundreds of ladders, made God knows where out of new, raw wood and hurried aboard the ships in England.

The little boats that ferried from the beach to the big ships in deep water listed drunkenly with the weight of men. The big ships slowly took on lists of their own with the enormous numbers crowded aboard. And always down the dunes and across the beach came new hordes of men, new columns, new lines.

On the beach was a destroyer, bombed and burned. At the water's edge were ambulances, abandoned when their last load had been discharged.

There was always the red background, the red of Dunkirk burning. There was no water to check the fires and there were no men to be spared to fight them. Red, too, were the shell-bursts, the flash of guns, the fountains of tracer bullets.

The din was infernal. The 5.9 batteries shelled ceaselessly and brilliantly. To the whistle of shells overhead was added the scream of falling bombs. Even the sky was full of noise —antiaircraft shells, machine-gun fire, the snarl of falling planes, the angry hornet noise of dive bombers. One could not speak normally at any time against the roar of it and the noise of our own engines. We all developed "Dunkirk throat," a sore hoarseness that was the hallmark of those who had been there.

Yet through all the noise I will always remember the voices of the young subalterns as they sent their men aboard, and I will remember, too, the astonishing discipline of the men. They had fought through three weeks of retreat, always falling back without orders, often without support. Transport had failed. They had gone sleepless. They had been without food and water. Yet they kept ranks as they came down the beaches, and they obeyed commands.

Veterans of Gallipoli and of Mons agreed this was the hottest spot they had ever been in, yet morale held. I was told stories of French troops that rushed the boats at first so that stern measures had to be taken, but I saw nothing like that. The Frenchmen I brought off were of the rear guard, fine soldiers, still fighting fit.

Having the Admiral on board, we were not actually working the beaches but were in control of operations. We moved about as necessary, and after we had spent some time putting small boats in touch with their towing boats, the 5.9 battery off Nieuport way began to drop shells on us. It seemed pure spite. The nearest salvo was about twenty yards astern, which was close enough.

We stayed there until everybody else had been sent back, and then went pottering about looking for stragglers. While we were doing that, a salvo of shells got one of our troopships alongside the mole. She was hit clean in the boilers and exploded in one terrific crash. There were then, I suppose, about one thousand Frenchmen on the mole. We had seen them crowding along its narrow crest, outlined against the flames. They had gone out under shellfire to board the boat, and now they had to go back again, still being shelled. It was quite the most tragic thing I ever have seen in my life. We could do nothing with our little park dinghy.

While they were still filing back to the beach and the dawn was breaking with uncomfortable brilliance, we found one of our stragglers—a navy whaler. We told her people to come aboard, but they said that there was a motorboat aground and they would have to fetch off her crew. They went in and we waited. It was my longest wait, ever. For various reasons they were terribly slow. When they found the captain of the motorboat, they stood up and argued with him and he wouldn't come off anyway. Damned plucky chap. He and his men lay quiet until the tide floated them later in the day. Then they made a dash for it, and got away.

We waited for them until the sun was up before we got clear of the mole. By then, the fighting was heavy inshore, on the outskirts of the town, and actually in some of the streets.

Going home, the Jerry dive bombers came over us five times, but somehow left us alone, though three times they took up an attacking position. A little down the coast, towards Gravelines, we picked up a boatload of Frenchmen rowing off. We took them aboard. They were very much bothered as to where our "ship" was, said quite flatly that it was impossible to go to England in a thing like ours. Too, too horribly dangerous.

OUT OF THE rescue boats onto the soil of England stepped an army of dirty, sleepy, hungry men, staggering with fatigue. Many of them were blood-covered and unrecognizable. One reporter noted that they brought with them half the canine population of Belgium and France. "Some of the dogs were shell-shocked; they whimpered; but the men didn't." Newsmen got some superb eyewitness stories from the ragged army which had lived to fight again:

A trooper: I never believed anything like the wall of fire our ships put up to screen troops was possible. Shells fell in a mathematically straight line behind our positions, while beyond the line British planes dropped bombs like hail. Jerry never had a chance to get us.

A sergeant major: Although we come back wounded, we have given them plenty to remember us by. At times the slaughter was wholesale. Column after column of Germans was mowed down by our Bren guns. The morale of our men was superb. When they were embarking, bombers raided the ships and one gun crew was put out of action. Wounded men went to take a share in feeding the guns.

A veteran of the last war: The British put up a barrage a mile long to stem the advance. I fought in the last war, but I have never seen anything like it. The Germans advanced right into it, disregarding danger. Their casualties must have been enormous.

An artilleryman: It's an inferno over there; a hell made by man. The Germans asked for a truce to bury their dead after a thirty-six-hour barrage had held up their advance. We replied: "There's no truce!" And we gave them another seven hours of barrage.

Another trooper: When we were hit by bombs we swam ashore, but when the ship didn't go down we swam back to her again to take her out of the harbor. Then she turned turtle and we had to swim again. Some of us were in the water for hours before we were picked up by a British warship.

Dunkirk was a turning point in World War II, with a devastating defeat turned into a magnificent moral victory. In the words of Divine, "it was a brutal, desperate adventure forced upon us by the most dire disaster, carried out under the eyes of an enemy flushed with victory, elated with the certainty of conquest. It was carried out in defiance of time, of circumstance, of death itself." The fact of Dunkirk inspired Britain's greatest voice to defiant challenge: "We shall fight on the seas and oceans," said Churchill, "we shall fight with growing confidence and growing strength in the air, we shall defend our island, whatever the cost may be, we shall fight on the beaches, we shall fight on the landing grounds, we shall fight in the fields and in the streets, we shall fight in the hills; we shall never surrender."

Quentin Reynolds Discovers "There Was No Dawn" as Germans Pound at the Gates of Paris

What has happened in France and Belgium is a colossal military disaster. The French army is weakened. Belgium is lost. The whole of the Channel ports are in Hitler's hands. We must expect another blow struck almost immediately at us or the French.

THUS SPOKE Winston Churchill in the House of Commons on June 4, 1940, after Dunkirk. A day later the Germans opened the Battle of France. The first phase of the drive began on the lower Somme. June 10 saw them at the Marne, the scene of the great French stands in World War I. But for the French history did not repeat itself. Overtaken by panic, overwhelmed by *Blitzkrieg,* the French armies dashed into headlong retreat. Hundreds of thousands of refugees jammed the roads from Paris south to Bordeaux for a distance of some four hundred miles, worsening an already confused situation.

Caught in the gigantic civilian exodus from the French capital was an ace American correspondent, Quentin Reynolds, onetime sports writer for the old *Evening World* and a Hearst correspondent in Germany during the Hitler revolution. For his carefully documented story for *Collier's* of the facts behind the killing of a German diplomat in Paris by Herschel Grynszpan, a seventeen-year-old Polish Jew, the Nazis had never forgiven him. After the fall of Norway Reynolds fretted to get his credentials cleared to cover the French army. From Paris he cabled F. D. R., urging him to speed things along. Signing the cable "Quent," he was asked by a French public-relations officer: "You are a nephew of the President?" Reynolds nodded casually: "Haven't you ever heard of Quentin Roosevelt?" * "But of course," said the Frenchman. "How stupid of me!"

When Reynolds finally reached the front, he saw plenty of action—but no longer any front. He lay in a field as Stuka bombers let their missiles fall all about him. In *The Wounded Don't Cry* (the royalties from which went to the British Red Cross) Reynolds described the terror and confusion of the evacuation of Paris. To his description one might add a comment by Elliot Paul, who, in *The Last Time I Saw Paris* (1942), has left us a memorable evocation of the folks in Rue de la Hachette. "And back on the Rue Saint-Séverin," Paul observed, "two dogs howled and howled, abandoned in an empty building."

* Theodore Roosevelt's son, a hero among the French, killed during World War I.

"And so Paris died"

Quentin Reynolds, *The Wounded Don't Cry,* (New York, 1941)

There was no dawn.

This was puzzling at first because it had been a clear night. Now the air was heavy with a smoky fog so thick that you could reach out and grab a piece of it in your hand. When you let it go your hand was full of soot. Then you realized that this was a man-made fog, a smoke screen thrown over Paris to hide the railroad stations from the bombers. But for the first time in its history Paris had no dawn.

The restaurants and the hotels were all closed. For nearly a week there had been no way of hearing from or communicating with the outside world. A reporter without means of communication is a jockey without a horse. No matter what story you wrote now, you would be its only reader. And now the Germans were pounding on the gates of Paris. Already their mechanized forces had encircled the city on three sides. Within a day the thing that couldn't happen was inevitably going to happen. They would be in Paris.

It was time to say farewell to Paris. Virtually everyone else had left. The government had left. The cable office and the wireless had moved south. With the exception of a few newspapermen who had been assigned to the deathwatch the entire press had left. They had to leave. They had to follow their communications. Hotels were closed. There were no telephones, and not a taxicab on the streets. Today Paris was a lonely old lady completely exhausted. The last of the refugees were leaving, some on bicycles, some on foot, pushing overladen handcarts.

I had stayed behind to write the story of the siege of Paris, confident that the army would hold out in the north. Now it developed that there would be no siege of Paris. The Grand Boulevard was almost deserted this morning. One middle-aged woman was sitting at a table at a sidewalk café, one of the very few where one could still get coffee and bread. She had driven into the city that morning in her small one-seated car. She wanted to sell her car. I bought it on the spot.

Now I was mobile.

We didn't catch up with the great army of refugees until we passed the city limits. From then on we were a member of this army. It is one thing to see thousands of weary refugees in the newsreels; it is something quite different to be one of them. We moved slowly, sometimes we would be held up for as long as three hours without moving. The road stretched from Paris to Bordeaux four hundred miles away, and it was packed solid that entire distance. Thousands of these people had come from the north, many had been on the road for two weeks. They had only one thought: move south. Move away from terror that swooped down from the skies. Move away from the serfdom that would be theirs under German rule. Few had any money. Few knew where they were going.

Some rode in open trucks and large, open wagons drawn by horses. Inevitably the sides of these would be buttressed by mattresses. These were not for sleeping. These were protection against machine-gun bullets. Refugees coming from Belgium and from Holland and refugees who had come from the north had been machine-gunned by Messerschmitts not once or twice but repeatedly. This is not rumor; it is fact.

Thousands in our army of refugees rode bicycles, and they made the best time. Often a military convoy came down the road against our tide of traffic. Then we would stop and wait interminably until it passed. Those on bicycles managed to keep going, winding in and out of the massed traffic.

Thousands were walking, many carrying huge packs on their shoulders. This was a quiet, patient army. There was little talk. The hours passed slowly. My uniform and military pass gave me priority. And yet in eight hours I had only covered fifty miles.

It started to rain as night fell. Now we began to be held up by trucks and automobiles that had run out of gasoline. There was no gasoline to be had. Women stood on the roadside crying to us for gasoline as we passed. We could only look ahead and drive on. The rain continued to fall softly and the night grew very dark, which made us breathe easier. Even German bombers can't see through a pall of blackness.

Individuals would emerge from the mass when we stopped. Here on the roadside was a woman lying asleep. Her head pillowed on her bicycle. Here was a farm wagon that had broken down. A man and woman with their three children, the youngest in the mother's arms, looked at the wreck. The rear axle had broken and when the wagon collapsed its weight had completely smashed one wheel. They stood there looking at it, their faces empty of everything but despair. The road was completely jammed now. A man went from car to car asking:

"Is my wife there? She has lost her mind. She has lost her mind."

Our army went on through the night. Hours later a whisper ran back: *"Alerte . . . alerte."* It had started perhaps miles ahead and had come back to us. The very few cars that had been showing lights snapped them off. Boche bombers were somewhere overhead in that black, unknown world above us. We were very quiet, thousands of us. I stepped out of my car. I flashed my light once to see where we were. I was in the middle of a bridge. Not a good place to be with German bombers overhead. But there was no place to go.

Occasionally a car crawled by or a silent bicyclist or a few on foot passed. From the thousands and thousands ahead and behind came an overwhelming silence that somehow had the effect of terrific, overpowering noise. This silent symphony of despair never stopped. It was impossible to sleep. We sat in our cars and our wagons and waited for the dawn. It took hours for it to come and when it arrived it was murky dawn. Without food or drink, we set forth south, always south.

We passed through small towns. Streams of cars half a mile long would be lined up at a gasoline pump that had run dry days before. Now we passed stranded cars every few minutes. Sometimes people pushed their cars, hoping that there would be fuel in the next town. There was no fuel in the next town.

At one town we passed a railroad station. A long freight train was just pulling in from Paris. The doors of the freight cars were open, and humanity poured out, spilled, overflowed. These were the cars on which the famous sign, "Forty men, eight horses," was scrawled during the past war. Forty men. There were at least one hundred men and women and children in each of these freight cars. At each station the doors were opened for five minutes. This train had been on the road nearly three days from Paris. Once the train had been machine-gunned. Not one, but everyone I spoke to, told me the same story. It had been machine-gunned by eight German planes. French fighters had come and driven them off. Had anyone been hit? No one knew.

The congestion increased the farther south we went. People looked even wearier.

They had to move on. They stumbled on south, bearing the cross of their despair with the same courage and stoicism with which another had borne a cross nearly two thousand years ago.

William L. Shirer Tells the Listening World of Hitler's Hour of Triumph

EIGHTY-FOUR-YEAR-OLD MARSHAL PÉTAIN, hero of World War I, stood before the microphone and told the people of France:

The continuation of the struggle against an enemy superior in numbers and in arms is futile. It is with a heavy heart I say we must cease the fight. I have applied to our opponent to ask him if he is ready to sign with us, as between soldiers after the fight and in honor.

Upon the news of the French collapse Adolf Hitler executed a horrible little war dance, which was duly recorded for posterity by a Nazi newsreel cameraman. It is a study in devilish joy—the stiff, intense Führer almost automatically breaking into an awkward tap dance to express his delight in victory over France. But Hitler did not reply to Pétain's petition for three days. On June 21, 1940, at exactly the same spot where on November 11, 1918, the Armistice that ended World War I had been signed in a little clearing in the forest of Compiègne, Hitler received three French envoys and handed them the German terms. The next day the French accepted defeat. Hitler ordered the German and French plenipotentiaries to meet in Marshal Foch's private car—the same railway car in which Foch had laid down his armistice terms to Germany in the previous war. As additional salt for the wounds of prostrate France Hitler insisted that the same table in the shaky old *wagon-lit* be used. Tasting the sweet fruit of revenge, he himself occupied the seat on which Foch had sat when the Frenchman had dictated terms to the Boche.

William L. Shirer, onetime foreign correspondent of *The Chicago Tribune*, was an eyewitness to this dramatic interlude of World War II. His broadcast for CBS from Compiègne on the meeting of the triumphant Führer and the humiliated French commission demonstrates how on some occasions oral, improvised reporting can be more effective in conveying a sense of immediacy than on-the-spot newspaper coverage. When reporting on the air waves the speaker must phrase his reactions quickly, without an opportunity to polish his story. Shirer's broadcast was improvised from notes, which accounts for the conversational style and the inconsistency in tenses.

The Nazi overlord tastes revenge and finds it sweet

Broadcast by William L. Shirer, Columbia Broadcasting System, June 21, 1940

ANNOUNCER—At this time, as the French government considers Germany's terms for an armistice, Columbia takes you to Berlin for a special broadcast by William Shirer in Germany. We take you now to Berlin. Go ahead, Berlin.

SHIRER—Hello, America! CBS! William L. Shirer calling CBS in New York.

William L. Shirer calling CBS in New York, calling CBS from Compiègne, France. This is William L. Shirer of CBS. We've got a microphone at the edge of a little clearing in the forest of Compiègne, four miles to the north of the town of Compiègne and about forty-five miles north of Paris. Here, a few feet from where we're standing, in the very same old railroad coach where the Armistice was signed on that chilly morning of November 11, 1918, negotiations for another armistice—the one to end the present war between France and Germany—began at 3:30 P.M., German summer time, this afternoon. What a turning back of the clock, what a reversing of history we've been watching here in this beautiful Compiègne Forest this afternoon! What a contrast to that day twenty-two years ago! Yes, even the weather, for we have one of those lovely warm June days which you get in this part of France close to Paris about this time of year.

As we stood here, watching Adolf Hitler and Field Marshal Göring and the other German leaders laying down the terms of the armistice to the

French plenipotentiaries here this afternoon, it was difficult to comprehend that in this rustic little clearing in the midst of the Forest of Compiègne, from where we're talking to you now, that an armistice was signed here on the cold, cold morning at five A.M. on November 11, 1918. The railroad coach—it was Marshal Foch's private car—stands a few feet away from us here, in exactly the same spot where it stood on that gray morning twenty-two years ago, only—and what an "only" it is, too—Adolf Hitler sat in the seat occupied that day by Marshal Foch. Hitler at that time was only an unknown corporal in the German army, and in that quaint old wartime car another armistice is being drawn up as I speak to you now, an armistice designed like the other that was signed on this spot to bring armed hostilities to halt between those ancient enemies—Germany and France. Only everything that we've been seeing here this afternoon in Compiègne Forest has been so reversed. The last time the representatives of France sat in that car dictating the terms of the armistice. This afternoon we peered through the windows of the car and saw Adolf Hitler laying down the terms. That's how history reversed itself, but seldom has it done so as today on the very same spot. The German leader in the preamble of the conditions which were read to the French delegates by Colonel General von Keitel, Chief of the German Supreme Command, told the French that he had not chosen this spot at Compiègne out of revenge but merely to right a wrong.

The armistice negotiations here on the same spot where the last armistice was signed in 1918, here in Compiègne Forest, began at 3:15 P.M., our time, a warm June sun beat down on the great elm and pine trees and cast purple shadows on the hooded avenues as Herr Hitler with the German plenipotentiaries at his side appeared. He alighted from his car in front of the French monument to Alsace-Lorraine which stands at the end of an avenue about two hundred yards from the clearing here in front of us where the armistice car stands. That famous Alsace-Lorraine statue was covered with German war flags, so that you cannot see its sculptured works or read its inscriptions. I had seen it many times in the postwar years, and doubtless many of you have seen it—the large sword representing the sword of the Allies, with its point sticking into a large, limp eagle, representing the old empire of the Kaiser, and the inscription underneath in front saying, "To the heroic soldiers of France, defenders of the country and of right, glorious liberators of Alsace-Lorraine."

Through our glasses, we saw the Führer stop, glance at the statue, observe the Reich war flags with their big swastikas in the center. Then he strolled slowly toward us, toward the little clearing where the famous armistice car stood. I thought he looked very solemn; his face was grave. But there was a certain spring in his step, as he walked for the first time toward the spot where Germany's fate was sealed on that November day of 1918, a fate which, by reason of his own being, is now being radically changed here on this spot.

And now, if I may sort of go over my notes—I made from moment to moment this afternoon—now Hitler reaches a little opening in the Compiègne woods where the Armistice was signed and where another is about to be drawn up. He pauses and slowly looks around. The opening here is in the form of a circle about two hundred yards in diameter and laid out like a park. Cypress trees line it all around, and behind them the great elms and oaks of the forest. This has been one of France's national shrines for twenty-two years. Hitler pauses and gazes slowly around. In the group just behind him are the other German plenipotentiaries—Field Marshal Göring, grasping his Field Marshal baton in one hand. He wears the blue uniform of the air force. All the Germans are in uniform. Hitler in a double-breasted gray uniform with the Iron Cross hanging from his left breast pocket. Next to Göring are the two German army chiefs, Colonel General von Keitel, Chief of the Supreme Command, and Colonel General von Brauchitsch, Commander-in-Chief of the German Army. Both are just approaching sixty, but look younger, especially General von Keitel, who has a dapper appearance, with his cap slightly cocked on one side. Then we see there Dr. Raeder, Grand Admiral of the German Fleet. He has on a blue naval uniform and the invariable upturned stiff collar which German naval officers usually wear. We see two nonmilitary men in Hitler's suite—his Foreign Minister, Joachim von Ribbentrop, in the field-gray uniform of the Foreign Office, and Rudolf Hess, Hitler's deputy, in a gray party uniform.

The time's now, I see by my notes, 3:18 P.M. in the Forest of Compiègne. Hitler's personal standard is run up on a small post in the center of the circular opening in the woods. Also, in the center, is a great granite block which stands some three feet above the ground. Hitler, followed by the others, walks slowly over to it, steps up, and reads the inscription engraved in great high letters on that block. Many of you will remember the words of that inscription. The Führer slowly reads them, and the inscription says, "Here on the eleventh of November, 1918, succumbed the criminal pride of the German Empire, vanquished by the free peoples which it tried to enslave." Hitler reads it, and Göring reads it. They all read it, standing there in the June sun and the silence. We look for the expression on Hitler's face, but it does not change. Finally he leads his party over to another granite stone, a small one some fifty yards to one side. Here it was that the railroad car in which the German plenipotentiary stayed during the 1918 armistice negotiations stood from November 8 to 11. Hitler looks down and reads the inscription, which merely says: "The German plenipotentiary." The stone itself, I notice, is set between a pair of rusty old railroad tracks, the very ones that were there twenty-two years ago.

It is now 3:23 P.M., and the German leaders stride over to the armistice car. This car, of course, was not standing on this spot yesterday. It was standing seventy-five yards down the rusty track in the shelter of a tiny museum built to house it by an American citizen, Mr. Arthur Henry Fleming of Pasadena, California. Yesterday the car was removed from the museum by the German army engineers and rolled back those seventy-five yards to the spot where it stood on the morning of November 11, 1918. The Germans stand outside the car, chatting in the sunlight. This goes on for two minutes. Then Hitler steps up

into the car, followed by Göring and the others. We watch them entering the drawing room of Marshal Foch's car. We can see nicely now through the car windows.

Hitler enters first and takes the place occupied by Marshal Foch the morning the first armistice was signed. At his sides are Göring and General Keitel. To his right and left at the ends of the table we see General von Brauchitsch and Herr Hess at the one end, at the other end Grand Admiral Raeder and Herr von Ribbentrop. The opposite side of the table is still empty, and we see there four vacant chairs. The French have not yet appeared, but we do not wait long. Exactly at 3:30 P.M. the French alight from a car. They have flown up from Bordeaux to a near-by landing field and then have driven here in an auto.

They glance at the Alsace-Lorraine memorial, now draped with swastikas, but it's a swift glance. Then they walk down the avenue flanked by three German army officers. We see them now as they come into the sunlight of the clearing—General Huntziger, wearing a brief khaki uniform; General Bergeret and Vice-Admiral Le Luc, both in their respective dark-blue uniforms; and then, almost buried in the uniforms, the one single civilian of the day, Mr. Noël, French Ambassador to Poland when the present war broke out there. The French plenipotentiaries passed the guard of honor drawn up at the entrance of the clearing. The guard snapped to attention for the French but did not present arms. The Frenchmen keep their eyes straight ahead. It's a grave hour in the life of France, and their faces today show what a burden they feel on their shoulders. Their faces are solemn, drawn, but bear the expression of tragic dignity. They walked quickly to the car and were met by two German officers, Lieutenant Colonel Tippelskirch, Quartermaster General, and Colonel Thomas, Chief of the Paris Headquarters. The Germans salute; the French salute; the atmosphere is what Europeans call "correct"; but you'll get the picture when I say that we see no handshakes—not on occasions like this. The historic moment is now approaching. It is 3:32 by my watch. The Frenchmen enter Marshal Foch's Pullman car, standing there a few feet from us in Compiègne Forest. Now we get our picture through the dusty windows of the historic old *wagon-lit* car. Hitler and the other German leaders rise from their seats as the French enter the drawing room. Hitler, we see, gives the Nazi salute, the arm raised. The German officers give a military salute; the French do the same. I cannot see Mr. Noël to see whether he salutes or how. Hitler, so far as we can see through the windows just in front of here, does not say anything. He nods to General Keitel at his side. We can see General Keitel adjusting his papers, and then he starts to read. He is reading the preamble of the German armistice terms. The French sit there with marblelike faces and listen intently. Hitler and Göring glance at the green table top. This part of the historic act lasts but a few moments. I note in my notebook here this—3:42 P.M.—that is, twelve minutes after the French arrived— 3:42—we see Hitler stand up, salute the three with hand upraised. Then he strides out of the room, followed by Göring, General von Brauchitsch, Grand Admiral Raeder is there, Herr Hess, and, at the end, von Ribbentrop. The French remain at the greentopped table in the old Pullman car, and we see General Keitel remains with them. He is going to read them the detailed conditions of the armistice. Hitler goes, and the others do not wait for this. They walk down the avenue back towards the Alsace-Lorraine monument. As they pass the guard of honor, a German band strikes up the two national anthems *Deutschland über Alles* and the *Horst Wessel Song.*

The whole thing has taken but a quarter of an hour—this great reversal of a historical armistice of only a few years ago.

CBS ANNOUNCER—You have just heard a special broadcast from the Compiègne Forest in France, where on the historic morning of November 11, 1918, representatives of the German army received from the Allies the terms of the armistice which ended the First World War, and where today, June 21, 1940, representatives of the French government received from Führer Adolf Hitler the terms under which a cessation of hostilities between Germany and France may be reached. As you know, the actual terms presented to the French plenipotentiaries have not yet been made public.

MUSIC—*Organ*

ANNOUNCER—This is the Columbia Broadcasting System.

THE GERMAN PRESS, thoroughly briefed by Dr. Goebbels, greeted the proceedings at Compiègne with a roar of approbation. The once-independent *Frankfurter Zeitung,* now completely co-ordinated, hailed the event as "a shame wiped out" and "a piece of great history." "This time the defeated nation has been struck down by weapons alone in a military catastrophe without parallel, and no friendly help stood at the victor's side. Germany, which was once without belief and hope, is today stronger than for many centuries. All eyes turn now to the gas-blinded lance corporal of 1918." Thousands of other newsmen throughout the Third Reich were thinking and writing in exactly the same terms.

Five Correspondents Cover Battle of Britain

O<small>N</small> JULY 19, 1940, Adolf Hitler, flushed with victory, magnanimously decided to give the British a last chance to surrender before their complete annihilation. "I am not the vanquished seeking favors," he said, "but the victor speaking in the name of reason." The British replied with contemptuous silence. Hitler countered with an all-out attack of the Luftwaffe on English ports, airfields, industrial centers, and London. This was the Battle of Britain, the first great air battle in history and the turning point of the war. It was also Britain's finest hour. Little did Adolf Hitler know the spirit and the fiber of the people he intended to beat down before his feet. "This wicked man," said Winston Churchill, "this monstrous product of former wrongs and shame, has now resolved to break our famous island race by a process of indiscriminate slaughter and destruction." As might have been expected, Churchill and the British people—to express it with typical British understatement—were not at all inclined to accept this state of affairs. "What kind of people do they think we are?" was Churchill's challenging question.

The Battle of Britain stimulated some of the finest reporting of this or any other war. Robert Bunnelle described the sensational air struggle as it developed on August 11-14 around Dover.

"It's a bit public not having windows": *Robert Bunnelle*

The New York Times, August 12, 15, 1940

From a balcony spattered with machine-gun fire and jarred by deafening bombardment I saw a new chapter in the Battle of Britain written today in a Sabbath sky thick with airplanes and spotted with mushroom puffs from antiaircraft shells.

Between attacks, we gathered shell-fragment souvenirs. We found machine-gun bullets embedded in the concrete a few feet from where we stood. Antiaircraft guns thundered a nerve-racking din one hundred yards away.

The raiders screamed down—sometimes from 15,000 feet—out of the early-morning sun, pouncing on coastal balloon barrages. From the ground and in the air the British gave them a hot reception. In one attack I saw four German planes bagged by British fighters and antiaircraft shells. Another correspondent farther down the coast counted one, and possibly two others, plummeting down from great height and trailing dense smoke.

The raid began as a surprise attack on the balloons, but developed into fierce dogfights, and was followed by repeated attacks by larger and larger waves, finally attacking the town as well as the water front. The gunfire rolled like thunder. One flight of raiders was split into two parts by antiaircraft fire, which kept one group performing aerial acrobatics while British pilots engaged the other.

Sometimes the planes were so high they looked like tiny specks of windblown paper. Some fought clear and streaked back toward the German-held coast of France. One of these trailed a great black plume of smoke. The battle raged so furiously it was impossible to keep accurate track of the planes that fell. A pilot of one destroyed plane drifted by parachute into the water two miles offshore. [Bunnelle was still reporting the battle on August 14.] I saw a lightship literally blown out of the water and sunk, her seams ripped open; I peered from a shelter while barrage balloons plunged into flames from the sky, their clashing cables falling almost at my feet; I saw a melee of perhaps 150 raiders and defenders surge through the clouds, and in my ears all day dinned the crash of antiaircraft and the dull thud of bombs behind me—inland.

The biggest cloud of German raiders—I counted about one hundred plainly visible, with others dotting the sky up higher—roared across the coast this forenoon from France, defiantly breasting a circle of twenty-seven British fighters. The British ringed them; then, one by one, dived on them. One vast, wild jamboree of twisting, flame-spitting planes developed. Four planes, then another, then others rocketed, burning, into the sea. We could not tell which side they belonged to.

In a crazy din of antiaircraft, machine-gun, and cannon explosions, six big Junkers screamed at the lightship, dropping two bombs apiece. They sent up geysers from the sea; others dropped on land.

A new swarm of raiders tore viciously at the barrage balloons moored from coastal barges. Some, in flames and shreds, came down—in a shower of spent machine-gun bullets, aerial cannon shells, and antiaircraft fragments.

While other planes were getting inland and up and down the coast to other targets, a low-flying German bombed one sea front near us, killing a Home Guard soldier, wounding several civilians, and wrecking three houses. In another town a Messerschmitt machine-gunned a railway station. Shelters saved the civilians there. In a house that had not a window left the family remained at the dinner table. A newspaperman poking his head through a gaping window, apologizing at the same time for the intrusion, was told by the father of the family: "You aren't the first one. It's a bit public not having windows, but the fresh air is nice."

HIGH ON Hitler's priority list was the bombing of London. By killing large numbers of civilians indiscriminately, he hoped to terrorize the British and distract their attention from the onslaught he was preparing. The Nazi airmen, who had smashed Warsaw and subjected Rotterdam (an open city) to a hideous air bombardment that took the lives of at least 30,000 civilians, were quite certain that they could annihilate London. Witness these cocksure words, dated August 18, 1940, from the diary of a German airman, Gottfried Leske, in *I Was a Nazi Flier* (1941): "Today I flew over this biggest city in the world. I knew with absolute certainty, as though I could foretell the future: This all will be destroyed. It will stand for but a few days more. Until the moment the Führer pronounces its death sentence. Then there will be nothing left but a heap of ruins."

The first all-out blow came on September 7, 1940, when 375 bombers— a huge flight at that time—dropped its load of bombs on the city in full daylight. "This is the historic hour," said Göring, "when our air force for the first time delivered its stroke right into the enemy's heart."

In her weekly "Letter from London," dated September 8, 1940, to *The New Yorker,* Mollie Panter-Downes described the reactions of the British people as the air *Blitzkrieg* started in earnest. "The calm behavior of the average individual," she wrote, "continues to be amazing. Commuting suburbanites, who up to yesterday had experienced worse bombardments than people living in central London, placidly brag to fellow passengers on the morning trains about the size of bomb craters in their neighborhoods, as in a more peaceful summer they would have bragged about their roses and squash." Day after day the Luftwaffe returned, hoping to repeat the damage it had done to Rotterdam.

Helen Kirkpatrick, the only woman member of the *Chicago Daily News* foreign staff, worked almost uninterruptedly in London under Nazi bombs. She later covered the North African and Italian fronts, and was one of the first correspondents to enter liberated Paris, from which she sent a thrilling dispatch of civil war inside Notre-Dame Cathedral. More recently she has been handling the *New York Post*'s Paris office. This brief story of the bombing of London substantiates Mollie Panter-Downes' conclusion that "the courage, humor, and kindliness of ordinary people continue to be astonishing under conditions that possess many of the merry features of a nightmare."

"London still stood this morning":
Helen Kirkpatrick

Chicago Daily News, September 9, 1940

London still stood this morning, which was the greatest surprise to me as I cycled home in the light of early dawn after the most frightening night I have ever spent. But not all of London was still there, and some of the things I saw this morning would scare the wits out of anyone.

When the sirens first shrieked on Saturday, it was evident we were in for something, but dinner proceeded calmly enough. It was when the first screaming bomb started on its downward track that we decided the basement would be healthier.

The whole night was one of moving

from the basement to the first floor, with occasional sallies to make sure that no incendiaries had landed on the rooftop.

That was perhaps more frightening than the sound of constant bombs punctuated by guns near and far. For the London air was heavy with the burning smell. The smoke sometimes brought tears to the eyes, and the glow around the horizon certainly looked as though the entire city might be up in flames any minute.

On one occasion I dropped off to sleep on a basement floor and slept probably forty-five minutes, when two screamers sounding as though they had landed right next door brought me, startled, to my feet. A few minutes later a couple of incendiaries arrived just around the corner, but the fire equipment came within seconds.

Most of the time we felt that the entire center of the city had probably been blasted out of existence and we ticked off each hit with "That must be Buckingham Palace—that's White-hall." It was staggering, to say the least, to cycle for a mile through the heart of London and fail to see even one pane of glass shattered and eventually to find one's own house standing calm and in one piece.

A later tour, however, showed that while none of the bombs hit any objectives we had picked out, they had landed squarely on plenty of places.

I walked through areas of rubble and debris in southeastern London this morning that made it seem incredible that anyone could be alive, but they were, and very much so. Fires for the most part were put out or were well under control by early morning.

It was a contrast to find one section of "smart London" that had as bad a dose as the tenement areas. Near one of many of Sir Christopher Wren's masterpieces, houses were gutted structures with windowpanes hanging out, while panes in a church were broken in a million pieces.

It is amazing this morning to see London traffic more like New York theater traffic than the slow dribble it had been during past months, but it is most amazing to see that there is any London to have traffic at all. It is pretty incredible, too, to find people relatively unshaken after the terrific experience.

There is some terror, but nothing on the scale that the Germans may have hoped for and certainly not on a scale to make Britons contemplate for a moment anything but fighting on.

Fright becomes so mingled with a deep almost uncontrollable anger that it is hard to know when one stops and the other begins. And on top of it all London is smiling even in the districts where casualties must have been very heavy.

* * *

London was stunned but defiant. The British fought back, their anti-aircraft organization functioning with skill and effectiveness and the RAF striking heavily at the invaders. On September 15 the Luftwaffe made another great mass attack on southern England and London. Definitely confirmed losses of German aircraft on that day amounted to 185, yet the *National Zeitung,* a newspaper controlled by Göring, insisted that "at an extraordinarily rapid rate, London drifts toward its fate." Although this attack must have wrecked Göring's hopes of dealing a death blow to the RAF, the German press maintained an air of optimism. The next day DNB, the German official news agency, reported this communiqué of the High Command:

Despite overcast skies the German Air Force continued retaliatory attacks yesterday and last night on military objectives in middle and south England, with especial attention to London. Dock and harbor facilities in the British capital suffered blows. Our fighters were successful in air battles over London.

The Luftwaffe paid dearly for this overconfidence. In *Their Finest Hour* (1949) Churchill listed aircraft losses in the Battle of Britain from July 10 to October 31, 1940, as follows:

British Fighters Lost by RAF (complete write-off or missing)   915
Enemy Aircraft Actually Destroyed (according to German records) 1,733
Enemy Aircraft Claimed by Us (Fighter Command, A.A., Balloons, etc.) 2,698

Throughout the ordeal in London Edward R. Murrow, chief of the Columbia Broadcasting System's foreign-news staff, broadcast to the people of the United States. Convinced that the Nazi attack had resulted in a kind of "revolution by consent," in which old power-politics notions were giving way to objectives of general welfare, Murrow won international acclaim for his on-the-spot reporting from Britain.

Britain's revolution by consent: Edward R. Murrow

Broadcast by Edward R. Murrow, Columbia Broadcasting System

September 15, 1940
During the last week you have heard much of the bombing of Buckingham Palace and probably seen pictures of the damage. You have been told by certain editors and commentators who sit in New York that the bombing of the palace, which has one of the best air-raid shelters in England, caused a great surge of determination—a feeling of unity—to sweep this island. The bombing was called a great psychological blunder. I do not find much support for that point of view amongst Londoners with whom I've talked. They don't like the idea of their King and Queen being bombed, but, remember, this is not the last war—people's reactions are different. Minds have become hardened and callused. It didn't require a bombing of Buckingham Palace to convince these people that they are all in this thing together. There is nothing exclusive about being bombed these days. When there are houses down in your street, when friends and relatives have been killed, when you've seen that red glow in the sky night after night, when you're tired and sleepy—there just isn't enough energy left to be outraged about the bombing of a palace.

The King and Queen have earned the respect and admiration of the nation, but so have tens of thousands of humble folk who are much less well protected. If the palace had been the only place bombed the reaction might have been different. Maybe some of those German bomb aimers are working for Goebbels instead of Göring, but if the purpose of the bombings was to strike terror to the hearts of the Britishers, then the bombs have been wasted. That fire bomb on the House of Lords passed almost unnoticed. I heard a parcel of people laughing about it when one man said: "That particular bomb wouldn't seriously have damaged the nation's war effort."

I'm talking about those things not because the bombing of the palace appears to have affected America more than Britain, but in order that you may understand that this war has no relation with the last one, so far as symbols and civilians are concerned. You must understand that a world is dying, that old values, the old prejudices, and the old bases of power and prestige are going. In an army, if the morale is to be good, there must be equality in the ranks. The private with money must not be allowed to buy himself a shelter of steel and concrete in the front-line trench. One company can't be equipped with pitchforks and another with machine guns. London's civilian army doesn't have that essential equality—I mean equality of shelter. One borough before the war defied the authorities and built deep shelters. Now people arrive at those shelters from all over town and the people who paid for them are in danger of being crowded out. Some of those outsiders arrive in taxis, others by foot. Since it's a public shelter they can't be barred by the people whose money went into the digging. This is just one of the problems in equality that London is now facing.

There are the homeless from the bombed and fire-blackened East End area. They must be cared for, they must be moved, they must be fed, and they must be sheltered. The Lord Mayor's fund, contributions from America, from unofficial agencies, are in the best tradition of Anglo-Saxon generosity and philanthropy, but no general would desire to rely upon such measures for the care and maintenance of injured troops. The people have been told that this is a people's war, that they are in the front lines, and they are. If morale is to be maintained at its present high level, there must be no distinction between the troops living in the various sections of London.

Even for those of us who live on the crest of London, life is dangerous. Some of the old buildings have gone, but the ghosts, sometimes a whole company of ghosts, remain. There is the thunder of gunfire at night. As these lines were written, as the window shook, there was a candle and matches beside the typewriter just in case the light went out. Richard Llewellyn, the man who wrote *How Green Was My Valley*, sat in the corner and talked about the dignity of silence while the guns jarred the apartment house. We went out to dinner, and the headwaiter carefully placed us at a table away from the window. "There might be," he said, "one of those blasts." In the West End of London, life follows some kind of pattern. The shops are still full of food; the milk arrives on the doorstep each morning; the papers, too, but sometimes they're a little late. Much of the talk, as you would expect, is about invasion. On that score there is considerable confidence. Everyone is convinced that it will be beaten back if it comes. There are some who fear that it will not come.

October 1, 1940

There is occurring in this country a revolution by consent. Millions of people ask only, "What can we do to help? Why must there be 800,000 unemployed when we need these shelters? Why can't the unemployed miners dig? Why are new buildings being constructed when the need is that the wreckage of bombed buildings be removed from the streets? What are the war aims of this country? What shall we do with victory when it's won? What sort of Europe will be built when and if this stress has passed?" These questions are being asked by thoughtful people in this country. Mark it down that in the three weeks of the air *Blitz* against this country more books and pamphlets have been published on these subjects than in any similar period of the war. Remember also that I am permitted to record this plan of political and social salvation at a time when this country fights for its life. Mark it down that these people are both brave and patient, that all are equal under the bomb, that this is a war of speed and organization, and that the political system which best provides for the defense and decency of the little man will win. You are witnessing the beginning of a revolution, maybe the death of an age. All these moves, Dakar, the pact with Japan, diplomats flying hither and yon, mean only that a large section of the world is waiting to be told what to do, as the Germans were waiting seven years ago.

Today, in one of the most famous streets in London, I saw soldiers at work clearing away the wreckage of nearly an entire block. The men were covered with white dust. Some of them wore goggles to protect their eyes. They thought maybe people were still buried in the basement. The sirens sounded, and still they tore at the beams and bricks covering the place where the basements used to be. They are still working tonight. I saw them after tonight's raid started. They paid no attention to the bursts of antiaircraft fire overhead as they bent their backs and carried away basketfuls of mortar and brick. A few small steam shovels would help them considerably in digging through those ruins. But all the modern instruments seem to be overhead. Down here on the ground people must work with their hands.

WE HAVE ALREADY mentioned Mollie Panter-Downes' reports of the cheerfulness and fortitude with which the ordinary "little people" of London did their jobs under nerve-racking conditions. Fire fighters, ambulance drivers, wardens, and relief workers labored around the clock as London was ringed and stabbed with fire. "We shall get used to it," they said.

One of these little people was Jock Evans, air-raid-precautions warden— "like the medieval leper, ringing his bell and shouting, 'Unclean! unclean!'" The story of Jock Evans was told by a great reporter, Robert J. Casey. "I salute Robert J. Casey," wrote Ben Hecht, "a member of the old *Chicago Daily News* staff, whom I knew as the dean of all the talented reporters hatched in that fabled local room."

"Jock Evans was on duty that night":
Robert J. Casey

Chicago Daily News, September 17, 1940

HOTSPOT, SOUTHEAST ENGLAND, SEP-TEMBER 17—In the larger matters of threatened invasion by aerial bombs and artillery fire people have given little thought to Jock Evans, upon whose thin breast nobody will ever pin any medals, even posthumously.

He will never have a public funeral with muffled drums, muted trumpets, and suchlike tokens of civic gratitude. It is most unlikely he will ever have any funeral at all.

In the years before the war he had done nothing to distinguish himself. He had some sort of dock job where the dust hadn't been too good for his lungs. Because of bad eyes and other deficiencies, he had been rejected for military service even at the end of the last war, when medical examiners hadn't been too particular.

In other words, though nobody noticed it at the time, he was made of the stuff heroes are made of.

So far as concerns the elements that have made England to date, he was an architect's model for the spirit of the British Empire.

Jock Evans, to get on with it, was in his most recent career an air-raid-precautions warden. In a year's drill on how to put on the gas mask, how to revive fainting women, how to direct people to the nearest shelter, he had never shown more than ordinary aptitude.

Jock Evans was on duty that night. He had been on duty most nights in the past month, as he would be now with warnings on all the time and never an all-clear. He had phoned to the central control at eleven P.M. that he had seen a bright light somewhere —his superiors, remembering Jock, suspected it might be somebody with a too-bright cigar.

He had stationed himself near the telephone kiosk near the edge of an outlying suburb where the artillery shells still land each day when the town is shelled. He had had no occasion to move from his post at midnight when the big crump fell.

The big crump was a dud. For a moment Jock felt glad of that. The shriek of it had been pretty nerve-racking. But after a while, when he remembered he had better go run over and look at it, he wasn't reassured. It wasn't a dud. He had looked at enough diagrams and sketches to know. It was a time bomb—and a big one.

He told all this to his chief in his report a minute later.

'Where is it?" inquired his chief.

"In the garden," said Jock.

Then the same order:

"Get people out, empty near-by houses, and keep people away!"

"Yes, sir," said Jock Evans.

Maybe it might be as well to mention here something of the nature of a time bomb, especially for Americans, who so far haven't had much experience with such things.

In the first place, it is not like the old-type torpedo with nose fuse which could be unscrewed by a handy man with a monkey wrench. This is more complicated. The timing device is a simple interior arrangement of acid working on metal.

By varying the thickness of the metal density, the acid rate of corrosion may be set for anything between one minute and one month. Eventually the acid reaches the fulminating charge and the neighborhood goes to pieces.

There have been some hints that in what followed after his report Jock didn't show any great judgment, but the same might have been said of Dewey if he had run into a mine at Manila Bay. He followed out his orders. In less than an hour he had evacuated the few homes in the immediate vicinity. Then he stationed himself to warn off traffic.

There wasn't much to do until about seven o'clock in the morning, when workers and sight-seers began to pass afoot, on bicycles, and in automobiles.

The odd feature of a community which is being continuously bombed is the inquisitive interest in lethal hazards. Jock Evans suddenly found himself alone in a two-man job. The bomb lay almost at the junction of two lanes, giving access to it from four directions.

Mr. Evans solved this problem as best he could. He roped off the street a hundred yards behind the bomb, then took up his post at the middle of the crossing.

Dozens of persons heard and heeded his call during the next two hours. "Time bomb here. Keep away, keep away."

One of those who passed was the priest of the neighborhood Anglican church, to whom is owing the best description of Jock Evans' last stand.

"He hardly needed to point out the bomb," said the padre. "It was lying there in a grass plot right behind him, and it was evident he knew all about it. His face was white and drawn, but there wasn't any tremor in his voice. I couldn't get it out of my head, as he sang out the warning and blew his whistle, that he was the psychological equivalent of the medieval leper, ringing his bell and shouting, 'Unclean! unclean!'"

"I had told him to get away from the corner, block off the streets with ropes. But he said, 'My duty is to stay here. Please go on, sir; don't set a bad example.' I went to telephone for help."

The bomb went off at 9:10, blew a crater forty feet wide. No trace has been found of Evans.

MADE HESITANT by heavy losses, the Nazis by the end of October, 1940, decided to shift from daylight to night bombing. London was not knocked out, but it was badly scarred. As late as the fall of 1944 visitors to the old imperial city were shocked speechless by the tremendous destruction caused by the German pilotless jet-propelled aircraft, the secret V-1—the *Vergeltungswaffe*—the "Reprisal Weapon," and V-2, the flying rocket that traveled faster than sound. S. N. Behrman, the noted playwright, wrote a vivid report for *The New Yorker* of his reactions as a visitor to London. "Mr. Behrman's suspended drawing room is among his finest work," commented Robert E. Sherwood. "It makes a superb showing." The author of *The Second Man* and *Serena Blandish* might well have called this piece *No Time for Comedy*.

The suspended drawing room: S. N. Behrman

An English editor I met on the plane had told me that the day after I arrived would provide one of the biggest news stories of the war: London, for the first time in five years, was to have light. That night, however, the blackout was still to be on, and I deposited my fifty-five pounds of luggage in Claridge's and went for a walk while there was still some daylight. I made for Berkeley Square. Soldiers and sailors, English and American, were walking with their girls in a faint, intermittent drizzle. Most of the women wore no stockings. I had been seeing this all summer in New York. But the American legs were tanned and agreeable, whereas these English ones were muddy and streaked bluish and red with the cold. (A young woman later told me that she was embarrassed at having to go without stockings. "I hate the unusual," she said. As she had been going barelegged for five years, I wondered how long it took for the unusual to become the usual.) The façades of the houses leading into the square have a strangely quiet look; at a casual glance, you might think the houses were shut up for the week end, but a closer inspection shows you that they have been shut up for longer than that. I peered in through a grimy, narrow, leaded window at the side of a fine oaken street door. Behind it was a great, obscene shambles of shattered brick and mortar and twisted iron. A huge sheet of what had been a fluted ceiling lay against a section of stairway, as if propped up on one elbow. I looked down the row. Several places in the long vista of wreckage

had been cleared for the pools—for emergency use against incendiaries—which are now a common feature of the London scene. These dark, liquid oblongs, fine-meshed in the rain, reflected jagged back walls and gargoyles of contorted pipes. I remembered going out to the set in Hollywood where Leslie Howard was making the motion picture of *Berkeley Square*. Those reproductions of eighteenth century façades had not much less behind them than this one had.

I looked up. On the third story of a house on the corner, following accurately the theatrical convention of the missing fourth wall, was an exquisite, suspended drawing room: delicately tinted blue walls, molded cornices, the curved, rifted ceiling, with a beautifully shaped oval where the center chandelier had been. All but the framework of the rest of the house was gone, but there it hung, this upstairs drawing room, elegant and aloof. I thought of Henry James. Here was his Mayfair, crisply anatomized. What would he have done with this room? With what malevolent ghosts would he have peopled it? What seedlings of social casuistry would have sprouted beneath that nonexistent chandelier, simmered along those pastel walls? An acute English critic speaks of James as the harbinger of decay and says that he described the final throes of a society he knew was done with. But James did not, I am sure, anticipate quite this finale. He must have visualized a long, slow inanition—the inhabitants of these drawing rooms giving up eventually because of their inability to sustain their own attitudes, to save face before their own pretensions. Certainly he could not have anticipated such rude visitations as there have been, cutting short the tortuous inhibitions, freezing the slow molds of refinement. Inescapably the Cassandra wails of our prophets, who are fond of reminding us that our civilization, like earlier ones, may disappear, somehow become very plausible. Ordinarily, when we become aware of moral rifts, we believe we can surmount them. Here disintegration was a physical actuality.

Later, I was to have this same feeling in drawing rooms still intact. I visited an august Englishman who has had a career of the highest distinction in English public life. He took me upstairs to show me his books—some of which he had written—and then into his shrouded drawing room. The long salon was musty and denuded. He lifted a linen hood from the head of a lovely statuette of a young girl. The girl smiled ravishingly, as if in sudden relief at her unveiling. He had bought her in Spain years ago. "We cannot, of course," he said, "keep these rooms open any longer." He walked about, uncovering other precious objects. "England," he said in the standard summary, "will never be the same again." He then made a rueful acknowledgment that there would be another England, but he felt that his had vanished. Fashionable London, upper-class London, is a vast, urban Cherry Orchard.

While I was still staring up at the Jamesian drawing room, I was gradually swallowed up by darkness. Before I knew it, the suspended drawing room had disappeared, together with the framework which suspended it. Suddenly there were no buildings, no streets, no squares. There was darkness. I started back to the hotel in something of a panic.

Three Newspaper Accounts of

"A Date Which Will Live in Infamy"

ON DECEMBER 6, 1941, President Roosevelt dispatched a personal message to Emperor Hirohito "in the fervent hope that Your Majesty may, as I am doing, give thought in this definite emergency to ways of dispelling the dark clouds." Next day, Sunday, the seventh, saw no reply from Tokyo. At one o'clock that afternoon Saburo Kurusu and Admiral Kichisaburo Nomura, General ("The Razor") Tojo's emissaries, requested an audience with Secretary of State Hull, who arranged to see them at 1:45. At 2:05 the two bland envoys arrived. Hull kept them waiting an additional fifteen minutes. At the exact moment when he received them the flash reached Washington that Japan had attacked Hawaii. The emissaries handed Hull a final Japanese reply charging the United States with scheming for an extension of the war. Hull responded with a verbal blasting in the best Tennessee tradition, unfortunately not preserved for posterity, but doubtless without precedent in the annals of diplomacy. "In all my fifty years of public service," said the white-haired Secretary of State, "I have never seen a document that was more crowded with infamous falsehoods and distortions on a scale so huge that I never imagined until today that any government on this planet was capable of uttering them."

The scene at Pearl Harbor was described in a superb report that appeared in the news magazine *Time* on December 15 and 22, 1941.

Pearl Harbor: "The mainland papers will exaggerate this"

The U. S. Navy was caught with its pants down. Within one tragic hour—before the war had really begun—the U. S. appeared to have suffered greater naval losses than in the whole of World War I.*

Days may pass before the full facts become known, but in the scanty news that came through from Hawaii in the first thirty-six hours of the war was every indication that the Navy had been taken completely by surprise in the early part of a lazy Sunday morning. Although the Japanese attackers had certainly been approaching for several days, the Navy apparently

---

* Between April 6, 1917, and November 11, 1918, the U, S., according to *Jane's Fighting Ships* for 1918, lost one armored cruiser, two destroyers, one submarine, three armed yachts, one coast-guard cutter, and two revenue cutters—but not a single capital ship.

had no news of either airplane carriers sneaking up or of submarines fanning out around Hawaii. Not till the first bombs began to fall was an alarm given. And when the blow fell the air force at Pearl Harbor was apparently not ready to offer effective opposition to the attackers.

In fine homes on the heights above the city, in beach shacks near Waikiki, in the congested district around the Punchbowl, assorted Japanese, Chinese, Portuguese, Filipinos, Hawaiians, and *kamaainas* (long-settled whites) were taking their ease. In the shallow waters lapping Fort de Russy, where sentries walked post along a retaining wall, a few Japanese and Hawaiians waded about, looking for fish to spear. In Army posts all over Oahu, soldiers were dawdling into a typical idle Sunday. Aboard the ships of the fleet at Pearl Harbor, life was going along at a saunter. Downtown nothing stirred except an occasional bus.

The clock on the Aloha Tower read 7:55.

The Japs came in from the southeast over Diamond Head. They could have been U. S. planes shuttling west from San Diego. Civilians' estimates of their numbers ranged from fifty to 150. They whined over Waikiki, over the candy-pink bulk of the Royal Hawaiian Hotel. Some were (it was reported) big four-motored jobs, some dive bombers, some pursuits. All that they met as they came in was a tiny private plane in which Lawyer Ray Buduick was out for a Sunday-morning ride. They riddled the lawyer's plane with machine-gun bullets, but the lawyer succeeded in making a safe landing. By the time he did, bombs were thudding all around the city. The first reported casualty was Robert Tyce, operator of a civilian airport near Honolulu, who was machine-gunned as he started to spin the propeller of a plane.

Torpedoes launched from bombers tore at the dreadnoughts in Pearl Harbor. Dive bombers swooped down on the Army's Hickam and Wheeler Fields. Shortly after the attack began, radio warnings were broadcast. But people who heard them were skeptical until explosions wrenched the guts of Honolulu. All the way from Pacific Heights down to the center of town the planes roared, leaving a wake of destruction.

With antiaircraft guns popping and U. S. pursuits headed aloft, pajama-clad citizens piled out of bed to dash downtown or head for the hills where they could get a good view. Few of them were panicky, many were nonchalant. Shouted one man as he dashed past a CBS observer: "The mainland papers will exaggerate this."

After the first attack Governor Poindexter declared an emergency, cleared the streets, ordered out the police and fire departments. Farrington High School, the city's biggest, was converted into a hospital. But the Japanese attackers returned.

Obvious to onlookers on the Honolulu hills was the fact that Pearl Harbor was being hit hard. From the Navy's plane base on Ford Island (also known as Luke Field), in the middle of the harbor, clouds of smoke ascended. One citizen who was driving past the naval base saw the first bomb fall on Ford Island. Said he: "It must have been a big one. I saw two planes dive over the mountains and down to the water and let loose torpedoes at a naval ship. This warship was attacked again and again. I also saw what looked like dive bombers coming over in single file."

Not all the civilian casualties occurred in Honolulu. The raiders plunged upon the town of Wahiawa, where there is a large island reservoir, sprayed bullets on people in the streets. Behind the Wahiawa courthouse a Japanese plane crashed in flames.

Incoming passengers on the American liner watched the planes swoop down over Pearl Harbor and Hickam Field, commended the U. S. Navy's thoughtfulness in staging a big-scale war game on Sunday morning. An American automobile salesman, en route to Tientsin, gawked admiringly as a bomb whooshed into the harbor a scant one hundred yards away: "Boy! What if that had been a real one?" The perspiring ship's officer who finally broke the bad news flubbed his lines: "It seems there's a state of undeclared war between Honolulu and the United States."

Even the *Christian Science Monitor*'s war correspondent, Joseph C. Harsch, was fooled: "I awoke my wife and asked her if she wanted to know what an air raid sounded like in Europe. 'This,' I remarked, 'is a good imitation.' We then proceeded to the beach for our morning swim, assuming with everyone else in the hotel that it was just another practice maneuver by the Navy. Only when the radio began telling the people what had happened could one grasp the incredible fact."

After the first stunning shock, the defenders swung into action. Spotters in the Navy Yard signal tower picked up the attackers, flashed air-raid warnings via visual signals. Working coolly under enemy bombs and machine-gun fire and shrapnel from defending antiaircraft batteries, the signalmen routed scores of orders to ships standing out to sea or fighting from berths.

A recruit seaman is credited with the first blow against the enemy. General Quarters had not yet sounded when he fought off an attacking plane singlehanded with a machine gun.

A battleship captain had his stomach laid open by a shrapnel burst as he went from conning tower to bridge to direct his ship's fight. He fell to the deck, disdained attempts to lift him to safety, continued to command until the bridge went up in flames. Two officers attempting to save him were themselves saved only after a third officer climbed above the fire, passed a line to an adjoining battleship, another to the trapped men, thus led them to safety.

Ten members of a five-inch gun's crew fell before a strafing attack. The lone remaining bluejacket took over: three times he grabbed a shell from the fuse pot, placed it in the tray, dashed to the other side of the gun, rammed it home, jumped into the pointer's seat, and fired. A terrific bomb blast finally carried him over the side. He was rescued.

When the brig door blew open a seaman confined earlier for misconduct dashed to his post at an antiaircraft gun. A hospitalized officer brushed aside his nurses when the first alarm was sounded, ran across the yard to his ship. So effectively did he fight, despite his illness, that his captain recommended promotion. One sailor, unable to find a mount for a heavy machine gun, fired the weapon from his arms despite terrific rapid-fire concussion.

A moored aircraft tender, blazing under repeated attacks, downed a Japanese plane on her own decks. Simultaneously her captain spotted a midget submarine's shadow within yards of his vessel. Hits were immediately scored and, as the sub's conning tower emerged, a destroyer administered the *coup de grâce* with depth charges. The tender then shot down a second plane. Motor launches from a vessel laid up for overhaul braved a steady hail of bullets and shrapnel, rescued scores of victims from the oil-fired harbor. Almost without exception officers and men exhibited quick thinking, coolness, coordination.

A CURTAIN of censorship quickly came down over Hawaii. Early ecstatic claims of Japanese newspapers culminated in the headline of the *Japan Times and Advertiser* for December 19, 1941: U. S. PACIFIC FLEET IS WIPED OUT! Asserting that Japan's claims to have reduced the United States "to a third-class power overnight" were based upon "the eyewitness accounts taken by the forces which carried out the attacks and photographic records subsequently obtained," the Nipponese journal claimed the sinking of five out of eight battleships. These losses were accurately reported, and, in addition, a target ship, a mine layer, and a floating drydock were sunk, and damage dealt out to three destroyers, the three other battleships in the harbor at the time, and other ships. Only Japanese claims to have set afire by bombing or machine-gunning some 450 planes and to have shot down fourteen proved exaggerated. In all, 187 U. S. planes were smashed. To destroy this fleet had cost the Japanese five two-men submarines and twenty-eight planes.

For the people of the United States it was a stunning shock. The Secretary of the Navy, Frank Knox, immediately flew to Honolulu to survey the damage and report to the American people. What he told them was not encouraging: "The air attack simply took us by surprise. We weren't on air alert." This admission astonished the entire nation, which had been told through its press and radio that its men were at battle stations from Manila to Pearl Harbor. Another report from *Time* described the reactions on the American mainland:

America's answer: "We'll stamp their front teeth in"

It was Sunday morning, clear and sunny. Many a citizen was idly listening to the radio when the flash came that the Japanese had attacked Hawaii. In Topeka they were listening to *The Spirit of '41* and napping on their sofas after dinner. In San Francisco, where it was not quite noon, they were listening to the news, Philharmonic, and *Strings in Swingtime*. In Portland, Maine, where it was cold but still sunny, they were lining up for the movies.

For the first time in its history, the U. S. at war was attacked first. Out on the Pacific and in the islands the great drama of U. S. history was coming to a climax. Over the U. S. and its history there was a great unanswered question: What would the people, the 132,000,000, say in the face of the mightiest event of their time?

What they said—tens of thousands of them—was: "Why, the yellow bastards!"

Hundreds of thousands of others said the same thing in different ways, with varying degrees of expression. In Norfolk, Virginia, the first man at the recruiting station said: "I want to beat them Japs with my own bare hands." At the docks in San Diego, as the afternoon wore on, a crowd slowly grew. There were a few people, then more, then a throng, looking intently west across the harbor, beyond Point Loma, out to the Pacific where the enemy was. There was no visible excitement, no hysteria, and no release in words for the emotions behind the grim, determined faces.

In Dallas, 2500 people sat in the Majestic Theater at 1:57 when *Sergeant York* ended and the news of the Japanese declaration of war was announced. There was a pause, a pin point of silence, a prolonged sigh, then thundering applause. A steelworker said: "We'll stamp their front teeth in."

In every part of the U. S. the terse, inadequate words gave outward and visible signs of the unfinished emotions within. Sometimes they just said, "Well, it's here." Sometimes they had nothing at all to say: Louisiana State University students massed, marched to the President, who came out in his dressing gown with no message except "study hard." Sometimes they laughed at something someone else had said, like the remark of the Chinese Vice-Consul at New Orleans, who announced: "As far as Japan is

concerned, their goose is overheated."

The statesmen, the spokesmen, the politicians, the leaders, could speak for unity. They did so. Herbert Hoover: "American soil has been treacherously attacked by Japan. We must fight with everything we have."

Alfred Landon (to President Roosevelt): "When the nation is attacked every American must rally to its support. All other considerations become insignificant."

Charles Lindbergh: "We have been stepping closer to war for many months. Now it has come, and we must meet it as united Americans regardless of our attitude in the past toward the policy our government has followed. Whether or not that policy has been wise, our country has been attacked by force of arms, and by force of arms we must retaliate. Our own defenses and our own military position have already been neglected too long. We must now turn every effort to building the greatest and most efficient Army, Navy, and air force in the world. When American soldiers go to war, it must be with the best equipment that modern skill can design and modern industry can build."

It was evening. Over the U. S. the soldiers and sailors on leave assembled at the stations. There would be a few men with their wives or their girls, standing a little apart from the people waiting for the train. The women would cry or, more often, walk away stiffly and silently. Slowly, the enormity of what had happened ended the first, quick, cocksure response.

Next morning the recruiting stations, open now twenty-four hours a day, seven days a week, were jammed too. New York had twice as many naval volunteers as its 1917 record.

Thus the U. S. met the first days of

the war. It met them with incredulity and outrage, with a quick, harsh, nation-wide outburst that swelled like the catalogue of some profane Whitman. It met them with a deepening sense of gravity and a slow, mounting anger. But there were still no words to express the emotions pent up in the silent people listening to the radios, reading the papers, taking the trains. But the U. S. knew that its first words were not enough.

FOLLOWING THE FORMAL Japanese declaration of war, couched in terms of medieval grandiloquence, Hitler declared to the Reichstag: "A historical revision of unique scope has been entrusted to us by the Creator." With only a single dissenting voice,* Congress, on December 8, declared its disagreement with the Führer. "We are now in this war," proclaimed President Roosevelt. "We are in it all the way."

So were the Japanese. Our determination was matched by their fanaticism. Reporting a raid over Manila, *Nichi Nichi,* a Tokyo newspaper, took occasion to illustrate *Yamatodamashi* (Do-or-die Jingoism).

Yamatodamashi *(Do-or-die Jingoism)*—
Nichi Nichi, *Tokyo newspaper, tells how
Nippon airman joins honorable ancestors*

Nichi Nichi (Tokyo), December 12, 1941

The weather was bad. As the planes approached the island, they were caught in electrical storm.

Undaunted, the "wild eagles," as the Army and Navy airmen are termed by the Japanese, flew inland; dropping bombs on enemy bases, and raking the ground equipment with machine-gun and aerial cannon fire.

As the squadron raided Clark Field, it was met by a swarm of enemy planes. A total of nine planes, mostly the Curtis Boeing type [*sic*], were downed over the airfield.

After fierce fighting the wild eagles gained mastery of the air. Leisurely, they bombed ground defenses, setting a number of hangars afire and destroying a total of fourteen planes on the ground.

Having achieved their objective, the wild eagles, in formation, returned to their base, leaving the ground defenses of the enemy airfield ablaze.

At this moment the plane piloted by Warrant Officer Hiratsuka was hit by machine-gun bullets. He began to lose speed, his motor having been hit.

As he was falling from the formation, he was pleasantly startled to see another plane of his group trying to slow down to keep abreast of his machine.

That plane was found to be the

---

* Without a single speech and without a wasted word, the Senate voted war with Germany, 88-to-0, and war with Italy, 90-to-0. The House voted war with Germany, 393-to-0, war with Italy, 399-to-0. "In both House votes," reported *Time,* "Republican Pacifist Jeannette Rankin cinched her footnote place in history piping 'Present'—a refusal to vote." The first woman ever to sit in the House of Representatives, the Montana Congresswoman was consistent—she had voted against war with Germany in 1917.

one occupied by the commander of the squadron. It was evident that the commanding officer had left the formation to see whether he could be of any help to Warrant Officer Hiratsuka trying in vain to catch up with his comrades. Seeing that smoke was pouring out increasingly from the warrant officer's engine, the commander of the squadron waved to him to cheer up.

Presently the Hiratsuka plane was enveloped in smoke. The warrant officer waved back to the commander.

The commander managed to bring his plane closer to that of his subordinate in trouble. His concern was how to save the Hiratsuka plane.

For a while the two planes, one of them enveloped in dense smoke issuing from its damaged engine, flew side by side.

Then the commander suddenly heard a voice. It was that of Warrant Officer Hiratsuka.

The warrant officer was seen to rise slowly from his seat. Now he was up, his face turned to the commander in his machine, which by this time had been dangerously close to him.

He stood at attention. Then his right hand went up. He was making a military salute.

In another second the Hiratsuka plane shot down toward the ground, leaving a trail of black smoke.

Four Accounts of Men Against the Sea

O N DECEMBER 7, 1941, while Pearl Harbor was under attack, Japanese bombers struck at Hong Kong and Singapore. Admiral Phillips, commander of the British Far Eastern Fleet, put out to sea in an effort to smash the Japanese transports and landing craft that were disembarking invading troops at Siam and Malaya. The plan was to strike the Japanese octopus before it could attack Singapore by land.

Two British capital ships, the great new 35,000-ton battleship *Prince of Wales*, and the battle cruiser *Repulse*, surrounded by a supporting destroyer screen, steamed northward. When only fifty miles off the coast of Malaya and only a hundred and fifty from Singapore, the battle wagons were spotted by Japanese reconnaissance planes. Yukio Waku, *Yomiuri* correspondent "at an undisclosed base," obtained from a Japanese naval airman this account of the battle from the skies:

Yukio Waku, Yomiuri *correspondent, reports the sinking of the* Prince of Wales *and the* Repulse

Tokyo *Yomiuri*, December 10, 1941, translation by Henry F. Graff

The air-current condition was quite unfavorable to flying that morning, with dark clouds hovering low over the South China Sea. It goes without saying that visibility was poor. While flying low over the Japanese transports, our planes continued a reconnaissance flight over the seas off the eastern coast of the Anambas Islands. Columns of black smoke were sighted far on the horizon. Careful reconnaissance told us that the smoke columns were those from the enemy fleet, which included the *Prince of Wales* and the *Repulse*. A wireless operator began to send out information to our bombing base on the location of the enemy fleet.

Imperial Naval Air Force bombers, on receipt of the wireless message, took off in a big formation, with torpedoes loaded, in defiance of bad weather. Our bombers caught sight of the British Far Eastern Fleet, which seemed to have noticed our attempt and started fleeing in zigzag at full speed of thirty knots under cover of the dark clouds. In the gathering twilight which prevented our further search for the enemy fleet, we were obliged to head for our base, with unexpressible regret.

The following morning the engines of the reconnaissance planes and bombers were readied for take-off with their throttles open. With firm resolve to wipe out the enemy fleet, the planes took off from their base. Visibility was better than the previous day, with less clouds.

We continued flying, and finally succeeded in locating the *Prince of Wales* and the *Repulse* a few miles off Kuantan. Both were targets of our torpedoing. Our formations of bombers fell on the two capital ships amidst antiaircraft fire from the enemy. Our torpedoes hit their mark with incandescent glow flashing amid dark smoke columns. In disorderly wakes ran the *Prince of Wales* and the *Repulse,* and in a moment they turned into columns of fire, going to the bottom.

AT FIVE A.M. on the morning of December 11, 1941, the newsroom of the Columbia Broadcasting System in New York heard a Tokyo news broadcast claim that the *Prince of Wales* and the *Repulse* had been sunk. "Another fantastic claim to spread confusion" was the general reaction. On the desk of Paul White, CBS director of news broadcasts, was a cable from Cecil Brown, Columbia's correspondent in Singapore, dated December 10: OUTTOWNING FOUR DAYS SWELL STORY. No one dreamed that there might be a connection between the Tokyo claim and the Brown cable.

A few hours later White heard from London that Brown and a British newspaperman had been aboard the *Repulse*. Then Brown's second cable came through, almost twenty-four hours to the minute from the Tokyo broadcast. It was broadcast from New York four times that day—at five A.M., eight A.M., 3:45 P.M., and 8:16 P.M.

Cecil Brown had sailed as a seaman to South America, Russia, and West Africa, and had gained wide newspaper experience as a reporter for Los Angeles, Pittsburgh, and Newark papers. He first came into international prominence when, as a CBS commentator, he was expelled from Italy in April, 1941, for his "continued hostile attitude toward Fascism." His sensational broadcast that follows was acclaimed by the Overseas Press Club, the National Council for Education by Radio, and several other groups, and, in the editors' opinion, the accolades were thoroughly deserved. The same night of the broadcast Paul White, not quite certain about the nature of British income-tax regulations and anxious to camouflage his message, cabled Brown in code Americanese: HAVE NOTIFIED YOUR BANK YOU DID ONE GRAND JOB. Upon receipt of this pleasant news Brown reacted normally: "My God! A thousand-dollar bonus!"

Cecil Brown's account: "All hands on deck, prepare to abandon ship. May God be with you!"

Broadcast by Cecil Brown, Columbia Broadcasting System, December 11, 1941

Here's the eyewitness story of how the *Prince of Wales* and the *Repulse* ended their careers in the South China Sea, fifty miles from the Malaya coast and a hundred and fifty miles north of Singapore.

I was aboard the *Repulse* and with hundreds of others escaped. Then, swimming in thick oil, I saw the *Prince of Wales* lie over on her side like a tired war horse and slide beneath the waters. I kept a diary from the time the first Japanese high-level bombing started at 11:15 until 12:31, when Captain William Tennant, skipper of the *Repulse* and senior British captain afloat, shouted through the ship's communication system, "All hands on deck, prepare to abandon ship. May God be with you!"

I jumped twenty feet to the water from the up end of the side of the *Repulse* and smashed my stop watch at thirty-five and a half minutes after twelve. The sinking of the *Repulse* and the *Prince of Wales* was carried out by a combination of high-level bombing and torpedo attacks with consummate skill and the greatest daring. I was standing on the flag deck slightly forward amidships when nine Jap bombers approached at ten thousand feet strung in a line, clearly visible in the brilliant sunlit sky. They flew directly over our ship, and our antiaircraft guns were screaming constantly.

Just when the planes were passing over, one bomb hit the water beside where I was standing, so close to the ship that we were drenched from the waterspout. Simultaneously another struck the *Repulse* on the catapult deck, penetrating the ship and exploding below in a marine's mess and hangar. Our planes were subsequently unable to take off. At 11:27 fire is raging below, and most strenuous efforts are under way to control it. All gun crews are replenishing their ammunition and are very cool and cracking jokes. There are a couple of jagged holes in the funnel near where I am standing.

It's obvious the Japs flew over the length of the ship, each dropping three bombs so that twenty-seven bombs fell around us at first in their attack. Brilliant red flashes are spouting from our guns' wells. The *Prince of Wales* is half a mile away. Destroyers are at various distances, throwing everything they have into the air. A splash about two miles off our port beam may be antiaircraft, but we are uncertain. At 11:40 the *Prince of Wales* seems to be hit. She's reduced her speed. Now they're coming to attack us. The communication system shouts, "Stand by for barrage." All our guns are going. We are twisting and snaking violently to avoid torpedoes. The Japs are coming in low, one by one in single waves. They're easy to spot. Amid the roar from the guns aboard the *Repulse* and the pom-poms of antiaircraft fire, we are signaled, "We've a man overboard."

Two Jap aircraft are approaching us. I see more of them coming with the naked eye. I again count nine. They're torpedo bombers and are circling us about a mile and half or two miles away. Eleven forty-five—now there seem to me more bombers but they are circling like vultures at about one-thousand-feet altitude. The guns are deafening. The smell of cordite is almost suffocating and explosions are ear-shattering and the flashes blinding. The officer beside me yells, "Here comes a tin fish."

A Jap torpedo bomber is heading directly for us, two hundred yards above the water. At 11:48 he's less than five hundred distant, plowing onward. A torpedo drops, and he banks sharply and his whole side is exposed to our guns, but instead of driving away he's making a graceful dive toward the water. He hits and immediately bursts into flame in a gigantic splash of orange against the deep-blue sky and the robin's-egg-blue water. Other planes are coming, sweeping low in an amazing suicide effort to sink the *Repulse*.

Their daring is astonishing, coming so close you can make out the pilot's outline. One coming in at 11:48 to our starboard just dropped a torpedo. A moment later I hear shouts of joy indicating that he was brought down, but I didn't see that. We also claim we brought down two high-level bombers previously, but I didn't see these crash. At least, for the moment I have no recollection of seeing them.

At 12:01 another wave of torpedo bombers is approaching. They are being met with everything we've got except our fourteen inchers. Beside me the signal officer flashes word from Captain Tennant to the *Prince of Wales:* "We eluded all torpedoes this second attack." It's fascinating to watch our tracer bullets speeding toward the Jap bombers. Twelve three: we've just shot down another torpedo bomber who is about four hundred yards away, and we shot it out. All of its motors are afire, and disintegrating pieces of the fuselage are flying about. Now it disappears over the surface of the water into scrap. The brilliant orange from the fire against this blue sky is so close it's startling. All the men are cheering at the sight. It's so close it seems you could almost reach out and touch the remains of this Jap bomber.

At 12:15 the *Wales* seems to be stopped definitely. I've been too busy to watch the attacks against her, but she seems in utmost difficulty. Her guns are firing constantly and we are both twisting. One moment the *Wales* is at our starboard, the next it's at our port. I'm not watching the destroyers, but they have not been subjected to

air attacks. The Japs are throwing everything recklessly against the two capital ships.

There's fire aboard us; it's not out. I just saw some firemen and fire-control parties. The calmness of the crews is amazing. I have constantly roved from one side of the flag deck to the other during the heavy firing and attacks, and the cool precision of all hands has seemed unreal and unnatural. Even when they are handing up shells for the service guns, each shell is handed over with a joke. I never saw such happiness on men's faces. This is the first time these gun crews have been in action in this war, and they are having the time of their lives. Twelve-twenty: I see ten bombers approaching us from a distance. It's impossible to determine whether this will be a high-level attack or another torpedo-bomber attack. "Stand by for barrage" comes over the ship's communication system.

One plane is circling around; it's now at three or four hundred yards, approaching us from the port side. It's coming closer, head on, and I see a torpedo drop. It's streaking for us. A watcher shouts, "Stand by for torpedo," and the tin fish is streaking directly for us. Someone says: "This one got us." The torpedo struck the side on which I was standing about twenty yards astern of my position. It felt like the ship had crashed into a well-rooted dock. It threw me four feet across the deck, but I did not fall and I did not feel any explosion. Just a very great jar. Almost immediately we began to list, and less than a minute later there was another jar of the same kind and the same force, except that it was almost precisely on the starboard side.

After the first torpedo, the communication system coolly announced:

"Blow up your life belts." I was in this process when the second torpedo struck, and the settling ship and the crazy angle were so apparent I didn't continue blowing my belt.

That the *Repulse* was doomed was immediately apparent. The communication system announced, "Prepare to abandon ship. May God be with you!" Without undue rush we all started streaming down ladders, hurrying but not pushing. It was most difficult to realize I must leave the ship. It seemed so incredible that the *Repulse* could or should go down. But the *Repulse* was fast keeling over to port and walking ceased to become a mode of locomotion. I was forced to clamber and scramble in order to reach the side. Men were lying dead around the guns. Some were half hidden by empty shell cases. There was considerable damage all around the ship. Some of the men had been machine-gunned. That had been unquestioned fact.

All around me men were stripping off their clothes and their shoes and tossing aside their steel helmets. Some are running alongside the three-quarter-exposed hull of the ship to reach a spot where they can slide down the side without injuring themselves in the jagged hole in the ship's side. Others are running to reach a point where they have a shorter dive to the water. I am reluctant to leave my new portable typewriter down in my cabin and unwilling to discard my shoes, which I had made just a week before. As I go over the side, the *Prince of Wales* half a mile away seems to be afire, but her guns are still firing the heaviest. It's most obvious she's stopped dead and out of control due to her previous damage.

The air attack against the *Prince of Wales* carried out the same scheme directed against the *Repulse*. The Japs

were able to send two British capital ships to the bottom because of, first, a determined air torpedo attack and, second, the skill and efficiency of the Japanese operations. It's apparent that the best guns and crews in the world will be unable to stem a torpedo-bombing attack if the attackers are sufficiently determined.

According to the best estimate obtainable, the Japs used in their operations against both the *Wales* and the *Repulse* eighty-six bombers; eighteen high-level bombers and approximately twenty-five torpedo bombers against the *Repulse* and probably an equal number against the *Prince of Wales*. In the case of the *Wales*, however, the Japs started the torpedo bombing instead of initial high-level bombing. In the first attack, one torpedo hit the *Wales* in the afterpart. Some survivors believe the *Wales* was hit twice in the initial attack, then followed two more torpedo attacks, both successful. The final attack on the *Wales* was made by high-level bombers around ten thousand feet. When that attack came, the *Wales* was sinking fast and everyone threw himself down on deck.

Most of the guns were unmanageable as a result of the list and the damage. I jumped into the water from the *Repulse* at 12:35. While I was in the water, the *Wales* continued firing for some time. The *Wales* suffered two direct hits by bombs on the deck. Like the attack on the *Repulse*, the Japs flew across the length of the *Wales* in a single line, each bomber dropping a stick. One officer said a child of six could see some of them were going to hit us. During the entire action Admiral Tom Phillips, Commander-in-Chief of the Far East Fleet, and Captain Leech, skipper of the *Prince of Wales*, were on the bridge.

While the torpedo bombers were rushing in toward the *Wales,* dropping tin fish and machine-gunning the decks, Phillips clambered up on the roof of the bridge and also atop the gun turrets to see better and to direct all phases of the action.

When it was apparent that the *Wales* was badly hit, the Admiral issued an order to the flag officer for the destroyer then lying alongside close by. "Signal to Singapore to send tugs to tow us." Evidently up to that moment, Phillips was not convinced that the *Wales* was sinking. The last order issued by Phillips came at approximately 1:15. It said, "Blow up your life belts."

Later the ship was underwater. Phillips and Leech were the last from the *Wales* to go over the side, and they slid into the water together. It's probable that their reluctance to leave the ship until all possible men had left meant their death, since it's most likely they were drawn down by the suction when the *Wales* was on her side and then settled at her stern with her bow rising into the air.

Swimming about a mile away, lying on top of a small stool, I saw the bow of the *Wales.* When Phillips signaled to ask Singapore to send tugs, the *Wales* already had four torpedoes in her. Like the *Repulse,* the *Wales* gun crews were very cool, and although many guns were no longer effective the crew stood beside them. When the final high-level-bombing attack came, only three guns were capable of firing, except the fourteen-inchers, which naturally did not go into action. I did not meet Phillips, but last week when I visited the *Wales* at the naval base I had a long talk with Captain Leech. He's a jovial, convivial, smiling officer who gave me the impression of the greatest kindness and ability. The *Wales* carried a complement of seventeen hundred; the *Repulse* twelve hundred and fifty officers and ratings. When the *Wales* sank, the suction was so great it ripped off the life belt of one officer more than fifty feet away. A fortunate feature of the sinking of both the *Repulse* and the *Wales* was that neither blew up.

Since the tide was strong and there was an extremely powerful suction from both ships, it was extremely difficult to make any progress away from the ship in the thick oil. The gentle, quiet manner in which these shell-belching dreadnoughts went to their last resting place without exploding was a tribute of gratitude from two fine ships for their fine sailors.

* * *

THE SINKING of the two capital ships resulted in a prompt revision of the notion that victory over Japan would be quick and easy. It meant the doom of Singapore. Winston Churchill spoke in grave tones to the House of Commons: "In my whole experience I do not remember any naval blow so heavy or painful as the sinking of the *Prince of Wales* and the *Repulse* on Monday last. These two vast, powerful ships constituted an essential feature in our plans for meeting the new Japanese danger as it loomed against us in the last few months. These attacks were delivered with skill and determination."

The second great sea story of World War II came from the Mediterranean, where an American reporter attached to a British ship had a sensational escape from death.

Born October 19, 1908, Lawrence Edmund Allen's first contact with the newspaper profession came in the traditional small-fry American fashion of selling and delivering papers. Accredited in May, 1940, as Associated Press correspondent to the British Mediterranean fleet, he sailed 100,000 miles with it and managed to be present wherever there was trouble and disaster.

On January 15, 1941, aboard the British aircraft carrier *Illustrious,* Allen described a fierce seven-hour pounding by fifty German aircraft, which dropped 100,000 tons of bombs in an unsuccessful attempt to sink the newest of Britain's carriers. "The German pilots dived so low," he wrote in a vivid dispatch, "that the markings could easily be seen on their big Junkers planes. They dropped bombs all around the deck. Bomb splinters flew about the bridge and the rest of the carrier like hailstones; near misses so shook her that it seemed they would hurl her over on her side. . . . I reached the bridge just as a big, German bomb struck the ship. There was a shattering blast. Almost simultaneously a thousand-pound bomb crashed alongside, and a blinding flash seemed to envelop the ship."

On December 16, 1941, Allen topped a long list of dramatic eyewitness reports of the sea war in the Mediterranean with a story of the destruction of the British cruiser *Galatea* and his own narrow escape from death after a forty-five-minute plunge into the sea.

For these graphic reports, in the best Richard Harding Davis and Floyd Gibbons tradition, Allen was awarded the 1942 Pulitzer Prize for distinguished telegraphic reporting.

*"The most agonizing experience of my life":
Larry Allen goes down with the dying* Galatea

The Associated Press, January 10, 1942

ALEXANDRIA, EGYPT, JANUARY 10— The British light cruiser *Galatea,* struck by three torpedoes from an Axis submarine, flopped over like a stabbed turtle and went down within three minutes off Egypt's Mediterranean coast in the inky darkness just after midnight the morning of December 16.

The torpedoes, fired from close range, smashed in swift succession against the *Galatea*'s after-port side, amidships, and forward, tearing into her interior with loud blasts and spurting flame.

On the dying cruiser's quarterdeck I clung tenaciously to the starboard rail until the list of the ship flung me into the cold, choppy sea. Then I battled through thick, oily scum for forty-five minutes before being rescued.

We had been dive-bombed for more than seven hours on December 14, while patrolling with a squadron of cruisers and destroyers off Libya, but the *Galatea* successfully beat off those attacks and headed eastward.

At midnight on December 15 the cruiser's announcer system warned: "First-degree readiness heavy armament." Gunners thus were ordered to stand by for expected action.

A marine sentry aroused me from a nap in the captain's cabin, and I ran to the commander's cabin and informed the Reuters naval correspondent, Alexander Massy Anderson.

Adjusting life belts, we stepped out into the inky blackness of the quarterdeck and raced toward the bridge.

We had barely started when the first torpedo smashed into the afterport side with a burst of flame, heavily rocking the *Galatea*. The time was 12:02 A.M.

Torpedoes seemed to chase us along the deck, for the second crashed through amidships with a blinding flash and the third struck forward, just under a six-inch gun turret.

The ship listed quickly and heavily to port, shuddering all over.

As the warship dipped quickly and deeply into the sea on the port side I caught hold of the starboard-deck rail, dropped my tin helmet, bomb-anti-flash gear, and raincoat, and with my free hand unscrewed the nozzle on the lifeboat hose hung around my neck.

I blew into it with all the breath I could summon, inflating it just as the cruiser flopped completely over on her port side. From that moment I went through the most dangerous and agonizing experience of my life.

The sharp keeling over of the ship flung me sliding down the starboard side into the sea. Hundreds of officers and seamen plunged into the water along with me.

Anderson had reached the starboard railing a little to the right of

me when the cruiser was hurled over. I heard him shout something to an officer as I slid into the sea. I never saw him again.

I could not swim and was fearful lest the pressure of a deep submersion collapse the old life belt which I had retrieved after the bombing of the *Illustrious* just one year ago today (January 10).

As I slipped under the water the cruiser disappeared with a tremendous suction, leaving a huge lake of oil on the sea. There was one muffled blast as she took her death plunge.

I swallowed large quantities of oily scum and water before I bobbed to the surface. The water all around was dotted with heads of hundreds of sailors.

Several sailors had succeeded in getting off a small motorboat. Trying to splash toward it I went under again. My lungs felt as if they were bursting, but I came up, and a sailor helped me aboard the boat.

But a score of others had the same idea. The boat's stern rapidly filled with water as the weight of more and more men pushed it down. Finally the motorboat tipped over, hurling us all into the sea.

I managed to reach the boat and pull myself into the front cockpit again. Then the boat sank.

With a lone sailor I hung to the very tip of the bow until it slipped beneath the waves. I even hung on until it pulled me under, and I got another large dose of oil and water.

I strained every muscle to force my head above the surface.

From beneath the waves a pair of hands reached up and pawed at my shoulders, then slipped away.

I collided with a small floating spar. Desperately I tried and succeeded in tucking it under my left arm, still carefully holding up the life belt with the right.

I joined with scores of others in crying for help, hoping in the pitch darkness to attract the attention of the destroyers. No one had a flashlight, so it was difficult for the destroyers to find us.

At that moment I saw a huge black silhouette of a destroyer about seventy-five yards ahead.

"Help, I'm drowning," gasped a sailor in the water near me.

"Keep going," I called weakly. "Look, there's a destroyer ahead."

That seemed to give him a new energy. He swam toward the destroyer. I tried, but couldn't get any closer.

The waves seemed to carry me farther away as I screamed for help.

A big wave swamped me again with a mouthful of oil. Then, as if miraculously, another wave pushed me forward almost directly under the propellers of the destroyer *Griffin*.

I called for help until my throat felt burned out. Suddenly, a long, oily rope was flung over the side. I grasped it, but there was no strength left in my hands.

"Hang on!" an officer on the ship shouted. "We'll pull you up."

"Can't!" I called as the rope slipped from my fingers.

"Try to get a little forward," the officer shouted. "We are putting over a rope ladder."

Somehow I managed to propel myself forward and hang onto the ladder, safe, but so spent that I couldn't pull myself up even the first rung unaided.

At that moment a life raft drifted against the destroyer's side. I repeatedly banged my head against the warship and I cried out time and again: "Stop it! You're killing me!"

Sailors on the raft grasped the rope ladder and clambered up safely while I fought desperately to keep from drowning. Several stepped upon my head, pushing me down into the water.

Only half conscious, I hooked my right arm through the rung of the ladder, which helped keep my head above water occasionally, and again I called out for help.

A young British sailor aboard the raft saved my life.

"I'll help you!" he shouted. "Get this rope under your arms!"

He passed a thick, heavy rope under my arms, tied it, and flung the end to the quarterdeck of the destroyer.

Three sailors slowly pulled me out of the oily mass and flopped me flat on the quarterdeck like a wet fish, completely covered with thick, oily scum.

"This fellow's an American," I dimly heard someone say as they read the words "American naval correspondent" on the sleeve of my oil-soaked coat while pressing the water from my lungs.

They cut off all my clothes and carried me to the mess deck below, where nearly one hundred other survivors were getting medical attention.

The ship's doctor gave me a countershock injection, and for the next ten hours, while the navy searched the sea for the submarine which torpedoed the *Galatea*, I lay on a mass of greasy rags and oil-soaked clothes, too weak to get on my feet.

RETURNING TO ALEXANDRIA, Allen walked ashore with the help of naval officers, cleaned off the oil, and went to bed for several days, suffering from shock and numerous bruises. The Germans immediately claimed that they had sunk a cruiser of the *Galatea* class, but not until January 9, 1942, did the British Admiralty announce that a submarine had sunk the 5220-ton cruiser, with no specification of date, place, or number of casualties.

For the fourth great sea story of World War II let us return to Far Eastern waters, where the United States was recovering rapidly from the blow at Pearl Harbor and was beginning the task of pulverizing the bantam-weight Japanese Empire.

Pearl Harbor, Bataan, Wake Island, Singapore, Java Seas—a steady procession of Japanese victories! In June, 1942, the Nipponese sent a vast armada of fifty-three warships and a score of transport and supply ships toward Hawaii, to deal a knockout blow against the American Navy.

This time, however, the Americans were not caught napping. Early on the morning of June 3, a patrol plane sighted the enemy fleet, a great armada outnumbering the American warships in the area. But the Americans had an air base at Midway, and they rushed all available air power to the island.

The great battle that followed during the next three days and nights was fought entirely by planes and submarines. The Japanese heavily bombed Midway but failed to immobilize the island's airfields. Then American naval aviation went to work on the Jap fleet. The battered enemy forces split up and fled westward, heavily punished by the pursuing American carrier forces. For America, a brilliant victory; for Japan, the first defeat suffered by her navy in 350 years. Midway was the turning point in the Pacific war.

An extraordinary eyewitness account of the engagement was given by a young American torpedo-plane pilot, Ensign G. H. Gay of Texas. Crashing his plane into the sea, he survived to tell the story of what a major naval engagement looks like from the "fish-eye view." Associated Press correspondent Walter Clausen got the story from the young pilot, who saw the battle at he floated helplessly by on the wreckage of his plane.

A pilot's fish-eye view of Midway,
as related to Walter Clausen

The New York Times, June 9, 1942

The first eyewitness account of the Battle of Midway Island, detailing its most violent stages, was related today by a wounded American naval aviator who told of floating in the sea and watching a line of burning Japanese ships pass by.

He told of a thunderous—and highly successful—attack by American dive bombers and torpedo planes on Japanese aircraft carriers. And from his "fish-eye" view he watched the desperate circlings of Japanese naval planes, unable to settle on their blazing and battered mother ships. The story was told by Ensign G. H. Gay, twenty-five-year-old torpedo-plane pilot of Houston, Texas. His wounds were not serious.

For ten hours the pilot, careful to conceal himself from vengeful Japanese fliers by hiding his head under a cushion from his wrecked plane, drifted in the sea and obtained one of the most amazing stories of a major naval engagement.

Ensign Gay occupied what naval men called "a fish-eye view" of the attack on three Japanese carriers. His squadron met fierce enemy fighter-plane opposition while driving home a torpedo assault on one of the larger Jap carriers. It occurred early on June 4, opening day of the battle. He was the only one of the crew of three to survive the crash of his ship.

Taking off from his fleet carrier with his squadron, Gay approached the objective in midmorning. Visibility was unlimited. Below lay three Japanese carriers, less than ten miles extending between the first and last of the enemy ships that were screened by a considerable force of cruisers and destroyers. Gay took stock of the drama below him. Two *Kaga*-class carriers had been taking on their aircraft. Another smaller carrier lay between them, also receiving planes. One of the larger carriers already burned fiercely, while enemy cruisers and destroyers wheeled around it, waiting to rescue personnel.

Twenty minutes later the American dive bombers rocketed into view. In the face of terrific antiaircraft fire and enemy fighter attack, they leveled for the assault. Gay heard his machine gunner say he had been hit. But the approach continued. Near the great Japanese carrier, Gay launched his projectile, then swung sharply over the target and sped astern as fast as his plane could carry him.

Suddenly an explosive shell from a Zero fighter ripped through his torpedo plane's rudder controls. The detonation seared Gay's left leg. Almost simultaneously, a small-caliber bullet struck his upper left arm. Coolly, he brought his heavy plane into a stall and pancaked into the sea several miles astern of the enemy carrier. His gunner was dead, and in the emergency landing his radioman was unable to pull free.

At eleven A.M. Gay, alone, watched the tail surfaces of his plane disappear. Then a bit of luck held with him. Out of the sinking wreckage floated the bag containing the deflated rubber life raft—and a black cushion on which the bombardier kneels while working. Gay figured his chances quickly and accurately. There had been reports of Japanese strafing helpless pilots bailing out by parachute, and of machine-gunning of men in such life rafts as had floated clear of his own plane. He declined to offer himself as such a victim. He ducked under the cushion as enemy fighters swarmed overhead. Not knowing the extent of his wounds, he felt cautiously at his arm. The bullet, which apparently had struck him at the spent end of its trajectory, dropped out in his hand.

"For some reason," Gay recalled, "I put it in my mouth. Maybe I wanted a souvenir. Anyhow, I lost it before long."

He bandaged his injured leg underwater. Then from his fish-eye view, he saw two other Jap carriers hit squarely by U. S. bombers. Tremendous fires burst from these vessels. Great billows of smoke churned upward with the flames billowing from the apex in dark columns. Internal explosions sent new gushes of smoke and fire belching from the carriers. As the ferocious Pacific-fleet attack ended, the second *Kaga*-class carrier was on fire from bow to stern.

Surface craft gave Gay some narrow brushes. One enemy destroyer appeared to be driving straight at him as she sped to 'aid a stricken carrier. He thought she would run him down, but at the last instant she plowed past. A heavy Jap cruiser steamed by less than five hundred yards away. He saw her crew lining the rail, their white uniforms gleaming against the battle paint, grimly watching the destruction of their force.

As the afternoon waned, the Japanese made frantic efforts to stem the damage. An enemy cruiser sought to stand alongside a crippled cruiser, but seemed unable to approach close enough. Gay observed this vessel's big guns commence to rake the wounded carrier, presumably to scuttle her. Sometime later a destroyer managed to come alongside the still-floating carrier to remove survivors. Overhead, Japanese planes appeared to be circling in a vain attempt to land on the smashed carrier. They would pass above her, then soar out of sight and return.

Darkness fell, and Gay never learned what became of them. In the twilight, "maybe a little earlier than was wise," he inflated his life raft from his carbon-dioxide bottle. He said he had his fill of salt water. He had to make emergency patches on several bulletholes in the rubber boat before it would sustain him safely. He clambered in. The long night began.

Far to the north, great glowing patches appeared in the sky. Gay thought these might have been the searchlights of Japanese rescue vessels seeking to pick up carrier personnel. There didn't seem to be much else to do, so he "tried to catch a few winks of sleep." Toward morning, he was awakened by three explosions, which he believed may have been demolition charges. Several hours after sunup a Navy patrol plane, winging out on a search, spotted his rubber boat and picked him up. A Navy doctor asked him what treatment he had had for his burns and he replied: "Well, I soaked 'em in salt water for ten hours."

Sergeant Hargrove Sees the Chinese Honor

a Dead American Flier

We had a job to do; we were moving. I forgot my tension. I began to think of what I had to do and of the redhead back home.

Suddenly I saw something moving in the brush about twelve yards away. My jaw froze. I felt like vomiting. It was a Jerry. Only one, I hoped. He was coming right up the waddy. He came out in the open, looked around, and turned to signal the others to come through. Another came in sight. I don't know what the hell I did. Instinctively I must have dropped my food and picked up my rifle. I was glad I'd traded my sharp-shooter rifle for an M-1; I could fire from the hip.

Without looking around, I saw that Gerhardt had seen them, too. I knew I should have held my fire, but my finger squeezed the trigger. Almost immediately Gerhardt fired at the second one. Both of the Jerries went down.

I heard a scream on my left. Nemo was standing up, his Tommy gun in his hands. He was hit in the chest. He ran at the Germans. A machine pistol opened up and tore the top of his head off. The rim of his helmet dropped down around his neck.

PRIVATE Justin Gray, who fought in Sicily and Italy with the Third Ranger Battalion, never published a line until *Yank, The Army Weekly* encouraged him to put his reactions on paper. His special kind of staccato reporting, of which a small sample is given above, is typical of the first-rate job done during World War II by the Army magazine. Written by and for enlisted men, *Yank* presented its stories in soldier shoptalk, whose significance was sometimes lost on the outsider. Most *Yank* reporters made no attempts to comment or editorialize in any way. Their job was "to portray effectively the strange, uncertain, frequently dangerous world in which we live." There were casualties. Sergeant John Bushemi was fatally wounded by Jap mortar fire at Eniwetok, in the Marshalls, and Sergeant Peter Paris met death on D-Day in Normandy, when he landed with the first wave of the First Division. Among those who survived were Sergeant David Richardson, who won the Legion of Merit for his front-line coverage of the New Guinea campaign; Sergeant Walter Peters, who was cited for bravery under fire at Saint-Lô; Sergeant Joe McCarthy, chief editor of all seventeen editions of *Yank,* who was the first GI to enter Athens when it was liberated; Sergeant Walter Bernstein, who scored a world-wide beat by obtaining an exclusive interview with Tito; Private Irwin Shaw, who crashed the best-seller lists with his novel *The Young Lions* (1948); and Private William Saroyan, who lived to become the daring middle-aged man on the flying trapeze.

Another reporter for *Yank,* Marion Hargrove, had scored a resounding success with a book that struck the American public straight on the funny-bone. During his training days at Fort Bragg, North Carolina, young Hargrove wrote for his old newspaper, the *Charlotte* (N. C.) *News,* a series of sketches designed to show the civilians back home what he was going through in the Army. The pieces, later published in book form under the title, *See Here, Private Hargrove* (1942), described a hapless GI who seemed to do everything wrong. Eventually promoted to sergeant, Hargrove was sent to China as a correspondent for *Yank.* As was to be expected, the lighthearted voice of training days gave way to a more serious tone. Here is Hargrove's moving story of the burial of an American pilot after a great sky battle in China.

Glory for Mei-Kua

The Best from Yank, The Army Weekly, (New York, 1945)

SOMEWHERE IN CHINA—There was a great battle in the sky, and the people stopped their work to look at it. And then the battle moved away until there was nothing left of it but one plane of the *Mei-Kua fi chi* (the American fliers), with its large white star with the red border around it, and two planes of the Japanese devils, the *Yi Bin Kwe-Tse.* There was much shooting, and then the first and then the second of the Japanese planes fell to the earth with much smoke and great noise.

And after this had happened the people saw that the little plane of the *Mei-Kua* was also greatly harmed. There was much noise such as one hears from trucks on the great road when they are using gasoline of pine roots and there are too many yellowfish riding on the top of the load. And finally the *Mei-Kua* came down to the earth, not smoothly but with a heavy crash, so that the great body of the plane was crumpled and the wide wings were twisted and bent

And the people found in the wreck-age of the plane the *fi chi* who had driven it in the air and beaten the *Yi Bin Kwe-Tse.* He was tall and large, as are all the *Mei-Kua,* and on the shoulders of his jacket were two narrow strips of white embroidery and on his back was sewn the flag of China, with the white sun of *Kuo Min Tang* in the corner, and the chop of the Gissimo himself was stamped below the writing that said this was one of the men who had come from across the wide waters to help drive the *Yi Bin Kwe-Tse* from the soil of China.

The people took him up gently and carried him to a house and attended to his wounds, although they knew he could not live for long. For his arm and his leg were broken and there were many wounds made by the bullets of the *Yi Bin Kwe-Tse* and his stomach was torn so that the guts of the man could be seen within it. But they did what they could to make him comfortable, although the *Mei-Kua fi chi* knew as well as they that he could not live for long.

And while they did the little that

they could for him, he laughed with them and made jests in a poor and awkward Chinese that they could not understand, for it was not the Chinese spoken in that village. But they could understand his labored laugh and they could see the greatness and the goodness and the strength and the dignity of the dying man.

And when he was dead, this man with the flag of Free China upon his back, they wrapped his body in white, for white is the color of the honored dead, and they laid it in the finest coffin in the village and they placed the coffin upon a barge in the river to take it to the people who would return it to the great general of the *Mei-Kua fi chi, Ch'e Ne T'e,* and the others of the *Mei-Kua.*

And in a box beside the coffin they put the clothing they had removed from him when he was in pain, and with the clothing they put the things that had been in his pockets. They put the little leather case with his money, and the pieces of heavy paper with his picture and the other pictures of the woman and the two children, the *Mei-Kua* cigarettes and the little silver box of self-arriving fire, the two small metal plates on a little chain, the knife that folded within itself, and the small brown *Mei-Kua* coin with the picture of a bearded man upon it.

And when this had been done four of the young men of the village took poles and poled the barge up the river to return the *Mei-Kua fi chi* to his own people.

And the news ran quickly all along the river that the dead hero was returning to his people. And all of the villagers along the river and all of the people who lived in the sampans tied along the banks of the river waited to see the barge go slowly by. And wherever it passed, the people lit long strings of firecrackers and honored the *Mei-Kua fi chi* who had fought for China and laughed and jested and died as a hero should.

* * *

A. B. Austin, of the London *Herald*, Lands with British Commandos West of Dieppe

CORPORAL HITLER, said Winston Churchill in his memoirs, was "a maniac of ferocious genius, the repository and expression of the most virulent hatreds that have ever corroded the human breast." How to bring this vicious killer at bay was the immediate problem of Allied commanders in early 1942. There was some difference of opinion. With a kind of frustrated persistence Churchill wanted to strike at the soft underbelly of Europe; * F. D. R. favored a direct frontal assault against the Germans from across the Channel; and Stalin, with monotonous insistence, demanded the opening of a second front to draw off the German hordes hammering eastward. In the summer of 1942, American and British leaders agreed on an exploratory combined-operations raid on France as a preliminary to the big show.

In mid-August a contingent of Canadian and British Commandos, assisted by a token force of American Rangers, struck at Dieppe, on the French coast. For several hours the Allied expeditionary force, protected by a strong air umbrella, held a precarious toehold on the Atlantic Wall.

Here is the story of that extraordinary raid as described by A. B. Austin, of the London *Daily Herald,* who covered the show for all the English newspapers.†

"Don't fergit the other bastards is twice as scared as you!"

London *Daily Herald*, August 21, 1942

We landed west of Dieppe at dawn.

The British Commando troops to whom I was attached, Lord Lovat's No. 4 Commando, were the first men of the Dieppe raid force to jump ashore.

They had been told a few hours earlier by Admiral Louis Mountbatten, Chief of Command Operations: "Your task is most vital. If you don't knock out the German howitzer battery, the whole operation will go wrong. You

---

* In 1915 Churchill, then first sea lord of the Admiralty, devised a bold stroke to capture Constantinople, put Turkey out of the war, and then drive against Austria and Germany in a smashing blow from below. This enterprise at the Dardanelles, also called the Gallipoli campaign, was a tragic fiasco, costing tens of thousands of British lives and not a little damage to Allied morale.

† Austin was later killed in the fighting in Italy.

have got to do it, even at the greatest possible risk."

They had heard their colonel, Lord Lovat, say: "This is the toughest job we've had. Remember that you represent the flower of the British army."

And as we nosed in under the Dieppe cliffs, I heard a Commando trooper whisper to his mate: "Don't fergit the other bastards is twice as scared as you!"

They knew that if they failed there would be a great disaster. They did not fail. The German guns were shattered, their ammunition dump blown up, and the German gunners were wiped out at the bayonet's point in hand-to-hand fighting.

Because of that and with superb support from the RAF, our detachments were able to land on their five appointed beaches. No German has ever been able to do that in England.

One question worried all of us in those last silent twenty minutes after the long, cramped voyage in the starlight: "Would the Germans be ready for us?"

The thought of it made me hang on, in my rising funk, to the thought that "the other 'bastards' were twice as scared as I."

A sergeant crouching up front of me kept a whispered running commentary:

"'Bout five hundred yards now . . . see the cliffs? . . . There's the crack we want. . . . Look at the Jerry tracer bullets. . . . Don't think they're firing at us, though! . . . A hundred yards now . . . fifty . . . God, there's a bloke on the cliff!"

So our question was answered. I could just make out a figure, silhouetted for an instant in the half-light. The next moment we grounded on the shingle at full tide, a few yards from the foot of the cold-looking, unscalable, one-hundred-foot overhanging chalk-white cliffs.

That was the worst moment.

The assault craft grounded, hesitated, nosed a little to port, grounded again, and stayed put.

As we blundered, bending, across the shingle to the cliff foot, a German machine gun began to stutter from up above. The oerlikon guns from our support craft answered.

Red-hot tracer bullets flashed past each other between clifftop and sea.

At the same moment the other half of No. 4 Commando, led by Lord Lovat himself, had landed a little farther west. They were to try to take the battery in the rear while our force, covered by its mortar fire, made the frontal attack.

There were only two cracks in the cliffs up which we could pass, and we found in a few minutes that one of these was so crammed full of barbed wire that we could not take time to risk it.

The second crack, a little to the left, ended in an almost vertical beach staircase for holiday bathers and fishermen, about twenty feet wide, between walls of chalk.

Had the Germans prepared their defense properly, we would not have had a chance. One platoon with a machine gun would have held it against a fair-sized army.

But the Commando leaders knew that there was just a chance that the Germans would not believe anyone could be fool enough to try such a suicidal approach.

It came off. In a few minutes the two banks of the barbed wire at the top of the steps had been blasted with explosives, and the Commando spearhead, followed by the mortar platoon, were creeping cautiously up the gully.

At that moment the howitzers fired. The light had grown just enough for any observers to spot craft a fair way out to sea.

For a few minutes I watched the soaring fireworks across the Dieppe approaches.

The naval bombardment, timed for twenty minutes after our landing, had begun. The shore batteries, and all the light German guns, were replying.

The sky was spotted with the tracks of incendiary shells, and the Dieppe basin was beginning to rumble and thud like the explosive growling of a volcano crater.

A formation of four-cannon Hurricanes dived out of the sky on the cliffs above us, spitting fire at the machine-gun posts.

Commando troopers under the cliffs yelled: "Give them hell!"

I passed several times up and down the gully, carrying messages or mortar shells. Snipers seemed to be the Germans' favorite defense.

Where the gully ended there was scrub, and beyond that a narrow road into the woods. A cow was grazing by it. She gave an occasional worried moo, but never budged—in spite of all the bullet whine and mortar crash—from the corner of the field which was on her grazing schedule for that morning.

Just as I got back from the gully stairs a bullet or two began to whistle past.

"That saucy sniper," said a Navy signaler, "is too bloody cocky."

A chain of mortar-shell carriers were winding up the gully and through the woods. I caught up with a load of shells and went with them.

"Lord, I'm in a muck," said a man in front of me.

"Never mind the sweat, mon," said a Scot behind him. "It'll thin ye off,

and think how much more beer ye'll be able tae soak in."

An explosion in front of us, louder and longer than any we had heard that morning, made us crouch suddenly.

Presently Major Mills Roberts, the leader of our part of the Commando force, came back from the trees, grinning with pleasure:

"We've got their ammunition dump," he said. "Mortar shell bang on top of it. Bloody fools, they'd got their ammunition all in one lot. Must have been drunk with power!"

A minute later I was running down the cliff gully again with another message to pass to England.

It read: "Flak gun demolished 0650."

Quickly after me came another message which said: "Assault has gone in."

This meant that Lord Lovat and his men had worked their way round and were swarming over the battery position from the rear.

In a pause of the firing I looked up to find Lord Lovat sitting against a rock beside me.

You could see that he was bubbling with happiness.

"By God, we did that job all right," he said. "Went in straight with the bayonet. Cut them in shreds. Not a man left in the battery. How glad I am I wasn't in the battery. But they fought hard."

He was easy to pick out anywhere in that day's battle. "Cool as a trout," as a trooper said.

The enemy mortars banged down a bit of cliff near us.

"Getting a bit hot," said Lord Lovat. "I'm going aboard," and he strolled into the sea up to his knees, following the long lines of men who were clambering into the assault landing craft.

"Hi," he yelled to the nearest craft some way out. "You come in here. Why should I get my knees wet?" *

On the long, weary voyage back our men shared their cigarettes, water, food, and blankets with the prisoners.

So busy were the Messerschmitts and the Focke-Wulf 190's kept by our fighters that they had no time to strafe our craft.

All through the afternoon I watched German and British fighters scribbling their quarrels across the sky. Many planes fell, whether German or British I could not see.

Once an American pilot in a Spitfire whirled down, bailing out as he fell. One of our craft picked him up. Then we attacked a German pilot, who parachuted down, and we stopped to pick him up, too.

After many hours, even watching one of the most significant air battles of the war palled. We huddled slackly down in our boat, dead-tired, filthy-looking, ragged, lolling, happy men—happy because we knew that the Commandos had made the battle of Dieppe possible.

* * *

THIS WAS, indeed, a great spot news story, but Reporter Austin may be forgiven for not having been able to give the entire overall picture—he was too busy remaining alive. The truth was that the raid on Dieppe was a tragic failure, despite the fact that the Allied commanders learned many lessons that were to prove useful in the big show on D-Day, June 6, 1944. The casualties were heavy. In all, 10,000 men engaged in the operation, including large naval personnel and RAF pilots, and of these more than one third were lost, killed, or wounded. One destroyer was sunk, and the RAF lost ninety-eight planes, but thirty pilots were saved. To counterbalance this, British fighters downed at least 150 German aircraft.

The Dieppe raid produced another magnificent story. While Austin accompanied the Commandos ashore Quentin Reynolds, roving correspondent for *Collier's*, was assigned to a fast destroyer from which he watched the entire Dieppe operation at considerable risk to his person. In his book, *Dress Rehearsal, The Story of Dieppe* (1943), he told how the barrage began and the air trembled and vibrated with sound:

The guns thundered and golden flashes cut the half-light of the dawn. For ten minutes this Wagnerian overture continued and then, as though it had been rehearsed by a master director, the curtain of the night rolled up, the sun chased a few wisps of mist away, and in front of us lay the city of Dieppe.

Quentin Reynolds went on to tell of the retreat from Dieppe. His destroyer caught up with the flotilla returning home—barges, self-propelled

---

* Another version of this already legendary story was given to Quentin Reynolds by one of the Commandos. "We were all in the barges. They were about fifteen feet offshore, so they wouldn't get stuck in case of a quick getaway. We all waded out and climbed in, and there was the Colonel on the beach, being sure everyone was aboard. They were giving us plenty of hell, too. Stuff was dropping all over and then, to make it worse, a Focke-Wulf dove at us and gave us plenty. The Colonel starts walking out in the water, and when it gets to his knees, he's still ten feet from our barge and he lets out a yell: 'Why the bloody hell should I get soaking wet because you blokes are too damned lazy to bring the barge in close to shore? Come and get me.' He is a hell of a man!"

and laden with men, darting motor-torpedo boats, barges towed by transports, flak ships, and all sorts of other ships lumbering along for home.

It was dark when we reached Portsmouth. By now wounds began to hurt; the merciful, deadening anesthetic of the shock had worn off. The organization was magnificent. No orders were necessary. Men slipped aboard silently, picked up stretchers bearing wounded, and walked down the gangplank. Nurses stood on the pier and, as the wounded walked off, each nurse grabbed an arm and led the tired men to waiting ambulances. There was no confusion.

The German press reported the news of Dieppe in a tone of superb self-confidence. The *Deutsche Allgemeine Zeitung* stated coldly: "As executed, the venture mocked all rules of military logic and strategy. The invasion recalls the fate of Dunkirk. It was forced by Stalin and as such was conceived under an unlucky star." Under the caption HANDS OFF EUROPE! the *Völkischer Beobachter,* the major organ of the Nazi party, crowed: "The collapse of the attack should remind Prime Minister Winston Churchill that every similar attempt will swiftly founder on German defenses."

George Weller Describes an Appendix Operation Performed by a Pharmacist's Mate while Japanese Destroyers Pass Overhead

FOR THIS GRAPHIC ACCOUNT of an emergency appendectomy aboard a submarine in enemy waters George Weller of the *Chicago Daily News* was awarded the Pulitzer Prize for distinguished reporting in 1942. The "surgeon" was a twenty-three-year-old pharmacist's mate who had himself suffered four shrapnel wounds when the Japanese bombed Cavite. While the bow and stern planesmen kept the submarine from varying more than half a degree vertically in 150 minutes below the stormy sea, the young seaman, assisted by his shipmates and utilizing a weird variety of surgical tools, saved the life of a stricken sailor as the craft hid from enemy ships.

During the war Weller was bombed and machine-gunned and, finally, captured by the Germans in Athens. His brilliant coverage of the Greek and North African campaigns was perhaps surpassed by his work in the Far East—Burma, Singapore, Java, New Guinea, and the early Pacific island fighting.

"Doc" Lipes commandeers a submarine officers' wardroom

Chicago Daily News, December 14, 1942

SOMEWHERE IN AUSTRALIA—"They are giving him ether now," was what they said back in the aft torpedo rooms.

"He's gone under, and they're ready to cut him open," the crew whispered, sitting on their pipe bunks cramped between torpedoes.

One man went forward and put his arm quietly around the shoulder of another man who was handling the bow diving planes.

"Keep her steady, Jake," he said. "They've just made the first cut. They're feeling around for it now."

"They" were a little group of anxious-faced men with their arms thrust into reversed white pajama coats. Gauze bandages hid all their expressions except the tensity in their eyes.

"It" was an acute appendix inside Dean Rector of Chautauqua, Kansas. The stabbing pains had become unendurable the day before, which was Rector's first birthday at sea. He was nineteen years old.

The big depth gauge that looks like a factory clock and stands beside the "Christmas tree" of red and green gauges regulating the flooding chambers showed where they were. They were below the surface. And above them were enemy waters crossed and recrossed by whirring propellers of Japanese destroyers and transports.

The nearest naval surgeon competent to operate on the nineteen-year-old seaman was thousands of miles and many days away. There was just one way to prevent the appendix from bursting, and that was for the crew to operate upon their shipmate themselves.

And that's what they did; they operated upon him. It was probably one of the largest operations in number of participants that ever occurred.

"He says he's ready to take his chance," the gobs whispered from bulkhead to bulkhead.

"That guy's regular"—the word traveled from bow planes to propeller and back again.

They "kept her steady."

The chief surgeon was a twenty-three-year-old pharmacist's mate wearing a blue blouse with white-taped collar and squashy white duck cap. His name was Wheeler B. Lipes. He came from Newcastle near Roanoke, Virginia, and had taken the Navy hospital course in San Diego, thereafter serving three years in the naval hospital at Philadelphia, where his wife lives.

Lipes' specialty as laboratory technician was in operating a machine that registers heartbeats. He was classified as an electrocardiographer. But he had seen Navy doctors take out one or two appendixes and thought he could do it. Under the sea, he was given his first chance to operate.

There was difficulty about the ether. When below the surface the pressure inside a boat is above the atmospheric pressure. More ether is absorbed under pressure. The submariners did not know how long their operation would last.

They did not know how long it would take to find the appendix. They did not know whether there would be enough ether to keep the patient under throughout the operation.

They didn't want the patient waking up before they were finished.

They decided to operate on the table in the officers' wardroom. In the newest and roomiest American submarine the wardroom is approximately the size of a Pullman-car drawing room. It is flanked by bench seats attached to the wall, and a table occupies the whole room—you enter with knees already crooked to sit down. The only way anyone can be upright in the wardrooms is by kneeling.

The operating room was just long enough so that the patient's head and feet reached the two ends without hanging over.

First they got out a medical book and read up on the appendix, while Rector, his face pale with pain, lay in the narrow bunk. It was probably the most democratic surgical operation ever performed. Everybody from box-plane man to the cook in the galley knew his role.

The cook provided the ether mask. It was an inverted tea strainer. They covered it with gauze.

The twenty-three-year-old "surgeon" had, as his staff of fellow "physicians," all men his senior in age and rank. His anesthetist was Communications Officer Lieutenant Franz Hoskins of Tacoma, Washington.

Before they carried Rector to the wardroom, the submarine Captain, Lieutenant Commander W. B. Ferrall of Pittsburgh, asked Lipes as the "surgeon" to have a talk with the patient.

"Look, Dean, I never did anything

like this before," Lipes said. "You don't have much chance to pull through, anyhow. What do you say?"

"I know just how it is, Doc."

It was the first time in his life that anybody had called Lipes "Doc." But there was in him, added to the steadiness that goes with a submariner's profession, a new calmness.

The operating staff adjusted gauze masks while members of the engine-room crew pulled tight their reversed pajama coats over their extended arms. The tools were laid out. They were far from perfect or complete for a major operation. The scalpel had no handle.

But submariners are used to "rigging" things. The medicine chest had plenty of hemostats, which are small pincers used for closing blood vessels. The machinist "rigged" a handle for the scalpel from a hemostat.

When you are going to have an operation, you must have some kind of antiseptic agent. Rummaging in the medicine chest, they found sulfanilamide tablets and ground them to powder. One thing was lacking: there was no means of holding open the wound after the incision had been made. Surgical tools used for this are called "muscular retractors." What would they use for retractors? There was nothing in the medicine chest that gave the answer, so they went as usual to the cook's galley.

In the galley they found tablespoons made of Monel metal. They bent these at right angles and had their retractors.

Sterilizers? They went to one of the greasy copper-colored torpedoes waiting beside the tubes. They milked alcohol from the torpedo mechanism and used it as well as boiling water.

The light in the wardroom seemed insufficient; operating rooms always have big lamps. So they brought one of the big floods used for night loadings and rigged it inside the wardroom's sloping ceiling.

The moment for the operation had come. Rector, very pale and stripped, stretched himself out on the wardroom table under the glare of the lamps.

Rubber gloves dipped in torpedo alcohol were drawn upon the youthful "Doc's" hands. The fingers were too long. The rubber ends dribbled limply over.

"You look like Mickey Mouse, Doc," said one onlooker.

Lipes grinned behind the gauze.

Rector on the wardroom table wet his lips, glancing a side look at the tea-strainer ether mask.

With his superior officers as his subordinates, Lipes looked into their eyes, nodded, and Hoskins put the tea mask down over Rector's face. No words were spoken; Hoskins already knew from the book that he should watch Rector's eye pupils dilate.

The twenty-three-year-old surgeon, following the ancient hand rule, put his little finger on Rector's subsiding umbilicus, his thumb on the point of the hipbone, and, by dropping his index finger straight down, found the point where he intended to cut. At his side stood Lieutenant Norvell Ward of Indian Head, Maryland, who was his assistant surgeon.

"I chose him for his coolness and dependability," said the Doc afterward of his superior officer. "He acted as my third and fourth hands."

Lieutenant Ward's job was to place tablespoons in Rector's side as Lipes cut through successive layers of muscles.

Engineering Officer Lieutenant S. Manning of Cheraw, South Carolina, took the job which in a normal operating room is known as "circulating nurse." His job was to see that packets of sterile dressings kept coming and that the torpedo alcohol and boiling water arrived regularly from the galley.

They had what is called an "instrument passer" in Chief Yeoman H. F. Wieg of Sheldon, North Dakota, whose job was to keep the tablespoons coming and coming clean. Submarine Skipper Ferrall too had his part. They made him "recorder." It was his job to keep count of the sponges that went into Rector. A double count of the tablespoons used as retractors was kept: one by the Skipper and one by the cook, who was himself passing them out from the galley.

It took Lipes in his flap-finger rubber gloves nearly twenty minutes to find the appendix.

"I have tried one side of the caecum," he whispered after the first minutes. "Now, I'm trying the other."

Whispered bulletins seeped back into the engine room and the crews' quarters.

"The Doc has tried one side of something and now is trying the other side."

After more search, Lipes finally whispered, "I think I've got it. It's curled way into the blind gut."

Lipes was using the classical McBurney's incision. Now was the time when his shipmate's life was completely in his hands.

"Two more spoons." They passed the word to Lieutenant Ward.

"Two spoons at 14.45 hours [2:45 p.m.]," wrote Skipper Ferrall on his note pad.

"More flashlights. And another battle lantern," demanded Lipes.

The patient's face, lathered with white petrolatum, began to grimace.

"Give him more ether," ordered the Doc.

Hoskins looked doubtfully at the original five pounds of ether now shrunk to hardly three quarters of one can, but once again the tea strainer was soaked in ether. The fumes mounted up, thickening the wardroom air and making the operating staff giddy.

"Want those blowers speeded up?" the Captain asked the Doc.

The blowers began to whir louder.

Suddenly came the moment when the Doc reached out his hand, pointing toward the needle threaded with twenty-day chromic catgut.

One by one the sponges came out. One by one the tablespoons bent into right angles were withdrawn and returned to the galley. At the end it was the skipper who nudged Lipes and pointed to the tally of bent tablespoons. One was missing. Lipes reached into the incision for the last time and withdrew the wishboned spoon and closed the incision.

They even had the tool ready to cut off the thread. It was a pair of fingernail scissors, well scalded in water and torpedo juice.

At that moment the last can of ether went dry. They lifted up Rector and carried him into the bunk of Lieutenant Charles K. Miller of Williamsport, Pennsylvania. Lieutenant Miller alone had had control of the ship as diving officer during the operation.

It was half an hour after the last tablespoon had been withdrawn that Rector opened his eyes. His first words were, "I'm still in there pitching."

By that time the sweat-drenched officers were hanging up their pajamas to dry. It had taken the amateurs about two and a half hours for an operation ordinarily requiring forty five minutes.

"It wasn't one of those 'snappy valve' appendixes," murmured Lipes apologetically as he felt the first hand-clasps upon his shoulders.

Within a few hours, the bow and stern planesmen, who, under Lieutenant Miller's direction, had kept the submarine from varying more than half a degree vertically in 150 minutes below the stormy sea, came around to receive Rector's winks of thanks. Rector's only remark was, "Gee, I wish Earl was here to see this job." His brother Earl, a seaman on the Navy submarine tender *Pigeon,* is among the list of missing at Corregidor, probably captured.

*   *   *

WHEN THE SUBMARINE surfaced that night, the ether-drunk submarine crewmen found themselves grabbing the sides of the conning tower and swaying unsteadily on their feet. Thirteen days later Rector, fully recovered, was at his battle station, manning the phones. In a bottle vibrating on the submarine's shelves was the prize exhibit of surgeon Lipes—the first appendix ever known to have been removed below enemy waters.

Ernie Pyle Supplies a Worm's-Eye View of Yank Infantrymen in North Africa

A SHY, GNOMELIKE little fellow with an almost bald pate, Ernie Pyle was the idol of GI's on a dozen fronts. He deliberately avoided the command post in favor of the foxhole. He wrote only about what he personally witnessed and experienced. He lived with the men who fought and he accompanied them into battle. He reported what the GI's felt, what the war meant to them, and what they were dreaming about.

Pyle's dispatches were filled with homely details—the GI's home town, his address, the names of members of his family. He noted little acts of kindness and unselfishness, the sadness, loneliness, and ennui of men bored to distraction behind the lines, the raw courage of boys who, in battle, became men. To the people at home he made it clear that for the average infantryman the war extended just about a hundred yards to either side.

The little reporter, with his worm's-eye view of the war, didn't write about military strategy, because he felt that he knew nothing about it. He pictured tired, dirty soldiers who didn't want to die, and he wrote of heroism, anger, wine, cussing, flowers, and many, many graves. This was the human side of the war.

For all this the GI's loved the bald little reporter from Indiana. He was one of them.

Here is Ernie Pyle's description of the final push of the First Infantry Division in the North African campaign. Written in the front lines before Mateur in early May, 1943, it shows the great reporter at his best.

"They are just guys from Broadway and Main Street"

New York World-Telegram, May 3, 5, 1943

We're now with an infantry outfit that has battled ceaselessly for four days and nights.

This northern warfare has been in the mountains. You don't ride much any more. It is walking and climbing and crawling country. The mountains are big, but they are constant. They are largely treeless. They are easy to defend and bitter to take. But we are taking them.

The Germans lie on the back slope of every ridge, deeply dug into foxholes. In front of them the fields and pastures are hideous with thousands of hidden mines. The forward slopes are left open, untenanted, and if the Americans tried to scale those slopes they would be murdered wholesale in an inferno of machine-gun cross fire, plus mortars and grenades.

Consequently, we don't do it that way. We have fallen back to the old warfare of first pulverizing the enemy with artillery, then sweeping around the ends of the hill with infantry and taking them from the sides and behind.

I've written before how the big guns crack and roar almost constantly throughout the day and night. They lay a screen ahead of our troops. By magnificent shooting they drop shells on the back slopes. By means of shells timed to burst in the air a few feet from the ground, they get the Germans even in their foxholes. Our troops have found that the Germans dig foxholes down and then under, trying to get cover from the shell bursts that shower death from above.

Our artillery really has been sensational. For once we have enough of something and at the right time. Officers tell me they actually have more guns than they know what to do with.

All the guns in any one sector can be centered to shoot at one spot. And when we lay the whole business on a German hill the entire slope seems to erupt. It becomes an unbelievable caldron of fire and smoke and dirt. Afterward, veteran German soldiers say they have never been through anything like it.

Now to the infantry—the Goddamned infantry,* as they like to call themselves.

I love the infantry because they are the underdogs. They are the mudrain-frost-and-wind boys. They have no comforts, and they even learn to live without the necessities. And in the end they are the guys that wars can't be won without.

I wish you could have seen just one of the ineradicable pictures I have in my mind today. In this particular picture I am sitting among clumps of sword grass on a steep and rocky hillside that we had just taken. We are looking out over a vast rolling country to the rear.

A narrow path comes like a ribbon over a hill miles away, down a long slope, across a creek, up a slope, and over another hill.

All along the length of that ribbon there is a thin line of men. For four days and nights they have fought hard, eaten little, washed none, and slept hardly at all. Their nights have been violent with attack, fright, butchery, their days sleepless and miserable with the crash of artillery.

The men are walking. They are fifty feet apart, for dispersal. Their walk is slow, for they are dead weary, as you can tell even when looking at them from behind. Every line and sag of their bodies speaks their inhuman exhaustion.

On their shoulders and backs they carry heavy steel tripods, machine-gun barrels, leaden boxes of ammunition. Their feet seem to sink into the ground from the overload they are bearing.

They don't slouch. It is the terrible deliberation of each step that spells out their appalling tiredness. Their faces are black and unshaved. They are young men, but the grime and whiskers and exhaustion make them look middle-aged.

In their eyes as they pass is not hatred, not excitement, not despair, not the tonic of their victory. There is just

---

* The profanity, deleted by the censor in the original newspaper report, appears in a revised version included in Pyle's book *Here Is Your War* (1943).

the simple expression of being there as if they had been doing that forever, and nothing else.

The line moves on, but it never ends. All afternoon men keep coming round the hill and vanish eventually over the horizon. It is one long tired line of antlike men.

There is an agony in your heart and you feel almost ashamed to look at them. They are just guys from Broadway and Main Street, but maybe you wouldn't remember them. They are too far away now. They are too tired. Their world can never be known to you, but if you could see them just once, just for an instant, you would know that no matter how hard people work back home they are not keeping pace with these infantrymen in Tunisia.

After four days in battle, the famous infantry outfit I'm with sat on its newly won hill and took two days' rest, while companion units on each side of it leapfrogged ahead.

The men dig in on the back slope of the hill before any rest begins. Everybody digs in. It is an inviolate rule of the commanding officers, and nobody wants to disobey it. Every time you pause, even if you think you're dying of weariness, you dig yourself a hole before you sit down.

The startling thing to me about those rest periods is how quickly the human body can recuperate from critical exhaustion, how rapidly the human mind snaps back to the normal state of laughing, grousing, yarn spinning, and yearning for home.

Here is what happens when a unit stops to rest:

My unit stops just after daybreak on Hill 394. Foxholes are dug, out-posts are placed, phone wires are strung on the ground, some patrol work goes on as usual. Then the men lie down and sleep till the blistering heat of the sun wakes them up.

After that you sit around in bunches, recounting things. You can't do much of anything. The day just easily kills itself.

That first evening is when life begins to seem like Christmas Eve. The mail comes up in jeeps just before dark. Then come the men's blanket rolls. At dark, hot food arrives—the first hot food in four days. This food is cooked in rolling kitchens several miles back and brought up by jeep, in big thermos containers, to the foot of the hill. Men carry the containers, slung on poles over their shoulders, up goat paths in the darkness to all parts of the mountain.

Hot food and hot coffee put life into a man, and then in a pathetic kind of contentment you lie down and you sleep. The all-night crash of the artillery behind you is completely unheard through your weariness.

There are no mosquitoes so far in the mountains, and very few fleas, but there are lots of ants.*

Hot food arrives again in the morning before daylight. Your breakfast is at four A.M. Then begins a day of reassembling yourself.

Word is passed that mail will be collected that evening, so the boys sit on the ground and write letters. But writing is hard, for they can't tell in their letters what they have just been through.

The men put water in their steel helmets and wash and shave for the first time in days. A few men at a time are sent to a creek in the valley to take

* Someone, perhaps a censor, eliminated Pyle's words at this point. "we discovered that our ridge was inhabited by a frightening menagerie of snakes, two-legged lizards, scorpions, centipedes, overgrown chiggers, and man-eating ants."

baths. The remainder sit in groups on the ground, talking, or individually in foxholes, cleaning their guns, reading, or just relaxing.

A two-month-old batch of copies of the magazine *Yank* arrives, and a two-week-old bunch of the *Stars and Stripes*. Others read detective magazines and comic books that have come up with their bedrolls.

At noon everybody opens cans of cold C ration. Cold coffee in five-gallon water cans is out in the sun to warm.

Soldiers cut each other's hair. It doesn't matter how it looks, for they aren't going anywhere fancy, anyhow. Some of them strip nearly naked and lie on their blankets for a sunbath. Their bodies are tanned, as though they had been wintering at Miami Beach. They wear the inner part of their helmets, for the noonday sun is dangerous.

Their knees are skinned from crawling over rocks. They find little unimportant injuries that they didn't know they had. Some take off their shoes and socks and look over their feet, which are violently purple with athlete's-foot ointment.

I sit around with them, and they get to telling stories, both funny and serious, about their battle. They are all disappointed when they learn I am not permitted to name the outfit they're in, for they are all proud of it and would like the folks at home to know what they've done.

"We always get it the toughest," they said. "This is the third big battle now since coming to Africa. The Jerry is really afraid of us now. He knows what outfit we are, and he doesn't like us."

Thus they talk and boast and laugh and speak of fear. Evening draws down, and the chill sets in once more. Hot chow arrives just after dusk.

And then the word is passed around. Orders come by telephone.

There is no excitement, no grouching, no eagerness either. They had expected it.

Quietly men roll their packs, strap them on, lift their rifles, and fall into line.

There is not a sound as they move like wraiths in single file down tortuous goat paths, walking slowly, feeling the ground with their toes, stumbling, and hushfully cussing. They will walk all night and attack before dawn.

They move like ghosts. You don't hear or see them three feet away. Now and then a light flashes lividly from a blast of our big guns, and for just an instant you see a long slow line of dark-helmeted forms silhouetted in the flash.

Then darkness and silence consume them again, and somehow you are terribly moved.

* * *

"IT MAY BE THAT the war has changed me," Pyle wrote later, "along with the rest. It is hard for anyone to analyze himself. I find more and more that I wish to be alone. I believe that I have a new patience with humanity that I've never had before. When you've lived with the unnatural mass cruelty that mankind is capable of inflicting upon itself, you find yourself dispossessed of the faculty of blaming one poor man for the triviality of his faults. I don't see how any survivor of war can ever be cruel to anything, ever again."

Ernie Pyle hated the entire dirty business of war, but he felt his place to be with the men at the front. He was killed by a Jap machine-gun bullet on the island of Ie Shima.

Disconsolate GI's who loved the wistful little newsman placed this inscription on a simple monument at the spot where he was killed:

AT THIS SPOT
THE
77TH INFANTRY DIVISION
LOST A BUDDY
ERNIE PYLE
18 APRIL 1945

John Hersey's Major Rings a Bell in Licata

Amgot it was called—the Allied Military Government of Occupied Territory.* The first task of the American and British armies as they fought their way up the peninsula was to strike down the enemy. The second was to set up a military government to administer Italian soil under joint Anglo-American supervision. For this purpose American and British officers were sent to govern the Italian villages and cities as long as they remained in the military theater. For some of these officers the assignment was a sinecure important only in terms of wine, women, and song. Others of a more conscientious mold appreciated the critical nature of the experiment—a heaven-sent opportunity to teach Italy self-government. In unhappy Sicily, as occupation troops soon discovered, the spirit of Garibaldi was quite dead.

The story of one of these officers with a mission and of the magnificent job he performed was told by a young journalist soon to be acclaimed as one of the outstanding writers of World War II. John Hersey was born in Tientsin, China, in 1914, the son of a YMCA worker engaged in administering Chinese famine relief. After his graduation from Yale in 1936, he became an editor of *Time* and also wrote articles for *Life*. As a war correspondent in the Far East he sent in some remarkable reports on his Guadalcanal experiences. Here is his report on democracy at work in Sicily.

"I thank you and I kiss your hand"

Reprinted by permission, from *Life,* August 23, 1943. Copyright, 1943

Army desk jobs are famous for dullness. And yet one of the most exciting things you can do in Sicily right now is to sit for a day by the desk of the Major who runs the town of Licata in the name of the Allies.

For a long time we have taken pleasure in the difficulties met by Germany and Japan in organizing the conquered lands. Here at the Major's desk you see difficulties, hundreds of them, but you see shrewd action, American idealism and generosity bordering on sentimentality, the innate sympathy of common blood that so many Americans have to offer over here. You see incredible Italian poverty, you see the habits of Fascism, you see a little

* Within a few weeks AMGOT took a 40% reduction in its name to AMG. When somebody discovered that AMGOT was an unprintable word in Turkish, the Axis radio made gleeful reference to it and American commentators criticized the unfortunate choice.

duplicity and a lot of simplicity and many things which are comic and tragic at one time. Above all you see a thing succeeding—and it looks like the future.

First look at the desk. It is no ordinary Army desk. It is oak and it is vast. Underneath it there is a little wooden scrollwork footstool. On each end of the desk are fasces and the inscription ANNO XV—for the fifteenth year of Fascism, 1937, when the desk must have been made. It sits at the end of a huge marble-floored room in the Palazzo Dicittà or Town Hall—a room obviously copied from the famous room of the recent Number One boy. Sitting at the desk you see pictures of King Victor Emmanuel, his Queen, Prince Umberto and his Princess, and scenes of the King driving through the town after it was bombed some time ago. Approaching the desk you see a huge and violent painting which the Major's fawning interpreter will tell you represents Columbus discovering America but actually is a scene from Sicilian Vespers, the bloody revolt against a previous invader.

The Major comes in at 7:45. His assistant, Corporal Charles Nocerini of Franklin, Kansas, is already at his improvised table at the opposite end of the huge room from the Major's desk. The corporal goes to a closet against the wall, takes out a big tin of orange juice, pokes holes in it with a bayonet, and pours out breakfast for the Major, which he takes at his desk. He is already deep in his account book, balancing fines and incomes from sales of seized equipment against home-relief payments and repair costs. Bent over his work, the Major appears furiously energetic in a La Guardia kind of way. His skin is dark. He has a mustache which he says he grew "because it makes me look more fitted for the

job." His dark-brown eyes are clear and quick in spite of the fact that he didn't sleep very well last night because he had so many things to think about for today.

After balancing his books he writes a couple of brief reports, and then the process begins which makes his day both killing and fascinating—a stream of visitors bring their problems to him. First come two women dressed in black. For some reason the women always come in pairs. The younger of these two has a baby in her arms. The Major sits them down. As the older one starts explaining trouble in fine circumlocutions the younger one pulls out a tit and starts nursing the baby, which is pathetically thin. It seems the family had nine goats, eight of which were killed by the bombing. It seems that the roof leaks. The girl's husband is in the Italian Army. Her brother deserted but is in Palermo. The family has always been against Fascism. There is much malaria in Sicily . . . and so the tale of woe rambles on until the Major says sharply, "You wish?"

"We wish," says the old lady, "permission to go to Palermo to find the brother of my daughter here, my son who fought for his country but still does not work for his family."

The Major politely explains that there is a war going on, that trains are not now carrying civilians, that everything is being done to hurry the war but that one must have patience

Next visitor is a lawyer, an unctuous man in a white suit and blue glasses who out of habit raises his hand in the Fascist salute and then, remembering, slides it over his forehead. With gestures which beggar description he describes the unhappy lot of an old man who is a client of his and who owns a five-room house.

Three of the rooms the old man has sold. He is dying. He wants permission to sell the other two rooms at once so that he will not die intestate still owning the rooms. Major grants permission.

An old fisherman comes in. His face is like the hills of Sicily and his hands are like good rope, though he is over sixty. He is very sad. The Major brought it about that Licata was the first Sicilian town to send out civilian fishing boats, for in the first days after the invasion people almost starved. Yesterday one of the seven boats hit a stray mine and all but one of the crew were killed. The old man tells what is known of the accident. The Major asks if the others are willing to go out today. The old man straightens himself up and says, "Yes, Mr. Major, we will go because our people are hungry."

A prosperously dressed man comes in complaining that he has perfectly good draft notes on the Bank of Sicily but that no one will advance cash against them. The Major explains that the Allies had to close the banks for a few days because it was feared that a panic might develop which would break all the banks. Allied funds, he says, will soon be forwarded to the banks, which will then be able to give out cash in controlled amounts. Meanwhile the man must get along as best he can.

An MP breaks into the room. He salutes snappily and says, "A problem for you, sir. We have here a diseased whore." The Major orders her brought in. A sorry procession comes in: a forty-five-year-old woman, in a pink blouse and black polka-dotted skirt, with the mouth of a mackerel, a scarecrow of a man in green slacks and white shirt, a soldier who caught the clap from this mockery of womankind,

and a witness. The evidence is clear and frank. The sick and frightened boy says, "I seen a GI who says he had a piece off this whore in a pink shirt and I says to him, 'She's the one who dosed me, Mac.' We had her took in by the MP's." The Major then asks the thin man if he is a pimp. He acts most offended and denies it. Major says, "I am a lover of truth. If you speak truly you will merely be a man in trouble, but if you speak lies you will go to jail." The Major has somehow made the truth seem an admirable thing to this thin, contemptible man, and he tells it—he pimped for this girl and three others whose names were . . . "Never mind," says the Major, "this is a case for the Carabinieri," and he turns the pair over to the local police, all of whom the Major has continued in office.

A merchant comes in. His shirt is buttoned, but he has no tie. He is a man who was recommended to the Major as honest. He says (as does everyone, including the notorious Squadristi, or Fascist thugs, in Licata) that he has been against the Fascists for many years and if there is anything he can do to help he will be glad. The Major says that his men have found certain clothing and stuffs which had been impounded by the Fascists and which he wishes now to sell since the people have had no new clothes for a long time. Will the merchant please prepare him a list of really fair prices on the understanding that all the merchants in town will be allowed to sell the goods at a small commission, proceeds to go to the town government for home relief? The merchant waves his hand from habit and says he will gladly do so.

It is time for lunch. As the Major leaves his office and makes his way through the big crowd of waiting beseechers outside you can hear the whisper, "Kiss your hand . . . kiss your hand . . . kiss your hand. . . ." This is a vestigial expression of respect left over from times when hands really were to be kissed. It embarrasses the Major, and he says he is going to pass the word that the expression ought not to be used any more.

You lunch in a little restaurant where for breakfast, lunch, and dinner the menu is *pasta* and eggplant, fried fish, red wine, and grapes. During lunch the Major tells you his own story, which is a thoroughly American history. His parents were peasants from Parma who went to the States when they were sixteen. His father has always worked in hotels and now is assistant steward in the Merchants Club in New York. Frank went to school through high school. When he was fourteen he began working nights. When he was sixteen he lied and said he was eighteen so that he could get a driver's license and a truck driver's job. For two years he drove trucks and lifted terrible weights—until they ruptured him. When he was well a friend suggested a job with the city. He was afraid he hadn't enough education, but on his exams he came out 177th out of 1100. They gave him a job as clerk in the Markets Department. When La Guardia was elected he was laid off. He married a daughter of one of the owners of a big trucking firm, borrowed money, bought a grocery store in the Bronx, and made out all right for two years. Then he sold out and went back to the city, where he worked up to be a second-class clerk in the Sanitation Department at forty-two dollars a week. Then he went into the Army.

He says, "I can't tell you how anxious I was to get on shore to see what this was all about. At first I looked around all the time at these people, their mannerisms, their expressions, their dress. I saw them barefooted and didn't believe white people could be in that state. I am the son of an immigrant. I have seen what I thought was poverty. But now I can just picture my father's family and how poor they were. I want to help these people out as much as possible, I don't want to see them suffer that way." Then he adds, "But we've got to go now. I'm holding trials this afternoon."

Back at the office the Major finds a note from Arturo Verdirami, eighty-two-year-old eccentric who owns most of Licata's sulphur business and has for many years been agent there for Lloyd's of London. He writes the Major many notes in an English for which he apologizes "because it is Shakespearean, I am sorry." The letter says:

"I beg to notify for the necessary steps: since four months the small people of Licata does not receive the Italian *razione tesspata* of olive oil or other fats, but the officials both of commune civil and military staff have been largely provided for the families and personal friends.

"I am informed that the small population is therefore compelled to pay at the black market any price up to lire 80 per liter equal to 800 grammes. The price fixed by the Fascist government for the supply is lire 15½ per kilo of 1000 grammes.

"You cannot allow any longer this tyranny against the poors. You should therefore stop this tyrannical sufferance for the poor inhabitants by giving dispositions on the subject of the Commissario at the municipality *dokt sapio,* inviting him to notify his guards that any preference for anyone in the distribution of ailments [*sic*] will be punished inexcrably and any official civil or communal is not allowed to take the quantity to which his family has a right before the poors have received their rations respectfully signed Arturo Verdirami."

The Major is acutely aware of the black market and he has already taken the steps which the ancient Verdirami suggests. He called all the municipal employees together one day. Most of them were in the same jobs they had held under the Fascists. The Major said to them, "Now that the Americans are here, Licata is a democracy. Democracy is this—it is that the people in its government are no longer the masters of the people. How are the government people paid? They are paid out of taxes which come from the people. And so the people are really masters of the government, not the government of the people. You are now servants of the people of Licata." And he warned them about standing in line for rations, among many other things.

Now the trials begin. The chief of the Carabinieri reads off the accusations and practically acts out the crime, so acute is his sense of drama. The culprits stand before the desk and all without exception give an absentminded Fascist salute, then the first is led in.

The first case is of a man who refused to take American dollars but, much worse, refused to sell bread on credit to the local people. His plea, supported by the unctuous lawyer in white suit and blue glasses, is ignorance. He says he never had time to read the proclamations. The Major is stern as he says that ignorance of the law is no defense, and he fines the man a stiff penalty.

The second case also concerns bread. A loaf is produced in evidence to show that it was badly baked of inferior flour. Major points at the baker's hands and tells him that filth is as great a crime as cheating, and he fines the man.

Next comes a pathetic old man who stole some clothing from an Italian military storehouse. He pleads guilty and says he can't read but hates Fascists. He is so patently poor that the Major sentences him to three months' suspended sentence and gives him a lecture on honesty.

Next, six peasants are brought forward. They are very slow of speech and mind and heartbreaking to look at. They are accused of having taken some hay from an abandoned warehouse. Again the Major gives only a warning.

The last case is both the funniest and saddest. The accused is an old cartman. He stands before the desk with his cloth cap clutched in his hand and as defiant as if his accusers are Fascists, whom he says he hates. The chief of the Carabinieri starts to read the accusation. It appears that the old cartman was driving through town when a train of American amphibious trucks approached. The old man was drowsing at his reins and blocked their way. Leaping about the room and roaring, the chief of Carabinieri describes how one of his men grasped at the reins of the horse and with towering strength got the cart aside and saved the honor of Licata. The old man stays silent.

The chief now describes how the old man jumped down from his cart and charged the Carabinieri and tried to fight with him. Finally the old man speaks.

He speaks slowly about the death of his wife and the number of his children and grandchildren with malaria. He describes in detail how the Fascists once took away a horse. Then he himself begins to act out the scene in question, and it really turns out after much swooping and shouting and another near fight that the reason he charged the Carabinieri was that he who loved his horse could not bear to see this rider of motorcycles attack his old animal. The Major dismissed the case.

After the trials an embarrassment walks up to the desk in the person of Signor Giuseppe Santi, owner of the house at Number 29 Piazzi San Sebastiano. Signor Santi's house had been requisitioned for billets. This, he says, pleased him because he hated the Fascists. But it did not please him, he says, to go into the house and find drawers broken open, glasses broken, and door panels split. The Major tells the man that the soldiers were not willfully destructive but that war had given them rough habits. The Major's explanation is a masterpiece of tact. He tells Signor Santi to file a claim for damages.

Now a girl comes in who is quite pretty but very frightened-looking. She says her sweetheart is in the Army and she has heard that he was captured by the Americans. The Major asks his name. He calls up the prisoner-of-war enclosure and asks if the man is there. He is able then to tell the girl that her man is indeed a prisoner. Tears come into her eyes. "Mr. Major, I thank you, I thank you and I kiss your hand," she says.

The Major says, "I think I'll go home. I like to end each day on a happy note if I can because there are so many unhappy ones." But before he leaves, if you ask him, he will tell you the ways in which the people of Licata are already, after only a handful of days, better off than they were under the Fascists, whom they say with varying degrees of honesty that they hated.

"Sure, they're better off," he says. "For one thing they can congregate in the streets any time they want and talk about whatever they want to. They can listen to the radios. They came to me and asked if they could keep their receiving sets. I said sure. They were surprised. They asked what stations they could listen to. I said any stations. They said, 'Can you mean it?' Now they prefer the English news to the Italian, and today a crowd of them laughed and whistled at an Italian propaganda broadcast saying Sicilians were being oppressed by Americans. They can come to the City Hall and talk to the Mayor at any time they want. The Fascist Mayor had office hours from twelve to one each day, and you had to apply for an interview weeks in advance. Their streets are clean for the first time in centuries. I have forty-five men with a water truck and eight wagons cleaning up the place. Oh, there are lots of ways and there will be lots more."

And then he adds, "We have a big job to do here. You see, I can't stop imagining what it must have been like for my father and his family."

* * *

THIS ARTICLE was the genesis of Hersey's Pulitzer Prize novel about the American occupation of a Sicilian town, *A Bell for Adano* (1944). One of the most popular books published during World War II, it sold some 100,000 copies within a year after its appearance. A highly successful stage version was produced on Broadway by Leland Hayward, and a suitably colossal film adaptation came from the studios of Twentieth Century-Fox.

Ilya Ehrenburg Is Haunted
by Ghosts of the Homeless as the
Germans Retreat in Russia

W ITH STALINGRAD, the turning point of the European phase of World War II, the Moscow-born Russian journalist, Ilya Ehrenburg, saw "the beginning of retribution." The most famous and most popular of Soviet reporters, Ehrenburg was born in 1891, left Tsarist Russia at the age of seventeen, returning home after the 1917 Revolution. Four years later he left again to work in France as a writer and journalist, but shortly before Germany invaded the Soviet Union he returned once more to his native land and became a war correspondent.

Ehrenburg's reporting is impressionistic rather than photographic. He mingles descriptions of kaleidoscopic scenes with lush oratory and a stream-of-consciousness narration, the reporter's staccato recital of facts with the novelist's omniscient pronunciamentos. His is highly subjective, tendentious reporting. This specimen, date-lined November, 1943, describes a tour through Russian villages just abandoned by the retreating Germans.

"A Tommy gun, not a pen, is needed"

Information Bulletin, Embassy of Union of Soviet Socialist Republics, Washington, D.C., November, 1943

I have just made a journey of over six hundred miles—from Orel to the Sozh, from Rylsk to Slobodka, a suburb of Kiev. I have no words adequate to describe the grief which the enemy has brought to our country.

Near Gomel one night we passed some villages recently abandoned by the Germans. The embers glowed. The Byelorussian villages of Vasilievka, Gornostayevka, and Terekhovka were dying amidst smoke and tears. I saw Chernigov one transparent autumn day. It looked like a phantom: charred stone against pale-blue sky. A woman whispered over and over again: "They brought people here, stripped them, and buried them."

I passed dozens of burned villages, one after another. Everywhere were the same signs of human misfortune. All through the cold nights homeless children warmed themselves by the glowing embers; in the daytime they rummaged in the rubbish, looking for broken household goods. They huddled for shelter in pits, in dugouts, in shacks.

The Germans slaughter the cattle as they retreat. They used to drive away the cows and eat the hogs and geese. But here the retreat was hasty, and so Tommy gunners shot the pigs. The Germans machine-gunned the herds. Dead cows with split bellies lie around the fields.

I spoke to Mefody Vaskovtsev. The Germans took him to the place of death, wounded him, but did not kill him. He looks at the world with terrible eyes which understand too much. He says: "I do not think I will be able to live. My spirit will not hold out." I saw Maria Selitskaya sobbing among the ashes: the Germans had killed her son Vanya. She stretched out her arms to the empty gray sky and in her black shawl, stricken with grief, she was Niobe, symbol of inconsolable motherhood.

The village of Vasilievka was put to death on September 26. Soldiers of the Sixth German Infantry Division, under the command of Lieutenant General Grossmann, burned and murdered. Prisoners say indifferently: "We had our orders." The Brovary district was a place of gardens and orchards: Kiev got its vegetables and fruit from there. Brovary exists no more: of 2300 houses, 160 escaped destruction. It is not easy to find any trace of life in this district. Here is the village of Bogdanovichi. One cottage and one seventy-year-old man. Here are the ashes of another village —Semipolki. This smell of burning, the ghosts of the homeless under the autumn sky, will haunt me as long as I live.

What else can I add? That a child saved by its mother remained alive in Rylsk? The mother lay on the little boy. She was killed by a bullet in the back of the head. The three-year-old boy remained alive under the dead body of his mother. Or perhaps that in Sumy, in the basement of School No. 5, three hundred Ukrainians were tortured to death? Or shall I recall how in Piryatin the mound over the grave of 1600 people moved? The people were not shot dead. They were buried alive.

Where are the apple trees of Ponyri? Where are the orchards of Poltava? Where is the theater of Sumy? Where are the antiquities of Chernigov? Where are the schools? Where are the tractors?

People huddle in pits. They plow with cows, or pull the plows themselves. There are no more gay girls in the Ukrainian villages—they are in Swinemünde, dying among heartless jailers.

It seems as if all the birds have deserted the orchards and the cherry trees have dried up. There are no more old Jews, quaint old men, and dreamers, tailors, and shoemakers in the Ukraine. Hundreds of thousands of children have been killed by the Germans. That army, equipped with the most up-to-date weapons, the officers with Zeiss field glasses, with Leica cameras, with monocles and fountain pens, murdered infants.

Perhaps people will forget this someday. But we who have seen will not be able to forget anything. The retreating Germans destroy everything. They do this methodically: such are the orders of the Supreme Command. "Torchbearers" are sapper detachments of the German army. "Torchbearers" are helped by infantry, by tankmen, by cart drivers.

I have a bundle of documents that seem to smell of smoke and blood. Here is an order of the commander of the Thirty-fourth German Infantry Division, dated July 30, 1943:

"All local residents from fourteen to fifty-five are to be seized and treated as prisoners of war. . . . The compulsory abduction of the remaining population is to be carried out in accordance with previously established rules."

Here is a letter from Private Johann Hauster, Field Post 11981: "Dear Wife—Retreating at night, we burn everything. Whole villages burn, the entire harvest in the field must also be burned. We ransack the houses as the residents leave the villages. What do you think—is it better to drag the goods around or send them to you?"

Here are excerpts from the diary of Otto Berger, staff lance corporal of the Second Security Battalion: "Stary Bykhov is completely demolished; 250 Jews were shot. We have eaten well. The prisoners of war dug their own graves. We lined them up and shot them, row after row. In the evening we shot two men. They dug their grave, kissed each other, and lay down. They were father and son. Fifty prisoners were brought here and given for us to use as target practice. The prisoners of war eat rotten potatoes. They have no strength at all."

Can one speak of retribution? All right, this staff lance corporal was killed. But can the black life of this stupid, vile murderer atone for everything he did?

I know the day will come when the dead towns and burned villages will rise again. But now a horrible crime is before us. It cries for retribution. I have heard people curse the Germans more than once, but the simplest word seems to me to be the strongest. I heard it from an old woman: the Germans had driven her granddaughter away and burned down her cottage. Hardly moving her dried lips, she kept repeating: *"Conscienceless."*

One could not say it better. The incensed conscience of the people has pierced the front of the powerful Hitlerite army, swept from the Volga to the Dnieper, and stepped across the wide river as across a little stream. The conscience of the people seethes day and night. In wrath and in sadness the Red Army men at Kiev think of the conflagrations, of the graves, of everything they have seen.

My generation has lived through much. This is not the first war I have seen. But I cannot write calmly about what I see here. A Tommy gun, not a pen, is needed. We do not dare to die, we older people, without saying to ourselves before death: this will not happen again. Conscience demands vengeance, expiation, the triumph of justice.

Edward R. Murrow of CBS Witnesses a Massive Blow of Retribution as the RAF Makes Berlin an "Orchestrated Hell"

WITH THE BATTLE OF BRITAIN the German Luftwaffe had shot its bolt. The Allied counteroffensive in the air was a study in devastating revenge. Harmonious co-operation between British and American air forces enabled round-the-clock operations, the former raiding by night, the latter by day. During 1943 forty major centers and fifty more of less significance were thoroughly pummeled. Berlin gained the unenviable distinction of being the most bombed city on earth.

One of the ace radio news reporters who witnessed an all-out attack on Berlin from the air was the same Edward R. Murrow who in 1940 told the American public how the little people of London had taken the Nazi air *Blitz*. Born in Greensboro, North Carolina, Murrow was graduated from Washington State College in 1930. The next year he was named president of the National Student Federation, and as such visited over three hundred colleges and universities in America and abroad. After three years in charge of the foreign office of the Institute of International Education, he became European director of the Columbia Broadcasting System and, in 1937, head of its foreign staff. During the war the London *Telegraph* called him "America's unofficial ambassador." To the American public his was one of the best-known voices of World War II. In the decade from 1938 to 1948 he won a dozen awards for outstanding radio news reporting, including the National Headliners' Club Award of 1944 for the following broadcast.

At 5:30 P.M. on the evening of Friday, December 3, 1943, millions of Americans heard the CBS announcer start the news broadcast:

CBS World News now brings you a special broadcast from London. Columbia's correspondent, Edward R. Murrow, was on one of the RAF bombing planes that smashed at Berlin last night in one of the heaviest attacks of the war. Forty-one bombers were lost in the raid, and only two of the correspondents who flew with the raiders returned to base. For Mr. Murrow's story of the attack, we take you now to London.

"The cookies—the four-thousand-pound high explosives—were bursting below like great sunflowers gone mad"

Broadcast by Edward R. Murrow, Columbia Broadcasting System, December 3, 1943

This is London. Yesterday afternoon, the waiting was over; the weather was right; the target was to be the big city. The crew captains walked into the briefing room, looked at the maps and charts, and sat down with their big celluloid pads on the knees. The atmosphere was that of a school and a church. The weatherman gave us the weather. The pilots were reminded that Berlin is Germany's greatest center of war production. The intelligence officer told us how many heavy and light ack-ack guns, how many searchlights, we might expect to encounter. Then, Jock, the Wing Commander, explained the system of markings, the kind of flare that would be used by the Pathfinders. He said that concentration was the secret of success in these raids.

I noticed that the big Canadian with the slow, easy grin had printed "Berlin" at the top of his pad and then embellished it with a scroll. Late in the afternoon, we went to the locker room to draw parachutes, Mae Wests, and all the rest. Walking out to the bus that was to take us to the aircraft, I heard the station loud-speakers announcing that that evening all personnel would be able to see a film, *Star-Spangled Rhythm*, free.

We went out and stood around the big, black, four-motored Lancaster—*D for Dog*.

A small station wagon delivered a thermos bottle of coffee, chewing gum, an orange, and a bit of chocolate for each man. Up in that part of England, the air hums and throbs with the sound of aircraft motors all day. But for half an hour before take-off, the skies are dead, silent and expectant. A lone hawk hovered over the airfield, absolutely still as he faced into the wind. Jack, the tail gunner, said, "It would be nice if we could fly like that." Jock looked at his watch and moved toward the aircraft. Nothing was said. We followed.

D for Dog eased around the perimeter track to the end of the runway. The green light flashed, and we were rolling—ten seconds ahead of schedule! The take-off was smooth as silk. As we came up through the clouds, I looked right and left, and counted fourteen black Lancasters climbing for the place where men must burn oxygen to live. The sun was going down, and its red glow made rivers of lakes of fire on top of the clouds. Down to the southward, the clouds piled up to form castles, battlements, and whole cities—all tinged with red.

Soon we were out over the North Sea. Dave, the navigator, asked Jock if he couldn't make a little more speed. We were nearly two minutes late. By this time, we were all using oxygen. The talk on the intercom was brief and crisp. Everyone sounded relaxed. For a while the eight of us in our little world in exile moved over the sea. There was a quarter moon on the starboard beam. Jock's quiet voice came through the intercom. "That'll be flak ahead." We were approaching the enemy coast. The flak looked like a cigarette lighter in a dark room—one that won't light. Sparks but no flame. The sparks crackling just above the level of the cloud tops. We flew steady and straight, and soon the flak was directly below us.

D-Dog rocked a little from right to left, but that wasn't caused by the flak. We were in the slip stream of other Lancasters ahead and we were over the enemy coast. And then a strange thing happened. The aircraft seemed to grow smaller. Jack in the rear turret; Wally—the mid-upper gunner; Titch—the wireless operator; all seemed somehow to draw closer to Jock in the cockpit. It was as though each man's shoulder was against the other's. The understanding was complete. The intercom came to life, and Jock said, "Two aircraft on the port beam." Jack in the tail said, "O.K., sir, they're Lancs." The whole crew was a unit and wasn't wasting words.

The cloud below was ten tenths. The blue-green jet of the exhausts licked back along the leading edge, and there were other aircraft all around us. The whole great aerial armada was hurtling toward Berlin. We flew so for twenty minutes, when Jock looked up at a vapor trail curling across above us, remarking in a conversational tone that from the look of it he thought there was a fighter up there. Occasionally the angry red of ack-ack burst through the clouds, but it was far away and we took only an academic interest. We were flying in the third wave. Jock asked Wally in the mid-upper turret and Jack in the rear turret if they were cold. They said they were all right, and thanked him for asking. Even asked how I was, and I said, "All right so far." The cloud was beginning to thin out. Up to

the north we could see light, and the flak began to liven up ahead of it.

Boz, the bomb aimer, cracked through the intercom, "There's a battle going on on the starboard beam." We couldn't see the aircraft, but we could see the jets of red tracer being exchanged. Suddenly there was a burst of yellow flame, and Jock remarked, "That's a fighter going down —note the position." The whole thing was interesting, but remote. Dave, the navigator, who was sitting back with his maps, charts, and compasses, said, "The attack ought to begin in exactly two minutes." We were still over the clouds. But suddenly those dirty gray clouds turned white. We were over the outer searchlight defenses. The clouds below us were white, and we were black. *D-Dog* seemed like a black bug on a white sheet. The flak began coming up, but none of it close. We were still a long way from Berlin. I didn't realize just how far.

Jock observed, "There's a kite on fire dead ahead." It was a great golden slow-moving meteor slanting toward the earth. By this time we were about thirty miles from our target area in Berlin. That thirty miles was the longest flight I have ever made. Dead on time. Boz, the bomb aimer, reported, "Target indicators going down." At the same time the sky ahead was lit up by bright yellow flames. Flares were spouting all over the sky—red and green and yellow—and we were flying straight for the center of the fireworks. *D-Dog* seemed to be standing still, the four propellers thrashing the air. The clouds had cleared, and off to the starboard a Lanc was caught by at least fourteen searchlight beams. We could see him twist and turn and finally break out. But still the whole thing had a quality of unreality about it. No one seemed to be shooting at us, but it was getting lighter all the time. Suddenly, a tremendous big blob of yellow light appeared dead ahead, another to the right, and another to the left. We were flying straight for them.

Jock pointed out to me the dummy fires and flares to right and left. But we kept going in. Dead ahead there was a whole chain of red flares looking like stop lights. Another Lanc was coned on our starboard beam. The lights seemed to be supporting it. Again we could see those little bubbles of colored lead driving at it from two sides. The German fighters were at him. And then with no warning at all, *D-Dog* was filled with an unhealthy white light. I was standing just behind Jock and could see all the seams on the wings. His quiet Scots voice beat into my ears, "Steady, lads, we've been coned." His slender body lifted half out of his seat as he jammed the control column forward and to the left. We were going down.

Jock was wearing woolen gloves with the fingers cut off. I could see his fingernails turn white as he gripped the wheel. And then I was on my knees, flat on the deck, for he had whipped the *Dog* back into a climbing turn. The knees should have been strong enough to support me, but they weren't, and the stomach seemed in some danger of letting me down, too. I picked myself up and looked out again. It seemed that one big searchlight, instead of being 20,000 feet below, was mounted right on our wing tip. *D-Dog* was corkscrewing. As we rolled down on the other side, I began to see what was happening to Berlin.

The clouds were gone, and the sticks of incendiaries from the preceding waves made the place look like a badly laid-out city with the street lights on. The small incendiaries were going down like a fistful of white rice

thrown on a piece of black velvet. As Jock hauled the *Dog* up again, I was thrown to the other side of the cockpit, and there below were more incendiaries, glowing white and then turning red. The cookies—the four-thousand-pound high explosives—were bursting below like great sunflowers gone mad. And then, as we started down again, still held in the lights, I remembered that the *Dog* still had one of those cookies and a whole basket of incendiaries in his belly and the lights still held us. And I was very frightened.

While Jock was flinging her about in the air, he suddenly flung over the intercom, "Two aircraft on the port beam." I looked astern, and saw Wally, the mid-upper, whip his turret around to port and then look up to see a single-engined fighter slide just above us. The other aircraft was one of ours. Finally, we were out of the cone, flying level. I looked down on the white fires, the white fires had turned red. They were beginning to merge and spread, just like butter does on a hot plate. Jock and Boz, the bomb aimer, began to discuss the target. The smoke was getting thick down below. Boz said he liked the two green flares on the ground almost dead ahead. He began calling his directions. And just then, a new bunch of big flares went down on the far side of the sea of flame and flare that seemed to be directly below us. He thought that would be a better aiming point. Jock agreed, and we flew on. The bomb doors were open. Boz called his directions, "Five left, five left," and then there was a gentle, confident, upward thrust under my feet, and Boz said, "Cookie gone." A few seconds later the incendiaries went, and *D-Dog* seemed much lighter and easier to handle.

I thought I could make out the outline of streets below. But the bomb aimer didn't agree, and he ought to know. By this time, all those patches of white on black had turned yellow and started to flow together. Another searchlight caught us but didn't hold us. Then through the intercom came the word, "One can of incendiaries didn't clear; we're still carrying it." And Jock replied, "Is it a big one or a little one?" The word came back, "Little one, I think, but I'm not sure. I'll check." More of those yellow flares came down and hung about us. I haven't seen so much light since the war began. Finally, the intercom announced that it was only a small container of incendiaries left, and Jock remarked, "Well, it's hardly worth going back and doing another run-up for that." If there had been a good fat bundle left, he would have gone back through that stuff and done it all over again.

I began to breathe and to reflect again—that all men would be brave if only they would leave their stomachs at home. Then there was a tremendous whoomp, an unintelligible shout from the tail gunner, and *D-Dog* shivered and lost altitude. I looked at the port side, and there was a Lancaster that seemed close enough to touch. It whipped straight under us, missed us by twenty-five, fifty feet, no one knew how much. The navigator sang out the new course, and we were heading for home. Jock was doing what I had heard him tell his pilots so often—flying dead on course. He flew straight into a huge green searchlight, and as he rammed his throttles home, remarked, "We'll have a little trouble getting away from this one." And again, *D-Dog* dove, climbed, and twisted and was finally free. We flew level then. I looked at the port beam

of the target area. There was a red, sullen, obscene glare. The fires seemed to have found each other—and we were heading home.

In a little more than half an hour, Berlin had received about three times the weight of bombs that had ever fallen on London in the course of a long winter night. For a little while, it was smooth sailing. We saw more battles. Then another plane in flames. But no one could tell whether it was ours or theirs. We were still near the target. Dave, the navigator, said, "Hold her steady, skipper, I want to get an astral sight." And Jock held her steady. And the flak began coming up at us. It seemed to be very close. It was winking off both wings. But the *Dog* was steady. Finally Dave said, "O.K., skipper, thank you very much." And a great orange blob of flak smacked up straight in front of us. And Jock said, "I think they're shooting at us." I'd thought so for some time.

And he began to throw *D for Dog* up, around, and about again. And when we were clear of the barrage, I asked him how close the bursts were, and he said, "Not very close. When they're really near, you can smell 'em." That proved nothing, for I'd been holding my breath. Jack sang out from the rear turret, said his oxygen was getting low, thought maybe the lead had frozen. Titch, the wireless operator, went scrambling back with a new mask and a bottle of oxygen. Dave, the navigator, said, "We're crossing the coast." My mind went back to the time I had crossed the coast in 1938, in a plane that had taken off from Prague. Just ahead of me sat two refugees from Vienna—an old man and his wife. The copilot came back and told them that we were outside German territory. The old man reached out and grasped his wife's hand.

The work that was done last night was a massive blow of retribution for all those who have fled from the sound of shots and blows on a stricken continent.

We began to lose height over the North Sea. We were over England's shore. The land was dark beneath us. Somewhere down there below, American boys were probably bombing-up Fortresses and Liberators, getting ready for the day's work. We were over the home field. We called the control tower, and the calm, clear voice of an English girl replied, "Greetings *D-Dog*. You are diverted to Mule Bag." * We swung around, contacted Mule Bag, came in on the flare path, touched down very gently, ran along to the end of the runway, and turned left. And Jock, the finest pilot in Bomber Command, said to the control tower, "*D-Dog* clear of runway."

When we went in for interrogation, I looked on the board and saw that the big, slow-smiling Canadian and the redheaded English boy with the two weeks' old mustache hadn't made it. They were missing. There were two reporter friends of mine on this operation who didn't come back either— Norman Stockton, of Australian Associated Newspapers, and Lowell Bennett, an American representing International News Service. There is

---

* Code for an airfield.

something of a tradition among reporters that those who are prevented by circumstances from filing their stories will be covered by their colleagues. This has been my effort to do so.

In the aircraft in which I flew, the men who flew and fought it, poured into my ears their comments on fighters, flak, and flares in the same tone they would have used in reporting a host of daffodils. I have no doubt that Bennett and Stockton would have given you a better report of last night's activities.

Berlin was a kind of orchestrated hell, a terrible symphony of light and flame. It isn't a pleasant kind of warfare—the men doing it speak of a job. Yesterday afternoon, when the tapes were stretched out on the big map all the way to Berlin and back again, a young pilot with old eyes said to me, "I see we're working again tonight." That's the frame of mind in which the job is being done. The job isn't pleasant; it's terribly tiring. Men die in the sky while others are roasted alive in their cellars.

Berlin last night wasn't a pretty sight. This is a calculated, remorseless campaign of destruction. Right now, the mechanics are probably working on *D-Dog*, getting him ready to fly again.

I return you now to CBS, New York.

*   *   *

Merle Miller of *Yank* Records a Surprise Party
at Eniwetok as the Last Enemy Stronghold
in the Marshalls Is Secured

BY EARLY 1944 the plan of U. S. assault on the Japanese Empire became clear: it was a series of leapfrog operations making possible stupendous advances up the Pacific ladder through the central Pacific—New Guinea, the Gilberts, the Marshalls, the Marianas, and Bonin and Ryuku islands. The pattern, arrived at in bloody fighting on Tarawa, was improved on at Kwajalein, in the Japanese archipelago of the Marshalls, and perfected in mid-February on Eniwetok, an atoll some four hundred miles northwest of Kwajalein. Here at the northwest corner of the Marshalls the Japs had siphoned their airplane supply to Pacific fronts.

Eniwetok was taken by the 22nd Marines and the 106th Infantry. Sergeant Merle Miller, a twenty-six-year-old correspondent for *Yank*, described in a remarkable dispatch the soldiers' beachhead landing and the bizarre fighting that followed. Miller, whose novel *That Winter* penetratingly reported the reactions and adjustments of a group of ex-GI's to postwar America, served briefly on *Time*'s editorial staff and was until recently an editor of *Harper's Magazine*.

> *"Underground! The sonsuvbitches are*
> *underground!"*

Yank, The Army Weekly, March 31, 1944

The aerial bombardment began soon after morning chow, which included fresh eggs because this was the day of battle.

From our troopships only a few hundred yards offshore, the entire island of Eniwetok seemed on fire. Red, yellow, and black smoke clung to the shattered trees and bushes. At dawn our destroyers moved closer, almost hugging the beach.

By the time our assault boats had gathered in the rendezvous area, coconuts and huge palm fronds were floating out from the beach.

Suddenly the bombardment ceased; for a single, incredible minute there was silence. That silence seemed to underline the question all of us were asking ourselves: Where were the Japs?

At no time had the enemy answered the Navy's surface and air bombardments. None of our observers had sighted a single Jap on the island—or any other living thing. Some of the men of the 106th Infantry wondered out loud whether Eniwetok was another Kiska, whether the Japs had fled without a fight.

There was nothing to make the infantrymen change their minds as the first two assault waves piled out of amphibious tractors and threw themselves over the steep fire trench that ran along the entire beach, then stood upright and moved inland. There was still no sign of Japs.

As troops under Lieutenant Colonel Harold I. (Hi) Mizony of Spokane, Washington, moved north and troops under Lieutenant Colonel Winslow Cornett of White Plains, New York, moved south, the guns of the destroyer force shifted their fire ahead of the moving troops, to clear the way north and south.

By this time the fourth wave had hit the beach. Sergeant John A. Bushemi of Gary, Indiana, *Yank* staff photographer, and I landed in this wave.

There was still no resistance. The only sounds were the sounds of our BAR and rifle fire, spraying every tree that might contain a sniper and every exposed shell crater.

Sergeant Mat Toper of New York City lay flat on his back on the fire trench and lit the first of twenty cigars he'd managed to keep dry through the landing operation. Private First Class Albert Lee, a Chinese-American tank gunner from Los Angeles, California, grinned and said: "This is the easiest one yet." Lee had made three previous assault landings.

Our rear elements, preceded by tanks, were moving up to the front. At 1010 a cooling rain began to fall, and in a few minutes you couldn't see more than a few feet ahead.

It was then that the Japs decided to let us know they were present and ready to fight. The high-pitched ring of Jap rifle fire sounded on all sides, our first warning that there were nearly as many Japs behind as in front of our own lines. Knee-mortar shells, from positions on both ends of the island, began to sprinkle the landing beach, just short of the incoming boats. A few shells hit the troops south of the beach party, killing six men and wounding eight.

As First Lieutenant John Hetherington of Mt. Vernon, New York, transportation officer, headed back for the beach in search of his motor sergeant, he saw some engineers blasting away at what looked like a small pile of mangrove leaves, evidently knocked down from a tree by a Navy blast.

Just ahead were some communications men, cleaning their rifles and sharing a D-ration chocolate bar. As the engineers moved out, Lieutenant Hetherington saw a Jap rise up from under the leaves, knife in one hand, grenade in the other. The lieutenant fired his carbine once and squeezed the trigger for a second shot. The carbine jammed, but that didn't matter; his first shot had plugged the Jap in the head. Under the palm fronds and dried leaves, Hetherington found a neatly dug square hole, four feet deep. Inside were three other dead Japs.

He saw hundreds of similar holes later on; we all did. Some were spider trenches, connected by carefully covered underground passages, a few with corrugated tin under the fronds and mangrove leaves. Many of the trenches had been built for a single Jap, others for two or three or four men. None of the holes was large enough to accommodate more than six Japs.

Sergeant Chris Hagen of Fairmont, Minnesota, a squad leader, and eight riflemen became separated from their platoon in the landing. Just as they walked over the fire trench, in the area through which almost the whole battalion had passed without encountering resistance, scattered Jap rifle fire came from their rear, barely clearing their heads. They dropped to the ground.

"Underground!" shouted Hagen. "The sonsuvbitches are underground!" This squad began throwing grenades into every pile of fronds. Three Japs darted out of one hole and ran for the beach. Hagen fired once and hit the first one before he'd gone fifteen yards. He hit the other two a few yards farther on. In the next twenty minutes, Hagen killed twelve Japs by pitching grenades into a dozen holes. Private First Class Joseph Tucker, a rifleman from Live Oak, Florida, accounted for at least nine more, and the entire outfit cleaned out about fifty in some twenty unconnected holes, all dug underground in an area about forty yards square.

As Colonel Mizony moved up with eighteen of his enlisted men, including battalion CP personnel, Captain Carl Stoltz of Binghamton, New York, commander of a heavy-weapons company, yelled: "Look out, Hi!" The colonel hit the ground, and Stoltz, a former Binghamton cop, got the underground sniper with a carbine. He found four others in a tin-and-palm-covered trench on the beach. As he started to walk over it, the captain stopped, looked down, and noticed a movement inside. He killed two Japs with the carbine and the other two with grenades.

When the company commanded by Captain Charles Hallden of Brooklyn, New York, reached a native village and the smoking ruins of some Jap concrete installations, a young native stuck his head up from a hole and shouted, "Friend!" The advance halted while the native guided First Sergeant Louis Pawlinga of Utica, New York, and a search party to other holes, where they found thirty-three natives—four men, twelve women, and seventeen children—only three injured. They were taken to the beachhead.

Just before noon the troops circled south, although there were some Japs still alive on the western side of the island. As First Lieutenant George Johnson of Sikeston, Missouri, moved up with his company, the leader of the second squad, Sergeant Earl Bodiford of Pocahontas, Tennessee, fired at a covered foxhole. The muzzle of a rifle moved in the shadows. Bodiford raced forward, grabbed the gun from a dazed Jap, and hurled it as far as he could. He killed the Jap and moved on.

By early afternoon we had run up against concentrated underground defenses and were held up by knee-mortar fire. Shells were falling on every side, in and around the CP and ahead and just behind the front lines. Colonel Cornett ordered the line held and called for reinforcements.

The sun was shining again, and the atmosphere was hot and muggy as hell. Black flies covered everything— guns, clothes, faces, and hands. Knee-mortar fire was falling throughout the area, no spot was safe from snipers, and there was Jap heavy-machine-gun fire up ahead. Colonel Mizony called for some Navy Avengers.

Johnny Bushemi and I crouched behind a medium tank with some other men to smoke our first cigarettes in several hours and tell one another what had happened since we'd become separated that morning. When the short, concentrated aerial strafing was completed, five of us, including Johnny Bushemi, started forward to take a look at the damage.

Just beyond the fire trench on the lagoon side of the beach, perhaps seventy-five yards behind the front lines, we stopped to examine a bullet-ridden chest filled with Marshallese books. That area had been under sporadic knee-mortar fire throughout the morning, but for two hours none of the 60-mm. grenades had fallen there.

Then, suddenly, the first shell landed in our midst. I ducked into an exposed hole, just below the chest of books, and the others threw themselves on the open ground. Shells burst all around us, pinning us in a diminishing circle of fire.

Each explosion kicked up dirt and sand as it landed; we thought each shell would be our last. No one knows how many bursts there were in all—probably five or six—but after two or three interminable minutes the explosions stopped. Johnny had been hit and was bleeding profusely. Three of us ran three hundred yards down the beach to get the medics.

By the time we returned to the shallow crater where Bushemi lay, Johnny had already lost a tremendous amount of blood from shrapnel wounds in his left cheek and neck and in his left leg. But he was still conscious, and as we returned through the sniper-infested area inland from the lagoon beach, he asked for his two cameras. He carried both of them until we reached the advanced aid station in a demolished coconut-log emplacement. There he was given more sulfanilamide and two plasma applications.

Johnny was conscious, joking with all of us, until after he had reached our transport. He died at 1750, a little less than three hours after he was wounded, while Navy surgeons were tying the arteries in his neck. His last words were: "Be sure to get those pictures back to the office."

During the night the advance continued on Eniwetok, the marines pushing seaward on the eastern end and the soldiers continuing northward. They moved barely fifteen yards at a time, tanks leading the way, flanked on each side by infantrymen—BAR men spraying every foot and riflemen throwing grenades into each mound.

There was no organized counterattack by the enemy, and only two attempts at resistance. At about 2000, an hour after the advance began, a dozen Japs tried to swim through the lagoon to reach the rear. Spotted by a destroyer searchlight, they were wiped out when they reached the beach.

The second attempt came at 0100, when forty Japs leaped from their holes about thirty yards from the marine lines and raced forward. Brandishing sabers, hurling grenades, and screaming, "Banzai! the f—— marines will die!" they leaped into the Marine foxholes. There was hand-to-hand combat, jujitsu, knifing, and bayoneting. In less than twenty minutes, forty Japs and twenty marines were killed on a line not more than thirty yards long.

Then the entire battalion was ordered back three hundred yards to mop up the southern, lagoon side of the island for the second time. They found almost as many live Japs hiding under their feet this time as during the first advance.

Dead Japs were being piled up on the beach, but many still remained where they had fought and died—

underground. At almost any spot on the island there were still some Japs alive, and occasionally rifle fire broke out around the aid station. Several times mop-up squads came back to clean out all the holes they could find. Then, after they had left, the fire would break out again in another spot.

A few Japs, not many, were taken prisoner. There had been a steady stream of American casualties flowing back to the aid stations the first day, but our casualties were lighter now.

By late afternoon of the third day, Eniwetok, last stronghold of the enemy in the Marshalls, was secured.

ACCORDING TO A correspondent of *Time,* the battle-hardened marines who helped take Eniwetok took time out to grin. On a bulletin board was a notice from one of the outfit's more sensible censors, addressed to a private. The message:

Letter at mail desk. Name on envelope: Dorothy. Name on letter: Bettye. Check, and if name is correct, mail.

Two Eyewitness Accounts of D-Day

> *And thence to France shall we convey you safe,*
> *And bring you back, charming the narrow seas*
> *To give you gentle pass . . .*

THROUGH THE MOUTHS of his chorus Shakespeare thus described the invasion of France by King Henry V's army in 1415, climaxed by the battle of Agincourt.

But for the Allied invasion forces of World War II the seas between Britain and France were by no means gentle. Because of the tides there were only three days in early June of 1944 when the invasion could be launched—June 5, 6, and 7. On Sunday, June 4, a gale blew, but there was a forecast of clear for Tuesday morning, with weather closing in by evening.

The decision was up to Eisenhower—whether to gamble that invasion operations could be sufficiently advanced before the newly threatening storms or to postpone the invasion for a considerable period. "I went to my tent alone and sat down to think," Eisenhower later recalled in his *Crusade in Europe* (1948). He took the gamble. D-Day was set for Tuesday the sixth. Reporting D-Day minus one, Charles Christian Wertenbaker, who headed *Time*'s news staff assigned to cover the invasion, cabled from headquarters ship *USS Acamar,* in the English Channel:

Monday morning at six o'clock the final confirmation came. The day was cloudy and cold. The staff officers looked at the sky, shrugged, and put their trust in the weatherman. A sleepy colonel said: "Win, lose, or draw—and there ain't no draw—they can't call it off now, thank God."

By late afternoon the command ship was gone. The small boats were gone. One by one the destroyers left the harbor. At ten o'clock, when the clouds broke and the low sun shone across the water, the harbor was almost empty. Then, gathering her flock of small boats around her and with two destroyers shepherding the flock, the *Acamar,* last big ship to leave, set out under full steam for the invasion of France.

On June 6, supported by an ingenious system of artificial harbors, breakwaters, and landing stages, the Allies hurled an armada of four thousand ships, eleven thousand planes, and whole divisions of air-borne troops across the Channel to France. It was the greatest invasion the world had ever seen.

The Germans, certain that it could not be done, were almost stupefied by the size, firepower, and organization of the invading forces. This was *Blitzkrieg* with a vengeance. Awaiting the striking force was the Atlantic Wall, which Hitler had constructed in four years and of which he had boasted: "No power on earth can drive us out of this region against our will."

During the invasion a soft-spoken radio reporter for the Blue Network made a recording on board the American naval flagship *Ancon* a few miles off the shores of France. George Hicks' eyewitness account was broadcast over and over again during the evening of D-Day. Millions of listeners heard the calm voice of the reporter against a background of combat crashes and explosions. Chief European war correspondent for the American Broadcasting Company, Hicks covered the invasion of Corsica, the campaigns from Naples to Cassino, and reported the movements of the First Army in Normandy until meeting the Russians on the Elbe in May, 1945.

"This is George Hicks speaking"

Broadcast by George Hicks, American Broadcasting Company, D-Day, June 6, 1944. All rights reserved by the American Broadcasting Company, Inc.

This is George Hicks speaking. I am speaking now from a tower above the signal bridge of an American naval flagship, and we're lying some few miles off the coast of France, where the invasion of Europe has begun. It's now twenty minutes to six, and the landing craft have been disembarked from their mother ships and are moving in in long irregular lines toward the horizon of France, which is very plain to the naked eye.

Our own bombardment fleet lying out beyond us has begun to blast the shore line, and we can see the vivid yellow burst of flame quite clearly, although the sound is too far away to be heard, and at the same time from the shore are answering yellow flames as the Nazi batteries are replying.

Overhead planes are high up in the thin cloud, which is a gray screen over the sky but which is not thick nor heavy, and is not low enough to be an inconvenience to bombing.

The LCT's and LCI's have begun to pass along the side of us. Those are the amphibious beach-landing craft that carry the tanks, trucks, the bulldozers, and finally the men ashore. They have been churning along and are bouncing along on the choppy channel sea now, and all around us on either side are stretched the vast transports at anchor, which have disembarked the small craft. All over the surface of the sea here they can be seen cutting and zigzagging and then falling into those somewhat irregular lines that make a black pencil point across the sea itself, heading toward the ribbon of land that's France and the coast of Normandy. . . .

It's now becoming quite near daylight as six A.M. approaches on June 6, 1944. . . . We can hear the thud of shells or bombs landing on the French coastline, perhaps eight or ten miles before us, and the steel bridge on which we stand vibrates from the concussion of the heavy guns that are firing on the American and British battleships and heavy cruisers on the long line right behind us. I can count twenty-two of the squat, square-nosed landing craft, carrying vehicles . . . as they turn and bounce in the choppy sea, awaiting the exact timing to form their lines and start in toward the beach.

On our first [*static*] . . . it was the shore batteries of the Nazis that had spotted us here at sea [*static*] . . . and our naval bombardment squad has replied to them.

One battleship is in as close as three miles, and one of the famous American battleships, the *Texas,* was [*static*] . . . finally in her firing position. [*static*] . . . battleships lying just a couple of miles off the French shore, and firing broadsides into the land. The Germans are replying from the land with flashes, and then the battleship lets go with its entire broadside again. The whole side of the battlewagon lights up in a yellow flare as a broadside goes off, and now we can see brown and gray smoke drifting up from her, from her gun barrels . . . and now batteries are firing from the beach . . . the broadsides of the battleship are pouring it back at them. Overhead, high, planes are roaring . . . they just came in and dropped a salvo of bombs. . . .

The [*static*] . . . one of America's famous cruisers, is in off the shore near [*static*] . . . as well as the *Texas,* the *Nevada,* and the *Arkansas;* old battleships. . . . They're just anchored offshore and blowing into the Nazi batteries on shore. . . . The first Allied forces are reaching the beaches in France. . . .

That baby was plenty low!

I think I just made the statement that no German planes had been seen, and I think there was the first one we've seen so far . . . just cleared our stack . . . let go a stream of tracers that did no harm. . . .

[*Sound of ship's whistle.*]

Our own ship has just given its warning whistle, and now the flak is coming up in the sky. . . .

It's planes you hear overhead now . . . they are the motors of Nazis coming and going. . . . The reverberation of bombs. . . .

[*Sound of crash.*]

That was a bomb hit, another one. That was a tracer line, shaped arching up into the darkness.

Very heavy firing now off our stern. . . . Fiery bursts and the flak and streamers going out [*several words drowned out by voice in background and static*] in the flak.

[*Sound of explosions.*]

Now, it's died down. . . . We can't see the plane. . . . Here comes a plane. . . . More antiaircraft fire . . . in more toward the shore . . . the Germans must be attacking low, with their planes off our stern, because the streamer fire of the tracers is almost parallel with the water. [*Noises in background.*] . . . Flares are coming down now. You can hear the machine-gunning. The whole seaside is covered with tracer fire . . . going up . . . bombs . . . machine-gunning. The planes come over closer [*sound of plane*], firing low . . . smoke . . . brilliant fire down low toward the French coast a couple of miles. I don't know whether it's on the shore or is a ship on fire.

Here's very heavy ack-ack now— [*heavy ack-ack*]—right . . . the plane seems to be coming directly overhead . . . [*sound of plane and machine-gun fire and ack-ack*].

Well, that's the first time we've shot our guns . . . directly right over our head . . . as we pick up the German bombers overhead.

VOICE: What was that—a bomb?

VOICE: Cruiser firing over there.

HICKS: Heavy fire from the naval warships . . . 20-mm. and 40-mm. tracer . . . was the sound you just heard. . . .

Well, it's quiet for a moment now. . . .

If you'll excuse me, I'll just take a deep breath for a moment and stop speaking. . . .

Now the air attack has seemed to have died down. . . . See nothing in the night. . . .

Here we go again! [*Noise.*] Another plane has come over . . . right over our port side . . . tracers are making an arc right over the bow now . . . disappearing into the clouds before they burst. . . .

Looks like we're going to have a night tonight. Give it to her, boys . . . another one coming over . . . a cruiser on . . . pouring it out . . . something burning is falling down through the sky and hurtling down . . . it may be a hit plane. [*Terrific noises in background.*] . . . Here he goes . . . they got one! [*Voices cheering.*] They got one! [VOICE: Did we?] Yeah . . . Great splotches of fire came down and are smoldering now just off our port side in the sea . . . smoke and flame there.

[*Various sounds and voices in background.*] . . . The lights of that burning Nazi plane are just twinkling now in the sea and going out. . . .

To recapitulate, the first plane that was over . . . was a low-flying German Ju-88 that was leading the flight and came on the convoy in surprise, we believe, because he drew up and only fired as he passed by, and perhaps he was as surprised as we were to see each other. . . . One bomb fell astern of this warship, 150 yards away, as the string of rockets were fired at a cruiser beside us on the port side. No damage was done, and gun No. 42 at our port, just beside the microphone, shot down the plane that fell into the sea off to the port side. . . . Scheiner [?] of Houston, Texas, who is the gunnery control officer, and seaman Thomas Snyder [?] of Baltimore, Maryland, handled the direction finder. It was their first kill for this gun, and the boys are all pretty excited about it. A twin-barrel 40-mm. antiaircraft piece.

They are already thinking of painting a big star on their chart and will be at that first thing tomorrow morning. . . . It's daylight. . . .

As GEORGE HICKS watched the invasion from the sea, Roelif Loveland, correspondent for the *Cleveland Plain Dealer,* flew overhead in a flak-dodging Marauder and saw the Channel jammed with assault ships. Here is a condensed version of his report:

"It's kind of scary, no fooling" — *Roelif Loveland*

Cleveland Plain Dealer, June 7, 1944

A NINTH AIR FORCE MARAUDER BASE IN ENGLAND, JUNE 6 We saw the curtain go up this morning on the greatest drama in the history of the world, the invasion of Hitler's Europe.

We saw it from a balcony seat high up in God's heaven, in a combat Marauder piloted by a Cleveland boy, First Lieutenant Howard C. Quiggle, 17118 Lipton Ave. S.E. Flak flew about us and tracer bullets missed us by uncomfortable margins, but our bombardier dropped sixteen 250-pound bombs on military installations near the area in which our troops later were to come ashore for the invasion.

Being only one of thousands riding the tail of a comet to see history in the making leaves a witness drained of all emotion and too numb to be very articulate.

With the chance to write something immortal, such a witness realizes that words sometimes are weak.

How can words describe properly the deathless bravery that the world saw on the shores of France? How can words describe properly a sky filled with planes, fighters, bombers, risking life itself to give the infantry the best possible chance to succeed. What magnificent teamwork!

The fliers did not wear shiny armor when they went out to their planes, the sleek, fast, deadly Marauders. They looked bulgy, and no man can look otherwise who is wearing a Mae West life preserver, a parachute, a flak suit, earphones, and a flak helmet. Before we got into the plane we had to remove all personal letters and such. I was assigned to Lieutenant Quiggle's plane, the *Dottie Dee,* named after his wife. When you start out on a strange adventure at that time in the morning you sort of like to be with a home-town boy. It's kind of scary, no fooling.

The moon was in the sky when we started, and it followed us all along, and presently we were riding over clouds which looked like cotton wool of a lavender color. I can't imagine that heaven could be more beautiful.

But angels would probably ride the clouds better than we could have done if the *Dottie Dee* had not been purring along sweetly.

Purring is a bad word. The *Dottie Dee* roars, but your earphones sort of dim the noise. When you are in a fighting plane advancing toward the enemy the plane becomes your one little world and none of the sweet things of life exist any more. And your fellows become the most important people in the world, even more important to you than Mr. Churchill or Mr. Roosevelt.

I stood up front behind the pilots and watched England fade from view. And not long afterward, so perfectly had the job been synchronized, we saw the invasion ships.

The sea—the Channel, if you prefer—was thick with them, as thick with ships as the sky was thick with clouds. In addition to the big landing craft were large naval vessels, and fighters were hovering over the ships, guarding them.

Nothing which could have been thought of to save life was spared. The lads had everything which it was humanly possible to give them.

We saw our own naval vessels shelling the daylights out of German installations on the French coast. We could see the red flashes as the shells struck home. They were big shells.

Flak began to come pretty soon, and tracer bullets shot in front of us like red-hot rivets, but the expression on the face of the kid from Cleveland who was piloting the plane did not change in the slightest degree. He followed the course to the target, and then the bombardier did his stuff, and the plane fairly leaped up in the air and down below flames shot up.

Then we started back. We had taken off at 4:45 A.M., but by now it was light. Guns shot at us again, but missed badly. The Allied battle wagon was continuing to pour in shells.

In a few minutes all danger seemed to be past. Later, when all danger was past, the sergeant with twenty missions to his credit remarked: "I'd sure hate to do this for a living."

Daylight showed strained faces, and we got back at breakfast time.

One will never forget the sight of the ships and the landing craft heading for France any more than a knight would have forgotten the appearance of the Holy Grail.

* * *

AMONG THE NEWSMEN who took the historic cross-channel trip was A. J. Liebling, who was assigned to an LCIL (Landing Craft, Infantry, Large). His series of dramatic eyewitness reports, published in *The New Yorker* on July 1, 8, and 15, 1944, caught the irrepressible humor of young Americans going into battle and the stark terror of the invasion itself. As the clumsy landing craft waited for the signal to start, Liebling observed the actions of the coast-guard crew and the infantrymen passengers of the First Division. Aware that the Germans might use poison gas, all were busily rubbing "impregnating grease" into their shoes. "This is the first time I ever tried to get a pair of shoes pregnant," one of the sailors called out sociably. "No doubt you tried it on about everything else, I guess," another sailor yelled. Crewmen complained loudly about the "ambiguous farce," their pet name for the amphibious forces. A little sailor with a Levantine face began to sing a song he had written especially for the occasion: "I'm going over to France, and I'm shaking in my pants!" Seaman Sisnitsky, washing clothes at a sink aft of the galley, observed sagely: "The fois' ting I'm gonna do when I get home is to buy my mudder a Washington machine. I never realize what the old lady was up against." A soldier from Brooklyn remarked: "My brother-in-law is an MP. He is six inches bigger than me. He gets an assignment in New York. I would like to see him here. He would be apprehensive."

In a matter of hours these men were facing exploding mines, shrapnel, and machine-gun bullets. Badly wounded GI's were swung wildly in baskets up the sides of the bobbing ship. "A coastguardman reached up for the bottom of one basket so that he could steady it on its way up. At least a quart of blood ran down on him, covering his tin hat, his upturned face, and his blue overalls. He stood motionless for an instant, as if he didn't know what had happened, seeing the world through a film of red, because he wore eyeglasses and blood had covered the lenses."

Back home President Roosevelt led the nation in prayer:

My Fellow-Americans:

Last night when I spoke with you about the fall of Rome I knew at that moment that troops of the United States and our Allies were crossing the Channel in another and greater operation. It has come to pass to success thus far.

And so, in this poignant hour, I ask you to join with me in prayer:

Almighty God: Our sons, pride of our nation, this day have set upon a mighty endeavor, a struggle to preserve our Republic, our religion, and our civilization, and to set free a suffering humanity.

Lead them straight and true; give strength to their arms, stoutness to their hearts, steadfastness in their faith. . . .

With Thy blessing, we shall prevail over the unholy forces of our enemy. Help us to conquer the apostles of greed and racial arrogance. . . .

Thy will be done, Almighty God.

Amen.

The Germans were literally bowled over by the scope and size of the invasion. Captain Ludwig Sertorius, DNB's military commentator, tried whistling in the dark: "The Allied landing in the West has put the German armed forces in a mood which they express with the laconic: 'They are coming!' " A German Foreign Office spokesman announced: "Roosevelt needs invasion for success of his election campaign." And again Dr. Goebbels: "The German nation is listening to one single command, and this is the Führer's command. Under his command we have overcome even the most serious crisis."

This time the little Minister of Propaganda was dead wrong. The invasion was a brilliant tactical success, but anything might have happened in the early stages of the operation, when the worst June gale in forty years lashed the invading forces, but the obstacles of weather and German defenses were overcome and two million American and Empire troops, supplied with sixteen million tons of matériel, crossed the Channel. By the end of the third week the Allies had captured the port of Cherbourg and most of the Normandy peninsula. Within a period of little more than two months, enemy casualties amounted to more than 400,000 killed, wounded, or captured. Within three months Allied motorized troops broke out of the Normandy beachhead and surged on to Paris.

A. J. Liebling Meets a Ghost of W. W. I

T HE *New Yorker*, that ultrasophisticated, gently satirical brainchild of a journalistic genius, Harold Ross, who had cut his newspaper teeth on *Stars and Stripes,* consistently published some of the finest reportorial pieces from the war fronts in World War II. Mollie Panter-Downes, Rebecca West, Janet Flanner, E. J. Kahn, Jr., Philip Hamburger, John Lardner, John Hersey, and others, never let their readers down. It is only fair to say that, were it not for space limitations, much more of their work would have been included in this volume. Outstanding among *New Yorker* war reporters was that self-styled "wayward pressman," A. J. Liebling, who covered the fall of France, the fighting in North Africa, the landings in Norway, and the liberation of Paris.

"My dear little Louise"

During our breaking-out offensive in Normandy, the division artillery headquarters I was traveling with occupied four command posts in five days. A French family was living in one wing of the first house we used, although most of the roof was gone and a couple of the bedrooms had only three walls, but the farmhouses in which we had our second and third command posts were deserted. The Germans had forced all the inhabitants to leave. In our fourth one, we found civilians again. The Germans, not expecting so quick an advance, had not evacuated people from what they still considered the rear area. In the barnyard of that place, we found a dead Panzer Grenadier of a Schutzstaffel division. His pay book said that he had been born in Essen, and on his body there was a typewritten form that he had filled out but obviously had not had time to hand in to his company commander,

asking for what we would call an emergency leave to go home. His reason was "Bombing deaths in family—urgent telegram from wife." He had been hit by a fragment of shell, but it had not torn him up much. A detail of our fellows buried him in back of the barn.

The dead cows were more of a problem. Now that we had moved on to Brittany, one of the things that make us happy is that we are out of dead-cattle country. The war moves more swiftly, and it isn't necessary to drop artillery shells on every field and crossroad. Besides, the cattle in Brittany are fewer and more scattered than in Normandy, where every pasture was full of them. You need a bulldozer to bury cows properly, unless you are going to take all day about it, and nobody had men to spare for a large-scale interment detail. They lay in the fields with their four legs pointing stiffly in the air, like wooden cows discarded

651

from a child's Noah's Ark, and their smell hung over the land as the dust hung over the roads. Men are smaller than cattle and they are always buried first; we lived in the stench of innocent death. At our fourth command post, there were more dead cows than usual, because, the people on the farm told us, eighteen extra cows had arrived with the Germans a couple of weeks before. There had been two sets of Germans in the farm buildings— ten paratroopers who had showed up driving eight cows, and forty SS men who had appeared driving ten cows. The paratroopers, one of whom was a captain, had got there first and taken up quarters in the farmhouse. The SS men, arriving later, had billeted themselves in the outbuildings, but only after a noisy argument, in which they had failed to get the paratroopers out of the big house. The captain had too much rank for them. The paratroopers had been fighting a long time and were very down in the mouth, the people of the house said. A soldier who served as interpreter had told the French family that the war was over, that Germany was beaten. But the SS fellows, who had come from soft berths in Warsaw and Brno, were still *gonflés en bloc* (blown up hard) and talked as if they owned the earth. That was less than two weeks ago, but even the SS men, to judge by those taken prisoner, have changed now. The SS soldiers had brought a refugee family with them to milk the cows, the people on the farm said. Every day the paratroopers drank the cream from their eight cows and threw the milk away. Both sets of Germans had departed abruptly, but the SS had left one man to guard the cows, presumably in case the reports of the Allied attack proved exaggerated. A shell had killed the cowtender.

I am sure that I will remember our two deserted command posts longer and more vividly than the two that were inhabited. Perhaps that is because you think more about people when they aren't there, and because you can be your own Sherlock Holmes and reconstruct them in accordance with your own hypothesis. The first deserted farm was a solid rectangle of stone and stucco buildings with walls nearly a foot thick. The farmyard, on which all the buildings fronted, could be reached only by narrow lanes that pierced the solid row of buildings at the front and at the back. It would have been a tough defensive position to crack if there had been any tactical reason to defend it. The farmhouse was very old and must have belonged to an aged, rich, crippled, bigoted woman or to a crippled man who had a fat old woman for a housekeeper. There was a crutch in the farmyard, lying as if it had fallen off a departing wagon, and in two of the bedrooms there was a pair of old, mended crutches that must have been discarded for newer ones. In the kitchen, by the great open hearth, there was a reclining chair with an extension on which to rest your legs, and in one bedroom there were several old and dirty corsets, whose whalebones, despite the garments' immense girth, had all sprung because of the continual effort to encompass a bulging body. There was a tall Norman clock in every room. Clocks of this sort are made in little towns, like Périers and Colombières and Marigny, which nobody outside Normandy ever heard of before this summer. Every crossroad seems to have had its clockmaker as well as its baker and its harness maker. The wooden cases of these timepieces are generally rather austere, but the dials are framed by hammered gilt sculpture; sheaves, golden apples, plows, and peasants in donkey carts are favorite motifs. The pendulums are vast, and they too are encrusted with ornament. A bride, I imagine, although no one has told me so, brings a clock as part of her dowry, and a house where there are many clocks has been ruled in turn by many women. This house was full of hideous modern religious images and of wax fruits and flowers under glass bells. There were no books except devotional ones and those that gave quick ways of making the computations a farmer must make in doing business with wholesalers. There were many of each kind.

The farmsteaders had left the place in a great hurry, and some soldiers, either German or American, had been there afterward and rummaged through the house, littering the floors with things, useless to them, that they had pulled from the cupboards— women's high-collared blouses, skirt hoops, dingy photographs of family outings and one of a man in a cuirassier's uniform, with breastplate and horsetail helmet, and three or four parchment manuscripts. One, dated 1779, was the deed of sale of a farm, another was a marriage contract dated the Year 3 of the First Republic. The contract enumerated the items the bride was to bring in her dowry, which included six pillowcases, one canopy for a bed, and ten handkerchiefs; the whole thing was to come to a thousand and fifty-seven francs. If the husband died before the wife, she was to be allowed to withdraw that much from the estate in consideration of her dowry. If the wife died first, the widower was to keep the pillowcases, handkerchiefs, and all the rest, probably to bestow on his next choice. I wondered, naturally, which of them had survived the other. There were canopies over

the beds in all the bedrooms; one must have been the canopy listed in the contract. The house had stone floors that did not shake even when some guns just across the road were being fired, which happened for one entire night we spent there.

The guns were only three thousand yards behind the front line, but they were firing at a target—a railroad station or road junction—eleven miles away. They belonged not to division artillery but to a remote, unfamiliar entity called Corps. The battery commander, a harassed-looking little captain, called on our artillery general as soon as we moved in and said he hoped the general did not mind guns; there were a lot of generals who couldn't sleep on account of the noise, and he had had to move twice already. He was like a man apologizing to his new neighbors for having noisy children; he was sensitive. Our general said that the guns were music to his ears, and we all smiled mechanically and obediently. The captain said, "I'm sure glad to hear that, because I feel I have an ideal setup here."

Across the yard from the house, in a small storeroom, lived a donkey so old that he had a gray beard. His hoofs were long and misshapen, like the nails of an old dog who gets no exercise, and he stayed in his gloomy cell, blinking out at the world, without enough energy to walk into the adjoining barn and eat the hay, although he would accept cabbages if they were brought to him.

From the crippled woman's, or man's, house we moved into a region that had been heavily bombed on the first day of the offensive and was completely deserted except for the surviving animals. An officer who had done some reconnoitering had found a hamlet, Chapelle en Litige (Chapel in Litigation), which was intact. Bombs had fallen into all the adjoining fields and bomb craters had made the roads into it almost impassable, but its half-dozen houses and the dependent barns stood untouched. One officer, who considers the Air Forces a form of artillery totally lacking in professional direction, said, "If they had dropped hundred-pound bombs instead of five-hundred, they'd have killed just as many cows without spoiling the roads." The facade of the granite house in which we set up shop was hidden by pear trees *en espalier*, laden with fruit and lush with leaves. An old hen had made a nest in a branch under the hayloft window and was rearing her chicks there; they were hard to find, buried among the pears, and produced a noise that was inexplicable to us until we discovered them. Some of the soldiers with us took up quarters in smaller houses, and once they had found niches for themselves, we all strolled about the village looking over the interiors of the houses. The owners had evacuated them in an orderly fashion, taking most of their belongings with them. There was not much left except furniture.

I found a pile of letters, most of them old, a few recent, lying on a dressing table in one of the houses. In a near-by cupboard was a long row of schoolboys' notebooks filled with exercises in drawing, arithmetic, and composition. All the books bore the inscription, written in a hand that became progressively less slack, "Cahier d'Albert Hédouin." A couple of recent business letters were addressed to Veuve Hédouin, and I assumed that Albert was the widow's son. There were also in the cupboard a number of the usual breviaries and cheap books of devotion, including a pamphlet of

prayers for prisoners of war. Idly, because as a camp follower I had nothing else at the moment to do, I took some of the letters and, sitting down on the threshold of the plain little house I was in, started to read them.

One was dated September 25, 1914. It began, "My dear little Louise: I utilize a little moment to send you news of me. I am in good health and hope my letter finds you the same. I'd rather be at Chapelle en Litige than where I am, for it isn't nice to sleep outdoors. If this thing ends soon, I won't be sorry. I am with Anatole and Désiré, and they are in good health, too. Probably the buckwheat has been harvested, if the weather is as good there as it is here. I'd like to help thresh it and drink a big bowl of cider instead of being here, but it's useless to think about it. When you geld the little colt, leave him in the barn for two days, then turn him into the fields of broom, where the donkey is. Put some branches on top of the gate, so he won't try to jump over it. When you get this letter, send me some news of what goes on at home. Have you made a barrel of cider for Pannel yet and have the cows turned out well? Excuse me for being brief, my dear little Louise and cherished babies. I write this letter in the open air, sitting on my knapsack, and now I must go. Your husband, who loves you and kisses you again and again, Louis Hédouin, 336th Infantry. P. S. Put the donkey in Fernand's field."

The next letter was dated in November, 1914, and began, "My dear little Louise: It is with great pleasure I learn that you are in good health. I too am in good health. Dear little Louise, I think you should make at least three barrels of cider, although I know it will give you a lot of trouble. Considering the price of apples and the price of cider, it pays better to make cider than to sell apples. And make a good barrel for us, so that we can have the pleasure of drinking it together when I come home." ("Come home," I thought. "That war had four years to go then.") "My dear little Louise, you tell me that you have planted some wheat. Good. Prices are going up. I hope you have sowed oats, dear one. Dear little Louise, I hope you are well. Also the cows and calves. Butter is selling at a pretty good price, if it can only continue. I was glad to hear you had someone help you thresh the buckwheat. Dear little Louise, I wish I could have been there, but it's useless to think about it. Here one is and here one stays—until when, nobody knows. Your husband, who loves and will never cease to love you and the dear little children, Louis."

Looking up, I saw that four or five cows, probably wanting to be milked, were staring hopefully at me, and I wondered how Louis Hédouin would have felt if he had known that in thirty years not even a woman would be left to care for the cattle in Chapelle en Litige. There was another letter, also written in 1914, in which he said he had been to Mass and then eaten some ham dear little Louise had sent him; he would rather have attended Mass at home, but it was "useless to think of it."

"Dear little Louise," he went on, "you say you have had a card from Aimable and he is in good health. So much the better, for you can't imagine how unhealthy it is where he finds himself. I couldn't either, unless I had been there, but don't worry, I'm all right. Dear little Louise, you say that Marie has had a letter from Pierre and he is a prisoner. So much the better. That way he is sure to survive. I know that threshing must be a lot of

trouble to you. I am sorry you are alone and have so much work to do. Do you remember, on that evening before I went away, Enée said that this business wouldn't be over before Easter? I am afraid he was right. It is sad when I think of it. Days are indeed long. Louis."

And on March 15, 1915, he wrote that he was sorry to hear that Louise was suffering but hoped she would soon be delivered—the first indication I had had that he knew she was pregnant. "My dear little Louise," he continued, "I had a letter from Papa the same time as yours. He says he has sold the old cow for three hundred and forty-five francs. It's not bad, when you think that she only had four teeth left. What about the black cow you thought was going to calve March 8 and what are you doing with the Jersey? Tell me in your next letter. Dear little Louise, you say you have threshed the oats. Good. There must have been some loss, but you did the best you could. The worst of it is we probably won't be home in time for the haying this season. Excuse me for not having written. We were taking ammunition up to the front lines. Lately things go badly. The regiment has refused to march to an attack. Everybody is sick of this business, and we lose courage and ask for an end of this terrible war. A sweet kiss from your husband, Louis."

Then, on the twenty-second of March, the latest date I found on any of his letters, Hédouin wrote, "My dear little Louise: I have received with great pleasure your letter of the eighteenth. Your mother writes to me that you have had a nine-pound boy and are doing well, and the boy, too. My dear little Louise, you did well to have a midwife from Remilly, and she didn't charge much, either—eight francs. My dear little Louise, I'd like to be with you, but it's useless to think of it. Distance keeps us apart. I hope God will help you in your troubles. My parents write me that at home people are saying this will end soon. So much the better. Dear little Louise, the boy will be called Albert. Before telling you, I waited to see whether you would have a boy or a girl. Your husband, who loves you, Louis. P. S. What about the black cow?"

Nineteen-fifteen. I did a bit of subtraction. Albert would have been twenty-four in 1939—just the right age. I thought of the graded notebooks and the pamphlet of prayers for prisoners of war.

*   *   *

Mark S. Watson of the Baltimore *Sun* Tells the Story of the Seven Martyrs of Arlon

IN LATE SEPTEMBER, 1944, Mark S. Watson, a *Stars and Stripes* veteran, who had been a major of artillery in World War I, attached to American headquarters at Chaumont, arrived once more at the same spot, this time as military correspondent of the Baltimore *Sunpapers*. Starting out on a two-day sentimental exploration of the area that had held the news headlines a quarter of a century before, he came across painful evidence of the conduct of retreating German troops, particularly the German Gestapo. "The Seven Martyrs of Arlon" was one of a series for which this veteran reporter and editor was awarded the 1945 Pulitzer Prize for distinguished telegraphic reporting on international affairs. It substantiates John Steinbeck's penetrating judgment, written in 1947, after the passions of war had subsided: "No savage tribe, no invader, ever was responsible for the stupid calculated cruelties and the destruction of the Germans. They raged through the country like frantic, cruel children." They slew with the ferocity of fear.

"Tragedy more dreadful than the brothers Grimm recorded in their fairy tales"

Baltimore *Sun*, October 1, 1944

CHAUMONT, HAUTE MARNE, SEPTEMBER 30—Here stood the first American headquarters during the First World War. From the converted French barracks at the edge of this historic town overlooking the still more historic valley of the Marne, General Pershing for a year and a half directed the training and supplying of his expeditionary force of 2,000,000 men—and then their admirable employment in battle.

Here the battles of the present world conflict paused only momentarily for rear-guard actions, for the enemy was in full retreat when he passed through Langres, Chaumont, Neuf-château, Gondrecourt, and that "quiet sector north of Toul."

It is almost unbelievable that even in recent days, when the German retreat made ultimate defeat seem inevitable and one might have expected less inhuman behavior, based on caution if nothing else, the German savagery toward civilians has been undiminished.

We had started from the vicinity of Aachen and pushed southward through the Belgian province of Luxembourg close to the Grand Duchy of Luxembourg itself, a region of extraordinary beauty when one flits over hilltops and escapes the great fir forests which stretch for miles.

These forests are admirably planted and scientifically harvested, as is the way with European forests, but their denseness and darkness make one understand they must have impressed the children through the ages and in the end developed the fairy tales in which all the mystery and tragedy take place "in the dark forest."

Today's war has spread tragedy far beyond the dark forest, however, and tragedy more dreadful than the brothers Grimm recorded in their fairy tales. In two Belgian villages on the route, we passed those tragic little processions of which we have seen so many in newly liberated lands.

In each case almost the entire village population was in attendance and in each case flags fluttered at the head of the parade and were spread over the caskets being carried toward the cemetery. Here were the latest victims of the German retreat. Sometimes they had fallen in open combat. Usually they had been murdered in cold blood without trial and without warning.

We were to see the ceremony which already had taken place in Arlon and to hear that little city's story of its losses. There had been many of these during the last five years, for the German invaders were particularly bitter in their relations with the border people. Roughly half are of German and half of Belgian blood.

The invaders seemed to think that because German is largely spoken there the thinking should also be largely German. It has not been so among the Chasseurs des Ardennes, and for that reason, it would seem, special fury had been visited upon these independent hill people of the region, which covers much of south-ern Belgium and eastern France.

Bastogne had its share, but Arlon fared especially ill during the German retreat.

The story of "The Seven Martyrs of Arlon" will long be remembered.

Most conspicuous perhaps was Dr. Jean Hollenflatz, village physician, who was known and loved all over the countryside as the only general physician. He had been an active worker in the Red Cross, which meant that he had displeased the Gestapo.

There were no charges, however, and of course no trial. At two o'clock in the morning the Gestapo agents took him from his bed, ordered him to dress and precede them up the village street. Two blocks away they shot him in the back and left him lying dead on the sidewalk. There he lay all night, and the next day the German guard forbade the family to remove the body.

It was not moved to shelter until the Germans pulled out. Today a great wreath hangs on the wall above the spot where this useful life was ended.

The fate of André Lucion, who had been the King's procurator, was more poignant. He too had been taken from his bed during the night and marched up the street and shot in the back as he walked. He was not so fortunate as to be killed outright. He lay there dying and unattended for several hours, shouting defiantly that he had made no attempt to escape but had simply been assassinated.

The Germans eventually took him away. His body was found two days later.

There was also the case of Noël Fernand, a twenty-four-year-old teacher. He had been a sergeant in the 1940 army and had been cited for gallantry. He had been a prisoner of war and on release had come back home to take his place back of the desk in the Arlon school. Perhaps his teaching had displeased the Gestapo agents.

Whatever the cause, he too was taken under arrest but was not removed from the house. Instead he was shot down there in the presence of his wife and father-in-law. They were ordered not to aid the poor fellow, who lay there dying for two hours.

When the wife tried to throw herself down beside him, the Gestapo agents beat her and pushed her away. The old father-in-law, past seventy, was taken presumably to Germany. He has not been heard from since.

The fate of the other four martyrs of Arlon is not sufficiently different to call for special recording. The little village still blazes with fury and still mourns a great many other citizens who have vanished during the earlier years.

Bodies found buried under the Gestapo headquarters doubtless are some of these missing men and women.

* * *

WATSON UNCOVERED additional evidence to prove that some of the martyrs of Arlon had been turned in by Belgian renegades whom the Germans hired as spies, paying sums as little as five hundred francs and promising as much as 500,000 for fugitives whom the Gestapo especially prized. The Gestapo paid a reward of 20,000 francs for the betrayal of four American aviators who had parachuted to temporary safety near Arlon; these four, however, were "confiscated" by German soldiers, who treated them correctly.

Hal Boyle Tells How "Shorty" Plotnick Came a Long Way to Die

IN 1945 Harold V. (Hal) Boyle, war reporter and columnist for the Associated Press, was awarded the Pulitzer Prize for distinguished reporting during the year 1944. In dispatches that appeared in more than four hundred afternoon newspapers, he depicted graphically the lives, hardships, and the humor of the American fighting man. One of his best stories, written while with the American troops in France, concerns Shorty, who, fighting the Germans for a second time, died a hero.

"Leave me tell you, I'll get those Germans"

The Associated Press, September 1, 1944

WITH AMERICAN TROOPS IN FRANCE—Shorty came a long way to die—and he came against the will of the Army he had served for twenty-seven years.

"Leave me tell you," he used to say, "I'll get those Germans."

That was back in the United States. Shorty had what most soldiers regard as a soft touch, a master sergeant's rating on the operations staff of an armored outfit's headquarters.

He had the reputation of eating young "shavetails" for breakfast, and every man in the unit was fond of this sawed-off, gray-haired little man with the salty voice and the tough manner.

He was a good poker player and after twenty-seven years of selective competition with cards he had put away enough buck privates' pay so that he and his wife could afford more than C rations any time he wanted to hang up his uniform.

But although his health was poor, Shorty had no wish to get out of the Army. He was only five feet four and he was all soldier.

When he learned his outfit was going overseas Shorty had to fight a personal campaign to go along. He was the oldest man in the unit, and his friends didn't think his health would stand up under the strain of field duty.

"He had 111 things wrong with him, from varicose veins to arteriosclerosis," said Lieutenant Edward Sasson, Los Angeles, "but he wasn't looking for a way out."

Shorty was Russian and hated the Germans. He hated them in the last war, too, and won the Purple Heart and three wound stripes fighting them in France. He waved those wound stripes to clinch his point—that he had earned a chance for a return at the enemy.

"Leave me tell you," he said with a deeply serious look on his gnomelike face, "I'll get those Germans."

Today a small group of officers who knew and loved the lionhearted little man stood around a jeep near the front lines and talked sadly of how the Germans finally got Shorty.

"We'd just taken a town," said his company commander, Captain James Kuhns, Greensburg, Pennsylvania, "and Shorty and two other men heard there still was a German machine-gun nest giving us trouble in one of the buildings.

"It wasn't the concern of the operations sergeant to knock it out, but you couldn't keep Shorty from going after those Germans. He was armed only with a pistol, but the two men with him had carbines. Shorty told them, 'OK, I'll go out and draw their fire, and then you boys give it to them.'

"He edged out, but the Germans caught him with the first burst and mowed him down. He died before he knew he had located and wiped out that machine-gun nest. That was like Shorty—sticking his own neck out."

"Poor old Shorty," one officer said. There was silence for a minute, then another officer laughed reminiscently.

"Remember the time that young lieutenant walked up to Shorty and told him to take his hands out of his pockets, and Shorty just looked at him and said, 'Listen, recruit——'?"

For a quarter of an hour they stood there within a few hundred yards of the front lines, telling legends of Shorty. He never knew his own age because he had no birth record.

"He was the best damned soldier in this division," said Major Nathan M. Quinn, Spencer, Massachusetts.

Shorty would rather have had that sentence over his grave than his own name plate—Sergeant Joe L. Plotnick, Baltimore, Maryland—because when he was alive he proudly thought so, too. He knew he was "the best damned soldier" in any division. He wouldn't have been Shorty if he didn't think so.

Those Wonderful Fiji Islanders Terrify the

Japanese and Fascinate *The New Yorker*

WE AGREE WITH the judgment of Robert E. Sherwood, the playwright, that Robert Lewis Taylor's story on the Fijian jungle fighters, published in *The New Yorker* on December 16, 1944, is a superb piece of writing. Perhaps Robert Louis Stevenson, who knew the South Seas best of all, would think so, too.

"Him fella go get lawn mower belong'm head"
—Happy talk from the South Pacific

At Bougainville, where I was on duty with the Navy not long ago, nearly everybody felt that the best fighters in those parts were the Fijians, who do much of our jungle scouting in the Solomons. The Fijians are tall and black and bushy-haired, and most of their time at home is spent at water sports of one kind and another. Consequently, the majority of men are built along the lines of Johnny Weissmuller, only more rugged. The wonderful enlarged photograph that hangs in the lobby of the Grand Pacific Hotel in Suva, the Fiji capital, called *Oliva, a Fisherman of Fiji*, depicts perhaps the typical Fiji male—graceful and muscular but not overdeveloped like some of our bar-bell addicts. A funny thing about the Fijians is that they are thicker than first seems apparent; they weigh more than you would think. For example, a man whose erect carriage gives an impression of slimness often turns out to weigh something like two hundred and thirty pounds, which the Japs find runs a little high for hand-to-hand fighting.

I have visited Fiji two or three times. In 1936, I was in Suva for a while and had a chance to watch the Fijians play Rugby. They generally play Rugby intramurally; that is, just among themselves. Their style of play is considered too vigorous for the English colonials there, or for anyone else, for that matter. A team from an Australian cruiser took them on one Sunday afternoon but played only one game. Owing to a brisk run on the ship's doctor, who treated about fifteen crewmen for assorted abrasions and contusions, the cruiser was tied up in port an extra four days. The Fijians don't play Rugby viciously; in fact, they play it happily and in the friendliest spirit. But they try very hard to win and they bowl over everything in their way.

The traffic policemen are one of the greatest sights of Suva. In the old days, tourists from the Matson ships would collect on the street corners and watch them, and nowadays the American troops who pass through find them a curiosity. Fiji policemen are chosen partly for their looks and physique. There is a mixture of races and some poverty in Fiji, but crime is no problem. The sunny, uninhibited policemen often have a dull time, so when an opportunity comes to nab a felon, they sometimes forget and imagine they are playing Rugby. A half-caste, say, warmed up by native beer, may snatch a string of cat's-eye beads from a sidewalk merchant and go sprinting off down the street. With many a joyous leap and wild cry, the cops will string out in pursuit. When they catch up, as they always do, they will try to bring him down in various ways. The policeman in the lead may elect to smack him from the side with a body block. If this happens, the others may dive or jump on the pair, landing head downward or in a sitting position. Again, the leading officer may just swing his bolo, or native billy. In this case, the delinquency authorities seldom find a regeneration program necessary. The offender has learned his lesson; if he ever gets out of the hospital, he goes straight.

All the Fiji police wear a blue serge skirt, a bright-red sash, and a white blouse, and go barefoot, and the traffic cops usually provide themselves with an extra fillip, such as gold earrings or gardenias in their hair. Standing on a little podium and under a huge umbrella, they go through amazing contortions. No symphony conductor fired by the genius of Beethoven has ever risen to greater muscular heights. At the approach of a two-wheeled cart pulled by a sick donkey, a Fiji traffic cop is likely to raise his left hand slowly, palm inward, then swing his right hand up in a beautiful arc and lay his head straight back, nose pointed to the sky. The gesture presumably means "Come ahead, if your donkey can make it," but an onlooker

from the Western world is apt to find himself listening for the opening strains of the "Pastoral" or *Tyll Eulenspiegel*. The Fiji traffic cops love their work. They get equal pleasure from a Chinese ricksha and the limousine of the governor general, and they have been known to do some of their best work on a perfectly empty street. Just practicing.

From birth, the Fijians are in and out of the jungle. They understand the tangled greenery that covers the South Pacific islands the way a New Yorker understands Times Square. Their senses are sharper than the white man's and their strength and endurance are greater. There is very little left for them to learn about the jungle. Certainly the news, a year or so ago, that they were to be "trained for jungle fighting" by the Allies must have struck them as comical, though none of them ever said so. In fact, I was recently told by a New Zealand captain stationed at the Fiji camp on Bougainville that the men there had been unfailingly deferential and kind to their white tutors. They are a people with an extraordinary sense of humor, but they have an almost pathological aversion to hurting the feelings of a friend. However, at the end of their training, which took place in the Fijis, they allowed their sense of humor a fairly free hand. The company of white soldiers who had trained them arranged to fight a mock battle with them in the bush. After dark, each side was to try to penetrate as far as possible into the other's lines. The main idea was to see how well the new Fiji scouts had learned their lessons. It turned out that they had learned them pretty well. During the night some of the white scouts worked thirty or forty feet into the Fiji lines, and figured they had the battle won, since they hadn't caught any Fijians behind *their* lines. When they came to check up at daylight, it developed that most of the Fijians had apparently spent the night in the white headquarters. They had chalked huge crosses on the tents and the furniture and had left one of the most distinct crosses on the seat of the commanding officer's trousers, which he had thrown over a chair around four A.M.

After the mock battle, it was felt that the Fijians were ready for the jungle. They were shipped up to Bougainville, several hundred strong, and introduced to the Japanese. At that time, as now, the Americans and New Zealanders held only a pin point of land on the big island. In this area we had several airstrips and from them we bombed Rabaul every day. The Japs occupied the rest of Bougainville; all around the perimeter of our small territory they were thick in the jungle, fanatically fighting to throw us out. There were times when it was touch and go with the Allied troops, who were generally outnumbered and frequently unskilled in bush warfare. The fighting on the perimeter went on continuously. In the daytime it was often limited to guerrillalike skirmishes and sniper activity, but before dawn every morning there was always a lively exchange of artillery. For a while the booming of the big guns woke up all the aviation people, but eventually they got used to the racket and slept right through it. "Quite a morning out on the perimeter" was a common breakfast observation back during the early artillery duels. The situation, though not desperate, called for experts in jungle reconnaissance, who could sift through the enemy's lines and keep us posted on what he was up to. The Fiji scouts rose hilariously to the occasion. It seemed that

they were homesick for the wildwood after their dreary ocean voyage and, besides, they had never liked Japs.

The jungle on Bougainville, and throughout the South Pacific, is a dark, unwholesome, hostile thing. Great, stifling webs of vegetation spread over the ground and crawl up the giant banyan and eucalyptus trees, forming big cones that look like green circus tents. Men unfamiliar with the jungle have burrowed fifty yards into it and been lost for a week. When airplanes crash in the jungle, even within sight of the ground units, a party of natives usually takes two or three days to find them. The planes penetrate the top layer of foliage and are swallowed up. Into this colorful natural hell the Fijians plunged with fine high spirits. Primarily they were after information, but they never neglected any stray Japs that were handy. In a very short time the enemy on Bougainville came to know the Fiji scouts and to regard them with terror. American and New Zealand troops emphatically verified this on several occasions.

Once, during my stay on Bougainville, a report came in from the perimeter that a pocket of two hundred American soldiers had been cut off. Gloom was heavy throughout the Allied camps; the men had many friends. That evening word got around that the Fijians were going out to have a look at the trouble. I walked along the road past their camp and stared through the high wire fence that surrounded it. There was no use going in, since at that time the New Zealanders in charge of the Fijians were a little reluctant to discuss them. The huge black men appeared to be in a rollicking mood, joking and laughing as they strapped on knives and made other preparations for the bush. Their assignment seemed to me particularly dismal—facing a heavily armed and numerous enemy in a cheerless jungle on a night as black as ebony —and I wondered how they could be looking forward to it so gaily. The next morning, however, when the news came in about the night's outing, their good humor seemed perfectly justified. The Americans, it appeared, had been rescued, all two hundred of them, and the Fijians were back in camp and sleeping soundly. Just how this miracle was accomplished was never announced, but later in the day I stopped the New Zealand captain I knew and asked him if there had been much trouble. "Why, yes," he replied, "the boys said they had to rough up the little bastards a bit." That was all the information I ever got out of him.

Some time after that I was quartered in a Quonset hut with an American Army photographer who had just had a singular and nerve-racking experience. He had been out in the bush for two weeks with a party of Fijians, having put in a request to take some motion pictures behind the enemy lines. Someone, he said almost bitterly, had taken him up on it. He had lost about twenty-five pounds and figured that he had aged somewhere between ten and fifteen years. It was not that the Fijians had treated him badly. On the contrary, they had been most solicitous, in their own way. But the photographer had nevertheless found the pace quite trying. His escorts carried all his photographic gear, but most of the time he had to run to stay with them. And he was always getting tangled in creepers and vines and tripping up. "They didn't seem to use any paths," he told me. "They kept disappearing into walls of stuff that a snake couldn't have got through with a bush knife." The disappearing was, in fact, one of the worst aspects of the trip, and the photographer couldn't explain it. "They must have been pulling my leg," he said over and over to me. "And yet, why would they? They were the nicest fellows you ever met. I don't understand it. We would be going along, me hardly daring to breathe—we'd run across two Jap patrols the first hour out—and all of a sudden I'd look around and I'd be alone, completely damned horribly alone, not a sign of them anywhere, no leaf stirring, no sound, nothing. I'd just stand there, thinking, 'O.K., sniper, let's have it, I'm right out in front of you and no place to go. Let's have it.' And then in a minute, all of those big black guys would be around again, and pretty soon my heart would start back up and things were all right. I don't know where they went and I don't know where they came from, but most of all I don't know why they did it. They *must* have been pulling my leg." He really seemed very concerned about it.

On the second day, the photographer said, the Fijians spotted a group of Japs in a clearing in a valley below them. He explained to them in some excitement that he wanted to take pictures, and started fitting a telescopic lens to his camera. The Fiji corporal in charge of the group gave an amiable nod; then he and his men disappeared again. It was ten minutes before the photographer was ready to shoot. When he got set up and had a look at the clearing, there were no Japs in sight. The Fijians reappeared shortly. "Where'd they go, fellows?" the photographer kept asking. "What about the patrol?" His questions seemed to amuse the scouts. "They laughed and laughed," he said to me. "Some of them slapped their knees. I began to get the general idea. There had been some misunderstanding.

The Jap patrol had quit patrolling—for good."

The Fijians, the photographer told me, carried no food. They ate herbs and roots and wild fruits and vegetables. Sometimes they cooked their meal, squatting over a quick, small fire, and sometimes they didn't. The photographer lived on some field rations he had started out with, and when they gave out he tried the Fiji diet, but it disagreed with him. Their sleeping habits distressed him, too. Several times they made camp in what seemed to the photographer the middle of the most populous Jap territory. He would roll up in a blanket, feeling exposed and uneasy, and perhaps a couple of hours later he would wake up and look around. The Fijians would be missing. "Not one left," he told me. "All gone—God knows where and God knows why. And me surrounded by the Japanese South Pacific Army. It was great." On none of these occasions did he see any of them return. They were always on hand early in the morning, though, always fresh and ready to move. In camp the Fiji scouts wear khaki clothing similar to that of other jungle troops, but they cached it soon after they left on this trip and proceeded almost naked. They had their own methods of camouflage, the photographer said a little ruefully, adding, "Not that they had been getting in my way as it was." By a skillful use of berry juices and miscellaneous greenery, they were able to surpass their customary efforts to become one with the jungle. They usually did this, I gathered, when they were going to be operating within a few feet of the enemy.

The photographer took a lot of pictures of Japs in action during the two weeks. The Fijians wove back and forth behind the Jap front, counting the troops, noting what kind of equipment they had and how it was brought in, and in general taking inventory. It was the photographer's impression that his colleagues were spending their mysterious nights visiting the Jap camps. In view of what we learned from various sources later, the visits must have been lively. The Fijians had side arms, but the photographer never saw any of them fire one. The scouts apparently depended on the knives and small hardwood bludgeons they carried. Also, he thought, they must frequently have used only their hands at close quarters. "You know," he told me, "I think everybody down here feels grateful to the Fijis. Soldiers watching them come in from a mission seem to be saying to themselves, 'Fine. Nice work, boys. We wouldn't be down here if it weren't for those nasty little Japs, and a lot more of us would be alive today. We don't know what you've been up to, and we're not especially bloodthirsty, but we hope there's quite a little group of ex-supermen lying around somewhere near by. They got better than they deserved. A nice clean death in the dark is too damn good for them.'"

Before I left Bougainville, I dropped into the Fijians' camp. The secrecy about them had been relaxed by then. Most of the scouts were sitting on the front steps of their huts, quietly talking and laughing. As soon as I got near enough for them to see that I was a lieutenant, they sprang to their feet and froze to attention. "Freeze" seems to be the only word that describes the stance they take in the presence of an officer. There is nothing in our services like it as a symbol of discipline; a Marine guard saluting a Marine general comes close. At the headquarters shack, I asked the Fiji guard on duty if the commanding officer was in. He saluted and answered promptly. He said, "Him fella go get lawn mower belong'm head." I thanked him, returned his salute, and struck out briskly down the path, headed for no place in particular. Some of the Fijians speak good English, some can't speak any, and most of them speak pidgin. I worked on the guard's reply for a while, then finally went over to the barbershop and asked for the commanding officer. He had already got a haircut and left for the perimeter.

On the way out of the camp, I stopped to talk to a Fiji sergeant. He was at least six feet five, he was wearing a skin-tight blouse and a pair of khaki shorts, and he had what appeared to be an orchid behind his left ear. I looked again; it was an orchid. "How have things been out in the bush lately?" I asked, not much impressed with my opening.

"It has been quiet of late, sir," he said, in a cultured voice.

"Not much doing, hey?" I asked.

"By and large, I should say quiet, sir," the sergeant answered.

I had a question in mind and I decided to come out with it. "I suppose you fellows have a lot of casualties out there, don't you?" I asked.

It seemed to be an ill-advised question. His attitude changed abruptly. His posture stiffened and his face took on an unmistakable look of pain.

"I'm sorry," I said. "They must be terribly high, of course."

"Sir," said the sergeant, "we have no casualties."

I muttered something polite and waited.

"We have no casualties," he repeated. "Sir, we are not seen by the enemy. It is a point of pride."

His feelings were plainly hurt. I felt very bad about it, and I have ever since.

Larry Newman Sees "Blood and Guts" at the Battle of the Bulge

IN FORTY HOURS I shall be in battle, with little information, and on the spur of the moment will have to make most momentous decisions, but I believe that one's spirit enlarges with responsibility and that, with God's help, I shall make them and make them right. It seems that my whole life has been pointed to this moment."

Such reflections, found in *War as I Knew It* (1947), were typical of General George Patton. Commanding general of the American Third Army, Patton was a professional soldier, one of a long line of scintillating American commanders like Winfield Scott, Robert E. Lee, and Stonewall Jackson, who pursued their duty in war with vigor and imagination. Every war produces legendary characters among the big brass, and General Patton, blessed with fierce courage and damned by eccentric behavior, was World War II's gift to the mythology of warfare. His fellow officers called him "Georgie" and his GI's affectionately nicknamed him "Blood and Guts." Master of the expletive, raucously pious, acerbate, and profane, he strode through western Europe like a streamlined version of a giant of old, riding atop his tanks, brandishing a pearl-handled revolver, and exuberantly performing such deeds as swimming across a stream in freezing weather to prove to his men that it could be done. German brass, nourished on Clausewitz and the elder von Moltke, did not quite know what to make of this flamboyant personality combining the flashier traits of Frank Merriwell, Henry V, and Leo Durocher. "For certain types of action," said Eisenhower, "he was the outstanding soldier our country has produced."

Patton's role in World War II was almost stifled in the very beginning when he made the grievous mistake of striking a wounded GI whom he suspected of feigning illness. Public opinion was against the battle-taut general, but General Eisenhower, who weighed hot temper against combat value, gave Patton a severe dressing down while retaining him on active duty. In the meantime, Patton, like a chastened schoolboy, apologized to his entire army.

Larry Newman, a veteran International News Service correspondent who covered the war on many fronts, accompanied General Patton on his frequent visits to front-line foxholes, observed him during the smashing Ardennes offensive, and later moved with Patton's famous Third Army on its sweep through Bavaria and into Czechoslovakia. Here is Newman's story, condensed from a series of biographical articles in the *New York Journal-American*, of the swashbuckling general during the crucial days of the Battle of the Bulge.

"What the hell is all the mourning about?"

New York Journal-American, December 24–29, 1944. International News Service.

The Germans' initial gains were staggering. The snow-covered forests of the Ardennes were soaked with the blood of American boys who never had a chance to fight.

Our forces were scattered, confused. [Seven thousand men of the 106th Infantry Division became captives.]

Tiny groups of men stood out against the Germans. Held out miles behind the most advanced Nazi units. Refused to yield even though ammunition was scarce, food supplies impossible to obtain.

Meanwhile, General Eisenhower and all his commanding generals met at Verdun to decide what had to be done.

After hours of discussion a decision was reached. Bedell Smith, Eisenhower's chief of staff, said to the assembled generals:

"Montgomery will contain them to the north.

"General Hodges [commander of the U. S. First Army] will hold them at the Meuse River.

"Georgie [General Patton], can you hold them on the south flank?"

Patton stood up, looking about the room, then said:

"Hold them! Why, I'll take von Rundstedt and ram him right down Montgomery's ——!"

Patton's Third Army was fighting the Germans in the Saar at the time and was taking a pasting from them. He wanted nothing more than to let go of the lion's tail and instead take a crack at von Rundstedt. When he got his orders to move north, he traveled personally to the command post of the Fifth (Red Diamond) Division and ordered its commander, General Irwin, to break contact with the enemy.

All day long on December 19 he drove his men. Then he shot the Fifth north. They traveled ninety miles and attacked the German flank. All within twenty-four hours.

Bastogne was surrounded by Germans who predicted over their radios that the arrogant 101st Airborne and remnants of the U. S. Armored Tenth Division would be annihilated unless they gave up.

Everything favored the Germans for a while. But Patton never was disheartened. In the midst of the battle—perhaps the most desperate a U. S. Army ever had to fight—Patton called a conference of correspondents. As we filed into the war room, the tenseness was depressing. But when Patton strode into the room, smiling, confident, the atmosphere changed within seconds. He asked:

"What the hell is all the mourning about? This is the end of the beginning. We've been batting our brains out trying to get the Hun out in the open. Now he is out. And with the help of God we'll finish him off this time—and for good."

He talked of his plans. Then he said:

"I have a little Christmas card and prayer for all of you."

On one side of a piece of paper was a simple Christmas greeting with his signature. On the other side this prayer was printed:

"Almighty and most merciful

Father, we humbly beseech Thee, of Thy great goodness, to restrain these immoderate rains with which we have had to contend. Grant us fair weather for battle. Graciously hearken to us as soldiers who call upon Thee that, armed with Thy power, we may advance from victory to victory, and crush the oppression and wickedness of our enemies, and establish justice among men and nations. Amen."

He said he had called Major General Otto P. Weyland, commanding general of the Nineteenth Tactical Air Force, and told him to be ready to throw everything at the Germans when the weather broke.

The following day the sun broke through. And then came nine perfect flying days.

Our air forces shuttled over and smashed the German tanks, riddled their infantry columns, left the roads littered with dead and dying.

Patton told us the following Friday:

"The war is all but over. The God of battles always stands on the side of right when the judgment comes."

In the meantime, the paratroopers and tankers turned infantry had held Bastogne and received the plaudits of the Allied world. The 101st Airborne and Bastogne took place alongside Valley Forge, Anzio, Cassino.*

But the Fourth Armored fighting up the road from Arlon to Bastogne had suffered more grievously than the paratroopers.

When Patton finally stood in the division CP † of the 101st Airborne Division, he told correspondents to remember:

"It's a helluva lot easier to sit on your rear end and wait than it is to fight into a place like this.

"Try to remember that when you write your books about this campaign.

"Remember the men who drove up that bowling alley out there from Arlon."

* * *

As THE OUTSTANDING figures of World War II begin to take on the varied hues of legend, more reports of Patton's amazing propensity for prayer begin to appear. Another Patton prayer for success was published in the Swedish Life Guard Grenadiers' regimental journal. "Sir," began this prayer delivered on December 23, 1944, on the eve of the Ardennes offensive, "this is Patton talking. Rain, snow, more rain, more snow—and I am beginning to wonder on which side they actually are in Thy headquarters. You must decide for Yourself on whose side You are standing." Four days later Patton prayed again, this time in a more optimistic mood: "Sir, this is Patton again, and I beg to report complete progress. Sir, it seems to me that You have been much better informed about the situation than I was, because it was that awful weather which I cursed so much which made it possible for the German army to commit suicide. That, Sir, was a brilliant military move, and I bow humbly to a supreme military genius."

Publication of these prayers aroused an ecclesiastical furor in Sweden. Dean Anderberg of Uppsala, chief of the Swedish army chaplains, com-

---

* When Brigadier General Anthony McAuliffe, acting commander of the 101st Airborne Division, received a surrender demand from the Germans, he countered with a historic reply: "Nuts!"

† Command Post.

mented: "For that kind of thing I can only use the old-fashioned word 'heresy.' "

On occupation duty in Germany after the war, General Patton was finally relieved of his command of the Third Army when he publicly announced that in his estimation the difference between Nazis and anti-Nazis was no more than that between Republicans and Democrats. This was too much for long-suffering General Eisenhower, who reluctantly transferred his problem general to another unit. A few months later General Patton was killed in an automobile accident in Germany.

The Working Press Reports F. D. R.'s Death

ARMY-NAVY
CASUALTY LIST

WASHINGTON, April 13—Following are the latest casualties in the military services, including next-of-kin.

ARMY-NAVY DEAD

ROOSEVELT, Franklin D., Commander-in-Chief, wife, Mrs. Anna Eleanor Roosevelt, the White House.

MILLIONS WERE plunged into grief by the sad tidings that the architect of victory had died on the eve of triumph. The people at first refused to believe it, then they had to accept it. All Robert E. Sherwood could think of when the realization finally did get through was, " 'It finally crushed him. He couldn't stand up under it any longer.' The 'it' was the awful responsibility that had been piling up for so many years."

The President had captured the hearts of his people. The mighty and humble alike had been fascinated by his cheerful smile and unfailing courage, his power "to soar above circumstances which would have held other men earthbound." Gently but firmly he had led Americans from bewilderment "to face evil and rise up and destroy it." It was hard to accept the fact that the warm radio voice with its heartening: "My friends!" would speak no more.

Not only Americans, but people throughout the civilized world mourned the passing of a great humanitarian and a very great President. This news story, which appeared in the newspaper *PM* on April 13, 1945, tells of the reaction of the people of New York City. It might have been Chicago, San Francisco, or New Orleans.

*A stunned people bids farewell to a war
casualty*

The heart of this whole, great city welled over with frank, unashamed grief at dusk last night as the news of President Roosevelt's death spread, by rumor, by radio, and by extra editions of the afternoon newspapers. People told the news to each other in hushed, choked voices. In every corner of the metropolis, people clustered about their radios, hurried into the streets, not wanting to believe it.

When it was true—palpably, hopelessly true—men and women wept open, honest tears at the dread news.

Shock and disbelief were stamped across the faces of the milling thousands in Times Square when they heard the news.

"Roosevelt is dead. Roosevelt is dead. Roosevelt is dead." The solemn, swelling whisper ran its course through the knotted, massed crowds which had gathered at first, as crowds do in New York, without knowing why.

First it had been those who had heard the news over office radios and had left their work in the vicinity to rush for confirmation by the newspapers. They, waiting for the extras at the newsstands in Times Square, had stopped passers-by, and, as the homegoing workers left the buildings, they joined the others solidly to block Broadway and Seventh Avenue from Forty-second to Forty-third Street and beyond.

Mounted cops kept the crowd in order, hemming in those on the safety island and the pavement surrounding the Times Building. Across the street, on Seventh, the pavement was jammed with persons peering up at the dead, blank electric bulbs of the Times Building as if expecting them suddenly to flash out a confirmation or denial.

They had heard about it over the radio, they had heard about it from friends or strangers, but obstinately they waited for the final word that would leave no doubt—the extras.

As those on the fringe heard the news, they stood in silent disbelief for the space of a pulsebeat, and then vehemently and from the heart denied

it—it was a hoax. And so they joined the others, waiting to be shown.

Two sailors shoved their way to the middle of the crowd before asking what it was all about.

"The President has died," a man told them.

They looked at each other quickly, gulped, looked away, and then back again, searching each other's faces for the truth.

"My God," said one, "it can't be true."

"Of course not," said the other.

And they stood there, waiting.

An old man, who emphasized his thickly accented words with twisted, gnarled hands, said to a young girl who did not listen:

"All the enemies, they had a respect for him, you know. It's hard to find such a man."

As the minutes dragged by conviction grew that this was not a fake rumor. Facing the national disaster, and each experiencing his own, personal loss, strangers gathered together in tiny islands of their own inside the crowd to talk to one another for solace.

"Where are those damned newspapers?" a man shouted. Then the first extras arrived. There was a mad rush for the stands; newsboys tore through the crowd, hawking the cruel headlines.

"He was a great and brave man," one quiet civilian told those near him, folding the paper under his arm.

"There was no one who could match him," a sailor said. "He used my ship, the one I worked on, mind you—to go to Malta. I didn't see him, but the President used my ship!"

A soldier took a *Journal-American* from a newsboy.

"That'll cost you a dime," the newsboy said. The soldier looked shocked

—not at the demand, but at the little profiteer—and demanded that the nearest cop arrest him.

Near the police information booth opposite the Forty-third Street subway kiosk, three Chinese women wept piteously, as if their hearts would break.

The news came more slowly to the neighborhoods. Up in Harlem and Little Italy, the news had not reached some street corners by 7:30. But with each new subway crowd, each busload of sobered, silenced people, the story came up from downtown.

As the word spread, little knots of people gathered on corners, in doorways, talking it over, questing for more details. A car stopped at a Harlem street corner, the radio going full blast. The people strained to listen. The driver shook his head sorrowfully.

"It's true," he said. "He's dead. He's really dead!"

Outside of a Lenox Avenue store, a Negro man talked calmly to the small crowd around him.

"Don't worry," he said. "He was a great man with great ideas, and he didn't let any grass grow under his feet. His plans are made and somebody's gonna carry them out."

On the subways and the bus lines, normal New York restraints disappeared. People compared versions of the news, told it to newcomers, joined in speculation about the future of the country. At Grand Central, an old Negro halted a young girl on the subway platform, tears streaming from his eyes.

"Miss, did you hear the news?" he asked. "What will we do now?"

On Bleecker Street, three girls in their young teens walked arm in arm. One of them spoke confidently to the others:

"You wait and see. You'll read about President Roosevelt in the history books. He suffered more for everybody, all the time."

A Jewish housewife on Rivington Street was asked if she had heard the radio.

"For what do I need a radio?" she asked. "It is on everybody's face."

On Mulberry Street, an Italian undertaker mourned:

"It is too bad—too bad this great man could not have carried his burden just a little while longer, to enjoy the peace he has won for us."

In Chinatown, the three-hundred-pound locality mayor, Kenneth ("Shavey") Lee, spoke for his community and his countrymen:

"We have lost a true friend and an honest one."

And from the fire escapes of two buildings at Lewis and Stanton Streets in the lower East Side, a group of young boys hung out what they called a "mourn sign," about three feet square, which read:

"We mourn the loss of our beloved President, Franklin Delano Roosevelt."

At the Veterans Hospital on Kingsbridge Road, the Bronx, seventy-two wheel-chair cases among the wounded servicemen had been guests at the Yankee-Dodger baseball game at Yankee Stadium. Back in their mess hall, they were chinning about the game, when another wounded man wheeled himself into the hall, accompanied by a nurse. He tried to speak, but the words would not come. Finally, the nurse said it for him.

"What he is trying to tell you," she said, "is that President Roosevelt has just died."

Throughout the city, to thousands of servicemen it was the toughest of blows. The canteens were solemn places. There was no music, no dancing. The men and women just talked. You heard the words "shocking," "great man," "noble soul."

"He has been an inspiration to the men overseas," said a corporal.

"He'll go down in history greater than Washington and Lincoln together," said a merchant seaman.

A boy from Jersey City summed it up.

"I don't want to believe it," he said, "but, if it really has happened, may God bless him!"

Two Foreign Correspondents Describe
the Nazi Death Factories

I HAVE NEVER FELT able to describe my emotional reactions when I first came face to face with indisputable evidence of Nazi brutality and ruthless disregard of every shred of decency." Thus spoke Dwight D. Eisenhower in his book *Crusade in Europe* (1948) about the first horror camp he saw near the town of Gotha. He visited every nook and cranny of the camp because he felt it to be his duty to be in a position from then on to testify at first hand in case there grew up at home the belief that "the stories of Nazi brutality were just propaganda."

Although the pattern of German concentration camps was exposed by Ilya Ehrenburg in a report in *PM* on August 13, 1944, the shocking story was not widely publicized until April, 1945, when the German juggernaut was stopped dead in its tracks by the sledgehammer blows of Allied power. Triumphant armies swarmed onto German soil from both east and west—unlike the end in 1918. Along with the cities that fell into the hands of the Allies were many concentration camps—Buchenwald, Auschwitz, Lublin-Maidanek, Dachau, Belsen, and other hellholes. Men hardened by battle were sickened by the sights, sounds, and stenches horrible beyond belief that they found in these German camps, cruelties so enormous as to be incomprehensible to the human mind.

Gradually it became clear to an appalled world that the Germans had deliberately inaugurated and systematically carried out a policy of genocide —biological warfare against civilians. The idea was to weaken the "inferior" peoples of Europe—Jews, Poles, Czechs, Frenchmen, Russians—so that even if Germany lost the war she would possess the necessary biological base for recovery and regeneration while the "inferior" folk were slaughtered in a campaign of terror and brutality unprecedented in the annals of civilization. This was not wartime propaganda, but diabolical atrocity clearly substantiated by camera and pen.

Who killed these people? It was the Nazis, said every German. And where were the Nazis? There were no Nazis left in Germany. It was always some other Fritz.

One of the worst of the Nazis death factories was at Buchenwald, near Weimar, celebrated as the home of German culture and famous because of its rich literary associations—Goethe, Schiller, Herder, and Wieland. The first prisoners to arrive at this camp came from Sachsenburg and Lichtenburg. In May and June, 1938, the death rate was ten per cent. After the German counselor von Rath was shot in Paris, some 12,500 Jews were transported to Buchenwald. When an attempt was made on the life of Hitler, twenty-one Jews were selected arbitrarily at Buchenwald and shot to death, while all other Jews were kept in darkness for three days without food. A thousand Poles were sent to the camp in August, 1940, of whom only three hundred survived the first five months. All had been murdered. During the summer of 1941, 104 prisoners were murdered by injections of evipan-natrium.

Buchenwald was liberated by the Eightieth Division on April 10, 1945. A few days later, on April 16, Gene Currivan sent a report to *The New York Times* of a forced tour of Weimar Germans to view the horrors of the death factory. Currivan's story has something of the macabre quality of Dante's *Inferno*.

Forced Tour at Buchenwald, by Gene Currivan

The New York Times, April 18, 1945

BUCHENWALD, APRIL 16, 1945—German civilians—1200 of them—were brought from the neighboring city of Weimar today to see for themselves the horror, brutality, and human indecency perpetrated against their "neighbors" at the infamous Buchenwald concentration camp. They saw sights that brought tears to their eyes, and scores of them, including German nurses, just fainted away.

They saw more than 20,000 nondescript prisoners, many of them barely living, who were all that remained of the normal complement of 80,000. The Germans were able to evacuate the others before we overran the place on April 10.

There were 32,705 that the "visiting" Germans didn't see, although they saw some of their bodies. It was this number that had been murdered since the camp was established in July, 1937. There was a time when the population reached more than 110,000, but the average was always below that. It included doctors, professors, scientists, statesmen, army officers, diplomats, and an assortment of peasants and merchants from all over Europe and Asia.

There was a group of British officers among those left behind and one of seven French generals, but this was obviously an oversight in the great confusion that followed the news of our approach.

Five generals died and one escaped. This government-controlled camp was considered second only to that at Dachau, near Munich, as the world's worst atrocity center.

It had its gallows, torture rooms, dissection rooms, modern crematoria, laboratories where fiendish experiments were made on living human beings, and its sections where people were systematically starved to death.

This correspondent made a tour of the camp today and saw everything herein described. The statistics and an account of the events that happened before our troops liberated the camp were obtained from a special committee of prisoners, some of whom had been in the camp since its inception and others who had been German prisoners for twelve years. Their information was documented and in most cases confirmed by the records.

This story has already been told in part, but not until today has the full import of the atrocities been completely felt.

One of the first things that the German civilian visitors saw as they passed through the gates and into the interior of the camp was a display of "parchment." This consisted of large pieces of human flesh on which were elaborate tattooed markings. These strips had been collected by a German doctor who was writing a treatise on tattoos, and also by the twenty-eight-year-old wife of the *Standartenführer,* or commanding officer.* This woman, according to prisoners, was an energetic sportswoman who, back in Brandenburg, used to ride to hounds. She had a mania for unusual tattoos, and whenever a prisoner arrived who had a rare marking on his body, she would indicate that that trophy would make a valuable addition to her collection.

In addition to the "parchments" were two large table lamps, with parchment shades also made of human flesh.

The German people saw all this today, and they wept. Those who didn't weep were ashamed. They said they didn't know about it, and maybe they didn't, because the camp was restricted to Army personnel, but there it was right at their back doors for eight years.

The visitors stood in lines, one group at a time passing by the table on which the exhibits were displayed. A German-speaking American sergeant explained from an adjacent jeep

what they were witnessing, while all around them were thousands of liberated "slaves" just looking on. Even the barracks roof was crowded with them. They watched silently. Some of them looked as if they were about to die, but this assemblage of "slaves" constituted the more healthy elements of the camp.

In barracks farther down the line were three thousand sick who could not move and 4800 aged who were unable to leave their squalid quarters. In addition, there were untold hundreds just roaming around, not knowing where they were or what was going on.

There were human skeletons who had lost all likeness to anything human. Most of them had become idiots, but they still had the power of locomotion. Those in the sick bay were beyond all help. They were packed into three-tier bunks, which ran to the roof of the barnlike barracks. They were dying there, and no one could do anything about it.

The German visitors were to see them, too—and much more—but at the moment they were merely seeing "Exhibit A" and fainting.

Some Germans were skeptical at first, as if this show had been staged for their benefit, but they were soon convinced. Even as they had milled along from one place to another, their own countrymen, who had been prisoners there, told them the story. Men went white and women turned away. It was too much for them.

These persons, who had been fed on Nazi propaganda since 1933, were beginning to see the light. They were seeing with their own eyes what no quantity of American propaganda

---

* Ilse Koch, who again attracted world-wide attention in 1948, when her sentence of life imprisonment was reduced to four years by a U. S. Army review board. This gentle treatment of the notorious "Bitch of Buchenwald" aroused deep resentment all over the world.

could convince them of. Here was what their own government had perpetrated.

But they hadn't seen anything yet. In a barracks building in front of them was a scientific laboratory where captured scientists worked with material supplied by their overlords. There were shelves of bottles filled with various organs of the human body. In one was half a human head. It had been cut longitudinally to show all its component parts. This head once belonged to a prisoner, as did all the other human parts so displayed. In another room were a dozen death masks, skulls, and shrunken human heads. A Czechoslovak scientist and surgeon who worked in the laboratory told us the history of each part, each head, each mask—because he had known the human beings to which they belonged. Some had been his own countrymen.

The German visitors saw this, too.

And then they were taken to another laboratory, where victims had been injected with typhus so that Germany could have typhus serum. There were still a score of "patients" who were still alive, although the Polish doctor left behind, who had been forced to give these injections even to his own people, said the death rate had been ninety-eight per cent.

This sight was too much for many German housewives, especially a little farther on, where only the children were kept. One nine-year-old boy, who had had only the first few injections, seemed quite chipper. He was Andor Gutman, a Hungarian Jew of Budapest. He had been in the camp three years. When asked where his parents were, he replied, without any emotion: "My father was killed and my mother was burned to death."

As one watched the Germans filing out of this building there was hardly a dry eye, although some tried to maintain their composure. There was real horror ahead, but some of them just couldn't go on.

From there they were taken to the living quarters. The stench, filth, and misery here defied description. Those human wrecks standing in the corridor were beyond the stage where any amount of hospitalization could restore them to normal, while others peering helplessly from their bunks would be fortunate when they died.

There was a still-lower grade in another barracks, where the prisoners were alive but could not rouse themselves. They were living skeletons. This was Barracks 58, and it was from here that they were taken to the crematory. This was the end of the road, and for them it was probably a godsend. The Germans saw this, too— and there was more to come.

The next exhibit was the most ghastly of all, although it was merely the disposal of the dead.

In a little one-story red brick building, with a red tile roof, was a crematory with the most modern ovens that science can provide. But before you enter, you see a trailer stacked high with withered, starved, naked bodies. A few moments ago you saw the same thing, but those still had life in them. On top of the pile was a big robust body, fully clothed. This one had been murdered brutally.

Next to him was the body of an SS guard who had hanged himself on the day of our arrival. Former prisoners who had felt the lash of his whip cheerfully pointed out his body, and it was easy to identify because it had one stump leg.

In the crematory itself were two batteries of three ovens, each prominently marked with the makers' name

—J. A. Topf & Söhne, Erfurt. This concern customarily manufactured baking ovens. These ovens were of extremely modern design and heated by coke. Narrow-gauge tracks were built into the concrete floor, and over these traveled steel contrivances resembling stretchers. Each oven had the remains of at least two bodies that had not yet been sifted into the chamber below. On a table near by were urns for the ashes. They looked like flowerpots and were packed within metal containers, which, in turn, were packed in cardboard boxes for shipment to relatives. The names on the boxes, however, indicated that only Germans' remains were shipped.

Diminishing columns of German civilians also saw this. Then they were taken to the rear of the building, where there was a gallows equipped for hanging five persons at a time. Just beyond was a pile of ashes from the furnaces.

The basement of the building was a torture chamber, where victims were forced to stand on low chairs, place a rope through a ring high on the wall, and fasten the noose around their necks. The next victim got the job of kicking the chair from under them.

The next exhibit was the dissection room, adjacent to the crematory. This was a small, well-equipped cubicle with a white tile operating table and cabinets filled with surgical instruments. On hooks were several rubber aprons, and on the floor piles of prisoners' clothing. This was the room where the original owners of the "parchments" had been stripped of their skin.

Before Buchenwald obtained its elaborate crematories, prisoners who no longer could work were sent to Auschwitz to die or be killed in gas chambers. Auschwitz also had great furnaces. Reliable statements claim that five thousand were disposed of there in three days. It was also at Auschwitz that Jewish women among the thirty thousand once here at Buchenwald were sent to be exterminated after they had become pregnant. "Aryan" women in this group who were in similar physical condition were sent to Ravensbrueck to have their children.

Buchenwald was bombed from the air on August 24 of last year because it was the site of a V-2 plant, which was just outside the main gates of the camp. It was here that many prisoners worked. The Nazis claimed that this bombing was the excuse for the murder of the German Communist party leader, Ernst Thaelmann, but records show that Thaelmann was never in the camp.

The camp was liberated April 10 by the Eightieth Division. Two days later President Roosevelt died, and the liberated prisoners unfurled a large black flag over the building at the entranceway. It still flies as a memorial to his death and to the dead within the camp. Those still living realize what he tried to do, and they doff their caps every time they see an American uniform.

* * *

SEVERAL DAYS LATER, on April 24, 1945, the Oxford historian, Patrick Gordon-Walker, BBC commentator and chief editor of Radio Luxembourg, went to the concentration camp at Belsen. These next words are his report as broadcast to the United States.

"I Went to Belsen," by Patrick Gordon-Walker

Courtesy War Department, Washington, D.C.

I went to Belsen. It was a vast area surrounded by barbed wire. The whole thing was being guarded by Hungarian guards. They had been in the German Army and are now immediately and without hesitation serving us. They are saving us a large number of men for the time being. Outside the camp, which is amidst bushes, pines, and heather, all fairly recently planted, were great notices in red letters: DANGER—TYPHUS.

We drove into what turned out to be a great training camp, a sort of Aberdeen, where we found the officers and Oxfordshire Yeomanry. They began to tell us about the concentration camp.

It lies south of the training area and is behind its own barbed wire. The Wehrmacht is not allowed near it. It was entirely guarded by SS men and women. This is what I discovered about the release of the camp that happened about the fifteenth. I got this story from Derek Sington, political officer, and from officers and men of Oxfordshire Yeomanry.

Typhus broke out in the camp, and a truce was arranged so that we could take the camp over. The Germans originally had proposed that we should by-pass the camp. In the meanwhile, thousands and thousands of people would have died and been shot. We refused these terms, and demanded the withdrawal of the Germans and the disarmament of the SS guards. Some dozen SS men and women were left behind under the command of Higher Sturmführer Kramer, who had been at Auschwitz. Apparently they had been told all sorts of fairy tales about the troops, that they could go on guarding, and that we would let them free and so forth.

We only had a handful of men so far, and the SS stayed there that night. The first night of liberty, many hundreds of people died of joy.

Next day some men of the Yeomanry arrived. The people crowded around them, kissing their hands and feet—and dying from weakness. Corpses in every state of decay were lying around, piled up on top of each other in heaps. There were corpses in the compound in flocks. People were falling dead all around, people who were walking skeletons. One woman came up to a soldier who was guarding the milk store and doling the milk out to children, and begged for milk for her baby. The man took the baby and saw that it had been dead for days, black in the face and shriveled up. The woman went on begging for milk. So he poured some on the dead lips. The mother then started to croon with joy and carried the baby off in triumph. She stumbled and fell dead in a few yards. I have this story and some others on records spoken by the men who saw them.

On the sixteenth, Kramer and the SS were arrested. Kramer was taken off and kept in the icebox with some stinking fish of the officers' home. He is now going back to the rear. The rest, men and women, were kept under guard to save them from the inmates. The men were set to work shoveling up the corpses into lorries. About thirty-five thousand corpses were reckoned, more actually than the living. Of the living, there were about thirty thousand.

The SS men were driven and pushed along and made to ride on top of the loaded corpses and then shovel them into their great mass open graves. They were so tired that they fell exhausted amongst the corpses. Jeering crowds collected around them, and they had to be kept under strong guard.

Two men committed suicide in their cells. Two jumped off the lorry and tried to run away and get lost in the crowd. They were shot down. One jumped into a concrete pool of water and was riddled with bullets. The other was brought to the ground, with a shot in the belly.

The SS women were made to cook and carry heavy loads. One of them tried to commit suicide. The inmates said that they were more cruel and brutal than the men. They are all young, in their twenties. One SS woman tried to hide, disguised as a prisoner. She was denounced and arrested.

The camp was so full because people had been brought here from East and West. Some people were brought from Nordhausen, a five-day journey, without food. Many had marched for two or three days. There was no food at all in the camp, a few piles of roots —amidst the piles of dead bodies. Some of the dead bodies were of people so hungry that though the roots were guarded by SS men they had tried to storm them and had been shot down then and there. There was no water, nothing but these roots and some boiled stinking carrots, enough for a few hundred people.

Men and women had fought for these raw, uncooked roots. Dead bodies, black and blue and bloated, and skeletons had been used as pillows by sick people. The day after we took over, seven block leaders, mostly Poles, were murdered by the inmates. Some were still beating the people. We arrested one woman who had beaten another woman with a board. She quite frankly admitted the offense. We are arresting these people.

An enormous buried dump of personal jewelry and belongings was discovered in suitcases. When I went to the camp five days after its liberation, there were still bodies all around. I saw about a thousand.

In one place, hundreds had been shoveled into a mass grave by bulldozers; in another, Hungarian soldiers were putting corpses into a grave that was sixty feet by sixty feet and thirty feet deep. It was almost half full.

Other and similar pits were being dug. Five thousand people had died since we got into the camp. People died before my eyes, scarcely human, moaning skeletons, many of them gone mad. Bodies were just piled up. Many had gashed wounds and bullet marks and terrible sores. One Englishman, who had lived in Ostend, was picked up half dead. It was found that he had a great bullet wound in his back. He could just speak. He had no idea when he had been shot. He must have been lying half unconscious when some SS man shot him as he was crawling about. This was quite common. I walked about the camp. Everywhere was the smell and odor of death. After a few hours you get used to it and don't notice it any more. People have typhus and dysentery.

In one compound I went, I saw women standing up quite naked, washing among themselves. Near by were piles of corpses. Other women suffering from dysentery were defecating in the open and then staggering back, half dead, to their blocks. Some were lying groaning on the ground. One had reverted to the absolute primitive.

A great job had been done in getting water into the camp. It has been pumped in from the outside and carried by hoses all over the camp with frequent outlet points. There are taps of fresh clean water everywhere. Carts with water move around.

The Royal Army Service Corps has also done a good job in getting food in.

I went into the typhus ward, packed thick with people lying in dirty rags of blankets on the floor, groaning and moaning. By the door sat an English Tommy talking to the people and cheering them up. They couldn't understand what he said, and he was continually ladling milk out of a caldron. I collected together some women who could speak English and German and began to make records. An amazing thing is the number who managed to keep themselves clean and neat. All of them said that in a day or two more, they would have gone under from hunger and weakness.

There are three main classes in the camp: the healthy, who have managed to keep themselves decent, but nearly all of these had typhus; then there were the sick, who were more or less cared for by their friends; then there was the vast underworld that had lost all self-respect, crawling around in rags, living in abominable squalor, defecating in the compound, often mad or half mad. By the other prisoners they are called Mussulmen. It is these who are still dying like flies. They can hardly walk on their legs. Thousands still of these cannot be saved, and if they were, they would be in lunatic asylums for the short remainder of their pitiful lives.

There were a very large number of girls in the camp, mostly Jewesses from Auschwitz. They have to be healthy to survive. Over and over again I was told the same story. The parades at which people were picked out arbitrarily for the gas chambers and the crematorium, where many were burned alive. Only a person in perfect health survived. Life and death was a question of pure chance.

Rich Jews arrived with their belongings and were able to keep some. There were soap and perfume and fountain pens and watches. All amidst the chance of sudden, arbitrary death, amidst work commandos from which the people returned to this tomb so dead beat that they were sure to be picked for the gas chamber at the next parade, amidst the most horrible death, filth, and squalor that could be imagined.

People at Auschwitz were saved by being moved away to work in towns like Hamburg and were then moved back to Belsen as we advanced. At Auschwitz every woman had her hair shaven absolutely bald.

I met pretty young girls whose hair was one inch long. They all had their numbers tattooed on their left arm, a mark of honor they will wear all their lives.

One of the most extraordinary things was the women and men—there were only a few—who had kept themselves decent and clean.

On the first day many had on powder and lipstick. It seems the SS stores had been located and looted and boots and clothes had been found. Hundreds of people came up to me with letters, which I have taken and am sending back to London to be posted all over the world. Many have lost all their relatives. "My father and mother were burned. My sister was burned." This is what you hear all the time. The British Army is doing what it can. Units are voluntarily giving up blankets. Fifty thousand arrived while I was there and they are being laundered. Sweets and chocolate and rations have been voluntarily given.

Then we went to the children's hut. The floors had been piled with corpses there had been no time to move. We collected a chorus of Russian girls from twelve to fourteen and Dutch boys and girls from nine to fifteen. They sang songs. The Russian children were very impressive. Clean and quite big children, they had been looked after magnificently amidst starvation. They sang the songs they remembered from before captivity. They looked happy now. The Dutch children had been in camp a long time and were very skinny and pale. We stood with our backs to the corpses, out in the open amidst the pines and the birch trees near the wire fence running around the camp.

Men were hung for hours at a time, suspended by their arms, hands tied behind their back, in Belsen. Beatings in workshops were continuous, and there were many deaths there. Just before I left the camp a crematorium was discovered. A story of Auschwitz was told to me by Helen—and her last name, she didn't remember. She was a Czechoslovak.

When the women were given the chance to go and work elsewhere in the work zones like Hamburg, mothers with children were, in fact, given the choice between their lives and their children's. Children could not be taken along. Many preferred to stay with their children and face certain death. Some decided to leave their children. But it got around amongst the six-year-old children that if they were left there they would at once be gassed. There were terrible scenes between children and their mothers. One child was so angry that though the mother changed her mind and stayed and died, the child would not talk to her.

That night when I got back at about eleven o'clock very exhausted, I saw the Jewish padre again and talked to him as he was going to bed. Suddenly, he broke down completely and sobbed.

The next morning I left this hellhole, this camp. As I left, I had myself deloused and my recording truck as well. To you at home, this is one camp. There are many more. This is what you are fighting. None of this is propaganda. This is the plain and simple truth.

* * *

It was not until some six months later, at the Nuremberg trials, that the world could appreciate fully the unbelievable enormity of the Nazis' crimes. The statistics were overwhelming. At Auschwitz alone, according to the testimony of its commandant, a total of three million persons died —both from gas and from disease.

Some thought that these figures were exaggerated, others claimed that they were too low. But it made no difference. Whatever the exact number of victims, it was only too clear that this was mass murder such as the world had never before seen, and hoped never to see again.

Mussolini and His Mistress, Petacci, Are Dumped Like Carrion on the Piazza Loretto of Milan, the City Where Fascism Was Born

BENITO MUSSOLINI, emotional Latin, egocentric demagogue, imitation Caesar, constructed a house of cards in Italy. Like the legendary toad, he attempted to huff and puff himself and Fascism to world grandeur. He gave Italy—the home of grand opera—the song *Giovinezza,* the myth that her trains ran on time, the weapon of castor oil, the odor of beastliness, and, finally, the odium of defeat.

In his *Glass Houses* (1938), Carleton Beals described how the Fascist dictator, intoxicated by the exuberance of his own verbosity, swayed multitudes with a kind of hypnotic eloquence. "His speaking gestures were compact, strong, but overly affected. He posed his body in driving home his ideas rather than using merely hand dexterity and the hair-pulling effervescence of most Italian orators. His favorite gesture was raising his left shoulder slightly and leaning forward, hands tense and close to the body, a sort of chip-on-the-shoulder attitude. This accentuated his large semibald skull and caused the whites of his eyes to gleam in almost darky fashion."

This Italian of Calvinistic determination and Cromwellian ego was the first of the totalitarian dictators to drink the heady wine of power and he was the first of them to lose it. On April 25, 1945, as the Allies marched on Milan, the Duce, under the protection of the Germans, slipped away northward toward the frontier. Quite by accident, Mussolini, his young mistress, Clara Petacci, and several of his followers were trapped by a squad of partisans in the town of Dongo, on Lake Como. On April 28, Lieutenant Colonel Valerio, a former metalworker and Communist, appeared with an expedition to "apply on the spot the decree of the North Italian Committee of National Liberation against those responsible for the catastrophe into which Italy had been led."

Valerio found Mussolini with his mistress in a bedroom of a farmhouse. Petacci was lying on the bed. Mussolini was up, wearing a brown mackintosh, a cap of the Republican Guard, and a pair of black boots.

When Mussolini expressed surprise at being disturbed, Valerio said quietly: "I have come to free you." Soon the two prisoners were pushed outside the room. Aware now that his life was in danger, Mussolini tried to bribe his captor: "I shall give you an empire." After a short automobile ride, Valerio said: "I heard a noise. I'd better see what it is." A few seconds later he called: "Get out quickly, both of you. Stand at that corner of the wall." With Petacci protesting that "you can't do that!" Valerio pumped bullets into the dictator and his mistress, with the comment: "I execute the will of the Italian people."

What happened after these summary executions was described by Milton Bracker, a correspondent for *The New York Times*. A graduate of the College of the City of New York and a product of the Columbia School of Journalism, Bracker had achieved a reputation for his consistently informative reporting of the North African and Italian fronts. "The greatest moment of my professional life," he wrote later, "was standing in the Piazza Loretto, Milan, on April 29, 1945, literally amid the bodies of Mussolini, Petacci, and the others. That moment, culminating more than two years of war experience, roared into and possessed my spirit, as indeed it must have done to anyone remotely sensitive to classic drama."

"A finish to tyranny as horrible as ever visited on a tyrant"

The New York Times, April 30, 1945

MILAN, APRIL 29, 1945—Benito Mussolini came back last night to the city where his Fascism was born. He came back on the floor of a closed moving van, his dead body flung on the bodies of his mistress and twelve men shot with him. All were executed yesterday by Italian partisans. The story of his final downfall, his flight, his capture, and his execution is not pretty, and its epilogue in the Piazza Loretto here this morning was its ugliest part. It will go down in history as a finish to tyranny as horrible as any ever visited on a tyrant.

At 9:30 A.M. today, Mussolini's body lay on the rim of the mass of corpses, while all around surged a growing mob wild with the desire to have a last look at the man who once was a Socialist editor in this same city. The throng pushed and yelled. Partisans strove to keep them back, but largely in vain. Even a series of shots in the air did not dissuade them.

Mussolini had changed in death, but not enough to be anyone else. His closely shaved head and his bullneck were unmistakable. His body seemed small and a little shrunken, but he was never a tall man. At least one bullet had passed through his head. It had emerged some three inches behind his right ear. There was another small hole nearer his forehead where another bullet seemed to have gone in.

As if he were not dead or dishonored enough, at least two young men in the crowd broke through and aimed kicks at his skull. One glanced off. But the other landed full on his right jaw, and there was a hideous crunch that wholly disfigured the once-proud face.

Mussolini wore the uniform of a squadrist militiaman. It comprised a gray-brown jacket and gray trousers with red and black stripes down the sides. He wore black boots, badly soiled, and the left one hung half off as if his foot were broken. His small eyes were open, and it was perhaps a final irony that this man who had thrust his chin forward for so many official photographs had to have his yellowing face propped up with a rifle butt to turn it into the sun for the only two Allied cameramen on the scene.

When the butt was removed the face flopped back over to the left. Meanwhile I crouched over the body to the left in order not to cut off the sun from his turned face. A group of us had been thrust by the enthusiastic Milanese, who had not yet seen any Americans, right into the circle of death. It was naturally one of the grimmest moments of our lives, but it will at least serve to give absolutely authentic eyewitness accounts.

Mussolini lay with his head on the breast of his mistress, Clara Petacci, who had sought to rise to movie fame through him. Younger even than his daughter, she had been executed with him in a suburb of the village of Como, on the shore of Lake Como, and now she lay in a ruffled white blouse, her dark hair curly and her relative youth apparent even now.

Some counts placed the total number of bodies at eighteen, but that left four unidentified, and even from my vantage point it was impossible to count accurately so tangled a mass of flesh.

New York Times dispatch, April 29, 1945, delayed

The degradation to which the bodies of Mussolini, his mistress, Clara Petacci, and his Fascist followers were subjected this morning did not end in the muddy gutter.

Soon after ten A.M., six of the corpses, including Mussolini's and Signorina Petacci's, were hung by the feet with wire from an exposed steel girder of a former gasoline station a few yards from the original dumping point. Black-lettered white signs bearing their names were plastered above them. Later the bodies were cut down and taken to the morgue, where a crowd gathered all over again, and men, women, and children climbed fences to get a final look.

Ed Kennedy of the Associated Press Breaks the News of the Nazi Surrender

THE LONDON STAFF of the Associated Press was sweating out the peace news in an atmosphere loaded with rumor. The Germans were finished —there was no doubt about it, but when would the flash come through?

At 3:24 P.M. London time (9:24 A.M. Eastern war time), May 7, 1945, one of the many telephones on the main news desk rang. Russell Landstrom, AP man who was herding copy to cable and radio channels, answered it.

"This is Paris calling," came a faint, muffled voice. Then it faded and came back. Landstrom turned the telephone over to Lewis Hawkins.

The dim voice said that Germany had surrendered unconditionally at Reims, Hawkins asked who was calling and was told that it was Morton Gudebrod of the AP Paris staff.

Unfamiliar with Gudebrod's voice, Hawkins began asking for details and authority, when Edward Kennedy, chief of the Paris bureau, broke in to say:

"This is Ed Kennedy, Lew. Germany has surrendered unconditionally. That's official. Make the date Reims, France, and get it out."

Since he was well acquainted with Kennedy's voice, Hawkins jotted down the flash and then called a woman traffic operator to take the call in a dictation booth and copy the story that Kennedy had ready.

Kennedy's voice faded again and again, until ten "takes" had been brought in, copied, edited, and cleared to New York. Then the connection faded entirely and communication was not re-established.

Since Kennedy's dispatch had originated abroad and was only being relayed through London, the British censors raised no questions and passed it. Moreover, they had been given no special instructions on surrender stories.

When the flash reached the AP foreign desk in New York it was held up for eight minutes and then sped through to the Allied world.

News beat or unethical double cross?

The New York Times, May 8, 1945

THE WAR IN EUROPE IS ENDED!
SURRENDER IS UNCONDITIONAL
V-E WILL BE PROCLAIMED TODAY

By Edward Kennedy

REIMS, FRANCE, MAY 7—Germany sur-rendered unconditionally to the Western allies and the Soviet Union at 2:41 A.M. French time today. [This was at 8:41 P.M. Eastern war time, Sunday, May 6, 1945.]

The surrender took place at a little

red schoolhouse * that is the headquarters of General Dwight D. Eisenhower.

The surrender was signed for the Supreme Allied Command by Lieutenant General Walter Bedell Smith, chief of staff for General Eisenhower.

It was also signed by General Ivan Susloparov of the Soviet Union and by General François Sevez for France.

General Eisenhower was not present at the signing, but immediately afterward General Jodl and his fellow delegate, General Admiral Hans Georg Friedeburg, were received by the Supreme Commander.

They were asked sternly if they understood the surrender terms imposed upon Germany and if they would be carried out by Germany.

They answered yes.

Germany, which began the war with a ruthless attack upon Poland, followed by successive aggressions and brutality in concentration camps, surrendered with an appeal to the victors for mercy toward the German people and armed forces.

After having signed the full surrender, General Jodl said he wanted to speak and received leave to do so.

"With this signature," he said in soft-spoken German, "the German people and armed forces are for better or worse delivered into the victor's hands.

"In this war, which has lasted more than five years, both have achieved and suffered more than perhaps any other people in the world."

THIS WAS IT—the end of World War II in Europe!

The observant reader will immediately comment: "What's great about that? Sounds like an ordinary news story to me!" True enough, it was indeed a routine report couched in that terse journalese familiar to every newspaper reader. But judged within the framework of what happened before and after, Kennedy's story assumes quite different proportions. His flash exploded like a bombshell and set off a wild victory celebration throughout the United States and the Allied world. The Associated Press ("we fill the news needs of eight hundred million people") served some thirteen hundred newspapers in the United States alone, nearly all of which printed the dispatch under banner headlines.

For four hours officials in Washington, London, and Moscow were silent. Then the British Ministry of Information announced that Prime Minister Churchill would make a formal V-E Day proclamation at nine A.M. and that King George would speak at three P.M., both Eastern standard time. In Washington it was announced that President Truman would broadcast a statement at the same time, and in Paris that General Charles de Gaulle would address the French people.

By this time it had become clear that Kennedy had scored a beat and that the leak had forced an official announcement. Immediately upon pub-

---

* This was an error which was factually unimportant but irritating to a good reporter. Kennedy informed the editors of this volume: "As I wrote the dispatch, and as it was published in Europe, Eisenhower's headquarters at Reims was described as 'the big red schoolhouse.' (It was a sort of industrial high school, covering a block.) This was changed to 'little red schoolhouse'—presumably by someone on the AP cable desk in New York who had that familiar phrase on his mind. Otherwise, the story was wholly correct."

lication of the dispatch SHAEF (Supreme Headquarters, Allied Expeditionary Forces) suspended the filing facilities of the Associated Press in Europe. It was an unprecedented action, which resulted at once in an outburst of protests. Roy W. Howard, president of the Scripps-Howard newspapers, defended the AP in a letter to President Truman: "I am writing to you as a correspondent in the last war who was pilloried personally and whose organization was condemned unjustly for a legitimate reporting job which, under identical circumstances, I would unhesitatingly repeat.* Six hours and twenty minutes after it had taken its action, SHAEF lifted its ban on the Associated Press, but continued it on all copy submitted by Kennedy.

What had happened? Sixteen reporters, including Kennedy, had been chosen to witness Germany's signing of the unconditional surrender and had been flown to Reims. On the plane Brigadier General Frank Allen, PRO (Public Relations Officer) of SHAEF, had addressed the newsmen: "You represent the press of the world. This story is entirely off the record until the heads of the governments have announced it. I therefore pledge each of you on your honor not to communicate the results of the conference or the fact of its existence until it is released on the order of the Public

---

* Then president of the United Press, Howard in November, 1918, had reported the Armistice of World War I four days before it happened. The two cases were almost an exact parallel, with the exception that Howard's report was wrong and Kennedy's right. On the morning of Thursday, November 6, 1918, Howard learned from Admiral Henry B. Wilson, Commanding Officer of all the United States Naval Forces in France, a bluff old sailor, that the Armistice had been signed. Howard, who had come to Brest with a precious travel order authorizing him to proceed aboard the first transport for New York, immediately dashed off his message:

UNIPRESS
NEW YORK
URGENT ARMISTICE ALLIES GERMANY SIGNED SMORNING HOSTILITIES CEASED TWO
SAFTERNOON SEDAN TAKEN SMORNING BY AMERICANS
HOWARD
SIMMS

No French censor ever passed on the message, for all of them to a man were in the streets, celebrating with the rest of the population. Howard later described the scene at Brest: "Doughboys, gobs, poilus, and hundreds of French girls and women who seemed to have sprung from the earth marched and danced, arms entwined, as they sang lustily the popular war songs." French shopkeepers began passing free bottles of wine to the crowd, an act which was to the American doughboys almost as sensational as the Armistice itself.

Howard had no idea that he had a beat. Entering a restaurant, he was appalled when a naval orderly rushed up to him and gave him a message from Admiral Wilson stating that the first dispatch was "unconfirmable." Howard immediately sent a second bulletin correcting the original error. Although it was filed approximately two hours after the first one, for some reason it was not delivered to the United Press in New York until shortly before noon of the following day.

It was too late, anyhow. The news had traveled with the speed of lightning. "Telephone exchanges became madhouses," Howard wrote. "Telegraph offices were swamped. Offices and businesses were deserted. New York's luncheon crowd never went back to business. Impromptu parades were started and grew to gigantic proportions." America awoke the next morning with probably the greatest headache in history.

The official signing was not announced until November 11. The public did not mind the premature news, but newsmen who had been scooped denounced Howard as a traitor to his country and as "the greatest faker in the long annals of journalism."

Relations Director of SHAEF." Apparently the news was to be synchronized in Washington, London, and Moscow.

On the return trip to Paris General Allen suggested that the correspondents write their stories in the plane in order to have them all ready for the censor when they hit Paris. A minute after they arrived Allen told them that someone "higher up" had ordered the stories held. When he heard the Absie (the Office of War Information's American Broadcasting Station in Europe) broadcast the surrender story, Kennedy went to an Army telephone and put in his call for London.*

The AP story touched off a violent controversy among newsmen, with Kennedy taking a merciless tongue-lashing from outraged reporters. As the hours flew by he was pushed further and further into the doghouse. The next day fifty-four correspondents accredited to SHAEF addressed a bitter letter to General Eisenhower: "We have respected the confidence placed in us by SHAEF and as a result have suffered the most disgraceful, deliberate, and unethical double cross in the history of journalism." Among the signers were such respected names as Mark S. Watson (Baltimore *Sun*), Edward W. Beattie, Jr. (United Press), Charles Collingwood (Columbia Broadcasting System), Carl Levin (*New York Herald Tribune*), and Harold Callendar, Drew Middleton, Gladwin Hill, and F. Raymond Daniell (*The New York Times*).

One American newspaper wrote that it "cannot condone Kennedy's broken faith. The newspaper profession cannot exist unless it has the confidence of the people with whom it deals." William L. Shirer noted in his *End of a Berlin Diary* (1947): "The stink about the AP's scoop is growing. . . . A poor scoop to boast about, it seems to me. . . . When the press of America thinks a headline and a scoop more important than its word of honor, then its hard-won freedom will have become an awful mockery and sooner or later the people will know it."

Other newspapers made a spirited defense of Kennedy. One said: "The AP lived up to the highest traditions of the American press." Another said: "Mr. Kennedy's now historic news 'beat' is no stigma: it is a distinction." Newsman A. J. Liebling, himself one of the great reporters of World War II, wrote that it just goes to show that "if you are smart enough you can kick yourself in the seat of the pants, grab yourself by the back of the collar, and throw yourself out on the sidewalk. This is an axiom that I hope will be taught to future students of journalism as Liebling's Law." The only parallel, said Liebling, was the case of Harold the Saxon, who was shipwrecked in the territory of William of Normandy at a time when Edward the Confessor was an old man. "William, taking Harold into protective custody, made him swear not to claim the English throne after Edward died, but when Harold got home he cocked a snook at William. Anglo-Saxon

---

* A. J. Liebling: "I suspect that that part of the other boys' indignation was because they had forgotten about that particular telephone line."

historians have since expressed a good deal of sympathy for Harold's point of view, but the Church held with William."

It is clear that had Kennedy refused to promise anything on the plane he would have made certain of missing the great event, which no newsman in his right mind would have done. Later he claimed that he had never promised to keep his mouth shut until it was opened officially and that instead of violating a fundamental tenet in journalism's code of ethics, he was proud of what he had done. One reporter quoted him as saying that the pledge should not have been exacted and that he did not feel bound by it. "My only pledge was not to break the story until after the surrender was signed. There was no security involved. I was simply doing my job and I was not interested in whether or not I had a beat." Another reporter insisted that far from imperiling the lives of any Allied soldiers, Kennedy had probably saved a few, because his prompt announcement made the shooting stop.

Fascinated by the controversy, the editors asked Kennedy, now managing editor of the Santa Barbara (California) *News-Press,* for his version of the story. Here it is:

After first saying that the news would be released without delay for its possible effect in saving lives, the Public Relations division of the Supreme Allied Command later informed correspondents that orders had been received "from a high political level" to withhold the news until three P.M. the following day, May 8.

The request for this delay was made by the Russians, who wanted to hold a surrender ceremony of their own in Berlin. This second surrender was meaningless, since Russia had already accepted the German surrender. Its purpose, and that of the request to suppress the news of the surrender until the Berlin ceremony had been held, was to further Soviet propaganda plans for making it appear that Russia had obtained the surrender of Germany on the eastern front, almost unaided by the war effort of the Western Allies.

Despite the instructions from Washington, the Supreme Command then ordered the German government to announce the surrender "by all possible means." This was to make sure that all German units and civilians would receive the news and cease fighting; German army communications were too disrupted to be relied upon. Shortly after noon on May 7 the German government, in compliance with this order, publicly announced the unconditional surrender over the radio at Flensburg, Denmark.

I then immediately informed the censorship that since the Supreme Command had itself released the news, I felt no longer obligated to accept the gag imposed on the correspondents. I also pointed out that the censorship in this case was admittedly political, in violation of the assurance that Allied censorship would be limited to matters of military security. I sent the story.

As we have seen, in doing so Kennedy incurred the wrath of the headquarters bureaucracy and of correspondents beaten on the story. On the other hand, he won overwhelming commendation at home, where the people felt that they had the right to know the news. The Associated Press did not support him, and he was discredited as a war correspondent. He obtained a hearing for the first time a year later. This resulted in the restoration of his credentials by General Eisenhower and his eligibility for reaccreditation if he should choose to apply.

After this vindication *Editor and Publisher* commented editorially: "Had we been in Kennedy's position we are inclined to believe we would have attempted to do just as he did. Kennedy's name has been cleared and we believe that his story will go down in the books as one of the greatest journalistic beats in history." *

May 8, 1945, was V-E Day in the United States, Great Britain, and Russia. But not on Okinawa! Here is the moving report sent that day from Okinawa via Navy radio by Gordon Cobbledick, war correspondent of the *Cleveland Plain Dealer*.

V-E Day? The enemy on Okinawa wouldn't wait

Cleveland Plain Dealer, May 9, 1945

We stood in the rain this morning and heard the voice from San Francisco, only half believing. There had been so many false reports. But this seemed to be the McCoy.

"Confirmed by General Eisenhower's headquarters," the voice was saying. "Prime Minister Churchill proclaimed May 8 as V-E Day."

Artillery thundered and the planes roared low overhead and we couldn't hear all that the voice was saying.

"President Truman . . . Marshal Stalin announced . . . the Canadian government at Ottawa . . . unauthor-

ized announcement . . . American news agency . . ."

So this was V-E Day. It was V-E Day in the United States and Great Britain and Russia, but on Okinawa the ambulances skidded through the sticky red mud and bounced over rutted, rocky coral roads. Some of the men who rode them gritted their teeth behind bloodless lips and let no cry escape them. Some stared skyward through eyes that were dull with the look of men to whom nothing mattered greatly. Some screamed with pain that the morphine couldn't still.

* That should have ended the matter, but it didn't. On April 12, 1948, Senator Arthur Capper of Kansas submitted to the Senate and Representative Edith Nourse Rogers of Massachusetts introduced in the House bills awarding a special decoration of a journalism medal to the group of war correspondents who witnessed the unconditional surrender of the Germans at Reims and who "kept the military secret of that event in the interest of saving American lives." Both Senator Capper and Representative Rogers spoke of the "great temptation to release the historic story without authorization." These correspondents "displayed the highest ideals of responsible journalism and brought credit to their profession and security to their respective countries by keeping inviolate the pledge of confidence and military secrecy imposed upon them."

Defenders of Kennedy promptly pointed out that this was the first proposal in the history of American journalism to decorate reporters who had been beaten on a vital news story.

And some lay very quiet under ponchos that covered their faces.

It was V-E Day all over the world, but on Okinawa two doughboys lay flat behind a jagged rock and one said, "I know where the bastard is and I'm going to get him."

He raised his head and looked and then he stood, half crouched, and brought his Garand into position. When he tumbled backward the rifle clattered on the rocks. The boy looked up and smiled sheepishly and said, "I hurt my arm when I fell," and the blood gushed from his mouth and ran in a quick torrent over the stubble of beard on his young face, and he was dead.

It was V-E Day at home, but on Okinawa men shivered in foxholes half filled with water and waited for the command to move forward across the little green valley that was raked from both ends by machine-gun fire.

It was V-E Day, but on Okinawa a staff officer sat looking dully at the damp earthen floor of his tent. A young lieutenant, his green field uniform plastered with mud, stood awkwardly beside him.

"I was with him, sir," the lieutenant said. "It was a machine-gun bullet, sir. He never knew what hit him." He paused. "He was a good marine, sir."

The staff officer said, "He was the only son we had."

On Okinawa a flame-throwing tank lumbered across a narrow plain toward an enemy pillbox. From a cave a gun spat viciously and the tank

stopped and burst into fire. When the crewmen clambered out machine guns chattered and they fell face forward in the mud and were still.

It was V-E Day everywhere, but on Okinawa the forests of white crosses grew and boys who had hardly begun to live died miserably in the red clay of this hostile land.

It was a day of celebration, but on Okinawa the war moved on. Not swiftly, for swift war cannot be waged against an enemy who burrows underground where bombs and shells and all the instruments of quick destruction can't touch him. Not gloriously, for there is little glory in any war and none at all in cold and mud. But the enemy wouldn't wait and the war moved on.

It was V-E Day, and on Okinawa a soldier asked, "What are they going to do back in the States—get drunk and forget about us out here?"

Another said, "So they'll open the race tracks and turn on the lights and give people all the gas they want and the hell with us."

Another said, "They'll think the war is over and they'll quit their jobs and leave us to fight these bastards with pocketknives."

You told them it wasn't so. You said the people would have their day of celebration and then would go grimly back to the job of producing what is needed so desperately out here.

And you hoped to God that what you were saying was the truth.

* * *

William L. Laurence of *The New York Times* Sees

Atom Bomb III Dropped Over Nagasaki

IT WAS THE MORNING of July 16, 1945. A great cloud of cosmic fire and smoke, the atomic version of the old Arabian story about a poor fisherman and a jinni imprisoned in a bottle, rose more than eight miles to the stratosphere over the New Mexico desert. At long last the secret weapon to put a quick end to World War II was found. Man, pigmy though he was, had invaded the sacred precincts of the cosmos.

Just fifty years earlier, the French physicist Henri Becquerel had observed that a piece of uranium left in his desk drawer caused the blackening of some photographic plates near by. This peculiar property of uranium to emit radiation was called radioactivity, and inspired the chief advance of nuclear physics during the last half century. To buttress the experimental evidence, Max Planck's quantum theory (1900) and Albert Einstein's special theory of relativity (1905) provided formulae to determine the amount of energy released by the atom. The answer was staggering, and already physicists began talking about atomic explosions.

To split the atom and turn loose the energy held within its core Rutherford, Bohr, Chadwick, Lisa Meitner, Frisch, and other great physicists, all bent their efforts. In 1932 Cockroft and Walton constructed in the physics laboratory at Cambridge University, England, an atom smasher, later improved by the cyclotron of E. O. Lawrence of the University of California. As early as 1934 Fermi, then at the University of Rome, began bombarding uranium with neutrons. His experiments paid off in the fall of 1938, when Hahn and Strassman, at the Kaiser Wilhelm Institute in Berlin, split the uranium atom, the full significance of which event was first revealed by Lisa Meitner and Frisch at Copenhagen. Working in Columbia University's physics laboratory, atom-smashers Fermi and Dunning elaborated these experiments in 1939. Then the probability of setting off a chain reaction was soon established by both Joliot-Curie and Szilard.

The international race was on to produce the atomic bomb. Spurred on by Einstein, F. D. R. set in motion a giant project which ultimately expended two billion dollars. On December 2, 1942, a controlled chain reaction was first produced on the University of Chicago's campus. Finally, the giant task of assembling the bomb was entrusted to J. Robert Oppenheimer, who directed operations at Los Alamos.

F. D. R.'s gamble paid off. On August 6, 1945, a B-29, a giant American Superfortress, flew over Hiroshima, a Japanese city of some 350,000 people, and dropped a small bomb with the destructive force of twenty thousand tons of TNT. Half of the city was wiped out in raging clouds of dust and smoke. One hundred thousand were killed.

What actually happened at Hiroshima was revealed a year later by John Hersey in a sensational thirty-thousand-word story, to which the editors of *The New Yorker* devoted their entire issue of August 31, 1946.* Hersey, who had only recently won acclaim for his moving and sensitive exposé of American military rule in Italy in his best-selling novel, *A Bell for Adano,* reported the experiences of six survivors at the moment when the atomic bomb flashed over Hiroshima. "They still wonder why they lived when so many others died," Hersey commented. The Reverend Mr. Kiyoshi Tanimoto, Methodist pastor, was saved because he was two miles from the center of the explosion, although houses collapsed all about him. Mrs. Hatsuyo Nakamura, a tailor's widow, 1350 yards from the center of the explosion, "seemed to fly into the next room over the raised sleeping platform, pursued by parts of the house." Dr. Masakayu Fujii, on the porch of his private hospital, 1550 yards away, was "squeezed tightly by two long timbers in a V across his chest, like a morsel suspended between two huge chopsticks." Jesuit Father Wilhelm Kleinsorge, stunned by the flash, found himself wandering around in the mission's vegetable garden in his underwear. His housekeeper near by kept crying in Japanese, "Our Lord Jesus, have pity on us!" The only physician in the Red Cross hospital to escape injury was Dr. Terufumi Sasaki, surgeon. Soon began an invasion of his hospital by maimed and dying citizens "that was to make Dr. Sasaki forget his private nightmare for a long, long time." Miss Toshi Sasaki, clerk in a tinworks plant 1600 yards from the center of the catastrophe, was crushed when her room suddenly collapsed, and her left leg was pinned down by a falling bookcase. "There, in the tin factory, in the first moment of the atomic age, a human being was crushed by books."

Hiroshima was instantly obscured by a huge rolling cloud of smoke and dust. Huge drops of water the size of marbles began to fall—drops of condensed moisture falling from the tower of dust, heat, and fission fragments miles above the stricken town. Streets were littered with parts of houses that had collapsed and sheets of flame whipped through the city. Thousands fled in panic. The eyebrows of some were burned off and skin hung from their faces and hands. Others, because of pain, held their arms as if carrying something in both hands. Some were vomiting as they walked. There was a strong odor of ionization, an "electric smell" given off by the bomb's fission. When the dust settled, an area of three square miles was completely leveled except for a few reinforced concrete walls.

Three days later another, improved bomb was released on Nagasaki,

---

* As it was found impracticable to include the complete story here, neither the editors nor Mr. Hersey felt that the narrative should be subjected to the hazards of excerpting. We do, however, subscribe to Henry Seidel Canby's comparison of the genius of Hersey's report with the pioneer journalism of Defoe.

with even more terrible results. The newsman who covered this assignment was born in Lithuania, educated at Harvard, and already nationally renowned as a science reporter. In 1937 William L. Laurence had been awarded a Pulitzer Prize for his coverage of the Harvard Tercentenary Conference of Arts and Science. He had followed the developments in nuclear physics with keen interest. In 1940 he wrote the first comprehensive story on the significance of the discovery of uranium fission as an explosive and a source of power. Selected by the head of the atom-bomb project to visit the secret war plants and to write a series of reports following the release of the bomb, Laurence was the only journalist present at the first test of the atom bomb in New Mexico, July 16, 1945, and was an eyewitness on the mission that dropped Bomb III on Nagasaki. For his account of that mission and a subsequent series of ten articles on the development of the bomb Laurence was awarded a second Pulitzer Prize.

A thousand Old Faithful geysers rolled into one blast

The New York Times, September 9, 1945

WITH THE ATOMIC-BOMB MISSION TO JAPAN, AUGUST 9 (Delayed)—We are on our way to bomb the mainland of Japan. Our flying contingent consists of three specially designed B-29 Superforts, and two of these carry no bombs. But our lead plane is on its way with another atomic bomb, the second in three days, concentrating in its active substance an explosive energy equivalent to twenty thousand and, under favorable conditions, forty thousand tons of TNT.

We have several chosen targets. One of these is the great industrial and shipping center of Nagasaki, on the western shore of Kyushu, one of the main islands of the Japanese homeland.

I watched the assembly of this man-made meteor during the past two days and was among the small group of scientists and Army and Navy representatives privileged to be present at the ritual of its loading in the Superfort last night, against a background of threatening black skies torn open at intervals by great lightning flashes.

It is a thing of beauty to behold, this "gadget." Into its design went millions of man-hours of what is without doubt the most concentrated intellectual effort in history. Never before had so much brain power been focused on a single problem.

This atomic bomb is different from the bomb used three days ago with such devastating results on Hiroshima.

I saw the atomic substance before it was placed inside the bomb. By itself it is not at all dangerous to handle. It is only under certain conditions, produced in the bomb assembly, that it can be made to yield up its energy, and even then it gives only a small fraction of its total contents—a fraction, however, large enough to produce the greatest explosion on earth.

The briefing at midnight revealed the extreme care and the tremendous amount of preparation that had been made to take care of every detail of the mission, to make certain that the atomic bomb fully served the purpose for which it was intended. Each target in turn was shown in detailed maps and in aerial photographs. Every detail of the course was rehearsed—navigation, altitude, weather, where to land in emergencies. It came out that the Navy had submarines and rescue craft, known as Dumbos and Superdumbos, stationed at various strategic points in the vicinity of the targets, ready to rescue the fliers in case they were forced to bail out.

The briefing period ended with a moving prayer by the chaplain. We then proceeded to the mess hall for the traditional early-morning breakfast before departure on a bombing mission.

A convoy of trucks took us to the supply building for the special equipment carried on combat missions. This included the Mae West, a parachute, a lifeboat, an oxygen mask, a flak suit, and a survival vest. We still had a few hours before take-off time, but we all went to the flying field and stood around in little groups or sat in jeeps talking rather casually about our mission to the Empire, as the Japanese home islands are known hereabouts.

In command of our mission is Major Charles W. Sweeney, twenty-five, of 124 Hamilton Avenue, North Quincy, Massachusetts. His flagship, carrying the atomic bomb, is named *The Great Artiste,* but the name does not appear on the body of the great silver ship, with its unusually long, four-bladed, orange-tipped propellers. Instead, it carries the number 77, and someone remarks that it was "Red"

Grange's winning number on the gridiron.

We took off at 3:50 this morning and headed northwest on a straight line for the Empire. The night was cloudy and threatening, with only a few stars here. and there breaking through the overcast. The weather report had predicted storms ahead part of the way but clear sailing for the final and climactic stages of our odyssey.

We were about an hour away from our base when the storm broke. Our great ship took some heavy dips through the abysmal darkness around us, but it took these dips much more gracefully than a large commercial air liner, producing a sensation more in the nature of a glide than a "bump," like a great ocean liner riding the waves except that in this case the air waves were much higher and the rhythmic tempo of the glide was much faster.

I noticed a strange eerie light coming through the window high above the navigator's cabin, and as I peered through the dark all around us I saw a startling phenomenon. The whirling giant propellers had somehow become great luminous disks of blue flame. The same luminous blue flame appeared on the plexiglas windows in the nose of the ship, and on the tips of the giant wings. It looked as though we were riding the whirlwind through space on a chariot of blue fire.

It was, I surmised, a surcharge of static electricity that had accumulated on the tips of the propellers and on the di-electric material of the plastic windows. One's thoughts dwelt anxiously on the precious cargo in the invisible ship ahead of us. Was there any likelihood of danger that this heavy electric tension in the atmosphere all about us might set it off?

I expressed my fears to Captain Bock, who seems nonchalant and unperturbed at the controls. He quickly reassured me.

"It is a familiar phenomenon seen often on ships. I have seen it many times on bombing missions. It is known as St. Elmo's fire."

On we went through the night. We soon rode out the storm and our ship was once again sailing on a smooth course straight ahead, on a direct line to the Empire.

Our altimeter showed that we were traveling through space at a height of seventeen thousand feet. The thermometer registered an outside temperature of thirty-three degrees below zero Centigrade, about thirty below Fahrenheit. Inside our pressurized cabin the temperature was that of a comfortable air-conditioned room and a pressure corresponding to an altitude of eight thousand feet. Captain Bock cautioned me, however, to keep my oxygen mask handy in case of emergency. This, he explained, might mean either something going wrong with the pressure equipment inside the ship or a hole through the cabin by flak.

The first signs of dawn came shortly after five o'clock. Sergeant Curry, of Hoopeston, Illinois, who had been listening steadily on his earphones for radio reports, while maintaining a strict radio silence himself, greeted it by rising to his feet and gazing out the window.

"It's good to see the day," he told me. "I get a feeling of claustrophobia hemmed in in this cabin at night."

He is a typical American youth, looking even younger than his twenty years. It takes no mind reader to read his thoughts.

"It's a long way from Hoopeston," I find myself remarking.

"Yep," he replies, as he busies himself decoding a message from outer space.

"Think this atomic bomb will end the war?" he asks hopefully.

"There is a very good chance that this one may do the trick," I assured him, "but if not, then the next one or two surely will. Its power is such that no nation can stand up against it very long." This was not my own view. I had heard it expressed all around a few hours earlier, before we took off To anyone who had seen this manmade fireball in action, as I had less than a month ago in the desert of New Mexico, this view did not sound overoptimistic.

By 5:50 it was really light outside. We had lost our lead ship, but Lieutenant Godfrey, our navigator, informs me that we had arranged for that contingency. We have an assembly point in the sky above the little island of Yakushima, southeast of Kyushu, at 9:10. We are to circle there and wait for the rest of our formation.

Our genial bombardier, Lieutenant Levy, comes over to invite me to take his front-row seat in the transparent nose of the ship, and I accept eagerly. From that vantage point in space, seventeen thousand feet above the Pacific, one gets a view of hundreds of miles on all sides, horizontally and vertically. At that height the vast ocean below and the sky above seem to merge into one great sphere.

I was on the inside of that firmament, riding above the giant mountains of white cumulus clouds, letting myself be suspended in infinite space. One hears the whirl of the motors behind one, but it soon becomes insignificant against the immensity all around and is before long swallowed by it. There comes a point where space also swallows time and one lives through eternal moments filled with an oppressive loneliness, as though all life had suddenly vanished from the earth and you are the only one left, a lone survivor traveling endlessly through interplanetary space.

My mind soon returns to the mission I am on. Somewhere beyond these vast mountains of white clouds ahead of me there lies Japan, the land of our enemy. In about four hours from now one of its cities, making weapons of war for use against us, will be wiped off the map by the greatest weapon ever made by man: In one tenth of a millionth of a second, a fraction of time immeasurable by any clock, a whirlwind from the skies will pulverize thousands of its buildings and tens of thousands of its inhabitants.

But at this moment no one yet knows which one of the several cities chosen as targets is to be annihilated. The final choice lies with destiny. The winds over Japan will make the decision. If they carry heavy clouds over our primary target, that city will be saved, at least for the time being. None of its inhabitants will ever know that the wind of a benevolent destiny had passed over their heads. But that same wind will doom another city.

Our weather planes ahead of us are on their way to find out where the wind blows. Half an hour before target time we will know what the winds have decided.

Does one feel any pity or compassion for the poor devils about to die? Not when one thinks of Pearl Harbor and of the Death March on Bataan.

Captain Bock informs me that we are about to start our climb to bombing altitude.

He manipulates a few knobs on his control panel to the right of him, and I alternately watch the white clouds and ocean below me and the altimeter on the bombardier's panel. We reached our altitude at nine o'clock. We were then over Japanese waters, close to their mainland. Lieutenant Godfrey motioned to me to look through his radar scope. Before me was the outline of our assembly point. We shall soon meet our lead ship and proceed to the final stage of our journey.

We reached Yakushima at 9:12 and there, about four thousand feet ahead of us, was *The Great Artiste* with its precious load. I saw Lieutenant Godfrey and Sergeant Curry strap on their parachutes and I decided to do likewise.

We started circling. We saw little towns on the coastline, heedless of our presence. We kept on circling, waiting for the third ship in our formation.

It was 9:56 when we began heading for the coastline. Our weather scouts had sent us code messages, deciphered by Sergeant Curry, informing us that both the primary target as well as the secondary were clearly visible.

The winds of destiny seemed to favor certain Japanese cities that must remain nameless. We circled about them again and again and found no opening in the thick umbrella of clouds that covered them. Destiny chose Nagasaki as the ultimate target.

We had been circling for some time when we noticed black puffs of smoke coming through the white clouds directly at us. There were fifteen bursts of flak in rapid succession, all too low. Captain Bock changed his course. There soon followed eight more bursts of flak, right up to our altitude, but by this time were too far to the left.

We flew southward down the channel and at 11:33 crossed the coastline and headed straight for Nagasaki, about one hundred miles to the west.

Here again we circled until we found an opening in the clouds. It was 12:01 and the goal of our mission had arrived.

We heard the prearranged signal on our radio, put on our arc welder's glasses, and watched tensely the maneuverings of the strike ship about half a mile in front of us.

"There she goes!" someone said.

Out of the belly of *The Great Artiste* what looked like a black object went downward.

Captain Bock swung around to get out of range; but even though we were turning away in the opposite direction, and despite the fact that it was broad daylight in our cabin, all of us became aware of a giant flash that broke through the dark barrier of our arc welder's lenses and flooded our cabin with intense light.

We removed our glasses after the first flash, but the light still lingered on, a bluish-green light that illuminated the entire sky all around. A tremendous blast wave struck our ship and made it tremble from nose to tail. This was followed by four more blasts in rapid succession, each resounding like the boom of cannon fire hitting our plane from all directions.

Observers in the tail of our ship saw a giant ball of fire rise as though from the bowels of the earth, belching forth enormous white smoke rings. Next they saw a giant pillar of purple fire, ten thousand feet high, shooting skyward with enormous speed.

By the time our ship had made another turn in the direction of the atomic explosion the pillar of purple fire had reached the level of our altitude. Only about forty-five seconds had passed. Awe-struck, we watched it shoot upward like a meteor coming from the earth instead of from outer space, becoming ever more alive as it climbed skyward through the white clouds. It was no longer smoke, or dust, or even a cloud of fire. It was a living thing, a new species of being, born right before our incredulous eyes.

At one stage of its evolution, covering millions of years in terms of seconds, the entity assumed the form of a giant square totem pole, with its base about three miles long, tapering off to about a mile at the top. Its bottom was brown, its center was amber, its top white. But it was a living totem pole, carved with many grotesque masks grimacing at the earth.

Then, just when it appeared as though the thing had settled down into a state of permanence, there came shooting out of the top a giant mushroom that increased the height of the pillar to a total of forty-five thousand feet. The mushroom top was even more alive than the pillar, seething and boiling in a white fury of creamy foam, sizzling upward and then descending earthward, a thousand Old Faithful geysers rolled into one.

It kept struggling in an elemental fury, like a creature in the act of breaking the bonds that held it down. In a few seconds it had freed itself from its gigantic stem and floated upward with tremendous speed, its momentum carrying it into the stratosphere to a height of about sixty thousand feet.

But no sooner did this happen when another mushroom, smaller in size than the first one, began emerging out of the pillar. It was as though the decapitated monster was growing a new head.

As the first mushroom floated off into the blue it changed its shape into a flowerlike form, its giant petals curving downward, creamy white outside, rose-colored inside. It still retained that shape when we last gazed at it from a distance of about two hundred miles. The boiling pillar of many colors could also be seen at that distance, a giant mountain of jumbled rainbows, in travail. Much living substance had gone into those rainbows. The quivering top of the pillar was protruding to a great height through the white clouds, giving the appearance of a monstrous prehistoric creature with a ruff around its neck, a fleecy ruff extending in all directions, as far as the eye could see.

*   *   *

IN THE SUMMER OF 1946, at a time when peace had not yet been made, the United States tested the effects of atomic bombing on sea power. On July 1, Bomb IV was dropped over the little crescent-shaped island of Bikini in the Pacific. Here seventy-three lifeless, still, and deserted ghost ships of all types awaited the macabre cloud of an atomic explosion. The results disappointed the man on the street who expected one atomic bomb to sink the entire Bikini fleet, kill all the animals aboard, and create tidal waves of enormous magnitude.

A few weeks later Bomb V was exploded beneath the surface of Bikini Lagoon. This time there was a dreadful toll of ships and animals as a huge geyser spurted up to five thousand feet, giving birth to the now familiar-shaped mushroom cloud.

In an attempt to awaken world opinion to the menace, President Truman's special evaluation committee for study of the Bikini atomic-bomb tests reported that the safety and security of the world in an age of atomic energy depended on elimination of war. The Bikini demonstrations "strongly indicate that future wars employing atomic bombs may well destroy nations and change present standards of civilization." And further: "Distance is the best defense against a weapon combining the terrific explosive power and deadly radioactivity of this bomb." David Bradley reiterated this warning in an eyewitness account of the Bikini tests, appropriately called *No Place to Hide* (1948).

The Japanese Drink Bitter Tea
Aboard the USS *Missouri*

THE WAR SITUATION has developed not necessarily to Japan's advantage." In this masterpiece of understatement Emperor Hirohito informed his people on August 14, 1945, that they would have to endure what was unavoidable and to suffer what was "unsufferable" in order "to pave the way for a grand peace for all the generations to come." Atom Bomb III had helped Hirohito make up his mind.

On September 2, 1945, representatives of the Japanese Imperial General Headquarters signed the instrument of surrender aboard the USS *Missouri* in Tokyo Bay. Sergeant Dale Kramer, staff correspondent for *Yank*, witnessed the ceremonies, and enlivened his account with a grand GI punch line.

V-J Day

Yank, the Army Weekly, October 5, 1945

ABOARD THE USS *Missouri*, TOKYO BAY —For a while it looked as though the proceedings would go off with almost unreasonable smoothness. Cameramen assigned to the formal surrender ceremonies aboard the battleship *Missouri* arrived on time and although every inch of the turrets and housings and life rafts above the veranda deck where the signing was to take place was crowded, no one fell off and broke a collarbone.

The ceremonies themselves even started and were carried on according to schedule. It took a Canadian colonel to bring things back to normal by signing the surrender document on the wrong line.

No one had the heart to blame the colonel, though. A mere colonel was bound to get nervous around so much higher brass.

The other minor flaw in the ceremonial circus was that it was something of an anticlimax. Great historic events probably are always somewhat that way, and this one, to those of us who had taken off three weeks before with the Eleventh Airborne Division from the Philippines, was even more so. We had started out thinking in terms of a sensational dash to the Emperor's palace in Tokyo, only to sweat it out on Okinawa and later off Yokohama.

When it did come, the signing aboard the *Missouri* was a show which lacked nothing in its staging. A cluster of microphones and a long table covered with a green cloth had been placed in the center of the deck. On the table lay the big ledger-size white documents of surrender, bound in brown folders.

The assembly of brass and braid was a thing to see—a lake of gold and silver sparkling with rainbows of decorations and ribbons. British and Australian Army officers had scarlet stripes on their garrison caps and on their collars. The French were more conservative, except for the acres of vivid decorations on their breasts. The stocky leader of the Russian delegation wore gold shoulder boards and red-striped trousers. The Dutch had gold-looped shoulder emblems. The British admirals wore snow-white summer uniforms with shorts and knee-length white stockings. The olive-drab of the Chinese was plain except for ribbons. The least decked-out of all were the Americans. Their hats, except for Admiral Halsey's go-to-hell cap, were gold-braided, but their uniforms were plain suntan. Navy regulations do not permit wearing ribbons or decorations on a shirt.

Lack of time prevented piping anyone over the side, and when General MacArthur, Supreme Commander for the Allied powers, came aboard he strode quickly across the veranda deck and disappeared inside the ship. Like the other American officers, he wore plain suntans. A few minutes later, a gig flying the American flag and operated by white-clad American sailors putted around the bow of the ship. In the gig, wearing formal diplomatic morning attire, consisting of black cutaway coat, and striped pants and stovepipe hat, sat Foreign Minister Mamoru Shigemitsu, leader of the Japanese delegation.

Coming up the gangway, Shigemitsu climbed very slowly because of a stiff left leg, and he limped onto the veranda deck with the aid of a heavy, light-colored cane. Behind him came ten other Japs. One wore a white suit, two more wore formal morning attire, the rest were dressed in pieced-out uniforms of the Jap Army and Navy. They gathered into three rows on the forward side of the green-covered table. The representatives of the Allied powers formed on the other side. When they were arranged, General MacArthur entered and stepped to the microphone.

His words rolled sonorously: "We are gathered here, representatives of the major warring powers, to conclude a solemn agreement whereby peace may be restored." He emphasized the necessity that both victors and vanquished rise to a greater dignity in order that the world may emerge forever from blood and carnage. He declared his firm intention as Supreme Commander to "discharge my responsibility with justice and tolerance while taking all necessary dispositions to insure that the terms of surrender are fully, promptly, and faithfully complied with."

The Japanese stood at attention during the short address, their faces grave, but otherwise showing little emotion. When the representatives of the Emperor were invited to sign, Foreign Minister Shigemitsu hobbled forward, laid aside his silk hat and cane, and lowered himself slowly into a chair. The wind whipped his thin, dark hair as he reached into his pocket for a pen, tested it, then affixed three large Japanese characters to the first of the documents. He had to rise and bend over the table for the others.

The audience was conscious of the historic importance of the pen strokes, but it watched for something else, too.

General MacArthur had promised to present General Wainwright, who had surrendered the American forces at Corregidor and until only a few days before had been a prisoner of war, with the first pen to sign the surrender. Shigemitsu finished and closed his pen and replaced it in his pocket. There could be no objection. He had needed a brush-pen for the Japanese letters.

When the big surrender folders were turned around on the table, General MacArthur came forward to affix his signature as Supreme Commander. He asked General Wainwright and General Percival, who had surrendered the British forces at Singapore, to accompany him. General Mac-Arthur signed the first document and handed the pen to General Wainwright. He used five pens in all, ending up with one from his own pocket.

Sailors have been as avid souvenir collectors in this war as anyone else, but when Admiral Nimitz sat down to sign for the U. S. he used only two pens. After that the representatives of China, the United Kingdom, Russia, Australia, Canada, France, the Netherlands, and New Zealand put down their signatures.

As the big leather document folders were gathered, a GI member of a sound unit recorded a few historic remarks of his own. "Brother," he said, "I hope those are my discharge papers."

* * *

AMONG THE INTERESTED spectators were four Japanese newspapermen, including two reporters, a photographer, and a newsreel cameraman. The factual story written by Masuo Kato, reporter for the Domei agency, was substantially the same as that of Sergeant Kramer, but the former did some heavy thinking while he jotted down his notes, and drank the hot American coffee in very large cups. "To me," Kato wrote, "it was the most impressive event of the day." He saw a vision of the "black ships" of Commodore Perry and what they had meant to Japan. He wondered how many years his country had been set back by this disastrous defeat. This much was clear—there could no longer be any thought of Japan's achieving her destiny through war. Totalitarianism had been tried and it had brought only ruin and destruction. Japan's fault was that she had overlooked the dignity of the individual and the rights of human beings, a lesson that she had learned the hard way. She had asked for trouble and she had gotten a fearful dose of it, enough to discourage her tendency toward blind materialism for some time to come. "We were lacking in a fundamental quality as a people, the understanding of the importance of individual liberty and the will to protect it.

"We now await the will of our new masters," Kato concluded.

Rebecca West and Kingsbury Smith Report on

the Nuremberg Trials and Executions

THE TRIUMPHANT Allies came out of World War II flushed with victory and divided upon all policies except one—the German war criminals were to be punished at long last. An agreement dated August 8, 1945, among the United States, Great Britain, and the Soviet Union to try the leaders was subsequently endorsed by nineteen member states of the United Nations.

The public trial of twenty-two German principals began at Nuremberg in November, 1945. Although special courts had been set up in the past to judge political crimes by extraordinary authority, no such court had ever obtained such universal recognition. Here was in effect the first step in the creation of an international court to judge crimes against peace, against humanity, and against defenseless minorities. The legality of the proceedings troubled many jurists (disturbed by the ex post facto implications of such trials) as well as professional dissenters like George Bernard Shaw. But as it became clear from the carefully compiled testimony of the court how mercilessly the Nazi leaders had treated their victims, fewer and fewer voices were raised against the proceedings. The evidence showed that between five and ten million people had been starved, beaten, and tortured to death in the concentration camps, a crime without parallel in history. At Nuremberg there was a parade of human vice and folly that furnished a devastating commentary on the German weakness for propelling midgets into the seats of the mighty.

What was it like, this arduous and exhausting trial lasting more than a year? Here is a brilliant description of the scene at Nuremberg by Rebecca West, one of the great women journalists of our generation. Her report, which first appeared in *The New Yorker* issue of September 7, 1946, bristles with the Rebecca West trade-mark—reporting in depth, with fine feminine regard for character, situation, and context, extraordinarily acute intuition, and a keen eye for detail.

To Rebecca West, Göring "recalls the madam of a brothel"

NUREMBERG, AUGUST 23—There rushes up toward the plane the astonishing face of the world's enemy: pine woods on little hills, gray-green, glossy lakes too small to be anything but smooth, gardens tall with red-tongued beans, fields striped with red-gold wheat, russet-roofed villages with high gables, and pumpkin-steepled churches that no architect over seven could have designed. Another minute and the plane drops to the heart of the world's enemy: Nuremberg. In not many more minutes, one is in the courtroom where the world's enemy is being tried for his sins, and immediately one forgets those sins in wonder at a conflict going on in that court which has nothing to do with the indictments it is considering. The trial is now in its tenth month, and the courtroom is a citadel of boredom. Every person attending it is in the grip of extreme tedium. This is not to say that the work at hand is being performed in a languid or perfunctory way. An iron discipline meets that tedium head on and does not yield an inch to it. But all the same, the most spectacular process in the court today is a certain tug of war concerning time. Some of those present are fiercely desiring that the tedium should come to an end at the first possible moment, and the others are as fiercely desiring that it should last forever.

The people in court who want the tedium to endure eternally are the twenty-one defendants in the dock, who disconcert the spectator by presenting the blatant appearance that

historical characters, particularly in distress, assume in bad paintings. They really do look what they are, even as Belisarius sitting by his beggar's cup or Napoleon brooding on St. Helena. They are crudely wreathed in suggestions of death. Not only are they in peril of the death sentence, but there is constant talk about millions of dead and arguments whether they died because of these men or not, and there now emanates from them a sense of corruption hardly less tangible than the smell which, as one walks through the old town of Nuremberg, sometimes rises from the rubble where one of the thirty thousand missing Nurembergers has not fully reacted to time and the disinfectant spray. Knowing so very well what death is like, these men prefer the tedium of the trial to its cessation. So they cling to the procedure through their lawyers and stretch it to the limits of its texture, and by the suggestions they make as to the handling of the witnesses they put the brakes on the proceedings, thus arousing in the rest of the court, the living people who have a prospect of leaving Nuremberg and going back to life, a savage impatience. This impatience is checked by the iron discipline which the court has imposed on itself, but it makes the air more tense.

It does, indeed, seem ridiculous for the defendants to try to stave off the end, for they admit by their appearance that nothing is to go well with them again on this earth. These Nazi leaders, dedicated to the breaking of all rules, break last of all the rule that the verdict of a court must not be anticipated. Their appearance announces what they believe. The death penalty has been asked for all of them; it is obvious that the defendants think that the prosecutors are going to get their wish. Believing that they are to lose everything, they hold on to nothing. Not the slightest trace of their power or their glory remains. None of them looks as if he could ever have exercised any valid authority. Göring uses imperial gestures, but they are so vulgar that it is as if there had always been quotation marks around the adjective—as if people said, "You know, he was the one they used to call 'the Emperor.' " But now the defendants are losing what is more fundamental than manner or gestures —the accustomed color and texture of their skins, and the molding of their features. Except for Schacht, who is white-haired, and Speer, who is swarthy, they are neither dark nor fair, and there is among them no leanness that does not sag and no plumpness that seems more than inflation by some thin gas. So completely obscure are their personalities that it is hard to keep in mind which is which, even after one has sat and looked at them for days, and such as stand out define themselves by oddity rather than by character.

At one end of the front row in the dock sits Schacht, twisted in his seat so that the back of his tall body, stiff as a plank, is propped against the panel which ought to be at his side. Thus he sits at right angles to his fellow defendants and looks past them and over their heads; it was always his argument that he was far superior to Hitler's gang. Thus, too, he sits at right angles to the judges on the bench before him; he is a leading international banker, a most respectable man,

and no court on earth can have a moral right to try him. He is petrified by rage at the indignities practiced on him. He might be a corpse frozen by *rigor mortis* into an attitude which would make it difficult to fit him into his coffin. Schirach, the Youth Leader, startles because he is like a woman. It is as if a neat and mousy governess sat there, not pretty but with never a hair out of place, and always to be trusted not to intrude when there are visitors—as if he was Jane Eyre. Streicher is pitiable, because it is plainly the community and not he who was guilty of his sins. He is a dirty old man of the sort that gives trouble in parks, and a sane Germany would have sent him to an asylum long ago. Speer, the architect, is the one defendant for whom the court has some liking and respect. He seems to have worked with the Nazis simply because he was a social creator and had to use whatever government was in power to get control of his medium. There is something baboonish about his sharp, dark face that explains how he came to forget that an artist, like anybody else, has to have some fastidiousness.

Though one has read surprising news of Göring for years, he still surprises. He is, above all things, soft. He wears either a German air-force uniform or a light beach suit in the worst of playful taste, and both hang loosely on him, giving him an air of pregnancy. He has thick brown young hair, the coarse, bright skin of an actor who has used grease paint for decades, and the preternaturally deep wrinkles of the drug addict; it adds up to something like the head of a ventriloquist's dummy. His appearance makes a pointed but obscure reference to sex. It is a matter of history that Göring's love affairs with women played a decisive part in the development of the

Nazi party at various stages, but he looks as one who would never lift a hand to a woman save in something much more peculiar than kindness. Nevertheless, he does not look like any recognized type of homosexual. Sometimes, particularly when his humor is good, he recalls the madam of a brothel. His like are to be seen in the late morning in doorways along the steep streets of Marseilles, the professional mask of geniality still hard on their faces, though they stand relaxed in leisure, their fat cats rubbing against their spread skirts. At other times, particularly when he is talking to his friends in the intervals, his gestures recall a tout in a Paris café offering some tourists a chance to see a Black Mass. Whatever was his field of experience, it seems certain that it lacked the element of consummation. There is a sense of desert thirst about him. No matter what superb aqueducts he built to bring water to his encampment among the sands, some perversity in the architecture let it run out and spill before it reached him. Yet even now his wide and woodenish lips sometimes smack together in smiling appetite. If he were given the chance, he would walk out of the Palace of Justice, take over Germany again, and turn it into a stage tor the enactment of his governing fantasy, which is so strong that it fills the air around him with its images, so madly private that those images are beyond the power of those who see them to interpret them.

But now, after these many months, even these men are giving up the effort of being themselves and are more and more cohering into a common pattern which reiterates the plea of Not Guilty. All the time they make quite unidiosyncratic gestures, expressive of innocence and outraged common sense, and in the intervals they stand up and chat among themselves, forming little protesting groups which, painted in a mural, could be recognized as the men who would have saved the world if it had let them. But all this they do more weakly every day. They are visibly receding from the field of existence and are perhaps no longer conscious of the recession. It is possible that they never think directly of death or even of imprisonment, and that there is nothing positive in them at all except their desire to hold time still. For they are praying with their sharpest nerves, "Let this trial never finish, let it go on forever and ever, without end."

They are as bored as anyone else, the lawyers in court, but because of their loyalty to their idea they work against the grain of their boredom, as climbers, distressed by the lack of oxygen in the upper air, nevertheless continue to climb, because they have mastered their technique to such an extent that it can take control of them when they lose grip, and because they continue to remind themselves of the importance of their aim. On the bench sit the eight judges, with the American and the British judges in the middle. Francis Biddle looks like a highly intelligent swan, occasionally flexing down to commune with a smaller waterfowl, for Sir Geoffrey Lawrence, English president of the court, who sits beside him, is much smaller, though of a dignity that keeps the German lawyers scuttling. Sir Geoffrey's father was a Lord Chief Justice, and he brings to legal procedure the quality that the second generation of a theatrical family brings to Shakespeare. He has the most charming voice in the world, and a silvery querulousness that can flay without drawing a single drop of blood. The alternate American judge, John J. Parker, of Charlotte, North Carolina, proves it true that a good local product can be sent the world over and do trade no harm. People living in the American countryside like an American judge to be this and that, and they have not low standards, and because those standards are set by human necessities, they are valid anywhere, and the man who satisfies them is liked better than any cosmopolitan with less defined standards. The alternate British judge, Sir William Norman Birkett, has a head of hair that tells his story. It is like a toupee made by a wigmaker, and he would have done something about it had he not been a person without vanity, happily preoccupied by intellectual things. He likes poetry and music and good food and wine, and is a fierce Liberal.

Between the English-speaking spectator and the four other judges there are veils. There is a veil of misleading familiarity, of odd and false association, between us and the French judges. Because they wear the robes of French lawyers, they immediately recall the drawings of Daumier and distract one with considerations of what a superb artist Daumier was. These judges are not in the least like the sharks and alligators that Daumier drew, being sober embodiments of the French tradition of learning and civilized living, but Daumier has made so many exciting patterns out of these white jabots and black gowns that at the sight of them the grateful memory involves his work. Costume, too, makes the veil that hangs between the English-speaking spectator and the Russian judges. They are in military uniform, the strangest choice for officers of a tribunal set up in the hope of superseding war by law. Yet both of them are liked—one of them, General

Nikichenko, as well as almost anyone in Nuremberg. Of the judges we can understand, it can be said that all realize very well the drawback of this trial. They all know very well that it is a pity that the defeated have to be tried by the victors, that it is impracticable to have judgment delivered by a neutral court. But they are all judges who know that every trial is flawed by the same imperfection, who are aware that every accused person is suffering the injustice of being tried by people who, in the economic and social struggles which have worsted him, have come off best, to the extent of being on the bench while he is in the dock. They believe that the imperfection can be remedied by strict adherence to a code of law, which they must force themselves to apply as if they were not victors but representatives of a neutral power. One has read of such idealistic efforts in history books. It is the charm of a visit to Nuremberg that one sees the effort being made and, in listening to arguments subtle as the serpent and slow as the snail, counts the immense cost of legality and wonders at the immense fortitude of those who are paying the cost. For however much a man loved the law, he could not love so much of it as lies about at Nuremberg.

At the tables where the prosecutors sit, there is the same national division as on the bench. Most of the Russian lawyers are in uniform, and those that are and those that are not are alike in dumfounding the court by their use of legal procedure. Cross-examination is the process by which a witness' story is checked by reference to probability and the statements of other witnesses. It is impossible to guess why a Russian lawyer should step up to the rostrum to cross-examine a witness and, squaring his shoulders as if he were going to address himself to an athletic feat, should shout words which it would be fair to quote as "Did you conspire to wage an aggressive war against the peace-loving democracies? Answer yes or no." Or why, on receiving the inevitable answer, "No," he should continue, "I accept your answer." If that cannot be understood, the cross-examination for which the French lawyers are responsible can be understood too well. The French prosecutors are headed by M. Champetier de Ribes, whose name, when it is first seen by strangers on the official lists, creates a feeling that the proceedings may at any time take a queer turn, for the most famous obstetrician in France also bears that name. Champetier de Ribes and all his team do fine work, pressing the case against the Nazis with precision and elegance, but they are too familiar with the case; they knew about it long before there were Nazis, they foresaw all as soon as the War of 1870 happened to them. The fire of their resentment has gone out; there are only ashes on their hearthstones. The American and the British are in a fortunate position for attack. They are like the sailor who was found beating a Jew because of the Crucifixion; when he was reminded that that had been a long time ago, he said that that might be, but he had just heard about it. This freshness of wrath gives them an advantage in dealing with the defendants, who are, with the exception of the generals and admirals and diplomats, too ignorant to realize the continuity of their own policy, too egotistical to know that they are the sons of their fathers.

The table at which the British prosecuting attorneys sit is spectacular in a manner that has offered Colonel Burton C. Andrus, the much beloved cavalry officer who is commandant of the prison and in charge of security, one of his few gratifications. Almost the whole of life strikes the Colonel as a departure from ideal military discipline, which God knows it is. He mourns over many abuses— such as the habit of calling American troops GI's instead of soldiers—which are unlikely to be immediately reformed. But he expresses great satisfaction at the impeccable decorum of the British prosecutors' clothes, which is indeed remarkable. Their suits seem to have been pressed, their ties to have been knotted, not by fallible human hands but by the decree of a divine will. This heavenly neatness transcends earthly political differences. Between Sir Hartley Shawcross, the British Chief Prosecutor, who is bright-red Labour, and his second-in-command, Sir David Maxwell Fyfe, who is a Conservative Member of Parliament and in line for the leadership of his party, there is not a pin to choose in elegance, and the third-in-command, Mr. Elwyn Jones, who is a Labour MP, is almost as grand.

Shawcross and Maxwell Fyfe produce an interesting situation. They are very different in physical type. Sir David is a dark and thick-set Highland Scot who could be mistaken by strangers for a Jew; Sir Hartley is slender and rather better-looking than it pays any man to be unless he is a film star. Sir David has the temperamental advantage. When the two men were photographed on their arrival at the Nuremberg airport, Sir David looked as if he were cross-examining the camera, Sir Hartley as if it were cross-examining him. But they have much in common. Both belong to the new England, where privilege is dead. Neither was at Eton or Harrow or any of the other great public schools,

neither had any private means to help
him in his career, and each received
his title recently, as a reward for public service. Both are good lawyers;
both are pleasant people who like
pleasant things. It happened that the
Nuremberg Tribunal was planned
during the time when the "caretaker
government" held power in England;
this was the government Winston
Churchill formed from the Conservative party to take charge of the country while the general election was
fought. Hence the chief prosecuting
attorney for the British was at first
the Attorney General in that government, who was Sir David Maxwell
Fyfe. When the Labour government
was formed, the new Attorney General was Sir Hartley Shawcross, who
therefore automatically became the
chief prosecuting attorney at Nuremberg. Sir David then volunteered
to carry on as second-in-command,
which meant giving up his bar practice
and his political career and settling
down to exile in Nuremberg and immersion in this sordid and repetitive
investigation. He has done all the
donkey work of the case and has had
little of the glory of making the opening and closing speeches for the British prosecution, besides being able to
spend the time between in London
and go on with his appearances in the
law courts and the House of Commons. There have been many attempts
to make bad blood between the two
men because of this sequence of
events, which does press harder on the
one than on the other. But there are
no two men who could handle such a
situation more handsomely. They
speak of each other generously, in the
unmistakable accents which mean
that they think generously of each
other.

This British team works well with
the Americans, who have their own
way of being spectacular. Justice
Jackson is what Europeans best love
an American to be, for he is as charming as any European could be but
carries with him a sense of dedication
to the aim of making life in America
simpler and happier than it has been
in Europe. It is good that these teams
work well together, for, so far as the
Germans are concerned, they are the
only ones that count. In the examination and cross-examination of witnesses, Sir David Maxwell Fyfe holds
the honors. This gentle and heavily
built man, who never exempts himself
from the discipline of fairness, drives
witness after witness backward, step
by step, till on the edge of some moral
abyss they admit the truth. But Justice Jackson's closing speech was a
masterpiece, exquisitely relevant to
the indictment, for its examination of
the charge of conspiracy laid against
the defendants was made with the
civilized good sense and beauty of
form against which they had conspired. It is to be regretted that one
phrase may be read by posterity as
invective of a not very high order, but
it has a significance to everyone who
has attended the Nuremberg trial.
"Göring," he said, "stuck a pudgy
finger in every pie." The courtroom is
not small, but it is full of Göring's
fingers. His soft and spongy white
hands are forever smoothing his curiously abundant hair, or covering his
wide mouth (while his plotting eyes
look facetiously around), or weaving
impudent gestures of innocence in the
air. Sir Hartley Shawcross' closing
speech was not so shapely, for it was
longer and covered more ground and
stopped more legal holes, but he re-
deemed the charges from the staleness
which has fallen on them during the
last ten months by his imaginative

realization of what some of the mass murders meant.

Justice Jackson, Sir David, and Sir Hartley alone got under the skin of the defendants. The Nazis seem not to care when a Russian lawyer cross-examines them, because they see he does not know how to do it; they seem not to care when a French lawyer cross-examines them, because they think he is working on a scheme more formal and subtilized than they can respect. But they are ashamed when Sir David proves them liars. At the end of Justice Jackson's speech, he pointed a forefinger at each of the defendants and denounced his specific share in the Nazi crime; almost all of them wilted. One exception was old Streicher, who munched and mumbled away in some private and probably extremely objectionable dream. The commonplace killer Kaltenbrunner, who was in charge of all the concentration camps, exchanged giggles with Rosenberg. Schacht became stiffer than ever, stiff as an iron stag in the garden of an old house. All the rest looked naïve in shame, and when Shawcross ended his speech in the same way the next afternoon, they were ashamed again. The feminine Schirach achieved a gesture that was almost touching; he listened attentively to what Shawcross had to say of his activities as Youth Leader, and when he heard him go on to speak of his responsibility for the deportation of forty to fifty thousand Soviet children, he put up his delicate hand and lifted off the circlet of his headphones, laying it down very quietly on the ledge before him. It seemed possible that he had indeed the soul of a governess, that he was indeed Jane Eyre and had been perverted by a Mr. Rochester who, disappearing into self-kindled flames, had left him disen-

chanted and the prey of prim but inextinguishable remorse. All these people hardly troubled to listen to the Russian and the French speeches for the prosecution.

So it appears in the Palace of Justice that it is only the Americans and the British who can hold up a mirror to Germany and help her to solve her own perplexing mystery—that mystery which, in Nuremberg and the countryside around it, is set out in flowers, flowers which disconcert by being not only lovely but beloved. All the little cottages which begin where the rubble ends have phlox in their gardens, white and clear pink, shining as if seen through water. In the windows of the steep-gabled houses, the pink and purple petunias are delicate containers of ardent light. In the villages, the clematis is trained in great purple knots over low posts, so that its beauty does not go straying up the walls but lies under the eye. It is difficult not to conclude that a people who so love flowers must love all beautiful and simple things. The further landscape continues this protestation of innocence, this artless seduction. Where the pine trees rise from the soft, reddish bed of scented pine needles, and dragonflies draw patterns of iridescence above the cloudy green trout stream, and the miller's little blond son plays with the gray kitten among the meadowsweet by the edge of the millpond, there can surely be no harm. There is, of course, evidence to the contrary. "The people where I live now send me in my breakfast tray strewn with pansies," says the French doctor who is custodian of the relics of atrocities at the Palace of Justice (the lampshade made of human skin, the shrunken head of the Polish Jew). "Beautiful pansies, arranged with the most exquisite taste. I have to remind myself that they supplied me with my exhibits, that they are of the same race that tortured me at Mauthausen." Not long ago, in London, a treachery case was tried by courtmartial—British prisoners of war who were induced by a combination of threats and bribes to become informers against their fellow prisoners. They were taken out of their camps and to a house not far from these pine woods, this trout stream, only a mile or two from this mill. The German authorities supplied them with girls, who were not prostitutes brought from the town but the daughters of peasants in the district, who apparently obeyed the summons without reluctance and probably were extremely fond of flowers.

Unquestionably, there is a German mystery, and certainly it needs to be solved, and a continued critical relationship with the American and the British people, such as has begun at Nuremberg, would help toward a solution. Such a relationship, however, needs the sanction of force. Before one of the eight judges could take his seat on the bench, some millions had to come to Europe. But now everybody wants to go home. The most significant sight in Nuremberg can be seen by those who find their way into one of the offices in the Palace of Justice that overlook the exercise ground of the jail behind 'it. There, at certain hours, can be seen the Nazi prisoners, padding up and down, sullen and puffy, young men or wrinkled old men, with a look of fierceness, as if they were missing the opportunities for cruelty as much as they miss the company of women or whatever their fancy is. They are watched by military guards, who stand, their young chins dropped, their hands joined behind them, slowly switching their white truncheons backward and forward in the very rhythm of boredom itself. If an apple falls from a tree beside them, they do not bend to pick it up; nothing that happens here can interest them. It would not be easy to tell that these guards were not the prisoners, so much do they want to go home.

* * *

"Tode durch den Strang!"—"Death by the rope!"

These words came in German through the headphones in the Nuremberg courtroom to eleven leaders of the Third Reich on the afternoon of October 1, 1946—to Göring (age fifty-two), Ribbentrop (fifty-three), Keitel (sixty-three), Kaltenbrunner (forty-three), Rosenberg (fifty-three), Frank (forty-six), Frick (sixty-nine), Streicher (sixty-one), Sauckel (forty-eight), Jodl (fifty-six), Seyss-Inquart (fifty-four). Bormann (forty-five), *in absentia,* was also sentenced to death. Three others were sent to prison for life—Hess (fifty-two), Funk (fifty-six), and Raeder (seventy). Four were condemned to terms of imprisonment—Dönitz (fifty-five) to ten years, Schirach (thirty-nine) to twenty years, Neurath (seventy-two) to fifteen years, and Speer (forty) to twenty years. To the surprise of a good many people, three were acquitted—Schacht (sixty-nine), von Papen (sixty-six), and Fritzsche (forty-six).

In the case of Schacht the Tribunal found it clearly established that although he was the central figure in Germany's rearmament program and many of the steps he took, particularly in the early days of the Nazi regime, were responsible for Nazi Germany's rapid rise as a military power, re-armament in itself was no crime. The judgment stated that Schacht had participated in the plan to get rid of Hitler, first by deposing him and later by assassination, and furthermore the inference had not been estab-lished beyond a shadow of a doubt that he had known of the Nazi plans for aggression. "You can't hang a banker," was one disgruntled reaction. The Russian member of the Tribunal, General Nikichenko, delivered a hot dissenting opinion asserting that the evidence indisputably established that Schacht actively assisted in the seizure of power by the Nazis, closely collaborated with Hitler for twelve years, provided the financial basis for the creation of Hitler's war machine, and prepared Germany's economy for the waging of aggressive wars. But the economic wizard of the Third Reich went free.

Historians of the twentieth century will record that after the arch-medicine men of Nazidom, Hitler and Goebbels, committed suicide in an orgy of Wagnerian self-immolation, ten other Nazis came to the end of their rope at Nuremberg. Here is the report of the executions by Kingsbury Smith, European general manager of the International News Service, who was chosen by lot to represent the combined American press at the pro-ceedings.

The Nazi Haman Julius Streicher's last words: "The Bolsheviks will hang you one day"

New York Journal-American, October 16, 1946, International News Service

NUREMBERG, OCTOBER 16—Ex-Reichsmarschall Hermann Wilhelm Göring succeeded in cheating the gal-lows of Allied justice by committing suicide in his prison cell a short time before the ten other condemned rem-nants of the Nazi hierarchy were hanged today.

Despite the fact that an American security guard was supposed to be watching his every movement, the crown prince of Nazidom managed to hide in his mouth, chew, and swallow a vial containing cyanide of potas-sium.

Goring swallowed the poison while Colonel Burton C. Andrus, American security commandant, was walking across the prison yard to the death-row block to read to him and the ten other condemned Nazi leaders the International Military Tribunal's sen-tence of death.

Within little more than an hour after the reading of this sentence to the condemned men in their cells, Göring was scheduled to be led out to a near-by small gymnasium building in the jailyard to lead the parade of death of the Nazi political and

military chieftains to the scaffold.
Göring had not previously been told
that he was going to die this morning,
nor had any of the other condemned
men.

How he guessed this was to be his
day of doom and how he managed to
conceal the poison on his person is a
mystery that has confounded the security forces.

With former Foreign Minister
Joachim von Ribbentrop taking the
place of Göring as the first to mount
the scaffold, the ten other condemned
princes of Nazidom were hanged one
by one in the bright, electrically
lighted barnlike interior of the small
gymnasium inside one of the prison
yards of the Nuremberg city jail.

The execution of von Ribbentrop
and the others took approximately one
hour and a half. The once-arrogant
diplomatic double-crosser of Nazidom
entered the execution hall at 1:11 this
morning. The trap was sprung at 1:16
and he was pronounced dead at 1:30.

The last to walk up the thirteen forbidding wooden steps to one of the
two gallows used for the execution was
Artur Seyss-Inquart, Austrian traitor
and Nazi *Gauleiter* for Holland. He
dropped to his death at 2:45 A.M. and
was pronounced dead at 2:57.

All ten of the Nazis attempted to
show bravery as they went to their
deaths. Most of them were bitterly defiant, some grimly resigned, and
others asked the Almighty for mercy.

All but Alfred Rosenberg, the pagan party theorist, made brief, last-
minute statements on the scaffold,
nearly all of which were nationalistic
expressions for the future welfare and
greatness of Germany.

The only one, however, to make any
reference to Nazi ideology was Julius
Streicher, the arch Jew-baiter. Displaying the most bitter and enraged

defiance of any of the condemned, he
screamed "Heil Hitler" at the top of
his voice as he was about to mount
the steps leading to the gallows.

Streicher appeared in the execution
hall, which had been used only last
Saturday night for a basketball game
by American security guards, at
twelve and a half minutes after two
o'clock.

As in the case of all the condemned,
a warning knock by a guard outside
preceded Streicher's entry through a
door in the middle of the hall.

An American lieutenant colonel
sent to fetch the condemned from the
death row of the cell block to the
near-by prison wing entered first. He
was followed by Streicher, who was
stopped immediately inside the door
by two American sergeants. They
closed in on each side of him and held
his arms while another sergeant removed the manacles from his hands
and replaced them with a leather cord.

The first person whom Streicher
and the others saw upon entering the
gruesome hall was an American lieutenant colonel who stood directly in
front of him while his hands were
being tied behind his back as they had
been manacled upon his entrance.

This ugly, dwarfish little man,
wearing a threadbare suit and a well-
worn bluish shirt buttoned to the neck
but without a tie, glanced at the three
wooden scaffolds rising up menacingly
in front of him.

Two of these were used alternately
to execute the condemned men while
the third was kept in reserve.

After a quick glance at the gallows,
Streicher glared around the room, his
eyes resting momentarily upon the
small group of American, British,
French, and Russian officers on hand
to witness the executions.

By this time Streicher's hands were

tied securely behind his back. Two guards, one to each arm, directed him to No. 1 gallows on the left entrance. He walked steadily the six feet to the first wooden step, but his face was twitching nervously. As the guards stopped him at the bottom of the steps for official identification requests, he uttered his piercing scream:

"Heil Hitler!"

His shriek sent a shiver down the back of this International News Service correspondent, who is witnessing the executions as sole representative of the American press.

As its echo died away, another American colonel standing by the steps said sharply:

"Ask the man his name."

In response to the interpreter's query Streicher shouted:

"You know my name well."

The interpreter repeated his request, and the condemned man yelled:

"Julius Streicher."

As he mounted the platform Streicher cried out:

"Now it goes to God!"

After getting up the thirteen steps to the eight-foot-high and eight-foot-square black-painted wooden platform, Streicher was pushed two steps to the mortal spot beneath the hangman's rope.

This was suspended from an iron ring attached to a crossbeam which rested on two posts. The rope was being held back against a wooden rail by the American Army sergeant hangman.

Streicher was swung around to face toward the front.

He glanced again at the Allied officers and the eight Allied correspondents representing the world's press who were lined up against a wall behind small tables directly facing the gallows.

With burning hatred in his eyes, Streicher looked down upon the witnesses and then screamed:

"Purim Fest 1946!" *

The American officer standing at the scaffold said:

"Ask the man if he has any last words."

When the interpreter had translated, Streicher shouted:

"The Bolsheviks will hang you one day."

As the black hood was being adjusted about his head, Streicher was heard saying:

"Adele, my dear wife."

At that moment the trap was sprung with a loud bang. With the rope snapped taut and the body swinging wildly, a groan could be heard distinctly within the dark interior of the scaffold.†

It was originally intended to permit the condemned to walk the seventy-odd yards from the cells to the execution chamber with their hands free, but they were all manacled in the cells immediately following the discovery of Göring's suicide.

The weasel-faced Ribbentrop in his last appearance before mankind uttered his final words while waiting for

---

* Purim is a Jewish holiday celebrated in the spring, commemorating the hanging of Haman, Biblical oppressor of the Jews.

† One morbid detail was omitted at this point from the account published in the *New York Journal-American*. In a later version appearing in *It Happened in 1946* (1947), the International News Service annual, edited by Clark Kinnaird, Kingsbury Smith reported that while Streicher was audibly strangling, the hangman disappeared into the dark interior of the scaffold. Streicher's groans almost immediately ceased. Apparently the hangman must have helped the process of death in his own fashion. "After it was over," Smith wrote, "I was not in a mood to ask what he did, but I assume that he grabbed the swinging body and pulled down on it. We were all of the opinion that Streicher had strangled."

the black hood to be placed over his head. Loudly, in firm tones, he said:

"God save Germany!"

He then asked:

"May I say something else?"

The interpreter nodded. The former diplomatic wizard of Nazidom who negotiated the secret German non-aggression pact with Soviet Russia on the eve of Germany's invasion of Poland, and who approved orders to execute Allied airmen, then added:

"My last wish is that Germany realize its entity and that an understanding be reached between East and West. I wish peace to the world."

The ex-diplomat looked straight ahead as the hood was adjusted before the trap was sprung. His lips were set tight.

Next in line to follow Ribbentrop to the gallows was Field Marshal Wilhelm Keitel, symbol of Prussian militarism and aristocracy.

Here came the first military leader to be executed under the new concept of Allied international law—the principle that professional soldiers cannot escape justice for waging aggressive wars against humanity by claiming they were merely carrying out orders of their superiors.

Keitel entered the death arena at 1:18, only two minutes after the trap was dropped beneath Ribbentrop and while the latter was still hanging at the end of his rope.

The Field Marshal could not, of course, see the ex-Foreign Minister, whose body was concealed within the first scaffold and whose rope still hung taut.

Keitel did not appear as tense as Ribbentrop. He held his head high while his hands were being tied, and walked erect with military bearing to the foot of the second scaffold, al-

though a guard on each side held his arms.

When asked his name he answered in a loud sharp tone, "Wilhelm Keitel!" He mounted the gallows steps as he might have climbed to a reviewing stand to take the salute of the German Army. He certainly did not appear in need of the guards' help.

When turned around at the top of the platform, Keitel looked over the crowd with the traditional iron-jawed haughtiness of the proud Prussian officer. When asked if he had anything to say he looked straight ahead and speaking in a loud voice said:

"I call on Almighty God to have mercy on the German people. More than two million German soldiers went to their deaths for the Fatherland. I follow now my sons."

Then, while raising his voice to shout, "All for Germany," Keitel's black-booted, uniformed body plunged down with a bang. Observers agreed he had shown more courage on the scaffold than he had in the courtroom, where he tried to hide his guilt behind Hitler's ghost.

Then he claimed that it was all the Führer's fault, that he merely carried out orders and had no responsibility.

This despite the fact that documentary evidence presented during the trial showed he "approved and backed" measures for branding Russian prisoners, directed "Draconian measures" to terrorize the Russian people into submission, and issued secret orders for invasion of Poland three months before the attack took place.

With both Ribbentrop and Keitel hanging at the end of their ropes, there was a pause in the grim proceedings.

The American colonel directing the executions asked the American general representing the Allied Control Commission if those present could smoke. An affirmative answer brought cigarettes into the hands of almost every one of the thirty-odd persons present.

These included two official representatives of the German government in the American zone—Dr. Wilhelm Hoegner, Minister-President of Bavaria, and Dr. Jacob Leisner, Chief Prosecutor of Nuremberg.

Officers and GI's walked around nervously or spoke a few words to one another in hushed voices while Allied correspondents scribbled furiously their notes of the historic, though ghastly event.

In a few minutes an American Army doctor accompanied by a Russian Army doctor and both carrying stethoscopes walked to the first scaffold, lifted the curtain, and disappeared within.

They emerged at 1:30 A.M. and spoke to a short, heavy-set American colonel wearing combat boots. The colonel swung around and, facing official witnesses, snapped to attention to say:

"The man is dead."

Two GI's quickly appeared with a stretcher, which was carried up and lifted into the interior of the scaffold. The hangman, a sergeant, mounted the gallows steps, took a large commando-type knife out of a sheath strapped to his side, and cut the rope.

Ribbentrop's limp body with the black hood still over his head was speedily removed from the far end of the room and placed behind a black canvas curtain. This all had taken less than ten minutes.

The directing colonel turned to the witnesses and said: "Lights out, please, gentlemen," and then, ad-

dressing another colonel he called "Norman," said, "O.K." The latter went out the door and over to the condemned block to fetch the next man.

This creature was Ernst Kaltenbrunner, Gestapo chief and director of the greatest mass murder Europe has seen since the Dark Ages.

Kaltenbrunner, master killer of Nazidom, entered the execution chamber at 1:36 A.M. wearing a sweater beneath his double-breasted coat. With his lean, haggard face furrowed by old dueling scars, the terrible successor of Reinhard Heydrich had a frightening look as he glanced around the room.

He was nervous and he wet his lips as he turned to mount the gallows, but he walked steadily. He answered his name in a calm, low voice. When he turned around on the gallows platform he first faced a U. S. Catholic Army chaplain attired in a Franciscan habit.

Kaltenbrunner was asked for his last words and answered quietly:

"I would like to say a word.

"I have loved my German people and my Fatherland with a warm heart.

"I have done my duty by the laws of my people and I am sorry my people were led this time by men who were not soldiers and that crimes were committed of which I have no knowledge."

This sounded like strange talk from a man, one of whose agents—a man named Rudolf Hess *—confessed at a previous trial that under Kaltenbrunner's orders he gassed three million human beings at the Auschwitz concentration camp.

As the black hood was about to be placed over his head Kaltenbrunner, still speaking in a low, calm voice, used a German phrase which translated means:

* Rudolf *Hoess,* not Hess. The name was probably garbled in transmission.

"Germany good luck!"

His trap was sprung at 1:39 A.M.

Field Marshal Keitel had been pronounced dead at 1:44 A.M., and three minutes later guards had removed his body. The scaffold was made ready for Alfred Rosenberg, master mind behind the Nazi race theories, who sought to establish Nazism as a pagan religion.

Rosenberg was dull and sunken-cheeked as he looked around the court. His complexion was pasty brown. But he did not appear nervous and walked with a steady step to and up the gallows.

Apart from giving his name and replying "No" to a question as to whether he had anything to say, this atheist did not utter a word. Despite his disbelief in God he was accompanied by a Protestant chaplain, who followed him to the gallows and stood beside him praying.

Rosenberg looked at the chaplain once, but said nothing. Ninety seconds after he entered the execution hall he was swinging from the end of a hangman's rope. His was the swiftest execution of any of those condemned.

Then there was a brief lull in the morbid proceedings until Kaltenbrunner was pronounced dead at 1:52 A.M. Hans Frank, the *Gauleiter* of Poland and former SS general, was next in the parade of death. He was the only one of the condemned to enter the chamber with a smile on his lips.

Although nervous and swallowing frequently, this man, who was converted to Catholicism after his arrest, gave the appearance of being relieved at the prospect of atoning for his evil deeds.

He answered to his name quietly and when asked on the platform if he had any last statement replied in a low voice that was almost a whisper:

"I am thankful for the kind treatment during my captivity and I ask God to accept me with mercy."

Frank then closed his eyes and swallowed again as the black hood went over his head.

The sixth man to leave his prison cell and walk with handcuffed wrists across the corner of the small yard separating the condemned block from the death house was sixty-nine-year-old Wilhelm Frick, former Nazi Minister of the Interior.

He entered the execution chamber at five and a half minutes after two, six and a half minutes after Rosenberg had been pronounced dead. He seemed to be the least steady of any so far and stumbled on the thirteenth step of the gallows. His only words were "Long live eternal Germany" before he was hooded and dropped through the trap.

Following Streicher's melodramatic exit and removal of Frick's corpse after he was pronounced dead at 2:20 A.M., Fritz Sauckel, the slave-labor director and one of the worst of the blood-stained men of Nazidom, was brought to face his doom.

Wearing a sweater with no coat and looking wild-eyed, Sauckel proved to be the most defiant of any except Streicher.

Here was the man who drove millions into a land of bondage on a scale unknown since the pre-Christian era. Gazing around the room from the gallow's platform, he suddenly screamed:

"I am dying innocent. The sentence is wrong. God protect Germany and make Germany great again. God protect my family."

The trap was sprung at 2:26 A.M., and, like Streicher, this hatred-filled man groaned loudly as the fatal noose snapped tightly under the weight of his body.

Ninth to come was Colonel General Alfred Jodl, Hitler's strategic adviser and close friend. With the black coat collar of his Wehrmacht uniform turned up at the back as though hurriedly put on, Jodl entered the death house with obvious signs of nervousness.

He wet his lips constantly and his features were drawn and haggard as he walked forward, not nearly so steady as Keitel in mounting the gallows steps. Yet his voice was calm when he uttered his last six words on earth:

"My greetings to you, my Germany."

At 2:34 Jodl plunged into the black hole of the scaffold's death. Both he and Sauckel hung together in that execution chamber until the latter was pronounced dead six minutes later and removed.

The Czechoslovakian-born Seyss-Inquart was the last actor to make his appearance in the ghastly scene of Allied justice. He entered the death chamber at 2:38½ A.M., wearing the glasses which made his face a familiar and despised figure in all the years he ruled Holland with an iron hand and sent thousands of Dutchmen to Germany for forced labor.

Seyss-Inquart looked around with noticeable signs of unsteadiness and limped on his left clubfoot as he walked to the gallows. He mounted the steps slowly, with guards helping him on his way.

When Seyss-Inquart spoke his last words his voice was very low but intense. He said:

"I hope that this execution is the last act of the tragedy of the Second World War and that the lesson taken from this World War will be that peace and understanding should be between peoples.

"I believe in Germany."

* * *

IN AN EDITORIAL published on October 17, 1946, the day after the executions, *The New York Times* held that these men of Nuremberg performed in death at least one service—their hanging was "a grim warning to all who would emulate them in the future that mankind has entered a new world of international morality and that in the end the angered forces of humanity must triumph over those who would outrage it."

Once more this revolution in international justice was underscored when, on December 22, 1948, at midnight after the winter solstice, Hideki Tojo, the wartime Premier of Japan, and six of his immediate circle of cocksure militarists mounted the thirteen steps to the gallows in Tokyo's quiet Sugamo prison and were hanged until dead. Tojo left a poem:

> *It is good-by.*
> *Over the mountains I go today*
> *To the bosom of Buddha.*
> *So, happy am I.*

To his wife he sent a lock of hair and a fingernail clipping as mementos, as well as his glasses and his false teeth. The reaction of the Japanese to these executions was *Kinodoku, kinodoku* (pity, pity).

Death could not undo the evil wrought by the men of Nuremberg and Tokyo, nor could it bring back to life a single one of the millions they slaughtered. But some very important boundary marks in the march of civilization were set up at Nuremberg in 1946 and at Tokyo in 1948. It is probable that these markers would have met with the approval of the great apostles of international law—Plato the Greek, Hugo Grotius the Dutchman, and Woodrow Wilson the American.

A Reporter Sees the Light of India Put Out

H E WAS A FRAIL, wizened, enigmatic little brown man, toothless and bald, bowed by the weight of seventy-eight years and the sorrows of mankind. But he was one of the fabulous figures of our time. For thirty years Mohandas Karamchand Gandhi, saint and mystic, had worked for a free and united India. "One of that unbroken line of saints and seers, running like the stitches of a golden thread through the tangled pattern of human affairs, who have insisted that man, like God, is spirit, and can achieve his ends, and thus fulfill his life," said John Haynes Holmes in tribute. Gandhi once said that he had "learned from Christ passive resistance and nonviolence, from Tolstoy nonco-operation, from Thoreau disobedience." "Never has there been a more absolute simplicity," said Vincent Sheean in tribute.

It was the irony of fate that one whose whole life was directed against violence should be snuffed out by the forces of violence personified by a fanatical Hindu youth. "It shows how dangerous it is to be good," was George Bernard Shaw's reaction to the news of the assassination. James Michaels, United Press staff writer, reported the murder and cremation of the Hindu saint in these two news stories. A more impressionistic account was written by Sheean, who in his *Lead, Kindly Light* (1949) claimed to have broken out in "psychosomatic" blisters at the moment the Mahatma was shot.

Gandhi's assassination: "Bapu [*father*] *is finished"*

New York World-Telegram, January 30, 1948, United Press Associations

NEW DELHI, JANUARY 30—Mohandas K. Gandhi was assassinated today by a Hindu extremist whose act plunged India into sorrow and fear.

Rioting broke out immediately in Bombay.

The seventy-eight-year-old leader whose people had christened him the Great Soul of India died at 5:45 P.M. (7:15 A.M. EST) with his head cradled in the lap of his sixteen-year-old granddaughter, Mani.

Just half an hour before, a Hindu fanatic, Ram Naturam, had pumped three bullets from a revolver into Gandhi's frail body, emaciated by years of fasting and asceticism.

Gandhi was shot in the luxurious gardens of Birla House in the presence of one thousand of his followers, whom he was leading to the little summer pagoda where it was his habit to make his evening devotions.

Dressed as always in his homespun,

723

sacklike dhoti, and leaning heavily on a staff of stout wood, Gandhi was only a few feet from the pagoda when the shots were fired.

Gandhi crumpled instantly, putting his hand to his forehead in the Hindu gesture of forgiveness to his assassin. Three bullets penetrated his body at close range, one in the upper right thigh, one in the abdomen, and one in the chest.

He spoke no word before he died. A moment before he was shot he said —some witnesses believed he was speaking to the assassin—"You are late."

The assassin had been standing beside the garden path, his hands folded, palms together, before him in the Hindu gesture of greeting. But between his palms he had concealed a small-caliber revolver. After pumping three bullets into Gandhi at a range of a few feet, he fired a fourth shot in an attempt at suicide, but the bullet merely creased his scalp.

The shots sounded like a string of firecrackers and it was a moment before Gandhi's devotees realized what had happened. Then they turned on the assassin savagely and would have torn him to bits had not police guards intervened with rifles and drawn bayonets. The assassin was hustled to safekeeping.

Gandhi quickly was borne back to Birla House and placed on a couch with his head in his granddaughter's lap. Within a few moments she spoke to the stricken throng, among them Pandit Jawaharlal Nehru, Premier of India: *"Bapu* [father] is finished."

Then Mani rose and sat cross-legged beside the body of the man whose life was forfeit for the cause of peace and humanity. She began to chant the two-thousand-year-old verses of the Bhagavad-Gita, the Hindu scripture.

Over all India the word spread like wildfire. Minutes after the flash was received in Bombay rioting broke out, with Hindu extremists attacking Moslems. A panic-stricken Moslem woman echoed the thoughts of thousands with a cry: "God help us all!"

In Delhi itself, in the quick-gathering gloom of the night, the news set the people on the march.

They walked slowly down the avenues and out of the squalid bazaars, converging on Birla House. There by the thousands they stood weeping silently or moaning and wailing. Some sought to scale the high walls and catch one last glimpse of the Mahatma. Strong troop contingents strove to keep order.

Tonight in response to the insistent demand of the people, his body was shown to them.

The balcony window of the house opened and the body was borne outside. The people gasped and surged forward as it was placed in a chair, facing them. A brilliant spotlight blazed on the wrinkled, brown face. The eyes were closed, the face peaceful in repose. A white sheet covered the bloodstained loincloth.

Within Birla House there was grief and mourning which at least for the moment fused the dissident sects of India—the Hindus, the Moslems, and the Sikhs—into a community of sorrow.

But there were grave fears, heightened by the savage outbreaks in Bombay, that without her saint to hold passions in check, all India might be whirled into strife.

* * *

Cremation: "Gandhi still lives!"

New York World-Telegram, January 31, 1948

NEW DELHI, JANUARY 31—The body of sainted Mohandas K. Gandhi today was committed to the flames of the burning ghat as violence touched off by his assassination flared anew in Bombay.

The ancient Hindu ceremonial was carried out on the banks of the Jumna, one of the five sacred rivers of India, in a demonstration of national grief.

Devadas Gandhi, eldest son of the slain leader, touched fire to the pyre to consume the earthly remains of India's great soul.

For the moment India's capital was unified by grief over Gandhi's death.

His body was borne through the streets of New Delhi and Old Delhi in such a procession as India had never seen. As the cortege passed, the hundreds of thousands of mourners left their places and followed the bier in a procession that wound more than five miles long behind Gandhi's body.

At the banks of the Jumna, the huge mass of humanity, wailing and weeping, packed around the newly bricked burning platform for as far as the eye could see.

Gandhi's body was placed on the pyre with wood heaped below and around it.

While the crowd raised a cry: "Gandhi! Gandhi! Gandhi!" Devadas began the ceremony.

First an unguent, a mixture of liquid butter and incense, was poured over the pyre. Then Devadas faced toward the sun, now lowering to the west, and began to chant the ancient verses of the Sanskrit Veda, holy book of the Hindus.

The verses committed Gandhi to the gods who will be responsible for his next reincarnation.

As the chanting ceased, Devadas took flame from the sacred lamp, which had burned all night beside Gandhi's body, and touched it to the pyre.

The day was clear and warm. But a light wind arose and swirled up the dust raised by the naked feet of the hundreds of thousands of mourners. The dust hung over the whole eight-mile route of the cortege from Birla House to the banks of the sacred river.

All of Delhi gathered at the pyre in final tribute to Gandhi. There were leprous beggars in the crowd and there were true nabobs with rubies as big as pigeon eggs gleaming in their feather-bedecked turbans.

The shouting of the crowd rose to thunder as the cremation proceeded. Again and again they shouted: "Victory to Gandhi! Gandhi still lives!"

The multitude watched as the flames licked up through the sandalwood pyre, consuming Gandhi's earthly remains.

* * *

IN A HEARTBROKEN broadcast in which he announced Gandhi's death, Pandit Jawaharlal Nehru, Prime Minister of India and close friend of the assassinated leader, said: "Now the light has gone out," perhaps an unconscious imitation of Homer's "The sun has perished out of the heav-

ens." "Just an old man in a loincloth in distant India," commented Louis
Fischer. "Yet when he died, humanity wept." In a moving editorial *The
New York Times* paid tribute to "the saint who will be remembered, not
only on the plains and in the hills of India but all over the world. He strove
for perfection as other men strive for power and possessions. He pitied
those to whom wrong was done: the East Indian laborers in South Africa,
the untouchable 'Children of God' of the lowest caste in India, but he
schooled himself not to hate the wrongdoer." "Now he belongs to the
ages," concluded the *Times'* tribute.

On February 12 near the city of Allahabad, amidst the frenzy of a traditional religious festival, three million awe-struck Indians watched as the
ashes of Gandhi were immersed in India's holiest waters. It was a strangely
incongruous sight: a wartime amphibious "duck" carried the remains;
airplanes, relics of war, swooped low over the floating white hearse; guns,
always hated by the deceased, boomed a farewell.

In Which Leo the Giraffe Dies, to Be Survived by Second Wife, Canine Buster Finkel Is Outfitted with False Teeth, and a Beer-bibbing Baboon Bathes, Pinches Mrs. Plummer's Pence

Twentieth-century animal crackers

JUST LIKE the rest of us, reporters are fascinated by what goes on in the animal world. Every now and then a crack newsman comes up with a really fine animal story that heads straight for the heart of the reading public. After happily wading through several thousand, the editors have rescued these three from oblivion.

First—Harold Faber, of *The New York Times*, wrote this story of the death of Leo the giraffe at the Central Park Zoo. The next day a huge bundle of laudatory mail covered the city editor's desk.

Leo the Giraffe dies; Survived by second wife

The New York Times, October 23, 1946

Leo the giraffe, one of the favorite attractions at the Central Park Zoo, died suddenly on Monday. He was sixteen years old.

He was born in Kenya, Africa, a member of the family *Giraffa camelopardalis*, which became well known in Tertiary times and spread all over southern Europe and India. In recent years, however, the family has restricted its activities to Africa, south of the Sahara.

Leo came to this country on July 14, 1937, when he was seven, with his first wife, Pauline. They immediately settled in the Manhattan zoo and began to earn their living as attractions for crowds of humans.

Pauline died in 1943.

"Leo was everybody's favorite," one of the keepers recalled. "They came from all over to see Leo."

The giraffe was discovered ill at eight o'clock Sunday morning. A veterinary was called, but before definitive medical treatment could be supplied he died. The cause of death was believed to be tuberculosis, with pneumonia complications.

Surviving are his widow, Pauline II, and two cousins at the Bronx Park Zoo, Jack and Jill. He had no children.

Interment was private, following cremation by the Department of Sanitation.

IN ANOTHER short news item Dan Smyth, of the *Chicago Times,* showed the disappointing effects of civilization on the canine world.

The dog with the false teeth

Chicago Times, February 8, 1939

Most dogs have upper teeth shaped something like this: VVVVVVVVV.

Buster Finkel, sadfaced pet of Max Finkel, 3333 W. Washington, has upper teeth something like this:

UUUUUUUUUU.

Buster came to the Finkel home three years ago with a healthy set of canine canines. He masticated the toughest steaks, chewed up the parlor rug, and enjoyed the rich walnut flavor of the dining-room table.

But, despite the urging of his master, a dental technician, Buster used the wrong dentifrice.

Acids formed by fermentation of tiny food particles lodged in the crevices between the teeth beyond reach of the ordinary brush did their deadly work.

He was lovely until he smiled.

Science hastened to the rescue. Over his worn-down teeth Finkel fitted an artificial plate. Not having any dog's teeth in stock the technician equipped Buster with a set of human teeth.

Buster, with two gold crowns already in his suffering gums, at first resented wearing a whole mouthful of phony tusks. Instead of leaving them in a glass for the night he tried to bury them in the back yard forever. But he doesn't mind them any more.

"I'll never make another set for a dog, though," said Finkel. "He wants to chew twice as much as ever before, including the hand that feeds him."

DATE-LINED Ipswich, England, July 15, 1948, this United Press story was calculated to take people's minds off tension in Berlin, high meat prices, and the fate of the Brooklyn Dodgers:

Beer-bibbing baboon bathes, pinches Mrs. Plummer's pence

United Press, July 15, 1948

An escaped baboon had a wonderful time at Mrs. Dorothy Plummer's house here recently drinking stout and eating, then taking a shower and going to bed, while the terrified woman cowered in the kitchen.

Elizabeth, a kindly six-year-old baboon, escaped from a fair and ambled a quarter of a mile to the home of Mrs. Plummer, who sat in the kitchen drinking coffee and did not hear Elizabeth let herself in by the front door.

The baboon went into the dining

room, helped herself to oranges and bananas, then spied a pint bottle of stout. After taking a swig, Elizabeth tucked the bottle under her arm and went upstairs, eating cherries and spitting the pits over the banister.

Still drinking the beer, she entered the bathroom, turned on all the water taps, and climbed into the bathtub. Then she sprayed the walls with the hand shower.

Mrs. Plummer, meanwhile, had gone out into the yard and looked up just in time to see Elizabeth waving cheerfully from the bedroom window. Mrs. Plummer locked herself in the kitchen while a neighbor phoned the police.

Elizabeth dusted herself with a powder puff and entered three more rooms before wrapping herself in a pink silk quilt.

When police arrived, she was propped up in bed, finishing off the stout. A worker from the fair led away the baboon without trouble, but Elizabeth had taken Mrs. Plummer's handbag.

"She was handing my money to everyone," said Mrs. Plummer bitterly.

* * *

Berlin Airlift: "Operation Vittles" Frustrates the Soviet Gamble to Throttle Berlin

H ARDLY HAD THE shooting war ended when a Cold War between former allies took its place. When the Soviet Union assumed an aggressive posture, the United States was impelled to take a stand for the military and economic support of Greece and Turkey, to initiate the Marshall Plan, and to reconstitute its Western military alliances.

Of all points of friction in the Cold War, Germany was the most critical. The Soviet Union envisioned a united Germany as a future communist state ("Who controls Germany controls Europe"—Lenin), whereas the West desired a democratic Germany operating under some form of the free-enterprise system. Friction was most evident in Berlin under the joint control of the former allies. The Kremlin regarded that city as a part of the Soviet zone. In fact only a single railway, a single auto road, and a twenty-mile corridor united the former German capital with the Western zones. These land routes could be closed at any time by the Russians.

On March 20, 1948, the Control Council met in Berlin for the last time. Marshal Sokolovsky read a long prepared statement of grievances against the West, declared the meeting adjourned, and stalked out of the room. Thus ended quadripartite government in Berlin.

Unable to come to an agreement with the Soviet authorities on currency reform for Berlin, the Western Allies on June 18, 1948, introduced a new currency in their zones. In retaliation the Russians closed all approaches to Berlin by rail, road, and water. Electrical power from the power stations in the Soviet sector was cut off. The Kremlin had taken a calculated gamble that the 2,250,000 Berliners, suffering from cold and hunger, would themselves request the Western powers to quit the city.

The response of the Western powers was immediate, daring, and extraordinarily effective. Almost at once a large-scale airlift was inaugurated to take supplies into Berlin. Huge cargo planes were loaded at Frankfurt and Wiesbaden with food, clothing, and even such bulk raw materials as coal, and flown to an airport in the United States sector in Berlin. When the airlift (or airbridge, as the Germans called it) moved into high gear, a loaded cargo plane landed at Tempelhof Airdrome every three minutes, day and night, and an ascending curve of supplies came down from the skies. First 3,000 tons a day, then 7,000, then as much as 8,000 tons a day.

For 320 days "Operation Vittles" was carried on, despite a severe north-German winter, despite accidents, despite innumerable difficulties. After the airlift had brought in more than a million and a half tons of supplies, the Russians acknowledged defeat by calling off the blockade. Contributing to the reluctant Russian decision was the Allied counterblockade, resulting in the virtual economic strangulation of East Germany, which was deprived of such essential items as coal, iron, and steel from the Western sector.

Many dispatches covering the Berlin blockade and airlift appeared in the press of the Western nations. One of the most vivid is that related by Karl Detzer.

"Thank you, thank you, and God be with you!"

Karl Detzer, "Riding the Berlin Airlift," in *Reader's Digest,* April 1949

One night recently, I rode the airlift to Berlin. In a few short hours I saw a million pounds of food and coal dive out of the rainy sky to feed and heat the hungry people in this dazed and battered city. I saw American and British boys perform the impossible, exultantly, to feed their enemies of three short years ago.

Today the enemy is starvation. The Russians are its allies. And if it weren't for the ingenuity and skill and the stupendous courage of these young airmen, starvation would long since have won this cold and gnawing war.

About three hundred miles from Berlin, beyond the last sullen outposts of the Russian zone, is the great American-built airport called Rhein-Main. There and at other flying fields an endless parade of trucks hauls in the food and fuel, and there the big four-motored planes take off on "Operation Vittles."

All day in nearby Frankfurt I had heard their roar overhead, and at six o'clock in the evening I rode to the port with a sergeant named Boyer from Michigan. Thin rain was falling and fog covered the earth. It would be eight o'clock before we could get off, they told me at the operations office. I drank coffee with a young American from San Francisco and his pretty Chicago bride. They'd both worked in Berlin and had gone out to be married and were on their way back. We shouted to one another over our coffee, for the endless roar was close by, ships taking off, ships landing, trucks of flour and raisins and canned foods rushing out to the loading strips.

Then word came in that our ship was ready. We'd have to hurry. The airlift waits for no man. We ran, lugging our flight bags. The plane stood on the apron, one of a score with engines turning over, eager to take to the dark night air. This was a cargo carrier, dusty with flour and coal, and there were no seats, only a narrow bench around the sides. We sat facing inward with mailbags piled at our feet, Americans, Englishmen and French army officers, all bound for jobs in beleaguered Berlin.

We moved out from the ramp, our nose nearly touching the tail of the plane in front, and behind us another ship nearly touching our tail. There's no time for caution on the airlift. I could look back through the small, round, dirty window and see thirty other ships loading or taking places in the line. The roar of motors was deafening.

Then we were off, a scant two hundred yards behind the ship ahead of us. And by the time our wheels lifted from the concrete there was another plane racing behind us to take to the air.

But then came a radio flash. A Navy plane had landed wrong on the slippery strip at Tempelhof, turned over, exploded. Men in asbestos suits were trying to rescue the crew. We could not land there. Nor would we turn back.

At Gatow Field in the British sector of Berlin, British York planes were depositing their cargoes at the rate of one every four minutes. We'd make for Gatow, there insinuate ourselves into the British line. It took extra precious minutes but there we swooped down, less than sixty seconds behind the plane ahead of us, a minute ahead of the plane behind. As we banked to land, our pilot had said, "Notice those people down there? They're always there, watching—day and night."

Next day I stood with those people; I saw them lift their threadbare caps to incoming ships and heard them say: "Thank you, thank you, and God be with you!" Hundreds stand at the airports from foggy dawn till late at night. When a flier dies—and in the first six months of the airlift 36 U.S. and British airmen did die in blazing wrecks—the Germans gather and pray for the souls of the dead young men. They write pathetic letters to the families of the fliers.

Berlin is an island in a sea of Russian troops. We have 2500 soldiers

there, and in a ring around them stand 100,000 of Russia's best fighting men with tanks and guns. If war came we could hold out perhaps half an hour. But we're there, and there we stay as long as a single German citizen depends on us for food and coal.

On the day when he started the airlift last June, General Lucius D. Clay, American Military Governor, had two four-motored C-54 transports, a handful of bombers and about two dozen twin-engine C-47's. Tonnage that first week was alarmingly small, and the 21-day stockpile of food and fuel began to shrink. Clay called for more planes, more pilots and ground crews. For millions of gallons of gasoline. For spare parts, repair shops, de-icers, extra radios and radar equipment.

From all over America big Air Force transport planes set off. Then came the C-54's of the Alaska Command, with their tall red tails, and ships from Panama, Puerto Rico, Honolulu, the Far East. The Navy sent planes to the airlift and relieved the Air Force on the transatlantic transport run. The British sent every ship they had; Australians and New Zealanders offered their handful of planes and many ground crews.

Today 240 big American Air Force and Navy planes, 100 British Yorks and Dakotas, and a few new "flying boxcars" with open rear ends to handle big machinery pour some 5000 tons of food, fuel and medical supplies into the beleaguered city every 24 hours. By January, Berlin's stockpile had grown from 21 days' backlog to 30, in spite of fog and winter weather.

All Europe on both sides of the Iron Curtain knows the story of the airlift's success. Eight thousand young Americans—pilots and engineers, radio and radar men, truck drivers and motor repairmen—are writing it across the German sky for the world to see. With them strive two thousand British airmen and a few hundred sturdy Australians and New Zealanders. The French, who do not have a powerful air force, have sent technicians to help.

The planes load at seven supply airports in the British and American zones. As they swoop down to land in Berlin in endless procession day and night, little yellow jeeps guide them to unloading stands. Each jeep has a bright-green neon sign on its tail: "Follow Me." The planes rush off the crowded runways and follow their jeeps to the stands.

As a ship approaches its place, a huge 16-wheel truck rumbles out to meet it. The plane's side door opens while the truck is backing into position. The precision is astounding; there's not a wasted second.

The plane's crew of three men hurry down a ladder or slide down a rope to the ground. An Air Force captain or first lieutenant is the pilot; the copilot is a lieutenant, the engineer a staff sergeant. They are young and sturdy—and terribly tired. Their faces are often black with coal dust from their cargos. They don't get enough sleep; they grab a bite to eat when and where they can.

A little truck meets each incoming ship. Inside its open windows are a German cook and two German waitresses. "Two hot dogs with plenty mustard," the pilot shouts above the roar of motors. "Coffee, black." The copilot takes a hamburger and a coke, the engineer hot chocolate and doughnuts. The crew stamp their feet on the frozen earth. On many a ship the heaters long ago burned out, but there's no time for nonessential repairs.

In ten minutes the truck pulls away with its cargo. The fliers, munching their sandwiches, have already climbed back aboard their ship. The copilot picks up his microphone. "Ready for take-off," he reports to the control tower.

"Get into line," the tower replies.

The tower at Tempelhof airport is one of the most important rooms in the world. Washington and London, Paris and Moscow watch it narrowly, and their decisions are guided by its effectiveness.

It's just a shack on tall wooden stilts high above the roof of the six-story headquarters building. Broad windows look down on the parallel white runways. Sitting at a long table, five young American soldiers with earphones clamped to their heads guide the endless procession of incoming planes, "talking them down," keeping them close enough together to prevent a wasted minute.

They call this room the "hot box," and it's easy to understand why. There is never a moment when one of these youngsters can allow his mind to wander from the exacting job on hand. The day I was there, the man in command was a 25-year-old Air Force lieutenant. Two sergeants and two corporals about 23 years old formed his immediate staff. A microphone hangs in front of each man and a row of loudspeakers on the table is making a fearful racket. In a room below, other soldiers are logging the flights on a dispatcher board.

Outside, a thick haze is gathering and the orange runway lights are a muddy ocher. Ships already are beginning to fall behind schedule; you can't bring them in as fast by radar as you can on a clear day. The men in the hot box talk into their microphones and the loudspeakers shout back. A corporal is saying, "Tempelhof to Flight 79. Come in, 79. What's your position?"

"Five miles out at two thousand feet," the ship replies.

Another loudspeaker says stridently, "Our number-three engine's out. Have a mechanic ready."

"Roger!" one of the sergeants answers and he cranks a telephone. The other sergeant has been repeating, "Tower to 92. Come in, 92." He turns to the lieutenant. "Flight 92 don't answer." The lieutenant grabs a microphone and calls the missing ship. No reply. The sergeant looks up into the darkening sky. "Maybe that's him up there," he says. "Looks as if he's in trouble." The ship banks to come in. The four soldiers shout warnings to all other planes to keep aloft. The lieutenant signals for crash truck and ambulance. The plane is heading for the runway, coming in fast. You feel the tightness in the hot box. The plane touches the runway, does not turn over. Everyone breathes again.

"Tower to Flight 63," a sergeant says casually. "Come in for landing. Number 51, follow 63. Close up distance."

Routine again. . . .

Although airlift planes were carrying thousands of tons last winter, the fog which shrouded the fields day after day gave the Russians temporary hope. The pilots flew blind through the worst weather in 32 years, and radarmen had to guide each ship down.

One evening while the fog was at its worst, a pilot received radio orders to make an instrument landing. A dozen ships were behind him. Their pilots, listening tensely for orders, heard the first flier's reply: "There'll be a slight delay. I can't find my oars!" The other pilots howled; the tension broke; they all came in safely. Not long afterward a cold wave froze away the fog.

Nearly four-fifths of the airlift tonnage is coal, but two-thirds of the bulk is food. Most of the food is dehydrated. The coal is used only to produce electric current and gas for cookstoves. The people of the city are chopping down shade trees in the parks for fuel to warm their homes. The average Berliner has lost 15 pounds since the blockade started. But he blames the Russians and counts his blessings. Eighty-five per cent of the eligible voters cast ballots last December, in that free election in the city under siege, and 99 out of 100 voted against Communism.

Besides the British airfield, there's a new field in the French sector. When General Clay decided to build the latter, the Russians were amused. They knew that there was not enough cement or asphalt in the whole city to build one runway. Besides, when they evacuated western Berlin and left it to the Allies, the Russians had taken away every bulldozer, concrete mixer and paving machine.

General Clay put 30,000 German men and women to work with pick, shovel and wheelbarrow, leveling the bomb craters. The flying boxcars flew in with big machines. If a steam shovel was too large to be carried whole, mechanics cut it apart with acetylene torches and welded it together in Berlin. The airlift carried millions of pounds of cement and asphalt to build the mile-long runways. Today, ships land on those runways, bringing in food.

Although the bulk of cargo moves eastward to the city, the planes have carried special cargo on their westbound flights. One month, for instance, they transported three thousand children who needed more milk and green vegetables than their Berlin ration allowed. These youngsters are now putting on weight and getting back their color in farmhouses in the British and American zones.

On the Sunday last January when the airlift was two hundred days old, Berlin decided, without telling the Americans, to celebrate the anniversary by paying respects to the fliers who brought them their daily bread. Early in the morning the streets around the airfield began to fill with people dressed in their shabby best. They brought modest gifts for the fliers—small hand-carved toys, old silver or china salvaged from the ruins of the city. All day they came by the grateful thousands; they broke through the police lines and rushed out on the field to present their gifts personally to the fliers.

When the Americans took over Tempelhof, a huge black Nazi eagle with a white swastika on its breast stood above the main entrance. The Americans didn't tear it down. They chopped off the swastika and substituted an American shield, then painted the eagle's head a glistening white. It's an American eagle now.

The kids who fly the lift, who guide the trucks, who run the control towers are farm boys and lads from our city streets. There's a swagger to their walk and they talk lightly of the risks they take. And if they carry a chip on their shoulder, who can blame them? For that chip is a bright thing called Democracy. They wear it well.

Triumph, Near-Disaster, and Stalemate:
Three Pulitzer Prize Winners Describe
the Progress of the Korean War

TECHNICALLY it was a "police action," but in reality the Korean War proved a grueling struggle which cost the participants as many casualties as some major wars. It was a military action marked by dramatic reversals in fortune, ending where it started, and resulting in a stalemate rather than a conclusive peace.

The year 1950 proved a year of critical testing both of the American policy of the containment of Communism and of the willingness and ability of the free world to halt aggressors. In the first half of that year three dates are important. On January 12 Secretary of State Dean Acheson drew a "defense perimeter" beyond which American forces would not venture. Beyond this line lay Korea, and it seemed to be the implication of Acheson's remarks that America accepted no responsibility for its defense. On February 14 the Soviet Union and the Chinese Communists entered into a formal alliance, and on June 24 North Korean troops crossed the 38th parallel.

That line had been set up soon after Potsdam, as a dividing line for the troops of the Soviet Union and the United States to maintain order and prepare the defenses for a liberated Korea. In fact, Russia opposed unification of North and South Korea and barred the UN commissioners from the area north of the 38th parallel. When Korea was proclaimed an independent state, the puppet Soviet Democratic People's Republic of North Korea announced that it too was a sovereign state.

The North Korean Communists and the powers behind them seemed prepared to take grave risks, because once it was clear that the UN and the United States would resist aggression—and that decision was made almost immediately—they moved ahead regardless of cost. Seoul, the Korean capital, fell on June 28, and Pohang on September 6, but the Red offensive failed to drive UN forces off the peninsula. Instead General Douglas MacArthur, the UN commander, launched a daring counteroffensive on September 15, when UN forces made an amphibious landing at Inchon far north of Red penetration and began an eastward sweep across the peninsula. The story of the landing of the American marines at Inchon, as well as other exciting front-line dispatches, was written by a pretty blond correspondent who shared with Homer Bigart the Korean War coverage for the *New York Herald Tribune*. Born in Hong Kong of an American father and a French mother, Marguerite Higgins had previously covered the entry of American troops into Berlin in World War II and was among the first correspondents to see the concentration camp at Dachau. For her front-line coverage of the Korean War she won a Pulitzer Prize for International Reporting in 1951, making her the only woman ever to win this award for war correspondence.

"My God! There are still some left"— *Marguerite Higgins*

New York Herald Tribune, September 18, 1950

WITH THE U.S. MARINES AT INCHON, KOREA, SEPTEMBER 15 (DELAYED)— Heavily laden U.S. Marines, in one of the most technically difficult amphibious landings in history, stormed at sunset today over a ten-foot sea wall in the heart of the port of Inchon and within an hour had taken three commanding hills in the city.

I was in the fifth wave that hit "Red Beach," which in reality was a rough, vertical pile of stones over which the first assault troops had to scramble with the aid of improvised landing ladders topped with steel hooks.

Despite a deadly and steady pounding from naval guns and airplanes, enough North Koreans remained alive close to the beach to harass us with small-arms and mortar fire. They even hurled hand grenades down at us as we crouched in trenches, which unfortunately ran behind the sea wall in the inland side.

It was far from the "virtually unopposed" landing for which the troops had hoped after hearing of the quick capture of Wolmi Island in the morning by an earlier Marine assault. Wolmi is inside Inchon harbor and just off "Red Beach." At H-hour minus seventy, confident, joking Marines started climbing down from the transport ship on cargo nets and dropping into small assault boats.

Our wave commander, Lieutenant R. J. Schening, a veteran of five amphibious assaults, including Guadalcanal, hailed me with the comment, "This has a good chance of being a pushover."

Because of tricky tides, our transport had to stand down the channel and it was more than nine miles to the rendezvous point where our assault waves formed up.

The channel reverberated with the earsplitting boom of warship guns and rockets. Blue and orange flame spurted from the "Red Beach" area and a huge oil tank, on fire, sent great black rings of smoke over the shore. Then the fire from the big guns lifted and the planes that had been circling overhead swooped low to rake their fire deep into the sea wall.

The first wave of our assault troops was speeding toward the shore by now. It would be H-hour (5:30 P.M.) in two minutes. Suddenly, bright-orange tracer bullets spun out from the hill in our direction.

"My God! There are still some left," Lieutenant Schening said. "Everybody get down. Here we go!"

It was H-hour plus fifteen minutes as we sped the last two thousand yards to the beach. About halfway there the bright tracers started cutting across the top of our little boat. "Look at their faces now," said John

Davies of the Newark *News*. I turned
and saw that the men around me had
expressions contorted with anxiety.

We struck the sea wall hard at a
place where it had crumbled into a
canyon. The bullets were whining
persistently, spattering the water
around us. We clambered over the
high steel sides of the boat, dropping
into the water and, taking shelter beside the boat as long as we could,
snaked on our stomachs up into a
rock-strewn dip in the sea wall.

In the sky there was good news. A
bright, white star shell from the high
ground to our left and an amber
cluster told us that the first wave had
taken their initial objective, Observatory Hill. But whatever the luck of
the first four waves, we were relentlessly pinned down by rifle and auto-
matic-weapon fire coming down on us
from another rise on the right.

There were some thirty Marines
and two correspondents crouched in
the gouged-out sea wall. Then another assault boat swept up, disgorg-
ing about thirty more Marines. This
went on for two more waves until
our hole was filled and Marines lying
on their stomachs were strung out all
across the top of the sea wall.

An eerie colored light flooded the
area as the sun went down with a
glow that a newsreel audience would
have thought a fake. As the dusk
settled, the glare of burning buildings
all around lit the sky.

Suddenly, as we lay there intent on
the firing ahead, a sudden rush of
water came up into the dip in the
wall and we saw a huge LST (Landing Ship, Tank) rushing at us with
the great plank door half down. Six
more yards and the ship would have
crushed twenty men. Warning shouts
sent every one speeding from the sea

wall, searching for escape from the
LST and cover from the gunfire. The
LST's huge bulk sent a rush of water
pouring over the sea wall as it
crunched in, soaking most of us.

The Marines ducked and zigzagged
as they raced across the open, but
enemy bullets caught a good many in
the semi-darkness. The wounded were
pulled aboard the LSTs, six of which
appeared within sixty-five minutes
after H-hour.

As nightfall closed in, the Marine
commanders ordered their troops forward with increasing urgency, for
they wanted to assure a defensible
perimeter for the night.

In this remarkable amphibious operation, where tides played such an
important part, the Marines were
completely isolated from outside supply lines for exactly four hours after
H-hour. At this time the outrushing
tides—they fluctuate thirty-one feet
in twelve-hour periods—made mud
flats of the approaches to "Red
Beach." The LSTs bringing supplies
simply settled on the flats, helpless
until the morning tides would float
them again.

At the battalion command post the
news that the three high-ground objectives—the British Consulate,
Cemetery Hill, and Observatory Hill
—had been taken arrived at about
H-hour plus sixty-one minutes. Now
the important items of business became debarking tanks, guns, and ammunition from the LSTs.

Every cook, clerk, driver, and administrative officer in the vicinity
was rounded up to help in the unloading. It was exciting to see the huge
M-26 tanks rumble across big planks
onto the beach, which only a few minutes before had been protected only

by riflemen and machine gunners. Then came the bulldozers, trucks, and jeeps.

It was very dark in the shadow of the ships, and the unloaders had a hazardous time dodging bullets, mortar fire, and their own vehicles.

North Koreans began giving up by the dozens by this time and we could see them, hands up, marching across the open fields toward the LSTs. They were taken charge of with considerable glee by a Korean Marine policeman, Captain Woo, himself a native of Inchon, who had made the landing with several squads of men who were also natives of the city. They learned of the plan to invade their home town only after they had boarded their ship.

Tonight, Captain Woo was in a state of elation beyond even that of the American Marines who had secured the beachhead. "When the Koreans see your power," he said, "they will come in droves to our side."

As we left the beach and headed back to the Navy flagship, naval guns were booming again in support of the Marines. "This time," said a battalion commander, "they are preparing the road to Seoul."

Having trapped the extended North Korean forces by the daring landing on the Pusan Peninsula, the UN forces swept eastward across the peninsula, capturing Seoul on September 26. MacArthur's troops pressed north, crossed the 38th parallel, and, after capturing the North Korean capital of Pyongyang on October 20, advanced toward the Manchurian border.

Now the vast manpower of Red China was hurled into the breach. As early as September 30, Foreign Minister Chou En-lai of Red China had implied that the Chinese Communists would intervene. Soon Peiping denounced the crossing of the 38th parallel, and on October 26, Red Chinese divisions openly intervened in Korea, crossing the Yalu River from Manchuria. Against General MacArthur's "end-the-war" offensive the Chinese launched on November 26 a massive counteroffensive in the Yalu Valley. Outnumbered many times, the UN troops withdrew to the 38th parallel, where they managed to stabilize a defensive line that has been roughly maintained since then. In short, the war ended where it began, but the aggressor had paid a frightful price for his adventure.

The story of the valiant defense put up by the United States Marines cut off in the Changjin Reservoir and of their gallant withdrawal from an icy hell was brilliantly reported by Keyes Beech of the *Chicago Daily News*. A seasoned war correspondent who had covered the Korean action from its opening moments, Beech was awarded a Pulitzer Prize in International Reporting in 1951 for his Korean War coverage, including this moving story written after he had flown deep into North Korea to cover the Marine breakout from the Changjin Reservoir.

"This was no retreat"—
Keyes Beech

Chicago Daily News, December 11, 1950

YONPO AIRSTRIP, KOREA—"Remember," drawled Colonel Lewis B. "Chesty" Puller, "whatever you write, that this was no retreat. All that happened was we found more Chinese behind us than in front of us. So we about-faced and attacked."

I said "so long" to Puller after three snowbound days with the 1st Marine Division, 4,000 feet above sea level in the sub-zero weather of Changjin Reservoir. I climbed aboard a waiting C-47 at Koto Airstrip and looked around.

Sixteen shivering Marine casualties—noses and eyes dripping from cold—huddled in their bucket seats. They were the last of more than 2,500 Marine casualties to be evacuated by the U.S. Air Force under conditions considered flatly impossible.

Whatever this campaign was—retreat, withdrawal, or defeat—one thing can be said with certainty. Not in the Marine Corps' long and bloody history has there been anything like it. And if you'll pardon a personal recollection, not at Tarawa or Iwo Jima, where casualties were much greater, did I see men suffer as much.

The wonder isn't that they fought their way out against overwhelming odds but that they were able to survive the cold and fight at all. So far as the Marines themselves are concerned, they ask that two things be recorded:

1. They didn't break. They came out of Changjin Reservoir as an organized unit with most of their equipment.

2. They brought out all their wounded. They brought out many of their dead. And most of those they didn't bring out they buried.

It was not always easy to separate dead from wounded among the frozen figures that lay strapped to radiators of jeeps and trucks. I know because I watched them come in from Yudam to Hagaru, 18 miles of icy hell, five days ago.

That same day I stood in the darkened corner of a wind-whipped tent and listened to a Marine officer brief his men for the march to Koto the following day. I have known him for a long time but in the semidarkness, with my face half-covered by my parka, he didn't recognize me. When he did the meeting broke up. When we were alone, he cried. After that he was all right.

I hope he won't mind my reporting he cried, because he's a very large Marine and a very tough guy.

He cried because he had to have some sort of emotional release; because all his men were heroes and wonderful people; because the next day he was going to have to submit them to another phase in the trial by blood and ice. Besides, he wasn't the only one who cried.

In the Marines' twelve-day, forty-mile trek from Yudam to the "bottom of the hill," strange and terrible things happened.

Thousands of Chinese troops—the Marines identified at least six divisions totaling 60,000 men—boiled from every canyon and rained fire from every ridge. Sometimes they came close enough to throw grenades into trucks, jeeps, and ambulances.

Whistles sounded and Chinese ran up to throw grenades into Marine foxholes. Another whistle and the Chinese ran back.

Then mortar shells began to fall. The 3rd Battalion of the 5th Marine Regiment was reduced to less than two companies but still was ordered to attack "regardless of cost."

"We had to do it," said Lieutenant Colonel Joe Stewart, of Montgomery, Alabama. "It was the only way out."

Fox Company, 7th Regiment, was isolated for three or four days—nobody seems to remember dates or days—but held at terrible cost.

One company killed so many Chinese the Marines used their frozen bodies as a parapet. But for every Chinese they killed there were five, ten, or twenty to take his place.

"What 'n hell's the use in killing them," said one Marine. "They breed faster 'n we can knock 'em off."

The Chinese had blown bridges and culverts behind the Americans. The Marines rebuilt them or established bypasses under fire.

No part of a division escaped, including headquarters sections composed of file clerks, cooks, and bakers. Bullets plowed through a Korean house in Hagaru occupied by General O. H. P. Smith.

Always the infantry had to take high ground on each side of the road to protect the train of vehicles that sometimes stretched ten miles.

When the Chinese attacked a train the artillerymen unhooked their guns from their vehicles and fired muzzle bursts from between trucks at the onrushing foe. This was effective, but rather rough on Marine machine gunners who had set up their guns on the railroad tracks fifteen or twenty yards in front of the artillery.

If there was an occasional respite from the enemy there was none from the cold. It numbed fingers, froze feet, sifted through layers of clothing, and crept into the marrow of your bones. Feet sweated by day and froze in their socks by night. Men peeled off their socks—and the soles of their feet with them.

Among the men of the 5th Marines, Lieutenant Commander Chester M. Lessenden, Jr., of Lawrence, Kansas, a Navy doctor, became a hero.

"Lessenden is the most saintly, Godlike man I've ever known," said Stewart. "He never seemed to sleep. He was always on his feet. He never said it can't be done. And yet he was suffering from frostbite worse than most of the men he treated."

In their struggle to keep from freezing, the Marines wrapped their feet in gunnysacks or pieces of old cloth scrounged from the countryside. When they could, they built fires, but this wasn't often, because fire gave away their positions.

When they came to Koto before the final breakthrough to the sea, they made tents of varicolored parachutes used by the Air Force to drop supplies. The red, white and green chute tents looked like Indian wigwams.

Some covered themselves with Japanese quilts dropped from the air. But they were warmest when they were fighting. Combat was almost welcome because they forgot about the cold.

The cold did strange things to their equipment. Because of sub-zero temperatures, artillery rounds landed as much as 2,000 yards short. Machine guns froze up. Men tugged frantically at their frozen bolts. The M-1 rifle generally held up but the Marines cursed the lighter carbine.

Communications gear broke down because equipment, like men, can stand only so much. Canteens burst as water froze inside them.

Despite all these things, the Marines who walked down from Changjin Reservoir still could laugh.

"It was impossible for us to get out, because we were surrounded, encircled, and cut off," said one lieutenant. "But we never got the word, so we came on out. That's us—we never get the word."

Once a front had been established along the 38th parallel, the Korean War settled down and became a grim struggle for mere inches of territory at a time. Consequently, a new kind of reporting developed—in which correspondents tried to give their readers back home some idea of what it was like to live along a line that rarely changed, but was never quiet. One of the best examples of this kind of journalism is Jim Lucas' account of "Our Town" on Pork Chop Hill. Written a little over six months before an armistice was signed at Panmunjon, it is one of the reasons why Lucas, a Scripps-Howard reporter, received the Pulitzer Prize in 1954 for his coverage of the Korean conflict.

"Our Town's business is war"— *Jim Lucas*

from Scripps-Howard newspapers, January 3, 1953

PORK CHOP HILL, KOREA, JANUARY 3 —Our Town atop Pork Chop Hill is in a world of its own.

Its contacts with the outside world are few—but imperative. Its immediate concern is the enemy on the next ridge. That's "His Town." To "His Town" Our Town gives grudging respect. But, if possible, "His Town" is going to be wiped out.

Our Town's business is war. It produces nothing but death. To exist, therefore, it must rely on others. Food, mail, clothing—even the weapons of destruction—are shipped in.

These items are sent in from that part of the outside world which the men of Our Town call "rear." As often—and far more passionately—

they are at war with "rear" as they are with enemy. "Rear," which includes anything beyond the foot of Pork Chop, is populated, Our Town is convinced, by idiots and stumble-bums.

Physically, Our Town—while hardly attractive—is not uncomfortable. Much municipal planning went into it.

The streets are six to eight feet deep. At times after dark, Our Town's streets are invaded by men from His Town. The citizens of Our Town invariably expel these interlopers. To assist in maintaining law and order on such occasions, the shelves along the streets of Our Town are liberally stocked with hand grenades.

There are thirty to fifty houses in Our Town. They are referred to as bunkers. Each street and each bunker is numbered. After a few days it's comparatively easy to find one's way.

Half of Our Town's bunkers are living quarters. The others are stores —storage bunkers, that is. From these you can obtain a wide assortment of ammunition, sandbags, candles, charcoal, or canned rations.

Our Town's buildings are sturdy. The typical building is at least six feet underground. It is made of four-by-ten-inch logs to which are added many sandbags. It's almost impervious to enemy shelling.

Our Town is not without its social life. I went visiting this morning at 19 Third Street in Our Town. Entering No. 19, one gets down on his hands and knees. The front door is low.

My hosts were First Lieutenant Pat Smith of Hollywood, California, Corporal Joe Siena of Portland, Connecticut, Private First Class Eddie Williams of Brooklyn, and Private Don Coan of Anadarko, Oklahoma.

Don had coffee brewing in an old ration can. He opened a can of sardines. Eddie was heading for the rear on a shopping trip. His list included candles, a coffeepot (which he'd had on order for a month already), and a reel of communications wire. He also was taking a field telephone for repairs.

Our Town, like others, enjoys small talk. Over coffee, the group discussed what a man should do if a grenade-wielding Chinese suddenly appeared at the door. There was no unanimous decision.

Our Town has its own banker— Warrant Officer James W. Cherry of Jackson, Tennessee. He came up the other afternoon. Within three hundred yards of the enemy, he distributed $23,411.

Many men didn't want their money, really. Money is an almost valueless commodity up here. Three days from now, the postal officer will come up the hill, selling money orders.

If money has no value, other things do. Things like candles, fuel, toilet tissue. There's never enough charcoal for the stoves which heat the bunkers. To stay warm you can climb into your sleeping bag—if you're a fool. The men refer to sleeping bags as "coffins." Too many soldiers have been killed before they could unzip their sleeping bags.

Our Town's Mayor is a tall, gangling Texan—Captain Jack Conn of Houston. He's company commander. The Vice Mayor is his executive officer—First Lieutenant Bill Gerald, also of Houston. Bill Gerald is a Negro.

The battalion commander, Lieutenant Colonel Seymour Goldberg of Washington, D.C., is convinced Our Town is a pigsty. Our Town's residents think Colonel Goldberg is a martinet.

Colonel Goldberg always arrives in a foul mood, to be expected, since high-up officials usually are blind to local problems. The Colonel expects miracles overnight. (Privately, he concedes this is an act—"If I didn't raise hell, they wouldn't take me seriously.")

Our Town endures this outsider stoically. The Colonel says the men need haircuts. "When would they have time to get haircuts?" say Our Town's citizens. He says the bunkers need cleaning. "They look all right to us," fume Our Towners. "We live here." He says ammunition isn't stored properly. "Let up on these all-night patrols and we'll store it right," retorts Our Town—not to the Colonel's face, of course.

Invariably the Colonel corrals a hapless private and demands he be court-martialed for one thing or another. Our Town's Mayor dutifully notes the boy's name and then throws away the notes when the Colonel leaves.

But the Colonel expects this.

There was much glee the other day when the Colonel issued an order that any man found outside a bunker without bulletproof vest on be punished. A moment later, the Colonel left the bunker—and forgot his vest.

There's method in the Colonel's madness. He deliberately sets out to make Our Town hate him. "If I didn't," he says, "it would go to pot."

You see, the Colonel once was a company commander who hated "rear." But on Bloody Triangle Hill, he won a promotion. Now he's part of "rear." He knows he must prod the men up front, so that their outfit will remain—despite the presence of death itself—a proud, disciplined, organized Army fighting unit.

Two Correspondents See the Russians Stifle
Satellite Hungary's Rebellion After
a Few Precious Days of Freedom

THE DEATH of Joseph Stalin in 1953 was followed by what Soviet journalist Ilya Ehrenburg called "The Thaw," which was the title of his book written outside Stalin's shadow. De-Stalinization was stepped up in February 1956 when Nikita Khrushchev denounced Stalin as "capricious and despotic" and a practitioner of "brutal violence."

"The Thaw" encouraged the Soviet satellites to demand greater freedom and independence of the Kremlin. In October of '56, patriotic Poles forced the Soviet government to accept as First Secretary Wladyslaw Gomulka, who, though a Communist himself, had been a victim of the Stalinist purges. As a result of a series of demonstrations in Warsaw, a nationalist communist government was set up, one presumably less subordinate to the Soviet Union than its predecessor.

One week later revolution broke out in Hungary. Starting as a general strike, the movement soon spread throughout western Hungary. Flushed by victory, the rebels put Imre Nagy in office as Prime Minister. Would the Soviets make the kind of concessions they had in Poland, or would this movement be put down ruthlessly? For a time the fate of the revolt was in doubt, as the Soviets appeared to accept the new regime and announced that they were withdrawing their troops. But on November 2, while the United States and the Soviet Union were both denouncing the Anglo-French-Israeli invasion of Egypt, reinforced Soviet army units encircled Budapest, sealed off the frontier with Austria, and proceeded to move in thousands of tanks to wipe out the poorly armed resistance groups, while the West stood by helplessly.

Graphic accounts of the Hungarian revolt were reported in the press of the free world. One of the most eloquent and moving was the report of Carl Gustaf Ströhm, correspondent of the Vienna weekly *Christ und Welt.*

"When the oppressors have·spoken, then will the oppressed speak" — *Carl Gustaf Ströhm*

Christ und Welt, November 1956

Translated by Louis L. Snyder

VIENNA, IN NOVEMBER—"Well, what are you going to write about Hungary when you get home?" I was asked by the Soviet political officer at the Russian command station in Ödenburg. "Will you perhaps say that Russian soldiers are murderers and barbarians?" I tried to smile, but I could not quite manage it. The humor of a commissar is just something different from that to which we are accustomed.

That was only a few hours ago. Now I am sitting in a friendly hotel room in Vienna and I am trying to collect my thoughts and decide what I really ought to say about Hungary. The reflections of electric-light signs blink in my window. If I hear the noise of automobile motors out there now, I know at least that they are not Soviet tanks. Even so I cannot be happy. I was only a witness to the battle for freedom by a small, courageous people. For four days I shared the surge of joy over their newly won freedom and then for eight days I had to look on as the people of Hungary were strangled. I had to escape, because my passport revealed that I was a foreigner. But hundreds of people, whom I saw and with whom I spoke, remained there. They stayed on to continue the struggle.

Never shall I forget the day when I saw the arrival of an Austrian Red Cross column in a small town on the road to Budapest. The modern auto-mobiles, packed with bandages and medicines, were immediately surrounded by hundreds of people. But these people, who knew that Soviet troops were only a few kilometers away, were not interested in medical supplies. With tears in their eyes they begged for weapons and ammunition. "Send us weapons instead of that stuff there," sobbed a worker, "otherwise we shall never get rid of the Russians. . . ." I didn't envy the Austrian Red Cross relief-column leader, who was besieged by the crowd and who could think of nothing else to say than: "Please, first of all we are from the Red Cross, and secondly, as Austrians we are neutral!"

In those days no one was frightened by the Soviet tank troops at Komorn, just halfway between the Austrian border and Budapest. Their speech showed them to be Ukrainian peasant lads. They seemed to be perplexed by the stream of freight and passenger cars which poured into the Hungarian capital. There didn't seem to be any front any more. Right in the midst of the Russian strong points were islands of Hungarian army detachments with improvised red-white-and-green cockades in their hats. Next to them were the auxiliary National Guardsmen—civilians with arm bands and tommy guns. One look was enough to reveal the inequality in strength. The few Hungarian tanks on the streets of the capital were ancient and apparently stemmed from the last war. "What we desperately need is tank-smashing artillery," said a young Hungarian officer who acted as controller on our train. "We can handle the T-34's in the streets of our capital, but on flat land in the countryside we are powerless." Even so he was full of optimism. In his view the Russians would have to get out.

I shall never forget how the Russians entered the city on the evening of October 30. On the sidewalks glowed the fires into which Communist literature and other propaganda materials had been thrown. An armistice had been arranged between the Soviets and the freedom fighters. We rode on the Margaret Bridge right through the middle of the front. On the one side there was a Soviet tank checkpoint, where we were searched for weapons. Less than two hundred meters farther on there were three railroad cars turned over, behind which the young boys and the broad-shouldered workers lay ready with their tommy guns and hand grenades. On the other shore of the Danube the Soviets had thrown a strong guard of tanks around the house of Parliament.

A Hungarian freedom fighter whom I had asked about lodgings put his weapon on the barricade, shoved his red-white-green arm band into his pocket, and said to me in German: "Come with me. You can live with me." Then he took me by the arm and marched quietly over the damaged bridge and through the rubble toward the Russian tanks. He steered me with much loquacity through several control points and finally brought me to his home near the War Ministry, which, just 24 hours ago, had

been the scene of hard fighting. This anti-Soviet freedom fighter, it turned out, lived right in the center of the Soviet positions.

When I asked him whether he was afraid to return home each evening into what amounted to Soviet imprisonment, he merely laughed. "The Russians are stupid. They notice nothing. When I want to get some sleep, I just put my weapon away over there and I go home as a civilian. And when I want to fight, I just put on my coat and I go to my weapon."

Then he opened the window, leaned out, and from the third story he yelled imprecations at the Russians, who were dozing alongside their tanks. Near them I saw some Hungarian soldiers. I asked my friend whether these were Communist Government troops—but he didn't quite understand me. "Do you know," he said, "they are first of all Hungarians. In the second place, they are Government troops. That is, they are Government troops only so long as they don't get orders to fire on the people. If they get such an order, then at worst they will share their weapons with the civilians, and at best they will fight on our side against the Russians."

The next morning he led me through the ghostlike streets of the city. At times it seemed to me that everything was peaceful. But then we would turn a corner and run straight into the mouths of weapons and machine guns. We would stumble onto a barricade and would have to get out of the way of half-grown boys and girls (they, too, were armed). The whole city was hunting for the hated members of the AVO, the Communist security police. I myself was a witness when a car with four secret police was stopped by freedom fighters in a western suburb of Budapest. Within five minutes not one of the AVO men was alive. I was at the tunnel near the Ketten Bridge when workers hauled down the great Red star. The crowd celebrated and applauded as the huge iron frame toppled to the ground. The Soviet troops looked on and did nothing. On railroad trains at the station, workers had written with white chalk in Cyrillic (old Slavic) letters such legends as "Hungary for the Hungarians," "Ivan, Go Home," "Russians, Get Out of Budapest." And on the walls were the placards which urged people to strike and go hunt out the AVO secret police.

The Soviet march into the city came as a surprise. Suddenly, seemingly out of a clear sky, a column of tanks appeared, lumbered through the streets, and then disappeared again. The people stared at them from the sidewalks and the armed Hungarian civilians turned their backs on them, for an order had gone out not to provoke the Russians. As a matter of fact, everyone hoped up to this very moment that Moscow would honor its pledged word. While the Russians were blocking the arterial roads, the revolutionary council was meeting in the former Communist Party building and was receiving the representatives of the foreign press. The last official word of a Hungarian anti-Communist politician that I heard was a despairing appeal to the West not to leave the fighting people of Hungary in the lurch.

Only a few days earlier there had been serious differences of opinion among the freedom fighters. But when the Soviet tanks began to move again, the whole nation placed itself

behind the new Budapest regime under the leadership of Imre Nagy and the young war minister, Colonel Maleter, who had distinguished himself as the courageous defender of the Maria Theresa barracks.

At one time I had the opportunity —no, the honor—to speak with young Hungarian officers of his stamp and his generation. I believe that most of them are now dead. But I know that all of them were ready to fight and did fight in hopeless situations.

Then came the day when the loudspeakers on City Hall Square blared forth a proclamation by the Soviet High Command to the people. Soviet tanks were drawn up before all public buildings, and under their protection the obedient Communists came out of their hiding places. As the crowds on the streets and squares heard the assertions of the Soviet General, that it was only a matter of an action against "Fascist elements" from which the Hungarian people had to be protected, there came this unexpected reaction: In the mouths of the Soviet cannon the Hungarians broke out into shrill laughter and derisive calls. They turned their backs on the Russians. In a minute the streets were empty of humans.

The Hungarian Revolution is not yet ended. It will never end. It will cost more bloody sacrifices than we dared to think about several days ago. Here a world-historical process inexorably goes on: not the revolution of a class or a rank, not a revolution of poverty and misery, but an elementary outbreak of the will to freedom. Not a single Hungarian answered my question as to why this revolution had taken place with the plea that living conditions had become unbearable—although they really were. The people of Budapest went to the barricades not for more bread or more money, but for human dignity and freedom.

My Budapest student of biology and freedom fighter showed me in his home a volume of poetry by Bertolt Brecht in the German language. I have not forgotten one very special sentence. It runs: "When the oppressors have spoken, then will the oppressed speak."

A few newsmen covered the thirty-seven-day Battle of Budapest from start to finish. Some of the most stirring reportage of the Hungarian revolt was dictated to the United Press bureau in Vienna over the telephone by its correspondent, Russell Jones, who was awarded the Pulitzer Prize for International Reporting in 1957 for his stories about the Hungarian rising.

"For the first time since I was a boy I wept"— Russell Jones

The United Press International, October 29–December 3, 1956

BUDAPEST, NOVEMBER 15 (UP)—Life as the only American correspondent left in shattered Budapest is sometimes frightening, sometimes amusing. But mostly it is a continuous feeling of inadequacy both as an American and as a reporter who helplessly watched the murder of a people.

For the first time since I was a boy I wept.

I saw a former British soldier break down completely. The situation was worse than the Warsaw uprising into which he was parachuted in 1944.

None of us are Hemingways and it needs a Hemingway to tell this story adequately.

Since a convoy of other newsmen left Budapest under Russian guard last weekend there have been five Western journalists left to tell the world what happens here. There are two British reporters, a Frenchman, a stateless person, and myself.

Except for the stateless person, who has continued to live in the shelter of the British legation, all of us are gathered in the Duna Hotel on the east bank of the Danube.

In the last few days our life has settled down to a routine struggle—checking with Western diplomats for their reports on the situation, futile attempts to interview the puppet regime of Janos Kadar, endless wandering through the city to find out what is going on, and hours-long struggles for telephone connections with the outside world.

Our average day: Sleeping in hotel rooms—unheated in near freezing weather—then rushing for a bath before the hot-water supply is cut off at 9 A.M. Then down to the hotel lobby where everyone is sitting family-style at two long tables. The dining room itself is unusable, since Russian shells have knocked out two of the huge windows.

The food—bread and bad coffee for breakfast—comes from the basement, as the kitchen was destroyed by a Soviet attack.

After a quick check of the situation we start our morning struggle to telephone. Sometimes we find ourselves with a story written but no telephone, and other times with a connection but no news.

Our tours of the town are punctuated by frequent checks by Soviet soldiers or Hungarian AVO—secret police.

Treatment at the checkpoints can vary from a polite salute and waving hands to the suspicious examination of all papers by an AVO man apparently unable to read. As the evening curfew at 7 P.M. local time nears, the checks become more rigorous—and more frightening. One correspondent was killed and three others wounded in the early stages of the revolt, and none of us is anxious to join the casualty list.

Walking through the city is made more difficult by masses of Hungarians streaming along in their search for food and wandering aimlessly through the wreckage, determined to continue their general strike until the Russians leave. They have nothing else to do.

Our meals are shared by a handful of prostitutes, elderly "class enemies" who returned from deportation after the revolt, a Swiss Red Cross man, a Czech businessman whose faith in Communism has been shaken, and a few ordinary Hungarians bombed out of their homes.

A strange multilingual community has been established, with the Hungarians watching for news, the prostitutes washing the correspondents' laundry, and correspondents completing less eagerly the normal work of the newsman.

One of the few bright spots in the city is the Grand Hotel on Margaret Island, isolated from the rest of the city by the Danube River. The Island might be a thousand miles away from the scene of death and destruction.

Yesterday I lunched there with Mrs. Tanya Rahmann, wife of the Indian chargé d'affaires in Budapest, and rarely have I had a more pleasant meal. But it was a brief interlude.

On leaving, as on entering the Island, I made a sharp right turn literally under the guns of a huge Soviet tank, which stood at a Soviet checkpoint on Margaret Island, and drove back to the tangle of fallen street-car wires, piles of rubble, and crowds of hopeless, desperate people.

.   .   .   .

BUDAPEST, NOVEMBER 21 (UP)—They ask the same whispered questions in the hurried conversations that spring up wherever the only American goes in search of news in Budapest.

"How do I get out? . . . What are the borders like?"

"How many times do the Russians check you before the borders?"

The news has come to this battle-torn city that President Eisenhower will allow 5,000 Hungarian refugees to enter the United States. Hungarians want to know how to get out, and this reporter is a busy man.

Already the U.S. legation has been besieged by dozens of Hungarians seeking visas under the "Eisenhower Plan."

While the fighting was going on, many a newspaperman received tearful pleas for help, for moral support from the freedom fighters—both men and women. Now there are the whispers, and the notes. Dozens and dozens of times, in three weeks in Budapest, you have found the notes.

You come back to your car and find a note stuck under the windshield wiper. You find them under your plate at lunch. They are slipped into your hand as you pass by.

Sometimes they want you to get word to relatives in America. At the Csepel Island Steelworks south of Budapest yesterday, a hand reached out of the crowd and pressed a dirty scrap of paper into my hand.

"To Louis Menyhert, 34–54 89th St., Jackson Heights (New York City)," a scratchy pencil had written. "We are all living. I also have uncles in San Diego and Detroit. We miss them."

It was signed "Louis."

To the Louis in Long Island, I can only say: Your friend or relative is safe. I did not see him, only the hand, but there is his message and God bless him.

.   .   .   .

LONDON, DECEMBER 10—The greatest shock to the Hungarian Communists and their Russian masters must have been the type of people who fought the hardest.

Believe none of the stories that this was a misguided uprising fomented to restore the great estate owners of the Horthy regency or the industrial magnates. I saw with my own eyes who was fighting and heard with my ears why they fought.

The first armed resistance came from students of the schools and universities, the youth who had been so carefully selected as the party elite of the future.

The fiercest fighters were the workers, the proletarians in whose name

Communism had ruled. Even the Hungarian army, purged and repurged a dozen times, joined the battle for freedom or sat on the sidelines.

The two big names that came out of the revolt were Communist—Imre Nagy, a lifelong Party member, and Lieutenant Colonel Pal Maleter, who had deserted to the Russians in World War II and returned as a Red partisan.

Wherever came the spark, it found its tinder among the common people.

The areas of destruction, the buildings most desperately defended and the dead themselves are the most eloquent proof of this. It was the workers' tenements that Soviet siege guns smashed, factory buildings that became forts and the tired shabby men with broken shoes and horny hands of the laborer who died by the thousands. The women with their hair bound with kerchiefs and the cheap and tawdry dresses of working people.

A seventeen-year-old girl, twice wounded at Corvin Theatre, told me she fought because "it isn't right that my father, with four children to feed, should get only nine hundred forints [$80] a month."

The chairman of the Workers' Council at the Csepel Iron and Steel plant with 38,000 workers, biggest in the country, said, "These are our factories. We will fight to the death to hold them. But we will continue plant maintenance because we want to work here again."

In Dorog, one of the coal centers, miners continued to work despite the general strike. But not to produce coal. They didn't want *their* mines ruined by flooding.

The same attitude is true in the

country. The farmers want to get out of the collectives but they do not want the restoration of the landlords. They think everyone should have the right to own and till his own land. Something like 100 acres a family would be fair, they think.

It was for these simple, basic things that the Hungarian people fought. These and the right to speak and think freely, to elect men of their own choice, and to raise their children in their own way.

They will go on fighting for them.

Even when the armed revolt had ended, a series of general strikes drove the new Communist regime in Hungary to virtual desperation. In Budapest alone this seven weeks' war was said to have rendered 40,000 families homeless, to have killed perhaps 30,000 Hungarians and 7,000 Russians, and to have forced by the end of 1956 over 150,000 refugees to seek asylum across the border of neighboring Austria. Thousands of suspected youths were deported to the U.S.S.R. and numberless executed, including Imre Nagy and General Pal Maleter.

In voting for a UN resolution condemning the Soviet Union's actions in Hungary a Burmese delegate said: "We do this to keep our self-respect. . . . There, speaking of Hungary, but for the grace of God go we."

Relman Morin Reports a Setback in the
Cold War: The Disgrace of Little Rock

A CENTURY after the Civil War had begun it was still apparent that some of the chief issues over which it was fought remained unsettled. True, freedom had been won for the Negro, but a nation whose watchword was equality of opportunity had signally failed to eradicate serious discrimination and to implement the guarantees of political and civil rights provided in the Constitution.

In 1896 the Supreme Court, in Plessy v. Ferguson, had interpreted the requirement of the Fourteenth Amendment that states give "equal protection of the laws" to mean that separate but equal facilities could be furnished to Negroes. This ruling recognized a policy of *apartheid* for the South, and an inferior public education for Negro children. That was how the law stood until May 1954, when Chief Justice Earl Warren, in the epoch-making decision of Brown v. Board of Education of Topeka, overthrew the "separate but equal" ruling. "We cannot turn the clock back," the Chief Justice declared. "We must consider public education in the light of its full development and its present place in American life throughout the Nation." To the question: "Does segregation of children in public schools solely on the basis of race, even though the physical facilities and other 'tangible' factors may be equal, deprive the children of the minority group of equal educational opportunities?" his answer was unequivocal. "We believe it does."

Although by the fall of 1957 large cities in the upper South and border areas managed to desegregate their schools quietly, the overwhelming majority of school districts in the South, notably in Virginia and the lower South, resorted to every possible legal device to avoid complying with the Brown decision. Some districts attempted desegregation on a token basis, giving the most literal meaning to the wording of the court's instructions to act "with deliberate speed." One of these was Little Rock, Arkansas. Under a desegregation plan of the School Board, nine Negro pupils were to be admitted into the formerly segregated Central High School. On the day before classes began, Governor Orval Faubus ordered National Guardsmen to surround the school and prevent the Negro children from entering. He did this professedly to prevent violence, but since no violence was imminent his act was an incitement to riot. When the Department of Justice obtained a federal injunction against the use of the National Guardsmen to prevent desegregation, Faubus withdrew them.

When the desegregated Central High School opened its doors on the morning of September 23, Relman Morin of the Associated Press, stationed in a glass-enclosed telephone booth opposite the school, began dictating his story. Eight Negro students were escorted into school, and it seemed as though the day might pass without incident despite the ugly mob gathered before the building. Suddenly Morin interrupted his routine story. "Hey, wait a minute!" he shouted into the phone. "There's a helluva fight starting!" Here follows the account of the "helluva fight" for which Morin was awarded a Pulitzer prize in 1958 for national reporting (he had previously received a Pulitzer award in international reporting for his coverage of the Korean War).

"Oh, God, the niggers are in the school!" —
Relman Morin

The Associated Press, September 23, 1957

LITTLE ROCK, ARKANSAS, SEPTEMBER 23 (AP)—A howling, shrieking crowd of men and women outside Central High School, and disorderly students inside, forced authorities to withdraw eight Negro students from the school Monday, three and one-half hours after they entered it.

At noon, Mayor Woodrow Wilson Mann radioed police officers on the scene, telling them to tell the crowd: "The Negro students have been withdrawn."

Almost immediately, the three Negro boys and the five girls left the school under heavy police escort. The officers took them away in police cars.

Crowds clustered at both ends of the school set up a storm of fierce howling and surged toward the lines of police and state troopers. They were beaten back.

The explosive climax came, after the school had been under siege since 8:45 A.M., when the Negroes walked quietly through the doors. Police, armed with riot guns and tear gas, had kept the crowd under control.

Inside, meanwhile, students re-

ported seeing Negroes with blood on their clothes. And some whites who came out—in protest against integration—pictured wild disorder, with policemen chasing white students through the halls, and attacks on Negroes in the building.

The break came shortly before noon.

Virgil Blossom, school superintendent, said he asked Gene Smith, assistant chief of police at the scene, if he thought it would be best to pull out the Negroes. Smith said he did.

Mann's announcement, ordering the police to notify the crowd, came minutes afterward.

Three newspapermen were beaten by the crowd before the sudden turn in the situation. They were Paul Welch, a reporter, and Gray Villette and Francis Miller, photographers. All three are employed by *Life* Magazine. A man smashed Miller in the face while he was carrying an armful of camera equipment. Miller fell, bleeding profusely.

Even after the Negroes left the school, the crowds remained. Teenagers in two automobiles cruised on the outskirts yelling, "Which way did the niggers go?"

During the hours while the Negroes were in the school an estimated thirty to fifty white students left. The crowd yelled, cheered, and clapped each time a white student left the school. "Don't stay in there with the niggers," people yelled.

Four Negroes were beaten and some arrests were made before the eight students went into the school.

The initial violence outside the school was a frightening sight. Women burst into tears and a man, hoisted up on a wooden barricade, roared, "Who's going through?"

"We all are," the crowd shouted. But they didn't.

The drama-packed climax of three weeks of integration struggle in Little Rock came just after the buzzer sounded inside the 2,000-pupil high school at 8:45, signaling the start of classes.

Suddenly, on a street leading toward the school the crowd spotted four Negro adults, marching in twos, down the center of the street. A man yelled, "Look, here come the niggers!"

They were not the students. One appeared to be a newspaperman. He had a card in his hat and was bearing a camera.

I jumped into a glass-windowed telephone booth on the corner to dictate the story. As the crowd surged toward the four Negroes they broke and ran.

They were caught on the lawn of a home nearby. Whites jumped the man with the camera from behind and rode him to the ground, kicking and beating him. They smashed the camera.

This, obviously, was a planned diversionary movement to draw the crowd's attention away from the school. While I was dictating, someone yelled, "Look! They're going into the school!"

At that instant, the eight Negroes —the three boys and five girls—were crossing the schoolyard toward a side door at the south end of the school. The girls were in bobby sox and the boys were dressed in shirts open at the neck. All were carrying books.

They were not running, not even walking fast. They simply strolled toward the steps, went up and were inside before all but a few of the two hundred people at that end of the street knew it.

"They're gone in," a man roared. "Oh, God, the niggers are in the school."

A woman screamed, "Did they get in? Did you see them go in?"

"They're in now," some other men yelled.

"Oh, my God," the woman screamed. She burst into tears and tore at her hair. Hysteria swept the crowd. Other women began weeping and screaming.

At that moment a tall, gray-haired man in a brown hunting shirt jumped on the barricade. He yelled, waving his arms: "Who's going through?"

"We all are," the people shouted.

They broke over and around the wooden barricades, rushing the policemen. Almost a dozen police were at that corner of the street. They raised their billy clubs.

Some grabbed men and women and hurled them back. Two chased a dark-haired man who slipped through their line, like a football player. They caught him in the schoolyard, whipped his coat down his arms, pinning them, and hustled him out of the yard.

Another man, wearing a construction worker's hard hat, suddenly raised his hands high in front of a policeman. It was only a dozen yards or so in front of the phone booth.

I couldn't see whether the officer had a gun in the man's stomach, but he stopped running abruptly and went back. Two men were arrested.

Meanwhile, a cavalcade of cars carrying state troopers, in their broad-brimmed campaign hats and Sam Browne belts, wheeled into the street from both ends. They came inside the barricades, and order was restored for a moment.

The weeping and screaming went on among the women. A man said, "I'm going in there and get my kid out."

An officer said, "You're not going anywhere."

Suddenly another roar—and cheering and clapping—came from the crowd. A white student, carrying his books, came down the front steps. He was followed by two girls wearing bobby sox. In the next few minutes, other students came out. Between fifteen and twenty left the school within the next half hour.

Each time they appeared, the people clapped and cheered. "Come on out," they yelled. "Don't stay in there with the niggers. Go back and tell all of them to come out."

Inside, it was reported, the eight Negro students were in the office of the principal. A moment later, two policemen suddenly raced into the building through the north door. When they came out, they were holding a girl by both arms, rushing her forcibly toward a police prisoners' wagon.

For an instant it looked as though the crowd would try to break the police lines again to rescue her. But the police put her in the car and drove swiftly down the street. Screams, catcalls, and more yelling broke out as the car raced down the street.

A man, distraught, came sprinting after it. "That's my kid in there," he yelled. "Help me get my kid out."

But the car was gone. Soon afterward four white students ran down the steps of the school and across the street. Policemen were chasing them.

One of the boys said they had caught a Negro boy outside the principal's office in the school. "We walked him half the length of the building and we were going to get him out of there," they said. They refused to give their names.

Meanwhile, on the streets, at both ends of the school, clusters of troopers took up their stations, reinforcing the police. The crowd heckled them, hurling insults and some obscenity.

"How you going to feel tonight when you face your neighbors?" a man shouted.

The people called the police "nigger lovers" and insulted them. The officers stood, poker-faced, making no response.

Then the crowd, lacking any other object, turned on the newspapermen and photographers. A boy jumped up, caught the telephone wire leading from one of the three booths to the main wire and swung on it, trying to break it. The booth swayed and nearly toppled to the street.

Someone said, "We ought to wipe up the street with these Yankee reporters."

"Let's do it right now," another replied.

But it was only words. Nothing happened. The same woman who had first burst into tears buttonholed a reporter and said, "Why don't you tell the truth about us? Why don't you tell them we are peaceful people who won't stand to have our kids sitting next to niggers?"

People in the crowd reported gleefully—and shouted it at the other officers—that one policeman had torn off his badge and thrown it on the ground.

"There's one white man on the police force," a burly slick-haired youth in a T shirt yelled at the policeman in front of him.

Sporadic tussles broke out, from time to time, when men tried to pass the police and trooper lines. The police wrestled one man to the street and then, taking him by the hands and arms, hauled him into the squad car and drove off.

A number of plainclothesmen— some reported to be FBI agents— kept circulating up and down in front of the school.

Inside there was no sign that this was different from any other school day. Students who came out at the 10:30 recess said that, in one class of thirty students, only one stayed in the classroom when a Negro entered.

The day of the Little Rock riot President Eisenhower warned that he would use the full power of the United States to carry out the orders of the Federal Court, and on the following day he called the Arkansas National Guard into federal service and dispatched the 101st Airborne Infantry to the scene. The federal troops were withdrawn in November, but the Guardsmen remained on duty under federal orders throughout the school year.

To the uncommitted peoples of the world, mostly people of color, the disgrace of Little Rock was a clear setback for the United States in the Cold War. To the credit of the newspaper profession, courageous Southern newspapermen raised their voices in protest against the South's program of massive resistance to desegregation. Harry S. Ashmore of the *Arkansas Gazette* led the fight for the restoration of sanity at Little Rock and mobilized public opinion against Governor Faubus and "the angry, violent and thoughtless band of agitators who rallied to his call." "Sooner or later," Ashmore sensibly pointed out, "we have got to make some adjustment of our legal institutions to comply with the public policy of the United States—or once again secede from the Union, which no one seriously contemplates."

A Pianistic Sensation Takes
Moscow by Storm

"THE THAW" which followed Stalin's death (see p. 745) had cultural as well as political consequences. To lessen political tension between East and West outstanding talent was exchanged. An American theatrical troup brought *Porgy and Bess* to Leningrad. The Moyseiev dancers and the Bolshoi Ballet thrilled New Yorkers. America transported to Moscow symphony orchestras and virtuosos like Isaac Stern and Yehudi Menuhin, and in turn the Soviet Union sent to the States Oistrakh, Gilels, and Richter.

Perhaps the outstanding single incident of the cultural exchange was the performance in Moscow in the spring of 1958 of a young American pianistic talent. Van Cliburn was a tall, slender, 23-year-old artist with a mop of wild hair. Born in Shreveport, Louisiana, he had lived for some years in Kilgore, Texas. Until he was 17, he was taught the piano by his mother. Then he came to New York's Juilliard School of Music, where he studied under Mme. Rosina Lhevinne and was graduated in 1954 with highest honors. Early in 1958, with funds contributed by the Institute of International Education, the modest young Southerner went to Moscow to compete in the renowned Tchaikovsky International Piano and Violin Festival.

What happened in Moscow was pithily reported in a *Time* Magazine story. The Russians were enchanted by the technical virtuosity and musicianship of this young American, by his masterful twelve-note span, and by his attractive personality. Van Cliburn proved an extraordinarily effective cultural ambassador. "He has taken Moscow not only by storm but by surprise," wrote Max Frankel of *The New York Times*. "The outcome of the contest seemed almost of secondary importance . . ." but perhaps not to Van Cliburn, who was awarded the first prize.

*"Cliburn is playing tonight; call back
tomorrow"*

Courtesy of *Time;* copyright Time, Inc., 1958

Texan in Moscow

The rage of Moscow this week was a lanky (6 ft. 4 in.), curly-haired Texan whose long, flashing fingers at the piano keyboard put a rare thaw into the cold war.

Van Cliburn, 23, blazed through the opening round of the first Tchaikovsky International Piano and Violin Festival with 49 other pianists from 19 countries, and his twelve-note span carried him triumphantly through the second round. By then the town's elite was on its ear. To hear him in the finals, standees jammed the aisles in the Moscow Conservatory's deep balconies. Soldiers held back enthusiastic crowds in the street outside. To the hundreds of callers who asked for tickets, the Conservatory's box office had a standard reply: "Cliburn is playing tonight; call back tomorrow."

In the finals, which matched him against eight other pianists—including three top-rated Russians and another American, Los Angeles' Daniel Pollack, 23—the good-looking young Texan chose to play Rachmaninoff's powerful *Concerto No. 3.* As required of all finalists, he also played Tchaikovsky's familiar *First* and a rondo by Soviet Composer (and contest judge) Dmitry Kabalevsky, who wrote it for the contest.

Despite a bandaged index finger (which he had cut during a grueling rehearsal), Cliburn displayed the tautly controlled technique, the steel-fingered power and booming romantic style that had dazzled audiences in the opening rounds. Toward the end of the rondo, a piano string snapped under his bold percussive attack. He piled through the rest of the piece without faltering, rose after the final Rachmaninoff to one of the most thunderous ovations ever accorded an artist in Moscow.

For nearly ten minutes the bravos echoed through the cavernous hall; finally the judges, in violation of the contest rules, permitted Cliburn to return to the stage for a second bow. Then the orchestra rose and joined the ovation. Backstage, the jurors, including famed Russian Pianist Emil Gilels, embraced Cliburn. Alexander Goldenweiser, octogenarian dean of Russian pianists, kept repeating one word: "Genius!" Hearing the news, the New York Philharmonic promptly signed Cliburn for four Manhattan concerts in the winter.

Still, with six of his rivals yet to play, Cliburn's victory was hardly assured; indeed, on his U.S. record, he could not have been expected to whip up such frenzy. Born in Shreveport, Louisiana, the son of an oil executive, Cliburn grew up in Kilgore, Texas, studied the piano with his mother, a onetime concert pianist named Rilda Bee. He had no other training until he enrolled at Manhattan's Juilliard School of Music in 1951 to study with Russian-born Teacher Rosina Lhevinne. He won the Leventritt Award for young pianists in 1954, and as a result made his debut with the New York Philharmonic to glowing reviews. But like many another promising young U.S. instrumentalist, he promptly dropped out of sight on the smalltime recital circuit, found himself playing successful but unheralded recitals in places from High Point, North Carolina to Coldwater, Michigan.

It was the Russians, still slightly incredulous that any U.S.-trained pianist could be so good, who decided that he was ready for the big time. The night before Composer Dmitry Shostakovich was to hand out the first prize—25,000 rubles, or $6,250 at the official rate—Moscow leaked the winner's name: Van Cliburn. Said Pianist Cliburn: "I can't believe it." Then, noting the 10 lbs. he had lost during his harrowing two weeks of competition, he added: "I'd like to go back to Texas. I'm just about to break down."

A. M. Rosenthal Reports No News
From Auschwitz

FOR ADOLF HITLER, product of Austria's *Waldviertel*, former Viennese tramp, half-blinded World War I veteran, now absolute dictator of Nazi Germany, it was a gnawing monomania. In the summer of 1941, master of a continent, he decided on a "Final Solution"—he would wipe out ten million Jews as well as countless Slavs, gypsies, and other "racial undesirables." It all started out with little more than an institutionalized dislike of the Jews. It ended with the most horrible story of unreasoning violence in the history of mankind. More than six million Jews and countless others of "inferior race" fell victims to Hitler's insane fanaticism.

Germany's main death camp was constructed just outside the remote farming town of Auschwitz in eastern Poland. Throughout Europe, province by province, town by town, Jews and others were rounded up by SS commanders, packed into boxcars, and shipped eastward. Night and day the packed boxcars rumbled into Auschwitz. Here the prisoners saw a sign over the huge iron entrance gate: ARBEIT MACHT FREI (Work Makes You Free). They entered the compound to the tune of lilting Viennese waltzes. Those who were strong enough worked for a few months in the camp's war-matériel factories.

Others, hundreds at a time, were ordered to undress and enter the "bath chambers" for delousing. Instead of water, they were covered with Zyklon B insecticide gas (provided by the chemical firm of I. G. Farben), which poured from the faucets. Then the bodies were stripped of hair and teeth—the hair was used for army mattresses and the melted gold was sent to Swiss banks.

The story of the monstrous murders at Auschwitz was soon forgotten by the civilized world. When the last century was about to end, the Dreyfus Affair—the mere jailing of one innocent Jewish officer—was enough to awaken the passionate wrath of humanity. But the slaughter of six million Jews in Hitler's gas ovens was too terrible to recall. On August 31, 1958, *The New York Times* published this poignant reminder by its correspondent A. M. Rosenthal.

"The sun is bright, and grass and daisies grow."

The New York Times Magazine, August 31, 1958

BRZEZINKA, POLAND—The most terrible thing of all, somehow, was that at Brzezinka the sun was bright and warm, the rows of graceful poplars were lovely to look upon and on the grass near the gates children played.

It all seemed frighteningly wrong, as in a nightmare, that at Brzezinka the sun should ever shine or that there should be light and greenness and the sound of young laughter. It would be fitting if at Brzezinka the sun never shone and the grass withered, because this is a place of unutterable terror.

And yet, every day, from all over the world, people come to Brzezinka, quite possibly the most grisly tourist center on earth. They come for a variety of reasons—to see if it could really have been true, to remind themselves not to forget, to pay homage to the dead by the simple act of looking upon their place of suffering.

Brzezinka is a couple of miles from the better-known southern Polish town of Oswiecim. Oswiecim has about 12,000 inhabitants, is situated about 171 miles from Warsaw and lies in a damp, marshy area at the eastern end of the pass called the Moravian Gate. Brzezinka and Oswiecim together formed part of that minutely organized factory of torture and death that the Nazis called Konzentrationslager Auschwitz.

By now, fourteen years after the last batch of prisoners was herded naked into the gas chambers by dogs and guards, the story of Auschwitz has been told a great many times. Some of the inmates have written of those memories of which sane men cannot conceive. Rudolf Franz Ferdinand Hoess, the superintendent of the camp, before he was executed wrote his detailed memoirs of mass exterminations and the experiments on living bodies. Four million people died here, the Poles say.

And so there is no news to report about Auschwitz. There is merely the compulsion to write something about it, a compulsion that grows out of a restless feeling that to have visited Auschwitz and then turned away without having said or written anything would somehow be a most grievous act of discourtesy to those who died here.

Brzezinka and Oswiecim are very quiet places now; the screams can no longer be heard. The tourist walks silently, quickly at first to get it over with and then, as his mind peoples the barracks and the chambers and the dungeons and flogging posts, he walks draggingly. The guide does not say much either, because there is nothing much for him to say after he has pointed.

For every visitor, there is one particular bit of horror that he knows he will never forget. For some it is seeing the rebuilt gas chamber at Oswiecim and being told that this is the "small one." For others it is the fact that at Brzezinka, in the ruins of the gas chambers and the crematoria the Germans blew up when they retreated, there are daisies growing.

There are visitors who gaze blankly at the gas chambers and the furnaces because their minds simply cannot encompass them, but stand shivering before the great mounds of human hair behind the plate-glass window or the piles of babies' shoes or the brick cells where men sentenced to death by suffocation were walled up.

One visitor opened his mouth in a silent scream simply at the sight of boxes—great stretches of three-tiered wooden boxes in the women's barracks. They were about six feet wide, about three feet high, and into them from five to ten prisoners were shoved for the night. The guide walks quickly through the barracks. Nothing more to see here.

A brick building where sterilization experiments were carried out on women prisoners. The guide tries the door—it's locked. The visitor is grateful that he does not have to go in, and then flushes with shame.

A long corridor where rows of faces stare from the walls. Thousands of pictures, the photographs of prisoners. They are all dead now, the men and women who stood before the cameras, and they all knew they were to die.

They all stare blank-faced, but one picture, in the middle of a row, seizes the eye and wrenches the mind. A girl, 22 years old, plumply pretty, blond. She is smiling gently, as at a sweet, treasured thought. What was the thought that passed through her young mind and is now her memorial on the wall of the dead at Auschwitz?

Into the suffocation dungeons the visitor is taken for a moment and feels himself strangling. Another visitor goes in, stumbles out and crosses herself. There is no place to pray at Auschwitz.

The visitors look pleadingly at each other and say to the guide, "Enough."

There is nothing new to report about Auschwitz. It was a sunny day and the trees were green and at the gates the children played.

Two *Times*men Cover America's
First Man-in-Space Flight

O N OCTOBER 5, 1957, America was aroused from a deep sleep. On that day the Soviets announced that they had successfully launched "Sputnik," the first man-made satellite. First to achieve an intercontinental ballistic missile, first to launch an earth satellite, soon first to launch an animal in outer space and to send a rocket to the moon, the Soviet Union demonstrated an ascendancy in the matter of rocketry and outer-space technology which was a source of deep concern to Americans.

"This is a grim business" was Walter Lippmann's comment on the portent of the Soviet moon. Twelve years after the close of World War II, the United States, which had been so far ahead in nuclear weapons and scientific technology, appeared to be losing that lead to the Russians, who at the end of the war were so nearly prostrate. Lippmann blamed prosperity, anti-intellectualism and McCarthyism for America's declining prestige and her scientific defeats. "With prosperity acting as a narcotic, with Philistinism and McCarthyism rampant, our public life," he declared, "has been increasingly doped and without purpose. With the President in a kind of partial retirement, there is no standard raised to which the people can repair. Thus we drift with no one to state our purposes and to make policy, into a chronic disaster like Little Rock. We find ourselves then without a chart in very troubled waters." Whether any or all of these factors were to blame for America's humiliating situation, it was clear that a totalitarian state, as contrasted with a democratic society, had a frightening capability to manipulate manpower, allocate materials and factory output and impose sacrifices to achieve a specific scientific and technological objective.

True, America made valiant efforts to catch up in the space race, and in fact launched far more satellites than the Soviet, even though they were much smaller. In addition, the United States led in the development of atomic-powered submarines, with epoch-making subpolar expeditions of the *Nautilus* and *Skate* in the summer of 1958. But the big question which now loomed up was: Who would put the first man into outer space? Under circumstances of considerable mystery the Soviet Union announced that an orbital flight had been successfully made by Yuri Gagarin on April 12, 1961. America's prestige seemed again in the balance when, on May 5th, it scheduled a suborbital flight by one of its own astronauts, Commander Alan B. Shepard, Jr. The accounts of this superb flight, accomplished in the hot glare of publicity, with all the attendant risks which the Russians had always studiously avoided in their space efforts, were reported by two *New York Times* reporters. Richard Witkin told the general story while John W. Finney gave the minute-by-minute, blow-by-blow account.

"Boy, what a ride!"—Richard Witkin

The New York Times, May 6, 1961

CAPE CANAVERAL, FLORIDA, MAY 5— A slim, cool Navy test pilot was rocketed 115 miles into space today.

Thirty-seven-year-old Alan B. Shepard, Jr. thus became the first American space explorer.

Commander Shepard landed safely 302 miles out at sea fifteen minutes after the launching. He was quickly lifted aboard a Marine Corps helicopter.

"Boy, what a ride!" he said, as he was flown to the aircraft carrier *Lake Champlain* four miles away.

Extensive physical examinations were begun immediately.

Tonight doctors reported Commander Shepard in "excellent" condition, suffering no ill effects.

The near-perfect flight represented the United States' first major step in the race to explore space with manned space craft.

True, it was only a modest leap compared with the once-around-the-earth orbital flight of Major Yuri Gagarin of the Soviet Union.

The Russian's speed of more than 17,000 miles an hour was almost four times Commander Shepard's 4,500. The distance the Russian traveled was almost 100 times as great.

But Commander Shepard maneuvered his craft in space—something the Russians have not claimed for Major Gagarin.

All in all, the Shepard flight was welcomed almost rapturously here and in much of the non-communist world as proof that the United States, though several years behind in the space race, had the potential to offer imposing competition.

Commander Shepard, a native of East Derry, N.H., was a long time starting his journey.

He lay on his contoured Fiberglas couch atop the Redstone missile— "the least nervous man of the bunch," the flight surgeon reported—for three and a half hours while the launching crew delayed the count-down because of weather and a few technical troubles.

Finally, at 10:34 A.M. Eastern Daylight Time, the count reached zero. A jet of yellow flame lifted the slender rocket off its pad as thousands watched anxiously from the Cape and along the public beaches south of here.

Hundreds of missiles had been launched here, but never before with a human being aboard. Only once before, so far as is known, had a human ridden a missile into space anywhere—and that was from the Soviet base at Tyura Tam, near the Aral Sea, last month.

The rocket, and the pilot in the Project Mercury capsule on top, performed flawlessly.

Commander Shepard kept up a running commentary with the command center during the flight. He experienced six times the force of gravity during the rocket's climb, then there were five minutes during which gravity seemed to have vanished. The abrupt re-entry into the atmosphere pressed him into his couch with a force of more than ten times gravity.

At 7,000 feet, his capsule descending by a red-and-white parachute, Commander Shepard radioed, as if returning from a routine flight by plane:

"Coming in for a landing."

The capsule, dropping then at a fairly gentle thirty feet a second, hit the water at 10:49 A.M. The commander, apparently as sound and healthy as when he had entered the capsule at 6:20 A.M., radioed that he would climb out immediately rather than ride inside it to the carrier.

A horse-collarlike sling was lowered from Marine helicopter 44 and he was pulled aboard, less than five minutes after hitting the gently rolling waves. His first words were:

"Thank you very much. It's a beautiful day."

A minute later, the capsule was hooked and flown, dangling below the helicopter, to a mattress-covered platform on the carrier. Moments later, as hundreds of sailors cheered, the astronaut, his silver space suit gleaming, debarked from the helicopter.

Instead of going directly to the admiral's quarters below, where he was to receive a thorough physical examination and pour out his fresh impressions of his journey, he jogged to the capsule to retrieve his space helmet.

The formalities below were interrupted when a call came into the carrier bridge from the White House. It was President Kennedy.

A naval officer who overheard the conversation quoted the astronaut as saying:

"Thank you very much, Mr. President. It was certainly a very thrilling ride. I'd like to thank everyone who made it possible."

While being checked by the doctors, Commander Shepard told one: "I don't think there's much you'll have to do to me, Doc."

In the twenty-four to forty-eight hours following the flight, Commander Shepard is to undergo the physical check-ups and interviews. He is resting tonight at Grand Bahama Island.

All aboard the carrier, except for two physicians, were under strict orders not to speak to the astronaut unless he asked a question.

The precaution was taken so that the astronaut's reactions could be recorded with the meagerest possible distortion by intervening discussions.

The chief physician on the carrier, Commander Robert C. Laning, reported the astronaut in "excellent physical condition."

Commander Shepard's first refreshment was a glass of orange juice. He told the doctor that he was "thrilled and experienced a great sense of humility."

The astronaut spent two hours and twenty-five minutes on the carrier, then was flown to a special clinic on Grand Bahama, where the examinations and questioning continued.

There, after an extensive examination, Colonel William Douglas, personal physician for the seven astronauts, found Commander Shepard in "excellent shape and health." He doubted that the further tests to be made would show any ill effects.

Plans are to fly Commander Shepard to Washington Monday for a hero's welcome and a meeting with President Kennedy.

What were the scientific contributions made by the fifteen-minute Mercury flight?

Chief among them, according to Dr. Hugh A. Dryden, Deputy Administrator of the National Aeronautics and Space Administration, was information on the reactions of the astronaut under the stresses of space flight.

Commander Shepard was reported to have performed no differently during the actual rocket flight than he had in dozens of practice flights in ground simulators and whirling centrifuges.

He was able to click off moment-by-moment reports on the operations of the complex array of mechanisms, without missing a beat. His voice remained normal except during the exposure to the maximum gravity force. Then it became strained, as had the voices of all astronauts during training.

In addition, Commander Shepard was able to control the attitude, or position, of the capsule in space by operation of a control stick that sent squirts of hydrogen peroxide rushing from sixteen strategically located jets.

In this way, Commander Shepard was able to change not the path of the capsule, which was determined by the ballistic trajectory established by the rocket, but the angle at which the capsule flew through space. Turning levers inside the capsule, he was able to control the pitch (nose up or down), yaw (right or left motion) and roll of the capsule.

The astronaut also regulated the attitude of the capsule for the firing of the retro or backward-firing rockets and fired the rockets as the capsule

started descending toward earth. For the suborbital flight the firing of the three retro rockets on the blunt nose of the capsule was only practiced. But in orbital flight, the retro rockets are necessary to slow down the capsule and start it returning to earth.

Commander Shepard talked about his experiences "flying" the capsule to Captain Ralph Weymouth, skipper of the *Lake Champlain.*

"He told me," the captain said, "that four or five years from now, we may look back at this as a pretty crude thing, but at this moment it seemed a tremendous event."

Dr. Stanley C. White of the Air Force said there had been very little change in the astronaut's pulse or respiration throughout the flight.

Temperatures both in the capsule and in the astronaut's airtight air-conditioned double-layer space suit rose only slightly during the friction-generating descent into the atmosphere.

According to Dr. White, the suit temperature rose from 75 to 78 Fahrenheit during re-entry and the cabin air temperature rose from 99 degrees to 102.

To indicate the decelerating impact of the atmosphere, it was calculated that the capsule, in one minute, slowed from a speed of 4,227 miles an hour at forty miles altitude to 341 miles an hour at twelve miles altitude.

The Mercury capsule was a compact, 2,300-pound steel-and-titanium craft shaped something like a television tube. The astronaut, lying on his couch against the blunt "picture" end of the tube, had about as much space as he would in the cockpit of a jet fighter plane.

Before him were panels containing

more than a hundred switches, buttons, and levers for performing such functions as firing retro rockets; switching radio channels; turning on and off the manual control jets; blowing out the escape hatch at the side; and extending or retracting a periscope with which he could monitor operations of devices not visible to the direct-view porthole down through his legs.

The barrel-shaped capsule bore the name of "Freedom 7" painted in white letters on the black side of the capsule. The name was thought up by the seven Mercury astronauts.

There were many emergency measures that the astronaut himself could initiate in case the automatic and ground-controlled systems both malfunctioned.

Perhaps most important was triggering of the escape tower, a rocket-powered pylon atop the capsule that would carry the capsule up and away from the Redstone booster if trouble developed anywhere from launch pad to burnout and separation of the booster.

Commander Shepard did report that he encountered several "unexpected sensations."

One was what he termed "a bit of roughness" during the early part of the flight, apparently when the Redstone nosed its way upward through the sonic barrier.

There also was a bit of wobbling when one of the retro rockets was fired.

Otherwise, the commander said, "everything went like clockwork."

Space-agency officials were asked whether any special insurance policies had been taken out to cover the astronaut in case he had been killed or injured.

The officials did not know of any.

"What a beautiful view!"—John W. Finney

The New York Times, May 6, 1961

CAPE CANAVERAL, FLORIDA, MAY 5—
"All systems go . . . Everything A-O.K. . . . Mission very smooth . . . What a beautiful view! . . . Coming in for a landing."

These were the reports of Commander Alan B. Shepard, Jr. as he rode the capsule "Freedom 7" 115 miles up into space today in the United States' first step toward manned exploration of space. His "A-O.K." is a rocket-engineer term meaning double O.K. or perfect.

In a calm, methodical way he reported back by radio on every detail of his fifteen-minute flight, even during the moments of greatest stress as his capsule accelerated from the launching pad and then quickly decelerated upon re-entering the earth's atmosphere.

And there were moments of excitement in his voice, such as when he viewed much of the eastern coast of the United States through a periscope from 115 miles up in space.

"What a beautiful view," he exclaimed into a microphone inside his visored space helmet and then, according to instructions, he returned to scientific observations to report that the cloud cover was three- to five-tenths and was obscuring much of the coast up through Cape Hatteras.

"Three- to five-tenths cloud cover"

is a description used by meteorologists to indicate how much of the sky is covered by clouds.

The clocklike precision with which the Redstone missile and capsule performed was matched by the calm performance of the 37-year-old astronaut from Derry, New Hampshire.

As Dr. Stanley C. White, medical support chief of Project Mercury, described Commander Shepard after the flight:

"He was probably the most unperturbed member of the crew."

The mission, however, started off in an atmosphere of tension that gripped the Mercury launching crew and the thousands of spectators standing on the sand dunes of Cape Canaveral to witness the launching.

The tension increased as the blast-off was delayed, first because of an early-morning cloud cover that swept in over the Cape and then fortunately dissipated, and then because of a faulty electronic part in the missile that had to be replaced.

For nearly three and one-half hours before the launching, Commander Shepard sat sealed in his black, barrel-shaped capsule atop the fuming eighty-three-foot-tall missile loaded with highly explosive fuels.

As he continued his lonely wait for the delayed blast-off, his tension visibly increased. Observers inside the Mercury control center reported that his heartbeat, recorded on an oscilloscope, increased perceptibly as the time dragged on and holds were called in the count-down.

But with the obviously near-perfect launching, the tension on the beach turned to elation, and Commander Shepard assumed the calm, crisp manner of an experienced test pilot off on another mission.

His reports came back loud and clear and covered, as had been ordered, all the details of the performance of the rocket and his space craft. Only for the first one minute and fifty seconds, as the capsule and rocket quivered passing through the sonic barrier, was the ride at all rough. After that, he reported, the mission was "very smooth."

Even when the capsule was re-entering the atmosphere and Commander Shepard was enduring his maximum stress of 10 G's—or ten times the force of gravity—he continued saying "O.K., O.K., O.K." into his microphone. For several seconds, while the stress was most severe, his words were mostly grunts, but then his voice came through loud and clear again.

The force of gravity, at sea level, is sufficient to accelerate a body roughly twenty-two miles an hour in every second.

Commander Shepard's day began at 1:05 A.M. Eastern Standard Time, when, along with Lieutenant Colonel John H. Glenn, Jr., the alternate astronaut for the flight, he was awakened by Dr. William K. Douglas, the personal physician to the seven astronauts. The two astronauts had gone to bed at 10:30 P.M. in Room 205 in Hangar S after a quieting evening watching television.

His day then went like this (all times in Eastern Daylight Time):

2:50—After showering and shaving, the two astronauts had a breakfast consisting of *filet mignon* wrapped in bacon, two poached eggs, dry toast with jelly and orange juice.

3:20—The astronauts received a complete physical examination. Dr. Douglas reported that "as usual they

were in superb physical condition"
and relaxed and optimistic.

3:50—Biochemical sensors are
attached to Shepard's body to record
his physical reactions during flight.

4:00—Shepard began wiggling and
squirming into his silvery, twenty-
pound pressure suit.

4:30—With Shepard reclining in
a contour couch, a pressure check of
the suit was conducted to make sure
there were no leaks.

4:59—Accompanied by his doctors,
Shepard left Hangar S. "Here I go,
Dee," he said to his nurse, Lieutenant
Dolores O'Hara, who watched him
from the second-floor window. He
walked briskly eleven steps from the
hangar into a waiting white van. He
looked neither to right nor left and
in his right hand he carried a portable
air conditioner to control the temperature inside the pressure suit.

Inside the van, he reclined in a
chair as the truck slowly made the
three-mile trip from the hangar to the
launching pad.

At the launching pad, the glare of
searchlights created an artificial glow
of dawn on the horizon and made the
white Redstone rocket glisten in the
pre-dawn darkness. Overhead there
was a yellow half-moon and on the
horizon glittered the planets Saturn
and Jupiter, which Shepard had bet
Glenn he would see during the flight.

5:27—Van arrived at launching
pad and backed up to within ten feet
of the elevator that would take the
astronaut to the capsule. He was
greeted by Captain Leroy G. Cooper,
a fellow astronaut who briefed him on
the count-down and the weather.

6:14—Shepard stepped briskly out
of the van and stopped briefly at the
foot of the steps from the van. Shield-
ing his eyes from the glare of the
searchlights, he looked up at the ice-
coated rocket for a couple of seconds
and then walked the few steps to the
elevator. He carried a clipboard with
papers in his right hand and in his
left the air conditioner. As applause
broke out among the technicians at
the foot of the rocket he smiled in
acknowledgment.

6:15—Along with Dr. Douglas he
took the sixty-five-foot elevator ride
up to the "greenhouse" surrounding
the capsule. Walking awkwardly in
his pressure suit, he looked over the
ten-foot-high capsule and talked with
technicians in the manner of a test
pilot checking out his plane. He
laughed at a comment made by Virgil
I. Grissom, a fellow astronaut.

6:20—He started climbing through
the capsule hatch, right foot first. He
received an encouraging pat. Glenn
leaned in to talk with Shepard, who
was beginning to check out the capsule. Below him the rocket fumed as
the liquid oxygen boiled off.

6:40—The count-down was at T
minus 100 minutes. Dawn, tinting
pink ribbons of clouds on the eastern
horizon, was beginning. Ground fog
shrouded the palmetto shrubs on
Cape Canaveral.

7:10—The hatch on the capsule
was sealed. Shepard began his long,
lonely wait for blast-off.

7:27—The count-down was at T
minus sixty minutes and a technician
in the greenhouse affectionately polished the capsule with a rag.

7:34—The gantry crane began
moving back, leaving the white missile and the black capsule standing
alone in the sunlight. The "cherry
picker," a mobile boom crane, moved
into position to snatch the astronaut
from the capsule in the event of
trouble.

8:00—The count-down was at T minus 29. Gray clouds began to cover the morning sky. The launching seemed to be turning into a race with the weather.

8:14—A hold was ordered in the count-down to permit a check on the weather. Anxiety gripped the Mercury control center.

8:47—The control center announced that during the hold some trouble had been discovered in an inverter in the missile that turned direct current into alternating current. The inverter had to be replaced, so the gantry crane rolled back around the rocket.

9:05—Shepard remained sealed in his capsule, but two pressure lines were attached to keep the capsule interior cool.

9:40—The gantry crane was pulled back again and the count-down was resumed at T minus 35 minutes.

10:00—A hold was ordered to check a computer. At the emergency recovery area Nurse O'Hara was visibly nervous as she fingered rosary beads.

10:17—Count was resumed at T minus 14½ minutes.

10:30—A hold was ordered at T minus 2 minutes 40 seconds to check on a pressure gauge.

10:31—Trouble was cleared up and count resumed.

10:32—"Cherry picker" removed. Now Shepard's only escape route was by having the capsule yanked off the rocket by the emergency escape tower atop the capsule.

10:34:13—Ignition and blast-off. The rocket slowly rose, a diamondlike flame spurting from its tail. For a moment it became lost behind a large cumulus cloud and then it reappeared, leaving a wiggling white contrail against the blue sky. Straight up it

went, the roar of its rocket engines still audible. Cheers arose from onlookers at the obviously successful launching.

10:35—Astronaut reported stability good, trajectory O.K., acceleration 3.5 G's and cabin pressure 5.5 pounds a square inch.

10:36—Shepard reported "all systems go."

10:36:12—Rocket burned out at 180,000 feet. Then ten seconds later the capsule was separated from the rocket. Shepard reported the escape tower had been jettisoned. He now had no alternative but to ride the capsule on its ballistic trajectory into space and back to earth.

10:37—The capsule was turned around to orbital attitude so that its blunt nose was pointed forward and slightly upward. Astronaut begins to take over manual control of capsule's attitude. First pitch, then yaw, then roll.

10:38—Ground monitors reported that astronaut's physical condition appeared excellent and trajectory looked "A-O.K." Pilot reported carrying out manual control in normal, planned fashion.

10:38:30—"What a beautiful view," Shepard reported as the capsule arched over the top of its trajectory. Reported a three- to five-tenths cloud covering obscuring the eastern coast up through Cape Hatteras, North Carolina.

10:39—Pilot reported mission very smooth. Began to tip capsule for firing of retro rockets.

10:40—Shepard reported retro rockets 1, 2 and 3 had fired and the retro-rocket package on the front of the blunt re-entry shield had been jettisoned.

10:41—Astronaut, using manual

controls and small air-jet control rockets, began putting the capsule into the re-entry attitude.

10:42—Capsule was beginning to re-enter earth's denser atmosphere. For first time in five minutes Shepard began to feel weight again, at first only 5/100 of a G.

10:43—Capsule in one minute had slowed down from 4,227 miles an hour to 341 miles an hour. With the rapid deceleration, the stress on the astronaut steadily mounted until for about four seconds he was enduring 10 G's. His weight seemed to be 1,600 pounds instead of the normal 160. He continued talking but his words turned more into groans or grunts.

10:43:45—The G-forces let up. Pilot reported he was at 30,000 feet on way down.

10:44—Drogue parachute reported deployed to stabilize capsule. Cheers break out on beach. Pilot reported all systems working "A-O.K." Medical monitor reported the pilot was "A-O.K." all the way.

10:45—Main parachute reported deployed. Pilot reported that he was at 7,000 feet and "coming in for a landing." The large red-and-white parachute was sighted by the Navy recovery task force and helicopters hovered near by as the capsule gently descended.

10:49—Capsule landed on the Atlantic Ocean 302 miles from the launching pad. Shepard had returned to earth after a fifteen-minute ride into space.

10:53—Shepard climbed out of the capsule and was hoisted into a hovering Marine helicopter. "Thank you very much. It's a beautiful day," he told the helicopter crew.

11:00—Shepard hopped out of the helicopter onto the flight deck of the carrier *Lake Champlain*, jogged over to the capsule to retrieve his space helmet and then went to the admiral's quarters for a preliminary medical check and to the bridge for a radio-telephone conversation with President Kennedy.

Jerusalem 1961: The Eichmann Trial Recalls the Faces of Six Million Dead

ADOLF HITLER's SS Bureau IVA4b had total charge of rounding up all Jews in Nazi-held Europe (in Nazi terminology, IV stood for the Gestapo, A for Internal Affairs, 4 for religion, and b for Jews). Chief of the Gestapo Bureau of Jewish Affairs was Adolf Eichmann, who received from the Führer himself the order to apply the Final Solution of the Jewish Problem. For Eichmann this was *Kadavergehorsam*—unquestioning obedience that makes even a corpse do what it is told. For him an order was an order.

After the war Eichmann vanished. It took fourteen years before Israeli agents tracked him down in Argentina and spirited him to Jerusalem. There, in April 1961, he was brought to trial. Once a dreaded SS colonel, he was now an unprepossessing, balding little man of fifty-five, with thin lips, protruding ears, a lined face, and a high, wrinkled brow. At the trial he was placed in a glass cage to protect him from assassination.

Many wondered about the legality of bringing a man to justice in one state who had been kipnaped from another, of placing him on trial for acts committed outside the jurisdiction of the court, and of trying him for offenses perpetrated even before Israel had emerged as an independent state. Despite criticism, the trial went on.

Eichmann pleaded Not Guilty. He denied that he was a mass murderer. He was, he said, "a man of average character, with good qualities and many faults." He could not stand the sight of blood. He never killed anyone, he insisted, although some testimony controverted this claim. He merely carried out orders to ferret out the Jews and bring them to the gas ovens. He was just "a little sausage."

To cover the "trial of the century," more than five hundred correspondents from forty countries (from West Germany forty-five alone) flocked to Jerusalem. The Israelis supplied them with $350,000 worth of new transmission facilities. The court proceedings were conducted in four languages—French, English, German, and Hebrew.

From the veritable torrent of prose which poured out of Jerusalem (280,000 words on the very first day alone), three remarkable accounts of the months-long trial have been selected. The first is from a series reported by Richard Starnes for the *New York World-Telegram*. In the second, Harry Golden, homespun philosopher, editor and publisher of the *Carolina Israelite* and author of three best-selling books, weighed the risks for Israel in the tragic revelations of the trial. Finally, Homer Bigart, an ace foreign correspondent for *The New York Times*, tells the almost unbelievable story of the woman who was buried alive in a common grave.

"At the entrance to the gas chambers each [child] was handed a sweet" — Richard Starnes

New York World-Telegram, April 19, 1961. Copyright, 1961

JERUSALEM, APRIL 19—The translation of Prosecutor Gideon Hausner's words came through the earphones clearly and persuasively, even though two of us had forsaken the courtroom for a brief respite in the sunshine.

It is difficult enough to believe the words heard inside—in the presence of the judges, prosecutor and Adolf Eichmann, the caged defendant—but the mind totally rejects Mr. Hausner's black book of horrors when one is sitting in Jerusalem's clear, clean air.

"In the spring of 1943," his words say, "Jewish deportees from Warsaw arrived at Maidanek [concentration camp], and immediately the killings were speeded up, reaching a climax in November when, in one day, 18,000 Jews were shot."

It is hard to relate the attorney general's words to numerical reality. If I could remember the capacity of Madison Square Garden, maybe I could see 18,000 humans in my mind's eye. But it's useless. The imagination refuses to try to picture 18,000 men, women and children being put to death in a span of 24 hours.

Then there was the fact the Maidanek camp teemed with disease.

"The Maidanek cure for typhus was execution by shooting," said Mr. Hausner.

Again, in the prosecutor's inexorable opening statement:

"In Maidanek there was only one place where children were treated kindly: At the entrance to the gas chambers each one was handed a sweet."

There was the story of one SS guard at the Treblinka camp near Warsaw. Franz had a big dog which he'd trained—much as suburbanite householders train dogs to fetch thrown objects. But Franz's dog was trained to pounce on victims at a single-word command: *"Jude"* (Jew).

Returning to the almost surgical atmosphere of the courtroom, we note the judges sitting attentive, inscrutable, gravely aware they are being asked to perform a superhuman job.

Eichmann is there, of course, and there's nothing left to say about Eichmann—except that his faintly tentative poise, occasionally betrayed by a nervous fidget, is still with him.

Dr. Hausner, the avenger, is on his feet reading, occasionally pointing his finger in the direction of the glass cage, his black robe strangely appropriate to the dossier of death he is reading.

Time after time his statement contained the words: "We will prove." If indeed he succeeds in proving one-tenth of the horrors he has outlined in the last two days, the judges' task will not be to judge but to punish.

The horror tales seem endless. Of an SS trooper dashing an infant to death before the mother's eyes. Of families herded naked into gas chambers so crowded the dead couldn't fall, and of the dying taking what comfort they could from holding the hand of a loved one. Of squads prying open the mouths of the dead with iron bars for gold teeth.

Fortunately the recital is relieved by two episodes of heroism. There is the story of the Danes, for example.

Almost alone among the nations of Europe, the Danes resisted Eichmann's murder squads successfully, organized a mass escape by sea and saved almost all Danish Jews from "the final solution."

Mr. Hausner, nearing the end of his marathon account, let this one faint ray of decent, honorable human behavior flicker through.

"The roundup [in Denmark] finally took place during the first two days of October 1943. The barbarians broke into Jewish homes, seized Jews in the streets and brought them in. But something occurred that stunned the assassins: Most of the Jewish homes turned out to be empty.

"The Danish people, having prior knowledge of the murderous plot, organized—at great risk, under the very noses of occupation authorities —an underground rescue operation which became known as a miniature Dunkirk.

"Fishing and excursion boats were mustered at ports. Jews were escorted to the coast by Boy Scouts, students and other volunteers, put on board and secretly transported to Sweden. In this way some 6000 Danish Jews were rescued; only a few hundred fell into the hands of Eichmann's accomplices."

"A stranger to the human race"— *Harry Golden*

Life, April 21, 1961, pp. 43–46

JERUSALEM—What is most remarkable about Adolf Eichmann, sitting in his booth of bulletproof glass, is that he is so ordinary-looking. He might be a waiter, a window cleaner, perhaps, or an insurance agent. But the defendant's very drabness might be an advantage for what the Israelis are seeking in this trial. A man of overwhelming personality such as the late Hermann Göring might intrude himself upon the story, and the Israelis are intent upon telling the story. It is a part of their 4,000 years of history. More than that, it is a religious obligation. "And thou shalt tell it to thy son."

Yet despite his ordinary appearance, this Adolf Eichmann is really a stranger, a stranger to the human race who has come among us as the central figure in the greatest of all murder trials. And what are the charges that bring this stranger into a courtroom in the Holy Land among people who for centuries have repeated the hopeful prayer—"Next year in Jerusalem"—and who are now willing to risk the prestige of their hard-earned sovereignty on this single process?

The indictment is staggeringly unlike any ever heard before in the courtroom of any nation. It alleges that Adolf Eichmann issued his instructions to Gestapo and other commanders calling for the extermination of the Jews of Europe, that he directed the use of poison gas for this purpose at Auschwitz, that he helped devise measures to prevent childbirth among the Jews and among the children of Jewish-Gentile marriages, that he robbed the Jews of untold millions, including the personal properties of the extermination camp victims: the gold from their teeth, their artificial limbs, their clothing, their shoes, all of which were sent back to Germany—presumably in the same freight cars which had brought the victims to the gas chambers and incinerators.

And now this stranger is on trial for these things, and Israel has turned over to his defense bales of documents, including the names of all prosecution witnesses, so that Eichmann will be defended in accordance with Anglo-Saxon law, upon which Israeli law is based.

One amazing fact about this event is that it marks the first time in centuries the Jews themselves have ever tried a man for persecuting and killing Jews. Eichmann is far from the first of his kind. Standing in ghostly array behind him in his bulletproof booth are the many godfathers of Auschwitz, the official persecutors beginning with the Roman emperors of the fourth and fifth centuries A.D. who decided that Jews must not marry Christians on pain of death, and imposed rigid restrictions on the conduct of their everyday life.

In the opening sessions of the trial both sides roughed out their positions in the case. The defense counsel, Dr. Robert Servatius, challenged the legality of Eichmann's capture in Argentina, disputed the law on which the trial is based, questioned the

court's jurisdiction on grounds that an alleged criminal could not be tried by his alleged victims, and indicated doubt about the partiality of the judges. He gave further indication of his strategy when he referred to the accused as a mere cog in the machinery of a "predecessor" state of the modern Germany.

The prosecutor, Attorney General Gideon Hausner, responded by citing a whole series of U.S. court decisions establishing that a court may try a defendant regardless of how he was caught or brought to trial. He cited particularly Pettibone *v.* Idaho, in which the court ruled that even though Mr. Pettibone was taken out of Colorado against his will and without the knowledge of that state's authorities, the courts of Idaho thereupon had a right to try him for murder. Colorado had a grievance, the U.S. court held, but Pettibone did not. As for the legality of the Israeli law under which Eichmann is being tried, Hausner noted that no less than 17 nations have passed similar laws since 1945 making crimes against humanity retroactive.

Yet the fact remains that the trial is not without its serious risks for Israel. (It reminds me of the warning the fathers gave their growing sons on the Lower East Side of New York concerning relations with the women of the streets: "It begins all right. But you never know how it will end.") One of the chief dangers for Israel is that the revelations of the trial are likely to prove embarrassing to some of her closest friends in the Western world. The defense will most certainly try to claim that a year before the war ended, Eichmann had offered to let hundreds of thousands of Jews out of German-occupied territory if they were accepted elsewhere. But (as the story goes) all the doors were shut tight and the only place where they could go, Palestine, was effectively sealed against them by Britain.

We may also expect testimony that as early as January 1944 carefully drawn maps and diagrams of the railroad facilities leading to Auschwitz were placed in the hands of the Allies. But the road beds over which the daily boxcars of Jews traveled to extermination were never bombed—because the Russians said that these railroad tracks were too important to their advancing armies.

Some of this is doubtless true, but a philosopher to whom I spoke in Israel was quick to discount much of it as hindsight. "Even we Jews did not produce any Jeremiahs between 1939 and 1945," he said, adding, "The Jews themselves, on their way to the gas chambers, could not quite get themselves to believe what was happening to them."

The point of the matter is that the Western allies were not aware that the Nazis were fighting two separate wars, with two separate general staffs —one war to conquer the world and the other war to kill all the Jews. Because the West was not aware of these two wars, the Jews could gather to themselves no allies.

In this regard one of the most important witnesses for the prosecution probably will be a Mr. Joel Brand. I spent a day with Mr. Brand recently and saw for myself what others had told me—that he is a man who lives in the shadows with a broken heart, haunted by the dream that if his mission had been successful, one million Jews who died in the gas chambers might be alive today.

Joel Brand was the representative of the Jewish community in Budapest. Eichmann gave Brand the mission of opening ransom negotiations with the Allies, through the Jewish Agency, a sort of shadow government of Palestine under the British Mandate: one million Jews in exchange for 10,000 trucks and a few carloads of coffee, tea and soap. But Brand was unable to make personal contact with anyone who could negotiate. The British took him into custody in Syria, brought him to Cairo and kept him incommunicado.

At this moment President Roosevelt heard of the possibility of saving some of the Jews from the gas chambers and he dispatched a personal representative, Ira Hirschmann, to seek out Brand. Mr. Hirschmann was given the runaround from Istanbul to Aleppo and finally to Cairo where only his personal credentials from President Roosevelt persuaded Lord Moyne—the British Resident Minister in the Middle East—to grant him a visit of one hour with Brand. Brand says that Lord Moyne's position was that the release of all those Jews "would pose a great problem." The Brand mission failed with Lord Moyne's final word that everything would have to be cleared with the Foreign Office in London and there was no telling how long that would take.

Another phase of the Eichmann trial takes place outside the courtroom in the reaction of the people of Israel, many of whom knew of Eichmann in another world twenty years ago. But in Israel there is a surprising lack of passion about the trial. A woman who survived Auschwitz expressed the opinion of many Israelis: "I was happy when they caught him.

But I was also very sad." Another said to me, "Our brains are being opened again." As these reminders of the past come back to these people they are forced to relive an experience which is beyond human understanding, even after the mountains of literature that have been written about it, and even after the testimony of the Nuremberg trials.

There is also in Israel a considerable body of conservative opinion. It expresses itself in terms of "don't rock the boat" and would have preferred that one of the commandos who captured Eichmann had shot him in Argentina, and thus avoided any further complications.

A cynic in a coffeehouse stopped his game of chess long enough to answer my question. "What do I think of the Eichmann trial? Well, the Gentile world will watch it carefully to see if we are liars—to see if maybe there were not six million Jews massacred by the Nazis but only 4,999,-400." And he turned from me and said to his partner, "Your move."

One segment of the Jews in Israel remains unimpressed with the whole procedure. I visited Meah Shearim, the ultraorthodox section of Jerusalem, and had an audience with Rabbi Avrom Blau. The rabbi was seated at a long bench in the old synagogue Beth Joseph. He was surrounded by some of his disciples, all of them wearing the traditional black gowns and round black fur hats. Speaking in Yiddish (these ultraorthodox Jews believe that it is blasphemous to speak Hebrew except when addressing God in prayer), I asked him what he thought of the Eichmann trial. There was a long pause while all the others looked toward the rabbi. Finally he said, "It does not matter who is the accused or who is the accuser. These affairs are beyond our understanding, which is only to read the law and await the Messiah."

But the prime minister himself expressed the opinion which seems to be the general atmosphere surrounding the Eichmann trial at this moment. "Our concern is not one of vengeance but only of documenting an era in which genocide became a policy of a political state." And on this basis the Israelis are willing to shoulder all the risks involved in the attempt to bring this ordinary-looking man to justice for the most incredible crime in history.

*"They could not understand why we were
all pushing nearer the grave"—
Homer Bigart*

The New York Times, May 9, 1961

JERUSALEM (ISRAELI SECTOR), MAY 8 —Today's testimony at Eichmann's trial for responsibility in the murder of six million Jews provided a ghoulish account of the mass execution of women and children.

Mrs. Rivka Yosselevska, who was buried alive in a common grave near Pinsk in White Russia, told in a choking voice of how she had struggled upward through a pile of corpses. Her face ashen, she told of dying victims who were "biting at my legs and trying to pull me down."

Mrs. Yosselevska's testimony was the most searing yet in the four-week-old trial. As they listened to her tale of unrelieved horror, spectators in the packed courtroom sobbed or squirmed uneasily. She is a little woman, middle-aged, with a gaunt and tragic face.

A heart attack kept her from testifying Friday, but she recovered over the weekend and her physician said she was well enough to take the stand today.

Once she had started her narrative, the words came with a rush. With a strength born of madness, she said, she had clawed her way out of the tangle of corpses. Later, realizing that she was alone in the world and that her young daughter had been buried in the pit, she returned to the grave and clawed at the fresh dirt that had been thrown over it.

"I was digging with my fingernails, but the grave would not open. I did not have enough strength. I thought: 'Why didn't they kill me? What was my sin? I saw them all being killed— why was I spared? I had no one to go to.' "

She began her story by recalling how the Jews of Zagrovski, a White Russian village of five hundred Jewish families near Pinsk, were driven to a mass execution in the autumn of 1942.

"Some fled to the woods," she said. "From the woods we heard firing in the village. By dawn the firing ceased and we again began to move back. In town the rabbi's wife told us what had happened.

"She said the Germans came to take the rabbi, told him to put on his prayer shawl, then ordered everyone to assemble in the market place.

"There they ordered the rabbi to preach a sermon and then started beating the people and driving them to a cemetery where a shallow grave was ready.

"The Jews were forced to lie down in fours in the grave and were shot dead," Mrs. Yosselevska said. "But this was only the first action against Jews. The real horror was to come later."

With trembling lips the witness recalled the holocaust that befell her village on the first day of the Hebrew month of Elul.

"Germans poured into the ghetto and ordered us out of our homes," she said.

"Suddenly a large truck appeared and Jews were thrown into it. When there was no more room in the truck, others were ordered to run behind it.

"I ran, carrying my daughter in my arms. There were other mothers running with two, three or four children. Those who stumbled and fell were shot."

When they had run about three miles, they reached their destination —a meadow freshly scarred by a trench, the witness said. Jews from the truck had already been lined up on a mound of dirt above the trench. They had been ordered to disrobe and were standing naked, awaiting execution.

"I turned my head and saw that about twelve people already had been shot," she said. "My daughter said: 'Mother, why did you make me wear my Sabbath dress? We are being taken to be shot.'

"And when we were near the grave she cried: 'Why are we waiting? Let us run!'

"Some of the young people did try to escape, but they were caught immediately and shot on the spot.

"It was difficult to hold on to the children. They could not understand why we were all pushing nearer the grave, nearer the end of torture for us and the children."

The witness told how her father and mother and grandmother had been shot down, and of how her sister had been shot after she had pleaded to be spared.

"Then my turn came," Mrs. Yosselevska said.

"We reached the edge of the pit and the German said: 'Whom shall I shoot first?'

"I didn't answer. I felt him tear the child from my arms. The child cried out and was shot immediately."

Mrs. Yosselevska sobbed. Then she went on.

"He grabbed me by the hair and turned my head around. I heard a shot and fell into the pit.

"Then I felt I was suffocating. People were falling on top of me. I discovered I was alive."

After she crawled out of the grave, Mrs. Yosselevska, who had been wounded in the head, was sheltered by a farmer, who took her to a forest where she joined a group of partisans.

As this book goes to press, there is still no verdict from the judges in Jerusalem. The fate of Adolf Eichmann is still in doubt. What is not in doubt, however, is the broad significance of his trial. In "The Faces of the Dead," a moving editorial that appeared after a day of particularly gruesome testimony in Jerusalem, *The New York Times* commented that the mystery and the meaning of the trial of Adolf Eichmann lay in the fact that "the nameless and faceless dead have received the blessing of remembrance and are again alive, vivid as a scream in the night, in the minds of men." The editorial concluded:

"Each person who reads the testimony brings the dead back to life and gives them faces. There was a boy in the crowd of Jews being flogged to the grave. He turns around in the mind of some living person and suddenly he has a face and is remembered.

"There was a father who wept when he told his son he could no longer give him a father's advice; he has a face. The teacher who rode with his children to death and on the way told them not what he knew was coming but that at last they would see woods and fields and flowers; he has a face, and the beauty and sweetness of his soul is, for others, a matter of tears and remembrance.

"But how long will they live in the memory now so newly fresh? How long before they are returned to the final grave of the forever forgotten, returned by men's desire to turn away from pain and by the very fact that their sufferings were so great and their number so many that sane men cannot—or will not—really retain comprehension of it all?

"How long before their resurrection ends? This will be the real verdict of the Eichmann trial and it will not be given by the judges in Jerusalem, but by each person who has read of the suffering and humiliation of the dead and heard their cries and seen their faces."

ACKNOWLEDGMENTS

MANY INDIVIDUALS and many institutions have contributed to the completion of this enterprise. The editors are especially indebted to Dean Carl W. Ackerman of the Pulitzer School of Journalism, Columbia University, to Herbert Bayard Swope, and to Dean Frank Luther Mott of the University of Missouri School of Journalism for their suggestions and encouragement.

In addition, the editors wish to express their deep sense of obligation to the following: S. P. Barnett, Managing Editor, Cleveland *Plain Dealer;* Prof. Herman Ausubel, Dept. of History, Columbia University; Roland Baughman, Head of Special Collections, Butler Library, Columbia University; Meyer Berger, *The New York Times;* Thornton Boulter, Managing Editor, San Diego *Tribune-Sun,* California; Turner Catledge, Assistant Managing Editor, *The New York Times;* Laura L. Cleverdon, Library Assistant, City College of New York; Dr. Sidney Ditzion, Assistant Librarian, City College of New York; Dr. Edward Mead Earle, Institute for Advanced Study, Princeton, N. J.; Calvin F. Eby, Kansas City (Missouri) *Star;* Barry Faris, Editor-in-Chief, *International News Service;* Dean James L. C. Ford, Montana State University School of Journalism; Professor Ira M. Freeman, Rutgers University; Ben W. Gilbert, City Editor, Washington *Post;* Harold S. Goodwin, Assistant Managing Editor, Baltimore *Sun;* Prof. Henry Graff, Dept. of History, Columbia University; Joseph G. Herzberg, City Editor, New York *Herald Tribune;* N. R. Howard, Editor, Cleveland *News;* Prof. John Paul Jones, University of Illinois School of Journalism; David H. Joseph, Assistant Managing Editor, *The New York Times.*

Also: Edward Kennedy, Managing Editor, Santa Barbara (California) *News-Press;* Clem Lane, City Editor, Chicago *Daily News;* Mrs. Charmion London; Louis M. Lyons, Curator, Nieman Foundation for Journalism, Harvard University; Prof. Curtiss MacDougall, The Medill School of Journalism, Northwestern University; George T. Matthews, Dept. of History, Columbia University; Henry L. Mencken; L. B. Mickel, Superintendent of Bureaus, United Press Associations; Sig Mickelson, Director News and Special Events, WCCO, Minneapolis; Basil Mitchell, Librarian, and Mrs. Mary V. Montgomery, Assistant Librarian, Pulitzer School of Journalism, Columbia University; Berenice Robinson Morris; Prof. Ralph O. Nafziger, University of Minnesota School of Journalism; Lieutenant-Colonel Robert G. Van Ness, Ordnance Department, Bureau of Public Relations, War Department; Everett Norlander, Managing Editor, Chicago *Daily News;* Hal O'Flaherty, Director, Chicago *Daily News* Foreign Service; Maclean Patterson, General Managing Editor, *The Sunpapers,* Baltimore; James E. Pollard, Director, Ohio State University School of Journalism; Prof. Sidney I. Pomerantz, Dept. of History, City College of New York; Capt. Robert S. Quackenbush, Jr., U.S.N., Quentin Reynolds; Donald B. Robinson; William L. Shirer; Eric Sevareid, Director of News Broadcasts, Columbia Broadcasting System; Ida Mae Brown Snyder; Keats Speed, Executive Editor, New York *Sun;* Leslie C. Staples, The Dickens House, London; Louis Stark, *The New York Times;* William F. Swindler, Director, School of Journalism, University of Nebraska; Charles A. Tyler, Chairman and General Manager, Philadelphia *Inquirer;* Edward R. Wallace, News Director, WTAM, Cleveland; and William C. Wren, Managing Editor, San Francisco *Examiner.*

Finally, the editors wish to express their thanks to M. Lincoln Schuster for his wholehearted co-operation and invaluable suggestions at all stages of the project, and to the publisher's staff, especially Henry Simon, of the editorial department, and Helen Barrow, production, for major assistance in the preparation of the book.

Index